Psychology

Fourth Edition
....

Psychology

Andrew B. Crider

George R. Goethals

Robert D. Kavanaugh

Paul R. Solomon

All of Williams College

HarperCollins*CollegePublishers*

Acquisitions Editor: Catherine Woods
Developmental Editor: Rebecca Kohn
Project Editor: Katharine Glynn
Art Director: Lucy Krikorian
Text and Cover Design: Lucy Krikorian
Cover, Part, and Chapter Opening Photos:
    Les Jörgensen
Photo Researcher: Sandy Schneider
Production Manager: Willie Lane
Compositor: Arcata Graphics/Kingsport
Printer and Binder: Von Hoffman Press, Inc.
Cover Printer: The Lehigh Press, Inc.

PSYCHOLOGY, Fourth Edition

**Library of Congress Cataloging-in-Publication
Data**

Psychology / Andrew B. Crider . . . [et al.]. — 4th ed.
        p.   cm.
    Includes bibliographical references and indexes.
    ISBN 0-673-46538-1 (student ed.)
    ISBN 0-673-46539-x (teacher ed.)
    1. Psychology.   I. Crider, Andrew.
  BF 121.P7915   1993
  150—dc20   92-30213
                                                CIP

93 94 95 96   9 8 7 6 5 4 3 2

Brief Contents

Detailed Contents

Preface

TEACHING PSYCHOLOGY: THE CHALLENGES AND GOALS

In our years of team-teaching introductory psychology, we have found that it is both the single most important course in the undergraduate psychology curriculum and the most difficult to teach.

The goals of the introductory course are ambitious: to introduce students to the structure of contemporary psychology, to present the central concepts and theories of the discipline, and to outline the empirical tools that psychologists use. In addition, the instructor wants to communicate a sense of the accomplishments, promises, and continuing vitality of a discipline that takes as its subject matter every aspect of human behavior and cognition.

Achieving these goals is difficult for two reasons. One is the challenge of presenting the richness of the discipline without overwhelming students with the vast and diverse number of terms and concepts traditionally covered in the introductory course. A second reason is that well-meaning efforts to simplify the material may lead students to regard psychology as a loose collection of distinct fields, rather than as a unified discipline.

The response to the first three editions of *Psychology* leads us to believe that our solutions to these challenges have been well received by both instructors and students. Our approach to presenting this complex body of material relies on two organizing principles. First, we focus on psychology as an integrated discipline and second, we give careful attention to pedagogical principles.

PSYCHOLOGY AS AN INTEGRATED DISCIPLINE

We believe that introductory psychology can and should be taught as a subject unified in the way psychologists frame questions and seek answers. We have accordingly organized the material in a manner that emphasizes the formation and testing of hypotheses, as well as the empirical methods that guide inquiry into the questions posed by human behavior and cognition.

In addition, a major aim of this text is to demonstrate in its exposition that the subfields of psychology are mutually supportive and overlapping. For example, the student will find neurochemistry discussed in the chapters on brain and behavior, psychological disorders, and treatment. Theory and research on learned helplessness informs discussions in the chapters on learning, health and stress, and psychological disorders. Hypotheses derived from psychoanalytic theory are discussed in fully half the chapters. Problems of human memory are addressed in the chapters on memory, development, and social cognition.

ORGANIZATION

The seventeen chapters of this edition are newly organized into five parts plus an introductory chapter on history, methods, and perspectives. This organization is designed to give the student an easily apprehended map of the major topic areas of psychology and their subdivisions. **Part One** discusses the relationship of biological processes to behavior and mental activity. Here we examine the central nervous system (Chapter 2), followed by chapters on sensation and perception (3), motivation and emotion (4), and states of consciousness (5). **Part Two** deals with learning and cognition, containing chapters on conditioning and learning (6), human memory (7), and thinking and language (8). **Part Three** focuses on social, cognitive, and intellectual development, with chapters on infancy and childhood (9), adolescence, adulthood, and aging (10), and intelligence (11). **Part Four** presents the area of social and personality psychology. Here chapters on social cognition (12) and social influence (13) are combined with a chapter on personality and assessment (14). **Part Five** surveys psychological disorders and treatment. It contains chapters on health and stress (15), psychological disorders (16), and treatment (17). Finally, we have provided an appendix dealing with research methods and statistics in psychology.

CONTENT CHANGES IN THE FOURTH EDITION

In preparing this edition, we have received a large number of helpful suggestions from users of the first three editions. More often than not, we have followed their advice to add or to delete, to simplify or to elaborate, to reorganize or to fine-tune. We thank them for helping us strengthen the book. Every chapter has been revised with the aim of enhancing accessibility, balance, and currency. Some examples of new or significantly revised material include:

- Recent developments on brain imaging and a new section on the endocrine system in Chapter 2
- A discussion of biological influences on the development of homosexuality and a discussion of research on the facial feedback hypothesis of emotion in Chapter 4
- A section on the applications of classical conditioning, including immune system conditioning, in Chapter 6
- Reorganizing Chapter 7 on memory around the processes of forming, retrieving, and forgetting memories
- Material on prenatal development and a greatly expanded section on gender differences in Chapter 9
- A discussion of the impact of AIDS on adolescent sexuality in Chapter 10
- New material on attribution and on prejudice in Chapter 12
- An expanded discussion of leadership in Chapter 13
- Sections on the five factor model of personality and on gender differences in personality in Chapter 14
- Expanded treatments of personality and health in Chapter 15
- New material on women and depression and a reorganized and expanded discussion of schizophrenia in Chapter 16
- We have also added some new features to introduce students to the applications of psychology in everyday life.

Psychology in the News **boxes** reproduce a current newspaper or magazine story related to the surrounding chapter material. The story is followed by a series of two or three questions. The news story helps students understand the significance of the material, and the questions allow them to analyze the story with newly acquired concepts. For example, an article from *The New York Times,* "Babies Learn the Sounds of Language by 6 Months" discusses new research on early language acquisition, followed by questions linking the article to language theory discussed in the chapter. An article from *The Wall Street Journal,* "Recession Fears Have Some People Depressed . . ." discusses the relationship between economic and psychological depression, and the questions ask students to critically evaluate the article based on their reading of the chapter material. We think students will not only respond favorably to the *Psychology in the News* boxes, but they will form the basis of interesting class discussions.

A Conversation with. . . . Each part opens with a conversation with a leading psychologist. This feature gives students an insider's view of the discipline.

We are confident that this fourth edition is as current as the first in reflecting advances in our knowledge and understanding.

SUPPLEMENTS

Psychology, Fourth Edition is accompanied by a variety of supplements for both instructors and students.

For the Instructor

Instructor's Resource Kit. Eve Conrad of San Bernadino Valley College and Mark Rafte of Chaffee College have compiled this generous collection of teaching ideas, demonstrations, hand-outs, and references. The instructor's kit is available in a three-ring binder for easier reproduction of student hand-outs and incorporating additional materials.

The Integrator. Bound into the instructor's edition of the text, this is a chapter-by-chapter cross-reference listing to all the instructional resources available for this text. The integrator is a valuable tool for use in coordinating elements of the supplements package and organizing class time.

Test Bank 1 and Test Bank 2. Written by Patrick S. Williams, University of Houston and Deborah R. McDonald, New Mexico State University, these two test banks contain a total of 3600 class-tested and reviewed test items. Each provides approximately 90 multiple-choice questions and 10 essay questions per chapter. Questions are referenced by topic, text page number, and type (interpretive or factual).

TestMaster Computerized Testing System. This is a flexible, easy-to-use computer test bank, containing all the questions from both Test Bank 1 and Test Bank 2. The software allows instructors to edit existing questions and add new questions. Tests can be printed in several formats, and include graphs and tables. TestMaster is available for both IBM and Macintosh.

Psychology Encyclopedia III Laserdisc. The laserdisc contains animated sequences showing biological and physiological concepts, over 200 still images, and a variety of motion clips. This new version of the laserdisc has been completely revised and updated. It is accompanied by an instructor's manual which includes a detailed list of contents and barcode directory for easier access to individual frames.

Transparency Package. One hundred full-color transparency acetates, most taken from sources other than the text, is available.

For the Student

Practice Tests. Each student who purchases a new copy of the text will automatically receive a free copy of this supplement which contains a sample test for each chapter. Written by Deborah McDonald of New Mexico State University, the sample tests contain multiple choice and essay questions. An answer section provides explanations that help the student learn why answers are correct.

Study Guide and Practice Tests. Each chapter of the study guide, written by Sarah Rundle, contains an introduction, learning objectives, vocabulary exercises, and two multiple choice practice tests.

SuperShell Computerized Tutorial. Developed by Patrick S. Williams of the University of Houston, this interactive program for the IBM reinforces important concepts through drill and practice exercises and diagnostic feedback. SuperShell provides immediate answers and references the text page on which the material is discussed.

Journey II Interactive Software. This newly revised and expanded program, developed by Intentional Educations, involves students in a variety of simulations and experiments on a variety of topics including the nervous system and learning development. This program is available for IBM and Macintosh users.

ACKNOWLEDGMENTS

We would like to thank the many professionals at HarperCollins who guided us through the planning and completion of this project. Anne Harvey, psychology editor, helped us reorganize the fourth edition of this project and oversaw the development of a creative, educationally valuable, supplements package. Rebecca Kohn, our developmental editor, gracefully refined the text, and helped immensely with the critical issues of pedagogy and style. Katharine Glynn, project editor, painstakingly managed the project through the complex production process. To all three, we express our sincere appreciation for their helpful guidance and willing forbearance.

We would also like to thank Keith Stanovich for his skillful revision of the statistics appendix.

Several colleagues at Williams College provided sage advice about particular issues. We wish to thank Laurie Heatherington, Betty Zimmerberg Glick, Saul Kassin, and Dan Willingham for their helpful suggestions. Finally, we would like to express our sincere appreciation to Marianne Congello, Angie Giusti, and Karen Ware for their assistance in preparing the manuscript and keeping us on schedule.

Over the course of four editions we have had the benefit of many academic reviewers. We would like to thank all of them. The reviewers for this edition were:

Fredrick M. Brown, Pennsylvania State University
Roseann Cappella, East Stroudsburg University
Paul J. Chara, Jr., Loras College
Michael A. Church, King's College
Eric Cooley, Western Oregon State
Robert Delmas, Northeast Missouri State
Janet Dizinno, St. Mary's University
Ann Dunn, Montgomery College
Donald L. Fields, University of New Brunswick
Judith D. Gentry, Columbus State Community College
Jeff Goodpaster, Gateway Technical College
Richard A. Griggs, University of Florida
Sherri Lynn Jackson, Jacksonville University
Robert Keefer, Mount St. Mary's College
Mark A. Koppel, Montclair State College
T. C. Lewandowski, Delaware County College
Angela McGlynn, Mercer County Community College
Edward Mosely, Passaic Community College
Ken Murdoff, Lane Community College
Dean Richards
Joyce R. Schaeuble, Sacramento City College
Lloyd H. Strickland, Ottawa University
Wanda A. Trahan, University of Wisconsin, Oshkosh
Yvonne Wells, University of Rhode Island
Daniel B. Willingham, Williams College
Stephen J. Zaccaro, George Mason University

Andrew B. Crider
George R. Goethals
Robert D. Kavanaugh
Paul R. Solomon

Psychology

1

···············

Welcome
to
Psychology

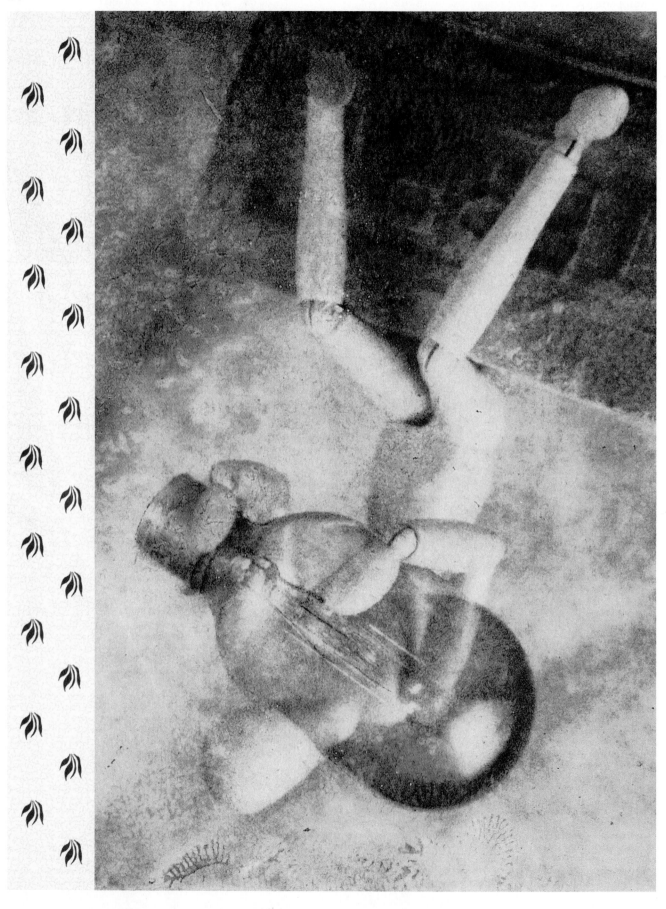

Welcome to the study of psychology. Psychology is an exciting field of knowledge that continues to grow at an accelerating pace each year, providing answers to basic questions about the human condition. Psychology offers us the hope of both understanding and improving our lives, our communities, and our planet. We are eager to share with you the knowledge that psychology has already uncovered and the initiatives that will help chart its course into the future.

Psychology is both a field of study and a means of improving the quality of life (Kimble, 1984). Its range of inquiry is enormous. Psychologists have searched for the precise spot in the brain where information in memory is stored, they have studied the mysteries of insight and creativity, and they have theorized about the way morality develops. They have outlined the conditions that foster cooperation and competition and the biological and environmental factors that contribute to depression and schizophrenia. Volumes of information have been generated on a wide range of subjects, and ideas are still being tested. While some psychologists continue to gather new data, others have taken what we know already and applied it. Through the application of psychology we have made strides in improving human learning and memory, reducing international tension, and relieving the misery of psychological disorder. Psychological knowledge has been used in measuring intelligence, designing school curricula, helping troubled marriages, controlling aggression, campaigning for the presidency, selling beer and toothpaste, and treating both the young and old with greater sensitivity and humanity. The promise of psychology is exhilarating and gives reason for optimism as we face the future.

We hope you will come to realize that psychology is and always will be a part of your life—at home, at work, in the media, and in your communities. Throughout this text and this course you will be asked to learn facts, but, equally important, you will be encouraged to understand the methods used to generate new knowledge. We want you to be aware of the way good research is conducted and reliable answers are generated. Only with a thorough knowledge of the methods of psychology, as well as its findings, can you be prepared to assess the numerous claims about psychological truth that will be presented to you.

We will begin with an overview of the field and then discuss its goals and methods. After we examine the intellectual background of psychology, we will look at the specialties that currently define the field. We will also consider the varied settings in which psychologists work. Then we will discuss the ethical principles that govern both the ways psychologists collect new information and the ways they put that knowledge to use.

Throughout your study of psychology you will come to see numerous ways in which psychology is part of your life.

WHAT IS PSYCHOLOGY?

Psychology is the scientific study of behavior and mental processes. This definition contains three key ideas: scientific, behavior, and mental processes. Like many familiar terms, each of these is used in a specific way by psychologists.

Scientific refers to the fact that the study of psychology is based on information collected through a set of systematic procedures known as the *scientific method*. The information collected is referred to as **data**, specifically defined as records of the observations or measurements in a study. Using the scientific method requires specifying a precise set of procedures for collecting data that others can use to collect data themselves or perhaps even improve on. For example, a psychologist studying dreams might specify that the subjects in sleep laboratories should be awakened and questioned about their dreams whenever during sleep their eyes make specific kinds of rapid movements. The psychologist follows a set of procedures for collecting dream data that are spelled out in enough detail for anyone else to question, reproduce, or improve. Thus knowl-

edge in psychology is based on inferences from data that are open to inspection and criticism.

Behavior is any activity that can be observed, recorded, and measured. This includes, first, what living beings do—that is, their actual movements in time and space. For example, smiling, sucking, and sleeping are all behaviors commonly seen in babies. Behavior also includes what people say or write. Their reports of their fears or their desires are behaviors. In addition, behavior includes physiological, or bodily, changes such as elevations in blood pressure or alterations in the electrical activity of the brain. For example, when equipment measuring electrical brain activity is attached to a person's head and it begins emitting more signals of the sort called alpha waves, we observe that a change in behavior has taken place.

Mental processes include thoughts, memories, emotions, motivations, dreams, perceptions, and beliefs. The study of these processes presents a special problem because they cannot be directly observed, recorded, or measured. Most contemporary psychologists feel that mental processes can be studied by observing changes in behavior in specific situations and then inferring that a change has also occurred in a mental process. For example, psychologists can study an individual's level of alertness by measuring changes in the electrical signals generated by the brain. Stress can be inferred by measuring changes in blood pressure and perspiration or changes in voice quality. Under certain conditions, attention in newborn infants can be inferred from decreases in heart rate and slower breathing.

The study of mental processes presents many challenges because they cannot be directly observed, recorded, or measured. For example, from simple observation we could not say whether this man is unhappy about the progress of the meeting he is attending or simply lost in thought.

The study of behavior and mental processes poses many puzzles that we can begin to solve using the scientific method. The practice of science requires intellectual curiosity, objectivity, determination, perseverance, and, above all, a willingness to look beyond common sense and obvious answers.

The Goals of Psychology

Science exists because people are curious, because they want to have accurate knowledge, and because they want to improve their lives. Psychologists attempt to meet these needs by setting four general goals: to describe, explain, and predict behavior and mental processes and to use the knowledge gained to promote human welfare.

The first and basic goal is to describe, that is, to observe and measure, behavior and mental processes. For example, if we wanted to study children at play, we might begin by watching, recording their interactions and the amount of time they spend at each game. If we wanted to study alertness, we might use an instrument called an *electroencephalograph* (*EEG*), a device that measures the electrical activity of the brain, to look at the brain's activity

The electroencephalogram, or EEG, is a device that can measure the electrical activity of the brain in a variety of circumstances.

in a variety of circumstances. The structure and functioning of the brain can be studied and measured through electronic brain scans. Personality and intelligence can be described and measured by administering specially designed tests. In each case, the primary purpose is to gather data in an objective and accurate manner.

The second goal of psychology is to explain what the data mean. Psychologists usually accomplish this goal by formulating a **theory**, a coherent group of assumptions and propositions that can explain the data. Forming theories in psychology is especially challenging because so many factors can influence behavior and mental processes. For example, many explanations are possible when a new neighbor doesn't answer if you say "good morning." Maybe your neighbor is an unfriendly person, or perhaps he doesn't hear well. Maybe he's angry at you for not keeping your home tidy on the outside, or perhaps a passing truck drowned out your voice. Maybe this particular person just doesn't "wake up" until midday. Any one of these reasons, or some combination of them, might explain his behavior. Psychologists continually generate theories to help them explain the most recent data about behavior and mental processes. However, before these theories are accepted they are subjected to rigorous tests based on the scientific method.

One test of a theory's accuracy and usefulness is its ability to predict behavior and mental processes. Given a particular set of circumstances, a theory should allow psychologists to meet their third goal: predicting what will happen in those circumstances. For example, a theory of cognitive development should be able to specify the kinds of thinking a child can manage at a particular age. In Chapter 10 we will discuss Jean Piaget's well-known theory of child development, an attempt to do precisely this.

Psychology's final, and some feel ultimate, goal is to apply knowledge to promote human welfare. The most obvious application is in a subfield of psychology known as clinical psychology, where our knowledge of behavior and mental processes is used to help individuals with psychological disorders. But even if you never see a psychologist for this kind of help, most of you probably have been affected by psychological research. Knowledge gained through psychological research touches almost every aspect of our lives. It ranges from the way we raise and teach our children to the tests you took to gain admission to college, from the advertising we see on television to the design of airplane cockpits, and from the way leaders make decisions to the way nations resolve conflicts.

The Scientific Method in Psychology

Psychologists are scientists who subject their theories to stringent empirical testing. They gather evidence that will tell them whether their theories are right or wrong. When you think of a scientist, you may think of a person in a white coat in a laboratory, surrounded by delicate and complex equipment. But the practice of science can take place anywhere, and the only tool needed is the scientific method.

The starting point of any scientific endeavor is simple curiosity—the desire to understand. But this curiosity produces results only when it is harnessed to the scientific method. Although each of the research methods we will discuss in the next section has its own unique procedures, the following key steps in the scientific method are common to all.

Specify the Problem Simple curiosity inspires scientific inquiry, but researchers must go beyond curiosity and identify specific issues they want to study. In other words, the question, or *hypothesis*, being investigated must be stated in a clear, focused, and *testable* manner (Aronson, Brewer, & Carlsmith, 1985). A researcher who is curious about memory and wants to study it must ask a specific question, such as how long people can remember a specific list of words under specific conditions.

Design the Study After a question has been stated in a specific and testable way, a study must be designed. In the memory example mentioned above, the researchers must work out such details as the words to be presented, whether they should be given to the subjects in writing or read aloud, the length of time the subjects have to rehearse the words, the length of time the subjects will have to hold the words in memory before being tested, and so forth.

Designing a study requires creating operational definitions of key elements of the study. An **operational definition** is a definition stat-ed in terms that can be observed and mea-

sured. Once we have defined an element in this way, we have *operationalized* it. For example, in order to study memory we operationalize it by defining it, for instance, as the percentage of the words on a list that subjects can recall 15 minutes after they have read them. In this instance, memory is defined in terms of a specific observable behavior that can be clearly understood and measured by any other researcher.

Bias in a research study, although it is usually unintentional or unconscious, can lead to misleading or erroneous conclusions that render the study worthless. Researchers use various techniques to help prevent bias from negatively affecting the results of their studies. Operational definitions are one such technique. They help achieve the overall goal of the scientific method, which is to generate believable data and reach convincing conclusions. An operational definition of memory makes claims about memory more objective and less biased by letting everyone who reads the study know exactly what is meant by the terms used in the study.

Sometimes the subjects in a study may behave in ways in which they think the researcher wants them to behave; thus, their performance in the study becomes biased. To prevent this from happening, researchers use a **single-blind procedure** in which the subjects are kept uninformed about the hypothesis of the study so that this knowledge does not unconsciously affect their behavior. **Experimenter bias** occurs when researchers who are aware of the hypothesis subtly influence the subjects to behave according to prediction (Rosenthal, 1966). Use of a **double-blind technique,** in which both the subjects and the researcher analyzing the data of the study are kept uninformed about the hypothesis, helps prevent experimenter bias from negatively affecting a research study.

COLLECT THE DATA
After the research has been fully planned and a satisfactory design has been devised, the actual collection of data can begin. The researcher must direct the **subjects,** or research participants, through the study. The procedures of the study must be designed to eliminate bias, and they must be carried out with meticulous care.

After the data have been collected, but before it is time to draw conclusions, the data will typically be subjected to thorough **statistical analysis,** a set of techniques borrowed from mathematics that can be used to describe data, determine the probability that results are due to chance, and guide the inferences that can be made from the data. Taken together, statistical methods give psychologists a clearer understanding of what their data actually mean. We discuss a number of these methods in the appendix, Methods and Statistics in Psychology, that follows Chapter 17.

REPORT THE CONCLUSIONS
If a study has been appropriately designed to answer a specific question and if the data have been collected in a careful, unbiased manner, then meaningful conclusions can be drawn from the findings. These conclusions, and the studies from which they are drawn, are typically reported in psychological journals or books. The citations you will see in this text, such as (*Asch, 1952*), refer to published reports of research. (Asch is the author's or researcher's name and 1952 is the year in which the report was published.) Because they are drawn from clearly defined methods and fully reported statistical analyses, the conclusions can be questioned or challenged by anyone who reads the publication in which they appear. Reporting the results of a study allows a researcher to present his or her work to the scientific community, where it can be judged by a jury of peers. Publishing a study allows other researchers to examine a study for errors, biases, and faulty logic. In addition, if a research study has been designed and executed carefully, another researcher should be able to duplicate the original results. **Replication,** repeating a study to see if the same results will be obtained again, is one of the hallmarks of science.

There is another important function of publishing studies. Reporting research allows psychologists to share their knowledge and contribute to the growing body of knowledge that is modern psychology. Often one study inspires another, thus ensuring the progress and growth of psychological knowledge (Aronson, 1977). **Table 1.1** (on page 8) is a summary of the steps of the scientific method.

Interim Summary

Psychology is the scientific study of behavior and mental processes. Its goals are to describe, explain, predict, and modify behavior and experience.

Table 1.1   **The Steps of the Scientific Method**

1. Specify the problem.
   State the hypothesis in a testable way.
2. Design and conduct the study.
   Create operational definitions.
   Eliminate bias.
3. Collect the data.
   Subject the collected data to statistical analysis.
   Draw conclusions.
4. Report the conclusions.
   Publish the results of the study.

The scientific method is a systematic procedure for defining problems, designing and conducting studies, and drawing conclusions that enables other scientists to have confidence in the data that are collected and the conclusions that are drawn.

The scientific method in psychology requires the use of operational definitions so that variables can be manipulated and measured. An operational definition is one that is stated in terms of observable and measurable events or behavior.

METHODS OF PSYCHOLOGICAL RESEARCH

If you glance at the table of contents of this book, you can see how diverse the science of psychology is. Psychologists must use many different methods to study topics ranging from the brain and learning to interpersonal attraction and psychological disorders. In this section, we will discuss the most important methods psychologists use to accomplish their goals. These are naturalistic observation, the case study, surveys, correlational studies, and experimentation. All of these methods are extremely useful in gathering data and in describing, explaining, predicting, and modifying behavior and mental processes. However, only the fifth method, experimentation, can identify cause-and-effect relationships. Identifying these relationships is essential to achieving psychology's goals. For this reason, many psychologists feel that experimentation is the most important method. In fact, a great deal of the information we will present in this book was gathered

through experimentation. However, all the methods of psychological study have made important contributions to our knowledge.

Naturalistic Observation

Much of what psychologists have learned about behavior in both human and animal subjects comes from studies performed in laboratories. But sometimes psychologists want to study how people or animals behave in their normal environments. To do this, psychologists use a method called naturalistic observation.

Naturalistic observation is a method of study in which (1) subjects are observed in their natural environments and (2) the observer does not attempt to interfere with the natural behavior of the subjects. In fact, in the best type of naturalistic observation the subjects are not aware that they are being observed. This method is very different from an experiment, in which the researchers purposely alter an environment and observe the effects of this alteration on behavior.

Many kinds of psychologists, and other social scientists, use naturalistic observation. For example, anthropologist Margaret Mead (1935) studied the relationship between gender and assertiveness in four different societies. She showed that assertiveness levels in men and women are strongly influenced by culture.

One group of scientists who emphasize the use of naturalistic observation is called ethologists. **Ethology** is the study of the behavior of animals in their natural environment (McGill, 1977). Much of what we know about aggressive behavior in animals comes from ethological studies. From these studies psychologists have learned that groups of animals have territories and will band together to fight off any intruders (Kruuk, 1966). Some researchers have proposed that by studying animals in their natural surroundings we will also learn about human behavior. The Nobel Prize–winning ethologist Konrad Lorenz (1966), for example, has proposed that, like other animals, human beings also band together to defend their territory and that this is one of the primary causes of human aggression.

Naturalistic observation does have some disadvantages. Researchers have less control over what happens in the natural environment, so they can study only those behaviors that happen to be taking place when they are watching. Furthermore, it is more difficult to

Naturalistic observation is one method scientists use to study behavior. Anthropologist Margaret Mead was a pioneer of this technique. Here Mead is shown in Samoa.

see the causal relationship among specific variables in a natural setting than in a laboratory. Thus, naturalsitic observation is often used in conjunction with other methods.

The Case Study

A **case study,** the extensive study of all or part of the life history of an individual, is like biography. In literature, biographies entertain, instruct, and inspire. In psychology, case studies also have three major uses. First, the case study is an essential part of understanding and helping people with psychological disorders. To treat a patient, a psychologist must know what sort of person the patient is and what sort of difficulties he or she is experiencing. In addition, the psychologist wants to know *how* the patient's difficulties developed. The psychologist therefore usually asks the patient about his or her childhood, family, schooling, hobbies, love relationships, career, and so forth. The psychologist then composes a case study describing how the patient's difficulties arose, how he or she copes with these difficulties, and what can be done to help.

An example of a case study is the book *The Three Faces of Eve* (1957), written by two therapists named Thigpen and Cleckley. Eve was the pseudonym for a woman living in Georgia who had a severe psychological disor-

The case study can help a psychologist understand and treat someone with psychological disorders. Case studies are also important teaching and research tools. Shown here is "Eve," subject of a famous case study, *The Three Faces of Eve.* Eve suffered from multiple personality disorder and each of these four paintings was done by a different personality.

der that manifested itself in a multiple personality. Most of the time Eve would show a shy, cautious, and inhibited personality called Eve White. At other times she became another personality, Eve Black. Eve Black was flirtatious, provocative, and assertive. In order to devise a suitable treatment for her unusual disorder, Eve's therapists attempted to discover as much about her past and present life problems as possible. Therapy resulted in a third personality, Jane, that seemed relatively well adjusted. Eventually Eve wrote her own book and described more than 30 personalities that she manifested at later points in her life (Sizemore & Pitillo, 1978).

A second major use of the case study is as a means of illustrating ideas and relationships in teaching. For example, in Chapter 2 we will see that people with damage to the frontal lobes of the brain generally lack foresight and become impulsive and irritable. This generalization is illustrated in a case study of Phineas Gage, a man who survived an accident in which an iron bar passed through his frontal lobes. The case method was also used to great advantage by psychologists John B. Watson and Rosalie Rayner (1920) in a famous study known as "The Case of Little Albert." Watson and Rayner illustrated how fears and phobias could be viewed as learned responses, by using principles of learning to make Little Albert fear a white rat. This famous case is discussed in more detail in Chapter 6.

Third, the case study is an important research tool. In research, the case study is used primarily to suggest theories or hypotheses about human behavior. For example, in a book entitled *The Nazi Doctors* (Lifton, 1987), intensive case studies of three German physicians who worked in Hitler's concentration camps and assisted in the selection of Jewish prisoners to be put to death generated hypotheses about the psychological mechanisms people use to deny their own evil behavior. The book also offers several intriguing propositions, based on the case studies, about the ways people can justify participating in genocide. It is a chilling study but one that deals with very important psychological and historical questions. Case studies pose questions but do not answer them. In scientific terms we say that case studies *generate*, but do not *confirm*, hypotheses. In order to test hypotheses, we have to turn to other research methods.

Social scientists often use surveys to measure attitudes and behavior patterns of a group of people.

Surveys

Often psychologists find it useful to investigate larger groups. Psychologists and sociologists often use a survey as a very effective way of measuring the attitudes and behavior patterns of a group of people. **Surveys** are questionnaires, conducted in person, over the telephone, or through the mail, that inquire into the ways a group of people think or act. In conducting surveys, researchers first attempt to identify the population, or group of subjects, they wish to survey. Then they use statistical methods to pick a random but representative sample of that population.

Surveys often reveal information that runs counter to common sense and prior beliefs. For example, during the 1940s and early 1950s Alfred Kinsey and his colleagues studied Americans' sexual behavior, including the percentage of men and women who engaged in premarital sexual intercourse. The researchers reported that 68 percent of college men and 60 percent of college women had engaged in premarital sexual intercourse (Kinsey, Pomeroy, & Martin, 1948; Kinsey, Pomeroy, Martin, & Gebhard, 1953). These figures surprised many people and may well have had the effect of liberalizing sexual attitudes. The data showed that premarital sex was more common than was generally believed. This led some people to believe that perhaps premarital sexual activity was not as immoral as many people claimed. Surveys conducted in the 1970s (Hunt, 1974; Tavris & Sadd, 1977) indicated that premarital sex was even more common a generation after the Kinsey reports. These reports indicated that 68 percent of unmarried women and 97 percent of unmarried men have had sexual intercourse by the age of 25. Subsequent survey research has helped to clarify some of the determinants of engaging in premarital sex. For example, one study indicated that both males and females who are more independent, less academically motivated, and less religious engage in earlier premarital sex (Jessor, Costa, Jessor, & Donovan, 1983).

Surveys have two important limitations. One is that the survey results can be generalized only to the population of persons from whom the sample was drawn. For example, if Kinsey had selected his sample from only blue-collar workers, his surveys could not have told us much about sexual behavior in other social groups. Second, surveys depend on subjects' verbal reports of their attitudes and behaviors. Whether people give completely honest answers to such surveys is difficult to know. One way researchers have attempted to deal with this problem is to ask each question on a survey in two or three different ways—how consistently subjects respond is one indication of their honesty.

Correlational Studies

Sometimes researchers analyze data from surveys to see what relationships exist among the variables. For example, a person studying premarital sex may try to determine whether there is a relationship between income level and sexual attitudes. Do people with higher incomes have more liberal attitudes about sex? **Correlation,** a statistical technique devised by Sir Francis Galton, is the method psychologists use to see if two variables are associated or related in some way. The relationship between the two variables is also referred to as a correlation. Although the mathematics involved in correlation are somewhat complex, the idea is very simple: two variables are *correlated* when changes in the value of one variable are associated with changes in the value of a second variable. For example, one recent correlational study supports the idea that heat can produce aggression. Data from major league baseball games show that there is a correlation between the temperature at baseball games and the number of batters hit by a pitch during the games. The higher the temperature at game time, the more hit batters (Reifman, Larrick, & Fein, 1991).

ANALYZING CORRELATIONAL DATA

One method of examining the correlation between two variables is to draw a graph known as a *scatter plot.* A **scatter plot** is a visual representation of the relationship between two variables in a group of subjects. **Figure 1.1** is a hypothetical scatter plot of the relationship between SAT scores and grade point averages (GPA's) in a group of 30 college students. Actual studies show a correlation between these two measures such that students who do well on the SAT tend to have higher GPA's, whereas those with lower SAT scores tend to have lower GPA's.

The horizontal axis of Figure 1.1 shows SAT score values ranging from 200 to 800. The vertical axis shows GPA values ranging from 0 to 4. Each point on the scatter plot represents

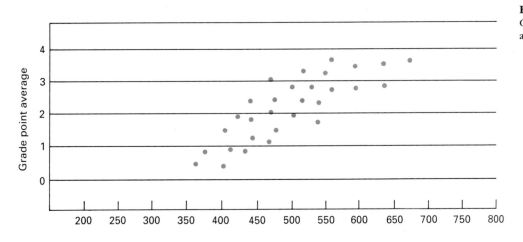

Figure 1.1
Correlation Between SAT Scores and Grade Point Averages.

the SAT score and GPA for one student. For example, there is a point for a student who had a SAT score of 550 and a GPA of 3.2. The scatter plot shows that students with higher SAT scores generally have higher GPA's.

This relationship is known as a *positive correlation*, meaning that high values for one variable (SAT) are associated with high values for the other (GPA). In a *negative correlation,* high values for one variable are associated with low values for the other. For example, people who score high on a measure of interest in money and practical affairs tend to score low on a measure of interest in sharing and giving to others (Allport, Vernon, & Lindzey, 1960).

A second method of examining the correlation between two variables is to compute a statistic known as a *correlation coefficient*. A **correlation coefficient** is a number that expresses the degree and direction of relationship between two variables. Correlation coefficients can take on any value between −1.0 and +1.0, depending on the degree of relationship between the variables and the direction, either positive or negative. The correlation coefficient is 0 when there is no relationship between the variables, as is undoubtedly the case for the correlation between shoe size and GPA, for example. The correlation coefficient is +1.0 when there is a perfect positive relationship between the variables. It is −1.0 when there is a perfect negative relationship between the variables. Correlation coefficients between 0 and +.30 or 0 and −.30 indicate *weak* positive or negative relationships between two variables. Coefficients between +.30 and +.70 or −.30 and −.70 indicate *moderate* positive or negative relationships, and coefficients between +.70 and +1.0 or −.70 and −1.0 indicate *strong* positive or negative relationships. The correlation coefficient for the data in Figure 1.1 is +.68.

INTERPRETING CORRELATIONAL STUDIES
In one particularly interesting correlational study, the researcher was interested in examining the deterrent effects of capital punishment (Ehrlich, 1975). First he considered the severity of punishment for various crimes in each state and then checked FBI data to see how often those crimes were committed in the different states. Sophisticated correlational analyses showed that the more severe the punishments for various crimes, the less frequently the crimes were committed. The researcher concluded that severe punishment, including the death penalty, can deter crime. As we shall see in a moment, however, this conclusion may not be justified.

Correlational studies give extremely important information about the relationship between two variables in the real world. However, correlational studies have one serious limitation. Simply because two variables are related or associated does not mean that one *causes* the other; it means only that they occur together. For instance, although variable A may cause variable B, it is also possible that the causal relationship between the two variables is the reverse. Consider the conclusion that harsh punishment is a deterrent to crime. Such a conclusion cannot be drawn from the data. Why not? Is there a reasonable alternative explanation for the correlation? There might be. Research in social psychology suggests that if a certain crime is uncommon in an area, judges and juries view it as particularly offensive. Thus they treat defendants who commit rare crimes harshly. Perhaps the rarity of a crime actually causes it to be severely punished. Does this severe punishment deter future crime? We can't tell from correlational data. Only an experiment, perhaps using mock juries and fictional crimes, could inform us about cause and effect.

Another possible explanation for the correlation between any two variables, A and B, is that a third variable, C, is the cause of both A and B. For example, research has shown a correlation between being authoritarian, dogmatic, and rigid and being prejudiced against minorities (Adorno, Frenkel-Brunswik, Levinson, & Sanford, 1950). Some researchers have taken this correlation as evidence that having an authoritarian personality causes people to be prejudiced. However, it is also possible that certain social class norms produce both authoritarian behavior patterns and ethnic prejudice. Again, it is impossible to tell by knowing only the correlation (Brown, 1965).

Experimentation

An **experiment** is a procedure in which a scientist treats an object of study in a specific way and then observes the effects of the treatment. The two key elements, then, are *treatment* and *observation* of the effects of the treatment. A chemist may heat a mixture to see if it changes. A biologist may inject a drug into a muscle to see if it paralyzes movement.

In psychology, experiments are performed on animals and humans. Let's consider two specific examples. The first experiment was conducted in the natural environment, or "in the field;" the second was conducted in the laboratory. The field experiment was conducted by psychologists Verlin Hinsz and Judith Tomhave, who were interested in the effects of one person's smiling or frowning on the facial expressions of another person. Is it true that when you smile "the world smiles with you," but that when you frown, you frown alone? Hinsz and Tomhave trained college students to smile, frown, or display a neutral expression as they walked past other individuals in public places such as shopping centers, grocery stores, libraries, and sidewalks. Walking five feet behind the college student was an observer who recorded the response of the individual who was smiled or frowned at. Smiling elicits smiling in return. Over half the passersby smiled when they were smiled at, compared to slightly more than one fifth when the student displayed a neutral expression. On the other hand, people do not return a frown with a frown of their own. Four percent of passersby frowned in response to a neutral ex-

pression, and that number increased to only 7 percent when the students frowned. There is an interesting implication of this study. Since people often experience positive emotions when they are smiling, smiling at other people has the potential to make them smile and then to feel good as a result (Hinz & Tomhave, 1991).

The laboratory experiment we want to consider was conducted by psychologists Robert Liebert and Robert Baron, who were interested in the effects of observing violence on children's aggressive behavior (see **Table 1.2**). Using two similar groups of children, they showed individual children from one group a segment of a violent television program, "The Untouchables." Children from the other group watched a program of nonviolent athletic competition, including races and jumps. Afterward, the children from both groups were observed playing in a room. Aggression was operationally defined as the number of 10-second time intervals during which a child played with aggressive toys (a gun or knife) or assaulted an inflated doll. According to this definition, children from the group who watched "The

Table 1.2   The Elements of an Experiment: An Illustration of Liebert and Baron's (1972) Study "Some Effects of Televised Violence on Children"

Form an Hypothesis	Classify Variables	Create Operational Definitions	Assign Subjects	Conduct Study and Collect Data
The experiments form a hypothesis, a proposition about the cause-and-effect relationships between variables	The experimenters determine the independent variables, the ones that are varied or manipulated, by the experimenters, and the dependent variables, the ones that are affected by manipulation of the independent variable.	The experimenters create operational definitions for key elements and variables in the experiment.	Some subjects are randomly assigned to the experimental group, the group exposed to the independent variable. Other subjects are randomly assigned to the control group, the group not exposed to the independent variable.	The experimenters measure the dependent variable, the number of aggressive play responses in the experimental and the control groups.
Subjects who view violence on television will behave more aggressively than those who view nonviolence.	The independent variable is the episode of the violent television program "The Untouchables" shown to subjects.	Televised violence is defined as the episode of "The Untouchables" shown to subjects.	Experimental Group: Subjects watch a violent television show ("The Untouchables")	Experimental Group: 4.63 aggressive responses in specified time period.
	The dependent variable is children's aggressive behavior.	Aggression is defined as the number of time intervals during which a child plays with a specific toy.	Control Group: Subjects watch a non-violent television show (a track meet)	Control Group: 3.55 aggressive responses in specified time period.

Untouchables" behaved more aggressively than children from the other group (Liebert & Baron, 1972).

One key element of experimentation that is well illustrated in this study is that an experiment allows a scientist to identify cause and effect. Liebert and Baron's experiment shows a relationship between observing violence on television and behaving aggressively. There is no ambiguity about what caused what. Aggressive behavior did not cause watching of televised violence, nor did some third factor cause both the behavior and the viewing. The experimental procedure, assigning some children to watch the violent program and others to watch the nonviolent one, required—or caused—particular children to observe violence. Watching that violent program led them to be more aggressive. Using this experiment as an example, let's look more closely at exactly what is involved in experimentation.

HYPOTHESES

An **hypothesis** in psychology is a proposition about behavior or mental processes that is subject to empirical testing. In experiments, an hypothesis is a proposition about cause-and-effect relationships. The goal of an experiment is to test an hypothesis. For example, Liebert and Baron's hypothesis was that observing televised violence would lead children to behave violently or aggressively.

INDEPENDENT AND DEPENDENT VARIABLES

In any situation of interest to psychologists there are important variables that need to be identified. A **variable** is any element in the situation that can vary or change from one time or individual to another. For example, in regard to the issue of TV violence and aggression, the amount of violence observed is one variable and the number of aggressive behaviors is another. There are potentially numerous others: the characteristics of the people studied, the specific setting in which they are studied, the manner of the experimenter, and so on. Can you think of any other variables in this study?

In experiments there are two distinct and important kinds of variables—independent variables and dependent variables. **Independent variables** are ones that are varied, or manipulated, by the experimenter. They are variables that are hypothesized to cause changes in a dependent variable. In the aggression example, the only independent variable was whether violence was portrayed in the television program shown to the children. **Dependent variables**

are the ones that are theoretically affected by the independent variables. They are *measured* by the experimenter. In the example we have been discussing, the dependent variable was the children's aggressive behavior. Both independent and dependent variables must be operationalized. Televised violence was operationally defined as the episode of "The Untouchables" shown to the subjects. Aggression, as noted earlier, was operationally defined as the number of time intervals during which the children played with specific toys. In any experiment it is critical to control—that is, hold constant—all elements of the experiment other than the independent variables. For example, in the aggression experiment the manner of the experimenter, the background of the children studied, the setting in which the study was conducted, and so forth were held constant. These factors were potential variables, but all of them were held constant so that they would not change from subject to subject. The only element that changed was the television program shown to the children. Because the other factors were held constant, the experimenters were able to conclude that the one factor that did vary, the television program itself, was responsible for the differences in the dependent variable, aggressive behavior, that were observed between the two groups of subjects. Thus, the independent variable was shown to cause the change in the dependent variable.

COMPARISON OF DATA

Experiments always involve some kind of comparison. Generally, the comparison is made between a control group and an experimental group or groups. The **control group** is made up of subjects who are not exposed to the independent variable being studied. The **experimental group** is made up of subjects who are exposed to the independent variable. For example, in the study on violent television programs and aggressive behavior, the control group was the one that was not exposed to the violent television program. The experimental group was the group that saw the violent program. Afterward, the behavior of the two groups during play was compared.

RANDOM ASSIGNMENT

Many experiments are complex and call for sophisticated statistical techniques to compare the effects of different treatments. However, in all experiments involving one or more experimental groups and a control group, the most important procedure is the random assignment of subjects to groups. **Random assignment** involves using a procedure such as flipping a coin or following a computer-generated list of random numbers to assign individual subjects to groups by chance so that each subject has an equal chance of being in any group in the experiment. For example, in their study of aggression, Liebert and Baron needed to assign children randomly to either the nonviolent program or "The Untouchables." Random assignment is usually the best way to ensure that all groups in the experiment are the same to begin with. If they were different from the start, no meaningful conclusions could be drawn from comparing the behavior of the two groups. In general, if groups of subjects are randomly assigned we can assume that each group is representative of all the people who are participating in the experiment and that all of the groups are similar to one another. Therefore, we can conclude that differences in the behavior of individuals in each group are due to the different conditions that they encountered in the experiment, not differences between them that already existed.

ADVANTAGES AND POTENTIAL PROBLEMS

Conducting a sound experiment is not easy. Various problems must be overcome to ensure that the conclusions drawn from the experiment are correct. One problem is that independent variables sometimes have unanticipated effects. For example, in the aggression experiment we have been discussing, children watching "The Untouchables" might be aroused by the action in the program. Perhaps their aggressive behavior should be attributed to being aroused rather than to having observed violence. However, this potential alternative explanation seems to have been ruled out. Children in the control group also watched an arousing program. Therefore, arousal was controlled and made equivalent in both the experimental group and the control group. If arousal had not been controlled, that is, if there had been more arousal in the experimental condition than in the control condition, we would have to say that arousal was *confounded* with, that is, mixed in with, observed violence, and we couldn't make any valid inferences about the effects of watching violence on children's aggression.

Ruling out all the confounds in an experiment can be difficult. However, if these problems are overcome we can say that the experiment has *internal validity*. This means that the

Are children more aggressive after watching a television show because of violence in the program or because they are simply aroused by watching television? An experiment to measure the effect of violent television would have to control for arousal.

experiment itself was sound and competently designed and conducted. If an experiment has internal validity, we are able to draw conclusions about causal relationships. Being able to understand causal relations is the main advantage that conducting experiments offers.

Perhaps the most difficult potential problem in experimentation is the problem of *external validity* or generalizability. How can we be sure how far we can generalize the results of any one study? For example, in the study on violence and aggression, we could not be sure that the results applied to all kinds of televised violence, including, for instance, cartoons. We could also not be sure that the results applied to children of all ages or to children in all kinds of communities. Only more research could solve this problem. For example, in another experiment the researchers might compare the effects of violence in live-action television shows to the effects of violence in televised cartoons.

Psychological knowledge is built bit by bit. Each experiment adds a little more to our store of information but is not sufficient in itself to establish sweeping generalizations.

The Multimethod Approach to Psychological Issues

When an issue under study is as important as the effects of television violence, it is often wise to use more than one method. Indeed, the issue of television violence is approached in many ways. First, parents answer surveys on

Many methods of investigation are necessary to answer a question such as the effects of violent television on children's behavior. For example, children may be observed in a playground, parents may be asked to complete surveys about their children's behavior, and subjects may be monitored over a long period of time to see if watching violent television programs affects behavior into adulthood.

the programs their children watch and how their children behave. The surveys also include questions on the family's background and attitudes. Correlational analyses of these surveys are made to see if a relationship exists between watching television violence and aggression and, if so, how general the relationship is. Some of these correlational studies have been *longitudinal* in design; that is, the same subjects have been observed over long time intervals, sometimes more than 10 years, to see if children who watch violent television at an early age behave aggressively as adolescents or young adults. Naturalistic observation is used to see how different children actually behave in the schoolyard, in their neighborhoods, and in their homes. In short, many different methods are used to investigate many aspects of the problem. Together they provide a more complete picture of the relationship among variables.

Interim Summary

Psychologists use many methods. For some problems, more than one method of study must be used. Naturalistic observation is a

method in which animals or people are observed in their natural habitat without interruption. The case study is a biographical account of a person's life and is used to generate hypotheses. Surveys are questionnaires administered to samples of people that ask about their attitudes or behavior. Correlational studies consider the relationship between two or more variables. They can show association but not causality.

Experiments treat objects of study and observe the effects of the treatment. They use both independent variables, or variables manipulated by the experimenter, and dependent variables, or variables measured by the experimenter. Independent variables are hypothesized to cause changes in dependent variables. An experiment is the only method that allows a psychologist to identify a cause-and-effect relationship.

THE ORIGINS OF A SCIENCE

The study of behavior and mental processes has not always been conducted scientifically. The background and development of modern psychology have clear roots in the humanities as well as the sciences. Psychology is actually a hybrid science, resulting from the combination of philosophy, with its questions about human nature, and physiology, the branch of biology that studies living organisms. We will review briefly the central ideas of these two fields, the work of the two men who launched the new science of psychology, and the development of psychology in America.

The Roots of Psychology

Philosophy and physiology are ancient fields of study. Philosophy is often traced to the Greek philosopher Socrates (470–399 B.C.). Socrates and his followers, such as Plato and Aristotle, struggled with questions about human nature. Are people inherently good or evil? Are they rational or irrational? Can they perceive reality correctly? What is consciousness, and how does it work? How do people think, reason, and plan? How do they create? Are humans truly capable of free choice, or is all action determined by forces in the environment?

These and other questions are still widely debated by philosophers. How one answers them depends, in part, on assumptions about

Psychology in the News

HEY, I'M TERRIFIC!

By Jerry Adler with Pat Wingert in Washington, Lynda Wright in Los Angeles, Patrick Houston in Minneapolis, Howard Manly in Atlanta, Alden D. Cohen in New York and bureau reports

If you're like most Americans, chances are you never thought you were at risk for low self-esteem. Sure, you felt bad at your kids' school's Career Day when you were the only parent who didn't own his own company. But unless your family psychometrician has administered a Coopersmith Self-Esteem Inventory or the Kaplan Self-Derogation Scale you probably never imagined that a negative self-image might be holding you back in life. You just thought you were no good.

But now you know that there are no bad people, only people who think badly of themselves. You know that "if you really joyfully accept yourself . . . nothing can make you unhappy," in the words of Father John Powell, a specialist in "psychotheology" at Loyola University of Chicago. You know that even famous, successful people like writer Gloria Steinem ("Revolution From Within: A Book of Self-Esteem") have to battle "inner feelings of incompleteness, emptiness, self-doubt and self-hatred." Negative thoughts afflict even paragons of achievement like athlete Michael Jordan, author of this poignant confession in the "self-esteem corner" of the Children's Museum of Denver: "I wish I came in first more often." Ordinary people obviously wish the same thing for themselves. Although only one in 10 Americans believes he personally suffers from low self-esteem, according to a NEWSWEEK Gallup Poll, more than 50 percent diagnose the condition in someone else in their families. And, of course, deviant behavior is prima facie evidence of self-image problems, as in the case of a man being sought in Montgomery County Md., for a series of rapes. Citizens have been warned by police to be on the lookout for a man in his 30s with a medium build and "low self-esteem."

As a concept, self-esteem can be traced to Freud, who used the term ego ideal. Shame, the emotional expression of low self-esteem, has been a hot topic among therapists in recent years, and is the subject of a new book ("Shame: The Exposed Self") by a prominent developmental psychologist, Michael Lewis. But as a paradigm for analyzing almost every problem in American society, self-esteem is clearly a product of today's relentless search for ever more fundamental and unifying laws of nature. Self-esteem is the quark of social science, a way to make sense of the wildly proliferating addictions, dependencies and 12-step programs jostling for air time on "Donahue." Low self-esteem is a meta-addiction, a state that seems to underlie afflictions as diverse as bulimia and performance anxiety. "People saw that self-esteem was a component of so many other things—teenage pregnancies, drop-outs, drugs, school success—and they were hoping we'd found one solution to many problems," says psychoanalyst Nancy E. Curry of the University of Pittsburgh. People always hope that; it's what keeps publishers going, not to speak of religions.

As the distinction between therapy and the rest of American life has eroded, the concept of self-esteem has established itself in almost every area of society. The bulletin of The National Council for Self-Esteem, Self-Esteem Today, lists 10 national and regional conferences this year aimed at extirpating negative self-images from society. Most people, thanks to "Doonesbury," know that California appointed a state commission to promote self-esteem. But the idea is also very big in places like Minnesota (home of the "Very Important Kid" program for "encouraging self-esteem in 3-6 year olds") and in Maryland, where a state task force counted more than 1,000 ways in which citizens were already working to improve the self-esteem of their fellow students, government workers, business executives and cellmates. An outfit called High Self-Esteem Toys Corp. has brought out a fashion doll named Happy To Be Me, whose scale measurements of 36-27-38 are intended to represent a more realistic ambition for a human being than Barbie's exotic mannequin's figure, with its 18-inch waist and 33-inch hips.

As a theory of behavior, self-esteem has intuition on its side, if not necessarily a monopoly on convincing research. It seems to make sense that people who have a low opinion of themselves are more likely to seek momentary pleasures in drugs or sex. Many criminologists believe that delinquency results from youth with low self-esteem trying to show off—a "performance for an audience," in the words of Martin Gold of the University of Michigan's Institute for Social Research. Inevitably, the evidence for this tends to be somewhat anecdotal. The best anecdote is Lewis's account of adolescent boys in a reform school who would punch the offender in the face when one of them passed gas. But does it necessarily follow that "people with low self-esteem confuse being in the presence of someone who farts with the different situation of actually being farted upon"? And what should the nation do about it, anyway?

As a general prescription for child-rearing, self-esteem is unassailable. To develop it, says child psychiatrist Dr. Stanley Greenspan, children need "a constant and loving caregiver . . . a fundamental sense of safety and security." Who could be against that? "A sense of self, grounded in a sense of personal competence and supported by people who think I am a valuable and worthy person, is a requisite for productive learning to occur," says Linda Darling-Hammond, a professor of education at Columbia Teachers College. That also seems intuitively obvious to most Americans today—although 70 years ago it was equally obvious to many educators that schools had to break down children's "sense of self," the better to fill their heads with facts.

But what is it? Like most things that are intuitively obvious, though, self-esteem can be hard to demonstrate empirically. A recent survey of the literature estimated that more than 10,000 scientific studies of self-esteem have been conducted. Researchers have measured it with more than 200 different tests. (Typically, respondents are asked to agree or disagree with statements such as, "On the whole I am satisfied with myself.") There isn't even agreement on what it is. Greenspan defines it, tautologically enough, as "the innermost sense of self-worth and value." "I think of it as related to three things: confidence, competence and relationships," says Rutgers University psychologist Maurice Elias, clarifying matters only somewhat. Even the National Council has been unable to agree on

a single definition, according to executive director LeRoy Foster, after polling 100 teachers and coming up with "27 distinctly different answers."

Self-esteem is a common prescription for African-American youth, who bear the particular burden of a heritage of racial prejudice. "The decks are really stacked against some minorities," says Dr. Alan Stoudemire, a psychiatrist at the Emory Clinic in Atlanta. "They receive powerful messages from family or teachers or society that they are not as good as everyone else." In the absence of real solutions to this problem, slogans and exhortations are being tried instead. Jesse Jackson's famous chant distills the philosophy of self-esteem to its minimalist essence: "I am . . . Somebody!" Others are a trifle more specific. When Jacqueline Ponder, the principal of Atlanta's East Lake Elementary School, noticed that the boys in her classrooms were neglecting to carry books and hold doors for their teachers, she diagnosed the problem as low self-esteem and prescribed a motto: "I Am a Noble African-American Boy!" "Once they have their self-esteem," Ponder asserts, "they don't need anything else. They *are*. And all they have to do is develop that which they are."

The man most responsible for putting self-esteem on the national agenda is not a clergyman or philosopher, but a California state assemblyman named John Vasconcellos, Democrat from San Jose. In his own life Vasconcellos, 59, is a walking advertisement for the importance of self-esteem. He was raised by strict, attentive parents who set high standards for him. This is one of the biggest risk factors for self- esteem problems, next to lax, indifferent parents who don't demand enough. He was college valedictorian, a successful lawyer and politician. Overachievement is a very common sign of low self-es-

teem, next to underachievement. Yet he was also a troubled legislator, going for three years without cutting his hair and engaging in hostile outbursts against colleagues. Self-esteem problems often contribute to aggression, except when they result in passivity.

The big picture: Psychotherapy helped Vasconcellos correct his own self-esteem shortfall. Then one day in 1983 he stumbled on a theory linking teen pregnancy with low self-esteem. "All of a sudden, the pattern just loomed large," Vasconcellos said. "Maybe violence, drug addiction, crime and other problems were also a product of the same thing."

Eager to share this insight, Vasconcellos helped create a state task force on "self-esteem and personal and social responsibility." Its conclusion—that "lack of self-esteem is central to most personal and social ills plaguing our state and nation"—has inspired five states and nearly all 58 California counties to set up self-esteem task forces. Several groups are urging national legislation. This is a remarkable instance of adopting as a goal of public policy something that is quintessentially private and introspective. It is one thing for the state to discourage welfare dependency, for instance, by requiring recipients to get jobs. It is a big—and thus far unexamined—step for the state to try to do the same thing by tinkering directly with citizens' psyches.

And if it does, it ought at least to be sure it knows what it's doing. Most of what people believe about the public-policy implications of self-esteem come from the task-force report, "Toward a State of Esteem." The report's "key finding" was that "self-esteem is the likeliest candidate for a *social vaccine* [emphasis in original], something that empowers us to live responsibly and that inoculates us against the lures of crime, violence, substance abuse, teen pregnancy, child abuse, chronic welfare dependency and educational failure."

A lot less attention has been paid to the scientific papers prepared for the task force, which were published separately as "The Social Importance of Self-Esteem." Can self-esteem cut drug abuse? The scientists concluded that "there is a paucity of good research, especially studies that could link the abuse of alcohol and drugs with self-esteem." Is it implicated in child abuse? "There is insufficient evidence to support the belief in a direct relation between low self-esteem and child abuse." Crime and violence? "Self-esteem may be positively *or*

negatively correlated with aggression." Teen pregnancy? Somewhat embarrassingly, two studies linked *high* self-esteem with increased sexual activity by teens. But there was evidence that girls with high self-esteem were more likely to use contraceptives. Admitting the findings were inconclusive, the authors went on to write that "our approach is to make the strongest case possible, given the research, for the existence of a causal link between self-esteem and teenage pregnancy. We conclude, therefore, that low self-esteem does contribute to the risk of an adolescent pregnancy."

That does seem a remarkable ad-

mission in an academic paper, and at least one of the task-force members refused to sign the final report in part because of the gap between the research results and the report's sweeping conclusions. Vasconcellos regards this as pettifoggery. Such criticism comes from "those who only live in their heads, in the intellectual." The research, he says, did what it was supposed to do; it "confirms our intuitive knowledge."

Questions

1. What does this article suggest about the increasing importance of psychological concepts in modern life?
2. Why is it important to develop good measures of self-esteem?
3. What does the research on self-esteem suggest about the importance of testing hypotheses with empirical data?
4. Does society always take the results of psychological research as seriously as it should?

---

human nature. These assumptions also underlie different perspectives on psychology. However, psychologists have attempted to go beyond these philosophical questions to study specifically when people behave in helpful, altruistic, and caring ways; how they are rational and irrational; and how much of their behavior is controlled versus how much is freely chosen. At the same time, psychologists push forward by trying to discover what can be known through the scientific analysis of other specific behaviors and events.

Physiology is as old as philosophy. The Greek physician Hippocrates (circa 460-377 B.C.), who lived at the same time as Socrates, is often referred to as the father of medicine. Hippocrates studied the workings of the body extensively and can therefore be considered the first physiologist. Like today's physiologists, Hippocrates was curious about human anatomy, the functioning of human organs, and biological systems. He anticipated today's biopsychologists by considering the relationship between the body and mind. He learned from his

observations that the brain was the most powerful organ of the human body because it controlled other organs and parts of the body including the eyes, ears, tongue, hands, and feet. He also saw the brain as the "interpreter of consciousness."

It was not until the nineteenth century, however, that researchers developed the techniques and methods needed to explore systematically the workings of the human body. One physiologist whose work was highly influential was Hermann von Helmholtz (1821-1894). A pioneering neural scientist, Helmholtz conducted groundbreaking research on the nervous system and on key aspects of vision, hearing, and perception. His breakthroughs contributed much to our knowledge of how humans take in information about the external world, a question that had puzzled philosophers for centuries.

Given the common interests of philosophers and physiologists, it should be no surprise that many of the early psychologists were both philosophers and physiologists.

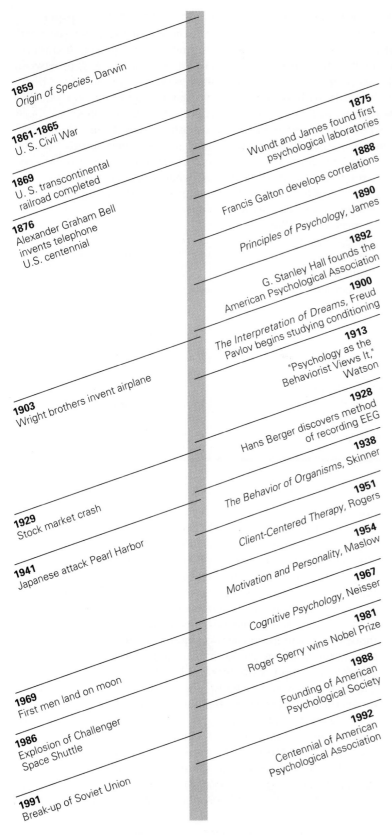

1859
Origin of Species, Darwin

1861-1865
U.S. Civil War

1869
U.S. transcontinental
railroad completed

1876
Alexander Graham Bell
invents telephone
U.S. centennial

1903
Wright brothers invent airplane

1929
Stock market crash

1941
Japanese attack Pearl Harbor

1969
First men land on moon

1986
Explosion of Challenger
Space Shuttle

1991
Break-up of Soviet Union

1875
Wundt and James found first
psychological laboratories

1888
Francis Galton develops correlations

1890
Principles of Psychology, James

1892
G. Stanley Hall founds the
American Psychological Association

1900
The Interpretation of Dreams, Freud
Pavlov begins studying conditioning

1913
"Psychology as the
Behaviorist Views It,"
Watson

1928
Hans Berger discovers method
of recording EEG

1938
The Behavior of Organisms, Skinner

1951
Client-Centered Therapy, Rogers

1954
Motivation and Personality, Maslow

1967
Cognitive Psychology, Neisser

1981
Roger Sperry wins Nobel Prize

1988
Founding of American
Psychological Society

1992
Centennial of American
Psychological Association

Figure 1.2
Major Milestones in the History of Psychology.

The Emergence of Psychology: 1875–1900

Wilhelm Wundt and William James are usually credited with founding psychology, independently, in 1875 (**Figure 1.2**). A quarter of a century later, in 1900, two other milestones in the history of psychology were passed: the Russian physiologist Ivan Pavlov began to study the learning phenomenon that came to be known as conditioning, and Sigmund Freud published his great work, *The Interpretation of Dreams.* In the 25 years between 1875 and 1900, psychology came into its own. In this section we will consider the lives and work of the founders, Wundt and James. Later in this chapter we will discuss the tremendously important contributions of Pavlov and Freud. Wilhelm Wundt was born in a small village in western Germany in 1832. A studious child, he began to study medicine as a young man, probably with the intention of becoming a scientist rather than a practicing physician. He was an active scholar and published extensively in both philosophy and physiology. At one point he was a student of Helmholtz. His main interest, however, was the branch of philosophy that dealt with psychological questions such as perception, attention, and feeling. In 1874 he wrote the first of six editions of *Principles of Physiological Psychology.* Then, in 1875, he became professor of philosophy at Leipzig and immediately opened one of the world's first two laboratories for psychological research.*

*There is some controversy about the exact date of the founding of Wundt's laboratory. The year 1879 is sometimes cited. The laboratory was first used in 1875, although it was not formally established until 1879.

Wilhelm Wundt (center) in his laboratory.

Within a few years he attracted many students from Europe and America to study with him. He was a popular lecturer with a talent for simplifying his material in order to make it interesting and clear to his audience (R. I. Watson, 1963). By 1881 he had established a psychological journal, which attracted even more students to an interest in psychology.

Wundt is most famous for his interest in **introspection,** a method of studying consciousness in which subjects report on their subjective experiences. Introspection involves long and difficult training. People were taught to achieve a state of "strained attention," in which they could closely examine their own conscious experience and report the smallest possible elements of awareness. The goal of introspection was to learn about the basic building blocks of experience and the principles by which they combined to give us our everyday consciousness. Although introspection was not used by many psychologists after Wundt, it helped him achieve his goal, to "work out a new domain of science." A man of many interests and abilities, Wundt was first and foremost a psychologist.

In 1875, the same year that Wundt opened his laboratory in Leipzig, William James founded psychology in North America at Harvard University. James, the brother of the noted novelist Henry James, was a physiologist, physician, and philosopher whose work touched on every area of psychology.

James was born in 1842. After finishing medical school he took a teaching appointment at Harvard. In 1875 he gave his first course in psychology, noting that the first lecture he ever heard on psychology was his own (R. I. Watson, 1963). He set up a psychological laboratory that same year. In 1889 his title was changed from professor of philosophy to professor of psychology. The next year he published his landmark two-volume text, *Principles of Psychology.* This work remains a highly readable classic with chapters on nearly every psychological topic ranging from vision and the brain to the self and will. It is interesting to note that in his later philosophical writings, James distinguished between individuals who were "tough-minded," or scientific, and those who were "tender-minded," or philosophical. Henry James' work in psychology was both.

PSYCHOLOGY IN AMERICA—YESTERDAY AND TODAY

Every new discipline needs an organizer to give it life and viability. In America, psychology's organizer was G. Stanley Hall. Hall was born in western Massachusetts in 1844 and graduated from Williams College in 1867. A scholar, he taught English literature at Harvard and became interested in psychology. He studied with James and others and took a Ph.D. at Harvard in 1878 in the new discipline of psychology—the first psychology Ph.D. in the country. After completing his degree, Hall went to Europe and became Wilhelm Wundt's first American student. He also studied with Helmholtz. On his return to the United States he taught at Johns Hopkins University and in 1887 founded the *American Journal of Psychology,* the first psychological journal in the United States. In 1892 he organized the American Psychological Association and was elected its first president. While Hall conducted important studies in the areas of childhood and adolescence, he also continued as an able and bold educational organizer and administrator. He became president of Clark University in Worcester, Massachusetts, and in 1909 arranged for Sigmund Freud's only visit to the United States. Freud and other students of his psychoanalytic viewpoint, including Carl Jung, visited Clark that year and lectured on their work to an American audience.

Hall's organization, the American Psychological Association, (APA), has just passed its 100th birthday. It has become a massive and diverse society. Not surprisingly, it has experi-

William James (1842–1910)

Sigmund Freud, G. Stanley Hall, and Carl Jung (front row, left to right) at Clark University in September, 1909.

Table 1.3   **Divisions of the American Psychological Association**

APA Division Number	APA Division Name
1	Division of General Psychology
2	Division on the Teaching of Psychology
3	Division of Experimental Psychology
5	Division of Evaluation and Measurement
6	Division of Physiological and Comparative Psychology
7	Division on Developmental Psychology
8	The Society of Personality and Social Psychology
9	The Society for the Psychological Study of Social Issues
10	Division of Psychology and the Arts
12	Division of Clinical Psychology
13	Division of Consulting Psychology
14	The Society for Industrial and Organizational Psychology, Inc.
15	Division of Educational Psychology
16	Division of School Psychology
17	Division of Counseling Psychology
18	Division of Psychologists in Public Service
19	Division of Military Psychology
20	Division of Adult Development and Aging
21	Division of Applied Experimental and Engineering Psychologists
22	Division of Rehabilitation Psychology
23	Division of Consumer Psychology
24	Division of Theoretical and Philosophical Psychology
25	Division for the Experimental Analysis of Behavior
26	Division of the History of Psychology
27	Division of Community Psychology
28	Division of Psychopharmacology
29	Division of Psychotherapy
30	Division of Psychological Hypnosis
31	Division of State Psychological Association Affairs
32	Division of Humanistic Psychology
33	Division of Mental Retardation
34	Division of Population and Environmental Psychology
35	Division of Psychology of Women
36	Psychologists Interested in Religious Issues (PIRI)
37	Division of Child, Youth, and Family Services
38	Division of Health Psychology
39	Division of Psychoanalysis
40	Division of Clinical Neuropsychology
41	Division of Psychology and Law
42	Division of Psychologists in Independent Practice
43	Division of Family Psychology
44	The Society for the Psychological Study of Lesbian and Gay Issues
45	Society for the Psychological Study of Ethnic Minority Issues
46	Division of Media Psychology
47	Division of Exercise and Sport Psychology
48	Peace Psychology

(*Note:* There are no Divisions 4 or 11.)

After APA (1991)

enced some growing pains. The APA has struggled to represent fairly the interests of its two biggest subgroups, practitioners and scholars. Practitioners are involved in applying psychological knowledge, usually as therapists helping people with personal problems and psychological disorders. Scholars include professors, researchers, and teachers, many of them involved in trying to find answers to basic psychological questions and discovering new applications of psychology. Although the APA was founded by scholars, practitioners have become more numerous and, within the past 25 years, more influential. As a result, in 1988, a new organization, the American Psychological Society (APS), was founded to advance psychological knowledge and research and "to encourage the 'giving away' of psychology in the public interest." In 1990 it published the first issue of its journal, *Psychological Science*.

Despite the importance of the APS, APA remains the largest and most diverse organization in psychology. There are over 100,000 APA members, and there are 46 divisions or associated societies representing such fields as psychotherapy, physiological psychology, social psychology, psychology and the law, media psychology, the psychology of women, the study of ethnic minority issues, and, most recently, peace psychology. Clinical psychology is the largest division of the APA. Psychotherapy and counseling psychology are also among the largest divisions. These are the divisions that represent practitioners. Among the largest divisions for academicians and researchers are the divisions on experimental, developmental and personality, and social psychology (see **Table 1.3**).

Interim Summary

Psychology has its roots in both philosophy and physiology. The questions of psychology derive from philosophy. Psychology's concern with biological systems and the scientific method derives from physiology.

Wilhelm Wundt and William James both founded psychological laboratories, independently of each other, in 1875. They are regarded as the founders of psychology. G. Stanley Hall, founder of the American Psychological Association, is credited with organizing the study of psychology in the United States.

MAJOR PERSPECTIVES WITHIN PSYCHOLOGY

Psychology has come a long way in the century or so since the early efforts of Wundt, James, and Hall. But even today, psychologists have different philosophical perspectives on their work. They have different ideas about the nature of humanity, the nature of science, and the topics and methods that psychologists should emphasize. For example, some psychologists believe we should study only behavior and leave "the mind" to philosophers. Others think that we must study human experience and feeling even if these are more difficult to observe and measure than action and reaction. In this section we will introduce the major *perspectives* or schools of thought in the field of psychology.

As you look at each perspective individually, keep in mind that to a large degree the perspectives are related. Often the limitations of one perspective have led to the creation of another. Then, at a later time, interest in the older perspective is frequently rekindled. Also, no single perspective is considered dominant or correct. Many psychologists incorporate the views of several perspectives into their thinking. Some perspectives may be more useful at one time than at another, but they all have something important to offer. Think of each perspective as a special vantage point for studying the complex puzzle of behavior and mental processes.

The Neuroscience Perspective

As the name implies, **neuroscience** is really a combination of disciplines. It combines physiology, especially the physiology of the brain, with psychology, the study of mental processes and behavior, and draws as well from the field of chemistry. The underlying assumption of neuroscience is that for every behavior, feeling, and thought, a corresponding physical event takes place in the brain. The goal of neuroscience is to understand the relationship between these two realms.

What changes occur in the brain during learning? What happens to the chemistry of the brain in mental illness? How do drugs such as Valium act on the brain to produce their tranquilizing effect? What happens in the brain when a person commits a violent act? These are the kinds of questions neuroscientists address. Similarly, neuroscientists want to know

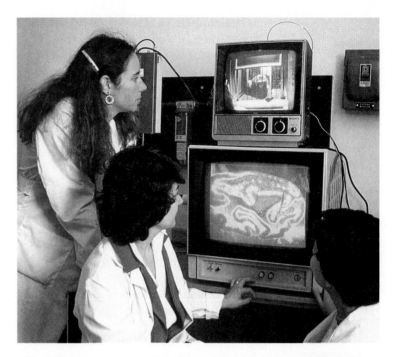

These neuroscientists are studying the metabolic activity of a monkey's brain.

why stimulation of certain areas of the brain causes rats who have just been fed to eat again, whereas surgery in other areas of the brain induces animals to starve to death even though food is available. They want to understand why certain brain operations cause previously aggressive monkeys to become tame and docile.

After Hippocrates, the study of the relationship between the brain on the one hand and behavior and consciousness on the other was largely ignored until the eighteenth century. This was partly due to religious dogma that insisted that the body was separate from the mind or soul. Since the eighteenth century, however, neuroscientists have once again pursued the remarkable insights of Hippocrates and have made dazzling discoveries about the functioning of the brain. Although much of their research has been conducted on animals, some of the most intriguing studies have involved surgery on the human brain, conducted in a daring effort to help patients with severe brain disorders.

In addition to operating on the brain in order to change behavior, neuroscientists study the changes that occur in the brain during certain behaviors. For example, they have identified electrical changes that occur in the brain during the learning process. They have also found that different patterns of electrical activity occur during relaxation, sleep, and waking. Still other researchers have found that certain drugs can control the symptoms of schizophrenia, suggesting that biochemical activity in the brain is related to schizophrenia. And in 1981 Roger Sperry was awarded the Nobel Prize for his work on the split brain. His research suggests that the two halves of the brain perform different functions.

To be sure, we are a long way from a complete understanding of the relationship of the brain to human behavior and mental processes. Indeed, the complexity of both the brain—with its billions of cells—and human behavior makes this a tall order. Nevertheless, the neuroscience perspective holds great promise for understanding behavior and perhaps bettering the human condition.

Freud argued that the highest achievements of civilization, including the arts, are motivated by sublimated drives.

The Psychodynamic Perspective

Sigmund Freud
(1856–1939)

The underlying assumption of **psychodynamic psychology** is that unconscious forces are important influences on human behavior. Although the psychodynamic perspective is made up of both Freudian and non-Freudian theories, it actually grew out of the work of Sigmund Freud and his followers, called neoFreudians. Freud's work is known as psychoanalytic theory (Freud, 1940/1964). *Psychoanalysis* is the term Freud used to describe his psychological theories and his method.

Freud's ideas are consistent with philosophical viewpoints that see human beings as irrational and motivated by biological drives, not all of which are noble. His central assumptions were that human beings are born with unconscious drives that seek some kind of outlet or expression from the very start. Many of the drives that young children have violate social conventions of proper behavior. For example, young children often enjoy smearing feces, masturbating, or hitting their playmates. Parents typically forbid these behaviors and punish their children for performing them. As a result of these restrictions, many innate drives are *repressed,* that is, pushed totally out of conscious awareness.

An important idea in psychoanalytic theory is that repressed drives continue to demand some kind of expression or satisfaction. Since they cannot be expressed in behavior or even admitted into consciousness, they are manifested indirectly. For example, Freud felt that

many drives for socially unacceptable behavior were *sublimated,* that is, channeled into some kind of approved or even highly praised behavior. He argued that the highest achievements of civilization, including painting, music, and architecture, were motivated by sublimated drives (Freud, 1930/1961). Thus, a young man's drive for a forbidden intimate relationship with his sister may lead him to marry a woman who closely resembles his sister. Similarly, dreams or slips in speech or memory may indirectly express repressed drives. For instance, sexual drives are often expressed in dreams. Hostile feelings may be expressed by forgetting a meeting with someone you do not like or whom you fear.

Freud was particularly interested in analyzing psychological disorders, and his writings stress the way parental treatment of children's behavior can lead to problems. At the same time, Freud was quite optimistic about the power of psychological treatment to relieve psychological disorders. His goal in treatment was to make the patient aware of his or her own unconscious feelings. In this way, patients would understand themselves better and would be freer to choose effective responses to the world they face.

Freud continued to refine and develop his theories throughout his lifetime. His ideas address human motivation, personality, personality development, psychological disorders, and methods of psychotherapy. Because his theories were based on the assumption that human nature is rooted in the unconscious, and some feel ignoble, drives, Freud's theories spurred much controversy.

The development of Freud's theories is itself an interesting story. As a young physician Freud became interested in patients with physical symptoms that seemed to have a psychological basis. One such patient was a woman called Anna O., whose symptoms included occasional paralysis of her limbs, nausea, and speech disturbances. Freud and a colleague, Josef Breuer, found that when Anna O. was under hypnosis she was able to speak much more freely about intense emotional experiences. The expression of these emotions seemed to provide a **catharsis,** that is, a cleansing or reduction of a feeling through the expression of that feeling, and led to a dramatic improvement in Anna O.'s physical symptoms.

Freud was fascinated with hypnosis and the "talking cure" and pursued it vigorously. He soon discovered an alternative to hypnosis— **free association,** a method in which the patient learns to discuss embarrassing or painful thoughts simply by reporting whatever comes to mind. Freud also found that it was useful to have patients free-associate about their dreams. Freud and the patient could then begin to unravel the tensions that were being expressed, often in disguised form, in these dreams.

Using the techniques of free association and dream analysis, Freud began to explore how forgotten or unexpressed emotional experiences might be related to patients' symptoms. He believed that critical problems for many patients were related to sex. Few people supported Freud in these ideas, but he continued developing them in his work with patients, then in his own self-analysis, for which he used his dreams as an important tool. In 1900, the same year that Pavlov began to study conditioning, Freud published his major work, *The Interpretation of Dreams.* In that book we see the origins of Freud's theories of human functioning, which would eventually fill 23 volumes. His theories not only have tremendous influence in psychology, they have influenced our culture as a whole. Because of Freud's influence, most educated people today believe that dreams reflect unconscious wishes, that slips of the tongue express hidden feelings, and that jokes betray hostile feelings. Similarly, we often assume that our feelings toward members of the opposite sex are related to our feelings about our mothers and fathers and that repressed childhood sexual feelings are responsible for sexual difficulties in adulthood. These ideas permeate our culture and strongly influence our interpretation of drama, literature, and the overall condition of society. They are a direct reflection of Freud's writings. In Part 4, when we consider personality, psychological disorders, and psychotherapy, we will discuss Freud's ideas in more detail. But throughout this text we will see many instances in which Freud's ideas have influenced the entire field of psychology.

The Behavioral Perspective

The behavioral perspective emerged in part as a reaction to Wundt's method of introspection. Behavioral psychologists felt that studying consciousness through introspection was too unscientific. The key assumption of **behavioral psychology** is that if psychology is to be a science, it must study only that which is observable, namely behavior. The followers of this perspective define psychology as the science of behavior and leave consciousness and other unobservable phenomena to the field of philosophy. Behavioral psychologists study behavioral responses and the way these responses are influenced by stimuli in the environment. In this section we shall consider some of the key people and ideas in the development of this perspective.

The behavioral perspective has its roots in the work that Ivan Pavlov began at the turn of the century. Pavlov was born in Russia in 1849, the son of a village priest. He was a promising student who studied animal physiology before attending medical school. Pavlov was, in his time, the most successful physiologist in Russia and made important advances in the study of digestion. His work on digestion was important enough to win him a Nobel Prize in 1904.

Ivan Pavlov
(1849–1936)

As we shall see in Chapter 6, Pavlov discovered one of the most important findings in the history of psychology quite by accident. Pavlov had implanted a tube in the salivary ducts of a dog in order to collect and measure saliva for a study on digestion. In order to stimulate such secretions, Pavlov gave meat powder to the dog. He soon discovered that the dog often began salivating *before* it actually received the meat powder. In fact, Pavlov noted that the dog would begin salivating when it heard Pavlov or his assistant walking down the hall toward the laboratory. Pavlov observed that the dog associated stimuli such as footsteps coming down the hall with the meat powder. By their association with meat powder, these other stimuli acquired the power to elicit salivation. Pavlov called this phenomenon the *conditioned reflex.*

At first Pavlov was unsure whether to pursue conditioned reflexes. He believed that an independent science of psychology was "completely hopeless," and he recognized that association and conditioning were psychological matters. However, in 1900 he decided to study conditioned reflexes for the remainder of his career, always holding that he was investigating the structure and physiology of the brain and simply using these unique responses as a tool.

A second important contribution to the behavioral perspective was the work of Edward Thorndike. Thorndike was one of William James' brightest students. In 1898, at the age of 24, Thorndike published a famous paper on learning in cats based on experiments he conducted in James' basement. Thorndike found that when certain behaviors were rewarded with food, the cats were more likely to repeat them in similar circumstances later on. Behaviors that were not rewarded were less likely to be repeated. On the basis of these findings Thorndike proposed the *law of effect,* which holds that when a behavior is followed by satisfaction it is "stamped in," and when it is not followed by satisfaction it is "stamped out." Thorndike's work dominated debate in the field of learning for half a century (Hilgard, 1956). The idea that the consequences of behavior, reward or punishment, are critical in determining future behavior remains vitally important today in the work of B. F. Skinner and other modern behavioral psychologists (see Chapter 6).

A third important figure in the development of the behavioral perspective was John B. Watson, a professor of psychology at Johns Hopkins University. Stimulated by the work of Pavlov and Thorndike, Watson launched in 1913 what is known today as **behaviorism,** a philosophy of psychological study which holds that only observable behavior is the proper subject for psychological investigation. In that year Watson published an article, "Psychology as the Behaviorist Views It," that revolutionized psychology and made him one of its most important figures. At that time the chief method for studying mental processes was introspection. Watson pointed out that Wundt's intro-

Edward L. Thorndike (1874–1949)

John B. Watson (1878–1958)

spective method had a serious flaw. When different people were asked to describe a certain conscious experience, they often disagreed. You can see this yourself by asking five different people what the conscious experience of happiness consists of. You are likely to get five different answers.

Watson's solution to this problem was simple and direct—banish the study of consciousness and the introspective method from psychology. Instead, define psychology as the study of behavior and of the ways in which humans and animals learn to adapt to their environments. Watson suggested that psychologists set up various environments in the laboratory and then observe how subjects react. In this way, both the environmental stimuli and the subjects' responses could be objectively described and measured. Instead of asking people to describe happiness, for example, the behaviorist might count the number of smiles or belly laughs while subjects watched an amusing film.

Watson felt that Pavlov's studies of conditioned reflexes and Thorndike's studies of learning in cats were both major successes of the behavioral method. By carefully controlling environmental stimuli, both scientists had shown how behavior could be modified in predictable ways. Behaviorism provided a method that made scientific psychology a possibility. Without it, psychology as a science might never have developed. In subsequent years, psychologists flocked to behaviorism's banner. Research on conditioning and learning flourished. Some psychologists developed elaborate theories of learning, while others applied behavioral methods to problems in education, child development, social psychology, and mental illness. We shall see many examples of these developments throughout the book.

The Humanistic Perspective

Just as the behavioral perspective developed as a reaction to introspectionism, so the humanistic perspective has developed over the last several decades as a reaction against perceived shortcomings in the psychoanalytic and behavioral perspectives. The argument is that these two perspectives have theoretical elegance and impressive explanatory power but that the *person* seems to get lost. Individuals are dissected into conditioned responses or unconscious drives, while the whole human being—his or her feelings, experiences, needs, and problems—seems to be pushed aside. This concern has given rise to a "third force," called **humanistic psychology,** which emphasizes the whole person and the importance of each person's subjective experience. Perhaps the central concept in humanistic psychology is the need for self-actualization. While recognizing that many motives affect behavior, humanistic psychologists believe the most important is the underlying need to develop our full potential. Freedom is another key concern in humanistic psychology. According to behavioral psychology, people's actions are determined by the external environment. In psychoanalysis, people are largely governed by unconscious, internal drives. Humanistic psychology rejects the emphasis on these internal and external determinants of action. Instead, it emphasizes the fact that people can choose and that, if society gives them more freedom, people will ably and gladly take responsibility for their own lives and make the best of them. Humanistic psychology also assumes that there is inner goodness in all human beings.

If it is true that people are inherently good, active, and responsible and if they really strive toward self-actualization, why are so many people aggressive, frightened, passive, and dissatisfied much of the time? Humanistic psychologists feel that the structure of society—its pressures and its restrictions—accounts for these problems. Consequently, people need help in discovering themselves and in starting on the path toward self-actualization. For this reason, many humanistic psychologists were active in the encounter group movement of the 1960s and early 1970s. An **encounter group** is a form of group interaction that emphasizes becoming aware of one's inner feelings and experience, taking responsibility for one's life, and pursuing life actively and productively. According to humanistic psychologists, honest communication and the sharing of feelings and experience in encounter groups facilitate the self-actualizing tendencies within each of us.

Two important figures in humanistic psychology are Abraham Maslow and Carl Rogers. Maslow is known for his comprehensive hierarchical theory of motivation. This theory emphasizes that basic motives such as the need for food, water, safety, and affection must be satisfied before people can develop their potentials (Maslow, 1954). Rogers (1961) has written ex-

tensively about how people can become themselves and how they can relate to others in helpful and constructive ways. We will study the ideas of Rogers and Maslow closely in Chapter 14.

The Cognitive Perspective

One of the newest trends in psychology is the intensive study of **cognition,** a broad term that refers to the ways we process or transform information about the world around us. Cognition includes the mental processes of thinking, knowing, perceiving, attending, remembering, and the like. The cognitive approach developed as a reaction to the behaviorists' exclusion of mental life and consciousness from their definition of psychology. It has its roots in Wundt's introspectionism and, before that, in Aristotle's ancient writings on images and experience. **Cognitive psychology** is the psychological perspective that is primarily concerned with mental processes or cognitions. Cognitive psychologists want to know how we organize, remember, and understand everything we experience. For example, how do we turn the small lines of ink on this page into meaningful sentences? How do we translate the sound waves produced by a friend into the complex questions and statements that are a part of adult conversations?

Cognitive psychologists view human beings as extremely active processors of information. Cognitive psychologist Ulric Neisser stated that "whatever we know about reality has been acted on . . . by complex systems which interpret and reinterpret sensory information" (Neisser, 1967). The goal of cognitive psychology is to specify the mental processes involved in this interpretation and reinterpretation. For example, in one important line of research, cognitive psychologists have used the computer to try to duplicate the features of human memory and problem solving (Kotovsky & Simon, 1973) in order to develop a model of how humans reason. To do this, researchers must produce a computer program that solves problems in the same sequence humans do.

How do cognitive psychologists study human behavior? Frequently they create small experimental tasks that allow them to determine how past experiences influence the way people think. For example, in one classic experiment subjects were given the objects pictured in **Figure 1.3:** a box of candles, a box of matches, some string, and some thumbtacks (Duncker,

Abraham Maslow

Figure 1.3
The Thumbtack Problem
This is a classic problem cognitive psychologists pose.
Mount the candle on the wall vertically, using any of the
objects in the picture.

Figure 1.4
The Solution.
Use the matchbox as a shelf.

1945). The subjects' task was to mount the candle on a wall vertically, using any of the objects they were provided with. Subjects typically had a difficult time solving this problem because they could not think of novel uses for the objects. One aspect that contributed to the task's difficulty was that the matches were presented in a box. This made subjects regard the box as a receptacle, rather than as a potentially important element in solving the problem. As you can see in **Figure 1.4,** using the matchbox as a shelf for the candle is the key to solving the problem.

What this brief experiment demonstrates is that the way people think about objects is strongly affected by the way they have thought about them in the past. The old ways can make it difficult to think in new ways. How people overcome familiar ways of thinking and devise creative solutions to new problems is one of cognitive psychology's central concerns.

Like the other approaches to psychology, the cognitive perspective has been applied to helping people overcome psychological problems. For example, a cognitive therapy known as *rational-emotive therapy* (Ellis & Harper, 1975) emphasizes exactly the difficulty seen in the matchbox problem we just discussed—becoming trapped by old, familiar ways of thinking. Sometimes people have irrational beliefs that adversely affect their entire view of themselves and their relations with others. Cognitive therapies emphasize changing these irrational beliefs so that people can achieve greater self-acceptance and improved interpersonal functioning. We will discuss these and other therapies in greater detail in Chapter 17.

Interim Summary

There are many approaches to understanding psychology. Five major perspectives are the neuroscience, psychodynamic, behavioral, humanistic, and cognitive approaches. The neuroscience approach considers how activity in the brain is related to behavior and experience. The psychodynamic approach, which stems from the work of Sigmund Freud, considers how human drives are modified by the demands of reality and moral restrictions.

The behavioral perspective, rooted in the work of Ivan Pavlov, Edward Thorndike, and John B. Watson, emphasizes the study of behavior and how it is affected by environmental stimuli.

The humanistic approach, sometimes called the "third force" in psychology, emphasizes people's strivings for self-actualization and freedom. Two important figures in humanistic psychology are Abraham Maslow and Carl Rogers.

The cognitive approach emphasizes the ways people process information, especially the ways in which perception, memory, thinking, and problem solving are interrelated.

PSYCHOLOGICAL SETTINGS AND SPECIALTIES

Clearly, psychologists approach the study of behavior and mental processes from different perspectives and use a wide variety of methodologies. To some extent the different methodologies and perspectives go together. Psychodynamically oriented psychologists, for example, often use the case study method as a research tool.

As beginning students of psychology, you might be curious about the range of settings in which psychologists work, the kinds of problems they work on, and the career opportunities open to people who have studied psychology. The work that psychologists do is probably more varied than in any other field of science. Psychologists work in schools, assessing the intellectual capacities of young students; in universities, teaching and conducting research; and in clinics, counseling people who are having problems in living. Just as there are many specialties within the field of medicine—surgery, pediatrics, and ophthalmology, to name just a few—there are many specialties in psychology. This book is based on the work of psychologists in all specialty fields.

Although psychologists do many different kinds of work in many different places, we can make one basic distinction between types of psychological endeavor. For the most part, psychologists are involved either in a combination of teaching and research in an academic setting or in putting theory and research into practice in various settings such as schools, hospitals, clinics, and businesses. We will consider academic psychology first, because the main focus of this book is the work produced by academic psychologists.

Academic Specialties

Academic psychologists include biopsychological, experimental, developmental, personality, and social psychologists. About 80 percent of these specialists work in colleges and universities, teaching and conducting research with undergraduate, graduate, medical, law, and business students. Let us consider the several different kinds of academic psychologists and the kinds of work they are concerned with.

Biopsychology is the specialty that examines physiological processes and how they are related to behavior and experience. Many biopsychologists study the effects of drugs and surgical procedures on behavior, usually in animals. Their goals are to understand as much as possible about the interactions between the body, the brain, and behavior. Their work is considered in detail in the next chapter.

Experimental psychology is the specialty that considers basic psychological processes such as sensation and perception, motivation and emotion, learning, memory, and cognition. The name *experimental psychology* is somewhat misleading because many academic psychologists—for example, biopsychologists, conduct experiments. But by tradition, and because many of the other academic specialties grew out of experimental psychology, the name *experimental psychologist* is used for those working in the basic areas listed above. The work of these psychologists is considered in Parts 1 and 2.

Another specialty in academic psychology is **developmental psychology,** the study of how individuals grow and change throughout life. Developmental psychologists often study children. Some of them consider social development, or how children learn to interact with other people, while others study cognitive development, or how children's intellectual and creative abilities grow and change. However, not all developmental psychologists study children. Some study development over the life span with special emphasis on changes in adolescence and adulthood. We will consider the work of developmental psychologists in Part 3 of this book.

Personality and social psychology are two closely related branches of academic psychology. Specialists in both of these fields study how normal people behave and interact in everyday life. **Personality psychology** is the specialty

Developmental psychologist Jerome Kagan is seen here observing a child play.

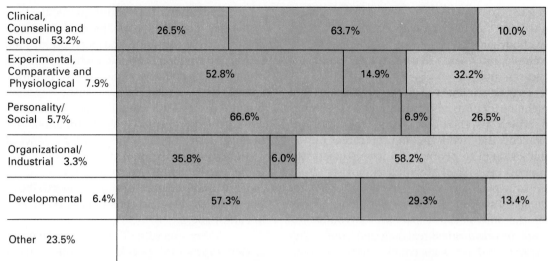

	Colleges, universities, schools, school systems, other academic settings	Hospitals, clinics, private practice, other organized human service settings	Business, government, and other
Clinical, Counseling and School 53.2%	26.5%	63.7%	10.0%
Experimental, Comparative and Physiological 7.9%	52.8%	14.9%	32.2%
Personality/ Social 5.7%	66.6%	6.9%	26.5%
Organizational/ Industrial 3.3%	35.8%	6.0%	58.2%
Developmental 6.4%	57.3%	29.3%	13.4%
Other 23.5%			

Figure 1.5
Where Psychologists Work. (Based on Howard et al., 1986)

concerned with how people differ and the traits that make individuals unique. **Social psychology** is the specialty interested in how people in general interact and how one individual affects another. We will consider the work of social and personality psychologists in Parts 3 and 4 of this book.

Practicing Psychologists

The majority of psychologists are not academic psychologists (see **Figure 1.5**). On the contrary, the majority are "in the field," often putting into practice the theories and research produced by academics. These practitioners include clinical and counseling psychologists, school psychologists, and industrial psychologists.

More than half (56 percent) of all psychologists are either clinical or counseling psychologists. **Clinical psychology** is the specialty involving the assessment and treatment of persons with psychological difficulties. **Counseling psychology** is the specialty that deals with the treatment of persons whose psychological disorders are usually less serious than those dealt with by clinical psychologists. Most clinical or counseling psychologists work in nonuniversity settings, such as hospitals and clinics, or in private practice. Their work centers on advising and treating people in need of help. The first step in working with a person with psychological problems is assessing the problem. Clinical psychologists have a wide range of assessment tools at their disposal.

Some of these are discussed in Chapter 14. Once there is some understanding of the person's disorder, a treatment program can be initiated. Individual psychotherapy, group therapy, drugs, hospitalization, marriage counseling, or other techniques may be used, sometimes in combination. Clinical and counseling psychologists see people with a wide range of psychological disturbances.

Another group of practicing psychologists are school psychologists. **School psychologists** work for the most part in primary- and secondary-school settings. Their job is to help assess the intellectual and personal capacities of students in schools and, at times, to counsel or otherwise help them. For example,

School psychologists help assess intellectual and personal capacities of students as well as provide counseling for students who need it.

school psychologists may give intelligence tests to students who seem to be unusually gifted or to students who are having difficulty learning. They may try to understand problems that students are having at home. In most cases, the school psychologist refers a student with serious problems to someone, perhaps a clinical psychologist, who can give further help. School psychologists often apply research conducted by developmental or educational psychologists. **Educational psychologists** work, for the most part, in colleges and universities, conducting research on the education process.

A third group of practitioners are **industrial psychologists,** who work primarily in business and government. Their work includes measuring potential employees' interests and aptitudes, assisting in personnel selection, consulting on problems that arise from interactions among employees in the workplace, or giving advice to companies about psychologically effective sales and business practices.

Interim Summary

Psychologists can be divided into academic psychologists, who conduct research, and practicing psychologists, who apply psychological knowledge. In each of these two broad areas there are many specialties, including biopsychology, experimental psychology, developmental psychology, personality psychology, social psychology, clinical psychology, counseling psychology, school psychology, educational psychology, and industrial psychology.

ETHICAL PRINCIPLES OF PSYCHOLOGISTS

As we have stated, the goals of psychology are to describe, explain, and predict behavior and to use this knowledge to promote human welfare. In pursuing these goals psychologists subscribe to a number of ethical principles. As you read about psychological study and consider how you might use psychological knowledge, you should keep these ethical principles in mind.

The psychologists' general ethical position is stated in the preamble of the American Psychological Association's statement of ethical principles. This preamble reads, in part, as follows:

Psychologists respect the dignity and worth of the individual and strive for the preservation and protection of fundamental human rights. They are committed to increasing knowledge of human behavior and of people's understanding of themselves and others and to the utilization of such knowledge for the promotion of human welfare. While pursuing these objectives, they make every effort to protect the welfare of those who seek their services and of the research participants that may be the object of study. (APA, 1981)

Among the ten specific principles declared by the APA, three are worth special mention. First, psychologists have an obligation to protect the *confidentiality* of information provided by others. This applies to information provided by persons seeking counseling or psychotherapy, to people who are studied in their place of work, to students, and to participants in psychological research. Second, a more general principle protects the *rights* of persons who participate in psychological research. This principle states that such research must always consider both the benefits to society and the dignity and welfare of the subjects themselves. There is a specific obligation to determine the advantages of and alternatives to any concealment of the purposes of an experiment or to any deception.

The principle of protecting the rights of persons who are research participants states that psychologists must consider the benefits of their studies. What are some of the practical benefits that have been derived from psychological research? The APA presented to Congress some of the benefits to society that have come from psychological research (Mezibov, 1981). A number of these benefits are quite interesting. For example, the application of research on perception has benefited aviation safety by helping pilots learn to recognize common optical illusions. This has contributed directly to a decrease in airplane accidents. Second, applications of research on personality and assessment have contributed to improved objective techniques of personnel selection in business. Third, techniques for changing attitudes and behavior have been applied to many health issues. Such techniques have helped people with high blood pressure change their diets. Other benefits include measuring consumer sentiment, motivating schoolchildren, and suggesting less stressful physical environments in hospitals.

Because issues of confidentiality and participant rights are so complex, in 1990 the APA named a new group, called the Committee on Standards in Research (CSR), to monitor ethical issues and to set standards for protecting the rights of participants in psychological research (Grisso et al., 1991). Among the issues the CSR considers are confidentiality, deception, coercion, and fraud. Most psychologists believe that the integrity of the discipline requires that such issues as these receive regular attention.

The third ethical principle deserving special comment concerns the care and use of animals in psychological research. There has been a great deal of discussion about using animals in behavioral research during the past several years. This discussion falls within the larger consideration of the use of animals in science and medicine. For example, in 1984 there was prolonged controversy about the morality of transplanting a baboon heart into the human infant known as Baby Fae. That same year, psychologists at the annual APA convention considered in great detail the ethics of research with animals. Psychologists pointed to the numerous contributions made through animal research—including studies pertaining to the rehabilitation of people suffering from stroke, anxiety control without drugs, and the use of biofeedback to reduce high blood pressure and the risk of heart attack (APA, 1984). The APA mandates that psychologists who conduct re-

search with animals safeguard the health, comfort, and humane treatment of their animal subjects. Furthermore, psychologists must make every effort to minimize the chances of pain, illness, or discomfort in the animals. In short, the APA strongly believes that research with animals is necessary in order to make scientific progress and to benefit the human condition, but it insists that such research be conducted as ethically and humanely as possible.

With psychology's emphasis on helping human beings, it may seem odd that psychology conducts so many experiments on animals. The reasons for using animals are actually good ones. There are many similarities between human and animal behaviors. Researchers can, however, manipulate the environments of animals in ways that would be repugnant and unethical for human subjects. Similarly, researchers can perform physical experiments on animals and gain much knowledge about the working of the brain.

There are tremendous benefits to be derived from psychological research. Still, such research must always be conducted with the welfare of both human and animal subjects carefully safeguarded.

Interim Summary

Psychologists' ethical principles emphasize protecting the rights and welfare of human and animal subjects and promoting human welfare.

● ●

THE PROMISE OF PSYCHOLOGY

No one knows what kind of future lies in store for psychology. There are encouraging signs that able young people will continue to study psychology and join the many researchers and practitioners already in its ranks. Furthermore, psychology increasingly promises to make contributions to important social issues.

What do we know about the numbers of students who are studying psychology? The number of undergraduate psychology majors reached just over 50,000 in 1976. Then the number declined steadily until 1985, when it dipped to 40,000. In 1987 the number increased to 42,000, and the trend seems to be upward (McGovern et al., 1991). We hope that many of you studying introductory psychology

The American Psychological Association mandates that psychologists safeguard the health, comfort, and humane treatment of animal subjects. However, there is still controversy over this issue. In the photo, animal-rights protesters dressed as monkeys demonstrate in front of the United States Department of Health and Human Services.

now will help swell the ranks of students majoring in psychology. You will find that psychologists are tackling an ever wider range of important social questions.

The range of questions psychology explores is illustrated by the topics that have been given special attention in the APA's journal, *The American Psychologist*. In 1991 there was a special issue of the journal on homelessness (Jones, Levine, & Rosenberg, 1991). In addition, the following issues were explored in depth: sexual orientation, problems in rural America, family support, children's rights, health objectives for the nation, and the law and social change (Crutcher, 1991; Hart, 1991; Loftus, 1991; McGinnis, 1991; Morin & Rothblum, 1991; Murray & Keller, 1991). Psychology is making strenuous efforts to continue doing basic reasearch on the principles that govern behavior and mental processes and, at the same time, applying that knowledge to critical public policy issues and social problems. We urge all of you to join our endeavor.

Interim Summary

The numbers of undergraduates majoring in psychology decreased from 1976 to 1985. In recent years the number has been increasing. Psychologists are addressing an ever widening range of public policy issues.

SUMMARY

1. Psychology uses the scientific method to study behavior and mental processes. Stating operational definitions is at the heart of the scientific method.
2. Methods in psychology include naturalistic observation, case studies, surveys, correlational studies, and experiments.
3. Psychology developed from philosophy and physiology. Its founders were William James and Wilhelm Wundt. G. Stanley Hall founded the American Psychological Association, called the APA, in 1892.
4. Five major perspectives within psychology are the neuroscience, psychodynamic, behavioral, humanistic, and cognitive perspectives.
5. Psychologists work in a variety of settings, as academic or research psychologists, or as practicing psychologists.

6. Psychologists' ethical principles emphasize the rights of human research participants and the welfare of animal research subjects.
7. Increasingly, psychologists deal with issues in the public forum.

KEY INDIVIDUALS

Sir Francis Galton
Hippocrates
Hermann von Helmholtz
Wilhelm Wundt
William James
G. Stanley Hall
Sigmund Freud
Ivan Pavlov
Edward Thorndike
John B. Watson
Abraham Maslow
Carl Rogers
Ulric Neisser
Elliot Aronson
Elizabeth Loftus
Roger Sperry

KEY RESEARCH

naturalistic observation studies conducted by an anthropologist
naturalistic observation study conducted by an ethologist
the case study of "Eve"
surveys of sexual behavior of American men and women
an experiment on the effects of televised violence
introspection
the development of psychoanalytic theory
conditioned reflexes in dogs
the law of effect
behaviorism
a problem-solving task used in cognitive psychology
the APA statement on the ethical principles of psychologists

KEY TERMS

psychology
data
behavior
mental processes

theory
operational definition
single-blind procedure
experimenter bias
double-blind technique
subjects
statistical analysis
replication
naturalistic observation
ethology
case study
surveys
correlation
scatter plot
correlation coefficient
experiment
hypothesis
variable
independent variables
dependent variables
control group
experimental group

random assignment
introspection
neuroscience
psychodynamic psychology
catharsis
free association
behavioral psychology
behaviorism
humanistic psychology
encounter group
cognition
cognitive psychology
biopsychology
experimental psychology
developmental psychology
personality psychology
social psychology
clinical psychology
counseling psychology
school psychologists
educational psychologists
industrial psychologists

Part One

....

BRAIN, BEHAVIOR, AND CONSCIOUSNESS

A Conversation With . . .

James L. McGaugh is the founding director of the Center for the Neurobiology of Learning and Memory and Professor of Psychobiology at the University of California, Irvine. His major research interest is the neurobiology of learning and memory and his research focuses on the role of neuromodulatory systems in the regulation of memory storage.

Q What can we learn about psychology by studying the relationship between brain, behavior, and consciousness?

A It seems obvious, but is perhaps worth emphasizing, that brain processes provide the mechanisms underlying behavior and consciousness. Thus, in order to understand the bases of our behavior and experiences, it is essential to examine the anatomical, physiological, and chemical machinery of the brain. Our interaction with the world around us involves the use of our sensory-perceptual systems. We see and respond to colors, shapes, and objects because of complex information processing occurring in the brain. We hear, locate, and identify sounds effortlessly because of highly efficient and effective neural processes. And, because of brain processes we can remember our experiences and change our behavior. In fact, our perception of a continuously flowing world of conscious experiences is based on brain changes enabling memory. After all, our lives consist of a series of very brief experiences. Experiences of even the immediately preceding moments linger only as memories. All of our expectations and plans, including our expectation that in the next instant the world will be much as we perceive it now is also only a memory—an expectation based on past experiences. Brain processes provide the bridge from the present to the past and future that makes our consciousness and behavior seem seamless. Brain damage pro-

duced by disease or injury can affect all aspects of our experience and behavior. Diseases, such as Alzheimer's Disease, that destroy the brain processes underlying memory disrupt the connection between past experiences and current experience and behavior. Drugs that alter the functioning of the nervous system can profoundly affect our consciousness and behavior. Clearly, knowledge of brain processes is absolutely essential for understanding disorders of experience and behavior.

Q Your work on brain mechanisms of learning and memory has been very important to the field. Please tell us about it.

A My research is based on findings (which I learned about when I was a graduate student) of studies of retrograde amnesia in humans and laboratory animals. It was known for perhaps centuries that brain injury can produce a selective loss of memory for experiences occurring shortly before the injury. A few years before I started graduate school, several researchers (including C. Duncan at Northwestern University and R. Gerard at the University of Chicago) reported that retrograde amnesia was produced in rodents given electrical stimulation of the brain (ECS) after they were trained on a simple learning task. These experimental findings provided strong support for the Perseveration Consoldiation Hypothesis of memory originally proposed in 1900 (by Mueller and Pilzecker). These findings and the Consolidation Hypothesis suggested that it might be possible to enhance memory by mild stimulation of the brain administered after learning. To explore this possibility I injected rats with low doses of stimulant drugs immediately after they were trained in a maze. To my astonishment (and delight) the drug treatments enhanced the

James L. McGaugh

rats' retention performance. I interpreted these findings, as well as those many subsequent studies, as indicating that the drugs enhanced retention by acting on post-learning processes underlying the consolidation of memory. Over the course of several decades the research in my laboratory (conducted in collaboration with many students and colleagues) has investigated the bases of neurochemical influences on memory consolidation. Our findings indicate that neuromodulatory systems (e.g., hormones and neurotransmitter systems) activated by learning experiences serve to regulate the storage of recently acquired information and that such effects are mediated by actions in specific brain systems. The role of this process appears to be that of creating strong memories of important (i.e., exciting) experiences. Our current research is examining the interactions of brain systems involved in regulating memory storage. The basic aim of this research is to learn more about the processes underlying learning and memory. However, if research of this kind is successful in increasing our understanding, such knowledge may prove useful in developing treatments for disorders of learning and memory. I must also confess that the major aims of this research are the excitement of collaboration with collegaues in research and the joy of discovery.

Q What are some of the other important applications of brain-behavior relationships?

A Knowledge of brain processes is essential for understanding of all aspects of our experiences and behavior, including our alertness, our motives, and our emotions and how these processes develop in infancy and childhood and continue to change with aging. Research of the past several decades has begun to provide understanding of the neurobiological bases of attention, sleep, hunger, thirst, and sex as well as anxiety, fear, and depression. We know that drugs can affect our motivational states: Drugs have been found effective in treating some types of emotional disorders including depression and anxiety.

Q What do you think the exciting new developments in the future will be?

A It seems highly likely that many new powerful techniques for studying the brain will be developed. Progress in understanding the brain has been accelerated by recently developed techniques for imaging the brain (e.g., PET, MRI, optical imaging). Techniques such as microdialysis and high performance liquid chromatography have greatly increased our ability to analyze brain chemistry in relation to behavioral states. Developments in molecular biology have led to the development of the new subfield of molecular neurobiology. Research in molecular neurobiology is rapidly increasing our understanding of genetic regulation of brain mechanisms. These techniques, and the knowledge that they create, will no doubt continue to accelerate progress in understanding brain processes underlying our experience and our behavior. And, by providing understanding, such developments should also accelerate our ability to prevent, alleviate, and treat debilitating diseases affecting our experience and behavior.

2 Brain and Behavior

CHAPTER OUTLINE

39

Psychologists approach the problem of understanding behavior and mental processes from a variety of perspectives. One area where these differences become apparent concerns how psychologists treat events that occur in the brain and nervous system. At one extreme are the behaviorists, who feel that events inside the organism need not be studied and that behavior can be understood by studying external events only. At the other extreme are biopsychologists, who feel that to understand behavior and mental processes it is necessary to examine the brain and nervous system.

These two points of view can be compared to how two students might approach learning about a computer. One student might try to understand the computer in terms of inputs and outputs—external events. This would be analogous to the behavioristic approach. This student would learn that giving the computer certain inputs in the form of commands and information (programs) produces a particular output. The student would attempt to understand which inputs produce which outputs while ignoring the internal workings of the machine. The second student might examine the internal circuits of the computer to see how the computer turns a particular input into a specific output. This would be analogous to the biopsychological approach.

It is important to realize that both approaches have merit. All psychologists are concerned with understanding human behavior and mental processes. Their different approaches are not in conflict—they represent different ways of studying the same problem. As we will see in other chapters, many psychologists have taken the behavioristic approach and focused on external events. In this chapter, however, we want to introduce you to the "inner workings" of behavior, the role of the brain and nervous system.

Contemporary psychologists studying the relationship between brain and behavior believe that all behavior and mental processes, from seemingly simple events such as walking to the complex processes involved in splitting an atom or writing a poem, are produced by the actions of the cells and chemicals in the brain. In this chapter we will examine much of the information that has led psychologists to this conclusion. Some of the topics we will examine are several thousand years old. For example, we will discuss acupuncture, the ancient Chinese method of controlling pain by inserting long needles into certain areas of the body. How acupuncture works has been a mystery for thousands of years, but recent research suggests that it may work by releasing natural painkillers in the brain. Other issues are quite contemporary and have the potential to affect all of us. For example, brain researchers have made rapid advances into understanding how the release of certain chemicals in the brain produces certain emotional states.

The ability to control behavior and mental processes in these and other ways will lead to some difficult decisions for society. Should a society allow brain surgery on violent people to control their aggressive behavior? Answers to questions like this are neither easy nor obvious. But as we will see, psychologists and other brain researchers have given us some fascinating insights.

In this chapter we will discuss some of these insights into the relationship between the brain and behavior. Besides discussing exactly what the brain is and how it functions, we will be looking at the different parts of the brain and how they are related to different kinds of behavior. We will also examine how the brain transmits information from one area to another. As we will see, the brain's communication system relies on electrochemical energy. This may be particularly important to the field of medicine, because many of the drugs that affect our behavior do so by affecting this electrochemical transmission in the brain. We will discuss methods for repairing the damaged brain and various techniques used to examine the activity of the living, intact brain. Finally, we will conclude this chapter by examining human consciousness and the split brain. But before we begin to address these topics, it would be useful to have an overview of what a brain is and what it does.

THE NATURE AND FUNCTION OF THE BRAIN

In the very simplest terms, the brain is an organ like the heart or lungs. The brain weighs about three pounds and, like other organs, it is made up of cells. There are two types of cells in the brain: neurons and glia cells.

Neurons, the cells that are the basic unit of the nervous system, are responsible for conducting information throughout the nervous system. Neurons give the brain its unique characteristics, such as the ability to sense the environment, to think and learn, and to control the muscles of the body. Although no one has ever counted the neurons in a single brain, researchers now estimate that the brain contains between 100 billion and 200 billion neurons. If this number sounds astounding, consider that each neuron can communicate with about 1000 other neurons. Thus the possible number of connections between neurons in the brain is practically infinite.

Neurons make up about half the volume of the brain. **Glia cells,** which supply support and transport nutrients to the neurons, make up the remaining half. Glia cells may be 10 times as numerous as neurons (Kalat, 1984). The word glia, meaning "glue," indicates one important function of these cells—to support or hold together the neurons. In addition to providing nutrients to the neurons, glia cells may even help neurons communicate with one another.

Understanding exactly how neurons and glia cells interact and communicate with each other may be the key to understanding how the brain controls behavior and mental processes. But for now we will focus on a more general description of what the brain does to guide behavior and mental processes.

The brain has three general functions. The first is to take in information. The brain senses light, sound, smell, taste, and how things feel. Taking in information is referred to as a *sensory process.* The brain's second general function is to interpret the information and make decisions based on it. These decisions can be influenced by what we already know (memory), by our likes and dislikes (attitudes), by how we feel (emotion), and by many other factors that make each of us unique. Once these decisions have been reached, the brain performs its third general function: commanding the muscles of the body to take action. If we think of sensory information as the input of the brain, then controlling the muscles or *motor behavior* is the output.

To see how these three general functions occur, consider this simple example. You are driving in your car and you approach a red light. The first function that the brain would be involved in is registering the important sensory information. In this case, the eyes would send impulses to the brain which the brain would interpret as a red light. Once this sensory infor-

The three functions of the brain can be seen in the way we respond to a red light. First, in a sensory process, the brain takes in the information that the light is red. The brain then interprets the information, determining what action should be taken. Finally, the brain commands the leg muscles to depress the brake.

mation has been conveyed, the brain's second task is to analyze the information and to make a decision as to how to act. Finally, the third general task of the brain is to send impulses to the muscles, commanding them to take the proper action. In this instance, impulses would be sent to the leg muscles commanding them to depress the brake. Thus the brain is involved in three basic processes: receiving sensory information, analyzing the information and making decisions, and commanding the muscles to take action.

THE RELATIONSHIP OF THE BRAIN AND THE NERVOUS SYSTEM

Although the brain is critical in controlling our most complex behaviors, it could not control these behaviors without interacting with the rest of the body. It does this through the nervous system. **Figure 2.1** is a simple outline of the parts of the nervous system.

The nervous system can be divided into two parts—the central nervous system (sometimes abbreviated the CNS) and the peripheral nervous system (the PNS). The **central nervous system** consists of the brain and spinal cord. The spinal cord is a narrow column that starts at the base of the back (at about hip level) and extends up through the neck and into the base of the skull. Here it joins the brain,

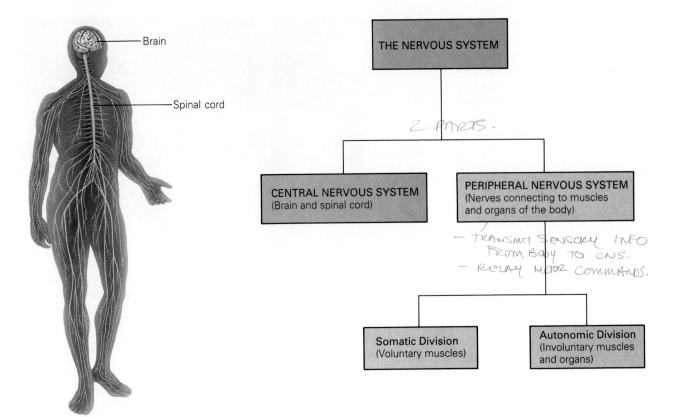

Brain

Spinal cord

Figure 2.1
Divisions of the
Nervous System.

which is completely housed in the protective skull.

The **peripheral nervous system** consists of groups of neurons called nerves, which transmit information between the CNS and the rest of the body. The PNS has two general functions: (1) to transmit sensory information from the body to the CNS and (2) to relay motor commands from the CNS to the muscles and glands of the body.

The peripheral nervous system is divided into two general systems: the somatic nervous system and the autonomic nervous system. Nerves in the **somatic nervous system** connect the brain and spinal cord with the voluntary muscles in the arms and legs. The nerves in the **autonomic nervous system** connect the brain and the spinal cord with the involuntary muscles and organs, such as the heart, stomach, and liver. The autonomic nervous system also transmits information from the CNS to the adrenal glands, which secrete hormones. We will discuss the autonomic nervous system in more detail in Chapter 4.

To understand how the central and peripheral nervous systems interact, consider the example of reaching into your pocket to find a quarter. Assuming you have several coins in your pocket, you might handle them one at a time until you finally grasped the quarter. But how does the nervous system register that you have grasped the correct coin and then send a message to muscles in your arm to withdraw your hand?

The pressure the quarter exerts on your hand stimulates the sensory receptors in the hand. The PNS nerves in your hand register the sensory information and carry it to the spinal cord (the CNS). The information then travels up the spinal cord to the brain. The brain interprets the sensory signal as "a quarter" and then sends a motor signal back down the spinal cord. The motor signal travels from the spinal cord through the peripheral nervous system until it reaches the muscles of the arm, commanding them to contract. In this manner the central and peripheral nervous systems interact to receive information from the environment and to control behavior.

Interim Summary

The brain is a complex structure. It is made up of 100–200 billion neurons, each with the capacity to communicate with up to

1000 other neurons. Brain researchers believe that the physiological and chemical events in the brain are responsible for our thoughts, feelings, and behavior.

The brain has three general functions: (1) sensory functions, or taking in information: (2) analysis and decision making; and (3) motor functions, or commanding the muscles and glands to take action.

The nervous system can be divided into two parts: (1) the central nervous system (CNS), which includes the brain and the spinal cord; and (2) the peripheral nervous system (PNS), which is further divided into the somatic and autonomic nervous systems. The brain communicates with the rest of the body through the spinal cord and the PNS.

THE NEURON—BUILDING BLOCK OF THE BRAIN

Up to this point, we have discussed in general terms what a nervous system does. We have only mentioned in very general terms what neurons do. In this section we will turn our attention to a more detailed discussion of the neurons' function. First, we will talk about how neurons interact to transmit information within the nervous system. Then we will examine a single neuron's role. Finally, we will discuss how individual neurons communicate with each other. As we will see, communication between neurons is accomplished through chemicals called neurotransmitters. Neuro-

Neural impulses involved in reflexes bypass the brain. So, if you touch a hot burner, it takes longer for the impulse to reach the brain than the muscle in your hand and you withdraw your hand before you actually feel pain.

transmitters may be extremely important in a number of psychological processes ranging from experiencing pleasure to feeling anxiety.

Three Types of Neurons

Most of you have probably made the mistake of placing your hand on a hot burner of a stove. The experience is painful and your reaction is quick—you jerk your hand back. This type of behavior is called a **spinal reflex** because all the neurons necessary to carry it out are located in the peripheral nervous system and the spinal cord. The brain itself is not involved. To execute the reflex, the nervous system must transmit information. This information is carried by the specialized cells of the nervous system called neurons. Like other cells, neurons have a cell body with a nucleus. But neurons can do something that no other cell in the body can do—they can transmit information. Let's return to our example to see exactly how this transmission is accomplished.

The simplest spinal reflexes, like the knee jerk, may involve only a sensory neuron and a motor neuron. In most cases, however, it takes at least three different types of neurons to carry out the simple spinal reflex behavior. First of all, we need a sensory neuron to receive information: our hand is in a very hot place. **Sensory neurons** respond directly to external stimuli such as light, sound, or touch. We also need a motor neuron to command the muscles in our arm to remove our hand from the hot place. **Motor neurons** carry messages to the muscles or glands. In addition, we need an association neuron to connect the motor and sensory neurons. All neurons not classified as sensory or motor neurons are **association neurons.**

When the nervous system actually carries out a reflex, thousands of sensory neurons are connected to thousands of association neurons, which in turn are connected to thousands of motor neurons. But the basic principle remains the same: (1) sensory neurons gather information about the environment and transmit it to (2) association neurons, which transmit the information to (3) motor neurons, which activate the muscles.

One interesting aspect of spinal reflexes is the speed at which they occur. Two factors contribute to this. First, although some neural impulses travel rather slowly (about 2 or 3 miles per hour), the impulses involved in reflexes are among the fastest in the nervous system and travel at speeds of over 200 miles per

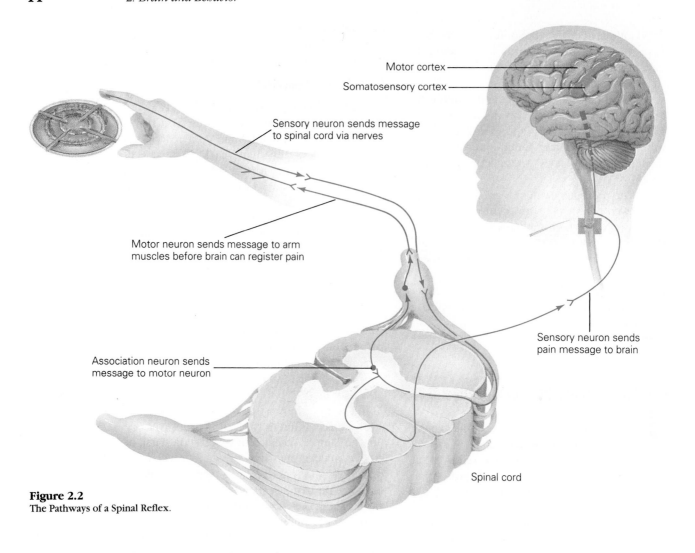

Motor cortex

Somatosensory cortex

Sensory neuron sends message
to spinal cord via nerves

Motor neuron sends message to arm
muscles before brain can register pain

Sensory neuron sends
pain message to brain

Association neuron sends
message to motor neuron

Spinal cord

Figure 2.2
The Pathways of a Spinal Reflex.

hour (Kuffler, Nicholls, & Martin, 1984). Second, the neural impulses involved in reflexes take a shortcut. They bypass the brain. In our example, when the hot burner triggers the sensory neuron in the hand, the impulse moves from the hand to the spinal cord and then right back to the muscle. Information about the painful stimulus, however, is sent to the brain at the same time. But because it takes longer for the impulse to reach the brain than for the impulse to complete the reflex arc and get back to the muscle, we withdraw our hand before we actually feel pain. This is a good system because it allows us to remove our hand quickly before the heat does much damage and it allows us to experience the pain so that we do not touch the hot stove again. **Figure 2.2** summarizes the pathways of a spinal reflex.

The Role of the Neuron

Neurons perform a very simple service. They receive information at one end (usually from another neuron), process the information, and transmit it to the opposite end. From there the information is transmitted to the next neuron and so on through the nervous system. The receiving end of the neuron is known as the **dendrite,** and the sending portion is called the **axon (Figure 2.3).** The **soma,** or cell body, lies between the dendrites and the axon. In addition to receiving and sending information, the soma is involved in keeping the axon and dendrites healthy by manufacturing nutrients and other necessary chemicals. In the photograph of a neuron we notice that there are often not just one but many dendrites. These enable each neuron to receive information from many other neurons. Early anatomists named these structures dendrites, the Greek word for "tree," because they looked like tree branches. Each neuron has only one soma, on which all of its dendrites converge, and only one axon protruding from the other side of the soma. In some neurons the axon splits, allowing one neuron to send information to several other neurons.

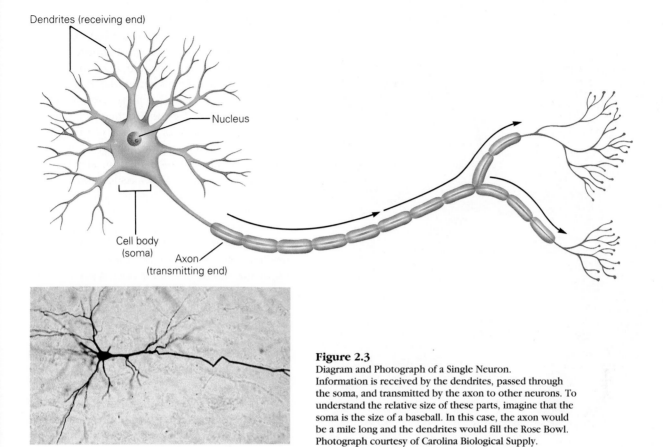

Dendrites (receiving end)

Nucleus

Cell body
(soma)

Axon
(transmitting end)

Figure 2.3
Diagram and Photograph of a Single Neuron.
Information is received by the dendrites, passed through
the soma, and transmitted by the axon to other neurons. To
understand the relative size of these parts, imagine that the
soma is the size of a baseball. In this case, the axon would
be a mile long and the dendrites would fill the Rose Bowl.
Photograph courtesy of Carolina Biological Supply.

The size of the axons of different neurons can vary enormously. To consider the extremes, there are neurons with cell bodies and dendrites located in the motor cortex whose axons extend all the way to the base of the spinal cord, a distance of about 3 feet. Other neurons have very short axons, often less than one thousandth of an inch. These axons typically connect adjacent neurons in the cortex.

The Neuron at Rest

Before we consider how a neuron might send information from the dendrites to the axon, let's look at the neuron when it is not sending information. In this state, the neuron is said to be at rest. When the neuron is at rest, an electrical difference or charge exists between the inside and the outside of the cell. This charge is much like that contained in a battery, only much smaller. It is *potential* energy, just waiting to be released. This electrical potential that exists between the inside and the outside of the cell when the neuron is at rest is referred to as the neuron's **resting potential.** How does this resting potential come about?

Like other cells, a neuron has a cell membrane. This membrane, or skin, keeps chemi-

cals inside the cell from escaping, and vice versa. But the membrane of every cell has a special characteristic. It is *semipermeable.* That is, it allows some chemicals to cross it, or go in and out of the cell, more easily than others. The two most important chemicals that cross the membrane are sodium and potassium *ions* (charged chemical particles). Although the membrane readily allows potassium ions to cross back and forth from the inside to the outside of the cell, it keeps sodium ions on the outside. As a result, there is more sodium outside the neuron than inside. The membrane also acts as a barrier for a second group of chemicals—proteins. But in this case, the proteins are permanently trapped *inside* the cell. How do these factors create a resting potential? The answer lies in the fact that sodium and potassium have positive electrical charges and that proteins have a negative electrical charge. Because there are more negative protein ions inside the neuron, the inside has a negative electrical charge relative to the outside. Because opposite charges attract (much like opposite poles of a magnet), the positive sodium ions try to cross into the negative inside of the cell but can't because of the semipermeable membrane.

A. Resting Potential   B. Action Potential

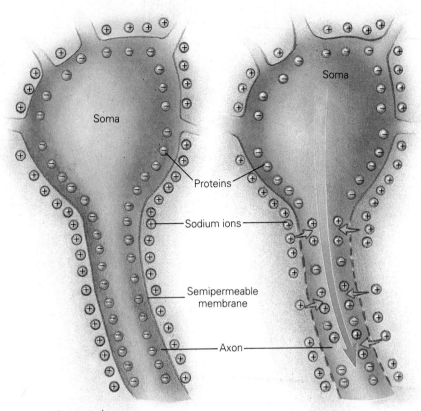

Figure 2.4
Resting and Action Potential.
a. Resting potential. The semipermeable membrane keeps the negative protein ions inside the axon and the positively charged sodium ions outside the axon. Because of this, there is a charge between the inside and the outside of the axon. This charge, much like the charge in a battery, is potential energy waiting to be released.

b. Action potential. When the axon becomes excited, the semipermeable membrane breaks down and allows the sodium ions to flow into the axon. Because positively charged sodium ions are attracted to negatively charged proteins as in magnetic poles, (unlike charges attract), the sodium ions rush into the cell. When this happens, the electrical charge moves down the axon. This is the action potential, which allows information in the form of electrochemical energy to move down the axon and on to the dendrites of the next neuron.

The Neuron Taking Action

The resting potential of a neuron is a very delicate state. Any slight disturbance will lead to a large chain reaction. For example, if something (usually an impulse from another neuron) excites the dendrites of a resting neuron, the semipermeable membrane breaks down and allows the waiting sodium ions to rush in. When this happens, a surge of electrochemical energy moves like a wave down the axon. This surge of energy is called the **action potential.** The action potential allows information, in the form of electrochemical energy, to be transmitted from the axon of one neuron to the dendrites of the next (see **Figure 2.4**).

Let's return to our example of touching a hot stove. When we place our hand on the hot surface, the heat causes the dendrites in the sensory neurons to become excited. This in turn allows sodium to enter the cell and an electrochemical charge to be transmitted down the axon. When the electrochemical information reaches the end of the axon of the sensory cell, the charge excites the dendrites of the association neuron. This excitation again allows sodium ions to enter the association neuron. The electrochemical charge is then transmitted from the axon of the association neuron to the dendrites of the motor neuron and finally down the axon of the motor neuron. When the electrochemical charge reaches the end of the axon of the motor neuron it does not excite the dendrites of another neuron. Instead, it excites a muscle. This excitation causes the muscle to contract, and we quickly pull our hand away from the stove's surface.

This very simple neural reflex requires only three kinds of neurons, but the same principle applies to even the most complicated behaviors. Suppose someone asks you how old you are and you answer "nineteen." This sounds like an easy task, but just think about how many different neurons might be involved. First, the sensory neurons in the ear must record the sound waves. The neurons in the auditory cortex must interpret the information. Neurons associated with memory are required to recall the answer. Neurons associated with language must then formulate the proper answer, and finally the motor neurons in the tongue and mouth must excite the correct muscle groups to produce the proper answer. This "simple" behavior is very complicated. As in the case of the reflex, all information must travel through the nervous system from neuron to neuron. In each case, the axon of one neuron stimulates the dendrites of another neuron, and so on. Even if a billion neurons were involved, the principle would be the same. The entire process starts with sensory neurons whose dendrites are excited not by an impulse from another neuron, but rather by sensory information from the outside world. (We will discuss sensory processes in Chapter 3.) The information then goes through one or billions of association neurons, which act together to integrate information and transmit "decisions" about appropriate behavior to motor neurons. As in the reflex, the axons of motor neurons excite muscles.

Communication Between Neurons— The Synapse

Imagine that you had the ability to watch a neural impulse travel down the neuron. You would see the impulse start at the dendrite, flash through the cell body, and then burst down the axon. The entire event would take place in a fraction of a second. But what happens to the impulse when it reaches the end of the axon? How does it get to the dendrites of the next cell? One way would be for the axon of one cell to touch the dendrites of the next cell. Then the electrochemical energy could be directly transmitted—almost like plugging two extension cords together. In fact, until about 50 years ago brain researchers thought this was exactly what happened. And although we know this is the case for a small number of neurons (Shepherd, 1988), we also know that for most neurons there is a tiny space (about 1/250,000 of an inch) between the axons and the dendrites. This space or gap between the axon of one neuron and the dendrites of another is called a **synapse** (from the Greek word meaning "point of contact"). Having a synapse between two neurons is similar to unplugging two extension cords: the electricity cannot flow. So how does the impulse bridge the synapse?

The synapse is bridged by chemicals called **neurotransmitters,** so called because they transmit energy from one neuron to the next. Neurotransmitters are found in a specialized place in the neuron known as the **axon terminal,** which is located at the end of the axon. Here the molecules of the neurotransmitters group together in the **synaptic vesicles,** small, hollow, pear-shaped structures located in the axon terminals to await the electrical impulse.

When the electrical impulse reaches the axon terminal, it causes these vesicles to crash through the axon terminal. This happens with such force that the vesicles break, and the transmitter is shot out into the synapse. It is almost like throwing a water balloon against a screen. The balloon bursts and the water rushes through the screen. Some of the transmitter thrown into the synapse reaches the dendrites of the next cell. Here it attaches to a **receptor,** the portion of the dendrite into which a neurotransmitter fits. The molecules that make up the transmitters fit the receptor much like a key fits a lock. When the transmitter attaches

to the receptor, it breaks down the semipermeable membrane, sodium flows into the neuron, and the electrochemical process in the dendrites starts. The impulse then flows across the soma and down the axon until it again reaches the axon terminal. From here, the entire process starts again. **Figure 2.5** on page 48 summarizes the steps in synaptic transmission.

Decision Making in a Single Neuron

We have seen that, through synaptic transmission, the firing of one neuron can cause a second neuron to fire. But the firing of one neuron will not *always* cause the second to fire. A number of factors determine whether this event occurs.

Recall that the dendrites of one neuron can be connected, through synapses, with the axons of up to 1000 other neurons. At any given instant, a neuron may be receiving messages from just a few or from hundreds of other neurons. Whether the neuron fires depends on the total of the messages that it receives. Some of the axons that synapse on the neuron are *excitatory.* When they fire, they release a transmitter into the synapse that excites the next neuron. The transmitter pushes the neuron toward the point or threshold of firing, an event called an **excitatory potential.** Its effect may be compared to that of squeezing the trigger of a gun. If we squeeze the trigger past a certain point—the threshold—the gun fires. But squeezing the trigger partway has no effect. In the case of the neuron, if it receives just one excitatory message, the "trigger" will be moved a small distance, but not to the firing point. If no other excitatory messages come within a very short period of time, the trigger returns to its normal position. But if several excitatory messages from different axons come together or are spaced very closely in time, they combine to push the trigger to the firing point, and the neuron fires. Thus it generally takes more than one excitatory message to cause a neuron to fire.

The firing point of a neuron is called the threshold. If the threshold is reached, the neuron fires an impulse down its axon. But increasing the stimulus above threshold will not increase the intensity or the speed of the neural impulse. The neuron always fires with exactly the same intensity and speed. The neuron's response is called an **all-or-none response.** The neuron is much like a gun: it does not matter if you squeeze the trigger gently or hard, the gun fires in exactly the same way—only a single bul-

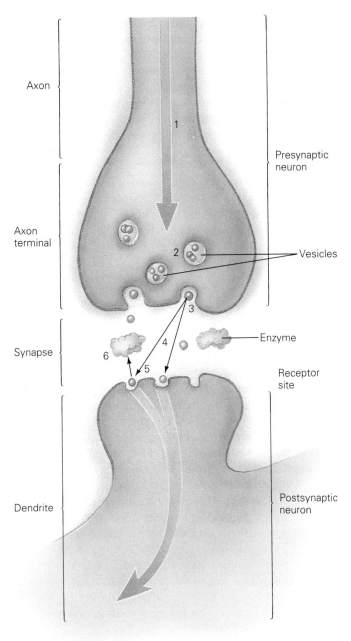

Axon

Axon
terminal

Synapse

Dendrite

Presynaptic
neuron

Vesicles

Enzyme

Receptor
site

Postsynaptic
neuron

Figure 2.5
Steps in Synaptic Transmission.
(1) The neurotransmitter is synthesized in the cell body of
the neuron (sometimes called the presynaptic—before the
synapse—neuron) and is then transported down the axon
to the axon terminal. (2) Neurotransmitters are stored in
small packets called vesicles. (3) When an electrochemical
impulse or action potential reaches the axon terminal, it
causes the contents of the vesicles to release into the
synapse. (4) The neurotransmitter crosses the synapse and
occupies the receptor sites on the dendrites of the next
neuron (sometimes called the postsynaptic—after the
synapse—neuron). (5) When the neurotransmitter
occupies the receptor sites, it allows sodium to enter the
postsynaptic cell, and the entire process begins again, (6)
The neurotransmitter is either recycled—that is, taken back
into the axon terminal of the presynaptic neuron and
stored in vesicles to be used again—or is inactivated by
enzymes in the synapse.

let is fired and it always travels at exactly the
same speed.

How, then, is information about the intensity of a stimulus transmitted by neurons?
How can they distinguish between touching a
warm stove and touching one that is very hot?
Although a strong stimulus cannot cause a neuron to fire with a stronger or faster impulse, it
can cause more neurons to fire. The more neurons that fire, the more intense the feeling.

But not all messages are excitatory. Some
of the axons release an inhibitory neurotransmitter. These transmitters produce inhibitory
messages, creating an **inhibitory potential**
that prevents the neuron from firing. Inhibitory
signals make it more difficult for the excitatory
messages to cause the neuron to fire. Inhibition
is an important process in the brain. When the
inhibitory synapses in the brain are blocked,
as happens with the use of certain drugs,
the brain can go into a seizure (Cotman &
McGaugh, 1980).

If similar numbers of excitatory and inhibitory potentials reach the neuron at about
the same time, they cancel each other out and
the neuron does not fire. Thus, each individual
neuron makes a "decision" whether to fire
based on the sum of the inputs it receives from
all the other neurons that synapse on it. Because this decision-making process occurs constantly at each of the billions of neurons in the
nervous system, we can see why the brain is
such a complicated organ with the capacity to
carry out so many complex functions at the
same time.

Neurotransmitters and Behavior

Why do we experience feelings such as pain
and anxiety? Why is it that some days we feel
happy and other days we feel depressed? No
one has the complete answer to these questions, but brain researchers believe that part of
the answer may have to do with the neurotransmitters of the brain (Barchas, Akil, Elliott,
Holman, & Watson, 1978; Krieger, 1983). Consider the following two examples:

A soldier has been badly wounded on the
battlefield. He is still conscious and in terrible pain. To make matters worse, it will
be several hours before he can be taken
to the hospital. To alleviate his pain, the
medics give him morphine.

A young woman has chronic back
pain. She has been to specialists all over

the world and no one has been able to help her. But when an acupuncturist inserts small electrified needles in her arm, she experiences the first relief she has had from pain in 5 years.

Both acupuncture and morphine relieve pain, but only recently have researchers discovered that both of these treatments may act by working on neurotransmitters at the synapse.

Several years ago, brain researchers Candace Pert and Solomon Snyder made a startling discovery. They found that some of the receptors in the brain, like those that attract neurotransmitters, also attract morphine. When animals were given morphine, the drug found its way to these receptors and attached itself to them (Pert & Snyder, 1973). Furthermore, when the morphine reached the receptor, it acted much the way a neurotransmitter does.

The discovery of morphine receptors in the brain was an important one. It showed how a drug could affect the brain. But this discovery also posed a mystery. Why should the brain have receptors for morphine? After all, morphine is not a neurotransmitter—or is it? Shortly after the discovery of the morphine receptors, brain researchers found the answer to this puzzle. The brain produces its own morphinelike substances. Known as **endorphins,** these chemicals also relieve pain, but they occur naturally in the brain. The term endorphin comes from *endogenous,* or internal, morphine (Hughes, Smith, Kosterlitz, Fothergill, Morgan, & Morris, 1975). This finding suggests that the brain has its own built-in mechanism for relieving pain. It may be that we experience relief from pain in some situations because endorphins are released (Akil, Watson, Young, Lewis, Khachaturian, & Walker, 1984; Snyder, 1977).

Brain researchers have only begun to understand the different circumstances that may cause endorphins to be released. One activity that may release endorphins is acupuncture (Goldstein, 1978). If this is true, it helps explain why acupuncture sometimes relieves pain. Similarly, some researchers believe that reinforcement by electrical stimulation of the brain is mediated by endorphins (Belluzi & Stein, 1981). Other researchers have even suggested that activities like jogging can release endorphins. This may explain why some people experience a "natural high" when they exercise (Carr et al., 1981).

In one interesting study involving endor-

Aerobic activities such as jogging may release endorphins, which can explain the "natural high" some people experience when exercising.

phins, researchers found that endorphin levels in the blood increased during pregnancy and then further increased during labor (Cahill & Akil, 1982). In a related study, researchers found that the pain threshold of pregnant rats increased sharply (meaning they could withstand more pain) one or two weeks before they gave birth (Gintzler, 1980). These results suggest that the body may naturally raise endorphin levels in response to painful situations and that this increase may help in the control of pain (Terenius, 1982).

Endorphins are only one of the neurotransmitters in the brain. Brain researchers have now identified more than 30 other chemicals that may help transmit information from one neuron to the next—and the list seems to grow longer every day. Some researchers suggest that there may be up to 300 neurotransmitters in the brain, each with the ability to affect both neurotransmission and behavior (Cooper, Bloom, & Roth, 1991; Snyder, 1984). **Table 2.1** is a summary of the major neurotransmitters and the behaviors they seem to affect.

Brain researchers are now faced with the difficult problem of determining the roles of these chemicals. Neurotransmitters appear to be involved in a wide range of processes, from basic regulation of temperature and blood pressure (Krieger, 1983) to complex psychological

Table 2.1   **Major Neurotransmitters and Affected Behaviors**

Neurotransmitter	Behaviors in which the neurotransmitter may be involved	Drugs that affect the neurotransmitter
Dopamine	Schizophrenia—An excess of dopamine may lead to schizophrenic symptoms. We will discuss this in greater detail in Chapter 16 Motor disorders such as Parkinson's disease—Lesions that damage parts of the brain containing dopamine produce this disorder of movement	Amphetamine—Increases the amount of dopamine released from the synapse; chronic high levels of amphetamine can produce states resembling paranoid schizophrenia Haloperidol—Blocks the postsynaptic dopamine receptor and prevents transmitter from having any action; alleviates the symptoms of schizophrenia by functionally reducing the amount of dopamine
Norepinephrine	Affective disorders—A norepinephrine deficiency may lead to a depressed state, and an excess may lead to a manic state; we will discuss this in greater detail in Chapter 16	Reserpine—Reduces the amount of norepinephrine by preventing it from being stored in the vesicles; has a potent tranquilizing effect Amphetamine—Also increases the amount of norepinephrine released; acts as a stimulant
Serotonin	Implicated in states of consciousness (e.g., sleep), mood, depression, and anxiety	Parachlorophenylalanine (PCPA)—Reduces the amount of serotonin by blocking its synthesis; can lead to insomnia LSD—Evidence suggests that this drug produces hallucinations by acting on the serotonin system, but the mechanism of action remains unclear
Acetylcholine	Learning and memory—Found in abundance in the cortex; drugs that increase acetylcholine seem to facilitate learning and memory and those that decrease it appear to disrupt learning and memory.	Scopolamine—Blocks the postsynaptic acetylcholine receptor and prevents the transmitter from having any action; disrupts learning in a variety of situations Choline—A substance found in our diets that increases the amount of brain acetylcholine; may facilitate learning and memory in some situations (see Chapter 7)
Endorphins	Hypothesized to be involved in a variety of behaviors including feeding, sexual activity, pain perception, and placebo effects	Naloxone—Blocks the postsynaptic receptor and prevents transmitter from having any action; blocks the ability of acupuncture to relieve pain (see Chapter 3)
GABA (gamma aminobutyric acid)	May be involved in the modulation of anxiety	Valium—Increases the activity of GABA; reducing anxiety

Many other substances may also be neurotransmitters. The student who wishes to know more about the rapid growing field should consult: Cooper, J. R., Bloom, F. E., & Roth, R. H. (1987). *The biochemical basis of neuropharmacology* (5th ed.). New York: Oxford University Press; Lickey, M. E., and Gordon, B. (1991). *Medicine and Mental Illness, the Use of Drugs in Psychiatry.* San Francisco: Freeman; *Psychopharmacology—The Third Generation of Progress,* A. H. Meltzer (ed.), New York: Raven Press.

processes such as learning and memory (McGaugh, 1983). They are also involved in psychological disorders such as depression and schizophrenia (Krieger, 1983). Current evidence even shows a direct relationship between these chemicals and motivational processes such as the control of hunger (Paul, Hulihan-Giblin, & Skolnick, 1982) and emotional processes such as anxiety and fear (Tallman, Paul, Skolnick, & Gallagher, 1980). Recently, researchers have discovered how neurotransmitters in the brain may modulate anxiety. These findings have important implications for the possible treatment of severe anxiety, which affects about 5 percent of the population (Taulbee, 1983).

One very useful drug in the treatment of anxiety is Valium. In fact, Valium is one of the most widely prescribed drugs in the United States, with over 8000 tons consumed yearly (Tallman et al., 1980). In 1977, researchers located a receptor in the brain for Valium and related substances. Following the logic used with endorphins, they reasoned that if there is a receptor, there must also be a substance in the brain that acts on the receptor—an endogenous Valium-like substance. Recently, researchers have found evidence for a naturally occurring Valium-like substance in the brain (Rothstein et al., 1990).

Through this work researchers have made progress toward understanding brain mechanisms of anxiety. Researchers now believe that drugs like Valium act in an indirect manner. Specifically, they bind to receptors in the brain, thus causing a second neurotransmitter, GABA (gamma aminobutyric acid), to become more active (Tallman & Gallagher, 1985). GABA, an inhibitory neurotransmitter in the brain, decreases the amount of neuronal activity. When it does this in a system involved with anxiety, it decreases anxiety levels. **Figure 2.6** shows how this process occurs (Nina, Insel, Cohen, Skolnick, & Paul, 1982). This research shows how several of the neurotransmitters in the brain may interact to control a complex psychological process such as anxiety. It also paves the way for finding more effective methods for controlling anxiety (Cooper, Bloom, & Roth, 1991).

Researchers have only begun to discover the relationships between neurotransmitters, behavior, and mental processes. Yet with the advances in this field, information about how the brain controls very complex processes through neurotransmitters should come at a rapid pace. For example, researchers have identified the brain receptors for alcohol, which are related to GABA receptors. Like Valium, alcohol decreases the amount of neural activity (Suzdak, Schwartz, & Skolnick, 1986). Could this be why alcohol has a sedating effect? This research also raises the fascinating and very important possibility that drugs could be developed that would knock the alcohol off the GABA receptor and help return the neuron to its normal state. Research such as this could eventually lead to a "sobriety" pill.

One of the most promising new areas of research on neurotransmitters and behavior involves addiction. One approach to drug addiction is to try to find substances that stop the craving. But before this can be accomplished, researchers must understand how the addictive drugs act on the brain. Recently, researchers have learned that the highly addictive drug cocaine acts on yet another neurotransmitter in the brain, dopamine. In the normal brain, one of the primary effects of dopamine is to help people experience pleasure. Under normal circumstances, dopamine is released from the ax-

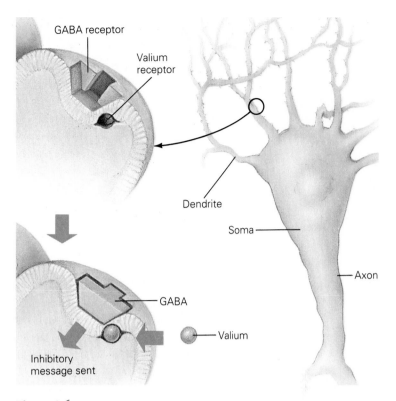

Figure 2.6
The Neurochemistry of Anxiety.
When Valium bonds to the Valium receptor, it allows more GABA to bond to the GABA receptor. The GABA is an inhibitory neurotransmitter which decreases the neuronal activity in systems that modulate anxiety. (After Taulbee, 1983)

on, crosses the synapse, and attaches to receptors on the dendrites of the next neuron. Leftover dopamine in the synapse is reabsorbed by the cell and stored for later use. When cocaine is used, it blocks the reabsorption process so that the dopamine floods the neuron and produces a feeling of euphoria **(Figure 2.7)** (Ritz, Lamb, Goldberg, & Kuhar, 1987). "Crack," a form of cocaine that is particularly potent because it is smoked and thus gets into the blood supply and to the brain very quickly, is probably the most powerful pleasure-producing drug. When people take cocaine they become euphoric, talkative, and active. They feel powerful and alert.

Researchers now believe that because cocaine causes dopamine not be recycled, neurons become depleted of the substance. When this happens, the addict loses the ability to experience pleasure, becomes depressed, and craves the euphoric effects of the drug. Researchers are trying to develop drugs that will fit the dopamine receptors, substitute for the missing dopamine, and help the addict experience normal pleasure (Gawin, 1991).

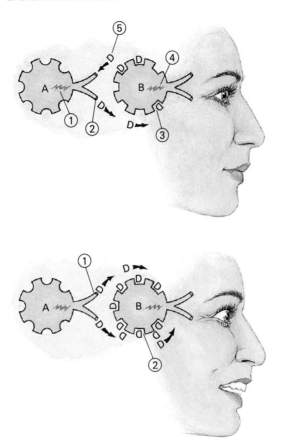

Figure 2.7
How Cocaine Causes Euphoria.
(Top) The healthy, drug-free brain. Dopamine is one of the chemical messengers in the brain that is involved in feelings of pleasure. An electrical signal in neuron A (1) causes release of dopamine from the nerve endings (2). Some of the dopamine attaches to special receptors (3) in neuron B, sending on the message (4). Leftover dopamine is reabsorbed by cell A and stored (5).
(Bottom) High on cocaine. Cocaine blocks the pumping mechanism in nerve endings responsible for reabsorbing leftover dopamine (1). The dopamine floods into neuron B (2), causing a feeling of euphoria.

This approach of understanding addictions at the synaptic level is now being used for a variety of addictive substances. For example, researchers know that the nicotine in cigarette smoke is addictive because of its actions on receptors in the brain. This finding may in turn help researchers develop better strategies for helping people who are addicted to tobacco (Marsh, 1990).

THE ENDOCRINE SYSTEM

We might consider the nervous sytem the great communication system. Its job is to transmit information from one part of the body to an-

other. But there is a second communication system in the body that performs similar functions. Chemical messages travel not only from nerve cell to nerve cell but also throughout the body. **Hormones** are chemical messengers that are produced in one part of the body, travel in the bloodstream, and affect distant parts of the body. These hormones are often secreted by the glands of the **endocrine system (Figure 2.8).** Unlike the nervous system, in which chemicals send messages short distances with lightning speed, the endocrine system can send messages long distances but much more slowly. It may take several seconds for the bloodstream to carry hormones from an endocrine gland to its target for action.

Hormones influence everything in our lives from growth, to sexual drive, to mood, to reactions to stress and danger. To begin to appreciate how the hormonal system may influence us, consider how hormones might come into play in a stressful situation. The adrenal gland located above the kidneys (see Figure 2.8) is the major gland for coping with stress in humans. Almost any type of sudden stress causes the adrenal medulla to increase its secretion of epinephrine (also known as adreneline) into the bloodstream. When this happens, the heart begins to pound, blood pressure is increased, the palms begin to sweat, and the blood sugar level goes up. The net effect is a surge of energy. As the emergency passes, the hormones subside and things return to normal.

If the nervous system and the endocrine system are the two great communication systems of the brain, it follows that they should work together. They do so through the **pituitary gland.** The pituitary gland is a pea-sized structure located in the base of the brain. It is sometimes referred to as the master gland because many if its secretions influence the release of hormones from other glands in the endocrine system. Lying just above the pituitary gland is the hypothalamus, a part of the brain. The hypothalamus is involved in behaviors such as aggression, sexual behavior, and feeding and drinking—the very processes that are regulated by the endocrine system. The location of the hypothalamus above the pituitary is not accidental. Its close proximity allows it to influence greatly the pituitary and the entire endocrine system. So we now complete the loop. Brain state influences the endocrine system, and the secretions of these glands in turn influence the brain.

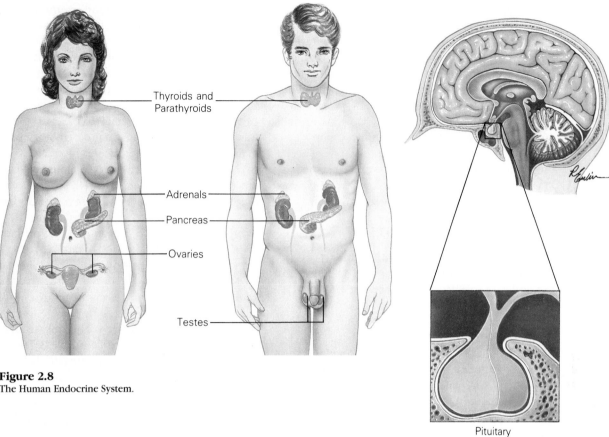

Figure 2.8
The Human Endocrine System.

Interim Summary

To understand precisely how the brain controls behavior, it is necessary to examine the single neuron—the building block of the brain. There are three types of neurons: sensory neurons, motor neurons, and association neurons.

Neurons are either in a resting state or conducting information. In the resting state, the neuron has potential energy waiting to be released. This potential energy is in the form of positively charged sodium ions that are held outside the neuron. When the neuron is stimulated (typically by an impulse from another neuron), sodium is allowed to enter the neuron. This results in an electrochemical current, which is transmitted down the axon to the axon terminal.

When the impulse reaches the axon terminal, it releases neurotransmitters across the synapse. Neurotransmitters have attracted a great deal of attention since research has shown that they are involved in many behaviors and mental processes. Researchers also believe that many drugs act by working on neurotransmitters at the synapse.

A second great communication system in the brain is the endocrine system. Hormones secreted by the glands in the endocrine system send messages through the blood to different parts of the body. These hormones influence a variety of processes including growth, sexual drive, mood, and reactions to stress.

THE ORGANIZATION OF THE BRAIN

At first glance, the human brain is not very impressive. Could this pale gray, three-pound mass that looks like an oversized walnut and has the consistency of soft gelatin really control our loftiest thoughts and most complex actions? A closer look at the surface of the brain, called the cortex (Latin for "bark" or "covering"), reveals that the brain has about the same appearance throughout. The top, bottom, front, and sides all look about the same. Because of this, many people once thought that all parts of the brain performed similar functions.

It was not until the nineteenth century that researchers began to realize that different parts of the brain might be involved in different behaviors. This realization spurred many questions. Are certain parts of the brain primarily responsible for receiving sensory information? Are other parts involved in memory and still others in emotion? Where are decisions made? Do certain parts of the brain control motor behavior? These were exactly the questions that early brain researchers and psychologists faced and it was this early work that gave the first hints as to how the brain was organized.

Phrenology — A False Beginning

Ironically, the pseudoscientific theory of a Viennese physician first led other scientists to wonder if there were specialization in the brain.

Franz Gall (1758–1828)

Franz Gall, a nineteenth-century Viennese physician, was interested in the brain. But in the early 1800s methods for "unlocking" the skull to examine the brain had not yet been developed. Gall wondered whether he could learn something about the brain by studying the bumps and protrusions on people's skulls. As a young boy he had noticed that a number of his friends who had particularly good memories also had large protruding eyes. Gall reasoned that people with good memories had large protruding eyes because the front of the brain was so well developed that it had pushed out the eyes. Thus, he concluded that the front of the brain must be involved in memory. "I was forced to the idea," Gall wrote in 1812, "that the eyes so formed are the mark of an excellent memory" (Blakemore, 1977, p. 5). If this were the case, could bumps on other parts of the skull signify other mental capabilities?

Gall and his followers examined thousands of people. Based on their observations, Gall proposed the theory of *phrenology* and assembled a catalog showing the relationship of bumps on the skull to human abilities. A bump on the back of the head signified a cautious person; a bump on the side of the head indicated a secretive person; a bump just above the ears meant a destructive person—often a criminal.

Although phrenology was quite the rage in the early nineteenth century, brain researchers soon realized that bumps on the head had no relationship to human abilities. But even though Gall was wrong, phrenology did make an important contribution to the study of the brain. It raised the possibility that different parts of the brain were indeed specialized for different abilities. And this idea stimulated more research.

Language and the Brain — Localization of Function

While studying the brain, Gall had concluded that the frontal lobes, the part of the brain closest to the top of the forehead, were specialized for speech. An admirer of Gall's work was so taken by this claim that he offered a reward of 500 francs (a large sum of money at that time) to anyone who could find a patient with damage to the frontal lobe who *did not* have a speech disorder. This challenge prompted a young neurosurgeon named Paul Broca to begin examining patients who suffered from loss of speech.

Broca's first case, in 1861, involved a man who was admitted to the hospital with a serious leg infection. The man had also suffered from loss of speech for many years. The patient was called "Tan" because this was the only word he could say. A day or two after Broca examined him, Tan died from the infection, and Broca was able to perform a postmortem examination of the brain. The autopsy revealed damage to the left side of the frontal lobe. Over the next three years Broca reported additional

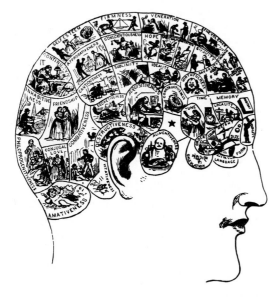

Phrenologists believed that an individual's abilities can be identified by the shape of the skull. They devised this complex map of specialization in the brain. This early theory, although incorrect, raised the possibility that different parts of the brain are specialized and has lead to much important research.

Broca's postmortem autopsy of Tan's brain revealed damage to the left side of the frontal lobe. In subsequent investigations, Broca came to learn that this area of the brain is critical to the production of speech.

cases. In each one, disorders of speech were accompanied by damage to the left frontal lobe. **Broca's area** was the name given to this area, which is critical to the production of speech.

Shortly after Broca reported his findings, Carl Wernicke identified a second area in the brain, now called Wernicke's area, that was also involved in language. **Wernicke's area** is located in the temporal lobe, a part of the brain located over the ear. What was startling was that Wernicke's and Broca's areas were involved in different aspects of language. A lesion (tissue damage) to Broca's area produced a language disorder characterized by slow and labored speech and poor articulation, making the words themselves difficult to understand. In this **aphasia,** or language disorder, the language may make sense but usually cannot be expressed as a complete sentence. For example, when asked about a dental appointment, a patient said: "Yes . . . Monday . . . Dad and Dick . . . Wednesday nine o'clock . . . ten o'clock . . . doctors . . . and . . . teeth" (Geschwind, 1979, p. 111). All the information seems to be there, but the words are difficult to understand and the sentences are incomplete.

Although patients with Broca's aphasia

have difficulty expressing themselves, they have no difficulty understanding language. Lesions in Wernicke's area produce a different type of aphasia. Sentences can be grammatically correct and speech itself is normal, but the sentences make no sense. When a patient with damage to Wernicke's area was asked to describe a picture of two boys stealing cookies behind a woman's back, the patient replied: "Mother is away here working her work to get her better, but when she's looking the two boys looking in the other part. She's working another time" (Geschwind, 1979, p. 111). The speech itself is normal and the words are strung together to resemble sentences, but the sentences do not make sense.

In addition to disrupting spoken language, lesions to Wernicke's area disrupt comprehension of language. Patients with severe Wernicke's aphasia cannot even understand single words (Goodglass & Kaplan, 1983).

The differences between Wernicke's and Broca's aphasias led Wernicke to formulate a model of how the brain produces language. Today, nearly 100 years later, this model is still widely accepted. According to this model, when a word is heard the signal passes to Wernicke's area, where it is understood as a verbal message. Spoken language originates in Wernicke's area. It is here that meaningful sentences are formed. The sentence is then transferred to Broca's area. Broca's area is responsible for programming the muscles in the face, tongue, and larynx to speak the sentence formed in Wernicke's area. Thus, damage to Broca's area affects speech, whereas damage to Wernicke's area leaves speech intact but disrupts the understanding of language and the formation of meaningful sentences **(Figure 2.9).**

The work of Broca and Wernicke provided some of the earliest evidence that there was localization in the brain. It also showed how several different areas of the brain interact to produce speech and comprehension. Their work also made a second important contribution. If we look at the brain, we see that it is divided into two halves, or **hemispheres.** Each hemisphere is approximately a mirror image of the other. This is very much in keeping with the right-left symmetry of the rest of the body (two arms, two legs, two eyes, and so forth). Before Broca's discovery, researchers assumed that since the two hemispheres of the brain were anatomically symmetrical, they must also be functionally symmetrical; each half must per-

Paul Broca
(1824–1880)

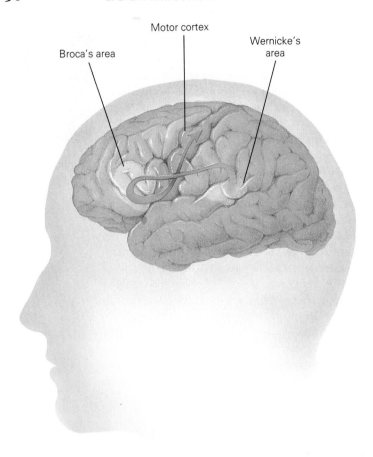

Broca's area   Motor cortex   Wernicke's area

Figure 2.9
Generation of Language.
Language originates in Wernicke's area. It is here that meaningful sentences are formed. They are then transferred to Broca's area, which is responsible for programming the muscles of the face, tongue, and larynx. This information is conveyed to the motor cortex, which in turn sends signals to the muscles.

form similar functions. But the work on language and the brain indicated that this was not the case. Both Wernicke and Broca discovered that the language centers in the human brain were almost always located in the left hemisphere. This is why patients who experience damage from stroke on the left but not the right side of the brain have language difficulty. We will consider some other functional differences between the two halves of the brain later in this chapter, when we discuss research on the split brain.

Thus, the early work on language and the brain indicated that the brain is not a giant uniform mass. Instead, different parts of the brain are specialized for different functions. With this

in mind, researchers began to explore the brain in the hope that they could understand the functions of the different areas. In the next section we will discuss the organization of the brain and some of the research that has shown the relationship between different parts of the brain and different behaviors.

The Three Major Systems of the Brain

In the nearly 200 years since phrenology, we have learned a great deal about how the brain is organized. Contemporary brain researchers organize the brain into three major systems: the brain stem, the limbic system, and the cerebral cortex. As we will see, each of these three systems contributes to different aspects of human behavior.

Figure 2.10 shows an exploded view of the brain. For our purposes, it might be useful to think about the major divisions of the brain as three overlapping layers. The innermost section is the *central core*. As the spinal cord enters the brain, it attaches to the bottommost portion of the central core, called the *brain stem*. This connection between the spinal cord and the brain stem links the higher brain centers with the rest of the body. From an evolutionary point of view, the brain stem is the oldest portion of the brain. Whereas other areas of the brain changed as humans evolved, the brain stem remained about the same (Gaither & Stein, 1979), controlling such primitive or automatic body functions as breathing and blood pressure.

Surrounding the central core is the *limbic system* (limbic means "border"). This system, which evolved after the brain stem, is concerned primarily with emotional behavior. The **cerebral cortex,** or simply **cortex,** is the third and most recently evolved layer of the brain. It surrounds the limbic system and, as we will see, is responsible for our most complex mental processes.

The layered structure of the human brain has prompted some researchers to describe it as being three brains in one (**Figure 2.11** on page 58). At the core is the "reptilian brain," composed of structures that were already well developed in primitive reptiles. This part of the brain roughly corresponds to the central core. Surrounding the reptilian brain is the "old mammalian brain," which corresponds to the limbic system. These structures are well developed in all mammals but much less developed in reptiles. Finally, surrounding the old mam-

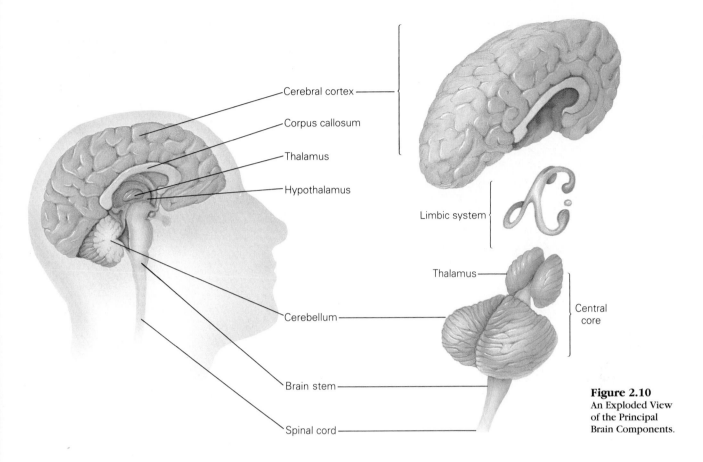

Cerebral cortex

Corpus callosum

Thalamus

Hypothalamus

Limbic system

Thalamus

Central core

Cerebellum

Brain stem

Spinal cord

Figure 2.10
An Exploded View
of the Principal
Brain Components.

malian brain is the "new mammalian brain," which consists of the cerebral cortex. This structure is absent in reptiles but is at least partially developed in all mammals. Only humans, other primates, dolphins, and whales, however, have a well-developed cerebral cortex (McClean, 1977). According to this view, then, the more recently evolved structures such as the cerebral cortex have developed to enable organisms to perform more complex and varied behaviors and mental processes.

It is important to keep in mind that we cannot simply assign one brain structure to each behavior. If we did, we would quickly run out of structures. Although some behaviors appear to be strongly influenced by a particular brain structure, most behaviors are controlled by the interaction of various brain structures. This complex interaction is one of many aspects of the brain that makes its study such a challenging puzzle.

The Cerebral Cortex

The most intriguing and massive structure in the human brain is the cerebral cortex. This crumpled outer layer of the human brain is re-

sponsible for the uniqueness and complexity of human behavior. The ability to sense the world in exquisite detail, to perform fine motor acts, to learn and remember, and to plan and judge, to mention a few, are all functions of the cerebral cortex. The rest of the human brain is very

This model shows what a man's body would look like if each part were proportional to the area of the cortex involved in its sensory perception.

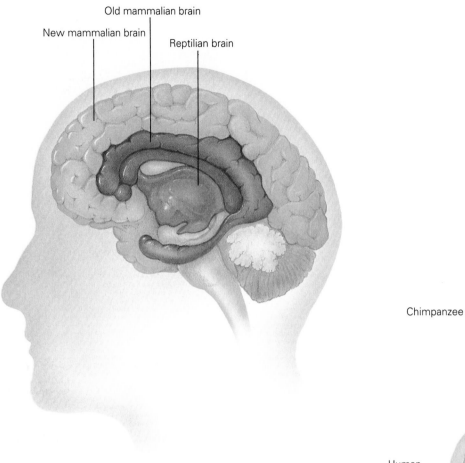

New mammalian brain

Old mammalian brain

Reptilian brain

Figure 2.11
Three Brains in One.

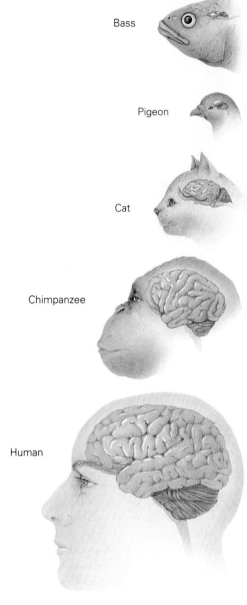

Bass

Pigeon

Cat

Chimpanzee

Human

Figure 2.12
The Increase in the Size of the Cerebral Cortex of
Organisms with Increasingly Complex Behaviors.
Note the appearance of convolutions in the more complex
organisms.

much like that of other animals; it is the cerebral cortex that sets humans apart.

If we examine the cerebral cortex of several species of animals, including humans, we notice two things **(Figure 2.12)**. First, as we go from comparatively simple to more complex animals, the size of the cortex relative to the rest of the brain grows. Second, in the more complex organisms, the cortex has a series of hills and valleys called **convolutions.**

Both the increased cortical size and the convolutions are products of evolution. As organisms became more and more complex and developed new abilities, the cortex grew. Many animals, such as the elephant, have brains much larger than those of humans; however, the ratio of brain weight to body size (the amount of brain per square inch of body surface) is greater in humans than in any other

species. Moreover, the increase in human brain size is due almost exclusively to our larger cortex (Parssingham, 1973).

While the human brain tripled in size during the past two million years, the cerebral cortex increased by at least tenfold. To a large extent, this has been accomplished by the development of convolutions. These convolutions allow a relatively large amount of cortex (2$\frac{1}{2}$ square feet—about the size of a 26-inch televi-

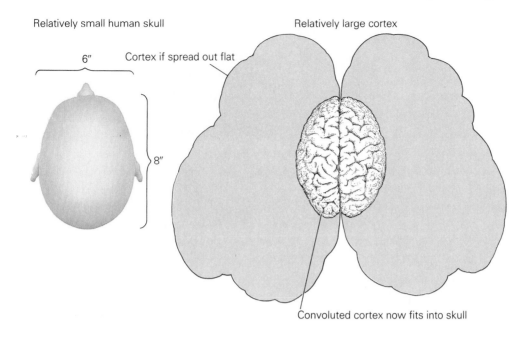

Relatively small human skull

6″

Cortex if spread out flat

8″

Relatively large cortex

Convoluted cortex now fits into skull

Figure 2.13
The Formation of
Convolutions in
the Human Brain.

sion screen) to fit into the relatively small skull **(Figure 2.13)**.

Some of the convolutions serve as landmarks that divide the cortex into four separate areas of lobes (**Figure 2.14,** page 60). The four cortical lobes are the frontal, parietal, temporal, and occipital lobes. The **frontal lobes** are the frontmost portion of the cerebral cortex, and the **occipital lobes** are the rearmost portion. The **parietal lobes** lie between the frontal and occipital lobes, and the **temporal lobes** are located on the side of the brain below the parietal lobes and in front of the occipital lobes. One of the first questions we might ask about these lobes is whether they perform different functions. As the work on language indicates, there is specialization in the cortex.

FUNCTIONS OF THE CORTEX

As early as the nineteenth century, brain researchers knew that certain areas of the cortex were specialized to receive sensory information and others were specialized to control motor acts (e.g., Frietsch & Hitzig, 1870). However, detailed knowledge of specialization in the human cortex came from the pioneering research of Wilder Penfield (1947). Penfield, a neurosurgeon at the Montreal Neurological Institute, was among the first brain researchers to study the human cortex directly.

Many of Penfield's patients had severe epilepsy. *Epilepsy* is a brain disorder in which abnormal electrical activity in the brain causes convulsions. In an attempt to help these people, Penfield often performed surgery to remove the damaged portion of the cortex. Penfield was very concerned about performing this type of surgery, because he knew that removal of part of the cortex would also disrupt some of the person's abilities. So he set out to "map" the cortex and find out exactly what parts of the cortex performed what functions. To accomplish this, Penfield used *electrical stimulation of the brain* (ESB). Penfield operated on conscious patients whose skulls had been treated with a local anesthetic. Once Penfield had exposed the brain, he used a small electric probe to stimulate different areas of the cortex. As he did this he noted the behaviors of the patient. After hundreds of these operations, Penfield was able to begin to assemble a map of the human cortex.

THE SENSORY AREAS

One of Penfield's first findings was that certain parts of the human cortex are specialized to receive sensory information. When Penfield placed the stimulating electrode on the occipital lobe in the back of the brain, the patients reported seeing different kinds of visual displays: "flickering lights, dancing lights, colors, bright lights, star wheels, blue, green, and red colored discs, fawn and blue lights, colored balls swirling, radiating gray spots becoming pink and blue, a long white mark, and so on" (Penfield, 1947). The displays never formed a

Wilder Penfield
(1891–1976)

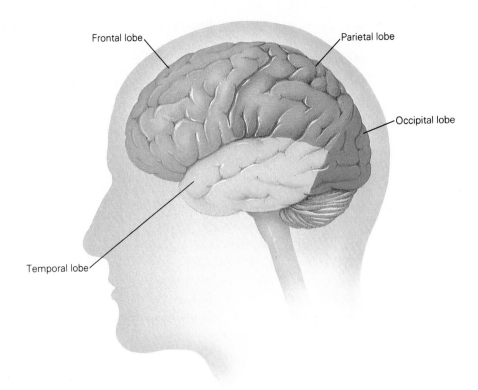

Frontal lobe

Parietal lobe

Occipital lobe

Temporal lobe

Figure 2.14
The Four Cortical
Lobes.

complete picture for the patient, but their presence nevertheless indicated that the occipital lobe is one part of the cortex that is important in vision. Since then, other researchers have indicated more precisely the role the occipital cortex plays.

Large lesions of the occipital lobe produce the disorder called **visual agnosia,** the inability to recognize visual objects (agnosia means "failure to know"). Although these patients can see objects, they do not recognize them (Alexander & Albert, 1983). For example, in a case reported by the neurologist Oliver Sacks, a patient could not even recognize his own wife. When his examination was over, the patient started to look around for his hat. He then reached out and took hold of his wife's head and tried to lift it off and put it on his head. He had apparently mistaken his wife's head for a hat (Sacks, 1985). Such evidence suggests that the occipital cortex is responsible for the conscious experience of visual recognition.

In other cases, Penfield confirmed earlier observations that the sense of hearing is represented in a small area of the temporal lobe.

When he stimulated this area, the patients often reported hearing sounds, such as the ringing of a doorbell or the hum of a motor. In still other patients, Penfield was able to locate the part of the human cortex where the sense of touch is represented. This sense is monitored in a narrow strip in the front of the parietal lobe called the somatosensory cortex (based on the Greek root *soma,* meaning "body," plus *sensory* or *sensation*). The **somatosensory cortex** lies at the border of the frontal and parietal lobes and receives sensory information from the touch receptors in the skin. Even before Penfield began his work, researchers had recorded the electrical activity of this area by placing small electrodes in the somatosensory cortex of animals. They found that when they touched different parts of the body, different areas of the somatosensory cortex showed increased electrical activity. If they touched the animal's paw, one area of the cortex was stimulated. Touching the animal's nose stimulated another area. The researchers reasoned that these excited areas monitored the sense of touch for particular parts of the body (Adrian, 1940; Woolsey, 1958).

Penfield continued the study of the somatosensory cortex in humans. Using the electrified probe, Penfield touched different parts of this cortical strip (Penfield & Rasmussen, 1950). He found that when he stimulated the top of the somatosensory strip, patients reported that someone had touched their leg. When he stimulated the bottom of the strip, patients reported that someone had touched them on the face. Keep in mind that these patients were not able to see their legs or faces and really thought that someone had touched them. They did not know that the sensations were caused by stimulating the cortex. As the result of testing many patients, Penfield confirmed in humans what was already known in animals: that the whole body is represented on the somatosensory cortex. Whenever something touches a certain part of our body, we feel it because the corresponding part of the somatosensory cortex is stimulated.

Damage to the somatosensory cortex produces deficits in the sense of touch. Patients who have extensive lesions of the somatosensory cortex and other parts of the parietal lobe on one side of the brain lose all awareness of the opposite side of the body (the left side of the somatosensory cortex receives information from the right side of the body and vice versa). This condition is sometimes referred to as the *sensory neglect syndrome* (Lezak, 1983). Patients with this syndrome shave only one side of their face and comb only half of their hair. They sometimes object to sharing a hospital bed with what they feel to be someone else's arms and legs (Heilman, Watson, & Valenstein, 1985; Mesulam, 1983). By losing the parietal cortex, the patients lose all sense of one side of their body. Thus, it seems that the somatosensory cortex not only receives touch sensations from the body but also interacts with the rest of the parietal cortex to represent the very existence of the body.

THE MOTOR AREAS

Just as certain parts of the cortex are specialized for sensory functions, others are specialized for motor functions (Evarts, 1979). Once again, our understanding of the motor areas of the human brain is in part due to Penfield's work. Penfield found that when he stimulated a strip of cortex in the very back of the frontal lobe (and right next to the somatosensory strip) his patients would twitch specific muscles. If he stimulated the top, the leg would

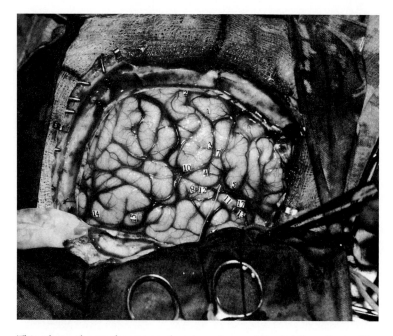

This photo shows the exposed cortex of one of Penfield's patients. The numbers indicate areas that Penfield stimulated with an electric probe. Using this method, Penfield was able to confirm that the entire human body is represented on the somatosensory cortex.

twitch. Stimulating the bottom of the strip produced tongue movement. As was the case with the somatosensory cortex, Penfield was able to map the representation of the entire body on the strip of motor cortex. The **motor cortex** is the area of the cortex located at the border of the frontal and parietal lobes that sends impulses to the voluntary muscles.

The importance of this strip in motor behavior has also been demonstrated in studies in monkeys. In one study, a monkey was taught to depress a telegraph key and then to watch for the appearance of a light. If the monkey released the telegraph key immediately after the light appeared, it received a squirt of fruit juice. While this was occurring, researchers recorded the electrical activity of the neurons in the motor cortex. In doing so they found that the motor cortex became excited (showed increased electrical activity) just before the monkey released the key (Evarts, 1972). This confirmed that the motor cortex is important in initiating muscle action.

Figure 2.15, page 62, shows the primary motor and somatosensory areas of the cortex. In general, the larger the area of representation on the cortex, the greater the sensitivity or degree of motor control. Note, for example, the relatively large areas devoted to the face and hands and the smaller areas for the legs and feet.

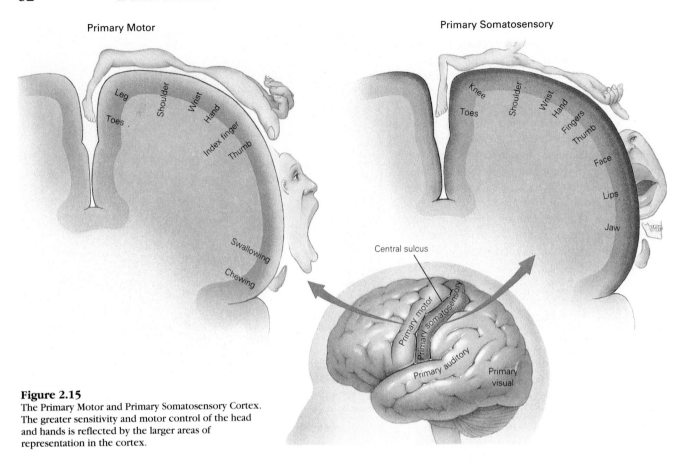

Figure 2.15
The Primary Motor and Primary Somatosensory Cortex.
The greater sensitivity and motor control of the head
and hands is reflected by the larger areas of
representation in the cortex.

THE ASSOCIATION AREAS

The areas of the cerebral cortex discussed thus far are specialized for either sensory or motor functions. These parts of the cortex either receive information from the environment or initiate muscle action. But we have left nearly three fourths of the human cortex uncharted. These areas, not directly involved in either sensory or motor functions, make up the **association cortex.** It is in the association cortex that the brain performs its most complex functions (Pandya & Seltzer, 1982). In this section we will examine the association areas of the frontal, temporal, and parietal lobes.

The frontal lobes are larger in humans than in any other species **(Figure 2.16).** Because of this, early researchers thought the frontal lobe was the seat of intelligence (Frietsch & Hitzig, 1870). But as many studies have since shown, there is no overall loss of intelligence in humans with frontal-lobe damage (Stauss & Benson, 1983). Instead, patients with frontal-lobe damage are sometimes described as lacking in planning and judgment (Luria, 1973; Milner & Petrides, 1984). These patients are unable to make and carry out plans. They are also

unable to change their behavior when a situation changes. For example, one such patient who worked in a carpenter's shop continued to sand a piece of wood until he had sanded completely through the wood and the workbench below (Cotman & McGaugh, 1980).

This lack of planning and judgment has also been clinically demonstrated through a card-sorting task. In these tests, the patient is given a series of cards, each with a different geometric shape on it (for example, crosses, stars, triangles, and circles). In addition, the shapes can be different colors, and there can be a different number of geometric shapes on each card **(Figure 2.17).** Initially, the patient is asked to sort the cards on the basis of color. After sorting 10 cards, the patient is then asked to sort them on the basis of shape. Most of the patients could do the first task, but when asked to shift strategies they were unable to do so. They continued to sort on the basis of color (Milner, 1963). The results of this experiment have several interpretations; however, when considered along with the clinical descriptions of patients, these results suggest that the frontal lobes are involved in the ability to adapt to new situa-

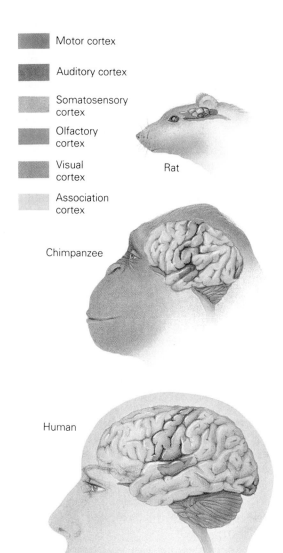

Motor cortex

Auditory cortex

Somatosensory cortex

Olfactory cortex

Visual cortex

Association cortex

Rat

Chimpanzee

Human

Figure 2.16
Association Areas of the Cortex.
The yellow areas represent the association areas of the cortex in rat, chimpanzee, and human. Notice that as we go from less to more complex animals, the amount of association cortex increases. (After Eccles, 1966)

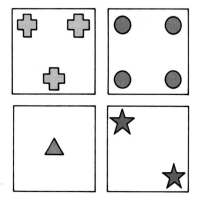

Figure 2.17
The Wisconsin Card-Sorting Test.
The cards in this task can be separated on the basis of several different criteria. They might be sorted on the basis of the geometric shapes on the card, color of the card, or the number of objects on the card. (After Warren & Akert, 1964)

tions and perhaps more generally in planning and judgment.

A second characteristic often seen in humans with frontal-lobe damage is a change in personality. Perhaps the most famous case of personality change following frontal-lobe damage is that of Phineas Gage (Harlow, 1868).

Phineas Gage was a railroad worker whose job was to blast large rocks that were blocking the tracks. One afternoon, Gage was packing gunpowder and sand into a crack in a rock in preparation for a blast. But a spark from the metal tamping rod ignited the gunpowder and a massive explosion followed. The metal rod, 3½ feet long and 1¼ inches in diameter, passed cleanly through Phineas' skull and brain, entering high on his left cheek and emerging from the top of his head. The rod did massive damage to his frontal lobe. To everyone's amazement, Gage survived. The doctors stopped the bleeding and packed the wound, and within a few months Gage went back to work. Although Gage showed no loss of mental abilities and no loss of memory, he did show some interesting personality changes. Before his accident, Gage had been a considerate and friendly person. The new Gage was irritable and inconsiderate and engaged in gross profanity, things he never did before. In fact, Gage's friends noticed such a change that they said he was "no longer Gage." Because of his personality change, Gage lost his job and began drifting around the United States and South America, exhibiting himself and the metal rod as a fairground attraction.

Since the case of Phineas Gage, many other case studies have reported personality changes in patients with frontal-lobe damage. These patients often show lack of restraint, profane language, promiscuous sexual behavior, and a general lack of social graces (Blumer & Benson, 1975; Damasio & Van Hoesin, 1983; Stuss & Benson, 1987). In summary, the available evidence suggests that the frontal lobe is

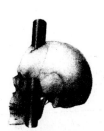

These drawings show three views of how the tamping rod damaged Gage's skull.

involved both in planning and judgment (flexibility of behavior) and in personality. It may be that different parts of the frontal lobe contribute to each of these.

Like the frontal lobe, parts of the temporal and parietal lobes are also involved in complex human functions. One of these functions is memory. Lesions to certain parts of the temporal lobes can impair memory (Milner, 1972). Similarly, neurosurgical patients whose temporal lobes are electrically stimulated often report having an almost dreamlike reliving of a past event. Some say it is like watching a motion picture of something that once happened to them. Upon stimulation of the temporal cortex, a 25-year-old man with a 6-year history of epileptic seizures produced the following responses: "Something brings back a memory, I could see Seven-Up bottling company—Harrison Bakery" (Penfield & Perot, 1963). We will have a more detailed discussion of the temporal lobe's role in memory in Chapter 7.

The association areas of the parietal lobes are important in the integration of complex sensory information. This type of sensory integration may be demonstrated by a simple exercise called *cross-modal matching*. In this task, an object, such as a ball, is placed in a person's hand but kept out of sight. The person is then asked to choose the object visually from among a group of objects. To be successful, the person must integrate visual and touch information. Although healthy people can easily do this task, patients with damage to the parietal association lobe have extreme difficulty (Butters & Brody, 1968).

This completes our tour of the human cortex. We have seen that certain areas are specialized to receive sensory information. Others guide our motor behavior. But most of the cortex—the association cortex—controls the very processes that make us human. In turn, we have looked at three of the association areas— the frontal lobe, which allows us to plan and judge; the temporal lobe, which appears to be involved in memory; and the parietal lobe, which is important in integrating sensory information.

The Limbic System

We have seen that the cortex is involved in our most complex behaviors. It allows us to collect and evaluate information about the world, to make decisions, and even to organize complicated motor behaviors. But in addition to these very complicated behaviors, humans (as well as animals) also exhibit more basic behaviors that are critical to our survival. These behaviors include eating and drinking, sexual behavior, fear and aggression, and experiencing pleasure. Interacting with other brain areas, the cortex plays a role in these behaviors, but other brain centers are primarily responsible for their control.

Directly below and completely surrounded by the cortex is a series of structures that interconnect to form a ring known as the limbic system. The **limbic system** is the set of related anatomical structures, including the hippocampus, amygdala, and hypothalamus, that surround the brain stem and are involved in a number of processes, including emotion, motivation, and aspects of memory. *Hippocampus* is Greek for "seahorse," and this structure is so named because it looks like a seahorse. *Amygdala* is Greek for "almond" and, as we might expect, the amygdala is almond shaped. The *hypothalamus* gets its name because it is located below (in Greek, *hypo*) the *thalamus.* We will discuss the thalamus as part of the central core in the next section. Now, having learned the names and locations of the structures in the limbic system, we can begin to discuss the behaviors with which they are involved.

PLEASURE CENTERS IN THE BRAIN—
THE HYPOTHALAMUS

Many experiences produce pleasurable sensations—a hot shower, a massage, a particularly good meal, or perhaps completing a 5-mile run, to mention a few. But what do all these things have in common? Do we experience pleasure, no matter what the source, because a particular center in our brain has been activated? Could there be a pleasure center? Or are there many pleasure centers in the brain? The following research provided some interesting clues to these questions.

In 1954, James Olds and Peter Milner made an accidental discovery that changed psychologists' views about what it means to say that something is pleasurable. Olds and Milner implanted an electrode in the hypothalamus of a rat's brain. The **hypothalamus** is a group of nerve centers sitting directly under the thalamus on the underside of the brain. Olds and Milner next attached the electrode to a stimulator and then let the rat run free in a 3-square-foot enclosure. Each time the rat entered one of the corners of the enclosure, Olds and Milner electrically stimulated the hypothalamus with a mild current. They wanted to see if the brain stimulation would be unpleasant and cause the rat to avoid that corner. Instead, just the opposite happened. The rat kept coming back to the very corner in which it received brain stimulation. In fact, the rat would go to any part of the box where it received hypothalamic stimulation. Olds and Milner recognized the importance of this discovery and suggested that they had found a "reward or pleasure" center in the brain. The experiments did not stop there. In other studies, Olds rewarded rats for pressing a small bar by giving them electrical stimulation of the hypothalamus. The behavior of these rats was astonishing. They pressed the lever at a rate of more than 2000 times an hour for 24 hours straight **(Figure 2.18)**. Although appearing near exhaustion, some of the rats managed to drag themselves to the bar and press. Still other rats were willing to cross an electrified grid **(Figure 2.19)** or do without food and water for the opportunity to bar press for stimulation (Olds, 1958).

Because brain stimulation can be so rewarding to animals, some critics have raised the possibility that brain stimulation could be misused to control human behavior. The effects of brain stimulation in humans, however, are not clear. Often the subjects in these human studies have a neurological disorder that can be treated only by direct brain stimulation. Some of these patients report that stimulation of the hypothalamus produces a pleasurable feeling, a sense of well-being. Others say it evokes memories of pleasant events (Heath, 1964). But other research indicates that, although humans will push a button for brain stimulation (much like a rat presses a bar), most people can "take it or leave it" and seem to initiate brain stimulation more out of curiosity: "What am I feeling, let me try it once more" (Sem-Jacobson, 1968).

Most researchers now agree that the hypothalamus is important in experiencing pleasure; they also recognize that many other structures in the brain are also important in experiencing "pleasure or reward" (Bozarth, 1986; Olds & Forbes, 1981; Wise & Bozarth, 1984). As is the case with most behaviors, reward is not controlled by one area of the brain. Instead, it is governed by an interaction of many structures. In the case of reward, the hypothalamus plays an important part.

In addition to reward, the hypothalamus is involved in many other critical survival behaviors, such as feeding, drinking, and sexual

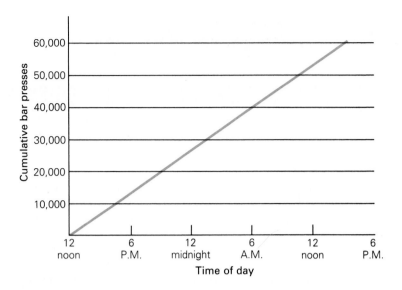

Figure 2.18
Bar Pressing for Brain Stimulation.
Total number of bar presses by a rat for brain stimulation. The animal started at noon and pressed for more than 24 hours at a rate of 2000 presses per hour.

behavior (Grossman, 1979; Pfaff, 1982). In fact, some very recent research suggests the hypothalamus may be related to homosexuality (see "Psychology in the News"). Once again, this is probably because the hypothalamus interacts with many systems in the brain. We will consider some of these other functions in more detail in Chapter 4.

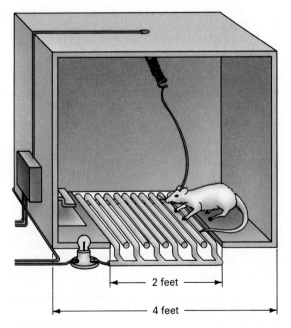

Figure 2.19
Rats and Brain Stimulation.
Research has shown that rats will cross an electrified grid for the opportunity to press a bar for brain stimulation.

Psychology in the News

BRAIN FEATURE LINKED TO SEXUAL ORIENTATION

By C. Ezzell

A comparison of 41 autopsied brains has revealed a distinct difference between homosexual and heterosexual men in the brain region that controls sexual behavior. The finding supports a theory that biological factors underlie sexual orientation, although it remains unclear whether the anatomical variation represents a cause or result of homosexuality, says neurobiologist Simon LeVay, who describes the study in the Aug. 30 SCIENCE.

LeVay, of the Salk Institute for Biological Studies in San Diego, found that a particular cluster of cells in the forefront of the hypothalamus was, on average, less than half as large in the brains of homosexual men as in their heterosexual counterparts. Although scientists have yet to identify the precise function of the clump, called the interstitial nuclei of the anterior hypothalamus 3 (INAH 3), the hypothalamus is known as the seat of the emotions and sexual drives.

LeVay obtained brain tissue from autopsies performed at seven hospitals in New York and California. His study included 19 homosexual men, 16 men presumed heterosexual, and six women presumed heterosexual. All of the homosexual men died of AIDS, as did six of the heterosexual

men and one of the heterosexual women.

As a group, the heterosexual men had larger INAH 3 regions than either the homosexual men or the heterosexual women, LeVay reports. The size difference remained statistically significant whether or not the subjects died of AIDS, ruling out the possibility that it resulted from the disease, he says.

"This proves that you can study sexual orientation at the biological level," LeVay asserts. "There are differences in the brains of adult gay and straight men." However, he warns, "my data don't say how that difference arose."

Previous investigations have turned up other contrasts. In 1984, scientists at the State University of New York at Stony Brook confirmed a German study showing that male homosexuals differ from heterosexual males or females in their response to injections of the sex hormone estrogen (SN: 9/29/84, p. 198). And last year, researchers at the Netherlands Institute for Brain Research reported that homosexual men had a larger suprachiasmatic nucleus than heterosexual men. The suprachiasmatic nucleus—which plays a role in day-night rhythms—also resides in the hypothalamus but

has no known part in sexual behavior.

Psychologist Sandra F. Witelson at McMaster University in Hamilton, Ontario, reported last year that lesbians show a higher incidence of left-handedness than the general population. Witelson, who studies handedness as a measure of brain organization (SN: 8/17/85, p. 102), told SCIENCE NEWS she has now found a similar incidence in homosexual men.

Together, the studies conducted to date "really show that there's something different in the [brain] anatomies of homosexuals and heterosexuals," she says.

Witelson and LeVay speculate that atypical levels of sex hormones may shape the brains of homosexuals in the womb or during childhood. This explanation does not rule out environmental influences, Witelson notes. "A certain brain structure could be a predisposition to homosexual behavior that requires a certain environment to be expressed," she says.

Questions

1. Do these results suggest that sexual orientation has a biological substrate?
2. Do these results mean that fewer cells in the hypothalamus cause homosexuality?
3. What might be the political and social consequences of a finding such as this?

THE HIPPOCAMPUS AND MEMORY

The **hippocampus,** the largest structure in the limbic system, lies between the thalamus and the cortex. Although researchers now believe that the hippocampus is involved in a number of different behaviors, one in which it plays an important role is memory. This is consistent with our earlier discussion of the importance of the temporal lobes in memory.

Surrounded by the temporal lobes, the hippocampus is intimately connected with them (Van Hoesin, 1982). As we will see in Chapter 7, humans with hippocampal damage suffer severe memory disorders.

THE AMYGDALA AND AGGRESSION

In 1937, Heinrich Kluver, a psychologist, and Paul Bucy, a neurosurgeon, reported that damage to the limbic system had a profound effect on the emotional behavior of monkeys. Whereas sexuality in these monkeys increased dramatically, their fearfulness and aggression toward each other were markedly decreased. Kluver and Bucy later reported that lesions limited to one part of the limbic system, the amygdala, changed wild, ferocious monkeys into tame, placid animals. The **amygdala** is the part of the limbic system that is located at the base of the temporal lobe and is involved in appetite, sexuality, and aggression.

Kluver and Bucy's findings were instrumental in the development of **psychosurgery**—the attempt to control human behavior by surgically altering the brain. If amygdala lesions produced a timid and docile monkey, could they do the same to an aggressive human?

One of the best-known cases of human psychosurgery involves the case of Julia, who came to Massachusetts General Hospital seeking help for a serious problem. On 12 separate occasions she had attacked other people without reason, the last time stabbing a woman in the heart with a penknife. Fortunately, the victim survived (Mark & Erwin, 1970). After a series of tests suggested that a diseased amygdala was responsible for Julia's aggressive behavior, Julia's family agreed to experimental psychosurgery. A small lesion was made in Julia's amygdala in the hope that destroying this diseased structure would reduce her aggressive behavior. As critics of this technique have pointed out, it is very difficult to determine the success of this type of treatment (Valenstein, 1980). However, Mark and Ervin reported in a

two-year follow-up that Julia's violent outbreaks had been greatly reduced (Mark, Sweet, & Ervin, 1972).

As you may have anticipated, psychosurgery for the control of aggression is a very controversial topic. On one side are proponents who argue that psychosurgery has produced beneficial effects (see Culliton, 1976). On the other side are critics who feel that it is neither morally nor ethically correct to control people's behavior by altering their brains. Peter Breggin, one of psychosurgery's most outspoken critics, argues: "If America ever falls into the hands of totalitarianism, the dictators will be behavioral scientists and the secret police will be armed with lobotomy and psychosurgery" (Breggin, 1973). This view may be extreme, but it does point out the dilemma of experimenting with the organ of our body that makes us human. If we change a heart or liver, we do not change the entire person; if we change a brain, we very well may.

We should hasten to point out that people who study the brain are interested in using their results to improve—not control—the human condition. In some cases, psychosurgery has produced beneficial effects (Culliton, 1976; Snodgrass, 1973).

The Central Core

The **central core** is the innermost portion of the brain and consists of the brain stem, the thalamus, and the cerebellum. The **brain stem,** the bottommost portion of the central core, is actually an extension of the spinal cord. As the spinal cord enters the skull it enlarges slightly to form the brain stem. The brain stem is specialized for very basic functions such as controlling breathing and blood pressure. Significant injury to this area often results in death. In addition, the brain stem relays sensory and motor signals to and from the rest of the brain. Sensory information coming from the spinal cord is relayed to higher brain areas such as the cortex via the brain stem. Similarly, motor commands from higher structures are relayed to the muscles of the body through the brain stem.

The **thalamus,** sitting like a ball directly atop the brain stem, serves as a sensory relay system, channeling sensory messages to the cortex. Sensory information from all the senses except olfaction (smell) is sent to the thalamus and then routed to the appropriate area of the cortex. In this capacity, the thalamus acts almost like a complex switchboard.

The **cerebellum** is attached to the brain stem and looks like a small brain in itself. The primary function of the cerebellum is coordination of complex motor movements. For example, when we first learn a complex motor act, such as juggling, we have to think about every movement. This often results in awkward, clumsy movements. But after we become proficient, we can perform the act smoothly and automatically. At this point, the cerebellum has taken over. In general, then, the cerebellum seems to be important in learning and programming motor responses (Anderson, 1983; Thompson, 1986).

Some researchers have likened the cerebellum to a computer that controls complex motor acts and thus frees the rest of the brain for conscious activity (Eccles, 1973). When the cerebellum is damaged, even the most common motor acts, such as walking, can no longer be performed automatically. (See **Table 2.2**).

Interim Summary

Some of the earliest attempts to study the relationship of the brain and behavior tried to determine whether different areas of the brain controlled different behaviors. Although phrenology was incorrect, it set the stage for the work of Broca and Wernicke, which established that distinct areas of the cortex were specialized for language.

The brain can be divided into three concentric layers. Each of these subdivisions is specialized for different types of behavior. The outermost layer is the cerebral cortex. This structure is composed of four lobes—frontal, parietal, temporal, and occipital. Certain areas of each lobe are specialized to receive sensory information. Other areas are specialized for motor responses. The remainder of the cortex is involved in associative processes such as planning, judgment, and memory.

Lying underneath and completely surrounded by the cortex is the limbic system. The limbic system is primarily concerned with emotion. Parts of it also play an important role in memory. The innermost segment of the brain, sometimes called the central core, consists of the brain stem, which is involved in controlling basic functions such as

Table 2.2   Organization of the Brain

Area	Function
Cerebral cortex	
Frontal lobe	Association areas—planning, judgment, flexibility
	Association areas—personality
	Motor areas—speech, Broca's area
	Motor areas—primary motor cortex
Parietal lobe	Association areas—sensory integration
	Association areas—sensory neglect syndrome
	Sensory areas—primary somatosensory cortex
Temporal lobe	Association areas—memory (in conjunction with hippocampus)
	Association areas—language, Wernicke's area
Occipital lobe	Sensory areas—Visual perception, lesions produce visual agnosia
Limbic system	
Hypothalamus	Survival behaviors—feeding, drinking, sexual behavior, experiencing pleasure
Hippocampus	Memory
Amygdala	Emotional behavior, a target of psychosurgery to control aggression
Central core	
Brain stem	Control of basic functions such as breathing and blood pressure; relay of sensory and motor information between spinal cord and brain
Thalamus	Sensory relay system to cortex
Cerebellum	Coordination and programming of complex motor movements

breathing and sleep; the cerebellum, which is involved in coordinating movement; and the thalamus, which relays sensory information to the cortex.

BRAIN, BEHAVIOR, AND COGNITION

Up to now we have been exploring the brain in bits and pieces. We have examined the different parts of the brain and discussed the kinds of behavior and mental processes in which they appear to be involved. We have also looked at the role of neurotransmitters and the building block of the brain—the neuron. In doing so, we have focused on relatively simple processes. But when we think about the remarkable capabilities of the human brain, an organ capable of creating Macbeth, the Constitution, and the atomic bomb, it becomes apparent that to fully understand this organ it will be necessary to understand how it functions during more complex processes, the very processes that make us human. Psychologists refer to these complex processes as cognitive processes. **Cognition** means the processing of information about the world around us and includes such mental events as thinking, attention, and memory. Each of these important psychological processes will be considered in later chapters. In this section we will examine some of the new and exciting techniques that brain researchers are beginning to use to better understand how the brain is involved in these cognitive processes.

The Electroencephalogram—Monitoring the Activity of the Brain

Toward the end of the nineteenth century, Hans Berger, a young German soldier, slipped from his horse and fell down an embankment, narrowly escaping serious injury. That evening he was astonished to receive a telegram from his father asking if he was well—his sister had had a feeling that he was in danger. Whether this event was mere coincidence or, as Berger thought, *telepathy*—the ability of someone distant to sense what is happening to another—it later led Berger to change his doctoral studies at the University of Jena from astronomy to psychiatry. Berger was particularly interested in the relationship between the brain and mental phenomena, in which he included telepathy. He knew from earlier research on animals that neurons in the brain communicated with each other through small amounts of electricity. Berger hoped to prove that the electrical responses in the human brain were correlated with consciousness and might even be the physical medium by which thoughts could be telepathically communicated. Berger began by trying to record the electrical activity of the brain.

Because of his primitive equipment, Berger worked unsuccessfully for many years. But in 1924 he discovered that if he placed two flat metal electrodes (about the size and shape of a quarter) on the skull of his son Klaus, he could record the electrical activity of Klaus' brain. Berger later reported that this electrical activity was indeed affected by conscious experience. He wrote, "In many experimental subjects, opening of the eyes caused an immediate change in the EEG and . . . during mental tasks, e.g., when solving a problem of arithmetic, the mere naming of the task caused the same change" (Blakemore, 1977).

What Berger recorded is now known as the electroencephalogram. The **electroencephalogram (EEG)** is a tracing of brain waves that is usually recorded by placing small disclike electrodes on the surface of the skull. Although Berger's dream of understanding telepathy has not been fulfilled, his more modest ambition of correlating human consciousness with EEG has been at least partially realized. The EEG has become both a valuable tool in clinical diagnosis and an often-used research technique for studying the relationship between brain and cognition. One of the first things revealed by an EEG record is that the electrical activity of the brain is not always the same. It changes depending on what the person is doing or even thinking at the time. It is different during waking and sleeping. The EEG may even be different in people with brain damage. Despite all of these differences, it is possible to identify certain distinct patterns of electrical activity that are often related to specific types of mental processes and behavior. The waves that Berger first recorded from his son had a very distinct pattern. Each of the waves was large, and they occurred at a rate of about 8 to 10 waves per second. These waves are called **alpha waves** and are associated with a relaxed but alert state. If we excite a person whose brain is exhibiting alpha waves, the alpha waves disappear and are replaced by smaller waves that occur much more frequently. This pattern of small, high-frequency waves is generally associated with an excited state. Many other types of EEG activity have been identified. Some of these are shown in **Figure 2.20.** But by just looking for the presence or absence of alpha waves, we can begin to tell something about the state of the person.

So far our discussion has focused on the EEG in healthy people. But one of the most useful and important applications of the EEG is to diagnose human brain damage. A damaged area of the brain—an area that contains an infection or a tumor, for example—can often be detected by looking at the EEG. To accomplish this, the neuropsychologist or neurologist might place EEG electrodes over different areas of the brain.

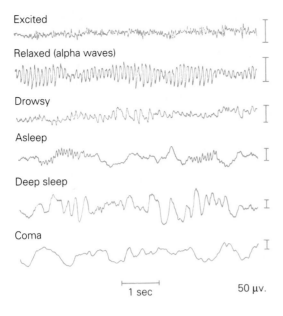

Excited

Relaxed (alpha waves)

Drowsy

Asleep

Deep sleep

Coma

1 sec   50 µv.

Figure 2.20
EEGs Characteristic of Various States in Humans.

When the electrodes are placed over a normal area of the brain, a normal EEG pattern, such as alpha waves, appears. When placed over a damaged portion of the brain, however, the electrodes register an abnormal or unusual EEG or perhaps no EEG at all. Sometimes the abnormal EEG waves take on a fast and almost violent form **(Figure 2.21)**. These signal a *seizure* in that part of the brain. Seizure activity is usually a good indicator that that part of the brain is damaged.

Most recently, researchers have begun to use sophisticated computer analysis of EEG recordings to help diagnose conditions ranging from depression to alcoholism (John, Prichep, Fridman, & Easton, 1988).

Imaging the Living Brain

The past decade has seen remarkable breakthroughs in technology. This technology has changed the way we live and has also changed the way we study the brain. Some of the most exciting and potentially useful ways to study the brain have only recently been developed. These methods make it possible to image or visualize the human brain as it functions inside the skull. Of great significance is that these imaging methods are noninvasive; that is, they do not require opening the skull or even placing electrodes on the skull. Moreover, they cause no pain or risk to the person. Because of this, they have the potential to be used in many situations and to provide a wealth of information about how the intact brain functions during a variety of cognitive processes.

Imaging methods use computer-assisted reconstructions of many individual views of the brain. It is almost as if thousands of photographers could take still images of a brain and then a computer could assemble the images into a three-dimensional model. The model, of course, would provide much more information than any individual snapshot. One imaging technique that is now familiar to most of us is **computer-assisted axial tomography,**

Figure 2.21
The EEGs of a Person With Epilepsy (Color Traces) and a Person Without Epilepsy (Black Traces).
The increased electrical activity occurring halfway through the color tracings indicates the onset of a seizure. Each tracing (AC, BF, and LO) shows electrical activity between two corresponding areas of the brain, as labeled on the diagram at left.

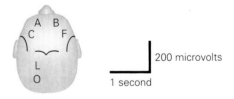

200 microvolts

1 second

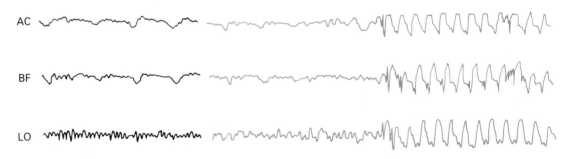

AC

BF

LO

which results in what is commonly known as a **CAT scan,** in which many individual images are obtained by passing X-rays through the head. The computer then assembles these individual pictures into an image. CAT scans are very useful in diagnosing disorders of the brain such as tumors.

MAGNETIC RESONANCE IMAGING

Magnetic resonance imaging (MRI) is another technique that allows us to look at the intact, functioning human brain without harming or endangering the individual. Its main advantage over the CAT scan is that it is more sensitive. That is, it produces pictures that are much clearer than CAT scans. It is like the difference between watching television on a regular set and a newer high-definition television. MRI takes advantage of the fact that nuclei of atoms in the brain respond to magnetic fields differently. By exposing the head to harmless magnetic fields of varying strengths, it is possible to produce a computer-assisted three-dimensional image of the brain. Research using MRI to investigate the brain is relatively new, but there are already some exciting findings. For example, Eric Courchesne has used MRI to show a link between autism and shrinkage of the cerebellum (Courchesne 1987) **(Figure 2.22).** Other researchers have suggested that MRI may eventually be useful in diagnosing a variety of brain diseases from shizophrenia (Andreasen, 1988) to Alzheimer's disease (Besson, Corrigan, & Foreman, 1985).

CAT scans and MRI have been valuable tools for looking at the human brain, but they do not tell us much about the relationship between brain activity and mental processes. These relationships are better studied by a technique called positron emission tomography (PET). If CAT scans and MRI provide snapshots of the brain at a particular time, then PET provides a full-length movie.

POSITRON EMISSION TOMOGRAPHY

Positron emission tomography (PET) takes advantage of the fact that, at any given time, some areas of the brain are more active than others (Phelps, Hoffman, Mullani, & Ter-Pogossian, 1975). For example, there is increased activity in the visual cortex when an individual looks at a painting, in the auditory cortex when an individual listens to a song, and in the cerebellum when a person shuffles a

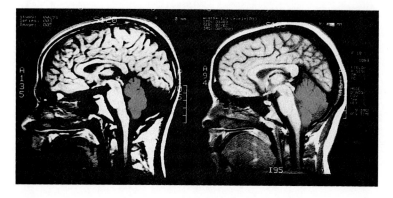

Figure 2.22
Magnetic Resonance Imaging Showing a Fully Functional Brain (right) and an Autistic Person's Brain (left).
The part of the cerebellum colored red is much smaller in the brain of the autistic person (left) than in the brain of a normal person. This area regulates responses to outside stimuli such as noises, heat, and cold, and may be involved in controlling motion and memory.

deck of cards. PET scans provide a way to visualize this activity. We will first briefly describe how a PET scan accomplishes this feat and then discuss some of the applications.

The brain's primary source of energy is glucose, a form of sugar. When an area of the brain becomes more active, it uses more glucose. Thus one way to measure the involvement of brain areas in a particular mental process is to measure the amount of glucose that area of the brain uses. In positron emission tomography, the scanner measures the amount of glucose used in thousands of small brain areas and then feeds this information to a computer that produces a picture of the level of activity throughout the entire brain.

Figure 2.23 is a PET scan of a normal, healthy person. To appreciate the scan, keep in mind that hotter colors—reds and oranges, for example—indicate more activity, whereas the cooler blues and greens indicate less activity. On the left-hand scan the person's eyes are closed. Notice how cool the occipital or visual cortex appears. In the middle panel, the person looks at a white dot of light. Note the increase of activity in the visual cortex. Finally, in the right-hand panel the person observes a complex picture, perhaps a painting. Here activity in the visual cortex increases dramatically. **Figure 2.24** shows a person either sitting in a silent room or listening to a Sherlock Holmes story. Notice how the auditory areas of the cortex in the temporal lobe light up when the mystery is read. Also notice that the hippocampus is active. This is because the person was told to try to remember the story (recall that the hip-

Figure 2.23
PET Scan of a Normal Person.

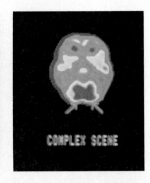

Figure 2.24
PET Scans of a Person Sitting in a Silent Room (top row) and A Person Listening to a Sherlock Holmes Story (bottom row).

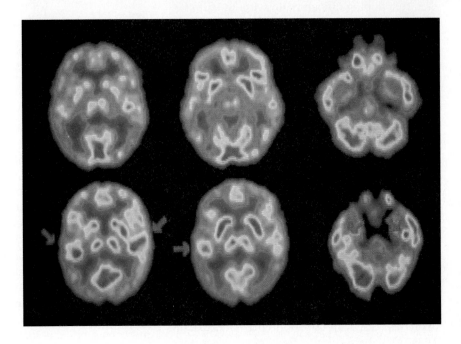

pocampus is involved in memory). Here, then, is an example of a PET scan showing the brain areas involved in an important cognitive process—memory (Martin & Brust, 1985).

Might PET scans be used to examine mental processes as complex as human thought? Consider the following experiment. In this study a subject was placed in a PET scanner and asked to move his right hand. This activated the frontal cortex and motor areas in the opposite (left) side of the brain. Next the subject was told just to "think about moving the hand." In this case, the motor areas were no longer activated and the PET scan revealed the basic neural activity pattern of the thought in the frontal cortex (Restak, 1984).

PET scans have already been used in a variety of situations. For example, they have helped identify the abnormal brain areas in patients with aphasia (Benson, Metter, Kuhl, & Phelps, 1983) as well as the damaged brain areas in patients with epilepsy (Engel, 1983). PET scans may also help to diagnose psychological disorders such as schizophrenia, depression, and mania (Benson, 1983; Andreasen, 1988).

These examples show the tremendous potential of PET scans to provide the much needed microscope for examining the intact, functioning human brain.

DAMAGE AND REPAIR OF THE HUMAN BRAIN

In a structure as complex as the human brain many things can go wrong. Indeed, it is amazing that for most people the brain functions effectively for more than 70 years. Nevertheless, disorders do sometimes occur. These disorders are due to a variety of causes. Some are due to genetics—they are inherited. Huntington's disease (sometimes called Huntington's chorea), which affects the brain centers concerned with movement, is one example of a genetically transmitted brain disorder (Burch, 1979). Other disorders are due to environmental factors such as viruses. Creutzfeldt-Jakob disease, a rare disorder that strikes middle-aged adults causing a steady decline in mental abilities, is produced by a virus (Kety, 1979). But most disorders of the brain do not have such clear-cut genetic or environmental causes. Instead, they are produced by a combination of genetic and environmental events. Strokes, which cause more deaths than any other brain disorder (WHO, 1980), have both genetic and environmental components. Psychological disorders such as schizophrenia and depression are now believed to be related to chemical disorders in the brain. Again, these chemical disorders have both genetic and environmental components. We will discuss the biochemical basis for schizophrenia and depression when we consider abnormal behavior in Chapter 16. In Chapter 11 we will examine the debilitating brain disorder known as Alzheimer's disease.

One of the most tragic aspects of brain damage is its permanence. Unlike the liver or kidneys, which have the ability to regenerate, the brain does not have the capacity to repair itself. Once neurons are damaged, they are lost forever, along with the mental processes they controlled. Therefore, developing a way to repair the damaged brain is one of the most important goals of brain research. In this section, we will examine the rapid and exciting progress in this area.

Brain Grafts

Although it would have sounded like science fiction only a few years ago, brain researchers have begun transplanting part of one brain into another in a surgical procedure known as a **brain graft.** Most of the work to date has been conducted in animals, but recently the first human brain grafts have been attempted.

One area of great promise for the use of brain grafts is in the control of Parkinson's disease, a neurological disorder that affects about 1 million people in the United States. Parkinson's disease disrupts coordinated movement. Even simple tasks such as walking across the room become an ordeal for victims of Parkinson's disease.

Although brain researchers do not yet know what causes Parkinson's disease, they do have a good understanding of what goes wrong in the brain as a result of the disorder (Calne et al., 1987). Parkinson's disease is the result of damage to an area in the brain stem called the *substantia nigra* (the "black substance"). Normally, neurons in this area secrete the neurotransmitter dopamine. In Parkinson's disease, these cells die and there is a shortage of dopamine. The typical treatment is to administer L-dopa, a chemical that the brain converts to dopamine. The problem with L-dopa therapy, however, is that over a period of 5 to 10 years the drug no longer helps many patients, and in some patients the drug causes severe convulsions and hallucinations.

The possibility of using brain grafts to treat Parkinson's disease has generated both excitement and research. The initial research was conducted in animals, but more recently attempts have been made in humans.

In the studies in animals, brain researchers began by destroying the substantia nigra of 12 adult rats. As expected, the lesion depleted the supply of dopamine and produced the symptoms of Parkinson's disease. Next, the researchers removed the substantia nigra from rat fetuses and implanted the tissue into the brain of the adult rats. Four weeks after the implants the researchers tested the rats and noted a 70 percent improvement in the rats' parkinsonian symptoms. Not only had the brain transplants survived, they were functioning. This was still true 9 months after the operation (Perlow, Freed, Hoffer, Seiger, Olson, & Wyatt, 1979).

Since this exciting experiment, grafts of several brain areas have been successfully attempted in animals (Bjorkland & Steveni, 1984). But perhaps the most exciting aspect of this technique is the possibility of using brain grafts to help human patients. The first human transplant was attempted by physicians at the Karolinska Institute in Stockholm in the spring of 1982. The patient was a man so seriously affected by Parkinson's disease that, without medication, he could not even move. He agreed to the operation, and the hospital's board of ethics gave its permission. The neurosurgeons first removed about two thirds of the man's adrenal medulla, a structure that rests above the kidneys and makes dopamine as a minor product. They then implanted this tissue directly into the man's brain. Unfortunately, the results of this study were disappointing (Backlund, Grandburg, & Hamberger, 1985).

In 1987 a group of Mexican researchers stirred a great deal of interest in brain grafts when they reported that transplanting a portion of the dopamine-secreting medulla into the brain of two patients dramatically improved their condition. One man, who could barely move before the operation, reportedly became well enough to return to his home, where he ran a small farm (Madarazo, Drucker-Colin, Diaz, Torres, Becerril, & Martinez-Mata 1987). This report prompted a widespread clinical trial in the United States. But the results here as well as subsequent studies in Mexico have not been nearly as successful. There has been only a modest improvement in about 30 to 50 percent of the patients (Lindvall, 1991). Nevertheless, researchers continue to be very excited about the prospects for this therapy. The most recent work in humans has been done in Sweden using an important variation in the procedure. The Swedish researchers have implanted tissue from a human fetus. The results have been quite encouraging, with all patients showing some improvement in the symptoms of Parkinson's disease (Lindvall et al., 1990).

Although the results of brain grafts for Parkinson's disease continue to be promising, they must be treated with caution until further tests are conducted and until the process by which the grafts work is better understood.

Ethical Considerations

Even if brain grafts prove successful, the procedure raises serious ethical issues. For example, some researchers believe that the best tissue for transplantation is from an unborn or aborted fetus. This raises the troubling possibility that some women will conceive children with the intent of aborting them either to aid a family member or to sell the fetuses for their brain tissue. There has already been a report in the popular press of a woman in California who asked a medical ethics expert whether she could be artificially inseminated with sperm from her father, who suffers from Alzheimer's disease. The resulting fetus would have been aborted for brain tissue to transplant into her father's brain (T. Lewin, 1987). Issues such as this will make brain grafts a highly controversial procedure in the years ahead (Hoffer & Olson, 1991). One promising solution to the problem of where to obtain human tissue is to grow neurons in test tube cultures. Progress in this exciting line of research is already under way (Ronnett et al., 1991).

What is the future of brain grafts? Some researchers believe that they will be commonplace in 10 years. Others caution that a significant amount of research is necessary before the technique can be useful. Nevertheless, the potential for brain grafts is startling. At present there is research to examine many possibilities, including grafting tissue that releases acetylcholine to improve Alzheimer's disease, grafting tissue into the hippocampus to improve memory loss, and even grafting entire eyes to help restore vision (Bjorkland, 1991).

Interim Summary

Several techniques have been developed to examine the functioning of the intact brain. The electroencephalogram (EEG) records the electrical activity of the brain. It is very useful in detecting seizures. Computer-assisted axial tomography (CAT) is an X-ray technique used to record brain structure. Magnetic resonance imaging (MRI) produces high-resolution pictures of the brain. MRI has been used to begin to understand how the brains of autistic children may be different. An imaging technique that permits measurement of brain activity during particular mental processes is positron emission tomography (PET). PET scans have allowed researchers to examine the brain mechanisms involved in complex human mental processes such as panic attacks.

Although the human brain does not have the capacity to repair itself, recent research indicates that it may be possible to transplant part of one brain into another. The results of such experiments on rats suggest that this technique may be valuable in treating disorders such as Parkinson's disease. Recent studies in human Parkinson's patients have been promising. There are, however, many ethical questions surrounding the issue of brain grafts.

HUMAN CONSCIOUSNESS AND THE SPLIT BRAIN

We now know a good deal about the human brain and how it controls behavior. We know quite a bit about the geography or anatomy of the brain. And we know something about its chemistry—about its neurons and synapses and how drugs and chemicals affect these components. We even know something about specialization in the brain and the areas and chemicals that are involved in behaviors like aggression and the experience of pleasure. We have also learned about techniques that can be used to look inside the living brain. But we still know very little about how the brain is involved in what is perhaps our most important and intriguing experience, the experience of consciousness—awareness of ourselves and the world.

Gustav Fechner was a German physicist and philosopher who was intrigued by the relationship between mind and body. One of the founders of experimental psychology, he was also one of the first to speculate about the relationship between consciousness and the brain.

Fechner knew that the brain is *bilaterally symmetrical.* That is, it has two sides or hemispheres that are apparent mirror images of each other. If we find a structure on one side of the brain, we find the same structure on the opposite side. There are two temporal lobes, two amygdalas, two frontal lobes, and so on for all the structures of the brain. With this knowledge in mind, Fechner (1860) proposed a seemingly impossible experiment. He asked what would happen to the train of human consciousness if it were possible to split the brain in half. Fechner believed that if this were possible, each half of the brain would have a different conscious experience. Two minds would live inside one brain. Fechner proposed this remarkable test over 100 years ago, never dreaming that it could actually be carried out. But the hypothetical experiment of Fechner has now actually been conducted with fascinating results.

The Split Brain in Humans

The test of Fechner's idea came about as a by-product of surgery performed on human patients to prevent epileptic seizures. An epileptic seizure usually starts in one small area of the brain and then spreads rapidly to other brain areas. Since about 1930, neurosurgeons have tried to control some cases of epilepsy by removing the disordered areas of the brain. These treatments have met with limited success, so they decided to try a more dramatic approach—to separate the two hemispheres of the brain. To do this the neurosurgeons cut the **corpus callosum,** a large bundle of axons ¹/₂ inch wide by 3¹/₂ inches long that connects the two hemispheres (see **Figure 2.25**). No one knew exactly what the corpus callosum did, but brain researchers were fairly certain that

this bridge of 200 million axons was somehow involved in transmitting information between the two hemispheres. The surgery was often successful in reducing the severity of epileptic seizures by limiting them to only one half of the brain. But what was the fate of these people with a bisected brain? Was Fechner right? Did they have two separate consciousnesses? The case history of a split-brain patient provides a partial answer to this separate-consciousness question.

A few years after a traumatic head injury, W.J. began to experience severe epileptic seizures. After attempting all conceivable remedies for W.J.'s problem, the neurosurgeons decided to cut through his corpus callosum (Bogen & Vogel, 1963). Beginning in the 1950s, a group of psychologists led by Roger Sperry were carrying out a series of experiments in split-brain animals (animals whose corpus callosum had been cut). They found some interesting results (Sperry, 1968), but the opportunity to examine a split-brain human was even more exciting. It provided the chance to answer Fechner's question.

At first observation, Sperry (1964) was unable to see anything unusual about W.J. In fact

Roger Sperry

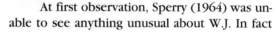

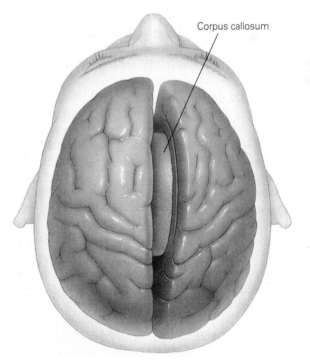

Figure 2.25
The Corpus Callosum.
The corpus callosum is a large band of about 200 million axons connecting the right and left hemispheres of the cortex. In this diagram the hemispheres have been separated so that the corpus callosum is visible.

he once commented, "In casual conversation over a cup of coffee and a cigarette, one would hardly suspect that there was anything at all unusual about him" (p. 46). But after more intensive testing, it became apparent that people with split brains were quite different (Gazzaniga, 1970; Sperry, 1974).

Before we can look at the unusual effects in split-brain humans we need an understanding of how information gets in and out of each side or hemisphere of the brain. There is a form of division of labor in the brain such that the right hemisphere receives information only from the left side of the body and the left hemisphere receives information only from the right side. So if we place an object in the left hand, only the right hemisphere senses it. Similarly, if we see an image in the right visual field, only the left hemisphere senses it. This poses no problem when the brain is intact, since all information can get to both hemispheres by crossing the corpus callosum. But in the split brain, each hemisphere gets information only from one side of the body (**Figure 2.26**). As we will see, this can pose some interesting problems for humans with split brains.

One of the first tests that Sperry and Gazzaniga conducted on the patients with split brains was a simple one. They showed a spoon to either the right visual field (left hemisphere) or the left visual field (right hemisphere) and asked what the subject had seen (Sperry, 1972; Gazzaniga & LeDoux, 1978). As shown in **Figure 2.27,** when the left hemisphere was tested, the subject replied "spoon." But when the right hemisphere was tested, the subject replied, "I don't know" or "There is nothing there." The researchers were initially puzzled, but additional tests provided the information necessary to solve the puzzle. As we indicated earlier, the left hemisphere almost always controls language. When shown the spoon, the left hemisphere recognized it and conveyed the information to the language center. The subject was thus able to say "spoon." But when the spoon was shown to the right hemisphere, there was no way for the information to be passed along to the language center in the left hemisphere since the corpus callosum was severed. The right hemisphere controls the left hand, and with the left hand the subject could identify the spoon by touch but could not convert this information into words. Since the left hemisphere had not seen anything and had no way of knowing what the right hemisphere had observed, the subject replied by saying, "There is nothing there."

From this and other studies, an interesting picture of the two hemispheres has emerged. The left hemisphere is specialized for verbal abilities, or the capacity for language, reading, and writing. It also seems to be involved with mathematical and analytical abilities. The right hemisphere is nonverbal but has other important abilities. It thinks in symbols, not words. It has excellent spatial abilities and may be related to the ability to draw (Springer & Deutsch, 1989).

The Major and Minor Hemispheres

The left hemisphere is sometimes known as the **major hemisphere** because it controls language, an important human skill. The right hemisphere, which controls spatial skills, has been treated as something of a second-class citizen and has often been referred to as the **minor hemisphere** (Nebes, 1974). However,

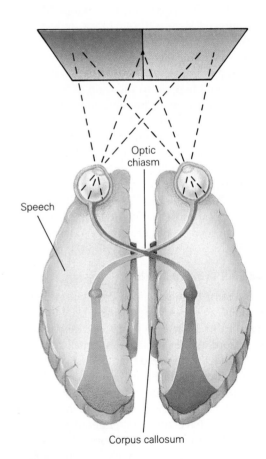

Figure 2.26
Visual Information in the Split Brain.
As this figure shows, in the split-brain patient, information from the left side of the visual field projects only to the right hemisphere and information from the right side of the visual field projects only to the left hemisphere. Because of this, it is possible to present stimuli to only one hemisphere of the split-brain patient.

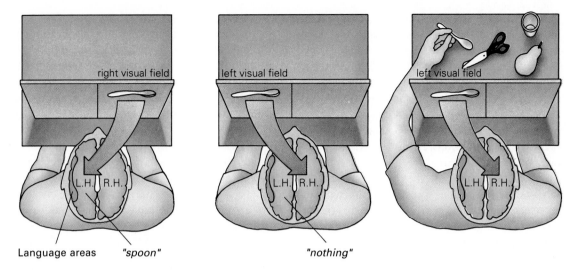

right visual field

left visual field

left visual field

L.H. R.H.

L.H. R.H.

L.H. R.H.

Language areas   *"spoon"*

"nothing"

Figure 2.27

Testing the Split-Brain Patient.
When a picture of a spoon is presented to the right visual field and thus registered in the left hemisphere, the subject is able to answer "spoon" when asked to identify the object. This is because language areas are located in the left hemisphere. When the same object is presented to the left visual field and thus registered in the right hemisphere, the subject is unable to verbally identify the object. Yet with the left hand, the subject can correctly identify by touch the object presented to the left visual field.

psychologists have begun to recognize the talents of the right or minor hemisphere. The left or language hemisphere may give us the ability to solve a brainteaser or tell a wonderful story, but without the right hemisphere we can't so much as copy a simple shape. Only the excellent spatial talents of the right hemisphere enable us to draw complex figures **(Figure 2.28).** In fact, one view stresses the idea that the reason many people are poor artists is that they are dominated by their left or verbal hemisphere (Edwards, 1979). Without the right hemisphere, we may have difficulty recognizing complex figures like a face. When the left hemisphere is damaged, people may lose their ability to speak and write, but they are still able to compose music. As you can see, it may not be fair to refer to the right hemisphere as the minor hemisphere. Although it is not specialized for language, it does perform some very important functions. In fact, Albert Einstein once said that he rarely thought in words at all, claiming that his concepts first appeared in symbols and images and were only later expressed in words. This raises the intriguing possibility that Einstein's brilliant theories were constructed in the right hemisphere and then shifted to the left hemisphere to be formed into written language.

Two Hemispheres Working Together

From the evidence, we might think that Fechner was correct. The two sides of the brain seem to have separate consciousnesses. One hemisphere is specialized for verbal functions. The other is involved with nonverbal or spatial functions. But before we draw this conclusion, we might ask why the two hemispheres perform different functions.

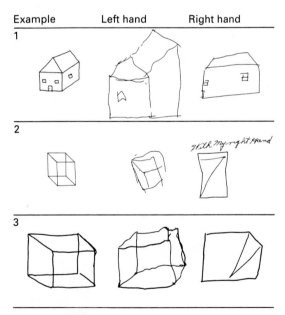

Example   Left hand   Right hand

1

2

3

Figure 2.28

Spatial Abilities of the Right Hemisphere.
The superior spatial talents of the right hemisphere are demonstrated by the drawing abilities of a split-brain subject. The subject was asked to produce the figures in the first column, using either the right or left hand. The left hand (controlled by the right hemisphere), though not as dexterous as the right hand, was better able to reproduce the spatial arrangement. The right hand (left hemisphere), though more coordinated, could not duplicate the 3-D forms.

To help answer this question, let's look at the results of one of the most unusual tests performed on patients with split brains (Levy, Trevarthen, & Sperry, 1972). In these tests, the subjects were asked to look at a face on a screen **(Figure 2.29).** The face, however, was actually a composite of two faces, with half of one face on each side. This is called a *chimeric,* or imaginary, stimulus because such a stimulus does not exist in the real world.

When the subjects viewed the screen, the face on the left half of the screen, the woman, was seen only by the right hemisphere, and the face on the right half of the screen, the man, was seen only by the left hemisphere. Thus, each hemisphere had a different image and each did not know what the other was seeing.

Now, what happened when the subjects were asked about the picture? When subjects were asked to describe the picture, the left or language hemisphere dominated. Subjects answered that they had seen a picture of a man with bushy eyebrows and a thin mustache. But if the subjects were asked to select from a group of photographs the one that matched the face on the screen, the right or nonverbal hemisphere dominated and the subjects selected the woman. Which hemisphere dominated depended on the type of information requested.

This tells us that the two hemispheres process different types of information about a stimulus. In the case of a face, the left hemisphere processes it in terms of language. It might remember deep-set eyes, a small nose, or a double chin. The right hemisphere, on the other hand, responds to the whole face as a total picture.

Based on evidence such as this, some researchers have characterized the left hemisphere as the "analyzer" and the right hemisphere as the "synthesizer" (Nebes, 1974). The left hemisphere best handles discrete information that can be stated as verbal statements or mathematical propositions. It analyzes the face in terms of its components. The right hemisphere is superior when information cannot be adequately described in words or symbols. It synthesizes all the information in the face and recognizes it as a whole. It is, however, important to keep in mind that these are not all-or-nothing abilities. Although the left hemisphere is specialized for language-analytical functions and the right for spatial-synthetic abilities, there is overlap. To a lesser degree, each hemisphere can perform some of the tasks for which the opposite hemisphere is specialized. For example, although the right hemisphere cannot speak, it does have some important language abilities and can understand simple language (Sperry, 1983).

Recent research suggests that the right hemisphere contributes the color to ordinary speech in much the same way that the color commentator in a sporting event contributes to the play-by-play announcer. Like the play-by-play announcer, the left hemisphere is primarily responsible for expressing and understanding basic language. But the right hemisphere makes possible the expression and understanding of emotions such as enthusiasm, joy, and sadness. It also helps us understand puns and sayings (Springer & Deutsch, 1985). Patients with damage to their right hemisphere are often incapable of expressing anger. If these patients are asked to speak in an emotional voice, for example, to say "Get the hell out of here," their voice is flat and unemotional. They sometimes emphasize their feelings by adding parenthetic statements. For example, to express anger they might say in an unemotional voice, "I am angry (and I mean it)" (Ross & Mesalum, 1979). These patients also have difficulty understanding familiar sayings such as "It takes one to know one" or "the truth, the whole truth, and nothing but the truth" even though they can understand otherwise very complex

Figure 2.29

Stimuli Used in the Chimeric-Stimulus Study.

The top photo is the face flashed on the screen. When the subjects are asked to verbally describe the stimulus, the left hemisphere controls the response and subjects answer, "A man with dark eyebrows and a mustache." But when asked to point to the photo they saw, subjects select the photo of the woman, indicating the response is controlled by the right hemisphere. (After Levy, Trevarthen & Sperry, 1972)

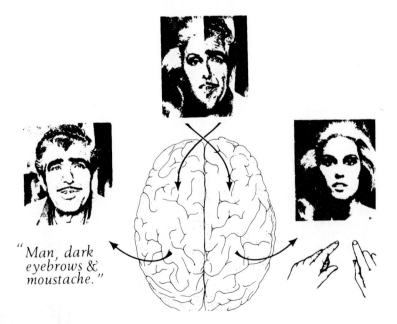

"Man, dark eyebrows & moustache."

language. To explain this finding, researchers have suggested that understanding familiar phrases requires a type of *pattern recognition,* a spatial ability in which individual stimuli are classified into meaningful categories. As in the case of other spatial abilities, the right hemisphere is specialized for pattern recognition (Kempler & Van Lancker, 1987). Studies such as these suggest that the right hemisphere plays an important, if underrated, role in language.

Before we conclude that the two hemispheres are separate conscious entities, we might consider how the two work together. Consider the case of recognizing a friend. The right hemisphere sees the face and, due to its superior ability to recognize complex patterns and figures, realizes that it is a friend. Now that you have recognized the face, you might want to call your friend by name. The right hemisphere, however, can't do this. So, it sends its information over the corpus callosum to the left hemisphere, where a name is associated with the face. This example shows how the two hemispheres work together and that they are specialized in the way they process information. This specialization allows us to perform many complicated tasks, like associating a figure or a face with a name.

In a sense, Fechner was right. When the brain is split, two separate streams of consciousness are created. But it may be more important to realize that in the intact brain these two streams of consciousness blend together to help us perform the complex functions that make us conscious, functioning humans.

The Split Brain—Cautions and Controversies

Research on split-brain patients has had a tremendous impact on how we think about the human brain. Indeed, Roger Sperry was awarded the 1981 Nobel Prize in Medicine and Physiology for his pioneering work in this field. But split-brain work has also brought forth controversy. Some researchers have suggested that we have taken the notion of a divided brain too far and recommended that we proceed with caution (Sperry, 1983). In this section we will examine two of these controversial areas.

Can We Generalize from the Damaged Brain?

We know a good deal about specialization in the two hemispheres. But pause for a moment and think about the source of this information. It comes from a relatively small number of patients who underwent neurosurgery for severe brain impairments. Many of these patients had

a long history of epileptic seizures before undergoing the split-brain operation. Can we conclude anything about the normal brain from studying these unusual patients?

To answer this question, studies of specialization in normal people are needed. Of course, split-brain operations are not performed on healthy people, but technology such as the PET scan has made it possible to study hemispheric specialization in the intact human brain. Consider an experiment in which people listen to music after being given some very specific instructions. The listeners are presented with two musical chords and asked, "Are they the same or different?" If they are asked to respond reflexively by pushing a button, the right hemisphere lights up. But if they are asked to mentally arrange the chords on a scale, a task that requires analysis and some musical sophistication, the left hemisphere lights up (Mazziota & Phelps, 1985) **(Figure 2.30)**.

One interpretation of this finding is that scaling the chords is an analytical task and is thus carried out by the analytical left hemisphere. Just determining whether the chords are the same or different is a nonanalytic or holistic task and is thus carried out primarily by the synthesizing right hemisphere. Studies such as this support the idea that the hemispheres are specialized much in the way that research on split-brain patients suggests.

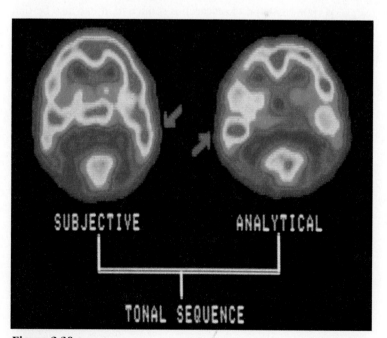

Figure 2.30
Specialization in the Intact Brain.
When subjects were asked merely whether the musical chords presented were the same or different, the PET scan indicates activity in the right hemisphere of the brain (A). When the subjects were asked to arrange mentally the chords on a scale, the PET scan shows more activity in the left hemisphere (B).

Brain and Sex Differences—Are They Real?

Although the studies are controversial, there is some research suggesting that men generally have better spatial abilities than women but women generally speak earlier and learn foreign languages more easily (Halpern, 1986). These findings have prompted some researchers to hypothesize that differences in the brain produce these differences in abilities. Specifically, the superior right hemisphere in men accounts for their superior spatial abilities, whereas the better-developed left hemisphere in women is responsible for their superior language abilities (De Lacoste-Utamsing & Holloway, 1982; Moir & Jessel, 1990). Although conclusions such as this fit nicely into what we know about specialization and the split brain, they have been sharply criticized.

The first line of criticism questions whether men really do have better spatial abilities. The critics point out that for every study that finds superior spatial abilities in males, there is another that finds no such difference (Caplan, MacPherson, & Tobin, 1985). Other critics argue that the evidence suggesting better development of the right hemisphere in men and the left hemisphere in women is also flawed (Bleier, Houston, & Byne, 1986).

What can we conclude? At this point all we can say is that this a controversial topic that must await further research. And although this type of research is seductive, it can also be dangerous. For example, some might use it as a rationale for channeling young boys and girls into different career tracks. Although the work on the split brain has been very influential, it is important to be cautious in making broad generalizations about the relationship between brain and behavior.

Interim Summary

One of the most intriguing questions faced by psychologists who study the brain is the brain's role in experiencing consciousness. Studies of the split brain have yielded important insights into this brain function and the issue of brain and behavior in general.

By severing the corpus callosum, researchers have determined that the two hemispheres are specialized for different functions. The left hemisphere is specialized for language, while the right hemisphere is primarily concerned with spatial abilities. Researchers have also gained insight into

how the two hemispheres work together to process information.

Some of the most recent work on the split brain raises cautions and controversies. For example, some of the research suggesting that men and women have different abilities based on different brain organization has been sharply criticized.

SUMMARY

1. The brain has three general functions: (1) sensory functions or taking in information; (2) analysis and decision making; and (3) motor functions or commanding the glands and muscles to take action.

2. Neurons are individual cells that can transmit information in the brain. When a neuron is stimulated, an electrochemical current is transmitted down the axon to the axon terminal. When the impulse reaches the axon terminal, it releases a neurotransmitter across the synapse.

3. A second great communication system in the brain is the endocrine system. Hormones secreted by the glands in the endocrine system influence a variety of processes including growth, sexual drive, mood, and reactions to stress.

4. The brain is divided into three concentric layers. The innermost is the central core which is involved in controlling basic functions such as breathing and sleep. Surrounding the inner core is the limbic system which is involved in processes such as emotion. The outermost layer is the cerebral cortex which is involved in higher cognitive processes such as thinking, reasoning, and memory.

5. CAT scans, PET scans, and MRI enable researchers to examine the functioning, intact brain. CAT scans and MRI provide pictures of the living brain. PET scans allow the measurement of brain activity during mental processes.

6. One of the reasons that brain damage can be devastating is that unlike other organs of the body, the brain does not have the capacity to repair itself. Recent research raises the possibility that it may be possible to treat disorders that produce brain damage such as Parkinson's disease by using brain grafts.

7. Studies in split brain patients indicate that the left hemisphere is specialized for lan-

guage while the right hemisphere is specialized for spatial abilities. Although research on split brain patients has provided useful information about how information is processed in the human brain, it has also raised controversies including the suggestion that men and women have different abilities based on different brain organization.

KEY INDIVIDUALS

Franz Gall
James Olds
Julia
Paul Broca
Peter Milner
Hans Berger
Carl Wernicke
Heinrich Kluver
Gustav Fechner
Wilder Penfield
Paul Bucy
Roger Sperry
Phineas Gage

KEY RESEARCH

endorphins and morphine receptors in the
  brain
cocaine's actions on the brain
the theory of phrenology
early studies on localization of language function in the brain mapping the human cortex
brain stimulation and the sensation of pleasure
the amygdala and aggression psychosurgery
the EEG—recording the electrical activity of
  the brain
imaging techniques for examining the intact,
  functioning brain
brain grafts and Parkinson's disease
split-brain studies
specialization in the intact brain

KEY TERMS

neurons
glia cells
central nervous system (CNS)
peripheral nervous system (PNS)
somatic nervous system
autonomic nervous system (ANS)
spinal reflex
sensory neuron
motor neuron
association neurons
dendrite
axon
soma
resting potential
action potential
synapse
neurotransmitters
axon terminal
synaptic vesicles
receptor
excitatory potential
all-or-none response
inhibitory potential
endorphins
hormone
endocrine system
pituitary gland
Broca's area
Wernicke's area
aphasia
hemispheres
cerebral cortex
cortex
convolutions
frontal lobe
occipital lobe
parietal lobe
temporal lobe
visual agnosia
somatosensory cortex
motor cortex
association cortex
limbic system
hypothalamus
hippocampus
amygdala
psychosurgery
central core
brain stem
thalamus
cerebellum
cognition
electroencephalogram (EEG)
alpha waves
computer-assisted axial tomography (CAT)
magnetic resonance imaging (MRI)
positron emission tomography (PET)
brain graft
corpus callosum
major hemisphere
minor hemisphere

3

Sensation and Perception

CHAPTER OUTLINE

hat color is the sky? Which is smoother, sandpaper or velvet? Is the sound of thunder louder than a whisper? Which tastes sweeter, sugar or a lemon? Although these questions may seem trivial and the answers obvious, understanding how we take in such information about the environment is a problem that has puzzled psychologists since the beginning of the discipline. When Wilhelm Wundt established the first psychological laboratory in Leipzig in 1875, two of the fundamental areas he set out to study were sensation and perception.

Sensation is the process by which the sense organs, such as the eyes and ears, gather information about the environment. **Perception** is the closely related process by which the brain selects, organizes, and interprets these sensations.

A psychologist interested in studying sensation might investigate phenomena such as how the eye registers light. The investigator might look at the structure of the eye and then try to determine how this organ can transform light into neural impulses that the brain can process. A psychologist studying perception might be interested in the subjective experience produced by these sensations. He or she would want to know how we form a conscious representation of the outside world.

Sensation and perception are important in psychology because they are our only link with the outside world. What we know of reality depends on the information we gather through our senses. And this information has a profound effect on our psychological functioning. Imagine, for example, how dramatically different your world would seem if you lost the use of your eyes or ears. If you try to list the changes this would make in your experience of the world and your behavior, you can appreciate the importance of understanding the basic processes of sensation and perception.

Furthermore, sensation and perception are not isolated phenomena but are part of the more general psychological process by which we gain knowledge about the world. This general process is known as *cognition* and, as we will see in Part 2, cognitive processes such as learning, memory, thinking, and language all interact with the information taken in through sensation and perception.

We will begin this chapter by discussing the six sensory systems: vision, audition, olfaction (smell), gustation (taste), the skin senses (touch, temperature, and pain), and the sensory systems for bodily position and movement. Although each of the sensory systems is specialized to register a different type of environmental stimulus, they all share certain common features. Thus, before discussing each of the senses individually, we will discuss some common characteristics of sensory systems. In the second half of the chapter we will focus on perception.

GENERAL CHARACTERISTICS OF SENSATION

The process of sensation begins with a stimulus in the environment. A **stimulus** is any form of energy (a light wave, heat, or an odor, for example) that is capable of exciting the nervous system. The stimulus first excites one of the sensory receptor cells, whose general function is to transform energy from the environment into neural impulses (i.e., action potentials) that can be processed by the brain. **Transduction,** the name given to the process whereby receptor cells transform stimuli into neural impulses, occurs in all the sensory systems.

Each of the sensory systems is specialized to respond to a different type of stimulation. The eye is responsive to light, the ear to the movement of molecules in the air, and the nose and tongue to chemicals. But in each case the sensory receptor cell performs the same general function: it transduces the environmental stimulus into a neural impulse. These neural impulses are then relayed from the receptor cell through the peripheral nervous system and then to the brain, where they are experienced as light, sound, smell, taste, or touch.

Two of the fundamental questions that psychologists studying sensation strive to answer are: Exactly how does transduction take place in each of the sensory systems? How do the sensory systems and the brain distinguish between the different types of stimuli in the environment? In addition to responding to a particular type of stimulus, each sensory system is responsive to two important properties of stimuli: quality and quantity. The quality of a stimulus refers to the kind of stimulation produced, for instance, the *color* of a light. Quantity refers to the amount of stimulation—how intense or bright the light is, for example.

Closely related to the concept of quantity is the idea of sensory thresholds. *Absolute threshold* refers to the quantity of stimulation necessary for an organism to sense a stimulus. *Difference threshold* refers to the degree of difference between two stimuli that is necessary for humans to tell the two stimuli apart. In the next section, we will examine thresholds in greater detail and see how they are determined.

Absolute Thresholds

How loud must a sound be before a person can hear it? How bright must a light be before a person can see it? To answer these questions we must determine the absolute threshold of the sensory system in question. The **absolute threshold** is the minimum amount of stimulation necessary to produce a sensation. As we will see, however, the absolute threshold is not a constant value but changes from person to person and from situation to situation.

The absolute thresholds for our senses are surprisingly low. For example, we can see a candle 30 miles away on a dark, clear night, and we can detect a single drop of perfume in a six-room apartment (Galanter, 1962). If our auditory systems were any more sensitive than they are, we would hear our blood rumbling through our veins and arteries. **Table 3.1** lists examples of the absolute thresholds for each of the five human sensory systems.

Table 3.1 **Approximate Absolute Thresholds for the Five Senses**

Sense	Threshold
Vision	A candle flame seen at 30 miles on a dark, clear night
Hearing	The tick of a watch under quiet conditions at 20 feet
Taste	One teaspoon of sugar in two gallons of water
Smell	One drop of perfume diffused into the entire volume of a six-room apartment
Touch	The wing of a fly falling on your cheek from a distance of one centimeter

From Galanter (1962)

A German philosopher, J. F. Herbert, first suggested the concept of an absolute threshold in the early 1800s. But it was Gustav Fechner, the father of threshold theory, who later provided researchers with a method of measuring absolute threshold. To determine the absolute threshold for light, Fechner (1860) performed the following type of experiment. One by one, subjects were seated in a totally dark room and were asked to stare straight ahead at a blank screen. The subjects were then told that an extremely dim dot of light was going to appear on the screen and that the dot would become progressively brighter. The subjects were instructed to indicate when they first detected the dot. This entire procedure was repeated a number of times. The absolute threshold was defined as the lowest intensity at which a subject detected the light 50 percent of the time.

As you may have gathered, the term *absolute threshold* is somewhat misleading. There is no single or absolute intensity at which a subject detects a light on every trial. The example presented in **Figure 3.1** shows this range. Notice that the subject was able to detect the light when it was set at eight units 75 percent of the time. The subject could detect the light at five units 50 percent of the time. And when the brightness was set at three units, the subject detected it only 25 percent of the time. Thus, the amount of stimulation necessary for detection changes from trial to trial. Because it is impossible to pinpoint the exact threshold, psychologists have agreed on the rather arbitrary definition of the point at which the subject can detect the stimulus 50 percent of the time. Thus, in the example presented in Figure 3.1, the absolute threshold is five units of light.

You can appreciate firsthand how a threshold changes from trial to trial by trying the following demonstration. You will need a wristwatch or alarm clock that ticks. Place the clock on a table in a quiet room and move across the room until you can no longer hear the ticking. Now approach the clock one small step at a time. Mark the point at which you hear the ticking. Repeat this procedure 10 times, each time marking the point where you first heard the ticking. You will probably notice that your threshold for hearing the clock was slightly different on each trial.

Psychologists have now identified several factors that help to explain why thresholds may vary at different times. One of the factors

Gustav Fechner
(1801–1887)

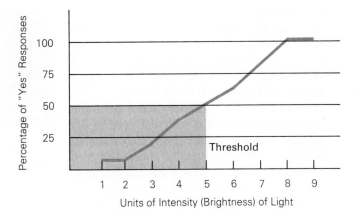

Figure 3.1
Absolute Threshold for Light.
The vertical axis shows the percentage of times the subjects responded, "yes, I saw the stimulus." The horizontal axis shows the intensity of the stimulus. The absolute threshold is the intensity at which a subject responds "yes" 50 percent of the time.

that can affect threshold is the number of sensations competing for our attention. In the laboratory, researchers try to eliminate other, distracting stimuli, but in real life this is rarely possible. You have probably experienced this yourself if you tried to hear a clock ticking in a busy office. **Noise** is the term used to define irrelevant and distracting stimuli. Noise need not refer only to auditory stimuli. It can affect the other senses as well, such as when you try to find the Big Dipper while standing on a brightly lit city street.

Another factor affecting threshold is the subject's motivation. For example, if subjects are told that they will receive a dollar each time they detect a light, they might be willing to adopt a lower threshold for detection. That is, they might say they see the light even if they are not entirely sure. On the other hand, if the subjects are told they will have to *pay* a dollar each time they give a wrong answer, they will probably raise their threshold to the point where they are absolutely sure they see the light. Similarly, a young child might have a higher threshold for pain from a stomachache when it's time to go out to play than when it's time to go to school.

Signal Detection

In view of these factors, some psychologists have denied the existence of sensory thresholds. These psychologists have proposed the

signal detection theory, which states that our ability to detect a stimulus depends not just on the intensity of the signal but on many internal factors (Egan, 1975; Green & Swets, 1966). Imagine that you were waiting for a very important telegram, perhaps about a job. You knew the telegram was due between 3:00 and 4:00 P.M. Within that 1-hour period your criterion for hearing a knock on the door might be quite low. In fact, you might even think you heard the knock on several occasions. In terms of the signal detection theory, the probability of the response "I hear a knock at the door" increases. This increase occurs for two reasons: (1) there is a good chance that there will actually be a knock during this time; (2) there are important benefits associated with answering the door and potential harm with not answering the door—the potential rewards and punishments associated with the response. According to the signal detection theory, the probability of detecting a stimulus at any given time depends on the intensity of the stimulus and on the observer's *response bias*—his or her decision to respond in a certain way. The response bias is influenced by the situation's potential rewards and costs. When the rewards are high and the costs for a false alarm are low, the observer will be biased to respond—to detect the stimulus. In our example, the potential reward for answering the door is high, so you will be biased to respond. You will answer the door each time you hear a knock or even think that you hear one. If, however, you had to pay a fine for each false alarm, you might not be so ready to respond.

The original method of establishing absolute thresholds assumed that the threshold was determined entirely by the stimulus. The newer method of signal detection recognizes that the individual brings certain biases to each situation, and these biases affect the threshold. These biases and the general idea of signal detection have important implications. For example, consider the air traffic controller who must detect blips on a radar screen. Here an error in detection could result in a midair collision.

Difference Thresholds

As the example of the air traffic controller suggests, detecting a stimulus can be a very important event, but equally important is the ability to detect very small differences between stimuli. For example, a chef must detect subtle differences in the taste of foods and an artist must be able to notice small differences in color and texture. Just as there must be some minimum amount of stimulation before a stimulus can be detected, there must also be a minimum degree of difference between two stimuli before they are perceived as being different. The **difference threshold** is the minimum amount of stimulus change needed for two stimuli to be perceived as different.

To study the difference threshold for light, a psychologist might show a subject two identical dots of light. The psychologist would keep one dot (the *reference stimulus)* at a constant intensity and increase the intensity of the second until the subject could detect a difference 50 percent of the time. The **just noticeable difference, or j.n.d.** for short, is the amount of stimulus change needed before a difference threshold can be detected. Perhaps the most important finding regarding the difference threshold is that, like the absolute threshold, it is not constant. As Ernst Weber first discovered in the mid-1800s, humans are able to perceive small changes if the reference stimulus is small, but as the reference stimulus grows larger, a greater change is necessary before the subject perceives a difference.

A common example of this involves price increases. If the price of a postage stamp were suddenly raised from 29 cents to 35 cents, virtually everyone would notice the difference. But if 6 cents were added to the price of a $12,000 automobile, hardly anyone would notice. Six cents is not a j.n.d. when the reference stimulus is 12,000 dollars.

Weber first noticed the relationship between the size of the reference stimulus and the size of the j.n.d., but it was his brother-in-law, Gustav Fechner, who formulated it into a general law. Fechner called this relationship Weber's law.

According to **Weber's law,** the ratio of the difference threshold or j.n.d. to the reference stimulus is a constant value. This value is called *Weber's constant.* Weber's constant for lifted weights is 0.02 or 2 percent. That is, no matter what the weight of the reference stimulus, it will have to be increased (or decreased) by 2 percent before a change is perceived. So if the reference stimulus weighed 100 ounces, it would have to be increased to 102 ounces before a difference was detected. If the reference stimulus weighed 500 ounces, it would also

Table 3.2 **Weber's Constant for the Sensory Systems**

Type of Stimulus	Weber's Constant
Visual brightness	2%
Loudness of a tone	10%
Lifted weight	2%
Pressure on the skin	14%
Smell	25%
Taste for table salt	20%

Ernst Weber
(1795–1878)

have to be increased by 2 percent, or to 510 ounces, before a difference could be detected. For a 1000-ounce weight, the increase would have to be to 1020. It is noteworthy that Weber's constant is not the same for all the senses. **Table 3.2** presents these values for the various senses.

You can easily demonstrate Weber's law by placing two quarters in one envelope and one in another. If you pick up each of the envelopes by the corner it should be easy to detect the difference. Now insert one envelope in one of your shoes and the second in the other, and pick up one shoe in each hand. Now can you tell the difference? Although the absolute difference between the two stimuli is the same (one quarter), it no longer represents a j.n.d. because the reference stimulus (a shoe) is now much heavier (Coren & Ward, 1989).

Interim Summary

Sensation is the process whereby the sensory organs transduce stimuli in the environment into neural impulses. Perception is the process by which we organize and interpret these sensations. Sensation and perception are not isolated processes but are part of the more general psychological process by which we gain knowledge about the world.

Each of the senses has an absolute threshold and a difference threshold. The absolute threshold is the minimum amount of stimulation that can be detected 50 percent of the time. The difference threshold is the minimum change in stimulation that can be detected 50 percent of the time. According to Weber's law, the just noticeable difference, or j.n.d., for each sense is a constant percentage of the intensity of the original stimulus.

• •

THE VISUAL SENSE

Organisms vary in their dependence on the different senses. Dogs rely heavily on their sense of smell, porpoises on their hearing, and certain insects on their keen sense of taste. But humans are primarily visual animals. We gather most of our information about the world through our eyes and, as we will discuss in later chapters, we often think and reason by using visual images and symbols. Perhaps it is for these reasons that psychologists study vision intensely.

In this section we will first look at light—the basis of all visual stimuli. We will then examine the visual receptor, the eye, and see how it is involved in transduction. We will conclude with a discussion of one of the most interesting and complex aspects of human vision—color vision.

The Visual Stimulus

The physical stimulus that the eye responds to is a form of electromagnetic energy that we call *light*. There are many forms of electromagnetic energy, ranging from X-rays at one end of the spectrum to television and radio waves at the other. But the receptors in the eye are sensitive only to the one small segment of this electromagnetic spectrum called light.

Light travels in waves. A physicist studying a light wave would describe it in terms of

Figure 3.2
The Electromagnetic Spectrum.
The human eye is sensitive to a relatively narrow band of electromagnetic radiation, shown here in color. Other types of electromagnetic radiation are shown, along with the size of their wavelengths in nanometers. A nanometer is one billionth of a meter.

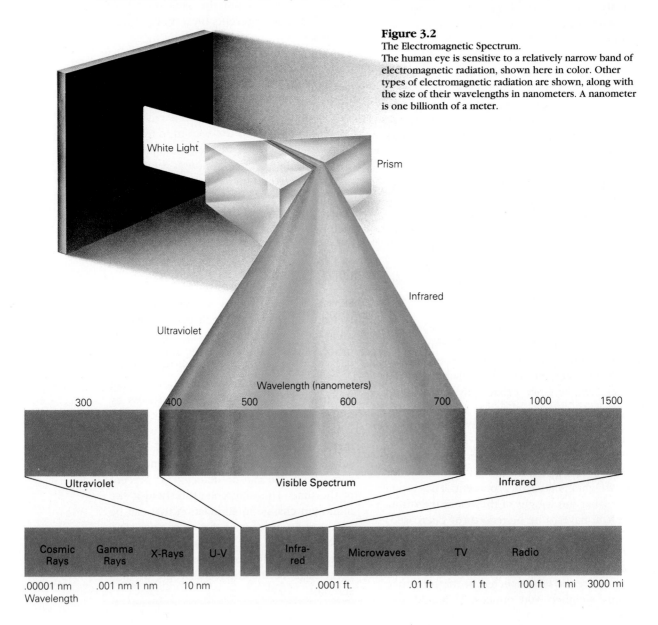

Table 3.3   **Properties of Light**

Physical Properties	Psychological Properties
Wavelength	Hue (color)
Amplitude	Brightness
Purity	Saturation

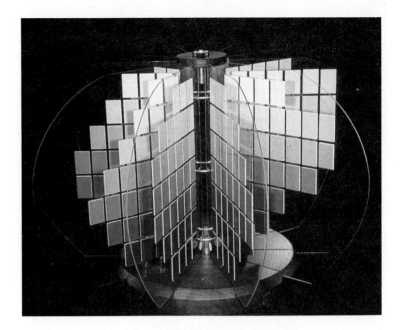

three basic characteristics: *wavelength, amplitude,* and *purity*. But when we see a light we describe it in terms of *hue* (color), *brightness,* and *saturation*. Each of these psychological properties of light corresponds to one of the physical characteristics: hue to wavelength, brightness to amplitude, and saturation to purity (see **Table 3.3**).

Wavelength is the distance from the crest of one wave to the crest of the next. Humans have the ability to see wavelengths between 380 and 760 nanometers (a nanometer is one billionth of a meter). Within this range, the different wavelengths correspond to different hues or colors (see **Figure 3.2**). **Hue** is the psychological dimension of light that corresponds to wavelength. We see wavelengths of about 400 nanometers as violet and wavelengths of about 700 nanometers as red. The other colors of the spectrum—orange, yellow, green, blue, and indigo—fall in between.

A second important characteristic of a light wave is **amplitude,** or the height of the wave. **Brightness** is the psychological property that corresponds to amplitude of a wave. The larger the amplitude of the wave, the brighter the light appears. So if we describe one light as bright red and another as dull red, we are indicating that both lights have the same wavelength but that the brighter one has a larger amplitude.

The third property of light is purity. By **purity** physicists mean the number of wavelengths that make up the light. **Saturation** is the psychological property that corresponds to purity. The fewer wavelengths that make up a light, that is, the purer it is, the more saturated we say it is. For example, a pure red light made up of only one wavelength (700 nanometers) would appear highly saturated. If another light, say white, were added, the light would take on a less saturated, pinkish appearance (see **Figure 3.3**). A pure light is quite rare and can be produced only by a laser beam. Most lights that we encounter are not totally pure but are a combination of many wavelengths.

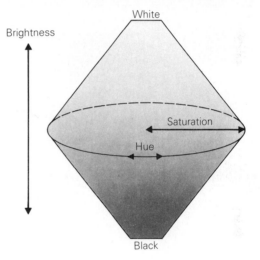

Figure 3.3
Munsell's Color Tree.
This device illustrates the three psychological characteristics of light. As shown in the small line drawing, hue, which corresponds to the physical characteristic of wavelength, is shown along the circumference of the tree. Brightness, which corresponds to the physical characteristic of amplitude, is shown by chips arranged from top to bottom. Saturation, which corresponds to the physical characteristic of purity, is shown along the radius. A single leaf from the tree shows differences in saturation and brightness for each hue.

The Human Eye

The human eye has two basic functions. The first, performed by the cornea, pupil, and lens, is to focus light on the retina. The second function is then performed by the retina when it transduces the light into neural impulses that can be relayed to the brain. In many ways, this process is like taking a picture with a camera.

The lens of the camera, like the lens, cornea, and pupil of the eye, focus light on the film. Then the film, like the retina, transforms or transduces the light into a visual image or picture (see **Figure 3.4**).

The **cornea** is the transparent outer covering of the lens and iris that allows light to enter the eye. From the cornea, light passes through the **pupil,** the opening in the iris that has the capacity to change size in order to control the amount of light that enters the eye. In very dark places, such as movie theaters, the pupil is wide open to allow the maximum amount of light to enter. Outside on a bright sunny day the pupil constricts to limit the

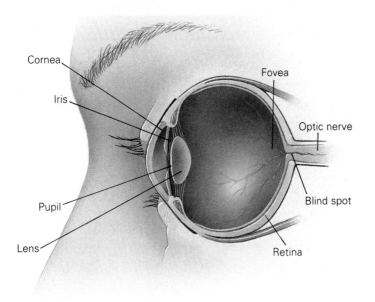

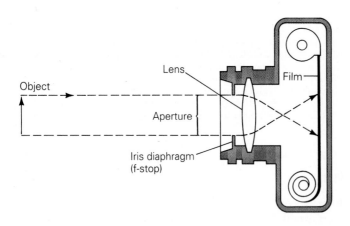

Figure 3.4
The Anatomy of the Eye.
The eye and its parts are in many ways like a camera. In the eye, the pupil, lens, and cornea all serve to focus the light on the retina. In the camera, the lens and iris (*f*-stop) serve to focus light on the film.

amount of light entering the eye. Directly behind the pupil is the **lens,** a transparent structure that bends the entering light so that it falls directly on the retina. The lens is a flexible substance (like a soft plastic) that can change shape to allow both near and far objects to come into focus. With age, the lens becomes less flexible, which is one reason why many older people must wear glasses.

The Retina and Transduction

The **retina** is a thin piece of tissue (about the thickness of a sheet of paper) in the back of the eye. It is lined with more than 115 million specialized nerve cells called rods and cones. The **rods** and **cones** are the cells responsible for transducing light into the neural impulses sent on to the brain (see **Figure 3.5**). The process of transduction occurs through a *photochemical* reaction that is slightly different in the rods and the cones. The rods contain a chemical called *rhodopsin.* When light strikes the rods, it breaks the rhodopsin down into its component parts. This breakdown causes the rods to generate a neural impulse. The impulse is then transmitted across a synapse to the next neuron in the retina, called the *bipolar cell,* and then on to the *ganglion cell.* The axons of the ganglion cells make up the *optic nerve,* which carries visual information to the brain (Masland, 1986; Tomita, 1986).

The optic nerve ends in the lateral geniculate nucleus of the thalamus, a relay center in the brain for visual input. From here, axons from neurons in the thalamus carry visual information to the visual cortex in the occipital lobe (see **Figure 3.6** on page 92). A very similar process occurs in the cones, where light breaks down a visual pigment called *iodopsin* (Schnapf & Baylor, 1987).

Although both the rods and cones transduce light into neural impulses through similar processes, each is active in different situations. Early clinical studies first suggested that the rods and cones played different roles. Individuals whose retinas contained no rods seemed to have normal vision under daylight conditions, but as soon as it became dark they became functionally blind. Individuals who had no cones had a different set of problems. These people found normal levels of light quite painful and they totally lacked color vision (Kries, 1895).

The rods, so named because of their long cylindrical shape, are extremely sensitive to light. (Rhodopsin breaks down with just a small amount of light.) Because of this property, they can function effectively at low illuminations and are thus used for night vision. The rods, however, do not transmit information about color. This explains why it is so difficult to distinguish color at night. The cones, shorter and more squat in appearance, are sensitive to color but require higher levels of illumination to function. Thus the cones are useful only during the day or in bright artificial light.

The rods and cones also differ in their location on the retina. The **fovea,** which is a small indentation in the center of the retina directly opposite the pupil, contains only cones—about 50,000 of them. Although estimates of these numbers vary, the rest of the approximately 6 million cones are distributed throughout the remainder of the retina, with a higher concentration near the center. All of the approximately 110 million rods are located near the outer edge or periphery of the retina. The **blind spot** is a small area of the retina containing neither rods nor cones. This area is where the axons (nerve fibers) of the ganglion cells converge and leave the eye as the optic nerve. (See **Figure 3.7** on page 92 for a demonstration of the blind spot.)

Many of the 6 million cones are connected by the bipolar and ganglion cells to their own optic nerve fiber. The 110 million rods, in contrast, share fewer than 1 million optic nerve fibers. In a sense, cones have a direct link to the brain, while rods share a party line. Since each cone has its own line, its signals are very sharp. Cones are thus able to record very fine detail. Because messages from the rods are combined, however, their signals are not as sharp. This explains why images we see at night, when we are using rod vision, appear fuzzy or hazy.

Understanding the different locations and functions of the rods and cones can help us see better in different situations. For example, the best strategy for seeing fine detail in an object would be to stare directly at the object, because the cones, which can record fine detail, are more concentrated in the center of the retina. To see a dim star at night you should look out of the corner of your eye, thus using the rods. **Table 3.4** summarizes the distinctions between rods and cones.

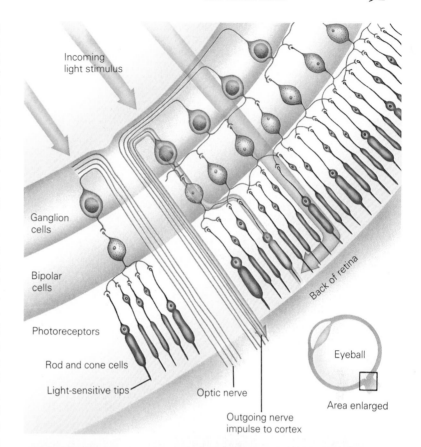

Figure 3.5
The Retina.
A close-up of the retina showing the rods, cones, bipolar, and ganglion cells. Notice that the light must actually pass through the ganglion and bipolar cells before it is tranduced in the rods and cones. The bottom figure is an electron microphotograph of the retina.

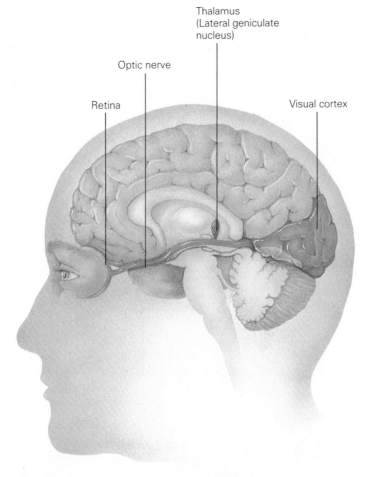

Figure 3.6
The Visual Pathway.
Light travels through the eye to the optic nerve and then to the lateral geniculate nucleus of the thalamus. From here, it is transmitted to the visual cortex in the occipital lobe.

Table 3.4   **Distinctions Between Rods and Cones**

Characteristic	Cones	Rods
Number	6 million	110 million
Location	More common in fovea	Absent from fovea; increasingly common toward periphery
Sensitivity to detail	High; many cones have a direct link to optic nerve fibers	Low; many rods funnel into a few optic nerve fibers
Sensitivity to dim light	Poor	Good
Sensitivity to color	Yes	No

Theories of Color Vision

Much of the richness of our visual world is due to color. Everyday decisions such as what combination of colors to wear, whether to stop at a traffic light, or whether we like a painting, for example, are greatly influenced by color. For most of us, it is difficult to imagine a world without color. Seeing an old movie produced in black and white may be the closest we'll ever come to this experience.

Although hue, brightness, and saturation all contribute to color sensation, hue is the most important factor. To understand how our eyes sense colors, researchers first looked at what happens when colored lights are mixed. To do this, they followed the artist's lead and arranged the color spectrum in a circle, called a color wheel, shown in **Figure 3.8**. **Primary colors** are the colors that are not a mixture of any other colors but can be combined to create other colors. In light, the primary colors are red, blue, and green. **Complementary colors** are colors appearing opposite each other on the wheel. They produce a neutral gray when combined. The two pairs of complementary colors we will be concerned with are blue-yellow and red-green.

This knowledge about color is reflected in both the trichromatic and opponent-process theories of color vision. The trichromatic theory holds that the eye is sensitive to the three primary colors (red, blue, and green) and that

Figure 3.7
Demonstration of the Blind Spot
To "see" the blind spot, hold the book at arm's length. Cover your left eye and focus the right eye on the apple. By adjusting the distance of the book from your eye, you can make the pear disappear. This indicates that the pear has fallen on the optic nerve, or blind spot, of the right eye.

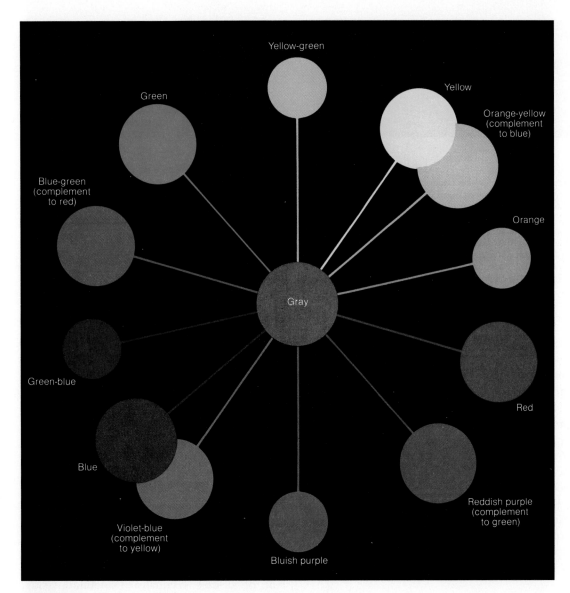

Figure 3.8
The Color Wheel.
In light, red, blue, and green are considered primary colors because they are not a mixture of any other colors, but they can be mixed to produce other colors. Colors opposite each other on the color wheel will, when mixed, produce the neutral gray in the center. For example, the complement of blue is an orange-yellow and the complement of red is a blue-green. This knowledge about color was reflected in both the trichromatic and opponent-process theories of color vision.

all other colors are produced by combining these three primaries. The opponent-process theory argues that the eye is sensitive to two pairs of complementary colors, red-green and blue-yellow. Although these two theories appeared to be in complete opposition for nearly 100 years, more recent findings suggest that the key to understanding how humans experience color lies in a combination of the two (Lennie, 1984).

THE YOUNG-HELMHOLTZ TRICHROMATIC THEORY
A British physician and physicist named Thomas Young proposed a theory explaining how our visual system distinguishes between the various wavelengths of light and how we actually code the experience of color (Young, 1802). In 1852 Young's theory was modified by Hermann von Helmholtz and is now called the Young-Helmholtz theory. The **Young-Helmholtz theory** postulates that the retina

Hermann von
Helmholtz
(1821–1894)

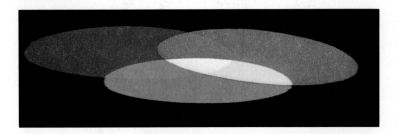

Figure 3.9
Trichromatic Theory.
If we examined the lighted screen of a television under a magnifying glass, we would see that it was composed of tiny dots arranged in groups of three, each group containing a red, blue, and green dot. Without magnification, the dots are too small to be distinguished and the eye blends them to produce all possible colors. The transformation of three colors into all colors is called additive color mixing. The same process is demonstrated here with color lights from three slide projectors—one produced through a blue filter, and one through a red filter. Mixing two colors produces a third. For example, red plus green makes yellow. Mixing all three produces white. The Young-Helmholtz trichromatic theory proposed that the same sort of color mixing takes place in the eye and the brain.

has three different types of cones, each sensitive to red, green, or blue light. Young reasoned that, just as colored lights could be mixed on a screen to produce different colors, colored lights could be mixed on the retina to produce different colors **(Figure 3.9)**.

Direct support for the Young-Helmholtz theory came from the Nobel Prize–winning experiments of George Wald (1964), who identified three different types of cones in the retina. just as the Young-Helmholtz theory predicted, each type was sensitive to one of the primary colors. Wald found that when the retina is struck by a wavelength of 700 nanometers, only the cones that are sensitive to red produce

neural impulses. Similarly, only the cones sensitive to blue or to green respond when the retina is struck by wavelengths in the blue or green bands. To produce colors other than red, blue, or green, different combinations of cones are excited. For example, the sensation of yellow is produced by stimulating both the red and green cones. White is produced by stimulating all three cones. The Young-Helmholtz theory of color vision is often referred to as the **trichromatic (three-color) theory** because it relies on three different types of color photoreceptors or cones.

Although the Young-Helmholtz theory could explain certain aspects of color vision, it had difficulty explaining others, such as color blindness and afterimages. Color blindness is a loosely used term that seems to imply that a person cannot see any colors. **Color blindness** is more accurately defined as a condition in which individuals lack the ability to discriminate among different wavelengths of light (colors). Total color blindness is quite rare; most color-blind individuals are unable to distinguish only certain colors. The most common form of color blindness, occurring in about 2 percent of men and less than 1 percent of women, is to the colors red and green (Goldstein, 1984). People with red-green color blindness may see both red and green as yellowish gray. Because of this, they often confuse the two colors. In fact, red-green color blindness is the reason that the red light is always placed at the top of a traffic signal. Blue-yellow color blindness is extremely rare and typically occurs only as a result of disease (Nathans, Piantanidu, Eddy, Shows, & Hogness, 1986).

People who can see all colors are called *trichromats* (three colors), people who have either a red-green or blue-yellow deficit are referred to as *dichromats* (two colors), and people with total color blindness are called *monochromats* (one color). Interestingly, people with color blindness often do not realize their problem until they take color-blindness tests like the one shown in **Figure 3.10**.

An **afterimage** is a sensation that persists after the stimulus is removed. Visual afterimages are quite common and often occur in pairs of complementary colors. Staring at red produces a green afterimage, staring at yellow produces a blue afterimage, and staring at black produces a white afterimage. To demonstrate this phenomenon to yourself, refer to **Figure 3.11**.

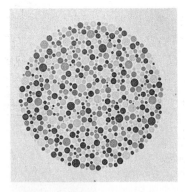 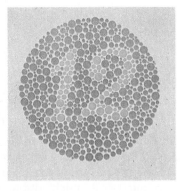

Figure 3.10
Test for Color Blindness.
These two plates are samples of those used to test people for color blindness. People with normal vision can see the number 26 in the plate on the left and the number 12 in the plate on the right. People with red-green color blindness see something different. They may see no numbers, parts of the numbers, or all of the numbers. Color blindness is a phenomenon that could not be explained by the Young-Helmholtz theory.

Both color blindness and afterimages contradict the trichromatic theory. According to this theory, cones are sensitive to either red *or* green. Thus, red and green color blindness should not necessarily occur together. Yet they *always* do. In the same way, the trichromatic theory does not explain why staring at red should produce a green afterimage. A theory that does seem to be supported by color blindness and afterimages is Ewald Hering's opponent-process theory of color vision (Hering, 1878).

HERING'S OPPONENT-PROCESS THEORY

Although Hering agreed that there are three types of receptors (Hering did not actually talk about cones) in the retina, he did not agree that each type is capable of detecting only one of the three primary colors. Instead, Hering's **opponent-process theory** proposes that one type of receptor is sensitive to both blue and yellow, the second type detects red and green, and the third type detects brightness ranging from black to white. Within each type, one color is produced when the receptor is positively stimulated (excited) and the second color is produced when the receptor is negatively stimulated (inhibited). Thus, the same receptor cannot produce, for example, blue and yellow at the same time. That is why, according to this theory, we never see bluish yellow or reddish green but often see bluish green or reddish yellow.

Some of the best evidence for the opponent-process theory comes from general information about color blindness and afterimages. For example, color blindness typically occurs in the pairs red-green or blue-yellow; these pairs correspond to Hering's theory. Afterimages also occur in pairs that correspond to Hering's color pairs: when we stare at yellow, the yellow receptor in the blue-yellow pair dominates. But when the yellow stimulus is turned off, the blue receptor rebounds and becomes dominant, producing the blue afterimage.

A COMPOSITE THEORY

Proponents of the trichromatic and opponent-process theories argued and experimented for almost 100 years trying to determine which was correct. But, as is so often the case in scientific debates, both theories had merit, and it was a combination of the two that produced

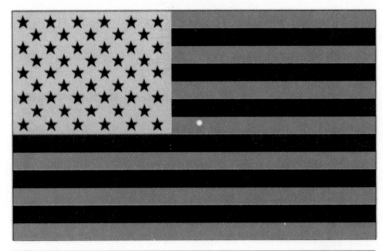

Figure 3.11
Demonstration of an Afterimage.
Stare at the American flag, focusing your eyes on the white dot. Try to stare at this point for one minute without shifting your gaze. At the end of the minute, look at the black dot in the white box below the flag. Did you see the green, black, and yellow flag turn into the more familiar red, white, and blue version? If so, you have just experienced an afterimage, a phenomenon that could not be explained by the Young-Helmholtz trichromatic theory of color vision.

the most satisfactory explanation of how we sense color.

According to the composite theory, color vision is a complex, two-stage process. In the first stage, cones in the retina take in visual information according to the Young-Helmholtz trichromatic theory. That is, there are three types of cones, one responsive to red, one to green, and one to blue (Mollon, 1982). The second stage involves the cells in the thalamus. By recording from single neurons, researchers have found that neurons in these areas function in accordance with the opponent-process theory. Certain neurons are excited (turned on) by red and are inhibited (turned off) by green.

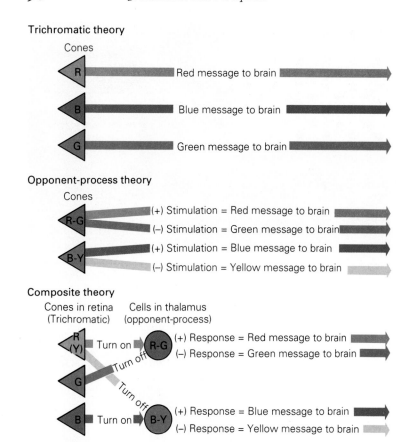

Figure 3.12
Theories of Color Vision.
In the trichromatic theory, each cone sends an excitatory message to the brain; the brain interprets this as a particular color. In the opponent-process theory, each receptor can send either an excitatory or inhibitory message. The brain interprets the excitatory message as one color and the inhibitory message as another. In the composite theory, both processes combine. In this theory, the red cone can both excite the red-green cell in the thalamus (thus sending a message of red to the brain) and inhibit the blue-yellow cell (thus sending a message of yellow to the brain).

Others are excited by blue and inhibited by yellow (De Valois, 1965; Svaetchin, 1956). It is this on-off firing pattern of the cells in the retina and brain that allows us to experience color (De Valois & De Valois, 1975; Hurvich & Jameson, 1957). **Figure 3.12** summarizes the three theories of color vision.

Interim Summary

Light can be described in terms of hue (color), which corresponds to wavelength; brightness, which corresponds to the amplitude of the wave; and saturation, which corresponds to the number of wavelengths that make up the light.

Light enters the eye through the cornea and pupil and is focused on the retina by the lens. When light hits the rods and cones in the retina, it is transduced into neural impulses that are carried by the optic nerve to the brain.

The rods and cones transduce light under different circumstances. The rods are sensitive to small amounts of light and are useful at night and in other situations when illumination is low. The cones have better acuity than the rods and can detect color but require more light to function.

There are two theories of color vision that, when combined, give a reasonable explanation of how humans sense color. The Young-Helmholtz trichromatic theory holds that there are three different types of color receptors, each sensitive to a different color (red, blue, or green). The Hering opponent-process theory postulates that there are two types of receptors, one sensitive to red-green and the other sensitive to blue-yellow. It now appears that color vision is a complex, two-stage process. The first stage takes place in the cones and adheres to the trichromatic theory. This information is then reorganized into an opponent-process system in the thalamus.

THE AUDITORY SENSE

In our discussion of the visual sense we saw how light waves entering the eye were transduced into neural energy and sensed as visual stimuli. In this section we will see that sound waves entering the ears are also transduced into neural energy, but this neural energy is experienced as sound. As with the visual sense, we will first look at the nature of the auditory stimulus and then at the human ear and transduction. We will conclude by examining several theories of hearing.

The Auditory Stimulus

All sounds, ranging from the noise produced by an automobile horn to the notes produced by a symphony orchestra, are caused by rhythmic vibrations of air molecules. To understand the nature of these vibrations, let's examine the relatively simple vibrations that can be produced by striking a tuning fork. When we strike a tun-

Table 3.5   Properties of Sound

Physical Properties	Psychological Properties
Frequency (wavelength)	Pitch
Amplitude	Loudness
Complexity (purity)	Timbre

ing fork, its prongs move in and out, or compress and expand. This movement causes the air molecules surrounding the fork to move in a similar way. This corresponding compression and expansion of air molecules around the fork produces a wave of movement called a *sound wave* (see **Figure 3.13**). Sound waves, like waves of light, have three important characteristics: frequency, amplitude, and complexity (see **Table 3.5**).

Each time the air expands and contracts it completes one *cycle*. The **frequency** of a sound is determined by the number of cycles that occur in one second. The frequency of sound waves is usually expressed in hertz, after the German physicist Heinrich Hertz. One **hertz** (abbreviated **Hz**) equals one cycle per second. Thus, a tone with a frequency of 2000 cycles per second is a 2000-Hz tone. Our ears sense the frequency of a sound wave as its **pitch,** the psychological property that corresponds to the physical property of frequency. For example, the lowest note of a bass singer is about 100 Hz, and the upper range of a soprano is about 1000 Hz. **Table 3.6** shows the frequencies of some common sounds.

Humans have the ability to hear frequencies between 20 and 20,000 Hz. (Interestingly, this corresponds to the frequency range of high-priced stereo amplifiers.) Our greatest sensitivity, however, is between 1000 and 4000 Hz, and most of the sounds we encounter in

Table 3.6   Some Common Sounds and Their Frequencies

Sound	Frequency (Hz)
Lowest note on piano	27.5
Lowest note of bass singer	100
Lowest note on clarinet	104.8
Middle C on piano	261.6
Conversation	200–800
Upper range of soprano	1000
Cat meowing	760–1520
Highest note on piano	4180
Limit of hearing	16,000–20,000

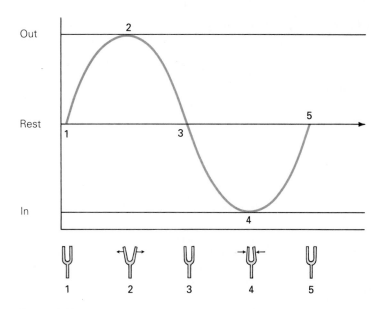

Figure 3.13
A Pure Sound Wave Produced by a Tuning Fork.
This wave has two important characteristics: the amplitude or height of the wave, which corresponds to its loudness, and the frequency or width of the wave, which corresponds to its pitch. Most sounds are made up of many such waves, with differing amplitudes and wavelengths.

our everyday experience fall within this range. Other species are sensitive to different ranges. For example, dogs can hear frequencies ranging from 15 to 50,000 Hz. This is why a "silent" dog whistle is not silent to a dog. It simply has a frequency that is above our range of hearing but well within a dog's.

A second physical characteristic of a sound wave is amplitude. **Amplitude** refers to the height of each sound wave and is a measure of how much air is expanding and compressing. We sense the amplitude of a sound wave as its **loudness,** the psychological property of hearing that corresponds to the physical dimension of amplitude of a sound wave. The higher the amplitude (the more air that is moving), the louder the sound. To express the amplitude or loudness of different sounds, scientists at Bell Laboratories created a unit of measurement called a *bel* (named after Alexander Graham Bell). Sounds, however, are measured in tenths of a bel or **decibels** (abbreviated **dB).** Zero decibels is the human threshold for hearing a 1000-Hz tone (Fletcher & Munson, 1933). Twenty decibels represents a very soft sound such as leaves rustling in a breeze. A conversation between two people occurs at about an 80-dB level, and the sound of a subway train registers about 100 dB. Decibel levels above 120, typically found at rock concerts and in

Table 3.7   **Decibel Ratings for Selected Sounds and Time of Exposure Considered Dangerous**

Typical Level (Decibels)	Example	Dangerous Time Exposure
0	Lowest sound audible to human ear	
30	Quiet library, soft whisper	
40	Quiet office, living room, bedroom away from traffic	
50	Light traffic at a distance, refrigerator, gentle breeze	
60	Air conditioner at 20 feet, conversation, sewing machine	
70	Busy traffic, office tabulator, noisy restaurant	Critical level begins
80	Subway, heavy city traffic, alarm clock at 2 feet, factory noise	More than 8 hours
90	Truck traffic, noisy home appliances, shop tools, lawnmower	Less than 8 hours
100	Chain saw, boiler shop, pneumatic drill	2 hours
120	Rock concert in front of speakers, sandblasting, thunderclap	Immediate danger
140	Gunshot-blast, jet plane	Any length of exposure time is dangerous
180	Rocket launching pad	Hearing loss inevitable

American Academy of Otolaryngology—Head & Neck Surgery, Inc., Washington, D.C.

certain industrial situations, are often experienced as painful. Sounds loud enough to cause pain can damage the ears, probably permanently (AMA, 1982; Henry, 1984). But even softer sounds can cause damage over a prolonged period of time. **Table 3.7** shows the decibel ratings of selected sounds and the time of exposure that is considered dangerous.

It is important to realize that measurements on the decibel scale do not correspond to our own perception of loudness. For example, the sound of a rock concert registering 100 decibels is much more than twice as loud as

the sound of a rushing stream registering 50 decibels. This is because sound level doubles with each increase of 6 decibels. Thus, while you might think an increase from 90 to 96 decibels is not very significant, it actually doubles the perceived loudness of the sound; an increase from 0 to 100 decibels is a 10 billion-fold increase!

So far we have discussed the frequency and amplitude of single sound waves, such as those produced by a tuning fork. It is as rare to encounter a pure sound made up of a single frequency, however, as it is to encounter a pure color made up of a single wavelength. Most sounds outside the laboratory are a combination of sound waves, each with a different frequency. Even the supposedly pure sound of middle C on a piano (262 Hz) contains other frequencies. **Complexity** is the term used to describe the combination of sound waves that make up a sound. **Timbre** is the term for the psychological property of hearing that corresponds to complexity. Because of timbre, we can distinguish a middle C produced by a piano and one produced by a flute.

When sounds of different frequencies are combined they can be perceived as either pleasant, as in the case of the blending of instruments in a symphony orchestra, or unpleasant, as in the case of noise. Whether a particular sound is considered pleasant or unpleasant is determined by the complex relationship between the various frequencies that make up the sound (Plomp & Levelt, 1965). **Figure 3.14** shows how sound waves of different pitch and loudness might look on an oscilloscope, an instrument that records sound waves as visible patterns on a cathode-ray screen.

The Human Ear and Transduction

The human ear is made up of three basic components: the outer, middle, and inner ear. The **pinna,** or outer ear, funnels sound waves. Although this structure plays only a small role in hearing, it is interesting to note that early hearing aids consisted of nothing more than funnels to "expand" the outer ear. Sound waves entering the pinna are channeled to the eardrum, or **tympanic membrane,** a thin membrane that separates the outer and middle ear. The sound waves cause the eardrum to vibrate. The inside of the eardrum is connected to the **ossicles,** the three small bones that make up the middle ear. These three bones are

Higher Frequency

Increased Amplitude

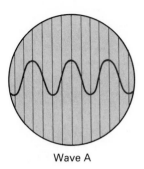

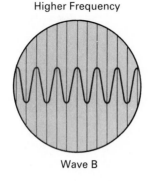

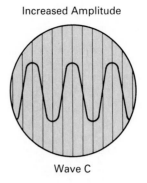

Wave A

Wave B

Wave C

Figure 3.14
Sound Waves of Different Pitch and Loudness.
Wave A represents a sound with a certain pitch. If the frequency of the wave is increased, as shown in wave B, a higher pitch results. If the amplitude is increased, as shown in wave C, a louder sound results.

the **malleus,** the **incus,** and the **stapes,** although they are often called the hammer, anvil, and stirrups because of their distinctive shapes. The function of the ossicles is to concentrate the vibration and thus amplify the sound. The vibration is passed from the stirrups to another thin membrane called the oval window. The **oval window** marks the entrance to the inner ear, the site of transduction. Here, the vibration from the oval window causes fluid in the cochlea to vibrate. The **cochlea** is a small, snail-shaped tube less than an inch long that contains the receptors for hearing. The **basilar membrane** is a long thin membrane that runs through the cochlea. Embedded in the basilar membrane are the **hair cells,** very fine hairs that bend as the fluid travels through the cochlea. It is this bending movement of the hair cells that transduces the sound vibration into neural impulses. The **auditory nerve,** which contains the axons of neurons in the cochlea, then conducts these neural impulses to the auditory portions of the brain. The structures of the human ear and the path of a sound wave through the ear are shown in **Figure 3.15** on page 100.

In summary, the physical stimulus of vibrating air produces vibrations in the eardrum, the ossicles, and finally the fluid in the cochlea. The vibrating cochlear fluid produces movement in the hair cells, which stimulates the neurons that make up the auditory nerve. Then the information travels from the auditory nerve to the thalamus and on to the auditory cortex in the temporal lobe.

Theories of Hearing

Any theory of hearing must explain how the ear transduces sound of different amplitudes and frequencies into the different neural messages that are interpreted by the brain as different sounds. Most theories of hearing agree that the loudness of a sound depends on how many hair cells, and thus how many neurons, are excited. The louder the sound, the more neurons that fire.

How we distinguish between sounds of different frequencies is more complicated. One of the earliest theories was first suggested by Hermann von Helmholtz in 1863 and later expanded on by George von Békésy, who won a Nobel Prize in 1961 for his work. According to the Helmholtz-Békésy **place theory,** different areas of the basilar membrane are sensitive to different frequencies (Békésy, 1960).

Békésy tested this theory by cutting tiny holes in the cochlea of guinea pigs and actually watching the basilar membrane while sounds of various frequencies were presented to the animals. He found that the hairs closest to the oval window showed maximum movement during high-frequency sounds, whereas hairs toward the middle of the membrane tended to move most during sounds with lower frequencies. It is interesting to note that the inability of elderly people to hear high-frequency sounds is associated with destruction of hair cells near the oval window (Corso, 1977; McFadden & Wightman, 1983). This finding is consistent with Békésy's place theory.

Figure 3.15
Anatomy of the Human Ear. The arrows show the direction taken by the sound wave as it travels through the outer, middle, and inner ear during the process of sound transduction.

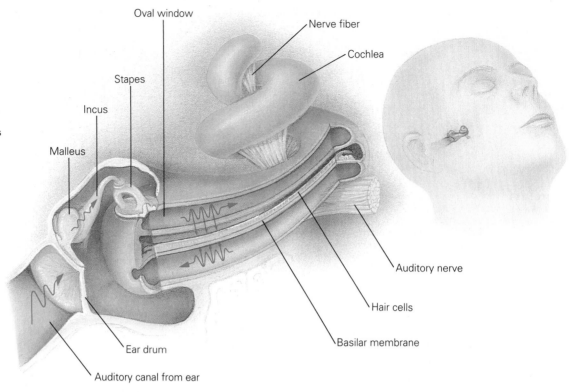

However, a major flaw in the place theory was revealed when Békésy could not identify a part of the cochlea that responded to frequencies below 400 Hz. It is at this point that the frequency theory steps in. The **frequency theory** states that the entire basilar membrane and attached hair cells vibrate at the same rate as the auditory stimulus. Thus, a 200-Hz tone causes the basilar membrane and hair cells to vibrate at 200 cycles per second. This in turn causes neurons in the auditory nerve to fire at a rate of 200 times per second. The problem with the frequency theory is that neurons can fire up to a rate of only 1000 cycles per second, yet we can hear frequencies up to 20,000 cycles per second. Part of this problem can be overcome by individual neurons combining to share the work. For example, five neurons, each with the ability to fire at the rate of 1000 times per second, could combine to code a sound with a frequency of 5000 Hz. There is evidence that neurons do indeed combine in this way (Zwislocki, 1981). But even with this combined effort, 5000 Hz is the maximum. This is where place theory takes over—to code frequencies from 5000 to 20,000 cycles.

It appears that a combination of the place and frequency theories can best explain how we sense different frequencies. According to this combined theory, low-frequency sounds stimulate the entire basilar membrane and the hair cells: frequency theory prevails. Sounds with higher frequencies stimulate only certain areas of the basilar membrane: place theory prevails. **Figure 3.16** summarizes the place, frequency, and combined theories.

Hearing Loss

As we have seen, the ear is a complex and delicate structure. Because of this, it is vulnerable to damage that can produce hearing loss. Hearing loss can be divided into two general categories: conduction deafness and nerve deafness. **Conduction deafness** or **middle ear deafness** occurs because the bones of the middle ear do not transmit sound waves properly. This can be caused by certain diseases and infections. Because the cochlea and auditory nerve are still normal, this type of hearing loss can be partially restored by a hearing aid that amplifies the sound waves.

Nerve deafness or **inner ear deafness** results from damage to the cochlea, the hair cells, or the auditory nerve. Unfortunately, because the neural tissue is destroyed, hearing

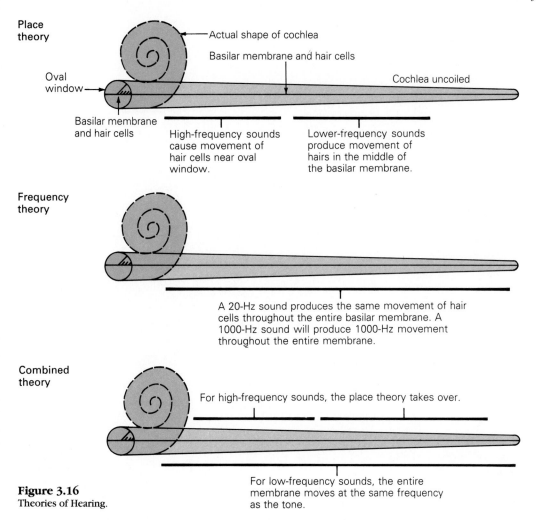

Place theory

Actual shape of cochlea

Basilar membrane and hair cells

Cochlea uncoiled

Oval window

Basilar membrane and hair cells

High-frequency sounds cause movement of hair cells near oval window.

Lower-frequency sounds produce movement of hairs in the middle of the basilar membrane.

Frequency theory

A 20-Hz sound produces the same movement of hair cells throughout the entire basilar membrane. A 1000-Hz sound will produce 1000-Hz movement throughout the entire membrane.

Combined theory

For high-frequency sounds, the place theory takes over.

For low-frequency sounds, the entire membrane moves at the same frequency as the tone.

Figure 3.16
Theories of Hearing.

aids do not help. Nerve deafness can be caused by three factors. Diseases during pregnancy such as rubella (German measles) can produce nerve deafness in the newborn. Nerve deafness also often accompanies old age. Interestingly, the nerve deafness associated with aging is usually more severe for the high frequencies (Corso, 1985). Many older people complain that they do not enjoy listening to music as much as they once did. This is because they cannot hear the high-pitched sounds of the piccolo, harp, and violin. A third and increasingly common cause of nerve deafness is exposure to loud sounds. As we saw in the previous section, prolonged exposure to loud noise can damage hearing. Researchers now believe that the loud noises move hair cells so violently that they damage them. For example, current estimates are that 8 million production workers in the United States are exposed to potentially dangerous sound levels (above 85 dB) and about 1.5 million have hearing loss (Harvard

Health Letter, 1986). A second potentially dangerous source of loud sounds is music. Rock musicians and people who regularly attend rock concerts, where sound levels can approach a very dangerous 120 dB, have hearing loss. Similarly, people who listen to large portable stereos, where dB levels can be well over 100, face a danger of hearing loss.

Although hearing aids do not help nerve deafness, there may be hope for people suffering from this type of hearing loss. The electronic ear works in cases in which the hair cells in the cochlea are damaged and cannot transduce sound waves into neural impulses. This remarkable device consists of a tiny microphone in the outside ear that picks up sounds and transmits them directly to a miniature electrode implanted directly in the cochlea (see **Figure 3.17**) (Loeb, 1985). The electrode then stimulates the cochlea, sending a message to the brain that a sound is present. Although this device does not yet allow people to distinguish

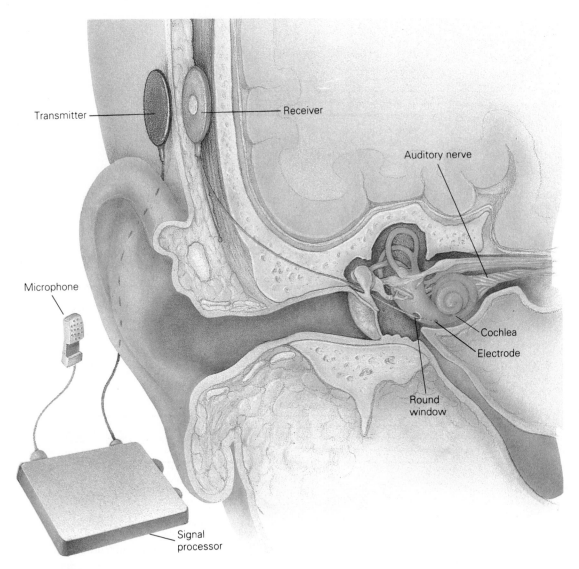

Figure 3.17
The Artifical Ear.
Adapted from "Tuning a Deaf Ear" by Patricia J. Wynne from *Science and the Citizen*, SCIENTIFIC AMERICAN, November 1984, p. 76. Copyright © 1984 by Scientific American. Reprinted by permission. All rights reserved.

words, it does allow them to detect changes in tone of voice and volume, distinguish between male and female voices, and to better monitor the loudness of their own words (Townsend, Cotter, Van Compernolled, & White, 1987).

Interim Summary

Sounds can be distinguished on the basis of pitch, which corresponds to the frequency of the sound wave; loudness, which corresponds to amplitude of the wave; and purity, which corresponds to how the different sound waves are combined.

Sound waves entering the human ear are funneled by the outer ear to the eardrum, which separates the outer and middle ear and causes the ossicles contained in the middle ear to vibrate. This vibration causes the oval window, which separates the middle and inner ear, to vibrate. This in turn moves the fluid in the cochlea of the inner ear. The movement of this fluid causes movement in the hair cells in the basilar membrane, which then produces neural activity.

The best explanation of how humans sense sounds of different frequencies is

Psychology in the News

NOW HEAR THIS—IF YOU CAN

By Anastasia Toufexis

Diane Russ of Evanston, Ill. never stays in the kitchen when the dishwasher is running. She wouldn't think of using power tools without wearing earplugs. And on weekends she keeps her windows closed. "Some mornings you can't walk outside because so many people are using their power mowers," she laments. "It's very noisy out there." Who would dispute it? From the roar of airplanes to the wail of sirens, the blast of stereos to the blare of movie sound tracks, noise is a constant part of American life. But few go to the lengths Russ does to avoid it. Noise is annoying and frustrating—and accepted.

That tolerant attitude needs to change—and fast. Increasingly, the racket that surrounds us is being recognized not only as an environmental nuisance but also as a severe health hazard. About 28 million Americans, or 11%, suffer serious hearing loss, and more than a third of the cases result from too much exposure to loud noise. Last week specialists testifying before a House committee documented an alarming new trend: more and more of the victims of noise-induced deafness are adolescents and even younger children. "We need to get people thinking the same way about protecting their ears as they now do about protecting their eyes," says Dr. James Snow Jr., director of the National Institute on Deafness and other Communication Disorders. "There is so much noise we're exposed to that we tend to become complacent about it."

Much of the clamor is unavoidable because it fills work sites or public places. As many as 10 million Americans are exposed daily to on-the-job noise that could gradually cause some degree of permanent hearing loss. Sixty million Americans endure other noise, including the cacophony of city traffic, that is louder than the level the Federal Government deems safe, and 15 million live close to busy airports or beneath heavily traveled air routes. In some neighborhoods of northern New Jersey, more than 1,000 flights thunder overhead each day.

Children lead some of the most raucous lives of all. Noisy activities range from playing with cap guns to practicing with school bands to riding the school bus. Of greatest concern, however, is youngsters' devotion to amplified music. Rock concerts can surpass 110 decibels, though they are more of a threat to musicians than to audience members, who endure the punishing pounding for only an hour or two.

The most endangered kids are those who wander around with cassette players blaring music into their skulls for hours. These personal stereos can funnel blasts of 110 decibels or more into the ear. "If you can hear the music from a Walkman someone next to you is wearing, they are damaging their ears," declares Dr. Jerome Goldstein of the American Academy of Otolaryngology. After years of such assaults, notes audiologist Dean Garstecki, head of the hearing-impairment program at Northwestern University, "we've got 21-year-olds walking around with hearing-loss patterns of people 40 years their senior."

The ear is an amazingly flexible organ, but it simply was not designed to withstand the strain of modern living. Hearing naturally deteriorates with advancing years, but not by much. Mabaan tribesmen in the Sudan, for example, who have never been exposed to industrial sounds, maintain their hearing into old age. Sudden intense noise, like a gunshot or dynamite blast, can damage hearing instantly by tearing the tissue in the delicate inner ear. Sustained noise from a jackhammer or disco music is more insidious. The prolonged barrage flattens the tiny hair cells in the inner ear that transmit sound to the nerves. As the hairs wilt, people often feel a fullness or pressure in the ears or a buzzing or ringing, known as tinnitus.

Such symptoms soon subside and the hairs regain their upright posture—if the ear gets some rest. But unrelenting noisy assaults can eventually cause the hair cells to lose their resilience and die. They do not regenerate, and the result is a gradual loss of hearing.

Those who cannot escape exposure to loud or prolonged noise should wear ear protectors, which can muffle sound by about 35 decibels. National Institute on Deafness director Snow contends that such protective gear should be as commonplace for children as bicycle helmets and infant car seats. His institute and other organizations are launching programs to educate children about hazards to hearing. And musicians who have suffered hearing loss, including Pete Townshend of the Who, are helping spread the message about the price of high-decibel rock. "We teach kids to

103

keep their hands off the hot stove," says Jeff Baxter of the Doobie Brothers. "Let's do the same with their hearing."

The ultimate hope, says Dr. Patrick Brookhouser of Boys Town National Research Hospital in Omaha, is that people will realize "when you lose hearing you lose, to some degree, one of our most vital attributes, the ability to interact with our environment." In other words, Americans should be making the most noise about noise itself.

—Reported by Barbara Dolan/ Chicago, with other bureaus

From "Now Hear This—If You Can" by Anastasia Toufexis, TIME, August 15, 1991. Copyright © 1991 The Time Inc. Magazine Company. Reprinted by permission.

Questions

1. In 1982 the Environmental Protection Agency closed its noise-control office and dropped noise emission labeling on such items as lawn mowers and power tools. In light of recent information, what changes in noise control do you think are appropriate for public policy?
2. How might we go about convincing young teenagers that portable cassette players operating at 110 dBs are dangerous to their health?

based on a combination of the place and frequency theories of hearing. The place theory, which can account for high frequency sounds, holds that different parts of the basilar membrane are sensitive to different frequencies. The frequency theory, which accounts for the sensation of low frequency sounds, postulates that the entire basilar membrane vibrates at the exact frequency of the sound.

Two types of hearing loss are conduction deafness, in which the bones of the middle ear do not transmit sound properly, and nerve deafness, which results from damage to the cochlea, hair cells, or auditory nerve. Conduction deafness may be corrected with a hearing aid; help for nerve deafness may be possible with an artificial ear.

THE OTHER SENSES

Much of the information we humans use to guide our behavior comes to us through our eyes and ears. Because of this and because both vision and hearing lend themselves to systematic study, psychologists have concentrated on these two senses. However, the senses of smell, taste, and touch also provide information that affects behavior and experience and, therefore, are important to the study of psychology.

The Chemical Senses—Smell and Taste

The human senses of smell and taste are closely related. This is readily apparent to anyone who has tried to appreciate the taste of a favorite food while suffering from a head cold. One reason for this close relationship is that both of these senses detect chemicals. The sense of smell is sensitive to chemicals that float in the air, while the sense of taste is sensitive to chemicals that can be dissolved in saliva. Despite the similarities in these two senses, they are distinct, and we will consider each separately.

SMELL

Although the sense of smell in humans is not as important as that of vision or hearing, it does provide important information. One of its primary functions is to warn us of potentially dangerous substances that we might eat or inhale. For example, we often first smell food to determine if it is spoiled, and the smell of smoke serves as a clear warning of fire. The sense of smell also plays an important role in other, more routine aspects of our lives. Without the sense of smell, foods such as meat, fruit, butter, and coffee would lose most of their flavor (Geldard, 1972). Research also indicates that the sense of smell may help babies recognize their mothers. When infants are only 6 days old, they can distinguish between their mother's scent and that of a strange woman

(Cernoch & Porac, 1985). In addition, the fact that Americans spend millions of dollars each year to add pleasant smells to their bodies with perfume and to eliminate unpleasant ones with deodorant certainly indicates that the sense of smell is important to us. Some of the most complete information regarding the sense of smell promises to come from a recently conducted survey reported in *National Geographic* magazine (Gilbert & Wysocki, 1987). Although the data from about 2.5 million people have been only partially analyzed, as **Table 3.8** shows, they have already produced fascinating results.

The human sense of smell, however, is not essential for life. Indeed, one of the pioneers of olfactory research, Lord Adrian (1928) suggested that losing the sense of smell would be roughly as serious as becoming color blind. Nevertheless, a recent study estimates that about 2 million Americans have smell disorders but only 10 percent seek help (Seiden, 1987). It is important to note, however, that other animals depend on smell for survival. They use odors to mark territories, signal danger, and attract mates (Gibbon, 1986).

Smell, or olfaction as it is often called, occurs when airborne molecules traveling up the nose strike the olfactory mucosa, which lies just above the roof of the mouth. The **olfactory mucosa** is the area in the nasal cavity that contains the receptor cells that transduce the stimulation from these molecules into neural impulses that travel along the olfactory nerve to the olfactory bulb in the brain (Getchell & Getchell, 1987). From here information about smell is distributed to other areas of the brain, including the limbic system as well as the temporal and frontal cortex (Tanabe, Iino, & Tagaki, 1975). The olfactory system is shown in **Figure 3.18** on page 106.

Although the site of transduction and the areas of the brain involved in smell have been identified, little is known about why certain airborne molecules produce specific odors. One theory of olfaction (Amoore, Johnston, & Rubin, 1964) suggests that there are seven types of primary odors, each with a characteristic molecular shape (see **Table 3.9** on page 106). According to this *stereochemical* theory, each shape fits a particular receptor in the olfactory mucosa much as a key fits a lock. Thus different odors excite different receptors, which in turn send different messages to the

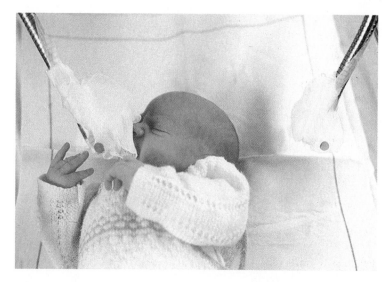

When an infant is only six days old, she can distinguish her mother's scent from that of a strange woman.

brain. Although Amoore has presented some evidence for his theory (Amoore & Venstrum, 1967), other studies have shown that there is not a perfect relationship between odor and molecular shape. For example, one study showed that two chemicals with nearly identical molecular shapes had very different smells: one smelled like musk and the other was almost odorless (Beets, 1978). Thus, although Amoore's theory is a good starting point, scien-

Table 3.8   **Preliminary Findings from the *National Geographic* Smell Survey**

- Women not only think they can smell more accurately than men, they generally can.
- Pregnant women, thought to be more smell sensitive, may actually experience a diminished sense of smell.
- Nearly 2 in 3 people have experienced a temporary loss of smell—usually due to a cold. (Imagine if this were the case for vision!)
- About 1 to 2 percent of the respondents cannot smell at all.
- Smoking diminishes sensitivity to certain odors.
- Smell sensitivity diminishes slightly with age.

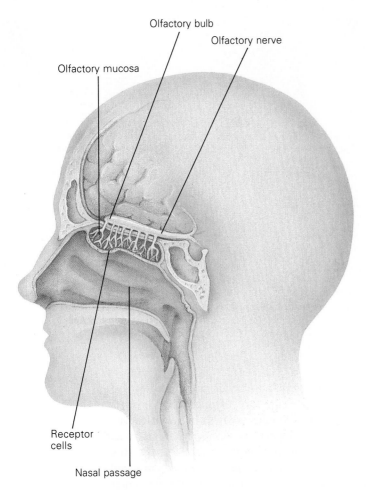

Figure 3.18
The Olfactory
System.

Wine tasters make subtle and complex taste distinctions that rely on smell and taste.

tists still have much to learn about the way we sense odors (Amoore, 1982; Erikson & Covey, 1980).

TASTE

Like the sense of smell, the sense of taste serves as an early warning system for the body. It warns us about dangerous substances before we swallow them and signals that other sub-

stances are safe to eat. Taste can also be a great source of pleasure and can affect our behavior in ways ranging from the foods we buy to the restaurants we frequent.

When we discussed color vision, we said our sensation of color came about by mixing three basic colors. A similar mechanism has been proposed for the sense of taste. According to this theory, first proposed by Aristotle nearly 2000 years ago, the four basic tastes are sweet, sour, salty, and bitter. The way a particular item tastes depends on how these four tastes are mixed (Beidler, 1978). We should, however, recognize that when we eat food, taste is only one of the characteristics that influences the food's flavor (Bartochuk, 1982). Smell, texture, and even color also appear to be important factors (Berridge & Fentress, 1985). For example, part of the reason that a steak has a pleasant flavor to many people is due to its aroma and texture. In fact, when the texture of a steak is destroyed by grinding, its taste is exactly the same as that of inexpensive hamburger. Most people would also have great difficulty eating a blue steak. Similarly, early studies on taste found that white chocolate is perceived as "milkier" and less "chocolatey" than brown chocolate, even though the basic ingredients are the same (Duncker, 1939).

If you examine your tongue in a mirror, you can see that it is covered with small bumps called **papillae.** Each of these papillae

Table 3.9   **Amoore's Primary Odors**

Primary Odor	Example
Ethereal	Dry-cleaning fluid
Camphoraceous	Moth repellent
Musky	Angelica root oil
Floral	Roses
Minty	Mint candy
Pungent	Vinegar
Putrid	Rotten egg

is separated from its neighbors by small valleys. Located on the walls of the papillae that form these valleys are the **taste buds,** the groups of cells that contain the receptors for taste (see **Figure 3.19**). Each of the approximately 9000 human taste buds contains 40 to 60 sensory receptor cells for taste. When substances enter the mouth they penetrate tiny pores in the papillae and stimulate these taste receptors. By a mechanism not yet fully understood, this stimulation produces a neural response (Pfaff, 1985). Unlike sensory cells in other systems, a completely new set of taste receptor cells is produced about every 11 days (Graziadei, 1969). This is why scalding a portion of the tongue with hot soup produces only a temporary loss of taste.

Although all areas of the tongue can sense each of the four different tastes, different areas of the tongue seem to be more sensitive to specific tastes. The front of the tongue is most sensitive to sweetness and saltiness, the back to bitterness, and the sides to sourness. The very middle of the tongue does not have taste buds and is insensitive to any taste (see Figure 3.19).

Skin Senses

Sensory receptors in the skin allow us to experience four basic types of sensations: touch, warmth, cold, and pain. These four types of sensation can also combine in various ways to produce other sensations, such as itching, vibration, and tickling. The sensation of tickling, for example, can be produced by gently stimulating adjacent touch spots on the skin in rapid succession.

Researchers initially thought that there was a separate receptor in the skin for each of the four basic sensations, but subsequent experiments failed to support this theory. Although researchers have identified a receptor that responds only to touch, the *pacinian corpuscle,* they have not been able to identify receptors for pain, warmth, or cold. In addition, the cornea of the eye contains only one type of receptor, yet it is sensitive to cold, touch, and pain. Because of such evidence, most researchers now believe that the skin contains many types of receptors, and the type of sensation that we experience depends not on the stimulation of a particular receptor but rather on the *pattern* produced by the stimulation of different combinations of receptors.

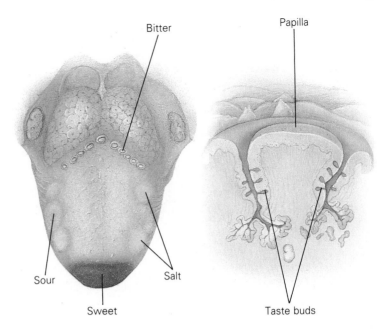

Figure 3.19
Taste Buds.
Left, areas of sensitivity. Right, diagram of a single papilla.

TOUCH

Our sensitivity to touch varies considerably over the surface of our bodies. One standard method used to measure the sensitivity of different skin areas is to touch the areas with varying amounts of pressure and ask subjects to report when they sense the touch. Such tests indicate that the most sensitive area of the body is the tip of the tongue (requiring only 2 grams per square millimeter to sense touch), whereas the least sensitive area is the sole of the foot (requiring 250 grams).

As we indicated, the pacinian corpuscles respond to touch. The pacinian corpuscles, like other receptors in the skin, consist of dendrites of a neuron with a covering over them. When pressure is applied to the skin, the dendrites become excited and send an impulse first to the axon, then on to other neurons, and eventually to the brain. Thus, direct mechanical stimulation of the dendrites appears to be one mechanism of transduction for touch.

TEMPERATURE

The sense of temperature is actually based on two separate senses—one for warmth and one for cold. Researchers first determined this by drawing a small grid on a subject's skin and touching each square in the grid first with a warm probe and then with a cold probe

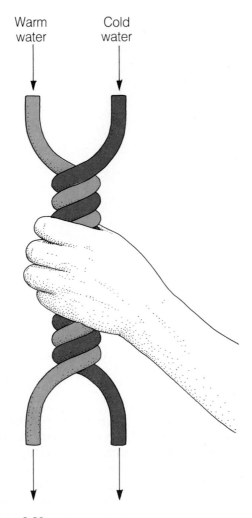

Warm water   Cold water

Figure 3.20
A Sensory Illusion.
When two metal pipes are braided together, one containing cold water and the other containing warm water, the person grasping the coil will experience the sensation of "hot" and will yank his or her hand away quickly.

(Dallenbach, 1927). The researchers found that the spots that were sensitive to warmth were not sensitive to cold, and vice versa. They also found that, for all parts of the body, the cold spots outnumbered the warm spots.

If the skin has only warm and cold spots, how do we experience the sensation of hot? A classic laboratory experiment provides the answer. In this experiment, two pipes, one with warm water running through it and the other with cold water, were braided together (see **Figure 3.20**). Surprisingly, when subjects grasped this device, they withdrew their hands quickly, claiming that very hot water was running through both pipes. This suggests that the sensation of hot is caused by a pattern of recep-

tor stimulation in which both warm and cold receptors are stimulated simultaneously. This makes good sense if we add the fact that cold receptors respond to cold temperatures, are insensitive to intermediate temperatures, but do respond to hot temperatures. Thus hot water stimulates both the warm and cold receptors. This pattern of stimulation produces the sensation of heat (see **Figure 3.21**).

PAIN AND ITS CONTROL
Pain, by definition, is an unpleasant experience. Yet the sensation of pain is extremely important to survival. Painful stimuli warn us that the body is in a potentially dangerous situation and that we must act to eliminate this danger and the accompanying pain.

Of all the skin senses, pain is both the most puzzling and the most studied. Many questions about the sensation of pain, such as the nature of painful stimuli and pain receptors, have not yet been fully answered.

What environmental stimuli produce pain? As we know from experience, extreme pressure, extreme heat, and a variety of other stimuli can produce pain. But this does not mean that pain is simply an overactivation of the skin senses. A hard, pulsating jet from a shower massage excites the pressure receptors but does not produce pain; conversely, a small paper cut in the skin causes very little neural activity but is painful nevertheless. As was the case with temperature, there is probably not a receptor for pain alone. Rather, a particular pattern of activity within several receptors probably produces the sensation of pain.

Although there is not yet a completely acceptable theory regarding pain, the pain-gating theory has helped to explain many of pain's phenomena (Melzack & Wall, 1965). This theory is unique in recognizing that the amount of pain is not simply related to the amount of damage to the body but can be affected by a variety of psychological factors. Beecher (1959) cited the example of seriously wounded American soldiers returning from the battle of Anzio who reported that they felt no pain from their wounds. Many of them did not even request medication. Similarly, studies have shown that 35 percent of the patients with pain caused by disease get relief by taking a *placebo*—a pill that the patients believe contains painkillers but which actually has no active ingredients (Weinsenberg, 1977). These examples indicate that pain cannot be caused simply by exciting pain receptors that send un-interrupted messages to the brain. It must be a more complex process.

Although pain acts as an essential early warning system, for many people chronic pain is a serious problem. This year some 40 million Americans will experience chronic and debilitating headache and 100 million will have a bout with backache (Budiansky, 1987). Pain from arthritis, cancer, and nerve disease will affect millions of other people. Fortunately, what psychologists and other scientists have learned about pain can also help in pain control.

BLOCKING PAIN PATHWAYS

According to the pain-gating theory, there are specialized axons that carry information about painful stimuli from the body to the spinal cord and brain. But before these stimuli can be relayed to the brain, they must pass through a "neuronal gate" in the spinal cord (see **Figure 3.22** on page 110). One way to control pain, then, is to close the gate.

There are many treatments that may close the gate. One relatively simple treatment involves stimulating the injured portion of the body. Vigorously rubbing your knee after you bang it on the corner of a table or putting a cold compress on a sprained ankle can provide some relief. Pain clinics now use more sophisticated techniques to produce similar effects. For example, an arthritis patient may wear a small device that electrically stimulates the pain pathways, thus replacing the pain with a tingling sensation (Murphy, 1982).

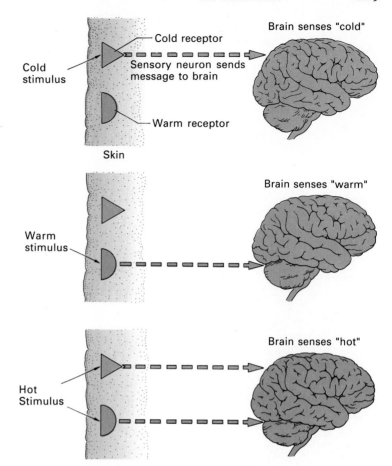

Figure 3.21
The Sense of Temperature.
The sensation of cold is produced by stimulating a cold receptor (top). The sensation of warm is produced by stimulating a warm receptor (middle). The sensation of hot, however, poses a problem since there are no hot receptors in the skin. Hot stimuli simultaneously stimulate the cold and warm receptors in the skin. This pattern of stimulation is interpreted by the brain as "hot." This is why subjects who grab the braided pipes report that the pipes are hot.

Endorphins. Recall from Chapter 2 that endorphins are pain-relieving chemicals that are released in the nervous system. There is now evidence that these chemicals relieve pain by acting on the spinal cord, perhaps on the pain gate. According to this theory, endorphins stimulate neurons in the brain that then send messages to the spinal cord which block the pain signal (Basbaum & Fields, 1984). Researchers believe that many treatments that relieve pain act through the endorphin system (Watkins & Mayer, 1982).

Acupuncture is a technique in which different parts of the body are stimulated in order to control pain. Typically, this is achieved by inserting electrified needles into the skin. Acupuncture has been used in China for over 2000 years to control pain in a variety of situations including tooth extractions, tonsillec-

tomies, and childbirth (Yang, 1979). In one series of studies, researchers at the University of Washington produced pain in volunteers by electrically stimulating a tooth. The volunteers reported that the pain was mild and that they felt as if they were biting into a frozen food or having a cavity filled. The volunteers were then divided into three groups. One group of volunteers received acupuncture. The procedure consisted of placing small electrified needles between the thumb and first finger at a point the Chinese call *Hoku*. Stimulation here is thought to relieve tooth pain. In a second group, the same electrified needles were inserted in another acupuncture point that is not considered effective for tooth pain. A third group received no acupuncture treatment. The

Figure 3.22
The Pain-Gating Theory.

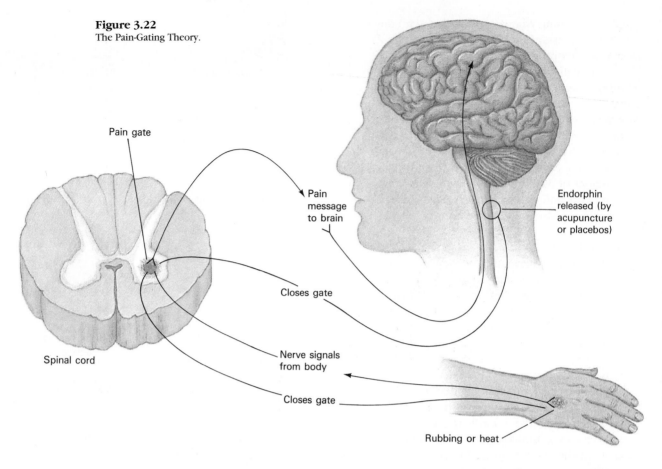

Pain gate

Pain message to brain

Closes gate

Nerve signals from body

Closes gate

Spinal cord

Endorphin released (by acupuncture or placebos)

Rubbing or heat

results indicated that the group who underwent acupuncture treatment at the Hoku point were much less sensitive to the pain than they were before the acupuncture. The two other groups reported no difference (Chapman, Wilson, & Gehrig, 1976). Additional research suggests that acupuncture may be mediated by endorphins. When patients are given naloxone, a drug that blocks the action of endorphins,

acupuncture no longer relieves the dental pain (Hassett, 1980).

Many other pain-relieving techniques may also act through endorphins. For example, stimulation of the vagina decreases pain in women (Komisurak & Whipple, 1986). Listening to loud "thrilling" music, the kind that makes people tingle all over, also decreases pain (Goldstein, 1984). Placebos, those little

Acupuncture is a technique that stimulates different parts of the body in order to control various types of pain.

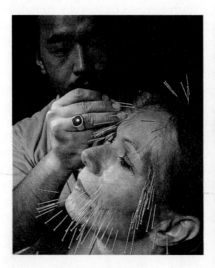

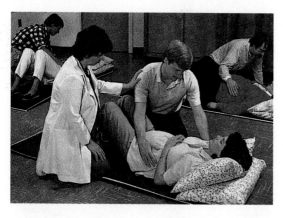

Psychological techniques are useful in controlling pain. These expectant mothers are preparing to cope with the pain of labor through deep breathing and other relaxation strategies.

red sugar pills, also have a powerful pain-killing effect. Researchers now believe that these manipulations act on the endorphin system because drugs such as naloxone that block endorphins also block the pain-killing actions of placebos and loud music.

Although the endorphins are important in the control of pain, they are not involved in all pain-controlling techniques. For example, hypnosis can sometimes be used to control pain; but the effects of hypnosis, unlike acupuncture and placebos, are not blocked by naloxone (Watkins & Mayer, 1982).

Psychological Control of Pain. Because pain is both a physical and a psychological phenomenon, psychological techniques are also quite useful in controlling pain. Techniques such as relaxation and distraction both help in alleviating pain. Prepared childbirth classes help expectant mothers cope with the pain of labor by teaching them to relax through deep breathing and by distracting them and encouraging them to imagine pleasant scenes (McCaul & Malott, 1984).

Attitudes about pain can also play a central role. Children who see their mothers receive an injection without expressing pain are less likely to cry when they get an injection. Similarly, if people believe that a certain medical procedure or illness is not painful, they are less likely to experience pain (DiMatteo & Friedman, 1984). According to the pain-gating notion, these techniques have the ability to send messages from the brain to close the gate (Melzack, 1973).

In summary, a message about a painful stimulus can get through to the brain depending on whether the pain gate is open or closed. A variety of techniques for controlling pain may work by closing the pain gate. Rubbing a painful area may send an ascending message to close the gate. Similarly, descending messages from the brain may also close the pain gate. Descending messages may be produced by the release of endorphins—sometimes caused by events such as acupuncture or placebos. Psychological factors may also play a role.

We must point out that the pain-gating theory is not without its critics (see Casey, 1973; Hentall & Fields, 1978). Yet even if it eventually requires modification, this theory still provides a useful model for studying and treating pain.

Body Position and Movement

We have been discussing sensory systems specialized to provide information about the world around us. But if we were limited to only these five senses, we would not be able to survive. We would not be able to walk, eat, or even reach out to touch someone. To accomplish any of these seemingly simple tasks, we need to know about internal sensory information, that is, the position of our body. Consider a task we take for granted, taking a drink from a glass. To accomplish this we need to know the position of our hand, how far to move our hand to reach the glass, and then how to move the glass smoothly to our mouth. This act requires that we know the position of our hand at all times and is accomplished by constant feedback from up to 200 muscles.

The sense of the position and movement of body parts is called **kinesthesis**. There are millions of receptors all over our body that constantly inform us about position and movement. These receptors are on our muscles, joints, and tendons. If we are to move with grace and coordination, these receptors must send millions of messages to the brain so that movement can be coordinated. To begin to appreciate what an elegant system this must be, consider the diver or gymnast who in a few seconds must change body position thousands of times. This system must operate with the speed and precision to make it the envy of the most sophisticated computer.

A sense closely related to kinesthesis is **equilibrium.** Equilibrium keeps us informed about the position of our whole body in space. The receptors for equilibrium are next to the cochlea in the inner ear (**Figure 3.23**). The

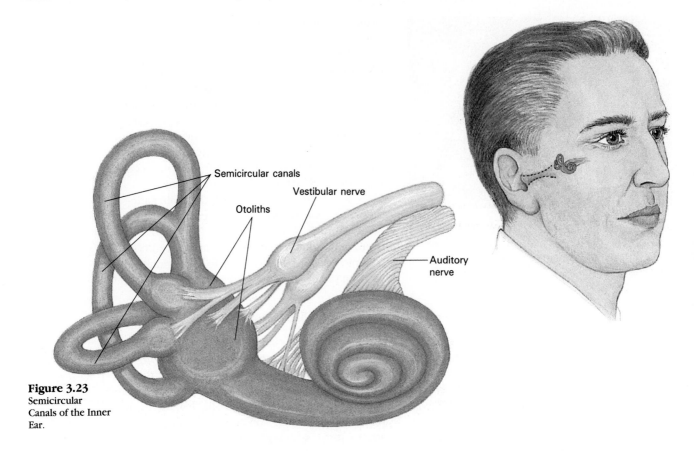

Figure 3.23
Semicircular
Canals of the Inner
Ear.

three semicircular canals look much like inter-connected pretzels and act like gyroscopes. These gyroscopes help keep the balance along three planes: left-right, front-back, and up-down. Nerve receptors in these closed canals are bathed with fluid that surges through the canal whenever the head drops, tilts, turns, ac-celerates, or stops. The receptors then flash a signal to the brain that tells us where the head is in relation to the rest of the body and to the outside world.

How the equilibrium system functions can best be appreciated by considering what happens when it is temporarily disabled by a virus or bacteria. This condition is called ver-tigo. Vertigo is characterized by spinning, blurred vision, and nausea. In its extreme forms it is very debilitating. We have probably all ex-perienced a mild form of vertigo (not caused by a disease) when looking up at moving clouds. In these cases the eyes report motion, but the vestibular system reports no motion (your head is still). This mismatch leads to verti-go. These signal mismatches are also involved in carsickness, seasickness, and the dizziness reported by astronauts in outer space. For ex-ample, in seasickness, there is disagreement be-tween your equilibrium which clearly senses

movement, and your visual system, which sees the ship as a stationary world. One way to com-bat this is to focus your gaze on the horizon, which will also seem move.

Table 3.10 lists the stimuli, receptors, and mechanism of transduction for each of the sensory systems we have examined in this part of the chapter. We turn now to the second ma-jor topic of the chapter, perception.

Interim Summary

The senses of smell and taste are referred to as the chemical senses. For smell, airborne molecules enter the nose and stimulate the olfactory mucosa. For taste, substances in the mouth are first dissolved in saliva. Molecules from these substances then stimu-late the taste receptors in the taste buds.

The skin senses are touch, warmth, cold, and pain. Unlike other senses, there is not a separate receptor for each skin sensa-tion. Rather, sensations such as heat and pain are the result of specific patterns of ac-tivity in the various receptors in the skin. One theory to explain pain is the pain-gating theory. Some methods that have proved use-

Table 3.10   **Summary of Sensory Systems**

Sense	Stimulus Properties and Sensation Produced	Receptors	Mechanism of Transduction
Vision	Light waves Amplitude—brightness Wavelength (frequency)—color Combination of different wavelengths (purity)—saturation	Rods and cones in retina	Photochemical reaction in rods and cones stimulate optic nerve
Auditory	Sound waves Amplitude—loudness (in dBs) Wavelength (frequency)—pitch Combination of different wavelengths (purity)—timbre	Hair cells in cochlea	Vibrating fluid in cochlea produces movement in hair cells, which stimulate the auditory nerve
Smell (Olfaction)	Airborne molecules	Hair cells in olfactory mucosa	Stimulation of hair cells
Taste (Gustation)	Acids—sour Salts—salty Sugar—sweet Complex molecules similar to sugar—bitter	Taste buds in tongue	Stimulation of taste buds; mechanism unknown
Skin senses Touch	Pressure to skin—touch	Pacinian corpuscles	Physical stimulation of corpuscles—mechanism unknown
Temperature	Stimuli of different temperatures—hot, warm, cold	Cold receptors (respond to hot and cold) Warm receptors (respond to warm)	Patterns of stimulation of cold and warm receptors; mechanism unknown
Pain	Variety of stimuli	Unknown	Pattern of stimulation of pain receptors as in pain-gating theory; mechanism unknown
Body position Kinesthesis	Body position and movement	Muscles, joints, and tendons	—
Equilibrium	Acceleration or changes in movement	Hair cells in semicircular canals of inner ear	Moving fluid in canals stimulates hair cells in the inner ear

ful in the control and relief of pain are blocking pain pathways, acupuncture, and psychological methods such as relaxation and distraction.

Another set of senses, kinesthesis and equilibrium, provide information about body position and movement. Kinesthesis tells us about the position of our body parts. For example, we need to know where our hand is relative to our mouth in order to get a piece of food to our mouth. Equilibrium keeps us informed about the position of our whole body in space. By monitoring the movement of fluid in the three semicircular canals in the inner ear, this sense tells us when the head drops, tilts, accelerates, or stops.

THE PROCESS OF PERCEPTION

If the primary function of sensation is to take in information, the primary function of perception is to help us make sense of that information. Perception allows us to impose a logic and order on the chaos of the millions of stimuli that bombard our senses. Even though our eyes detect lights and colors and our ears react to tones of different loudness, pitch, and timbre, we do not see or hear the world as a random array of light, dark, and colors, nor do we hear random tones of different loudness and pitch. Instead, perception allows us to make sense of these sensations.

Figure 3.24
What Do You
See?

Although psychologists do make a distinction between sensation and perception, it is not always clear where sensation ends and perception begins. In fact, some researchers have argued that it is impossible to make such a distinction (Goldstein, 1984). Our eyes, for example, do not register or transduce all waves in the electromagnetic spectrum. As we saw earlier in the chapter, our eyes are sensitive only to the so-called visible light waves; we are unable to see, for instance, radio waves or X-rays. By being selective, our eyes in a sense interpret what we see. Thus, vision, generally considered a sensory process, might also be considered a perceptual process (Gibson, 1966).

To understand what psychologists mean by the process of perception and how it differs from sensation, try this demonstration. **Figure 3.24** is a poster for a trained seal act. Look at the figure for 10 seconds and then describe what you saw. If you are like most people, you probably saw a man, a seal, a whip, a ball, and a fish. Now look at the poster again, but this time think of it as a poster for a costume ball. Now what do you see? Suddenly, the seal becomes a woman, the whip a sword, the fish a hat, and the ball a woman's head. In both instances, the stimulus and sensation remained the same—only your perception changed.

Psychologists divide perception into three processes: selection, organization, and interpretation. Most research in perception has focused on organization and interpretation, and so will we. Before we discuss these processes,

however, we will briefly mention the selection process.

The first step in perception is the *selection* of specific sensations. As we monitor the thousands of sensations in our environment, we focus on some and disregard others. **Attention** is the process by which we determine which sensations will be perceived. Attention is just one aspect of our state of awareness or consciousness, one that we will discuss in more detail in Chapter 5. We will devote the rest of this chapter to the perceptual processes of organization and interpretation.

ORGANIZATION AND PERCEPTION

Organizing sensations is a fundamental perceptual process. In this section, we will discuss the three basic types of perceptual organization. The first, form perception, refers to how stimuli are organized into meaningful shapes and patterns. For example, how do you organize the pattern of lines on this page into meaningful letters and words? A second type of perceptual organization deals with depth and distance perception. How are we able to organize the world into three dimensions when our retina records only two-dimensional images? A related issue is how we perceive depth in a two-dimensional picture. A third aspect of perceptual organization deals with perceptual constancies. For example, why do we perceive the shape of an object to be constant, even though the shape of the image that strikes our retina is affected by the angle from which the object is viewed? The image of a plate is perfectly round only when we stare directly down at it. Viewed slightly from the side, the plate produces an oval image. But we still perceive the plate as round.

Form Perception

Form perception—how sensory stimuli are organized into meaningful shapes and patterns—was one of the first topics studied by psychologists. As we saw in Chapter 1, Wilhelm Wundt is generally given credit for establishing the first psychology laboratory, at the University of Leipzig in 1875. In the course of his experiments on conscious experience, Wundt also made some important discoveries about form perception.

In one experiment, Wundt asked his subjects to describe the experience of listening to

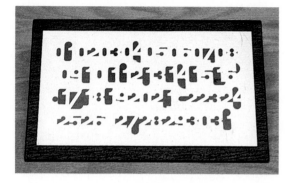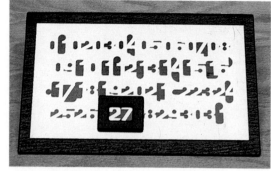

This black on metal drawing looks like an abstract design until you can determine what is figure and what is ground. As the panel at the right shows, it is a calendar. Can you pick out the other numbers?

a metronome. The metronome played a simple pattern of regularly repeated ticks. Each tick produced the same sound and the ticks occurred at evenly spaced intervals, one right after the other. Yet when Wundt asked his subjects to describe what they had heard, almost all reported hearing patterns more complex than the simple repetition of individual ticks. Some subjects heard paired beats. Others grouped the ticks into even more complex—and irregular—rhythms. Wundt's simple study was one of the first clues that we tend to organize sensory information into specific forms and patterns.

Perhaps the first group of psychologists to systematically study form perception were the Gestalt psychologists (Wertheimer, 1912). *Gestalt* is a German word that may be loosely translated as "whole." The Gestalt psychologists felt that to understand human perception it was necessary to understand how humans organize many stimuli into a single, meaningful, whole image. Their view was that "the whole is greater than the sum of its parts." Based on the results of many experiments performed in the 1920s and 1930s, the Gestalt psychologists proposed basic laws of form perception (Rock & Palmer, 1990).

FIGURE-GROUND RELATIONSHIPS

One of the basic laws proposed by the Gestalt psychologists is the principle of **figure-ground relationships,** which states that we organize stimuli into figures and grounds. For example, when we look at this page the words (the black ink) stand out as a figure against the ground, or background, of the white page. Similarly, we see a picture on a wall as a figure

and the wall as a background. In general, the figure in a figure-ground relationship takes on a meaningful form, and the background is perceived as formless and neutral (Coren, 1969).

Although the relationship between figure and ground is clear in most situations, in certain situations the relationship is ambiguous. For example, in **Figure 3.25a** on page 116, do you see green silhouettes on a white background or a white vase on a green background?

SIMILARITY

Another law proposed by the Gestalt psychologists is that of **similarity**—that similar elements within a perceptual field tend to be grouped together. For example, most people see **Figure 3.25b** as horizontal rows of dots and squares, not as vertical columns that contain dots and squares alternately. Similar things are grouped together: squares with other squares and dots with other dots.

PROXIMITY

The law of **proximity** (nearness) states that objects near each other tend to be grouped together. Most people see the left pattern in **Figure 3.25c** as a set of columns, not a set of rows. This occurs because the dots are closer to one another on the vertical dimension. In the right pattern, however, the dots are closer horizontally and are perceived as a set of rows.

CLOSURE

The Gestalt law of **closure** states that we tend to fill in the gaps in incomplete stimuli (see **Figure 3.25d**). If part of a familiar pattern or shape is missing, our perceptual processes complete the pattern and allow us to perceive

a. Figure-ground
relationships

b. Similarity

c. Proximity

d. Closure

e. Good continuation

f. Simplicity

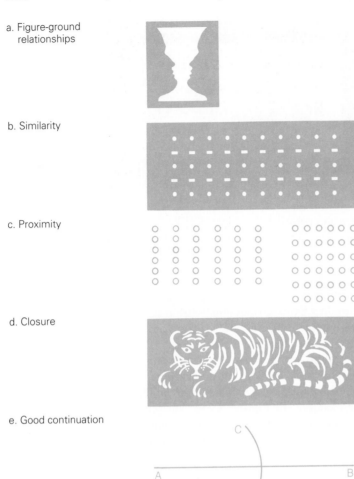

Figure 3.25
Gestalt Laws of
Form Perception.

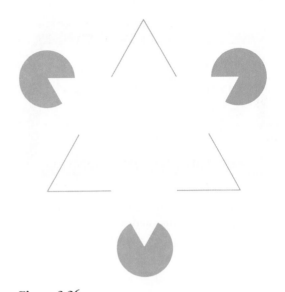

Figure 3.26
Subjective Contour.
The contour of a second triangle is perceived even though
it does not exist. (From Bradley & Petry, 1977)

the whole form. You may have experienced this yourself if you have ever observed how artists can suggest a well-known face just by sketching a few lines.

An interesting phenomenon that is closely related to closure is *subjective contour* (see **Figure 3.26**). This is a contour that is perceived even though it does not physically exist. Some researchers interpret subjective contours as special instances of closure (Kanizsa, 1976).

GOOD CONTINUATION

The Gestalt law of **good continuation** states that we tend to organize stimuli into continuous lines or patterns. For example, we tend to think of **Figure 3.25e** as the intersection of the

two lines AB (straight) and CD (curved). We do not break down the figure into lines AD and CB, or into AC and BD, because the lines created by such an arrangement are not continuous. We expect the curved line to be curved throughout the figure and the straight line to be straight.

SIMPLICITY

The law of **simplicity** predicts that we will organize a stimulus pattern into its simplest components. For example, **Figure 3.25f** is usually perceived as a rectangle with an overlapping triangle and not as a complex and nameless geometric shape.

The laws of perceptual organization are apparent in many situations. For example, the laws of proximity and similarity are often used by advertisers (Zaika, 1975). Consider an ad for an air conditioner that shows a rounded cat curled up next to the rounded corners of the rounded grid on the air conditioner (see **Figure 3.27**). According to Zaika (1975), the viewer would tend to group the cat and the air conditioner because of the law of similarity (the rounded corners). This grouping would then encourage the association between the quietness of the sleeping cat and the implied quietness of the air conditioner.

Form Perception and the Brain

The Gestalt psychologists assumed that the brain was designed to organize stimuli in a par-

David Hubel and Torsten Wiesel won the Nobel Prize for their work on how the brain codes our perception of form.

Figure 3.27
The Laws of Proximity and Similarity.
An advertisement that grouped a sleeping cat and an air conditioner would convey an association between the quietness of the cat and the quietness of the air conditioner.

ticular way. But it was not until 50 years later that researchers began to provide the first clues to how the brain codes our perception of form. To be sure, this research has not yet explained all the complexities of form perception, but it has provided an important start.

In these studies, which earned the researchers a Nobel Prize in 1981, David Hubel and Torsten Wiesel set out to determine if the millions of neurons in the visual cortex responded differently to different forms. Would one type of neuron respond only to horizontal lines and another only to vertical lines? Moreover, could the responses of these individ-

ual cells combine to produce the overall perception of a figure?

In order to answer these questions, Hubel and Wiesel implanted a microelectrode in the visual cortex of a cat. They then showed the animal a series of lines and shapes and recorded the activity of individual neurons (see **Figure 3.28**).

Hubel and Wiesel found that there were three types of specialized neurons in the visual cortex: *simple cells, complex cells,* and *hypercomplex cells.* **Simple cells** responded to lines that were located in a particular place and a particular way. For example, some of the simple cells would respond only to a vertical line in the middle of the screen. Other simple cells would respond only to a horizontal line on an-

Figure 3.28
Hubel and Wiesel's Apparatus for Recording Neuronal Activity in the Visual Cortex of the Cat.
As the cat observes different stimuli projected on a screen in front of it, a microelectrode records how often neurons in the visual cortex fire. Since these are very small signals, they must be amplified (much like a signal from a record) before the experimenter can observe them on an oscilloscope.

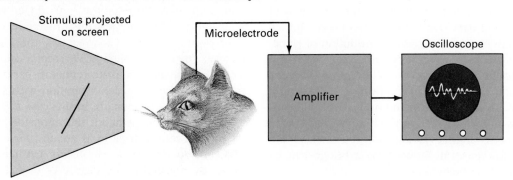

other part of the screen. Still others would respond only to a line at a 45-degree angle, and so on.

According to Hubel and Wiesel, a **complex cell** receives input from many simple cells and responds to lines of a particular orientation located anywhere in the visual field. A **hypercomplex cell** receives input from many complex cells and responds to particular shapes. In this way, information about different lines in the environment can be combined to form a single image. For example, one simple cell may be excited by the line "/"; a second by the line "\"; and a third by the line "__." If the information from these three simple cortical cells eventually converged on a complex and then a hypercomplex cell, all the lines could combine to form the letter "A" (Hubel & Wiesel, 1962).

As Hubel and Wiesel point out, we cannot explain how we see forms in the environment solely on the basis of these specialized cells, but it is possible that we perceive a particular form because a certain group of hypercomplex cells are stimulated through a building-block system.

Are there specialized cells for more complex stimuli? Studies with monkeys indicate that there are cells in the visual cortex that fire when the animals are shown slides of the faces of other monkeys (Bayliss, Rolls, & Leonard, 1985). Indeed, recent studies suggest that there may even be groups of cells that help us visualize illusions such as the subjective contours we discussed in the previous sections. Researchers have now identified groups of cells in the visual cortex of the brain that become excited when a subject looks at an illusory contour like the one seen in Figure 3.26 (Peterhans & von der Heydt, 1991).

Although these result are fascinating, the exact nature of the building blocks that make up the visual system is under debate. Some researchers argue that the building blocks may not be cells that respond to bars but rather cells that respond to more complex patterns of light and dark (De Valois, Albrecht, & Thorell, 1982). Nevertheless, the contribution of Hubel and Wiesel remains very important because it explains how patterns of firing of neurons could lead to the perception of form, color, movement, and depth and how all this information could be united in the brain to allow us to perceive objects (Livingstone & Hubel, 1988). In this sense, it shows how a bridge can be made from brain to mind.

Depth and Distance Perception

Up to this point, our discussion of perceptual organization has focused on two-dimensional objects such as the drawings on the pages of this book. But we perceive the world in three dimensions. Not only do objects have width and height, they also have depth.

Although depth perception is automatic and we often take it for granted, it is quite important. We depend on our ability to perceive depth and distance for judgments ranging from the trivial, such as how far down the curb is, to the important, such as whether we can run across the street before an oncoming car reaches us.

BINOCULAR CUES FOR DEPTH PERCEPTION
You may know someone who has lost vision in one eye. Although such people are still able to see, they do have a special problem with depth perception. This is because many of the cues that we have for depth perception are **binocular cues,** cues that rely on both eyes working together.

Binocular cues for depth perception result from two general processes: convergence and retinal disparity. **Convergence** refers to the process whereby the eyes point more and more inward (converge) as an object gets closer. As the eyes converge (or diverge), they send a message to the brain. The brain interprets this message to mean that the more the eyes are pointed inward, the closer the object. To experience this, hold your finger out at arm's length and then slowly move it toward your nose. As you move your finger closer you may notice that in order to follow it, your eyes must point inward.

A second binocular cue is retinal disparity. **Retinal disparity** refers to the fact that, because the eyes are in slightly different locations, a slightly different or disparate view of an object falls on each retina. You can demonstrate retinal disparity by holding your finger about 6 inches from your nose and closing your right eye. Now look at your finger with your left eye alone. Repeat this procedure with your right eye alone. Each eye saw the image of your finger in a slightly different position. You can virtually eliminate retinal disparity by performing the same demonstration with your finger held at arm's length. In this case the image of your finger is about the same for both eyes. Thus retinal disparity is greatest for close objects and decreases as objects get farther away. By registering the degree of retinal dis-

Aerial haze

Relative size

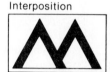

Linear perspective

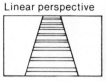

Interposition

Figure 3.29
Monocular Cues for
Depth Perception.

parity, the brain gains another cue about the depth of an object.

MONOCULAR CUES FOR DEPTH PERCEPTION

Although people with vision in only one eye do not have binocular cues for depth perception, they are still able to perceive depth. This is because some of the cues we use for depth perception are **monocular cues,** cues that can be registered by each eye working independently.

Figure 3.29 shows some of the monocular cues for depth. **Aerial haze** refers to the fact that objects that are hazy are perceived to be at a distance, whereas objects that are in focus are perceived to be close. **Relative size** refers to the perception that larger objects are close and smaller objects are farther away. **Interposition** refers to the fact that close objects block our vision of objects that are farther away. A fourth monocular cue is **linear perspective,** a cue by which parallel lines, such as railroad tracks, appear to converge as they get farther away.

Perceptual Constancies

Perceptual constancy refers to our ability to perceive objects as relatively stable in terms of size, shape, and color despite changes in the sensory information that reaches our eyes. Once we form a perception of an object, we can easily recognize the object from almost any distance, at almost any angle, and in almost any illumination. We recognize this textbook's color, its rectangular shape, and its size regardless of how far away from the book we are, from what angle we observe the book, or how much light is in the room. The types of constancy that allow us to do this are *size and shape constancy* and *color constancy*.

SIZE AND SHAPE CONSTANCY

Emmert's law states that the closer an object is to us, the larger the image it casts on our retina. Thus, an object that is 6 inches away casts a retinal image that is twice as large as the image cast by the same object 12 inches away. Based on this, we might expect to perceive that an object 6 inches away is twice as large as the same object 12 inches away. But we know from our experience that this does not happen. If we observe two men, one across the street and the other directly in front of us, the man across the street casts a much smaller retinal image. But we do not perceive him as a midget. Instead, he appears to be a normal-sized individual who is at a distance. Similarly, as an automobile approaches us, the size of the retinal image increases. Yet, we do not perceive the car as growing in size; instead, we know that the car maintains a constant size but is getting closer. **Size constancy** is the tendency for the size of familiar objects to be perceived as constant even though the retinal image changes (see **Figure 3.30**).

Figure 3.30
Demonstration of Size Constancy.
In the left photo, we perceive the man as being normal size because he is at a distance even though the size of the retinal image is identical in the photo at right, where the man appears to be the size of a small doll.

Figure 3.31
Demonstration of Shape Constancy.
As a door is opened we perceive its shape as constantly rectangular, even though the shape of the image striking our retina changes (black outline).

Closely related to size constancy is **shape constancy,** the perceptual process that allows objects to maintain a constant shape even though their orientation or position might change. To demonstrate this, hold your textbook at arm's length and turn it around. Each time you move the book it casts a slightly different image on the retina. Yet despite the different sensation, you always perceive a rectangular book (see **Figure 3.31**).

How do we resolve the discrepancy between the retinal image an object casts and its actual shape and size? Familiarity with the object plays an important role. If we are very familiar with the size of an object, such as a friend's height, we perceive the size as constant no matter how far away it is. Similarly, if we are familiar with the shape of an object, we perceive its shape as constant no matter what our vantage point. Size constancy is further aided by distance cues. Even when we are not familiar with an object, if there are cues to indicate distance, we still see it as a constant size. However, in situations in which the object is not familiar and there are no distance cues, the retinal image prevails. Thus, size and shape constancies seem to be due to experience with various objects. Support for this view comes from studies showing that adults have better size constancy than children (Leibowitz, 1974).

COLOR CONSTANCY

A third form of constancy that adds order to our perceptual world is color constancy. **Color constancy** refers to the ability to perceive the color of familiar objects as constant even though the sensation of color may change. This means that an orange will appear orange even when you have a green light bulb in your lamp. Color constancy is particularly good for familiar objects (Delk & Fillenbaum, 1965), presumably because what we know about the object influences our perception. When we do not already know the color of an object, however, color constancy is not as effective. For example, studies have shown that fluorescent lighting alters our perception of color (Helson, Judd, & Wilson, 1956). Anyone who has purchased new clothes that appeared to be one color in the fluorescently lit store, only to become a different color at home, will certainly agree. Thus, although there is some degree of color constancy for unfamiliar objects (Goldstein, 1984), there is a higher degree for objects of familiar color.

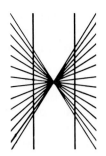
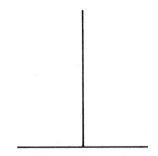
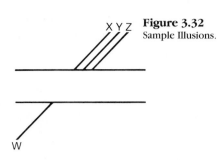

Figure 3.32
Sample Illusions.

a. Shape illusions. Although the two vertical lines are parallel, they appear to bend outward.

b. Size illusions. Which is the longest— the horizontal or vertical one? Although most people pick the vertical line, both lines are actually the same size.

c. Illusions of direction. Which line, X, Y, or Z, is a continuation of W? Most select X, but it is actually Y. Check it with a ruler.

In summary, form perception allows us to see objects as coherent wholes, depth and distance perception allows us to locate an object in space, and constancies allow us to recognize objects without being deceived by changes in size, shape, or color. These processes allow us to organize stimuli so that we can accurately perceive the world around us.

Illusions

Although perception is usually a reliable process, there are some instances when our perceptions actually misrepresent the world. When this occurs, we experience the sometimes annoying but often fascinating phenomenon of illusion. An **illusion** occurs when our perception of an object does not agree with the true physical characteristics of the object. For example, in **Figure 3.32a,** despite what you perceive, the vertical lines are actually straight. **Figures 3.32b** and **3.32c** are other examples of illusions.

Illusions fall into two basic categories: those due to physical distortion of stimuli and those due to our misperception of stimuli (Coren & Girgus, 1978). Illusions due to distortions of light are a common example of the first category. A group of researchers demonstrated that when light is refracted (i.e., bent) in a particular way, a stick floating on the water can appear as a "lake monster" (Lehn, 1979). This might explain sightings of the Loch Ness monster as well as early sailors' reports of large ocean monsters. Similarly, desert mirages of water occur due to refracted light.

Although illusions produced by distortions of light and other stimuli are fascinating,

psychologists have been more concerned with illusions caused by distortions in perceptual processes. By studying these misperceptions, psychologists have learned a good deal about normal perceptual processes.

One illusion that has greatly contributed to the understanding of size constancy is the Ames room. Look at **Figure 3.33** and determine which person is taller. Most people select the person on the right. In actuality, both people are the same size. This illusion is created by the unusual construction of the room. Even though it appears to be a normal, rectangular

Figure 3.33
The Ames Room.

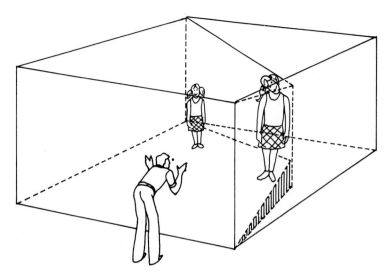

Figure 3.34
Explanation for the
Ames Illusion.

down in normal perception. Rather, the illusion occurs because we try to apply the standard perceptual process of size constancy to an extraordinary situation.

Another example of illusion due to misperception is the impossible figure. This illusion reveals interesting information about how we organize the parts of a figure into a meaningful whole. Examine **Figure 3.35.** At first glance it probably looks like an ordinary figure, but on closer inspection you will notice that the figure cannot exist in reality. Why does it take a few seconds to realize that the figure is impossible? According to one view, it takes this long to fully examine or scan the figure and organize the parts into a meaningful form (Hochberg, 1970). The process by which this scanning takes place is related to eye movements. Although you are probably not aware of it, when you look at a figure your eyes move from place to place on the figure at a rate of about three changes per second (Yarbus, 1967). Thus, when we look at the impossible figure it takes several seconds (the more complex the figure, the longer it takes) to scan the picture and perceive the form. Only after scanning can we appreciate the impossible nature of the figure. Now look at **Figure 3.36,** which is a painting by the well-known artist M. C. Escher. It too is an impossible figure, but because it is complicated it will take you a bit longer to scan it and to realize that it is impossible.

room, it is not. As **Figure 3.34** shows, the left corner of the room is nearly twice as far away from the viewing point as the right corner.

If we combine the knowledge of the unusual shape of the room with the principle of size constancy, we begin to understand why this illusion works. Recall that Emmert's law states that the farther away an object is, the smaller the retinal image. Because the person on the left is actually much farther away, she casts a smaller retinal image. Under normal conditions, size constancy would correct for this. We know by experience that most people are about the same size, so we would assume that the person on the left is not smaller but rather farther away. But the Ames room prevents us from doing this. Because the Ames room is constructed to appear rectangular, the distance cues in the Ames room create the impression that both women are the same distance away. Thus, we assume that the woman who casts a smaller retinal image, the one on the left, is much smaller. The illusion produced by the Ames room does not result from a break-

Illusions also play an important role in perception in natural settings. Consider the natural occurrences of the horizontal-vertical illusion (Figure 3.32b). People have a tendency to overestimate the size of vertical objects such as lamp posts and buildings; thus a tree looks shorter when it is cut down than it does when it is standing (Coren & Girgus, 1978). One of the most famous architectural examples of this illusion is the Gateway Arch in St. Louis (see **Figure 3.37**). Only by measuring can you convince yourself that the height and width are equal. They are both 630 feet.

Sometimes misperceptions based on illusions can have disastrous effects. Imagine you are an air traffic controller looking at a radar screen like the one in **Figure 3.38**. Glancing at the screen, it appears that the two planes are on entirely different paths and would not collide. But now take a ruler and trace the paths. You will immediately see that they are in store for a midair collision. This illusion is the same as the one demonstrated in Figure 3.32c.

Figure 3.35
An Impossible Figure.

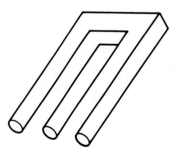

For the past 100 years, psychologists have used illusions, such as the Ames room and the impossible figure, to help understand perceptual processes (see also Coren & Girgus, 1978; Robinson, 1972; Solomon, 1980).

• •

INTERPRETATION AND PERCEPTION

The third process in perception is interpretation. The change you saw in the trained seal act/costume ball poster (Figure 3.24) is an example of perceptual set, or seeing what you were "set" to see. Although the poster did not change, your interpretation of it changed based on what you *expected* to see. Our expectation is just one of the factors that can affect our interpretation of a sensory stimulus. In this section we will examine this and other factors that affect how we interpret sensory stimuli.

Perceptual Set

Perceptual set is the tendency for our perception of an object to be influenced by what we expect to see (or hear, touch, smell, or taste). One of the earliest and most vivid demonstrations of perceptual set is a picture originally

Figure 3.36
Ascending and Descending, by M. C. Escher.

Figure 3.37
Demonstration of the Horizontal-Vertical Illusion.
The height of the Gateway Arch in St. Louis, Missouri, is equal to its width.

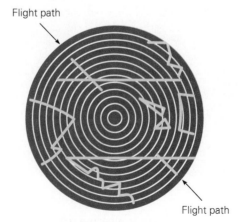

Figure 3.38
Misperceptions on a Radar Screen.

Figure 3.39
Old Woman or Young Woman?
Whether we perceive this ambiguous figure as an old woman or as a young, fashionable woman can be influenced by perceptual set.

published in *Puck* magazine in 1915 (see **Figure 3.39**). But it was not until 1930 that the psychologist Edwin Boring recognized it as an instance of perceptual set. Whether the picture is seen as an old woman or a young woman can be influenced by what we see before it. If we see a picture that is clearly a young woman before we see the ambiguous figure, we see the ambiguous figure as a young woman; if preceded by the picture of an old woman, we perceive the ambiguous figure to be an old woman.

A striking example of perceptual set is demonstrated in **Figure 3.40.** Look at this pair of photographs. What do you see? Most people see two pictures of former British Prime Minister Margaret Thatcher. Now turn the pictures right side up and look again. Because we do not expect to see a distorted mouth and eyes, they are easy to overlook.

Closely related to perceptual set is the idea of perceptual context. In perceptual set, we perceive an ambiguous figure in a particular way based on *previous* information. In **perceptual context,** other stimuli that are present at the *same time* affect our perception of a

Figure 3.40
Perceptual Set.
Upside down, the two pictures look pretty much alike. What happens when you turn the pictures right side up?

stimulus. For example, read the message in **Figure 3.41.** You probably read it as "My phone number is area code 604, 876-1569. Please call!" Now go back and carefully examine the message. Note that the two characters in the word *is* and the number *15* are identical. In addition, the "h" in the word *phone* and the "b" in the word *number* are identical, as are the "d" in the word *code* and the "l" in *call*. But in each instance you interpreted these identical stimuli as different because of the context in which they appeared (Coren & Ward, 1989).

The work on perceptual set and perceptual context demonstrates that we often see what we expect to see. The role of expectancy in perception has some important applications, such as in eyewitness identification. Our general expectation is to see people of average height and average weight. This might explain why almost all eyewitness accounts describe people as average in these two characteristics (Buckout, 1975). Because of this, some researchers investigating eyewitness testimony feel that the perceptions of eyewitnesses may be unreliable (Loftus, 1980).

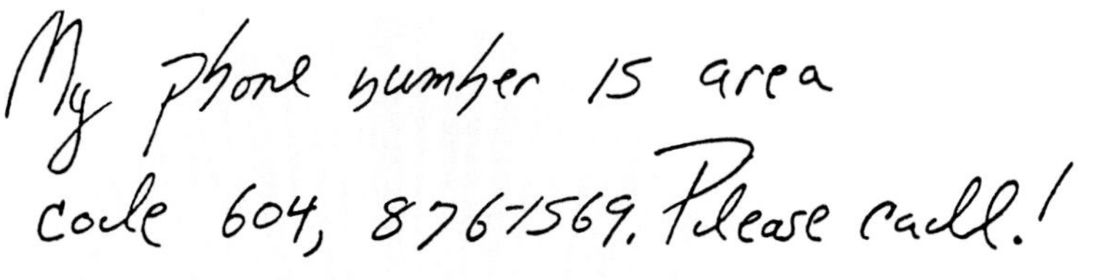

Motivational Factors

A second factor that can influence our perceptions is motivational state. Are hungry people more likely to perceive an ambiguous figure as food? Do we perceive people we admire as being taller? In general, motivational factors can cause us to perceive what we need or want.

One of the first evaluations of the effects of motivation on perception was carried out by R. H. Sanford (1935), who studied the effect of hunger on the perception of ambiguous figures. Sanford presented figures to 10 children both before and after they had eaten. In each case he asked the children what the figures looked like. The children responded that the figures looked like food twice as often before they had eaten than after.

Children commonly perceive their parents to be larger than other people, and adults show similar distortions when they estimate the size of people. Apparently, bigger is better. People with more status or value are judged to be taller. For example, Kassajarjian (1963) questioned California residents prior to the 1960 presidential election about how they intended to vote. They were also asked which of

Figure 3.41
Demonstration of the Effect of Perceptual Context.

the candidates, Kennedy or Nixon, was taller. Although Kennedy was 1/2 inch taller than Nixon, Nixon supporters saw them as being about the same height, while Kennedy supporters overwhelmingly believed that Kennedy was taller. Apparently, children are not alone in overestimating the size of people they admire.

Are things of greater value generally perceived to be larger? In an attempt to answer this question, Baker, Rierden, & Wapner (1974) asked people to compare the size of coins to the size of valueless metal discs. The researchers found that people judged the coins, considered valuable, to be larger than the plain metal discs. Furthermore, the more valuable the coins, the greater the overestimation—the size overestimate of the half-dollar was usually greater than the overestimate of the quarter.

Early Experience

Another factor that affects interpretation is early experience. Evidence from both humans and animals indicates that sensory experience in early life can alter the way an organism perceives the world.

Most Western people have slightly better acuity for horizontal and vertical lines than they do for lines oriented at an angle. One hypothesis to explain this is that Westerners have grown up in a *carpentered environment* of objects such as buildings and roads with horizontal and vertical lines and right angles. Thus our experience with these stimuli could actually sharpen our perception of them. To test this hypothesis, Robert Annis and Barrie Frost (1973) checked perceptual acuity in a group of Canadian Cree Indians who live in a noncarpentered environment consisting of summer tents and winter lodges with lines of all different orientations. They found that the acuity of these Indians was about the same for lines of all orientation. This suggested that the differences in visual acuity between the Canadian Cree and

Figure 3.42
The Striped Tube Used in Blakemore and Cooper's Experiment.
Within the tube, the kitten stood on a glass floor that did not interrupt the pattern of vertical stripes. The stiff collar prevented the kitten from seeing its own body. As a result, the kitten became insensitive to horizontal lines.

other Westerners may be due to early visual experience.

The most convincing evidence for the effects of early experience on perception comes from studies in animals. These studies show that early visual experience not only alters perception but can also alter the brain's visual centers. In one experiment, kittens were raised in vertically striped tubes like the one shown in **Figure 3.42.** After 5 months of this type of rearing, the kittens' vision was tested. The most significant finding was that the kittens

were insensitive to horizontal lines. When the experimenters held a rod in a vertical position and shook it, the kittens tried to play with it. But when they shook the rod in the horizontal position, the kittens completely ignored it. The experimenters also recorded neural activity from the kittens' visual cortex using a procedure similar to the Hubel and Wiesel procedure described earlier. They found that many of the cortical cells were sensitive to lines with a vertical orientation but that none responded to horizontal lines (Blakemore & Cooper, 1970). Since this experiment, many other studies have also shown that perceptual ability is directly related to the environment in which an organism is raised (Blakemore, 1977; Pettigrew, 1978).

Do humans show the same effects of early visual experience on perception? The answer to this question comes from people who have an *astigmatism* early in life due to a distortion in the shape of their eye. This results in an image that is out of focus in either the horizontal or vertical dimension. Thus, people with astigmatism see an environment that is in focus for lines of one orientation; for example, vertical lines may be clear but horizontal lines may be blurry (see **Figure 3.43**). In many respects they are like the kittens raised in an environment with only vertical lines.

To evaluate the effects of these early astigmatisms, researchers determined how well the individuals could see horizontal and vertical lines after their vision had been optically corrected. Even with their vision corrected, these people still saw the vertical lines clearly but saw blurs in the horizontal lines. This finding suggests that, much as with the kittens, abnor-

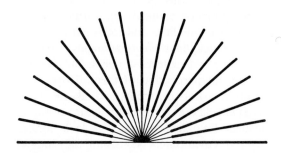 

Figure 3.43
Demonstrations of Astigmatism.
The fan chart on the left is used to test for astigmatism. At any one time, people who have astigmatism can focus for lines of only one orientation. Thus, an astigmatic person may see the fan chart as it is shown at the right: in this case, only the vertical lines are sharply defined; all other lines are blurred.

mal vision early in life had a permanent effect on the brain and, consequently, on perception (Mitchell & Wilkinson, 1974).

Interim Summary

Three important aspects of perceptual organization are form perception, depth and distance perception, and perceptual constancy. Form perception is the process whereby stimuli are organized into meaningful shapes and patterns. The six general laws of form perception formulated by the Gestalt psychologists are (1) figure-ground relationships, (2) similarity, (3) proximity, (4) closure, (5) continuation, and (6) simplicity. Brain researchers have begun to understand how the neurons in the visual cortex register different forms.

Depth perception and distance perception are based on both binocular (two-eye) and monocular (one-eye) cues. The third aspect of perceptual organization, constancy, refers to our ability to perceive the world as being relatively unchanging despite changing sensory stimuli. Perceptual constancies are dependent on both experience and other stimuli in the environment.

Illusions occur when our perception does not agree with the true physical characteristics of a stimulus. Illusions can be due to distortions in the physical stimulus or to misperceptions. The study of misperceptions has provided important clues to the nature of the perceptual process.

Three factors that which can affect perceptual interpretation are perceptual set and perceptual context, motivation, and early experience.

SUMMARY

1. Each sense has an absolute threshold and a difference threshold. Weber's law states that the amount of stimulation that it takes to notice when the intensity of a stimulus has changed, a just noticeable difference or j.n.d., is not constant, but rather a percentage of the intensity of the original stimulus.

2. Light can be described in terms of wavelength (color), amplitude of waves (intensity), and number of wavelengths that make up the light (saturation or pureness).

3. Light enters the eye through the cornea and is focused on the retina. On the retina are two different types of receptors, rods and cones, that transduce light into neural impulses. Rods are useful at night because they can transduce small amounts of light. Cones require more light but also have better acuity and can detect color.

4. If we combine the Young-Helmholtz trichromatic theory, which holds that there are different types of cones for red, green, and blue, with the Hering opponent-process theory, which holds that there are two types of receptors (red-green and blue-yellow), we come up with a reasonable explanation of how humans perceive color.

5. Sound can be described in terms of frequency of sound waves (pitch), amplitude of sound waves (loudness), and combination of sound waves (purity).

6. One important aspect of the auditory system is how it allows us to distinguish between sounds of different frequencies. Place theory, which holds that different parts of the basilar membrane of the cochlea are sensitive to different frequencies, can account for how we hear high-frequency sounds. The frequency theory accounts for low-frequency sounds by stating that the entire basilar membrane vibrates at the exact frequency of the sound.

7. The chemical senses are smell and taste. The skin senses are touch, warm, cold, and pain. A final set of senses are for body movement and position. Kinesthesis tells us about the position of our body parts. Equilibrium keeps us informed about the position of our whole body in space.

8. Form perception, depth and distance perception, and perceptual constancy are three important aspects of perceptual organization. Form perception is governed by the six laws of Gestalt psychology. Depth perception and distance perception are based on both binocular and monocular cues. Perceptual constancy is based on both experience and cues in the environment.

9. Perceptual set, perceptual context, motivation, and early experience all influence how we interpret our perceptual world.

KEY INDIVIDUALS

Wilhelm Wundt
Gustav Fechner
Ernst Weber
Thomas Young
Hermann von Helmholtz
George Wald
David Hubel
Ewald Hering
Torsten Wiesel
Heinrich Hertz
Edwin Boring
George von Békésy
J. E. Amoore

KEY RESEARCH

determination of the absolute threshold
signal detection
relationship between the reference stimulus
  and the just noticeable difference
theories of color vision: trichromatic theory,
  opponent-process theory, composite theory
identification of three types of cones in the
  retina
theories of hearing: place theory, frequency
  theory, combined theory
pain-gating theory
Gestalt laws of form perception
neural activity and form perception in the
  visual cortex of the cat
effects of motivational factors on perception
effects of early visual experience on perception

KEY TERMS

sensation
perception
stimulus
transduction
absolute threshold
noise
signal detection theory
difference threshold
just noticeable difference (j.n.d.)
Weber's law
wavelength
hue
amplitude
brightness

purity
saturation
cornea
pupil
lens
retina
rods
cones
fovea
blind spot
primary colors
complementary colors
Young-Helmholtz theory
trichromatic (three-color) theory
color blindness
afterimage
opponent-process theory
frequency
hertz (Hz)
pitch
loudness
decibels (dB)
complexity
timbre
pinna
tympanic membrane
ossicles
malleus
incus
stapes
oval window
cochlea
basilar membrane
hair cells
auditory nerve
place theory
frequency theory
conduction deafness (middle ear deafness)
nerve deafness (inner ear deafness)
olfactory mucosa
papillae
taste buds
kinesthesis
equilibrium
attention
form perception
figure-ground realtionships
similarity
proximity
closure
good continuation
simplicity
simple cells
complex cell
hypercomplex cell

binocular cues
convergence
retinal disparity
monocular cues
aerial haze
relative size
interposition
linear perspective

perceptual constancy
Emmert's law
size constancy
shape constancy
color constancy
illusion
perceptual set
perceptual context

4

Motivation and Emotion

CHAPTER OUTLINE

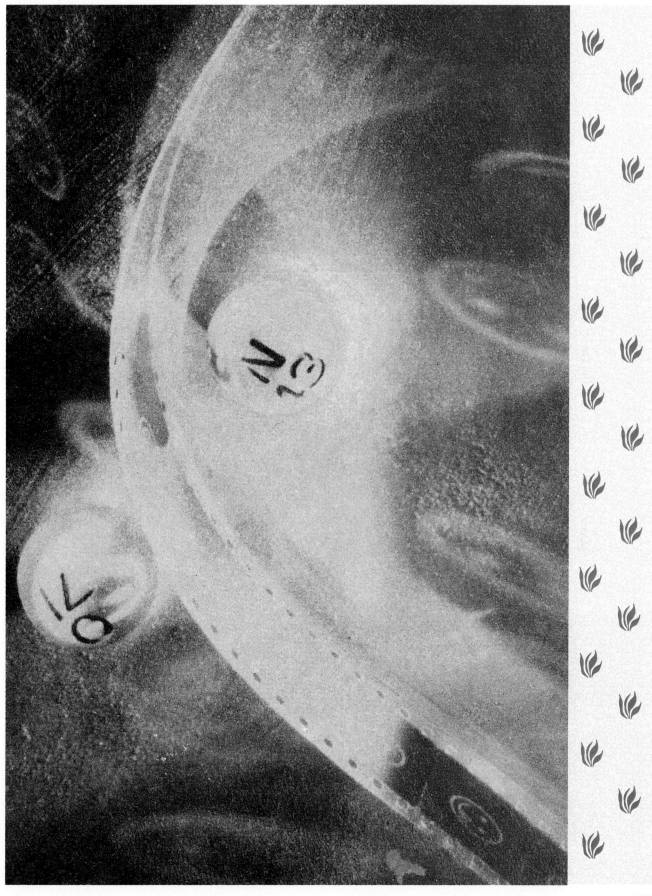

We are all familiar with the basic idea of motivation. Television and newspapers often describe athletes who spend years training for the Olympics, scientists who spend long hours searching for a cure for cancer, or entrepreneurs who seek to make their first million before age 30. The common denominator in each of these activities is the need, desire, and determination to strive for a specific goal or accomplishment. In everyday terms, we would say that these are the actions of highly *motivated* individuals.

Motivated behavior is often accompanied by strong emotions. For example, a person who spends many hours on a single task, such as searching for a cure for cancer, often experiences feelings of tedium and frustration until the goal is achieved. On the other hand, feelings of joy and happiness accompany even a partial solution to such a long-standing goal. Because of this interdependence between motivation and emotion, we consider the two topics together. To clarify the key issues, we give separate treatment to motivation and emotion in this chapter, but you should keep in mind that the two are often inseparable.

● ●

THE NATURE OF MOTIVATION

We can define **motivation** as the desires, needs, and interests that *arouse* or *activate* an organism and direct it toward a specific *goal*. Consequently, we would expect the behavior

Runners who are training for a marathon will be more motivated to train vigorously than a casual runner.

of a motivated organism to differ sharply from that of an unmotivated organism. For example, a runner who wants to complete a marathon will train more vigorously than an individual who has only a casual interest in distance running. Similarly, a hungry rat placed in a complex maze will search for food more purposefully than a rat that has not been deprived of food.

Motivation can arise from either internal or external sources. The desire for food and water arises from internal, physiological needs. On the other hand, the desire for approval and recognition results from external, social circumstances. Sometimes motivation results from the interaction of both internal and external factors. For example, we all have the need to eat, but environmental variables and prior learning determine what we eat and how much we eat.

In the discussion that follows, we will first look at five major theories of motivation, each of which gives different weight to internal and external factors. These five theories are *instinct theory, drive theory, arousal theory, opponent-process theory,* and *incentive theory.* Then we will look at three specific examples of motivation: hunger, sexual motivation, and social motivation.

Instinct Theory

One way to explain why organisms act the way they do is to propose the existence of instincts. An **instinct** is an innate or genetically predetermined disposition to behave in a particular way when confronted with certain stimuli. For example, if a squirrel finds a nut on the ground, it will bury the nut for future consumption. This behavior does not seem to require much prior learning. Simply discovering the nut is enough to set the behavior in motion.

The idea that instincts control certain behaviors is one of the oldest notions in psychology. At the turn of the century, instinct theory was popular in both North America and Europe. There was a considerable effort, especially in American psychology, to identify the basic instincts that governed survival. At first, 10 basic instincts were suggested, including aggression, reproduction, and flight (McDougall, 1908). However, the list soon began to grow and within a short time more than 100 instincts had been proposed, many of which had little to do with survival (for example, cleanliness, modesty). As the number of proposed instincts grew, many critics objected that the word *instinct* had lost its meaning. It had become a convenient way of labeling, rather than explaining, complex human behavior.

ETHOLOGY AND INSTINCT THEORY

Instinct theory was revised in the 1930s by a group of scientists known as ethologists. **Ethology** is the study of how animals behave in their natural habitats. A modified notion of instinct became a central part of ethology.

By observing animals closely, ethologists noted the presence of fixed-action patterns. A fixed-action pattern is really a synonym for the term *instinct*, but ethologists wanted to avoid some of the problems associated with the earlier use of this word. So they carefully defined a **fixed-action pattern** as an unlearned behavior, universal to a particular species, that is elicited or *released* in the presence of naturally occurring events. The events that elicit fixed-action patterns are known as **sign stimuli.**

Ethologist and Nobel laureate Nikolaas Tinbergen described a classic example of a fixed-action pattern in a species of fish known as the three-spined stickleback (Tinbergen, 1951). Aggressive behavior in this fish is released whenever it spots the red belly of a male stickleback. In a series of clever experiments, Tinbergen· demonstrated just how important the sign stimulus was to the release of aggression. Using wooden models of male sticklebacks, Tinbergen discovered that aggression would not occur in the presence of a perfect replica of a male intruder unless the belly was painted bright red. On the other hand, even a poorly constructed replica elicited aggression if it had a painted red belly. These experiments led Tinbergen to conclude that a red belly was the critical sign stimulus for the release of aggression in the stickleback (see **Figure 4.1**).

MODERN INSTINCT THEORY

By carefully studying the fixed-action patterns of different species, ethologists revived the idea that instincts are motivators. However, the original concept of fixed-action patterns has been modified considerably in contemporary ethology. The current view is that instinctual behavior follows an inborn plan that allows substantial flexibility in the course of development (Bowlby, 1969; Eibl-Eibesfeldt, 1975). For example, the greylag goose has an inborn tendency to retrieve an egg that rolls from its nest. However, this behavior may change if the egg

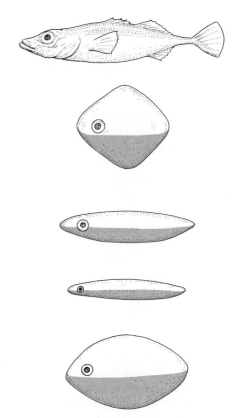

Figure 4.1
Five Models used to Elicit Fighting in the Male Stickleback. The red bellies of the lower four models "released" aggression even though the models themselves were not shaped like a stickleback. The top model, which is shaped like a stickleback, failed to release aggression because it lacked the critical sign stimulus of a red belly. (Based on Tinbergen, 1951)

rolls to a place that is dangerous for the goose. Similarly, human infants have a tendency to form a strong emotional bond with their biological mothers, but they can also form a bond with a surrogate mother. Modern theorists view instinctual behavior as innate or preprogrammed but subject to modification in the face of environmental demands (Eibl-Eibesfeldt, 1989).

Contemporary instinct theory is not without its critics, however. One point of debate is whether instincts should really be considered innate. Some psychologists believe that the term innate is misleading because it implies that environmental experiences play no role in the development of "instinctual" behavior patterns (Gottlieb, 1970; Lehrman, 1970). These critics feel that many of the behaviors that ethologists call instinctual are influenced by a variety of different experiences, including experiences that occur before birth. As one example, this group cites the behavior of newly hatched ducklings, who can detect the difference between the maternal call of their species and the call of the mothers of certain other species of birds. This discrimination is virtually impossible for humans to make. That ducklings can recognize their mother's call immediately after birth is very impressive and suggestive of an unlearned behavior. However, painstaking research has shown that experiences that take place just *before* hatching are responsible for the duckling's ability to discriminate maternal calls. One important event occurs when the duckling's bill penetrates the interior membrane of the egg, and the duckling begins to "talk to itself." Experiments have shown that this self-vocalization *within the egg* is critical to the duckling's subsequent ability to identify the maternal call of its species (Gottlieb, 1975).

SOCIOBIOLOGY

The most provocative and controversial view of instinctual motivation comes from a relatively new discipline known as **sociobiology** (Wilson, 1975). Sociobiologists believe that the primary motivation of all organisms, humans included, is to ensure the future survival of their basic hereditary mechanism—the genes. From this perspective, human behavior is basically selfish because it is designed to protect the genes from extinction. Sociobiologists even suggest that behavior that appears absolutely selfless, such as altruism, is motivated by the principle of gene survival.

For example, sociobiologists define *altruism* as an act that increases the fitness of another at the expense of one's own fitness. *Fitness* is specified by the number of offspring who survive the individual. In other words, an altruistic act is one which increases the probability that an individual's close relatives will survive. From this perspective, evolutionary pressures do *not* favor the survival of the individual *if* this is incompatible with the survival of the group. What matters, in the words of sociobiologist Edmund Wilson, is "the maximum average survival and fertility of the group as a whole" (Wilson, 1975, p. 107).

Wilson contends that there is a strong genetic component to human altruism which he sees as little more than "genetic selfishness." Although humans may perform heroic and self-sacrificing acts, such as risking their own lives to save their children's, the outcome of this heroism is always the same—many of the individual's genes remain with the surviving offspring or relatives (Wilson, 1975). Wilson downplays the usual social explanations of altruism, such as empathy and caring for others, in favor of a largely genetic explanation of why people behave altruistically.

Sociobiology has generated a great deal of interest as well as its share of criticism. Many people object to a treatise on altruism that does not address the social context in which altruism takes place. Even though Wilson feels that only about 10 percent of human social behavior can be explained through genetics, his reluctance to comment on the nature and importance of the other 90 percent has led many critics to charge that sociobiology is misleading. The principal objection of these critics is not that altruism is without a genetic basis but that sociobiology oversimplifies the concept by ignoring the situational and personal variables that affect altruistic behavior.

Drive Theory

Another biologically based theory of motivation involves the concepts of *drive* and *drive reduction.* These two related concepts, like the concept of instinct, have figured prominently in motivation research for many years. As we will see later in this chapter, Freud theorized that human behavior was motivated largely by sexual and aggressive drives. But it was a learning theorist, Clark Hull, who undertook the first systematic study of the concepts of drive and drive reduction (Hull, 1943).

Hull and his students believed that organisms were motivated to eliminate or reduce bodily tension. A common example is the discomfort that arises from deprivation of food or water. If a rat is deprived of water for 24 hours, it develops a strong physiological need for water. In turn, this need creates a state of tension or arousal. **Drive** is the term used to define the state of tension that occurs when a need is not met. Hull believed that drives motivate organisms to reduce tension. In Hullian terms, organisms in a high state of arousal are motivated to engage in the process of **drive reduction,** a set of behaviors designed to reduce or eliminate bodily tension. In our example, the rat is motivated to perform behaviors that will reduce its level of thirst.

Hull's theory provided some distinct advantages for the study of motivation. Perhaps the most important of these was the opportunity to operationalize the key concept of drive.

Because a drive cannot be observed directly, a psychologist must infer the existence of a drive from the behavior of an organism. For example, if a hungry animal searches for food more rapidly than an animal who has recently eaten, we can hypothesize that the need for food has created a state of tension known as the hunger drive.

Because a drive cannot be observed directly, psychologists must infer from the behavior of an organism that a drive exists. For example, if we observe that a hungry animal searches for food more rapidly than a satiated animal, we can hypothesize that the need for food created a state of tension known as the hunger drive. With the term drive operationalized in this way, investigators could measure drives by manipulating the physiological needs that gave rise to them. This is precisely what Hull and his students did in setting forth their principles of motivation (Hull, 1943; Spence, 1951).

DRIVES AND HOMEOSTASIS

As we noted above, the concept of drive is closely related to an organism's internal state of tension or arousal. For this reason, psychologists are interested in how organisms react to changes in their internal states. One possibility is that both humans and animals attempt to maintain certain internal states on a constant or even keel. To do this, organisms seek **homeostasis,** or the optimal level of physiological functioning that maintains an organism at a balanced or constant internal state.

Body temperature in humans provides a good example of homeostasis. Normal body temperature is approximately 98 degrees. If it begins to deviate more than a few degrees in either direction, the body compensates automatically, either by shivering or perspiring. Shivering and perspiring are the body's automatic homeostatic mechanisms for controlling body temperature.

Homeostasis is particularly useful in explaining the motivation for physiologically based activities such as eating and drinking. But unlike temperature, the homeostatic mechanisms that control eating and drinking can be maintained only by voluntary effort. For instance, food alleviates hunger, but organisms acquire food only by eating. There is no automatic, internal mechanism to correct for the continued absence of food. If we are deprived of food for several hours, we are motivated to restore balance by eating.

The principle of homeostasis, then, is closely related to the concept of drive. In order to maintain certain bodily functions at a steady-state level, organisms must eliminate or reduce high and unpleasant levels of tension or, in Hullian terms, engage in the process of drive reduction.

PERSPECTIVES ON DRIVE THEORY

Drive theory made a valuable contribution to the study of motivation. Questions arose in the 1950s, however, when psychologists recognized that some of the motivated behaviors they were studying could not result from a reduction of tension or arousal. Rats, for example, consumed the artificial sweetener saccharin for hours, even though saccharin has no nutritive value and cannot reduce the physiological basis for hunger or thirst (Sheffield & Roby, 1950). Similarly, monkeys were observed solving complex problems simply for the opportunity to look at interesting events, such as a toy train moving around a track (Butler, 1954). Results of this kind were difficult for drive reduction theorists to explain.

Arousal Theory

As the popularity of drive theory waned, psychologists began to reflect more broadly on motivation, particularly in humans. One common observation was that on many occasions people seemed to desire an increase in their level of tension or excitement, referred to as **arousal** (Routtenberg, 1968). Some contemporary examples of activities that suggest a need to increase arousal are roller coaster rides, sky diving, and horror movies. Whereas these examples point to the need to increase arousal, on other occasions people seek to decrease arousal. In other words, we may have a preference for an optimal level of arousal that is nei-

Some people, like these roller coaster riders, tend to seek an increase in tension or arousal.

ther too high nor too low (Berlyne, 1960, 1971).

Many psychologists are favorably impressed with the idea that the nervous system seeks a balance—an optimal level—of arousal (Berlyne, 1971; Hebb, 1949). Some have suggested a theoretical relationship between level of arousal and degree of efficiency in performing certain tasks (see **Figure 4.2**). For example, if you are in a low state of arousal (very tired or just awakening from sleep), your performance is likely to be impaired because of insufficient attention to the task at hand. However, a very

high level of arousal (extreme anxiety and nervousness, for instance) also interferes with performance because you are distracted from the task. Between the two extremes is an optimal level of arousal. Note that the curve depicting this relationship (see Figure 4.2) resembles an inverted U. For this reason, the arousal-performance relationship is often referred to as an inverted-U function.

The inverted-U relationship has one important qualification. The optimal level of arousal may vary from one task to another. In general, people perform best on easy or well-learned tasks when they are operating at a relatively high level of arousal, while optimal performance on difficult tasks usually requires a lower level of arousal. The classroom provides one example. If you are taking class notes, you will do better if you maintain a relatively high level of arousal, but if you are taking an exam in your most difficult subject, your performance is likely to deteriorate if your arousal level is too high. You will need to relax somewhat to achieve your best score on a difficult test (Sarason, 1984).

Do people differ in how much arousal they seek? Personality theorist Hans Eysenck, whose work we will discuss in Chapter 14, believes that optimal levels of arousal differ from one person to another. In Eysenck's view, outgoing individuals (extroverts) are likely to seek stimulating and even risky situations more often than others. By contrast, people who are somewhat shy and withdrawn (introverts) avoid highly stimulating and potentially hazardous experiences (Eysenck & Eysenck, 1985). What is exciting and stimulating to one person may be quite overwhelming to another.

Opponent-Process Theory

We can speak of some motives as acquired. The love of power, the need for achievement, the tendency to engage in thrill-seeking activities are all examples of acquired motives. On occasion, these acquired motives become driving forces in our lives. Witness the terrified parachutist who tumbles from an airplane miles above ground, or the addict who risks life and limb for a drug high. What motivates people to behave this way?

Richard Solomon (1980) believes that many acquired motives bring a basic or primary pleasure but that each pleasurable experience eventually triggers some kind of discomfort.

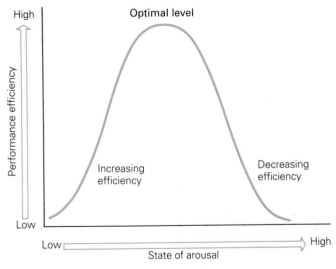

Figure 4.2
The Inverted-U Function of Arousal.
Between the two extremes is an optimal level of arousal for performing various tasks.

The pleasure of a high from heroin eventually brings the discomfort of withdrawal symptoms. Likewise, Solomon noted that emotional highs often compensate for initial suffering. The terror experienced by first-time parachutists seems to be offset by the elation they feel after conquering their fear of falling.

These observations led Solomon to propose the opponent-process theory of acquired motivation. The essential claim of **opponent-process theory** is that every emotional experience leads to an opposite emotional experience that persists long after the primary emotion has passed. The opposite emotion, which develops immediately after the primary emotion, lingers for a longer period of time and diminishes the intensity of the primary emotion. So the fear of parachuting should decrease with each successive jump while the exhilaration of the afterexperience should persist.

Solomon predicts that behavior is influenced by what happens in the long run rather than the short term. Repeated aversive experiences, such as parachuting from an airplane, eventually lose their unpleasant effect and dispose the individual to seek new avenues of pleasure and excitement. Likewise, repeated pleasurable experiences, such as a drug high, eventually lose much of their pleasantness and open up new sources of discomfort. This is particularly true of drugs that bring about intense withdrawal experiences. So why does the addict continue to abuse drugs? Repeated use of drugs may be the addict's attempt to avoid the discomfort of withdrawal, or the opposing emotional experience.

Incentive Theory

Although they differ in several important ways, the instinct, drive, arousal, and opponent-process theories of motivation share a common perspective. Each of these theories addresses the internal state of the organism. Some level of tension or arousal motivates the organism to perform certain actions. Put somewhat differently, the organism is "pushed" in certain directions by internal or biologically based states.

A contrasting idea is that external goals motivate organisms to perform certain actions (Bolles, 1972; Rescorla & Solomon, 1967). The external stimuli in the environment that "pull" the organism in certain directions are called **incentives.** The basic assumption of incentive theory is that if we anticipate a desirable outcome following the completion of a particular

action, we are motivated to perform that action. Conversely, anticipation of an undesirable goal—something aversive or unpleasant—motivates the organism not to perform the action. In short, incentive theorists ask what induces or inhibits behavior by focusing on the environment rather than on internal states.

Incentive theorists can make useful distinctions in evaluating the factors that influence human performance. For example, grades are an obvious incentive for students. However, students are more likely to study for high grades if they anticipate that studying will have a positive effect on the outcome. Alternatively, students might believe that studying has little relationship to high grades. In this example we can distinguish between the *value* of a particular goal (high grades) and the *expectation* of attaining that goal. Incentive theorists often make such distinctions as they focus closely on the (external) environmental events that underlie motivated behavior. (Lawler, 1975; Rescorla, 1978).

So far in this chapter we have examined five different ways of addressing the question of *why* organisms behave as they do. However, we should emphasize that no single theory offers a "correct" solution. Rather, each theory offers a unique perspective, a different way of looking at the reasons for motivated behavior. Because motivation is such a complex issue, we may see evidence for more than one theory in various behaviors. We will first see this interrelationship between theories in discussing the motives that govern hunger and sexual behavior.

Interim Summary

There are five major approaches to the study of motivation: (1) instinct theory, (2) drive theory, (3) arousal theory, (4) opponent-process theory, and (5) incentive theory.

Instinct theory holds that some behaviors are controlled by genetic factors, which dispose an organism to respond in a particular way when confronted with certain stimuli. *Drive theory* holds that organisms are motivated to eliminate states of tension or arousal, such as hunger or thirst, and to return to a state of balance known as homeostasis. *Arousal theory* suggests that there is a preferred or optimal level of arousal that is neither too high nor too low. If arousal is too low, organisms will seek to increase tension; if arousal is too high, they will seek to decrease tension. *Opponent-process* theory holds that acquired motives, such as thrill-seeking or drug addiction, are maintained and strengthened when a primary emotion triggers an opposite emotional response, which lasts longer than the primary emotion. *Incentive theory* proposes that motivation is determined by stimuli in the environment that "pull" the organism in certain directions. Incentive theory focuses not on the internal state of the organism, but rather on the external conditions that induce certain responses.

HUNGER

Hunger is a motivator that affects all living organisms. Humans who go without food for as little as several hours begin to experience hunger. Once this occurs, humans, as well as all other living organisms, will attempt to satisfy their need for food.

Hunger is a complex process. We will begin this section by examining how the body and brain interact to produce hunger. But the motivation to eat is not this simple. Although

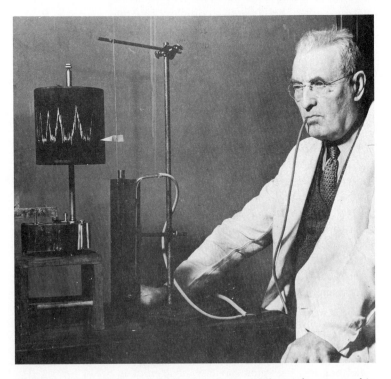

The scientist is using a stomach bag apparatus similar to the one used in the Washburn study to measure stomach activity.

organisms certainly eat to satisfy the physiological need for nutrients, other factors also affect eating. For example, humans will often continue to eat even after they have satisfied their nutritional needs. External factors also have to be taken into account. After discussing physiological mechanisms of hunger, we will discuss some of the factors that can lead to overeating and obesity.

Physiological Mechanisms of Hunger

Two basic questions puzzled the first psychologists who studied hunger. What mechanisms tell the organism when to start eating? Do the same mechanisms tell the organism when to stop? Researchers who studied hunger first addressed these questions by focusing on the role of bodily factors such as stomach activity, the taste of food, and blood sugar levels. From these investigations, they went on to study how the brain uses this information to control eating.

SIGNALS FROM THE BODY

For most people, hunger is experienced as "stomach pangs." This suggests that when the body is deprived of food, the empty stomach sends messages to the brain. Early researchers also thought that these stomach pangs, or contractions, might be related to the experience of hunger. In a classic study, an experimenter named A. L. Washburn swallowed a balloon specially designed to rest in his stomach. His partner, physiologist Walter Cannon, looked on. Whenever Washburn's stomach contracted, the balloon compressed. These investigators found that contractions of the stomach were closely related to Washburn's reports of hunger (Cannon & Washburn, 1912). However, subsequent research failed to support Cannon and Washburn's theory. Other researchers learned that the stomach was not only unimportant but also unnecessary for signaling hunger. For example, rats continue to show hunger even though all the nerves from the stomach to the brain are cut (Morgan & Morgan, 1940). Similarly, humans whose stomachs have been surgically removed because of cancer or severe ulcers still report feeling hungry (Ingelfinger, 1944). However, even though an empty stomach may not be critical in signaling hunger, a *full* stomach does seem to play a role in signaling *satiety* (fullness). It seems that receptors in the stomach send signals to the brain when the stomach is full (Gonzalez & Deutsch, 1981).

How might the stomach and digestive system signal the brain when enough food has been eaten? One possible body-to-brain signaling system involves the hormone cholecystokinin (CCK). Researchers have suggested that CCK is released when food enters the digestive system. The CCK serves as a "stop eating" signal to the brain. Indeed, if the CCK system is blocked, animals eat more (Dourish, Rycroft, & Iverson, 1989).

How might the stomach and digestive system signal the brain to start eating? One mechanism for accomplishing this involves blood sugar, or glucose, levels. As blood sugar levels drop, organisms are motivated to replace nutrients by eating (Friedman & Stricker, 1976). Apparently, by monitoring its own blood supply, the brain can detect low blood sugar levels. Thus low blood sugar levels serve as a signal to initiate eating. In fact, hungry rats postpone meals if they have had glucose injected into their veins (Campfield, Brandon, & Smith, 1985).

THE ROLE OF THE BRAIN

How might the brain use the signals from the body to control eating? As is so often the case, clinical observation gave researchers the first clue about the brain structure important in eating. Alfred Frolich, a Viennese physician, noted that patients afflicted with tumors near the hypothalamus became obese (Frolich, 1902).

The hypothalamus actually comprises a number of smaller areas (see **Figure 4.3**). The two areas that were initially identified as important in eating are the lateral hypothalamus, which is the outside area, and the ventromedial hypothalamus, which is the lower middle area. The **lateral hypothalamus (LH)** has been identified as a "start eating" center; destruction of this area causes an animal to stop eating. The **ventromedial hypothalamus (VMH)** has been identified as a "stop eating" center; destruction of the VMH produces excessive eating.

By destroying a small portion of the VMH of a rat, researchers were able to produce the kind of obesity seen by Frolich in his human patients (see **Figure 4.4**). The VMH was thus identified as the "stop eating" or satiety center (Brobeck, Tepperman, & Long, 1943). Later, Brobeck discovered that lesions to the LH of rats caused the animals to stop eating and eventually to starve. Because destruction of this area produced an animal that would not eat, re-

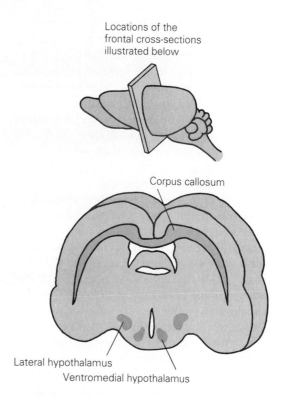

Locations of the frontal cross-sections illustrated below

Corpus callosum

Lateral hypothalamus
Ventromedial hypothalamus

Figure 4.3
The Lateral and Ventromedial Hypothalamus in a Rat's Brain.

Figure 4.4
The Role of the Ventromedial Hypothalamus in Obesity. After lesions were made in its ventromedial hypothalamus, this rat overate and gained more than three times its normal weight.

searchers called the LH the "start eating" or hunger center (Anand & Brobeck, 1951). Scientists concluded that the VMH and LH received information about nutrient levels in the body and then acted together to control eating.

Could the control of eating be regulated simply by an off-on switch in the hypothalamus? Probably not. Careful analysis of the eating habits of obese rats with VMH lesions showed that, although these rats eat voraciously for the first 3 weeks after the lesion is made, at the end of this period their food intake is only slightly higher than that of normal rats. These VMH-lesioned rats also become "finicky" eaters and overeat only if the food is palatable, that is, tasty (Weingarten, 1982). The VMH rats actually undereat if the food is made bitter by adding quinine (Teitelbaum, 1955). If the VMH is really the satiety center, why do rats with damage to the VMH eventually reduce their intake of food, and why do they become selective about what they eat?

Similarly, although rats with LH lesions initially do not eat, they can be coaxed into eating by first being tube fed. After this they eat by themselves as long as they are given palatable food, such as moistened chocolate-chip cookies (Teitelbaum & Epstein, 1962). Such results seem to indicate that the drive to start eating is not controlled solely by the LH.

Thus, scientists have started to look for other brain areas that might also be involved in the regulation of eating. Attention has focused on brain areas that send and receive neural impulses to and from the hypothalamus. The current view is that the hypothalamus is just one part of a system in the brain that regulates eating and that other areas, especially in the brain stem and limbic system, are also involved (Stricker, 1990).

In summary, the most widely accepted theory of why organisms eat holds that the brain monitors the amount of chemicals, including blood sugar, in the body. When these levels become too low, the hypothalamus and related brain structures control the onset and cessation of eating (see **Figure 4.5**).

Human Obesity

What we know of the physiological mechanisms of hunger suggests that organisms eat in order to replace nutrients. If this is so, why do people overeat and become obese? Generally, obesity occurs when the amount of food a person consumes far outweighs his or her nutritional needs. This raises the possibility that factors in addition to nutritional balance may motivate eating.

Although many people may be 5 or 10 pounds overweight at some point in their lives, true obesity is defined as a body weight that exceeds the average for a given height and sex by 20 percent. How can we determine our average or desirable weight? One way is to consult standard height-weight tables, such as those provided by the Metropolitan Life Insurance Company. Another way is to calculate your body mass index, the method described in **Table 4.1**.

A report by the National Institutes of Health concluded that obesity contributes to a number of health problems including coronary heart disease, diabetes, and high blood pressure (Kolata, 1985). As many people know, obesity can also be a source of social problems (Wadden & Stunkard, 1985). For these reasons obesity has been the focus of much research. In this section we will consider several factors that may contribute to the problem of human obesity. Then we will examine what each of these factors tells us about losing weight.

FAT CELLS

One common misperception about obese individuals is that they have physiological disorders. Except in very rare instances, this is not

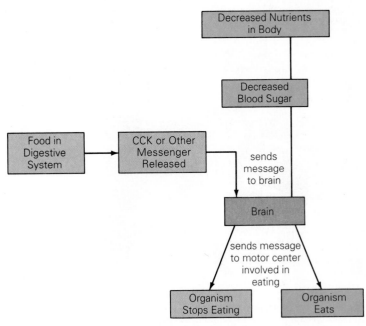

Figure 4.5
A Simplified Diagram of the Control of Hunger and Feeding.

Table 4.1 **Body Mass Index**

Body mass is the figure obtained by dividing your weight in kilograms by the square of your height in meters. You can calculate your body mass by following the three steps below.

1. To convert your weight to kilograms, divide the pounds (without clothes) by 2.2:
   _____ .

2. To convert your height to meters, divide the height in inches (without shoes) by 39.4
   (_____), then square it: _____ .

3. Divide 1 by 2. Body mass = _____ .

For men, desirable body mass is 22 to 24. Above 28.5 is overweight. Above 33 is seriously overweight.

For women, desirable body mass is 21 to 23. Overweight begins at about 27.5. Above 31.5 is seriously overweight.

These rats demonstrate the relationship between genetics and body weight. The larger rat is genetically obese and will become fat even if it is not permitted to overeat.

the case. Obese people do, however, differ physiologically from nonobese people in one important way: the obese have more fat cells. In one group of obese individuals, researchers found three times more fat cells than in a nonobese control group (Knittle & Hirsch, 1968). Researchers now suspect that an increased number of fat cells can lead to obesity.

What factors produce excess fat cells? One view is that heredity is the major influence in determining the number of fat cells an individual has (Bennett & Gurin, 1982). Breeding experiments in animals support this view because fat animals are more likely to give birth to offspring whose birthweight is above average (Schemmel, Michelson, & Gill, 1970). Similarly, there is now considerable evidence that human obesity tends to run in families (Milstein, 1980; Stunkard et al., 1986).

Other views hold that the number of fat cells is determined by environmental factors such as overeating during childhood (Knittle, 1975). Perhaps this is why a recent study found that many of the infants reared in middle-class homes were actually undernourished (Pugliese, Weyman-Daum, Moses, & Lifschitz, 1987). The parents, in an effort to keep their children thin, were not providing them with sufficient calories. But the notion that an overfed infant will develop new fat cells and grow up to be obese is controversial. Results of a 15-year study conducted at the University of California at Berkeley found that babies who were obese at 6 months to 1 year of age were most likely to be thin or normal weight by age 9. Lean toddlers also did not necessarily grow up to be slender children (Shapiro et al., 1984).

Fat cells pose a difficult problem for the dieter. The typical adult has about 30 million to 40 million fat cells. What determines whether someone is obese is both the number and the size of fat cells. In obese people, fat cells swell to two to three times their normal size and then multiply. Unfortunately, fat cells last forever. Once produced, a fat cell cannot be destroyed. Dieting adults do not lose fat cells, they simply shrink them (Sjostrom, 1980). This is one reason why it may be so difficult to lose weight. Some researchers believe that shrunken fat cells continue to send hunger messages to the brain until they are again filled. This may help explain why some overweight dieters are chronically hungry.

SET POINT

One intriguing theory of human obesity holds that each person has a set point that determines his or her weight. The **set point theory** holds that each individual has a predetermined weight which the body tries to maintain. The concept of a set point for body weight is much like a setting on a thermostat. If the thermostat in a house is set at 65 degrees, the set point, the heating system will do whatever is necessary to maintain the temperature. On an extremely cold day, the heating unit may have to consume a substantial amount of fuel to maintain this temperature. On a warm spring day, very little if any fuel will be consumed. Similarly, if the body's set point for weight is 180 pounds, the body will consume enough food to maintain that weight. When the person is very active, the body consumes a substantial amount of food; on relatively inactive days, less food is necessary to maintain the set weight.

What determines the set point? No one is sure as yet, but there are some interesting possibilities. One contributing factor appears to be heredity. Some of the most convincing evidence for a genetic factor in weight control comes from a study conducted in Denmark. This study took advantage of the Danish adoption register, which lists an adopted child's biological and adoptive parents. When 540 adoptees were measured, the researchers found a strong similarity between the adult weights of the adopted children and those of their biological parents, whom they never lived with (see **Figure 4.6**). No such relationship was found between adoptees and their adoptive parents (Stunkard et al., 1986).

A second factor that contributes to set point is metabolic rate. (Bouchard, 1989). Why is it that one person who eats only a moderate amount of food will gain weight while another person who consumes much more food will remain thin? The answer to this paradox comes from an understanding that weight is determined by a combination of the number of calories consumed and the number of calories burned. Exercise burns calories; thus, exercise will contribute to weight loss. But exercise does not account for most of the calories burned by people. About two thirds of the calories are used for basal metabolism, the basic process of maintaining heat in the body. Some people burn more calories than others to accomplish this task; these people are said to have a high metabolic rate. It is these people who are able to eat more and gain less weight. As many dieters have discovered, weight loss can be substantial during the first few weeks of dieting, but then things get more difficult. This is because the body adjusts its metabolic rate to compensate for the reduced calorie intake (McMinn, 1984). Although the experience is frustrating for the dieter, the body is acting in a very adaptive manner. The body is being starved and it reacts by reducing its metabolic rate and thus conserving calories.

Set point and metabolic rate are closely related. In a sense, the body tries to maintain its set point by adjusting its metabolic rate. Individual differences in set point and metabolic rate tell us why two people of identical height, age, activity level, and diet may have very different weights. Although a lowering of the metabolic rate while dieting sounds like a conspiracy to keep the person from losing weight, as we will see later, there are ways to overcome this.

SOCIAL AND ENVIRONMENTAL FACTORS

The tendency to overeat may be controlled not only by internal physiological factors such as set point but also by social and environmental factors such as the clock striking twelve, the sight or smell of food, stress, or even the presence of other people.

Research by John DeCastro has shown that just the presence of other people is related to how much we eat. DeCastro and DeCastro (1989) simply asked people to keep diaries that listed all the food they ate during a seven-day period and the number of other people who were present when they were eating. They found that the more people who were present, the more the people ate.

Stress is another factor that may contribute to overeating and human obesity. Stress,

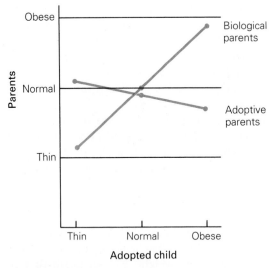

Figure 4.6
Relationship Between the Weight of Adopted Children and Their Biological and Adoptive Parents.
As the biological parents get heavier, so do the children. But there is no relationship between adoptive parents and children—children of obese adoptive parents are just as likely to be of normal weight as children of thin adoptive parents. (Based on Stunkard et al, 1986)

which we will discuss in detail in Chapter 15, may be defined as a state that occurs when an organism is faced with a threatening situation that is difficult to cope with.

In one study designed to test whether stress may lead to overeating in obese humans, Joyce Slochower (1976) had two groups of subjects, one obese and one of normal weight, participate in an experiment to test the "psychophysiology of thought." Actually, the experiment tested the relationship between stress and eating. Each subject heard clicks over a loudspeaker and was told that the clicks precisely mimicked his or her heartbeat. Slochower induced stress in these subjects by increasing the rate of the clicks, which the subjects thought indicated that their hearts were beating rapidly. Slochower then measured how many cashew nuts each subject ate under stress for a 3-minute period. Obese subjects showed a substantial increase in eating relative to control groups, while normal-weight subjects showed a decrease (see **Figure 4.7**). Apparently, stress produced an increase in eating in obese subjects and a decrease in normal-weight subjects.

Losing Weight

Dieting seems to be an American obsession. A recent poll in a popular magazine found that nearly 90 percent of Americans think they are overweight. Another survey in 1984 found that 30 percent of American women and 16 percent of men were on a diet. A Gallup poll released in November 1986 found that 31 percent of women between 19 and 39 years of age diet at least once a month. In 1990 Americans spent nearly $32 billion on diet foods, diet drugs, and diet books and this number is expected to rise to 50 billion by 1995.

Society seems to send the message to people that thin is desirable (Polivy, Garner, & Garfinkel, 1986). Over the past 30 years most *Playboy* "playmates" and fashion models have become much thinner (Garner, Garfinkel, Schwartz, & Thompson, 1980; Silverstein, Peterson, & Perdue, 1986). Unfortunately, becoming thin is very difficult. Most dieters eventually gain back all the weight they have lost (Johnson & Denrick, 1977). What is the point, then? Is losing weight a hopeless cause? Difficult, yes; hopeless, no. What we have discussed so far about the causes of obesity can be useful in losing weight.

WEIGHT REDUCTION IS A LONG-TERM PROPOSITION

Dieting and then regaining weight, the so-called yo-yo syndrome, is a common problem. In fact, binging, eating large quantities of food, is more common among dieters than nondieters (Polivy & Herman, 1985). Unfortunately, it is exactly this cycle that brings disaster. First,

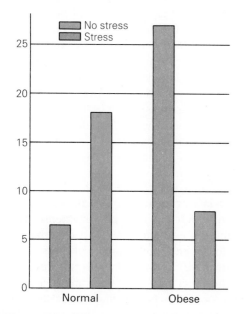

Figure 4.7
The Effect of Mild Stress on Eating. (Adapted from Slochower, 1976)

Binging is more common among dieters than nondieters. Binging carries a risk of producing additional fat cells and reducing metabolic rate.

if the weight after binging exceeds the weight at the beginning of the diet, there is the risk of producing additional fat cells. As we discussed, once produced, these fat cells last forever. Second, the more that weight fluctuates, the faster the body will begin to reduce metabolic rate to save energy when a diet is started. Recall that this reduction in metabolic rate makes weight loss even more difficult (Polivy & Herman, 1985). These factors suggest that we avoid fad diets that promise quick weight loss and instead change habits for the long run, attempting to maintain a stable weight pattern.

EXERCISE CAN CHANGE THE METABOLIC RATE

Exercise is often prescribed as the key to weight loss. This makes intuitive sense because exercise burns calories. For example, running one mile at a moderate pace burns 400 to 500 calories. A slice of chocolate cake with chocolate icing can wipe out the mile run in just a few bites. But, as we said earlier, basal metabolism accounts for two thirds of the calories that the body burns every day. Thus, simply burning calories may not be the most beneficial aspect of exercise. Fortunately, exercise has a second very important function: it raises the metabolic rate and may also lower the set point (Thompson, Jarvie, Lakey, & Cureton, 1982).

A second way to raise metabolic rate is through the use of appetite suppressants. The problem with this method is that once the dieter stops taking these drugs, metabolism returns to normal and the weight is regained (Stunkard, 1982). These pills thus contribute to the dangerous yo-yo effect.

CERTAIN FOOD TYPES CAN ALTER THE DEGREE OF HUNGER

Research by Judith Rodin (1985) suggests that both hunger and metabolic rate can be changed by the foods you eat. The key to which foods are most beneficial to weight loss lies in their effect on the hormone insulin. Insulin regulates blood sugar level. After sugar is consumed, insulin levels rise. Insulin then removes sugar from the blood, causing blood sugar levels to fall and causing hunger. The cycle takes about 2 to 3 hours. If the sugar that is ingested is glucose, the type of sugar in a jelly donut, for example, the rise in insulin and the resulting fall in blood sugar are very steep. If the sugar is fructose, the kind found in fruit, the rise in insulin and fall in blood sugar are

much less pronounced (see **Figure 4.8**). A donut for breakfast, then, not only means more calories than a grapefruit, but eating the donut also produces more insulin, thus making you hungrier at lunch! It seems that the more high-calorie foods we eat, the more we want.

Given the complexity of the control of food intake, it is not surprising that we do not have a simple way to help people lose weight. Although we eat to maintain a homeostatic balance of nutrients, how much we eat and how much weight we gain are controlled by a complex interaction of many factors. Heredity, metabolic rate, and environmental factors such as stress, anxiety, and societal pressures all contribute. But as we learn more about each of these, we can use this valuable information to maintain an optimal weight.

Eating Disorders

While weight loss may be a problem for many people, for some it becomes a psychological disorder that can become severe enough to be life threatening. Consider the following case:

> Jennifer is a popular 18-year-old college student who comes from a family where her mother and aunt are overweight. But Jennifer is anything but overweight, she is 5'9" tall and weighs 110 pounds. Despite this, she decides that she needs to lose weight to become even more attractive. She eventually reduces her food intake to three Cheerios for breakfast, skips lunch entirely, and eats only a small portion of vegetables for dinner. She becomes preoccupied with her body size and often looks at herself in the mirror. She continues to feel fat, even though she is rapidly losing weight. An avid runner, Jennifer has now increased her mileage from 2 to 5 miles per day. She feels depressed and is having difficulty sleeping. Her menstrual cycle has become irregular.

Jennifer is suffering from a disease called **anorexia nervosa.** Anorexia nervosa is a disease in which a person has an intense fear of becoming obese and there is a disturbance of body image and significant weight loss (25 percent or more). Individuals with this disease say that they feel fat when they are at a normal weight or even when they are emaciated. They often do not recognize that they have a problem and are very resistant to therapy. Yet, they

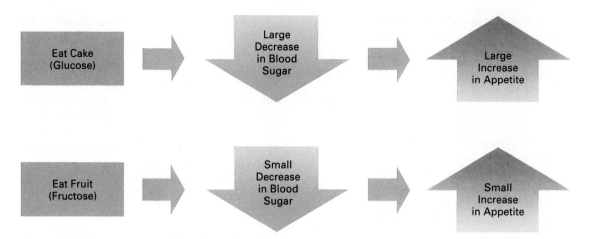

Figure 4.8
The Relationship Between Insulin, Blood Sugar, and Hunger.

Figure 4.9
Perceptions of Body Shape. Women, but not men, misperceive men as preferring a figure much thinner than their own.

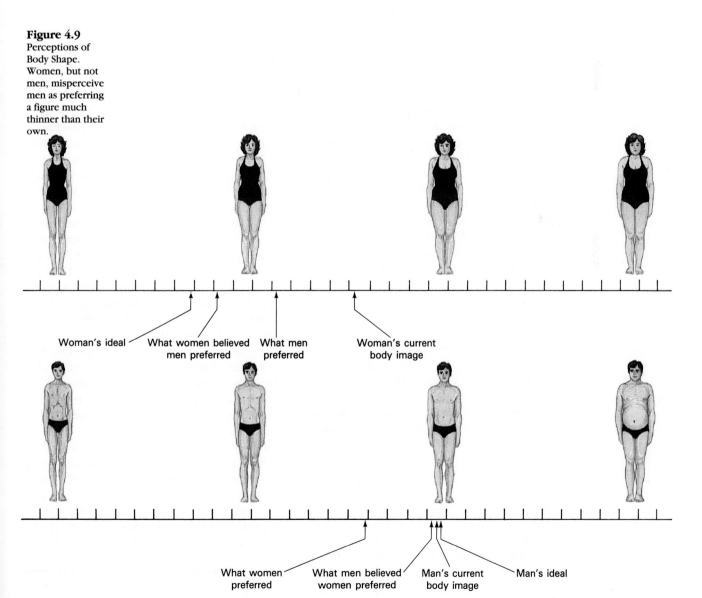

have a life threatening disease that kills up to 18 percent of those suffering from the disorder (American Psychiatric Association).

Susan is a twenty-year-old college junior of normal weight. Since coming to college, her eating patterns have been dominated by binges that consist of eating enormous amounts of sweets, followed by vomiting. In private, she will eat an entire chocolate layer cake, a half gallon of ice cream, and a half dozen donuts and then vomit. She becomes depressed following these binge and purge episodes. Because she alternates these episodes with periods of normal eating, her weight fluctuates greatly over the course of the year.

Susan is suffering from **bulemia.** Bulemia is a disease characterized by alternating periods of normal food consumption with binging and purging. Often these binges are planned.

Neither anorexia nor bulemia can be accounted for by any known physical disorder, although some have suggested that they may be due to a hypothalamic dysfunction. What then causes these diseases? Some clues come from those whom it affects. Anorexia and bulemia are diseases of young women. Ninety-five percent of anorexics are women, most between the ages of 15 and 30. In many cases the two diseases occur together with about 50 percent of anorexics also suffering from bulemia.

Because anorexia and bulemia are disorders of young women, some researchers have suggested that these eating disorders are social diseases brought about by a cultural obsession in women that "fat is bad" and it is "necessary to be thin to be attractive." A landmark study by April Fallon and Paul Rozin supports this view. Fallon and Rozin (1985) had 475 male and female undergraduates look at male and female figure drawings ranging from very thin to very heavy **(Figure 4.9).** They then asked them a number of questions regarding the drawings including:

1. The figure that looked most like the subject's current shape.
2. The figure they most wanted to look like.
3. The figure they felt would be most attractive to the opposite sex
4. The figure of the opposite sex to which they were most attracted.

The men chose very similar figures as representing their ideal figure, their current figure, and the figure most attractive to women. The women, in contast, chose a heavier figure as representing their current figure and a much thinner one as their ideal. Additionally, they thought men would prefer a thinner figure than the men said they actually preferred. Thus most of the women in the study, but not most of the men, were in some way dissatisfied with their current figure. These characteristics may predispose certain women to eating disorders.

Interim Summary

One reason that organisms eat is to maintain a homeostatic balance of nutrients. The most widely accepted theory of how organisms maintain this balance is that the brain monitors the amount of stored nutrients in the body. The brain then controls the onset and cessation of eating through the hypothalamus and related structures.

In some instances humans continue to eat even though the need for nutrients has been satisfied. Such behavior can eventually lead to obesity. Research indicates that many factors can contribute to obesity including the number and size of fat cells, the set point, metabolic rate, and social and environmental factors.

Although losing weight is difficult, an understanding of the causes of obesity gives some insight into effective means to control weight. For example, exercise has the dual benefit of burning calories and raising metabolic rate. In addition, the type of food eaten can affect the metabolic rate and the degree of hunger felt.

In some cases losing weight can become an obsession and develop into a life-threatening disorder. One such disorder is anorexia, which is characterized by an intense fear of becoming obese, disturbance of body image, and weight loss of 25 percent or more. A second disorder is bulemia, which is characterized by alternating periods of normal food consumption and binge-and-purge episodes. No one knows what causes these disorders, but one view holds that they are brought about by a cultural obsession in women that "it is necessary to be thin to be attractive."

SEXUAL BEHAVIOR AND MOTIVATION

The motivational basis for eating is clear: we eat to satisfy a basic need. Sexual behavior is also tied to a basic need, and, like eating, it is affected by biological, psychological, and cultural factors. However, sex and eating differ in important respects. People must eat to stay alive. If we do not eat, we die. On the other hand, not all human beings engage in mature sexual behavior. Some are unable, and even among those who are able, many survive quite well without engaging in sex. In recent years we have learned a great deal about complexities of sexual behavior and how it is affected by genetic factors, hormones, and experience. We will begin this section by examining human sexual behavior and how it has changed dramatically over the past 40 years. We will then consider some of the factors that motivate sexual behavior in both humans and other species. We will conclude with a discussion of sexual orientation.

Human Sexual Behavior

Human sexual behavior has been studied systematically for more than 40 years. The study of sex began when students of Alfred Kinsey, a biologist at Indiana University, asked him questions about human sexuality that he could not answer. Kinsey launched a series of investigations that culminated in his books *Sexual Behavior in the Human Male* (Kinsey, Pomeroy, & Martin, 1948) and *Sexual Behavior in the Human Female* (Kinsey, Pomeroy, Martin, & Gebhard, 1953). Studies since Kinsey's have looked at many aspects of human sexual behavior, and at the same time a great deal of important research has been done on the sexual behavior of other species. We will first discuss some of the highlights of Kinsey's findings and more recent studies of human sexuality and then look at a broad range of research on sexual motivation that helps us understand these findings.

CHANGES IN HUMAN SEXUAL BEHAVIOR

Although Alfred Kinsey and his colleagues found that sexual activity was more frequent and varied than most people in postwar America believed, later surveys (Hunt, 1974; Tavris & Sadd, 1977) showed that by the 1980s

it had become more so. We can point to three specific indications. First, as noted in Chapter 1, there was an increase in premarital sex. The percentage of both men and women who engaged in premarital sex had risen. The increase was especially dramatic for women, so that rates for men and women were much closer than in the past (Clement, Schmidt, & Kruse, 1984). Among college students, it was generally expected that sex would be part of an intimate relationship. In one mid-1980s survey, only 17 percent of college students had not had sex (Christoper & Cate, 1985).

Another change was found among married couples. Although the frequency of sexual intercourse declines with age, recent surveys indicate that married couples are engaging in sex more frequently than did couples of the same age 50 years ago. The increase has been about the same for all age groups. A final change we can note is that oral sex has become much more common among married couples. Hunt's surveys found that among couples 25 years old or younger, 90 percent had engaged in both cunnilingus, oral stimulation of the female genitals, and fellatio, oral stimulation of the male genitals.

The results of all these studies reflect what has been called the "sexual revolution" of the 1960s and 1970s. In recent years, however, the threat of AIDS (acquired immunodeficiency syndrome) has clearly changed sexual behavior. Now abstinence and sexual fidelity are increasing (Maugh, 1990). Some studies suggest a decline in premarital sex (Gerrard, 1987). People are much more careful about having sex and about who they have sex with.

THE HUMAN SEXUAL RESPONSE

Although studies of human sexual behavior began in the 1940s, detailed studies of the physiology of human sexuality did not take place until the 1960s. Research by William Masters and Virginia Johnson (1966) demonstrated that the physiological changes that accompany the human sexual response are remarkably similar for all men and women. Sexual behavior and experiences may differ widely, depending on such factors as previous sexual experience, social norms, maturation, internalized parental standards and other attitudes, external stimuli associated with sexuality in a given situation, and physiological factors. Yet the commonalities in male and female sexual responding are striking.

Alfred Kinsey
(1894–1956)

William Masters
and Virginia
Johnson

Psychology in the News

IS SEX REALLY NECESSARY?

By J. Madeleine Nash

Birds do it. Bees do it. But dandelions don't. The prodigious spread of these winsome weeds underscores a little-appreciated biological fact. Contrary to human experience, sex is not essential to reproduction. "Quite the opposite," exclaims anthropologist John Tooby of the University of California at Santa Barbara. "From an engineer's standpoint, sexual reproduction is insane. It's like trying to build an automobile by randomly taking parts out of two older models and piecing them together to make a brand-new car." In the time that process takes, asexual organisms can often churn out multiple generations of clones, gaining a distinct edge in the evolutionary numbers game. And therein lies the puzzle: If sex is such an inefficient way to reproduce, why is it so widespread?

Sex almost certainly originated nearly 3.5 billion years ago as a mechanism for repairing the DNA of bacteria. Because ancient earth was such a violent place, the genes of these unicellular organisms would have been frequently damaged by intense heat and ultraviolet radiation. "Conjugation"—the intricate process in which one bacterium infuses genetic material into another—provided an ingenious, if cumbersome, solution to this problem, although bacteria continued to rely on asexual reproduction to increase their numbers.

Animal sex, however, is a more recent invention. Biologist Lynn Margulis of the University of Massachusetts at Amherst believes the evolutionary roots of egg and sperm cells can be traced back to a group of organisms known as protists that first appeared some 1.5 billion years ago. (Modern examples include protozoa, giant kelp and malaria parasites.) During periods of starvation, Margulis conjectures, one protist was driven to devour another. Sometimes this cannibalistic meal was incompletely digested, and the nuclei of prey and predator fused. By joining forces, the fused cells were better able to survive adversity, and because they survived, their penchant for union was passed on to their distant descendants.

From this vantage point, human sexuality seems little more than a wondrous accident, born of a kind of original sin among protozoa. Most population biologists, however, believe sex was maintained over evolutionary time because it somehow enhanced survival. The mixing and matching of parental genes, they argue, provide organisms with a novel mechanism for generating genetically different offspring,

---

Specifically, Masters and Johnson found that men and women go through the same four stages of sexual response when they are aroused. These four stages are the excitement, plateau, orgasm, and resolution stages.

The *excitement* stage of sexual arousal begins when some internal or external stimulus causes the person to think about or feel sexual arousal. Heart and respiratory rates increase. Men usually experience an erection of the penis. In women swelling of the breasts and lubrication of the vagina occur. The duration of this stage varies greatly, from a few minutes to more than an hour.

Next comes the *plateau* phase, characterized by increased arousal, firmer erections, and more vaginal lubrication. There is a sense that arousal cannot increase more without bringing on the next phase, orgasm. *Orgasm* is a feeling of intense pleasure and release from building tension. Women experience rhythmic contractions of muscles around the vagina. Men experience similar contractions in and around the penis. These contractions in men lead to the ejaculation of semen. For both men and women, the contractions are spaced approximately every $8/10$ of a second, and usually the first five or six contractions are the most pleasurable.

In the *resolution* phase the body gradually returns to normal. During this phase, men

thereby increasing the odds that their progeny could exploit new niches in a changing environment and, by virtue of their diversity, have a better chance of surviving the assaults of bacteria and other tiny germs that rapidly evolve tricks for eluding their hosts' defenses.

However sex came about it is clearly responsible for many of the most remarkable features of the world around us, from the curvaceousness of human females to the shimmering tails of peacocks to a lion's majestic mane. For the appearance of sex necessitated the evolution of a kaleidoscope of secondary characteristics that enabled males and females of each species to recognize one another and connect.

The influence of sex extends far beyond the realm of physical traits. For instance, the inescapable fact that women have eggs and men sperm has spurred the development of separate and often conflicting reproductive strategies. University of Michigan psychologist David Buss has found that men and women react very differently to questions about infidelity. Men tend to be far more upset by a lover's sexual infidelity than do women: just imagining their partner in bed with another man sends their heart rate soaring by almost five beats a minute. Says Buss: "That's the equivalent of drinking three cups of coffee at one time." Why is this so? Because, Buss explains, human egg fertilization occurs internally, and thus a man can never be certain that a child borne by his mate is really his. On the other hand, because women invest more time and energy in bearing and caring for children, they react more strongly to a threat of emotional infidelity. What women fear most is the loss of their mates' long-term commitment and support.

The celebrated war between the sexes, in other words, is not a figment of the imagination but derives from the evolutionary history of sex —from that magic moment long, long ago when our unicellular ancestors entwined in immortal embrace.

From "Is Sex Really Necessary?" by J. Madeleine Nash. TIME, January 20, 1992. Copyright © 1992 The Time, Inc. Magazine Company. Reprinted by permission.

Questions

1. What is the evolutionary value of sexual reproduction? How does this help explain the power of the sex drive?
2. According to David Buss why do men and women have such different concerns about sexual versus emotional infidelity?
3. How could the difference between men and women's concerns about sexual versus emotional infidelity be explained by social factors instead of by evolutionary factors?

---

enter a *refactory* phase in which they are not capable of sexual orgasm again until some time has passed. Women, however, are capable of several orgasms in a short period of time.

Masters and Johnson's studies were important in determining the physiological aspects of the human sexual experience. Although all humans go through the same four stages of physiological response, there are substantial differences among individuals in the character of their sexual responses and the pleasure they experience from these responses. These differences are determined by the broad range of factors that affect sexual motivation. We will consider some of these factors in the next section.

Sexual Motivation

Four different kinds of factors that affect sexual motivation and sexual response in both humans and nonhuman animals are genetic and hormonal factors, early experience, external stimuli, and attitudes. As we shall see, the relative importance of each of these factors depends on the species. The sexual behavior of less complex organisms, such as rats and dogs, is governed to a large extent by genetics and hormones; experience and learning play a central role in human sexual behavior.

GENETIC AND HORMONAL FACTORS
Genetic and hormonal factors interact to determine whether an individual will develop as a

male or female. Humans and other mammals are *sexually dimorphic,* meaning that they develop in two forms, male and female. The determination of gender occurs at conception, when the mother and father each contribute one sex chromosome. Although this genetic basis for gender is important, it is only the first step in the chain. Another essential factor is hormones (Feder, 1984). Early in fetal life the sexual organs or gonads look very similar in males and females. But at about 8 weeks after conception, the sex chromosomes trigger the development of either testes in the male or ovaries in the female. In the case of the male, once the testes are partially developed, they begin to secrete **androgens,** which is the general name for the male sex hormones. The most important of the androgens is *testosterone.* This hormone further guides the development of the male reproductive system. If the androgens are not present, the fetus then develops ovaries and a female reproductive system. In a sense, nature predisposes the fetus to be female unless androgens are added.

Researchers have studied the relative roles of genetics and hormones in determining gender and sexual behavior by altering hormones in developing animal fetuses. In one such study, researchers gave pregnant monkeys the male hormone testosterone. When the offspring were born, the genetic females (monkeys with female chromosomes) had both male and female sex organs. For example, they had a small but well-developed penis, but they also had a female reproductive system (ovaries and a uterus) (Goy, 1968). The behavior of these "androgenized" female monkeys was also more like that of males. They were more likely than normal female monkeys to engage in rough-and-tumble play and make playful threat gestures (Goy & Goldfoot, 1973).

Similar effects were seen in humans when in the early 1950s some pregnant women were given a drug to prevent miscarriage. Although physicians did not know it at the time, the drug acted like an androgen and had an effect on human fetuses similar to the effect of testosterone on fetal monkeys. The female offspring of these mothers often had both male and female sexual characteristics but they always had a female reproductive system (Money & Ehrhardt, 1972). Fortunately, through surgical correction of the genitalia and hormone therapy, the physical characteristics of these children were made female.

The importance of hormones in determining sexual behavior is not the same for all species or for both genders. Secretion of sex hormones is fairly constant in males of most species, so they are willing to engage in sexual behavior at almost any time. In females, however, hormones circulate cyclicly, and in many species so does interest in sexual behavior. Female dogs, for example, are receptive to sexual advances only when they are in *heat,* the part of their cycle that corresponds to the period of greatest fertility. The notable exception to this is the human female. In women, sexual arousal seems more dependent on external cues and experience.

EARLY EXPERIENCE

In many animals, the ability to have normal sexual relations in adulthood depends on early experience. For example, adult male dogs raised in isolation (having no physical contact with other dogs for the first year of life) have difficulty mating with females. They try to mount the female as often as do normal dogs, but their efforts are clumsy and they often try to mount the female's front or side. This suggests that genetic and hormonal factors alone are not enough to produce normal sexual behavior. Nowhere is this more apparent than in Harry Harlow's research on monkeys.

In a series of now-classic studies, Harlow raised male and female rhesus monkeys in total isolation for the first 12 months of life. When the males and females were finally placed together, they not only avoided sexual contact but also often fought viciously (Harlow & Harlow, 1965). To explain these results, Harlow suggested that most normal sexual motivation is dependent on an affectional bond between the two mates. This ability to make an affectional bond is based on earlier bonds between the monkey and its parents and peers (Harlow, 1971). Harlow also pointed out that much of young monkeys' play behavior is necessary for successful sexual behavior later in life. For example, months before they are sexually mature, young monkeys wrestle with their peers and display the grasping and thrusting response that is characteristic of adult sexual behavior (see **Figure 4.10**).

Early experiences are equally important to the human capacity for normal sexual behavior. Throughout life people learn skills and develop psychological capacities that enable them to interact and socialize with others and

Figure 4.10
The Wrestling of Young Monkeys Is an Important Part of Their Sexual Development.

to experience intimacy. In addition, they learn about some of the specific skills involved in sexual relations. In fact, one form of sexual therapy focuses on teaching people the physical skills of sexual behavior (Masters & Johnson, 1970). All of these experiences contribute to adult sexuality, an awareness of oneself as a sexual being.

THE ROLE OF EXTERNAL STIMULI
In both animals and humans, many external stimuli can produce arousal. These include tactile (touch), olfactory (smell), and visual (sight) stimuli. In humans, tactile and visual stimuli are especially important. One aspect that makes the human sexual experience much more varied than that of animals is the greater variety in the kinds of touching and caressing that men and women find arousing.

The range of arousing visual stimuli was demonstrated in a study of human response to erotic photographs (Miller, Byrne, & Fisher, 1980). In this study, the researchers asked male and female college students to indicate how arousing they found various erotic photographs. These photographs varied in their degree of sexual explicitness. In general, the more explicit the photo, the more arousal the

subjects reported. Other studies show that both men and women are highly aroused by films depicting sexual behavior, such as a couple undressing and engaging in heavy petting (Fisher & Byrne, 1978). There are many kinds of visual stimuli that humans find sexually arousing.

THE ROLE OF ATTITUDES
Attitudes are extremely important in determining an individual's response to sexually arousing stimuli, to the sexual desires of others, and to his or her own sexual feelings. **Attitudes** are people's positive or negative evaluations of objects, behaviors, people, or ideas. Individuals with positive attitudes toward sex in general and toward specific sexual practices are apt to enjoy sexual feelings more and to engage in more frequent and varied sexual behavior. For example, people who have negative attitudes about masturbation are less aroused by erotic stimuli (Fisher & Byrne, 1978). This was shown in a series of studies using skin temperature as a measure of sexual arousal. In one of these studies, women who had negative attitudes toward masturbation were less aroused when reading an erotic story than women with positive attitudes toward masturbation (Abrahamson, Perry, Rothblatt, Seeley, & Seeley, 1979; Seeley, Abrahamson, Perry, Rothblatt, & Seeley, 1980).

As noted earlier, during the 1960s and 1970s sexual attitudes became much more liberal than they had been in earlier decades. Hunt's (1974) surveys showed that younger people had more positive attitudes about sex in general and about specific sexual behaviors, such as premarital sex and homosexuality, than did older people. The attitudes of these younger people were formed during the more permissive climate of the 1960s and 1970s. However, data clearly show that attitudes have become notably less liberal in the 1990s. AIDS and the publicity that has been attached to it are major factors. For example, AIDS and the human immunodeficiency virus (HIV) that causes it received a great deal of attention in 1991 when professional basketball star Magic Johnson of the Los Angeles Lakers contracted the HIV virus. The mass media in North America subsequently increased the emphasis on "safe sex." Now condoms are discussed—and dispensed—in ways unheard of just a few years ago, and people are becoming much more careful about casual sex. It is difficult to forecast how attitudes and behavior will

Through sex education programs, many communities hope to stem the tide of AIDS.

change during the rest of this century, but it seems likely that we will remain for some time in an era of more conservative, responsible sexuality.

SEXUAL ORIENTATION

Sexual orientation refers to the direction of one's sexual interest (Storms, 1980). A heterosexual orientation, sexual interest in partners of the opposite sex, is much more common than a homosexual orientation, that is, sexual interest in partners of the same sex. **Homosexuality,** defined as preference for partners of the same sex, has generated a great deal of research and concern in recent years, especially because AIDS is much more prevalent among homosexuals than among heterosexuals. Early surveys of sexual behavior showed that 4 percent of men and 3 percent of women reported they were exclusively homosexual. At least one homosexual experience was reported by 37 percent of men and 28 percent of women (Kinsey et al., 1948; Kinsey et al., 1953). Hunt's (1974) studies reported similar figures. A more recent study confirmed these general findings, showing that 20 percent of men had had one homosexual experience but only 3 percent had occasional homosexual or frequent homosexual experiences after the age of 19 (Fay, Turner, Klassen, & Gagnon, 1989). In recent years, atti-

tudes toward homosexuality have changed and homosexuality has become more accepted. For many years, for example, the American Psychiatric Association considered homosexuality a mental disorder. In 1973, however, it voted to delete homosexuality from its list of disorders.

In a 1979 study, Masters and Johnson found that homosexual couples often reported greater sexual satisfaction than heterosexual couples. Masters and Johnson observed that homosexual couples communicated more effectively with their partners and engaged in more gentle caressing. This may be because there are no cultural expectations for how homosexuals should behave and therefore no obligation to meet particular performance standards.

What causes homosexuality or, more generally, what leads people to have a homosexual orientation, a heterosexual orientation, or some combination of both? Investigations of this question have considered a range of factors, including classical and operant conditioning, psychodynamic conflict, the sex of the person with whom an individual had his or her first sexual encounter, hormone levels in adulthood and before birth, and genetics (Brown, 1986). There is no easy answer to the question of cause, but more and more evidence is suggesting that biological factors play a strong role.

Research has shown that homosexual couples often communicate more effectively and report greater sexual satisfaction than heterosexual couples.

There is a wide range of studies investigating biological contributions to sexual orientation. One study showed that male homosexuals and heterosexuals had different physiological responses to injections of an estrogen preparation (Gladue, Green, & Hellman, 1984). Other research on the effect of hormones in rats suggests that experiences of the mother during pregnancy can affect sexual orientation (Svare & Kinsley, 1987; Ward, 1972). Similarly, a study with human beings shows that mothers stressed in the middle term of their pregnancies were more likely to have homosexual sons (Ellis, Ames, Peckham, & Burke, 1988). As noted in Chapter 2, recent research has suggested that a region of the anterior hypothalamus in human beings is related to sexual orientation and that region is more than twice as large in heterosexual men as in homosexual men (LeVay, 1991). Another recent study considered genetic factors and showed that 52 percent of the identical twins of male homosexuals are also homosexual. Only 22 percent of the nonidentical, or fraternal, twins of homosexuals are also homosexual (Bailey & Pillard, 1991). The authors concluded that genetic factors account for 30 to 70 percent of male homosexuality. These studies have generated controversy and will generate more research. They do not indicate conclusively that genetics or physiology causes sexual orientation. They are highly suggestive, but more research is needed.

There is some evidence that family factors contribute to homosexuality in both men and women. Some studies have shown that lack of intimacy between parents, poor relationships with the parent of the same sex, and, in the case of men, lack of encouragement of traditional male behavior are related to homosexuality (Evans, 1969; Saghir & Robins, 1973; Stephan, 1973). On the other hand, a 1981 study found no family or experiential factors that are causally related to homosexuality (Bell, Weinberg, & Hammersmith, 1981).

One intriguing theory of homosexuality suggests that the key causal factors are the age at which sex drives develop and the gender of the persons involved in sexual fantasies or images during masturbation (Storms, 1981). According to this theory, if individuals develop sex drives early, when most of their interactions are with same-sex peers, they are more likely to imagine same-sex friends in sexual fantasies and during masturbation and thus are more likely to become homosexual. This theory is supported by studies showing that homosexual preference is more common among individuals who reached sexual maturity earlier (Goode & Haber, 1977). More research is clearly needed, not only on the specific question of homosexual orientation but also on the question of sexual orientation in general. The more we learn about motivation toward heterosexual orientation, the more we will come to understand the special case of homosexual orientation.

Interim Summary

Systematic study of human sexual behavior began with Kinsey's investigations in the 1940s and 1950s. More recent studies have reported changes in the incidence, frequency, and variety of sexual activity.

Masters and Johnson's studies of the human sexual response showed that men and women go through four stages of sexual arousal: excitement, plateau, orgasm, and resolution. Men, but not women, go through a refractory period during resolution in which they are temporarily incapable of sexual arousal.

When and how an organism engages in sexual behavior depends upon an interaction of genetic and hormonal factors, external stimuli, experience, and attitudes. The sexual behavior of less complex organisms, such as rats and dogs, appears to be largely dependent upon hormones. The sexual behavior of humans, in contrast, is more dependent upon experience and learning.

Attitudes strongly affect responses to erotic stimuli. For example, women with negative attitudes toward masturbation are less aroused by reading erotic stories than are women with positive attitudes. Recent studies suggest that the fear of AIDS has made attitudes about sex less liberal than they were in the 1960s and 1970s.

Recent research on homosexuality suggests that homosexuals may attain greater sexual satisfaction than heterosexuals, perhaps because they are less bound by cultural expectations for sexual performance. Research has explored both biological and experiential differences between homosexuals and heterosexuals, but it has not clearly identified the causes of sexual preference. The most recent research on sexual orientation has focused on possible brain structures and genetic factors related to homosexuality.

● ●

SOCIAL MOTIVATION: THEORY AND RESEARCH

Thus far we have discussed what are sometimes called primary, "tissue-based" motives, which grow out of physiological conditions and lead to behaviors that maintain the organism or species. Such motives are found in all forms of animal life, including human beings. However, a great deal of human behavior is under the control of the type of motivation that we will consider in this section—social motivation.

Unlike biological drives, social motives are not directly based on physiological conditions. Instead, they are acquired during interactions with other people. Many psychologists who discuss human motivation use the term *need* to refer to both human biological drives and social motives.

In the first part of this section we will discuss several past attempts by psychological theorists to list or classify human motives. Some of these theorists emphasized biological drives while others emphasized social motives, such as the need for acceptance by others. Today, psychologists recognize that both kinds of motives are important. In the second part of this section we will examine research on important social motives.

Classifications of Human Motives

In classifying human motives, some psychologists suggested that one or two major needs dominated human action. Others felt that many needs played important roles in motivating behavior. Such thinking about human motivation has been dominated by the theories of Sigmund Freud and by reactions to his ideas.

FREUD'S THEORY OF MOTIVATION

Sigmund Freud was trained to be a physician, and, as a psychological theorist, he believed strongly in the biological basis of human behavior. His original view was that all of human behavior had its roots in **eros,** the drive for bodily pleasure (Freud, 1917/1950). The strongest such pleasure was sex, but Freud believed that people sought a variety of pleasurable bodily sensations. Why, then, do people perform many behaviors that seem to have no relation to physical pleasure? Freud argued that, be-

cause of various constraints, people either delay the expression of their desire for pleasure or express it in altered forms. According to Freud, there are two types of constraints. First, there are constraints imposed by reality. For example, a person ordinarily needs to work to afford pleasurable activities. In this case, pleasurable activities are delayed until the work is completed. Second, there are constraints imposed by morals. For example, many people may feel that merely pursuing pleasure is immoral or at least that certain pleasures are immoral. These values can restrict the expression and the extent of people's desires for pleasure.

Freud argued that because the drive for pleasure conflicts with reality and morality, it is often channeled, or *sublimated,* into behaviors that are realistic and moral but still give some satisfaction of the need for pleasure. For example, a Freudian psychologist might argue that a man's interest in fashion is a sublimation of his sexual drive.

In his later work, Freud argued that human behavior was also directed by another strong drive. This was **thanatos,** the self-destructive or "death" drive. Freud believed that because thanatos conflicts with eros, it is often channeled outward in the form of aggression or destructiveness toward others. Freud proposed the idea of thanatos after World War I. He felt that some kind of destructive drive was needed to explain the massive devastation he observed during the war. He believed that destructive urges, like erotic ones, are constrained by reality and morality.

Freud's views were controversial when he proposed them, and they have remained that way. Many later psychologists rejected Freud's theory of human motivation for three reasons. First, a comprehensive account of human motivation must recognize that humans have many motives, interests, needs, and desires. Second, at least some of these motives are directed toward positive or noble behaviors, such as artistic creation. Third, not all motives are based on physiological needs. Some are acquired through social interaction. Two theorists who share these views are Henry Murray and Abraham Maslow, who both discussed the multiplicity of needs that guide human behavior.

THE NEED THEORIES OF MURRAY AND MASLOW

Henry Murray (1938) used many methods to study a small number of individuals intensively over a period of several years. From these studies, Murray compiled a list of 20 needs that motivate most behavior. The list of needs, with brief descriptions, is presented in **Table 4.2.** As you can see, the list is quite varied. It includes some needs that are direct opposites, such as nurturance (the need to give care) and succorance (the need to receive care). There are also intellectual and aesthetic needs. You may not be surprised that Murray lists a need for play.

Like Murray, psychologist Abraham Maslow (1954) believed that a range of needs motivates human behavior. Unlike Murray, however, Maslow believed the number of needs is relatively small. He classified human needs into seven major groups. Maslow's key contribution was the idea that these seven needs can be ranked in a hierarchy, ranging from the physiological needs (lowest) to the highest human need, the need for self-actualization (see **Figure 4.11** on page 156). Maslow felt that individuals would not be motivated by higher needs until they had satisfied the lower ones. Thus, according to Maslow, individuals are motivated throughout life to scale the ladder of needs, but only a few individuals reach the top, the highest rung of self-actualization. We will discuss Maslow's perspective in greater detail in Chapter 14 on personality.

Important Social Motives

As we can see from theorists as diverse in their thinking as Freud, Murray, and Maslow, motives related to social conditions as well as to physiological conditions affect human behavior. There has been a great deal of research on a number of these motives. Here we will consider two of them, the need for social approval and the need for achievement.

THE NEED FOR APPROVAL

Most human beings have a need for positive reactions from other people. Murray proposed a need for affiliation; Maslow discussed the need for belongingness. Similar to these needs is a desire simply to gain approval, or some kind of sign that others like us and think we are good. One interesting aspect of the need for approval is that there are marked individual differences in the degree to which people need approval. Some people are relatively indifferent to what others think of them. Others act as if they would do almost anything to gain approval or, perhaps more important, avoid disapproval.

The characteristics of people with a high need for approval have been investigated through the use of a Social Desirability Scale

Table 4.2   Murray's List of Needs

Need	Description
Abasement	To surrender. To comply and accept punishment. To apologize, confess, atone. Self-depreciation. Masochism.
Achievement	To overcome obstacles, to exercise power, to strive to do something difficult as well and as quickly as possible.
Affiliation	To form friendships and associations. To greet, join, and live with others. To co-operate and converse sociably with others. To love. To join groups.
Aggression	To assault or injure another. To murder. To belittle, harm, blame, accuse or maliciously ridicule a person. To punish severely. Sadism.
Autonomy	To resist influence or coercion. To defy an authority or seek freedom in a new place. To strive for independence.
Blamavoidance	To avoid blame, ostracism or punishment by inhibiting asocial or unconventional impulses. To be well-behaved and obey the law.
Counteraction	Proudly to refuse admission of defeat by restriving and retaliating. To select the hardest tasks. To defend one's honor in action.
Defendance	To defend oneself against blame or belittlement. To justify one's actions. To offer extenuations, explanations and excuses. To resist 'probing'
Deference	To admire and willingly follow a superior allied other. To co-operate with a leader. To serve gladly.
Dominance	To influence or control others. To persuade, prohibit, dictate. To lead and direct. To restrain. To organize the behavior of a group.
Exhibition	To attract attention to one's person. To excite, amuse, stir, shock, thrill others. Self-dramatization.
Harmavoidance	To avoid pain, physical injury, illness and death. To escape from a dangerous situation. To take precautionary measures.
Infavoidance	To avoid failure, shame, humiliation, ridicule. To refrain from attempting to do something that is beyond one's powers. To conceal a disfigurement.
Nurturance	To nourish, aid or protect a helpless other. To express sympathy. To 'mother' a child.
Order	To arrange, organize, put away objects. To be tidy and clean. To be scrupulously precise.
Play	To relax, amuse oneself, seek diversion and entertainment. To 'have fun,' to play games. To laugh, joke and be merry. To avoid serious tension.
Rejection	To snub, ignore or exclude another. To remain aloof and indifferent. To be discriminating.
Sentience	To seek and enjoy sensuous impressions.
Sex	To form and further an erotic relationship. To have sexual intercourse.
Succorance	To seek aid, protection or sympathy. To cry for help. To plead for mercy. To adhere to an affectionate, nurturant parent. To be dependent.
Understanding	To analyze experience, to abstract, to discriminate among concepts, to define relations, to synthesize ideas.

From Murray (1938).

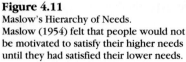

Figure 4.11
Maslow's Hierarchy of Needs.
Maslow (1954) felt that people would not
be motivated to satisfy their higher needs
until they had satisfied their lower needs.

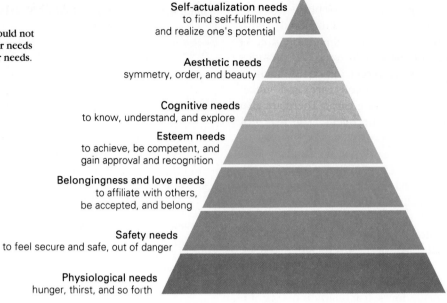

Self-actualization needs
to find self-fulfillment
and realize one's potential

Aesthetic needs
symmetry, order, and beauty

Cognitive needs
to know, understand, and explore

Esteem needs
to achieve, be competent, and
gain approval and recognition

Belongingness and love needs
to affiliate with others,
be accepted, and belong

Safety needs
to feel secure and safe, out of danger

Physiological needs
hunger, thirst, and so forth

developed by Douglas Crowne and David Marlowe (1964). This scale measures the extent to which people try to gain others' approval by behaving in socially desirable ways. It contains items such as the following:

> It is sometimes hard for me to go on with my work if I am not encouraged. (true or false)
>
> I am always courteous, even to people who are disagreeable. (true or false)
>
> I have never deliberately said something that hurts someone's feelings. (true or false)

Persons who agree with these statements tend to have a higher need for approval than those who disagree.

Studies by Crowne, Marlowe, and others have shown interesting differences between people with high and low needs for approval. One difference is that people with a high need for approval conform more. In one study, a group of subjects was shown a series of slides. Each slide contained two clusters of dots. One of the clusters was clearly larger than the other. Subjects were simply asked to state which cluster was larger. However, assistants to the experimenter, posing as subjects, gave obviously wrong answers on some of the clusters. Crowne and Marlowe counted how many times the real subjects agreed with the assistants, even though the assistants' judgments were clearly wrong. The subjects with a high need

for approval conformed 59 percent of the time, while those with a low need for approval conformed only 34 percent of the time. Thus, people with a high need for approval more frequently go along with the opinions of others in order to avoid disruptive or embarrassing disagreements (Crowne & Marlowe, 1964).

People with a high need for approval often change the way they behave if others can observe them. People with a low need for social approval are more likely to act the same whether they are observed or not. For example, in a study by Satow (1975), subjects were told that they could donate to a research fund part of $1.50 they had been paid for participating in an experiment. Subjects in one group were told they could do this in private during the course of the experiment. Subjects in another group were told that they would be observed through a one-way mirror. When subjects were unobserved they gave very little money, whether they had a high or low need for approval. The average donation was about 5 cents. When the subjects thought their behavior was being observed, they all tended to donate more, but this tendency was much stronger among subjects with a high need for approval. Those with a low need for approval gave about 25 cents. Those with a high need gave nearly 60 cents (see **Figure 4.12**).

It is clear, then, that people with a high need for approval will do what they believe is expected of them to gain approval or to appear desirable to others. Unfortunately, these efforts

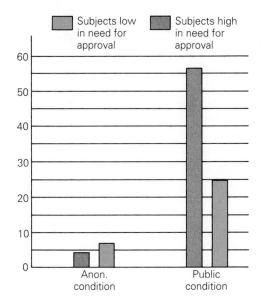

Figure 4.12
The Effect of Anonymity and Observation on Donations. (After Satow, 1975)

to gain approval are not generally successful. College men with a high need for approval tend to be liked less than their peers with a lower need. They also tend to expect rejection. Perhaps they try too hard to be accepted and appear to have little strength of character (Gergen & Marlowe, 1970).

THE NEED FOR ACHIEVEMENT

Like the need for approval, a great deal of research has been conducted on the need for achievement. The **need for achievement,** commonly called **n Ach** by psychologists, is the need to accomplish something difficult, to meet a standard of excellence, or to excel. Understanding achievement motivation is difficult because it is complex. The manner in which people strive for achievement is affected by the need for achievement, fear of failure, and perhaps even fear of success. In this section we shall consider the determinants of achievement strivings and the complexities of the fears of failure and success.

One important determinant of how much a person strives to achieve is the strength of that individual's need for achievement. Work by David McClelland, John Atkinson, and their associates has advanced our understanding of achievement motivation (Atkinson, 1977; McClelland, Atkinson, Clark, & Lowell, 1953). McClelland's method for measuring achievement motivation is an unusual one. He analyzes

stories subjects make up in response to pictures. McClelland states:

> If you want to understand motives behind . . . actions, find out what's on a person's mind. If you want to find out what's on a person's mind, don't ask him, because he can't always tell you accurately. Study his fantasies and dreams. If you do this over a period of time, you will discover the themes to which his mind returns again and again. And these themes can be used to explain his actions. (McClelland, 1971, p. 5)

The picture in **Figure 4.13** is one that McClelland has used to elicit such fantasies. A subject looking at this picture is asked to make up an imaginative story about it. Then the researcher analyzes the themes in the story, using a complex scoring system to identify the person's underlying needs. For example, consider a person who tells the following story about the picture: "This young architect would like to design an award-winning building. He knows this will be difficult because of family responsibilities, but he will persevere and ultimately reach his goal." This emphasis on competing

Figure 4.13
Sample Card from McClelland's Test for Achievement Need. McClelland used ambiguous pictures like this to analyze subjects' achievement motivation. (McClelland & Steele, 1972)

with a standard of excellence and succeeding would be considered evidence for an achievement need.

Using this and related methods of measuring achievement motivation, McClelland discovered that there are reliable differences in achievement motivation among individuals and also among groups of individuals. For example, some college students have a strong need to achieve relative to their peers. These students tend to do better at tasks such as anagrams and arithmetic problems than other students of equal intelligence. They are also more likely to go into occupations in which they own or manage their own business (McClelland et al., 1953). McClelland has also found that some groups have higher levels of achievement motivation. For example, middle-class boys have been shown to have higher n Ach scores than lower-class boys (Rosen, 1961). Also, junior executives in the United States have higher n Ach scores than comparable junior executives in Turkey (Bradburn, 1963). In short, within any group some individuals have a higher need for achievement than others, and the average score varies from group to group. What might account for these differences?

The need for achievement depends on social and cultural factors, which in turn affect child-rearing practices. In a culture that values achievement, parents demand self-sufficiency and independence in their children. Such parents tend to be less protective of and to remove restrictions on their children when the

children are relatively young. For example, it has been found that boys with a high need for achievement have mothers who are concerned that their sons learn to be independent at an early age (Winterbottom, 1958).

While parents' emphasis on independence and self-sufficiency is important, whether it leads to a high need for achievement is determined in part by how parents react to the child's efforts to succeed. If parents react positively to success and if they are supportive and affectionate, they are likely to instill the motivation to gain success. If they are unsupportive or cold, or if they punish failure, their children are likely to develop a fear of failure (Teevan & McGhee, 1972).

The two motives, to achieve or to avoid failure, can guide behavior differently. For example, people with a high need for achievement generally choose tasks of moderate difficulty for which there is a moderate probability of success. They seem greatly gratified by success but not upset by failure at such tasks. Individuals with a high fear of failure often choose very difficult or very easy tasks. They are assured of success at the easy ones and they cannot be blamed for failure at the very difficult ones. Thus the two motivational factors can produce different actions (Atkinson & Litwin, 1960).

Another factor that affects how much individuals strive to succeed is their desire to maintain a positive self-evaluation. People will put extra effort into tasks that are important to their self-definitions. Their tendency to do this is explained by a model of self-evaluation maintenance (SEM) (Tesser, 1988).

The SEM model proposes that self-evaluation may sometimes be raised or lowered through a comparison process (Masters & Kiel, 1987). This happens when a personal performance is compared with the performance of a close friend on a skill or task that is important to one's self-definition. Suppose, for example, that being a good piano player is important to Joan's self-definition. If her performance is judged to be better than that of her close friend Kay, Joan's self-evaluation will be raised. If her performance is judged worse than Kay's, Joan's self-evaluation will be lowered. According to the model, Joan's self-evaluation will be affected by these comparisons only if piano playing is important to Joan's self-definition. If it is not, and Kay is better, Joan might bask in Kay's glo-

Positive and warm parental support is a strong factor in the healthy development of a child's success motivation.

ry, thereby experiencing a rise in self-evaluation through her association with Kay.

Let us assume that piano playing is important to Joan. How will she react to information that suggests Kay is better, since this threatens her desire to maintain her self-evaluation? Studies have shown that Joan may derogate Kay's performance or even try to interfere with her performing well under some circumstances (Tesser, 1984). Another reaction would be for Joan to put more effort into her own practicing and performing. One study shows that high school students get higher grades when their friends do, provided that academic achievement is important for their self-definition. When academic achievement is not important to these students, they do not match their friends' higher grades (Tesser, Campbell, & Campbell, 1985). In general, people strive to achieve a level that other people who are close to them achieve when an unfavorable comparison with those other people threatens their desire to maintain a positive self-evaluation.

REWARD AND INTRINSIC MOTIVATION

One of the questions that has grown out of the extensive work on achievement motivation is how achievement strivings can be increased. McClelland and his associates have attempted the ambitious approach of increasing achievement motivation in societies where it is low. Training programs for business executives in such societies have led to increased achievement motivation and increased economic success for their companies (McClelland & Winter, 1969).

Another approach to increasing achievement strivings is simply to reward them. Following Thorndike's law of effect, this approach assumes that reward can increase behaviors (see Chapter 6). However, in *The Hidden Costs of Reward*, Lepper and Greene (1978) suggest that rewarding achievement strivings can in the long run decrease such strivings. This hypothesis is based on the concept of "intrinsic motivation."

What is intrinsic motivation and how can reward diminish it? Deci and Ryan (1980) state that "intrinsically motivated behaviors are those behaviors that are motivated by the underlying need for competence and self-determination." They argue that these needs are innate and that the intrinsically motivated behaviors that derive from them are rewarding in and of themselves.

These behaviors are performed in the absence of any apparent external reinforcement. In short, intrinsic motivation is the inner need to be competent and to choose one's own activities.

What evidence is there that reward can undermine intrinsic motivation? Consider an illustrative study. College students were asked to work on a series of puzzles that they found intrinsically interesting. Some students were paid one dollar for solving each of four puzzles. Others were not paid. At a later point in the experiment, subjects were left to occupy themselves in a room where they could work on more puzzles, read magazines, or engage in other activities. The subjects who had been paid for completing puzzles spent less time working on them during this free-time period. Apparently, the monetary reward made the students less interested in the puzzles (Deci & Ryan, 1980).

Similar effects have been found with young children who were given "good player" awards for playing with attractive art materials and for adults who escaped from a noxious buzzer for successfully completing interesting puzzles (Deci, 1975; Lepper, Greene, & Nisbett, 1973).

The explanation for these results focuses on people's perceptions of why they are engaging in the activities. When people are given a reward for doing something they find intrinsically satisfying, their perceptions change. At first they perceive themselves as seeking inner satisfaction. Then they come to perceive themselves as working for money. In a sense, the enjoyable activity becomes "work."

One study (Deci, 1975) found some intriguing differences in the reactions of men and women to reward. This study investigated the effects of praise on subjects' interest in working on puzzles. Women who were praised showed the typical decrease in intrinsic motivation, whereas men responded to the praise with increased intrinsic motivation (see **Figure 4.14** on page 160). How can we account for these results? The most probable explanation is that the men regarded the praise as a means of conveying information about their competence. Because the praise made them feel more competent, they became more interested in working on the puzzles. Women, on the other hand, saw the praise as causing or controlling their behavior. In short, praise can be viewed

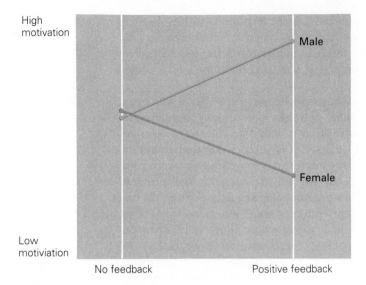

Figure 4.14
The Effect of Praise on Intrinsic Motivation (Deci, 1975)

in two different ways: as a means of control or as a means of giving information.

Why should men and women regard praise in different ways? One explanation is the difference in the ways males and females are socialized. Females are more often trained to be dependent, while males are socialized to be independent and achievement oriented. Because of learned dependence on others, women may be more sensitive to the controlling aspects of praise. They may take it as a directive about how they should behave and what they must do to please others. Men, on the other hand,

A sense of common purpose on the job can increase intrinsic motivation, job satisfaction, and productivity. This quality control team is discussing ways to reduce scrap when making cans.

may have learned to take praise as a signal that they have an area of competence and skill. Such information may make work in that area more enjoyable and may thus increase intrinsic motivation (Wheeler, Deci, Reis, & Zuckerman, 1978).

This explanation of the sex difference in response to praise is tentative. More research is needed before we get a firm idea of all that is involved. However, these studies alert us to some of the complex and unpredictable effects of using reward to increase the motivation for achievement. Parents, educators, and others responsible for teaching and caring for children will have to take these effects into account in the complex process of socializing children.

WORK MOTIVATION AND JOB SATISFACTION
The research on the need for achievement and intrinsic motivation has important applicability in the workplace. For many years industrial and organizational psychologists have asked what motivates people to work hard and effectively on the job and what gives people job satisfaction. The answers to these questions are as important to the welfare of the worker as they are to the profitability of the company. Research on worker productivity indicates that the same characteristics of the job setting that make workers happy also increase productivity in the workplace. It should come as no surprise that contented and enthusiastic workers are more productive.

Approaches to work motivation emphasize many of the motives that we have already discussed in this section. For example, one approach distinguishes three classes of work motives: *rational-economic* motives, *social* motives, and *self-actualization* motives (Schein, 1980). Rational-economic motives refer to the worker's concern with making money and maintaining a reasonably secure and comfortable source of income. Clearly, there are extrinsic reasons, namely money, for working, and economic incentives are a powerful source of motivation to work.

Schein also discusses social motives. People come to work because they enjoy affiliating with other people, having an opportunity to engage in social comparison, and, in general, satisfying the needs we all have to make contact with others. Finally, self-actualization motives, that is, intrinsic motivation, play a key part in motivating work. People strive to feel competent and they strive to achieve. To the extent that they can satisfy these motives they are likely to work hard and raise their level of productivity.

There has been considerable concern recently that workers in our society do not have high levels of job satisfaction and that productivity has fallen as a consequence. What steps might be taken to improve job satisfaction and therefore productivity? Theory Z, a theory derived from a fascinating report on Japanese managers and workers, emphasizes the importance of overcoming an adversarial relationship between labor and management (Ouchi, 1981). Some specific techniques that managers can use to overcome the antagonism between managers and workers are spending time with workers, sharing lunch with them, and asking for and using their suggestions. A sense of common purpose emerges that can increase intrinsic motivation, job satisfaction, and productivity.

Other important steps toward increasing job satisfaction, and therefore productivity, have also been suggested (Katzell & Guzzo, 1983). The most common suggestion calls for training and instruction. Workers are happier and perform better when they know clearly what is expected of them. Appraisal and feedback are also important, especially feedback that supports desirable behaviors rather than punishing undesirable behaviors. A third factor is goal setting. Workers respond well when they have goals to strive for. These goals should be high, but not out of reach. As we have seen before, striving to meet difficult but attainable goals engenders strong motivation. Last, financial compensation, especially financial compensation that is given on the basis of good performance, enhances job satisfaction and worker productivity. These are but a few of the findings from the fields of industrial and organizational psychology that show how basic research on human social motivation can be applied in an extremely relevant aspect of everyday living.

Interim Summary

Freud believed that human beings have two basic drives: eros, the drive for pleasure, and thanatos, the drive for self-destruction. Because reality and morality can conflict with the direct expression of these drives, they are often sublimated into socially acceptable and realistic forms of behavior.

Murray proposed that 20 major needs motivate human behavior. Maslow proposed a hierarchy of 7 kinds of needs that motivate human behavaior. In Maslow's theory, lower needs must be satisfied before higher needs can be satisfied.

McClelland developed a measure of the need for achievement based on the themes in people's imaginative stories in response to ambiguous stimuli. Achievement motivation is affected by child-rearing practices. Parents who demand self-sufficiency and independence and who react positively to their children's efforts to succeed are most likely to instill achievement in their children. Another factor affecting achievement strivings is the desire to maintain a positive self-evaluation.

Rewarding achievement strivings may undermine intrinsic motivation. Reward can make people feel that they are simply striving for reward rather than seeking to satisfy their own intrinsic interest in being competent.

The need for achievement and intrinsic motivation affect behavior in the workplace. The same factors that contribute to job satisfaction also motivate workers to work hard and effectively and thus promote productivity. Workers can be motivated by rational-economic motives, social motives, and self-actualization motives. Factors that can increase job satisfaction are instruction, training, appraisal, feedback, goal setting, and financial compensation given on the basis of good performance.

THE NATURE OF EMOTION

Humans are emotional beings *par excellence.* Our language is replete with powerful metaphors of the centrality of emotion in our lives: we may be *dissolved* in tears, *petrified* by fear, *consumed* with jealousy, or *transported* with ecstasy. Emotion continuously colors our experience—our likes and dislikes, as well as our joys and aversions. A being that perceives, thinks, and behaves but is devoid of emotion comes close to the popular conception of a robot. For these reasons, the study of emotion has always held a prominent place in psychology.

Emotion and motivation are distinct psychological processes that can occur independently of each other but that often converge.

As we noted at the beginning of the chapter, emotion and motivation are closely linked phenomena. In the first place, emotions often accompany motivated behavior. For example, feelings of love and affection generally accompany sexual behavior and feelings of anger generally accompany aggressive behavior. Note, however, that the linkage is not absolute: sexual activity can occur in the absence of tender emotion and aggression in the absence of anger. Conversely, love may be experienced in the absence of sexual activity and anger in the absence of aggression. The frequent uncoupling of emotion and motivation justifies studying them as separate phenomena.

Emotion and motivation are also linked in more complex ways. Emotions may serve as incentives for motivated behavior. We may engage in behavior sequences in order to produce positive emotional states or to avoid negative ones. We sometimes seek out the company of particular people to put ourselves in a good mood or go to great lengths to avoid situations that make us feel uneasy.

In addition, emotion may be produced when motivated behavior is blocked or frustrated. For example, when the environment interferes with attaining important goals, people often experience stressful negative emotions such as anxiety, anger, and depression. This particular relationship between motivation and emotion is part of the psychology of stress, which we explore in more detail in Chapter 15.

In sum, emotion and motivation are distinct psychological processes that can occur independently of each other but that often converge. Emotion can accompany motivated behavior, can act as a motivator, or can be provoked when motivated behavior is blocked.

What Is Emotion?

The word *emotion* literally means a stirred-up or excited state. An **emotion,** as defined by psychologists, usually includes three components: (1) a characteristic feeling or subjective experience, (2) a pattern of physiological arousal, and (3) a pattern of overt expression. The *subjective* component is conveyed in the labels we attach to our emotions, such as fear, anger, joy, or sadness. The *physiological* component includes all of the bodily changes that occur in emotion. Our language contains many phrases that express these physiological experiences. For example, we speak of "butterflies in the stomach" when fearful, "a lump in the throat" when sad, or "tingling" with pleasure. As we shall see, such sensations derive from changes in the internal or *visceral* organs, such as the heart and stomach, that accompany emotion. Finally, the *expressive* component includes the body postures and facial expressions characteristic of different emotions. For example, stooped shoulders and a downcast expression often betray sadness, while tense muscles and a wide-eyed stare often express fear. Sometimes emotional feelings can be induced simply by assuming the characteristic posture and facial expression: compare how you feel when you tense your body and facial muscles with the feeling induced by relaxed muscles and a broad smile.

Classifying Emotions

Because emotions exist in such a variety of forms and intensities, the task of classification is difficult. Many different systems of classification have been proposed, but there is as yet no universal agreement among psychologists on any single classification. Nevertheless, a number of distinctions are commonly used. These include distinctions between (1) positive and negative emotions, (2) primary and mixed emotions, (3) opposite emotions, and (4) degrees of emotional intensity. We will consider these four distinctions and then show how they have been combined in a classification suggested by Robert Plutchik.

POSITIVE VERSUS NEGATIVE EMOTIONS

Emotions can be divided into positive emotions like joy, love, and happiness and negative emotions like fear, anger, and sadness. In general, positive emotions tend to enhance one's sense of well-being and promote constructive relationships with others. Negative emotions tend to decrease one's sense of well-being and create disturbed relationships with others (Izard, 1971).

PRIMARY VERSUS MIXED EMOTIONS

Many psychologists liken emotions to colors, dividing them into a limited number of primary emotions and a larger number of mixed emotions constructed from combinations of primaries. The primary emotions include, at a minimum, happiness, disgust, surprise, sadness, anger, and fear. Some psychologists recognize additional primaries such as contempt and shame. A complex emotion such as disappointment is often considered a mixture of sadness and surprise, while jealousy is considered a combination of love and anger (Izard, 1971, 1979; Plutchik, 1980b).

OPPOSITE EMOTIONS

Many emotions exist as pairs of polar opposites. Thus we recognize joy as the opposite of sadness and love as the opposite of hate. Generally speaking, opposite emotions cannot be simultaneously experienced in mixed form. As we will see in Chapter 17, this principle is often used in psychotherapy when clients are taught to experience a positive emotion in order to block a negative emotion.

EMOTIONAL INTENSITY

Emotions vary in their degree of intensity. Different words used to describe emotion sometimes simply reflect different intensities of a common underlying emotion. For example, fear can be described in increasing degrees of intensity as follows: uneasy, fretful, tense, apprehensive, tremulous, agitated, panicky, and terrified (Buss, 1966).

A THREE-DIMENSIONAL CLASSIFICATION

Figure 4.15 shows a model, devised by psychologist Robert Plutchik, that combines the foregoing four distinctions among emotions. The model is composed of eight primary emotions—fear, surprise, sadness, disgust, anger, anticipation, joy, and acceptance. Each of these is represented as a vertical slice of the solid.

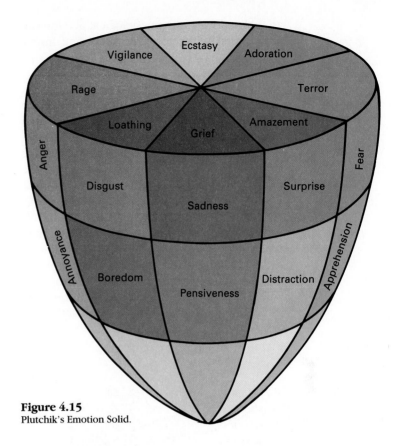

Figure 4.15
Plutchik's Emotion Solid.

Within each slice, each primary emotion varies in intensity from its mildest expression to its most extreme. For example, annoyance, anger, and rage are three levels of intensity of a single primary emotion. The solid contains both positive emotions (such as ecstasy and adoration) and negative emotions (rage, loathing, and grief, for example). Emotions that are close together on the solid are similar to each other, while emotions that are positioned directly across from one another are polar opposites, such as grief and ecstasy. You should remember that psychologists have not settled on any final classification of emotions. Therefore, this model is best considered a convenient way of thinking about the relationships among different types of emotions (Plutchik, 1980a, 1980b).

Bodily Changes in Emotion

As we have seen, any emotion is a complex state consisting of subjective, expressive, and physiological components. As a prelude to discussing how these components may be related to each other, we must first understand how the nervous system regulates physiological arousal and how this physiological activity can be assessed with electronic recording instruments.

THE AUTONOMIC NERVOUS SYSTEM

In Chapter 2 we discussed the division of the nervous system into the *central nervous system* (the brain and spinal cord) and the *peripheral nervous system* (the nerves outside the CNS). We further described the division of the peripheral nervous system into the *somatic nervous system* and the *autonomic nervous system*. The somatic nervous system controls the activity of the skeletal muscles. The autonomic nervous system, or ANS, controls the activity of the visceral organs such as the heart, stomach, and intestines. It also controls the constriction of small blood vessels throughout the skin and muscles, as well as the activity of

the sweat glands. The ANS is thus a communication network linking the brain and spinal cord with the visceral organs, blood vessels, and sweat glands. When we speak of the physiological component of emotion, we are referring to the body systems controlled by the ANS. Thus, when our hands are cold and clammy in fear or when we are blushing with embarrassment, it is because the ANS has been activated.

Figure 4.16 is a somewhat simplified diagram of the ANS. Notice that the ANS has two major divisions: the *sympathetic division* and the *parasympathetic division*. The neurons of the sympathetic division leave the central nervous system from the middle portion of the spinal cord. The neurons of the parasympathetic division connect with the central nervous system either at the lowest segment of the spinal cord or at the brain stem. The prefix

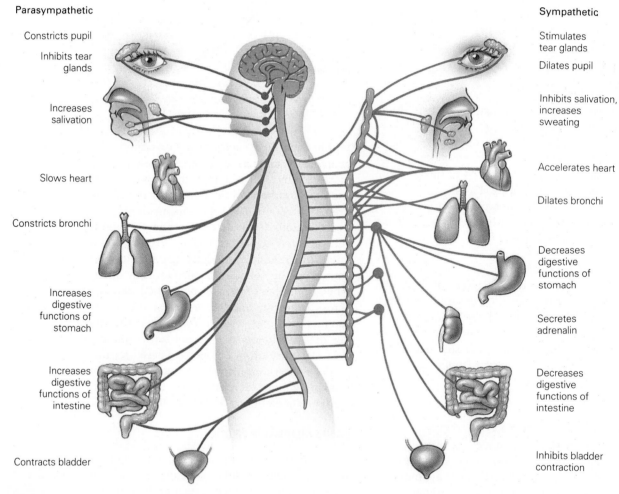

Parasympathetic

Constricts pupil

Inhibits tear glands

Increases salivation

Slows heart

Constricts bronchi

Increases digestive functions of stomach

Increases digestive functions of intestine

Contracts bladder

Sympathetic

Stimulates tear glands

Dilates pupil

Inhibits salivation, increases sweating

Accelerates heart

Dilates bronchi

Decreases digestive functions of stomach

Secretes adrenalin

Decreases digestive functions of intestine

Inhibits bladder contraction

Figure 4.16
A Diagram of the Autonomic Nervous System.
Functions of the parasympathetic nervous system are shown on the left, and the sympathetic nervous system is shown on the right.

para means "outside of"; the parasympathetic division lies outside the sympathetic division.

Most of the visceral organs are controlled by both sympathetic and parasympathetic neurons. The exceptions are the sweat glands and blood vessels, which receive only sympathetic control. Because the sympathetic and parasympathetic divisions tend to have opposing effects, the activity of the visceral organs can be rather finely tuned, or modulated. Important examples of this are seen in the pupil, the heart, and the intestines. Sympathetic activity acts to dilate the pupils, accelerate the heart rate, and inhibit intestinal activity. On the other hand, parasympathetic activity causes constriction of the pupils, deceleration of the heart, and normalizes intestinal activity. In general, sympathetic activity increases physiological arousal in order to prepare the organism for vigorous activity, whereas parasympathetic activity tends to reduce physiological arousal and return the organism to homeostatic balance.

MEASURING PHYSIOLOGICAL ACTIVITY

Psychologists interested in studying the physiological correlates of emotion often use an electronic recording instrument known as a **polygraph.** A polygraph (from *poly* meaning "many" and *graph* meaning "write") can simultaneously record several channels of physiological information from electrical signals generated by autonomic nervous system activity, skeletal muscle activity, or brain activity. A polygraph is composed of several amplifiers that detect and boost physiological signals much as a stereo amplifier boosts electrical signals picked up from discs or tapes. A stereo system converts audio signals to sound by driving an electromagnet in a speaker. In contrast, a polygraph converts physiological signals into a visual record by activating electromagnets that move pens back and forth over a continuous length of recording paper. The body's physiological signals are picked up by sensors attached to the subject and are sent to the polygraph via wire cables.

A polygraph can contain as few as two or as many as a dozen separate recording channels. Some of the more widely used channels, which are illustrated in **Figure 4.17,** are:

1. *Electroencephalogram (EEG).* The EEG reflects the brain's electrical activity. It is recorded through metal electrodes attached to the scalp.
2. *Respiration.* The rate and depth of breathing can be recorded by placing sensors around the chest. One form of respiration sensor is a rubber tube filled with mercury through which a current is passed. As the tube stretches and compresses with each breath, changes in the electrical resistance of the mercury are recorded on the polygraph.
3. *Finger pulse volume.* Each time the heart beats, blood surges through the blood vessels. These surges can be sensed at the fin-

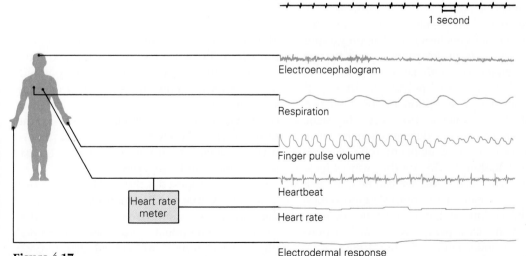

Figure 4.17
Some of the Bodily Functions That Can Be Monitored by a Polygraph. (From Gale & Coles, 1969)

gertips with a device known as a *plethysmo-graph*. This device generates an electrical signal that is proportional to the amount of blood in the finger at any one time.

4. *Heartbeat*. The heart is a strong muscle that generates an electrical signal each time it contracts. This signal, known as the *electrocardiogram* (ECG), is picked up from metal electrodes placed on the chest. The heart rate can be recorded with a meter that measures the time between successive heartbeats. The elapsed time is displayed on a polygraph channel separate from the ECG.

5. *Electrodermal response (EDR)*. The EDR reflects the electrical activity generated by the sweat glands in the hand. It is recorded by metal electrodes placed on the palm or fingertips. The EDR is often referred to by an older term, *galvanic skin response (GSR)*.

Although a polygraph is primarily a scientific research instrument, small, portable polygraphs are often used in police investigations as "lie detectors." This use of the polygraph is quite controversial, however, and most psychologists are skeptical that polygraph tests can in fact distinguish between truthfulness and deception. The use of the polygraph to detect deception assumes, first, that deceptive statements regarding a crime will create embarrassment or anxiety for the subject and second, that these emotions will be reflected in increased physiological reactivity to the statements.

A good deal of basic research, as well as field studies of police interrogations, have attempted to test the validity of these assumptions. A general conclusion is that polygraphs are more accurate in determining guilt than in proving innocence. Both laboratory and field studies show that the polygraph, in expert hands, can detect deception in about 90 percent of guilty subjects. However, the same techniques also detect deception in between 10 and 50 percent of innocent subjects (Lykken, 1979; Raskin, 1987). Another way of looking at the same data is that we can be quite certain that a person who "passes" a polygraph test is indeed innocent, but we cannot be nearly as certain that a person who "fails" a polygraph test is indeed guilty (Raskin, 1988).

Why do polygraph examiners often erroneously conclude that suspects are deceptive when in fact they are innocent of any crime? A likely reason is that innocent suspects are as threatened by the consequences of "failing" a polygraph test as are guilty suspects. To the extent that this threat is accompanied by increased physiological reactivity to questions regarding the crime, truthful subjects may also be judged to be deceptive by the examiner. The essence of the controversy surrounding the use of the polygraph to detect deception lies in the relatively high proportion of innocent subjects who are deemed guilty. Because most courts require proof of guilt "beyond a reasonable doubt," many psychologists are opposed to use of the polygraph in criminal investigations. However, other psychologists argue that the polygraph can provide useful information if testing is carried out by trained investigators and if the information is supplemented by other types of evidence of guilt or innocence (Lykken, 1981; Raskin, 1988; Saxe, Dougherty, & Cross, 1985).

Theories of Emotion

Theories of emotion attempt to specify exactly how emotion-provoking events and physiological arousal interact to produce subjective emotional experience, or emotions as we feel them. The question has been debated by psychologists for over a century. Our discussion begins with the classic theory of emotion proposed by William James in his *Principles of Psychology* (1890). We then consider criticisms of this theory, as well as research related to important issues raised by it. Finally, we examine the contemporary two-factor theory of emotion.

JAMES' EMOTION THEORY
The first comprehensive theory of emotion was formulated by William James in the late nineteenth century. As we have previously noted, James' work continues to be a source of many stimulating ideas for psychologists. James' theory of emotion is sometimes known as the **James-Lange theory** because a similar theory was introduced about the same time by Danish physiologist Carl Lange (1887).

James proposed a theory of emotion that was quite contrary to commonsense notions of the time. The commonsense view held that subjective emotional experience preceded physiological arousal: we feel sad, therefore we cry; we feel afraid, therefore our heart races; we feel happy, therefore we laugh; and so

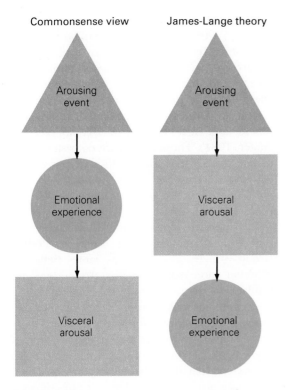

Figure 4.18
The Commonsense Versus James-Lange View of Emotion.

forth. James turned this formulation on its head by suggesting an opposite sequence of events: we feel sad *because* we cry, afraid *because* our heart races, and so forth. In other words, an emotionally arousing event triggers a specific pattern of visceral activity that is then experienced as a specific emotion. If we were to meet a bear in the woods, according to James, our heart would begin to race, our hands would become cold and clammy, and then we would feel afraid. In James' words, "Bodily changes follow directly the perception of the exciting fact.... Our feeling of the same changes as they occur is the emotion" (1890, p. 449). The contrast between the commonsense and James-Lange views of emotion is diagrammed in **Figure 4.18**.

CANNON'S CRITICISM

James' theory of emotion contains two major assumptions: (1) each emotion is accompanied by its own specific pattern of visceral arousal, and (2) people label their emotional states by perceiving the patterned feedback from their visceral activity. These assumptions were severely criticized a generation later by Walter B. Cannon, a prominent physiologist.

Cannon (1927) argued first of all that the anatomy of the autonomic nervous system did not allow the possibility of patterned visceral arousal. He believed that the sympathetic division of the ANS was so constructed that only a generalized state of arousal was possible in any and all emotional situations. In other words, Cannon believed that the ANS would respond in a unitary manner to any emotional stimulus and, therefore, that patterned arousal could not be the basis of emotional experience. Cannon thought that all emotions would be accompanied by a similar pattern of visceral activity.

Second, Cannon argued that the activity of the visceral organs was extremely difficult to perceive accurately. To emphasize his argument, Cannon chose an extreme case, pointing out that most people have only the vaguest knowledge of the spleen and, even if aware of this anatomical structure, are unlikely to recognize changes in its activity. In sum, Cannon argued that the subjective experience of emotion could not depend in any specific way on patterned visceral activity.

As part of his critique of James' theory, Cannon proposed an alternative possibility. Whereas James felt that visceral arousal was the basis of emotional experience, Cannon emphasized instead the role of brain mechanisms in generating emotional experience. Specifically, Cannon theorized that the thalamus, located at the top of the brain stem, was a crucial integrative center for emotion. According to Cannon, information from an emotion-provoking event is first relayed from sense organs to the thalamus. From the thalamus, this information is relayed both downward via the autonomic nervous system to produce visceral arousal and upward to the cerebral cortex to produce conscious emotional experience. This hypothesis, which was also proposed and expounded upon by American physiologist Philip Bard (1928), is known as the Cannon-Bard theory of emotion. It asserts that there is no one-to-one relationship between visceral arousal and subjective emotional experience. Although the two events occur simultaneously, they are linked only in that both are controlled by a common brain center.

RESEARCH FINDINGS

The difference of opinion between James and Cannon has stimulated a great deal of research on the roles of visceral patterning and of visceral feedback in emotion. The question of visceral patterning has been investigated by placing subjects in real or imagined situations designed to elicit different emotions and recording, usually with a polygraph, the accompanying visceral changes. The results of such studies suggest that the ANS is capable of greater patterned activity than Cannon believed.

In one study, subjects were asked to recall as vividly as possible the feelings associated with specific events in their lives that had produced happiness, sadness, anger, or fear. During the recreation of each emotion, the experimenters measured subjects' heart rate, systolic blood pressure (blood pressure at the heartbeat), and diastolic blood pressure (blood pressure between heartbeats). If, as Cannon thought, different emotions are accompanied by a unitary pattern of physiological arousal, we would expect the four emotions to produce similar effects in each of the three physiological measures. On the other hand, differences in the physiological effects associated with each emotion would support the idea of visceral pat-

terning. The results, shown in **Figure 4.19** indicate that the four emotions tended to be accompanied by different patterns of physiological arousal. Heart rate was lowest during happiness and highest during anger and fear. Diastolic blood pressure was highest in anger, lowest in sadness, and intermediate in happiness and fear (Schwartz, Weinberger, & Singer, 1981). These results are consistent with earlier studies that found different physiological arousal patterns when comparing anger with fear (Ax, 1953) and sadness with happiness (Averill, 1969).

It appears, then, that visceral activity is differentially patterned—at least in certain strong primary emotions—as James believed. Whether more subtle or mixed emotions are similarly patterned is still an open question. These findings make sense if we remember that motivated behavior often accompanies emotional states. Organisms may attack a source of anger or flee a source of fear, for example. To the extent that these behavior patterns differ, we might also expect underlying physiological arousal patterns to differ (Davidson, 1978; Schwartz et al., 1981).

James' second assumption—that people label their emotional states by perceiving the patterned feedback from visceral activity—is more controversial. On the one hand, people often speak of a "lump in the throat," "butterflies in the stomach," or a "racing heart" during various strong emotions. On the other hand, research indicates that people are not very accurate in perceiving less intense changes in the activity of specific visceral organs. Psychologists have studied this problem by recording visceral activity on a polygraph and asking subjects to indicate when a particular visceral organ (for example, the heart) is increasing or decreasing its rate of activity. Even after prolonged training, subjects do not learn to perceive their own visceral activity with any degree of accuracy (Handler, 1975). It therefore appears that Cannon was correct in questioning the degree to which visceral arousal is the primary basis for subjective emotional experience.

THE TWO-FACTOR THEORY

Contemporary psychologists emphasize, more than did James, the role of cognitive factors in determining subjective emotion. The current view is that people have some ability to perceive their own visceral arousal but that this

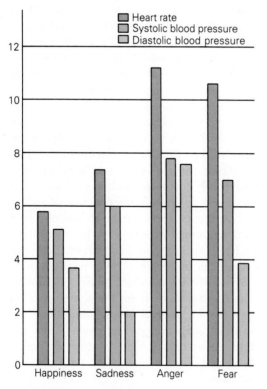

Figure 4.19
The Physiological Effects of Emotions.
Schwartz and his colleagues found that the recall of happiness, sadness, anger, and fear tended to be accompanied by different patterns of heart rate, systolic blood pressure, and diastolic blood pressure. (Adapted from Schwartz, Weinberger, & Singer, 1981)

perception is vague and imprecise. In addition to visceral arousal, emotional experience depends on the person's evaluation of external stimuli as emotion-provoking or not. In other words, full-fledged emotional experience requires a combination of two factors: (1) visceral arousal and (2) recognition that the visceral arousal is due to an emotion-provoking event. To return to James' example of meeting a bear in the woods, the two-factor theory holds that the experience of fear requires both a stirred-up physiological state and a perception that one is in danger. Neither factor is in itself sufficient to produce the emotion of fear. The **two-factor theory** thus accounts for the fact that a state of visceral arousal produced by nonemotional means, such as by physical exercise, will not usually give rise to emotional experience.

Although subjective emotional experience probably cannot be explained as a *direct* result of visceral arousal, this does not mean that visceral arousal plays no role in determining our subjective experience. A good deal of evidence suggests that visceral arousal functions as a sort of amplifier of emotional experience. That is, the intensity of emotional experience increases with the degree of accompanying visceral activity.

One source of evidence supporting this idea comes from studies of emotion in paraplegics—people whose spinal cord has been accidentally severed. The result of such an accident is to disconnect sensory neurons flowing from visceral organs back to the brain, so that internal bodily sensations are eliminated. Paraplegics often report that they continue to experience the same emotions as they did before their accident but that the emotions are less intense. In addition, people whose spinal cord is severed higher up on the back report greater loss of emotional intensity than those whose cord is severed lower on the back. Obviously, the higher the break, the greater the number of sensory neurons that are disconnected from the central nervous system (Hohmann, 1962).

A second source of evidence for the amplification function of visceral arousal comes from experiments showing that emotional responses to situations are enhanced if visceral activity is artificially increased. In one series of studies, researchers first had an annoying person provoke the subjects and then asked the subjects to engage in strenuous physical exercise, which increased their visceral activity.

Following the exercise, they were again confronted with the annoying person. These subjects experienced more intense feelings of anger and were more likely to act aggressively against the annoyer than control subjects who were provoked but did not engage in arousing physical exercise (Zillmann, 1978, 1983). Prior physical exercise has also been shown to enhance sexual excitement in response to erotic films as well as to increase males' romantic attraction to an attractive woman and reduce their attraction to an unattractive woman (Reisenzein, 1983). In brief, visceral arousal from nonemotional sources can combine with visceral arousal from emotional events to augment the intensity of the experienced emotion. The two-factor theory thus stands somewhere between the theories of James and Cannon. While holding with Cannon that visceral arousal is not the sole basis of emotional experience, the two-factor theory nevertheless assigns an intensity function to such arousal.

THE CASE OF UNEXPLAINED AROUSAL

In everyday emotional states, the cues that trigger physiological arousal also provide us with an explanation for our aroused condition. According to the two-factor theory, arousal combines with our cognitive interpretation of the reasons for this arousal to produce subjective emotional experience. But what would happen if the cognitive and physiological components were uncoupled and we felt aroused for no apparent reason? Consider, for example, waking one morning with cold, clammy hands and a racing heart but having no adequate explanation for these symptoms. Would we feel emotional? This question was raised in a famous experiment by Stanley Schachter and Jerome Singer (1962), who proposed that people in this condition would be motivated to seek an appropriate explanation for their aroused condition. In seeking an explanation, these people would then interpret their stirred-up condition in terms of any number of possible emotions. They might decide they were happy, sad, sexy, afraid, or anxious depending on the situation in which they found themselves. For example, they might feel sexy if in the company of an attractive person or anxious if anticipating a stressful event.

Schachter and Singer tested their hypothesis by injecting volunteer subjects with epinephrine, a drug that causes sympathetic nervous system arousal. They informed some subjects of the precise effects of the injection, thus giving these subjects an adequate explanation for their symptoms and no need to seek an emotional explanation for their stirred-up condition. These "informed" subjects constituted the control group. Other subjects were not given an adequate explanation for their physiological arousal. They were either given no explanation or actually were misled regarding the drug's effects. These "uninformed" subjects constituted the experimental group. Schachter and Singer hypothesized that the uninformed subjects would seek an explanation for their physiological arousal by searching their social environment for an appropriate emotional label. To test this hypothesis, they created two social environments with the help of two confederates. The first confederate was trained to feign anger at the appropriate time; the second was trained to act in a euphoric and happy manner. The behavior of each confederate established each social environment. After receiving the injection, subjects from the control and

experimental groups were placed in one of these two social environments. Schachter and Singer's hypothesis stated that the uninformed subjects would label their aroused state in terms of the behavior displayed by the confederate.

Unfortunately, the results of the Schachter and Singer study were somewhat equivocal. The hypothesis was confirmed for subjects placed with the angry confederate. Presumably searching for a reason for their arousal, uninformed subjects did in fact behave more angrily than did control group subjects who had previously been given a rationale for their sympathetic arousal. However, no differences between informed and uninformed subjects were observed in the euphoric environment. Subsequent studies by other researchers with the same interest have also failed to confirm the Schachter and Singer hypothesis. These later studies have found that subjects experiencing unexplained arousal generally feel somewhat uncomfortable regardless of the emotional quality of the social situation in which they are placed (Marshall & Zimbardo, 1979; Maslach, 1979).

It now appears that Schachter and Singer underestimated the role of physiological factors per se in determining the subjective experience of emotion. However, Schachter and Singer's provocative hypothesis has generated a great deal of research, which in turn has led directly to the two-factor theory of emotion. The Schachter and Singer experiment is thus a good example of how the specific findings of scientific research are sometimes less important than the ideas the research generates.

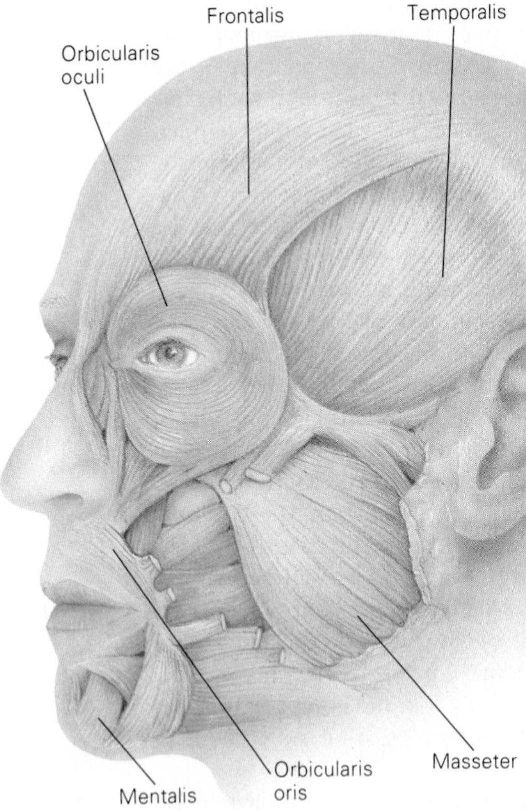

The Expression of Emotion

Emotions can often be read from a person's "body language"—his or her posture, bearing, and gestures. Facial expression is particularly important in this regard. The face contains a large number of separate muscles that can contract in a wide variety of different patterns to produce the smile of joy, the wide eyes of fear, the sneer of disgust, and so forth. **Figure 4.20** conveys the complex mosaic of the face by illustrating some of its major muscles.

The importance of facial expression in emotion was first suggested over a century ago by Charles Darwin in a book entitled *The Expression of the Emotions in Man and*

Figure 4.20
Major Muscles of the Face. (Adapted from Izard, 1971)

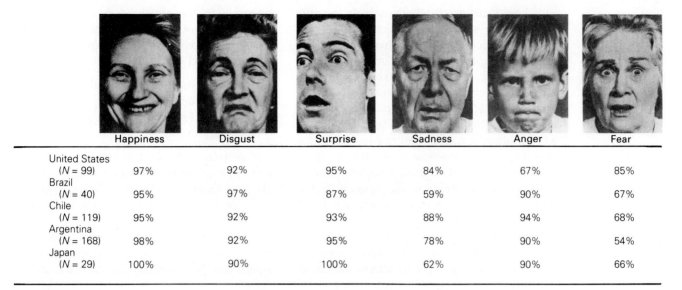

	Happiness	Disgust	Surprise	Sadness	Anger	Fear
United States (N = 99)	97%	92%	95%	84%	67%	85%
Brazil (N = 40)	95%	97%	87%	59%	90%	67%
Chile (N = 119)	95%	92%	93%	88%	94%	68%
Argentina (N = 168)	98%	92%	95%	78%	90%	54%
Japan (N = 29)	100%	90%	100%	62%	90%	66%

Figure 4.21
Percentage of Agreement on Judgments of Emotion in Five Cultures. (From Ekman, 1973)

Animals (1872). In this important work, Darwin argued that emotions had developed in human evolution because they promoted adaptation of the individual to his or her environment. Darwin saw emotions as an integral part of behavior patterns that had evolved to help ensure individual survival. For example, fear can be seen as the emotional accompaniment of the behavior of fleeing in response to danger, and joy as an accompaniment to courting and mating. More specifically, Darwin argued that the facial expression of emotion was adaptive because it signaled to others how the individual felt and therefore what kind of behavior was most likely to occur. In sum, facial expression of emotion served as an important means of communication among members of the social group (Chevalier-Skolnikoff, 1973).

Darwin's views on the expression of emotion have been the focus of much research. If emotions developed in human evolution, as Darwin thought, then facial expressions of different emotions should be similar from culture to culture throughout the world. This intriguing idea is in sharp contrast to the more commonsense notion that facial expressions of emotion are *culture specific;* that is, that the way in which emotions are expressed varies from culture to culture. Darwin's hypothesis has been tested by asking people in different countries to identify the emotions expressed in photographs of people's faces (Ekman, 1973;

Ekman & Friesen; 1971; Izard, 1971). For example, Ekman and Friesen showed facial photographs that expressed six primary emotions to university students in five different countries. They asked the students to describe each photograph with a word in their language for the emotion depicted. **Figure 4.21** shows some of the photographs used, as well as the percentage of agreement across cultures in identifying the specific emotion being expressed. As you can see, the amount of agreement in identifying the emotions being expressed varied somewhat from emotion to emotion, although there was a great deal of overall agreement across cultures. This high level of agreement confirmed Ekman and Friesen's hypothesis that characteristic facial expressions are associated with specific emotions across cultures. These findings therefore support Darwin's evolutionary theory of emotion.

Charles Darwin (1809–1882)

THE FACIAL FEEDBACK HYPOTHESIS

Psychologists have more recently taken Darwin's theory a step further by asking if subjective emotional experience is somehow dependent on specific facial expressions. According to the **facial feedback hypothesis,** the muscles of the face not only express a given emotion but also contribute to the feeling that characterizes that emotion (Adelmann & Zajonc, 1989; Izard, 1977; Tomkins, 1980).

The facial feedback hypothesis actually encompasses several specific research questions. One question is whether a subjective emotional experience will be more intense if we show the characteristic facial expression than if we show some other expression. In one simple but clever experiment, subjects were merely asked to hold a pencil in their mouths while looking at cartoons. In one condition the pencil was held crosswise in the teeth, which caused the subjects to draw back the corners of the mouth, as occurs when we smile. In the other condition, the pencil was held across the lips, which resembled a frown. When asked to rate how funny the cartoons were, the "smile" condition produced higher ratings of funniness than the "frown" condition (Strack, Martin, & Stepper, 1988). In general, research on this question shows that adopting a facial expression that is consistent with an emotion-producing stimulus produces more intense feelings than either inhibiting the expression or adopting an inconsistent expression. Expressing an emotion can amplify our experience of the emotion, and inhibiting the expression can dampen it (Adelmann & Zajonc, 1989). You can easily test this hypothesis for yourself by manipulating your facial expressions the next time you experience a particular emotion.

A second question arising from the facial feedback hypothesis is whether adopting the expression characteristic of a given emotion will produce a subjective emotional experience *even if no emotion-producing stimulus is present.* That is, will we experience emotion when there is no reason to be emotional if we simply mimic an emotional expression? Note that this question is very close to William James' theory of emotion: James believed that emotional feeling was due to our perception of heightened physiological activity, especially internal visceral activity, and that different emotions would be associated with a different pattern of physiological activity. The facial feedback hypothesis differs from James' theory mainly in emphasizing facial muscle patterns, rather than visceral activity, as the critical physiological component underlying emotional experience.

The foregoing question was investigated in a series of experiments by Ekman and his colleagues (Ekman, Levenson, & Friesen, 1983; Levenson, Ekman, & Friesen, 1990). The basic approach used in these experiments was to teach subjects to contract their facial muscles to produce the different facial expressions characteristic of several different emotions. For example, to pose the facial expression of anger, the subject was asked to:

1. Pull your eyebrows down and together.
2. Raise your upper eyelid.
3. Push your lower lip up and press your lips together.

The subjects were not asked to experience any particular emotions; they were simply asked to contract facial muscles in different patterns. After each emotional expression was posed, the subjects were asked to describe any feelings they had experienced. In addition, a battery of physiological measures like those described in Figure 4.17 was recorded during each pose.

The major results of these experiments were threefold: (1) a majority of subjects reported emotional feelings while posing emotional expressions, even though no emotionally arousing stimulus was present; (2) the different posed expressions tended to be associated with qualitatively different emotional feelings; and (3) the different posed expressions were also associated with different patterns of physiological response. These results therefore supported the facial feedback hypothesis by showing that subjective emotional experience can be produced by posing emotional expressions even in the absence of an emotional stimulus and that the particular emotional feeling depends to some extent on the particular facial expression adopted. In addition, these results supported William James' theory that different emotions are associated with distinct patterns of internal physiological activity.

In broader terms, the facial feedback hypothesis suggests that subjective emotional experience is "hard-wired" in the sense that it is strongly influenced by facial expressions, which in turn are part of our evolutionary heritage. Does this mean that there is no role for learning and culture-specific influences in the development of emotion? In answering this question, we should remember that the facial muscles involved in expressing emotion are voluntary muscles that we can learn to contract or relax at will. Because we can voluntarily control our facial muscles, we have the ability to inhibit or modify the universal stereotype. It is possible to learn from one's culture or experience *not* to express one's emotions. For example, the relatively stoic attitude in Germanic and Anglo-American cultures during funerals is in marked contrast to the more expressive attitudes found in Latin cultures. By the same token we can learn to communicate our feelings in culture-specific ways. Thus, in China, sticking out one's tongue is a way of showing surprise, whereas the same gesture in North American has a quite different meaning (Klineberg, 1938). In sum, the expression of certain primary emotions is a universal human trait that appears to have evolved as a means of communication. But these universal patterns of expression can be modified in culture-specific ways by learning.

SUMMARY

1. Motivation is essentially the study of why organisms behave the way they do.
2. There are five major approaches to the study of motivation: (1) instinct theory, (2) drive theory, (3) arousal theory, (4) opponent-process theory, and (5) incentive theory.

    Instinct theorists hold that some behaviors are controlled by genetic factors, which dispose an organism to respond in a particular way when confronted with certain stimuli. Drive theory holds that organisms are motivated to eliminate states of tension or arousal, such as hunger or thirst, and to return to a state of balance known as homeostasis. Arousal theory holds that there is a preferred or optimal level of arousal that is neither too high nor too low. If arousal is too low, organisms will seek to increase tension; if arousal is too high, they will seek to decrease tension. Opponent-process theory holds that acquired motives, such as thrill-seeking or drug addiction, are maintained and strengthened when a primary emotion triggers an opposite emotional response, which lasts longer than the primary emotion. Incentive theory proposes that motivation is determined by stimuli in the environment that "pull" the organism in certain directions. This theory is concerned with the objects or events that reward certain behaviors and punish others.
3. Hunger is a motivator that affects all living organisms. Hunger motivates organisms to

eat. The most widely held theory about eating holds that the brain monitors the amount of stored nutrients in the body. When nutrient levels fall below a certain point, the hypothalamus related brain structures control the onset, and later the cessation, of eating.
4. In some instances, organisms continue to eat even though nutrient levels have been restored. In extreme cases this can lead to obesity. There are several theories of obesity including too many fat cells, a higher set point, and the roles of social and environmental factors.
5 Losing weight can be a difficult process, but an understanding of the possible causes of obesity can provide useful information. The best weight-loss strategies take into account that: (1) despite the claims of fad diets, successful weight loss is a long-term proposition; (2) exercise can be helpful by both burning calories and raising metabolic rate; and (3) certain types of food, such as sugars, add large amounts of calories and can actually increase hunger.
6. In some cases, an obsession with food can lead to the eating disorders of anorexia and bulimia. Anorexia is characterized by reduced eating and significant weight loss, while bulimia is characterized by periods of enormous intake of calorie-rich foods followed by vomiting. These disorders, primarily found in young women, may be caused by poor body image and the view that it is necessary to be thin to be attractive.
7. The four phases of the human sexual response in both men and women are excitement, plateau, orgasm, and resolution. Human sexual behavior is affected by genetic and hormonal factors, external stimuli, experience, and attitudes. AIDS has made many people more cautious about casual sexual behavior.
8. Homosexuals may attain greater sexual satisfaction than heterosexuals. Research on the causes of sexual orientation suggest that genetics and brain structure, as well as experiential factors, may be involved in homosexuality.
9. Freud proposed that two drives, eros and thantos, direct human behavior. Murray identified twenty important needs. Maslow distinguished 7 needs, arranged in a hi-

earchy. The highest need in Maslow's system is self-actualization.

10. McClelland found that parents who demand self-sufficiency and independence are most likely to instill the need for achievement in their children. Rewarding achievement strivings may undermine intrinsic motivation.

11. The same factors that produce job satisfaction also motivate workers to word hard and effectively.

12. Emotions involve subjective, physiological, and expressive components. The physiological components of emotion can be measured by means of a polygraph. However, the use of polygraphs as "lie detectors" is controversial because innocent subjects are often judged to be guilty.

13. William James originally suggested that physiological feedback determined the subjective component of emotion. The contemporary two-factor theory holds that emotional experience depends on both physiological arousal and a cognitive evaluation or environmental stimuli as emotion-provoking.

14. Charles Darwin proposed that emotions are accompanied by distinct facial expressions that are innate and universal. Contemporary research has shown that feedback from facial expressions helps determine subjective emotional experience.

KEY INDIVIDUALS

Nikolaas Tinbergen
Virginia Johnson
Robert Plutchik
Edmund Wilson
Harry Harlow
William James
Clark Hull
Sigmund Freud
Carl Lange
Richard Solomon
Henry Murray
Philip Bard
A. L. Washburn

Abraham Maslow
Stanley Schachter
Walter Cannon
Douglas Crowne
Jerome Singer
Judith Rodin
David Marlowe
Charles Darwin
Alfred Kinsey
David McClelland
William Masters
John Atkinson

KEY RESEARCH

fixed-action patterns and the three-spined
  stickleback stomach
contractions and hunger pangs
hypothalamus and hunger
stress, obesity, and overeating
degree of hunger, metabolic rate, and type of
  food eaten
surveys of human sexual behavior
human sexual response cycle
role of early experience in normal sexual
  behavior
Freud's theory of motivation
need theories of motivation
Social Desirability Scale
need for achievement (n Ach)
a three-dimensional classification of emotions
James-Lange theory of emotion
Cannon-Bard theory of emotion
unexplained arousal
facial expression of emotion

KEY TERMS

motivation
instinct
ethology
fixed-action pattern
sign stimuli
sociobiology
drive
drive reduction
homeostasis
arousal
opponent-process theory
incentives

lateral hypothalamus (LH)

ventromedial hypothalamus (VMH)

set point theory

anorexia nervosa

bulemia

androgens

attitudes

homosexuality

eros

thanatos

need for achievement (n Ach)

emotion

polygraph

James-Lange theory

two-factor theory

facial feedback hypothesis

5 States of Consciousness

CHAPTER OUTLINE

177

hen psychology was first established as a separate discipline a little over a century ago, it was defined as the science of human consciousness. The goal of this new science was to isolate the basic elements of conscious experience—such as sensations, feelings, thoughts, and mental images—much as chemists identified the basic elements of the physical world. Psychologists also hoped to analyze how complex states of consciousness are built up from combinations of these basic elements. In fact, these early psychologists acquired the name of "mental chemists."

Among the most famous of the early psychologists was William James, who in 1875 established the first laboratory of experimental psychology in North America, at Harvard University. Two of James' books, *The Principles of Psychology* (1890) and *The Varieties of Religious Experience* (1902), are still required reading for any serious student of human consciousness.

James made many profound observations about conscious experience. For example, he proposed that consciousness is an ability that evolved because it had survival value for the human organism. According to James, consciousness aided survival by limiting the amount of information we must deal with at any one time and thereby facilitating voluntary activity. We will explore this important concept later in our discussion of consciousness and attention.

Another of James' most important ideas was that our everyday conscious experience—what he called *normal waking consciousness*—is only one of many possible forms of consciousness. James argued that there are uncharted regions of human consciousness that can be explored by studying phenomena such as mental illness, dreams, religious ecstasy, and drug use. According to James, these other forms of consciousness are hidden in all of us and are separated from normal waking consciousness by only the "filmiest of screens" (James, 1902).

Unfortunately, early psychologists like James were never able to develop a valid scientific method for investigating consciousness. The method of study they used most often was known as introspection, which means literally "looking inward." In **introspection**, subjects were presented with a particular stimulus or task and asked to describe their mental state as thoroughly as possible. For example, subjects might be asked to report on their conscious experience while solving a problem in logic. Subjects usually reported that they became conscious of sensations from their body, of various mild feelings, and of thoughts and images related to the question. They might also report that after a period of time the solution came into consciousness as a flash of understanding (Woodworth, 1938).

The introspective method ultimately came to a dead end because there was no way to determine the validity of subjects' introspective reports. If, for example, subjects reported feeling sleepy during a certain task, it was impossible to confirm this statement with an objective measure of sleepiness. Scientific methods require objective measurements of phenomena. The introspective method yielded only subjective evidence and was therefore scientifically questionable.

By the early twentieth century, psychologists recognized the shortcomings of introspection. This had two major consequences. First, psychologists began to develop other research methods, such as the behavioral method, that did not rely on subjective reports of inner experience. Second, the goal of establishing a science of human consciousness was virtually abandoned for several decades.

However, by the 1960s, prompted in part by a growing popular interest in subjects such as hypnosis, meditation, and the consciousness-altering effects of drugs, psychologists once again began seriously to explore the many forms of conscious experience. This rekindled interest also reflected psychologists' confidence that the research methods developed after the decline of introspection could be fruitfully applied to the abandoned study of conscious experience.

In this chapter we will examine this new psychology of consciousness. We begin with a discussion of what James called "normal waking consciousness." We then explore research and theory on the changes in consciousness that occur during sleep and dreaming. Contemporary approaches to meditation and hypnosis, two psychological states that lie between waking and sleeping, are then discussed.

We conclude by examining a variety of alterations in consciousness produced by psychoactive drugs.

NORMAL WAKING CONSCIOUSNESS

Consciousness can be defined as the sum total of all the external stimuli and internal mental events of which we are aware at any given time (Natsoulas, 1978; Ornstein, 1977). As William James first pointed out, consciousness is rarely fixed on any one event for any length of time. In fact, James thought it was psychologically impossible to focus attention on any one stimulus for more than a few seconds at a time. He felt that concentration would inevitably be broken by the distracting flow of changing sensations, thoughts, images, and events. James called this kaleidoscopic flow of awareness the *stream of consciousness*. The stream of consciousness is especially noticeable when we are in a relaxed or drowsy state. However, even when we make an effort to concentrate, our concentration is repeatedly broken by competing stimuli and mental events. How long can you focus on an external stimulus or concentrate on your reading without interruption from competing thoughts or sensations?

In the early twentieth century, a number of writers, including James Joyce and Virginia Woolf, used the stream of consciousness as a literary technique in an attempt to convey the multiple sensations, thoughts, memories, and feelings of a character at a given point in time, regardless of logical sequence. Consider, for example, the following passage from Joyce's *Ulysses* (1934), which represents the stream of consciousness of a man outside at dusk as he muses about gardening, the color spectrum of light, stars, shapes, and his native Ireland:

> Best time to spray plants too in the shade after the sun. Some light still. Red rays are longest. Roygbiv Vance taught us: red, orange, yellow, green, blue, indigo, violet. A star I see. Venus? Can't tell yet. Two, when three it's night. Were those nightclouds there all the time? No. Wait. Trees are they? An optical illusion. Mirage. Land of the setting sun this. Homerule sun setting in the southeast. My native land, goodnight. (pp. 369-70)

An important aspect of the stream of consciousness is the continual fluctuation between external and internal events. As every teacher knows, a classroom of students is like the randomly blinking lights of a Christmas tree. At different times, each student "tunes out" momentarily while awareness is captured by internal mental events. One researcher found that two thirds of a group of surgeons admitted to daydreaming during the less demanding and routine parts of surgical operations. Of course, the degree to which we can afford to tune out the external environment depends on the importance of what we are doing. Nevertheless, even under the most demanding conditions, awareness fluctuates between inner and outer worlds to some degree (Singer, 1977, 1984b).

Subconscious Mental Activity

A great deal of our behavior and mental activity takes place subconsciously. **Subconscious processes** are mental or behavioral activities that take place outside conscious awareness. Many psychologists break subconscious mental activity down into preconscious and unconscious processes, a distinction first made by Sigmund Freud. **Preconscious processes** are those subconscious activities that can be brought into awareness by paying attention to them. **Unconscious processes** are subconscious mental activities that are more or less permanently unavailable to consciousness.

Our ability to process information from external and internal environments is limited. Through the process of selective attention we can select only those stimuli we need to be aware of at the moment. Of course sometimes this is more difficult than others!

PRECONSCIOUS PROCESSES

Many of our everyday behaviors and mental activities are carried out on a preconscious level. Consider the case of driving an automobile along a familiar route. Many people have had the somewhat unsettling experience of arriving at a destination without "knowing" how they got there. They seem to awake suddenly with no memory of the details of the preceding period of time (Reed, 1972). In such cases, driving has become so undemanding and predictable that conscious awareness is directed to other activities, such as listening to the radio or conversing.

In contrast to unconscious processes, preconscious processes are always capable of becoming conscious. For example, the commuter who daydreams while driving to work is able to do so only after many hours of conscious practice with the details of shifting, steering, braking, and accelerating. These activities then recede to a preconscious level. However, an unfamiliar sound from the car's engine will bring the driver back into full consciousness of the task at hand.

UNCONSCIOUS PROCESSES

Large segments of our behavior and mental activity exist at an unconscious level that is more or less permanently unavailable to conscious awareness. For example, we are unaware of many body functions, such as the continuous secretion and circulation of hormones throughout the bloodstream, as well as the electrochemical activity of our nervous system. Many psychological phenomena are also unconscious: we are all able to recite our telephone number when asked, but we are unable to describe exactly how we are able to remember it. One of the enduring contributions of the introspectionists was the finding that people are often unable to describe the mental chain of events leading to the solution of difficult problems. In many cases, solutions seem to pop into our minds some time after we have given up on the problem:

> Ghiselin (1952) has collected into one volume a number of essays on the creative process by a variety of creative workers from Poincaré to Picasso. As Ghiselin accurately described the general conclusion of these workers, 'Production by a process of purely conscious calculation seems never to occur.' Instead, creative workers describe themselves almost universally as bystanders, differing from other observers only in that they are the first to witness the fruits of a problem-solving process that is almost completely hidden from conscious view. (Nisbett & Wilson, 1977, p. 240)

Unconscious mental processes are a prominent feature of the psychoanalytic theory developed by Freud. He likened conscious and preconscious mental activity to the tip of an iceberg and unconscious processes to the great mass of ice that lies under water. As you already know, Freud focused especially on the unconscious mental processes associated with sexual and aggressive drives. He shocked his own generation by suggesting that these unconscious processes exert a profound influence on our conscious mental activity and behavior. Although contemporary psychologists would tend to agree with Freud on the importance of unconscious mental processes, they would disagree that these processes are exclusively concerned with sexual and aggressive motives.

According to Freud, unconscious processes can be detected behind brief lapses and errors in our everyday use of language—sometimes referred to as "Freudian slips." **Table 5.1** lists some everyday errors of language use that might be interpreted in terms of the unconscious processes behind them. As we shall see later in this chapter, Freud felt that dreams also provide insight into unconscious mental processes.

Table 5.1   **Notes to the Teacher**

Please excuse Gloria. She has been sick and under the doctor.

My son is under the doctor's care and should not take P.E. Please execute him.

Please excuse Jimmy for being. It was his father's fault.

Mary Ann was absent December 11–15 because she had a fever, sore throat, headache, and upset stomach. Her sister was also sick, fever, sore throat, her brother had a low grade fever and ached all over. I wasn't the best either, sore throat and fever. There must be something going around—her father even got hot last night.

Compiled by the Graduate School of Education, Northern Illinois University.

Consciousness and Attention

Most people think of their conscious experience as a fairly accurate reflection of their environment. This might be called the photographic theory of consciousness. In fact, we are conscious at any one time of only a limited portion of all the stimuli impinging on our senses. If consciousness were not limited, we would be overwhelmed by constant sensory bombardment from all kinds of energy, such as heat, light, and sound, as well as ever changing patterns of stimulation from muscular, visceral, and mental activity. Becoming simultaneously aware of all these stimuli would make us as helpless as the hypothetical centipede which found it could no longer walk when it became aware of all its 100 legs. In sum, our ability to process information from the external and internal environments has a *limited capacity*—we can process only so much at one time (Glass, Holyoak, & Santa, 1979; Ornstein, 1977).

The cognitive (or mental) process that limits the amount of information allowed into consciousness is known as **selective attention.** William James referred to attention as the "searchlight of consciousness." By this he meant that attention is the means by which we scan the environment and select only those stimuli we wish or need to be aware of at the moment while ignoring the remainder.

The process of selective attention can be illustrated by the so-called cocktail party phenomenon. Imagine that you are at a party and have been talking with a boring person. In an effort to be polite, you continue to listen and even respond. But the situation grows worse. The two people standing next to you are engaged in a provocative conversation. You try to keep up with both conversations but soon discover you cannot. The best you can do is shift back and forth, taking in bits and pieces of each conversation. This situation often ends in embarrassment when the first person realizes you have not been paying attention.

The cocktail party phenomenon has been studied in the laboratory using a method known as *dichotic listening* (Cherry, 1953). In these studies the subject wears a pair of headphones that play a different message to each ear. The subject is told to attend only to the message in one ear. To assure that the subject is performing the task correctly, he or she must repeat or "shadow" the message as it is heard.

The results of such experiments document what we already know from the cocktail party: we can pay attention to only one train of information at a time. When paying attention to the shadowed message, subjects remember little about the message played to the other ear; they are unable to recall the meaning or the content of the unshadowed message (Moray, 1959). In fact, subjects do not even notice if the unshadowed message consists of a single phrase repeated over and over, nor do they recall whether the unshadowed message was in the same or a different language. There are exceptions to this one-track mind phenomenon. For example, subjects often remember hearing their names or sexually explicit words in the unshadowed message (Nielsen & Sarason, 1981). But, in general, consciousness requires an effort of selective attention. You can observe the phenomenon of selective attention for yourself by reading the paragraph in **Figure 5.1.**

Unconscious Information Processing

Shadowing experiments demonstrate that unattended information does not usually enter consciousness. Does this mean that information of which we are unaware has no influence on our behavior? Not necessarily. Research strongly suggests that we are able to monitor information at an unconscious level and that this unconscious information processing can affect our conscious behavior. In an interesting extension of the shadowing technique, subjects

Figure 5.1
Shadowing. (From Lindsay & Norman, 1977)
In the passage that appears below, there are two messages, one in black and one in color. Your job is to read the black-ink message aloud as quickly as possible. This procedure is similar to shadowing.

In performing an experiment like this one on man attention car it house is boy critically hat important shoe that candy the old material horse that tree is pen being phone read cow by book the hot subject tape for pin the stand relevant view task sky be red cohesive man and car gramatically house complete boy but hat without shoe either candy being horse so tree easy pen that phone full cow attention book is hot not tape required pin in stand order view to sky read red it nor too difficult

Now that you have finished, remember all you can about the message in color without looking back. Like the subjects in the shadowing experiment, you probably did not recall anything about the message in color, even though it contained the same words over and over.

Figure 5.2
Use of the Shadowing Technique To Demonstrate Unconscious Information Processing.
In this example, the subject is asked to summarize an ambiguous message delivered to the *attended* left ear. The message might be something like "visiting relatives can be such a bore." At the same time, a clarifying message is delivered to the *unattended* right ear. The subject's summary of the message is influenced by the message to the right ear, even though the subject was not conscious of hearing it. (From Gilling & Brightwell, 1982)

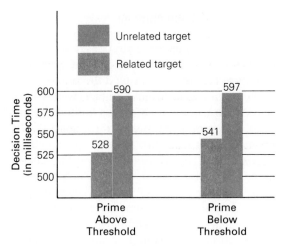

Figure 5.4
Results of Marcel (1983) Priming Study.
Even if the prime word is not detectable (it is below the threshold of awareness), it can influence decisions about the target word.

were asked to attend to and then summarize ambiguous sentences delivered to one ear. For example, "Visiting relatives can be a bore" is an ambiguous sentence because it can refer either to one's relatives or to the activity of visiting them. In this experiment short sentences containing clues about the meaning of the ambiguous sentence were simultaneously delivered to the *unattended* ear. Thus, the clue sentence "I don't like to visit relatives" clarifies the ambiguous sentence. The results showed that clue sentences delivered to the unattended ear influenced the subjects' summary of the ambiguous sentence delivered to the attended ear. As illustrated in **Figure** 5.2, subjects might summarize the ambiguous sentence as follows: "Going to visit relatives is a bore" (Lackner & Garrett, 1972; McKay, 1973).

Although some psychologists argue that the foregoing results may be due to brief shifts of attention from the attended to the unattended ear, other experiments also point to the possibility of unconscious information processing. One demonstration used a technique known as

priming. With this technique a word called a *prime* is presented on a screen and followed by a second word called the *target*. The subject's task is simply to decide whether the target is a meaningful word. It can be shown that the time the subject requires to decide whether the target is a word is shorter if the prime is a related word than if it is an unrelated word (see **Figure 5.3**). For example, the time required to decide if infant is a word is shorter if the prime is *child* than if the prime is *street*. In a demonstration of unconscious priming, Marcel (1983) presented prime words *below* subjects' threshold of awareness. That is, subjects were unable to detect whether a prime or a blank screen preceded the target word. Marcel found that even though prime words could not be consciously identified, they nevertheless influenced subjects' judgments of the target word: related primes produced faster reaction times than unrelated primes (see **Figure 5.4**). These results indicate that conscious information processing can be influenced by external stimuli of which we are unaware (Dixon, 1981).

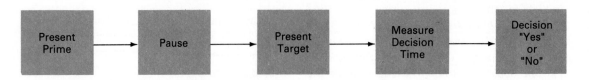

Figure 5.3
The Priming Procedure.
The subjects must decide as rapidly as possible if the target is a meaningful word.

At present many psychologists are willing to assert boldly that consciousness is not necessary for complex psychological functioning. Consciousness *may* accompany various forms of information processing, but it is not *required* for such processing to occur (Kihlstrom, 1987). As Posner and Snyder (1974) put it, "Consciousness is reserved for special processing." Other psychologists argue that a full understanding of unconscious information processing has yet to be achieved, and they therefore maintain a more cautious attitude about the role of unconscious information processing in our behavior and mental activity (Holender, 1986; Klatzky, 1984).

Effortful Versus Automatic Information Processing

We can think of the shadowing experiments using ambiguous and clue sentences as illustrating two forms of information processing. The ambiguous message delivered to one ear is detected by an *effortful process* that is consciously and voluntarily controlled—subjects are aware of the message and can presumably ignore it any time by directing their attention elsewhere. The clue sentence delivered to the unattended ear is detected by an *automatic process* that is subconscious and involuntary—subjects are unaware of being influenced by the unattended message. Many everyday tasks have the same characteristics. In reading this passage, you rapidly detect letters and words automatically, while conscious attention is directed toward comprehension of the meanings of sentences. A pianist automatically processes the notes and their relationship to hand and finger movements while consciously attending to the output of his or her performance.

In general, unfamiliar tasks require effortful processing, while tasks that have been extensively practiced are processed automatically. Consider the difference between a novice driver and a skilled driver. The novice driver is painfully aware of controlling the accelerator, brake, and steering wheel while attempting to process a multitude of visual and auditory stimuli. The skilled driver, on the other hand, can allocate all of his or her attention to a conversation while driving automatically. Effortful processing is slow and controlled by the limited amount of information we can attend to at any one time. Automatic processing is fast, effortless, and not limited by attentional capacity. Conscious awareness characterizes effortful

processing but not automatic processing (Fisk & Schneider, 1984; Klatzky, 1984).

The movement from effortful processing to automatic processing requires extensive practice. For example, Shiffrin and Schneider (1977) trained subjects to search for a target letter within a display of several letters. The target letters always came from the same set of nine possible letters. On any given trial, subjects might be given one letter to find, for example, "the letter *L*," or given one of several possible letters to find, for example, "the letter *L, M,* or *Y*" (see **Figure 5.5**). Early in the task, subjects required a good deal more time to detect one of several possible letters than to detect a single letter. Obviously, the greater the number of possible targets, the more attention is required to search out the one that actually appears. After practicing the task for more than 2000 trials, however, this difference disappeared. Subjects were able to identify one of four target letters in a display as rapidly as they could detect a single letter. The process of detecting targets had become automatic. Interestingly, the process had also become involuntary because subjects continued to detect letters from the original set even when given new targets to detect and instructed to ignore the well-practiced targets. (See **Figure 5.6** for another illustration of automatic processing.)

Mindlessness Versus Mindfulness

What are we to make of the findings that much of our behavior and mental activity occurs automatically and unconsciously? On the one hand, we can argue that automatic information processing is often adaptive. It would be hard to imagine how any skilled performance—a musi-

Figure 5.6
Do You See Anything Wrong with This Sign? Because of automatic processing, many people do not see anything wrong with this sign.

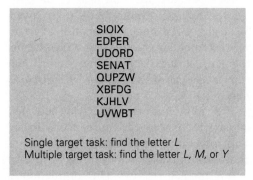

Single target task: find the letter *L*
Multiple target task: find the letter *L, M,* or *Y*

Figure 5.5
A Multiple Letter Display. (From Glass, Holyoak, & Santa, 1979)

cal recital, an athletic contest, or even an engaging psych lecture—could proceed if the performer were required to be conscious of the total flow of information processing underlying the activity. Indeed, we practice our skills so that they *will* become more or less automatic and effortless.

On the other hand, automatic behavior can also become what Langer (1989) calls "mindless" behavior. **Mindlessness** occurs when we unthinkingly follow routines or carry out orders simply because we have learned how to perform certain tasks too well:

> Once, in a small department store, I gave a cashier a new credit card. Noticing that I hadn't signed it, she handed it back to me to sign. Then she took my card, passed it through her machine, handed me the resulting form, and asked me to sign it. I did as I was told. The cashier then held the form next to the newly signed card to see if the signatures matched. (Langer, 1989, p.24)

Mindlessness can have disastrous consequences, as when an accident is caused by a driver who has failed to notice a slick road or when we automatically stereotype a member of an ethnic group different from our own. Fortunately, mindlessness can be avoided simply by making an effort to be "mindful". **Mindfulness** occurs when we choose to be more fully aware of our environment and our responses to it. In the final analysis, we all have the option of "putting it on automatic" when the situation allows or of becoming mindful when novel circumstances require careful, conscious attention and thought.

Interim Summary

Consciousness is the sum total of all internal and external events that we are aware of at any given time. Consciousness exists as a continuous succession of sensations, thoughts, images, and feelings, which William James called the *stream of consciousness.*

A good deal of our behavior and mental activity is carried out subconsciously. Many psychologists distinguish between preconscious and unconscious forms of subconscious mental activity. The distinction is based on the degree to which different mental activities are available to consciousness.

We are aware at any given time of only a selected portion of the external and internal stimuli potentially available to consciousness. Consciousness is governed by attentional capacity, which is limited. However, stimuli that are outside conscious awareness can influence our behavior.

Our ability to process information does not necessarily depend on conscious awareness. With highly practiced tasks, like reading or driving, information can be processed automatically and preconsciously. Mindless behavior can occur if we allow automatic information processing to proceed when the situation requires effortful and attentive information processing.

● ●

SLEEP AND DREAMS

We spend almost one third of our lives asleep, an average of about 7½ hours in each 24-hour period. But throughout most of human history this important aspect of life was locked in mystery, a subject for speculation but lacking a method of study. After all, how could scientists hope to observe psychological activity in sleeping subjects?

The major breakthrough in sleep research was the development in the 1930s of EEG machines for recording the brain's electrical activity, or electroencephalogram. EEG records of sleeping subjects showed that sleep was a multifaceted, patterned, and complex activity. Since the advent of EEG machines, thousands of subjects have been observed in sleep research laboratories. In this section we will introduce the major findings of this research and the theories of sleep and dreaming they have generated. Our discussion will include the EEGs produced during sleep and dreams, the patterns that occur in a night's sleep, sleep disorders, and major hypotheses of the functions of sleep and dreams.

Stages of Sleep

Sleep is far from being a uniform state that we enter into shortly after retiring and then exit from upon awakening. We all know through our own experience that sleep ranges from a light, dozing sleep, from which we are easily awakened, to the state of "sleeping like a log," from which we are awakened with difficulty. We need only watch a sleeping person to get

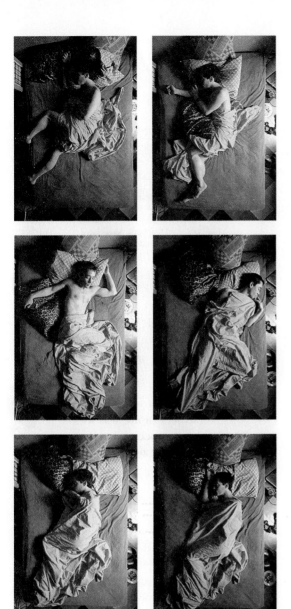

Figure 5.7
A Night's Sleep Is Characterized by Much Variability in Activity.

some idea of the variability of sleep. During some periods, sleepers are extremely restless. At other times they may spend more than an hour virtually motionless. **Figure 5.7** shows how active a sleeper can be over the course of a night.

The EEG allows sleep researchers to identify the depth, or *stage,* of sleep with considerable accuracy. The EEG records the electrical activity of the brain from small electrodes placed on the scalp. Because the brain generates only a few millionths of a volt of activity,

this activity must be amplified with a device like a stereo amplifier in order to be detected. The amplified voltage then activates a pen on a moving sheet of paper. The result is a pattern of electrical waves that changes with the different stages of sleep. With the EEG, researchers have identified four distinct stages of sleep, each of which has specific characteristics (see **Figure 5.8** on page 186).

Stage 1, the lightest level of sleep, occurs just as we drift off to sleep. The EEG shows irregular waves of relatively low voltage.

Stage 2, a deeper level of sleep, is identified by the appearance of very rapid waves from time to time. These bursts of rapid EEG waves resemble the thread wrapped around a sewing spindle and thus are known as **sleep spindles.**

Stage 3 marks a transition from relatively light to very deep sleep. The EEG begins to show periods of low-frequency, high-voltage waves known as **delta waves.**

Stage 4 is the deepest level of sleep. Here delta waves appear almost constantly in the EEG.

Yet something is missing from this picture—something that is the most dramatic of all changes that take place during a night's sleep. It is that special state of consciousness we call dreaming.

Dreaming Sleep

Periodically throughout the night, a curious set of changes comes over the sleeper. The EEG patterns show a shift from the deep levels of sleep into stage 1 activity. The steady breathing of deep sleep becomes choppy and irregular. The sleeper's heart rate and blood pressure begin to fluctuate rapidly. Penile and clitoral erection occur. Finally, the sleeper's eyes begin to move rapidly back and forth under the closed eyelids (see **Figure 5.9** on page 186).

What causes these effects? The answer came only in the 1950s when two sleep researchers, Eugene Aserinsky and Nathaniel Kleitman of the University of Chicago, awakened sleeping subjects when rapid eye movements occurred. When subjects were asked what they had been experiencing, about 80 percent of them reported that they had been dreaming. When awakened at other times, subjects sometimes reported dreamlike experiences, but their descriptions usually lacked the vivid visual images and fantastic themes of in-

Figure 5.8
EEG Tracings
Associated with
Each Sleep Stage.

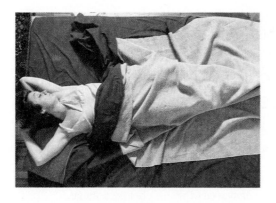

Stage 1

Stage 2   sleep spindles

Stage 3   delta waves

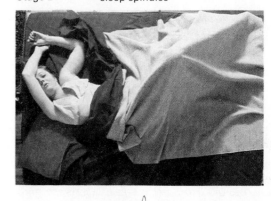

Stage 4   delta waves

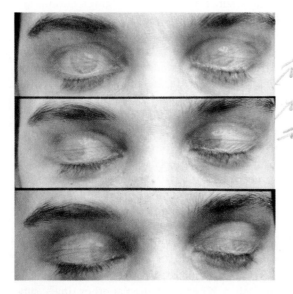

Figure 5.9
REM During Dreaming.
This double-exposure photograph shows the rapid eye
movements associated with dreaming.

tense dreaming (Aserinsky & Kleitman, 1953). Because the most easily recognized sign of dreaming sleep was the darting eye movements, this entire pattern of activity soon became known as rapid-eye-movement sleep, or simply **REM sleep.** By contrast, all other states of sleep became known as non-REM, or **NREM sleep.** This discovery enabled researchers to identify periods of dreaming sleep independently of the person's introspective reports.

Exactly what is our state of consciousness during REM sleep? We might suspect that during the REM period, we are close to being awake. After all, we are in a state of heightened EEG and physiological arousal. Yet we also know that it is relatively difficult to awaken a sleeper during REM sleep. The reason is that during REM periods the sleeper is effectively isolated from the external environment. Not only are the sleeper's eyes closed, but also sensory information from the skin, joints, and mus-

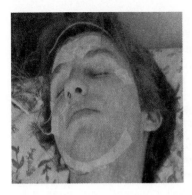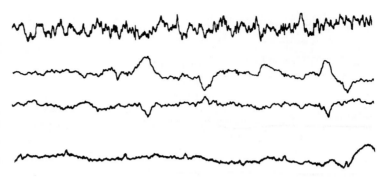

Figure 5.10
REM Sleep.
During dreaming, the brain and the internal organs are highly activated, even though the muscles are highly relaxed. In the polygraph tracings shown here, the volunteer's EEG (top) shows brain waves similar to those in the waking state. The two middle tracings indicate rapid eye movements, and the bottom tracing indicates virtually no activity in the chin muscles. The photograph shows the electrode placements that produce the various tracings on the right.

cles is inhibited by the brain. At the same time the brain inhibits the motor neurons required for muscular activity, leading to loss of muscle tone throughout the body (Hobson, 1989). In sum, the brain and the internal organs are highly activated, but the sleeper is immobilized as if locked in a cocoon. For this reason, sleep researchers often refer to REM periods as *paradoxical sleep* (see **Figure 5.10**).

In sum, we see that sleep is made up of two distinct states. NREM sleep contains four stages, ranging from light to deep sleep. REM sleep, which occurs periodically through the night, is a paradoxical state in which vivid dreams and increased brain and internal activity are accompanied by sensory isolation and muscular immobility. Without waking the subject, we can identify these changing states by observing different patterns of physiological activity, such as the EEG, eye movements, and muscle tension over the course of a night's sleep.

A Night's Sleep

Given our ability to measure REM sleep and the four stages of NREM sleep, we can ask another important question: do these periods occur randomly and unpredictably over the course of a night's sleep, or are they patterned in some way? As you might expect, the pattern of a night's sleep varies from person to person and also from night to night in the same person.

Yet despite this variability, the events of a night's sleep are remarkably predictable. A diagram of this typical pattern is shown in **Figure 5.11.**

This diagram illustrates a number of important general findings about sleep. As you can see, the typical sleeper enters stage 1 about

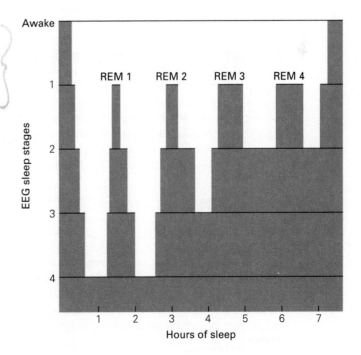

Figure 5.11
A Typical Night of Sleep. (From Cartwright, 1987)

20 minutes after retiring. He or she then begins a rapid but orderly descent through the sleep stages, reaching stage 4 within the first hour. After about 30 minutes of deep sleep, the sleeper rapidly ascends through stages 3 and 2 and then pauses at stage 1. At this point, about 90 minutes after retiring, the first REM period of the night occurs. This REM period is quite brief and is followed by another descent into a second, lengthy period of deep, stage 4 sleep. The pattern then repeats itself, with the second REM period occurring about 90 minutes after the first. In sum, the course of a typical night's sleep is marked by a series of descents and ascents through different sleep stages, and this pattern is regularly punctuated by REM periods.

The diagram also illustrates three other important findings. First of all, most deep sleep occurs in the first half of the night. Second, most REM sleep occurs in the second half of the night. Third, each succeeding REM period is longer than the preceding one, so that the fourth REM period may last as long as an hour. The average person wakes up after about $7\frac{1}{2}$ hours of sleep, and it is common for this to happen during a final period of REM sleep. How many times have you awakened not knowing for a minute where dreaming left off and normal waking consciousness began?

Many people are convinced that they seldom, if ever, dream. Yet no subject of the thousands observed in sleep laboratories has ever failed to show REM sleep. How can we explain this contradiction? The answer seems to be that dreams are difficult to remember in our waking state and that some people simply have better memories for their dreams than others. The easiest dreams to recall are those occurring in the last REM period of the night because we often capture them upon awakening. The memory of earlier dreams tends to disappear unless we awake during or soon after a REM period.

The Need to Sleep

The answer to the question of why we sleep would seem to be simple: we need sleep to restore and revitalize our bodies and minds for the next waking day. Unfortunately, this simple answer is not borne out by the facts. Literally hundreds of studies have looked for physical and mental deterioration in people deprived of sleep for long periods but have discovered very few adverse effects. Lack of sleep causes only minor changes in the body's physiological and biochemical functioning. There is some deterioration in the performance of lengthy tasks, especially if they are repetitive and boring. But if the task is interesting, or if the subject is encouraged to do his or her best, sleep deprivation does not impair performance. Intellectual abilities and problem-solving abilities show almost no change (Webb, 1975).

Can we assume that sleep is not necessary? No, we cannot. The longer people are deprived of sleep, the more difficult it is to keep them awake. Unless constantly encouraged to remain awake, they rapidly doze off in almost any position or any place. They resent being kept awake and, regardless of the evidence, they are convinced that their physical and mental activity is adversely affected. In other words, there seems to be a powerful need to sleep even though sleeplessness is not particularly harmful. We are left with the rather unsatisfactory conclusion that people sleep in order to avoid feeling sleepy!

It is helpful to view sleep as part of a sleep-wake cycle that mirrors the night-and-day cycle of our world. Daily cycles in behavioral or physiological activity are known as **circadian rhythms,** from the Latin meaning "around a day." Circadian rhythms can be observed in many physiological functions, such as the ebb and flow of hormone levels and variations in body temperature (see **Figure 5.12**). Circadian rhythms continue even when subjects are placed in enclosed environments without clocks or light-dark cues. In such environments, people spontaneously develop a 25-hour cycle of waking and sleeping activity. Thus much of our activity is influenced by internal mechanisms, known as *biological clocks,* that closely resemble the light-dark period of the day (Coleman, 1986).

Many sleep researchers now see sleep as a circadian rhythm developed in our evolutionary history. According to this view, our nightly feeling of sleepiness is programmed into us because enforced inactivity at night promoted human survival in the distant past. Why would this be so? First, early human beings were hunters and gatherers who foraged widely for food. Because the probability of finding food at night was markedly reduced, more energy was likely to have been spent hunting than would have been gained by the search. Therefore, sleeping at night helped early humans conserve energy. Second, an enforced period of inactivity at night would reduce the possibility of death by accidents or at the hands of predators. And finally, some kind of rest is obviously necessary to restore body tissues after strenuous physical exertion during the day. Although this rest need not be in the form of sleep (simply relaxing is also restorative), enforced sleep ensured that the necessary rest would occur. Thus sleep may be a deeply rooted biological program built into the human species because enforced inactivity at night promoted survival. Even though nighttime activity no longer threatens our survival to the degree it did our ancestors, we continue to act out the daily rhythm established by natural selection many thousands of years ago (Cohen, 1979; Webb, 1975).

Sleep Disorders

Normal patterns of sleep and waking can be disturbed for many reasons. In one survey, 52 percent of the respondents complained of a current or past sleep disorder (Kales, Soldatos, & Kales, 1981). The most common sleep disorder is insomnia. Other sleep disorders include sleepwalking, narcolepsy, and sleep apnea.

INSOMNIA

Insomnia is the long-term inability to obtain adequate sleep because of (1) lengthy time to sleep onset, (2) frequent wakening during the night, and/or (3) early morning wakening—waking up 2 to 3 hours before normal rising time.

Insomnia is sometimes caused by psychological disorders. People with anxiety disorders, for example, often complain of sleep onset insomnia. They are unable to relax or to rid their minds of anxious thoughts and images. Patients with severe depression often suffer from early morning wakening. The best solution for insomnias associated with psychological disorders is to treat the underlying disorders themselves with appropriate psychological or medical therapy (Soldatos & Kales, 1986).

Psychoactive drugs also interfere with the sleep process. Heavy alcohol consumption may decrease the time needed to fall asleep but interferes with various sleep stages as well as with REM sleep. Stimulant drugs, including caffeine, produce an alert state that interferes with falling and staying asleep. Some sleeping pills are also known to disturb normal sleeping patterns. People who use sleeping medications on a regular basis usually experience troubled and

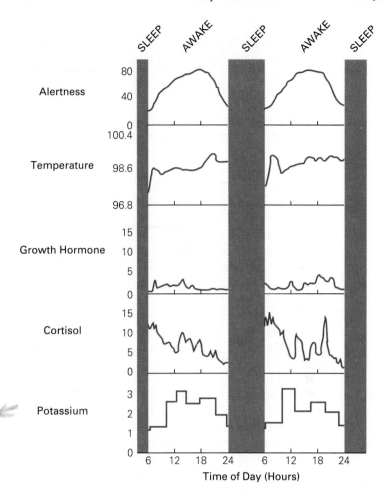

Figure 5.12
Circadian Rhythms.
The figure shows circadian rhythms in the sleep-wake cycle and in four physiological functions over two days. (From Coleman, 1986)

fitful sleep in the long run. Giving up sleeping pills abruptly after long-term use can also create problems. For several days or weeks the person may suffer from the effects of withdrawal, including anxiety, nightmares, and frequent wakenings. Most physicians now prescribe sleeping medications for only a few days to help overcome insomnia caused by temporary periods of stress.

People with chronic insomnia not due to a drug problem or a major psychological disorder are usually mildly depressed or anxious. During the day, they tend to internalize their concerns, worries, and feelings rather than express them outwardly. At night, as external distractions wane and attention is directed inward, these concerns enter conscious awareness. The insomniac typically suffers from uncontrollable thoughts and feelings described as a "racing mind." This mental alertness blocks sleep, causes muscular tension and physiological arousal, and leads to an escalating pattern of fearing to go to bed because of expected insomnia. Treatment usually requires dealing with the underlying worries and concerns as well as teaching relaxation techniques to reduce bodily tension and control intrusive thoughts and feelings (Borkovec, 1982).

SLEEPWALKING

Sleepwalking is a sleep disorder in which complex behaviors such as walking about are performed in a state of sleep. This disorder occurs with greatest frequency in children, and most outgrow the problem. In a typical episode of sleepwalking, the child arises from bed and walks around in a poorly coordinated, automatic manner for up to half an hour. He or she may also perform complex activities, such as opening doors, eating, or going to the bathroom. While sleepwalking, the child stares blankly and is unresponsive to others' efforts to communicate with him or her. The episode may end when the child returns to bed or wakes in a confused state. Upon awakening, whether this takes place the next morning or directly from sleepwalking, the child has no memory of what transpired during the episode.

The sleepwalker is not in REM sleep, as might be assumed. Rather, an episode begins during relatively deep stage 3 or stage 4 sleep, usually several hours after retiring. Sleepwalking shows characteristics of both waking and sleeping activity. Generally, no special treatment is required for sleepwalking. However, appropriate safety measures, such as locking windows and doors, should be taken (DSM-III-R, 1987).

NARCOLEPSY

Narcolepsy is a sleep disorder characterized by sudden, irresistible attacks of sleep during normal waking hours. In less severe forms, the sleep attacks occur in monotonous, low-stimulation situations. In more severe forms, the attacks may occur in exciting circumstances such as sports activities or even sexual intercourse. Some forms of narcolepsy resemble REM sleep: the person may have a loss of muscle tone and experience vivid, emotionally charged images while passing into sleep. In such cases, attacks are about as long as typical REM periods. Narcolepsy is generally treated with stimulant drugs to keep the patient awake during the day as well as by restriction of potentially danger-

ous activities like lengthy periods of monotonous driving (Kales et al., 1981, Siegel et al., 1991).

SLEEP APNEA

In **sleep apnea** sleep is repeatedly interrupted by cessation of breathing (apnea) due to obstruction of air flow in the throat. Breathing may be suspended for about 10 to 40 seconds, followed by loud snorting sounds; this may occur hundreds of times per night. Because sleep is continually disrupted, the victim usually suffers from excessive daytime sleepiness. Curiously, victims usually do not recognize the cause of their chronic sleepiness because attacks of apnea do not completely waken them. Middle-aged men who are also overweight are the most common victims.

Attacks of apnea occur when muscles in the upper throat relax, causing the airway at the back of the mouth to close. Treatment is aimed at ensuring that the upper airway remains open during sleep. Removing fatty tissue from the airway, either through weight loss or through surgery, is often helpful. The most widely used treatment is to have a small bedside air compressor deliver a steady stream of air to a mask worn over the nose. The airflow keeps the airway open continuously throughout the night (Kales et al., 1981, Palca, 1989).

The Nature of Dreams

We have seen that we can usually identify dream periods by REM sleep. But how exactly would we describe the dreamer's state of consciousness? Consider an example:

> She walked down the steps of the public library wearing her nightgown and cradling a bowl of raspberry Jell-O in her arms. At the foot of the long staircase she could distinguish the dim figure of her high-school algebra teacher. His right arm was upraised and he seemed to be shouting at her, but she could not make out the words. She hurried toward him, straining to hear. . . . Suddenly the scene shifted. Now she found herself traveling through a dense forest. The sun was setting ahead of her and the forest deepened in darkness. She felt afraid. An unseen menace seemed to be following her, dodging from tree to tree, but when she glanced back in fear she saw no one. She tried to run faster, but her legs would not re-

spond. The pursuer drew nearer, gaining on her, but she was powerless to escape and . . . (Kiester, 1980, p. 36)

Most psychologists agree that dreams have four easily recognized characteristics. First of all, they are made up of a succession of usually vivid and colorful *visual images*. Second, dreams are *fantastic* in that the space-time relationships of waking consciousness are distorted. Time may speed up or slow down, one scene may shift quickly into another without regard for logical relationships, and normally distinct concepts are condensed into unusual images. In the example above, a bowl of Jell-O, a staircase, and an algebra teacher are woven into one theme. The third characteristic of dreams is that they are often charged with emotion. The emotions of dreams can range from the intensely pleasurable, as in sexual dreams, to the intensely frightening, as in nightmares of being helplessly pursued. Finally, dreams have a *delusional quality*. That is, dreams are products of our imagination, yet we believe them to be real when they occur (Hobson, 1988).

The Need to Dream

Is there a need to dream, just as there is a need to sleep? The best way to answer this question is to deprive people of dreaming sleep and observe what happens. These *dream-deprivation studies* are carried out by awakening subjects whenever they pass into REM sleep. After one to two nights of this procedure, subjects are allowed to recover by sleeping without interruption.

The results of dream-deprivation studies seem to indicate that we do have a need for a certain amount of dreaming sleep. First of all, in the course of these studies it becomes increasingly difficult to awaken subjects during REM periods. Second, REM periods begin to occur more frequently, so that more awakenings are required. And third, subjects have a REM "rebound" when they are finally allowed to sleep without interruption. On recovery nights, subjects spend a greater than usual percentage of their total sleep time in REM sleep. Thus, we seem to need a certain amount of dreaming sleep. If this need is blocked, we try harder and harder to enter into dreaming, and we make up for dream deprivation by more frequent dreaming on subsequent nights (Dement, 1978).

Although dream deprivation is not psychologically harmful, subjects do not appreci-

The emotions in dreams can range from pleasurable to frightening. This painting by Fuseli is called "Nightmare."

ate being dream deprived and may become somewhat irritable. They may even try to compensate by daydreaming more than usual. However, subjects are generally able to adjust to dream deprivation much as people can learn to adjust to not eating for several days (Webb, 1975).

Dream Theories

Assuming that we have a need to dream, exactly *what* need does dreaming fulfill? Although there is no final answer to this question, just as there is no final answer to the question of why we sleep at all, there are many interesting theories. In this section we will examine two major theories and the evidence for both.

DREAMS AS WISH FULFILLMENT

Sigmund Freud was the first modern theorist to consider seriously the psychology of dreaming. Freud felt that dreams, like slips of the tongue, are derived from unconscious drives, or *wishes.* During the day, these unconscious wishes undergo repression; that is, they are actively excluded from consciousness. But during sleep, repression is relaxed and unconscious wishes are more likely to emerge into consciousness. They do not emerge directly, however. Freud postulated a mental *censor* that transforms and disguises unconscious wishes so that the person's sleep is undisturbed. The resulting dream is a product of this transformation. Freud used the term **manifest content** to describe the conscious and remembered aspects of a dream. The manifest content is symbolic of unconscious wishes. **Latent content** is the term used for the unconscious wishes or drives expressed in the manifest content. For Freud, the reason that dreams are difficult to understand is that their true latent content is distorted by the censor in order to maintain sleep. He believed that dreams must be interpreted to be understood (Freud, 1900/1953).

Freud's theory predicts that symbolic representations of sexual and aggressive wishes will appear in people's dreams. This hypothesis can be tested by analyzing the thematic content of dreams collected from groups of subjects. As it happens, aggressive themes appear in about 50 percent of dreams; however, pleasant encounters among people occur almost as frequently. Sexual themes characterize only a small portion of all dream themes. Interestingly, penile and clitoral erection occur as part of REM sleep independently of the content

of the concurrent dream (Hall & Van de Castle, 1966; F. Snyder, 1970). Many psychologists feel that these observations offer only weak support, at best, for Freud's theory. Skeptics are more likely to regard dream content as an extension of the problems, concerns, and experiences of the day, distorted in the vivid context of REM sleep (Cartwright, 1978).

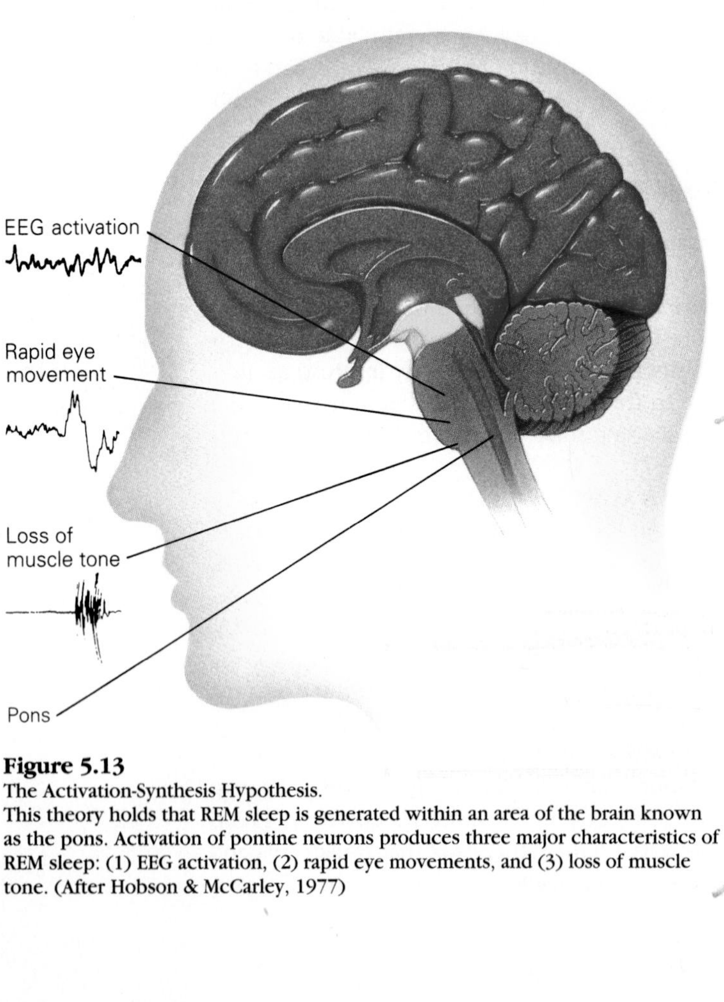

DREAMS AS BRAIN ACTIVITY

Two eminent sleep researchers, J. Allan Hobson and Robert McCarley, have proposed a neuropsychological theory of dreaming, which they call the *activation-synthesis hypothesis* (Hobson & McCarley, 1977, Hobson, 1988). The term *activation* refers to the state of the brain during REM sleep. Hobson and McCarley argue that the "dream state" of REM sleep is generated in an area of the brain stem known as the pons (see **Figure 5.13**). They further argue that this dream state generation occurs spontaneously in a periodic rhythm throughout the sleep cycle.

Spontaneous generation of the dream state activates the cortex in a more or less random pattern. This random activation is responsible for the shifting and fragmentary images of dreams. The cortex acts to *synthesize* these essentially random images by drawing on stored information in memory. The process of synthesis does impose some order on dream images, but the dream itself is, according to Hobson and McCarley, only "the best of a bad job."

The activation-synthesis hypothesis differs from Freud's theory in two major respects. First, it regards dreams as mere by-products of periodic brain activation, rather than as the result of unconscious wishes. Second, it regards dreams as inherently random and meaningless, rather than as a window into the deeper reaches of personality. Critics of this theory take exception to such radical conclusions. They point out, for example, that dream content is influenced by waking experience and therefore not as random and psychologically meaningless as Hobson and McCarley suggest (Foulkes, 1985). Nevertheless, the hypothesis does present a sharp neuropsychological alternative to purely psychological theories of dreaming. **Figure 5.14** summarizes the psychoanalytic and activation-synthesis theories of dreaming.

But why is the brain periodically activated during sleep? Some researchers think that REM sleep is analogous to recharging a battery. Brain activation during sleep may restore supplies of

EEG activation

Rapid eye movement

Loss of muscle tone

Pons

Figure 5.13
The Activation-Synthesis Hypothesis.
This theory holds that REM sleep is generated within an area of the brain known as the pons. Activation of pontine neurons produces three major characteristics of REM sleep: (1) EEG activation, (2) rapid eye movements, and (3) loss of muscle tone. (After Hobson & McCarley, 1977)

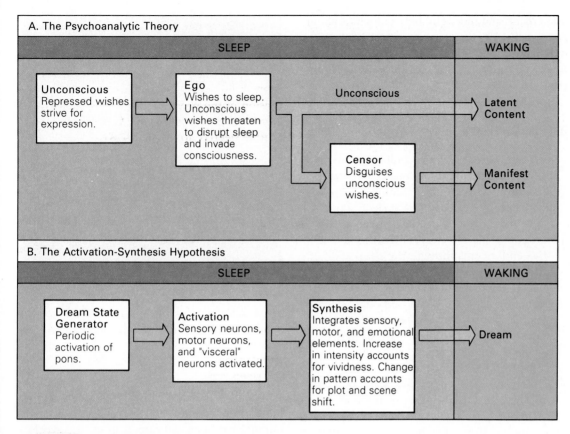

Figure 5.14
Comparison of the Psychoanalytic Theory of Dreaming and the Activation-Synthesis Hypothesis. (After Hobson & McCarley, 1977)

neurotransmitters depleted during waking activity (Cohen, 1979; Hartmann, 1973). Other evidence suggests that REM sleep may be important in the development and maturation of brain neurons. **Figure 5.15** shows that the proportion of REM to total sleep decreases as we get older. Newborns spend 50 percent of their sleep in REM periods, infants between 30 and

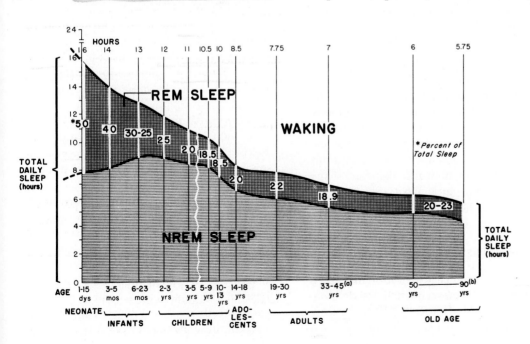

Figure 5.15
Changes in NREM and REM Sleep Over the Life Span. (From Roffwarg, Muzio, & Dement, 1966)

40 percent, and older children and adults about 20 percent. The greater amount of REM sleep in newborns and infants shows that REM is particularly important to the developing brain (Hobson, 1989).

Interim Summary

Sleep is far from being a uniform activity. EEG recordings reveal four stages of increasing depth of sleep. In addition, sleep is punctuated by periods of REM sleep, during which vivid dreaming usually occurs. The course of a night's sleep is marked by descents and ascents through the sleep stages, with REM periods occurring about every 90 minutes. Sleep deprivation studies have established a need for sleep, although sleeplessness is not particularly harmful. Sleep occurs as part of a circadian rhythm, perhaps developed in our evolutionary history because it promoted survival.

Dreaming is an altered state of consciousness that also appears to fulfill an important need, as established by REM deprivation studies. However, there are competing theories concerning exactly what psychological or physiological requirement this need fulfills. The study of dreaming, like the study of sleep itself, continues to pose many intriguing possibilities.

MEDITATION

Meditation is a method for voluntarily producing a state of consciousness distinct from both sleep and normal waking consciousness. To reach the meditative state, the meditator focuses his or her attention on a simple image, phrase, or sound, thereby reducing awareness of all other external and internal stimuli. In this section we consider both the elements of the meditative method and what psychologists have discovered about its effects on consciousness.

Elements of Meditation

Many people are familiar with a form of meditation known as Transcendental Meditation. **Transcendental Meditation, or TM,** is a secular adaptation of a meditation technique used

People who meditate usually report a sense of calmness and well-being that often continues into their daily activities.

in Yoga, a Hindu spiritual discipline dating back thousands of years. Similar forms of meditation have been developed in all the world's great religions, including Buddhism, Islam, Taoism, Judaism, and Christianity. For example, some Roman Catholics practice a meditative technique known as the "Prayer of the Heart."

Herbert Benson, who has conducted extensive research on meditation, analyzed the meditative techniques developed over the centuries by various religions (Benson, 1975). He found that all forms of meditation include four essential ingredients:

1. *A quiet environment.* In order to reduce external distractions, meditators usually practice in a quiet location with their eyes closed.
2. *A comfortable position.* A comfortable posture induces a feeling of relaxation and helps eliminate potential distraction from cramped muscles. The Yoga "lotus" position is often employed.
3. *A mental device.* In TM, meditators are instructed to repeat a special Hindu word, or mantra. The Prayer of the Heart uses the repeated phrase, "Lord Jesus Christ, have mercy on me." A form of Buddhist meditation uses the device of mentally focusing on the base of the nose and becoming aware of each breath as it is inhaled and exhaled. Each of these mental devices provides an at-

tentional focus that helps impede the normal stream of consciousness.

4. A *passive attitude.* Novice meditators find it extremely difficult to concentrate solely on the mental device. Consciousness becomes flooded with competing external stimuli and mental activity. When this happens, the meditator does not actively strive to suppress the distractions. Instead, he or she returns passively to the mental device and allows the distractions to pass from awareness. By practicing as little as 20 minutes twice a day, the meditator becomes increasingly able to focus attention and eliminate the stream of consciousness.

Psychological Effects

Meditators usually report a sense of calmness, detachment, and well-being while meditating that may continue into their daily activities. While meditating, some may also experience sensations of floating or even of being detached from their bodies. As one novice meditator reported:

> In the afternoon of the second day I had, for some minutes, a strong felt sense of being above and beyond the stream of breaths, thoughts, and bodily pulsings going on within "me." There was a delightful sense of detached freedom, a sense of living only in the "herenowness" of those moments, without past or future. (King, 1961, p. 57)

Such shifts in consciousness are not always pleasant. For some people, the thoughts and images that well up from the subconscious mind may be threatening and upsetting. Others may find it difficult to tolerate the sensations of floating and mind-body separation or the loss of the stream of consciousness. It is always advisable to learn meditation from someone experienced in dealing with negative reactions.

Physiological Effects

The most consistent physiological change produced by meditation is a shift in the usual patterns of brain-wave activity. When people are alert and active, the electroencephalogram shows an irregular wave pattern known as the *beta* rhythm. During periods of relaxed alertness such as occur in meditation, the EEG shifts into a pattern characterized by the presence of alpha waves, known as the *alpha* rhythm.

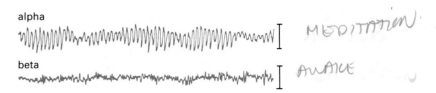

Figure 5.16
EEG Tracings of Alpha and Beta Waves. (From Blakemore, 1977)

Unlike beta waves, alpha waves occur very regularly, about 10 times per second (see **Figure 5.16**).

In addition to the alpha rhythm, some meditators may show temporary bursts of EEG activity characteristic of deep sleep. Other consistent physiological changes include a decrease in breathing rate, a decrease in oxygen consumption, and often a decrease in heart rate. In sum, meditation is accompanied by a state of reduced physiological arousal (Schuman, 1980).

Clinical Uses of Meditation

Many people believe that meditation is justified simply because it is distinct from sleeping or normal waking consciousness. But meditation is also used in medicine and clinical psychology as a therapy for anxiety and stress-related disorders such as headaches and hypertension (Shapiro & Shapiro, 1980). For example, one study investigated the effects of TM in a group of people who suffered from long-standing anxiety that had not been controlled by other methods of treatment. After six weeks of meditating twice a day, 40 percent of the subjects reported a significant decrease in their anxiety (Raskin, Bali, & Peeke, 1980). We will discuss the use of meditation for stress-related disorders in Chapter 15.

The factors responsible for the clinical effectiveness of meditation are not entirely understood. One factor is the ability of meditation to reduce physiological arousal. For example, meditation, like relaxation, produces a decrease in physiological arousal, which counteracts stress and anxiety (Holmes, 1984; Shapiro, 1985). A second factor appears to be the temporary respite from the demands of external reality that accompanies meditation: studies show that people who benefit most from meditation are also good hypnotic subjects who easily becomes absorbed in imaginative experiences and can resist distraction (Delmonte, 1985). Thus meditation appears to be similar to other therapies, such as relaxation and hypnosis, that promote reduced physiological arousal and a temporary suspension of normal waking consciousness.

Interim Summary

Meditation is a voluntary alteration in consciousness that is based on a highly selective form of attention. Meditators report a sense of calmness, detachment, and well-being that is correlated with a physiological state of low arousal. This state can sometimes be useful as a treatment for anxiety and stress-related disorders.

HYPNOSIS

Hypnosis can be defined as a psychological state, induced by a ritualistic procedure, in which the subject experiences changes in perception, memory, and behavior in response to suggestions by the hypnotist. Whether hypnosis also represents a state of consciousness distinctly different from normal waking consciousness is a matter of debate among psychologists.

Hypnosis has been studied and debated for about 200 years. The key figure in bringing hypnosis to public and scientific attention was Anton Mesmer, an Austrian physician who practiced in Paris in the late eighteenth century. Mesmer believed that illness was caused by an imbalance of invisible magnetic fluids in the body and that illness could be cured by reestablishing the proper balance. To achieve a cure, Mesmer would pass his hands across a patient's body, touch or massage the affected part, or wave a wand at the source of discomfort. Patients would often pass into a trancelike state, after which their symptoms would disappear. Mesmer's view of illness became known as the theory of *animal magnetism* and his therapeutic procedure as *mesmerism.*

Mesmer's unorthodox methods aroused the suspicions of the scientific and medical establishment of the day. In 1784, a commission of inquiry appointed by the king of France and chaired by Benjamin Franklin concluded that the theory of animal magnetism was erroneous and that Mesmer's cures were due mainly to

Anton Mesmer
(1734-1815)

Mesmer and his followers believed that restoring a free flow of "animal magnetism" through the body would restore psychological harmony and cure nervous complaints.

touch and imagination. Mesmer gave up his practice amid scandal, but mesmerism laid the groundwork for the development of today's hypnosis.

Since Mesmer's day, scientific interest in hypnosis has waxed and waned. In periods when interest runs high, hypnosis is hailed as a powerful method for exploring consciousness and for relieving both psychological and physical ailments. In periods when interest declines, hypnosis is dismissed as a minor curiosity, if not an outright sham. Today the pendulum is swinging toward a renewed interest in hypnosis. The nature, uses, and limitations of hypnosis are being examined more extensively and critically than at any previous time. In this section, we will discuss the process of inducing hypnosis, the effects of hypnotic suggestions, hypnotic susceptibility, and theories of hypnosis.

The Hypnotic Induction

The hypnotic procedure is composed of two segments: the *hypnotic induction* and *hypnotic suggestion*. The purpose of the hypnotic induction is to enhance the subject's response to subsequent hypnotic suggestions. There is no single method for inducing or guiding the subject into hypnosis. Rather, each hypnotist tends to have a preferred style. Nevertheless, all methods aim to prepare the subject for suggestions by (1) focusing attention, (2) reducing reality testing, and (3) increasing imaginative involvement.

FOCUSED ATTENTION

Hypnosis requires subjects to concentrate on the words and other stimuli presented to them by the hypnotist and simultaneously to ignore all other aspects of the external environment. As we saw in the last section, focusing attention in such a highly selective manner is also a core element in meditation. In hypnosis, however, attentional focusing is guided by the hypnotist. Old-fashioned induction techniques included asking the subject to stare into a flame or to follow a slowly swinging pendulum. Today the hypnotist is more likely to ask the subject to stare at a spot on the ceiling. The subject's eyes will inevitably become tired, and as the eyelids flutter and close, the hypnotist will suggest that the subject is becoming very calm and relaxed. The purpose is to have the subject enter a state of relaxed alertness.

REDUCED REALITY TESTING

Reality testing is the process by which we weigh our perceptions and beliefs against information from the external world. For example, if we think we see a friend in a crowd but believe he is out of town, we search for information to resolve the discrepancy. In hypnosis, the subject temporarily suspends normal reality testing and accepts the hypnotist's suggestions uncritically. This is not as unusual as it may sound. A similar process is at work when we read a compelling novel or watch a good film. On one level we know we are looking only at words on a page or images projected on a screen. But on another level, we feel as involved in the characters and events as if they were real.

IMAGINATIVE INVOLVEMENT

As the subject's normal reality testing recedes, his or her imaginative abilities come to the fore. The hypnotist guides the subject's imaginative involvement with detailed word pictures. For example, the hypnotist might present a relaxing image of lying on a quiet ocean beach by completely describing the associated sights, sounds, smells, and tactile sensations. Responsive hypnotic subjects often experience a vivid fantasy that is every bit as compelling as the deep involvement in a good book or film.

This imaginative heightening releases the subject's hold on external reality and promotes acceptance of the hypnotist's suggestions.

Hypnotic Suggestion

If focused attention, reduced reality testing, and imaginative involvement are successfully induced, the subject becomes deeply involved in the hypnotic experience and very responsive to suggestions from the hypnotist. The hypnotist can then guide the subject through often dramatic shifts in normal perception, behavior, and memory.

PERCEPTION

A deeply hypnotized subject following the hypnotist's instructions may be able to experience the smell of roses in a crumpled piece of paper or to see a friend sitting in an empty chair. These perceptual-like experiences occurring in the absence of adequate external stimuli are known as *positive hallucinations.* They are best understood as imaginative recreations of past experiences. Responsive hypnotic subjects are also often able to experience *negative hallucinations,* or an inability to perceive stimuli actually in the environment. If so instructed, these subjects will feel no pain when the skin is punctured with a sharp needle and will not wince when sniffing a bottle of ammonia. In negative hallucinations, the subject's imagination is strong enough to override normal perceptual functioning (Kihlstrom, 1979).

By altering normal perception, hypnosis can often be used to control pain. Cases of controlling the pain of surgical and dental opera-

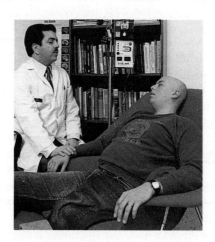

Psychologist Harold Wain uses hypnosis to help this cancer patient tolerate his chemotherapy treatment.

tions through hypnosis have been reported for over a century. In addition, hypnosis can sometimes by used to relieve long-standing, or chronic, pain. Some patients may be able to block out their pain sensations altogether. Others are able to lessen these sensations by transforming them into a feeling of pressure or tingling. Still others can benefit by simply learning to relax deeply when pain becomes intense (Hilgard & Hilgard, 1975). Experimental studies of hypnotic pain reduction have shown that subjects with good hypnotic ability can, on average, reduce the pain of holding an arm in ice water by about two thirds (Knox, Gekoski, Shum, & McLaughlin, 1981).

BEHAVIOR

Hypnotized subjects will usually behave in ways suggested by the hypnotist. This phenomenon is often exploited in stage hypnosis, where the hypnotist gets laughs from the audience by asking subjects to engage in silly behavior such as crowing like a rooster. It is, of course, unethical to ask people to perform under hypnosis in ways they would not perform in their normal waking state.

A less controversial form of hypnotic suggestion helps people control addictive behavior like smoking and overeating. The hypnotist might suggest alternative behaviors when the urge to smoke or overeat strikes. The hypnotist might also suggest vivid images of the adverse effects of these habits on health and appearance. Such suggestions are technically known as **posthypnotic suggestions** because, although received under hypnosis, they are carried out after the hypnotic session is terminated. The effectiveness of hypnosis in changing addictive behavior has not been thoroughly evaluated. Although many people benefit, others do not seem to be helped.

To what extent is the subject under the hypnotist's control? Although many people think hypnosis involves a loss of self-control, this does not seem to be the case. Interestingly enough, the hypnotized person is quite capable of deciding whether a suggestion is consistent with his or her ethical and moral standards. For example, people who have been hypnotized often later report that they "knew" they could resist the hypnotist's suggestions but that they either did not feel like making the effort or were quite willing to have the hypnotist temporarily take charge of their behavior and mental functioning. However, research has shown that if a hypnotist makes an unethical suggestion, subjects react in accordance with their normal waking values (Orne, 1972).

MEMORY

After being awakened from hypnosis, subjects are often unable to recall some or all of their hypnotic experiences. This phenomenon is known as *spontaneous amnesia.* **Amnesia** is a condition in which memories for certain events are unavailable to recall. Amnesia can also be induced by specific hypnotic suggestion. For example, the hypnotist may suggest that the subject forget the number 3 until told to remember it. When asked to count from 1 to 10, subjects may respond "1, 2, 4, 5, . . ." or even decide that they have 6 fingers on each hand (Orne, 1966). Although hypnotic amnesia rarely lasts long, ethical practice requires the hypnotist to remove all suggestions of amnesia by the end of the session.

Note that hypnotic amnesia does not obliterate memories. With the passage of time or with specific suggestion from the hypnotist, hypnotic amnesia can be removed and the memories retrieved. Hypnotic amnesia represents only a temporary inability to retrieve memories, not a permanent memory loss.

If hypnosis can produce amnesia, can it also produce the opposite effect—**hypermnesia,** or a heightened ability to recall past experiences? Could hypnosis help a student remember course material during an exam or an eyewitness recall the details of a crime more precisely? This question has received a great deal of popular and scientific attention in recent years because of the increasing use of hypnosis in police investigations.

Police often turn to hypnosis after a witness to a crime has produced as many details about the event as he or she can recall. In many cases the hypnotized witness seems able to recall further details. A famous case along these lines concerned the 1976 hijacking of a busload of schoolchildren who were hidden at a remote site and held for ransom. Fortunately, the bus driver was able to escape and contact the police. The driver had tried to memorize the license plate numbers of the vans used by the kidnappers but was unable to recall them when questioned by the police. However, when later hypnotized and asked to recall the events of the crime, he suddenly called out two numbers. One proved to be almost identical to the license plate number of one of the vans, leading to the arrest and conviction of the kidnappers (M. C. Smith, 1983). Reports like this have led many to conclude that hypnosis can be a powerful investigative tool.

In sharp contrast to such reports, however, a great deal of controlled research has failed to find any enhancement of memory with hypnosis (Orne, Whitehouse, Dinges, & Orne, 1988). Subjects under hypnosis often provide information on past events that they were unable to recall in the normal waking state, but most of this information is found to be inaccurate. The process by which imagined events are perceived by the subject as true memories is known as **confabulation.** One study used a group of subjects and 60 slides of common objects. The slides were shown to the subjects three times in a row. They were then asked to recall as many of the items as possible immediately after the showings and on each of seven subsequent days. These repeated attempts to recall the information led to some hypermnesia—there was a 27 percent increase in recalled items by the end of the week. On the eighth day, subjects were asked to relax and focus all their attention on the slides seen the week before. Half of the subjects did this with hypnosis and half did it without hypnosis. As seen in **Figure 5.17**, the hypnotized subjects recalled more previously unreported objects than did the control group. However, the great majority of this newly recalled information had not been presented on the original slides and was therefore erroneous. Thus we see that hypnosis does lead subjects to report events not previously reported in the waking state, but most of these reports are confabulated memories (Dywan & Bowers, 1983).

There are two further reasons that psychologists are concerned with the use of hypnosis as an investigative tool. The first is that hypnotized subjects are usually unaware that their confabulated memories are inaccurate. They generally fail to realize that their made-up memories derive from imagination rather than from actual events. In fact, subjects believe in the reality of confabulated memories as strongly as they believe in the reality of memories based on fact. In criminal trials this can be a problem because jurors are likely to believe witnesses who are confident about their testimony, even if the testimony is inaccurate (Kassin, 1986; M. C. Smith, 1983).

The second reason for concern is that, as we have already discussed, hypnotized subjects are very responsive to suggestions from the hypnotist. Even if subjects do not spontaneously confabulate memories, the hypnotist may subtly suggest memories for events that did not in fact take place. For example, investigative hypnotists sometimes ask hypnotized subjects to "zoom in" on a past event surrounding a crime as a means of recalling the details of the event. If the subject was not close enough to the original event to see it clearly, the instruction to "zoom in" is simply an indirect suggestion to confabulate the details of the event (Laurence & Perry, 1983). The ability of hypnotic instructions to influence subjects' memories has been demonstrated in laboratory studies. Laurence and Perry (1983) asked 27 highly hypnotizable subjects to remember events occurring on a previous night. While under hypnosis, the subjects were asked if they had heard loud noises that had awakened them and, if so, to describe the noises. After hypnosis, the subjects were again asked about their memories for the night in question. Of the 27 subjects, 13 reported that they had been awakened by noises. Even when these 13 subjects were told that the noises had been suggested to them under hypnosis, about half of them still maintained that the noises had occurred. One subject replied, "I'm pretty certain I heard them. As a matter of fact, I'm pretty damned certain. I'm positive I heard these noises."

In sum, the use of hypnosis to retrieve

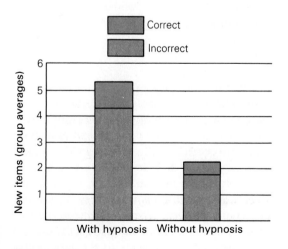

Figure 5.17
The Effects of Hypnosis on Recalling New Items of Information.
Hypnotized subjects recalled more items not previously reported than did nonhypnotized control subjects. However, most of this information consisted of incorrect, or confabulated, memories. (From Dywan & Bowers, 1983)

past events is fraught with difficulties. Subjects may spontaneously confabulate memories or may accept direct or subtle suggestions to remember events that did not really occur. Moreover, subjects are often quite confident of the reality of these false memories. In criminal trials such confidence is a major factor in determining whether jurors will regard witnesses' testimony as credible.

Hypnotic Susceptibility

Given the same hypnotic-induction procedure, some people may become deeply hypnotized, whereas others experience few if any effects. Ten to 20 percent of the population is highly susceptible to hypnosis, 5 to 10 percent cannot be hypnotized, and the remainder show varying degrees of susceptibility (E. R. Hilgard, 1965).

There is no simple way to predict a person's ability to be hypnotized. The only sure test is to perform a hypnotic induction and see if the subject responds. **Hypnotic susceptibility tests** are standardized procedures used to determine a person's responsiveness to hypnosis. For example, the Stanford Hypnotic Susceptibility Scale consists of a brief induction procedure and a series of test suggestions of increasing difficulty. Suggesting to subjects that their extended arms will move slowly apart is an example of an "easy" test suggestion. Most subjects respond to this suggestion. In a difficult test suggestion, to which most people do not respond, subjects might be told that they will be unable to detect a strong odor, such as ammonia, when it is presented. Subjects are assigned a hypnotic susceptibility score depending on the number of test suggestions to which they respond (Weitzenhoffer & Hilgard, 1962).

Psychologists have found that people who score high on such tests also have the ability to become deeply involved in imaginative areas of experience, such as reading a novel, listening to music, and enjoying nature or adventurous activities like mountain climbing or airplane flying. When engaged in such activities, they become totally absorbed with what they are doing, are able to dissolve the boundaries between themselves and the object of their experience, and are able to ignore distractions (J. R. Hilgard, 1970). One highly susceptible subject reported the following reaction to reading Orwell's *1984:*

> I identify myself with the character in *1984,* with Winston Smith, who was tortured at the end, fearing rats. His head

was in a cage and he felt he would have to submit. I felt the fear that he felt as it came closer, closer. Walking back from the Union after finishing the book I had a problem relating myself to my present environment, to the stuff around me, for I was so entangled in the story that I had become exhausted. (J. R. Hilgard, 1970, p. 26)

Thus, the capacity for spontaneous involvement in imaginative activities and the ability to enter deeply into the hypnotic experience are related. Indeed, we might say that a hypnotic induction is a fairly structured situation that allows certain people to adopt a state of consciousness similar to one that they spontaneously cultivate in their everyday lives. An important implication of hypnotic susceptibility is that many people will not be able to achieve deep hypnosis. This obviously limits the usefulness of hypnosis as a therapeutic tool in psychology and medicine.

Theories of Hypnosis

Theories of hypnosis attempt to account for the often dramatic responses of susceptible subjects to hypnotic suggestions. There are two major explanations for hypnosis. **Nonstate theories** hold that hypnotic responsiveness can be explained by psychological processes that do not involve a special state of consciousness. **State theories** hold that hypnotic responsiveness is the result of an alteration in consciousness that is fundamentally distinct from normal waking consciousness (Barber, 1979; Sheehan & Perry, 1976).

Nonstate Theories

In general, nonstate theorists aim to demonstrate that hypnotic responsiveness is due to the combination of motivation to comply with the hypnotist's requests and ability to become imaginatively involved with specific suggestions (Spanos, 1986). In one study, which focused on the motivational factor, the response to hypnotic suggestions was assessed following three types of instructions. Subjects in the hypnotic-induction group were given standard hypnotic instructions. Subjects in the task-motivation group were not given an induction but were encouraged to cooperate with the suggestions and urged to do their best. Subjects in the control group were simply told they would be taking a test. The results were that the hypnotic-induction and task-motivation groups performed equally well in response to the suggestions, both performing better than the control group. The researcher concluded that motivation to comply with suggestions is a major factor in hypnotic responsiveness (Barber, 1965).

Coe and Sarbin (1977) liken hypnotically susceptible subjects to dramatic actors who become so involved in their roles that they lose all distinction between themselves and their performance. Hypnosis is thus a form of "role enactment" in which the subject comes to believe totally in the imaginative experiences suggested by the hypnotist. According to this theory, people who have talent and experience in imaginative role enactments should also be good hypnotic subjects. In a test of this prediction, Sarbin and Coe (1972) demonstrated that drama majors scored higher on tests of hypnotic susceptibility than did science majors. The evidence that hypnotically susceptible people also show great imaginative involvement in everyday events is also consistent with this theory.

STATE THEORIES

State theorists insist that hypnosis is more than motivation combined with imaginative role enactment, although these are accepted as important factors. According to the state view, hypnosis represents an altered state of consciousness. Evidence for this view stems from people's reports of their subjective experience when deeply hypnotized. They report, for example, that responses to suggestions have an automatic and effortless quality. It is as if the subjects temporarily assign control over their behavior to the hypnotist (Bowers, 1976).

If hypnosis is a distinct state of consciousness, we might expect this state to be correlated with a specific pattern of EEG and physiological activity, as is the case in sleep and dreaming. However, EEG studies have shown that the brain wave patterns of hypnotized subjects are indistinguishable from patterns of nonhypnotized subjects (Barber, 1969). The absence of distinct physiological patterns does not disprove the state hypothesis, but it does make it more difficult to maintain.

Attempts have also been made to show that hypnosis is correlated with mental events different from normal waking consciousness. For example, Ernest Hilgard and Josephine Hilgard (1975) have proposed that deeply hypnotized subjects experience a division, or dissociation, of consciousness not seen in the normal state. **Dissociated consciousness** can be defined as a state in which two conscious activities are simultaneously carried out with little

or no communication between the two. For example, hypnotized subjects may describe their experience in terms of a hypnotized self that complied with the operator's suggestions and a second, nonhypnotized self that more or less monitored the hypnotized self. This second self has been called "the hidden observer" by the Hilgards.

The Hilgards discovered an interesting example of the "hidden observer" in the course of experiments on the hypnotic control of pain. In these experiments, subjects held one hand in a tank of ice water for about a minute in order to induce pain. Every 10 seconds, they rated their pain on a scale from 0 to 10, where 0 meant no pain and 10 meant pain so severe they wanted to remove their hand from the ice water.

The top curve in **Figure 5.18** shows that nonhypnotized subjects reached a pain level of 10 within 25 seconds. The bottom curve shows how highly susceptible subjects rated their pain when hypnotized and given suggestions that they would feel no pain. Their pain ratings reached a level of 2 after 25 seconds and then showed no further change.

Then, in an interesting variation on this experiment, the Hilgards asked their hypnotized subjects to indicate whether "some part" of them was in fact aware of the pain by pressing a key with their free hand. The middle

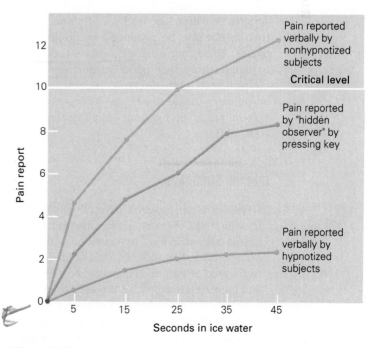

Figure 5.18
Pain Intensity Reported by Nonhypnotized Subjects, Hypnotized Subjects, and the "Hidden Observer." (From Hilgard & Hilgard, 1975)

curve of Figure 5.18 shows what happened. While the hypnotized self was reporting low pain levels, the other self or "hidden observer" experienced fairly intense pain, but less pain than in the nonhypnotized state. In other words, the hypnotized subjects were simultaneously aware of two different levels of pain. These two selves communicated with the experimenters in two different, dissociated response channels.

Here is how one of the Hilgards' subjects described his experience after the experiment:

> Both parts were concentrating on what you said—not to feel pain. The water bothered the hidden part a little because it felt it a little, but the hypnotized part was not thinking of my arm at all. (Hilgard & Hilgard, 1975, p. 173)

In brief, state theories of hypnosis derive primarily from subjects' reports of altered consciousness while deeply hypnotized. But such reports are viewed with skepticism by many psychologists because they raise all the old problems of introspection. For example, some psychologists feel that the "hidden observer" is no more than a suggestion accepted as valid by highly suggestible subjects (Spanos, Gwynn, & Stam, 1983; Spanos, 1986). Nonstate theorists, rather than accept hypnosis as an altered state of consciousness, prefer to interpret responsiveness to hypnotic suggestions in terms of motivational and ability factors. These theorists suggest that there are no hypnotic phenomena that cannot also be produced by nonhypnotic means. The major goal of nonstate theorists is to demonstrate that good imaginative ability, coupled with motivation to comply with another person's suggestions, can account for the known range of hypnotic phenomena (Wagstaff, 1981).

Interim Summary

Hypnosis is an induced psychological state in which the person is responsive to suggested alterations of perception, behavior, and memory. It is induced by a combination of focused attention, reduced reality testing, and increased imaginative involvement.

Hypnosis can be used to alter people's perceptions of external objects and internal sensations and so has proved useful in relieving pain. Although people often behave in ways suggested by the hypnotist, the use of hypnosis to change addictive behavior has not been thoroughly evaluated. Hypnosis can also be used to induce a temporary amnesia, but there is no good evidence that hypnosis can induce hypermnesia.

There is a wide range of individual differences in susceptibility to hypnosis. Highly susceptible subjects, roughly 10 to 20 percent of the population, often have a capacity for deep absorption in imaginative activities during their daily lives.

Theories of hypnosis attempt to explain the responsiveness of susceptible subjects to hypnotic suggestions. Nonstate theories hold that this responsiveness, or suggestibility, is due primarily to enhanced motivation and the ability to become imaginatively involved with the hypnotic procedure. State theories hold that hypnosis is an altered state of consciousness distinct from normal waking consciousness.

PSYCHOACTIVE DRUGS

When William James (1902) first wrote about states of consciousness hidden from ordinary consciousness by the "filmiest of screens," he may have been thinking of the many forms of altered consciousness produced by psychoactive drugs. A **psychoactive drug** is a compound that produces a change in conscious experience by altering the chemical activity of the brain. Many such drugs were known even in James' day, including alcohol, cocaine, marijuana, and nitrous oxide ("laughing gas"). Today we know of an ever-increasing number of consciousness-altering drugs.

Why are psychoactive drugs important to understanding the psychology of consciousness? First of all, we can learn about the elements and structure of normal waking consciousness by studying the way in which drugs alter our perception, emotions, cognitive processes, and behavior. Second, by studying the way psychoactive drugs work in the brain, psychologists and other neuroscientists hope ultimately to understand how consciousness is related to electrical and chemical events in the brain. Thus, studying the effects of psychoactive drugs helps unravel the nature of conscious experience in both its psychological and physical dimensions.

Many psychoactive drugs are derivatives of plants with psychoactive ingredients. These plants have been used for centuries for medicinal and recreational purposes. The psychoactive ingredients are usually liberated by smoking, brewing, or eating the plants. In modern times chemists have been able to isolate the active chemical agents in many of these plants, which has led to the laboratory development of entirely new psychoactive compounds. These synthetic compounds are often used as therapeutic drugs in medicine. In addition, they often become drugs of abuse, both by people with drug prescriptions and by others who obtain drugs illegally. Drug abuse, in turn, leads to restrictive laws, which lead to the development of black markets and drug subcultures.

The history of heroin is a case in point. *Heroin* is a powerful analgesic, or painkiller, used in medical practice. An **analgesic** is an agent that produces insensitivity without loss of consciousness. Heroin is derived from morphine, which is the active ingredient in opium, a natural substance derived from the opium poppy. In addition to their analgesic properties, opium, morphine, and heroin often produce euphoric (pleasurable) and detached feelings that temporarily banish worries and tensions.

Opium has been used medically and recreationally for hundreds of years. Morphine and heroin were developed from opium in the nineteenth century as medical analgesics but soon became drugs of abuse. Thus, in 1914 the U.S. Congress prohibited the nonmedical use of all three compounds. Today, however, there are probably about 500,000 heroin addicts who use the drug illegally (Ray, 1983).

We will have more to say about the problem of drug abuse in Chapter 16. At this point we will concentrate on the alterations in consciousness produced by the four major classes of psychoactive drugs. They are (1) **sedatives,** which decrease activity levels, induce calmness, and produce sleep, (2) **stimulants,** which increase activity levels, enhance positive feelings, and heighten alertness; (3) **psychedelics,** which produce alterations in perception, thought, and imagination; and (4) miscellaneous drugs, such as marijuana and PCP, which produce a mixture of sedative, stimulant, or psychedelic effects.

Sedatives

There are three major types of sedatives. The oldest, *ethyl alcohol,* was probably produced as long ago as 6400 B.C. in the form of wine and beer. The process of distilling fermented grains and fruits to produce a purer form of alcohol was introduced about A.D. 1000 and remains the basis for the manufacture of *spirits* like whiskey, gin, and vodka.

A second class of sedatives, the *barbiturates,* was discovered by chemists about 100 years ago. Some 2500 barbiturates have since been developed and are now commonly used both in medical practice and as street drugs (Ray, 1983).

Finally, the *benzodiazepines,* such as Librium, Valium, and Halcion were developed beginning about 1960. Sometimes known as minor *tranquilizers,* the benzodiazepines are today among the most widely prescribed drugs in North America.

Although ethyl alcohol, the barbiturates, and the benzodiazepines are chemically different compounds, they have very similar psychological effects, as illustrated in **Figure 5.19**. Low doses reduce anxiety and tension. At slightly higher doses, and with a further decrease in anxiety, people tend to become less inhibited, more talkative, and more sociable. This is, of course, one of the chief motivations for the social drinking of alcoholic beverages. At still higher doses, sedation occurs. **Sedation** is a calm, tranquil state of consciousness in which the person is fully awake but somewhat detached from the environment. This state is often the goal of those who use barbiturates for recreational purposes. Sedation quickly passes into **intoxication,** a state in which the body is literally poisoned and behavior begins to become uncoordinated, reaction time is slowed, skilled activities are increasingly difficult, and speech is slurred. In the next stage, the person experiences a loss of waking consciousness and falls asleep. This sleep stage may progress into **anesthesia,** in which there is a loss of sensation. In the anesthetized state, the person fails to react to even painful stimuli. Finally, the person may pass into **coma,** a state of unconsciousness below normal sleep. It is extremely difficult to arouse the person in a state of coma. At even higher doses the body's physiological processes may cease altogether and death may occur.

Sedatives are central nervous system depressants. Although the exact details of this process are still unknown, it is widely presumed that the sedatives affect chemical transmission at specific brain synapses (Barchas, Berger, Ciaranello, & Elliot, 1977). For example, we know that the benzodiazepines increase the activity of GABA, a neurotransmitter that inhibits, or damps, neural activity in postsynaptic neurons. Thus, the brain may contain its own

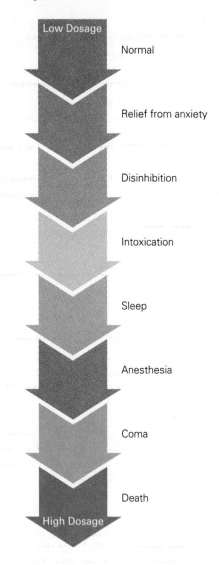

Figure 5.19
The Effects of
Increasing Doses
of Sedative-
Hypnotic Drugs.

benzodiazepine-like neurotransmitter. Taking a benzodiazepine may simply supplement this "natural sedative" when it is incapable of sufficiently calming the central nervous system. However, other sedatives such as alcohol probably exert their effects by other mechanisms.

The chief medical uses of sedatives are (1) as minor tranquilizers, to combat anxiety and tension; (2) as a sleeping potion, to combat insomnia; and (3) as an anesthetic during surgery. Alcohol was used for these purposes until about 100 years ago, when it was replaced by the more easily administered and faster-acting barbiturates. The chief problem with barbiturates is the potential for overdose. Until recently, several thousand deaths occurred each year because of intentional or accidental barbiturate overdose (Cooper, 1978). Fortunately, it is virtually impossible to overdose with the more recently developed benzodiazepines, and

these compounds have virtually replaced the barbiturates as antianxiety and sleep-inducing medications. The major disadvantage of benzodiazepine use is an intensification of the sedative effect if alcohol is imbibed at the same time, leading to intoxication. This can present a serious hazard if the person attempts to drive or use machinery (American Psychiatric Association, 1991).

Stimulants

The stimulants include caffeine, cocaine, and the amphetamines. Caffeine is the most widely used of the stimulants. It is derived from the bean of the coffee plant, whose psychoactive effects were discovered in the Middle East more than 3000 years ago. Although most caffeine is consumed in the form of coffee, it is also present in tea and cola drinks, as well as many over-the-counter (nonprescription) cold remedies and painkillers. Caffeine is generally considered a mild stimulant, yet many medical problems have been traced to its use. Excessive consumption of caffeine can cause anxiety, insomnia, headaches, irregular heartbeats, and stomach irritation.

Cocaine is the active ingredient of the coca plant. The use of cocaine as a stimulant was discovered centuries ago by the Peruvian Indians, who chewed the leaves of the coca plant to increase stamina and to relieve fatigue and hunger. Cocaine in powder form is usually "snorted" through the mucous membranes of the nose, which produces an intense but relatively brief "rush." A very powerful form of cocaine known as "crack" is smoked in a pipe, which has become the preferred route of administration of cocaine abusers.

Amphetamines are a group of drugs first synthesized in the 1920s. They were widely used by combat troops on both sides during World War II to reduce fatigue and increase feelings of self-confidence. After the war, the ready availability of amphetamines led to major epidemics of amphetamine abuse in Japan, Western Europe, and, later, in North America. A form of amphetamine known as "ice" (methamphetamine hydrochloride) has become a new drug of abuse because of its potency and because its effects last for several hours (Cho, 1990).

The use of cocaine and amphetamines produces an increase in brain activation. This effect is due to heightened activity at synapses that utilize norepinephrine or dopamine as neurotransmitters, particularly in the brain stem and limbic system (see Chapter 2).

At low and moderate doses, cocaine and amphetamines have three major psychological effects:

1. *Euphoria.* Stimulants replace the blues with a feeling of well-being. The positive mood colors the user's perceptions, so that external reality seems exciting and wondrous. The person's own self-perception is also enhanced, creating a sense of self-confidence and competence.
2. *Increased alertness.* Stimulants counteract the fatigue that comes with long hours of work. They are therefore sometimes used by students cramming for exams, truck drivers on long hauls, and athletes in grueling competitions. Stimulants do not create energy, nor do they make people smarter or more talented. But, by masking the symptoms of fatigue and enhancing confidence, they encourage users to go beyond normal levels of endurance.
3. *Enhanced attention.* Stimulants appear to enhance the ability to maintain focused attention on stimuli relevant to the task at hand. For this reason, stimulants are sometimes prescribed for hyperactive children who have short attention spans and difficulty concentrating in school.

Many users become dependent on stimulants because of these effects. Unfortunately, stimulant use carries potentially severe hazards. When stimulants are discontinued after even a relatively short period of use, a rebound effect occurs—depression replaces euphoria and fatigue replaces alertness. Taken in high doses over several days, amphetamines can produce an alteration in consciousness known as *amphetamine psychosis.* In this state abusers may experience frightening changes in the appearance of objects and delusions of being persecuted by mysterious forces. It is not unusual for hospital emergency room personnel to mistake a temporary amphetamine psychosis for a case of schizophrenia, a severe psychotic disorder we will discuss in Chapter 16. Thus, the same drug that, at low doses, creates feelings of well-being can, at high doses, create a temporary mental disorder of the utmost severity.

Psychedelics

The psychedelics produce marked alterations in consciousness. The term *psychedelic* was coined from two Greek words meaning "mind expanding." Another term frequently used for these drugs is *hallucinogens,* a reference to their ability to distort perception.

Scientific interest in psychedelic drugs dates from the discovery of LSD (lysergic acid diethylamide) by a Swiss chemist, Albert Hofman, in the late 1930s. Hofman produced LSD from a fungus known to have mildly psychoactive properties. The discovery of LSD led to the discovery of many other psychedelic compounds and to renewed interest in plants with psychedelic properties. These plants include the peyote cactus, from which *mescaline* is derived, and the *Psilocybe mexicana* mushroom, the source of *psilocybin.*

Even at low doses, the psychedelics produce striking changes in perception. Objects take on a shimmering outline or aura; textures become deep and rich; colors become vivid and intense. The perception of time slows dramatically so that a brief glance at an object is experienced as a long and careful study. With the eyes closed, fantastic images appear. These may consist of swirling designs, patterns of colors that shift like a kaleidoscope, or imaginary scenes of people and places that unroll like a technicolor movie. These images are sometimes pleasant and enjoyable and at other times grotesque and frightening (S. H. Snyder, 1974).

A user's perception of his or her own body may also be affected. Users frequently report a feeling of **depersonalization,** a state in which the body is experienced as separate from the self. Thus, users may feel that they are able to observe themselves from afar. Sometimes, even the sense of self as a separate object begins to disintegrate into a mystical feeling of union with the universe.

Psychedelics also seem to unlock long-forgotten or avoided thoughts, feelings, and attitudes. As these memories come into consciousness, some people feel they have gained new insights into themselves and their relationships with others. For this reason, there is some interest among researchers in the potential use of certain psychedelics in psychotherapy. Other users may become anxious and despondent when they discover or rediscover negative aspects of their personalities. Thus the emotional reactions caused by psychedelic use may vary from uplifting euphoria to despair (Grinspoon & Bakalar, 1990a).

Neuroscientists are interested in the psychedelics because their chemical structure closely resembles the structure of some of the brain's own neurotransmitters (see Chapter 2).

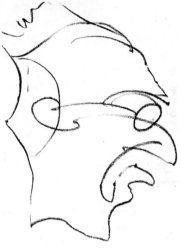

These drawings are self-portraits done while under the influence of LSD. They show the progressive effects of the drug experience.

Some psychedelics are closely related to dopamine, and others are similar to serotonin. Many researchers now believe that LSD, for example, produces its effects by competing with the normal activity of serotonin in the brain.

Miscellaneous Drugs

Marijuana and *PCP* fall into a fourth, miscellaneous category of psychoactive drugs that have mixed sedative, psychedelic, or stimulant effects. The marijuana plant, *Cannabis sativa*, probably originated in China and has been cultivated for at least 5000 years in many areas of the world (R. T. Jones, 1980). Its psychoactive ingredient, tetrahydrocannabinol (known as *THC*), is found primarily in the resin of its small, upper leaves and flowering tops. Throughout the centuries, marijuana has been smoked, eaten, and taken in a brew of fairly mild potency. Although marijuana is an illegal substance in North America, the cultivation of marijuana is a billion-dollar-a-year industry in California and Oregon and probably generates more income in Hawaii than the sugar industry (Drinkall & Martin, 1980; Pierce, 1985).

The amount of THC in the average "joint" smoked by North Americans produces a fairly mild high with both sedative and psychedelic effects. Among the former are relaxation, a degree of intoxication, some loss of social inhibitions, and an upbeat, humorous mood. Speech is somewhat slurred and coordination is impaired. Like alcohol, marijuana definitely decreases driving ability and undoubtedly contributes to many automobile accidents (NIDA, 1982).

During the marijuana high, concentration alternates between the external environment and more introspective concerns. Psychedelic-like shifts in perception occur, giving objects a depth, vividness, and sharpness not experienced in normal perception. This is especially true of auditory perception, such as listening to music. Among the more pronounced effects of marijuana is a distortion of memory. As one user described it:

My memory span for conversation is somewhat shortened, so that I may forget what the conversation is about even before it is finished. I think I've said something when actually I've only thought about saying it. My memory of what went on when I was stoned is poor afterwards. I can continue to carry on an intelligent conversation even when my memory span is so short that I forget the beginnings of what I started to say. (S. H. Snyder, 1971, p. 51)

A great deal of experimental research has shown that marijuana use interferes with the ability to recall previously learned information. This impaired recall may be due to the disruption of normal activity in acetylcholine-utilizing neurons in the limbic system of the brain (Miller & Branconnier, 1983). The role of acetylcholine in memory is further discussed in Chapter 7.

Strongly negative experiences with marijuana are fairly uncommon. Chief among these are feelings of anxiety that sometimes escalate into a feeling of panic, especially if users are apprehensive about the experience to begin with.

As with any other drug, increased doses lead to increased effects and overdoses may lead to temporary mental disorganization and loss of control (R. T. Jones, 1980).

Experts are not in complete agreement concerning the health hazards of marijuana. Studies of long-term marijuana users in Jamaica, Costa Rica, and Greece have found no evidence that regular use of marijuana impairs health. These studies lead some experts to regard marijuana as a relatively benign substance (Grinspoon & Bakalar, 1990a). However, these studies were limited to adult male users who smoked a relatively mild form of marijuana. Critics of these studies are concerned with the potential health hazard to children and adolescents and to women, especially in light of the increasing use of relatively potent forms of marijuana in North America (Petersen, 1984). Laboratory studies with animals have also raised questions about the effect of marijuana on the respiratory, reproductive, and immune systems. Given the lack of definitive information in this area, the U.S. National Academy of Sciences has advised that "marijuana has a broad range of psychological and biological effects, some of which, at least under certain conditions, are harmful to human health." Their report called for intensified study of the mental and physical health effects of marijuana, stating that what is known or suspected justifies "serious national concern" (National Academy of Sciences, 1982).

THC is known to stimulate specific postsynaptic receptors in the cortex, the limbic system, and the cerebellum (Matsuda, Lolait, Brownstein, Young, & Bonner, 1990). Because the brain contains specific THC receptors, there must be a "natural THC" neurotransmitter in the brain. Researchers hope to discover how this natural chemical works, what its effects are, and how the natural substance avoids producing the unwanted side effects of marijuana. This knowledge would open the possibility of developing a synthetic marijuana having desirable psychological and medical uses without harmful side effects.

PCP (phencyclidine) was first synthesized in the 1950s for use as a surgical anesthetic. The use of PCP as an anesthetic was soon discontinued in humans, however, because of the psychoactive side effects. As a recreational drug, PCP (in powder form) is usually combined with tobacco or marijuana and smoked as a "joint."

PCP causes a mixture of stimulant and psychedelic effects (Petersen & Stillman, 1978).

In the relatively low doses available in a joint, PCP causes a mild euphoria and a feeling that one's problems have been left behind. Like the psychedelics, PCP causes distortions in body image and depersonalization experiences. Unlike the psychedelics, however, PCP does not cause striking distortions in visual perception. As you might expect, this mixture of effects is accompanied by widespread changes in a variety of neurotransmitter systems. Like amphetamines, PCP increases brain levels of norepinephrine and dopamine; like the psychedelics, it affects activity at serotonin synapses; like marijuana, it appears to impair activity at acetylcholine synapses (Johnson, 1987).

The major effect sought by most PCP users is a dreamlike state accompanied by a sensation of floating or "walking on clouds." Some users experience mystical feelings of self-dissolution and unity with the universe. Users must learn to tolerate certain negative experiences as well: feelings of being numb or paralyzed, decreased ability to think clearly or to speak coherently, and periods of anxiety, paranoia, and restlessness. After a high lasting several hours, users often feel quite depressed (Grinspoon & Bakalar, 1990a).

Medical authorities consider PCP an extremely dangerous drug because of the severe reactions caused by overdose or long-term use. Possible effects of overdose, described as the four "Cs," include (1) *combativeness,* such as agitated or violent behavior, *(2) catatonia,* or a paralysis-like rigidity of the body, (3) *convulsions,* or epileptic-like seizures, and (4) *coma,* a deep, unresponsive sleep (Smith, Wesson, Buxton, Seymour, & Kramer, 1978). Long-term users often report having difficulty thinking clearly and complain of emotional blandness. Abuse of PCP is clearly a serious drug problem (Petersen & Stillman, 1978).

Table 5.2 summarizes the types of psychoactive drugs, their psychological effects, and the duration of those effects.

Interim Summary

A psychoactive drug is a compound that changes conscious experience by altering the chemical activity of the brain. Although most psychoactive drugs are legally limited to medical uses, illegal recreational use is not uncommon.

The major types of drugs include (1) sedatives, which induce calmness and sleep; (2) stimulants, which induce euphoria, in-

Table 5.2   Psychoactive Drugs

Classification	Examples	Psychological Effects	Duration of Effects (in hours)
Sedatives	Alcohol (ethyl alcohol)	Relaxation; reduced inhibitions	3 to 6
	Barbiturates (e.g., Amytal, Seconal)	Relaxation; disorientation; sleep	1 to 16
	Benzodiazepines (e.g., Librium, Valium, Dalmane)	Reduced anxiety; relaxation; sedation	4 to 8
Narcotics	Opium Morphine Heroin	Analgesia; euphoria; drowsiness; nausea	3 to 6
Stimulants	Amphetamines (e.g., Benzedrine, Dexedrine)	Increased alertness; excitation; decreased fatigue	2 to 4
	Caffeine (coffee, cola, tea)	Increased alertness; excitation; decreased fatigue	2 to 4
	Cocaine	Euphoria; excitation; alertness; decreased fatigue	2 to 3
Psychedelics	Lysergic acid diethylamide (LSD) Mescaline Psilocybin	Distortions; illusions; hallucinations; time disorientation	1 to 8
Miscellaneous	Marijuana PCP (phencyclidine)	Euphoria; relaxed inhibitions; increased sensory sensitivity; disorientation	2 to 4

Adapted from Oakley Ray, *Drugs, Society, and Human Behavior* (3rd. ed.). St. Louis: Mosby, 1983.

crease alertness, and enhance attention; (3) psychedelics, which produce alterations in visual perception, memory, and mind-body relationships; and (4) miscellaneous drugs such as marijuana and PCP, which combine sedative, stimulant, or psychedelic effects.

The study of the effects of psychoactive drugs helps psychologists map out major dimensions and categories of consciousness. By understanding how drugs act in the brain, psychologists hope to unravel the relationship between forms of consciousness experience and central nervous system activity.

SUMMARY

1. Consciousness exists as a continuous succession of sensations, thoughts, images, and feelings, which William James called the *stream of consciousness*. We are aware at any given time of only a selected portion of the external and internal stimuli potentially available to consciousness. Stimuli that are outside of conscious awareness can influence our behavior. In addition, our ability to process information does not necessarily depend on conscious awareness. With highly practiced tasks, information can be processed automatically and subconsciously.

2. EEG recordings reveal four stages of increasing depth of sleep. Sleep is also punctuated by regular periods of REM sleep, during which vivid dreaming usually occurs. Sleep occurs as part of a circadian rhythm, perhaps developed in our evolutionary history because it promoted survival. Dreaming is an altered state of consciousness that appears to fulfill an important need. However, there are competing theories concerning exactly what psychological or physiological requirement dreaming fulfills.

3. Meditation is a voluntary alteration in consciousness that is based on a highly selective form of attention. Meditators report a sense of calmness, detachment, and well-being that is correlated with a state of low physiological arousal. This state can sometimes be useful as a treatment for anxiety and stress-related disorders.

4. In hypnosis the person is responsive to suggested alterations of perception, behavior, and memory. Hypnosis has proved useful in relieving pain, but the use of hypnosis to change addictive behavior like smoking has not been validated. Good hypnotic subjects have a capacity for deep absorption in imaginative activities during their daily lives. So-called nonstate theories of hypnosis hold that hypnosis is due primarily to an ability to become imaginatively involved with hypnotic suggestions. State theories hold that hypnosis is an altered state of consciousness distinct from normal waking consciousness.

5. A psychoactive drug is a compound that changes conscious experience by altering the chemical activity of the brain. The major types of drugs include: (1) sedatives, which induce calmness and sleep; (2) stimulants, which induce euphoria, increase alertness, and enhance attention; (3) psychedelics, which produce alterations in visual perception, memory, and mind-body relationships; and (4) miscellaneous drugs such as marijuana and PCP, which combine sedative, stimulant, or psychedelic effects. By understanding how drugs act in the brain, psychologists hope to unravel the relationship between forms of conscious experience and central nervous system activity.

KEY INDIVIDUALS

William James
Sigmund Freud
Ellen Langer
Eugene Aserinsky
Nathaniel Kleitman
J. Allan Hobson
Robert McCarley
Herbert Benson
Anton Mesmer
Ernest and Josephine Hilgard
Albert Hofman

KEY RESEARCH

the introspective method of investigating consciousness
shadowing technique for studying attention
priming procedure
studies of effortful and automatic information processing
development of EEG machines and sleep research
REM and NREM sleep
sleep deprivation studies
dream deprivation studies
Freud's theory of dreaming
the activation-synthesis hypothesis of dreaming
the ingredients of meditation
hypnosis and memory
the "hidden observer"

KEY TERMS

introspection
consciousness
subconscious processes
preconscious processes
unconscious processes
selective attention
mindlessness
mindfulness
sleep spindles
delta waves
REM sleep
NREM sleep
circadian rhythms
insomnia
sleepwalking
narcolepsy
sleep apnea
manifest content
latent content
meditation
Transcendental Meditation (TM)
hypnosis
posthypnotic suggestions
amnesia
hypermnesia
confabulation
hypnotic susceptibility tests
nonstate theories
state theories
dissociated consciousness
psychoactive drug
analgesic
sedatives
stimulants
psychedelics
sedation
intoxication
anesthesia
coma
depersonalization

Part Two

LEARNING AND COGNITION

211

A Conversation With . . .

Elizabeth F. Loftus is Professor of Psychology at the University of Washington. Dr. Loftus is a cognitive psychologist who specializes in the study of memory.

Q What can we learn by studying memory? Why is it an important area of psychology?

A When people typically think about memory, they usually think about it as a receptacle for facts. People who can remember lots of facts are said to have a good memory while those who cannot remember very many are said to have a poor one. But memory is much more than a mental warehouse stuffed with facts and with one's personal collection of experiences. It involves complicated processes that get the information in and other equally complicated processes that get the information out.

Memory is something we usually take for granted, but life would be impossible without it. Everyday we would have to learn everything all over again. We would wake up in the morning and have to figure out anew how to get dressed, how to make toast, how to drive to work. Life would be a never-ending discovery, exhausting us before we had lasted a single day. It is important to understand memory because it forms the basis of just about everything else we do. . . .

Q Your work on eyewitness testimony has been important to this field. Can you tell us about it?

A A major sustaining factor in my work on eyewitness testimony has been a longstanding concern with cases in which an innocent person has been falsely identified, convicted, and even jailed. The most common reason for such wrongful convictions is faulty eyewitness testimony. About 20 years ago, I began to wonder whether the study of memory would be able to contribute to the solution of this social problem.

At that time, much of the field of memory consisted of studies of fairly artificial materials—lists of words or sequences of unrelated objects. A few studies—but very few—used materials that bore a reasonable resemblance to real-life experiences. In my experiments I showed subjects films of automobile accidents and crimes and then studied their memories for the details of those events. My principal concern focused on the effects of events that occur while the to-be-remembered information was in the memory system. In several studies, I demonstrated that the way a question is phrased and the assumptions it makes have a subtle yet profound effect on the stored information.

In one study, for example, witnesses were shown a movie of an automobile accident and afterward were questioned about it. One of the questions, the critical one, was phrased in two different ways to two different groups of witnesses. One group was asked, "How fast were the cars going when they smashed into each other?" The other group was asked, "How fast were the cars going when they hit each other?" A week later all witnesses returned and were asked "Did you see any broken glass in the accident?" Actually, there had been no broken glass, but witnesses who were originally queried with the verb "smashed" were substantially more likely to report wrongly, that is, to remember the presence of broken glass than were subjects originally queried with the verb "hit."

This result raises obvious issues about the whole process of questioning witnesses, whether by the police prior to trial or by counsel during trial. In either case, the questions asked may deposit information in memory that radically alters subsequent testimony.

Elizabeth F. Loftus

A large degree of memory distortion has now been found in scores of studies, involving a wide variety of materials. People have not only recalled nonexistent broken glass, but also tape recorders that never existed, a clean-shaven man as having a mustache, straight hair as curly, and even something as large and conspicuous as a barn in a bucolic scene that contained no buildings at all.

In short, misleading postevent information can alter a person's recollection in a powerful, even predictable manner. I proposed that memory is highly malleable and subject to distortion by events that occur later on. For example, when people who experience the same event talk to one another, overhear each other talk, or gain access to new information from the media, interrogators or other sources.

Others have disagreed with this theoretical interpretation, arguing instead that once information is acquired by the memory system, it is unchangeable. Errors in memory result from an inability to find stored information or from errors made during the original perception of the events. A lively controversy is now occurring over this issue.

Q What are some of the exciting new developments in the field of memory?

A One exciting new development that will continue in the future concerns the work by Harry Bahrick on the loss of information that is acquired in school. Bahrick has studied memory for Spanish learned in high school or college. Some of his subjects learned Spanish less than a year ago, while others learned it long in the past—up to 50 years earlier. An interesting question is how quickly material, like Spanish, fades from memory when a person doesn't use it. Bahrick has concluded that a good deal of Spanish is lost quickly, but some portions of the originally acquired material remain accessible for over 50 years, in spite of the fact that the information is not used or rehearsed. A debate has arisen about this work: Is the apparent permanence of memory for Spanish due to the long survival of some memory traces, or is it due to the fact that people have an overall schema for Spanish from which a few correct responses can be generated?

The research has also spawned other studies inquiring into how long education lasts. . . .

Another exciting development that will continue in the future concerns the role that the brain plays in memory storage. We have known for some time that surgical removal of parts of the temporal lobes can lead to problems with the storage of new information into long-term memory. More recent research by Stuart Zola-Morgan and Larry Squire expands our knowledge of the role of the hippocampus in memory formation. They destroyed a portion of the hippocampus in monkeys and found that the monkeys could remember something they had learned four months before their surgery significantly better than similar information learned only one month before. This result means that the hippocampus is involved in the storage of new information in memory, and also that memories are gradually reorganized and consolidated in a way that eventually they can be recalled without much involvement of the hippocampus.

6 Conditioning and Learning

215

uman beings are very complicated organisms. We live for a comparatively long time in environments that are constantly changing. To survive in these environments, we must adapt. **Adaptation** is the process of changing behavior to fit changing circumstances. Learning is an adaptive process because it enhances our ability to change. Finding food and shelter, avoiding danger, reading, making friends—all these activities require learning. In fact, it is difficult to think of many activities that do not require some sort of learning.

Because learning is so important to our survival, psychologists have devoted much time to its study. Learning also plays an important role in many other areas of psychological inquiry. For example, in the area of social psychology, learning may explain why children who watch televised violence tend to be more aggressive. Learning may also play a role in acquiring certain types of fears. Interestingly, therapy designed to eliminate these fears often applies learning principles to help "unlearn" the fear. Learning may also play a role in developmental processes such as identifying with the appropriate sex and acquiring language.

• •

WHAT IS LEARNING?

Learning can be defined as a relatively permanent change in immediate or potential behavior that results from experience. This definition has three critical aspects: (1) learning involves a change in either immediate or potential behavior, (2) the change must be relatively permanent, and (3) the change must be due to experience. To fully appreciate this definition, let's consider one of psychology's favorite examples, that of a hungry rat learning its way through a maze.

Figure 6.1 shows the type of maze typically used. The rat is placed in the start box and allowed to run to the choice point in the maze. Here, the rat must learn to turn either right or left to obtain a small pellet of food. The first few times it runs the maze, the rat sometimes turns to the right and sometimes to the left. But as it gains more and more experience, the rat begins to turn right on every try. At this point, the rat is said to have learned.

Let's see how this process fits the three criteria of learning. The first criterion is that

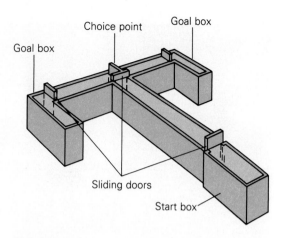

Figure 6.1
A Simple T-Maze.
Sliding doors keep the rat from retracing its steps once it has made a choice to turn left or right. A food cup can be placed in either goal box.

learning leads to a change in immediate or potential behavior. Because it is impossible to observe the internal process of learning, psychologists infer that learning has taken place only if behavior changes. The rat in the maze meets this criterion. Although it initially ran both to the left and to the right, the rat now runs only to the right. It is apparent that the rat has changed its *immediate behavior*.

It is possible, however, for learning to occur without an immediate change in behavior. Consider the student who fails an exam. The student may have learned well but performed poorly. Perhaps the student was tired and nervous during the exam. On another day, when the student is rested and confident, performance might improve dramatically.

Similarly, the rat might have learned to turn right to get food but may be ill and fail to perform. Even though both the rat and the student had learned, there was no *immediate* change in behavior. But in both cases, the organism does have the capacity to change its behavior at some future time. In these instances, there is a change in the *potential behavior*.

The second criterion is that the change in behavior must be relatively permanent. We could determine this by checking to see if the rat still ran to the right an hour or even a week later.

The third criterion of learning is that the behavior change must be due to experience. Experience includes practice, repetition, or training. The rat's change in behavior is due to experience because the animal had to be trained to turn right. By specifying that learning must be due to experience, we discount changes in behavior that are due to drugs, maturation, or illness.

How organisms learn has been a central question in psychology for over 100 years. In an attempt to understand learning, early psychologists broke down the process into simpler components, in much the same way as physicists studied the nature of matter by breaking it down into smaller components such as molecules and atoms.

One of the earliest theories of learning was based on the concept of association. Associating, that is, relating two different stimuli or events in the environment, may represent the simplest type of learning. Associative learning can be broken down into two types: classical conditioning and operant conditioning (Rescorla & Holland, 1982). According to the associative theory of learning, **classical conditioning** is learning that results from the association of two stimuli in the environment. For example, at a very young age a baby learns to associate the smell of its mother with food. Because of this association, a hungry baby will often stop crying when its mother picks it up. **Operant conditioning** is defined as learning that occurs when an organism learns to associate its behavior with the consequences, or results, of that behavior. A dog learns that shaking hands, a behavior, produces a dog biscuit, the consequence of the behavior. Similarly, a college student learns that working hard usually produces good grades, and a politician learns that promising to lower taxes and increase services often produces votes.

In the next sections we will examine classical and operant conditioning. Later in the chapter we will see that there may be more to learning than the simple association of two events. Psychologists now recognize that certain types of learning may involve more complex processes. These complex processes are called cognitive processes and include memory, thinking, and reasoning.

Interim Summary

Learning is a process by which organisms adapt to a changing environment. It is defined as a relatively permanent change in immediate or potential behavior due to experience. This definition reflects the fact that

learning must be long-lasting and must be due to experience. It also indicates that the learned behavior is not necessarily exhibited at the time of learning but may be demonstrated at a later time.

Psychologists have generally approached the study of learning by examining two simple types of learning—classical and operant conditioning.

CLASSICAL CONDITIONING

In the early 1900s, the Russian physiologist Ivan Pavlov began a series of experiments that have had a lasting influence on the way psychologists view the learning process. Pavlov's experiments were the first systematic study of the simple type of learning that came to be labeled classical conditioning.

Pavlov was not interested in studying learning when he began his research. Instead, he was studying the physiology of the dog's digestive system, a line of research that had already earned him the Nobel Prize in Medicine and Physiology.

As part of his experiments, Pavlov caused dogs to salivate by placing meat powder in their mouths. In the course of these studies, he noticed a remarkable phenomenon. The meat powder was not the only stimulus that caused the dogs to salivate. Stimuli that came just *before* the dogs received the meat powder, such as the sight of the food dish, also produced salivation. Pavlov recognized the importance of this accidental discovery. He reasoned that the dogs had learned to associate the sight of the

Ivan Pavlov and his co-workers.

dish with the delivery of the meat powder. With this in mind, Pavlov set aside his work on digestion and devoted full effort to the study of this phenomenon (Pavlov, 1927).

Pavlov's Experiments

To measure accurately how much a dog salivated, Pavlov performed a minor operation in which he implanted a small tube inside the

dog's mouth near its salivary glands and then passed the tube through its cheek. Whenever the dog salivated, the saliva ran through the tube and was collected outside the dog's mouth.

As before, Pavlov found that whenever he placed meat powder in the dog's mouth, the dog salivated. Pavlov recognized that this response to the meat powder was simply a reflex. A **reflex** is a specific and involuntary response to a stimulus and does not require any learning. To reflect the nature of this response, Pavlov named the dog's natural response to a stimulus—salivating in the presence of meat powder—the unlearned or **unconditioned response (UR).** The stimulus (the meat powder) that produced the unlearned response (salivation) was termed the **unconditioned stimulus (US).**

Next, Pavlov placed the animal in an apparatus like that shown in **Figure 6.2** (Goodwin, 1991). Once the animal was in place, Pavlov rang a bell. The bell was a neutral stimulus because it did not produce salivation. Pavlov then began to condition the dog to associate the bell with the meat powder by first ringing the bell and then presenting the meat powder. Each time the bell and meat powder were presented together, or *paired,* one *trial* occurred.

After about 12 trials, Pavlov simply rang the bell and did not present any meat powder. This time, the previously neutral bell caused

Figure 6.2
Pavlov's Experiment. In Pavlov's experiment, the dog was harnessed to the wooden frame and a tube conducted its salvia to a measuring device.

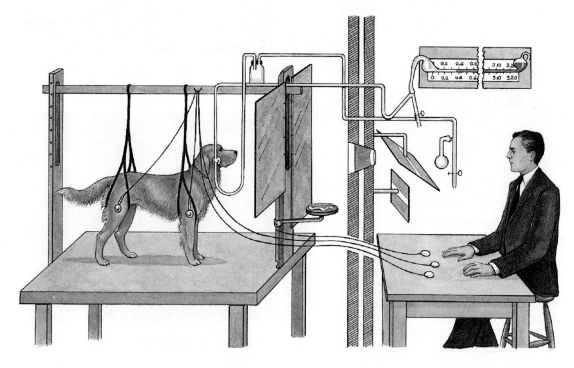

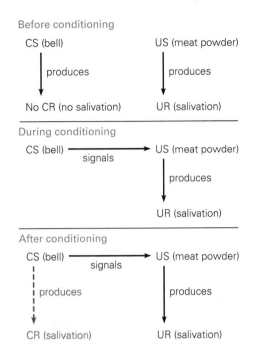

Figure 6.3
The Relationship Between Stimuli in Classical Conditioning.

the dog to salivate. Because the dog had learned to salivate in response to the bell, Pavlov called the bell the learned or conditioned stimulus (the CS). Salivation in this instance was called a conditioned response (a CR). In classical conditioning, the **conditioned stimulus (CS)** is the neutral stimulus that is paired with the unconditioned stimulus (US) and eventually comes to elicit the conditioned response (CR). The **conditioned response (CR)** is the response that results from the pairing of the CS with the US. The relationship between the various stimuli in classical conditioning is diagrammed in **Figure 6.3.**

To appreciate how classical conditioning might enter into a human learning situation, imagine you had a friend who had the habit of greeting you with a loud "hello" and then slapping you hard on the back. Whenever your friend slapped you (the US) you would reflexively flinch (the UR). After a number of trials—pairing the "hello" with the slap—you would probably flinch just from hearing your friend say "hello." In this instance, "hello" became the CS and flinching to "hello" became the CR.

Processes in Classical Conditioning

In Pavlov's simple experiment, the dog acquired a conditioned response. **Acquisition**, or learning of a new response, is one of the five

major processes that can occur during classical conditioning. The others are extinction, spontaneous recovery, generalization, and discrimination.

ACQUISITION OF THE CONDITIONED RESPONSE

One important goal of classical conditioning is to determine how many pairings or trials are necessary for the organism to acquire the CR. One general statement we can make is that the CR is acquired gradually. During the first few pairings of the CS and the US, there is no CR. After additional trials the CR begins to occur and, as the number of trials increases, the CR continues to strengthen until it reaches a maximum level. **Figure 6.4** shows a typical acquisition curve for Pavlov's experiments.

A second important aspect of the acquisition process is the time relationship between the CS and the US. For optimal conditioning should the CS be presented before or after the US? To begin to answer this question we might ask why organisms classically condition. Why did Pavlov's dogs salivate before they were fed? Researchers now believe they salivated to prepare them for the food. Why did you cringe before your friend slapped you on the back? As you may have reasoned, it was to prepare you for the slap; perhaps cringing makes it less painful. In general, conditioning occurs because the conditioned response prepares us for the unconditioned stimulus. Now let's return to the question of the time relationship between the CS and the US. If the purpose of conditioning is to prepare the organism, then conditioning should be best when the CS occurs before

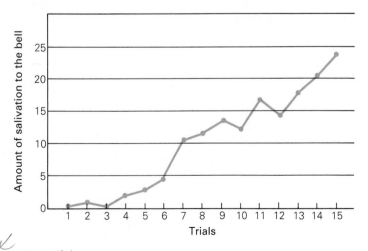

Figure 6.4
An Acquisition Curve Typical of Pavlov's Experiments.

Forward conditioning

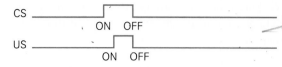

Backward conditioning

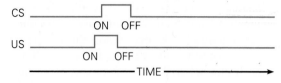

Figure 6.5
The Temporal Relationship Between Stimuli in Two Types
of Classical Conditioning.

the US. This is typically called *forward conditioning*. Conditioning can do little to help us prepare for the US if the CS occurs after the US, a process called *backward conditioning*. **Figure 6.5** summarizes forward and backward conditioning.

GENERALIZATION

Once an organism has been conditioned to give a CR in the presence of a particular CS, other stimuli similar to the original CS will also produce the same CR (Pearce, 1987). In Pavlov's experiments, for example, if dogs were conditioned to salivate in response to a bell with a middle-C tone, they would also salivate in response to bells with tones above and below middle C. Through this process of **generalization,** stimuli similar to the original CS also evoke the CR.

Results similar to those Pavlov obtained are shown in **Figure 6.6.** The figure shows the

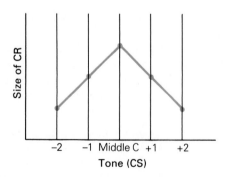

Figure 6.6
A Typical Generalization Curve.
In this case, the organism gives the CR tones that are both above and below middle C.

two important aspects of stimulus generalization: (1) the animals do generalize and respond to CSs that are similar to the original stimulus, and (2) as the CSs become less similar to the original CS, the strength of the CR decreases.

Generalization is an important process in human behavior. For example, ambulances use a variety of sirens to warn other drivers and pedestrians of their approach. Despite the variety, we come to associate the sirens with the approach of an ambulance. Of course, if any siren is too different, we might not readily associate it with an approaching ambulance. Another form of generalization occurs whenever we listen to the music accompanying a film. The music may be slightly different from film to film, but we soon learn to associate certain rhythms and instruments with danger or romance. Thus, generalization allows us to extend already existing associations to new situations, as long as the stimuli do not change too much.

DISCRIMINATION

Although generalization is an extremely useful process, it is not always beneficial and may even be harmful in some situations. Consider the young child who is frightened by a large, barking dog. Such a child might generalize and fear all dogs. Similarly, a young child who is startled by a man with a beard might generalize and fear all men with beards–even if one of them is Santa Claus. In such situations, the child must learn to *distinguish* between similar stimuli. This is **discrimination,** a process in which the organism learns to respond to certain stimuli but not to others. If Pavlov wanted his dogs to respond to the original middle-C tone only, he would have had to give them discrimination training. In this process the original middle-C tone (CS) is paired with the meat powder (US) until the CR is well established. Next, other CSs above and below middle C are presented but never followed by the meat powder. Initially the animal responds, or generalizes, to the similar CSs. But as training continues, the animal gradually learns that only the middle-C tone predicts food and gives the CR only when this stimulus occurs. At this point, the animal is said to show discrimination (see **Figure 6.7**).

Generalization and discrimination are sometimes thought of as opposite sides of the same coin. Generalization is a reaction to similarities, and discrimination is a reaction to differences.

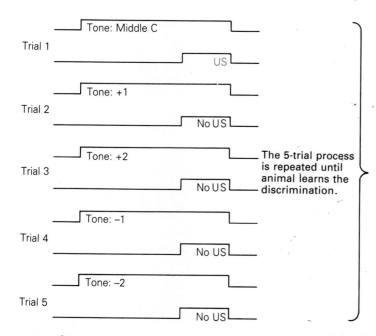

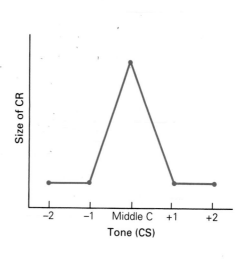

Figure 6.7
Discrimination.
A typical discrimination curve, right, results from the process diagrammed on the left. In this situation, the size of the CR sharply increases for the middle-C tone, the only tone that reliably predicts food.

EXTINCTION AND SPONTANEOUS RECOVERY

As we have discussed, classical conditioning, like most other forms of learning, is adaptive. Salivating in response to a CS that consistently predicts food may help an organism prepare to chew and digest the food. But if the environment changes, it is just as important for the organism to unlearn the association between the CS and the US. If the bell had ceased to signal meat powder for Pavlov's dogs, it would not have been to the dogs' advantage to continue to salivate in response to the bell.

Thus, just as organisms learn to salivate in response to a bell, they also learn to stop salivating when the bell no longer signals food. In this process of **extinction,** the CR gradually disappears when the US is removed. Pavlov's dogs stopped salivating in response to the bell after it was presented a number of times without any meat powder.

Extinction, like acquisition, is a gradual process. Each time the bell (CS) is presented and not followed by the meat powder (US), the strength of the CR, or the amount of salivation, decreases. As you can see in **Figure 6.8** (page 222), after five extinction trials, the strength of the CR is cut about in half.

Responses rarely completely extinguish after one extinction session (a series of extinction trials). Usually, a number of these sessions are necessary to completely eliminate the CR. But as these sessions progress, we encounter a phenomenon called **spontaneous recovery,** a process in which the CR recurs after apparent extinction.

After the first daily extinction session, the animal is returned to its home cage overnight and then put back into the conditioning apparatus for a second extinction session the next day. The strength of the CR at the beginning of day 2 is actually greater than it was at the end of day 1 (see Figure 6.8). This happens even though the animal has received no additional CS-US pairings in the meantime. This increased response at the beginning of day 2 is the spontaneous recovery. As extinction trials continue on day 2, the strength of the CR again decreases, but it usually takes many extinction sessions before spontaneous recovery no longer occurs and the response is completely extinguished.

Classical Conditioning and Human Behavior

Psychologists have demonstrated that classical conditioning is a widespread phenomenon that can be produced in both animals and humans, including infants. There are even reports of classical conditioning in simple organisms such

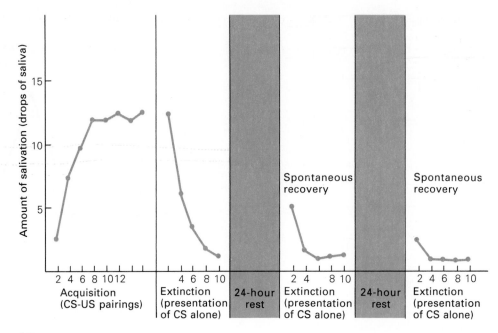

Figure 6.8
The Process of Extinction.
The increased responding following each of the 24-hour rest periods (colored
bars) represents the phenomenon of spontaneous recovery.

as fish, snails, and garden slugs (Hawkins &
Kandel, 1984; Matthies, 1989).

Because stimuli are often paired in day-to-
day experiences, the potential for classical conditioning is high. For example, the sound of a
dentist's drill (the CS) makes many people nervous (the CR), probably because it has been associated with pain (the US). In fact, there is
research to suggest that the sound of the dentist's drill is actually more unpleasant than the
drilling itself.

The producers of horror movies also recognize the effects of classical conditioning. In
this case, a gruesome event is frequently preceded by a theme song (you may remember the
music that signaled the coming of the shark in
the movie *Jaws*). If we consider the gruesome

event as the US and our reaction to this event,
perhaps fear, as the UR, then pairing the previously neutral music, the CS, with the gruesome
event (US) will lead to classical conditioning.
We know this has occurred when the music
alone (CS) now makes us fearful, the CR.

Experimental evidence also supports the
idea that fear can be learned through classical
conditioning. The first and most famous demonstration of this phenomenon was conducted by John B. Watson and Rosalie Rayner in
1920. In this study, a 9-month-old boy, "Little Albert," was conditioned to fear a white
rat.

The ethics and methods used in this study
have been criticized by contemporary psychologists and it is doubtful that this type of study

In 1920, Watson and
Raynor conditioned this 9-
month-old boy ("Little
Albert") to fear a white rat.
Albert's fear of the white rat
generalized to other furry
animals such as the rabbit
in the photo. (Photo
courtesy of Professor
Benjamin Harris.)

would ever be carried out today. But the study is a classic in psychology and its main conclusion that phobias can be learned is well accepted.

Before the conditioning began, the researchers established two important facts. First, they determined that Albert was not initially afraid of the rat, since he would play with the furry creature. Second, they determined that Albert *was* afraid of a loud clang produced by hitting a bar with a hammer, since the noise caused Albert to cry and crawl away.

To condition Albert, the researchers paired the white rat (CS) with the loud noise (US). Each time Albert touched the rat, the researchers struck the bar with the hammer. After seven pairings, Albert cried whenever the rat was presented. According to Watson and Rayner, Albert had learned to fear rats. Later in their study, Watson and Rayner demonstrated that Albert's fear of the rat generalized to other similar stimuli by showing that the sight of other animals, such as a rabbit or a dog, also made Albert cry.

Whatever happened to little Albert? Did his fear of white furry objects last? Unfortunately, we do not know. Watson and Rayner reported that they hoped to use conditioning techniques to extinguish Albert's fears, but Albert was taken from the hospital before Watson and Rayner had the opportunity (Harris, 1979). We shall see in Chapter 17, though, that other psychologists did eventually develop conditioning techniques for helping patients "unlearn" the extreme fears called *phobias*.

Classical conditioning has many other applications. Researchers have suggested that the conditioning process may help explain drug addiction, changes in the body's cardiovascular system, learning of certain sexual behaviors, and even allergic reactions (Turkkhan, 1990). For example, one study published long before Pavlov's experiments found that a person who had an allergy to roses sneezed when he was exposed to an artificial rose (Mackenzie, 1886). But perhaps one of the most interesting and potentially useful applications of classical conditioning concerns the human immune system.

One of the most devastating diseases of our time is AIDS (acquired immunodeficiency syndrome). Estimates indicate that there are now 75,000 diagnosed cases of AIDS in the United States alone; almost 2 million Americans are infected with HIV, the virus that causes AIDS, and perhaps more than 10 times that number are infected worldwide (Backer,

Batchelor, Jones, & Mays, 1988). As you may know, AIDS causes extreme suppression of the body's immune system and leaves individuals vulnerable to often fatal "opportunistic infections" that rarely strike healthy people. But not all people who are infected with the virus have this potentially fatal immunosuppressive response, and of those who do experience immunosuppression there is great variability in the severity of their symptoms. Because of this, AIDS researchers, including psychologists, have devoted considerable effort to trying to understand how the immune system is affected in AIDS. One avenue of research involves classical conditioning.

In 1982 Robert Ader and his co-workers made a striking discovery. They found that the immune response of a rat could be classically conditioned. They gave rats a taste CS (saccharin) and followed it with a drug US (cyclophosphamide) that suppressed the immune system. After pairing of the CS and US, the animals would show a suppressed immune system when they were given saccharin alone (Ader & Cohen, 1982) **Figure 6.9** shows how this conditioning takes place. Much like AIDS patients, the conditioned animals who were given only saccharin became much more vulnerable to germs in the laboratory environment and were much more likely to become ill and even die. Based on this research, Ader reasoned that the immune system may be responsive to learning. If this is true, it also may be possible to use conditioning to enhance the immune system and it may ultimately be possible to use conditioning procedures to help fight diseases such as AIDS in which the immune system is deficient (Ader, 1985; Kielcolt-Glaser & Glaser, 1988). Although conditioning procedures have not yet been tried in AIDS patients, several promising studies in animals have shown an

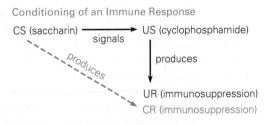

Figure 6.9
Conditioning of an Immune Response.

increase in the immune response following conditioning (Ghanta, Hiramoto, Salvason, & Spector, 1985; MacQueen, Marshall, Perdue, Siegal, & Bienenstock, 1989).

Contributions and Limitations of Classical Conditioning

Classical conditioning is a simple form of associative learning that helps the organism adapt to its environment (Rescorla, 1988). It occurs in a variety of species and situations and has a number of applications in human behavior. But can classical conditioning explain all types of simple learning? Consider the following example.

One trick that almost all pet dogs can learn is "shaking hands." This is a relatively simple trick that dogs can often acquire with very little training. To teach this trick through classical conditioning, we would begin with a US that is capable of producing the desired response of shaking hands. But what is the US that reflexively causes a dog to shake hands? There is none. Shaking hands is not a reflex, and there is no stimulus that automatically produces it. Because there is no US, the dog cannot learn to shake hands through classical conditioning. It is clear, therefore, that classical conditioning cannot account for all learning. To understand how a dog learns to shake hands on command, as well as how a number of other behaviors are learned, we will have to examine a second type of learning called *operant conditioning.*

Interim Summary

Pavlov's experiments revealed much of what we now know about classical conditioning. In classical conditioning an unconditioned stimulus (US) reflexively produces an unconditioned response (UR). If a second neutral stimulus (the conditioned stimulus or CS) is then paired with the US, it also produces a response. Pavlov called this learned response the conditioned response (CR).

The CR is acquired gradually over many pairings of the CS and the US. Once the CR is established, if the CS is no longer followed by the US, the CR ceases to occur. This is called extinction. Like acquisition, extinction occurs gradually. Furthermore, the CR will recur after apparent extinction. This is known as spontaneous recovery.

In classical conditioning, organisms may give conditioned responses to stimuli that are similar but not identical to the original CS. This is known as generalization. Organisms may also learn to discriminate between the original CS and other similar stimuli.

Classical conditioning can be used with humans as well as with other animals. One well-known experiment that demonstrated classical conditioning in humans was the experiment with "Little Albert" conducted by Watson and Rayner. More recent research has shown that classical conditioning may be involved in the immune response. This has implications for fighting diseases of the immune system such as AIDS.

OPERANT CONDITIONING

The basic assumption of operant conditioning is that behavior is influenced by its consequences. A dog will learn to shake hands if a certain consequence, such as getting food, follows the response. Similarly, a seal can learn to balance a ball on its nose if the consequence of this behavior is receiving a fish, and a child might learn to clean up his or her room if doing so produces a trip to the ice cream parlor. B. F. Skinner coined the term *operant conditioning* to describe this type of learning because the organism produces a consequence by *operating* on its environment.

There are two important distinctions between classical and operant conditioning. The first distinction concerns the organism's control over the situation. In classical conditioning, the organism has no control over the situation. For Pavlov's dogs, the meat powder (US) always followed the bell (CS). The dog did not have to give the CR of salivating to receive food. On the other hand, in operant conditioning the organism's behavior determines the outcome of the situation. The dog will receive food only if it shakes hands. Because of this, some psychologists prefer the term **instrumental conditioning** to operant conditioning, indicating that the organism's response is *instrumental* in determining the response's consequence. We will use the term *operant conditioning* throughout this chapter, but it is helpful to keep in mind that the two terms can be used interchangeably.

The second distinction between classical and operant conditioning involves the type of

According to the principles of operant conditioning, behavior that produces a positive response will occur most frequently. So, if a child receives a hug whenever she smiles, she will probably smile frequently.

response that can be conditioned. In classical conditioning, responses are limited to reflexes, or automatic responses to specific stimuli. As we saw in the example of a dog learning to shake hands, unless there is a preexisting US that automatically produces a UR, classical conditioning cannot occur. In operant conditioning, responses are not limited to reflexes but include an entire array of voluntary behaviors. For example, a young child in a playpen can exhibit any of a number of different behaviors. The child can smile, crawl, stand up, or cry, to mention a few. Which of these behaviors will occur most frequently? According to the basic principle of operant conditioning, the behavior that occurs most frequently is the one that produces a positive consequence. If the baby's parents always hug the child whenever she smiles, the baby will probably smile a great deal.

At first glance, operant conditioning appears straightforward and perhaps even simple-minded. It is no surprise that people perform certain acts because these acts produce positive consequences. But simple as it may appear, operant conditioning may explain how a good deal of behavior is learned. In this section we will explore the basic principles of operant conditioning and then see how they apply to certain types of human behavior.

Thorndike's Puzzle Box

At about the time when Pavlov was conducting his classical conditioning experiments, an American named E. L. Thorndike was carrying out a related set of experiments on cats. Thorndike was greatly influenced by Darwin's theory of evolution and his ideas about animal intelligence. In an effort to understand how animals learn to adapt to their environment, Thorndike decided to study, in a controlled laboratory setting, a form of learning that an animal might also use in its natural environment. To accomplish this, Thorndike studied how hungry cats learn to escape from a "puzzle box" in order to get food.

Thorndike placed hungry cats inside a wooden puzzle box like the one shown in **Figure 6.10** on page 226. To escape from the box and get a piece of fish, the cat had to learn to open a latch inside the box. During the first trial, the animal explored, sniffed, clawed, meowed, and howled. Eventually, the cat accidentally tripped the latch, opened the door, got out of the box, and ate the fish. The next time the cat was placed in the box it exhibited many of the same behaviors but took less time to escape from the box and get the food. After several additional trials, the cat immediately opened the latch to get the food.

Thorndike reasoned that responses such as exploring and clawing at the walls, which did not lead to a satisfying consequence (the fish), were "stamped out," whereas the behavior of opening the latch was "stamped in" by the resulting satisfaction. Based on these experiments, Thorndike proposed the **law of effect,** which states that acts followed by a satisfying state of affairs are more likely to recur than acts followed by an annoying state of affairs. In the case of Thorndike's cat, since opening the latch led to the satisfying state of eating, the behavior occurred more frequently (Thorndike, 1898). With these experiments, Thorndike had paved the way for operant conditioning.

The Consequences of Behavior

Although Thorndike is given credit for the first laboratory studies of operant conditioning, B. F. Skinner's work has provided most of what we know about this form of learning.

Skinner's insights into the *consequences of behavior* are perhaps his most important contribution. Building on Thorndike's law of effect, Skinner noted that when a particular be-

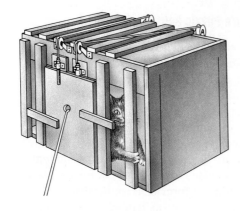

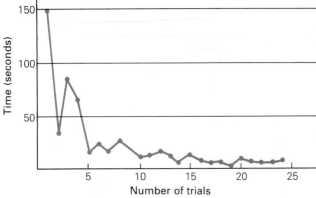

Figure 6.10
Thorndike's Puzzle Box.
Cats placed inside Thorndike's "puzzle box" had to learn to trip a latch to escape and get a piece of fish. As the graph shows, the cats learned to make this response more quickly after a number of trials. (After Thorndike, 1898)

havior is performed, it may have one of two general consequences: *reinforcement* (a positive outcome) or *punishment* (a negative outcome). Skinner reasoned that reinforcement would increase the probability that a behavior would recur, whereas punishment would decrease the probability a behavior would recur.

To test this hypothesis, Skinner studied the behavior of rats in an operant chamber. An operant chamber is a small cage with a lever, often called a bar, protruding from one wall (see **Figure 6.11**). Below the bar is a chute for delivering a food pellet. Operant chambers are typically used to study bar-pressing behavior in rats. To determine how the consequences of bar pressing affected the animal's behavior, Skinner monitored the rate at which the rat pressed the bar.

Through his experiments, Skinner identified three specific consequences of behavior that would affect the rate at which the rat bar pressed: positive reinforcement, negative reinforcement, and punishment (Skinner, 1938).

POSITIVE REINFORCEMENT

A **positive reinforcer** is any stimulus whose presentation increases the probability that a behavior will occur. An excellent example is a rat bar pressing in an operant chamber for the presentation of food. Because bar pressing then occurs more often, we know that food is a positive reinforcer. **Positive reinforcement** is the procedure used to increase the probability of a response by following that response with a positive reinforcer.

The use of positive reinforcement to guide human behavior is quite prevalent. When a second-grader completes a homework assignment (a behavior the teacher would like to occur more often), the teacher gives the student a gold star as a positive reinforcer. When a corporate executive increases her productivity, the boss gives her a bonus. When a gymnast successfully completes a difficult vault, the judges award him a high score.

NEGATIVE REINFORCEMENT

A **negative reinforcer** is a stimulus whose removal increases the probability that a behavior will occur. A rat is placed in an operant chamber and a low-level shock is turned on. The shock is an unpleasant or *aversive* stimulus. When the animal presses the bar, the shock is terminated. Here, the behavior of bar pressing is followed by the removal of an aversive stimulus. Consequently, the frequency of bar pressing *increases*. **Negative reinforcement** is the procedure used to increase the probability of a response by removing an aversive stimulus after the response occurs. With positive rein-

B. F. Skinner (1904–1990)

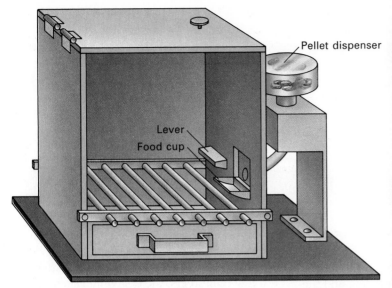

Figure 6.11
An Operant Conditioning Chamber.
The operant chambers used to condition rats usually have a bar for pressing and a chute for delivering food. The operant chamber allows the experimenter to control the animal's environment and eliminate any distracting stimuli.

forcement, the organism emits a behavior to obtain a reward. With negative reinforcement, the organism emits a behavior to secure relief from an aversive stimulus.

One common example of the use of negative reinforcement to increase a behavior in humans is the seat-belt buzzer in a car. When we start a car without first fastening the seat belt, a loud, aversive buzzer sounds. To remove this aversive stimulus, we increase the behavior of putting on our seat belts. A child crying is another aversive stimulus; crying often increases the parent's behavior of picking up the child to stop the crying.

PUNISHMENT

A **punisher** is a stimulus whose presentation *decreases* the probability that a behavior will occur. If a rat presses a bar and is shocked immediately afterward, the behavior of bar pressing will occur less often. The term for this process is **punishment,** defined as the procedure used to decrease the probability that a response will recur by presenting an aversive stimulus after the response. As you can see, the effects of punishment are just the opposite of those of reinforcement. Another type of punishment, called *negative punishment*, is defined as removal of a pleasant stimulus that has the effect of decreasing the probability of a behavior. For example, a teenager is grounded for staying out past curfew. The grounding, or removal of privileges (removal of a pleasant stimulus), has the effect of reducing the teen's behavior of staying out past curfew.

The use of punishment to change human behavior is widespread. Prison, fines, and spankings are just a few common examples. But, as we will see, the use of punishment to change human behavior also raises many questions. Graphic summaries of the differences between reinforcement and punishment are shown in Figures 6.12 and 6.13. **Figure 6.12** shows the consequences of behavior that is re-

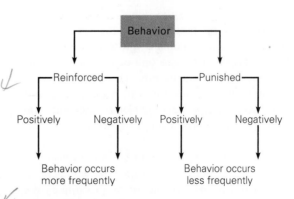

Figure 6.12
The Consequences of Behavior.

Figure 6.13
Types of Operant
Conditioning.

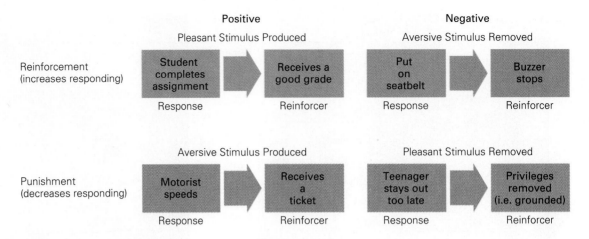

Processes in Operant Conditioning

inforced or punished, and **Figure 6.13** summarizes the types of operant conditioning and the effects on behavior of each type.

Processes in Operant Conditioning

Many of the processes that occur in operant conditioning are similar to those that occur in classical conditioning. For example, operantly conditioned responses show extinction, spontaneous recovery, generalization, and discrimination, as do classically conditioned responses. In operant conditioning, however, it is sometimes difficult to get an organism to make the first, reinforceable response. One solution to this problem is the process of shaping.

SHAPING

In operant conditioning, an experimenter must wait for a behavior to occur before it can be reinforced. But what happens if the behavior doesn't occur spontaneously? In this situation it becomes necessary to shape the behavior. **Shaping** involves reinforcing behaviors that are increasingly similar to the desired behavior until finally the desired behavior occurs. To illustrate the shaping process, let's see how it might be used to train a dog to ring a doorbell.

Several years ago one of the authors was having dinner at a friends. The doorbell rang, but our friend just ignored it. It rang again and she said, "don't be concerned, its only the dog." How do you teach a dog to ring a doorbell?

The first step would be to reinforce a spontaneous behavior that in some way is related to the desired behavior. For example, we might watch as the dog sniffed around the house and give the dog a reinforcer whenever

it came within 20 feet of the doorbell. After only a few reinforcers, the dog would spend most of its time near the bell. We could then give the dog a reinforcer for coming within 10 feet of the bell, then for coming within 5, and then only for standing right next to the bell. Next, we could give the dog a reinforcer for holding its head up in the direction of the bell and then only for sniffing at the bell. Finally, we would give the dog a reinforcer for actually pushing the bell with its nose. **Figure 6.14** illustrates this process of shaping.

Training a rat to bar press is a very similar process. When a rat is placed in an operant chamber, it will explore, sniff, and groom, but it will rarely press the bar. Operant conditioners say that bar pressing has a *low baseline rate,* meaning it doesn't occur very often. To circumvent this problem, researchers use a shaping procedure. Initially, the rat is given a food pellet whenever it is in the same half of the cage as the bar. Next, the animal's behavior is reinforced only when the rat is within 2 inches of the bar, then only for touching the bar, and finally only for pressing the bar.

Shaping is such a common process in human learning that we may not even be aware of it. When we teach children to dress themselves, to ride a bicycle, or to read, we begin with simple, easily executed components and gradually build to the complete response.

EXTINCTION AND SPONTANEOUS RECOVERY

If a rat has learned to press a bar for food but the experimenter changes the situation so that a bar press no longer produces food, the rat will eventually stop responding. As in classical conditioning, this extinction process occurs gradually. Also, a rat that has undergone an ex-

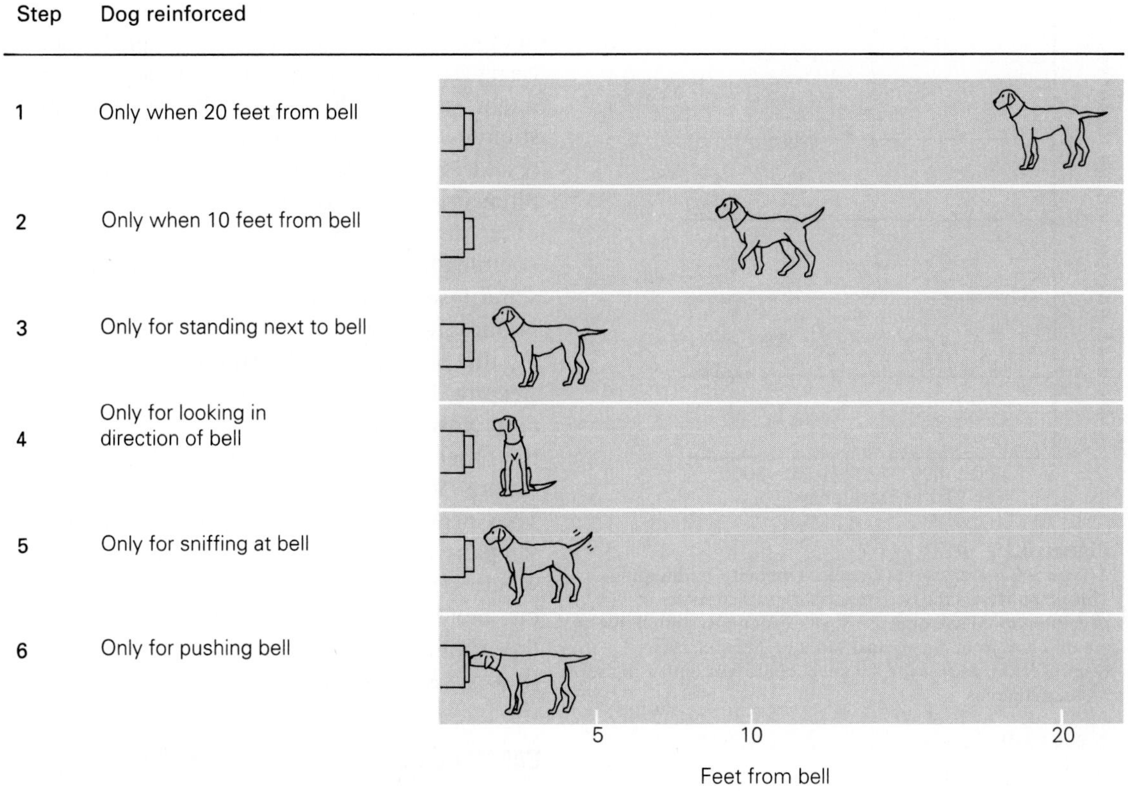

Step	Dog reinforced
1	Only when 20 feet from bell
2	Only when 10 feet from bell
3	Only for standing next to bell
4	Only for looking in direction of bell
5	Only for sniffing at bell
6	Only for pushing bell

5   10   20

Feet from bell

Figure 6.14
The Process of Shaping a Dog to Ring a Doorbell with Its Nose.

tinction session and has been returned to its home cage overnight will show spontaneous recovery when placed in the operant chamber the next day. That is, it will press the bar at a higher rate at the beginning of the second extinction session than at the end of the first.

Extinction of operantly conditioned responses can occur in a variety of situations. When parents no longer pick up a baby who throws a temper tantrum or when a teacher ignores children who show off in the classroom, they are allowing the behavior to occur without the resulting reinforcer. In each instance, the undesirable behavior will eventually be extinguished.

GENERALIZATION AND DISCRIMINATION

As was the case in classical conditioning, generalization and discrimination are important aspects of operant conditioning. Once a rat learns that pressing a bar will produce a food pellet, we can teach the rat to discriminate by changing the situation slightly. During discrimination, the animal learns that bar pressing will produce food only when certain stimuli are present. This is often done by sounding a par-

ticular tone. The rat will receive a food pellet for bar pressing only when the tone is on. Gradually, the rat learns to discriminate and will bar press only when it hears the tone. A **discriminative stimulus** is a stimulus that signals that a particular response will be reinforced.

What would now happen if the pitch of the tone changed? In this case, the rat would generalize and would press the bar in response to the new tone. As in classical conditioning, generalization of operantly conditioned responses has two important characteristics: (1) organisms will respond to stimuli that are different from the original stimulus; and (2) as stimuli become less similar to the original stimulus, the response decreases (see **Figure 6.15**).

Generalization and discrimination of operantly conditioned responses play an important role in human behavior. For example, even though we might have learned to drive in a 1988 Chevrolet, we can generalize this behavior to other, similar cars. In the case of discrimination, we quickly learn that many behaviors are reinforced only if they occur in the presence of a discriminative stimulus. Consider the

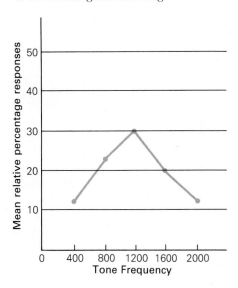

Figure 6.15
A Typical Generalization Curve for Operant Conditioning. This graph shows the two important characteristics of generalization. First, organisms will respond to stimuli that are different from the original stimulus. Second, their response decreases as the stimuli become less similar to the original stimulus.

case of a third-grader who works only when the teacher (the discriminative stimulus) is watching.

Generalization and discrimination are sometimes referred to under the single title of *stimulus control,* indicating that certain stimuli often gain control over behavior. The third-grader's behavior of working is under the stimulus control of the teacher. Stimulus control is an important concept in understanding certain human behaviors. Consider the case of a per-

son who cannot sleep, an insomniac. For most people, the stimulus of a bed signals sleep. Using terms from operant conditioning, we might say that the bed is the discriminative stimulus, sleep is the behavior, and being well rested is the reinforcer. Insomniacs, however, often use their beds for a variety of activities other than sleeping. Turning their beds into a combination office, living room, and kitchen, some insomniacs eat, read, write, talk on the phone, and watch television there. In these cases, the bed has lost its stimulus control over sleeping because it signals many other behaviors. Now when the person tries to sleep, all the other behaviors associated with the bed interfere. What is the solution to this problem? The insomniac should use the bed only for sleeping and do all the other activities elsewhere (see **Figure 6.16**). Although insomnia has multiple causes, research has shown that the application of stimulus control can help (Bootzin & Nicassio, 1978).

Operant Conditioning and Human Behavior

The principles of operant conditioning have probably had a greater impact outside the laboratory than any other field in psychology. Psychologists interested in operant conditioning have applied principles developed in the laboratory to a variety of situations including the classroom, mental institutions, diet workshops, athletic fields, corporate headquarters, and prisons, to mention a few (Kalish, 1981). Operant conditioning techniques have been used to increase productivity in the workplace, to help parents toilet train their children, and, as we will see in Chapter 17, even to help people learn to relax. In this section we will examine three of the more interesting applications of operant conditioning.

In one particularly gratifying example, the application of operant conditioning procedures allowed a severely disabled person to lead a more productive life. Robert Foster was in a serious automobile accident that left him completely paralyzed from the neck down. As you might imagine, Foster had great difficulty with simple, everyday tasks and needed constant care. But since his accident, Foster has attained a good deal more independence due to a small capuchin monkey named Hellion and the application of operant conditioning procedures.

Mary Willard, a psychologist and former student of B. F. Skinner, used shaping, positive

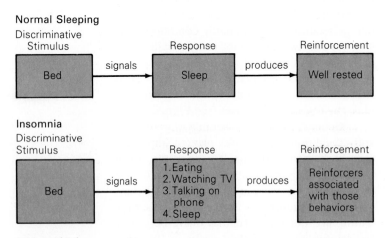

Figure 6.16
Stimulus Control and Insomnia.

Using shaping, positive reinforcement, and the use of discriminative stimuli, Hellion has been trained to help Foster lead a more productive life.

reinforcement, and discriminative stimuli to train Hellion to help Foster with everyday tasks such as turning lights on and off; opening, closing, and locking doors; fetching magazines; taking records out of their jackets and placing them on the turntable; and eating. To train Hellion to perform a complex task such as playing a record, Willard and Foster used a shaping procedure much like the one described to train a dog to ring a doorbell. Foster uses an optical pointer, a small laser beam that he operates with his mouth, to point to objects he wants Hellion to fetch. The optical pointer acts as a discriminative stimulus. Mounted to Foster's chair is a food dispenser, which Foster also operates with his mouth. Whenever Hellion performs the proper behavior, Foster dispenses a food pellet to reinforce the behavior. Hellion has learned that she will receive a pellet only if she fetches what the beam is pointing to (Mack, 1981).

A second application of operant conditioning principles involves teaching at the college level. In 1968, Fred Keller, a fellow graduate student of B. F. Skinner, wrote an article that had an immediate impact on college and university teaching. The article, entitled "Goodbye Teacher," introduced a method for applying operant conditioning principles to higher education. Keller noted that in the traditional college course, students work through material as a group. They hear lectures and take exams on a schedule set by the professor. Keller's method, called the "Personalized System of Instruction" or "PSI," took the traditional course and repackaged it to take advantage of the principles of reinforcement. The PSI method breaks down the course into many small units, each of which must be mastered by the student before he or she can move on to the next. Grades are based not on the score attained on two or three exams, but rather on the number of units the student completes. Students study a unit and, when they are ready, take an exam on that unit. The exams can be taken at almost any time and are graded immediately after the student completes the test.

How is PSI an application of operant conditioning? Much like the rat bar pressing in the operant chamber, the student under the PSI plan can respond whenever he or she wants. Responding in this case is mastering a unit (perhaps a chapter in a text) and taking an exam. When the exam is completed the student, like the rat, gets immediate feedback—the grade. A passing grade serves as a reinforcer and increases the behavior of mastering the next unit and taking an exam. Whether students learn more in the PSI plan than in traditional courses is somewhat controversial, but there is some evidence that they retain more information and that they enjoy this method of instruction (Lloyd, 1978; Lloyd & Lloyd, 1987).

Operant conditioning procedures have also been applied in the workplace. One well-known example comes from the best-selling book *One Minute Manager,* by Ken Blanchard and Spencer Johnson (1984). This book advised managers to use praise and constructive criticism in the workplace, in other words, to use the principles of positive reinforcement. The authors advised managers to (1) set clear goals, (2) catch people doing something right, and (3) praise them immediately in these situations. Although these principles seem remarkably simple, they prove to be very effective. **Table 6.1** summarizes these principles.

Table 6.1   **The One Minute Manager's Game Plan**

—Set new goals

—Praise the behavior (with true feelings)

—Do it soon

—Be specific

—Tell the person what they did right, and how you feel about it

—Encourage the person (with true feelings)

(Adapted from Blanchard & Johnson, 1982).

HOW DO YOU TELL A CHAIR FROM A CAT? SCIENTISTS SAY YOU COULD ASK A PIGEON

By Malcolm W. Browne

The humble pigeon, scarcely noticed as it pecks a livelihood from its sidewalk environment, may have more in common with human thinkers than generally realized.

In behavioral psychology experiments at the University of Iowa, Dr. Edward A. Wasserman and his colleagues have turned up what he called surprising evidence that "the conceptual abilities of pigeons are more advanced than hitherto suspected."

The pigeon mind, moreover, probably offers important clues as to how the human mind evolved and functions, Dr. Wasserman said in an interview.

"Darwin raised the possibility of a continuity in mental development from animals to human beings," he said "And it certainly looks as though he was right."

In a series of related experiments, the Iowa group is investigating the ability of pigeons to assign pictures of objects to such logical categories as "cats" or "automobiles." After being familiarized with the testing apparatus, the pigeons respond to questions by pecking at keys representing possible answers. A computer controls and records all experiments, and when a pigeon pecks a correct answer the bird is automatically rewarded with a pinch of grain.

"Pigeons commit new images to memory at lightning speed." Dr. Wasserman said, "but the remarkable thing is that they organize images of things into the same logical categories that human beings use when we conceptualize."

Experiments devised by Dr. Wasserman, his former graduate student, Dr. Ramesh S. Bhatt, and others in the Iowa group have built upon pigeon research begun in the 1960's by Dr. Richard J. Herrnstein of Harvard University. Dr. Herrnstein and other investigators have shown that pigeons can distinguish between images that contain some type of object and images that do not.

Dr. Wasserman carried this discovery a step further by showing that pigeons can distinguish among at least four categories of objects and, he said, "probably vastly more than that." He also found no difference in a pigeon's ability to distinguish "natural" objects like flowers and artificial ones like chairs.

Different Perspectives

The four categories Dr. Wasserman's group used in the experiments, which were recently reported in the Journal of Experimental Psychology, were cats (or in some cases, human beings), chairs, automobiles and flowers. Objects were shown from different perspectives, in altered lighting or settings and sometimes partially hidden.

In one test, 500 slides from each category were mixed in random order and shown to pigeons. Ten images from each category were repeatedly flashed on the screen until the subjects had learned to classify them correctly. The remaining slides were then presented with no repetitions. If a pigeon pecked the key corresponding to the correct category, it was rewarded; otherwise, the next slide was presented.

Dr. Wasserman said the birds achieved an accuracy rate of about 70 percent in this test. Since random pecking at the keys would have yielded a score of about 25 percent, he regards the result as highly significant.

"It's not just a matter of rote learning," he said. "Once a pigeon has realized that various objects resemble each other enough to constitute a category, the bird can accurately identify new pictures of different objects that belong to that category."

Skinner Box Is Main Tool

The main tool in Dr. Wasserman's experiments is the Skinner box, a device named for B. F. Skinner, the trailblazing psychologist who demonstrated in the 1930's and 1940's that behavior can be modified in complex ways by reinforcing desired behavior with judicious rewards. Among Dr. Skinner's achievements was teaching pigeons to play table tennis.

The variant of the device invented by Dr. Wasserman and his group is a box about the size of a microwave oven with a three-inch-square frosted-glass projection screen at one end. A slide projector controlled by a computer is mounted outside the box and projects images on the screen.

Near each corner of the screen are four round keys, each a different color. Behind each of the keys and the projection screen is a sensitive electrical switch that sends a signal to the computer if the key is pecked.

Just below the screen is a tray of grain that remains retracted out of reach of the pigeon unless the computer controlling the experiment recognizes that the bird is due a reward. The tray then pops out for about two seconds, gives the bird a quick snack, and then retracts to keep the bird interested in the experiment.

The pigeons themselves, trapped on Iowa farms, are fed only 85 percent of what they would normally consume. They are therefore always hungry and eager to hop into the box to work for rewards.

'Seed of Intelligence'

As Dr. Wasserman explained his work to a visitor, wild pigeons that had nothing to do with his experiments perched on the windowsill of his laboratory and looked in. "Pigeons are not just opportunistic creatures like rats," he said. "They're really part of the human environment and they have some striking features in common with us, acute vision, for one."

Many psychologists have theorized that the development of the visual area of the brain in animals is closely related to intelligence.

"Intelligence is really dependent on sensory organs like the eyes that operate over distance and permit an organism to plan what it will do before it makes contact with something," Dr. Wasserman said. "An amoeba can only sense its immediate chemical environment and cannot plan ahead. The evolution of long-distance sensory receptors was the seed of intelligence."

Pigeons also have a keen ability to distinguish the relative size of numbers and the duration of time, he said. In one set of experiments the birds were trained to register their answers by pecking the projection screen a number of times corre-

sponding to a category. Shown a cat, for instance, the bird was supposed to peck about 20 times, or shown a chair, the bird was to peck 140 times.

"Pigeons can't count," Dr. Wasserman said. "But they slow down when know they will have to peck many times before getting their reward. By timing the pecking rate we find that they give answers consistent with the relative size of the numbers."

One peculiarity of pigeon perception, he said, results from the fact that their eyes have two foveas rather than the one in human eyes. The fovea is a light-sensitive region at the back of the eye that converts images into electrochemical signals.

Looking for Life Vests

The double fovea gives the pigeon a good stereoscopic view of objects straight ahead as well as another view taking in a much wider angle that does not offer stereoscopic vision.

Whatever pigeons see, their visual acuity may be useful to humans. In a Coast Guard experiment Dr. Wasserman described, pigeons were trained to peck a key when they spotted the bright orange color used for life vests. Three of the birds were placed in a transparent box suspended from a helicopter flying over the ocean. Dr. Wasserman said the birds were adept at spotting the vests.

The legendary navigational abilities of pigeons, believed to be largely dependent both on keen vision and a superlative memory of topographic details, are still useful to humans. Although they are rarely used to carry messages any more, the birds are sometimes used for emergency flights in London to carry blood samples from hospitals to laboratories.

Dr. Wasserman sees his work with pigeons as closely related to somewhat similar experiments with

chimpanzees and human infants. In particular, he believes pigeons exhibit some of the abilities of chimpanzees that were reported by Dr. R. Allen Gardner and his wife, Dr. Beatrice T. Gardner.

In experiments in 1985 the Gardners trained chimpanzees to make sign language gestures of the kind used by deaf people. The primates were then trained to use the gestures to identify categories of objects they were shown, and to classify and identify new objects.

The title of the Gardners' paper, "A Vocabulary Test for Chimpanzees," helped to fuel a controversy among psychologists as to whether animals really use the equivalent of words in the same way people do.

Similarity in Teaching

Dr. Wasserman is undecided on the issue. He suggested that the Iowa pigeon research "formally resembled the chimpanzee study," and that this could imply that "pigeons also acquired a vocabulary." But, he added, "it is important to note that this 'vocabulary' may differ from the kind associated with human languages."

At the same time, he said, "there is a striking resemblance between the way pigeons learn the equivalent of words and the way we do."

"We teach pigeons in the same way I teach my baby daughter with the help of a picture book," he said.

Dr. Wasserman believes it is foolish to anthropomorphize pigeons or to imagine that they have anything approaching the mental capacity of humans. "We don't name our test birds," he said. "We just give them numbers."

At the same time, the pigeon's brain, "smaller than a fingertip," can perform some tasks that remain far beyond the ability of any existing or planned computer, he said.

"We're a very long way from explaining how either a pigeon brain or a human brain can do the things they do," he said. "But by studying their modes of mental behavior we are getting closer to knowing what intelligence is and how it came into existence."

From "How Do You Tell a Chair from a Cat? Scientists Say You Could Ask a Pigeon" by

Questions

1. What operant conditioning procedures might the researchers have used to train their pigeons?
2. Do you think that concepts can be developed by using operant conditioning processes?
3. Do you think that humans develop concepts in a similar manner to these pigeons or do we use fundamentally different processes? (Hint: The last section in this chapter and material in the next chapter will provide you with an alternative view.)

The Nature of Reinforcement

Reinforcement is the most important aspect of operant conditioning because it determines which behaviors will be increased. In this section, we will discuss one method for identifying reinforcers. We will then examine the distinction between primary and conditioned reinforcers and see how reinforcement can be used to produce very complex sequences of behavior.

THE EXPERIMENTAL ANALYSIS OF BEHAVIOR
One way to determine whether a stimulus is a reinforcer or a punisher is to observe its effect on an organism's behavior. If the stimulus increases the frequency of a response, it is a reinforcer. If a stimulus decreases the frequency of a response, it is a punisher. The method used to determine the function of a stimulus by examining its effect on behavior is closely identified with the experimental analysis of behavior. The *experimental analysis of behavior,* a movement led by B. F. Skinner, studies conditioning by focusing only on observable changes in behavior. This approach is much different from using common sense to determine what is a punisher and what is a reinforcer. A case that we observed involving a third-grader named Wendy illustrates this point.

The teacher complained that Wendy spent too much time out of her seat, even though the teacher punished her for this behavior. In fact, the teacher reported that the more Wendy was punished, the more Wendy stayed out of her seat. The school psychologist decided to observe Wendy and found that she spent 80 percent of the time out of her seat. The psychologist also observed that the teacher

punished Wendy by scolding her. At least the teacher meant this as punishment. But according to the experimental analysis of behavior, a punisher should *decrease* the frequency of the behavior that it follows. Thus, scolding was not a punisher at all. Indeed, since it actually *increased* the amount of time Wendy stayed out of her seat, scolding fit the definition of a reinforcer. But how could scolding be a reinforcer? One possibility is that the scolding gave Wendy attention, often a powerful reinforcer.

To make Wendy stay in her seat, the psychologist instituted a program whereby the teacher ignored Wendy whenever she was out of her seat. Only when Wendy sat down would the teacher pay any attention to her. After three weeks of this program, Wendy was out of her seat only 20 percent of the time.

Thus, a punisher or reinforcer may not always be what it appears to be. The experimental analysis of behavior allows us to determine which stimuli are punishers and which are reinforcers by observing their effects on behavior.

PRIMARY AND CONDITIONED REINFORCERS
As we have seen, a variety of stimuli can serve as reinforcers. Some stimuli are called **primary reinforcers** because they are necessary for survival. But why are stimuli such as money, diplomas, trophies, and good grades also reinforcers? The answer to this question lies in the concept of conditioned reinforcement.

A **conditioned reinforcer** is a stimulus that becomes reinforcing when it is paired with a primary reinforcer. For this reason, conditioned reinforcers are sometimes called *secondary reinforcers.* If a light flashed each time a rat received a food pellet, the light would be-

In a study by Wolfe, chimps were taught that coins inserted in the "chimpomat" would yield grapes. Wolfe found that the animals would perform a number of behaviors to receive the coins.

come a conditioned reinforcer. This is because the light was paired with the primary reinforcer of food. To determine if the light was now actually a reinforcer, we would see if the animal increased a particular behavior, perhaps pressing a bar, just to see the light. If so, we would then know that the light had become a conditioned reinforcer.

Conditioned reinforcement plays a central role in many human behaviors. Perhaps the most common conditioned reinforcer is money. A classic study by Wolfe (1936) demonstrated how money can take on reinforcing properties even for animals. In this study, chimps first learned that putting a coin in a slot would produce a grape. The coin was thus paired with the grape and became a conditioned reinforcer. Later, Wolfe found that he could get the chimps to perform several tasks, including lifting a lever, just to get a coin.

CHAINING

One of the most interesting applications of the conditioned reinforcers is chaining. **Chaining** is a procedure in which operant conditioning techniques are used to produce a complex sequence of responses. This process is often used by animal trainers to teach an animal a complicated sequence, or chain, of behaviors.

Consider the rat who performed the following sequence of behaviors flawlessly. When a light went on the rat responded by climbing a wire mesh staircase. After reaching the platform it pushed down a bridge and crossed to another platform. It then climbed a tall ladder. Next, it pulled a string connected to a small cart, climbed inside and moved it along a track by treading a paddle wheel with its front paws. At the end of the ride, it climbed up a flight of stairs and squeezed through a tunnel leading to a small elevator. For the grand finale, the rat raised the Columbia University flag and lowered itself to ground level. This turned on a buzzer, and the rat then pressed a bar to obtain food (Pierrel & Sherman, 1963).

How can a rat learn such a complex chain of behaviors? Although it looks as if the entire task was learned at once, the animal has really learned a series of separate behaviors that are reinforced with conditioned reinforcers. In chaining, the last behaviors in the chain are learned first. Thus, the rat first has to be shaped to bar press for a food pellet. Next the animal learns a simple discrimination: if the buzzer is on, a bar press will produce a food pellet; if it is off, a bar press will have no effect. After a few days of training, the rat learns to bar press only in the presence of the discriminative stimulus—the buzzer. Since the buzzer is always paired with the food, it takes on the properties of a conditioned reinforcer. At this stage, the rat will perform a task just to turn on the buzzer. The next task that the rat learns is pulling the string to lower the elevator and raise the flag. Now, since the string is paired with the buzzer and thus the food, it too becomes a conditioned reinforcer. We can now get the animal to exhibit a behavior just to get access to the string. By continuing in this way, we can train the animal to perform the sequence of behaviors we have described (see **Figure 6.17** on page 236).

Schedules of Reinforcement

In a **continuous reinforcement schedule (CRF),** a behavior is reinforced each time it occurs. Such a schedule is possible in the laboratory, but in situations outside the laboratory it is unusual for any behavior to be reinforced all the time. Studying is not always reinforced by a good grade, and even the best basketball player

Figure 6.17
Chaining.
Chaining can be used to teach an animal a complicated sequence or chain of
behaviors. This rat has learned to climb a ladder to a platform, pull a weighted
chain to raise the ladder to the next level, and then climb the ladder to the second
platform where a piece of food can be obtained.

does not score a basket every time he or she
shoots. Nevertheless, these behaviors still persist. When a behavior is reinforced only part of
the time, it is said to be on a **partial reinforcement schedule.**

Psychologists have identified two basic
types of partial reinforcement schedules. In the
first type, called **ratio schedules,** the reinforcer is delivered after the organism responds
a certain number of times. In the second type,
called **interval schedules,** the reinforcer is
delivered after a certain interval of time has
passed. One of the most important features of
these different types of partial reinforcement
schedules is that they produce different rates of
responding. In this section we will examine the
effects of partial reinforcement schedules on
behavior both in and out of the laboratory.

RATIO SCHEDULES
There are two basic types of ratio schedules:
fixed and variable. In a **fixed-ratio (FR)
schedule,** the response must occur a specific
number of times before the reinforcer is delivered. A rat on an FR-5 schedule would have to
press the bar 5 times before a pellet would be
delivered. On an FR-50 schedule, the rat would
have to press 50 times for each pellet.

Fixed-ratio schedules can produce a lot of
work for very little reinforcement. Pigeons will
peck a disc up to 2000 times just to receive
one reinforcer (Reynolds, 1975)! Of course, in
these situations the animal doesn't start out on

an FR-2000 schedule. This schedule is developed gradually by first training the animal on
CRF and then slowly shifting to FR-5, FR-10,
and so on.

Fixed-ratio schedules are quite common
outside the laboratory. One example is piece-
work. A worker who is paid 1 dollar each time
he or she completes 20 transistors is on an
FR-20 schedule. As you might have reasoned,
workers on an FR schedule cannot afford to
take breaks because this will decrease the
amount of reward (in this case money) they
obtain. Because of this, unions have discour-
aged FR arrangements and encouraged hourly
wages.

On a **variable-ratio (VR) schedule** the
response must occur a certain number of times
before a reinforcer will be delivered, but the
number of responses required for each reinforcer will vary. A rat on a VR-5 schedule will
receive a pellet, *on the average,* after every 5
bar presses. For example, the first reinforcer
might come after 3 bar presses; the next, after
8 bar presses; the next, after 1 bar press; and
the last one, after 8 bar presses. In all, the animal has received an average of 1 reinforcer for
every 5 bar presses. (The average is computed
by dividing the total number of bar presses, or
20, by the total number of reinforcers, which is
4.)

Perhaps the best example of a variable-ratio schedule outside the laboratory is gambling.
A slot machine may pay off an average of once

every 100 times a dollar is deposited—a VR-100 schedule (and no doubt the payoff is less than $100). But the gambler does not know when it will pay. It may pay off twice in a row and then not again for 200 trials. This, of course, is much to the dismay of gamblers who try to beat the odds.

Both FR and VR schedules produce extremely high rates of behavior. In other words, responses such as bar pressing will occur in rapid succession on these schedules. However, if the ratio in an FR schedule (remember the pigeon on the FR-2000 schedule) is very high, the animal will pause after each reinforcer. Higher ratios produce longer pauses.

With VR schedules, the pause disappears. VR schedules produce the most rapid rates of responding. Rats bar press hundreds of times per hour on these schedules, and humans on the VR schedule of a slot machine often deposit money at a furious rate.

INTERVAL SCHEDULES

In contrast to ratio schedules, which deliver reinforcers after a certain number of responses, interval schedules deliver reinforcers for the first response after a certain period of time has passed. On a **fixed-interval (FI) schedule**, a reinforcer is delivered for the first response after a set period of time. A rat on an FI-30 schedule will receive a reinforcer for responding only after 30 seconds have elapsed. If the rat were to respond 500 times during the 30-second period, it would make no difference. Only the first response after the end of the 30-second period would be reinforced. Then, a new cycle would begin. In this situation, the most efficient strategy would be for the rat to wait 30 seconds, give one response, get the reinforcer, and wait another 30 seconds.

This is exactly what a well-trained rat will do. Once a trained rat has learned an FI schedule, it will wait after each reinforcer is delivered. The animal appears to have learned that responses given immediately after a reinforcer will not be reinforced. As the end of the interval approaches, however, the rat again begins to bar press and will continue to do so until it receives the next food pellet. When this pattern of responding in bursts is graphed, it produces a "scalloped" curve (see **Figure 6.18**). One common example of an FI schedule that is familiar to most students is a weekly quiz. In this case studying is the behavior and the quiz (assuming you do well) is the reinforcer. Like

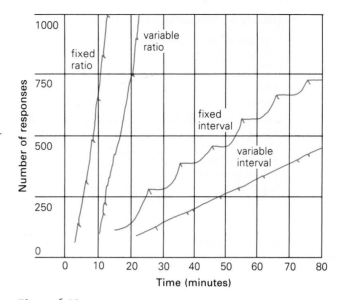

Figure 6.18
Reinforcement Schedules.
As the graph shows, each partial reinforcement schedule produces a curve with a distinctive shape. The fixed-interval schedule shows a "scalloped" curve because the organism stops responding for a time after each reinforcement, then responds rapidly as the time for delivery of the next reinforcer approaches. The hash marks indicate the point at which the reinforcer was delivered.
"Typical Curves for Different Reinforcement Schedules" from "Teaching Machines" by B. F. Skinner, SCIENTIFIC AMERICAN, November 1961, p. 96. Copyright © 1961 by Scientific American, Inc. Reprinted by permission. All rights reserved.

the rat in the Skinner box, students also exhibit the scalloped curve. Studying greatly increases the night before the quiz and drops off dramatically on the day after the quiz.

On a **variable-interval (VI) schedule** a reinforcer is delivered for the first response after a period of time, but the time period varies. A rat on a VI-30 schedule will receive a reinforcer for bar pressing on an average of once every 30 seconds. For example, a bar press might produce a food pellet only after 15 seconds have elapsed. The rat might then not receive a pellet for bar pressing until 30 seconds have elapsed and then not until 45 seconds have elapsed. This would add up to a total of three reinforcers in 90 seconds, for an average of one reinforcer every 30 seconds. These unpredictable VI schedules produce more steady rates of responding than FI schedules. Quizzes can also be given on a VI schedule. In this case the quiz would come on the average once a week, but it would be a "surprise" quiz in that the student never knows when it will be given. As you know, this will produce a more steady rate of studying. **Table 6.2** presents a summary of reinforcement schedules.

Table 6.2   **Summary of Schedules of Reinforcment**

Type of Schedule	When Reinforcers Are Delivered	Effect on Rate of Behavior	Examples
Ratio			
Fixed	After a fixed number of responses	High rate of behavior with a pause after each reinforcer	Piecework in a factory
Variable	After a variable number of responses	High and steady rates of behavior	Playing a slot machine
Interval			
Fixed	For first response after a fixed amount of time has elapsed	Low rates of behavior at the beginning of the interval and high rates toward the end (scalloped curve)	Studying for weekly quizzes
Variable	For first response after a variable amount of time has elapsed	Slow and steady rates of behavior	Studying for surprise quizzes

THE PARTIAL REINFORCEMENT EFFECT

The **partial reinforcement effect** states that behaviors that are reinforced only part of the time take longer to extinguish than behaviors that are reinforced continuously. In a typical experiment, one rat is placed in an operant chamber and given a food pellet each time it bar presses. This is continuous reinforcement. A second rat is reinforced only some of the time that it bar presses, perhaps after every tenth bar press—an example of partial reinforcement. When both animals are placed on extinction, the experimenters measure how many times each rat bar presses before ceasing to respond. The results show that the animal that was partially reinforced bar presses many more times.

The partial reinforcement effect has widespread implications for human behavior. Consider parents who reinforce their child's temper tantrums by paying attention to the behavior only some of the time as opposed to parents who reinforce the child's tantrums all of the time. The child who has been only partially reinforced will be very persistent in these tantrums even when the parents try to extinguish this behavior by completely ignoring it.

Why does the partial reinforcement effect occur? There are many explanations (Mackintosh, 1974). The most generally accepted one is that when an organism undergoes continuous reinforcement and is then placed on extinction, it is made immediately aware of the changed situation and that its behavior will no longer be reinforced. When an organism has been on a partial reinforcement schedule, how-

ever, and is then switched to extinction, it is not immediately aware that the situation has changed. After all, it has already had some experience with its behavior not being reinforced. The gambler playing a broken slot machine may put in dozens of coins before realizing that the machine is no longer working. But the same gambler would probably put only one quarter into a broken coffee machine because he or she expects the machine to deliver a cup of coffee each time a coin is deposited.

Behavior conditioned through a partial reinforcement schedule is hard to extinguish. A gambler playing on a broken slot machine may put in dozens of coins before she realizes that the machine is no longer working.

SUPERSTITIOUS BEHAVIOR

To now, we have been discussing schedules of reinforcement in which a reinforcer is delivered whenever a behavior occurs. But what happens if reinforcers are delivered at random, independent of what the organism is doing? This is exactly the question that B. F. Skinner asked in a now-classic set of experiments (Skinner, 1948). Skinner placed eight pigeons in operant chambers set to deliver food every 15 seconds no matter what the pigeon was doing. Pigeons are active birds, so each was doing *something* when the food was delivered. And it was this "something" that was reinforced. Apparently, the birds associated their behavior immediately prior to being fed with the delivery of the food. Even though the behavior was reinforced completely by chance, the frequency of the behavior—whatever it happened to be—increased. Thus when Skinner observed his pigeons, he found that one was bobbing its head up and down, one was swinging its head forward and back, and another was turning in counterclockwise circles. Skinner argues that this accidental reinforcement could account for many superstitious behaviors.

Some of the most interesting examples of superstitious behaviors come from athletes (Zimmer, 1984). For instance, we have all heard of basketball players who always bounce the ball three times before taking a free throw, baseball players who always tap the bat on the plate twice, and coaches who always wear their lucky sweater to important games. One study indicated that one third of college athletes admitted to having superstitions (Zimmer, 1984). Some cases of superstitious behavior can become quite elaborate. One example is former Boston Bruin's hockey player Phil Esposito. Before each home game Esposito drove to the game wearing a black tie. He always passed through the same toll booth that he had gone through before his last winning game. When he arrived at the locker room, he put on the same black turtleneck that he had worn years before in a game in which he had been the highest scorer. He then put on his gear in exactly the same order: underwear, pants, skates, laces. He then placed a pack of gum plus one stick next to him and arranged his equipment in a precisely predetermined order. During the national anthem he always said a Hail Mary and the Lord's Prayer. Only after he had completed this incredible ritual was he ready to start the game (Zimmer, 1984).

What might superstitious behavior such as Esposito's have to do with Skinner's pigeons? According to Skinner, when an athlete is reinforced for a particular behavior, the frequency of that behavior increases. A baseball player who strikes the bat on the left-hand corner of the plate three times and then hits a home run is more likely to perform this same behavior during the next time at bat. Despite performing the same behavior, however, the baseball player does not hit a home run on every at bat. So why don't these superstitious behaviors extinguish? Recall the previous section on the partial reinforcement effect. As we stated there, behaviors that are partially reinforced are most resistant to extinction.

The Use of Negative Reinforcement

So far, our discussion of operant conditioning has focused on the effects of positive reinforcement. As we indicated earlier, negative reinforcement also increases the frequency of behavior but, unlike positive reinforcement, uses an aversive or unpleasant stimulus, such as shock, to accomplish this. Two examples of negative reinforcement are escape learning and avoidance learning.

ESCAPE LEARNING

Another name for operant conditioning with negative reinforcement is escape learning. In **escape learning** an organism increases a particular behavior to terminate or escape from an aversive stimulus. We escape from a cold house by putting more wood on the fire. In this instance, cold is the aversive stimulus and the behavior we increase is putting wood on the fire.

In the laboratory, escape learning is generally studied by means of a two-way shuttle box. Developed by O. H. Mowrer and Neil Miller in the 1940s, the shuttle box consists of two identical compartments that are separated by an opening just large enough for a rat to fit through (see **Figure 6.19** on page 240). The bottom of each compartment consists of closely spaced metal rods that are used to deliver shock. The rat is placed in one compartment and a short time later a shock is presented. The rat can escape the shock by running (shuttling) to the opposite compartment. In keeping with the definition of negative reinforcement, the animal increases the behavior of running in order to escape the aversive stimulus of shock.

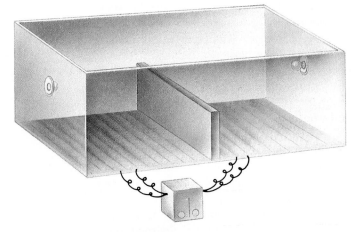

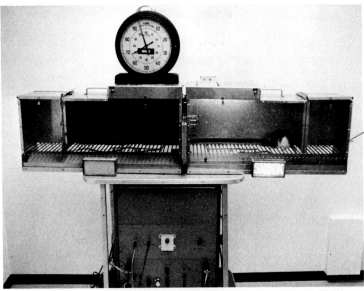

Figure 6.19
A Two-Way Shuttle Box Typically Used To Study Escape Learning.
The opening between the two compartments allows the rat to pass through.

AVOIDANCE LEARNING

Avoidance learning is similar to escape learning, except that the organism doesn't simply escape but learns to avoid the aversive stimulus completely. In **avoidance learning** a warning stimulus signals an aversive stimulus, and the organism learns to avoid the aversive stimulus by emitting the appropriate response to the warning stimulus. Avoidance learning can be demonstrated in the lab by making a small alteration in the escape-learning procedure. The modification consists of presenting a warning stimulus, usually a tone, 5 seconds before the shock occurs. During the first few tone-shock presentations, the animal exhibits escape learning; that is, it shuttles to the opposite compartment after the shock occurs. But after a number of trials, an interesting change occurs. The animal learns that the tone predicts the shock and avoids the shock altogether by shuttling to the opposite compartment when it hears the tone.

Humans show avoidance learning in many situations. For example, have you ever known people whose behavior you simply could not tolerate? Such people might be so unpleasant that whenever you speak with them you expect to be either insulted or embarrassed. After several encounters with such people, you might go the other way whenever you see them. That is, you avoid them. In terms of avoidance learning, the behavior of these people is the aversive stimulus (like the shock) and the sight of them or the sound of their voice is the warning stimulus.

One explanation of avoidance learning is the **two-process theory,** which states that both classical and operant conditioning are involved in avoidance learning (Mowrer, 1947). According to this theory, the animal initially develops a fear response to the stimulus of the tone. This response occurs through classical conditioning as illustrated in **Figure 6.20.**

Once this occurs, the animal becomes fearful whenever the tone is presented. Then, the operant conditioning phase begins. The unpleasant state of fear acts as an aversive stimulus and the animal increases a behavior, such as shuttling to the opposite compartment, to escape the fear. This response reduces the fear because shuttling terminates the fear-producing tone. It also allows the animal to avoid the shock.

The Use of Punishment

Both positive and negative reinforcement are used to increase the frequency of behavior. Punishment, on the other hand, is used to decrease the frequency of a behavior. When a punishing stimulus follows a behavior, that behavior is less likely to occur again.

The use of punishment is quite prevalent in our society. It is very much a part of our legal system and is frequently used by schools and parents to eliminate certain behaviors in children. Because of its frequent use, understanding the effects of punishment on learning is as important as understanding the effects of reinforcement.

Skinner originally thought that punishment was not effective and that positive reinforcement was a superior way to control behavior (Skinner, 1938). But psychologists now know that, under certain circumstances, punishment can be an effective means of decreasing the frequency of particular behaviors (Fantino, 1973).

In this section we will first examine what laboratory experiments have shown about the use of punishment and then discuss whether it is possible to apply these research results to human behavior.

LABORATORY EXPERIMENTS ON PUNISHMENT

Most of what psychologists know about punishment is based on studies conducted in the laboratory. In a typical experiment rats are first trained to press a bar in order to obtain food. Once they are pressing at a steady rate, they are punished with a shock each time they press the bar. To determine how effective the punisher is, the experimenter monitors how quickly the rats stop pressing the bar. Experiments like this have enabled psychologists to formulate several guidelines that must be followed if punishment is to be effective. Keep in mind that this does not mean that psychologists advocate the use of punishment. Rather, they have recognized that since punishment is often used, it is important to know exactly under which conditions it will work.

1. The punishing stimulus must be as intense as possible. This often limits the effectiveness of punishment because it is unethical to use intense punishers. One alternative to delivering a harsh punishment is to punish the response initially with a mildly aversive stimulus and to keep raising the intensity of the stimulus until the undesirable behavior decreases. Unfortunately, this method is not effective. Laboratory experiments have shown that if rats are shocked at a low level, they adapt to the shock and it has little effect on their behavior. As the shock level is gradually increased, the rats continue to adapt to the aversive stimulus until even high shock levels have no effect on behavior. But if a high shock level is used from the outset, the behavior is suppressed (Azrin & Holtz, 1966). Thus it actually may be more humane to use an intense punisher on the first trial. In this way, the behavior is eliminated and the organism receives no further punishment.

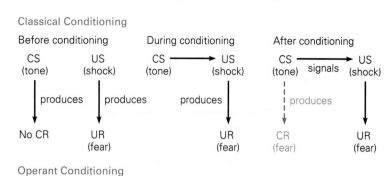

Figure 6.20
The Classical Conditioning Phase of Avoidance Learning.

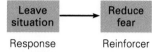

2. The stimulus should immediately follow the behavior. Just as in the use of a reinforcer, a punisher is most effective when it immediately follows the behavior. For example, mothers who attempt to punish their misbehaving children by saying, "Wait until your father gets home, then you'll get it," may not be very successful in improving their children's behavior. Similarly, the "punishment" for eating calorie-rich foods, excess weight, is usually not immediately apparent. What would happen if a piece of chocolate layer cake produced an immediate bulge in your stomach!

3. An alternative response should be provided. This last guideline is perhaps the most important. If we want to stop a dog from urinating in the house, we could punish the behavior, but this would not eliminate it unless we provided the dog with another place to urinate. Typically, this involves teaching the dog to urinate outside. In fact, the most successful method for housebreaking a dog is to punish urinating in the house and reinforce urinating outside. This guideline indicates that punishment is most effective when an undesirable behavior is punished and a desirable behavior is reinforced.

In summary, punishment can be an effective way to eliminate undesirable behavior; however, to be effective, punishment must be intense, immediate, and an alternative behavior must be positively reinforced (Schwartz, 1989).

PUNISHMENT AND HUMAN BEHAVIOR

It seems clear that if punishment is used correctly it can be effective, but does this mean that it should be used as a means of controlling human behavior? Not necessarily. Although punishment can be effective, its use can produce some undesirable side effects.

1. Punishment can lead to withdrawal. In the laboratory, some animals that are punished freeze and generally refuse to do anything. Similarly, some children who are punished become withdrawn and inhibited (Martin, 1977).
2. Punishment can trigger strong emotional responses. Through classical conditioning, punishment can become associated with a person or even a place. This can lead to fear of certain people and places.
3. Punishment can lead to aggression. Children who are punished often become aggressive and, as we have seen, punishment can lead to fear. It is possible that these factors may help explain why so many physically abused children become abusive parents.

Should punishment ever be used to decrease the occurrence of certain undesirable behaviors in humans? This is certainly a difficult ethical issue. Psychologists do not advocate the indiscriminate use of punishment, although in some cases the use of punishment has been justified. It is important to note that two conditions were present in most of these cases. First, efforts to use positive reinforcement had failed. Second, the behavior that was to be punished was more dangerous than the punishment. In addition, the subject or someone responsible for the subject's welfare gave permission to use punishment techniques in each instance.

Among the applications of punishment is the use of electrical shocks to help eliminate excessive alcohol consumption (O'Leary & Wilson, 1975) and to treat certain forms of sexual deviation (Marks & Gelder, 1967). Punishment has even been used to help people stop smoking (Hunt & Matarazzo, 1973). One of the most interesting and successful uses of punishment has dealt with self-injurious behavior in autistic children.

Childhood autism is a severe psychological disorder. In some cases, autistic children injure or mutilate themselves. In a pioneering study, Tate and Baroff (1966) worked with Sam, a 9-year-old autistic child. Tate and Baroff reported that Sam banged his head against the wall and other hard objects at a rate of up to seven times a minute. He also slapped and punched his face and kicked himself. In the hope of eliminating this dangerous behavior, Sam was first told about and then given a half-second electrical shock every time he hit himself. After several months of this therapy, Sam's self-injurious behavior was eliminated.

As Sam's case indicates, even though punishment might be distasteful, it is often the best way to eliminate undesirable behaviors—especially when the behavior is more dangerous to the person than the punishment itself.

Interim Summary

Although classical conditioning can account for a good deal of learning, it is not capable of accounting for all types. A second type of learning is operant conditioning. In operant conditioning the organism either increases or decreases the rate of a particular behavior depending on the consequences of that behavior.

According to Skinner, if an organism exhibits a behavior and receives a positive reinforcer, the rate of the behavior will increase. Similarly, if a particular behavior causes an aversive stimulus to be removed, that behavior will also increase. This is known as negative reinforcement. If the organism exhibits a behavior and receives a punishment, the rate of the behavior will decrease.

In instances where the organism does not spontaneously give the desired behavior it is necessary to shape the behavior. This involves reinforcing behaviors that occur and are similar to the desired behavior until the organism finally gives the desired behavior.

As is the case for classical conditioning, operantly conditioned behaviors show extinction, spontaneous recovery, generalization, and discrimination.

Some ways in which operant conditioning principles have been applied outside the laboratory include training of animals to assist disabled persons, development of the personalized system of instruction, and development of management techniques to increase productivity in the workplace. The experimental analysis of behavior is a method for identifying which stimuli are reinforcers and which are punishers by observing their effects on behavior. Reinforcers can be primary (necessary for survival) or conditioned by being paired with a primary reinforcer.

Most behaviors are reinforced on a partial reinforcement schedule. In ratio schedules the reinforcer is delivered after a certain number of responses. In interval schedules the reinforcer is delivered after a certain period of time has elapsed. Different types of partial reinforcement schedules produce different rates of responding. Behaviors that are reinforced only part of the time are more difficult to extinguish than behaviors that are continuously reinforced, a phenomenon known as the partial reinforcement effect.

With negative reinforcement, an organism increases the frequency of any behavior that terminates an aversive stimulus. This is sometimes called escape learning. In avoidance learning, the organism learns to avoid the aversive stimulus altogether by emitting the appropriate response to a warning stimulus. With punishment, an organism decreases the rate of a particular behavior because it is followed by an aversive stimulus. If used correctly, punishment is an effective way to decrease certain behaviors. However, certain precautions must be taken when using punishment to change human behavior.

THE INTERACTION OF BIOLOGY AND CONDITIONING

The early work on both classical and operant conditioning suggested several rules that must be followed for effective conditioning to occur. For example, in classical conditioning the US must closely follow the CS. Presenting Pavlov's dogs with the meat powder (US) 10 minutes after the bell (CS) would never produce a CR. Similarly, in operant conditioning the behavior must be followed immediately by a reinforcer or a punisher. Most researchers also believed that conditioning occurred gradually over many trials.

More recent research, however, indicates that an organism's natural, biological reaction to various aspects of the learning situation may determine how well the organism learns the task. This research has greatly influenced how

contemporary psychologists view the basic principles of learning.

In this section we will first see that in certain situations, organisms learn associations very easily. Second, we will see that certain associations are impossible for some animals to learn. We will then look at what this has taught us about effective conditioning. Finally, we will examine how learning may be important in explaining an organism's behavior in its natural environment.

Preparedness and Taste-Aversion Learning

Martin Seligman (1970) suggested that there are certain associations that organisms are best suited to make. He proposed that through natural selection, organisms have a built-in, genetic bias or *preparedness* that allows them to learn readily associations that have the greatest impact on their survival. To illustrate this point, let's examine one of the earliest experiments in this field, the taste-aversion studies conducted by John Garcia (Garcia, 1984, Garcia, Brett, & Rusiniak, 1989).

Garcia and his co-workers presented a thirsty rat with a saline solution and measured the amount the rat drank. Next, they exposed the animal to a high dose of X-rays, which made the animal quite nauseated, but not until 12 hours later. After the rat had recovered from the illness and was again thirsty, they presented the animal with the saline solution. This time the rat drank very little. Apparently, the animal had learned to associate the illness with the taste of the saline (Garcia, McGowan, & Green, 1972). There are three important results of this study. First, taste aversion took place, even though there was a 12-hour delay between drinking the saline and feeling nauseated. Second, the association between the saline and feeling ill was learned in one trial. A third significant factor was that only the taste of the saline water was associated with the illness, even though many stimuli could have been associated with feeling ill. For example, the rats did not show any aversion to the place in which they became ill. These results suggest the existence of the built-in bias Seligman calls preparedness.

How might preparedness have developed? Perhaps, as animals evolved, only those that could make this type of association survived. For example, consider an animal that drinks from a polluted water hole and becomes

This coyote has been exposed to taste-aversion conditioning and is showing species-specific disgust to its prey.

ill several hours later. To survive, the animal must associate the taste of the polluted water with illness and never drink from that water hole again. Thus, by natural selection, animals now may be prepared to make this type of association readily.

Garcia's work on taste-aversion learning has made an important contribution to the study of learning. Taste aversion also has had some rather interesting applications, such as in the control of coyotes who kill sheep. One of the most persistent problems facing a sheepherder is loss of sheep to coyotes. Sheepherders have been involved in a project in which they inject dead sheep with a toxic chemical. When a coyote eats the meat from the injected sheep, it becomes ill but does not die; in fact, it fully recovers within a few hours. But it never again touches sheep. Apparently, coyotes associate the taste of sheep with the illness, resulting in taste aversion to sheep. This solution seems to be an amicable one for both the sheepherder and the conservationist. It simultaneously allows the sheepherder to protect the sheep from the coyotes and avoids mass slaughter of the coyotes (Gustavson, 1977).

Taste-Aversion Learning in Human Behavior

Since the pioneering work of Garcia, researchers have identified a number of associations that animals seem prepared to make (Shet-tleworth & Jeurgensen, 1980). One question still remains: do humans also show taste-aversion learning and other forms of preparedness?

Like the animals in Garcia's experiments who learned to associate the taste of certain foods with illness, many people have had the experience of eating at a restaurant, becoming sick to the stomach several hours later, and blaming the illness on something they had eaten. This suggests that humans experience taste-aversion learning. The results of an experiment to discover why cancer patients undergoing chemotherapy often stop eating also indicate that humans experience taste-aversion learning.

Many cancer patients regularly experience nausea and loss of appetite from chemotherapy. These patients often refuse to eat enough and thus lose weight and strength. As a result, they are more vulnerable to infections and other problems that complicate their recovery. Since this is such a severe problem, researchers have spent considerable effort trying to understand the processes underlying this loss of appetite. One promising approach suggests that the loss of appetite may be due to a learned taste aversion.

A study by Ilene Bernstein demonstrated that children undergoing chemotherapy developed aversions to an unusual flavor of ice cream, Mapletoff (prepared with maple and black-walnut flavor extracts). The children in the experiment had eaten this ice cream shortly before the nausea-producing chemotherapeutic drugs were given. As Bernstein points out, the procedure of presenting a food with a nausea-producing drug is much like the procedure Garcia used to produce taste aversions in rats. The results in humans were much like those in rats. Patients who ate Mapletoff and then became nauseated due to chemotherapy avoided the Mapletoff ice cream the next time it was offered. It is interesting that these patients avoided the ice cream even though they knew that it was the chemotherapy and not the ice cream that made them ill (Bernstein, 1978).

This finding does not appear to be limited to one unusual food. Other research has indicated that chemotherapy patients develop aversions to foods that are eaten up to several hours before treatment. These studies also support the idea that the loss of appetite in chemotherapy patients may in part be due to learned taste aversions. This work also suggests that it may be possible to minimize or eliminate this problem if proper procedures are used.

Do humans also show preparedness for other types of learning? Some evidence indicates that humans may learn certain fears more readily than others (McNally, 1987). In one study, college students were shown pictures of snakes or of horses and asked to rate them from 1 to 9 on a "discomfort" scale. Then the conditioning phase began. Half of the students saw a picture of a snake; this was followed by a mild shock. The rest of the students saw a picture of a horse; this, too, was followed by the shock. After the conditioning, the students were once again asked to rate the snakes and the horses on the discomfort scale. Interestingly, the discomfort rating went up for the snakes but did not change at all for the horses (Ohman, Eriksson, & Olofsson, 1975). This result suggests that the students were prepared to associate snakes, but not horses, with unpleasant events (the shock). The fact that a fear of snakes is quite common may be related to this preparedness (Ohman, Dimberg, & Ost, 1985).

A second area of human learning in which preparedness may be a factor is language. Many researchers argue that humans acquire language rapidly because there is a biological preparedness for learning this complex behavior (Chomsky, 1975). We will examine this theory more closely in Chapter 8.

The Misbehavior of Organisms

Just as an organism can learn to make certain associations very easily, other associations appear impossible for the organism to learn. Two former associates of B. F. Skinner, Marion Breland and Keller Breland, used their expertise in operant conditioning to train animals for television shows. But sometimes things did not work out as expected. In 1960 they wrote an article based on this work called "The Misbehavior of Organisms." What they meant by *misbehavior* was the failure of positive reinforcement to increase certain behaviors. Although this article was not a serious research paper, it offered for the first time evidence that not all behaviors can be controlled by reinforcement.

One of the examples of "misbehavior" the Brelands described was that of the miserly raccoon. The Brelands had tried to teach the raccoon to place a coin in a piggy bank through positive reinforcement. However, some difficulty arose.

> Raccoons condition readily, have good appetites, and this one was quite tame and an eager subject. We anticipated no trouble. Conditioning him to pick up the first coin was simple. We started out by reinforcing him for picking up a single coin. Then the container was introduced, with the requirement that he drop the coin into the container. Here we ran into the first bit of difficulty: he seemed to have a great deal of trouble letting go of the coin. He would rub it up against the inside of the container, pull it back out, and clutch it firmly for several seconds. However, he would finally turn it loose and receive his food reinforcement. Then the final contingency: we put him on a ratio of 2, requiring that he pick up both coins and put them in the container. Now

Raccoons can be conditioned to perform a variety of tasks but instinctual drift may interfere with the conditioning process.

the raccoon really had problems (and so did we). Not only could he not let go of the coins, but he spent seconds, even minutes, rubbing them together (in a most miserly fashion), and dipping them into the container. He carried on this behavior to such an extent that the practical application we had in mind—a display featuring a raccoon putting money in a piggy bank—simply was not feasible. The rubbing behavior became worse and worse as time went on, in spite of nonreinforcement. (Breland & Breland, 1960, p. 682)

Why was it so difficult to train the raccoon to perform this task? The Brelands suggested it was due to *instinctual drift,* meaning that the animal's instinctual behavior (its natural biological reaction to the situation) interfered with learning the task. It is instinctual for raccoons to wash their food meticulously before eating it. Apparently, since the coins had been paired with food, much like a CR, the raccoon treated the coins like food. In the Brelands' task, then, the instinctual behavior of washing the coin prevented the animal from depositing it in the slot. Under these circumstances, conditioning is difficult and sometimes impossible.

Ethology and Learning

Ethologists are scientists who study the behavior of organisms in their natural environment rather than in a laboratory setting. In fact, research such as that on taste-aversion learning and the misbehavior of organisms has led ethologists to question the validity of using a laboratory setting for the psychological study of learning.

Ethologists argue that it is most beneficial to study how organisms learn in a natural environment where the organisms' powerful natural biological reactions can occur. For example, in a natural setting, organisms can associate illness with the taste of polluted water even when the two are separated by several hours. But when the same association is studied in a laboratory setting, where the experimenter can control the CS and US so that they always occur within a second of each other, all aspects of the organisms' natural power of association may not be brought out. For instance, the strict control in the laboratory would not allow for an "accident" that would show that even when the time between the CS and the US stretched

to several hours, the association was still formed effectively. Therefore, ethologists hold that this learned association may have been found much sooner through research done in the natural environment. They feel that a highly controlled laboratory setting masks some of the phenomena that can occur during learning.

Does this mean that the principles of classical and operant conditioning discovered in the laboratory may not operate in the real world? Some research provides an interesting insight into this issue (Fox, 1983; Miller, 1983).

Research by Karen Hollis has suggested that laboratory learning principles such as those derived from classical conditioning may be very valuable in the natural environment (Hollis, 1991). To make this point, Hollis has studied conditioning in tropical fish called blue goramies. The male of this species is very territorial and will attack any other male who enters its territory. In a classical conditioning experiment with these fish, Hollis paired a red light (the CS) with a rival male (the US). The purpose of this was to elicit aggressive behavior in the male whenever it saw the red light. A control group did not receive these pairings. She then tested subjects from the two groups of fish in a natural environment. During testing, she placed a previously conditioned male in the tank—his territory. He was then shown a red light, immediately followed by the presentation of another male fish. Hollis found that fish that had undergone classical conditioning won territorial contests significantly more often than did the control fish (Hollis, 1984; Overmier & Hollis, 1990).

According to Hollis, the red light for fish in the conditioning group allowed these fish to prepare better for the fight to come in the same way that salivation by Pavlov's dogs allowed them to prepare to digest the meat powder.

How is this research related to the debate between the ethologists and psychologists about how to study learning? Research such as Hollis' suggests that both approaches have merit. It suggests that the principles of learning developed in the laboratory can operate in the natural environment and it is up to researchers from a variety of disciplines to determine exactly how laboratory learning principles might operate in the real world.

Although researchers have been studying conditioning for nearly a century, they have only recently begun to recognize the importance of its biological aspects. An awareness of these biological influences should put psychologists in a better position to explain the very complex process of learning.

Interim Summary

The concept of preparedness states that certain associations are learned more easily than others. For example, animals learn to associate the taste of a liquid with illness even after just one trial and even when the delay between tasting the liquid and becoming ill is as long as 12 hours. This is called taste-aversion learning, and it has been demonstrated with humans as well as other animals. The concept of preparedness may also help explain why humans easily learn certain fears, such as fears of snakes.

In contrast, some behaviors are impossible for certain animals to learn, as demonstrated in the Brelands' work on the "misbehavior of organisms." The Breland's found, for example, that racoons could not be taught to put a coin in a bank to receive food. The research on preparedness suggests that biology and the genetic history of an organism do have an effect on the organism's ability to learn.

THE COGNITIVE APPROACH TO LEARNING

The focus of this chapter thus far has been the associative approach to conditioning. Its pioneering researchers, such as Pavlov and Thorndike, believed that conditioning occurred in a very mechanistic way. When a response occurred in the presence of a particular stimulus and that response was reinforced, a stimulus-response (S-R) connection was formed. As the response was reinforced more and more, the S-R connection was "stamped in" until the behavior became automatic. Thus, a rat that presses a bar or a dog that salivates is showing an automatic S-R pattern. This approach, sometimes referred to as the S-R approach to learning, has contributed much of what psychologists know about learning (Rescorla & Holland, 1982). But more recently, some psychologists have argued that this view may be too simplis-

tic. These psychologists have adopted the cognitive approach to learning. The *cognitive approach* to learning holds that learning is not simply an automatic process. Rather, the cognitive approach maintains that important cognitive, or mental, processes occur between the stimulus and the response (Rescola, 1988; Kesner & Olton, 1991). One of the first proponents of the cognitive approach was Edward Tolman. Tolman proposed the cognitive view of learning as a reaction to Thorndike's law of effect (Tolman, 1948). According to Tolman, all organisms, including animals, are capable of thinking and this capacity must be considered in any explanation of learning. It is too simple to regard an organism like a vending machine—put in a stimulus and expect a response. Rather, psychologists must recognize that in learning the organism takes in information about its surroundings and attempts to use this information to adapt to its environment. This is true for all behaviors, even a seemingly simple one like a rat learning to bar press (Hulse, Fowler, & Honig, 1978; Spear & Miller, 1982). The cognitive approach holds that it is important to examine these mental processes during conditioning.

To help appreciate the distinction between the S-R and cognitive approaches to learning, let's consider a now-classic experiment conducted by O. L. Tinklepaugh in 1928. In this experiment, a monkey was allowed to observe Tinklepaugh place a banana under one of two cups. When the monkey was then allowed to select one of the cups, it selected the one hiding the banana. In the next phase of the experiment, the monkey again watched Tinklepaugh place the banana under the cup. But this time, while the cups were out of the monkey's view, Tinklepaugh exchanged the banana for a piece of lettuce. When the monkey was allowed to choose, it selected the correct cup. But when the monkey found lettuce instead of the banana, it showed surprise and frustration, rejected the lettuce, and began searching for the banana.

Using evidence such as this, Tolman argued that the monkey did not simply make an automatic connection between the stimulus and the response. Rather, its behavior was guided by cognitive processes such as memory and expectancy. That is, the monkey *remembered* that a banana was placed under the cup and *expected* to find it there.

Edward Tolman
(1886–1959)

S-R Learning

Stimulus   Organism   Response

Bell ─────────→ | Automatic Association | ─────────→ Salivation

Cognitive Learning

Stimulus   Organism   Response

Bell ─────────→ | Perception / Memory ↻ Expectancy | ─────────→ Salivation

Figure 6.21
The S-R and Cognitive Approaches to Learning.

Expectancy, the view that an organism comes to expect a reinforcer, has also been used to explain very simple forms of learning such as classical conditioning. For example, when Pavlov's dogs salivated at the sound of the bell, it was because they expected food to follow, not simply because they made an automatic connection between the bell and meat powder. Salivating was a way to prepare to eat the expected food (Mackintosh, 1983). **Figure 6.21** contrasts the cognitive and S-R views of learning.

In this section we will examine some of the other evidence that suggests a cognitive view of learning. We will begin with some of the very early work of Wolfgang Köhler, who studied insight learning in chimps. We will then examine a phenomenon called observational learning, and we will conclude this section with some research that has far-ranging implications for human behavior, the phenomenon of learned helplessness.

Insight Learning in Chimps

Most of us have had the experience of studying a difficult problem for a long period of time with little progress toward the solution and then suddenly having an "aha" experience and realizing in a flash how to solve that math prob-

Wolfgang Kohler
(1887–1967)

lem, fix the stereo, or finally get the computer program to run. Is this type of insightful learning unique to humans?

In the 1920s, German psychologist Wolfgang Köhler was on the island of Tenerife, off the west coast of Africa near the equator. Apparently, Köhler was a German spy whose job was to monitor shipping (Ley, 1991). But Köhler was also a psychologist, and while on Tenerife he decided to take advantage of the local population of primates to study insight learning in chimps. His results directly challenged the S-R view of Thorndike.

According to Thorndike's law of effect, intelligent behavior is the result of random trial and error. A cat does not "figure out" how to escape from the puzzle box. Rather the cat produces a wide range of unintelligent behavior until it stumbles on the one behavior that allows it to escape from the box. This behavior then is "stamped in." Thus, Thorndike viewed learning as the automatic process of connecting the stimulus and the response. Köhler, however, had other ideas. He felt that at least sometimes the animal's behavior was intelligent right from the start.

To support his view, Köhler cataloged some examples of insight learning in the chimp. In one situation the chimps could see some tempting bananas above them, but the fruit was just out of reach. Köhler then distributed an assortment of boxes and sticks throughout the chimps' play area. Köhler (1925) observed that a chimp might first try to reach the fruit by jumping at it. Eventually, the chimp would give up and begin pacing back and forth. Suddenly the pacing would stop. The chimp would then act quite purposively in a way that would allow it to obtain the bananas. One chimp gathered boxes and stacked them, then climbed them to obtain the fruit. Another chimp took two hollow bamboo sticks and made one long stick by inserting one into the other. He then used the stick to retrieve the banana. Yet another chimp used a box and a stick, climbing on the single box and using the stick to swat at the banana. It looked as though the chimps had thought about the problem and suddenly arrived at the solution.

Köhler took these findings as evidence that chimps, like humans, showed insight learning. More generally, findings of this type are taken as evidence of cognitive learning in animals (Riotblat, 1987).

Photos from Kohler's early study of chimps and insight learning.

Observational Learning

A second area of research suggesting evidence for a cognitive view of learning is observational learning. **Observational learning, or modeling,** as it is sometimes called, is learning that results from watching the behaviors of others and observing their consequences. Research on observational learning questions the S-R view of learning because in these situations the learner neither directly experiences the stimuli nor makes the responses (Bandura, 1986).

The fact that humans learn a great deal by watching others probably comes as no surprise. In a typical experiment to examine the effects of observational learning, the subject will watch another person, the model, respond to a certain situation in a particular way. Later, the subject will be put in the same situation and the experimenter will determine how much the subject imitates the model's behavior. Often, the behavior of the model will have a profound influence on the subject's behavior. In one study, children who had won money in a table bowling game had the opportunity to donate some of this money to the March of Dimes. Before playing the game, the children saw a television sequence in which a model either made a donation, while commenting that it is good to donate, or spoke against donating

and gave no money. The children who saw the model donate contributed much more money (Bryan & Walbeck, 1970).

Do animals learn by observation? There has been some controversy over this point. Thorndike (1898) was interested in determining if cats could learn to escape from a puzzle box by observing a previously trained cat perform the escape response. He was unable to show that any of his animals learned by observation. But other experimenters have reported positive results. Kinnaman (1902) placed a monkey in a box from which it could escape by pulling out a plug that secured the lid. The monkey failed to work the mechanism and eventually gave up. Later, the unsuccessful monkey watched another monkey solve the problem by biting the end of the plug and pulling it out with his teeth. When the unsuccessful monkey was given another try, it solved the problem immediately. Following this study, many other experimenters have reported that animals, like humans, can learn by observation (see, for example, Green & Osborne, 1985; Menzel, 1978).

As we will see in later chapters, the research on observational learning has been very influential and has been applied to such diverse issues as how children may learn aggressive behavior from watching television and how to help people deal with phobias. For now, it is important to realize that observational learning does not support the view that all learning is simply an automatic S-R process.

Learned Helplessness

In our discussion of expectancy in Tinklepaugh's monkeys, we saw that when an organism expects a positive reinforcer and does not get it, it can react with disappointment. But how does an organism react when its behavior does not terminate an aversive stimulus as expected? The result in this situation is one of the most interesting phenomena in conditioning—the organism learns to be helpless. Let's first examine the experiment in which this principle was discovered and then discuss its implications.

In the experiment, dogs were divided into three groups. One group underwent standard escape learning. The dogs were restrained in a hammock and given shocks to their hind legs. They could terminate (escape) the shock by pushing a button with their noses. Dogs in the second group, the helpless group, also were suspended in a harness and received shocks to their hind legs but could not terminate the shock by pushing a button. Dogs in the third group, the control group, were placed in hammocks but did not receive shocks (Seligman & Maier, 1967).

In the second phase of the experiment, Seligman and Maier put each dog in a compartment of a two-way shuttle box and delivered shocks to the dog. As you might expect, dogs in the escape and control groups had no difficulty learning to run to the opposite compartment to escape the shock. But dogs in the helpless group never learned to shuttle to the opposite compartment.

> The behavior of the preshocked dogs was bizarre. When they received the first shock in the shuttle box, they initially looked like the naive dogs: they ran about frantically, howled, defecated, and urinated. However, unlike naive dogs, they soon stopped running around and quietly whimpered until the trial terminated. After a few trials, they seemed to "give up" and passively "accept" the shock. On later trials, these dogs failed to make any escape movements at all. A few dogs would get up and jump the barrier, escaping or avoiding shock; yet surprisingly, on

the next trial such a dog would go back to taking shock. It did not seem to learn that barrier-jumping produced shock termination. (Seligman, Maier, & Solomon, 1971, p. 355)

Seligman and Maier reasoned that during the first stage of the experiment, dogs in the helpless group learned that they had no control over their situation. No matter what they did, they could not escape the shock. Since these dogs had learned to be helpless, they didn't try to escape even when placed in a situation where escape was possible. **Learned helplessness** is the name given to this phenomenon whereby an organism does not attempt to escape an aversive stimulus after the organism has previously been subjected to a similar, inescapable aversive stimulus.

Learned helplessness also occurs in humans. In one experiment, college volunteers were presented with an aversive stimulus in the form of a loud, unpleasant noise. They were told that they could stop the noise by moving a control device. But actually these devices did not control anything. Later, when the volunteers were placed in a situation in which moving a lever *would* stop the noise, the volunteers made no attempt to do so. Instead, they tolerated the noise until the experiment was over. Like the dogs, they had learned to be helpless (Hiroto & Seligman, 1975).

The principle of learned helplessness shows that when organisms are placed in a situation over which they have no control, they develop the expectation that their behavior will not have any effect (Maier, 1989). This expectation then transfers to new situations where it may not be true. As we will see in Chapter 16, this important principle can be applied to a variety of situations.

Cognitive or Stimulus-Response Learning?

The research that we have described in this section questions the S-R view of learning. Does this mean that the S-R theory is wrong and should be abandoned? Probably not.

Rather than trying to call one theory right and the other wrong, it may be more fruitful to think of them as being complementary. Some forms of learning seem better explained by an S-R point of view, whereas others are better suited to the cognitive approach. Still others may require aspects of each. It is likely that we will need to use principles and theories from both points of view in order to understand the complexity of human learning.

For example, certain learned behaviors do seem very automatic. Consider driving a car. Most experienced drivers are able to perform this complex task while paying little or no attention to it. They respond automatically to stimuli such as green lights, stop signs, or children running into the street. Although cognitive processes may have come into play when these people first learned these reactions, the task now seems very automatic. Now contrast this with trying to learn to write a computer program. In this instance the programmer must reason about many facts, rules, and complex relationships to be successful. It seems that cognitive processes play a large role here. Nevertheless, as the programmer becomes proficient, some aspects may become automatic.

Both S-R and cognitive learning may interact in a variety of situations. This dual approach is now held by many psychologists (Premack, 1983). Nevertheless, cognition has taken on an increasingly important role in psychology. Indeed, some psychologists have referred to the past 20 years as the "cognitive revolution in psychology" (Gardner, 1985). In the next two chapters we will take a closer look at some of the topics that cognitive psychologists have studied, including memory, thinking, and language.

Interim Summary

The cognitive approach to conditioning argues that in order to understand learning it is necessary to study more than just stimuli and responses. The cognitive approach assumes that learning results from thinking and other mental processes such as memory and expectancy.

Support for the cognitive approach comes from several lines of research, including Köhler's work on insight learning in chimps, observational learning, and research on learned helplessness. Köhler's work on insight learning found that chimps could solve problems in ways other than trial and error, the method used by Thorndike's cats. The research on observational learning or modeling has shown that both humans and animals can learn by watching others. In the learned-helplessness studies, dogs who were unable to escape an aversive stimulus (a

shock) learned to be helpless. They developed the expectation that their behavior had no effect. Later, they did not try to escape the shock even though escape was possible.

Each of these studies suggests that simple S-R associations may not be sufficient to explain all types of learning, but it does not mean that we should abandon S-R learning. Each approach to the study of conditioning provides valuable information. The study of simple associations in classical and operant conditioning has provided the basic information about learning. The biological approach has shown that not all tasks are learned equally well and that the differences may be due to biological factors. The cognitive approach has shown that in some instances the learner may learn more than S-R associations.

SUMMARY

1. Learning is a relatively permanent change in immediate or potential behavior due to experience. It is the process by which organisms adapt to an ever changing environment.
2. Psychologists approach learning by studying two fundamental processes—classical and operant conditioning.
3. In classical conditioning, an unconditioned stimulus reflexively produces an unconditioned response. If a neutral, or conditioned, stimulus is then paired with the unconditioned stimulus, it will produce a conditioned or learned response.
4. In operant conditioning, the organism first exhibits a behavior and then that behavior has a consequence that determines whether or not the behavior will continue to be emitted. If the organism receives a positive reinforcement for emitting the behavior, the rate of the behavior will increase. This is called positive reinforcement. If the behavior causes an aversive stimulus (e.g., a shock) to be removed, this will also increase the rate of the behavior. This is called negative reinforcement. If the organism emits a behavior and this produces an aversive stimulus, the behavior will occur less often. This is called punishment.
5. Both classical and operant conditioning show extinction, generalization, and dis-

crimination. In extinction, in classical conditioning, the CS is no longer followed by the US and eventually the CR no longer occurs. In operant conditioning, the behavior is no longer followed by the reinforcer, so it also stops occurring. In generalization, the organism responds to stimuli that are similar to the CS (classical conditioning) or discriminative stimulus (operant conditioning). In discrimination, the organism learns to respond to only the original stimulus and not to similar stimuli.

6. Organisms seem better able to learn certain associations than others. For example, humans and animals readily learn to associate the taste of a particular substance with illness even after just one exposure and with a very long time between tasting the food and becoming ill. In contrast, some associations seem impossible to learn. Recall the case of the "miserly racoon." This concept, called preparedness, suggests that the genetic history of the organism better enables the organism to learn certain associations that are important to survival and shows the important relationship between biology and conditioning.

7. The cognitive approach to learning comes not only from automatic stimulus-response associations, but from mental processes such as expectancy, thinking, and memory. Support from the cognitive approach comes from research on insight learning in chimps, observational learning in children, and the work on learned helplessness in dogs.

8. The various approaches to learning, classical and operant conditioning, preparedness, and cognitive learning all demonstrate that learning is a complex process and is best understood by combining information from a variety of perspectives.

KEY INDIVIDUALS

Ivan Pavlov
Neil Miller
John B. Watson
Martin Seligman
Rosalie Rayner
John Garcia
"Little Albert"
Ilene Bernstein
B. F. Skinner
Marion and Keller Breland
E. L. Thorndike
Karen Hollis
Fred Keller
Edward Tolman
O. H. Mowrer
O. L. Tinklepaugh
Wolfgang Köhler

KEY RESEARCH

Pavlov's dogs and conditioned reflexes
"Little Albert" and conditioned fear
classical conditioning and the immune system
Thorndike's puzzle box and the law of effect
Skinner and the consequences of behavior
the experimental analysis of behavior
taste-aversion learning in animals and humans
the "misbehavior" of organisms and instinctual drift
the cognitive approach to learning
evidence for expectancy in studies with monkeys
insight learning in chimps
learned helplessness

KEY TERMS

adaptation
learning
classical conditioning
operant conditioning
reflex
unconditioned response (UR)
unconditioned stimulus (US)
conditioned stimulus (CS)
conditioned response (CR)
acquisition
generalization
discrimination
extinction
spontaneous recovery
instrumental conditioning
law of effect
positive reinforcer
positive reinforcement
negative reinforcer
negative reinforcement
punisher
punishment
shaping

discriminative stimulus
primary reinforcers
conditioned reinforcer
chaining
continuous reinforcement schedule (CRF)
partial reinforcement schedule
ratio schedules
interval schedules
fixed-ratio (FR) schedule
variable-ratio (VR) schedule

fixed-interval (FI) schedule
variable-interval (VI) schedule
partial reinforcement effect
escape learning
avoidance learning
two-process theory
expectancy
observational learning
modeling
learned helplessness

7 Human Memory

CHAPTER OUTLINE

254

One of the most remarkable aspects of human memory is that it takes just a few seconds to form a memory that can last a lifetime. How does this happen? How will you remember tomorrow what you learn today? What is memory? These are but of few of the questions that we will try to answer in this chapter.

In its very simplest form, **memory** is the ability to store information so that it can be used at a later time. Defined this way, memory is not limited to humans or even to living organisms. By this definition, tape recorders, videotape machines, and computers all have memory. Information can be recorded and stored on videotape to be used at a later time just as information can be stored in human memory to be used at a later time. But even though these two types of memory have much in common, human memory is a far more complex process. For example, the most sophisticated videotape can store only 8 hours of information. In a comparable amount of space, the human brain can store a lifetime's worth of knowledge. Even the most advanced computer cannot approach this capacity. To find a single piece of information on a videotape (one frame) it is necessary to search the entire tape, a process that may take hours. Finding a single piece of information in human memory, such as where you were born, usually takes a fraction of a second. And while videotapes have the ability to store only visual and auditory information, human memory can store information from any of our senses. Finally, human memory has the extraordinary capacity to mix, intermingle, and combine information in a way that no artificial memory system can approach.

Even this short look at human memory tells us that it is a rich, complex, and exciting process. In this chapter we will examine the abilities and capacities of human memory. We will focus on three basic questions regarding human memory: How do we place information into memory? How do we keep information in memory? How do we find information already stored in memory? Psychologists have been attempting to find the answers to these seemingly simple questions for over a century, and understanding what they have learned about these three processes is the key to unlocking the mystery of human memory.

Although we tend to talk about placing information into memory, keeping it there, and finding it, psychologists use somewhat more precise terms. Placing information into memory is called **encoding**. This often means changing the form of the information. To encode information into a computer's memory, we type symbols on a keyboard. As we will see, for humans encoding might involve forming a memory code of how an object looks or how it sounds or what it means. **Storage** refers to how a system maintains or remembers information. For the computer, this means modifying small electrical circuits. **Retrieval** refers to getting the stored information out of memory. Both computers and humans retrieve information by searching the contents of memory for the desired information. (**Figure 7.1**)

FORMING MEMORIES

Have you ever been to a party where you didn't know many people? If so, chances are you were introduced to many new people during the course of the night. And if you are like most of us, you probably did not remember many of their names. You may even have had the embarrassing experience of meeting one of these "new acquaintances" the next day only to find you did not know their name. Why can't you remember the person's name? Probably because you never formed the memory to begin with. In the next sections we will examine the two processes that allow us to form memories: encoding and storage.

Encoding

The first step in forming a new memory is encoding. Each day we are bombarded with thousands of pieces of new information—names of people we have met, names of authors from literature classes, new terms in psychology classes, equations in chemistry classes, phone numbers and dates to remember. How is this information encoded into memory? Psychologists now realize that there are several different ways that information can be encoded. Some

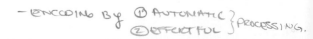

Figure 7.1
A Simplified View of Human Memory.

Diagram: Encoding (Forming Memories) → Storage (Maintaining Memories) → Retrieval (Recalling Memories)

Handwritten margin notes:

Memory: ABILITY TO STORE INFO TO BE USED LATER (NOT LIMITED)

- INFO RETRIEVED IN SECONDS
- STORE INFO FROM OUR SENSES.
- Fig 7.1

→ BASIC PARTS:
① ENCODING: PLACING INFO INTO MEMORY, (By CHANGING THE FORM OF INFO)
② STORAGE: HOW A SYSTEM MAINTAINS / REMEMBERS INFO.
③ RETRIEVAL: GETTING STORED INFO OUT OF MEMORY.

- 2 PROCESSES THAT ALLOW US TO FORM MEMORIES: ① ENCODING ② STORAGE

TO FORM MEMORY

- ENCODING BY ① AUTOMATIC ② EFFORTFUL } PROCESSING.

information is encoded with little or no effort. This is called automatic processing. You can probably remember what you had for breakfast today, even though you did not work at encoding this information. Other types of information require substantial effort, or what some psychologists call effortful processing or "mental work" (Klatzky 1980).

AUTOMATIC PROCESSING — NO EFFORT

Students probably appreciate as well as anyone that encoding some types of information requires effort. Learning the material in this chapter for an upcoming test will require practice, rehearsal, and other types of mental work. But does this mean that only rehearsed information can be encoded? Recently, psychologists have discovered that some information can be automatically encoded. *Automatic processing* is the effortless encoding of information. If you could automatically encode the information in this chapter, you would simply read it and have it stored. But only certain types of information can be stored automatically (and, unfortunately for students, not the type of information found in textbooks) (**Figure 7.2**).

Automatic processing is not under conscious control. For example, you do not actively rehearse the places you have visited during the day so that you can recall them later. But you probably can recall quite accurately the places you went yesterday. Perhaps the best example of this type of effortless recall occurs when you must mentally retrace your steps to find something you have lost.

Automatic processing has also been demonstrated in the laboratory. Lynn Hascher and Rose Zachs showed subjects a long list of words. Subjects in one group were told that they would be asked to remember how many times a particular word occurred. Subjects in a second group were given no such instructions, yet they remembered as well as the subjects who were warned (Hascher & Zachs, 1979). These studies suggest that certain information, such as how often something occurs, does not require effortful processing to remember; it is automatically encoded in memory.

EFFORTFUL PROCESSING

Effortful processing requires attention and mental work. It is the kind of mental work that we all go through when we have to learn new information such as the terms and concepts in this chapter. Students call this studying; psychologists call it effortful processing.

The study of human memory involves three process similar to the way computers process and store information. These are encoding, storage, and retrieval.

[handwritten: Fig 7.2 → ENCODING → (A) AUTOMATIC (NO PROCESSING : EFFORT)]

[handwritten: — NOT UNDER CONSCIOUS CONTROL. — NO REHEARSAL. — AUTOMATICALLY ENCODED.]

Just as there is more than one way to study, their is more than one way to effortfully process information. Moreover, just as all forms of studying are not equally successful, all forms of effortful processing are not equally successful in encoding information. A study by Fergus Craik and Endel Tulving (1975) pointed out some of the ways we effortfully process information and, more important, how some forms of effortful processing are better than others. Fergus and Craik distinguished between two types of effortful processing, elaborative rehearsal and maintenance rehearsal. **Maintenance rehearsal** is the simple repetition of information. This type of rehearsal, however, is not the most effective way to encode information (Greene, 1987). In order to accomplish encoding, a second type of rehearsal, elaborative

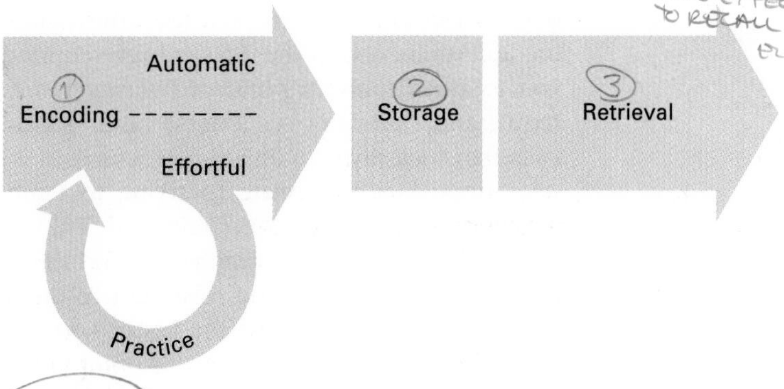

*[handwritten: (B) EFFORTFUL PROCESSING : — REQUIRES ATTENTION + MENTAL WORK (EG. STUDYING). — 2 TYPES: (a) MAINTENANCE REHEARSAL: REPETITION OF INFO (NOT → really effective) (b) ELABORATIVE REHEARSAL: ANALYSING MEANING OF NEW INFO + RELATING IT TO OLD INFO IN LONG TERM MEMORY. * MORE EFFECTIVE TO RECALL USING ELABORATIVE]*

Figure diagram:
① Automatic Encoding - - - - - Effortful
② Storage
③ Retrieval
Practice

Figure 7.2
Encoding—Automatic and Effortful Processing.

rehearsal, is best (Horton & Mills, 1984; Nelson, 1977). **Elaborative rehearsal** involves analyzing the meaning of the new information and relating it to information already in long-term memory.

A study by Craik and Tulving (1975) demonstrated that the more elaborate the rehearsal, that is, the more we analyze the material for meaning, the better the recall. To demonstrate this to yourself, try the following experiment, which is very much like Craik and Tulving's.

First, read the list of words in the margin. Then answer the following questions about the top four words in the list. Answer each question only once, and when you have finished a question do not go back to it.

1. Is each word printed in capital or small letters?
2. How many letters does each word have?
3. Does each word rhyme with care?

Now answer the next three questions about the bottom four words in the list.

1. Is the word a noun or a verb?
2. Give a synonym for the word.
3. Does the word fit into any of the following sentences?
   The child spun the_____.
   She took the _____ to school.
   He wore a _____ hat.

Now, without looking back at any of the words, recall as many as you can.

If you behaved like the subjects in Craik and Tulving's experiment, you probably recalled more words from the second group than from the first (see **Figure 7.3**). This is because the questions about the second list required you to attend to the *meanings* of the words. These questions involved identifying parts of speech, synonyms, and whether the words made sense in a sentence. On the other hand, the questions about the first group required you to attend only to *physical characteristics* (type and number of letters) and sound (whether they rhyme with another word).

How does this relate to trying to study new material? Just as the Craik and Tulving study suggests, the more time you spend thinking about new material and relating it to other information that you know, the better you will remember it. We will return to this point in the section on improving memory.

tape
TREE
CAR
bear
TOP
book
PEN
red

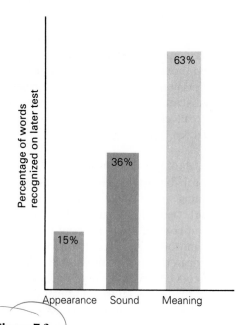

Figure 7.3
How Recall from Long-Term Memory Is Affected by Analyzing Words by Appearance, Sound, and Meaning. (After Craik, 1977)

ENCODING BY MEANING AND IMAGES

Try to remember what the person sitting next to you in your last class was wearing. Now try to remember the main point of the lecture or discussion in the same class. Chances are your memory of what your classmate was wearing is in the form of an image, a mental picture. But your memory of the content of the last class is probably in the form of words, probably a summary of the meaning of the lecture or discussion. This simple demonstration points out that two distinct types of encoding exist—encoding by images and encoding by meaning.

Encoding by meaning is called semantic encoding. **Semantic encoding** is remembering the general meaning of words and sentences. For example, a few minutes after hearing a sentence, all we can recall is the meaning or the main idea of the sentence, not each word. Jacqueline Sachs (1967) demonstrated this phenomenon by having subjects listen to the sentence "The good guy shot the bad guy." A few minutes later, after hearing a series of other sentences, the subjects were presented with slightly different forms of the original sentence to see if they could recognize the changes. Sachs found that the subjects could not tell the difference between the original sentence, "The good guy shot the bad guy," and a rearranged sentence with the same meaning,

Mary had a little lamb,
  Its fleece was white as snow;
And everywhere that Mary went,
  The lamb was sure to go.

He followed her to school one day—
  That was against the rule;
It made the children laugh and play,
  To see a lamb at school.

So the teacher turned him out,
  But still he lingered near,
And waited patiently about,
  Till Mary did appear.

Then he ran to her, and laid
  His head upon her arm,
As if he said, "I'm not afraid—
  You'll keep me from all harm."

"What makes the lamb love Mary so?"
  The eager children cry.
"Oh, Mary loves the lamb, you know,"
  The teacher did reply.

Sarah Josepha Hale

Figure 7.4
Words to "Mary's Lamb."

"The bad guy was shot by the good guy." This indicated that the subjects were not storing the sentence verbatim (word for word), rather they were only storing the meaning. You might demonstrate this to yourself by trying to recall the poem "Mary's Lamb" (you may know it as "Mary Had a Little Lamb"). You probably cannot recall the entire poem (see **Figure 7.4**) word for word, but you can recall the meaning, or gist, of what happened.

A second way to encode meanings is **imagery coding,** or creating a mental image of an object or a scene. Evidence indicates that we use both semantic and imagery coding (Paivio, 1986; Paivio & Desrochers, 1980). It is not clear, however, whether semantic or imagery coding is more effective. A series of experiments conducted by Alan Paivio (1971) suggests that images may be easier to recall than words. The following demonstration is quite similar to Paivio's experiments. Try to memorize the seven pairs of words given in list A below. You should spend no more than 5 seconds memorizing each pair. Once you have examined a pair, do not return to it. After you have memorized the list of pairs, cover the second column and try to remember the words that are paired with each word in the first column.

List A

calculator — bookshelf
poster — check
book — pencil
lamppost — shutter
knife — fireplace
stamp — ribbon
shoe — notebook

Now try the same for the pairs in list B, but this time use the following imagery system to improve your recall. For each pair, conjure up an image that contains both items in the pair. For example, for the pair *typewriter-wall,* you might think of a typewriter hanging on a hook on a wall, or perhaps a picture of a typewriter painted on a wall. Because some evidence indicates that the more unusual an image the better the recall, you could be even more creative and see, for example, a typewriter being splattered into pieces against the wall (see **Figure 7.5**). Again, allow only 5 seconds per pair, and be sure to create images.

After memorizing the pairs, cover the first column and test yourself. If you performed like the subjects in Paivio's experiments, you probably did better on the list in which you used imagery (Paivio, 1971). Experiments like this suggest that imagery is a more effective memory system.

List B

typewriter — wall
television — magazine
notebook — crayon
telephone — roof
fork — table
coin — dresser
shirt — frying pan

Imagery has also been used outside the laboratory to help remember things in everyday situations. One of the most interesting examples of the use of imagery in memory concerns John Conrad, a waiter in Boulder, Colorado, who once took 19 complete dinner orders, never wrote down a single item, and delivered each order to the right person without error. Conrad had to remember all the entrees, salad dressings, types of potatoes and vegetables, how each cut of meat should be cooked, as well as all the special requests (hold the salt and bring some extra mushrooms, please). Moreover, this feat was not an isolated instance. Conrad always works with his memory alone—never a pencil or pad.

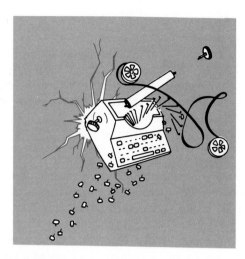

Figure 7.5
Imagery Coding.
This is a visual image that might help you recall the word pair typewriter-wall.

Can Conrad do this because he has a superior memory? Laboratory research using Conrad as a subject indicates that he has just an average memory but has learned to use it very efficiently (Ericsson & Polson, 1985). One of the techniques that he routinely uses is imagery. When memorizing an order, he begins by using imagery to associate the entree with the customer's face. For example, when taking an order for a Boulder steak, Conrad might take note of the customer's beefy set of jowls; combining the steak with the "beefy" jowls, he forms an image (Singular, 1982). He then goes on to make further associations, often through imagery, between other parts of the meal and the entree. By doing this he is able to use an average memory in a highly efficient manner.

We should point out that not all psychologists agree that imagery is the key to better recall (Anderson & Bower, 1973). Similar improvements in recall for word pairs can be obtained without using imagery. In a variation of Paivio's experiment, subjects were instructed

to connect each word pair by remembering a sentence that used both words. For example, for the word pair "typewriter-wall," the subjects might remember the sentence "The typewriter was hanging on the wall." The results of this experiment indicated that this method helped recall to the same extent that imagery did (Bower, 1972). Thus, although psychologists do not agree on whether images or sentences are a better way to encode lists of words (both help), they do agree that the critical factor is forming relationships or associations among the material to be learned (Maraschark, Richman, Yuille, Hunt, 1987; Paivio, 1986).

Interim Summary

The first process in memory is the formation of new memories is encoding. This is the process whereby new information is placed into memory. Some information is encoded automatically or effortlessly. For example, you can probably recall the places you visited yesterday even though you did not actively rehearse these places. A second method of encoding information is called effortful processing. This requires attention and mental work. Studying is one example of effortful processing. Psychologists have discovered that certain types of rehearsal are best for encoding information. Maintenance rehearsal, simply repeating a list of words over and over, is not a good way to encode information. Elaborative rehearsal, which involves analyzing the words for meaning and relating the words to other information already stored in memory, works much better. Finally, psychologists have discovered that some information is encoded by meaning or words; this is called semantic encoding. Other information is encoded as images or pictures; this is called imagery encoding. **Figure 7.6** summarizes the encoding process.

Storage

Once an event is placed or encoded in memory it must somehow be maintained there. *Storage* is the process by which a system maintains or remembers information.

Although psychologists have been studying memory for only a little over 100 years, speculation about how memories could be

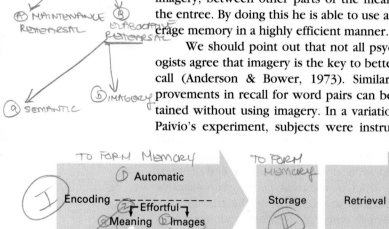

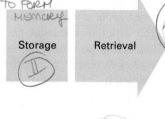

Figure 7.6
The Encoding Process.

stored have dated back to the ancient Greeks. Aristotle speculated that memory was like a block of wax. When memories were stored, they made an impression on the wax. As long as the impression lasted, the memory remained stored. A more contemporary analogy to how memory might be stored involves the computer (as technology has grown more sophisticated, so have our analogies). Today psychologists interested in memory storage often discuss the storage process in terms of how a computer might store information. This approach has come to be known as the information processing model of memory (Atkinson & Shiffern, 1968; Klatzky, 1980; Neisser, 1967). In this approach, psychologists try to trace a piece of information, a telephone number for example, as it passes through human memory.

INFORMATION PROCESSING APPROACH

By using the information processing approach, psychologists consider how memory might be stored in three separate memory systems, sensory memory, short-term memory, and long-term memory. To begin to appreciate how information might be stored in each of these systems, consider the following example. It is 11:30 on a Friday night and you are famished. You decide to order a pizza, so you look up the number of the local pizza parlor, 555-8486, in the phone book. You close the phone book, dial the number, and place the order. Let's trace this phone number through the three memory systems.

Sensory memory registers information that enters through one or more of the five senses. It holds a nearly literal image of the sensory stimulus for a very brief period of time. In our example, the phone number is presented visually, so it enters through the eyes. Sensory memory holds an enormous amount of information. When you look up the phone number in the book, the number 555-8486 gets stored along with many other names and numbers on the page. Although sensory memory can store an enormous amount of information, it is not very useful in remembering the phone number, because the memory lasts less than 1 second. To remember the phone number long enough to dial, you have to transfer it from sensory memory into a somewhat longer-lasting memory system called short-term memory.

Short-term memory is a temporary storage system that lasts less than 20 seconds and has the capacity to store only about seven separate pieces of information. In our example this is ideal because the phone number is only seven digits and we need to remember it only long enough to dial the phone—about 15 to 20 seconds. Once we have finished using the information in short-term memory it can either be transferred to a permanent memory system or it can be lost (forgotten). We forget information that we do not feel we will need again. This is perhaps best illustrated when, 5 minutes after ordering the pizza, we decide to add mushrooms and onions and once again have to look up the phone number. If, however, when we initially looked up the phone number we decided we would use it many times in the future, we might have placed it in long-term memory. In contrast to short-term memory, which is a temporary memory system, **long-term memory** is a relatively permanent storehouse of knowledge. It has the capacity to store enormous amounts of information over long periods of time, perhaps a lifetime. When discussing sensory, short-term, and long-term memory, psychologists treat them as separate systems. They even diagram them as separate boxes. When first learning about memory, you may find it easier to think of memory systems as actual physical objects and to envision short-term memory as a little "box" residing somewhere in the brain.

Although the three memory storage systems we will discuss are very useful in helping to organize and understand what psychologists know about human memory, it is important to recognize that this is only a model of how psychologists think memory might work. A model is an analogy for or a representation of reality. For example, in Chapter 2 we likened the brain to a computer. The computer is an analogy, a model we use to describe how we think the brain works. In the same way, the memory systems we describe here are models, representations of how we think human memory works.

SENSORY MEMORY

To appreciate what a sensory memory is, try the following: turn off all the lights in your room except the desk lamp (or any fairly bright lamp). Close your eyes and hold up three fingers a few inches away from the light bulb. Now open and close your eyes once as quickly as possible. After you close your eyes you should notice that the image of your fingers lasts briefly and then quickly fades. This image is a visual sensory memory.

Handwritten margin notes:
DETAILS:
① SENSORY MEMORY:
– 2 CHARACTERISTICS:
  Ⓐ STORE LARGE AMT. OF INFO FROM SENSES
  Ⓑ STORE THIS INFO FOR A BRIEF PERIOD OF TIME.

→ GEORGE SPERLING EXPERIMENTS:
– VISUAL SENSORY MEMORY LASTED 1 SECOND, & IT'S CAPACITY WAS LARGE
– FIG 7.7, 7.8
– LETTER RECALL
– INFO STORED IS SO BRIEF THAT SOME INFO WAS LOST BEFORE SUBJECTS WERE ABLE TO RECITE IT.
– AFTER 1/10 OF A SECOND MEMORY STARTS TO FADE & AFTER 1 SECOND IT IS GONE. (∴ FORGOTTEN)
     — co —
– AUDITORY MEMORY HAS A LONGER DURATION THAN VISUAL SENSORY MEMORY.

Sensory memory has two important characteristics: (1) it can store an enormous amount of information, almost everything that we see or hear, and (2) it can store this information for only a very brief period of time.

What is the capacity of sensory memory? That is, how much information can be stored? And how long can this information be stored before it is lost or forgotten? The answers to these questions came from a series of ingenious experiments performed by George Sperling of Bell Laboratories (Sperling, 1960). Sperling's research showed that visual sensory memory started to decay after only one tenth of a second and was completely gone after 1 second. His experiments also indicated that the capacity of visual sensory memory was surprisingly large.

In his experiments, Sperling presented subjects with a card containing nine letters as shown below:

D L R
K T G
M L B

Subjects were allowed to view the card for only 50 milliseconds (1000 milliseconds equal 1 second). Sperling then asked the subjects to repeat all the letters they could remember. The most any subject could recall was four or five letters. In fact, no matter how many letters were on the card, the subjects could report only four or five letters (see **Figure 7.7**). However, many subjects indicated that they initially remembered (saw) many more than four or five letters, but the memory faded so quickly that by the time they recited the first few letters, they had forgotten the others. In an attempt to verify these reports, Sperling modified his initial experiment. Once again he presented the nine-letter card to the subjects for 50 milliseconds. But instead of asking for a full report, Sperling asked for a *partial report* of only the first, second, or third row. However, the subjects did not know *which* row they would be asked to report before the card had been removed. To indicate to the subjects which row they were to report, Sperling presented either a high, medium, or low tone immediately after the nine-letter card was turned off. The subjects were instructed that a high tone signaled they were to report the top row, a medium tone signaled the middle row, and a low tone signaled the bottom row (see **Figure 7.8a**.

To report a given row accurately, Sperling reasoned, the subjects' sensory memories would have to include all nine letters. The results of the experiment showed that subjects had near-perfect recall no matter which row was signaled. These results verified Sperling's suspicion that all the information was actually stored in sensory memory but so briefly that some of the information was lost before the subjects were able to recite all the letters (recall how quickly the image of your fingers faded).

With the knowledge that visual sensory memory was quite brief, Sperling next conducted a study to see exactly how long this sensory memory lasted. To accomplish this, he modified the partial-report procedure by varying the time between the presentation of the nine-letter card and the presentation of the tone indicating which line was to be recalled (see Figure 7.8b). If the tone occurred immediately after the nine letters, the entire image or sensory memory was signaled available. But as the tone was delayed and the image faded, the recall of the letters became worse. Sperling found that even after one-tenth of a second the memory started to fade. After 1 second the sensory memory was gone (see **Figure 7.9**). This fading or decay represents forgetting in sensory memory.

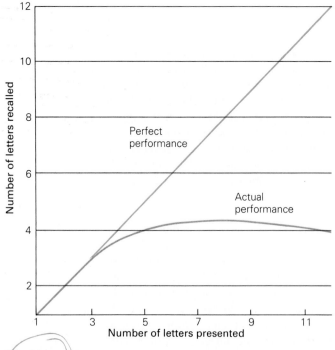

Figure 7.7
Sperling's Forgetting Curve for Sensory Memory. (Based on Sperling, 1960)

The Importance of Sensory Memory

Why should we have a memory system that lasts only a few tenths of a second? Consider what would happen if we did not have this system. Without visual sensory memory, we would experience a pause in the stream of visual information each time we blinked. Without auditory sensory memory we would also have some difficulty understanding language. Consider the case of a foreigner who is listening to a conversation and confuses the word *seal* with the word zeal. In order to clear up the confusion someone says, "No, not seal, zeal." The foreigner could not benefit from this information unless he or she could store the sound of the *S* in seal in auditory sensory memory long enough to compare it with the *Z* in zeal (Neisser, 1967). To accomplish this, auditory memory must have a longer duration than visual sensory memory (Darwin, Turvey, & Crowder, 1972). Estimates range from a few seconds to 10 seconds or longer (Cowan, 1984).

2 Short-Term Memory

Short- and long-term memory may be compared to a kitchen in which a chef is preparing a feast. All the ingredients necessary to prepare the feast—more than the chef can use at any one time—are neatly organized and stored in the cupboards and refrigerator. Only the items that the chef is working with, such as the soup ingredients, are on the worktable. When the chef begins to prepare the main course, the ingredients for the soup are placed back in storage and the main course ingredients are placed on the table. The cupboards and refrigerator represent a relatively *permanent storage* system for all the ingredients in the kitchen, while the worktable is a *temporary storage* system for the ingredients the chef is using at any one time. The shelves have an enormous storage capacity, but the capacity of the worktable is limited (Klatzky, 1980).

In this analogy, the shelves in the kitchen are something like long-term memory, and the chef's worktable is like short-term memory, a temporary system that has the capacity to hold only the limited number of items being worked with at a particular time. For this reason, short-term memory is sometimes called *working memory* (Baddeley, 1989).

In summary, short-term memory is a temporary storage system with the capacity to store a limited amount of information for a limited length of time or duration.

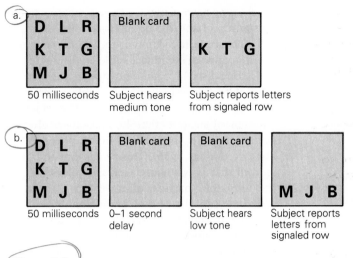

Figure 7.8
Sperling's Partial Report Method (a) and Partial Report Method with Delay (b).

Capacity

Read each of the following digits aloud once at a rate of about one per second. When you have finished, look up and try to repeat them in order.

7   4   9   3   6   7   1

If you have an average short-term memory, you probably got them all correct. Now try the same experiment with a slightly longer list:

7   4   9   4   7   2   5   8   9   4   6

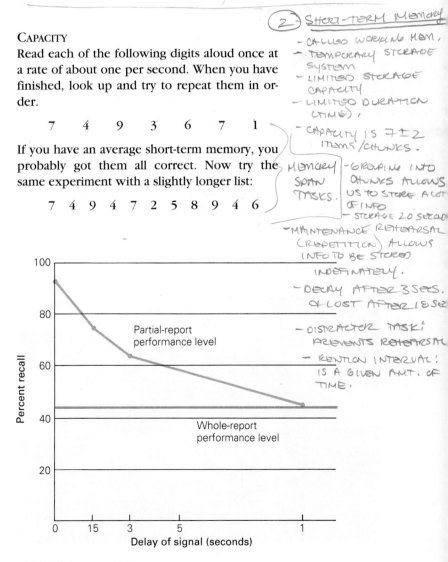

Figure 7.9
Forgetting in Sensory Memory. (After Sperling, 1960)

Unless you have a highly trained memory system, you probably did not do too well.

These tasks, known as *memory-span tasks,* involve presenting a subject with increasingly long lists of digits and noting the point where the subject is no longer able to repeat the digits in order without error. This simple experiment suggests that the capacity of short-term memory is about seven items, plus or minus two (Miller, 1956). This rule seems to hold so well that psychologist George Miller coined the term the "magical number 7 ± 2" to describe the capacity of short-term memory.

What constitutes one item in short-term memory? Consider the following two lists. Read the letters in list 1 once and then see how many you can recall.

12 CHUNKS

List 1: MT   VFB   IU   SAI   BM
        12   345   67   8910   1112

Now try the same for list 2.

CONTAINS FEWER CHUNKS. (4.)

List 2: MTV   FBI   USA   IBM
         1   2   3   4

You probably were not able to recall much of list 1 but had no trouble with list 2. Even though list 2 contains the same number of letters as list 1, it contains fewer *chunks,* or items, of information. A chunk is any piece of information that is represented as a single, meaningful item. Because the letters appear to be unrelated in list 1, each individual letter is stored in short-term memory as 1 chunk of information. This makes 12 chunks, which far exceeds the capacity. Retention of list 1 is thus poor. List 2 also contains 12 letters, but in this case the let-

Chunking allows us to store several sentences in short-term memory. This allows us to follow conversations or lectures.

ters can be combined into 4 chunks of information (Bower, 1970; Bower & Springston, 1970).

Grouping information together into chunks allows us to store a good deal of information in short-term memory. One chunk of information might include a group of words (a phrase) or even a sentence. Chunking allows us to store several sentences in short-term memory, an ability that helps us readily follow conversations or lectures.

DURATION

If we repeat information in short-term memory over and over, it will remain there indefinitely. **Maintenance rehearsal** is the process of keeping information in short-term memory by repeating it. Without maintenance rehearsal, information remains in short-term memory for only about 20 seconds.

We can all see maintenance rehearsal operating when we go on a shopping errand. A typical shopping list might include bread, milk, eggs, butter, soda, lettuce, and potatoes. Since there are only seven chunks of information to remember, you should be able to keep the list in short-term memory. Assume you have a 10-minute walk to the store. On the way to the store you keep repeating the list to yourself (maintenance rehearsal), and upon arriving you gather all the items on the list. Does this mean that short-term memory can always last 10 minutes? Not necessarily.

Consider a slightly different scenario. On the way to the store you run into a friend who tells you about a terrific party taking place over the weekend. Eager to find out where and when, you stop rehearsing to talk to your friend. Even though the conversation is shorter than a 30-second commercial, you suddenly cannot remember the shopping list. It has been lost or forgotten from short-term memory.

Experiments have shown that unrehearsed information remains in short-term memory for less than 20 seconds. These studies showed that if subjects were allowed to rehearse constantly, they could maintain information in short-term memory indefinitely. But if they were not allowed to rehearse, the subjects began to lose information after only 3 seconds and forgot almost all the information after 18 seconds (Peterson & Peterson, 1959).

To measure the duration of short-term memory, Lloyd and Margaret Peterson used a *distractor task,* which prevents rehearsal. In this task, subjects performed the following series of trials. First, the subjects listened to a sequence of three consonants (a trigram), such as *TMS*. Next, they heard a three-digit number, such as *271*. As soon as they heard the number, subjects were to begin counting backward from the number by threes: 271, 268, 265, and so forth, for a certain period of time called the *retention interval*. The retention interval in this experiment ranged from 3 to 18 seconds. At the end of the interval, a signal indicated that the subjects were to stop counting and recall the three letters. Because the distractor task kept the subjects from rehearsing the three-letter trigram, this experiment provided an accurate measure of the length of time unrehearsed information remains in short-term memory.

The results of the Petersons' experiment are shown in **Figure 7.10.** As the figure shows, recall decreased even after an interval as short as 3 seconds; by 18 seconds recall was minimal.

LONG-TERM MEMORY

Although sensory and short-term memory systems are essential, we usually think about memory as the ability to store a tremendous amount of information for a very long period of time. This capacity is known as long-term memory.

Long-term memory is often compared to a reference book or even to a reference library—it holds a storehouse of information. It enables us to remember events that occurred as recently as 5 minutes ago or as far back as our early childhood. Everything we store for future reference is encoded into long-term memory. Thus, it is easy to understand why psychologists have devoted so much effort to understanding this memory system.

CAPACITY

How much information can be stored in long-term memory? Personal experience suggests that the capacity must be enormous. Except for people who are struck with disorders of memory such as Alzheimer's disease, individuals live into their 80s and 90s with a good ability to store new memories. Does this mean that the capacity of long-term memory is endless? Unfortunately, this is not a question that we can currently answer. But what we can safely conclude is that the capacity of long-term memory is quite large. By one estimate, an average adult has about one billion bits of information in memory (Landauer, 1986). If this number

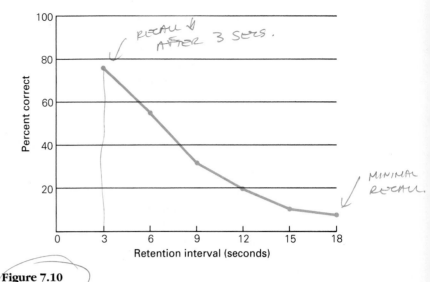

Figure 7.10

Results of an Experiment on the Duration of Short-Term Memory. (From Peterson & Peterson, 1959)

sounds enormous, when we consider that this information must constantly be stored and retrieved and related to other information, the capacity of memory may be thousands of times greater than this number.

DURATION

A second important question regarding long-term memory is how long information resides in it. Again, this is not an easy question to answer. Personal experience certainly suggests that some information lasts a lifetime. Most people late in life can readily recall experiences from their childhood even though they have not thought about them for years. Research suggests the same. Harry Bahrick found that people recognized the names and faces of former high school classmates even though in some cases they had not seen or thought about them in 35 years (Bahrick, Bahrick, & Wittlinger, 1975). But does this mean that *all* or even most information lasts a lifetime? To try to answer this type of question, researchers have used some ingenious techniques.

One line of evidence that may lend support to the idea of permanent memories comes from hypnosis. There are numerous reports of hypnotized subjects who have been taken back to early childhood and have recalled in vivid detail childhood events that they could not begin to recall when they were not hypnotized (Spiegal & Speigal, 1985). Because of the view that hypnosis can be used to reactivate memories that have been dormant for many years, law enforcement agencies have used hypnosis to help solve crimes. For example, in his book *Hypnosis: A New Tool for Crime Detection*, Eugene Block (1976) tells us how hypnosis has successfully played a role in such famous cases as the Boston Strangler case. These hypnosis-aided memories suggest that all the information is stored, but we just can't retrieve it.

A second line of evidence suggesting that all information is permanently stored comes from the brain stimulation work of Wilder Penfield that we discussed in Chapter 2. Recall that in these studies Penfield was able to stimulate the brain of awake patients during neurosurgery. He found that when he stimulated the temporal lobe, an area very much involved in memory, patients reported vivid recall of events that were long forgotten. One woman stated: "I think I heard a mother calling her little boy somewhere. It seemed to be something that happened years ago . . . in the neighborhood where I live." When the electrode was moved a little she said: "I hear voices. It is late at night, around the carnival somewhere—some sort of travelling circus. I just saw lots of big wagons that they used to haul animals in" (Penfield & Perot, 1963). These reports were taken as evidence that memory was like a permanent videotape just waiting to be played back.

This type of evidence is exciting, but does it mean that all memories are stored permanently? Unfortunately, no—there are problems with each of these lines of evidence. The work on hypnosis has proved to be controversial. More recent research has shown that memories recalled under hypnosis are not very accurate (Smith, 1983). In one study, subjects spent a week trying to recall 60 pictures that they had seen earlier. At the end of the week, half the subjects were hypnotized and again asked to try to recall the pictures. Although the hypnotized subjects were able to recall more items than the nonhypnotized subjects, they also made three times as many errors (Dywan & Bowers, 1983). One explanation for this is that hypnotized subjects are more willing to report whatever comes to mind, accurate or inaccurate (Orne et al., 1984).

What about the work on brain stimulation? The recollections of Penfield's patients could be explained in several ways. For example, the "memories" often seem to have a dreamlike character. They are more like the synthesis of many memories than a videotape playback of a particular memory (Neisser, 1967). A second problem is that very few patients experience these stimulation memories; in fact, only about 3 percent had this experience (Loftus & Loftus, 1980). Finally, some of the memories are clearly wrong, such as that of the woman who remembered being in a lumberyard and then added that she had never in her life been in a lumberyard (Loftus & Loftus, 1980).

Although it is tempting to speculate that all of our memories are stored away permanently just waiting to be recalled, there is no compelling reason to believe that this is the case.

Figure 7.11 summarizes the characteristics of sensory, short-term, and long-term memory.

DIVISIONS IN LONG-TERM MEMORY

Because long-term memory stores so much information, one question that has intrigued psychologists is how information in this warehouse of knowledge is stored. Although this is a difficult question to answer, psychologists have begun to unravel the puzzle. We now believe that information stored in memory can be broken down into two basic types: procedural and declarative (Squire, 1987).

PROCEDURAL AND DECLARATIVE MEMORY

Procedural memory, sometimes called "skill" memory, is our knowledge of *how* to do things. Examples of procedural memory include riding a bicycle or touch-typing. These memories are memories of actions and are acquired by practice or observation (Bandura, 1986). Procedural memories are pieces of information in long-term memory that cannot be inspected consciously. Riding a bicycle is a complex skill that most of us can perform, but if we try to explain how we do it, we give a sketchy description at best. Similarly, we speak grammatically correct English, but most of us cannot state the grammatical rules that allow us to do so. Indeed, describing the task is usually much more difficult than performing it. You may have had the experience of approaching a combination lock that you had not opened for some time. You experience a brief moment of panic because you cannot recall the numbers in the combination. But when your fingers touch the lock, they turn automatically to the correct numbers. The combination was stored as a procedural memory. Although the combination was not consciously available, you had the skill or procedural memory necessary to open the lock.

In contrast, **declarative memory,** sometimes called fact memory, is memory for specific information. How did you celebrate your six-

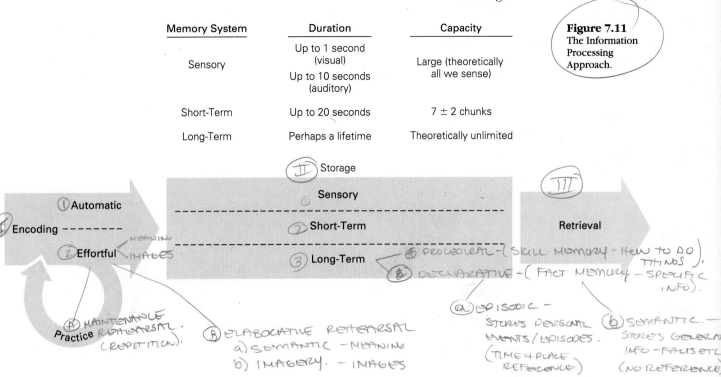

Memory System	Duration	Capacity	
Sensory	Up to 1 second (visual) / Up to 10 seconds (auditory)	Large (theoretically all we sense)	**Figure 7.11** The Information Processing Approach.
Short-Term	Up to 20 seconds	7 ± 2 chunks	
Long-Term	Perhaps a lifetime	Theoretically unlimited	

Storage

Encoding — Automatic / Effortful

Sensory
Short-Term
Long-Term

Retrieval

Practice

(Handwritten annotations):
- I Encoding; 1 Automatic; 2 Effortful — MEANING / IMAGES
- A MAINTENANCE REHEARSAL (REPETITION).
- B ELABORATIVE REHEARSAL a) SEMANTIC — MEANING b) IMAGERY — IMAGES
- II Storage; Sensory; Short-Term; Long-Term
- A PROCEDURAL — (SKILL MEMORY — HOW TO DO THINGS).
- B DECLARATIVE — (FACT MEMORY — SPECIFIC INFO).
- a) EPISODIC — STORES PERSONAL EVENTS/EPISODES. (TIME & PLACE REFERENCE)
- b) SEMANTIC — STORES GENERAL INFO — FACTS ETC (NO REFERENCE)
- III Retrieval

teenth birthday? Who was the first president of the United States? Canadian psychologist Endel Tulving has suggested that declarative memory can be broken down into two types: episodic and semantic (Tulving, 1972, 1985).

Episodic memory is an autobiographical memory system responsible for storing a record of the events of our lives. It allows us to answer such questions as what movie did you see last Saturday night? or what did you have for lunch today? As its name suggests, it notes individual episodes of your life. This memory system stores internal representations of personal events. Its distinguishing characteristic is that each event is identified by the time and place that it occurred. This memory system allows us to travel back in time to remember our fifth birthday party or our first roller coaster ride.

Semantic memory stores more general information about the world, such as rules, concepts, and facts. The crucial distinction between semantic and episodic memory is that, whereas episodic memories are linked to a particular time and place, the date and place of your fifth birthday party for example, semantic memories contain knowledge, but with no reference to when or where it was acquired. For example, most of us know what the capital of Russia is, but chances are you do not know when or where you learned this fact. This is a semantic memory—a piece of information that you have but cannot tell where or when you learned it.

As we will see later in the chapter, not only do procedural and declarative memories contain different kinds of information, but also they may be stored in different areas of the brain and may be differently affected by amnesia (Squire, 1987). **Figure 7.12** on page 268 summarizes some of the distinctions among these three types of long-term memory.

Interim Summary

Storage is the process by which a system maintains or remembers information. One useful model for how we store information is the information processing model, in which psychologists consider how memories might be stored in three separate memory systems: sensory memory, short-term memory, and long-term memory. For each memory system, psychologists have asked two basic questions: How much information can the system store (capacity)? How long does it last (duration)? Sensory memory has a large capacity, storing almost everything that we see or hear, but has a very short duration, less than 1 second. Short-term memory is a temporary storage system with limited capacity; it can store 7 ± 2 items for up to 20 seconds. Long-term memory is a permanent storage system that can hold enormous amounts of information for long periods of time. Information in long-term memory can be stored as procedural or skill memory

Figure 7.12
Three Types of Long-Term Memory.

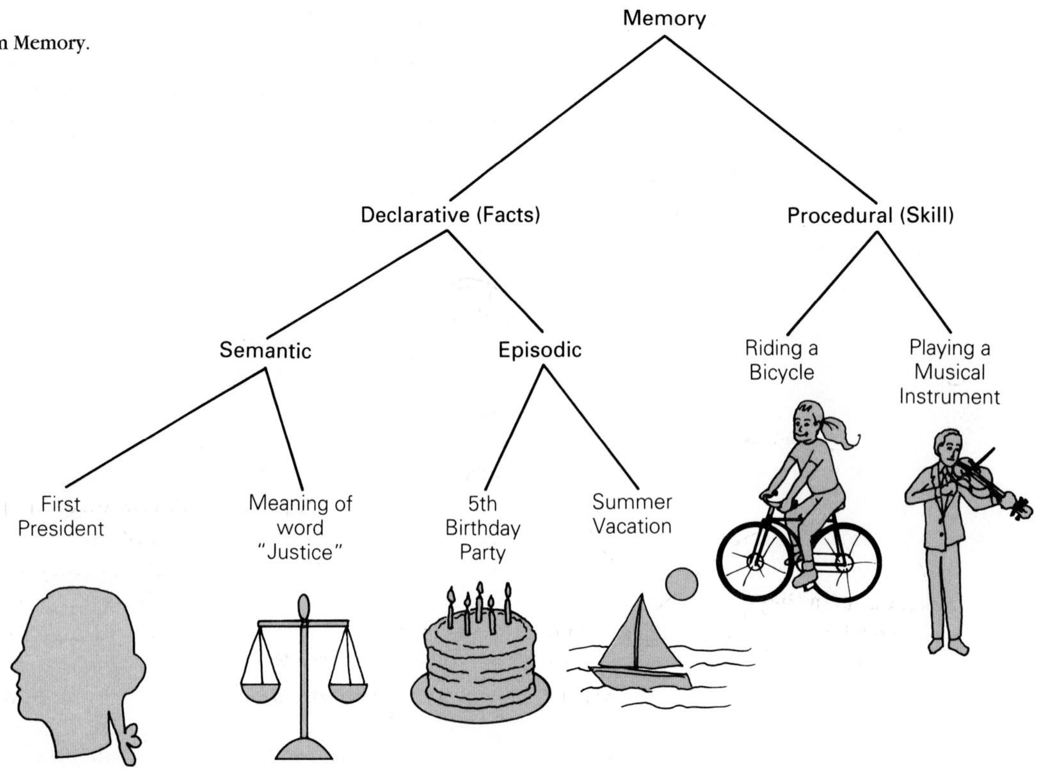

(memory of how to do things) or declarative or fact memory. Declarative memory may be broken down further into episodic or semantic memory. Episodic memory is an autobiographical memory system; semantic memory is a more general knowledge of rules, concepts, and facts.

RETRIEVING MEMORIES

Each of us has stored a tremendous amount of information, perhaps millions (even billions) of items, in long-term memory. One of the most intriguing questions regarding this vast memory storehouse is how we find any one piece of information.

One strategy for searching memory would be to examine each item, one by one. But considering the amount of information in long-term memory, if we used this strategy it could take days, weeks, or even years to locate a single piece of information; one source estimates that it would take 400 years to answer the question "What is your name?" There must be a more efficient strategy for searching long-term memory.

The ability to find information relies on two important principles, the organization of long-term memory and the use of retrieval cues.

Organization

Let's consider long-term memory as a library of personal information. This analogy is helpful because generally libraries contain a highly organized collection of books. But imagine for a moment a different type of library: one in which books were placed on the shelves according to when they were received or even at random. Imagine trying to find any particular book in such a library. With no organizing principles for this storehouse of knowledge, we would have to search through the books one at a time, growing old before we finished many term papers. Fortunately, material in a library is organized in a way that simplifies retrieval. First, the library is organized so that related materials are stored in the same general location. Second, the card catalog organizes information by author, title, and subject. We now have good evidence that long-term memory is organized in a similar way—related material is stored together or associated. This organization is what makes rapid recall possible.

In an early study on memory, subjects were given a list of 60 words to memorize (Bousfield, 1953). The subjects were not told that the words fell into four categories: animals, vegetables, professions, and names. The 60 words were given to the subjects in a random order. When the subjects were asked to recall the list in any order they liked, they grouped the words into the four categories. Other studies have shown that even when the items in the list to be remembered did not fall into natural categories, subjects created their own (Tulving, 1968).

This research showed that information was stored in a highly organized way and that this facilitated recall. Additional evidence that memory is stored in a highly organized way comes from a fascinating clinical case. Two years after suffering a stroke, the patient M.D. appeared to have made a complete recovery except for one curious problem. He could not remember the names of fruits or vegetables. Moreover, he could sort pictures of animals, types of food, or vehicles into proper categories, but he could not do the same for fruits or vegetables (Hart, Berndt, & Caramazza, 1985). This case provides further evidence that related information in memory is stored together, perhaps in specific areas of the brain. Indeed, there are now entire models of memory that show precisely how related information may be linked in long-term memory (Anderson, 1984; Chang, 1986; Collins & Quillian, 1969).

Retrieval Cues

If information is organized so that related information is stored together, certain cues called retrieval cues should help in recalling information. **Retrieval cues** are defined as stimuli that help locate information in long-term memory. For example, what if you were asked to remember the names of all the states? You might use a number of strategies to accomplish this. One way in which you *would not* go about doing this is to search through every item in your memory until you found the 50 states. Rather, you would use a strategy to search your memory. You might begin by identifying a geographical area, the Northeast, for example, and trying to identify all the states there. This would be followed by all the other geographical areas. Another strategy might be to pick one state and

then try to remember all the states that border it and then all the states that border those states. Indeed, you might use any number of strategies to search long-term memory. But these strategies all have one thing in common: they require that memory be well organized. In the case of remembering states, all the states in the Northeast may be stored together. Remembering one makes it easy to recall the rest. In an organized system like this, once we have a starting point or *retrieval cue,* it is relatively easy to remember related information. Let's now examine some of the research on the role of retrieval cues in facilitating memory search.

In one study, experimenters read category names along with words that fit into them to the subjects. For example, the category ANIMAL might include the words horse, pig, dog, and mouse, and the category PRESIDENTS might include Washington, Harding, Roosevelt, Jackson, Kennedy, and Bush. Each subject was given a total of 48 words, divided into 12 categories. The subjects were told that they did not have to remember the category names, only the words. Later, half of the subjects were asked to write down all the words that they could remember. The remaining half of the subjects were also asked to recall all the words they could but they were given the list of the categories. Subjects who were given the category names, a retrieval cue, recalled many more words (Tulving & Pearlstone, 1966).

The results of such studies indicate that we can facilitate retrieval by the way we store information in memory. By carefully organizing material when it is stored, the information becomes easier to retrieve, provided we are given a place to start our search.

Context and Retrieval

It is easier to remember a particular event if you try to recall it in the context in which it was learned. The late novelist Nabokov told of a surprise visit he paid to his former tutor at Cambridge University. The tutor had absolutely no idea who Nabokov was until Nabokov knocked over a tea tray, just as he had done when they first met. The tutor's memory of Nabokov and everything about him returned instantly (Talland, 1968).

Context can take on many forms. Places can serve as a context and can thus become a retrieval cue. If you learn material in a particular place, the best way to try to recall that material would be to return to the place. For example, if you wanted to remember the name of the person who sat next to you in second grade, you would go to your second-grade classroom. Interestingly, students perform better on tests if they are tested in the same room in which they were taught (Wingfield, 1979). An important study shows that if you can't take the test in the place where you studied, it is even helpful to imagine that you are in that place as you try to recall the information (Smith, 1979). Eyewitnesses also recall more information if they imagine the setting in which they saw a crime (Geiselman, 1988).

Drugs can also produce context. Studies have shown that if rats learn a maze while under the influence of a drug such as caffeine, they show poor retention if they are tested after the drug has worn off. Such studies might suggest that if you drink a lot of coffee (and thus caffeine) to stay up late and study, you should also drink coffee while trying to recall the material during the test. Unfortunately, there is not as yet enough research on human subjects to draw this conclusion (Swanson & Kinsbourne, 1979).

Construction and Distortion During Recall

As we have seen, memories are not simply stored like a library of videotapes. When we retrieve memories we do not simply play back

the appropriate section of the videotape. Instead, memories are often sketchy reconstructions of events. In some cases we recall more information than was actually given; this is called memory construction. In other cases our recollections change or distort the actual event.

CONSTRUCTIVE MEMORY

Constructive memory is the process by which we add to information stored in memory. When sentences are presented, listeners store not only the meanings of the sentences but also the implications the sentences suggest. They integrate the information in the sentences or story with their general knowledge about the world. In order to appreciate the processes by which memories are constructed, read the passage from *Aesop's Fables* in **Figure 7.13**. Now, without looking back at the passage, recall what you just read. Most people who are asked to perform this task give a summary of the article in their own words. It would be very unusual to recite the entire article word for word. It would even be unusual to recite a few key sentences of the article word for word.

If we remember only the general idea of a passage, how do we fill in the details? Because we have not memorized every small detail, we have to *construct* these memories. These constructed memories are based on both what we remember from the original passage (our summary) and what we already knew about the material in the passage *before* we read it (our general knowledge of the world). Now, without referring to the passage, try to answer the following questions:

1. What did the boy call out to attract the attention of the villagers?
2. Was the base of the mountain a grassy meadow or a forest?

Reread the story to check the accuracy of your answers. The answer to the first question is in the fable and you probably answered correctly. The answer to the second question, however, is not in the fable. To answer this question it was necessary for you to construct a memory, using both the information in the article and what you already know about sheep and grazing. The fable indicated that sheep were grazing at the bottom of the hill. You might already know that sheep typically graze where there is grass. If you combined the information from the fable that sheep were grazing at the bottom

---

"The Shepherd's Boy" from Aesop's Fables.

There was once a young shepherd boy who tended his sheep at the foot of a mountain near a dark forest. It was rather lonely for him all day, so he thought upon a plan by which he could get a little company and some excitement. He rushed down towards the village calling out "Wolf, wolf," and the villagers came out to meet him, and some of them stopped with him for a considerable time. This pleased the boy so much that a few days afterwards he tried the same trick, and again the villagers came to his help. But shortly after this a wolf actually did come out from the forest, and began to worry the sheep, and the boy of course cried out "Wolf, wolf," still louder than before. But this time the villagers, who had been fooled twice before, thought the boy was again deceiving them, and nobody stirred to come to his help. So the wolf made a good meal of the boy's flock, and when the boy complained, the wise man of the village said:

"A liar will not be believed, even when he speaks the truth."

Figure 7.13
"The Shepherd's Boy."

of the hill with what you already know about sheep, you could have constructed the memory that there was grass at the bottom of the hill.

Memory constructions are often quite useful in helping us fill in missing pieces of information. But sometimes they can be used to convey a false piece of information. For example, several years ago an aspirin manufacturer presented a television commercial promoting Aspirin A. The announcer stated that studies from a university and a leading hospital showed Aspirin A was more effective for pain *other than headache*. The commercial went on to present some other information about the product, and then the announcer reappeared saying, "So, the next time you have a headache, take Aspirin A." Even though we were not told that Aspirin A was more effective for headache, most of us probably combined the information in the announcer's two statements to conclude that it was (see **Figure 7.14**). In fact, experimental evidence indicates that subjects who listen to commercials often draw false conclusions about the advertised products (Harris & Monaco, 1978).

DISTORTION

Unlike constructions, **distortions** do not add information to memory; rather, they produce inaccuracies or changes in the material remembered. Distortions often occur when the incoming information is illogical or unusual. In these instances distortions produce memories that are more logical than the original input.

One of the best-known examples of distortion comes from a pioneering study performed by Frederick Bartlett (1932). Bartlett had subjects attempt to reproduce a story they had read. The story, called "The War of the Ghosts," was a legend about a tribe of North American Indians. When Bartlett's subjects, who were not Indians, tried to reproduce the story from memory, they made many predictable errors. Because the Indian legend seemed unusual and illogical to the subjects, they tended to reorganize the story into what they considered to be a logical and orderly pattern (see **Figure 7.15**).

According to Bartlett, the subjects distorted the memory because it did not fit into any existing *schema* that the subjects had. When individuals are placed in a situation many times they become familiar with various aspects of the situation. This general knowledge about that particular situation is called a **schema** (the

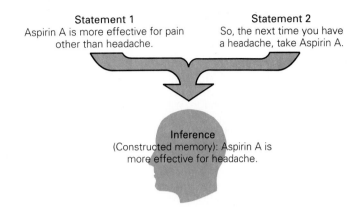

Figure 7.14
The Use of Inferences on a Television Commercial.
The advertiser hopes that the constructed memory is the one we store in long-term memory.

plural is **schemata).** In Bartlett's study, the subjects' schema for war was completely different from the account in "The War of the Ghosts." When they tried to recall the information in the story they distorted certain aspects of the legend that were incompatible with their schema.

Bartlett's views on distortion were well ahead of their time. But since his pioneering work, other studies have also shown distortion in memory (Smith & Graesser, 1981; Spiro, 1980). In one such study, subjects read a story about two friends of the experimenter, Bob and Margie, who were engaged to be married. The story concerned Bob's desire not to have children. He had not yet told Margie about these feelings because he was afraid that she wanted children. When he finally told Margie, she stated that she did indeed want children very much. Thus, her wishes were incompatible with Bob's. Later, the subjects were casually told that Bob and Margie did marry and were happy. The information that they were happily married was, of course, *inconsistent* with their disagreement over having children. This in turn did not fit the schema that people who disagree on important, basic issues are unable to remain happily married.

To assess memory for the story, the experimenters had the subjects return to the lab after intervals ranging from 2 days to 6 weeks and asked them to recall the story. Interestingly, the subjects recalled the initial disagreement over having children as less severe than it actually was. The subjects in this study had distorted the story so that the initial

Text and subject's reproduction in "War of Ghosts" experiment by Bartlett (1932).

The War of the Ghosts

One night two young men from Egulac went down to the river to hunt seals, and while they were there it became foggy and calm. Then they heard war-cries, and they thought: "Maybe this is a war party." They escaped to the shore, and hid behind a log. Now canoes came up and they heard the noise of paddles, and saw one canoe coming up to them. There were five men in the canoe, and they said.

"What do you think? We wish to take you along. We are going up the river to make war on the people."

One of the young men said: "I have no arrows."

"Arrows are in the canoe," they said.

"I will not go along. I might be killed. My relatives do not know where I have gone. But you," he said, turning to the other, "may go with them."

So one of the young men went, but the other returned home.

And the warriors went on up the river to a town on the other side of Kalama. The people came down to the water, and they began to fight, and many were killed. But presently the young man heard one of the warriors say: "Quick, let us go home: that Indian has been hit." Now he thought: "Oh, they are ghosts." He did not feel sick, but they said he had been shot.

So the canoes went back to Egulac, and the young man went ashore to his house, and made a fire. And he told everybody and said: "Behold I accompanied the ghosts, and we went to fight. Many of our fellows were killed, and many of those who attacked us were killed. They said I was hit, and I did not feel sick."

He told it all, and then he became quiet. When the sun rose he fell down. Something black came out of his mouth. His face became contorted. The people jumped up and cried.

He was dead.

Subject's Reproduction

Two youths were standing by a river about to start seal-catching, when a boat appeared with five men in it. They were all armed for war.

The two youths were at first frightened, but they were asked by the men to come and help them fight some enemies on the other bank. One youth said he could not come as his relations would be anxious about him; the other said he would go, and entered the boat.

In the evening, he returned to his hut, and told his friends that he had been in a battle. A great many had been slain, and he had been wounded by an arrow; he had not felt any pain, he said. They told him that he must have been fighting in a battle of ghosts. Then he remembered that it had been queer and he became very excited.

In the morning, however, he became ill, and his friends gathered round; he fell down and his face became very pale. Then he writhed and shrieked and his friends were filled with terror. At last he became calm. Something hard and black came out of his mouth, and he lay contorted and dead.

Figure 7.15
Actual Text and Subject Reproduction in Bartlett's "War of the Ghosts" Experiment (1932).

inconsistency was resolved and the story fit their schema (Spiro, 1977).

Before leaving the topic of schemata, we should point out that schemata do not always contribute to distortions of memory. In certain instances they actually help us remember. For example, stories may be difficult to understand unless we can fit them into their proper schema (Bransford & Johnson, 1973). To demonstrate this, read the following passage once.

> The left end is placed over and then under the right end. The left and right ends are then pulled. Next, the left end is folded over itself. The right end is then wrapped around the left end and folded over itself. The left and right ends are then once again pulled.

Try to recall whatever you can about the paragraph. You probably did not do too well. But if we provide one critical piece of information that gives you a schema and then ask you to reread the paragraph, your memory for the information would improve dramatically. The critical piece of information is that the paragraph describes tying a shoelace. A second area in which schemata can have a beneficial effect has been demonstrated by studying people with excellent memories in a particular area— the expert memorizers.

SCHEMATA AND EXPERT MEMORIZERS
Sometimes experts in a particular area seem to have remarkable memories for information in their own specialty. For example, the famous conductor Toscanini is reported to have had an extraordinary memory for music. Just before the start of a concert, an agitated musician appeared before him. The musician reported that the key for the lowest note on his bassoon was broken—how would he play the concert? Toscanini shaded his eyes, thought for a moment, and then said, "It's all right—the note does not occur in tonight's concert." Not only did Toscanini know every note for every instrument in that concert, but it has been estimated that he knew by heart every note for every instrument in about 250 symphonic works, the words and music for 100 operas, plus a volume of chamber music, piano music, cello and violin pieces, and songs (Marek, 1982). How could Toscanini memorize so much information? One view holds that experts can memorize information in their field because they already have well-developed schemata or frameworks in which to place the information (Alba & Hasher, 1983; Horton & Mills, 1984).

A study by Chiesi, Spilich, and Voss (1979) demonstrated the role of schemata in memory. This experiment showed that people who knew a lot about baseball could remember more about a fictitious baseball game than those who knew less about the sport. Baseball knowledge was first assessed by a test used to divide subjects into high- and low-knowledge groups. Both groups were given an account of one half of an inning in a fictitious baseball game and were then asked to recall the information. Presumably because they could more easily map the new information onto their existing knowledge structure or schema, the high-knowledge subjects remembered significantly more.

Schemata may also be helpful to students. For example, you may have noticed that when you are first studying a subject it is difficult to learn and remember the new terms and concepts. Yet the more you study the subject, the easier it becomes to learn additional information. Perhaps you have developed schemata for the material that help you to organize and remember the new information.

Although studies on schemata represent a new area of research in memory, you may recognize that the process is very much like the relationship between organization and retrieval in long-term memory. Schemata may be another method of storing information in highly organized ways.

CONSTRUCTION AND DISTORTION IN EYEWITNESS TESTIMONY

One of the most interesting applications of the role of construction and distortion in memory comes from the courtroom. The use of eyewitness testimony is based on the assumption that witnesses can accurately store and recall information about a crime they have seen. This assumption may be one of the reasons that few types of evidence have more impact in a court of law than the testimony of an eyewitness. But in most cases the eyewitness is not like a videotape recorder, capable of recording and playing back an event exactly as it occurred. As we have seen, construction and distortion produce inaccuracies in memory. Research by Elizabeth Loftus and her co-workers has shown that these processes can raise serious questions about the accuracy of eyewitness accounts.

One study conducted by two of Loftus' students involved enacting a fake crime (Loftus, 1979). In this experiment, two female students entered a Seattle train station. They left a large bag on a bench and then went away to check the train schedules. While they were gone, a male student reached in the bag, pretended to

pull out an object and place it under his coat, and then quickly walked away. Upon returning, one of the female students cried out "Oh my God, my tape recorder is missing." She went on to say that her boss had loaned it to her for a special reason and that it was very expensive. The two women then began to talk to eyewitnesses who were in the vicinity. Most eyewitnesses cooperated and were willing to give their phone numbers in case their testimony was needed.

One week later, another student posing as an insurance agent called each of the eyewitnesses. The "insurance agent" asked the witnesses for whatever details they could remember and concluded the interview by asking "Did you see the tape recorder?" Although there was no tape recorder, half of the eyewitnesses remembered seeing it and most of them were able to recall details about the color, shape, and even the height of the antenna. Apparently, these witnesses had constructed a memory based on what had actually occurred and what they already knew about expensive tape recorders. The eyewitnesses also claimed they would be able to recognize the thief again.

In a related study, Loftus and Zanni (1975) showed that eyewitnesses' memories could also be distorted. In this study, 45 subjects were shown a short film depicting a car accident. After viewing the film, each of the subjects answered questions about what they had seen. One critical question involved estimating the speed of the cars. One group was asked, "About how fast were the cars going when they hit each other?" Another group was asked "About how fast were the cars going when they *smashed into* each other?" For other groups, the verb *hit* was replaced with *collided, bumped,* or *contacted.* Subjects who heard the verb *smashed* gave the highest speed estimates (40.8 mph), while subjects who heard *collided, bumped,* and *hit* gave progressively lower speed estimates (39.3, 38.1, and 34.0 mph). Those questioned with the word "contact" gave the lowest estimates (30.8 mph) (see **Figure 7.16** on page 274).

Some psychologists have been critical of applying principles derived from laboratory studies to the courtroom (Konečni & Ebbesen, 1986), and others have suggested that the experimental results themselves can be interpreted differently (McCloskey & Zaragoza, 1985; Lindsay & Johnson, 1987). Nevertheless, these and other studies (see Loftus, 1979, Loftus &

Because of mistaken identity, the man shown on top was wrongfully imprisoned for crimes the other man committed.

Figure 7.16
Eyewitness Recall.
If an eyewitness sees a car accident such as the one depicted on the left (a), he or she might recall a more serious accident (c), depending on the external information supplied. Subjects who heard the word "smashed" to describe the accident gave the higher estimates for the speed at which they thought the cars were going.

Hoffman, 1989) are important and influential because they suggest that the same construction and distortion that occur in laboratory situations may also be factors in natural settings.

Interim Summary

The ability to retrieve information depends on two factors: the organization of long-term memory and the use of retrieval cues. In retrieval from long-term memory, the individual searches only those portions of memory that are likely to contain the desired information. This search process takes advantage of the high degree of organization in long-term memory, in which related material is stored together. Retrieval cues provide a "place" to begin searching. One useful retrieval cue is context.

Research on retrieval has demonstrated that memories are not simply stored like a library of videotapes. When we retrieve memories, we do not play back a portion of the video. Rather, memories, are often sketchy reconstructions of the past. In some cases we recall more information than was actually given. These memory constructions can be useful in helping us fill in missing information, but they can also be used to provide false information as in some television commercials. In other instances our recollections distort the actual event, these are called distortions. Unlike constructions, distortions do not add information, but instead produce inaccuracies. Bartlett's famous case of the "War of the Ghosts" shows how distortions produce memories that are more logical (and inaccurate) than the original input. One area in which both constructions and distortions seem to occur frequently is in eyewitness testimony. **Figure 7.17** summarizes the processes in retrieval.

IV FORGETTING

Where were you on August 8, 1985? In February 1987, then President Ronald Reagan challenged reporters at a press conference: "Everybody who can remember what they were doing on August 8, 1985 raise your hand." On August 8, 1985, two of Reagan's advisors briefed him on a proposal to sell arms to Iran. After the arms deal was disclosed to the press, Reagan claimed to have no memory of the meeting.

Do most people remember what they were doing on a particular day? If not, why do they forget? Interestingly, a study done at Fordham University by Robert Reynolds and Harold Takooshian (Reynolds & Takooshian, 1988) about a month after Reagan's challenge revealed that most students could remember at

Figure 7.17
The Retrieval Process.

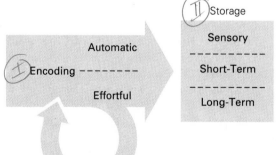
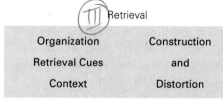

least something about where they were on August 8, but what about all the information they forgot?

Ebbinghaus's Pioneering Studies

The earliest studies on forgetting were done by Herman Ebbinghaus. He performed his studies over 100 years ago, using himself as the only subject (Ebbinghaus, 1885). Ebbinghaus studied *nonsense syllables*—three-letter syllables consisting of a vowel sandwiched between two consonants. By carefully constructing these syllables to avoid forming words, he hoped to minimize the effects of previous knowledge. Ebbinghaus constructed 2300 nonsense syllables, read them aloud at a fixed pace in groups of 7 to 36, and then tried to recite them from memory. He continued with each list until he could recite them all correctly. He then waited varying amounts of time and tested his memory. Ebbinghaus found that even after 20 minutes he could remember only 58 percent of the list, and after 48 hours he could remember less than 40 percent (see **Figure 7.18**). Ebbinghaus documented what we all know: we can forget large amounts of information over relatively short periods of time.

Does this rapid rate of forgetting also hold true for the information we learn in school? Apparently so. Continuing in the tradition of Ebbinghaus, Harry Bahrik (1984) compared a knowledge of Spanish vocabulary among people who had just taken a Spanish course and those who had studied Spanish up to 50 years ago. Compared with students who had just taken the course, those who had taken it 1 to 3 years ago had forgotten much of what they had learned. But after about 3 to 5 years forgetting stopped, even if the subjects had not taken Spanish at all for 50 years.

Why, like Ebbinghaus and the students in Bahrik's study, do we forget? Psychologists have suggested that forgetting can take place in encoding, storage, or retrieval. Recall our example from the beginning of the chapter in which you were at a party, were introduced to a number of people, and then encountered one of these people the next day only to be embarrassed because you could not remember their name. We suggested that you could not remember the person's name because you never formed the memory. That is, either you never encoded the name or something was faulty in the storage process. But it is also possible that

the name was encoded and was stored, but you can't retrieve the name. Psychologists have proposed four major views of forgetting.

1. *Encoding failure.* Memories cannot be recalled because they were never stored to begin with. It is as if a book in a library cannot be found because it was never placed in the library.
2. *Decay theory.* Memory of an item spontaneously fades or decays with the passage of time. Nothing other than the passage of time is necessary. It is as if the print on the pages of a book in a library have faded. This is a failure of storage.
3. *Interference theory.* Other memories interfere with the memory we are trying to recall. It is as if other books have been piled on the library book we are looking for. This is a failure of recall.
4. *Retrieval failure.* The information is there but cannot be located because the proper cues are not present. It would be like searching for a book in a large library without the proper aids, perhaps because the signs directing you to the proper shelf have been removed.

Let's now examine each of these views.

Encoding Failure

Sometimes we cannot remember information because we never stored the information in memory to begin with. You can easily demonstrate this to yourself by trying an experiment initially performed by Raymond Nickerson and

Herman
Ebbinghaus
(1850–1909)

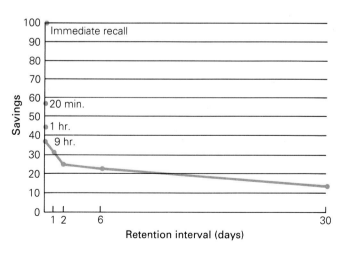

Figure 7.18
The Forgetting Curve. (After Ebbinghaus, 1885)

Figure 7.19
Which Is the Real Thing?
See answer on page 278. (From
Nickerson & Adams, 1979)

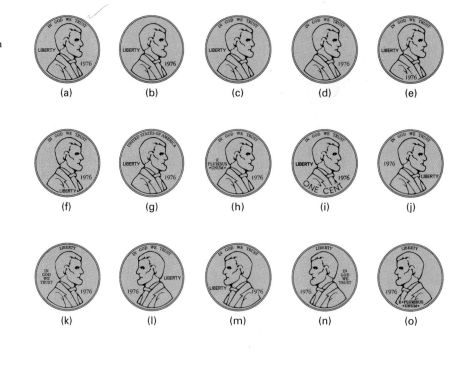

Marilyn Adams (1979). Each of you has seen a Lincoln penny thousands of times; you probably have one in your pocket right now. But do you know what Lincoln's head looks like on the penny? Try to select the real penny from those shown in **Figure 7.19**. If you couldn't select the correct penny, you are not alone. Nickerson and Adams found that most people could not select the correct penny. As we indicated earlier in the chapter, although some information is encoded automatically, other information requires effortful processing. Without this effortful processing information is never encoded.

Decay Theory

The **decay theory** of forgetting states that memory spontaneously fades or decays with the passage of time. The Greek philosopher Plato was one of the earliest proponents of the decay theory. Plato likened the initial formation of the memory to a fresh imprint of a seal on a block of wax. Plato argued that, just as the wax imprint loses its shape over time, so does the memory trace. At first the memory trace loses its sharp detail, and eventually it fades beyond recognition.

In the ideal experiment to study the role of decay in forgetting, we would have the subject learn information and then do nothing (either mentally or physically) for a certain time period. We would ask the subject to recall the material. Because the subject performed no activity and thus nothing could interfere with the information, any forgetting would be due to decay. As you might imagine, this ideal experiment is impossible (just try to stop thinking—to mentally do nothing—for even 30 seconds). Nevertheless, psychologists have attempted to approximate it in order to study forgetting.

One of the most interesting attempts to conduct such a study was an early experiment by John Jenkins and Karl Dallenbach (1924) in which two subjects were tested several times. Each subject first learned a list of 10 nonsense syllables like those used by Ebbinghaus. In one condition, each subject then went to sleep immediately, a situation that Jenkins and Dallenbach felt approached the ideal "do nothing" state. In a second condition, the subjects continued with their normal waking activities. After varying retention intervals of 1, 2, 4, or 8 hours, each subject was asked to recall the nonsense syllables. As **Figure 7.20** shows, when the subjects went to sleep they could recall much more information. Based on this study, Jenkins and Dallenbach concluded that "forgetting is not so much a matter of decay of old impressions and associations as it is a matter of interference, inhibition, or obliteration of the old by the new" (p. 612).

These results certainly do not mean that decay plays no role in forgetting. Subjects who

---

Handwritten margin notes:

DETAILS!

- ① ENCODING FAILURE!
  - CAN'T REMEMBER B/C INFO WAS NEVER STORED TO BEGIN WITH
  - B/C THERE IS NO EFFORTFUL PROCESSING OF INFO.

- ② DECAY THEORY!
  - MEMORY FADES W/ PASSAGE OF TIME a.'. DECAYS
  - OTHER FACTORS! INTERFERENCE, INHIBITION ETC OF THE OLD BY THE NEW.

③ INTERFERENCE THEORY!
  - OTHER MEMORIES INTERFERE W/ RETRIEVAL
  Ⓐ RETROACTIVE INTERFERENCE! NEW INFO INTERFERES W/ OLD INFO.
  Ⓑ PROACTIVE INTERFERENCE! OLD INFO INTERFERES W/ NEW INFO.

④ RETRIEVAL FAILURE!
  - AGREES W/ INTERFERENCE THAT INFO IS STILL AVAILABLE, BUT CAN'T BE RECALLED B/C PROPER RETRIEVAL CUES ARE NOT AVAILABLE
  - EG! TIP-OF-TONGUE EXPERIMENT BY BROWN & MCNEILL.
  - RETRIEVAL CUES FACILITATE RECALL.
  - BEST RETRIEVAL CUES HAVE THE FEWEST MEMORIES ATTACHED TO THEM. → NEED DISTINCTIVE EVENTS
  - FLASHBULB MEMORIES SIGNIFIES THE DISTINCTIVENESS THAT RECALL CUE OF AN IMPORTANT EVENT HAS.

Fig 7.23

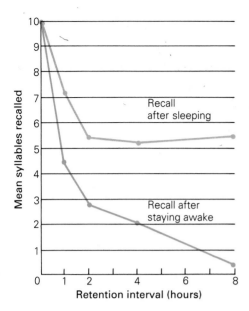

Figure 7.20
How Sleep Affects Recall.
The graph shows the mean number of nonsense syllables subjects recalled as a function of number of hours asleep or awake after learning. (After Jenkins & Dallenbach, 1924)

went to sleep did forget some of the material. However, it appears as though factors other than decay are primarily responsible.

Interference Theory

According to **interference theory,** other memories interfere with the retrieval of the particular memory we are searching for. Imagine that you are at a party and a very attractive person gives you his or her phone number. You can't find a pen to jot down the number, so you try to remember it. You rehearse it and place it in long-term memory. In the course of the

evening you see other friends. One of them knows of a place on the beach that you can rent next semester for only 50 dollars a month. She gives you the phone number and again you store it in long-term memory. The next evening you decide to call the person you met at the beginning of the party. You try to remember the phone number, but you can remember only the phone number of the beach house. The beach house phone number has interfered with recall of the other number. This type of interference is called **retroactive interference,** meaning that new information interferes with the recall of old information. In our case, the newer information of the beach house phone number interfered with your ability to recall the person's phone number (see **Figure 7.21a).**

A second type of interference, **proactive interference,** occurs when old information interferes with recalling new information. For example, many of you have probably had the experience of living in one place for a long time and then moving to a new neighborhood. One of the first tasks is memorizing your new telephone number. But the first time you try to recall your new number, all you can remember is your old number. In this case, the older telephone number interfered with the recall of the new number (see Figure 7.21b).

Retroactive interference and proactive interference have also been studied in the laboratory. In one task to measure retroactive interference, an interference group and a control group are used. Both groups learn one list of nonsense syllables (usually 10 syllables), which we will call list A. Subjects in the interference group then learn a second list of nonsense syllables, list B, while the control group performs a task that should not interfere with list A, such as listening to music. Both groups are then asked to recall list A, as diagrammed below:

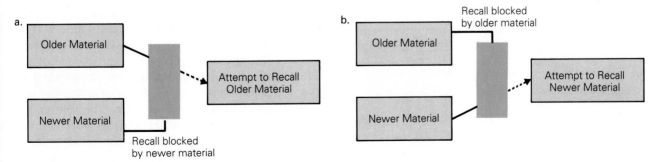

Figure 7.21
Schematics of Retroactive (a) and Proactive (b) Interference.

(a)

The answer is (a).

Interference	Control
Learn A	Learn A
Learn B	Perform unrelated task
Recall A	Recall A

Interference theory holds that learning list B should interfere with recalling list A and, as expected, the control group does much better when asked to recall list A (Briggs, 1957, Ceraso, 1967). Presumably this is because the control group did not experience retroactive interference.

In a typical task to study proactive interference, the interference group learns list A, then learns list B, and then recalls list B. The control group listens to music, learns list B, and then recalls list B, as shown below:

Interference	Control
Learn A	Perform unrelated task
Learn B	Learn B
Recall B	Recall B

As in the case of retroactive interference, the control group is much more successful during recall (Underwood, 1957). Results of laboratory studies on proactive interference are shown in **Figure 7.22.**

Retrieval Failure

A fourth theory of forgetting, retrieval failure, agrees with interference theory that all the information in memory is still available. But it differs from interference theory in specifying why the memories cannot be recalled. Interference

theory states that memories cannot be recalled because other memories interfere. **Retrieval failure** theory holds that memories cannot be recalled because the proper retrieval cues are not available. This view suggests that if the proper retrieval cues are provided, the missing information can be located. The Tulving and Pearlstone (1966) study (p. 269), in which subjects were able to recall more words in a particular category when they were provided with the name of the category, supports the retrieval-failure theory. In this instance, the category name served as the missing retrieval cue.

That retrieval cues are extremely important in recalling information was demonstrated in a now-classic study by Roger Brown and David McNeill (1966) that investigated the *tip-of-the-tongue phenomenon.* We have all experienced this phenomenon, but no one has described it better than William James (1890) in the first textbook of psychology:

> Suppose we try to recall a forgotten name. The state of our consciousness is peculiar. There is a gap therein: but no mere gap. It is a gap that is intensely active. A sort of wraith of the name is in it, beckoning us in a given direction, making us at moments tingle with a sense of our closeness, and then letting us sink back without the longed for term. (James, 1890, Vol. 1, p. 251)

To study this frustrating phenomenon in the laboratory, Brown and McNeill presented college students with dictionary definitions of unfamiliar words and then asked the students to provide the words. For example, subjects were read the definition: "a navigational instrument used in measuring angular distances, especially of the sun, moon, and stars at sea." Most of the subjects either knew the word or knew that they did not know it. But some experienced the tip-of-the-tongue phenomenon: they were sure they knew the word but could not recall it. Brown and McNeill found that in about 50 percent of the cases these subjects could give the first letter and the number of syllables in the word, but they could not recall it. They often offered words that sounded like the correct word, such as secant or sexton, or words that had similar meanings, such as compass or protractor, but not the actual word—sextant. These data suggest that the information is in memory and that it could be recalled with the proper retrieval cue.

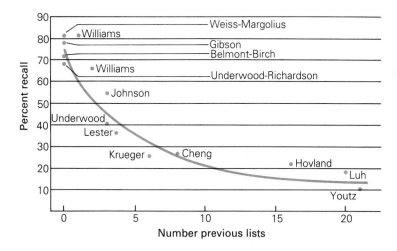

Figure 7.22
Proactive Interference When the Number of Previous Lists Varies.
The graph shows a summary of the results of many laboratory studies on proactive interference in which the number of previous lists varied. The names on the curve refer to the researchers. (From Underwood, 1957)

We have seen that retrieval cues facilitate recall. But what are the best retrieval cues? According to one theory, the best retrieval cues have the fewest memories attached to them. If this theory is correct, then *distinctive events* should serve as the best recall cues (Watkins, 1975). For example, if you were given a list of 20 fruits to remember, one of which was apple, the retrieval cue "fruit" would not be of much help in recalling apple. The cue is not distinctive. It is linked to all fruits in the list, not just the apple. But if the list consisted of 19 presidents and only 1 fruit—apple—then the retrieval cue "fruit" would be very effective. Fruit is now a distinctive cue. It is associated with only one thing.

One of the most vivid examples of the association between distinctive cues and accuracy of recall concerns memory for everyday occurrences that are associated with important events. For example, in a study conducted in 1899, subjects had remarkable recollections of what they were doing when they heard that President Lincoln was shot (Colegrove, 1899). Similarly, many people remember where they were and what they were doing when President Kennedy was shot. Julia Child reported that she was "in the kitchen eating soup de poisson." Tony Randall remembered being in the bathtub (Brown & Kulik, 1982). Brown and Kulik have called these *flashbulb memories* to signify the distinctiveness that the recall cue of an important event can have.

Although many of you were not alive when Kennedy was shot, you may be able to experience flashbulb memories by trying to remember where you were and what you were doing when you heard that the space shuttle *Challenger* had exploded (McClosky, Wible & Cohen, 1988). In this case, the important event serves as a distinctive recall cue.

Benefits of Forgetting

We tend to think of forgetting as a problem. Forgetting the name of someone we met a few weeks ago can be embarrassing, and forgetting information on a test can be disastrous. But in some cases forgetting may not be so bad. As James noted in his first textbook of psychology, "If we remembered everything, we should be on most occasions as ill off as if we remembered nothing" (James, 1890). To appreciate the benefits of forgetting, let's look at the case of someone who could not forget.

Soviet psychologist Alexander Luria describes the case of a journalist "S" who could remember long lists of words and giant grids of numbers (Luria, 1968). S had the uncanny ability to remember details of books he had read and conversations he had, even in childhood. But S's remarkable memory was also a problem. He could not forget. He remembered strings of numbers and other irrelevant information even when he did not want to. Images of lists of numbers and words distracted him and interfered with his working. Eventually, S was unable to work at his profession and supported himself by demonstrating his abilities for audiences.

This case highlights the dangers of what many of us would like to have—a perfect memory. But a perfect memory would not only help us remember things we would like to remember, it would also allow us to recall things that are better off forgotten. A certain amount of forgetting may be a very good thing.

To recap our discussion of the causes of forgetting, we note that forgetting can be attributed to four processes: encoding failure, decay, interference, or retrieval failure. Although experimental evidence indicates that encoding failure, interference, and retrieval failure are the primary causes of forgetting, decay also appears to play a role in some instances. Rather than attempting to determine which of these is the *cause* of forgetting, it might be better to realize that they all can be sources of forgetting. We can then try to understand under what circumstance each process is likely to be operating.

Interim Summary

Forgetting is the inability to recall a particular piece of information accurately. The pioneering work of Herman Ebbinghaus showed how much information was forgotten and how rapidly this occurred. Psychologists have proposed four theories of forgetting: (1) encoding failure, in which memories cannot be recalled because they were never stored to begin with; (2) decay theory, in which memories fade with the passage of time; (3) interference theory, in which old (proactive interference) or new (retroactive interference) information interferes with recall; and (4) retrieval failure, in which forgetting is due to inability to recall

Psychology in the News

WHEN CAN MEMORIES BE TRUSTED?

By Anastasia Toufexis

Less than two weeks ago, Americans were spellbound before their television sets, watching Anita Hill and Clarence Thomas clash over their recollections of events a decade past. The Senate Judiciary Committee hearings are still fresh in our minds, but how many of us remember exactly what the two adversaries said, what they wore, the expressions on their faces and the tone of their voices? And 10 years from now, when we think back, how faithful will our memories be? Will we remember Hill's tears at one particularly painful disclosure of sexual harassment, and Thomas thumping the table as he decried the hearing as a high-tech lynching of an uppity black?

Those with sharp memories will have noticed two errors in the preceding paragraph; Hill's voice may have sometimes wavered, but she never cried, and Thomas may have thundered with his voice but never with his fist. Even if memory fails to retain these details, how many Americans will accurately retain the essence of the events? Will our memories reflect the truth?

Psychologists and lawyers are finding that more and more cases turn on the question of how reliable memory is. Last November in Redwood City, Calif., George Franklin was convicted of killing an eight-year-old girl in 1969; the case was based largely on the testimony of his daughter Eileen Franklin Lipsker, who had repressed the memory of her playmate's murder for 20 years. This month in Pittsburgh, Steven Slutzker is scheduled to go on trial for the 1975 fatal shooting of John Mudd Sr. Slutzker was charged after the victim's son, who was 5 when his father died, claimed he had a flashback memory of the murder.

Fueling the debate over the certainty of memory has been the parade of men and women—among them Roseanne Arnold and former Miss America Marilyn Van Derbur—with newly surfaced recollections of being sexually abused as children. Many of the victims are suing their alleged molesters, including parents, relatives and therapists. Paula Pfiefle of Monroe, Wash., this spring received $1.4 million from her church-run school in settlement of her claim that a teacher repeatedly raped and sodomized her two decades ago. As if often the case with repressed memories, the events came flooding back during an emotional, evocative moment. For Pfiefle, it was while making love to her husband on their wedding night five years ago.

The validity of such memories has divided psychological and legal circles. "By and large, long-term memory is extremely credible," maintains Jill Otey, a Portland, Ore., attorney whose office receives five calls a week from women saying they have suddenly remembered childhood abuse. "I find it highly unlikely that someone who can remember what pattern was on the wallpaper and that a duck was quacking outside the bedroom window where she was molested by her father when she was four years old is making it up. Why in the hell would your mind do this?" Reflecting that faith, at least a dozen states since 1988 have amended their statute of limitations for bringing charges to allow for delayed discovery of childhood sexual abuse.

People—not to mention juries—place unwavering trust in the human ability to recall events, especially those that have had a strong emotional impact. But such confidence is often misplaced. "Our memory is not like a camera in which we get an accurate photograph," says psychologist Henry Ellis of the University of New Mexico.

Consider the *Challenger* explosion. As with the assassination of John F. Kennedy, most people claim to remember where they were when they heard the news of the shuttle disaster. Ulric Neisser, a psychologist at Emory University tested that assumption. The day after the 1986 accident he asked 106 students to write down how, when and where they learned the news. Three years later, he tracked down nearly half the group and asked them to describe their memories of the explosion. Though many claimed to recall it clearly, "often the memories were completely wrong," says Neisser. Many students said they had received the news from television, though they had actually heard it elsewhere.

. . . One of the many controversies concerning memory is how far back people can remember. TV star Roseanne Arnold, for example, claims that she has a vivid memory of being sexually abused as an infant by her mother. This summer Tina Ullrich, 36, a Chicago design-firm executive, abruptly recalled images from her infancy of her grandfather sexually molesting her while he changed her diapers. "I didn't have any words to describe the experience, so I began drawing my feelings," says Ullrich, who has created 35 surreal pictures. But many researchers are skeptical of such early recall. Most people's earliest clear recollections date back to around age 4 or 5. Before that, they believe, the mind holds at best primitive pictures but no coherent memory. "Under a year, a child doesn't have the mental structure to understand

how events hang together," says Neisser. "I wouldn't give you a nickel for memory in the first year of life."

. . . Experiences can be altered as they are hauled out of memory. Remembering is an act of reconstruction, not reproduction. During the process, normal gaps and missing details often get filled in. When Senators asked law professor Joel Paul to describe how Hill sounded years ago when she first told him about being sexually harassed by Thomas, Paul hesitated and then said Hill had sounded embarrassed. "He could have been falling back on a scripted memory of how he would expect someone to act in that circumstance," explains psychologist Douglas Peters of the University of North Dakota. On the other hand, experts are not the least bit disturbed because Hill's story grew and became more detailed as the hearings proceeded. Remembering incidents is an accretion process, psychologists say, and one image evokes another.

Memory integrates the past with the present: desires, fantasies, fears, even mood can shade the recollection. People have a tendency to suppress unpleasant experiences and embellish events to make themselves feel more important or attractive. "Some of us like to see ourselves in a rosier light," observes psychologist Elizabeth Loftus of the

University of Washington, "that we gave more to charity than we really did, that we voted in the last election when we really didn't, that we were nicer to our kids than we really were."

. . . Suggestion is a potent disrupter of truth, as Jean Piaget once noted. The renowned child psychologist wrote that for years he recounted the memory of how his nurse foiled an attempt to kidnap him from his carriage when he was two years old. But years later, the retired nurse sent his parents a letter saying she had made up the incident to impress her employers. The young Piaget had heard the story so often that he had created his own memory of the event.

Alas, there is no easy way to distinguish fact and fiction in many memories. The best method is to find corroborating evidence, from witnesses or written records, say, diaries or hospital charts, that can document the event. Years from now, videotapes of the Hill-Thomas hearings may verify the sights and sounds of their testimony, but the heart of their dispute is likely to remain unresolved. Whose memory told the truth?

Questions

1. What does the report that people have difficulty remembering details of the *Challenger* explosion suggest about the concept of flashbulb memories?
2. How might have constructive memory processes contributed to the testimony during the Clarence Thomas nomination hearings?
3. Do you think it will ultimately be necessary to have psychologists testify as expert witnesses on memory during trials and other legal proceedings?

Figure 7.23
The Process of Forgetting.

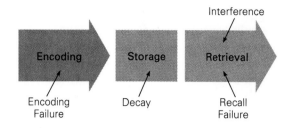

Encoding — Storage — Retrieval

Interference

Encoding Failure   Decay   Recall Failure

the information. Psychologists also recognize that each of these potential causes of forgetting might contribute in different situations and in some situations more than one could be operating. Finally, by studying clinical cases such as "S," the man who could not forget, psychologists have come to realize that in some situations, forgetting may be a useful process. Figure 7.23 summarizes the process of forgetting.

IMPROVING MEMORY

William James, a pioneer in psychology and one of the earliest students of memory, believed that memory might be like a muscle that could be strengthened and improved through exercise. To test this idea, he first determined how long it took him to memorize a series of passages from a book. After noting the results, he "exercised" his memory by memorizing Milton's *Paradise Lost!* He then retested his memory on a series of passages. The result—no improvement.

James' heroic demonstration indicates that simply using memory will not necessarily improve it. But psychologists now know that using memory in certain ways will help. One method we have already considered is chunking information to aid short-term memory. In this section we will consider several other techniques for improving memory.

Using Elaborative Rehearsal

We have already presented evidence showing that the more elaborate the rehearsal, the greater the chance of retrieval. When we think about the meaning of a word or try to associate it with other information already in long-term memory, we have a much better chance of recalling it than if we simply repeat the word or count the number of letters in it. Have you ever read a section in a book (perhaps four or five

pages) only to realize that even though you read the words, you do not remember a thing about the material? This is probably because you did not rehearse the information elaborately enough. One way to help guarantee elaborative rehearsal is to review the information. After each paragraph or section, try to restate what you have just read in your own words. You might even ask yourself questions about the material. This will guarantee that you have thought about the meaning and processed the information.

Periodic Retrieval

Reviewing the information as you are learning will help place the material in long-term memory but is probably not sufficient to ensure retention. Periodic retrieval of the material helps ensure that you will be able to recall the stored information accurately when it is needed. Periodic retrieval requires you to rehearse the material whenever the occasion arises. For example, if the term *attention* appeared in the next chapter, it would be beneficial to take a moment then and recall what you know about attention. This will not only facilitate recall at a later time but also indicate if you need to review the material.

One recent study shows a dramatic effect of periodic review. Harry Bahrick and Lynda Hall found that students who took college math courses retained most of their knowledge of high school algebra or geometry 50 years later (Bahrick & Hall, 1991). They concluded that when we learn material spaced out over several years and when each subsequent session involves broader applications of previously learned material, retention is greatly facilitated, even 50 years later.

Organization and Mnemonics

As we have seen, one way to facilitate recall is to store information in a highly organized manner. Categories often help accomplish this. For example, one study has shown that organizing a list of words into categories enables subjects to recall nearly twice as many words (Bower, Clark, Lesgold, & Winzenz, 1969).

Organization can also be used to remember the contents of a chapter in a book, perhaps this chapter. After finishing this chapter, outline the material in a tree diagram similar to the one shown in **Figure 7.24**. This activity will place the material in long-term memory in a highly organized manner and facilitate recall.

(handwritten margin notes)

IMPROVING MEMORY!

① CHUNKING INFO TO HELP SHORT TERM MEMORY

② ELABORATIVE REHEARSAL (SEMANTIC-MEANING IMAGERY)

③ PERIODIC RETRIEVAL
- REHEARSE INFO WHEN OCCASION ARISES.

④ ORGANIZATION & MNEMONICS:
- STORE IN ORGANIZED MANNER USING CATEGORIES
- MNEMONICS ORGANIZE INFO INTO:
Ⓐ RHYMES
Ⓑ METHOD OF LOCI
Ⓒ KEYWORD METHOD.

Ⓑ METHOD OF LOCI!
IMAGINING ITEMS TO BE REMEMBERED & ASSOCIATING THEM W A PLACE ALREADY STORED IN MEMORY EG. LIVING ROOM W SHOPPING LIST & TAKING A MENTAL TRIP THROUGH THE LIVING ROOM.

Ⓒ KEYWORD METHOD! RELATIVE PARTS OF "SPANISH" WORD TO "ENGLISH" WORD... & IMAGINE A BONE IN A MEATBALL → ∴ ASSOCIATE MEANING W IMAGE

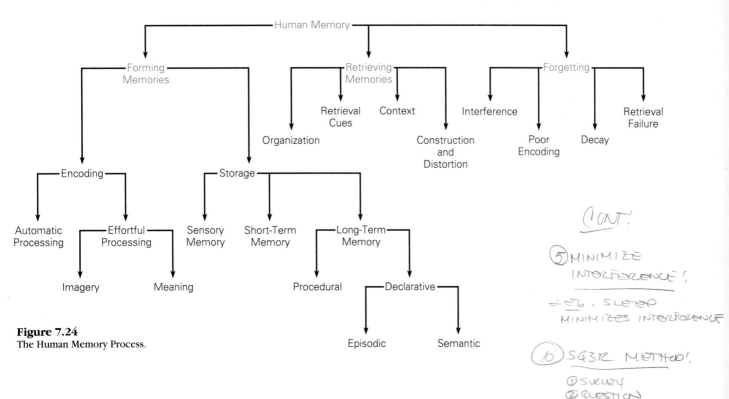

Figure 7.24
The Human Memory Process.

[Handwritten notes in right margin:]
CONT!
⑤ MINIMIZE INTERFERENCE!
± EG. SLEEP MINIMIZES INTERFERENCE
⑥ SQ3R METHOD!
① SURVEY
② QUESTION
③ READ
④ RECITE
⑤ REVIEW

Yet another way to help organize material is through the use of a mnemonic. A **mnemonic** (from Mnemosyne, the Greek goddess of memory) is a technique for organizing information in long-term memory. Certain mnemonics are familiar to almost everyone, such as the rhyme "*i* before *e* except after *c*" to help remember a rule of spelling. Another is "Thirty days hath September, April, June, and November. . . ." These mnemonics work because they organize the material into a logical framework—a rhyme—that is stored in memory as an organized unit. Rhyme is just one of the mnemonics that can help organize material. Two other methods are the *method of loci* and the *keyword method.*

THE METHOD OF LOCI

Although psychologists have begun to study mnemonics only recently, stage performers have been using them for hundreds of years. The following is a typical demonstration using mnemonics. The mnemonist asks each member of the studio audience to name an item they have in their pocket. One such list might be:

Person 1—lighter
Person 2—pen
Person 3—wallet
Person 4—lipstick
Person 5—nail file
Person 6—nickel
Person 7—photograph of grandma

Once the mnemonist has spoken to 20 people or more, he or she goes on to perform the rest of the act. Sometime later (perhaps an hour or so) the mnemonist tells each person in order the item he or she has named. One method that the mnemonist might have used to accomplish this feat is the **method of loci.** This method involves imagining items to be remembered and associating each image with a place already stored in memory. Imagine that you are walking through your house. The first thing you might see is the door, followed by a coat rack, a mirror, a chair, a brass lamp, a red velvet sofa, and so on. What we have just described is a trip through a fictitious house, but it is relatively easy for you to do the same for your own house. In doing so, you should identify the items in the order in which you would see them. You now have a list already stored in long-term memory that can be used as the logical framework. Next, you must associate one new piece of information with each item on the list. One efficient way to do this is through imagery. To associate the first new piece of information, for example a lighter, with the first location in the house (door), conjure up an image of a lighter setting fire to the door. The next image might be a 5-foot pen (remember, the more unusual the image the better the recall) hanging on the coat rack (see **Figure 7.25**). You could continue this method until you had associated each item on the second list

Figure 7.25
The Method of Loci.
The method of loci provides a logical framework for remembering a number of unrelated items.

with something in your house. To recall the information on the second list, you simply take a mental trip through your house, recalling the images associated with each item in your house. This way, it is possible to recall 20 or 30 items in order, even after hearing each item just once (Bower, 1972).

Most mnemonics can be broken down into several steps:

1. There is a known list of cues, or logical framework, to work from (in this case, things in your house).
2. New items are associated with these known cues.
3. Associations are made by images.
4. The known cues aid recall of the new information.

The Keyword Method
Mnemonics have also been used to help students learn the vocabulary of a foreign language. In this study, the students used the keyword method to associate Spanish words with their English equivalents (Atkinson, 1975; Atkinson & Raugh, 1975). For example, the word *albondiga* is Spanish for meatball. To remember this the students could form an image containing both an albondiga and a meatball. But this would be difficult since the student has no idea what an albondiga looks like. This is where the **keyword method** comes in. First, the student pronounced the foreign word (albon-dee-ga) and then tried to think of an English equivalent (the keyword) that sounds similar—the word bone, for example. Next, the student formed an image containing a bone and a meatball, perhaps a meatball the size of a

beach ball with a 3-foot bone through it. Although this may seem like a strange way to learn foreign words, research indicates that students who used this method did over 200 percent better than students who learned in the traditional manner (Atkinson & Raugh, 1975). With a little ingenuity, this method could be used to help learn almost any technical vocabulary. You might also use the keyword method to help you learn terms from this book. For example, by first using the keyword "hypo" and then forming an image of a hypodermic needle stuck in a hamburger, you might remember that the hypothalamus is an area of the brain that is involved in the control of feeding.

Mnemonics were once seen as a type of "memory trick" not to be used by serious students (and certainly not to be taught in the classroom). Perhaps this is the reason that despite the accumulating evidence that mnemonics facilitate memory, relatively few students use them. Surprisingly, a study by Margaret Intons-Peterson and JoAnne Fournier (1986) found that introductory psychology students rarely used mnemonics. Nevertheless, the study of mnemonics has become an important part of the study of memory (Harris, 1980; Harris & Morris, 1984). And mnemonics are being used as memory aids in groups ranging from brain-damaged patients with memory impairments (Wilson, 1987) to business executives (Hilton, 1986).

Minimizing Interference

We have seen that interference causes forgetting. To improve the chances of remembering material, then, you should minimize interference. Recall the Jenkins and Dallenbach study (1924) in which the group that slept immediately after learning had much better recall. Apparently sleep minimizes interference.

If you have a history test tomorrow, you should study only history tonight. (Of course, this is a bit of a problem during finals' weeks when you have five exams and three papers in three days.) And when you have finished studying, the best thing to do is to go to sleep.

The SQ3R Method

Have you ever been reading a text, perhaps this one, and found that you cannot recall anything about the last 3 or 4 pages? Most students have had this experience, most likely because they were not attending to the material. One technique to help you attend and store information in texts is the **SQ3R method** (Robinson, 1970). SQ3R refers to (1) survey, (2) question, (3) read, (4) recite, and (5) review. Before you read a textbook chapter you should survey its contents by reading and thinking about the title, outline, and main subject headings. This will provide a framework (or schema) for you to organize the material. Before you begin to read each section, formulate a question or two that you expect to be able to answer as you read the section. Next read the chapter, attempting to answer the questions you formulated (ensuring elaborative rehearsal). This will force you to be an active reader. When you have finished reading the section, glance back over the material to be sure you have stored the information and answered your questions. Finally, when you finish the chapter, review the entire chapter and try to organize the material. By doing this you will store the information in a highly organized manner and make it easier to recall.

Interim Summary

Although memory is not a muscle that can be strengthened through exercise, there are ways to improve memory. Mnemonics are techniques for organizing information in long-term memory. Three useful mnemonics are rhyming, the method of loci, and the keyword method. Although there are many different types of mnemonics, they all share a common strategy in which there is a known or logical framework to which new items are associated using imagery. The already known cues then assist with the recall of information. Using elaborative rehearsal, periodically retrieving information, minimizing interference, and using the SQ3R method are other ways to improve memory.

. . . .

MEMORY AND THE BRAIN

One of the most important and puzzling aspects of the study of memory is understanding how the brain stores information. Most researchers studying this process would agree that when new information is stored, there is an accompanying physical change in the brain. The physical change is called the **engram.** In searching for the engram, researchers face two difficult problems: identifying the area or areas of the brain that might be involved in memory, and discovering the nature of the changes that might occur in these areas.

Some of the best clues to how the brain stores information come from patients with memory disorders. In this section we will examine some of the progress that has been made in understanding how the brain stores information by looking at disorders of human memory. We will be particularly interested in cases where humans lose the ability to store new information. This memory disorder is called **anterograde amnesia.**

The Anatomy of Amnesia

The pioneering work on memory and the brain was done by Karl Lashley. Lashley devoted much of his career to studying which parts of the brain might be involved in memory in rats. His research consisted of making lesions in different areas of the rat's brain and observing the effect of these lesions on the rat's memory for a maze. Lashley's goal was to find a brain area or areas that, when damaged, would produce amnesia for the maze. But after nearly 30 years of research, he was unable to identify a single brain area that was critical. Lashley concluded in a tongue-in-cheek manner, "I sometimes feel, in reviewing the evidence on the localization of the memory trace, that the necessary conclusion is that learning just is not possible" (Lashley, 1950, pp. 477–78).

Shortly after Lashley published his conclusion, a Canadian neurosurgeon, William Scoville, and a neuropsychologist, Brenda Milner, reported a very important finding regarding the localization of memory in the human brain

Engram is the term used by Lashley to describe the physical change in the brain that occurs when new memories are formed.

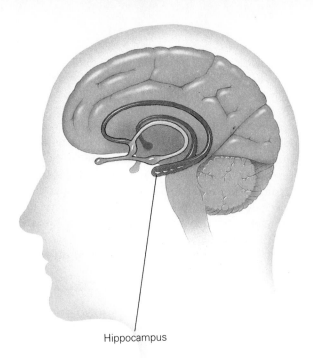

Figure 7.26
The Role of the Hippocampus in Memory.
In an effort to relieve H.M.'s severe epileptic
seizures, Scoville removed a portion of the brain
that included the hippocampus. The result was
severe amnesia.

Hippocampus

(Scoville & Milner, 1957). Their research involved a patient called H.M. H.M. had been suffering from severe epileptic seizures that, despite high doses of medication, grew worse. In an attempt to help H.M., Scoville removed a portion of the brain that he believed was the source of the seizures.

During the surgery, Scoville removed two thirds of H.M.'s temporal lobe and along with it a structure called the hippocampus (see **Figure 7.26**). The surgery was very successful in controlling H.M.'s seizures but also produced an unexpected effect—severe anterograde amnesia. Although H.M. could remember events that occurred *before* his surgery, he was unable to remember anything that happened after it. For example, 10 months after his operation, H.M.'s family moved. When he was examined nearly a year after the move, H.M. had still not learned the new address. Similarly, H.M. read the same magazine articles over and over again without finding their contents familiar and could not remember the names of people he saw every day (Milner, 1966). For all practical purposes, H.M. behaved as if he had never seen the people or magazines before. To put H.M.'s amnesia in the context of the information-processing model of human memory, it appears that even though H.M. was able to recall events that occurred before the surgery, he was unable to store any new information in long-term memory.

Aside from his memory disorder, H.M.'s other intellectual abilities were normal. His IQ remained unchanged and his speech was normal. In addition, H.M.'s *short-term memory* remained intact. In one test of short-term memory, the researchers asked him to remember the numbers 5, 8, and 4. As long as he was allowed to rehearse these numbers he could remember them, presumably by maintaining them in *short-term* memory. But once he was interrupted, even for less than a minute, he could not remember the numbers. He did not even know that he had been given any numbers to remember (Milner, 1966).

The case of H.M. was important for several reasons. It was the first study in humans to show that localized lesions in the brain could disrupt memory. It also showed that a lesion in one area of the brain could affect the ability to store information in long-term memory without affecting short-term memory. This suggests that different areas of the brain may be involved in the two memory systems.

The case of H.M. is a striking example of how a particular area of the brain can be involved in memory. But we must be cautious when interpreting these results. For example, we cannot assume from H.M.'s experience that all memories are stored in the hippocampus. One problem with this generalization is that damage to other brain areas produces different

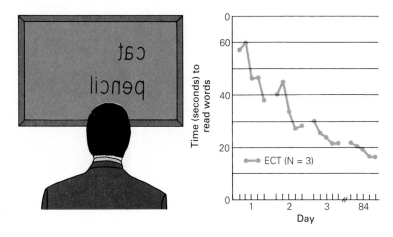

Figure 7.27
Amnestics' Ability to Learn a Mirror-Reading Task.
Over a 3-day period, amnestics show improvement at this task. They remember
how to read words in a mirror as long as 3 months later. (After Cohen & Squire,
1980)

types of amnesia (Squire, 1987). Also, large hippocampal lesions in animals do not always produce memory deficits (Moore & Solomon, 1980; Solomon, Solomon, Vander Schaaf, & Perry, 1983; Berger, Berry, & Thompson, 1986). Still a third difficulty is that even in cases of severe amnesia like H.M.'s, some types of memory are retained.

Psychologists have found that H.M. and other amnestics have the ability to remember certain things (Benzing & Squire, 1989, Parkin, 1987). For example, amnestics can remember how to perform skills such as navigating through a maze or learning to read words in a mirror (Squire, 1982). Learning to read words in a mirror is initially a difficult task that normal subjects can learn with practice (see **Figure 7.27**). Surprisingly, amnestics also show improvement at this skill. Over a 3-day period they read the words faster and faster (Cohen & Squire, 1980). These results indicate that amnestics do have the ability to remember how to read words in a mirror.

What is fascinating is that, even though they get better at the task every day, they never remember having done it. When presented with the apparatus at the beginning of each day, many of the amnestics deny ever having seen it before.

You may recognize tasks such as navigating through a maze or mirror reading as examples of memory for skills or procedural memory. Remembering the specific words in a mirror-reading task, in contrast, is an example of fact or declarative memory. Procedural memo-

ry is remembering *how* to do something and declarative memory is remembering *that* you did it. Based on studies of patients with amnesia such as H.M., neuropsychologist Larry Squire has hypothesized that the hippocampus is crucial for declarative memory, but other brain structures are involved in storing procedural memories (Squire, 1987; Squire & Zola-Morgan, 1988, Mishkin & Appenzeller, 1987).

In summary, although the hippocampus is important in memory, it is not essential for all memories, nor is it the only structure in the brain involved in memory. Rather, it is part of a larger system in the brain that is involved in certain types of learning and memory.

The Chemistry of Amnesia

While one group of researchers has focused on the possible location of the engram within the brain, another group has focused on the nature of the engram. One of the most promising lines of research in this latter area involves the chemical events in the brain that occur when an individual stores new information in memory (McGaugh, 1989).

Most of the chemical changes that are likely to be involved in storing new memories occur at the synapse. Recall from Chapter 2 that the synapse is the small gap between two adjacent neurons. For neural impulses to get from one neuron to the next, a neurotransmitter is released from the first or presynaptic neuron and travels to the second or postsynaptic neuron. This neurotransmitter then starts the neural impulse in the postsynaptic neuron. One

 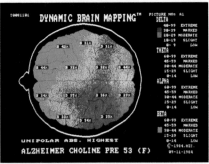 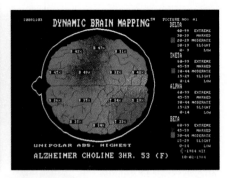

In the first photo on the left, an electrode headset picks up signals from the brain of this 58-year-old woman and a computer turns them into the brain map on the screen. The violet shading indicates a borderline case of Alzheimer's disease. The center and right maps show the brain of an Alzheimer's patient before and after the administration of the memory-boosting substance acetylcholine.

widely held theory states that when new memories are stored there is a change that makes the synapse (or more likely a whole series of synapses) more efficient.

One neurotransmitter that has attracted a great deal of attention is *acetylcholine*. Psychologists are interested in acetylcholine because it appears to be related to memory disorders that accompany Alzheimer's disease (Mann, 1988; Olton & Wenk, 1987). Patients with Alzheimer's disease often suffer from memory disorders similar to those seen in H.M. (Corkin, 1982). Their memory for events early in life is good, but they seem to have difficulty remembering new information. Brain researchers have discovered that patients with Alzheimer's disease have a decrease in brain acetylcholine (Coyle, Price, & Delong, 1983; Collerton, 1986). According to this discovery, then, raising the levels of acetylcholine in the brain could facilitate memory.

Drugs to Improve Memory

Several drugs now exist that can increase the levels of acetylcholine in the brain. One of these drugs, THA, has drawn widespread attention because of reports that it improved memory in Alzheimer's patients (Summers, Majovski, Marsh, Tachiki, & Kling, 1986). This study has prompted the National Institutes of Health to test the drug in a national clinical trial, but it is too soon to determine if it really has a beneficial effect (Pendleburg and Solomon, 1992).

Acetylcholine is not the only chemical in-

volved in the memory process. A second class of drugs that have received considerable attention as possible memory-improving agents are hormones. For example, research by psychologist James McGaugh has shown that the hormones vasopressin and norepinephrine can both improve memory in animals (Liang, Juler, & McGaugh, 1986; McGaugh, 1988). It is interesting that both of these hormones are released in stressful situations. This raises the interesting possibility that the flashbulb memories discussed earlier (p. 280) may be so vivid because they are formed in stressful situations and thus are formed in the presence of these hormones (Squire, 1987).

One difficulty with understanding the role of hormones in improving memory is that they do not directly enter the brain. Thus, they must be affecting the brain indirectly, through another chemical that can enter the brain. Studies by Paul Gold suggest that this chemical messenger may be a form of sugar called glucose. Gold has found that glucose can improve memory in animals (Gold, Vogt, & Hall, 1986) and he has begun to test the effects of glucose in humans. Early results from these studies indicate that glucose can improve memory in older subjects (Gold, 1988).

The work on the chemistry of memory is exciting and has enormous potential. Because memory disorders are very common, accompanying disorders ranging from Alzheimer's disease to depression, drugs that could improve memory are potentially very important (Goethals & Solomon, 1988). But the chemical basis of memory is complex and there are likely to be many neurotransmitters and hormones involved. Because of this, unraveling the puzzle and developing drugs that truly facilitate memory will be a difficult undertaking.

Interim Summary

One of the most puzzling aspects of memory is where and how the brain stores information. Research on the anatomy of amnesia suggests that a structure in the limbic system called the hippocampus plays an important role in storing new memories. The best evidence for this comes from the clinical case of H.M., who suffered hippocampal damage and lost the ability to store new information. A second focus of research on brain and memory is what chemical events occur in the brain that help form memories. Researchers believe that acetylcholine is one chemical (neurotransmitter) in the brain that may be involved in storing memories. There is some evidence that a shortage of acetylcholine may be involved in the memory deficit seen in Alzheimer's patients. Because of this, many of the experimental drugs used to treat Alzheimer's patients boost acetylcholine levels. Other substances that have been used to improve memory include hormones and glucose.

SUMMARY

1. Memory is the ability to store information so it can be recalled and used at a later time. Memory can be broken down into three processes: encoding, storage, and retrieval.
2. The first process in the formation of new memories is encoding. This is the process whereby new information is placed into memory. Some information is encoded automatically or effortlessly; other information requires work or effortful processing. Some information is encoded in the form of words and meaning; this is called semantic encoding. Other information is encoded in the form of images; this is called imagery encoding.
3. Storage is the process by which a system maintains or remembers information. One

useful model for how we store information is the information processing approach in which psychologists consider how memories might be stored in three separate memory systems, sensory memory, short-term memory, and long-term memory. For each memory system, psychologists have asked two basic questions: how much information can the system store (capacity) and how long does it last (duration)?

4. Sensory memory has a very large capacity, storing almost everything that we see or hear, but lasts for less than a second. Short-term memory is a temporary storage system with capacity of 7 ± 2 items and a maximum duration of 20 seconds. Long-term memory is a permanent storage system that can hold an enormous amount of information over long periods of time.
5. Information in long-term memory may be stored as procedural, or skill, memory (memory for how to do things) or declarative, or fact, memory. Declarative memory may be broken down further into episodic and semantic memory. Episodic memory is an autobiographical memory system; semantic memory is more general knowledge of rules, concepts, and facts.
6. Because tremendous amounts of information are stored in long-term memory, it is not possible to search all of the memory system each time we wish to recall a piece of information. Rather, retrieving memories depends on the high degree of organization in long-term memory, in which related material is stored together and retrieval cues are used to select a place to begin searching.
7. Storage in memory can be affected by two process: construction and distortion. Construction involves adding to information stored in memory, and distortion involves changing information stored in memory. Both processes may lead to inaccuracies, as has been demonstrated by research on eyewitness testimony.
8. Forgetting is the inability to recall a particular piece of information accurately. Psychologists have proposed four theories of forgetting: (1) encoding failure, which refers to failure to place information accurately in memory; (2) decay theory, which holds that memories fade with the passage of time; (3) interference theory, which

states that either old (proactive interference) or new (retroactive interference) information interferes with recall; and (4) retrieval failure, in which forgetting is due to inability to recall the information.

9. Although memory is not a muscle that can be strengthened through exercise, there are ways to improve memory. Mnemonics are techniques for organizing information in long-term memory. Three useful mnemonics are rhyming, the method of loci, and the keyword method. Using elaborative rehearsal, periodically retrieving information, and minimizing interference are other ways to improve memory.

10. One of the most puzzling aspects of memory is where and how the brain stores information. Research on humans suffering from amnesia suggests that one important brain area involved in memory is the hippocampus. Research on memory disorders that accompany Alzheimer's disease suggests that the neurotransmitter acetylcholine is important in memory. Other recent studies point to certain hormones as memory-improving agents.

KEY INDIVIDUALS

George Sperling
George Miller
Lloyd and Margaret Peterson
Fergus Craik
Endel Tulving
Lynn Hascher
Rose Zachs
Jacqueline Sachs
Alan Paivio
Herman Ebbinghaus
John Jenkins
Karl Dallenbach
Roger Brown
David McNeill
Frederick Bartlett
Elizabeth Loftus
Karl Lashley
William Scoville
Brenda Milner
H.M.
Larry Squire

James McGaugh
Paul Gold
Harry Bahrick

KEY RESEARCH

automatic and effortful processing in the storage of information
semantic encoding
imagery encoding
procedure for testing capacity of visual sensory memory
the "magical number 7 ± 2"
duration of long-term memory
differences between procedural and declarative memory
differences between semantic and episodic memory
organization of long-term memory
retrieval cues and long-term memory
"The War of the Ghosts" and distortion
construction and distortion in eyewitness testimony
Ebbinghaus' studies of forgetting
test of decay theory of forgetting
test of interference theory of memory
"tip-of-the-tongue" and retrieval failure
localization of memory in the brain
drugs as memory-improving agents

KEY TERMS

memory
encoding
storage
retrieval
effortful processing
maintenance rehearsal
elaborative rehearsal
semantic encoding
imagery encoding
sensory memory
short-term memory
long-term memory
maintenance rehearsal
procedural memory
declarative memory
episodic memory
semantic memory
retrieval cues
constructive memory

distortions
schema
decay theory
interference theory
retroactive interference
proactive interference
retrieval failure

mnemonic
method of loci
keyword method
SQ3R method
engram
anterograde amnesia

8

Thinking and Language

CHAPTER OUTLINE

Each (ēch), a. or a. pron...
number considered separate...
Ea'ger (ē'gẽr), a. Keenly desir...
Ea'gle (ē'g'l), n. Rapacious bird of p...
con family; gold coin of the United St...
worth $10; Roman or French standard...
Ea'glet, n. Young eagle.
Ear (ēr), n. Organ or sense of hearing, a...
tention; heed; sense of melody.
Ear (ēr), n. Spike of grain, containing the... Ears...
v.i. To form ears (of corn).
Earl (ẽrl), n. English nobleman next below... Ea...
Earl'dom, n. Jurisdiction or...
... without ears; deaf...

293

hinking is a universal human activity that has long captured the imagination of philosophers, poets, playwrights, and psychologists. Often the central question is how to understand the human intellect. We are capable of clear-headed logical thinking that has led to enormous improvements in the human condition. But we are also capable of destructive, even irrational thoughts that endanger our very survival. How can we explain this apparent paradox?

Part of the answer lies in the complexity of thinking. **Thinking** involves many different cognitive functions: organizing what we know, creating categories or concepts, formulating logical deductions, solving problems, and making clear decisions. If any part of this complex process goes awry, the actions that follow may be illogical or even irrational.

The picture is complicated somewhat further when we consider that our thoughts are often expressed through language. Like thought, language has a dual potential: it can clarify or confuse, explain or obscure what we intend to communicate. Thought and language often go hand in hand, and this close relationship is one reason we consider the two topics jointly in this chapter.

The complexity of thought and language, as well as the question of their interrelationship, have intrigued scholars for centuries. Does thought precede and guide the development of language, or does language give structure and definition to our thoughts? Why is thinking not always rational and logical? Does human thought resemble a computer program? Clearly, these questions have practical implications, but psychologists are also interested in them because of the fundamental issues they raise about the human condition.

In this chapter, then, we examine thinking and language, as well as the relationship between the two. We begin with an analysis of thinking—what it is and why it sometimes leads us to false or misleading conclusions.

Thinking involves organizing, categorizing, planning, reasoning, and problem solving.

How do concepts work? Imagine that you have just heard a new melody for the first time. To appreciate what you have heard, you need to know how it is similar to or different from other melodies you have listened to in the past. To do this, you automatically categorize the melody as belonging to a certain class of music. It becomes part of your concept of melodies.

Thinking also involves problem solving. For example, try to connect the dots in **Figure 8.1** by drawing only four straight lines without lifting your pencil from the paper. If you find this difficult, you are not alone. As **Figure 8.2** demonstrates, the solution to this vexing little problem is to extend the lines outside the boundaries of the square. As we will see, many problems are like this. They require the problem solver to put aside old ways of doing things and to think creatively.

Two other aspects of thinking are *reasoning* and *decision making*. Reasoning is an important skill that is widely applicable, both when you listen to the arguments of others and when you formulate your own positions. We will inquire about the nature of reasoning, including the somewhat surprising errors that people make. We will then consider decision making, perhaps the most practical aspect of thought, examining both the choices involved in a decision and the factors that influence (and interfere with) the decision-making process.

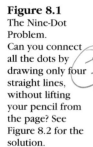

Figure 8.1
The Nine-Dot Problem. Can you connect all the dots by drawing only four straight lines, without lifting your pencil from the page? See Figure 8.2 for the solution.

THE NATURE OF THINKING

Thinking is a complex process, with many diffrent components. For example, thinking involves organizing objects and events into specific mental categories known as concepts.

CONCEPTS

A **concept** is a way of categorizing or classifying the people, objects, and events in the environment (Anglin, 1977). Consider, for example, the concept of *dog*. We know that certain things in the world belong to this concept, while others do not. However, this concept, like many others, is not acquired immediately. Rather, we gradually learn the identifying characteristics or *features* of a dog. We learn that a dog has four legs, a tail, a distinctive facial appearance, and that it makes a barking sound. These features help us distinguish a dog from other animals, such as a cat (no barking sound) or a horse (longer legs, no barking sound). We also learn that there are different *types* of dogs—dalmatians, golden retrievers, Irish setters, etc. Over an extended period of time, we make progressively more refinements in our concept of dog. Eventually, we know what should be included and excluded from the concept dog.

Dog represents a particular kind of concept, known as a *natural concept*. Natural concepts help us categorize the objects and events found in our everyday environment. A very different kind of concept is a logical or *artificial concept*, most often encountered in psychological experiments designed to discover the way in which people form or acquire new concepts. To illustrate, look at the array of stimuli in **Figure 8.3**. Imagine that your task is to use the objects shown there to devise an artificial concept that a friend must discover. Quite arbitrarily, you decide that your concept will be defined by the logical rule "shaded and square are instances (examples) of the concept." Now ask your friend to discover what the rule is. Each time the friend points to a stimulus that is both shaded and square, you would say "yes," indicating that the friend has discovered an "instance" of the concept. For all other choices you would say "no," indicating that the choice was a "noninstance" of the concept. In this way, you can observe and record the cognitive processes involved in the acquisition of your artificial concept.

For many years, investigators used this type of methodology to learn a good deal about concept formation. However, beginning in the 1970s, the work of Eleanor Rosch and her colleagues inspired psychologists to move away from the study of artificial concepts. Rosch (1973, 1975) argued convincingly that artificial concepts failed to capture the richness and complexity of the ideas that people acquired in their everyday lives.

One of Rosch's most compelling arguments was that in the real world many things do not divide neatly into "instances" and "noninstances" of a concept. Whereas some concepts, such as *dog*, have clearly defined features, other concepts have vague or ill-defined boundaries. For example, consider the concept *vehicle*. No doubt you will have little trouble thinking of good examples of this concept. Words such as truck and car come to mind quickly. But suppose you were asked whether an elevator is a vehicle. You would probably respond "maybe" or "sort of." This is because the exact boundaries of the concept *vehicle* are poorly defined. Concepts like *vehicle* are called "fuzzy" because it is sometimes difficult to make decisions about what qualifies as an instance of the concept (Smith & Medin, 1981).

Acquiring Concepts

Natural concepts are difficult to teach. A parent could teach some of the critical features of certain concepts, such as *brother* or *friend*, but the child would have to learn other features through experience. How? Rosch (1973) suggests that we acquire natural concepts by identifying *prototypes*, which are the best examples of the concept. We then use prototypes to decide whether less obvious objects belongs to the concept. For instance, many people consider chair the best example of the concept *furniture*, and *orange* or *apple* the best example of the concept *fruit* (Rosch, 1975). These prototypes then serve as a useful reference point in deciding whether less conspicuous examples belong to the concept. So if you were considering whether a telephone is an example of the concept *furniture*, you might compare a telephone with a chair because chair is a prototypical example of furniture.

Research on natural concepts has shown that people have a very strong intuitive sense about what is prototypical. For many concepts we seem to have a graded inventory of what constitutes an appropriate instance, extending

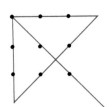

Figure 8.2
Solution to the Problem in Figure 8.1.

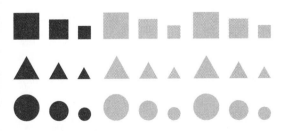

Figure 8.3
Array of Stimuli Used to Create an Artificial Concept.

This child may have acquired his concept of how a doctor acts from his parents, television shows, or his own experience.

Table 8.1	Good and Bad Examples of Eight Concepts	
Concept	**Good Example**	**Bad Example**
Furniture	Chair	Rug
Fruit	Apple	Boysenberry
Vehicle	Car	Wheelchair
Weapon	Pistol	Fist
Bird	Robin	Penguin
Sport	Football	Chess
Toy	Doll	Sandbox
Clothing	Pants	Purse

After Rosch (1975)

In short, most natural concepts include members that have a number of different features. The prototypical example is helpful and instructive because it bears the strongest similarity to other members of the concept and the least similarity to members of different concepts.

Integrating Concepts

Unfortunately, we do not have the memory storage to keep track of an infinite array of ideas. We need to simplify our lives by integrating concepts. This permits us to learn and recall information more easily.

One way that we integrate concepts is to form hierarchies. For example, consider the hierarchical organization of concepts shown in **Figure 8.4.** The most abstract concept, animal, is at the top of the hierarchy, with the more specific concepts (bird, fish, and so on) shown below. Each concept has some associated features listed alongside it. This is an interesting

from the best or prototypical example to the worst or nonprototypical (Barsalou, 1985). You can gain some sense of this by examining the list of concepts in **Table 8.1**. It is easy to tell the difference between the good and bad examples of each concept. In fact, this list represents the actual responses that subjects gave when asked to rank examples of furniture and other natural concepts (Rosch, 1975).

Over the course of a lifetime, we develop a sense that some examples of natural concepts are better or more prototypical than others. We expect apples to be red, even though they can be green, and we think that flying is prototypical of birds, even though some birds, such as penguins, do not fly.

Figure 8.4
The Hierarchical Organization of Concepts.
The closer two concepts lie in the hierarchy, the more readily they are retrieved from memory. (Adapted from Collins & Quillian, 1969)

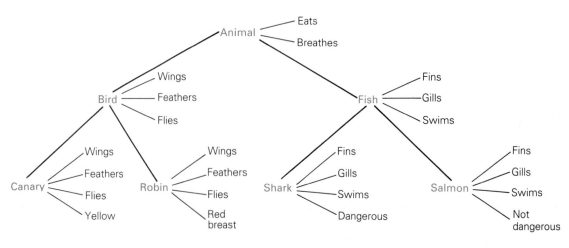

model, but how can we tell if people actually organize concepts in this way?

Suppose we design an experiment that requires people to *infer* the presence of properties not directly associated with a particular concept. For example, if we pose the questions "Does a bird eat?" and "Does a canary eat?" we are asking people to decide about a feature (*eating*) not directly associated with either bird or canary. If the hierarchical model is correct, it should take people longer to answer the question about the canary. To do so, they must move through two paths, canary to bird, bird to animal. When Allan Collins and M. Ross Quillian (1969) presented questions like these to adult subjects, they discovered that the hierarchical model accurately predicted response times. It took people longer to answer questions that were further apart in the hierarchy. Subsequent research has supported this basic idea. We learn the features associated with concepts, and over the course of time these features become integrated into networks that help us to organize and remember events (Collins & Loftus, 1975).

Interim Summary

Concepts are ways of categorizing the people, objects, and events in our environment. *Artificial concepts* are studied in the laboratory to help determine the cognitive processes involved in concept formation. By contrast, *natural concepts* are those we encounter more frequently in our everyday lives. Often, natural concepts have imprecise or "fuzzy" boundaries. In acquiring these concepts, we identify the best examples of each concept, known as *prototypes*. We then use prototypes as a reference point when evaluating new concepts. Once we have acquired concepts, we integrate them by forming hierarchies that help us to organize otherwise disparate notions.

PROBLEM SOLVING

Problem solving is one of the most inescapable aspects of our daily lives. We problem solve when we confront relatively simple tasks, such as finding a new way home when our normal route is blocked, and when we face more involved tasks, such as planning a cross-country trip that will take us to many different locations. Of course, problem solving can also involve finding solutions to highly complicated social and political problems, as well as solutions to difficult scientific and medical dilemmas. So, while problem solving is not unique to humans, there can be little doubt that it is an extremely complex skill that sometimes tests the limits of human intelligence (Chi & Glaser, 1985).

The Nature of Problem Solving

Problem solving begins when we have an end point or goal in mind but no apparent way to achieve the goal. For example, you may wish to cross a river but see no bridge, ford, or navigable means of transport. One solution, among many, is to fashion a raft from available driftwood. In doing so, you have solved the problem by constructing a "path" from the beginning to the end point.

What are the mental processes involved in problem solving? Alan Newell and Herbert Simon (1972) suggest that there are three distinct stages in solving complex problems. First, people try to divide the problem into smaller, manageable segments. Second, they look for a rule or hypothesis that will solve the particular segment they are considering. Finally, they evaluate their hypothesis. **Figure 8.5** shows how this model works. Note the presence of "feedback loops" that show how the stages continue to cycle until the problem is solved.

Now look at **Figure 8.6**. The figure shows a circle with letters of the alphabet placed on either the inside or the outside. The task is to determine why the letters shown in the figure are placed either inside or outside the circle and to determine where the remaining letters of the alphabet belong.

The solution to this type of problem usually conforms to Newell and Simon's three-stage model. People often begin by considering the relationship among the six letters shown in the figure. This segments the problem and makes it manageable. The second step is to search for a rule (a hypothesis) that explains why some letters go inside the circle and others outside. Finally, this hypothesis must be evaluated by determining whether it explains the placement of a subsequent group of letters inside or outside the circle.

Figure 8.7 shows the solution to the problem. As you can see, letters with straight

(handwritten margin notes)

II) PROBLEM SOLVING:
- COMPLEX
- HAPPENS WHEN WE HAVE A GOAL, BUT NO WAY TO ACHIEVE IT.
- SOLVE PROBLEMS BY CONSTRUCTING A "PATH" FROM BEGINNING TO END.
→ NEWELL & SIMON!
- 3 STAGES IN PROBLEM SOLVING!
① DIVIDE PROBLEM INTO SMALLER SEGMENTS/UNITS
② FIND A RULE or HYPOTHESIS THAT WILL SOLVE PARTICULAR UNIT
③ EVALUATE HYPOTHESIS.
- Fig 8.5
- FEEDBACK LOOPS! SHOW HOW STAGES CONTINUE TO CYCLE UNTIL PROBLEM IS SOLVED.
- USE STRATEGIES FOR PROBLEM SOLVING.
- STRATEGIES!
ⒶALGORITHM - PROCEDURE WHERE ALL POSSIBLE SOLNS. ARE CONSIDERED.
- REQUIRES A LOT OF TIME
- DOES FIND AN EVENTUAL SOLN.
ⒷHEURISTIC!
- SELECTIVE STRATEGY W HIGH PROB. OF PRODUCING A CORRECT SOLN.
- LIKE "RULE-OF THUMB"
- DON'T ALWAYS WORK
- PROVIDE SPEEDY SOLNS.
- 2 TYPES OF HEURISTICS!
ⓐ SUBGOAL ANALYSIS! - REDUCING PROBLEM INTO SMALLER PARTS → MOVE FORWARD
- EG. TOWER OF HANOI (RINGS)

b) WORKING BACKWARD!
- MOVE BACKWARD TO SOLVE
- IMAGINE END POINT & THEN FIND INTERMEDIATE STEPS

PROBLEM

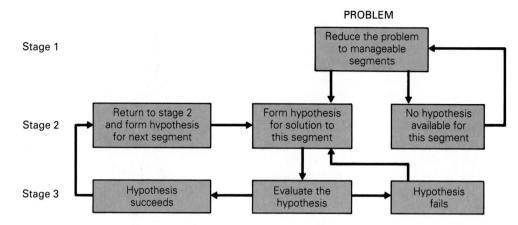

Figure 8.5
The Three-Stage Process
of Problem Solving.

Stage 1

Stage 2

Stage 3

lines belong inside the circle, while those with curved lines belong outside. If you began by analyzing the relationship between vowels and consonants, or by looking for a geometric pattern such as the first letter inside, the next three outside, and so forth, you were forced to discard these hypotheses and begin again. Many problems require this type of recycling before a correct solution is achieved.

Strategies for Problem Solving

Some problems are solved when people suddenly restructure the way they perceive a situation. Unfortunately, this kind of insight is rare. Most problems require a longer and more sequential solution. A game of chess is a good example of a more involved problem-solving situation. Each move is met by an opponent's countermove, which in turn requires a reanalysis of the situation. Typically, no sudden insight will determine the outcome of the game.

Problems like those found in a game of chess are open to a number of different options or *strategies*. One general strategy is to try to consider all possible solutions in order to pick the best one. However, this strategy may conflict with a need for a more rapid and efficient solution. Problem solvers are sensitive to both demands. They want to ensure a correct solution, but they are also aware of the time and mental effort involved in investigating every possible solution. Let us look in detail at two major strategies problem solvers use, bearing in mind their conflicting demands.

ALGORITHMS
One way to solve a complex problem is to use a method that will always produce a solution. In the language of cognitive psychology, this is

Figure 8.6
A Complex Problem.
If A, E, and F are inside the circle, and B, C, and D are outside, where do the remaining letters of the alphabet belong? See Figure 8.7 for the solution.

known as choosing an **algorithm**, a systematic procedure in which the problem solver considers all possible solutions to a problem. An algorithm guarantees the discovery of an effective solution, but it may require an inordinate amount of time. Imagine using an algorithm to solve a crossword puzzle or to unscramble the following letters so as to make an actual word.

M   A   S   R   E   B   C   L

Solving this problem with an algorithm requires arranging the letters in all possible combinations. With an eight-letter word that has no duplicate letters, you must try out 40,320 possible combinations! Even if your knowledge of the English language allows you to eliminate some potential combinations, you are still faced with a daunting task. Such is the nature of algorithms. They are often plodding and inefficient, but bound to produce an eventual solution. You may well feel, however, that they are better suited to a computer that can be programmed to evaluate all possible alternatives quickly.

HEURISTICS
When faced with a complex task, such as unscrambling eight letters, we need a shortcut that provides a reasonable chance of success. This is what cognitive psychologists refer to as a **heuristic**, or a selective strategy with a high probability of producing a correct solution. Heuristics are really "rules of thumb" or bits of knowledge that have helped you to solve problems in the past. One that you might use with scrambled letters is the relationship of consonants and vowels. You rarely find three consonants at the beginning of an English word, so you probably won't consider that possibility at

the outset. In fact, research has shown that subjects initially focus on letter combinations that have a high probability of occurrence (Bourne, Dominowski, & Loftus, 1979). A slightly different heuristic is to search for a partial solution involving only a few of the letters, then try to construct the longer word using all the letters. Although heuristics do not always work, they provide speedy solutions that can be quickly evaluated. The answer to this problem, incidentally, is SCRAMBLE, which points out another useful heuristic. Never underestimate the deviousness of people who construct scrambled-letter problems, better known as anagrams.

Heuristics are obviously a vital part of problem solving. They provide people with an opportunity to generate a number of different solutions in quick order. Below, we discuss two very different types of heuristics that problem solvers often use. The first, known as subgoal analysis, demonstrates how people work toward an overall solution by first dividing a problem into smaller segments. The second describes the somewhat curious phenomenon of working "backward" toward a solution.

Subgoal Analysis

Subgoal analysis is a problem-solving strategy commonly found both in the verbal descriptions of human problem solvers and in the operations of a computer program (Newell & Simon, 1972). Essentially, it is a method of reducing a complex problem to a series of smaller problems, or subgoals. For example, the ultimate goal in chess is to put the opponent's king in checkmate, but as every chess player knows, this is a long-range goal that must be preceded by a series of smaller moves. Similarly, when adult subjects confront the Tower of Hanoi problem shown in **Figure 8.8,** they must search for meaningful subgoals that will lead to the eventual solution. Take a moment to examine the Tower of Hanoi problem. All the rings on peg A must be moved to peg C, under two restricting conditions: (1) only the top ring on a peg can be moved, and (2) a ring cannot be placed on top of a smaller ring. What solution can you devise? Try the problem first; then consider the following analysis provided by Glass, Holyoak, and Santa (1979).

The restricting conditions dictate that ring 3 must be placed on peg C first. This becomes a subgoal in a successful solution to the problem, though it cannot be achieved immediately. Before ring 3 can be moved, rings 1 and 2 must be cleared away. Now a second subgoal

Heuristics can be used as shortcuts to solving problems when playing games like Scrabble or doing crossword puzzles.

arises. Ring 1 must be moved first, but to which peg, B or C? Here the integration of subgoals is important. If ring 1 is moved to peg B first, then ring 2 must go to peg C. But if that occurs, then the first subgoal (move ring 3 to peg C) will be impossible. However, if ring 1 goes to peg C, and ring 2 to B, then the following subsequent moves will be possible:

> ring 1 to peg B
> ring 3 to peg C
> ring 1 to peg A
> ring 2 to peg C
> ring 1 to peg C

Note that this approach to the problem involves a hierarchy of subgoals, all of which must be carefully integrated (Glass et al., 1979). Failure to see the integration among subgoals can produce a situation in which the problem solver feels stumped. As you would expect, subjects find it increasingly difficult to integrate

Figure 8.7
Solution to Figure 8.6.
Letters with straight lines belong inside the circle, while those with curves go outside.

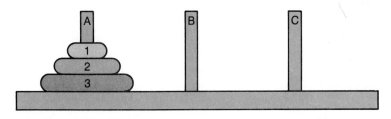

Figure 8.8
The Tower of Hanoi Problem.
Initial position of three seriated rings in the Tower of Hanoi problem. (From Glass, Holyoak, & Santa, 1979)

subgoals in the Tower of Hanoi problem as the number of rings increases (Egan & Greeno, 1974).

WORKING BACKWARD

Subgoal analysis is a systematic method that propels the problem solver in a "forward" direction. However, it is also possible to work "backward" toward a solution, that is, to envision what the end point or solution should look like and then to decide on the intermediary steps. You might well use this method when the problem involves an open-ended task, such as deciding how to spend a 1-week vacation. The starting point in your reasoning may actually be the final choice (I would like to spend a week in Austria). The intermediary "backward" steps may involve pariticular sites you want to see, lodgings in those areas, transportation, documents for travel abroad, and estimates of how much the vacation will cost.

Obstacles to Problem Solving

Many factors influence problem solving. One of the most important is the individual's experiences, both immediate and past. Experiences guide our problem-solving abilities by establishing expected outcomes. Often without realizing it, we adopt subtle hunches—what psychologists would call biases—as we attempt to solve difficult problems. But what served us well in one situation may be our undoing in another. Sometimes past experience leads us to analyze problems in a very confining and unhelpful way.

MENTAL SET

When we face a problem, especially one that is familar to us, we often adopt a particular way of thinking about the problem. What we are doing is forming a **mental set.** Mental sets can be helpful, but not if they become too inflexible. Unfortunately, this is exactly what happens in many situations. Consider the classic water-jar problems devised by Abraham Luchins (1942).

In Luchins' experiment (see **Table 8.2**), the subjects were asked to determine how to measure a required amount of water with the three jars labeled A, B, and C. For example, in problem 1, the task is to measure exactly 100 units of water. Jar A measures 21 units; jar B, 127; and jar C, 3. Many subjects puzzle over the problem momentarily but then discover a sim-

Table 8.2   **Luchins' Water-Jar Problems**

Problem	Jar A	Jar B	Jar C	Required Amount of Water
	AMOUNT OF WATER MEASURED BY EACH JAR			
1	21	127	3	100
2	14	163	25	99
3	18	43	10	5
4	9	42	6	21
5	20	59	4	31
6	23	49	5	16
7	10	36	3	7
8	28	76	3	25

After Luchins (1942)

ple rule that will produce the required amount: jar B minus jar A, minus twice jar C. With the solution in hand, they proceed to the second problem and discover that once again the same rule works. The subjects then apply this rule to problems 3 through 6 and discover that it continues to produce the correct answer. Now the subjects confront problems 7 and 8, and suddenly they are stumped; the rule no longer works. Many subjects cannot find a way to solve these two problems. Why? Because the mental set they have formed while solving the first six problems interferes with the solutions to problems 7 and 8. In this case, past experience with a particular rule now becomes an obstacle to finding a new solution. Perhaps you have also experienced the effects of mental set. Can you solve the last two problems? The solution, as it turns out, is actually simpler than the solution to the earlier problems. The rule "jar A minus jar C" leads to the correct answer.

FUNCTIONAL FIXEDNESS

One cogent example of the influence of mental set on problem solving is a phenomenon known as **functional fixedness,** a term used to describe how past experiences limit people's ideas about the way objects can be used (Duncker, 1945; Maier, 1931). For example, through everyday experience we develop notions of how objects are typically used. We expect to use hammers to drive nails, to use scissors for cutting, and so forth. Over time, these ideas become so strong and inflexible that we tend to overlook the fact that many different actions can be performed with the same object. The "string problem," shown in **Figure**

8.9, provides a good example. Two strings hanging from a ceiling are positioned so that no one can reach both of them at the same time. The room is otherwise empty except for a table with a pair of scissors lying on the top. The problem is figure out a way to tie the two strings together while remaining in one place on the floor.

The solution is simple enough once you overcome a strong tendency to think of the scissors simply as a cutting tool (see **Figure 8.10**). By tying the scissors to one of the strings and then setting that string in motion, you can grasp both strings at the same time and tie them together.

CONFIRMATION BIAS

Imagine that you have trouble starting your car on a cold winter morning. Like most people, you will probably hazard a guess as to what is wrong. A dead battery is a likely choice, because it is a known cause familiar to many people. The telltale sign of the engine failing to "turn over" may well confirm your suspicion. At that point you are likely to telephone the service station to request a new battery. You may be right, but you are also lucky because your strategy has failed to eliminate other possible difficulties. Cars are complex machines and often the same symptom (failure to start) can have many different causes (e.g., starting motor, solenoid switch). However, people often find it difficult to abandon their original hypotheses. Instead, they search only for evidence that will support their initial ideas. Psychologists call this common human failing the **confirmation bias**.

In a variety of different experiments, people have shown a strong tendency to seek evidence that will *verify* their initial hypotheses and, just as importantly, to fail to consider evidence that will *disprove* their initial ideas (Johnson-Laird & Wason, 1977). To illustrate, first try the problem shown in **Figure 8.11**. Most people quickly form a possible solution, but they also fail to try to disprove other possible solutions. Consequently, a common choice is E and 6, or just E alone. These appear to be clear-cut solutions. However, the correct choice is E and 7. Why? You cannot verify the truth of the proposition in Figure 8.11 unless you prove that there is no vowel on the other side of a card with an odd number. You must first disprove what for many people is the most obvious solution.

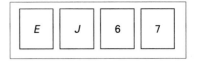

Figure 8.11
Verifying a Proposition.
Imagine that each of the squares shown here represents a card. What card(s) must you turn over to verify the truth of the following proposition? "If a card has a vowel on one side, it has an even number on the other side."

Psychologists have observed the confirmation bias at work in many different areas of our lives. Job interviews, medical diagnoses, and engineering decisions are but a few of the occasions when individuals fail to consider alternatives that violate their initial hypotheses. Clearly, the consequences of the confirmation bias can be serious, as when it leads to an incorrect medical diagnosis or selection of the wrong person for an important job.

Interim Summary

Problem solving involves selecting a solution or goal and then devising a strategy to reach that goal. In the three-stage model of problem solving, the first step is to divide the problem into smaller segments. The next step is to look for a rule or hypothesis to solve each individual segment. The final step is to evaluate each hypothesis. The cycle continues until the problem is solved.

Some problems, like a chess game, involve a long and sequential solution. In these situations, people devise problem-solving strategies. One strategy, known as an algorithm, is to consider all possible steps involved in a solution. Because this is very time-consuming, most people use heuristics. Heuristics are rules of thumb that shorten the solution time considerably, though they do not guarantee a correct solution.

Both immediate and past experiences can present obstacles to problem solving by establishing expected outcomes. For example, a misleading mental set can prevent people from finding a new way to solve a problem because they are relying on past methods that are no longer effective. Similarly, a tendency to seek only information that will confirm a hypothesis can lead people to faulty conclusions.

Figure 8.9
Demonstration of Functional Fixedness. Subject is asked to tie the strings together but is unable to reach both strings at the same time. The solution is shown in Figure 8.10. (Based on Maier, 1931)

Figure 8.10
The Solution to Figure 8.9. By tying the scissors to the end of one string and setting the string in motion, the subject is able to grasp both strings. The solution requires the subject to think of a novel use for the scissors. (Based on Maier, 1931)

Handwritten margin notes:

III REASONING!
- 2 TYPES!
① DEDUCTIVE
② INDUCTIVE

① DEDUCTIVE:
- DRAWING LOGICAL CONCLUSIONS FROM AVAILABLE EVIDENCE
- HAS BIASES THAT INFLUENCE OUR ABILITY TO DRAW LOGICAL INTERFERENCES.

Ⓐ SYLLOGISM! ARGUMENT OF 2 STATEMENTS ASSUMED TO BE TRUE (PREMISES) & A CONCLUSION THAT FOLLOWS PREMISES.
- ∴ TASK TO DECIDE IF CONCLUSION IS VALID/ VALID/ POSSIBLE.
- INFLUENCED BY STRUCTURE OF SYLLOGISM.
- DRAWN TO A LOGICAL ERROR WHEN PRESENTED ABSTRACTLY.

② INDUCTIVE REASONING!
- DISCOVERY OF A GENERAL RULE THAT IS DERIVED FROM SPECIFIC OBS.

EG: YOU HAVE SYMPTOMS + DOC. MAKES CONCL.
- SERIES COMPLETION PROBLEMS - FINISH SERIES
- ANALOGIES - FIND RELATIONSHIP.

REASONING

Reasoning is a more complex process than most of us imagine. To understand how reasoning works, we need to consider both how people reason and what factors interfere with sound reasoning skills. Two important kinds of reasoning, deductive and inductive reasoning, illustrate these issues.

Deductive Reasoning

We are called on to reason in several different ways. In some circumstances, we must emulate the skills of the great detective Sherlock Holmes and arrive at a conclusion after sifting through all the pertinent clues. When we do so, we engage in **deductive reasoning,** drawing logical conclusions from available evidence.

In practice, deductive reasoning usually involves careful analysis of one or two key statements, followed by a conclusion that is drawn logically from the information presented in the statements. For example, consider what conclusions you would draw from the following statement:

If you get an A on the final exam,
you will get an A in the course.

One conclusion is obvious. An A on the final exam overrides any other grades received during the semester and guarantees an A in the course. But this conclusion is so compelling that it forces some people to form a second conclusion that does not follow logically, namely that you *must* obtain an A on the final to receive an A in the course.

This is just one example of the pitfalls in deductive reasoning. We tend to have biases—particular ways of looking at a problem—that influence our ability to draw logical inferences. These biases are not always apparent, but on occasion we confront problems that are so counterintuitive they actually lead us toward logical errors. Perhaps the best example is found in one type of deductive reasoning problem, the syllogism.

A **syllogism** is an argument consisting of two statements assumed to be true (called premises) and a conclusion that follows logically from the premise. The task is to decide whether the conclusion is valid or invalid or whether a conclusion is even possible. The argument below provides a classic example of a syllogism:

All men are mortal.

Socrates is a man.

Therefore, Socrates is mortal.

This is an example of a straightforward and relatively easy syllogism. Most people do quite well when confronted with syllogisms like these. However, our ability to reason deductively is quite fragile. Often the form or *structure* of the syllogism influences our judgment. Consider the following example:

All As are Bs.

All Cs are Bs.

Therefore, all As are Cs.

Logically, this is quite similar to the first syllogism. However, dealing with more abstract terms in the premise makes the problems somewhat trickier. We are not used to symbols (As, Bs) as substitutes for words. Consider the same problem stated differently.

All bassoon players are musicians.

All flute players are musicians.

Therefore, all bassoon players are flute players.

Clearly, the conclusion is invalid. But note that in its more abstract form, the conclusion seems to follow naturally from the premise. We are drawn more easily toward a logical error when the syllogism is presented abstractly.

Deductive reasoning is a complex process. Subtle aspects of the structure of an argument can lead people toward faulty conclusions. Yet, these errors are not random mistakes. On the contrary, they reveal interesting dimensions of our deductive skills.

Inductive Reasoning

On some occasions, we must reason by taking a few observations and working our way "upward" toward a general conclusion. This is what a doctor does when you arrive at the office with some vague symptoms. This type of reasoning is known as **inductive reasoning** because it involves the discovery of a general rule or principle that is derived from specific observations.

Inductive reasoning is really one form of hypothesis testing. We begin with one or more observations and try to reach a general conclusion. Again take the example of a car that won't start. Is the battery dead? Are the spark plugs worn out? Is the starting motor disabled? The skilled mechanic listens to the car, makes some observations with appropriate tools, and reaches a conclusion.

Psychologists often study inductive reasoning by creating small problems that can be solved in the laboratory or classroom setting. Two familiar examples are *series completion problems* and *analogies*. In a series completion problem, subjects are asked to examine an incomplete series and determine what elements come next. An example is

3, 7, 15, 31, ___ , ___ ,

Analogies require subjects to induce a relationship among known elements. A verbal analogy is typical:

> *apple* is to *orange* as *hammer* is to: *chisel, tool, stick, hat*

You may have encountered both types of problems on tests taken during high school. Analogies, in particular, are often found on exams used for admission to colleges and graduate schools.

Interim Summary

To understand the process of reasoning, we need to know how people reason and the factors that interfere with sound reasoning. Two important kinds of reasoning are deductive reasoning and inductive reasoning. Deductive reasoning is drawing logical conclusions from available evidence. A common example of deductive reasoning is the syllogism, an argument consisting of two statements (premises) assumed to be true and a conclusion that follows logically from the premises. The structure of a syllogism can interfere with sound reasoning. For example, the use of abstract terms in the premises can lead people to faulty conclusions.

In inductive reasoning, we begin with a few specific observations and try to reach a general conclusion. Two types of problems often used to study how people use inductive reasoning are series completion problems and analogies.

DECISION MAKING

Decision making is something we do all the time, but most decisions are relatively minor, such as what to have for supper tonight or which movie to see this weekend. However, on occasion we face major decisions, such as what career to pursue, that may well have a lasting impact on our lives.

Here, we will consider two basic elements of decision making: (1) the factors that influence the choices people make and (2) the factors that bias or interfere with decision making.

Choices in Decision Making

Because a decision involves a choice, it presents us with a potential conflict. Should a couple have a child and derive the pleasure that comes from parenting, or should they retain the greater personal freedom they may enjoy without children? Should you begin writing your term paper this weekend, or should you visit a friend and postpone writing for a few days?

Researchers find that two factors influence the outcome of these and other decisions. One is the *utility,* or value, that people assign to the choices involved in the decision. If you feel that a weekend away from schoolwork is an absolute necessity, you are likely to choose that over beginning your term paper. Time away has greater utility to you. However, you will also calculate the *probability* that each choice will be fully realized. How likely is it that the weekend will be enjoyable if you visit your friend, and how likely is it that you can complete the term paper at some other time? Both utility and probability influence the decision-making process (Janis & Mann, 1977).

Heuristics in Decision Making

Decisions also involve judgments. Which political party is most likely to avoid war? What is the safest form of energy? Where is the best place to live? In making these decisions, people often rely on heuristics, the useful "rules of thumb" that help us solve many different types of problems. Unfortunately, heuristics can also lead us astray. Nowhere is this more apparent than in the decision-making process. Below we

review three different types of heuristics, all of which can lead people to erroneous judgments.

THE REPRESENTATIVENESS HEURISTIC

Consider the following description of an individual named Steve:

> Steve is very shy and withdrawn, invariably helpful, but with little interest in people, or in the world of reality. A meek and tidy soul, he has a need for order and structure, and a passion for detail. (Tversky & Kahneman, 1973, p. 1124)

People were presented with this description and then asked to decide how likely it was that Steve was involved in one of a number of different occupations, such as musician, salesperson physician, pilot, or librarian. The experimenters, Amos Tversky and Daniel Kahneman, were interested in what factors people considered in making a judgment about Steve's occupation. As it turned out, most considered only one factor—the personality characteristics given in the description. Because Steve was described as shy, introverted, and withdrawn, people frequently guessed that he was a librarian and rarely suggested that he was a salesman (Tversky & Kahneman, 1973). In doing so, the subjects in this experiment were relying on the *representativeness* heuristic. They held certain stereotypes about the typical or representative member of each of the occupations, and they matched these to the information available on Steve. Notice that by using this heuristic, the subjects ignored other factors that would have helped to predict Steve's occupation. For example, they might have inquired about the percentage of people in the population at large who are involved in each of the occupations mentioned by the experimenters.

THE ANCHORING HEURISTIC

Sometimes decisions involve estimates. If you are planning a trip to a new destination, you may want to estimate how far you are going to travel, or what is the likelihood of rain during your stay. Cognitive psychologists have found that when people address questions like these, they often use an **anchor** or starting point that is based on some recent experience. For example, consider the estimation problem shown in **Table 8.3.** The answer to the problem (40, 320) is unaffected by the first number in the se-

Table 8.3	The Anchoring Heuristic
Estimate the answer to (a) and (b) within 5 seconds	
A. 8 x 7 x 6 x 5 x 4 x 3 x 2 x 1	
B. 1 x 2 x 3 x 4 x 5 x 6 x 7 x 8	

ries. Yet, when high school students were asked to provide estimates of the correct answer to this problem, the average estimate for those who were given series A was 2,250, while the average for those who were given series B was 512 (Tversky & Kahneman, 1982). Clearly, the anchor in this problem was the first number in the series, and it had a major impact on the subjects' estimates.

Once people have established an anchor point, they are very reluctant to modify it. For example, Tversky and Kahneman (1974) found that even the promise of money for more accurate estimating failed to induce subjects to adjust their original anchor points. The implications of this result are quite profound, especially when we think about the ways in which people can manipulate our original anchor point. A prosecutor's description of a suspect, for example, provides an opportunity to establish a firm probability in the minds of jurors about whether the defendant could have committed a particular crime.

THE AVAILABILITY HEURISTIC

In making estimation and probability decisions, we tend to rely on examples that are easily available in our memories. If you are trying to decide if bad weather will ruin your summer picnic, you are likely to be influenced by the weather pattern over the past few days. A recent spate of afternoon thunderstorms may lead you to overestimate the likelihood of rain. Quite often, vivid and memorable experiences influence our decisions about the frequency or probability that some event will occur.

To demonstrate this phenomenon, ask a friend to estimate whether the letter *k* is more likely to appear as the first or third letter of words with more than three letters. Words beginning with *k* are easy to remember, and if your friend reasoned out loud, you probably heard examples like *know, kick, knot*, and so forth. Consequently, most people guess that words beginning with *k* occur about twice as often as words with *k* in the third position. In fact, the reverse is true (Tversky & Kahneman, 1973).

We should note, however, that the availability heuristic can be quite useful. As in the example above, recent weather is often a good predictor of weather in the immediate future. Nevertheless, our own experiences sometimes distort reality. When asked to guess the national divorce rate, people who have many divorced friends and acquaintances tend to overestimate the actual rate (Kozielecki, 1981). Furthermore, both vividness and repetition of key examples may unduly influence our judgments. Students who hear a graphic description of a professor's teaching skills often overlook large-scale, systematic evaluations when choosing a new course (Borgida & Nisbett, 1977), and physicians are more likely to order unnecessary tests to detect diseases that are frequently described in the medical journals (Schwartz & Griffin, 1986). Of course, the potential to create memorable and misleading examples is not lost on politicians. Many elections have turned on a politician's ability to sway public opinion by using a particularly vivid example, such as a single case of welfare fraud or violent crime, that misrepresents the true state of affairs.

Framing

One of the most intriguing features of decision making is the way in which the wording of a question affects our judgment. To illustrate, imagine that you had to decide what to do when confronted with the problems described in **Table 8.4.** When Kahneman and Tversky asked people how they would handle these situations, less than half of those who considered problem 1 said they would pay for another theater ticket. By contrast, almost 90 percent of those asked to consider problem 2 said they would purchase a ticket. Note that the cost to the theatergoer is exactly the same in both situations, but the two problems establish different *decision frames*, or ways to evaluate equivalent information.

We are all surprisingly vulnerable to decision frames, even when evaluating crucial information. For example, we tend to respond more favorably to a proposed medical treatment if we are told that it has a 50 percent chance of success as opposed to a 50 percent chance of failure. Consequently, physicians

Table 8.4   **Framing a Decision**

1. You have paid $10 for a theater ticket. Upon entering the theater you discover that you have lost the ticket. Would you pay $10 for another ticket?

2. You have decided to see a play with the admission price of $10 per ticket. As you enter the theater, you discover that you have lost a $10 bill. Would you still pay $10 for a seat?

must be careful about the way they frame choices because their words can unwittingly influence a patient's decisions (Payne, 1985). Perhaps not surprisingly, people who want to sell you something are likely to consider your decision frame very carefully. So should you. Which are you more likely to buy, ground beef that is advertised as "75% lean" or containing "25% fat" (Levin, 1987)?

Interim Summary

Decision making involves choices and often presents people with a potential conflict. Two factors seem to influence the resolution of the decision-making conflict: (1) the utility, or value, of each of the choices and (2) the individual's judgment about the probability that each choice will actually occur.

As with problem solving, people often use heuristics to make decisions. Unfortunately, in decision making heuristics sometimes lead us astray by providing us with partial or faulty information. Research on decision making has also shown that the way a problem is presented or *framed* for us can have a major impact on the decisions we reach.

• •
ARTIFICIAL INTELLIGENCE (AI)

In the summer of 1956, a group of scholars gathered at Dartmouth College in Hanover, New Hampshire to write a computer program that would "think" like a human (Gardner, 1985). From this early endeavor emerged the now burgeoning field of **artificial intelligence (AI).**

AI is the science of programming computers to simulate how humans act intelligently. For example, if a computer is programmed to

Computers are able to employ many of the same problem-solving strategies as humans. However, they cannot duplicate the breadth and complexity of the human mind.

One slight mistake and the computer program will fail.

Do computers really think? Psychologists have argued this question for nearly 30 years. Of course, much depends on what is meant by thinking, and to date we do not have complete agreement on that point. What is clear is that computers perform many problem-solving tasks very fast and efficiently. They play a major role in our lives now, and that role is likely to increase. But computers do not work on their own. They must be programmed intelligently. And no computer to date can do some of the things that humans do almost effortlessly—recognize a melody or a face, attach meaning to words, or distinguish a rose from a tulip (Longnet-Higgins, 1987).

Computers are impressive machines. They have a capacity for exact operation and storage of data that often outstrips the human mind. But they require programs that operators must create, and even with these instructions, they cannot duplicate the breadth and complexity of the human mind.

Interim Summary

Artificial intelligence (AI) is the science devoted to writing computer programs to simulate the way humans think. AI researchers have successfully programmed computers to carry out some of the mental tasks that humans perform, but to date no computer program has simulated the most creative elements of the human mind.

LANGUAGE

Language plays a very important role in our lives. On a daily basis, we use language to communicate our thoughts and feelings to others. But we have a fascination with language that goes well beyond the practical. For centuries, philosophers and psychologists have speculated about the very nature of language. Is language innate, that is, do children the world over learn the same basic elements of language? Is language such a powerful force in our lives that it actually determines the way we perceive the world around us? Finally, is language a uniquely human trait, or do animals have language as well?

solve difficult algebraic equations, we not only learn the solution to those problems but also gain some important insights into human problem solving. The computer becomes a model of how we think (Stillings, Feinstein, Garfield, Rissland, Rosenbaum, Weisler, & Baker-Ward, 1987).

Why try to make a machine think like a human? You may recall from Chapter 1 that psychologists have long wondered about mental states. In using computers to simulate human thought, AI researchers are revisiting old territory with new techniques. By altering and improving computer programs, AI investigators hope to represent what cannot be directly observed—the inner workings of the human mind (Stillings et al., 1987).

Computers can be programmed to deploy some of the same problem-solving strategies that humans use. For example, it is relatively easy to write a computer program that uses heuristics to solve the anagrams (scrambled-letter problems) that we discussed earlier in this chapter. Once programmed correctly, the computer is often much faster and more efficient in solving these problems. But the program must be precise. As you may well know from your own experience, computers do exactly what they are told! They do not make inferences.

The Nature of Language

Language may be a commonplace occurrence in our everyday lives, but it is nonetheless very complex. For example, consider what answer you might give to a friend who poses the question, "What is language?" The truth is that scholars have struggled with this question for many years without complete agreement. Nevertheless, we can identify some of the major criteria that linguists use to describe the essential characteristics of language.

MEANING

Virtually all of our words and sentences convey meaning. For example, the sentence "The man drove the car" conveys useful information about the relationship between a person and an object. However, if the words in this sentence were rearranged to read, "The car drove the man," the sentence would no longer make sense. Meaningfulness is one of the most fundamental characteristics of language. We can safely assume that if a species does not communicate meaningful information, no language is present in that species.

GENERATIVITY

Human language is creative. In the course of a day we rarely express the same sentence more than once. Over a lifetime, we use thousands of different sentences. Linguists refer to this aspect of human language as *generativity*, or the ability to use a finite number of words, along with rules for combining words, to produce an almost infinite number of sentences. Consider the following sentence:

The boy hit the ball.

This simple idea can be changed into a number of different ideas by rearranging the elements of the sentence and adding one or two additional words. Notice that each of the following sentences is generated quite easily from the basic underlying notion of the boy hitting the ball:

The ball was hit by the boy.

The boy did not hit the ball.

What did the boy hit?

Generativity is important because all organisms, both human and animal, have limitations on what they can remember. If we could not use rules to generate new sentences, but instead had to commit to memory all of our past sentences, we would be severely restricted in what we are able to say.

DISPLACEMENT

We often talk to one another about the events in our immediate surroundings. But we are not limited to talking about the here-and-now. We have the ability to talk about people and objects that the listener has not seen and to describe past and future events.

Psychologists refer to this skill as *displacement*, or the ability to convey information about events that occurred at another time or in a different place. As a consequence, we can learn a great deal through the experiences of others. Displacement is an important characteristic of language because it permits the rapid transmission of complex information from person to person and from generation to generation (Brown, 1973).

The three criteria just described provide a broad definition of language. Note that these criteria do not restrict the term *language* to a particular mode of expression, that is, to the spoken word, nor do they define language as a uniquely human faculty. The precise form that a language takes remains an open question. For example, deaf people, who often communicate through signs made with the hands, use a true language expressed in a different modality (Quigley & Kretschmer, 1982). To most of us these signs look like a confusing blur of rapid

These members of a deaf chorus are using sign language to "sing" to an audience.

hand movements, but those who know sign language recognize them as the basic units of a rich and expressive language. They allow the signer to "speak" effectively and even create poetry and music (Bellugi & Klima, 1972). Is it possible that chimpanzees, who communicate through signs and symbols, as well, also possess a true language? We will return to that question after we describe the characteristics of a spoken language.

Spoken Language

The world's many and diverse cultures have at least one thing in common—they all use some form of an oral or spoken language. Each of these spoken languages has three major components: *phonology, syntax,* and *semantics,* with each component making a distinct contribution to the sentences we speak and understand. But these components do not operate in isolation. Instead, they function together to form a set of rules known as the **grammar** of a language.

Ⓐ Phonology

Phonology refers to the study of how sounds are combined to produce words and sentences. It may surprise you to learn that words are not the most basic unit of language. Words are actually formed from a class of smaller sounds known as phonemes. A **phoneme** is the smallest unit of sound in a spoken language that influences the comprehension and production of a larger unit, such as a word. There are approximately 45 distinct phonemes in English that correspond roughly to the consonants and vowels of the alphabet. They must be combined with one another to produce generally recognizable sounds. In the English language, phonemes include such sounds as the *t* at the beginning of *tea* and the *k* at the beginning of *key* (Dale, 1976). Note that *tea* and *key* sound exactly the same except for the initial *t* and *k* of each word. The difference in the meaning of the words *tea* and *key* is expressed through a single phoneme. This is the primary function of phonemes: they are sounds that help us distinguish the meaning of one word from another.

The smallest *meaningful* elements of a spoken language are **morphemes.** Words are morphemes, though not all words are single morphemes. When a speaker uses the word *pictures,* for example, he or she is actually using two morphemes. One is *picture* and the other is the plural ending *s*. The first morpheme tells us that the speaker is referring to a drawing or photograph. The second morpheme tells us that the speaker is referring to more than one of these objects. The plural ending *s* is a morpheme because it adds new information, and therefore new meaning, to what the speaker is trying to convey.

Other examples of morphemes include suffixes, such as *ing*, and prefixes, such as *anti*. The difference between *run* and *running*, or *establishment* and *antiestablishment* illustrates the importance of suffixes and prefixes. In each case, the addition of the suffix or prefix produces a change in meaning.

Phonology is important because it allows us to distinguish between acceptable and unacceptable sound combinations. For example, each of the following sequences of letters is probably unfamiliar to you, but you can use your knowledge of English to determine which one is actually a word:

kferg

knout

kbear

The sequences beginning with kf and kb can be ruled out because you know intuitively that English words do not begin with these letters. The sequence knout, though probably very unfamiliar, is still a possibility because English permits kn at the beginning of words (such as in *knight* and *knot*). Incidentally, knout is an English word for a whip with long leather thongs.

Ⓑ Syntax

Syntax is the set of rules that determines how morphemes are combined to form grammatically correct sentences. All languages have rules specifying what is and is not an acceptable sentence. Consider the following two sentences:

The boy ran away.

Boy the ran away.

Adult speakers of English know that the first sentence is grammatically correct and that the second is incorrect. The rules of English do not permit a noun phrase (*the boy*) to be formed by placing the article (*the*) after the noun (*boy*).

It is worth noting, however, that syntactic rules are arbitrary. English generally does not allow the adjective to follow the noun, but other languages, such as Spanish and French, do. Furthermore, even within cultures, certain dialects use syntactic rules that differ from the standard form (Labov, 1970). Psychologists must be aware of this point when assessing the syntactic skills of individuals from communities that have substantial nonstandard dialects, such as some black or Latino communities (Baratz, 1970).

SEMANTICS

Semantics is the study of how meaning is expressed through words and sentences. Meaning is a very complex aspect of language. Words, for example, can refer to concrete objects (such as *ball* or *horse*), to abstract qualities (such as *beauty* and *love*), and to relationships among objects (such as *more* or *better*). In addition, some words can have both a *denotative* and a *connotative* meaning. The denotative meaning of a word is its literal meaning; the connotative meaning of a word is its emotional or affective meaning. For example, the literal or dictionary meaning of *house* and *home* is about the same: they both can be defined as a building in which people live or a residence for human beings. But the connotative meanings are slightly different. The word *home* conjures up an image of a warm, relaxing, and pleasant place, whereas *house* seems to be a more impersonal term.

But the complexity of word meaning does not end at the level of individual words. Meaning is often determined by subtle differences in the way something is said, or even the context in which it is said. If, for example, a police officer stops you for speeding and says, "May I see your license, please," you would be foolish to interpret the remark as a polite inquiry. It is a command, not a question, as you would soon find out if you answered, "No thank you, officer." The role of contextual meaning in particular and the social uses of language more generally form a special branch of semantics known as *pragmatics* (Macauley, 1980).

Interim Summary

A language has three defining criteria: meaning, generativity, and displacement. All languages must convey meaningful information. In addition, a language must be generative, that is, use a small number of rules to produce an infinite number of statements. Displacement means that a language must have some way of referring to past and future events. These three criteria give a broad overview of language and do not restrict language to any particular modality, such as the spoken word, or to any particular species.

A spoken language has three basic components: phonology, syntax, and semantics. Phonology is the study of the sound system—how vowels and consonants are combined to produce words. Syntax refers to the way words are combined in order to produce sentences. Semantics is the study of meaning expressed through words and sentences. Together, these three components form the grammar of a language, that is, the set of rules that allow us to produce and comprehend the words and sentences we know.

DEVELOPMENT OF LANGUAGE

Children acquire much of their native language in the first 5 or 6 years of life. Many progress from babbling to recognizable words before the age of 1. By the time they are 2 years old, most children have begun to combine words

Children begin to speak somewhere around their first birthday. Pronunciation may be erratic, but adults who spend time with the child will often notice that the same sound is used consistently to refer to an object (e. g., "soo" for shoe).

BABIES LEARN SOUNDS OF LANGUAGE BY 6 MONTHS

By Sandra Blakeslee

Babies learn the basic sounds of their native language by the age of 6 months, long before they utter their first words, and earlier than researchers had thought, a new study suggests.

The findings indicate that recognition of these sounds is the first step in the comprehension of spoken language. As a result, the researchers suggest, babies whose hearing is damaged by chronic ear infections may have lifelong language problems, and the way parents speak to their infants exerts important influences on language learning.

Previous studies suggested that infants' sound perception changes by about 1 year old, when children begin to understand that sounds convey word meanings.

The new research reported in the current issue of Science, was conducted by Dr. Patricia Kuhl of the University of Washington in Seattle and colleagues at Stockholm University in Sweden, the Massachusetts Institute of Technology and the University of Texas in Austin.

Adaptability of Newborn

Newborns are language universalists, Dr. Kuhl said. Able to learn any sound in any language, they can distinguish all the sounds that humans utter. But adults are language specialists, she said. Exposure to their native language reduces their ability to perceive speech sounds that are not in that native tongue. Thus Japanese infants can hear the difference between the English sounds "la" and "ra," but Japanese adults cannot because their language does not contrast those sounds.

Dr. Kuhl said she and her colleagues set out to discover when, during language development, experience alters sound perception and to explore the nature of the change. She said she had thought it could be earlier than other researchers believed.

Recognizing Slight Differences

To test her idea, she used the concept of phonetic prototypes: idealized mental representations of the key sounds in a given language. An English prototype sound is the vowel linguists write as "i," pronounced as in the word "fee."

into primitive sentences. Shortly thereafter, language begins to develop rapidly. Vocabulary size increases dramatically, phrases become noticeably longer, and children begin to produce and comprehend complex sentences. However, it would be misleading to suggest that children learn their entire native language by age 6. Many of the subtleties of language develop in the primary grades (ages 6 through 12) or even beyond (Menyuk, 1983). Nevertheless, any theory of language development must account for the considerable progress children make before they begin their formal schooling.

① Babbling

Infants produce many sounds before they say their first words. They cry, they laugh, and they yell in anger. They even sneeze and hiccup. But until 5 or 6 months of age, they do not produce sounds that resemble a human language. The first sounds that do resemble language occur during what is called the **babbling stage** and seem to be a mixture of the phonemes adults use (de Villiers & de Villiers, 1978). During this stage, infants produce such sounds quite frequently, sometimes with no one else around.

All infants, regardless of their nationality, begin to babble at about the same age and with many of the same sounds (Jakobson, 1968). If you were to listen to a tape recording of infants from many different countries babbling, you would not be able to distinguish the sounds of one infant from the sounds of another (Atkinson, MacWhinney, & Stoel, 1970). At the outset, babbling seems to be under the control of biological or maturational factors. Although the course of babbling in children with certain disabilities, such as deafness, is uncertain (Gilbert, 1982), in general we may assert that neither the physical condition of the child nor the cul-

When an adult English speaker hears something very close to this "i" sound (as when the sound is spoken by someone with a head cold), Dr. Kuhl said, the listener will hear the prototype "i" and not the slight variation. The prototype sound acts like a magnet, she said, pulling all similar sounds into one mental slot for language processing.

But the same is not true of foreign languages. Because English speakers have not memorized the prototype for a foreign vowel—like the Swedish vowel "y" (an EE-sound pronounced with front-rounded lips), they can discern when the vowel is pronounced slightly differently. They have no "magnet" that makes the sounds identical.

Using identical computer equipment to generate prototype Swedish and English sounds, Dr. Kuhl and her colleagues tested the mag-

net effect on 64 6-month-old babies in Sweden and the United States. During the experiment, each baby sat on its mother's lap and listened to pairs of "i" and "y" sounds. Babies were trained to look over their left shoulders when they heard a difference in the sounds (they would see a cute puppet bang a drum) and to ignore any sound pairs that seemed the same.

American babies routinely ignored the different pronunciations of "i" because they heard it as the same sound, Dr. Kuhl said. But they could distinguish slight variations in the "y" sounds.

The exact opposite was true of the Swedish babies, she said. They ignored the variations in "y" because they sounded the same, while they noticed the variations in "i."

The experiment confirms that linguistic experience in the first half

year of life alters an infant's perception of speech sounds, Dr. Kuhl said. Infants show a significantly stronger magnet effect for their native language prototypes.

The research calls attention to the language tutoring role of parents, Dr. Kuhl said. By talking "motherese" with its high pitch, exaggerated intonation and clear pronunciation, she said, parents help babies acquire phonetic prototypes that are building blocks to language.

The study also underscores the importance of treating chronic ear infections in infants, Dr. Kuhl said. There is evidence that such infections may impair language development later in life.

Questions

1. Do the findings of this study support one or more of the theories of language development discussed in this chapter?
2. Should doctors, especially pediatricians, know about the results of this study?
3. Does this research have implications for the way parents talk to infants?

---

ture in which the child is reared influences the course of early babbling.

What happens to those delightful babbling sounds? Gradually infants begin to shape babbling into the phonemes of their particular language environment. This means that Chinese infants begin to make sounds that resemble Chinese words, French infants begin to produce sounds that resemble French words, and so forth. In most cases, this shaping process takes place through infants' interactions with their parents. As parents and children begin to play and vocalize with each other, babbling sounds become progressively similar to the parents' native language.

Single Words

Sometime around their first birthday, children begin to talk. Words come slowly at first. A child might say "ball" at one moment and then

not use the word again for several weeks. Pronunciation is also erratic. Some children speak clearly, while others are difficult to understand. However, in terms of the development of *language*, pronunciation is not important. A child knows a word as long as he or she produces the same sound *consistently* when referring to an object (de Villiers & de Villiers, 1978). For example, if a 2-year-old produced the sound "soo," you might be puzzled at what the child said until his mother explained, "Oh, that's just Jamie's word for shoe."

What do children talk about when they produce their first words? **Table 8.5** on page 312 shows a typical sample of speech from children who are just beginning to talk. Apart from the fact that they are all nouns, what do these words have in common? What aspect of their environment is so noticeable to these children that they comment on it through their first words? All of these words refer to objects

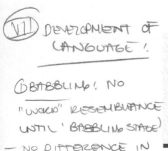

Table 8.5 **Examples of Children's First Words**

shoe
car
dog
sock
ball
Daddy

that have a dynamic quality—objects that *move* or *change* in the course of the children's interaction with them. Socks go on and off the foot. A ball rolls toward and then away from the child. Daddy is a person who comes and goes, picks up the child and puts him down, and so forth. A very large percentage of the child's first words refer to objects that have a dynamic quality (Nelson, 1973). This is all the more impressive because children do *not* talk about many objects in their environment that are *static* or unchanging. They are not likely to say words such as *chair, table, couch,* and the like even though they have equal opportunity to do so. Something about movement and action is important to 1-year-old children. Because the child's actions are also important in the development of intellectual skills, we can hypothesize that language and thought are closely related. We will return to the language-thought question later in this chapter.

Word Combinations

Between the ages of 1 and 2, children begin to combine words. A typical example might involve an 18-month-old who says "big truck" while looking out the window at a passing truck. The child is referring to an event that is plainly visible and thereby illustrating an important feature of children's early word combinations: much of what children say in their early language development is a comment on objects and people in the immediate environment. Only later on do they start to talk about events that are not immediately visible to them (Brown, 1973). For example, by the age of 2, a child might begin talking about "Mommy" even though his or her mother is nowhere in sight. Only a few months later, at roughly 2½ years, children extend this skill even more by referring to events that have happened days or even weeks earlier (Sachs, 1979). Talking about past

events is an example of the importance of displacement in the language of young children.

Do children the world over follow the same basic sequence of language development? Look at **Table 8.6,** which presents a sample of the two-word combinations of children from six different cultures (Slobin, 1970). Notice that children in each culture express certain basic facts about their environment. For example, 1- to 2-year-old children are fond of talking about *possession* ("Mama dress"), that is, the fact that an object belongs to a particular person. They talk about action in two ways: sometimes they note the *object* of an action ("hit ball"), and at other times they comment on the *agent* or person performing the action ("Bambi go"). What is most striking about these early word combinations is that children from very different cultures comment on precisely the same features of their environment (Brown, 1973). This suggests that language, or perhaps the thought processes that underlie language, are a universal feature of human development. As we shall see, the similarity in children's language may be a reflection of a common path in their intellectual or cognitive development.

Children's early language is also striking because it reveals an awareness of *word order*. English-speaking children say "big truck" and not "truck big" as they watch a truck pass by. As Mommy leaves the room, the response is "Mommy go" and not "go Mommy." Children are using word order to express the way they observe the events in their environment unfolding. Perhaps more important, word order is part of the *syntax* of a language. By using word order appropriately, children are taking their first steps toward mastering the rules of syntax.

Sentences and Complex Constructions

Many of a child's early word combinations are not really sentences. But at some time between the ages of 2 and 3, children begin producing sentences with subjects and predicates. They say such things as "Daddy go out," "Where truck go?" or "Mommy pick me up." Notice that these sentences are still incomplete and do not include certain words or morphemes that an adult would use. Still, the child's utterances are becoming progressively longer and more adultlike.

Although language develops rapidly at this stage, the *rate* of acquisition from one child to the next varies considerably. One 3-

Table 8.6   **Two-Word Combinations from Children in Six Different Cultures**

English	German	Russian	Finnish	Luo	Samoan
more milk	mehr Milch (more milk)	yesche moloka (more milk)	lisää kakkua (more cake)		
big boat	Milch heiss (milk hot)	papa bol-shoy (papa big)	rikki-auto (broken car)	piypiy kech (pepper hot)	fa'ali'i pepe (headstrong baby)
mama dress	Mamas Hut (mama's hat)	mami chashka (mama's cup)	täti auto (aunt car)	kom baba (chair father)	paluni mama (balloon mama)
Bambi go	Puppe kommt (doll comes)	mama prua (mama walk)	Seppo putoo (Seppo fall)	chungu biro (European comes)	pa'u pepe (fall doll)
hit ball		nasbla yaechko (found egg)		omoyo oduma (she dries maize)	
where ball	wo Ball (where ball)	gdu papa (where papa)	missa pallo (where ball)		fea pupafu (where Punafu)

After Slobin (1970)

year-old may produce sentences that are far longer and more complex than those of another 3-year-old. Because age is not a good indicator of children's language development, a far better index, known as the **mean** (or average) **length of utterance** (MLU), was developed (Brown, 1973). MLU is determined by first counting the number of words or morphemes in each sentence the child says, then dividing this number by the total number of sentences the child actually produces. For example, if a child produced 100 sentences, and these sentences contained a total of 300 words and morphemes, the child's MLU would be 3.00.

MLU is an excellent indication of how rapidly the child's language is developing. **Figure 8.12** shows the MLU values for three different children from roughly 18 months to 4 years of age. Notice the dramatic differences in the *rate* of language development for these three children.

One consistent way that language develops is through the addition of new morphemes. The sentence "Daddy go out" becomes "Daddy go*ing* out." "There is Mommy shoe" becomes "There is Mommy*'s* shoe." Children acquire these morphemes in a very predictable order. For example, the suffix *ing*, which can be added to many verbs (go*ing*, run*ning*, and the like) appears in the child's vocabulary before the apostrophe *s*, which is used to denote the possessive form (Daddy*'s* shoe). The possessive form in turn appears before the suffix *ed*, which is used to denote the past tense of many verbs (Brown, 1973; de Villiers & de Villiers, 1973).

Children's language becomes noticeably more complex between the ages of 3 and 5. In part, this occurs because children's sentences continue to lengthen and because new words appear in their vocabulary. But what is more striking than either sentence length or vocabulary size is the *type* of sentences children produce. By roughly age 5, children are using two types of sentences that are characteristic of adult speech: the *embedded sentence* and the *tag question*. Each is illustrated below.

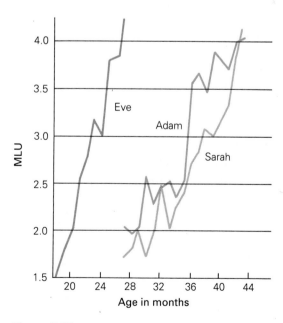

Figure 8.12
Mean Length of Utterance and Chronological Age of Three Children. (After Brown, 1973)

Look closely at the following sentence spoken by a 4-year-old. The child was watching her mother bake a cake when she said, "I see what you made." What is important about this sentence is that the child has actually combined two different sentences into one. At an earlier age, the child would have said, "I see cake," and a little later, "You make cake." But rather than produce two different statements, the child has combined them into one **embedded sentence,** that is, a sentence formed by inserting one simple sentence within another. Embedded sentences are important because they allow the child to convey a good deal of information in a precise and efficient manner.

Children also begin to produce complex questions between ages 3 and 5. One particularly impressive feat occurs when the child takes a simple sentence such as "Daddy is here" and adds a phrase to the end that converts the sentence to a question, "Daddy is here, isn't he?" This is called a **tag question** because the minor addition or *tag* at the end of the declarative statement ("Daddy is here") converts it to a question. Tag questions may appear quite simple, but they actually demand a good deal of grammatical sophistication. Think of what is required to change each of the following sentences into an appropriate tag question:

The boy is here.

They don't eat oranges.

In the first instance, the child must say, "The boy is here, isn't *he?*" The phrase "isn't she" or "isn't it" would be wrong because the pronoun in the tag *(he)* must match the subject of the sentence (the boy). The second example is even more complex. The child must say, "They don't eat oranges, do they?" and not, "They don't eat oranges, don't they?" The negative verb "don't" must be changed to the positive verb "do." The fact that young children produce correct tag questions is an indication of their mastery of the subtle rules that govern the syntax of language.

Interim Summary

Language develops rapidly. Between the ages of 6 months and 6 years, children progress from babbling, to single words, to two-word combinations, and finally to well-formed and complex sentences. Language does not develop completely in the first 6 years, but theories of language must account for the rapid development early in life.

Some major highlights of language development are (1) the similarity in the onset and structure of babbling in children from many different cultures; (2) the tendency for the child's first word to refer to objects that have a dynamic or changing quality; (3) the similarity in the content (semantics) of children's early word combinations, suggesting that children the world over attempt to express many of the same notions; and (4) the development of complex sentences (at roughly 3 years of age) as children move beyond the early stages of language development.

THEORIES OF LANGUAGE DEVELOPMENT

How do children acquire their native language? Let us begin by considering three major facts that a theory of language development must take into account. First, as we noted earlier, many of the basic elements of language appear to be universal. Children from a variety of cultures acquire language in much the same way. Second, children learn language in the absence of formal teaching. All children know a good deal of language before they ever attend school, even though their parents do not provide them with anything akin to formal language lessons. Finally, the language and thought of the child are closely related. Children do not speak mindlessly. They talk about things that are salient and comprehensible to them.

We can now use these facts to examine the contributions of three major theories of language development.

Theory 1: Language Is Acquired Through Imitation

This theory begins with the commonsense assumption that children learn language by imitating their parents. For example, language researchers have shown that young children learn to name novel objects, such as *hook* or *rack*, by first hearing and then repeating the names that adults use for the same objects (Leonard, Chapman, Rowan, & Weiss, 1983). Imitation theorists believe that this process occurs over and again during childhood and is the mechanism by which parents provide a rich linguistic model for their children to copy. From this perspective, children's language becomes progressively more sophisticated as they learn new words and phrases through imitation (Moerk & Moerk, 1979).

How successfully does theory 1 explain the development of language? Briefly, this theory accounts for part of the puzzle of early language development. When young children are observed at home talking to their parents, investigators find that imitation occurs, but it is quite variable from one child to the next. Approximately 30 children have been studied carefully, with the results revealing that roughly one fifth of the children imitated between 30 and 40 percent of what their parents said. The rest of the children imitated less than 10 percent of what they heard (Snow, 1981). However, there is little question that when children imitate, they intend to communicate something meaningful (Snow, 1983). This means that imitation is important, but it cannot account completely for the rapid acquisition of language discussed earlier.

We should note that imitation of parental speech is but one way that parents might influence the child's development of language. Parents also talk to their 1- and 2-year-old children in short, easy-to-understand sentences (Hoff-Ginsberg & Shatz, 1982). This simplified manner of talking to children makes the child's task of learning a native language much easier and more efficient (Furrow, Nelson, & Benedict, 1979). *How* parents talk to children is an important part of the child's own language development.

Theory 2: Language Is Innate

This theory assumes that humans have an innate disposition to acquire language rapidly. Proponents of this theory believe that despite wide variations in their environments, children learn the same basic rules of syntax and semantics because humans are biologically "prepared" to learn language in a particular way (Chomsky, 1975).

What evidence supports this theory? Lenneberg (1967) provided an extensive account of the biological basis of language. He showed that certain characteristics of the brain, the larynx (voice box), and the face (specifically the teeth and mouth) distinguished humans from other primates and allowed our species to develop language. Although using the larynx and face as evidence for this theory is somewhat controversial because to do so restricts the concept of language to speech, other researchers have tended to agree that specialization within the human brain makes language a uniquely human trait (Geschwind, 1970).

Proponents of an innate theory of language development often cite two other well-documented findings that we have already encountered: (1) children make rapid progress during their first 5 or 6 years in the development of language, and (2) they do so in the absence of explicit or formal language lessons. These findings have suggested to Noam Chomsky (1968, 1975), a well-known linguist, that we must have an inborn disposition to learn language. Were it otherwise, Chomsky argues, we would never be able to acquire language as quickly as we do without any formal instruction.

Theory 3: Language Is Dependent upon Cognition

This theory assumes that there is an important cognitive basis for language development. Cognitive theorists believe that language is a tool through which children express their basic understanding of the world (Bruner, 1983). Jean Piaget, a major theorist whose work we will consider in detail in Chapter 9, is perhaps the best-known advocate of this position. Piaget contends that language is dependent on thought (Piaget & Inhelder, 1969). By this he means that certain words or phrases can appear in the child's vocabulary only after the child has mastered the corresponding cognitive principle. For example, Piaget would predict that a child can begin to talk about objects that are not present in the immediate surroundings only *after* the child has developed the ability to *find* objects that are hidden from view. In other words, the child must first have the understanding (cognition) that hidden objects still exist before he or she can use language to talk about these "absent" objects.

Theory 3 is most useful in providing a broad context for language development. In essence, it postulates that language acquisition emerges from the child's understanding of the environment. As one group of cognitive theorists stated, language is the process of "learning how to do things with words" (Bates, Benigni, Bretherton, Camaroni, & Volterra, 1979).

Evaluating Theories of Language Development

Which of the theories that we have just reviewed provides the most plausible account of language development? As in most scientific endeavors, no single theory provides all the answers. Rather, each theory answers some of the fundamental questions about language.

The first theory, which focuses on the nature of the child's linguistic environment, addresses the question of how children acquire language in the absence of formal teaching. One way they do so is by imitating their parents. However, because imitation occurs infrequently, proponents of this theory have turned to another aspect of the linguistic environment—the nature of the speech addressed to young children. Parents speak to their children in short, redundant, and grammatically correct sentences that facilitate language learning. In doing so, parents simplify the child's task of understanding the basic elements of language.

The second theory addresses the question of why many elements of language are universal. We noted earlier that children from many different cultures express the same basic notions in their first words and phrases. If language development is innate, we should expect to find some universal elements of language. Consequently, this theory is most useful in explaining the similarities in the language development of children from widely different backgrounds.

The third theory holds that the growth of language can be predicted from an understanding of the child's cognitive skills. It addresses the relationship between thinking and language and is most helpful in showing how the child's language is part of a broader set of cognitive skills.

● ●

LANGUAGE AND THOUGHT

One assumption about the language-thought relationship is that thought structures language. Piaget adopted this position when he suggested that advances in language depend on the development of thought. However, one could also make the opposite case, namely that language structures or determines thought. From this perspective, thought becomes "relative" to the language in which it is expressed. This is the essence of the **linguistic-relativity hypothesis** proposed by Benjamin Whorf (1956).

English has only one word for snow, but the Eskimo language has different words to identify different types of snow.

Whorf believed language determines the way people of a particular culture perceive and understand the world they live in.

The implications of Whorf's hypothesis are sobering. The linguistic relativity hypothesis would predict that people who speak different languages should understand the world in very different ways. Might world leaders, for example, misunderstand one another because their different languages dispose them to think about global problems in radically different ways? Naturally, such a far-reaching proposal has led to considerable research and lively debate.

Whorf based his hypothesis on the observation that people in different cultures often have very different ways of talking about the same phenomenon. Perhaps his most famous example is the difference between English and Eskimo languages. While English has one word for snow, Eskimo has many different words. Whorf believed that this linguistic difference made it much easier for Eskimos to perceive actual differences in snow. Likewise, the Hopi Indians, who do not mark verb tense with special endings, such as *ed,* for past tense, should have a more difficult time thinking about past events.

How can we test the validity of this intriguing hypothesis? Psychologist Eleanor Rosch decided to look at a concept that is important to all cultures, such as the perception of color, and then examined both the color distinctions made by people in different cultures and the words used to describe those distinc-

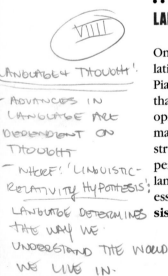

[Handwritten margin notes:]

VIIII

LANGUAGE & THOUGHT:
- ADVANCES IN LANGUAGE ARE DEPENDENT ON THOUGHT
- WHORF: 'LINGUISTIC-RELATIVITY HYPOTHESIS':
LANGUAGE DETERMINES THE WAY WE UNDERSTAND THE WORLD WE LIVE IN.
"PEOPLE WHO SPEAK DIFFERENT LANGUAGES HAVE A DIFFERENT UNDERSTANDING OF THE WORLD.

NOTE: EASIER TO EXPRESS SOMETHING IN LANGUAGE (FRENCH VS. ESKIMO) BUT DOES NOT MEAN LANGUAGE DETERMINES THOUGHT

tions. If, for example, culture A has many different color words while culture B has only a few, it follows that people in culture B should have difficulty perceiving some of the color distinctions common to culture A. The linguistic-relativity hypothesis would predict that a limited number of color words leads to a restricted number of color discriminations. However, this is not what Rosch found. The Dani, for example, who have only 2 color words, can make color distinctions identical to those of native English speakers, who have 11 basic color words (Rosch, 1974).

Results such as these have led psychologists to suggest that, while languages may reflect environmental distinctions important to a particular culture, they do not *create* those distinctions, nor do they prevent people from making them (Slobin, 1979). English provides one illustration of this point. Although English has only one word for snow, speakers of English (especially skiers) can perceive many differences in snow if the occasion demands.

What is the current state of the linguistic-relativity hypothesis? Few people subscribe to the hypothesis as originally formulated. Instead, psychologists believe that languages differ in the *ease* with which they embody certain distinctions about the environment (Dale, 1976). In other words, it may be easier to express a concept in one language than in another, but this does not mean that language determines thought.

Interim Summary

There are three major theories of language development. One school suggests that language is acquired primarily through imitation of adult models. A second school suggests that language is innate; that is, infants are "preprogrammed" to learn language in a rapid and systematic manner. A third school suggests that language is dependent on thought. In other words, the child learns certain words and constructions only after the corresponding thought processes have developed.

The intriguing question of whether language actually structures our thoughts lies at the heart of the linguistic-relativity hypothesis. The strong form of this hypothesis suggests that people who speak different languages may perceive the world in very

different ways. This hypothesis, as originally stated, is not widely accepted today, though many psychologists do believe that it may be easier to express a concept in one language than in another.

LANGUAGE IN OTHER SPECIES

Human beings are not the only animals who communicate. Honeybees communicate the direction and distance to a food source through bodily movements (von Frisch, 1974). Songbirds produce songs by combining different sounds (McNeil, 1970). And dolphins communicate with each other at great depths by using a combination of clicks, whistles, and barks (Lilly, 1967). The communicative skills of these species are impressive, but do they have language? Let us look at the honeybee as one interesting example.

Honeybees

Honeybees have a unique way of communicating. When a worker bee discovers a source of nectar, it returns to the hive and directs the other bees to the precise location of the food. In a series of clever experiments, for which he eventually won the Nobel Prize, biologist Karl von Frisch discovered that worker bees communicate what they know through an elaborate "dance" performed on the wall of the hive (von Frisch, 1974). By using different types of dances, worker bees can indicate both the approximate *distance* to the food and the proper *direction* for the other bees to travel (See **Figure 8.13** on page 318).

Although the dance of the honeybee is quite remarkable, there are major limitations on what can be communicated from one bee to another. For example, if a worker bee must fly uphill and thereby exert extra effort to reach the nectar, it will indicate that the food is much farther away than it actually is (McNeil, 1970). This overestimation occurs because honeybees have only a limited semantic system. They cannot use their dance to provide subtle and detailed information. Furthermore, the dance of the bees, however fascinating, lacks the additional elements required for a language—generativity and displacement.

Until recently, many of these limitations seemed characteristic of all animals, regardless

[handwritten margin note: Honey Bees communicate by 'Dance'. Chimps by sounds & facial expressions. Sign-language (AL).]

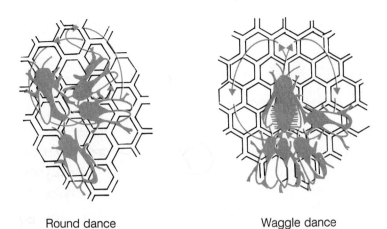

Round dance   Waggle dance

Figure 8.13
Dance of the Honeybees.
Bees communicate with one another through a series of elaborate dances on the
wall of the hive. The "round dance," left, indicates that a source of food is less
than 100 yards away. The "waggle dance," right, is used to signal that a food
source is greater than 100 yards away.

of their evolutionary proximity to humans.
However, through some fascinating studies
with chimpanzees psychologists have raised
anew the question of language in nonhuman
species.

The Linguistic Chimps

In their natural habitat, chimps use both facial
expressions and vocalizations to communicate
with each other. They use their vocalizations to
signal that a dangerous foe is approaching or to
indicate that a food source is nearby. Most often their facial expressions are used simply to
exert dominance over one another. However,
because chimps are close to humans in the
history of evolution, psychologists have often
wondered whether these intelligent animals
could do more. Could they, in fact, learn to
talk?

The earliest attempts to teach chimps to
talk were a resounding failure. One research
team, Keith and Cathy Hayes (1951), spent
many years trying to teach their chimp Viki to
speak. Despite their efforts, Viki acquired only
a four-word vocabulary that was often difficult
to understand. Other investigators mounted
major efforts to teach chimps to talk, but the
outcome was always the same. The chimps
were willing and cooperative subjects, but they
could not learn to speak (Kellogg, 1968).

Our conclusions about language in
chimps would undoubtedly be quite negative if

the story ended here. But in 1969, another husband and wife team, Allen and Beatrice Gardner, reported some remarkable findings about
the ability of a chimp named Washoe to learn
American Sign Language (ASL), the communication system used by many deaf people. In ASL,
words and sentences are constructed by forming distinct shapes (signs) with the fingers of either hand and by holding the hands in certain
positions. When Washoe was about a year old,
the Gardners began teaching her the ASL system. To do this, they used many of the principles of operant conditioning discussed in Chapter 6. At the outset, they modeled appropriate
signs and guided or "molded" Washoe's arms
and hands into the correct positions. Next,
Washoe was reinforced with food and the approval of her trainers for successive approximations to a correct sign. Finally, Washoe was
required to produce perfect signs as she communicated with her trainers. The trainers addressed Washoe only in sign language and, in
Washoe's presence, communicated among
each other exclusively in sign language. For the
first 5 years of her life, Washoe was literally surrounded by people who were using ASL (Gardner & Gardner, 1969).

Washoe's accomplishments startled the
scientific world. In her first 2 years Washoe
learned 38 different signs. Very often her use of
signs resembled the progress that children
make in the early development of a spoken language. Washoe made many of the same observations about her environment that 1- and 2-
year-old children frequently make. She used
signs to comment on the location of objects in
her environment, whom the objects belonged
to, certain qualities or properties of these objects, and so on. Washoe also generalized her
signs to a variety of related objects, just as
children generalize the meaning of their first
words. For example, Washoe's sign for dog
eventually was used not only in the presence of
a dog but also when Washoe saw a picture of a
dog, or even when she heard a dog barking.
Furthermore, Washoe continued to make advances as she grew older, often continuing to
show a striking parallel to children. By the time
she was 4 years old, Washoe had learned 85 different signs. More important, she could combine up to 4 or 5 different signs to make a single "sentence." And her combinations were
sometimes both unique and creative. Upon seeing a swan for the first time, Washoe signed
"water bird," a combination that no one had

ever modeled in her presence. By age 5, when Washoe had become so physically strong that she had to be moved to a primate colony, she had learned more than 160 distinct signs. She had also learned how to combine signs to make a number of interesting statements (Gardner & Gardner, 1977).

Washoe was the first and perhaps the best known of the "linguistic chimps," but she is by no means the only primate to learn a manual communication system. Psychologist Roger Fouts (1973) taught four young chimpanzees 10 different signs from the ASL system through the process of molding. Fouts also conducted experiments to see if chimps could use sign language to communicate with each other. It appears that once chimps become proficient in sign language, they will indeed sign messages to one another. More impressive still are the interactions of Washoe and a young chimp named Loulis, whom Washoe has "adopted." Observations of this pair reveal that not only will Loulis imitate Washoe's signs, but Washoe will on occasion teach signs to her young friend (Fouts, Hirsch, & Fouts, 1983).

Other chimps also have impressive linguistic credentials. Sarah, a chimp who learned to use plastic symbols as words, responded to questions and commands from her trainers by manipulating these symbols in appropriate fashion (Premack, 1971) The first "computer" chimp, Lana, learned how to begin, complete, and eventually form her own sentences by typing messages on a geometric symbol keyboard connected to a computer. Lana also showed that she could respond to questions. If Lana's trainers place different colored objects before her and type the message, "What is the name of the object that is green?" Lana can answer correctly (Savage-Rumbaugh, Pate, Lawson, Smith, & Rosenbaum, 1983). Even more provocatively, two chimps named Sherman and Austin, who mastered the same symbol system as Lana, have typed messages that parallel the child's tendency to comment on objects in their environment that vary or change (Greenfield & Savage-Rumbaugh, 1984). Finally, a gorilla named Koko has shown that she can learn over 200 distinct signs in just under 2½ years (Patterson, 1978). Like some of her compatriots, Koko showed human characteristics in her use of signs. She learned to combine two or more signs in a meaningful way and to invent new combinations for unfamiliar objects and events, such as using "white tiger" to refer to a zebra.

Washoe's linguistic advances with American Sign Language showed a striking resemblence to language development in human children.

Koko has also learned to express emotions (for example, happiness) and to refer to past and future events (Patterson, 1980).

Do Apes Have Language?

What do these studies say about language in nonhuman species? Can we conclude that apes like Washoe and Koko, for example, are capable of acquiring language? Clearly, these apes come much closer to meeting the criteria used to define language than any other nonhuman species. They use signs to express meaning, and their use of signs is creative. Futhermore, they are capable of making statements about objects or events outside their immediate environment. Furthermore, the clear parallel between the accomplishments of apes like Washoe and Koko and a child's development of linguistic skills provides further support for the claim that these animals have language (Gardner & Gardner, 1977).

Yet, some psychologists remain skeptical. They point out that no ape has progressed beyond the level of a 3-year-old child, particularly in forming complex syntactic constructions (Limber, 1977). Children of 4 and 5 years of age, including the deaf who learn ASL as a native language, regularly outpace Washoe and the other apes in their ability to ask questions, to form negative sentences, and so on. Children do this, the critics argue, despite the fact that they are given nowhere near the level of explicit training in language that the apes received. Furthermore, according to one analysis of the sign language of a young chimpanzee, almost all the signs were imitations of the trainer's prior signs (Terrace, Petitto, Sanders, & Bever, 1979). The authors of this study suggest that such a high proportion of imitative utterances provides strong evidence that apes are not capable of the generativity that is so vital to language.

For the moment, then, psychologists cannot agree on the question of whether apes have language. The solution may emerge from new research findings, but it is quite possible that results alone will not answer the question. Instead, psychologists may be forced to ask a more theoretical question: how do apes and humans differ in their use of language and symbols? For example, before children begin talking, they have acquired an impressive and effective system of pointing and gesturing to communicate with adults. This gestural system seems to dispose children to use their first words in an interactive and communicative fashion. Apes do not have the same gestural system, and as a result they are slower to understand the way signs can be used to promote conversation (Savage-Rumbaugh et al., 1983). Through training, however, apes can acquire this conversational ability. Presumably this difference in language usage tells us something about the way apes and humans have evolved, the survival value of language for each species, and the manner in which the two species deploy language in adapting to the demands of their environment. Perhaps the question we should be addressing is not whether apes have language, but how communication skills enhance the development of each species.

Interim Summary

Psychologists have now raised questions about language in other species. Chimps, in particular, are adept at learning a manual language known as American Sign Language (ASL). Some psychologists believe that chimps have shown the capacity to acquire language, but others challenge this notion. They believe chimps cannot acquire the syntactic rules that would satisfy the criterion of generativity.

SUMMARY

1. Concepts are ways of categorizing the people, objects, and events in our environment. Artificial concepts are studied in the laboratory to help determine the cognitive processes involved in concept formation. By contrast, natural concepts are those we encounter more frequently in our everyday lives.

2. Problem solving involves selecting a solution or goal and then devising a strategy to reach that goal. One strategy, known as an algorithm, is to consider all possible steps involved in a solution, but more commonly people rely on heuristics, or "rules of thumb," that shorten the solution time considerably. Both immediate and past experiences can present obstacles to problem solving by establishing expected outcomes. Mental sets induce people to rely on past methods that are no longer effective, and confirmation biases lead people to seek only selective information that can lead them to faulty conclusions.

3. Two important kinds of reasoning are deductive reasoning and inductive reasoning. Deductive reasoning involves drawing logical conclusions from available evidence. A common example of deductive reasoning is the syllogism, an argument consisting of two statements (premises) assumed to be true and a conclusion that follows logically from the premises. Inductive reasoning is a different process, in which people begin with a few specific observations and try to reach a general conclusion.

4. Two principal factors influence the decision-making process: the utility, or value, of the choices involved, and the individual's estimate about the likelihood that each choice will actually occur. As with problem solving, people often use heuristics to make decisions. However, heuristics are sometimes misleading, providing people with partial or faulty information. The way a problem is presented or *framed* can also have a major impact on the decisions people make.

Artificial intelligence is a subfield of cognitive psychology that attempts to make computers simulate the way humans think. Researchers have written programs that successfully mimic some cognitive functions, but no one has yet programmed a computer to simulate the most creative elements of human thought.

5. All languages must convey meaningful information, use a small number of rules to generate a large number of statements, and have the capacity to refer to past and future events. These criteria do not restrict the form of language, nor do they imply that only humans use language. Oral or spoken languages have three basic components: phonology, syntax, and semantics. Together, these three components form the grammar of a language, that is, the set of rules that allow us to produce and comprehend the words and sentences we know.

6. Between the ages of 6 months and 6 years, children progress from babbling, to single words, to two-word combinations, and finally to well-formed and complex sentences. Language does not develop completely in the first 6 years, but theories of language must account for the rapid development early in life.

7. There are three major theories of language development. One suggests that language is acquired primarily through imitation of adult models. A second suggests that language is innate, while a third holds that language is dependent on thought. The linguistic-relativity hypothesis suggests that people who speak different languages may perceive the world in very different ways. This hypothesis, as originally stated, is not widely accepted today, though many psychologists do believe that it may be easier to express a concept in one language than in another.

8. Psychologists have now raised questions about language in other species. Chimps, in particular, are adept at learning a manual language known as American Sign Language (ASL). Some psychologists believe that chimps have shown the capacity to acquire language, but others challenge this notion. They believe chimps cannot acquire the syntactic rules that would satisfy the criterion of generativity.

KEY INDIVIDUALS

Eleanor Rosch
Abraham Luchins
Amos Tversky
Daniel Kahneman
Allen Newell
Noam Chomsky
Herbert Simon
Jean Piaget
Benjamin Whorf
Karl von Frisch
Allen and Beatrice Gardner

KEY RESEARCH

artificial concepts
natural concepts
hierarchical organization of concepts
three-stage model of problem solving
water-jar problems
functional fixedness
factors influencing reasoning and decision making
"round dance" and "waggle dance" of the honeybee
imitation theory of language development
innate disposition to acquire language
cognitive basis of language development
linguistic-relativity hypothesis
teaching language to chimps and apes

KEY TERMS

thinking
concept
algorithm
heuristic
mental set
functional fixedness
confirmation bias
deductive reasoning
syllogism
inductive reasoning
framing
anchor
artificial intelligence (AI)
grammar
phonology
phoneme
morphemes
syntax
semantics
babbling stage
mean length of utterance (MLU)
embedded sentence
tag question
linguistic-relativity hypothesis

Part Three
· · · · · · · · · · · · · · · · · · ·

HUMAN
DEVELOPMENT

Chapter 9
Infancy and Childhood

Chapter 10
Adolescence, Adulthood, and Aging

Chapter 11
Intelligence

Sandra Scarr is Commonwealth Professor of Psychology at the University of Virginia, Charlottesville, VA. Her research on behavior genetics, intelligence, and child development has been published in more than 150 articles and 4 books on intelligence, child care, and family issues. In 1985, she won the National Book Award of the American Psychological Association for *Mother Care/Other Care.*

Q Your work on heredity, race, and intelligence has been very important in the field. Please tell us about it.

A My interests in behavior genetics began when, as an undergraduate, I was told that genetic differences among people did not exist. I knew this had to be wrong, but it was the 1950s, the heyday of rabid environmentalism, and all people were supposed to be politically equal, which was misunderstood to mean that all people were biologically identical.

Even a slight acquaintance with evolution would tell you that individual humans cannot be genetically identical, because our human species, and all other species, evolved to be what we are today by virtue of **natural selection** and **genetic variation.** Our human brains, emotions, and cognitions result from individually variable, genetically-transmitted traits that gave our ancestors certain reproductive advantages over other members of the species who reproduced less frequently. Thus, in short, human behaviors must be genetically variable.

And human **development** is also the subject of selection and variation. Developmental patterns are themselves genetically variable, a fact that is most dramatically seen in the exquisitely similar developmental patterns of identical twins, who share all of their genes. Some children are slower developers than others; all children have their unique patterns of ups and downs, spurts and lags in physical, intellectual, and social growth. Only identical twins have very similar spurts and lags in development.

Along with the doctrine of no genetic individual differences came the ideology of racial identity—despite observable physical differences among world populations, there could be no racial differences in anything behavioral, especially anything so important as intelligence or aggression. Anyone who dared suggest the possibility of racial differences in behavior was attacked, quite literally.

Two courses for research seemed open. One, to document again the many observable differences among racial populations in IQ test scores, school achievement, rates of criminal conviction and so forth. Or, two, to explore *why* these differences exist. A naturally-occurring experiment presented itself in transracial adoption, where children with African-American (black) ancestry were adopted by European-American (white) families. Rather than comparing children of different ethnic groups reared in different cultures—where behavioral differences could arise for many reasons—transracial adoptive families presented children of different ethnic origins reared in the same, majority-group, American culture. The major question was, "How well do black children reared in white homes score on IQ test and achieve in school?"

Richard Weinberg and I first tested the children and their families in the early 1970s and have followed them into mid-adolescence. A principal finding is that transracially-adopted black children score about as well on IQ tests and achieve as well in school as white adoptees. Being reared in the culture of the tests and the culture of the schools enabled these black children to perform about as well as other adopted children and far better than children reared in the black community. This result raises many issues about cultural differences between rearing in the African-American, minority community, the nature of schooling, and the nature of tests designed to predict school success (which they do well for all groups). But this result does support the idea that black children *can* learn the knowledge and skills sampled by IQ tests and required for success in schools today.

Q What are some applications arising from the study of human development?

Sandra Scarr

A Applications of developmental psychology range across the life span, across cognitive, social, and emotional development, and across many, many settings. Here are just a few examples. New knowledge about development changed newborn care in hospitals in the 1970s. Instead of being snatched away from mothers in delivery rooms and isolated in hospital nurseries, babies were given to their mothers (and often fathers) at birth and kept with them. Research on what infants can see, feel, and do revolutionized the toy industry, changed how parents interact with their babies, and gave rise to concerns about what is appropriate infant day care. Growing knowledge about preschool intelligence gave rise to the early educational curricula we have today, based on the work of Jean Piaget and many others.

Research on the importance of play and peer relationships influences how schools arrange classrooms, work assignments, and intervention programs for children who are rejected by their peers. Research on early sexual behavior and substance abuse has been influential in designing effective programs to reduce teenage pregnancies, and drug and alcohol problems (which research applications have been hindered by moralists who think that "just say no" is a sufficient response). Of course, research on learning and cognition has changed school curricula, for better and for worse, depending on how well educationists applied the knowledge.

In adulthood, research on the importance of work, for both men and women, has spawned programs for the unemployed, for women returning to the labor force, for adult education, and for retirees who feel lost without their jobs. Developmental research across the life span has fostered better programs for nursing home residents, for healthy elderly persons with too much leisure time, for the rehabilitation of injured and ill adults. Such practical applications of developmental research take into account the developmental status of the people, their social and biological needs, and arrive at practical solutions to problems. There are many, many successful applications of developmental research to human welfare from birth to death.

Q What are some of the most exciting new developments in the field?

A I think that the single most exciting change in developmental psychology is a shift in theoretical perspective from a predominant emphasis on environments to a recognition that people are genetically and biologically different, and that development depends on *both* biological and social influences. Developmental psychology today recognizes that, from birth, people are different from one another and that individuals make their own environments, both in what they attend to and in what meanings they give to their experiences. In fact, many psychologists have come to the conclusion that environmental differences are influenced by genetic differences among people—people who like sports spend their time on sports rather than listening to Bach, while people who are musical find musical opportunities and are less likely to hang out at ball games. The recognition that people influence their own development brings about a revolution in thinking about parents' influences on children (different for each child) and on every aspect of environments across the lifes pan.

This perspective of nature *and* nurture—how they work together—extends to how development occurs. What changes developmentally is the organization of behavior—two-year-olds think, feel, and act differently from 12- or 22-year-olds. It is not just one kind of difference that matters (for example, how many words you know or how fast you can count). At each age behavior is organized into a coherent system that works for that stage of development. Even at birth, newborns' behaviors are highly organized to get adult attention and to survive.

9 Infancy and Childhood

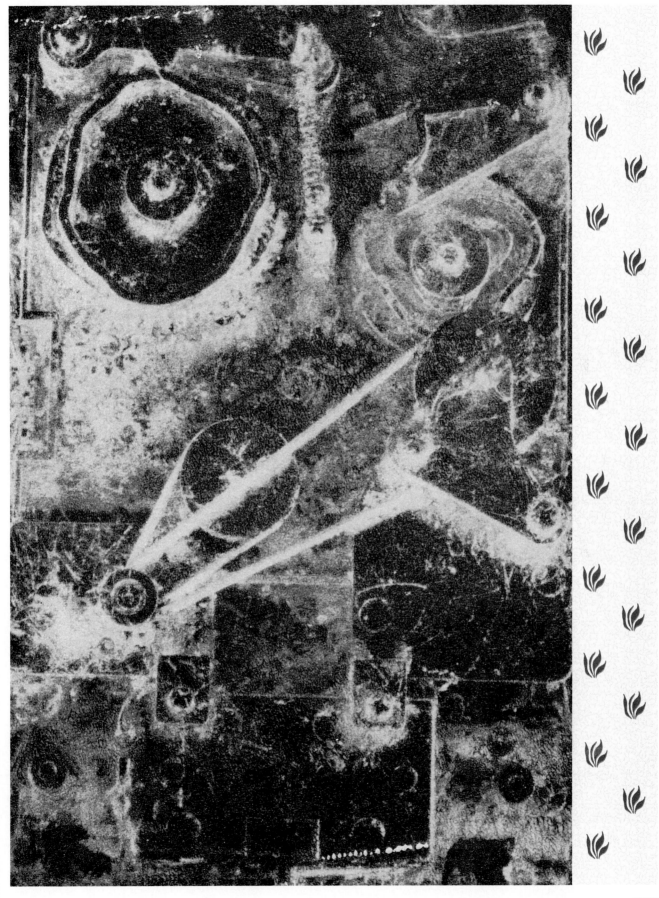

327

T he early years of life seem to fascinate everyone. Who is not captivated by the infant's first smile, the explorations of the happy toddler, or the whimsical comments of the eager preschooler? In today's child-oriented society, we celebrate these milestones in the growth and development of infants and children. But things were not always this way. The concept of childhood has a remarkably short history. Prior to the fifteenth century, people did not conceive of childhood as a separate and distinct period of life. Children played many of the same games as adults, were frequently present at taverns and places of work, and were largely unsegregated by age in the classroom. Early portraits reveal that artists did not think of children as physically different from adults, nor did they discriminate among children of different ages. Children were simply depicted as little adults.

The concept of childhood began to emerge in the aftermath of the intellectual and religious events of the fifteenth and sixteenth centuries. Both the Renaissance and the Pro-testant Reformation helped focus attention on the child as an "innocent" who had to be protected from the corrupting influences of the world. Parents were encouraged to watch over their children carefully, to discipline them when necessary, and to insulate them from adult activities. In the United States, by the late nineteenth century, education for children had become compulsory in some states, and a powerful movement to protect children from the hazards of the workplace had begun.

The growing interest in children had its first real impact on psychology in the form of *baby biographies.* These were detailed accounts of the everyday activities of the biographer's own children. The baby biographies were an important first step in documenting the process of **development,** which we can define as the changes in physical, intellectual, and social abilities that occur throughout life. By the beginning of the twentieth century, the first research center for the study of child development had been established at Yale University. Here, Arnold Gesell began to chart *norms* (average ages) for physical and motor development. Later, Gesell extended his work into the areas of social and emotional development.

With the tradition of child research firmly established, psychologists turned their attention to a variety of questions. How do children think? What is the nature of parent-child relationships? How do children play and interact with their peers? These and other questions became part of a new discipline focusing on the general issue of how behavior changes during the childhood years and how people continue to develop during adolescence and adulthood. Today, psychologists refer to that discipline as the study of *life-span development.*

Arnold Gesell
(1880–1961)

AN OVERVIEW OF DEVELOPMENT

Human development is both mundane and mysterious. At first glance, development is something that simply happens. We grow older and wiser, or so we believe. We notice that our bodies change, our personalities take shape, and our intellects begin to broaden. The whole process seems effortless and inevitable. And yet there is mystery involved. What guides the process of development? At the moment of conception, we inherit a genetic "blueprint" from our parents. Is this what steers us unwaveringly

Only in the last two centuries has childhood been considered a separate period of life. As this painting shows, children were previously considered to be "little" adults.

from infancy to adulthood? Or are we buffeted and molded by our environment—by the many and different experiences we encounter during a lifetime?

In this chapter and in the next, we will attempt to unravel some of the mystery of development. We will examine the factors that influence physical growth, personal and social development, and intellectual or cognitive development from conception until death. Our discussion in this chapter will focus on the central question of how behavior changes during the early years (infancy and childhood). In the next chapter, we will explore how people continue to develop during adolescence and adulthood.

Perspectives on Development

Three enduring questions confront all students of human development: (1) Is development a slow, gradual, and continuous process of change or does it occur abruptly in a series of discontinuous (distinct) stages? (2) Is development relatively stable and unchanging after the first few years of life or is there a great deal of change in later life that cannot be predicted from the early years? (3) Is development governed primarily by genetic influences or does the environment play a central role? In this section, we will examine the different approaches that psychologists have taken in attempting to answer these basic questions.

CONTINUITY VERSUS DISCONTINUITY

People change dramatically in the course of a lifetime. Consequently, a major question for psychologists is how to characterize change. Some theorists believe that development is a slow and steady process in which experiences gradually accumulate to produce meaningful change. These psychologists argue, for example, that children learn the facts of addition through a process of drill and repetition that is guided and reinforced by the teacher. Generally speaking, psychologists who adhere to a behaviorist tradition are likely to view development in this fashion. They believe that change occurs in a smooth, gradual, and continuous fashion.

Other theorists believe that change occurs rather suddenly in stagelike fashion. Advocates of this position note, for example, that children often do not understand a particular concept (e.g., the mathematical notion of greater than versus less than) for a long period of time despite the best efforts of dedicated teachers. Then, quite suddenly, the child's reasoning powers change and what was formerly a difficult concept becomes simple. This sudden reorganization of the intellect represents what some theorists call a new *stage,* that is, a qualitatively different way of understanding the world. We shall see that Jean Piaget, a Swiss psychologist, was a major advocate of this *discontinuity* position.

STABILITY VERSUS CHANGE

An important question for psychologists is how stable or unchanging are behaviors that first appear in infancy and childhood. Does the infant who talks a blue streak at age two become the gifted public speaker in high school? Did the mean-spirited bully you knew in grade school become an aggressive and antisocial adult? In short, do we become grown-up versions of what we once were, or do we acquire new characteristics that cannot be predicted from our behavior during childhood?

NATURE VERSUS NURTURE

You are no doubt familiar with a classic problem in psychology: Do we act and feel the way we do because of our biological nature, or does our environment shape and nurture us to become who we are? This question has many serious implications. If nature governs development, then it will be relatively difficult for people to change. We would not expect intervention programs, such as classes for special needs children or rehabilitation programs for

Human development is shaped by a combination of biological and environmental factors.

hardened criminals, to have much impact. On the other hand, if life experiences determine our fate, then we can be quite optimistic about the possibility of helping people change by providing everyone with the best possible environment.

Another possibility exists, however. Neither nature nor nurture alone may exert such a dominating influence on development. Rather, it may be more accurate to speak of the interaction between biological (nature) and environmental (nurture) factors. As we shall see, this interactionist position is the preferred, modern-day view of the nature-nurture controversy.

Methods of Studying Development

The focal point in the study of development is the question of how behavior changes over time. Psychologists use two basic research designs to measure behavioral changes. One method is known as the *cross-sectional method;* the other is referred to as the *longitudinal method.*

THE CROSS-SECTIONAL METHOD

The **cross-sectional method** allows researchers to observe or test people of various ages at approximately the same point in time. By comparing the responses of people in more than one age group, the investigator can determine whether there are differences in behavior at different ages. Do 10-year-olds, for example, show a different understanding of number concepts than 8-year-olds, who may in turn show a different understanding than 6-year-olds? Do young adults have different personal values than adolescents? Do the elderly have different memory capacities than middle-aged adults? One way to answer such questions is to compare the responses of a cross section of people belonging to each of the relevant age groups.

For example, suppose that we want to learn about the development of children's understanding of basic math facts. To do this, we construct a test of mathematical operations such as addition, subtraction, and simple multiplication. We administer this test to children in three different age groups: 10-year-olds, 8-year-olds, and 6-year-olds. Each group is tested at roughly the same point in time by a different experimenter. In this study we have employed the two essential elements of the cross-sectional method: (1) we have compared the performance of subjects representing different age groups, and (2) we have tested all the subjects at approximately the same point in time.

The cross-sectional method has the advantages of speed and simplicity. In the example above, we can assess quickly the performance of children who are several years apart in age. We do not have to wait 4 years until the 6-year-olds reach age 10. But while the cross-sectional method has the advantage of providing prompt results, it also has significant limitations, and for this reason psychologists often employ the longitudinal method to answer questions about human development.

THE LONGITUDINAL METHOD

With the **longitudinal method,** researchers measure change in behavior by following the same group of subjects over an extended period of time. For example, in the hypothetical study of math facts, we could select a group of 6-year-olds and test them immediately at age 6, again at age 8, and once more at age 10. Such a study would enable us to assess the changes that occur in children's understanding of math facts, as did the cross-sectional study. The essential features of the longitudinal design are quite different, however. In a longitudinal study (1) a single group of subjects is assessed and (2) this group is followed for a number of years.

It is obvious that a longitudinal study takes a great deal of time to complete. So why would psychologists ever use such a design? Because the cross-sectional method has one major limitation: It does not permit psychologists to evaluate how *individual* children change and develop. For example, suppose we wish to know whether the child who can count and add at age 6 is the same child who is most knowledgeable about subtraction at age 8 and simple multiplication at age 10. In other words, does knowledge of simple math facts at age 6 predict more sophisticated knowledge at ages 8 and 10? Only a longitudinal study permits us to answer this question. If we want to know whether one skill or behavior leads to another, we must use the longitudinal method.

Interim Summary

Three important perspectives on development center around the issues of continuity versus discontinuity (does development occur at a slow and steady rate, or in sudden spurts?), stability versus change (do our actions as children predict what we will be like as adolescents and adults, or do the early years fail to foretell what comes later?), and nature versus nurture (is development guided by hereditary influences, or shaped by the environment?).

Two frequently used methods for studying development are the cross-sectional method, in which people of various ages are studied at the same point in time, and the longitudinal method, in which the same group of people is followed over an extended period of time.

• •

INFLUENCES ON DEVELOPMENT

Earlier, we noted that two basic factors influence development: heredity and environment. Heredity refers to the genetic "blueprint" that we inherit from our biological parents. Environment is the broad range of experiences that an individual encounters over a lifetime, and even before, during the period of prenatal development. Although each of these factors makes a unique contribution to development, often the two are so closely interwoven that it is difficult to separate their effects. That is why psychologists speak of the *interaction* between heredity and environment when proposing a comprehensive model of human development.

Hereditary Influences

Hereditary influences begin at conception when we receive millions of **genes** from our biological parents. Genes, the basic building blocks in development, are actually segments of a crucial molecule known as DNA (deoxyribonucleic acid). Through a complex biochemical proces, DNA directs the myriad cellular reactions that eventually produce the tissues, nerves, and organs necessary for life.

Do genes work alone or in aggregrate? Although some relatively simple physical characteristics, such as eye color or hair loss, are under the direct control of one or two genes, virtually all complex human behaviors, such as language, temperament, and intelligence, are influenced by many genes. To illustrate how genes work, we will consider first an example of a simple physical characteristic. Then we will discuss the more complicated question of the genetic influence on intelligence.

In human cells, genes come in pairs. But the two members of the gene pair are not always alike. Occasionally, one gene will be dominant and the other one recessive. A *dominant gene* is one that controls the expression of a physical trait regardless of the nature of the other member of the gene pair. A *recessive gene* controls the expression of a physical trait only if it is paired with a similar gene. Genes determining eye color, for example, show the dominant-recessive pattern. The gene for brown eyes is dominant, whereas the gene for blue eyes is recessive.

If two brown-eyed parents each transmit a dominant gene for brown eyes, they will produce a brown-eyed child. However, one or both of the parents may also carry a recessive gene for blue eyes. If a child inherits a dominant gene from one parent and a recessive gene from the other, the dominant gene is still expressed. In this case, the child will have brown eyes. However, two brown-eyed parents could produce a blue-eyed child if each parent carried a recessive gene for blue eyes and the child inherited both recessive genes. A recessive characteristic will be expressed only if the child inherits both recessive genes.

The Interaction of Heredity and Environment

We have deliberately chosen a simple example to illustrate how genes work. However, many aspects of development are far more complex. Intelligence, for example, refers to a group of characteristics that are controlled by many different genes. Furthermore, these characteristics are subject to considerable modification by the environment.

When considering complex behavior patterns, it is helpful to make a distinction between *genotype* and *phenotype*. At conception we inherit many different genes. This total genetic inheritance is known as the genotype. It must be distinguished, however, from the phenotype—the physical characteristics and observable behaviors that eventually develop. For many human characteristics, genes do not establish the precise form (phenotype) of the behaviors that emerge. Rather, they set broad boundaries within which behavior will vary according to the influence of the environment. Put somewhat differently, genes establish a potential *range of reaction* rather than a fixed pattern of behavior.

Let us take intelligence as an example. Assume for a moment that we assess the intellectual ability of three children with very different genetic potentials. To do this, we use an in-

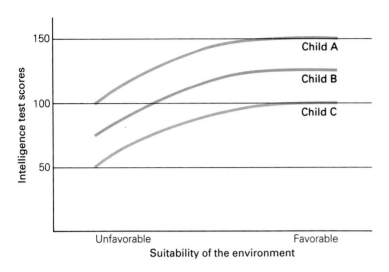

Figure 9.1
The Range of Reaction.
Illustration of the range of reaction. While genes establish the upper and lower limits of behavior, such as performance on intelligence tests, behavior may vary within these limits according to the suitability of the environment. (Gottesman, 1963)

telligence test with scores that range from a low of 50 to a high of 150. Let us assume further that we can vary the environment of each child from one that is very favorable to one that is very unfavorable. The relationship between genetic potential and environmental influence can then be illustrated as shown in **Figure 9.1.** When the environmental conditions are similar, child A, who has the greatest genetic potential, always receives the highest test score, followed by child B, and finally by child C. But each child also has a range of possible scores de-

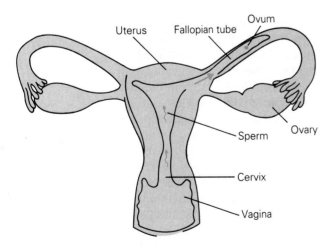

Figure 9.2
The Female Reproductive Organs.
The egg, or ovum, is moving through the fallopian tube, where it may be fertilized by the male sperm.

pending on the suitability of the environment. Child A's score, for example, might vary from 100 (average) to 150 (superior) depending on the influence of the environment. On the other hand, someone with a lesser genetic potential, such as child C, will always perform below average. However, this child also has a range of possible scores varying from 50 to 85.

Heredity and environment, then, share an intricate relationship. Genes may predispose an individual toward a range of responses, but the environment will help to determine which behavior patterns actually develop. Furthermore, it is important to note that heredity and environment interact from the moment of conception. Although we often think of the environment in terms of experiences that occur after birth, the child's prenatal or prebirth environment also makes an important contribution to development.

Interim Summary

Two major factors that influence development are heredity and environment. Heredity refers to the genetic code that we inherit from our biological parents. Environment refers to the broad range of experiences that we encounter living in a particular family and culture.

The genetic code is inherited at the moment of conception when we receive thousands of genes from each parent. Genes are present in pairs in the nucleus of every human cell, and are responsible for controlling the cellular reactions necessary for life.

Complex human behaviors, such as those involved in cognitive and social development, emerge as a consequence of the interaction between heredity and environment. Genes establish broad limits for behavior, but the environment shapes development within those limits.

PRENATAL DEVELOPMENT

Prenatal development begins at conception when a sperm from the father fertilizes the mother's ovum and creates a new human cell, known as a *zygote*. Fertilization occurs in one of two narrow structures called *fallopian tubes* (see **Figure 9.2**). Following fertilization, the newly formed zygote travels through the fallopian tubes and eventually attaches to the uterine wall. This process takes about 2 weeks. During that time, cell division occurs rapidly with dozens of cells forming even before the zygote is firmly implanted in the uterine wall.

What follows next is the period of the **embryo**, the term for the developing human organism from the second through the eighth week of prenatal life. Cell division continues to progress rapidly during this period, but now the cells become increasingly specialized, leading eventually to the development of vital structures and organs. For example, though little more than the size of a pin, the human embryo assumes a recognizable form around the third week, when an oval-shaped trunk with a discernible head and tail emerges. By the end of the fourth week a primitive heart is beating, and by 8 weeks many facial features, such as the mouth, eyes, and ears, can be distinguished.

From the third month (9 weeks) after conception until birth the developing human organism is referred to as a **fetus**. During this period, vital organs continue to develop and specialize. Internal organs—the heart, liver, kidneys, and stomach—become ever more functional. As the fetus grows, the hands, face, feet, and genital organs become more differentiated. In fact, so impressive is the development of the fetus that by the sixth month survival is possible if birth occurs prematurely.

The Delicate Prenatal Environment

The mother and the fetus are linked by an *umbilical cord* that extends from the fetus to a portion of the uterine wall known as the *placenta.* The placenta has two important functions. It filters the mother's blood passing on oxygen and vital nutrients to the growing fetus, and it acts as a protective barrier against potentially harmful substances, such as bacteria. Unfortunately, the placenta does not provide perfect protection for the fetus. A group of toxins, known collectively as **teratogens**, are able to pemeate the membranes of the placenta and disrupt the development of the embryo and fetus. Teratogens come in many forms. Drugs, radiation, pollutants, and certain diseases can all disturb the normal growth of the fetus. For example, if a pregnant mother is a morphine or heroin addict, she may give birth to an addicted infant who will show the withdrawal symptoms of vomiting, trembling, and rapid breathing in the first few days of life (Householder Hatcher, Burnes, & Chasnoff, 1982).

However, it is substances not generally regarded as addictive, such as cigarettes and alcohol, that vividly demonstate the delicate nature of the prenatal environment. For example, women who smoke regularly during pregnancy are likely to bear infants who have a greatly reduced birth weight (Spady, Atrens, & Syzmanski, 1986), thereby increasing the infant's susceptibility to serious infections and, in extreme cases, to impairment of intellectual abilities later in childhood (Fried & Watkinson, 1990). The effects of alcohol consumption during pregnancy are even more dramatic. Expectant mothers who drink heavily and continuously often bear children with birth defects (Stechler & Halton, 1982). This outcome is so predictable that scientists have now identified a particular disorder, known as **fetal alcohol syndrome (FAS)**, that frequently appears in the offspring of alcoholic women. The major manifestations of FAS are deformities of the heart, kidneys, face, and fingers (Abel, 1980). Even more striking, however, is the effect of moderate or "social drinking" during pregnancy. Expectant mothers who regularly consume two glasses of alcohol per day are far more likely than either abstainers or occasional drinkers to bear infants who are smaller than average and have serious physical problems, such as bodily tremors. Furthermore, researchers have found that regular moderate drinking can have long-term consequences for the mother's offspring. At age 4, children whose mothers consumed two glasses of alcohol daily while pregnant often have difficultiy concentrating and show clear signs of impaired intellectual ability (Landesman-Dwyer, Ragozin, & Little, 1981; Streissguth, Barr, Sampson, Darby & Martin, 1989). The effects of alcohol appear so powerful that at the moment it is unclear whether there is any safe level of regular alcohol consumption during pregnancy.

Critical Periods

Throughout the prenatal period, the developing embryo and fetus encounter moments when the risk to particular organs of the body is greatest. These **critical periods**, as they are called, are actually indicators of how teratogens work. As **Figure 9.3** on page 335 demonstrates, the period of greatest risk is quite predictable, though it varies considerably for different organs. For example, the central ner-

Psychology in the News

COCAINE-USING FATHERS LINKED TO BIRTH DEFECTS

An experiment using human semen has found that cocaine may attach itself to the sperm of men who use the drug, entering an egg at the moment of conception and damaging the fetus.

If the effect is proven true, cocaine-using fathers may have to share more of the responsibility with cocaine-using mothers for birth defects in children, said Dr. Ricardo Yazigi of the Temple University School of Medicine.

Other toxins such as lead and mercury to which fathers are exposed could also be hitchhiking on sperm in the same fashion. Dr. Yazigi added, affecting the fetus even before organ development begins.

Dr. Yazigi and his former colleagues at Washington University in St. Louis published their findings in the current issue of The Journal of the American Medical Association.

"We have heard for all these years that it is the mothers who are responsible for abnormalities, not just cocaine but with other substances such as alcohol, mercury, lead and so on," Dr. Yazigi said in an interview.

"In addition we have always thought exposure to the female occurred at a critical time when organs develop, from 3 or 4 to 12 weeks" into pregnancy, he said.

Premature Birth Common

"If these findings project into a clinical setting we will be talking not only about the male being a participant but in addition the abnormalities occurring at a much earlier time than we have so far expected" before fetal implantation in the uterus, he said.

The study, said researchers, has "clearly demonstrated the binding of cocaine to human spermatozoa. Binding was optimal after 20 minutes of incubation, with a decline following longer incubation periods."

The concentrations of cocaine used in the study "may be easily achieved in serum with doses of co-caine commonly used by human addicts," the study added.

Among the most common problems suffered by cocaine babies are premature birth and low birth weight. In addition. Dr. Yazigi said, the drug has been linked to detachment of the placenta, a life-threatening problem, as well as hyperactivity and abnormal neurologic reactions.

He said it was not yet known whether the latter problems are reversible or will persist through life.

Earlier studies found cocaine linked to decreases in the sperm count and the mobility of sperm, the study said, as well as to abnormal forms in sperm.

The new report seems to indicate that the effect on offspring may not be due to damage to the sperm but to the fact that it actually carries the drug itself into the female reproductive tract.

Questions

1. How does this report alter our views of the effects of teratogens on prenatal development?
2. What are the implications of this study for those involved in the field of prenatal health care?
3. How does this study illustrate the complex relationship between heredity and environment?

---

vous system is most sensitive to disruption during the early weeks of prenatal development, whereas the maximum risk of impairment to the ears and palate is considerably later. Knowing when these critical periods occur helps to explain why the same teratogen may pose an enormous danger at one moment but little or no peril at a different time.

PHYSICAL DEVELOPMENT

Physically, humans are unlike other species. Birds, for example, are mobile soon after birth. Other species, such as guinea pigs, are born with a brain that is almost fully developed. And in many species, the young communicate just

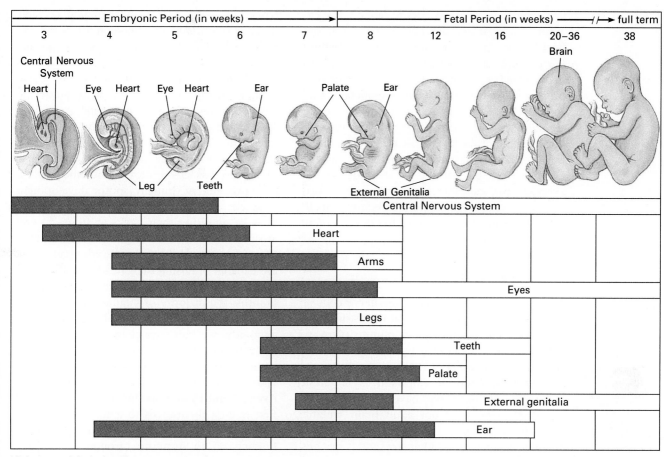

Figure 9.3
Critical Periods in Prenatal Development.
Body organs are most vulnerable to teratogens during particular periods of
prenatal development.

as effectively as adults. But we are different. The human infant is born in a relatively immature state. It takes many months before the infant can walk, still more before he or she is able to talk, and several years before the infant's brain is fully developed.

What this tells us is that during the early years humans undergo tremendous physical changes. At birth, the newborn infant lies immobile. But during the first year, the same infant begins to crawl, then creep, and shortly thereafter walk without support. During this period, neural networks in the brain develop swiftly. The child begins to master language. In just a few short years, a number of remarkable physical changes take place.

Norms for Physical Development

No two humans are exactly alike, but at birth the average infant weighs about 7 ½ pounds and is roughly 20 inches long. Two years later, at the end of the **infancy period**, the average child weighs approximately 25 to 29 pounds and is roughly 33 to 35 inches tall. Although these statistics give us some idea of how quickly infants develop, they are somewhat misleading. We must remember that the "average" infant exists only on paper. Real infants come in all different shapes and sizes.

So why should we bother about what is the average or expected level of physical development? This information may prove quite valuable in exceptional circumstances. For example, suppose we are concerned about the health of an infant who has fallen well behind her peers. Does the child need special care? In making such a judgment, we would rely heavily on norms. **Norms** are statistical guidelines that indicate both what is average and how much variation around the average one can expect. For example, if we know that the average newborn weighs 7 ½ pounds and that 90 percent of newborns weigh within 2 ½ pounds of the average, we can conclude that a newborn who weighs less than 5 pounds is quite small. Norms provide a vital view of the developmental landscape.

Brain and Motor Development

In the 9 months before birth, the nerve cells or *neurons* in the brain develop at the astonishing rate of 250,000 neurons per minute (Cowan, 1979). Small wonder that by the time we are born all the neurons of the brain are present. Nonetheless, brain development is far from complete. At birth we have achieved only about 25 percent of our adult brain weight. Over the next 6 months, brain weight doubles to about 50 percent of adult size, and it reaches 75 percent of final weight by 2 years of age (Tanner, 1978).

If all the neurons in the brain are present at birth, how else does the brain develop in the first 2 years? For one thing, nerve cells change shape and grow in size during infancy. But just as importantly, the connections among nerve cells, which begin to form even before birth, become denser and more numerous during infancy (**Figure 9.4**). As these neural connections develop, the transmission of nerve impulses among brain cells increases dramatically (Cowan, 1979).

What are the consequences of these changes in the brain? They help to guide the development of important mental capacities, such as memory and language, and to improve infants' motor development. By **motor development** we mean the ability of infants to use their arms and legs to move about and explore the environment. Initially, motor development proceeds slowly. During the first month, infants lie on either their backs or stomachs and are not capable of any significant movement. However, around the fifth or sixth week, most are capable of raising their head to a 45-degree angle when lying on their stomachs. By about 3 months, the majority of infants can roll from a front (stomach) to a back position. At roughly 4 months we can expect to see an infant sit with support; by 6 months most infants can sit alone. Sometime between 7 and 12 months infants begin to crawl and creep. Finally, between 7 and 15 months they master walking by first pulling themselves to a standing position (around 7 months), then sidestepping while holding on to furniture (around 9 months), then standing alone (around 11 months), and eventually walking without assistance (around 12 months).

In **Figure 9.5** we see an illustration of each of these milestones. Note how the *norms* in this figure show both the average age and the wide variations around the average for these important achievements in motor development.

Figure 9.4
Neural Connections in the Infant's Brain. The number and density of neural connections increase rapidly during the first 18 months of life.

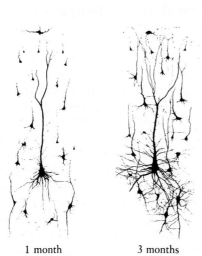

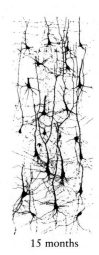

1 month   3 months   6 months   15 months

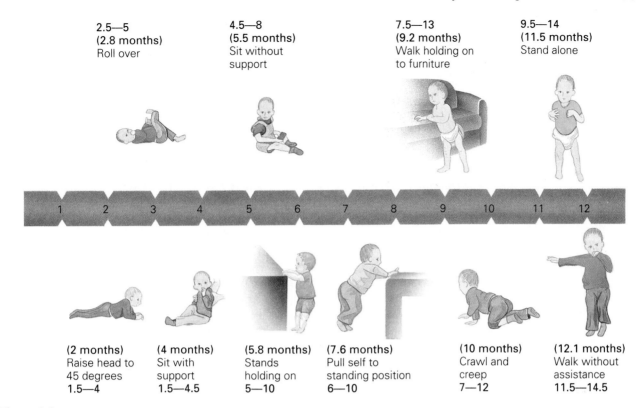

| 2.5—5
(2.8 months)
Roll over | 4.5—8
(5.5 months)
Sit without
support | 7.5—13
(9.2 months)
Walk holding on
to furniture | 9.5—14
(11.5 months)
Stand alone |

| (2 months)
Raise head to
45 degrees
1.5—4 | (4 months)
Sit with
support
1.5—4.5 | (5.8 months)
Stands
holding on
5—10 | (7.6 months)
Pull self to
standing position
6—10 | (10 months)
Crawl and
creep
7—12 | (12.1 months)
Walk without
assistance
11.5—14.5 |

Figure 9.5
Milestones in Motor Development.
The figure shows average age and variations (25th to 90th percentile) around the
average for major milestones in motor development. (After Frankenburg & Dodds,
1967; Shirley, 1931)

Sometime toward the end of the first year, children learn to stand on their own and take their first steps.

Interim Summary

Prenatal development consists of three distinct periods during which rapid growth occurs. During this early period in development, the environment plays a crucial role in protecting the developing embryo and fetus. Unfortunatley, the protection is not perfect, and the embryo and fetus are vulnerable to toxins known as teratogens, which have the potential to seriously disrupt the course of prenatal development.

Physical and motor development occurs rapidly in the first 2 years of life. Brain development is particularly impressive; by age 2 the brain has achieved nearly 75 percent of its adult size. As the brain matures, it guides the development of both physical and mental abilities.

PERCEPTUAL DEVELOPMENT

In the first few weeks following birth, infants appear to understand little of what is going on around them. They spend time staring at their surroundings, they cry loudly and vigorously, and they sleep. However, in reality, infants display sophisticated perceptual abilities, many of which are present immediately after birth. What they hear (*auditory perception*) and see (*visual perception*) is more than a blend of meaningless sounds and shapes.

How do psychologists study perceptual abilities in such young organisms? Because newborns cannot talk or follow directions, they are hardly ideal subjects. But they do display a number of vital responses. Newborns breathe, suck, cry, kick, turn their heads from side to side, and the like. If these behaviors are measured in the context of certain research designs, it is possible to understand a great deal about the perceptual abilities of infants.

Auditory Perception

Young infants hear remarkably well. Within minutes of birth, newborns turn their heads in the direction of a loud noise (Muir & Field, 1979). But will they notice the difference between two similar sounds? Suppose we have a newborn listen to a single note played on a piano 10 times in a row. At the same time we monitor the infant's heart rate. At first we ob-

serve a decrease in heart rate, a sign of attention in young infants. However, after eight or nine repetitions of the same note we observe no change in heart rate at all. The infant has lost interest in the familiar sound and no longer pays attention.

What happens now if we play a new note on the piano? If heart rate decreases once again, we can conclude that the infant noticed the difference between the new and the old sound. Using methods similar to this, investigators have discovered that newborn infants can easily detect the difference between sounds that are only one note apart on the musical scale (Aslin, Pisoni, & Jusczyk, Jusczyk, & Pisoni, 1983). Furthermore, newborns seem to be particularly sensitive to high-pitched sounds (Aslin, 1987). This is an interesting discovery because it is well known that parents often speak to infants in high-pitched, exaggerated tones. Could it be that this form of "baby talk" is universal precisely because it is well suited to hold the infant's attention (Sachs, 1977)?

Visual Perception

Infants are born nearsighted. They see at 20 feet what an adult with normal vision sees at roughly 800 feet (Cornell & McDonnell, 1986). So objects must be close at hand for the newborn to see them clearly, hardly a serious problem for someone who is often held by a doting parent. And while the newborn's eyes do not adjust well to varying distances (Banks & Salapatek, 1983), parents often bring objects into focus by placing them about a foot away—just the right interval for the newborn.

What do infants attend to? One of the sights they find most interesting is the human face. Perhaps by evolutionary design, the face contains many of the visual elements that attract an infant: movement (eyes and mouth), areas of contrast (eyebrows and hairline), and varying contours or edges (Olson, 1981). As parents interact with infants, all of these elements come into play. Parents speak, laugh, move their heads, and change expressions. While all this is going on, infants gaze back intently. With the help of specialized cameras, investigators have discovered precisely what parts of the face are most interesting to infants (**Figure 9.6**). Not surprisingly, this changes as infants develop. One-month-old infants scan the periphery of the face and search for points of high contrast, such as the hairline. But by 2

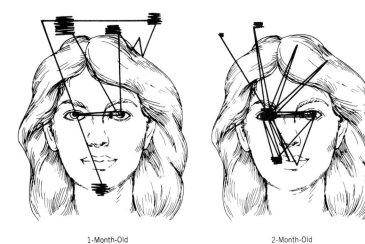

1-Month-Old   2-Month-Old

Figure 9.6
How Infants Scan the Human Face.
One-month-old infants look at the outside of the face and search for areas of high contrast. But 2-month-old infants look at the internal features of the face, especially the eyes.

months of age, infants are looking elsewhere. Now they scan the interior parts of the face, especially the eyes (Maurer & Salapatek, 1976). Shortly thereafter, infants perceive the face as a whole unit and begin to distinguish familiar from unfamiliar faces (Olson & Sherman, 1983). Toward the end of the first year, infants can even discriminate emotional expressions, such as happiness and anger, conveyed through facial expressions (Klinnert, Campos, Sorce, Emde, & Svedja, 1983). Clearly, infants learn a great deal about their world from staring intently at faces.

Depth Perception

For a moment, imagine that you could not judge how far away you are from the nearest door, or gauge the distance to the steps that allow you to exit the building you are in right now. You would be trapped in a confusing and dangerous world. Is this the fate of young infants, until they have literally learned the hard way, or is depth perception an innate ability present from birth onward? Psychologists Eleanor Gibson and Richard Walk (1960) set out to answer this question through a clever experiment involving the *visual cliff*, an apparatus shown in **Figure 9.7**. Note that the "cliff" has two distinct sides, one that is "deep" and the other "shallow." As soon as they are able to crawl, infants show a fear of the "deep" end of the table. If placed on the "shallow" side, they will not cross over to the "deep" end, even when beckoned by their mothers.

Subsequent research has shown that depth perception is a complicated phenomenon that may involve two distinct stages: perceiving depth and developing a fear of high places. For example, depth perception seems to exist even in infants who are not yet old enough to crawl. By recording changes in heart rate of infants placed face-down on either side of the visual cliff, a team of investigators determined that 6-week-old infants can distinguish the "deep" from the shallow "end" (Campos, Langer, & Krowitz, 1970). However, actual *fear of heights* develops only after infants begin to crawl and move about (Campos, Svedja, Bertenthal, Benson, & Schmid, 1981). Infants seem to need some real-world experiences—such as encountering a steep precipice and even falling down—before they develop a true fear of heights (Campos, Bertenthal, & Caplovitz, 1982).

Figure 9.7
The Visual Cliff.
The visual cliff, used by Gibson and Walk (1960), is really a patterned table covered with clear glass and divided in half by a center board. The difference in the two halves of the table is that the "shallow" end lies about an inch below the glass, while the "deep" end lies about 40 inches below.

Interim Summary

Perceptual abilities emerge early in infancy. Even newborn infants can discriminate minute differences in the visual and auditory stimuli of their surroundings. In a very short span of time, infants begin to further refine these remarkable skills. They acquire the capacity to discriminate subtle changes in facial expressions and they learn to perceive depth.

COGNITIVE DEVELOPMENT

Cognition refers to knowing and understanding. To study cognition, psychologists pose questions about the way people gather, process, and use information. But how does cognition develop? What are the steps that lie between an infant's first attempt to understand the outside world and the adult's ability to find solutions to complex problems?

No one has addressed this question more thoroughly than the late Swiss psychologist

Jean Piaget
(1896–1980)

Jean Piaget. Piaget is unique among psychologists in proposing a theory of cognitive development that spans the period from infancy to adulthood. In Piaget's view, there are four distinct periods of cognitive development: *sensorimotor, preoperational, concrete operational*, and *formal operational.* We have presented a brief description of each of these periods in **Table 9.1.**

The fundamental assumption of Piaget's theory is that, over the course of a lifetime, cognitive skills undergo major *qualitative* changes. This means that during each period of development people know and understand the world in a distinctly different way. Piaget believed that people do not simply acquire more information as they grow older; rather, they think and reason in a *unique* fashion at each successive period of development.

Piaget made an enormous contribution to the study of cognitive development. However, some psychologists believe that recent discoveries challenge some of Piaget's notions and require a modification of his theory. To understand this debate, we will examine both Piaget's theory and the research of those who believe the theory should be modified. Our discussion proceeds chronologically, beginning with a description of cognitive development during the sensorimotor period.

The Sensorimotor Period

The **sensorimotor period**, lasting from birth until approximately age 2, is the first of Piaget's four major periods of cognitive development. Piaget felt that infants understand their world by physically manipulating the objects around them. In the sensorimotor period they learn, quite literally, by pushing, banging, and poking.

Piaget began his study of infant cognition through detailed observations of his own three children (Piaget, 1952). These observations convinced Piaget that during the first month of life, infants focus almost exclusively on their own bodies. They show little interest in or awareness of the world around them. In Piaget's view, the primary accomplishment at this time is progressive refinement of some simple responses present at birth, such as sucking and grasping. What happens next is a shift from interest in self to an interest in objects outside the self. Piaget believed that this occurs because infants learn to coordinate one sensory skill with another. For example, 3-month-olds will gaze at an object and then move their hands toward it, while continuing to alternate their gaze between hand and object. As their interest in the outside world grows, infants begin to explore what they can *do to* objects. For

Table 9.1   **Description of Piaget's Four Periods of Cognitive Development**

Period	Approximate Age Range	Characteristics
Sensorimotor	Birth to 2 years	Infant begins to separate self from others. Explores the physical properties of objects in the environment. Learns that objects exist even when they are no longer in view. Begins to imitate others and to speak and understand simple words.
Preoperational	2 to 7 years	Language develops rapidly but is often used egocentrically, without an awareness of the listener's perspective. Cognition is limited. Child believes, for example, that the amount of water in a glass changes when the water is poured into a container of a different shape.
Concrete Operational	7 to 11 years	Cognition becomes more logical and adultlike. Child no longer believes that the shape of a container determines the amount it holds. Child reasons accurately about the qualities of objects.
Formal Operational	11 years through adulthood	Cognition becomes fully flexible. People reason abstractly. Can form hypotheses and evaluate them mentally, sometimes in the absence of concrete objects.

Based on Piaget & Inhelder (1969).

Figure 9.8
Object Permanence.
Piaget proposed that the typical 6-month-old will attend to an attractive toy, as in the top photo, but will quickly lose interest if the toy is blocked from view, as in the bottom photo. He believed that this occurs because the 6-month-old does not understand the concept of object permanence.

quent interaction with objects leads eventually to the development of **object permanence,** the notion that an object continues to exist even after it disappears from view. Piaget proposed that infants, somewhere between the ages of 8 and 11 months, can search for and retrieve an object hidden in a single location. Before that time, infants behave as though an object that is out of their sight is also "out of mind" (see **Figure 9.8**).

Piaget felt that during the second year infants become progressively more sophisticated in their understanding of the physical properties of objects. In his view, the infant's exploration of objects becomes more purposeful, deliberate, and systematic after the age of 12 months. For example, many 15-month-olds often look like young physicists as they purposefully manipulate the objects around them. Piaget has described in detail how this systematic experience with objects leads to an improved understanding of the physical world. As one example, he argued that during their second year, infants are capable of discovering a hidden object even after it has been moved from one hiding place to another.

Piaget believed that the sensorimotor period culminated with the development of *sym-*

During their second year, children become progressively more sophisticated in their understanding of physical properties of objects.

example, 6-month-olds will push, poke, mouth, and bang whatever is within reach. Curiously, Piaget observed that this activity begins almost by accident. A typical 6-month-old might grasp and shake a new toy. Unexpectedly, the toy (a rattle) makes a distinct rattling sound. Delighted with this outcome, the infant responds by shaking the rattle again. Soon the action is repeated, but it is no longer by chance.

At first glance, these observations may seem commonplace. Certainly, others have noticed that infants push, pull, and poke at objects. But Piaget was the first to suggest that this physical exploration of the environment is cognitively productive and not just aimless play. For example, Piaget proposed that fre-

bolic thought. This is the capacity to construct a mental representation of an object—a symbol—and to deal with the symbol as though it were the object. Pretending that one object is another (for example, a spoon is a small racing car) is one example of symbolic thought; using language—that is, designating words for objects—is another.

Piaget saw considerable development in cognition during the sensorimotor period. From an initial interest in their own body, infants progress to an interest in external objects, first in a somewhat haphazard fashion and then ever more systematically as they move into the second year. Eventually, infants become so comfortable and sophisticated in their object exploration that they can mentally represent, through symbols, objects that are not physically present.

The Preoperational Period

By the end of the sensorimotor period, the child has accomplished a great deal. Life is no longer confined to the here and now. People come and go, objects appear and disappear, but the 2-year-old is surprised by none of this. At age 2, most children can remember past events, engage in pretend play, and, as we saw in Chapter 8, begin to use language effectively.

But for all their sophistication, young children still demonstrate thought processes that are dramatically different from those of adults. It is difficult to imagine an adult protesting that a sandwich cut into four pieces contains more

to eat than the same sandwich cut into two pieces, but more than one 5-year-old has registered such a complaint. This unique perspective often leads the young child to make statements that adults find amusing. Witness the 3-year-old who answers the telephone and is asked, "Is your Mommy home?" "Yes," says the child, and then hangs up the phone.

Piaget believed that this type of reasoning is part of the preoperational period of development. The **preoperational period,** which others refer to as *early childhood,* extends from approximately age 2 until age 7. It is during this period that the child makes great strides in using and understanding language. However, Piaget's research led him to believe that there were definite limits on the preoperational child's reasoning skills. These limitations can be seen clearly in the young child's performance on one of Piaget's classic problems: the conservation task.

Conservation, as Piaget defined it, simply means that any quantity—number, volume, length, weight—remains the same despite physical changes in the arrangement or shape of an object or objects. A good illustration of this concept is the conservation of liquid problem shown in **Figure 9.9**. A child is presented with two identical glasses containing equal amounts of water. In full view of the child, the experimenter pours the water from one of the glasses into a third glass that is both taller and thinner than the two identical glasses. The experimenter than asks whether the two glasses that now contain water hold equal amounts, or whether one glass has more than the other.

A preoperational child, that is, one who has not mastered the concept of conservation, believes that the taller glass now contains more water. Why is this so? Piaget believed that preoperational children reason intuitively rather than logically. They are influenced by what they see. Thus, the preoperational child believes that because the water level is higher in the tall glass, it must contain more water. Intuitively, this may be correct (taller objects often do contain more), but according to Piaget, such reasoning ignores the logical principle of *reversibility.* Reversibility implies that every action has a logical opposite. Something that can be done can also be undone *without any gain or loss.* Thus, if water is poured from one glass to another, logically it can be returned to the first container without any change in quantity.

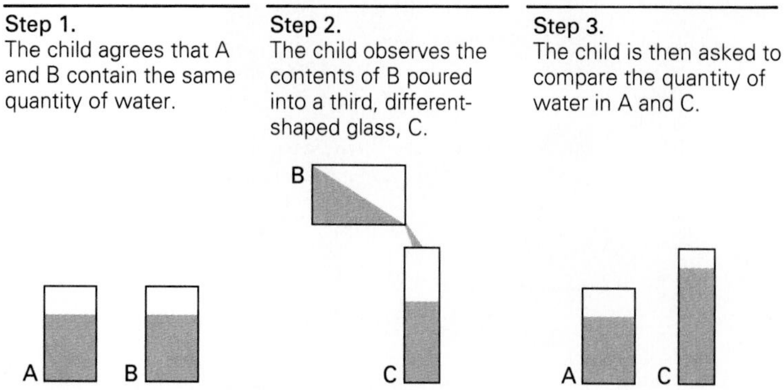

Step 1.	Step 2.	Step 3.
The child agrees that A and B contain the same quantity of water.	The child observes the contents of B poured into a third, different-shaped glass, C.	The child is then asked to compare the quantity of water in A and C.

Figure 9.9
A Simple Conservation Task.
A preoperational child will respond that the taller glass contains more water. A concrete operational child, however, understands the concept of conservation of liquid and will respond that the two glasses (A and C) still contain equal amounts of water.

The Concrete Operational Period

Piaget believed that at approximately age 7 the child becomes capable of logical reasoning. This capacity signals a new phase of development which Piaget designated the **concrete operational period,** the period during which the child begins to understand logical concepts. The concrete operational period extends from age 7 until roughly age 11 and corresponds to the period that other psychologists refer to as *middle childhood.*

The concrete operational child understands the concept of conservation. For example, this child asserts that after the water is poured into the tall glass (see Figure 9.9), the two glasses that now contain water hold equal amounts. When asked to justify their choice, concrete operational children often verbalize their understanding of the principle of reversibility with comments such as, "You could just pour it back and it would be like before."

Although Piaget believed that all conservation problems require an understanding of reversibility, he did acknowledge that the concept of conservation develops slowly. In fact, there is a definite sequence to the child's understanding of conservation. Conservation of number is acquired first, somewhere around age 5 or 6. It is followed in turn by conservation of liquid, the problem we have just described, which is followed by conservation of weight and then by conservation of length. The entire process is not completed until approximately age 11. For each of these problems, the testing procedure is essentially the same as the one described for the conservation of liquid (see **Figure 9.10**).

Piaget believed that a major change in cognition occurs when the child begins to master the concept of conservation. Now the child is thinking logically. With an understanding of the concept of reversibility, the child no longer makes judgments solely on the basis of how things appear (Piaget & Inhelder, 1969). Nevertheless, Piaget saw limitations in the child's reasoning. In the concrete operational period, children reason logically when the problem is displayed before them. In the presence of objects that can be viewed and sometimes manipulated, they demonstrate a practical, concrete form of intelligence. It is not until the next period of development, however, that children begin to demonstrate more abstract forms of thinking.

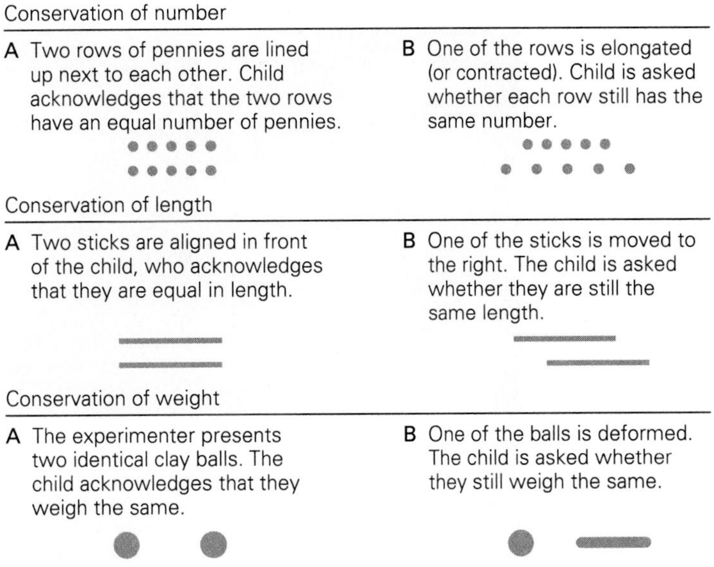

Conservation of number

A Two rows of pennies are lined up next to each other. Child acknowledges that the two rows have an equal number of pennies.

B One of the rows is elongated (or contracted). Child is asked whether each row still has the same number.

Conservation of length

A Two sticks are aligned in front of the child, who acknowledges that they are equal in length.

B One of the sticks is moved to the right. The child is asked whether they are still the same length.

Conservation of weight

A The experimenter presents two identical clay balls. The child acknowledges that they weigh the same.

B One of the balls is deformed. The child is asked whether they still weigh the same.

Figure 9.10
Conservation Tasks: Number, Length, and Weight. (After LeFrancois, 1980)

The Formal Operational Period

Beginning at approximately age 11 and continuing through adulthood, people acquire new reasoning skills which Piaget labeled *formal operational thinking.* In the **formal operational period,** the essence of thought is the ability to reason hypothetically—to consider beforehand all possible solutions to a problem. Unlike the concrete operational child, the formal operational thinker can reason about *what could be* as well as *what actually is.*

To illustrate, consider the responses of a 9-year-old and a 14-year-old to one of Piaget's classic problems of formal operational thought (Inhelder & Piaget, 1958). In this experiment, children are shown four different beakers, each containing a colorless chemical solution (see **Figure 9.11** on page 344). The examiner hands each child a small dropper filled with the chemical potassium iodide and a small dish to mix the liquids. The child is told that when the potassium iodide is combined with one colorless liquid or with a combination of colorless liquids, a bright yellow solution will appear. The child's task is to determine how the yellow solution is produced.

The typical 9-year-old subject will mix the potassium iodide with the colorless liquids in random fashion. Frequently one combination is

Figure 9.11
A Classic Problem in Formal Operational Thought.
Beaker G contains the potassium iodide. The child's task is
to discover which combination of liquids from beakers 1
through 4 will, when combined with G, produce a yellow
solution.

tried, then forgotten, and then tried again a few
moments later. This child may happen upon
the correct solution, but success will result
from persistence rather than from insight. By
contrast, a typical 14-year-old will plan a course
of action that involves a systematic test of the
possible solutions. If the 14-year-old first combines the potassium iodide with the liquid in
each container and no color results, on the
next attempt he or she will combine the potassium iodide with the liquid in the first two containers. If a colored solution now appears, the
14-year-old will deduce that although the liquids in the first two containers did not produce
the color individually, they did produce the col-
or when mixed together with the contents of
the dropper (Inhelder & Piaget, 1958).

This experiment illustrates two of the distinctive features of formal operational thought:
(1) the ability to consider beforehand a variety
of hypothetical solutions to a problem and (2)
the ability to reason about the possible as well
as the actual. Piaget believed that the ability to
think in this fashion was critical to higher
forms of human reasoning. He viewed the formal operational period as the culmination of a
process of thinking and reasoning that began in
infancy.

Interim Summary

Cognition refers to the ability to gather, process, and store information about the environment. Swiss psychologist Jean Piaget noted four distinct periods in cognitive develop-

ment from infancy to adolescence. In each
period, Piaget believed that the individual
gathers and processes information in a qualitatively different way.

Piaget referred to infancy as the sensorimotor period of cognitive development.
Two major accomplishments of this period
are the development of object permanence,
or the recognition that objects continue to
exist even if they are no longer in view, and
symbolic thought, or the ability to represent (through language or play) objects and
events that are not immediately present.
Piaget's second period of cognitive development is the preoperational period, which
extends from approximately age 2 to age 7.
During this period the child makes great
strides in using and understanding language
but has not yet acquired logical reasoning
skills, as demonstrated by the child's failure
to master the concept of conservation.

The concrete operational period extends from age 7 to roughly age 11. During
this period, the child begins to understand
logical concepts. One example is conservation, which includes an understanding of
the concept of reversibility—the recognition
that something that can be done can also be
undone without any gain or loss.

Piaget's fourth stage of cognitive development is the formal operational period,
which begins at approximately age 11 and
continues through adolescence and adulthood. During this period, people acquire
the ability to think abstractly and to reason
hypothetically—to consider beforehand various solutions to a problem.

CRITICISM OF PIAGET'S THEORY

Piaget made an enormous contribution to the
study of human development. No other theorist has proposed such an insightful account of
how thinking and reasoning develop from infancy to adulthood. Nonetheless, more recent
research has demonstrated that Piaget's theory
needs some critical rethinking. Many psychologists feel that Piaget's methods were unneces-
sarily complex, leading him to underestimate
the abilities of young children (Gelman & Baillargeon, 1983).

To illustrate, let us return to Piaget's notion of object permanence. Piaget believed that
young infants fail to find hidden objects because they lack the capacity for *mental repre-*

sentation. They cannot imagine that an object hidden from view continues to exist (Piaget, 1952). However, it is possible that young infants know full well that hidden objects exist, but do not know how and where to *search* for these objects (Harris, 1983). If this is so, then slight changes in Piaget's standard test—such as varying where the object is hidden—will influence the outcome. This appears to be true. For example, infants are more likely to find an object if it is hidden under some very distinctive landmark (Harris, 1983).

Psychologists have made similar criticisms of Piaget's ideas about preschool children's understanding of logical reasoning. Piaget believed that preschoolers (3- to 5-year olds) failed to master the critical concept of conservation because they did not understand the principle of reversibility, the idea that something which is done can also be undone without any gain or loss. But a number of investigators have challenged this interpretation. Recall the conservation of number task shown in Figure 9.10. The experimenter places two parallel rows of five pennies before the child. Once the child agrees that the two rows contain an equal number of pennies, the experimenter extends one of the rows and asks, "Do the two rows still contain the same number of pennies, or does one row have more?" According to Piaget, children who say the extended row has more pennies have not understood that *number* remains the same, only the appearance of the rows changes. But suppose the child thinks that the word *more* refers to the *length* of each row instead of the *number* of pennies. The child would respond "yes," meaning that the extended row is longer. The child's "failure" might show only that the experimenter and the child have a different understanding of the problem.

To overcome these difficulties, investigators have taught children to attend to number rather than length. For example, before the experimenter extends one of the rows, children are instructed to count the number of pennies in each row. The results of this simple procedure are striking. Preschool children who receive this kind of "training" do far better than expected on Piaget's standard test of conservation (Gelman, 1982; Gold, 1978). Apparently, once they know the rules of the game, many preschool children can demonstrate an understanding of number conservation.

The issues raised here highlight the concerns of many investigators who believe that children often possess abilities that Piaget failed to uncover (Gelman & Baillargeon, 1983). In short, while many psychologists agree with the broad outlines of Piaget's theory, they are beginning to question whether children know more, and at an earlier age, than Piaget realized.

INFORMATION PROCESSING

Piaget took a broad and sweeping look at cognition. He believed that each of his four major periods in development ushered in a new and different way of understanding the world. Over and again Piaget emphasized *qualitative* change, the idea that we think and reason in uniquely different ways as we grow older.

But we could view cognition differently. Suppose we think of the child's mind as working very much like a computer. The child must take in information from the environment, attend to it carefully, remember it, and then make critical comparisons and judgments. As children grow older, they become more proficient in each of these areas. Perception becomes more accurate, attention increases, memory improves, and rules for problem solving emerge. This model of cognitive development is known as **information processing**. Rather than searching for qualitatively different modes of thinking, as Piaget did, information processing theorists view cognitive development as the gradual acquisition of the skills and rules necessary to solve complex problems (McShane, 1991). Researchers from this tradition focus on the "how" questions that are addressed only vaguely in Piaget's theory: How does the child select and attend to information in the environment, and how is that information processed and remembered (Siegler, 1991)?

Attention

As children grow older, they become more focused, less distractable, and better able to control their attention (Flavell, 1985). This is one reason why television becomes more appealing. To the dismay of many parents, children's ability to attend to television shows increases dramatically during the first 5 years (Anderson, Lorch, Field, Collins, & Nathan, 1986).

Attention also improves in other important ways, particularly through the appearance of strategies that aid learning. For example, children learn to attend carefully to the most complex parts of a problem and to ignore things that are irrelevant to the solution (Flavell, 1985). But this process of *selective attention*, as it is known, develops slowly. Not until first or second grade do children learn to use selective attention strategies effectively (Miller, Haynes, & DeMarie-Dreblow, 1986). Before that time, children are likely to attend to something irrelevant, such as the color of pieces of candy, when trying to remember the number of pieces that are hidden from view.

Memory

Children's memory improves as they grow older, but more importantly for information processing theorists, children develop strategies for remembering. They learn techniques that help them to remember more efficiently. For example, consider a problem we all face from time to time—trying to memorize a list of words. What do you do? Most likely you would use a common memory strategy, known as *rehearsal*, that involves saying the words over and again until you have memorized the list. But young children do not recognize the value of rehearsal. Faced with the problem of remembering words in a list, 5-year-olds almost never rehearse what they need to recall, and 7-year-olds rehearse only occasionally. Not until age 10 do children regularly use rehearsal as a memory strategy (Flavell, Beach, & Chinsky, 1966).

Can young children be taught to use memory strategies? In some situations they can (Pressley, Heisel, McCormick, & Nakamura, 1982). But before the age of 6, children rarely use memory strategies consistently, even if they have been show how effective they are in one situation. Only through repeated experiences do children recognize the value of memory strategies (Harnishfeger & Bjorklund, 1990).

Interim Summary

Piaget made an enormous contribution to the study of cognitive development, but critics feel that his methods underestimated the ability of young children.

Information processing is an alternative approach for studying cognitive development in children. This approach focuses on the skills and rules that children acquire as they master mental problems. By examining areas such as attention and memory, information processing theorists have added considerably to our knowledge of how cognition develops.

SOCIAL DEVELOPMENT IN INFANCY

Throughout infancy and childhood, children make enormous strides in the development of cognition. But there is more to human development than knowing how to process and remember information. Children also learn how to live and interact with others. They form a series of close relationships, first with parents and later with peers. Children learn how to relate to others in formal settings, such as the classroom, and in informal settings, such as the playground. Along the way, they acquire a knowledge of gender—a sense of the similarities and differences between boys and girls. This process of developing as a person and learning how to relate to others is known as *social development.*

Social relationships begin in infancy. As early as the first few months of life, infants begin to smile, vocalize, and even laugh as they interact with their parents. Most parents play an active role in this process. They talk to their infants, hold and touch them playfully, and care for their basic needs. In these first few months, parents and infants establish a close emotional bond that will last for many years. In psychological terms, they develop an *attachment* relationship.

ATTACHMENT

Attachment refers to an intense emotional relationship between parent and child that begins in infancy an endures over a long period of time. Attachment relationships have special emotional qualities. Physical proximity to an attachment figure produces joy and happiness; prolonged separation from that person is often accompanied by stress and sorrow (Bowlby, 1982; Kagan, Kearsley, & Zelazo, 1978). Quite simply, attachment is the first of the many love relationships that humans experience.

Both parents and infants play a role in the development of attachment. Although the roles are different, each partner contributes mean-

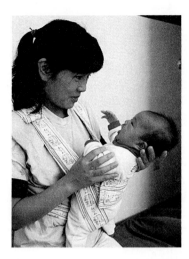

In the first few months of life, infants establish close emotional bonds with their primary caregivers.

ingfully to the relationship. That is why psychologists refer to the *interactive* nature of attachment.

The Parents' Role in Attachment

How do parents promote a good attachment relationship? An obvious answer is that they satisfy the infant's basic needs, which in turn leads the infant to develop positive feelings for the parents. Infants require feeding, clothing, bathing, and the like. In addition to these physical needs, infants also need attention, affection, stimulation, and comfort. But which of these needs is most important? Do infants form an attachment relationship because parents care for their basic needs? Or is holding, caressing, and stimulating the infant also crucial? Perhaps some combination of the two is required for a strong attachment bond. Interestingly, this question was first addressed in a series of classic studies of rhesus monkeys conducted by Professor Harry Harlow of the University of Wisconsin. Harlow first separated infant monkeys from their mothers. Then he provided each infant monkey with two different artificial "mothers." These substitute mothers were actually wire mesh cylinders with a wooden head attached to the top. One was covered with a soft terry-cloth lining while the other was left uncovered (see **Figure 9.12**). Either artificial mother could provide nourishment through a bottle attached at the center of the cylinder. When Harlow measured how much time the infant monkeys spent in contact with each of the substitute mothers, he found that all the infants preferred the terry-cloth substitute, including those who received their nourishment exclusively from the wire mother (Harlow, 1958). Subsequent research revealed that infant monkeys also preferred substitute "mothers" that were warm (heated with coils) and rocked back and forth (Harlow & Suomi, 1970).

Harlow's research established that infant monkeys needed more than nourishment from their mothers. They required rocking, warmth, and, most of all, contact with something soft. In Harlow's words, they had an inborn need for "contact comfort"—the desire to cling to and be near a soft, comforting object.

Are there implications for human infants from these intriguing results? Although we must be cautious in generalizing from animal experiments to the human experience, Harlow's findings suggest that simply caring for an infant's basic needs may not be sufficient for the development of a strong attachment relationship. Recent research appears to confirm this idea. Attachment relationships are often strongest and most secure for infants whose mothers who hold them frequently, are tender and affectionate with them, and engage in playful face-to-face interactions (Anisfeld, Casper, Nozyce, & Cunningham, 1990; Isabella & Belsky, 1991).

Figure 9.12
Wire and Cloth Surrogate Mothers Used by Harlow (1958).
Even when the wire mother was the sole source of nourishment, infant monkeys showed a preference for the terry-cloth mother.

Research has shown that children who are securely attached to both parents are more sociable than other children.

We have spoken rather exclusively of mothers, but what about fathers? Contrary to the popular stereotype, psychologists have shown that fathers have a strong interest in their children's development. Fathers like to hold, touch, and caress their infants, and they feel protective toward them (Parke, 1981). Fathers' caregiving—changing, clothing, and feeding the baby—is also quite effective, though rather infrequent. Fathers are far more likely to play with infants than to engage in caregiving (Lamb, 1981). Fathers' play also has a special quality. In contrast to mothers, who tend to stimulate infants verbally, fathers are more apt to play physical games, such as tickling, patting, and tossing the baby in the air (Power & Parke, 1983). Infants seem to enjoy these interactions with fathers and by 18 months will even show a preference for fathers over mothers when given the opportunity to play with either parent (Clarke-Stewart, 1978). But we should not lose sight of the most important point. Despite differences in mothers' and fathers' styles of interaction, infants form strong attachments to *both* parents (Main & Weston, 1981).

The Infant's Role in Attachment

How do we know if an infant has formed an attachment relationship? The answer is quite simple. Infants act differently toward attachment figures. They are likely to stay physically close to people with whom they have formed an attachmnent relationship, to explore unfamiliar places and objects in the presence of that per-

son, and to cry or fuss if they are separated from an attachment figure (Kagan, Kearsley, & Zelazo, 1978). Somewhere between 6 and 12 months of age, most infants begin to behave this way in the presence of their parents. For example, a 10-month-old girl may use her father as a secure base from which she ventures out to explore a strange room outfitted with novel toys, or a 1-year-old boy playing quietly may suddenly burst into tears if his mother leaves the house for even a brief period of time.

But what happens before 6 months of age? During this time, infants help to draw their parents into a close relationship, often through behaviors that are intrisically rewarding. Smiling is a good example. Parents tend to interpret smiling as an indication that the infant is happy and content and that their caregiving is effective (Stern, 1977). Paradoxically, crying is also important to the attachment relationship because it frequently brings parents and infants together. Two other infant behaviors effective in promoting attachment are gazing and vocalizing. As we noted earlier, the human face contains many of the visual features that are appealing to infants. Looking or gazing at parents literally comes quite naturally. Not surprisingly, parents and infants find mutual gazing very rewarding (Stern, 1977). Likewise, infant vocalizations often produce a positive response from parents. When an infant coos or vocalizes, parents tend to smile or vocalize in return, setting in motion yet another round of positive social interactions.

The Significance of Attachment

Is a strong attachment relationship important for later social development? Using the longitudinal research method, investigators have found that infants who develop a positive emotional relationship with their mothers early in life are often well adjusted as toddlers and young children. For example, 1-year-olds who are securely attached to their mothers are more compliant and cooperative at age 2 than children who failed to develop a strong attachment relationship (Londerville & Main, 1981). And by 3 years of age, children who as infants formed a secure attachment bond with their mothers are more confident and outgoing than those who did not develop a strong attachment relationship. They are often seen by other children their age as very attractive playmates (Jacobson & Wille, 1986; Sroufe, Fox, & Pancake, 1983).

Although psychologists generally regard a strong attachment relationship as an optimal first step in development, there is less agreement about the consequences of *not* forming such a relationship. Some theorists have suggested that if a stable and secure attachment relationship does not develop in infancy, the child's future social and emotional development is seriously jeopardized (Bowlby, 1980). Others believe that adverse early experiences are potentially reversible. People have the capacity to recover from a poor start in life (Clarke & Clarke, 1976; Lerner, 1984).

To examine this question, investigators have studied the lives of people who spent their childhood years in institutions that met only their basic physical needs, providing little in the way of emotional support. Quite frequently only a few adults were available to care for many different children, and the institutions themselves were dreary and unattractive places to live (Casler, 1967; Provence & Lipton, 1962). There is no question that this kind of upbringing is harmful. Children raised in such an emotionally deprived environment quickly become withdrawn, apathetic, and fearful of adults (Provence & Lipton, 1962). Later in life, they may have difficulty forming close relationships with others (Quinton, Rutter, & Liddle, 1984). Fortunately, under the right circumstances children can recover from the trauma of early deprivation. Chances for recovery are best when children are adopted into loving, supportive homes, but emotional scars may still persist (Clarke & Clarke, 1976; Rutter, 1979).

What, then, can we conclude about the significance of attachment? It appears that attachment to one or two people is an optimal way for social development to begin. In the words of Erik Erikson, a prominent theorist whom we shall discuss in more detail in the next chapter, the primary social accomplishment of infancy is a basic sense of either "trust or mistrust." That is, the outcome of the attachment bond is either a hopeful, trusting attitude that disposes the child toward positive relationships with others, or a fearful and anxious attitude that tends to disrupt social development. However, we cannot conclude that future development is completely determined by the outcome of the attachment relationship. The experiences of later childhood and, as we shall see, those of adolescence and adulthood have a major impact on social and emotional development.

Interim Summary

Social development begins in infancy with the formation of an attachment relationship between parent and infant. Parents promote attachment by providing physical care and a secure and interesting environment. Infants' behaviors, such as crying and smiling, bring parent and infant together and foster the attachment relationship.

A strong attachment relationship provides an optimal start to social development. If children have a poor or nonexistent attachment relationship, recovery is still possible but emotional scars may remain.

SOCIAL DEVELOPMENT IN CHILDHOOD

Attachment is just the beginning of social development. Relationships with parents continue to develop and become more complex during the childhood years. Consciously or unconsciously, parents impart values and beliefs to the child. Much of this is accomplished through the process of childrearing. Often this process involves parents in many different aspects of their children's lives. Nurturing, playing with, and disciplining children all come under the heading of childrearing.

CHILDREARING

One way to study childrearing is to take a broad view of how parents interact with their children. Apart from specific actions, such as feeding or dressing children, how do parents praise, punish, and communicate with their children?

In an influential study, psychologist Diana Baumrind identified four dimensions of childrearing. These were (1) *control*, or parental attempts to shape and modify expressions of dependent, aggressive, and playful behavior; (2) *demands for maturity*, or pressures on children to perform up to their ability; (3) *clarity of communication,* or seeking out children's opinions and using reason when demanding compliance from children; and (4) *nurturance,* or expressions of warmth toward children and pride in their accomplishments (Baumrind, 1967).

Baumrind observed that parents differed considerably on these dimensions. Furthermore, she noted a relationship between parental childrearing practices and children's behavior. By observing children both at home and at school, Baumrind identified three different groups who had experienced three different patterns of parenting. Children in the first group were self-reliant and socially competent in their dealings with peers and teachers. As **Figure 9.13** shows, their parents received high ratings on all four dimensions of childrearing. Children in the second group were confident and self-reliant but also socially withdrawn and generally distrustful. These children had parents who were highly controlling but not very warm or affectionate and who only rarely expressed an interest in their children's opinions. The third group was quite immature. These children were very dependent and passive, and their parents scored low on all dimensions except nurturance. The parents of these children were warm and affectionate, but their discipline was lax and inconsistent and their children received little encouragement to think and act for themselves.

In subsequent research, Baumrind used the longitudinal method to follow her original subjects until they were adolescents. The results of this investigation confirmed that socially competent and mature adolescents have par-

ents who are both nurturing and solicitous of their children's opinions, yet at the same time very firm about what is appropriate and acceptable behavior (Baumrind, 1983).

What do these results tell us about childrearing? One point comes through clearly: *how* parents communicate is as important as *what* they communicate. If rules are imposed without any explanation, the child's self-esteem suffers. On the other hand, there is a clear message that love is not enough. Warmth and nurturance alone do not direct children toward social maturity. Children are also looking for clear standards and open communication with parents.

But a note of caution is in order. Earlier we observed that social development is a two-way street. Parents are not the only ones who have influence in childrearing. The child's behavior can just as easily affect what the parent does. Could it be, then, that some children are by temperament and personality easier to rear? If so, these children would be more likely to elicit the most effective parenting skills that Baumrind observed. This is a real possibility, as is the middle ground position that both parents and children influence the childrearing process (Bell & Harper, 1977). Within the same family, two children may respond very differently to their parents' childrearing practices. This in turn influences how the parents respond to each of those children. When it comes to something as complex as childrearing, determining cause and effect is no simple matter.

Maternal Employment

Many of today's families have working mothers. Although some mothers have always worked, maternal employment has increased dramatically over the past two decades, particularly among women with young children. In 1960 only 20 percent of mothers with children under 6 years of age worked outside the home, but by 1980 this figure had risen to 50 percent (Barglow, Vaughn, & Molitor, 1987). The trend continues upward. Experts believe that by 1995 nearly 66 percent of mothers with preschool children will be employed at least part-time (Lamb & Sternberg, 1991).

How does family life differ when mothers work? In two-parent families, maternal employment seems to foster a less traditional household. When mothers work, fathers are more likely to participate in child care and to per-

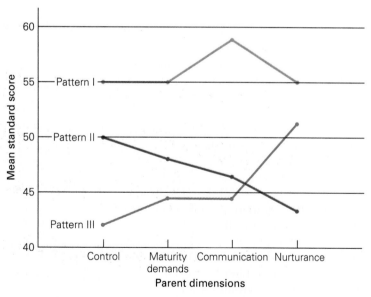

Figure 9.13
Relationship Between Childrearing Practices and Children's Behavior. Baumrind observed a relationship between childrearing practices and children's behavior. This chart shows four dimensions of parenting that were related to three distinct patterns of behavior among young children. (Baumrind, 1967)

form some household chores, although working mothers still bear the lion's share of both of these domestic obligations (Biernat & Wortman, 1991). Maternal employment also affects children. Once they are old enough to work, children typically have more chores and duties when their mothers work outside the home. Even more striking, however, is the difference in attitudes of children of employed mothers. Both sons and daughters of working mothers hold fewer stereotyped beliefs about men and women. They show greater respect for the competence of women, and are more likely to believe that women are entitled to professional opportunities, than are the children of women who do not work outside the home (Hoffman, 1984).

Day Care

In many societies, childrearing is not solely the responsibility of parents. Mothers in both China and Russia are encouraged to work full time while their children are cared for in state-supported institutions. Some children begin attending these programs as early as 2 months of age, so that even their early care and development is partially the responsibility of someone else. In Israel, child-care professionals provide much of the daily care for the children living on collective farms or *kibbutzim.*

In North America, however, child care has traditionally occurred in the home, with mothers bearing the primary responsibility. But as we have seen, the situation is changing. Many mothers with young children are now at work for at least part of the day. Where do children go when mothers work? Approximately 53 percent of children under 5 are cared for by nonrelatives for some portion of the day, 29 percent in a home day-care setting (a private home with an adult caregiver) and 24 percent in a nursery school or day-care institution (Bureau of the Census, 1987). Does this dramatic rise in day care have implications for the social and emotional development of young children?

In general, day care does not seem harmful and may well be a positive influence for children. For this to occur, however, day-care arrangements must be of high quality, providing children with a safe and stimulating environment and with a low caregiver-to-child ratio (Scarr & Weinberg, 1986). Under these circumstances, children develop warm and affectionate bonds with their caregivers. However, they continue to prefer their own parents and do not, as was once feared, form a stronger relationship with their temporary caregivers (Rutter, 1982). By age 5 children who have been in day care since they were infants are more sociable and outgoing, and perform better on measures of intellectual development, than children who have not had day-care experience (Clarke-Stewart & Fein, 1983). Furthermore, longitudinal research conducted in Sweden suggests that the positive effects of day care may be even more long lasting. Swedish children who entered day care before the age of 1 performed better in school and were judged more sociable by their teachers at age 13 than those who entered day care at a later age or not at all (Andersson, 1992).

Still, there is controversy about day care, particularly for children who spend a good deal of time in the care of others before their first birthday. Because the attachment bond is forming during this period, do children who are separated from their mothers for long periods of the day experience disruption in the *quality* of the attachment relationship? Will extended time away from their mothers lead to a less secure and more anxious attachment relationship? Some investigators believe this is true. They find that children less than 1 year old who are separated from their mothers for more than 20 hours per week develop insecure attachment relationships (Barglow, Vaughn, & Molitor, 1987; Belsky & Rovine, 1988). Others, however, feel it is premature to reach any conclusions about the relationship between attachment and day care. They note that psychologists have only limited ways to measure the quality of the child's attachment, and these may not be appropriate for children in day care (Weinraub, Hoffman, & Jaeger 1988). Furthermore, because maternal employment is on the rise, some experts feel that the critical question is not whether children should be in day care but how to make the day-care experience as beneficial as possible for children and their parents (Clarke-Stewart, 1989).

Interim Summary

Parents' childrearing practices have a major impact on children's social development. A warm nuturing style combined with firm expectations and open communication leads toward independence and social maturity in children. But children's temperament affects parental behavior and makes the process of childrearing a complex two-way street.

Mothers are joining the work force in increasingly large numbers. One outcome of this is a different family stucture that seems to affect the attitudes and beliefs of children growing up in families where mothers work. A second consequence of maternal employment is that more children are enrolled in day care. In general, high-quality day care does not adversely affect children and may have positive effects on intellectual and social development. There is a continuing debate about whether extensive day-care experience affects the quality of the attachment relationship between mother and infant.

GENDER

One of the major achievements of the childhood years is the development of a sense of **gender**, an awareness of yourself as male or female. To know your gender is to have a powerful sense of who you are and how others will respond to you. But long before you were aware of your gender, it was important to others. When parents announce the birth of a child, the first question that friends and relatives ask is whether the baby is a boy or a girl (Intons-Peterson & Reddel, 1984). Even parents are not immune from the expectations that

Through sex typing children acquire knowledge about the expected attitudes, beliefs, and behaviors associated with their gender in their culture.

gender evokes. When asked to describe their newborn boy or girl infants, who are objectively similar in the eyes of the attending doctors and nurses, parents say that girls are softer, have finer features, and are less attentive than boys (Rubin, Provenzano, & Luria, 1974).

Not surprisingly, gender continues to have a major influence on development. You need only a moment's reflection to think of the decision makers in government—in the Congress and Senate of the United States and in parliamentary forums all over the world—to see one of the most conspicuous reflections of gender. Men hold the lopsided majority of these positions. And though times are changing, much the same is true of other dominant societal institutions—business, law, medicine, and academia. But in all likelihood you have experienced the effects of gender at a more personal level. What happens at home is one example. If they were like most parents, your mother and father divided domestic duties unevenly, with your mother assuming far more responsibility for child care and household chores (Fuchs, 1986). Your relationship with peers, especially those involving interactions with the opposite sex, is another example of the pervasive influence of gender. As a rule, men have more difficulty than women in accurately perceiving what goes on in social interactions. They often misperceive friendly overtures from women as a sign of sexual or romantic interest (Abbey, 1987). Perhaps partly as a consequence of this, women are far more likely than men to experience unwanted sexual advances.

No doubt there are gender differences. But precisely what are they, and how do they arise? Does biology contribute to these differences, or are they the inevitable outcome of the varying socialization practices that males and females experience? As we address these questions, we should not lose sight of one important caveat. There are similarities, as well as differences, between the sexes. Gender does not always divide and distinguish.

GENDER DIFFERENCES

Psychologists have investigated gender differences intensely. In the past two decades alone, thousands of articles have appeared in the literature. Two major books have synthesized what is known about the topic (Maccoby & Jacklin, 1974; Hyde & Linn, 1986). What has all this scholarship revealed? As you might expect, the picture is complex. Here are some of the important conclusions.

Intellectual Ability

Beginning in adolescence, average scores for males on certain tests of mathematical and spatial abilities are higher than the average scores for females, while the opposite is true for average scores on certain tests of verbal abilities (Maccoby, 1990). But these average differences are not very large and not as impressive as the individual differences among men and women (see **Figure 9.14**). Furthermore, even these average differences may not be long-lived. Recent findings indicate that gender differences in cognitive abilities have diminished considerably over the past 25 years (Feingold, 1988).

There is one exception to this profile of similarity between the sexes. Males are over-represented in the extremes. As infants, they are more vulnerable to illness and abnormalities, many of which have a negative effect on their cognitive abilities. During childhood, problems in speaking and reading occur more often among boys, who are more likely than girls to experience learning difficulties in school. But investigators also find a disproportionate number of males among the most mathematically talented teenagers (Benbow, 1988). To date, there is no satisfactory explanation for this particular pattern of gender differences.

Personality Characteristics

Aggression toward others, both physical and verbal, occurs more often in males than in females (Eagly, 1987). This difference appears by 2 years of age and continues throughout the childhood and adolescent years. It is among the most stable and enduring of the gender differences, having been observed in many of the world's cultures (Maccoby & Jacklin, 1980).

Whereas aggression is associated with clear gender differences, behaviors from the opposite end of the spectrum, such as empathy and altruism, present a far more complicated picture. Empathy is the ability to appreciate and understand another person's feelings. When interviewed, women are more likely than men to describe themselves as empathic. If a distressing situation is created in the labora-

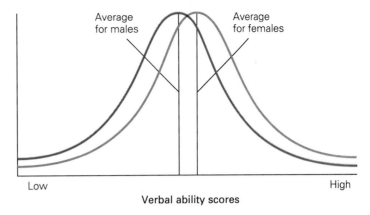

Figure 9.14
Verbal Ability Scores of Male and Female Adolescents. Beginning in adolescence, average scores for females on tests of verbal ability are higher than average scores for males. But like most gender differences in intellectual abilities, the average difference is small. Individual differences among both males and females are more striking than the average difference between the sexes.

tory, women are also more likely to cry or to report feeling upset. But when they witness a distressing situation, men and women do not differ on physiological measures of emotion, such as a change in heart rate, or on nonverbal indicators of empathy, such as facial expressions (Eisenberg & Lennon, 1983). How should we interpret this? It appears that women are more comfortable in expressing empathy. They may also be more in touch with their feelings. But we have no convincing evidence that men and women differ in their *capacity* for empathy.

What of other personality differences? Very few are evident. Women are somewhat better than men at understanding nonverbal cues and messages, but the differences are small and do not appear in all situations (Eisenberg & Lennon, 1983). Women are also more likely to offer help to others, which is one way of measuring altruism. But for the most part males and females demonstrate very similar personality profiles (Huston, 1985). Gender is but a small factor in the great variety of personality characteristics that we observe in people.

If gender differences in ability and personality are not striking, the same cannot be said of gender roles. A role is a way of behaving—a script really—that tells us what is appropriate or inappropriate. Gender roles indicate how males and females should behave and feel in everyday situations. They often prescribe very particular ways of interacting with others.

• •

GENDER ROLES

All societies have carefully defined gender roles. You have probably grown up expecting men to be more dominant and assertive than women and expecting women to be more nurturing and supportive. This division of gender roles is common to a number of societies but is by no means universal. Among the Tchambuli of New Guinea, for instance, women are independent and aggressive while the men are obedient and nurturing (Mead, 1935). Clearly, societies can differ a great deal in the roles they prescribe for women and men.

In most societies, children acquire gender roles very rapidly. Often this is reflected in their play. In the North American culture, beginning at roughly age 2, boys show a preference for trucks, airplanes, and other toys that they can move about and manipulate. Girls, on the other hand, show a strong interest in toys that evoke domestic themes, such as pretending to cook or clean (O'Brien & Huston, 1985). By preschool age, children's play begins to reflect traditional distinctions in men and women's roles. When opposite-sex 4- and 5-year olds play together, boys consistently choose roles such as Daddy, bus driver, and doctor, while girls prefer Mommy, teacher, and nurse (Grief, 1977). This preference for traditional roles is very difficult to change. In one convincing demonstration of this point, young children watched a film about a female physician assisted by a male nurse. When later asked to recall what they had seen, both boys and girls remembered the film as a story about a male *doctor* and his *female* nurse (Cordua, McGraw, & Drabman, 1979).

How do children acquire such powerful and inflexible notions about gender roles? Beginning in infancy, a process known as **sex typing** imbues children with a strong sense of the attitudes, beliefs, and behaviors that are appropriate for males and females. Below we review four prominent theories that address the question of how sex typing shapes the child's notion of gender.

Freudian Theory

One of the earliest theories of sex typing appears in Sigmund Freud's writings on childhood sexuality (Freud, 1905/1957). Freud believed that between 3 and 6 years of age children develop an unconscious sexual desire for the opposite-sex parent. By age 6 these feelings become very uncomfortable and threaten to bring the child into conflict with the same-sex parent. To resolve the conflict, children adopt many of the characteristics of the same-sex parent through a process known as **identification**. Identification allows the child to experience vicariously the love and affection that the opposite-sex parent expresses for the same-sex parent.

Identification may well promote sex typing, but critics of Freud note that children are aware of gender roles long before the age of 6 (Frieze, Parsons, Johnson, Ruble, & Zellman, 1978). As we noted earlier, even as toddlers boys become partial to stereotypically masculine toys, such as trucks, and girls develop a preference for stereotypically feminine toys, such as dolls. Other mechanisms must play a role in sex typing.

Social Learning Theory

Proponents of this theory assume that children are directed or socialized toward particular attitudes and beliefs about gender. Sometimes socialization is obvious and intentional. Parents may encourage their sons to play baseball, but encourage their daughters to pursue ballet. When this occurs, the social learning theorist would say that parents *reinforced* different gender roles for their sons and daughters. But on other occasions socialization is more subtle. Teachers in the upper grades of an elementary school, where science is first taught, may be predominantly male, secretaries who work in schools and offices predominantly female. To the social learning theorist, this provides an opportunity for *observational learning*. Children acquire gender roles by observing, and sometimes imitating, what they see in the world at large. Adults, and eventually peers, demonstrate or *model* what is appropriate behavior for males and females. Social learning theorists contend that the processes of reinforcement, modeling, and observational learning are among the most powerful means of sex typing.

Are social learning theorists describing a bygone era, or do children continue to observe traditional gender roles both within and outside the home? Although there may be winds of change, psychologists find little evidence that traditional sex typing is eroding. In providing play materials for young children, parents are likely to give more sports equipment, more toy animals, and more educational toys to boys, while girls receive more dolls and other domestic toys (Rheingold & Cook, 1975). Parents are also more apt to orient boys toward professional careers and to stress the importance of academic achievement for boys, particularly in the areas of math and science (Block, 1983, Eccles, 1985). Gender even affects the child's sense of autonomy and independence. Investigators find that parents reward risk taking and self-reliance in boys, while girls receive subtle encouragement to be more conforming and accepting (Huston, 1983; Ruble, 1984).

Social learning theorists also cite the importance of the mass media in reinforcing traditional gender roles. Although there has been some slight change in recent years, the vast majority of television programs and commercials portray males and females in stereotyped gender roles (Bretl & Cantor, 1988; Signorelli, 1989). The effect on children is just as social learning theorists would predict: Those who watch the most television hold the most traditional views of gender roles (McGhee & Frueh, 1980).

Social learning theory offers an important perspective on sex typing. It demonstrates how principles of learning theory can be applied to the development of gender roles. But critics of the theory point to a missing link—the child's understanding of the concept of gender. They argue that gender, like other important concepts, must emerge from the child's developing cognitive skills.

Kohlberg's Cognitive Developmental Theory

Lawrence Kohlberg was the first person to address this issue directly. Relying heavily on Piaget, Kohlberg proposed a cognitive theory of gender-role development (Kohlberg, 1966; Kohlberg & Ullian, 1974). Kohlberg believed that during the preschool years children acquire an understanding of the concepts *male* and *female* in three distinct stages.

The first stage, known as *gender identity,* occurs somewhere around age 3 when children recognize that they are either male or female. Kohlberg believed that knowing one's gender was an important achievement that helped children understand and categorize their world. But Kohlberg hypothesized that the 3-year-old's knowledge of gender was fragile. At this age, the child does not realize that boys invariably become men and that girls always become women. Then, between the ages of 4 and 5, children enter a new stage known

as *gender stability.* Now children understand the reality of gender. They know, for example, that girls and not boys become mothers. Still, there are limitations. At this stage, children rely on superficial signs—the length of someone's hair or whether they wear pants or a dress—to determine gender. Not until children reach the stage of *gender constancy,* somewhere between 6 and 7 years of age, do they realize that gender is immutable. Now children recognize, for example, that a girl is still a girl even if she dresses in a cowboy outfit or joins a Little League baseball team.

Kohlberg's theory is provocative, suggesting that the child's understanding of gender roles is fundamentally a cognitive process. Children should not begin to show a preference for the behaviors and attitudes of their own sex until they have a firm sense of gender. In other words, children must grasp the concept "I am a boy" or "I am a girl" before they begin to adopt male or female attitudes and behavior patterns.

To test this hypothesis, psychologists have constructed experiments like the following. A group of 4- to 6-year-old children were first asked a series of questions to determine their awareness of the stability and constancy of gender. For example, the experimenter asked a young girl, "When you grow up, will you be a mommy or a daddy?" or "If you played football, would you still be a girl?" Answers to these questions were used to classify children as having either a well-developed or a poorly developed sense of gender. Later, the same children watched a commercial that showed a child of the *opposite sex* playing with a gender-neutral toy (a movie viewer). After viewing the commercial, the children were given the opportunity to play with a group of toys that included the movie viewer. What should happen? If the cognitive-developmental theory is correct, children with a well-developed sense of gender should avoid playing with the movie viewer because the commercial identified it as a toy appropriate for members of the opposite sex. Conversely, children with a poorly developed sense of gender should not be influenced by the commercial. This is precisely what the experimenters found (Ruble, Balaban, & Cooper, 1981).

As Kohlberg's theory would predict, cognitive processes influenced the gender-role play of young children. However, the theory would also predict little or no expression of gender-appropriate behavior before children achieve gender constancy (age 6 or 7). This is clearly not true. As we noted earlier, even in infancy boys are more physical and aggressive than girls, and as early as 2 years of age both sexes show a preference for stereotyped male or female toys. This element of early sex typing is absent from Kohlberg's theory.

Gender-Schema Theory

Gender-schema theory seeks a middle ground between the cognitive-developmental and social learning perspectives. In agreement with Kohlberg, it stresses the importance of concepts or schemas for male and female, which first develop during the preschool period. However, gender-schema theorists also emphasize that as these concepts develop, social learning comes to the fore. Over and again society provides many cues that highlight the importance of gender and sharply distinguish male and female roles. This makes the concept of gender both relevant and easily identifiable (Bem, 1981). As children become more aware of their own gender, they begin to act in ways consistent with the roles that society assigns to males and females. Not surprisingly, then, when preschoolers play together, boys overwhelmingly prefer the role of doctor, while girls prefer the role of nurse.

In short, gender schema theory emphasizes that as children acquire the concepts of male (boy) and female (girl), they also begin to assimilate the roles that society assigns to these concepts. To the extent that traditional roles are modeled and reinforced, children will develop stereotyped ideas of what it means to be male or female. Note, however, that the outcome could be quite different. If parents, and society more generally, adopted less traditional gender roles, children would develop very different gender schemas (Bem, 1985).

BIOLOGY AND GENDER

Does biology contribute to gender differences? Although no one would dispute that males and females differ physically, strong arguments have arisen over the claim that biologically based differences account for the variations we observe in the behavior of males and females and in the roles they assume in society. We are accustomed to thinking about gender differences in cultural and societal terms. Recently, these assumptions have been challenged.

Sociobiology

As we noted in Chapter 4, sociobiologists believe that nature has endowed each of us with the selfish desire to see our genetic code survive and flourish (Wilson, 1975). They suggested that although we may not be consciously aware of it, we are all engaged in the genetic equivalent of loading the dice: we want to do everything we can to ensure the survival of our genes (Wilson, 1978).

But how does this help us understand gender differences? Sociobiologists argue that to ensure the survival of their genes, men and women should behave quite differently. Take the sexual double standard as an example. In many societies, sexual infidelity is frowned on in women, but is permissible, even encouraged, in men. The usual cultural explanation for this is that males are rewarded for a swashbuckling "man about town" attitude, but society wants females to be faithful spouses and dutiful mothers. Sociobiologists turn this explanation on its head, claiming that it is the survival of our genes, not our cultural heritage, that prompts men and women to behave so differently. From a sociobiological perspective, men are veritable sperm machines, producing thousands of sperm a day. With so many sperm available, a man increases the possibility that his genes will survive by copulating with as many fertile women as possible. (Buss, 1989). But for women, nature has prescribed a different formula for genetic success. A woman produces but one ovum a month. Because even a single act of intercourse can lead to 9 months of pregnancy, her genetic interests are best served by a cautious and selective approach to sexual intercourse. A woman should seek to mate with a man who will increase the likelihood that her offspring will survive (Buss, 1988).

What is the response of behavioral scientists to this provocative analysis of gender differences? The great majority are unimpressed. Psychologists, for example, acknowledge that genes contribute to behavior. Intelligence, personality, and mental health are all areas where genetics is known to play an important role. But sociobiologists go much further. They seek to reduce something as complex as human sexuality to a simple genetic principle—survival of the genes. Nowhere do we find room for the rich variety of cultural prescriptions that affect sexual practices: societies that demand premarital celibacy for both males and females, communities that encourage multiple wives or multiple husbands, and arranged marriages between strangers. Nor can sociobiology account for the changes that may come about when people are motivated to alter their sexual behavior.

In the view of most psychologists, sociobiology offers a provocative but incomplete account of gender differences. What is missing from the sociobiological perspective is the idea that complex human behaviors, such as gender roles, are shaped and molded by culture and experience.

Hormones and Behavior

Hormones are powerful chemicals that regulate growth and development. During the prenatal period, a genetically male fetus begins to develop testes that produce the male sex hormone testosterone. A genetically female fetus develops ovaries that produce the sex hormones estrogen and progesterone. Do these hormones, which are responsible for the development of the genitalia and reproductive organs of males and females, also contribute to gender differences in behavior? Let us consider aggression, an area of clear difference between males and females.

Recall that in a wide variety of cultures, from age 2 onward, males are more aggressive than females. This has led some investigators to suggest that aggression does not result solely from social and cultural practices (Maccoby & Jacklin, 1980). Biological differences between males and females might also play a role. How? The most frequent suggestion is that testosterone promotes aggressive behavior. Work with animals is particularly revealing. In many species, aggression between males is correlated with high levels of testosterone (Albert, Dyson, Walsh, & Wong, 1988). Furthermore, if the female of certain species undergoes removal of the ovaries coupled with daily injections of testosterone, she will become noticeably more aggressive (van de Poll, Taminiau, Endert, & Louwerse, 1988). For ethical reasons, experiments of this sort are not permissable with humans, but it is possible to correlate levels of

testosterone in the blood with aggressive behavior. Here we find parallels to the animal literature. For example, among teenage boys, elevated levels of testosterone are correlated with highly aggressive behaviors (Susman, Inoff-Germain, Nottelmann, Loriaux, Cutler, & Chrousos, 1987).

What is the essential point of this research? Are psychologists claiming that hormones determine behavior—that biology is destiny? Not at all. In contrast to sociobiology, the argument here is that hormones *interact* with socialization practices to produce gender differences in aggression (Huston, 1983). Male sex hormones may predispose toward aggression, but social practices often reward and encourage the same outcome. Researchers who support this viewpoint would argue that much the same process is at work for other gender differences.

Interim Summary

A major achievement of the childhood years is the development of a sense of gender. Research on actual gender differences in behaviors reveals that males and females are often quite similar. In the areas of intellectual ability and personality traits, investigators find only a few stable and consistent differences between the sexes.

Gender roles are the attitudes, beliefs, and behavior patterns that people associate with being male or female. Children acquire knowledge about gender roles through the process of sex typing. Four prominent theories of sex typing are the Freudian perspective, which holds that children acquire gender roles through the process of identification; the social learning perspective, which argues that parents model and reinforce behaviors they consider appropriately masculine or feminine; Kohlberg's cognitive-developmental theory, which proposes a three-stage process of gender-role development involving an understanding of gender identity, gender stability, and gender constancy; and gender-schema theory, which asserts that as children begin to understand the concepts of male and female, they assimilate the roles that society assigns to these concepts.

Suggestions of a biological basis for gender differences have ranged from the strictly genetic perspective (sociobiology) to an interactionist position (hormonal influences). Sociobiologists have suggested that men and women adopt different roles to ensure the survival of their genes. Sociobiological theories generally ignore the role of culture and socialization and reduce gender differences to a simple principle—ensuring one's genetic legacy. A different argument is put forth by those who suggest that hormones may contribute to gender differences. These theorists believe that hormones interact with socialization practices to produce some of the differences we observe in the behavior of men and women.

SUMMARY

1. Three issues in the study of human development are: (1) continuity versus discontinuity (Does development occur in sudden spurts or at a slow steady rate?), (2) stability versus change (Do the early years predict what comes later in development?), and (3) nature versus nurture (The role of heredity and environment in development).

2. The most frequently used methods for studying development are: the cross-sectional method, in which people of different ages are studied at roughly the same time, and the longitudinal method, in which one group of people is studied over an extended period of time.

3. Both heredity and environment influence development. Complex human behaviors always involve a delicate interaction between heredity and environment. Heredity (genes) appears to establish broad limits for behavior, but the environment shapes development within those limits.

4. The prenatal period is a time of rapid growth during which the embryo and fetus are vulnerable to teratogens which have the potential to seriously disrupt the course of development. Following birth, rapid physical growth continues during the first two years. Brain development, which guides the growth of both physical and mental abilities, is particularly impressive during the first two years.

5. Perceptual abilities, both auditory and visual, emerge early in infancy. Infants refine these skills quickly and within a short time period acquire the ability to make subtle discriminations in facial expressions, as well as the capacity to perceive depth.

6. Cognition is the ability to gather, process, and store information about the environment. Swiss psychologist Jean Piaget argued that cognition changes dramatically from birth to adulthood, progressing through four major periods: sensorimotor, preoperational, concrete operational, and formal operational. During each period, the child gathers and processes information in a unique and qualitatively distinct fashion.

7. Information processing is an alternative to Piaget's theory. It focuses on the skills and rules which children acquire as they solve mental problems. Information processing theorists often focus on the way attention and memory influence children's abilities to solve difficult problems.

8. Social development begins in infancy with the development of an attachment relationship between parents and infants, with both parties contributing to this important relationship. However, while a strong attachment relationship provides an optimal beginning to social development, children who have a poor or nonexistent attachment relationship may still recover, though emotional scars may endure.

9. Parental childrearing practices influence children's social development. In general, a warm nurturing style, combined with clear expectations and open communication, lead to independence and social maturity. However, children's temperament affects parental behavior and makes causal statements very difficult and complex.

10. Maternal employment is becoming increasingly more common. One outcome of this is a difference in the attitudes and beliefs of children who grow up in a family where mothers work. A second outcome is a growing number of children who are enrolled in day care. Research indicates that high-quality day care does not adversely affect the social and cognitive development of young children, though debate continues over the effect of day care on the quality of the infant's attachment relationship.

11. The development of a sense of one's gender is a major achievement of the childhood years. Research on actual gender dif-

ferences in intellectual ability and personality characteristics reveals that males and females are quite similar. Where gender differences have arisen, psychologists have considered the controversial position of sociobiologists who argue that males and females adopt different behavior patterns to ensure the survival of their genes. A more accepted biologically based proposal holds that hormones may interact with socialization practices to explain some of the difference we observe in the behavior of males and females.

Gender roles are the attitudes, beliefs, and behavior patterns associated with being male or female. Four prominent theories—the Freudian perspective, the social learning perspective, the cognitive-developmental perspective, and the gender-schema perspective—have been advanced to suggest how children acquire gender roles.

KEY INDIVIDUALS

Arnold Gesell
Harry Harlow
Eleanor Gibson
Diana Baumrind
Richard Walk
Sigmund Freud
Jean Piaget
Lawrence Kohlberg

KEY RESEARCH

effects of teratogens on prenatal development
visual scanning in infants
the "visual cliff"
Piaget's theory of cognitive development
test for mastery of object permanence
the conservation task
test for mastery of formal operational thinking
Gelman's method for test of number conservation
memory strategies in children
studies with rhesus monkeys and surrogate mothers
patterns of parenting and dimensions of childrearing
gender differences in intellectual ability
effects of socialization on gender roles

KEY TERMS

development
identification
sex typing
embryo
conservation
fetus
cross-sectional method
fetal alcohol syndrome (FAS)
longitudinal method
infancy period
teratogens
genes
norms
attachment
critical period
motor development
information processing
sensorimotor period
preoperational period
concrete operational period
formal operational period
gender
object permanence
gender constancy

10

Adolescence, Adulthood, and Aging

Ideas about development change slowly. For centuries people did not recognize childhood as a distinct period of life. Then gradually the idea took hold that children were different from adults. Soon the thoughts and feelings of the child became areas of intense scrutiny. But as psychologists began to look closely at the childhood years, a new notion emerged. Experts suggested that the experiences of childhood left an indelible mark. Who we are, what we do, what we become—all the critical choices of adulthood—have their roots in our earliest experiences. The childhood years chart an irrevocable course of development.

This idea—what we might call the primacy of childhood development—soon led to a commonsense notion. Psychologists assumed that childhood experiences could accurately forecast what would happen in adult life. To know the history of the child was to know the future of the adult.

But is this theory or myth? Psychologist Bernice Neugarten, who has conducted an intensive study of over 2000 adults, argues that adult experiences are very difficult to foresee (Neugarten, 1980). Like others who have studied the postchilhood years carefully, Neugarten finds that adult lives are more diverse and less predictable that anyone ever imagined. The elderly provide one example. What happens beyond age 65, the traditional entry into old age, is very difficult to predict. Unless they are suffering from ill health, an elderly population is likely to be a very diverse group with a wide range of interests, many of which developed later in life (Neugarten, 1980). It is not uncommon for new interests to emerge after people retire from lifelong jobs. Some retirees begin part-time work in a new field, some engage solely in leisure activities, and some return to school.

Of course, old age is but one example of postchildhood development. In this chapter, we will also consider the period of adolescence as well as the periods of young adulthood and middle age. We will examine these periods separately, but where possible we will show the relationship *between* periods. It is important to bear in mind that we are studying the human capacity for change throughout the adolescent and adulthood years.

ADOLESCENCE

Adolescence can be loosely defined as the time between childhood and adulthood. However, not all societies recognize adolescence. Some non-Western cultures have no distinct period to mark the transition from childhood to adulthood. Children simply assume what responsibilities they can as early as possible and eventually become independent of their parents.

From the outset, then, we should recognize that adolescence is not a universal state. Rather, it is an invention of modern industrial societies that emphasize a transition between the more carefree childhood years and the more complex responsibilities of adulthood. In most industrialized societies, young people must acquire training or schooling to develop a specialized set of skills. They must also acquire the emotional maturity to make personal decisions on their own. These first steps toward adulthood are accomplished in adolescence.

Perspectives on Adolescence

Adolescence is usually defined as the period that begins with the onset of puberty and ends somewhere around age 18 or 19. Several distinct physical changes signal the onset of puberty, principally menstruation in the female and the production of sperm in the male. Changes in height and shape of the body are also signs of pubescence. These physical changes can occur anywhere between the ages of 10 and 18, although puberty typically begins between 11 and 13 (Tanner, 1970).

In some cultures, there is no distinct period between childhood and adulthood. Children assume serious responsibilities as soon as possible.

But adolescence is more than a time of rapid physical development. It is a time of adjusting to bodily changes, of new relationships with members of the opposite sex, and of emerging intellectual powers. How well adolescents adjust to these changes is a matter of some debate. G. Stanley Hall, a pioneer in the study of postchildhood development, referred to adolescence as a period of great "storm and stress" (Hall, 1904). Hall believed that the teenage years, filled with youthful idealism and concerns about sexual development, were destined to be a turbulent period. Many other psychologists have agreed with Hall, arguing that the teenage years are especially stressful. For example, when 30-year-old adults reflected on their life experiences in an open-ended interview, many remembered their adolescent years as a time of confusion and despair. They spoke of conflicts with parents, anxiety about scholastic performance, and pressures for peer recognition (MacFarlane, 1964).

Yet, other psychologists remain unconvinced that adolescence is a uniquely troublesome period. In their view, the majority of adolescents do not encounter serious problems in personal adjustment, nor do they hold sharply negative attitudes toward their parents (Offer & Offer, 1975; Coleman, 1980l). These investigators have concluded that the image of the troubled and confused adolescent is erroneous and misleading. In their research, the typical adolescent, even in the stormy period of the 1960s, was actually quite well adjusted (Offer, 1969).

These conflicting opinions may result from the different ways that adolescents respond to the physical and psychological changes of the teenage years. Some react by challenging and testing authority, whereas others adjust relatively easily. Whatever the outcome, we can be certain that all adolescents are responding to a myriad of physical, cognitive, and social changes.

Physical Development

The first clear signs of adolescence are the distinct changes in height and weight known as the *growth spurt*. In girls, the growth spurt usually begins around age 10 1/2, reaches its peak at age 12, and begins to slow around 13 to 13 1/2 years. Boys have a similar 2- to 3-year spurt, but it generally occurs later. Typically, boys begin to spurt around 13, peak at 14, and then return to a slower rate of growth for the next year or two. As **Figure 10.1** shows, boys grow at a faster rate during the growth spurt, eventually achieving a greater average height than girls (Tanner, 1981).

The growth spurt occurs about the same time as the development of primary and secondary sex characteristics. **Primary sex characteristics** are the reproductive sex organs—the ovaries, uterus, and vagina of the female and the testes, scrotum, and penis of the male. While adolescents are aware of the development of primary sex characteristics, they are more likely to take note of nonreproductive physical changes, or **secondary sex characteristics**, such as the enlargement of breasts and widening of the hips in girls, chest hair and change of voice in boys, and pubic hair in both sexes.

Perhaps the most important physical event of adolescence is the beginning of the menstrual cycle for girls and the first ejaculation of semen for boys. The timing of both events can vary widely. The onset of menstruation, for example, can occur any time between ages 8 and 18, though for most girls it takes place between ages 11 and 13 (Tanner, 1978). The first menstrual cycle is a very memorable and important event for all girls. For some, it is a difficult experience, one that they may even

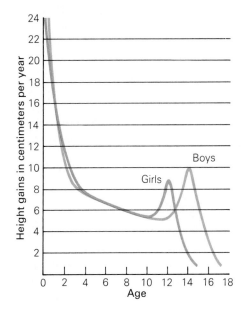

Figure 10.1
Annual Gains in Height.
Note the dramatic increase in height during the adolescent growth spurt, which occurs approximately 2 years earlier in girls than boys. (After Tanner, Whitehouse, & Takaishi, 1966)

try to keep secret. However, girls who are well prepared for their first menstrual cycle and feel that it is a normal part of their life cycle often have positive memories of the event (Greif & Ullman, 1982).

The timing of the physical changes of adolescence often has psychological consequences. In many Western cultures, boys have a distinct advantage if they experience an early pubescence. They become physically stronger and more athletic than their slower-maturing classmates, and they tend to develop a considerable degree of poise and self-confidence in their social activities. Boys who mature early are highly regarded not only by their peers but even by adults (Conger, 1977). But for girls, the consequences of early pubescence are more complex. Changes in the height and shape of the body sometimes interfere with early social adjustment, particularly if the girl suddenly becomes sexually attractive (Brooks-Gunn, 1986). This problem tends to diminish, however, as girls grow older. Girls who mature early have an advantage in social situations by the time they reach the pre–high school years.

Interim Summary

Adolescence is not a universal phenomenon but a period of development most common in industrialized societies. It is usually defined as the period that begins with puberty and ends at approximately age 19. Rapid physical development is one of the identifying characteristics of adolescence. Both boys and girls experience a substantial growth spurt. Maturation of the sex or reproductive organs also occurs during adolescence, accompanied by changes in the shape and size of the body.

Cognitive Development

In adolescence, we see the emergence of new powers of thought. Adolescents can reason abstractly, develop hypotheses about complex situations, and even reflect on their own thinking. These new-found intellectual skills frequently dispose adolescents to question existing moral and social values. Often, ideals are high as adolescents ponder how the world *might* be.

Moral Reasoning

Moral reasoning is an integral part of human development. Beginning in childhood, parents seek to instill moral values. How these values develop and change is a question that has intrigued psychologists for many years. While parental attitudes are no doubt important, several prominent psychologists have suggested that moral reasoning is tied closely to cognitive development. If so, we should expect to see major changes in moral reasoning during adolescence when intellectual powers are reaching their peak.

Piaget's Theory of Moral Reasoning. Jean Piaget, the cognitive-developmental theorist whom we discussed in Chapter 9, was the first to propose a link between the way people think and their ability to reason about moral dilemmas. Through his interviews and conversations with children, Piaget observed two stages in the development of moral reasoning (Piaget, 1932). The first, which occurs during the preoperational period, is called **moral realism.** In this stage the young child believes that rules are sacred and unchangeable and that those who violate sanctions must be punished according to the magnitude of their offense. To a 6-year-old, stealing 10 cookies is much worse than stealing 2 cookies. But during the concrete operational period, children shift toward **autonomous morality** or the **morality of cooperation.** A child in this stage believes that rules and regulations are the product of social agreements rather than sacred and unchangeable laws. Such a child will also consider the motives behind someone's actions and not just the consequences of the offense. Stealing cookies to give to a hungry friend is different from sneaking a forbidden dessert (Piaget, 1932).

In sum, Piaget emphasized that children's thinking influenced their moral judgments. He noted that while preoperational children consider only one dimension of a moral dilemma, concrete operational children consider two dimensions—the motives and the consequences of the offender's actions. Thus, Piaget's research established a definite link between thinking and morality.

Kohlberg's Theory of Moral Reasoning. Piaget conducted his research on moral reasoning in the early 1930s. This topic lay dormant for many years until Lawrence Kohlberg conducted a seminal study of moral reasoning in 7-

to 16-year-old boys (Kohlberg, 1963, 1969). Like Piaget, Kohlberg saw a relationship between cognition and moral judgments. However, Kohlberg believed that there were six different levels to moral reasoning. Kohlberg's method was to ask his subjects to listen to a series of stories involving a clear moral dilemma. After each story, the subjects would answer questions that forced them to choose between obedience to rules and concern for the welfare of others. The stories, though hypothetical, often portrayed gripping personal problems. Imagine you are one of Kohlberg's subjects as you read the following story:

> In Europe, a woman was near death from cancer. One drug might save her, a form of radium that a druggist in the same town had recently discovered. The druggist was charging $2000, 10 times what the drug cost him to make. The sick woman's husband, Heinz, went to everyone he knew to borrow the money, but he could only get together about half of what it cost. He told the druggist that his wife was dying and asked him to sell it cheaper or let him pay later. But the druggist said, "No." The husband got desperate and broke into the man's store to steal the drug for his wife. Should the husband have done that? Why? (Kohlberg, 1969, p. 379)

After listening to this story, Kohlberg's subjects answered a series of questions, such as, "Should Heinz have taken the drug?" and "What was right or wrong about what he did?" Kohlberg was interested not in whether the incident was judged right or wrong, but in the reasons people gave for their decisions. Based on their responses to this story and several other moral dilemmas, Kohlberg determined that there were six stages in the development of moral reasoning. He grouped these stages into three broad levels of moral development as shown in **Table 10.1** on page 366.

Kohlberg found that the moral judgments of children who were roughly 7 years old conformed to the premoral level (Level I). These children evaluated actions in terms of their consequences. They felt people should obey rules in order to avoid punishment (stage 1). However, the somewhat older stage 2 subjects were more selfish and more oriented toward

their own pleasure. At this stage, children believed that acts were morally acceptable if they were personally gratifying.

But Kohlberg observed that at age 13, or roughly the beginning of adolescence, there is a shift to the morality of conventional role conformity (Level II). This change is due in large measure to the greater cognitive skills of adolescents, who are better able to judge and evaluate the world around them (Kohlberg, 1969). At Level II, young people first become concerned with obedience to authority in the hope that others will approve of their actions. This is what Kohlberg called the stage of "good boy" morality (stage 3). However, this stage soon gives way to a respect for authority and a genuine concern with maintaining social order (stage 4). During stage 4, adolescents often talk about the importance of duties and obligations and stress the value of maintaining social order for its own sake.

The third level of Kohlberg's theory, the morality of self-accepted principles, is closely tied to the development of formal operational thinking. People who reach this level must demonstrate an awareness of highly complex and abstract ethical principles. However, as Piaget (1972) observed, not everyone is capable of formal operational thought, a fact which led Kohlberg to conclude that many people will not achieve Level III (Kohlberg, 1969). Those who do reach Level III first subscribe to the value of democratically accepted laws and agreements (stage 5). At this stage, people recognize that laws may sometimes be unjust or arbitrary, but they believe that in the long run society benefits from adherence to democratically agreed upon principles. However, in stage 6 there is a notable shift toward individual principles of conscience. People who reach this stage are keenly aware of the importance of laws and social customs, but they balance these obligations against their understanding of the civil and moral rights of individual citizens.

Challenges to Kohlberg's Theory. Kohlberg, like Piaget, viewed moral development from a cognitive perspective. He spoke of adolescents becoming "moral philosophers" whose advancement through the stages of moral development should occur in a regular and predictable fashion. Kohlberg's longitudinal research seems to support his point. After following his original sample for 20 years, Kohlberg and his associates discovered that all

Table 10.1   Kohlberg's Stages of Moral Development

Levels	Description of Stages		Examples of Each Stage in Response to Heinz's Dilemma	
			Response in Favor of Stealing Drug	**Response Against Stealing Drug**
I. Premoral	Stage 1	Obedience to rules so as to avoid punishment.	If you let your wife die, you'll be blamed for not spending the money to save her.	You shouldn't steal the drug because you'll be caught and sent to jail.
	Stage 2	Obedience to rules so that rewards or favors may be obtained.	If you get caught, you could give the money back and you wouldn't get much of a jail sentence.	You may not get much of a jail sentence, but it won't do much good because your wife will die before you get out.
II. Morality of Conventional Role Conformity	Stage 3	Seeking and maintaining the approval of others. Adhering to a "good-boy" morality.	Your family will think you're an inhuman husband if you don't steal the drug.	If you steal the drug, you'll feel bad thinking how you dishonored your family
	Stage 4	Conforming to norms so as to avoid censure or reprimands by authority figures	You'll always feel guilty that you caused your wife's death if you don't do your duty to her.	After you're sent to jail, you'll always feel guilty for your dishonesty and lawbreaking.
III. Morality of Self-Accepted Moral Principles	Stage 5	Obedience to democratically accepted laws and contracts.	If you don't steal the drug, you'd lose self-respect and probably the respect of others too.	If you stole the drug, you would lose standing and respect in the community and violate the law.
	Stage 6	Morality of individual conscience.	If you don't steal the drug and let your wife die, you'd always condemn yourself for it afterward. You wouldn't have lived up to your own conscience.	If you stole the drug, you wouldn't be blamed by others but you'd condemn yourself for not living up to your own standards of honesty.

Adapted from Kohlberg (1967, 1969).

the subjects proceeded through the stages of moral development in the predicted sequence, with no subject ever skipping a stage (Colby, Kohlberg, Gibbs, & Lieberman, 1983).

However, Kohlberg's perspective has not received universal acceptance. Other psychologists believe that moral judgments are influenced by social as well as cognitive factors. They note that the rewards and punishments dispensed by parents, the values of the peer group, and even the type of television programs watched are factors that contribute to moral standards (Bandura & Walters, 1963).

But perhaps the most crucial issue in the study of moral development is the relationship between moral *judgments* and moral *behavior*. Kohlberg measures what people *say* they will

do in certain hypothetical situations, not what they actually do. This raises the serious question of whether the resolution of actual, "real life" moral dilemmas is related in any meaningful way to the answers people give to Kohlberg's stories (Fischer, 1983). While Kohlberg acknowledged a potential problem, he pointed to studies that show that an individual's moral judgments are a strong predictor of his or her actual behavior in ethically difficult or ambiguous situations (Gilligan & Belenky, 1980; Kohlberg, 1969). Nevertheless, other psychologists are either skeptical or unconvinced, and they suggest that the potential discrepancy between moral judgments and moral behavior is a serious problem for Kohlberg (Blasi, 1980).

Finally, Kohlberg's critics have raised the question of bias. Does Kohlberg's theory implicitly assume that a certain kind of moral reasoning is superior? Some researchers believe that it does. They note that Kohlberg's postconventional stages (5 and 6) are usually found only among the well-educated members of industrialized countries (Edwards, 1982). Could it be that Kohlberg's stages represent a particular kind of moral reasoning, as opposed to universally accepted moral principles?

Most certainly, according to Kohlberg's colleague Carol Gilligan. In her provocative book *In a Different Voice* (1982), Gilligan criticized Kohlberg for constructing a theory based on an all-male sample. Noting that women rarely attained the highest level in Kohlberg's system, Gilligan began her own studies of moral reasoning. She compared the views of men and women on a series of moral and ethical problems, such as whether women should have the right to an abortion. These studies convinced Gilligan that men and women often differ in their conceptualization of moral problems. Women demonstrate a "morality of caring" that is characterized by a concern for the feelings of others and the relationships between the principals in a moral dilemma. While such reasoning might lead Kohlberg to place women at the conventional level of moral development (stages 3 and 4, which emphasize social concerns), Gilligan believes this is not a deficiency in women. Rather women are demonstrating a *different kind* of moral reasoning that contrasts with the "morality of justice" often exhibited by men. The deficiency lies not in women but in Kohlberg's failure to detect the full range of moral reasoning (Gilligan, 1982).

So there is both consensus and disagreement about Kohlberg's theory. The point of agreement is that cognition influences the development of a series of stages of moral reasoning. However, these stages may have cultural determinants and do not appear to be universal. Furthermore, there is a real question about whether moral reasoning is consistent with moral behavior.

INSIGHT AND JUDGMENT

By virtue of schooling and disposition, adolescents often find themselves pondering and debating major social and political issues. Should there be a legal drinking age? Are nonprescription drugs harmful? Is premarital sex wrong?

Adolescents often engage in discussion and debate about social and political issues. This group of teenagers is discussing alcoholism.

With great passion and a probing intellect, adolescents debate these issues endlessly. And as many a parent can ruefully attest, adolescents have both the logical ability to detect inconsistencies in other people's arguments and the moral conviction to point them out.

But there is a compelling paradox here. This clear-headed, logical thinker often acts irrationally, even to the point of self-injury or death. Researchers at the National Institutes of Mental Health find that adolescence is the only age group in which mortality rates have risen since 1960 (Goleman, 1987). More important, the great majority of these deaths could be prevented. Accidents, homicide, and suicide account for roughly 75 percent of all deaths in adolescence. As psychologist Lewis Lipsitt observes, adolescents are "dying of their own reckless behavior" (Goleman, 1987).

What would prompt adolescents to behave this way? One reason is that risk taking seems to be a natural component of the teenage years. Adolescents often maintain an unrealistic sense of their own vulnerability. They believe that little enduring harm will come their way. Death and disability are things for older people to worry about. Even more curious, however, is the tendency of adolescents to assess incorrectly the likelihood that misfortune will befall them. For example, researchers have found that when adolescents are asked to predict whether certain outcomes become more or less prevalent over time, they erroneously conclude that risks such as pregnancy following unprotected intercourse, or addiction from drug abuse, are *less* likely to occur (Goleman, 1987). That is, contrary to known facts, adolescents assume that if tragedy does not occur the first time, it is unlikely to occur later.

From a cognitive standpoint, the adolescent is something of a paradox. While the teenage years bring new-found cognitive skills, including the ability to engage in sophisticated moral and political arguments, there is also evidence that personal needs cloud the adolescent's ability to evaluate many social risks. Insight and judgment do not seem to go hand in hand during adolescence.

Interim Summary

Adolescents develop impressive new intellectual skills and new powers of moral reasoning. Jean Piaget proposed two stages of moral development, a stage of moral realism and a stage of autonomous morality. Psychologist Lawrence Kohlberg suggests that the highest levels of moral reasoning involve an understanding of abstract ethical principles. Kohlberg believes that these principles emerge for the first time during adolescence because they are closely tied to the development of formal operational thinking.

Despite their logical abilities, adolescents often act irrationally, even to the point of endangering their own lives. Personal needs sometimes cloud the judgment of adolescents and lead them to engage in extremely risky actions.

Social and Personality Development

Perhaps the most important task facing a teenager is forming a strong sense of self to cope with the many changes that surround the adolescent years. In psychological terms, this is known as establishing an identity. But at the same time that adolescents search for their own identity, they must also manage relationships with both their parents and their peers. Relationships with parents change throughout life, but they are particularly fluid during the teenage years, when parental influence is rivaled by peer influence. Peer relationships, for their part, add new dimensions to personal growth during the adolescent years. Hetero-

sexual friendships develop, and adolescents confront an awareness of their own sexuality.

All of these changes contribute to the personal and social development of the adolescent. To understand this process, we will look at four major components: (1) identity formation, (2) relationships with parents, (3) relationships with peers, and (4) sexuality in adolescence. We then conclude with a discussion of one of the consequences of sexuality in adolescence, teenage pregnancy.

ESTABLISHING AN IDENTITY

Two prominent theorists have stressed the importance of developing a clear and independent sense of self during the adolescent years. One was Sigmund Freud, who emphasized that adolescents must reduce their dependence on parents and begin to function autonomously. He predicted that this change would not occur smoothly and that parent-child conflicts would inevitably result (Freud, 1910/1953). The other is Erik Erikson, a prominent personality theorist whom we encountered briefly in Chapter 9. Erikson, in his extensive writings about the adolescent's search for identity, suggests that identity formation is really the fifth stage in a theory of personality formation that extends from birth to old age (Erikson, 1963).

Erikson postulates eight stages in personality development. As shown in **Table 10.2**, each stage is focused on a particular interpersonal relationship and involves a crisis or conflict. Erikson envisions two possible outcomes of the conflict at each stage, one of which promotes far greater personal adjustment than the other. In the first stage, for example, infants discover through relationships with their parents that their environment is either basically safe and secure or threatening and insecure. But the outcome at each stage is not irreversible (Erikson, 1963). According to Erikson, a child who is treated in a harsh and inconsistent manner in infancy can experience a normal adulthood if he or she receives a great deal of affection and care in the later stages of life.

In adolescence, the fifth stage in Erikson's developmental scheme, the conflict is between the formation of a new identity and **role confusion,** or the failure to synthesize past experiences and develop a clear and consistent sense of self. Why should adolescence prompt a search for identity? Erikson believes that the sudden biological changes of puberty, the awakening of sexual desires, and the formation

Table 10.2   Erikson's Stages of Life

Stage	Personal and Social Relationships	Crisis or Conflict	Possible Outcome
Birth to 1 year	Mother	Trust vs. mistrust	Trust and faith in others or a mistrust of people.
2 years	Parents	Autonomy vs. shame and doubt	Self-control and mastery or self-doubt and fearfulness.
3 to 5 years	Family	Initiative vs. guilt	Purpose and direction or a loss of self-esteem.
6 to 11 years	Neighborhood and school	Industry vs. inferiority	Competence in social and intellectual pursuits or a failure to thrive and develop.
Adolescence	Peer groups and outgroups; models of leadership	Identity vs. role confusion	A sense of "who one is" or prolonged uncertainty about one's role in life.
Early adulthood	Partners in friendship, sex, competition, cooperation	Intimacy vs. isolation	Formation of deep personal relationships or the failure to love others.
Middle age	Divided labor and shared household	Generativity vs. stagnation	Expansion of interests and caring for others or a turning inward toward one's own problems.
Old age	"Mankind" "My kind"	Integrity vs. despair	Satisfaction with the triumphs and disappointments of life or a sense of unfulfillment and a fear of death.

After Erikson (1963).

of new values and beliefs trigger the identity crisis. He detects in adolescents a need for continuity with the past, yet at the same time an intense concern for what lies ahead—jobs, careers, and new interpersonal relationships. For Erikson, this delicate task of balancing the past and the future gives rise to the fundamental question that defines the identity crisis, "Who am I and where am I going?"

Erikson sees a number of difficulties associated with the fifth stage of personality development. He suggests that if adolescents fail to synthesize past experiences with future expectations, no clear resolution of the identity crisis is possible. Instead, role confusion results. According to Erikson, role confusion can take several forms. Sometimes it is manifested in aimless drifting through a series of occupational and social roles. But it can also have more serious consequences, leading the adolescent into delinquent or abnormal behavior. Erikson refers to this type of role confusion as the formation of a **negative identity,** the choice of those adolescents who, unable to successfully resolve the identity crisis, adopt an extreme position—delinquency, drug abuse, or even suicide—that sets them apart from the crowd. They find this preferable to the loneliness and isolation that comes with the failure to achieve a distinct and more adaptive role in life.

Erikson formulated his theory of psychosocial development many years ago and without the benefit of systematic research. What have subsequent studies revealed? James Marcia (1967) classified adolescents in terms of their resolution of the identity crisis. He developed four different "status" categories that characterize the search for identity: (1) *achievement status,* when an individual has resolved the identity question and is committed to a particular course; (2) *moratorium status,* when an individual is still searching and experimenting; (3) *foreclosure status,* when an individual has avoided the identity crisis by aligning completely with his or her parents; and (4) *identity diffusion status,* when an individual is totally absent of direction or commitment. Unlike Erikson's stages, however, Marcia's iden-

Eric Erikson

tity statuses are not necessarily progressive. One individual might fall just short of achievement status; another might never move beyond identity diffusion. Marcia and his colleagues (Constantinople, 1969; Marcia & Freedman, 1970), in their research with college students, have found that during the college years there is a tendency to move from identity diffusion to identity achievement. Even within a single school year, some students show considerable movement toward the achievement status (Constantinople, 1969).

These results lend empirical support to Erikson's views on adolescence. However, other psychologists have raised specific questions about the difficulty of assessing the status categories that Marcia has described as well as more general objections to the sweeping nature of Erikson's theory. They note that Erikson formulated his opinions based on observations of a restricted group of individuals (largely middle-class, white males) and that the theory must be understood within that context. Carol Gilligan, who criticized Kohlberg for making broad generalizations about moral development, has levied a similar charge against Erikson. Erikson assumes that adolescents want to forge a separate identity, but Gilligan believes that this is more characteristic of males than females. Females are more interested in developing warm and nurturing relationships and less interested in the ideal of separateness (Gilligan, 1982). In short, Gilligan sees a common error in both Erikson's and Kohlberg's theories—the tendency to promulgate universal stages in the absence of confirming data.

Relationships with Parents

If adolescence is a time to develop a separate identity, does this mean an inevitable clash between parents and teenagers? Will adolescents rebel against parental values in their struggle to become independent? To be sure, parents and teenagers do not always see eye to eye. But how serious are their conflicts? The popular stereotype is that adolescents and parents clash frequently, but research actually supports the opposite conclusion. Most teenagers say they have a positive relationship with their parents. By a wide majority they agree with statements such as "My parents are patient with me," "I can count on my parents," and "I have a part in family decisions" (Offer, Ostrov, & Howard, 1981). Nor is this a new phenomenon. Even during the tumultuous period of the late 1960s, when youthful countercultures were emerging,

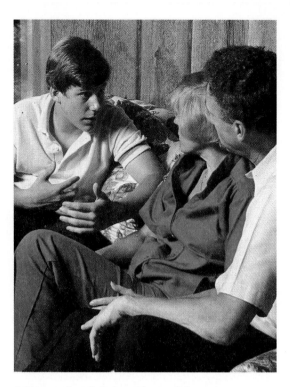

Self-assured and independent adolescents are more likely to engage in open communication with their parents.

the great majority of parents and adolescents did not experience a "generation gap" in basic ideals and values (Harris, 1971). Most adolescents hold social, religious, and political views that are quite similar to those of their parents (Gallatin, 1980).

This is not to say that peace and harmony always reign. As adolescents begin to assert their autonomy, conflicts arise around issues such as obedience to family rules, assistance with household chores, and completion of school work (Montemayor, 1982). Arguments about sexuality and drug use are also fairly common (Payne, Summers, & Stewart, 1973). For the most part, however, these are temporary squabbles—signs that adolescents and parents are renegotiating their relationship. Adolescents want greater freedom, but the majority also want the respect and approval of their parents. They seek to maintain a close personal relationship even as they separate from their parents (Youniss & Smaller, 1985).

Relationships with Peers

In childhood, parents are typically the sole reference point for ideas and values, but in adolescence the peer group competes for this role.

Peers have a strong influence on an adolescent's preferences for music, fashion, and recreation.

During adolescence, many young people look to their parents for answers to questions about basic values and attitudes. Although there is some disagreement between parents and adolescents in matters of personal taste, psychologists have consistently found that most adolescents enjoy a positive relationship with their parents.

Peers help to define the adolescent's personal interests and preferences. Music, clothes, hair style, and social events are all part of the domain of peer influence. In these areas, peer influence is often quite important, affecting such choices as whether or not to use recreational drugs.

Who do teenagers listen to? In truth, both sides, but from each they seek different advice. Peers tend to influence such lifestyle decisions as how to dress, what clubs to join, or what social events to attend. Parents are most influential in basic social and vocational decisions, such as which occupation to select, whether to attend college, or what to value in life (Sebald, 1986).

Peer influence is not trivial, however. Adolescents often make personal lifestyle decisions largely on the basis of what their peers are doing. Drugs provide one example. Among adolescents whose parents smoked marijuana but whose friends did not, only 17 percent used the drug themselves. But among those whose friends smoked but whose parents abstained, 56 percent reported using marijuana or other psychoactive drugs (Kandel, 1973). By high school age, the number of friends who smoke marijuana is the single best predictor of whether an adolescent will begin to use it (Oetting & Beauvais, 1987).

Interim Summary

Adolescents confront new challenges in personal and social development. One of these is what Erik Erikson refers to as establishing an identity. Erikson believed that the sudden biological changes of puberty and the formation of new heterosexual relationships create the need for a redefined sense of self. Erikson suggested that most adolescents successfully establish an identity. Those who are not successful experience role confusion.

SEXUALITY IN ADOLESCENCE

During adolescence, we develop the capacity for sexual behavior. We learn not only how to be sexual but also with whom we prefer to have sexual relationships. Learning our sexual orientation is one of the principal accomplishments of adolescence. For many adolescents this is clear from the outset. But an estimated 10 percent of adolescents experience some uncertainty about their sexual orientation throughout the teenage years (Gordun & Gilgun, 1987).

Although the great majority of adolescents are heterosexual, homosexual behavior is not uncommon, particularly among young teens. Approximately 14 percent of boys and 11 percent of girls report some homosexual experience before age 15. But much of this may be experimental rather than a sign of a lasting homosexual orientation. Among adult males, for example, only 4 percent profess to be exclusively homosexual (Rosenhan & Seligman, 1984).

What of heterosexual activity among adolescents? Large-scale studies reveal two important trends. First, sexual intercourse among teenagers is increasing quite rapidly, particularly since the 1970s. Second, the increase is more pronounced for girls than boys. Why? The most obvious answer is a gradual reversal of the sexual double standard. Historically, boys were freer to engage in sexual intercourse. Estimates from the 1940s to the 1960s suggest that between one third and two thirds of adolescent males were sexually active (Hofferth & Hayes, 1987). During roughly the same time period, only 10 percent of adolescent girls engaged in sexual intercourse (Dreyer, 1982). But over the past 30 years teenage girls have become much more sexually active. A recent national survey found that 60 percent of both boys and girls engaged in sexual intercourse by age 19 (Hofferth & Hayes, 1987).

What are these early sexual experiences like? Many teenagers do not plan to have intercourse. Often they feel that sex is something that happened to them, not something they chose to do (Brooks-Gunn & Furstenberg, 1989). Perhaps this is one reason why a sizable percentage of teenagers have negative feelings about sexual experiences, particularly their first. Only 25 percent of teenage girls report feeling excited about their first act of intercourse, and 63 percent said they were afraid. Although only 17 percent of boys experienced fear, less than 50 percent said they were excited about their first sexual encounter (Sorenson, 1973).

TEENAGE PREGNANCY

For most teenagers, one of the unintended consequences of sexual intercourse is the risk of pregnancy. In the United States alone, approximately 10 percent of teenage girls—more than 1 million in total—become pregnant each year. Thousands of adolescent girls face the difficult choice of terminating their pregnancies or giving birth with little in the way of emotional or financial support. For roughly 40 percent, some 400,000 teens altogether, pregnancy ends in abortion (Hayes, 1987).

Many of the teen pregnancies that occur each year are unwanted and cause tremendous hardship for those involved.

For teens who give birth, there is often a difficult road ahead. Teenage mothers are more likely to leave school early and to experience difficulty finding adequate employment than women of similar economic backgrounds who delay childbirth (Furstenberg, Brooks-Gunn, & Chase-Lindale, 1989). Often facing parenthood before they are emotionally prepared and without the support of a spouse, these young mothers are also likely to encounter problems in early parent-child relationships (Morrison, 1985). But on the plus side of a very difficult situation, we should note that researchers find a certain degree of resilience among teenage mothers. Later in life many show the capacity to recover both emotionally and economically (Furstenburg et al, 1989).

SEXUAL PRACTICES AND AIDS

At first glance, the frequency of teenage pregnancy is perplexing because contraceptives are more available than ever before. Why do adolescents, both boys and girls, fail to use them? Teenagers are sometimes remarkably unaware of how conception occurs. Many simply do not understand that pregnancy is related to sexual intercourse and a woman's menstrual cycle. Not surprisingly, then, abortion rates are lower in societies that provide information and access to contraceptive devices. In the United States, where there is less general acceptance of sex education, the abortion rate is higher than the *combined* rate of Canada, England, Wales, Sweden, and the Netherlands, all countries that provide systematic education about birth control and ready access to contraceptive devices (Gordon & Gilgun, 1987).

When adolescents do not have good information, they tend to engage in sexual practices that can lead directly to pregnancy. They may practice birth control infrequently or not at all, or seek the counsel of peers, who often provide incorrect information (Zelnick & Cantor, 1980). Parents offer much more reliable information about pregnancy, but most adolescents do not learn about sex from their parents. When parents are the primary source of information, however, investigators find that adolescents both use contraceptives more consistently and postpone sexual intercourse until a later age (Fox, 1981).

Unprotected sex has always involved the risk of pregnancy, but we now know that it can also lead to AIDS, the life-threatening immune disorder for which there is no known cure. Has the threat of AIDS changed the sexual practices of adolescents? So far, adolescents have shown few signs of practicing "safe sex" on a large scale (Carroll, 1988). Unfortunately, this has led experts to predict that this deadly disease will become an even greater threat as today's adolescents become young adults (Gardner, Millstein, & Wilcox, 1991). As with other aspects of adolescent sexuality, sound education may be the best hope for an effective solution.

Interim Summary

Today's adolescents are increasingly sexually active. While the great majority are heterosexual, homosexual experiences are not uncommon, particularly among young adolescents. Among heterosexuals, the largest change over the past 50 years is the number of adolescent girls who have become sexually active.

One frequent consequence of adolescent sexual activity is teenage pregnancy. Teenage mothers face a range of difficult problems, including interruption of their education and limited financial support. Although they may recover later in life, most experience considerable difficulty in adjusting to the demands of parenting.

Teenage pregnancy is most likely to occur in societies that afford little in the way of sex education and provide only limited access to contraceptives. In those societies, adolescents are also more likely to ask peers how to prevent pregnancy, and peers are often a very unreliable source of information.

Unprotected sex also exposes adolescents to the risk of AIDS, a life-threatening disease for which there is no known cure. So far, there is little evidence that the threat of AIDS has led adolescents to change their sexual practices.

• •

ADULTHOOD

It is difficult to pinpoint precisely when adulthood begins. Most experts speak of age 20 as the approximate starting point, but age alone is an imperfect landmark. Rather, the transition from adolescence to adulthood is defined by important psychological events. Two well-known theorists, Freud and Erikson, chose similar psychological criteria when characterizing the adult personality. To Freud, an **adult** was someone who could assume the responsibility of daily work and committed love. Erikson (1963) spoke of *intimacy* and *generativity* in defining adulthood, by which he meant something very close to the capacity for work and love. It is possible, of course, to choose other criteria, but most experts would agree with the psychological focus on adulthood as a period of maturity and responsibility in the vital areas of work and love.

Physical Development

In the young adult years, we reach the peak of our physical abilities. Strength, coordination, agility, and speed all peak before age 30. In most sports, athletes attain their maximum levels of skill and efficiency during their 20s. Unless illness intervenes, we are at the height of our physical health and endurance in early adulthood (Hershey, 1974).

While the peak of physical health occurs before age 30, declines from the peak are usually gradual. Most people experience only a slow decline until age 50, when physical changes become sharper and more easily perceived (Troll, 1975). Furthermore, we now know that personal fitness (diet, exercise) can help sustain physical vigor throughout the adult years, providing each of us with some measure of control over our body's response to growing older.

Nonetheless, eventually we all experience at least some of the telltale signs of ag-

Physical strength, coordination, agility, and speed all peak in the young adult years.

ing—graying hair, wrinkled skin, unflattering weight gains, and loss of physical stamina. How people react to these signs of aging is apparently due in part to their sense of self. One investigator found that people who derive their self-worth primarily from the condition of their bodies (such as models, athletes, and dancers) tend to *feel* old as soon as their physical attributes begin to decline. On the other hand, people who take pride in nonphysical attributes, such as intelligence or wit, tend to feel young and vigorous long after their bodies have lost their youthful appearance (Bühler, 1972).

Changes in physical appearance are but one sign that the body is growing older. For women, **menopause,** or the cessation of the menstrual cycle, is a more definitive sign. Menopause is a rather abrupt physiological change, brought on by a reduction in the hormone estrogen, that renders women infertile and is sometimes accompanied by such physical symptoms as hot flashes and sweating. There is no direct parallel to menopause in men. Men do experience a gradual decline in sperm production, but this does not make them infertile, nor is it accompanied by any physical symptoms.

Although menopause has achieved wide-spread recognition as a period of great emotional difficulty for women, research has shown that the psychological consequences of menopause are actually quite variable. Although some women experience emotional problems such as anxiety, irritability, or depression, statistics do not support the cultural stereotype of menopause as a universal time of great upheaval. Roughly 60 percent of middle-aged women experience hot flashes—sudden feelings of heat throughout the body followed by chills. However, this *physical* symptom is the most common experience among women who report difficulties with menopause. Roughly one in five women encounters no menopausal symptoms at all (Paschkis, Rakoff, Cantarow, & Rupp, 1967). In general, menopause does not seem to create significant emotional problems for women, nor does it lead to a significant decline in sexual desire (Newman, 1982).

Cognitive Development

We hear little about cognition during the adult years. While it is commonplace to read about dramatic advances in cognitive development during infancy and childhood, you would probably be hard-pressed to recall the last time you read about progress in learning, memory, and language among adults. Is this because there is no progress? Do we merely "hold on" during the adult years, trying to fend off the inevitable decline in cognition? Or is adulthood simply a forgotten period in the development of reasoning and problem solving?

Problem Solving

Contrary to popular belief, adulthood appears to be a time when existing cognitive skills are consolidated and sharpened. In contrast to adolescence, when personal and social concerns sometimes cloud cognitive judgments, adulthood is typically a period when abstract thought and rational thinking dominate. Metacognitive skills—the ability to monitor and evaluate one's thinking and reasoning—actually improve in adulthood (Newman & Newman, 1983). The capacity to plan, evaluate, and be reflective may well peak in adulthood.

Learning and Memory

Judgment and reasoning may excel during adulthood, but what about new learning? Do adults maintain the capacity to acquire novel information? Throughout most of the adult years, there appears to be little decrement in learning. Even when the material is not particularly relevant, such as learning the association between nonsense syllables, adult subjects perform well. However, elderly subjects, in their sixth and seventh decades, do show some declines when the material becomes more difficult (Botwick & Storandt, 1974). The elderly are also likely to demonstrate a lower level of abstraction in a game such as 20 Questions (Denney, 1980). But these "negative" findings may be due in part to greater caution and anxiety among older subjects, particularly when they are asked to deal with laboratory-type problems. In any event, we should recognize that as people grow older, they do not experience a general decline in the ability to learn new material (Schaie & Willis, 1986).

Memory follows a similar course. There is no overall decline in memory during the adult years, but as you know from Chapter 7, memory is a complex process. There are different types of memories, such as short-term and long-term memory, and different ways to measure what people remember. One such distinction is between *recall* and *recognition*. For example, if you were to take the next 5 minutes to write down the names of people in your high school graduating class, you would be engaged in a recall test. Alternatively, if you were to look at a large number of pictures of 18-year-olds, some of whom were members of your graduating class, and then try to determine which people actually were in your class, you would be engaged in a recognition test. Why is this distinction important? Some investigators have found that while there is little change in recognition memory during adulthood, recall memory declines in the later adult years (Bahrick, Bahrick, & Wittlinger, 1975).

But this generalization also needs qualification. Memory decline is neither pervasive nor incapacitating during adulthood. In fact, memory loss usually occurs on experimental, laboratory tasks that are not directly related to everyday life (Waddell & Rogoff, 1981). Memory loss does not impair either personal or professional responsibilities during the adult years.

Interim Summary

There is no precise agreement on when adulthood begins. Psychological criteria for defining adulthood are maturity and responsibility in the areas of work and love.

People reach the peak of their strength, health, and endurance in the young adult years before age 30, and declines from the peak are gradual until around age 50. During middle age women experience menopause, or cessation of the menstrual cycle. There is no direct parallel to menopause in men, although men do experience a gradual reduction in sperm productivity.

During adulthood cognitive skills, including the ability to plan, evaluate, and reflect on one's own thinking and reasoning, are consolidated and sharpened. Throughout most of the adult years there is no general decline in the ability to learn new material or in memory. The elderly may show some declines in these areas, but most of these findings are based on studies that involve laboratory tasks that may not be related directly to everyday life.

Social and Personal Development

We noted earlier that psychologists believe the adult years are characterized by two consuming interests: work and love. During adulthood, people make important decisions about jobs and careers, whether to marry, and what type of family life is most satisfying. These are not trivial choices. Most people spend the better part of their adult years dealing with these basic issues.

MARRIAGE AND FAMILY LIFE

Perhaps the most important lifestyle decision of adulthood is whether to marry. Although we often hear that marriage is on the decline, surveys show that by age 35 nearly 95 percent of adults have married at least once (Bureau of the Census, 1982). Furthermore, among those who marry and divorce, remarriage remains a popular choice. Marriage is a very compelling option for most adults.

How do people choose a marriage partner? The decision is a complex one. It appears to evolve as people pass through a series of stages during which they progressively narrow a potential group of mates (Lewis, 1973; Udry, 1971). This is sometimes known as a "filtering" process. **Figure 10.2** on page 376 shows some of the potential steps in mate selection according to the filter theory.

As Figure 10.2 indicates, mate selection is a combination of practical and personal decisions. To begin with, people who marry are

Research shows that most couples who want children begin their family shortly after marriage.

Figure 10.2
The Filter Theory
of Mate Selection.
(After Udry, 1971)

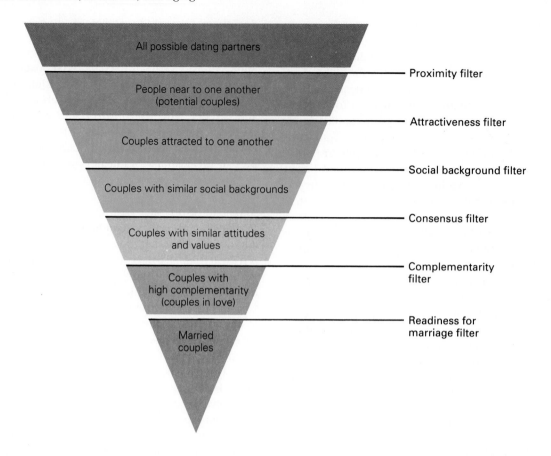

very likely to have lived near each other for a considerable period of their lives (Udry, 1971). Extended long-distance relationships are difficult to maintain. Beyond simple proximity, a number of factors determine whether we view someone as attractive. The height, weight, and facial and bodily features of a potential mate are all important. Somewhat surprisingly, age is an exceedingly strong factor in the choice of a marriage partner (Carter & Glick, 1976). In the United States, implicit age norms define an "acceptable" mate. Few young men, for example, will consider marrying women who are more than 3 years their senior (Blood, 1972). Finally, a group of social and personal factors help us screen potential mates. People who marry are usually quite similar in political and religious beliefs. They are almost universally members of the same social class; that is, they are alike in educational background and their parents are from similar occupational and economic levels (Udry, 1971). Marriage partners are very likely to share similar hobbies and interests. These are the activities that initially bring people together and later sustain a marriage

(Murstein, 1972a; Udry, 1971). The old adage that "opposites attract" does not turn out to be true.

Most couples begin a family shortly after marriage. This may seem surprising because of frequent references in the popular press to childless couples, but surveys show that the vast majority of couples want children and want them early in their marriage (Veevers, 1973). After just 2 years of marriage, two thirds of American women have given birth to their first child (Hill, Foote, Aldous, Carlson, & McDonald, 1970).

How can we characterize family life? No simple formula applies. There is really no such thing as a typical family. The "traditional" two-parent family (children living with their married parents) does exist, but only about 63 percent of families fit this configuration. The rest are divided among divorced couples and their children (roughly 22 percent), remarriages involving one stepparent (10 percent), and families headed by adoptive parents, grandparents, and nonrelatives—roughly 5 percent (Committee on Children, Youth, and Families, 1983).

Perhaps even more impressive is the changing nature of families. The birth of a child, for example, changes the structure of a family. Research has shown that becoming a parent alters the marital relationship in dramatic fashion. Marital satisfaction may actually decline as parents confront the reality that childrearing is a time-consuming and exhausting task (Rollins & Galligan, 1978). However, children are not simply a burden. They are often cited as one of the major sources of satisfaction in a marriage (Luckey & Bain, 1970). Furthermore, as children grow older the intensity of childrearing tends to diminish, leaving more time for couples to be involved with each other (Udry, 1971).

As children grow older, the family structure continues to change. One very significant development occurs when children leave home and parents are confronted with an "empty nest." Contrary to popular opinion, psychologists have discovered that the transition to a life without children is generally pleasant and uneventful. Although parents sometimes miss the day-to-day contact with their children, they do *not* miss the responsibilities and daily chores associated with childrearing (Neugarten, 1968). Women are often pleasantly surprised at the decrease in their daily work, but men also adapt well to the change in family structure. Greater personal freedom and a lessening of financial and childrearing responsibilities seem to outweigh the loss of daily contact with children (Deutscher, 1968). A number of studies show a pattern of expressed marital satisfaction similar to the one presented in **Figure 10.3**. Note that satisfaction with marriage reaches its lowest point just before children leave home. After this point, most couples experience a steady increase in marital satisfaction (Rollins & Feldman, 1970).

JOBS AND CAREERS

Work is a significant dimension of adult life. Adults work for a variety of reasons; income, personal satisfaction, and opportunity for social advancement are among the most common. But what people value in their work depends very much on the type of job they hold. Although income consistently surfaces as one of the most important characteristics of a job, it is more highly valued among people who hold low-status positions. Research has consistently shown that the lower people are in the occupational hierarchy, the more they value income

Many couples experience a steady growth in marital satisfaction after their children leave home.

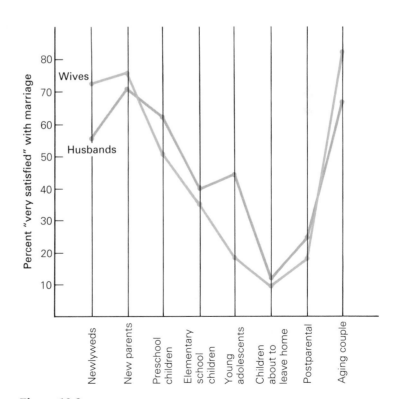

Figure 10.3
Marital Satisfaction in Various Stages in Family Life. (After Rollins & Feldman, 1970)

Psychology in the News

SURVEY: REPORTS OF MEN'S ROLE IN HOUSEHOLD 'EXAGGERATED'

Depite changes in the work force, wives spend much more time taking care of household duties than their husbands, even when both hold full-time jobs, a survey shows.

Work/Family Directions, a Boston-based consulting company collected the data from 60,000 employees at 15 major companies between 1986 and 1991.

"Women continue to bear an unequal burden when it comes to household and child care responsibilities," Charles Rodgers, the company's chief researcher, said Tuesday.

"Men are feeling the conflict between their careers and their families more than ever, but their behavior has not yet changed appreciably," he said.

Rodgers said the report's data shows that wives spend nearly twice as many hours per week on child care and household duties as do their husbands, even when both work full-time outside the home.

The average working mother spends 44 hours at work and 31 hours on family responsibilities each week, he said. In comparison, her spouse spends 47 hours weekly on the job and 15 on child care and household tasks.

The study indicated that many couples equally divided domestic responsibilities early in their relationships. But once children enter the picture, the wife carries a greater share of the burden, Rodgers said.

In addition, nearly two-thirds of the professional and executive men with young children also had a wife who was a full-time homemaker.

"Virtually no professional women have a similar situation," Rodgers said.

Those time constraints illustrate why women consider control over their working hours so important, he said.

"Working women simply can't compete on a level playing field with men at the workplace when a key requirement is physical presence for longer and longer hours," he said.

"Survey: Reports of men's role in household 'exaggerated.'" Reprinted by permission of Associated Press.

Questions

1. Applied to gender roles, what principles of social learning theory are illustrated in this study?
2. Why should couples change the allocation of domestic responsibilities after they have children? What does this tell us about gender roles?
3. What are the broadest implications for society if household responsibilities are not shared equally among working couples?

---

and job security (Crites, 1969; Kornhauser & Reid, 1965).

An equally important dimension of job satisfaction is the age of the worker. Older people are considerably more satisfied with their jobs than are younger workers. In one study, roughly 75 percent of the workers under 21 expressed satisfaction with their work, but 84 percent of those in their 20s and better than 90 percent of those over 30 expressed similar feelings (Troll, 1975). One possible explanation for these findings is the greater vulnerability of the older worker to unemployment. Young adults are active and mobile members of the work force, but older people experience greater difficulty finding new employment commensurate with their training and education. Workers who are unemployed at any age beyond the young adulthood period can anticipate fewer referrals to new employers and less success in securing a job than their similarly qualified but younger counterparts (Troll, 1975).

How stable are jobs today? Although people change jobs more frequently today than in the past, radical changes become less likely as workers grow older. Most middle-aged adults prefer to remain with the same employer unless their income is insufficient (Troll, 1975).

Older workers tend to be more satisfied with their jobs than younger workers.

One reason for this is that in North America middle-aged workers are becoming increasingly concerned with the personal benefits that accompany their job. White-collar workers, for example, are showing a reluctance to accept promotions that force a relocation of their family. They are no longer willing to make any personal sacrifice for promotion to a higher job (Beckhard, 1977; Van Maanen, 1977).

Apart from the dimensions of work that produce job satisfaction, psychologists have inquired about the variables that influence job selection. Although little is known about why young adults choose a particular firm or industry for their first job, responses to vocational-interest tests provide some clues about who is likely to be most successful in a particular job. A vocational-interest test is a measure of the activities that a person likes or dislikes. Typically, the test consists of several hundred statements describing a wide range of activities—for example, everything from writing a book on economics to freshwater fishing. The respondent must indicate whether he or she likes, dislikes, or is indifferent about the activity described in each statement. From this pattern of responses, a profile is drawn of the individual's work preferences.

Two of the best-known vocational-interest tests are the *Kuder Preference Test* and the *Strong-Campbell Interest Inventory*. These tests are quite successful in predicting who will be happy and productive in a particular job. For example, research has shown that if workers are divided into two groups, those who stay with their jobs and those who leave, the latter group tends to score lower on the Strong-Campbell Inventory for the particular occupa-

tion involved. Furthermore, the occupation of those who decide to change jobs is easily predicted from the original scores on the Strong-Campbell Inventory (Mussen, Conger, Kagan, & Geiwitz, 1979).

Interim Summary

One important decision of adulthood is whether to marry. Research on the selection of a marriage partner has demonstrated the utility of a filter model, in which people progressively narrow a large group of prospective mates. Important factors in the process are the proximity and age of the partner, the perceived physical attractiveness of this person, and his or her social background.

Most couples begin a family soon after marriage. The arrival of a first child increases the level of stress within the family, but parents also report that children are one of the major sources of satisfaction in a marriage.

Work is a significant aspect of adult life. Psychologists have developed several vocational-interest tests that accurately predict whether a person will be happy and productive in a particular job. Dimensions of job satisfaction include income, security, and opportunity for advancement. Income and security are more highly valued by those who are lower in the occupational hierarchy. Young adults may change jobs frequently, but older workers prefer to remain with the same employer as long as their income is sufficient.

THE LATER YEARS

At one time, living beyond age 65 was a rare occurrence. In 1790, only 2 percent of the United States population was 65 or older. By 1900, this group had increased to only 4 percent. But in 1981, 25 million people, fully 11 percent of the population, were 65 or over. Yet this was only the beginning of a phenomenal growth in the elderly population. In less than 50 years, by the year 2030, roughly 20 percent of the United States population will be 65 or older (Kalish, 1982).

It is important to understand that what has increased the survival rate of the over-65 population is not dramatic new advances in genetic engineering but rather a gradual victory over the illnesses that imperil a long life. As the incidence of heart attacks, strokes, cancer, and other life-threatening diseases declines, a greater percentage of the population will live to old age. And as an ever-increasing number of people join the ranks of the elderly, psychologists are asking what life is like in the "golden years." What are the rewards and challenges of old age?

Physical Development

There is no question that the body shows signs of weakening in old age. Bones become softer and more susceptible to fracture, coronary arteries narrow, blood pressure increases, kidney function and lung function decrease, and the digestive system is disrupted by gradual deterioration of the intestinal tract (Garn, 1975; Rockstein, 1975). Yet, many old people are in good health and lead active and vigorous lives. How can this be?

The answer seems to lie in understanding the great variability of old age. We noted earlier that the elderly, contrary to popular stereotype, are a very heterogeneous group. Health is one excellent example. Although chronic illness limits the daily activity of approximately half of the over-65 population, the remaining half is in generally good health (Hendricks & Hendricks, 1975). Many of these people enjoy a full and active life. Even though their visual acuity, strength, and stamina have decreased from the peak years of early adulthood, they are able to maintain a daily regimen of exercise and activi-

People in their late adulthood can often remain active. This 68-year-old woman is demonstrating her martial arts skills.

ty. Furthermore, the elderly are actually *less* likely to suffer from short-term illnesses, such as colds and influenza, giving them even more freedom to enjoy their leisure time (Palmore, 1981).

Can we predict which of the elderly will maintain good health and a positive outlook on life? This is a complicated problem with many unknowns. Genetic influences undoubtedly play a role. So too does lifestyle. There is growing evidence that people who work to maintain their physical and mental health throughout the early and middle adult years are likely to retain their good health and emotional well-being in old age (Perlmutter & Hall, 1985). The adage "use it or lose it" seems to apply aptly to the process of healthy aging.

Cognitive Development

What happens to the intellect in old age? Virtually everyone has an opinion. Many people, particularly the young, believe that older adults suffer some loss in their intellectual abilities. After all, the elderly appear to be physically less fit. Some are noticeably slower on motor tasks, such as driving a car or just walking down the street. Doesn't it follow that the mind would be less nimble in old age?

Not really. As we have seen over and over again, the human intellect is very complex and defies simple characterization. For example, the elderly do show some decline, particularly beyond the age of 70, on tasks that measure perceptual-motor speed and coordination (Woodruff, 1983). But this is only one way to gauge the strength of the intellect. Equally important are the verbal and reasoning skills that people acquire throughout life. Here the elderly are quite impressive. Assuming good health and freedom from debilitating illness, older adults retain their verbal and reasoning skills well into their eighth decade (Horn, 1982).

Much of what we know about cognition in old age comes from an analysis of intelligence tests. Initially, psychologists used the *cross-sectional method* to measure changes in intelligence across the years. This involved administering intelligence tests to people of different ages at the same point in time (see **Figure 10.4**). As Figure 10.4 demonstrates, this method revealed a steady decline in intelligence from age 50 onward. The conclusion from such studies seemed obvious: mental abilities lessen as we grow older.

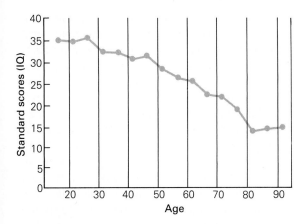

Figure 10.4
Pattern of IQ Scores Using the Cross-Sectional Method.
Note the progressive decline in scores from age 30
onward.

In science, however, everything depends on methodology. And in this case, the cross-sectional method is problematic. Although it allows the investigator to compare different age groups, it overlooks the fact that people born many years apart have dramatically different life experiences. For example, if we compare a 20-year-old to an 80-year-old, we are comparing people who grew up in two vastly different eras. The 20-year-old has the benefit of educational and cultural opportunities that the 80-year-old never dreamed of. If we then compare the two on an intelligence test, we must acknowledge that we are measuring more than a difference in age. In a very real sense, we are testing the effects of changes in education and cultural learning that have taken place over the past 60 years. It should come as no surprise if older subjects do not perform as well as younger subjects.

Older adults do not necessarily suffer a loss in their intellectual capabilities.

How, then, do we assess changes in intelligence across the years? The solution is to measure the same subjects over an extended period of time (the *longitudinal* method). Such a procedure allows the investigator to determine whether individuals actually decline in intelligence as they grow older. This is precisely what one group of investigators did when they began an intriguing study in the late 1950s. In actuality, this study *compared* two methods, by measuring the IQ scores of one group of subjects cross-sectionally and the scores of another group longitudinally. The cross-sectional method produced the expected results (see **Figure 10.5**). People showed a decline in IQ scores beginning at roughly age 50. However, as Figure 10.5 demonstrates, the longitudinal method yields a very different result. Using this type of analysis, investigators found that people maintained their intellectual abilities well into their 70s (Schaie & Labouvie-Vief, 1974). The idea that we decline in intellectual ability as we grow older appears to be a myth born of a particular method.

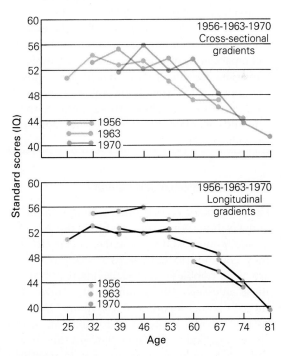

Figure 10.5
Contrasting Patterns of IQ Scores.
Note that the cross-sectional method reveals a declining pattern beginning at roughly age 30. The longitudinal method demonstrates that people maintain, or even increase, their IQ scores well into their seventh decade.
(Adapted from Schail & LaBouvie-Vief, 1974)

In short, the intellectual skills of the elderly typically do not diminish appreciably. Verbal skills, in particular, seem to hold well into the seventh decade. Although some perceptual-motor abilities begin to decline after age 60, few people will even notice the slippage. Often it takes precise, laboratory testing to reveal these deficits. Moreover, older adults may well possess an untapped form of intelligence—what one investigator called "wisdom." A test of wisdom would measure judgment, expertise, and insight and might well reveal an advantage for older adults (Baltes, 1983). Perhaps we can be "young of mind" as well as young of heart.

Interim Summary

The proportion of the elderly in the population is increasing as scientific and medical advances achieve victories over life-threatening illnesses. Although visual acuity, strength, and endurance decline from the peaks of early adulthood, healthy aging is not impossible. Many elderly people, especially those who have worked to maintain physical and mental health throughout adulthood, enjoy an active and vigorous life.

A common stereotype is that the elderly experience a decline in cognitive skills comparable to the decline in their physical abilities. Recent studies, particularly those employing the longitudinal method, do not support this idea. These studies indicate that people maintain their intellectual abilities well into their 70s.

Social and Personal Development

Life in the later years is often a favorite topic of conversation. What can the elderly do? Are older adults interested in an active social life? Do they continue to have sexual relations? What are their hobbies and special interests? All of these questions are genuine, of course, but they do reflect a particular viewpoint. Many of us have grown accustomed to thinking of old age as a period of gentle decline—a time when the elderly gradually lose interest in everyday activities. Research on old age, however, presents a different picture.

LIFE SATISFACTION
If there is a generalization to be made about old age, it is contrary to what most people would predict. The later years often represent the peak of personal happiness. For example, recall the data on marital satisfaction (Figure 10.3), which showed that couples are most content during old age. More direct evidence comes from surveys comparing personal happiness during different periods of the life span. Investigators consistently find higher levels of happiness and contentment among the elderly than among adolescents and younger adults (Herzog, Rogers, & Woodworth, 1982). Richard Kalish, an expert on late adult development, has suggested that personal happiness may be high because old age brings many hidden advantages. Among these are an increase in leisure time, a reduction in many day-to-day responsibilities, and the ability to pay attention only to matters of high priority (Kalish, 1982). This latter attitude may not be immediately obvious, but research has shown that older people respond to the reality of a finite future by ignoring many of the inconsequential details of life. They focus their energy on matters of true importance (Kalish, 1979).

It may seem surprising to speak of the advantages of old age, but only because all of us—psychologists and laypeople alike—have implicitly accepted the notion that aging is burdensome. The early models of old age were strikingly negative (Kalish, 1982). Experts tended to view old age as a time of loss—a period when health, awareness, intelligence, and vitality slowly ebbed away. But this notion of inevitable decline, known as the *decrement model* of old age, has not been confirmed in research with the elderly. Psychologists have therefore substituted a *personal-growth model* that stresses the potential of the old-age period. The later years can be a time of great personal development, even in the face of debilitating losses, such as the death of a spouse or loved one. Or old age can be a time of loneliness and withdrawal from the outside world. The personal-growth model stresses the open-ended quality of old age.

In old age, the single greatest threat to personal happiness is ill health. Although illness, particularly chronic illness, can occur at any point in the life span, it is a more acute problem for the elderly. We noted earlier that a sizable percentage of older adults endure some limitation in daily activity due to physical problems. Because restrictions on what people can do often contribute to feelings of unhappiness, health becomes a particularly important predictor of personal development during old age.

Apart from health, what factors influence personal adjustment in old age? Research has shown that the elderly have a strong tendency to focus on their inner lives (Neugarten, 1977). In the process of reviewing life's accomplishments, some people accept their past as a worthy and meaningful experience. They view their life with pride and look forward with optimism to the future. A sense of a productive and fruitful life contributes to positive personal adjustment in old age (Erikson, 1963).

Effective use of leisure time is also important. Most elderly people have retired from full-time employment. Beyond age 65, only 20 percent of men and 6.5 percent of women are likely to continue working (Kalish, 1982). This increase in leisure time following retirement is one of the major benefits of old age. People are free to pursue favorite activities or to take up new interests. Today the elderly are enjoying many different activities, including enrolling in college courses to study new subjects (Ingalls, 1980).

FAMILY LIFE

The relationship between husband and wife is a vital dimension of family life in old age. Because children leave the household and friends either move away or die, the spouse often becomes the single greatest source of support and friendship. This does not mean, however, that those without a spouse inevitably experience loneliness. Roughly 5 percent of the population over age 65 has never married, but research has demonstrated that these people are not particularly lonely or unhappy (Troll, 1975). They have apparently grown so accustomed to living on their own that old age poses no special problem. Furthermore, a small but not insignificant number of people marry for the first time in old age. In one annual period, nearly 3000 people began their first marriage after age 65 (Kalish, 1982).

A final dimension of family life in old age is the relationships the elderly have with their children and grandchildren. Approximately 80 percent of the elderly have children who are living, and some 75 percent have grandchildren (Harris et al., 1975). As we noted earlier, most children continue to maintain contact with their parents even after leaving home. In general, the relationship between the elderly and their full-grown children is positive. Most children upon reaching adulthood provide emotional and, if needed, financial support for their elderly parents (Kalish, 1982).

Grandparents tend to enjoy younger children more than older children.

Elderly people enjoy the role of grandparenting, though perhaps not quite so much as we might think. The great majority of elderly couples enjoy visits with their grandchildren, but they want these contacts to be relatively brief (Troll, 1971). Extended time with grandchildren can be burdensome for many older couples. Furthermore, the age of the grandchild is an important element in the older person's enjoyment of the visit. Grandparents tend to enjoy younger children much more than older children or adolescents (Kahana & Coe, 1969).

Interim Summary

The elderly often report greater feelings of happiness and contentment than young adults or adolescents, perhaps because older people have increased leisure time, reduced day-to-day responsibilities, and the ability to pay attention only to matters of high priority. Good health, a sense of pride in one's accomplishments, and effective use of leisure time are factors that contribute to satisfaction in the later years.

Family life takes on new dimensions in old age. The elderly usually have contact with their own children and their grandchildren. Psychologists have found that most older people enjoy brief but not extended time with grandchildren.

Challenges of Aging

The later years can be both rewarding and productive. But as the personal-growth model suggests, there are special challenges to happiness during old age. In this section, we examine three challenges that confront the elderly.

HEALTH

We noted earlier that good health cannot be taken for granted in old age. The human body is remarkable for its adaptability and endurance, but it does show signs of weakening in old age. The elderly are more susceptible to serious bone fractures, such as a broken hip, and accidents caused by diminished eyesight, such as a stairway fall. Partial hearing loss and reduced stamina are also quite common in old age (Hendricks & Hendricks, 1975).

Nevertheless, ill health is not the inevitable consequence of growing old. To the contrary, the elderly are quite capable of maintaining good health, and many do. *On average, it is a greater challenge for older people to remain healthy, but one that many elderly meet* (Rowe & Kahn, 1987). Less than 5 percent of the over-65 population requires nursing home care, and among those who live to 65, life expectancy rises to nearly 80 for males and even longer for females (Rockstein, 1975). Good health in old age is a goal that can be achieved.

DEMENTIA

A common worry for many people in our society is the fear of becoming a "burden" during old age. While some people fear a debilitating physical illness, others worry about "losing their mind." They fear that old age will bring an inevitable decline in mental abilities. In psychological terms, we would say they are concerned about dementia.

Psychological tests are often used to help diagnose Alzheimer's disease. In this instance, an Alzheimer's patient is taking a test of visuospatial abilities.

Dementia is a psychological disorder characterized by impairment of abstract thinking, memory, and judgment. It may be accompanied by confusion and disorientation. Dementia can occur at any time in adulthood, but it is most likely to appear after age 65. About 5 percent of the over-65 population suffers from some form of dementia (Hyman, Damasio, Damasio, & Van Hoesin, 1989).

For years, *senility* was the word used to describe the condition we now call dementia. But the term *senility* had unwanted consequences. It implied that as people grow older, they become forgetful, confused, and intellectually impaired as a matter of course. This is simply untrue. Dementia is not part of the normal aging process. It is the outcome of a variety of specific diseases that disturb brain chemistry. Chief among these is Alzheimer's disease, but on occasion chronic alcoholism and strokes can also cause dementia. Dementia is not a naturally occurring process, but the result of an abnormal deterioration of the brain.

Alzheimer's disease is by far the most common cause of dementia, accounting for 50 to 70 percent of all cases. Alzheimer's disease is a progressive disorder that can begin as early as age 40 but typically does not appear before age 60. Although the course of the disease can vary from one person to another, it often begins with memory impairment, attentional problems, and deteriorating mathematical abilities. As the disease progresses, there is an ever-widening loss of mental abilities. Alzheimer's patients may have difficulty learning new skills or mastering tasks that require abstract reasoning. They often have difficulty finding the right word to express their thoughts. In the final stages of the disease, Alzheimer's patients may become confused and disoriented, show uncharacteristic bursts of anger, and suffer personality changes. Eventually, Alzheimer's victims are unable to meet their daily needs, and most die within 7 to 10 years of the onset of the disease (Heston & White, 1983).

If Alzheimer's disease, like other forms of dementia, is not inevitable, can we predict who will be afflicted? Unfortunately, we do not have a complete answer to the puzzle as yet. We know that Alzheimer's victims suffer from a particular form of brain disease, first identified by the German physician Alios Alzheimer in 1907. Typically, there is an unusual loss of cells in the frontal and temporal cortex and the hippocampus. Although no one is certain why

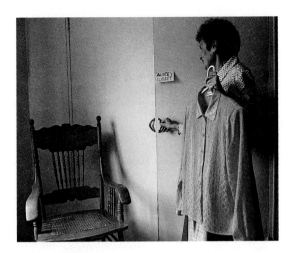

Victims of Alzheimer's may benefit from memory re-training programs in the early stages of the disease.

these cells die, some researchers have suggested that a virus, like those that cause influenza or the measles, might invade the nervous system. The virus might live within the nervous system for long periods of time and then become activated by changes in the internal environment. Other researchers have suggested that the cell death is related to changes in specific brain neurotransmitters. One neurotransmitter that has been implicated in Alzheimer's disease is acetylcholine, found in large quantities in the cerebral cortex (Corkin, Davis, Growdon, Usdin, & Wurtman, 1982). Postmortem (after death) analysis of the brains of Alzheimer's patients has revealed significant decreases in this transmitter. Another theory suggests that Alzheimer's disease is related to toxins, such as aluminum, invading the brain (Pendlebury, Beal, Kowall & Solomon, 1987). Still other theorists believe that the formation of abnormal proteins in the brain is the cause of the disease (Kowall, McKee, Yanker, & Beal, 1992.)

Although there is as yet no cure for Alzheimer's disease, there are many programs to help victims and their families. Adult Day Health Centers are one example. These centers, which provide a place for Alzheimer's patients to go during the day, bring some relief to the family from the habitual care required by Alzheimer's patients. They also offer special programs for the patients. For example, patients who are in the early stages of Alzheimer's disease may benefit from memory-retraining

programs. These programs use mnemonic devices and other memory aids much like those described in Chapter 6 (Wilson, 1987). Some centers offer programs in reality orientation. These programs help the more advanced Alzheimer's patients maintain an awareness of who they are and where they are. The centers also conduct support groups for the family. In these groups, family members meet to learn more about the disease and to share ideas on how best to care for the patient (Aaronson, Levin & Lipkowitz, 1984).

DEATH AND BEREAVEMENT

Confronting our own death and mourning the loss of loved ones are part of life. They are not unique to the elderly. However, due largely to the progress of modern medicine, people are living longer and healthier lives. And while research has shown that people are vulnerable to death at certain periods of life, such as infancy and middle age, the greatest vulnerability occurs in old age (Kalish, 1982).

The elderly seem to adjust to the prospect of their own death quite well. Interview studies have shown that although older people think about death more often than younger people, they have less fear of death (Kalish, 1979). Apparently, people work through some of their fears of death as they age. However, in old age many people must confront not only their own death but also the death of a spouse. In the United States, roughly 50 percent of women 65 years of age and older are widows and 15 percent of the men are widowers (Carter & Glick, 1976). The experience of confronting one's own death is not as well understood. Elisabeth Kubler-Ross, a former psychiatrist at the University of Chicago, provided one description by interviewing hundreds of terminally ill patients (Kubler-Ross, 1969). Although not all of these people were elderly, each knew of his or her impending death. Kubler-Ross observed five stages in the terminally ill patient's attitude toward death. The first stage is *denial*. The person wants to avoid what is happening. *Anger* follows denial, with questions such as, "Why is this happening to me?" As anger and resentment diminish, the *bargaining* stage emerges. The individual now accepts the reality of death but is anxious to have more time to enjoy life. Bargaining is followed by the fourth state, *depression,* in which the individual feels a tremendous loss in the face of his or her impending death. It is a time of profound grief and sorrow. This grieving prepares the way for the final stage, *acceptance* of death. The dying person achieves a "quiet victory" by facing death with neither happiness nor unhappiness. People recognize that their time "is very close now and it's all right" (Kubler-Ross, 1969).

It is important to understand both the strengths and limitations of Kubler-Ross' research, which had a major impact on health professionals who work with the terminally ill. Kubler-Ross managed to provide a supportive framework for understanding the highly charged emotions surrounding death. Nonetheless, psychologists have objected to the rather loose methodology that Kubler-Ross employed. She did not concern herself with the kind of systematic observation and statistical analysis that most researchers demand. Furthermore, Kubler-Ross' observations may apply only to those who face a prolonged illness. It is unlikely that they are a universal sequence that everyone experiences. Indeed, other investigators find somewhat different stages, though a period of denial is apparently common to many who face death (Schulz & Aderman, 1974; Shneidman, 1973). It is clear, however, that psychologists still have much to learn about variations in the attitude and behavior of those who face the immediate prospect of their own death.

Interim Summary

Although old age can be a time of great potential, the elderly face special challenges. The single greatest threat to happiness is ill health, but ill health is not an inevitable consequence of aging. Fear of decline in mental abilities, or dementia, is another frequent worry. Dementia occurs among about 5 percent of the elderly, with most suffering from Alzheimer's disease, a progressive disorder involving loss of mental abilities. Alzheimer's patients show loss of cells in the frontal and temporal cortex and the hippocampus regions of the brain, but the reason for the cell death is unknown.

A final challenge confronting the elderly is death, both the possibility of their own death and the death of loved ones. Elisabeth Kubler-Ross has provided one description of the attitudes of the terminally ill toward death. She outlines a five-stage process of de-nial, anger, bargaining, depression, and finally acceptance of death. Psychologists acknowledge the importance of Kubler-Ross' work, but not everyone agrees that these stages are universal.

SUMMARY

1. Adolescence is a culturally specific phenomenon that is observed most commonly in industrialized societies. It is usually defined as the period that begins with puberty and ends at approximately age 19. During this time, the size and shape of the body changes, and adolescents undergo the development of primary and secondary sex characteristics.

2. During adolescence, new and deeper intellectual skills and powers of moral reasoning appear. Two theorists, Jean Piaget and Lawrence Kohlberg, have detailed the changes in the adolescent's logical thinking and moral reasoning. Kohlberg proposed a link between the highest levels of moral reasoning and the more abstract intellectual skills that emerge during adolescence.

3. Erikson suggests that the adolescent's personal and social development is characterized by the search for identity, or the need to redefine one's sense of self in the face of the many changes that occur during the teenage years. He believes that those who fail to resolve the identity question experience role confusion.

4. Relationships between adolescents and their parents are often quite positive, with the exception of disagreements over matters of personal taste. In this area, adolescents are more likely to agree with and seek support from their peers.

5. A large percentage of contemporary adolescents are sexually active. One consequence of this is a rise in teenage pregnancies, often associated with interruption of education and limited financial resources to care for the offspring. A second consequence of teenage sexuality is the growing risk of contracting AIDS. To date the threat of AIDS has not prompted major changes in the sexual practices of adolescents.

6. Maturity and responsibility in the areas of work and love are the defining criteria of adulthood.

7. People reach the peak of their physical strength and endurance around age 30, but declines from this peak are very gradual until age 50. In the area of cognitive development, planning, consolidating ideas, and reflecting on one's thinking and reasoning skills all occur during adulthood. There is no general decline in memory or in the ability to learn new material during the later years of adulthood.

8. Marriage is a common lifestyle choice for many adults. Research on how people choose marital partners shows that a filter model, in which people progressively narrow a large group of prospective mates, generates good predictions about marital partners.

   Work is a significant aspect of adult life. Psychologists have developed several tests that help to predict whether a person will be happy and productive in a particular job. Investigators have also discovered what dimensions of a job contribute to a sense of job security.

9. Contrary to popular stereotypes, the elderly often report greater feelings of happiness and contentment than young adults or adolescents, provided that they remain in good health. The elderly often experience a change in family life as well, particularly in their role as grandparents. Research has shown that most grandparents enjoy brief visits with their grandchildren.

10. The single greatest threat to happiness in old age is poor health. Dementia, or a decline in mental abilities, is a common worry among the elderly, but it affects only about 5 percent of the old age population. Death is another challenge facing the elderly. Elisabeth Kubler-Ross has outlined a theory of how people accept their own death, though critics suggest that the stages offered in this theory may not be universal.

KEY INDIVIDUALS

Bernice Neugarten
Erik Erikson
G. Stanley Hall
James Marcia
Jean Piaget
Richard Kalish
Lawrence Kohlberg
Alios Alzheimer
Carol Gilligan
Elisabeth Kubler-Ross
Sigmund Freud

KEY RESEARCH

Piaget's theory of moral development
Kohlberg's stages of moral development
criticisms of Kohlberg's theory and methodology
eight stages of psychosocial development
status categories of the search for identity
a filter theory of mate selection
measurement of intelligence among the elderly
factors related to personal happiness in the later years
a five-stage model of dealing with death

KEY TERMS

adolescence
morality of cooperation
primary sex characteristics
role confusion
negative identity
secondary sex characteristics
adult development
moral realism
menopause
autonomous morality
dementia

11

Intelligence

ince the turn of the century, psychologists have been at the forefront of one of the most controversial human endeavors—the measurement of intelligence. At the heart of this often troubling issue are fundamental questions about scientific and human values. Should we attempt to compare one person to another on the ill-defined dimension known as intelligence? Do intelligence tests play any useful role in selecting people for positions in society? If so, how can we be assured that intelligence is measured objectively, and not according to the standards and values of one particular segment of society? In short, what assurance do we have that intelligence tests fairly and accurately assess the intellectual ability of people from all walks of life?

These questions, long the source of vigorous debate within the academic community, have taken on a renewed sense of urgency as a more pluralistic society questions the power and objectivity of intelligence tests. Two examples illustrate the point. One is a class action lawsuit filed on behalf of a group of black children whose parents believed that intelligence tests were responsible for assigning them unfairly to special education classes for the mentally retarded. A federal district court agreed with the parents, arguing that intelligence tests are both "racially and culturally biased," and subsequently upheld the decision on appeal (Opton, 1979; Landers, 1986). A second illustration of the controversy surrounding intelligence tests is a lively debate about the value of college entrance examinations (a variation on intelligence testing) in predicting academic achievement in college. The basic question, still hotly contested, is whether entrance exams provide an equitable assessment of the intellectual capabilities of all applicants, particularly women and minorities (Stewart, 1987).

These issues have important implications for the scientific study of intelligence. They also serve as a vivid reminder to psychologists that intelligence testing is a crucial public policy matter. If intelligence tests are going to play an important role in people's lives, the public wants assurances that the tests are fair and accurate. That is also the central question of this chapter, which we will explore by examining the nature and measurement of intelligence.

THE NATURE OF INTELLIGENCE

Although intelligence tests have existed for over 75 years, disagreement about the nature of intelligence persists. Why is this so? One problem is that people can behave intelligently in many different ways. Think for a moment about what intelligence means to you. As a student, you probably feel that academic excellence is a good measure of intelligence. But you may know people whom you regard as intelligent who were not particularly successful in school. The problem is only complicated further when we consider what different societies value as intelligent. In North America, we often think of intelligence in terms of verbal and quantitative abilities. But in certain African societies, intelligence means expert hunting, while Pacific Islanders think of intelligence as the ability to navigate the seas skillfully (Mussen, Conger, & Kagan, 1979).

Confronted with such diversity in what people regard as intelligent behavior, it is small wonder that psychologists have often failed to agree on a comprehensive definition. Years ago, the editors of the *Journal of Educational Psychology* invited 17 leading scholars to express their opinions on the nature of intelligence. Although they achieved some minimal agreement, in truth nearly 17 different definitions of intelligence emerged from this symposium (Thorndike et al., 1921). Some 60 years later, Robert Sternberg and Douglas Detterman

Many critics have challenged the accuracy of intelligence tests. They are concerned that such tests are biased toward the knowledge and values of particular segments of society and therefore not a fair measure for the overall population.

Thomas Edison was a poor student, yet he went on to make discoveries about the transmission of electricity that revolutionized the way we live. What does this say about the relationship between intelligence and school performance?

convened a different group of experts to consider the same question. Once again, diversity of opinion prevailed, though three general manifestations of intelligence were identified: intelligence within the individual, intelligence within the environment, and intelligence within the interaction between the individual and the environment (Sternberg & Detterman, 1986).

Is there any hope for a comprehensive definition of intelligence? Perhaps, but only if we take a very broad perspective. Many years ago David Wechsler, the author of several widely used intelligence tests, suggested that we define intelligence as *the capacity to act purposefully, to think rationally, and to deal effectively with the environment* (Wechsler, 1958). By this broad standard, people act intelligently when they learn from past experience, seek effective solutions to everyday problems, and adapt to the world around them.

But this hardly settles the issue and, in the view of some experts, only raises anew the question of values. Wechsler's key terms—coping, resourcefulness, and rationality—are often linked to skills such as reading, vocabulary building, and test taking. But as we noted earlier, many of the world's cultures do not share this emphasis on school-like abilities as indica-

tors of intelligence. Furthermore, even *within* cultures that tend to emphasize academic excellence, different circumstances demand different types of coping and resourcefulness. The demands placed on an ambitious college student are quite different from those placed on an unemployed teenager living in an impoverished urban environment. That is why the word *intelligence* always represents a value judgment (Wechsler, 1975). To call someone intelligent is to say that the individual possesses qualities that *you* believe are adaptive and resourceful.

With this overview in mind, we turn to the question of how intelligence is operationalized or measured. Since the turn of the century, psychologists have relied almost exclusively on one instrument—the famous (and sometimes infamous) intelligence test. Like any test, it is influenced by the assumptions and biases of the test constructor. As you read about the development of intelligence tests, you should be aware of how prevailing views about the nature of intelligence affected the kinds of tests that psychologists constructed.

Interim Summary

Intelligence is a complex concept that demands a broad and general definition. Experts have not agreed on any single set of criteria. However, there is a growing awareness of the relative nature of intelligence. It may be viewed as the capacity to adapt in purposeful and resourceful fashion to the demands of the environment, but these demands can differ widely, not only from one culture to another, but also within cultures.

INTELLIGENCE TESTS

Sir Francis Galton, cousin of the evolutionary theorist Charles Darwin, first explored the measurement of intelligence in 1884. Galton held two strong convictions: (1) that intelligence was largely a matter of superior perceptual and physical attributes and (2) that intelligence was inherited, with some families showing clear biological superiority over others. Galton reasoned that if he could link certain physical attributes with intelligent behavior, he could

Francis Galton
(1822–1911)

demonstrate how intelligence was passed from one generation to the next.

To test his ideas, Galton established a laboratory in London where, with the help of his American collaborator James Cattell, he tested the perceptual and physical abilities of thousands of volunteers. Galton's research design called for people to detect subtle changes in a variety of different senses, such as hearing, smell, taste, and touch. For example, participants might be required to discriminate between objects of very similar weight, or asked to detect subtle differences in pitch.

The results of this extensive investigation were extremely disappointing. Galton's tests showed little correlation with each other and, in a crucial blow to his hypothesis, were unable to discriminate among people of known differences in intellectual ability (Sternberg, 1990).

Galton's failure signaled the end of an era. By the beginning of the twentieth century, psychologists abandoned the notion that perceptual and physical skills were the best indicators of intelligence. However, a far more promising idea soon surfaced.

Alfred Binet

Alfred Binet
(1857–1911)

Modern tests of intelligence emphasize the measurement of *mental abilities,* such as reasoning, remembering, and imagining. These abilities were first identified in the pioneering work of Alfred Binet, a French psychologist with a strong interest in how mental abilities differ from one person to another. Binet's fascination with individual differences stemmed in part from observations of his own two daughters, to whom he administered some of his first tests of mental ability.

During the period when Binet was developing his first tests, the French government became increasingly concerned with the education of mentally retarded children. The government wanted to establish special classes for these children, but feared that teachers would be unable to make an objective evaluation of which children needed help. So, in 1904, the Ministry of Education in Paris called on Binet to develop an objective assessment procedure. In 1904, Binet and his collaborator, Theophile Simon, responded with a 30-question test that became the forerunner of all modern tests of intelligence. The Binet-Simon test successfully distinguished mentally retarded from normal children, confirming Binet's idea that abilities such as memory, imagination, and reasoning were better indicators of intelligence than were the perceptual-physical tests developed by Galton.

The original Binet-Simon test presented questions in order of increasing difficulty. For example, a question in the first part of the test might simply require the child to discriminate between a square of chocolate and a square of wood. Later in the test, a child would have to determine which of two lines of slightly different length was actually longer. At first, Binet and Simon did not classify questions in terms of their difficulty for children of different ages. As surprising as it may seem, one of the first findings to emerge from Binet and Simon's test was the discovery that older children passed more questions than younger children. However obvious this now appears, it was an important step forward in the development of the concepts of *mental age* and the *intelligence quotient (IQ).*

Mental Age and IQ

As Binet and Simon revised their test, they began to learn about the average performance of children of different ages. For example, the typical 9-year-old could pass the following questions from the 1911 revision: name the months of the year, make change for 20 cents, and define five words at an abstract level (Binet & Simon, 1916). Through repeated revisions of

Intelligence testing has been an important tool in our understanding of intelligence but like any test, intelligence tests are influenced by the assumptions and biases of the test constructor.

Table 11.1 **Questions from the Binet-Simon Test**

Age Level	Question
3	Repeat two digits. Point to nose, eyes, and mouth
4	Identify own sex. Repeat three digits.
5	Copy a square Repeat a sentence with 10 syllables.
6	Copy a diamond. Count 13 pennies.
7	Show right hand and left ear. Name four colors.
8	Count backward from 20 to 0. Note omissions from pictures of familiar objects.
9	Recognize nine common coins. Name the months of the year in order.
10	Arrange five blocks in order of weight. Copy two drawings from memory.
12	Discover the meaning of a disarranged sentence. Define three abstract words.
15	Name three rhymes for a given word in 1 minute. Interpret pictures.

their test, Binet and Simon eventually classified questions according to age level ranging from 3 to 15 years (see **Table 11.1**). In so doing, they created the concept of **mental age (MA),** an index of the child's problem-solving ability that is independent of the child's actual or **chronological age (CA).** The distinction between MA and CA allowed Binet and Simon to determine how well a child had performed. Children who answered questions above their age level were performing better than expected, while those who could only answer questions below their age level were performing worse than expected.

The Binet-Simon test made such an enormous contribution to the study of intelligence that it was subsequently revised and used worldwide. Lewis Terman, a psychologist at Stanford University, was the principal author of the first major revision in 1916. This test became known as the Stanford-Binet and was further revised in 1937, 1960, 1972, and most recently in 1986.

Although Terman was responsible for a number of major changes in the Binet-Simon test, his greatest contribution was to institute a numerical index that expressed intelligence as a ratio of mental age (MA) to chronological age (CA). This index, first suggested by the German psychologist William Stern, became known as the **intelligence quotient** or **IQ.** Below is Terman's formula for calculating IQ:

$$IQ = \frac{MA}{CA} \times 100$$

As you can see, when MA and CA are equal, the formula yields an IQ score of 100, designated as the average IQ. When MA exceeds CA, the test taker's performance is above average, whereas a CA greater than an MA yields a below-average performance.

Although the MA/CA formula was an important step forward, difficulties eventually arose. One particularly nettlesome problem is that mental age cannot continue to grow indefinitely. Intuitively, this makes sense because the growth of intelligence, like other human characteristics, must eventually begin to slow. However, as most adults will ruefully admit, there is no way to prevent a steady rise in chronological age. But if CA keeps increasing while MA levels off, IQ (defined as MA/CA) cannot help but decline as people grow older. You can rest assured that this difficulty was not lost on the adults who create intelligence tests.

The solution was to develop a new procedure that classified people into groups of roughly the same age. Any individual who took an intelligence test was then compared to others in the same age bracket. In this way, IQ became a *relative* measure comparing the test taker to people of the same chronological age. To achieve this, IQ is calculated by first setting a score of 100 as the average level of performance for each age group. An individual's score is then converted into a *percentile* that indicates how much he or she deviates from the average. **Figure 11.1** on page 394 shows how this works by presenting scores on the present-day Stanford-Binet and their percentile equivalents.

David Wechsler

David Wechsler, one of the most prominent psychologists in the field of intelligence testing, began his work over 40 years ago by disagreeing with Binet on one crucial point. In Binet's original test, and in subsequent revisions of the

Figure 11.1
Percentile Distribution of Stanford-Binet Scores.
Note that the scores assume a regular proportion or "normal curve." The average
score of 100 represents the 50th percentile.

Number of cases

Stanford-Binet IQ		52	68	84	100	116	132	148	
Percent of scores in each interval	< 1	2	14	34	34	14	2	< 1	

3rd   16th   50th   84th   97th

Percentiles

Stanford-Binet until 1986, questions were not organized into separate skill areas. This meant that an individual who took one of the earlier versions of the Stanford-Binet (prior to the 1986 revision) received only a single score.

Wechsler had a different idea about the measurement of intelligence. He believed test constructors should acknowledge explicitly that intelligence is a complex trait composed of

The revised Wechsler Adult Intelligence Scale (WAIS-R) measures both verbal and performance abilities.

a number of different abilities. Wechsler was particulaly concerned that most questions on existing intelligence tests measured only verbal abilities. Although Wechsler acknowledged that verbal abilities were important, he felt that a broad definition of intelligence should encompass spatial reasoning, visual memory, and other nonverbal abilities.

Wechsler's interest in nonverbal intelligence arose from his work with patients at Bellevue Hospital in New York City. For the most part, these people were poorly educated adults, and Wechsler feared that a test that relied solely on verbal abilities would underestimate their intelligence. After extensive field work, he produced a new test, known as the Wechsler Adult Intelligence Scale, or WAIS (pronounced *wace*), that measured both verbal and nonverbal abilities. A subsequent test measuring intelligence in 6- to 16-year-olds was called the Wechsler Intelligence Scale for Children, or WISC (pronounced *wisk*). These two tests are among the most widely respected intelligence tests in use today. Each has subsequently undergone revision, the WAIS in 1981 and the WISC twice, in 1974 and again in 1991. The most recent revised versions are known as the WAIS-R and WISC-III, respectively.

We can use the WAIS-R to illustrate the basic format of all the Wechsler tests. Each question in the WAIS-R belongs to a single subscale that is designed to measure a distinct ability (see **Table 11.2**). You can see from this table that subscales in turn belong to one of two major scales, known as the Verbal Scale

Table 11.2 — Description of the Subscales of the WAIS-R

Scale	Sample Task
Verbal	
Information	Answer questions of general knowledge, such as, "What is a ruby?"
Digit span	Repeat a series of numbers, such as 5, 1, 8, 2.
Vocabulary	Define a list of words.
Arithmetic	Solve mathematical problems without the aid of paper and pencil.
Comprehension	Respond to verbal-reasoning problems such as, "Why do people keep money in the bank?"
Similarities	Respond to verbal analogies such as, "In what way are air and water alike?"
Performance	
Picture completion	Find the missing element in a picture of a common object.
Picture arrangement	Arrange pictures displayed on different cards so that they tell a coherent story.
Block design	Arrange multicolored blocks so that they conform to a particular design.
Object assembly	Arrange pieces of a specially constructed puzzle in proper order.
Digit symbol	Copy nonsense symbols as rapidly as possible.

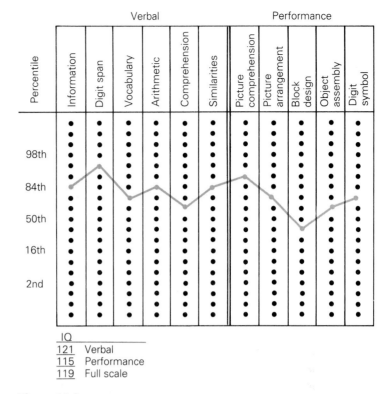

IQ
121 Verbal
115 Performance
119 Full scale

Figure 11.2
A Simplified Version of the WAIS-R Profile.
This hypothetical profile reveals a pattern of relative strengths and weaknesses. For example, note that the subtest scores on the Verbal Scale generally exceed those on the Performance Scale and that within each scale, some scores are higher than others. Most actual test profiles also show a pattern of relative strengths and weaknesses.

and the Performance Scale. Questions belonging to the Verbal Scale measure abilities such as general information, word knowledge, and verbal analogies, whereas questions from the Performance Scale measure spatial reasoning, perceptual and motor skills, and visual memory. People who take the WAIS-R receive a Verbal IQ score, a Performance IQ score, and an overall composite score known as a Full Scale IQ (see **Figure 11.2**).

Wechsler's notion that intelligence is composed of different abilities has received widespread acceptance among psychologists. The most recent (1986) revision of the Stanford-Binet explicitly acknowledges this point by grouping questions into four broad categories: *verbal reasoning, quantitative reasoning, short-term memory*, and *abstract/visual reasoning* (similar to some of Wechsler's performance subscales). As we will see, psychologists are generally more comfortable with tests that recognize the multifaceted nature of intelligence.

Interim Summary

Following Galton's unsuccessful attempt to measure intelligence, Alfred Binet, with the help of his colleague Theophile Simon, developed the first modern intelligence test. Unlike his predecessor, Binet concentrated on the measurement of higher mental abilities such as reasoning, imagination, and memory.

The Binet-Simon test was eventually revised and used worldwide. One of the best-known revisions is the Stanford-Binet, completed under the direction of psychologist Lewis Terman of Stanford University. Terman instituted a numerical index that expressed intelligence as a ratio of MA to CA. Eventually, this formula was replaced by a relative measure of IQ that compared the test taker to people of the same age.

In something of a break with the Binet-Simon tradition, David Wechsler argued that intelligence tests should reflect the fact that intelligence is composed of a number of different abilities. The tests that Wechsler developed, the WAIS for adults and the WISC for children, divided questions into subscales, each measuring a specific ability. These subscales were then grouped into two major scales, the Verbal Scale and the Performance (nonverbal) Scale. Wechsler's notion of grouping questions by category proved to be quite popular and was eventually incorporated into the revised version of the Stanford-Binet.

Test Construction

Before a test is accepted for use in the public domain, it must meet some very specific criteria. In this section we will consider three of the most important criteria: *standardization, reliability,* and *validity.*

STANDARDIZATION
It takes a great deal of time and effort to construct an intelligence test. Over the course of many months, an original list of questions is administered to people of varying ages, races, and social backgrounds to determine which questions are suitable for the final version of the test. This process is known as the **standardization** of a test, and it serves several important functions. Standardization eliminates ambiguous or unfair questions, establishes guidelines for administering the test, and provides a standard or **norm** for comparing an individual's score with the scores of others from a similar background.

Norms are particularly relevant to the all-important issue of fairness. Potential test questions must be pretested or tried out in advance on people who are similar to those for whom the final version of the test is intended. For instance, if the test is to be used in a country where 20 percent of the population is black, then blacks should constitute roughly 20 percent of the standardization sample. Because intelligence tests are administered to both males and females, test constructors also want to eliminate, or at the very least reduce to a minimum, sex differences in performance. This goal is often accomplished by including equal numbers of males and females in the standardization sample and by carefully analyzing their responses to potential test questions. A well-standardized test will also be sensitive to geographical differences (varying regions of a country) and urban versus rural lifestyles. Proportionate numbers of people from different geographic regions and from urban and rural homes should be included in the standardization sample.

RELIABILITY
One important quality of a well-standardized test is consistency. For example, if within a relatively short span of time you take the same test twice, you should receive roughly the same score each time the test is administered. If this occurs, we can conclude that the test you have taken has good **reliability**. It provided a consistent, reproducible measure of a your performance.

One way to measure reliability is to test people on two different occasions separated by a relatively short period of time. This method, known as *test-retest reliability,* has figured prominently in the development of intelligence tests. Although an individual will not obtain exactly the same score on two different occasions, there should be relatively little variation in scores if the test is well constructed. On both the Stanford-Binet and Wechsler scales, the test-retest correlation for two scores obtained less than 1 year apart is approximately +.90. This high correlation (recall that the highest correlation coefficient is 1.00) indicates that both tests are reliable.

There are other ways to measure reliability. Prominent among them is the method known as *split-half reliability,* in which the test constructor correlates the answers to the odd- and even-numbered questions on a test. This procedure checks the internal consistency of the test. Once again, a high (positive) correlation is a mark of reliability.

VALIDITY
Imagine that you are told that you are about to take an intelligence test. The first question asks you to recall a recent dream, the second asks about the number of friends you have, the third

calls for a list of your favorite hobbies. You are understandibly perplexed. What does all this have to do with intelligence? Very little, of course, and this mythical test violates one of the most fundamental requirements of test construction. If a test is designed to assess intelligene, the questions on the test must measure problem solving and not, for example, personality or some other characteristic that may be independent of intelligence. Public confidence requires that intelligence tests have **validity**. They must measure what they are intended to measure.

How do psychologists determine if a test is valid? One way is to determine the *predictive validity* of a test, or how well it forecasts some future event. This is perhaps the best-known example of validity, primarily because intelligence tests were originally developed to predict one event in particular—success in school. The original Binet-Simon test was successful primarily because it distinguished those who did well in school from those who did not. Subsequent intelligence tests, such as the Stanford-Binet and the Wechsler scales, are also highly successful in predicting school performance. We can safely say that these tests have good predictive validity.

Before a new intelligence test is introduced, it must fulfill a second criterion known as *concurrent validity*. This means that any new test must show a positive relationship to a similar test with a proven record. For example, if a new intelligence test and a Stanford-Binet were administered to a large number of children, those who obtain high scores on the new test should obtain high scores on the Stanford-Binet, and those who perform poorly on the new test should perform poorly on the Stanford-Binet. The implications of this are quite sobering. In effect, all intelligence tests trace their origins to Alfred Binet, whose intention was to create a test that identified children who were failing in school. It is no accident that many of the questions on modern intelligence tests tap the skills needed to do well in the classroom.

Group Intelligence Tests

Tests like the WAIS-R and the Standford-Binet are individual intelligence tests administered to only one person at a time. In contrast, group intelligence tests can be given to a large number of people simultaneously.

Group tests do not provide as much detailed information as individual tests, but they are more efficient. Although strictly speaking the Scholastic Aptitude Test (SAT) is not an intelligence test, it is a well-known example of a group test designed to measure both verbal and quantitative ability. Much like an individual intelligence test, the SAT has the goal of predicting future scholastic performance. Many colleges and universities require prospective applicants to take the SAT, or the very similar American College Test (ACT).

Aptitude Versus Achievement

Intelligence tests are designed to measure *aptitude*, or your ability to learn something new. Aptitude tests are often contrasted with *achievement* tests, which are designed to measure what you already know. Theoretically, aptitude tests measure your *potential* for future learning whereas achievement tests measure your mastery of old learning.

But the distinction is not quite so clear, as anyone who has taken a college entrance exam knows. The SAT, for example, attempts to measure your mathematical aptitude by asking you to solve a number of problems involving algebra and geometry. If you do not have an adequate background in these two areas of mathematics, you will find that section of the SAT very difficult. Much the same is true of the verbal section of the SAT. It presumes a certain level of vocabulary and reading ability that clearly falls within the realm of achievement.

The blurred distinction between aptitude and achievement is important to bear in mind. The two are so closely intertwined that any test trying to measure future potential is measuring both aptitude and achievement. What you can learn in the future is always related in some way to what you have learned in the past.

Test Performance

Test construction is one important element in understanding how intelligence is measured. But equally important is test performance, or what people actually do when confronted with an intelligence test.

Two factors play an important role in the outcome of any testing situation: competence and performance. **Competence** is the knowledge or skill that a person possesses. It is the sum total of what an individual knows. **Per-**

Psychology in the News

S.A.T. COACHING RAISES SCORES, REPORT SAYS

By Anthony DePalma

Commercial coaching courses that train students to take standardized tests can raise scores significantly, according to a new report, and give students who can afford such courses an advantage over poorer students in getting into college or receiving a scholarship.

The report by the National Center for Fair and Open Testing, a not-for-profit group in Cambridge, Mass., that also goes by the name FairTest, asserts that studies done over the last 20 years prove that coaching courses can raise a student's score by 100 points on the Scholastic Aptitude Test, a multiple choice examination with a top score of 1600 that many colleges and universities use in making admission decisions.

More than 100,000 students a year pay fees that can exceed $500 each for coaching courses, the report said.

The College Board, which administers the S.A.T. to more than 1.5 million students a year, and the Educational Testing Service, which devises the test, have consistently held that cramming and drilling do not reliably improve test scores.

Officials said the strategies and shortcuts taught by the coaching companies can sometimes hurt a student's performance.

Debate Over Coaching

The report, to be issued tomorrow, reopens an old argument about the equity of standardized tests. It says coaching courses can add 100 points to a student's score on the SAT whose score ranges from 400 to 1600 points.

FairTest, a longstanding critic of standardized tests, contends that since a coaching course offered by companies like The Princeton Review or Stanley H. Kaplan Educational Center costs more than $500, poor students who cannot afford such fees are put at an even greater disadvantage than already exists with the way the test is structured.

FairTest contends that the test is biased because certain questions deal with ideas and terms—like dividends, deeds and heirlooms—that students from low-income families are not likely to know.

"Coaching adds to a long list of flaws that the S.A.T. already has," said Cinthia H. Schuman, executive director of FairTest.

College Board officials said a rigorous academic background was the best long-term preparation for taking the test. In the short run, they encourage study of a booklet with sample questions prepared by the College Board and distributed to every test taker. Taking the test a second time also generally improves scores by about 30 to 40 points.

There is a correlation between family income and test performance, said the board's executive director of admissions and guidance services, Gretchen W. Rigol, but not because of bias in the test.

"The unfortunate reality in this country" Ms. Rigol said, "is that many students from low-income families are in schools where they are not encouraged to take rigorous academic courses or the courses are just not offered."

From "S.A.T. Coaching Raises Scores, Report Says" by Anthony DePalma, THE NEW YORK TIMES, December 18, 1991. Copyright © 1991 by The New York Times Company. Reprinted by permission.

Questions

1. How might coaching hurt a student's performance?
2. Should we ban coaching courses because they provide an unfair advantage to higher income students?
3. If taking rigorous academic courses helps people do well on the SAT, what does this tell us about the distinction between aptitude and achievement?

formance, on the other hand, is the knowledge a person actually demonstrates in a particular setting at a given moment in time. This distinction is quite analogous to what athletes face when they enter a major competition, such as the Olympic games. They may possess the ability (competence) to win a medal in their sport, but they have only a brief moment to demonstrate their ability. As many an Olympic hopeful knows, performance can sometimes underestimate ability.

Psychologists have taken a special interest in *performance factors*—the personal characteristics of an individual, or the circumstances surrounding the administration of a test, that can cause someone to perform below his or her ability level. Some examples are low motivation, uncertainty about what is demanded in the testing situation, or fear of the examiner.

Performance factors can influence any individual's test score, but they are particularly likely to depress the scores of people who are unfamiliar or uncomfortable with testing situations (Zigler, Abelson, & Seitz, 1973). Economically disadvantaged children are among those who fall into this category, and their performance on intelligence tests is sometimes adversely affected by their wariness of the examiner (Zigler, Abelson, & Seitz, 1973; Zigler & Butterfield, 1968). However, small adjustments can often undo these negative effects. For example, a short play period with the examiner prior to the administration of an intelligence test often leads to a significant improvement in the test scores of disadvantaged children (Zigler, Abelson, & Seitz, 1973).

Interim Summary

A sound intelligence test must meet three specific goals: standardization, reliability, and validity. A test is standardized by giving the original list of questions to people of various ages and social backgrounds. Through this process, the test constructor eliminates some questions and refines others. Reliability is achieved when the test yields a consistent measure of an individual's performance. Validity is achieved when the test actually measures what it was designed to measure.

Individual intelligence tests can be contrasted with group intelligence tests, which are administered to a large number of people simultaneously. The Scholastic Aptitude Test (SAT) is a well-known example of a group intelligence test. Like all aptitude tests, the SAT is designed to measure future potential, but aptitude is often closely linked to achievement or past learning.

In evaluating the way people perform on intelligence tests, psychologists must be mindful of the distinction between what a person knows (competence) and the expression of that knowledge in a particular situation (performance).

THE STRUCTURE OF THE INTELLECT

So far we have focused on two rather practical topics: how intelligence tests are constructed and how people perform on these tests. We turn now to a more theoretical question. What skills are measured on an IQ test? When people take an intelligence test, do they draw on one general source of knowledge, or are many different abilities involved?

General Versus Specific Abilities

One long-standing view is that intelligence reflects a general capacity for reasoning and problem solving. People who are intelligent will demonstrate their superior cognitive abilities in virtually any situation. An opposing viewpoint emphasizes that intelligence is primarily a set of individual abilities rather than one general trait. People will show greater strengths in some areas than others.

To understand these two positions, we need to know something about *factor analysis*, a statistical technique that allows the test constructor to determine if the various questions on an intelligence test are related to one another. To accomplish this, the investigator computes the correlation of each question with every other question on the test. Some questions will correlate highly with each other but very weakly with other questions. Those that correlate highly with each other are said to belong to the same dimension, or *factor*.

Charles Spearman's single-factor theory of intelligence provided the strongest support for the idea that intelligence reflects a general capacity for reasoning and problem solving (Spearman, 1904). Spearman believed that intelligence was composed largely of one major

Table 11.3   **Thurstone's Primary Mental Abilities**

Ability	Description
Verbal comprehension	Knowledge of words and word usage.
Word fluency	The ability to generate words quickly and accurately, for example, solving a crossword puzzle.
Numerical calculation	Computational skills used in a variety of situations involving number problems.
Spatial visualization	Awareness of the similarities and differences in objects presented in varying spatial orientations, for example, the ability to recognize a cube after it has been rotated 180°.
Memory	Recall of familiar words and sentences.
Perceptual speed	Rapid recognition of visual detail.
General reasoning	The ability to deduce general rules and principles governing particular problems, for example, identifying the next number in an incomplete series: 5, 11, 23, ?, 95.

factor, which he labeled general intelligence, or simply *g* for short. In Spearman's view, all individuals possess *g* in varying amounts. Whether a person is bright or dull, that is, performs well or poorly on an intelligence test, is a function of *g*. Spearman acknowledged that most people have particular intellectual strengths, or special abilities as he called them, but he stressed the importance of *g* as the single overriding factor in determininig intellectual ability.

Louis Thurstone took issue with Spearman's emphasis on a single factor of general intelligence. When Thurstone analyzed intelligence tests, he discovered seven different factors, which he labeled *primary mental abilities*. These **primary mental abilities** are verbal comprehension, numerical skills, word fluency, spatial visualization, memory, reasoning, and perceptual skills. **Table 11.3** briefly de-

scribes each of these abilities. Eventually, Thurstone developed a series of tests to measure these skills, known as the Test of Primary Mental Abilities. This test is still widely used, but in some ways it contradicts Thurstone's original hypothesis. The primary abilities, as Thurstone himself discovered, are not completely independent of one another. Instead, there are modest correlations among these abilities such that performance on one is somewhat correlated with performance on the others.

Other psychologists have also pursued the study of basic mental abilities (Ekstrom, French, Harman, & Derman, 1976; Guilford, 1959; Horn, 1978). However, their estimates of the number of separate abilities vary considerably, depending on the investigator's procedures and the questions selected for analysis. In each case, however, the separate abilities show some relationship to each other, a result that tends to support a position that is something of a compromise between Spearman's and Thurstone's original viewpoints. This modern view of factor analysis holds that people do possess some form of general intelligence, but each individual will show a particular cluster of strengths and weaknesses. Practically speaking, this means that relatively small differences in IQ are not very meaningful. Two people whose overall IQ scores differ by only 5 to 10 points may be virtually indistinguishable from one another. The person with the lower score may actually outperform the other in a number of situations. But when the difference in IQ becomes very large, for example 25 to 30 points, the person with the higher score can be expected to outperform the other individual on most tasks. A very large difference in overall test performance is usually an indication that two people differ considerably in their general problem-solving ability.

Triarchic Theory

The advantage of the factorial approach is that it offers psychologists a reasonably clear-cut model of the human intellect. However, it does not address directly the question of how people actually solve complex problems. Over the past two decades the *information-processing, approach*, which we discussed in Chapter 9, has examined how people encode, retrieve, and process information while solving difficult problems. Unlike the factorial approach, the goal of information processing is to determine what people do when confronted with complex problems—what strategies they use, what mental processes they evoke, and how rapidly they achieve solutions.

Adopting the information-processing perspective, Robert Sternberg suggested that the traditional intelligence test captures only one important aspect of intellectual functioning and should not be considered the sole indicator of how well people think (Sternberg, 1985). Sternberg argued that intelligence actually comprises three different abilities, which he described in his triarchic theory (Sternberg, 1985, 1986).

Sternberg proposed that people demonstrate one form of intelligence when they solve verbal and spatial reasoning problems similar to those found on an intelligence test. Sternberg referred to this as *componential* intelligence because it involves mastery of the sequence of steps, or components, that underlie the solutions to difficult problems. Componential intelligence is highly adaptive in school situations, although, as Sternberg notes, it does not necessarily correlate with creativity and insight.

A different kind of intelligence involves the ability to perceive novel and creative solutions to complex situations. Sternberg refers to this as *experiential* intelligence and suggests that it is quite separate from componential abilities. Sternberg feels that some individuals who possess only modest analytical skills (componential ability) are nevertheless highly creative and capable of very original work. Experiential intelligence is the kind of reasoning that is most likely to produce a sudden breakthrough in scientific research or a novel form of artistic expression.

Sternberg also noted that some people are particularly adept at knowing how to deal effectively with their environment. He referred to this as *contextual* intelligence because it involves a kind of street-wise knowledge critical to the practical problems that confront all of us. Contextual intelligence may be demonstrated by the individual who seems to have a knack for finding the perfect job, or the person who senses just the right time to ask for a promotion.

Multiple Intelligences

Howard Gardner shares Sternberg's view that the factorial approach fails to capture the breadth and scope of the human intellect.

However, in his provocative book *Frames of Mind,* Gardner (1983) departs from the information-processing approach by including in his view of intelligence problem-solving strategies that fall outside the traditional realm of mental abilities. Unlike information-processing theorists, Gardner believes that even nonmental abilities, such as music and motor coordination, should be considered if one wishes to delineate the full range of intelligent behavior.

Gardner proposed a theory of multiple intelligences, using the plural form of the word quite deliberately. He acknowledged the importance of the traditional manifestations of intelligence, *linguistic, logical-mathematical,* and *spatial* abilities, that are frequently measured on an intelligence test. But Gardner also recognized three other types of intelligent behavior that he felt were equally important though generally less valued: *musical intelligence, personal intelligence,* and *bodily-kinesthetic intelligence* (Gardner, 1983). Gardner believes that Western industrial societies have overemphasized the importance of the first three forms of intelligence while virtually ignoring the last three.

While critics dismiss some of Gardner's intelligences as "talents," Gardner's stated goal is to "democratize the range of the human faculties" by stressing the value of nontraditional forms of intelligent behavior (Gardner, 1983). Gardner includes in his theory the kind of sensitivity to pitch and rhythm that leads to the

Psychologist Howard Gardner identified three additional types of intelligence: musical, personal, and bodily-kinesthetic.

ability to recognize and construct harmonious patterns (musical intelligence); bodily control and fine motor coordination, such as a surgeon or a ballet dancer might display (bodily-kinesthetic intelligence); and the facility both to perceive and to understand the needs of others as well as to evaluate and monitor one's own emotions (personal intelligence).

The theories of Sternberg and Gardner represent a move away from the factorial analyses of intelligence that dominated psychological thinking through most of this century. It is too early to know the fate of these new theories, but it seems clear that Sternberg and Gardner speak for a growing number of psychologists who are interested in discovering the *processes* involved in human problem solving.

Interim Summary

Some psychologists have suggested that intelligence is largely a matter of a single factor or ability, labeled general intelligence or simply *g*. Other experts have disagreed, suggesting that intelligence is composed of a number of independent factors or separate abilities. The contemporary theories of Robert Sternberg and Howard Gardner stand in sharp contrast to both of these factorial approaches.

Sternberg believes that there are three forms of intelligence: componential intelligence, or the mastery of the steps used to solve complex problems; experiential intelligence, or the ability to perceive novel and creative solutions to complex problems; and contextual intelligence, or the ability to deal effectively with the environment.

Gardner's theory of multiple intelligences suggests that we view intelligence as a multifaceted phenomenon, including not only such traditional measures of intelligence as linguistic, logical-mathematical, and spatial abilities but also musical, personal, and bodily-kinesthetic skills. Gardner's critics dismiss these latter abilities as talents, but Gardner argues that they are true manifestations of intelligence largely ignored by most industrialized societies.

Stability and Change in IQ

One of the questions most frequently asked of psychologists is whether intellectual performance is fixed and unchanging. Both parents

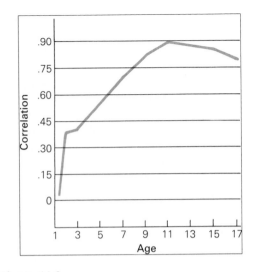

Figure 11.3
Correlation Between IQ Scores at Each Age and IQ Scores at Age 18.
By the time the children are 7 years old, there is a high correlation with their IQ at age 18. (After Bloom, 1964)

and educators want to know if a child's IQ score can change substantially and, if so, what experiences contribute to any changes that may occur.

The longitudinal research design, discussed in Chapter 9, provides an ideal way to answer this question. **Figure 11.3** shows the results of a large-scale longitudinal study in which children were given intelligence tests yearly from infancy through adolescence. IQ scores from age 1 onward were correlated with IQ scores obtained at age 18. Note that correlations with test performance at age 18 do not become stable (approximately +.45) until roughly age 4. From this point on, the relationship becomes increasingly strong, and by age 7 there is a very high correlation (roughly +.70) with performance at age 17. An individual's IQ at age 7 is a fairly good predictor of that person's IQ at age 18 (Bloom, 1964).

Whereas most people follow the pattern shown in Figure 11.3, some individuals show major changes in their test performance over a long period of time. In some studies, children who were tested from birth into adulthood showed shifts of 15 IQ points or more even after age 7 (Bayley, 1970; McCall, Appelbaum, & Hogarty, 1973). Although we do not completely understand why these changes occur, home experiences seem crucial. For example, a group of investigators identified two groups of children who showed marked changes in IQ scores. One group, whose parents often attempted to accelerate development by training children in various mental and motor skills, showed increased scores during the preschool years. By contrast, the parents of the second group of children, whose scores decreased sharply in the same period of time, rarely attempted to accelerate development. (McCall et al., 1973).

One recent development may alter the way we view the question of stability and change. New methods of measuring young infants' reactions to pictures and sounds have raised the intriguing possibility that attention to novel auditory and visual stimuli, as well as memory for these stimuli, may forecast how well children perform on intelligence tests (Bornstein & Sigman, 1986). For instance, Susan Rose and Ina Wallace (1985) found a .56 correlation between the visual memory skills of 6-month-old infants and the IQ scores of the same children at 6 years. Although many questions about this line of research remain unanswered, psychologists continue to investigate the possibility that infants' attention and memory can predict future IQ scores (DiLalla, Thompson, Plomin, Phillips, Fagan, Haith, Cyphers, & Fulker, 1990).

Interim Summary

Performance on intelligence tests is relatively stable from age 4 onward. By the time children are 7 years of age, IQ scores show a strong positive correlation with scores obtained at age 17. However, there are notable exceptions to this pattern. Some children experience gains or losses of 15 IQ points or more during the childhood years. The home environment seems to be the pivotal factor in these major shifts in IQ.

New ways of measuring attention and memory in infants have allowed researchers to predict how well children will perform on intelligence tests taken years later. However, it is too early to know how useful this research will be in determining the factors that affect performance on an intelligence test.

• •

EXTREMES OF INTELLIGENCE

A score of 100 is the average performance on most intelligence tests. However, because very few people obtain this exact score, it is impor-

tant to consider variations around the average. For example, on the Wechsler tests the scores of 68 percent of the population fall between 85 and 115. Almost the entire population (95 percent) receives a score between 70 and 130. Beyond these two extremes lies a small number of people who represent two distinct groups: the mentally retarded and the intellectually gifted.

The Mentally Retarded

Historically, mental retardation has been defined by the score that a person obtains on a standardized intelligence test. The exact score, however, is somewhat arbitrary. In 1959, the American Association on Mental Deficiency, recently renamed the American Association on Mental Retardation (AAMR), used an IQ of 85 as the cutoff point for normal intelligence. Anyone below this level was considered mentally retarded. However, in 1973 the cutoff score was lowered to 70. In this way, millions of people who would have been considered mentally retarded by the old criterion no longer were classified as such. These shifting criteria demonstrate that the dividing line between normal intelligence and mental retardation is somewhat flexible.

More important, the AAMR now recognizes that low intelligence is but one indicator of mental retardation. An equally significant criterion is a deficiency in adaptive behavior (H. J. Grossman, 1983). To be considered mentally retarded, an individual must have an IQ below 70 and demonstrate an inability to meet the standards of personal and social responsibility expected of his or her age group. Moreover, this intellectual and social deficit must occur for the first time before age 18. People who become incapacitated in adulthood through brain injury or disease are not considered mentally retarded.

The AAMR recognizes four distinct levels of mental retardation: mild, moderate, severe, and profound. These are defined by a combination of an intelligence-test score and the judgment of a psychologist about the individual's adaptive functioning. To judge adaptive functioning, psychologists often refer to a set of general guidelines that help identify the level of retardation (H. J. Grossman, 1983; Van Osdol & Shane, 1977). **Table 11.4** provides a sample of the kinds of criteria that a psychologist would use in classifying the adaptive behavior of a retarded adolescent. These criteria are then com-

Table 11.4   **Characteristics of Mental Retardation**

Level of Retardation	Characteristics
Mild	May hold a job involving semiskilled work, but needs help in managing income. Has some friends. Can deal adequately with many social situations.
Moderate	If employed, requires a sheltered work environment with considerable supervision. Has some friends, but encounters problems in many social situations.
Severe	Rarely employed. May need assistance even for simple errands. Typically has few friends and little social interaction.
Profound	Usually needs constant care. Not capable of true social interaction.

After Van Osdol & Shane (1977); Grossman (1983).

Table 11.5   **The AAMR Classification of Mental Retardation**

Level of Retardation	IQ Range	Expected Mental Age (in Years)
Mild	52–69	8–12
Moderate	36–51	3–7
Severe	20–35	0–3
Profound	below 20	—

After Cleland (1978).

bined with IQ scores to yield a classification system for mental retardation. One such system, based on norms provided by the AAMR, is outlined in **Table 11.5.**

Before turning to the question of what causes mental retardation, we want to consider an important point about the four levels of retardation we have just described. There is a widespread misunderstanding of mentally retarded individuals that borders on a stereotype.

Many people equate mental retardation with serious impairment in everyday functioning. In fact, the great majority of mentally retarded people are classified as having only mild retardation. In practical terms, this means that while the mentally retarded are deficient in academic skills, most are capable of holding jobs and can deal adequately with many social situations. The term *mental retardation* should not conjure up an image of a helpless and incapacitated person.

Generally speaking, the causes of mental retardation can be divided into two categories: *organic retardation* and *psychosocial retardation*. The basic distinction between the two is that organic retardation has a physiological basis (such as chromosomal damage, metabolic disorders, or injury to the brain), while psychosocial retardation has no obvious physiological cause but still afflicts more than one member of the same family.

Perhaps the best-known example of organic retardation is Down syndrome, so called because the physical characteristics associated with this disease were first described by the English physician Langdon Down. **Down syndrome,** which affects roughly 1 of every 700 infants, results from a chromosomal abnormality in which the child has one more chromosome than normal. The most obvious physical characteristics of Down syndrome are a rounded face with a low-bridged nose, a thick tongue that often protrudes slightly, and almond-shaped eyes that slant upward. Children afflicted with this disorder typically begin to walk late (around 2 1/2 years), and many have congenital heart problems that can result in an early

This Down Syndrome child is working with a therapist to improve speech skills.

death. Intellectually, they have a rather wide range of below-normal IQ scores, while on an interpersonal dimension they tend to be outgoing and friendly.

The other major form of mental retardation, psychosocial, is associated with living conditions that depress the expression of intelligence. Several independent studies have shown that children raised in deprived and impoverished conditions have low IQ scores, often in the 50–70 range (Provence & Lipton, 1962; Skeels, 1966). Although such findings suggest that an inhospitable environment is the essential cause of psychosocial retardation, some psychologists have pointed out that other children from similarly deprived backgrounds have normal IQ scores (Kugel, 1967). This suggests that the environment per se may not be the sole cause of mental retardation. Subtle organic or genetic factors may still play a role in the development of psychosocial retardation (Kugel, 1967).

The Intellectually Gifted

On the opposite end of the intellectual continuum is a small group of people who are of superior intelligence. These people have IQ scores that equal or exceed 130, and, like the mentally retarded, they represent roughly 2 to 3 percent of the population as a whole. In addition to a high IQ, the intellectually gifted often have a particular talent that clearly sets them apart from others.

Lewis Terman, who was involved in the development of the Stanford-Binet intelligence test, began a monumental study of gifted children in 1921. Terman selected over 1500 subjects between the ages of 3 and 19 whose IQ scores exceeded 135. With the help of a number of associates, Terman conducted follow-up studies on these subjects every 5 to 10 years (Terman, 1925; Terman & Oden, 1947, 1959). The most recent observations were made in 1972, when these gifted subjects were entering their 60s.

From this wealth of data, Terman made some discoveries that contradicted commonly held beliefs about highly intelligent people. Contrary to popular belief, he found that high intelligence is not routinely associated with an odd or eccentric personality or with a frail or weak constitution. Quite to the contrary, when these intellectually gifted people were compared to age-mates of average intelligence, they were superior in health, physical size, social ad-

Terman's study found that intellectually gifted people are often superior in health, physical size, social adjustment, and achievement.

justment, and achievement. Furthermore, superiority on these dimensions was a stable phenomenon that continued throughout the adult years. As you would expect, many gifted individuals graduated from college and secured successful positions in professional fields, but their marital and social lives were no more tangled than those of their normal counterparts. Life adjustment for the gifted was about the same as it was for the general populace.

Although few people dispute Terman's findings, the *interpretation* of the findings has caused considerable disagreement. Some psychologists believe that the relationship Terman discovered between high IQ and general success in life demonstrates the value of the intelligence test in predicting future accomplishments. Arthur Jensen, a staunch defender of intelligence tests, argues this point when he suggests that Terman's data firmly establish the power of intelligence tests to measure characteristics of great importance to our modern technological society. Jensen (1972) wrote, "To say that the kind of ability measured by intelligence tests is irrelevant or unimportant would be tantamount to repudiating civilization as we know it" (p. 9).

Psychologists on the other side of the issue are less in awe of the intelligence test. David McClelland (1973), a prominent member of this group, directly challenged Jensen:

> I do not want to repudiate civilization as we know it, or even to dismiss intelligence tests as irrelevant, but I do want to state, as emphatically as possible, that Terman's studies do not demonstrate that it is the kind of ability measured by intelli-

gence tests that is responsible for (i.e., causes) the greater success of high IQ children. (p. 5)

One of McClelland's primary concerns was the particular sample of people Terman chose to study. They were predominantly white, middle- to upper-middle-class individuals who came from superior social and economic backgrounds. Quite apart from their native intelligence, these people enjoyed access to the professional and social networks that are conducive to success in life (McClelland, 1973). In short, McClelland believed that Terman had failed to control for opportunity, and therefore nothing of consequence could be said about the value of IQ scores in predicting life's accomplishments.

Because the disagreement between Jensen and McClelland involves a basic question about the role of intelligence tests, it cannot be resolved completely through a single study. Nevertheless, it is worth noting that one aspect of Terman's data supports McClelland's argument. Terman had noted that not all of the gifted children were successful and had divided his sample into "more successful" and "less successful" groups. Although the IQ scores of these two groups were very close (average adulthood IQ of 139 for the more successful and 133 for the less successful group), there was a considerable difference in one aspect of their family backgrounds. Many more people from the successful group had a stimulating intellectual environment during childhood and had fathers who were college graduates. Such a finding implies that family background was an important factor in determining who belonged to the more successful group.

Nonetheless, the debate continues. Those who believe in the power of intelligence tests in predicting economic prosperity dispute key elements of McClelland's analysis, such as the claim that job success is based on social status and family background. The critics argue that tests of intellectual ability accurately foretell how well people from a variety of different backgrounds will perform in a wide range of occupations (Barrett & Dipinet, 1991).

Interim Summary

The mentally retarded and the intellectually gifted are two small but important groups who define the extremes of intelligence.

Mental retardation is indicated both by a score on an intelligence test (usually an IQ below 70) and an inability to meet age-appropriate standards of personal and social responsibility. The causes of mental retardation are usually divided into organic retardation and psychosocial retardation.

The intellectually gifted are people whose IQ equals or exceeds 130. Lewis Terman conducted a major study of intellectually gifted children and found that high intelligence was generally associated with superior health, social adjustment, and life achievement. However, because Terman's subjects came from the higher social and economic backgrounds, some psychologists have questioned whether the privileges of high social class more than intelligence contributed to the success of these gifted people. Others challenge this criticism, noting that tests of intellectual ability predict occupational success for people from many different backgrounds.

HEREDITY, ENVIRONMENT, AND INTELLIGENCE

Some years ago, a very portly young pitcher for the Detroit Tigers baseball team was questioned about his rotund figure. "I can't help it," he protested, "large bellies run in my family." There is, of course, some truth in this tongue-in-cheek response. Obesity does run in families, as do height, athleticism, and other traits. But what should we make of the fact that certain human characteristics, including intelligence, are commonly demonstrated in similar ways by members of the same family? Is this evidence for the genetic or inherited basis of human faculties, as Galton believed, or is a shared environment the principal reason for the similarity among family members?

Family Resemblance Studies. As it turns out, the study of intelligence is particularly well suited to address this age-old cunundrum. Over the years, psychologists have collected intelligence-test scores of hundreds of different blood relatives. These family resemblance studies, as they are known, permit researchers to examine the correlation in intelligence-test scores among people who vary in genetic similarity. Bouchard and McGue (1981) carried out a worldwide literature review that identified 111 family resemblance studies.

Table 11.6 Correlation in IQ Scores of People Varying in Genetic Similarity

Cousins	+.15
Parents and children	+.40
Siblings reared apart	+.24
Siblings reared together	+.47
Fraternal twins reared together	+.60
Identical twins reared apart	+.72
Identical twins reared together	+.86

Average correlation coefficients obtained from a survey of 111 studies. (Based on Bouchard & McGue, 1981)

Table 11.6 presents a summary of the results of this extensive review.

A striking feature of the data in Table 11.6 is that as genetic similarity between people increases, so does the correlation in their IQ scores. Cousins, who share roughly 12½ percent of their genes, have a correlation in IQ scores of +.15. The next three entries in the table—parents, siblings, and fraternal twins (who develop from separate eggs)—all share roughly 50 percent of their genes. Note that the correlation in IQ scores for each of these groups is close to +.50, except when siblings are reared apart. But identical twins, who develop from a single fertilized egg and share 100 percent of their genes, have a correlation of +.86 when reared together and +.72 when reared apart. This pattern of results suggests that heredity makes a strong contribution to an individual's performance on an intelligence test.

But environmental influences are also at work, and though it may be less obvious, the results in Table 11.6 demonstrate this fact as well. Note that for each of the relationships in this table the average correlation coefficient is higher when individuals are reared together. This finding suggests that the home environment contributes meaningfully to the development of intelligence. Furthermore, it is quite possible to *overestimate* the role of heredity based on the results shown in the table. For example, suppose the individual environments of twins reared apart are really quite similar. This frequently happens because twins are usually separated when the need for adoption arises and adoption agencies typically place twins in-

to similar adoptive homes. So twins who are reared apart may still experience very comparable intellectual environments, and this will contribute to the similarity in their IQ scores.

Adoption Studies. Adoption studies are what psychologists sometimes call experiments in nature. Without conscious design, adoption studies provide an opportunity to examine the heredity-environment relationhip. For example, investigators can determine the correlation between the IQ scores of adopted children and their two sets of parents: natural (biological) and adoptive (foster). If children are adopted shortly after birth, this correlation is potentially quite revealing. If later in life adopted children's IQ scores resemble those of their *natural* parents, whom they have virtually never seen, then heredity, the only real link between the two, must be an important factor. On the other hand, because there is no genetic similarity between adopted children and their *foster* parents, a strong correlation in IQ scores between the two would suggest a major role for the home environment.

One large-scale project, the Texas Adoption Study, has collected data that permit an analysis of the relative contribution of heredity and environment. Approximately 300 families with adopted children have participated in this project (Horn, 1983). The biological mothers of these children were all unwed women who were separated voluntarily from their children within a week of giving birth. **Table 11.7** shows the correlation in IQ scores of two different types of family members: those whose only common link is genetic (adopted children and their biological mothers) and those whose only common link is a shared environment (adopted children and their foster mothers). Note that adopted children who spent less than 1 week with their biological mothers still

Table 11.7 Correlation in IQ Scores of Adopted Children and Their Biological and Foster Mothers

Mother–child Combination	Correlation
Adopted child and biological mother	.25
Adopted child and foster mother	.15

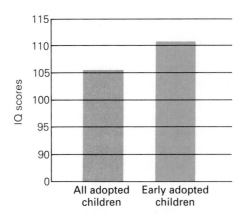

Figure 11.4
IQ Scores of Black Children Adopted by White Families.
(After Scarr & Weinberg, 1976)

showed a closer resemblance in IQ scores to these women than to their foster mothers.

Although these results seem to indicate that heredity plays the stronger role, we cannot draw such a conclusion without examining environmental influences more closely. To do this, psychologists have studied both the intellectual environment of foster homes and the length of time that adopted children have lived with their foster parents (Scarr & Weinberg, 1976; Skodak & Skeels, 1949). For example, Scarr and Weinberg conducted a "transracial" study of 101 white families who adopted black children. The parents in these families were well above average in intelligence, income, and social class. As **Figure 11.4** shows, the children adopted into these homes scored considerably above the average IQ of 100. Furthermore, children who were adopted early in life (within the first year) had higher IQ scores than those adopted later. Such findings suggest that when adoptive homes provide a superior intellectual climate, they can have a substantial effect on intelligence.

Heritability

Family resemblance and adoption studies make one point clear: both heredity and environment influence intelligence. But is there a way to gather information on the *relative* contribution of these two variables? For example, can we determine to what degree heredity and environment contribute to intelligence? Keeping in mind some crucial limitations, the answer is yes.

By drawing on studies of identical and fraternal twins, whose genetic relationship is well established, psychologists are able to estimate the proportion of the variability (roughly speaking the range) in IQ scores that can be attributed to genetic factors. In effect, this is an estimate of the **heritability** of intelligence. However, estimating heritability is far from a precise science, and estimates range from a high of 80 percent to a low of 40 percent (Jensen, 1980). Experts differ in which figure they accept, but the consensus seems to be an estimate of roughly 50 percent (Henderson, 1982).

Whatever estimate we accept, it is imperative to remember that heritability applies only to a *group* of people and never to any single individual. No one can say that 80 percent, or even 40 percent, of an individual's intelligence is determined by heredity. It is equally important to remember that the term heretability does not imply that intelligence is fixed and unchanging. Rather, it is a measure of the relative contribution of genetic factors for a particular *group of people* at a *given point in time*. Thus, if the heritability ratio of the adopted children in the Scarr and Weinberg (1976) transracial study was computed at two points in time, just after adoption and many years later, we could expect two different outcomes. The experience of living in a superior intellectual environment might very well alter the ratio.

Race and Intelligence

Racial differences in intellectual performance are a provocative topic. In the United States, comparisons between whites and blacks have often dominated the headlines, but other group or racial differences are also striking, though often overlooked. For example, Japanese school children have shown marked superiority over their American counterparts in mathematics, and compared to other ethnic groups, including whites, Asian Americans have demonstrated consistently superior performance in science (Stevenson & Lee, 1990).

Nevertheless, historically, one comparison—a difference in the *average* performance of blacks and whites on standardized intelligence tests—has been the focal point of some of the most intense and passionate debates about racial differences. A number of studies have shown that the average IQ score for the white population is approximately 10 to 15 points higher than the average for the black population (Jensen, 1980; Kamin, 1974). What is controversial, however, is not the difference, but how the difference should be interpreted.

Perhaps no single paper has done more to keep the controversy alive than Arthur Jensen's (1969) monograph on intelligence and educational practice. Jensen's long and scholarly argument was principally a discussion of genetic and environmental components of intelligence. Only a small portion of the paper was devoted to racial differences in intelligence, but what Jensen said about these differences made the paper a major target of criticism from biologists and psychologists alike (Bodmer & Cavalli-Sforza, 1970; Kagan, 1969, 1973; J. McV. Hunt, 1969). In his paper, Jensen reviewed a series of twin studies similar to those we discussed earlier. On the strength of this review, Jensen concluded that the best estimate of the heritability of intelligence was +.80. As we have seen, this is a high-end estimate, but the real controversy was not over the estimate but over Jensen's hypothesis that the difference in the average performance of blacks and whites on standardized intelligence tests might be due to average differences in genetic endowment between the races. (e.g., Chomsky, 1976; Jensen, 1973; Kagan, 1973; Kamin, 1976; Shockley, 1972).

Jensen's opponents were quick to point to life experiences common to many black individuals that have a strong potential for adversely affecting performance on a standardized intelligence test. For example, researchers have

Both heredity and environment contribute to an individual's intelligence. Here, Japanese high school students put in very long hours of study which in part accounts for their academic achievements.

Between Fields: Environmental factors (variations in soil) produce differences in the height of the corn

corn seed   corn seed
FERTILE FIELD   **BARREN FIELD**

Figure 11.5
Heritability and Environment.
Even when genetic factors contribute to differences *within* a group, they may have little to do with differences *between* a group.

observed differences between blacks and whites in family structure, educational background, and perceived opportunity for success (Deutsch, 1967; Kagan, 1973; Kamin, 1976). Black children are known to show greater levels of anxiety in formal test-taking situations than white children (Zigler, Abelson, & Seitz, 1973), report less motivation to do well on the tests (Katz, 1968), and show marked improvement in their test performance when the examiner takes longer than usual to establish good rapport (Kagan, 1969).

In addition to arguments about comparable life experiences, Jensen faced a torrent of criticism about the proper interpretation of the heritability ratio (Bodmer & Cavalli-Sforza, 1970; Feldman & Lewonton, 1975). In effect, Jensen used the heritability ratio to make comparisons between two different populations, blacks and whites. However, the heritability ratio actually says nothing whatever about differences *between* groups or populations. Psychologist Leon Kamin offers an intriguing analogy that highlights this point (see **Figure 11.5**). Kamin (1981) asks us to imagine a situation in which a farmer fills two sacks with a mixture of two different genetic varieties of corn seed.

The seed from one sack is then planted in a fertile field; the seed from the other sack is planted in a barren field. *Within* each field, we will observe considerable variation in the height of the corn that grows. This variation is due largely to genetic factors, that is, differences in the seed that was planted. However, we will also observe difference *between* the two fields: the average height of the corn in the fertile field will exceed the average height of corn in the barren field. But this variation is due entirely to environmental factors—differences between the soil in the two fields. Kamin argues that much the same process is at work with human intelligence. Variations in IQ scores *between* different racial groups may have little or no genetic basis even if heritabilty is high *within* each group.

In short, Jensen's critics contend that the heritability ratio must be computed separately for each population that is studied. While it may provide useful information about a given group or population, in the eyes of many psychologists it is an inappropriate tool to use for comparisons between races.

Interim Summary

Studies of people who vary in genetic relatedness reveal that as the genetic similarity between people increases, so does the correlation in their test scores. However, the same studies also demonstrate that for a given degree of genetic similarity, such as that between identical twins, the correlation between scores is higher when people are reared together in the same environment. Such studies have indicated that both heredity and environment contribute to intelligence.

The heritability ratio is a way of estimating the relative contribution of heredity and environment to the development of intelligence. It does not apply to any given individual but is instead an estimate of the relative contribution of genetic factors for a particular group of people at a given point in time. The heritability ratio does not imply that intelligence is fixed and unchangeable.

Arthur Jensen drew on the heritability ratio in advancing the hypothesis that the average difference in IQ scores between blacks and whites might be due to genetic differences between the two groups. A number of psychologists disagreed with Jensen, arguing that inequities in life experiences, more than genetic differences, contributed to an average difference in IQ scores between blacks and whites. Experts have also challenged Jensen's interpretation of the heritability ratio.

CULTURAL BIAS IN TESTS

What does it mean to speak of bias in testing? Essentially, a test is biased if it favors one group of people more than others. So when people speak of **cultural bias** in tests, they are raising the fundamental issues of fairness. For instance, if we agree with David Wechsler that intelligence involves the capacity to think rationally, then an intelligence test should measure this ability as objectively as possible. People from all social and economic backgrounds should have an equal opportunity to demonstrate rational thinking on an intelligence test.

In principle, there is no disagreement with this line of reasoning. In practice, however, a test must have a particular definition or objective. Because intelligence tests continue to reflect their historical objective—to identify the skills needed to succeed in school—many of the questions embody values and experiences more common to some people than to others. For example, certain questions about general information on the WAIS-R (such as, "Who wrote Hamlet?" and "What is the capital of Italy?") seem to fall into this category. Other questions involving verbal reasoning also reflect particular cultural expectations (Kagan, 1971). A very poor person who is asked, "Why is it better to pay bills by check than by cash?" may be required to reason about a concept (banking) that is quite unfamiliar.

Some experts believe that questions like these are *prima facie* evidence for cultural bias. In their view, such questions reflect white, middle-class values that are inaccessible to large segments of the population (Mercer, 1984). To overcome the problem, these researchers feel that psychologists must develop intelligence tests that tap basic cognitive processes dependent on experiences common to all people, rather than school-related or academic experiences common to the middle class (Kaufman, 1983). **Figure 11.6** shows several examples of one kind of problem that is usually not taught directly in school and should therefore be less affected by particular cultural experiences.

Other psychologists take a different view. They argue that middle-class subjects show superior performance even on problems, such as those in Figure 11.6, that are the most neutral or "culture fair." Furthermore, they point out that traditional intelligence tests do what they were intended to do—predict who will do well in classroom situations—and that they accomplish this equally for all racial and social groups (Jensen, 1980).

So what can we conclude? Obviously, cultural bias is a complicated issue that depends very much on definition and perspective. In one sense, traditional IQ tests are not biased. They predict school performance, and to a lesser extent job performance, for people from all racial and social groups (Holden, 1982). On the other hand, intelligence tests prescribe a rather narrow, school-related perspective on intelligence. They omit a great deal from the realm of what might be called intelligent behavior. In so doing, they place artifical limits on the human potential for personal growth and development (Gardner, 1983).

IQ test given to immigrants in the early part of this century were not fair assessments of intelligence because they did not account for language skills or cultural differences.

Test 1 Series
Select the item that completes the series.

Test 2 Classification
Mark the one item in each row that does not belong with the others.

Test 3 Matrices
Mark the item that correctly completes the given matrix, or pattern.

Figure 11.6
Examples of Neutral or Culture-Fair Problems.
(Taken from Culture-Fair Intelligence Test, Scale 2, Form A test booklet. © 1949, 1960, R 1977 by the Institute for Personality and Ability Testing, Inc. Reproduced by permission.)

Interim Summary

Cultural bias is a serious issue because it raises the possibility that intelligence tests are unfair to certain segments of the population. To correct the problem, some investigators believe that intelligence tests should be modified to include questions that measure problem-solving capabilities common to all people, rather than questions that depend on school-related experiences, which may be better known to some people than others. However, other experts dispute the idea that intelligence tests favor any one group. They believe that intelligence tests play an important role in determining school and job performance for people from all racial and social groups.

INTELLIGENCE TESTING—USES AND ALTERNATIVES

Before concluding our discussion of intelligence, we should turn to one very compelling question: what are the proper uses of the intelligence test? This is a simple but far-reaching question about the role of IQ testing in society.

It is all the more compelling when we contemplate some early misuses (and misinterpretations) of intelligence tests.

Early Uses of Intelligence Tests

At the turn of the century, a large number of European immigrants arrived in the United States. By the year 1912, the Public Health Service became concerned about the problem of allowing unselected masses to enter the country. In response to this concern, psychologist Henry Goddard was called upon to screen the immigrants using the newly developed mental tests (Kamin, 1974). Although there was an obvious difficulty with language and cultural barriers, Goddard believed that the tests could be translated and then used effectively as screening devices. In the years that followed, a number of potential immigrants were deported or refused admission because they were classified as "feeble minded" on the basis of these entrance tests. Authorities failed to recognize the very real possibility that the tests in no way measured the immigrants' true abilities.

A similar unhappy chapter in the history of intelligence testing can be found in several early discussions of the IQ data collected by the U.S. Army during World War I. During the war, the Army tested millions of draftees, including large numbers of immigrants from many different European countries. When prominent psychologists of the day analyzed these test results, they were looking for patterns that would show national superiority rather than the performance factors that might have influenced the outcome. They spoke about the superior intelligence of people from Scotland, England, and northern and western European countries and the rather inferior abilities of those from southern and eastern Europe, such as Italians and Russians (Kamin, 1974). Overlooked in this analysis was the question of how long the immigrants had lived in the United States before they were tested and thus how familiar they were with the American language and culture. In fact, when the scores of immigrants who had lived in the country 20 years or more before testing were compared with those of native-born Americans, no meaningful differences were found. But psychologists of that era ignored a cultural interpretation in favor of one that stressed the superiority of certain "blood" lines, such as Nordic blood over Mediterranean blood (Kamin, 1974).

Although such flagrant abuses and misin-terpretations of the intelligence test no longer occur, some psychologists remain concerned that IQ testing, particularly as part of a selection process, is less fair to some people than to others. This is one reason for the caution and concern that surround the contemporary use of intelligence tests.

Contemporary Uses of Intelligence Tests

In today's society, one of the most positive uses of an intelligence test is to help people resolve difficulties and make decisions about their lives. For example, an individual might approach a psychologist about a specific problem, such as reading difficulties in the classroom. In such a case, the psychologist may need to know something about the individual's general intellectual capabilities and may use an intelligence test as one part of the diagnostic procedure.

A far more controversial use of the intelligence test involves selecting people for a particular station in life, such as whether to take college preparatory or general courses in high school, or whether to pursue a particular job or career. One reason such uses of the intelligence test are controversial is that the consumers, those who are being tested, have usually not requested the test. In these instances, the psychologist is really acting on behalf of someone else. A second and more compelling concern is the fairness of the intelligence test to all those competing for a particular educational or vocational opportunity. As we noted earlier, many psychologists question whether the intelligence test provides an accurate assessment of the intellectual capabilities of people from all economic and racial backgrounds, especially when the goal is to select individuals for particular jobs (McClelland, 1973). These experts believe that in cases where assessment is required, a more equitable tool must be found. While some psychologists defend the use of intelligence tests as objective instruments that remove the potential for personal bias from the selection process (Jensen, 1973), there does not appear to be sufficient confidence in the tests to warrant their *exclusive* use when choosing people for particular educational or vocational positions.

In this regard, it is interesting to note the findings of a 4-year study of standardized tests by the National Academy of Sciences. This prestigious body concluded that standardized tests, including intelligence tests, show strong predictive validity and can often be quite helpful in forecasting how well a person will do in school or on the job ("NAS calls tests fair," 1982). However, the Academy qualified this cautious support for testing with the warning that tests should never be considered the sole measure of a person's ability. The report stated that although tests have "severe limitations," they create a fairer and more objective climate than would a situation in which no tests were used. The essential argument of the report is that tests must be used wisely. For example, in most school systems intelligence tests are now used primarily to determine if a student needs remedial help. The Academy suggests that this is a legitimate use of intelligence tests but warns that test scores alone should not be used to classify a student as below normal. Information from other sources, such as teacher reports, should also weigh in the decision. In addition, any classification of a child based even partially on test results should be subject to periodic review (Holden, 1982).

The question that confronts psychologists today is how to use intelligence tests effectively. Do they have any social value or should they be abolished altogether? The answer seems to be qualified support for intelligence tests. In situations where individuals need help, particularly with school-related activities, intelligence tests can be useful as one part of a broad-based assessment. They should not be regarded as the sole measure of intellectual capability, as the National Academy of Sciences report suggests, but they can provide a helpful profile of an individual's strengths and weaknesses. In this regard, we note that in many situations psychologists do not focus exclusively on a person's overall or full scale IQ (recall the WAIS-R profile on p. 395) but examine the *pattern of scores* on the various subtests. Often the psychologist's goal is to provide an extensive evaluation of an individual's abilities, not simply a single number that represents an estimate of general intelligence. In short, when used sensibly and interpreted cautiously, the intelligence test can play a productive role in the decisions people make about modern-day problems.

Interim Summary

Intelligence tests have many uses. Perhaps the least controversial use occurs when an individual requests help from a psychologist for a specific problem and the psychologist needs information on the individual's general intellectual capacities. A far more controversial situation is the use of intelligence tests to select people for educational or vocational placement. Not all psychologists agree that intelligence tests play a useful role in this process, particularly in assessing the skills of people not familiar with the knowledge and values of the majority culture.

SUMMARY

1. Experts have failed to agree on a comprehensive definition of intelligence. However, there is growing awareness that the problem-solving skills thought to reflect intelligence differ widely from one culture to another. Furthermore, even within the same culture, intelligence can have very different manifestations.

2. Binet and Simon developed the first modern intelligence test, which, in contrast to Galton's efforts, concentrated on the measurement of higher mental abilities such as reasoning, imagination, and memory. The best-known revision of Binet and Simon's test is the Stanford-Binet, which first incorporated the formula that led to an overall IQ score. David Wechlser subsequently developed a somewhat different intelligence test that measures both verbal and nonverbal intelligence.

3. A well-developed intelligence test must meet three specific criteria: standardization, reliability, and validity. A test is standardized by giving the original list of questions to people of varying ages and social backgrounds. Through this process, the test constructor eliminates some questions and refines others. Reliability is achieved when the test yields a consistent measure of an individual's performance. Validity is achieved when the test actually measures what it was designed to measure.

4. Individual intelligence tests can be contrasted with group intelligence tests, which are administered to a large number of people simultaneously. The Scholastic Aptitude Test (SAT) is a well-known example of a group intelligence test. Like all aptitude tests, the SAT is designed to measure future potential, but aptitude is often closely linked to achievement, or past learning.

5. In evaluating how well people perform on an intelligence tests, psychologists distin-

guish what a person knows (competence) from the expression of that knowledge in a particular situation (performance). Factors such as anxiety, unfamiliarity with the test situation, and low motivation can lead to poor performance, or underestimation of an individual's competence.

6. Some psychologists have suggested that intelligence is largely a matter of a single factor or ability, labeled general intelligence or simply *g*. Other experts have disagreed, suggesting that intelligence is composed of a number of independent factors or separate abilities.

7. The contemporary theories of Robert Sternberg and Howard Gardner stand in sharp contrast to both of these approaches. Sternberg believes that there are three forms of intelligence: componential intelligence, or mastery of the steps used to solve complex problems; experiential intelligence, or ability to perceive novel and creative solutions to complex problems; and contextual intelligence, or ability to deal effectively with the environment.

8. Gardner's theory of multiple intelligences suggest that we view intelligence as a mutifaceted phenomenon, including not only such traditional measures of intelligence as linguistic, logical-mathematical, and spatial abilities but also musical, personal, and bodily-kinesthetic skills. Gardner's critics dismiss these latter abilities as talents, but Gardner argues that they are true manifestations of intelligence largely ignored by most industrialized societies.

9. Performance on intelligence tests is relatively stable from age 4 onward. By the time children are 7 years of age, IQ scores show a stong positive correlation with scores obtained at age 18. However, there are notable exceptions to this pattern. Some children experience gains or losses of 15 IQ points or more during the childhood years. The home environment seems to be the pivotal factor in these major shifts in IQ.

10. New ways to measure attention and memory in infants have allowed researchers to predict how well children will perform on intelligence tests taken years later. However, it is too early to know how useful this research will be in determining the factors that affect performance on an intelligence test.

11. The mentally retarded and the intellectually gifted are two small but important groups who define the extremes of intelligence. Mental retardation is indicated both by a score on an intelligence test (usually an IQ below 70) and an inability to meet age-appropriate standards of personal and social responsibility.

12. The intellectually gifted are people whose IQ equals or exceeds 130. Lewis Terman conducted a major study of intellectually gifted children and found that high intelligence was generally associated with superior health, social adjustment, and life achievement. However, because Terman's subjects came from higher social and economic backgrounds, some psychologists have questioned whether the privileges of high social class more than intelligence contributed to the success of these gifted people. Others challenge this criticism, noting that tests of intellectual ability predict occupational success for people from many different backgrounds.

13. Studies of people who vary in genetic relatedness reveal that as the genetic similarity between people increases, so does the correlation in their test scores. However, the same studies also demonstrate that for a given degree of genetic similarity, the correlation between scores is higher when people are reared together in the same environment. Such studies have indicated that both heredity and environment contribute to intelligence.

14. The heritability ratio is a way of estimating the relative contribution of heredity and environment to the development of intelligence. It does not apply to any given individual but is instead an estimate of the relative contribution of genetic factors for a particular group of people at a given point in time.

15. Arthur Jensen drew on the heritability ratio in advancing the hypothesis that the average difference in IQ scores between blacks and whites might be due to genetic differences between the two groups. A number of experts challenged Jensen's interpretation of the heritability ratio.

16. Cultural bias is a serious issue because it raises the possibility that intelligence tests are unfair to certain segments of the population. Some investigators believe that intelligence tests should be modified to include

questions that measure problem-solving capabilities common to all people, rather than questions that depend on school-related experiences, which may be better known to some people than others. However, other experts dispute the idea that intelligence tests favor any one group. They believe that intelligence tests play an important role in determining school and job performance for people from all racial and social groups.

17. Intelligence tests have many uses. Perhaps the least controversial use occurs when an individual requests help from a psychologist for a specific problem and the psychologist needs information on the individual's general intellectual capacities. A far more controversial situation is the use of intelligence tests to select people for educational or vocational placement. Not all psychologists agree that intelligence tests play a useful role in this process, particularly in assessing the skills of people not familiar with the knowledge and values of the majority culture.

KEY INDIVIDUALS

David Wechsler
Arthur Jensen
Sir Francis Galton
David McClelland
Alfred Binet
Charles Spearman
Theophile Simon
Louis Thurstone
Lewis Terman
Robert Sternberg
Howard Gardner
Henry Goddard
Langdon Down

KEY RESEARCH

Galton's attempts to measure intelligence
the Binet-Simon test and the concept of mental age
the Stanford-Binet test and the intelligence quotient (IQ)
The WAIS-R and WISC-III tests
the effects of performance factors on test performance
Terman's longitudinal study of the intellectually gifted
the factor analysis approach to understanding the intellect
Thurstone's primary mental abilities
the triarchic theory of intelligence
Gardner's multiple intelligences
arguments concerning the relationship between race and intelligence

KEY TERMS

reliability
competence
mental age (MA)
validity
performance
chronological age (CA)
Down syndrome
intelligence quotient (IQ)
standardization
primary mental abilities
norm
heritability
cultural bias

Part Four
• •

SOCIAL PSYCHOLOGY AND PERSONALITY

Chapter 12

Social Cognition

Chapter 13

Social Influence

Chapter 14

Personality and Assessment

A Conversation With . . .

Claude Steele is Professor of Psychology at Stanford University. He has been at Stanford since 1991. Previously, Steele taught at the University of Michigan and the University of Washington. He is on the Board of Directors of the American Psychological Society and is past Chair of the Executive Committee of the Society of Experimental Social Psychology.

Q What is a major benefit of studying social interaction?

A Social psychology—as the scientific field that focuses on the relationship between the individual and society—has a particularly powerful ability to help understand the major social issues and problems of our time. One of the founders of the field, Kurt Lewin, said there is nothing as practical as a good theory. I take tremendous gratification in trying to be scientific about important social problems—bringing the insights of theory to bear on a problem and allowing the problem to expand theory. It is an exciting two-way street. One can have the sense of working on something practical at the same time that one is expanding scientific understanding. The world has no shortage of challenging problems: ethnic conflict in Eastern Europe, corrosive racial conflict at home, the challenge of educating a heterogeneous population. Many of these problems have important social psychological dimensions, and by using theory and research with great care, there is room for people to make exciting contributions to bettering problems

Q Your work on self-affirmation has been very important to the field of social psychology. Can you tell us a little about it?

A It is nice of you to characterize the theory that way. Like all theories, its aim is to explain as much as possible with as few assumptions as possible. We started with the simple assumption that people are motivated to see themselves as generally good and

competent, that is, as morally and adaptively adequate. In terms of everyday experience, this state is probably experienced as feelings of positive self-esteem, or of "being up to the challenge." The motive to maintain this perception, the theory reasons, pressures us to interpret ourselves, and to behave in ways that confer self-esteem.

Up to this point our theory isn't much different from other self-esteem theories going all the way back to William James. But two things, I believe, distinguish it. First, it explains what it means to be identified with something, say with being a swimmer, or a psychologist, or a good student. To be identified is to have one's sense of adequacy depend on how well one does with the activity or in the domain. This is another simple idea that, as I hope to show soon, can explain some important things about school achievement.

The theory also explains the tremendous flexibility we have in coping with threats to our self-esteem. This flexibility is an important source of human resilience and it is rooted, we reasoned, in a simple fact: that when threatened, our goal is restoration of an overall image of self-integrity, not necessarily refutation of each threatening event that comes along. This means that in responding to threat one can do things that affirm—thus the name of the theory—overall self-integrity as well as things that counter the threat itself. Consider the esteem-maintaining resilience of the cigarette smoker. When virtually every rationalization for smoking has been disqualified by society, smokers can still cope with its threat to their self-esteem by affirming something else about themselves that demonstrates their overall adequacy—for example, recalling a "parent of the year award," or working harder for sales bonus.

This idea has been tested most extensively as an alternative to cognitive dissonance theory, a theory that assumes people

Claude Steele

seek consistency in their behavior, thoughts and beliefs, such that when they become aware of an inconsistency they try to rationalize it away. We agreed that people are rationalizers, but see the goal of rationalization not as self-consistency but as an image of self-adequacy. To make this point, our research has shown that people can easily tolerate inconsistency—if they are allowed to affirm their overall worth. It is the war of global self-integrity, not the battle against specific inconsistencies, that drives our rationalizations.

Q What are some potential applications of your research?

A Recently, I have tried to understand some of the difficulties women and minorities experience in schooling in terms of this theory. The idea is this: that in some settings (for example, math and sciences for women, and a broader set of academic areas for black Americans) these groups are often vulnerable to stereotype-based judgments of inadequate ability. Failure in these areas, then, for members of these groups, carries a double threat; it impugns the specific ability for that kind of work—as it would for anyone—but it can also confirm the broad, group-based inferiority they are suspected of in the stereotype. Such vulnerability, we reason, makes it difficult for these students to identify with these areas of achievement in the sense of allowing performance in the area to become a basis of self-esteem. Many, of course, do identify and succeed. But all too many—pressured by this vulnerability—may give in disidentifying with achievement, and correspondingly, letting their efforts diminish. The good news from this analysis—supported in our own research, as well as many successful intervention programs—is that blocking this sense of vulnerability greatly improves achievement among these students. Schooling climates that assure them about their abilities, that challenge them rather than "remediate" them (challenge implies respect for their abilities, ascribes failure to task difficulty and success to the self) and that integrates them and their cultural perspective into the mainstream of school life, all show real achievement gains for these students. It does this, we argue, by reducing the vulnerability that is their default experience in too much American schooling.

Q What do you think some exciting new developments in the future will be?

A I believe an exciting area of future research in social psychology will be that of understanding the way in which people function collectively. Although it is an age-old problem in the social sciences, I believe we are just beginning to understand the processes through which the collective—i.e., the groups with which we identify and interact—functions to shape our beliefs, values, even our personality and sense of personal identity. We tend to think of ourselves as self-determining organisms, relatively immune to social influence. Yet it is becoming increasingly clear that much of the information processing that underlies our beliefs, values, and identities, is done not so much as individuals unconnected to others, but through interaction and conversation with others, through media influences and other means of public, not private discourse. Understanding these processes—especially in light of their importance to such self-defining internal states as personal goals, standards of conduct, stereotypes, social values, etc.—will become an increasingly important focus of social psychology.

12 Social Cognition

CHAPTER OUTLINE

ocial psychology is the study of social interaction—the way people affect and relate to each other. It considers how attitudes are shaped by parents and peers, how people come to love or hate each other, and how human beings influence each other's judgments, feelings, and opinions. Helping people in trouble, forming first impressions of individuals we have just met, conforming to group pressure, and deciding to make war or peace are all examples of topics that social psychologists study.

We can divide social psychology into two areas. **Social cognition** is the study of the ways human beings process information about their social world, including themselves, other people, and social issues. **Social influence** is the study of the ways people influence each other's judgments, actions, and decisions. This chapter looks at social cognition and Chapter 13 takes up social influence.

Social cognition seeks to understand and make sense of people (Fiske & Taylor, 1991). We live in a world full of numerous individuals and groups, a wide variety of lifestyles and opinions, and a complex assortment of feelings and relationships. Social cognition is concerned with how we perceive or interpret this social information, how we remember it, and how we make inferences about unknown aspects of people from what we do know.

Our first impression of a person can be strongly affected by a few key elements.

In the first section of this chapter we consider the ways we organize information about other people into an overall impression and the ways we make inferences about the causes of our own and other people's behavior. The next section considers forming and changing attitudes and beliefs. In the third section we apply what we know about impression formation, attribution, and attitudes to understanding a fundamental social problem the world over, prejudice and stereotypes. How do we account for the hostility that exists between groups of people, and what hope is there for a future with more harmonious intergroup relations? Finally, we will turn to a happier side of social cognition, those positive perceptions and evaluations of other people that lead us to feel attraction and love.

• •

IMPRESSION FORMATION AND ATTRIBUTION

The field of impression formation and attribution, also known as *person perception,* studies how we put together the various pieces of information we have about other people to come to a full understanding of their behavior. Suppose we know that a neighbor is friendly and intelligent, but also that he has told lies to close friends and bullies people who are less confident. How do we integrate these pieces of information? How do we form an overall impression and how do we explain his behavior? To answer these questions, we will consider principles of impression formation, the operation of schemata in social cognation, and the ways we make attributions about the causes of people's behavior.

Forming First Impressions

A classic study of impression formation shows that we organize coherent impressions from disparate pieces of information and that our overall first impression of a person can be strongly affected by a few key elements (Asch, 1946). Some subjects in this study were told to form an impression of a person who was described as intelligent, skillful, industrious, warm, determined, practical, and cautious. (What kind of impression would you form of such a person?) In contrast, others were told to form an impression of someone who was intelligent, skillful, industrious, cold, determined, practical, and cautious. Notice that the list of words is the same except that in the second list the word *cold* is substituted for *warm*. As you might imagine, the resulting impression was much more positive for those who heard the word warm than for those who heard the word cold. Even though warm or cold was only one trait out of seven, it gave the subjects in the study the only information they had about whether the person was friendly or unfriendly and therefore strongly affected the overall perception.

Asch's "warm-cold" study shows that people do form overall impressions based on the various pieces of information they have. A further question of great importance is what effect these initial impressions have during later interactions with the person. If we believe that a person is warm, does that impression have any impact on the way we interpret the person's later behavior? We can answer this question by employing the concept of *schema*.

The Concept of Schema

In Chapter 7, we defined a *schema* as our general knowledge about a particular situation. Generally, we can say that a **schema** is our general knowledge acquired from experience about any object, event, person, or group, including our knowledge about ourselves and others. The word *schema* is derived from the Greek word for "form" and thus refers to the form or outline of our knowledge, stored in memory, of any person, object, situation, and so on. Included in our schemata (the plural form of schema) may be specific beliefs about people, general impressions of them, or expectations about how they will behave. Although what people "know" may or may not be accurate, their schemata are the knowledge they have, right or wrong. The concept of schema is very helpful in understanding the ways we attend to, interpret, and remember the people and events we encounter in our day-to-day lives.

In the Asch study, subjects were asked to form an impression of a person based on a list of seven adjectives. These impressions are good examples of schemata. Let us consider a hypothetical subject, Tom, who heard the list of adjectives that included the word warm and who formed a generally positive impression of the person described. Tom's impression constitutes a schema that might include the specific beliefs that the person is warm, friendly, and

approachable. How would such a schema play a role in Tom's thinking about and interaction with the person?

A study related to Asch's experiment suggests that Tom's initial schema about the person can affect his expectations about the person's future behavior, his interpretation of the person's actual behavior, and Tom's own behavior. In this study (Kelley, 1950) some students in an economics class were told that a guest lecturer was "a very warm person, industrious, critical, practical, and determined," and others were told that he was "a rather cold person, industrious, critical," and so forth. After the class period students were asked about their impressions of the guest lecturer. As you might expect, the students had very different feelings depending on whether they were told the lecturer was "very warm" or "rather cold." That is, their schemata created an expectation of how he would behave and they interpreted his behavior according to their expectation. Students who were given the cold description rated the lecturer as more self-centered, formal, proud, unpopular, humorless, irritable, and ruthless than people who were told he was warm. Furthermore, they also tended to ask fewer questions and generally interacted in a more distant manner. In short, the initial schemata led to different expectations, different interpretations, and, finally, different behavior.

Thus we see that people form impressions on the basis of small amounts of information and that these impressions constitute schemata that affect both expectation and interpretation. Other research suggests our schemata affect what we pay attention to and what we remember (Crocker, Fiske, & Taylor, 1984; Hamilton, 1988).

There are many different kinds of schemata. In addition to schemata about persons, people have schemata about roles and groups, such as schemata about women, bankers, and Italians. These group schemata function as stereotypes pertaining to particular groups. Finally, people have schemata about events. These schemata are known as scripts. **Scripts** are the general knowledge that we have about what happens in particular situations. For example, many people have a script for what happens when they walk into a restaurant. A host or hostess will show them to their table, a waiter or waitress will fill their glasses with water and hand them menus, etc. Each of these different kinds of schemata contains general knowledge about the person, group, or event they pertain to.

Incongruent Information and Schema Change

Schemata are resistant to change. When we encounter information in the environment that is inconsistent with our schemata, however, our schemata can change. How does this happen?

Usually, information that is inconsistent with our schemata undergoes a process of assimilation. **Assimilation** occurs when we fit incongruent information into an existing schema by shaping or distorting the information during interpretation or recall so that it is seen as consistent with the schema. Take for example a young woman, Nancy, whose initial schema about President Bill Clinton during the 1992 presidential primaries was generally favorable. Before the New Hampshire primary, she saw him as a competent and honorable person. She might have perceived the information that came out during the campaign about an extramarital affair and his efforts to avoid the draft as false charges created by Republican campaign workers to discredit a formidable challenger to President George Bush.

Occasionally, however, schemata do change to fit incoming information. In this situation, we deal with the incongruent information through the process of *accommodation*. **Accommodation** occurs when schemata are revised completely or when they are simply developed further and made more complex. If Nancy had decided that Bill Clinton was a competent, promising politician who made some youthful mistakes, we would say that she had made her schema more complex. If she decided that Clinton was an untruthful opportunist who does not deserve the nation's support, we would say that she had revised her schema completely. We assimilate new information into existing schemata more often than we accommodate our schemata to fit new information. Because of this we say that schemata are resistant to change.

An experiment by Lord, Ross, and Lepper (1979) shows clearly how people assimilate information into their schemata. The subjects in the experiment were either strongly in favor of or strongly opposed to capital punishment. All subjects read two studies, one indicating that capital punishment was an effective deterrent to crime and one indicating that it was not. Subjects perceived the study that supported their position as being much more valid and believable, and subjects on both sides of the issue actually became more extreme in their attitude. Both groups assimilated the conflicting information into their schemata and strengthened them.

Although our schemata are resistant to change, our attention is drawn to novel or incongruent stimuli (Taylor & Fiske, 1978). Whether we act on this information once we've noticed it depends, in part, on three factors. We need to (1) have the time to think about the new information, (2) have the ability to understand its relation to our schema, and (3) have the motivation to process the information and either assimilate it or change our schema. If one of these conditions is not present, we will simply stop thinking about the new information.

Given that we have begun processing the information, however, what determines whether it changes our schema? One important factor is how discrepant the information is with our preconceptions. Moderately discrepant information is most likely to be accommodated, and highly discrepant information is simply dismissed. In addition, the information must be both unambiguous and memorable (Crocker, Fiske, & Taylor, 1984). The impact of memorable incongruent information was demonstrated in an experiment by Crocker, Hannah, and Weber (1983).

Assimilation occurs when we fit incongruent information into an existing schema. For example, many Clinton supporters, whose initial schema about the character of the 1992 presidential candidate was positive, felt that information about his personal life and efforts to avoid the draft were false charges designed to discredit him.

Subjects in this experiment had formed the schema that John was a friendly person. Then they were given incongruent information: "John cut in line in front of three people at the bank." The study showed that subjects changed their impressions of John depending on whether the behavior was attributed to external factors—"He did this because he was paged for an emergency"—or to his character—"He did this because he didn't care what others thought." When the incongruent information was attributed to the external factors, subjects did not remember it and did not change their schema about John. However, when the incongruent information was attributed to John's character, it was highly memorable; and the more subjects remembered it, the more they changed their schema about John. In short, subjects changed their schema to accommodate the incongruent information when that new information was attributed to John's character and therefore highly memorable.

Primacy and Recency Effects in Impression Formation

People form coherent impressions of others from disparate pieces of information, and their schema about an individual can change when they are confronted with incongruent information about that person. How do people form an overall impression when they are confronted with inconsistent information? When people behave in a way that is inconsistent with our first impression, is our final impression based more on the early information about the person or the later information? For example, when a friend whom we thought was extremely intelligent starts getting grades of Cs and Ds, what overall impression do we form of his or her intelligence? When people hold strongly to their first impressions, we refer to a *primacy effect*. A **primacy effect** is defined as an impression more heavily weighted by first information than later information. An impression more heavily weighted by later information is known as a **recency effect**. In the example above, if we conclude that our friend is not very bright, we are showing a recency effect.

Which effect is more common, primacy or recency? In one study (Luchins, 1957), subjects were asked to read one of two paragraphs about a boy named Jim. Some subjects read the following:

Jim left the house to get some stationery. He walked out into the sun-filled street with two of his friends, basking in the sun as he walked. Jim entered the stationery store, which was full of people. Jim talked with an acquaintance while he waited for the clerk to catch his eye. On his way out, he stopped to chat with a school friend who was just coming into the store. Leaving the store, he walked toward school. On his way out he met the girl to whom he had been introduced the night before. They talked for a short while, and then Jim left for school. After school, Jim left the classroom alone. Leaving the school, he started on his long walk home. The street was brilliantly filled with sunshine. Jim walked down the street on the shady side. Coming down the street toward him, he saw the pretty girl whom he met on the previous evening. Jim crossed the street and entered a candy store. The store was crowded with students, and he noticed a few familiar faces. Jim waited quietly until the counterman caught his eye and then gave his order. Taking his drink he sat down at a side table. When he had finished his drink he went home. (pp. 34-35)

In the first part of this paragraph, Jim seems extroverted and friendly. But starting with the sentence "After school . . ." Jim sounds much more introverted. One group of subjects read the paragraph as it was presented to you and came to the conclusion that Jim was very friendly. However, another group of subjects read the two parts of the paragraph in reverse order, starting with "After school . . ." and finishing with the part you read first. These subjects concluded that Jim was introverted. Thus, subjects in both groups formed final impressions that were consistent with their first impressions and gave less weight to later information.

In another study demonstrating the primacy effect, subjects observed a young woman taking a test. The woman always answered 15 of 30 problems correctly, but in one condition she answered more correctly at the beginning. In the other condition she did poorly at the start but well at the end. Subjects perceived the young woman as brighter when she had done better at the beginning (Jones, Rock, Shaver, Goethals, & Ward, 1968).

What about recency effects? They are less frequent, but recency effects can be obtained under particular circumstances. For example, if there is a long time between the early and later information, we are more influenced by the information we just received. Also, if we infer that the later information reflects changes in a person's character, we show recency effects (Schneider, Hastorf, & Ellsworth, 1979).

Making Attributions for Behavior

When a person behaves inconsistently, we usually ask why. Why has she changed? What is she really like? Does her initial behavior reflect her true personality, or is the most recent behavior more representative? How do we explain the discrepancies? These are questions of *attribution*. **Attribution** is the process of explaining the causes of behavior. At the heart of the attribution process is deciding whether a person's behavior is caused by something in the person (an internal attribution) or by something in the situation or environment (an external attribution). In our earlier example about John who cut in line at the bank, the question of causality was important. Whether subjects changed their schema about John was strongly affected by whether there appeared to be an internal or external cause for his behavior.

We have suggested that questions of causality and attribution arise when perceivers are puzzled by behavior and undertake to resolve the mystery. In fact, there is great debate about when we make attributions. Some believe that we make attributions deliberately and only under special circumstances, such as

when we encounter unexpected behavior or when we are dependent on the person whose behavior we are observing (Hastie, 1984). On the other side are those who suggest that attribution is spontaneous and automatic and occurs whenever we acquire information about a person's behavior (Uleman, 1987; Winter & Uleman, 1984). It now seems clear that causal reasoning occurs nonconsciously and spontaneously, but that people make more careful attributions when circumstances require them to think about why someone acted as she did and what she is really like (Bassili & Smith, 1986; Winter, Uleman, & Cunniff, 1985).

Principles of Attribution

Despite the controversy about *when* we make attributions, we have a clear idea of *how* we make them. The important distinction between internal and external causes of behavior was first discussed by Fritz Heider (1944, 1958). More recently, other attribution theorists have specified how people actually decide whether a behavior is attributable to internal or external causes (Jones, 1990; Kelley, 1973). They have identified two key attribution principles, the covariation and discounting principles.

THE COVARIATION PRINCIPLE

According to the **covariation principle,** people tend to attribute a person's behavior to events that are present when the behavior occurs and absent when the behavior does not occur. The covariation principle assigns cause and effect to events that *covary,* or occur together. Suppose, for example, that we want to know whether Joan laughed at a certain movie because of her good sense of humor or because the movie is very funny. If Joan's response, laughter, is present only if she watches this movie, her laughter covaries with this movie. We conclude that the movie is funny. If Joan's laughter is frequently present, whether or not she watches this movie, the response covaries with Joan. She is a person with a good sense of humor. To discover how Joan's response covaries, we have to do a little detective work and find out about three characteristics of Joan's reaction: its distinctiveness, its consistency, and its level of consensus.

Distinctiveness refers to how unusual or unique Joan's response to the movie is compared to past responses. Does she laugh often,

According to the covariation principle, we would attribute this person's behavior to his excitement about graduating.

High distinctiveness		High consistency		High consensus		External attribution
Joan laughs just at this movie.	+	Joan usually laughs at this movie.	+	Many other people laugh at this movie.	=	The movie is funny.

Low distinctiveness		High consistency		Low consensus		Internal attribution
Joan laughs often.	+	Joan usually laughs at this movie.	+	Few people laugh at this movie.	=	Joan is easy to amuse.

Figure 12.1
Kelley's Covariation Principle.

or just at this movie? *Consistency* refers to whether Joan's response is the same whenever she sees this movie. If she were to see it again, would she still find it funny? *Consensus* refers to how other people respond in the same situation. Do many other people laugh at this movie, or is Joan the only one?

Using information from the three criteria of distinctiveness, consistency, and consensus, we attempt to make an attribution about, or explain the cause of, Joan's behavior. In general, we attribute a response to an external cause—in this example the film that Joan saw—if the response has high distinctiveness, high consistency, and high consensus. On the other hand, if the response has high consistency but low distinctiveness and low consensus, we tend to attribute the response to some trait of the person. If the response has low consistency, low distinctiveness, and low consensus, we generally attribute it to a special circumstance or temporary mood. **Figure 12.1** illustrates how combinations of these three criteria lead to different attributions for behavior.

In a study showing the importance of the covariation principle, subjects were given information such as the following: "Sue is afraid of the dog. She is not afraid of almost any other dog. In the past Sue has always been afraid of that dog. Almost everyone is afraid of the dog." According to Kelley's criteria, should subjects attribute Sue's fear to an internal cause (she is a fearful person) or to an external cause (the dog is frightening)? First, Sue's response is distinctive. Her reaction to this dog is unique. Second, her response is consistent. She is always afraid of the dog. Third, her response has high consensus. Others are afraid of the dog too. Subjects should make an external attribution to this distinctive, consistent, and consensual re-

sponse. The results of the experiment show that they do and that subjects' attributions in general are consistent with the covariation principle (McArthur, 1972).

THE DISCOUNTING PRINCIPLE
The **discounting principle** holds that behavior cannot be attributed to any one cause if other, equally plausible causes for the behavior exist (Kelley, 1972). For example, we would discount the internal cause of a behavior if we learned of plausible external causes for the behavior. Consider the celebrity endorsement of a particular brand of cornflakes. If we know that the celebrity is being paid handsomely for his endorsement, we discount the internal cause of his making the commercial—that he really likes this brand of cornflakes. The money he is being paid is a plausible external cause for his behavior. Similarly, we discount intelligence (an internal cause) as the reason for a person's doing well on a test if the test was very easy (a plausible external cause).

In one study showing how people use the discounting principle, subjects read: "When Dan came to the city hall and was told by the clerk he couldn't be helped because of a strike, Dan was very itchy and almost screamed at the clerk." Though Dan's behavior is angry, he is not seen as an angry person. Angriness, an internal cause, is discounted because the strike, an external cause, can also explain the behavior. On the other hand, when subjects read: "As Dan came home, his little son jumped on him and hung onto his neck, Dan was very itchy and almost screamed at him," they do not discount. They see Dan as an angry person because his son's jumping is not seen as a plausible external cause for Dan's angry behavior (Trope, Cohen, & Moaz, 1988).

Biases in Attribution

People commonly use both the discounting and covariation principles. But this does not mean that we *always* use them. Correctly applying attribution principles, especially the covariation principle, takes time, energy, and intellectual effort. However, people are not always rational, deliberative, and scientific. In all too many cases, we shortcut the principles that would lead to accurate perceptions and jump to incorrect conclusions. These errors can lead to harmful mistreatment of individuals and groups. Two important and related biases in attribution are the correspondence bias and the actor-observer bias. Both biases suggest we often fail to take full account of all the factors affecting other people's behavior.

THE CORRESPONDENCE BIAS

The **correspondence bias,** also known as the **fundamental attribution error,** is the tendency for observers to underestimate the role of external causes and to overestimate the role of internal or dispositional causes of other people's behavior. It is a failure to use the discounting principle. For example, we might conclude that a young boy is unintelligent (internal cause) when his poor performance in school is really due to his unsettled home life (external cause). Or we might assume that a salesperson is very helpful (internal cause) when her kindness is caused by her efforts to close a deal (external cause). Finally, we might assume that a police officer is a hostile person when in fact carrying out his job requires aggressive behavior. In short, we err in the direction of paying too little attention to external causes of behavior (Gilbert & Jones, 1986).

We might assume that these policemen are hostile people when in fact aggressive behavior is a necessary part of their responsibilities.

One study demonstrated the use of the correspondence bias (Napolitan and Goethals, 1979). College students individually discussed their views of a case study with a young woman who was either very friendly and supportive or very cold and critical. Some of the students were told that the woman was practicing various styles of interacting with others and some were told that she was being herself. Later, when students were asked what they thought the woman's personality was really like, they inferred she was the way she had acted, either friendly or unfriendly, regardless of whether they had been told her behavior was forced or spontaneous. However, if they met her twice and saw her act friendly one time and unfriendly the other, they began to consider situational forces that might have caused her behavior. In this situation they formed impressions that more accurately considered why she might be acting friendly or unfriendly.

When do people show the correspondence bias, and when do they follow the discounting principle? Several studies show that subjects are more likely to show the correspondence bias when they have a lot to think about, such as having to plan a difficult interaction with another person (Gilbert, Pelham, & Krull, 1988; Osborne & Gilbert, 1992). For example, in one study subjects were busy devising ways to present themselves positively to other people. When the other people presented themselves positively in return, the subjects thought those people must have very high self-esteem. Subjects were too busy to remember that the other person's positive self-presentation was induced by their own. As a result they failed to discount and fell victim to the correspondence bias (Baumeister, Hutton, & Tice, 1989). Very often being cognitively busy means that we jump to conclusions about what people are like. If we had the time to give full consideration to their situation we would be much more cautious about making such inferences.

These studies of the correspondence bias suggest that when we judge the behavior of *other* people, it is easy to make internal attributions. We do not, however, make this error in explaining our own behavior, as we shall see in the next section.

THE ACTOR-OBSERVER BIAS

Jones and Nisbett (1971) have proposed that attributions are influenced by an **actor-observer bias.** This is the tendency to attribute our own behavior to external causes and the behavior of others to internal causes. **Figure 12.2** illustrates the actor-observer bias.

In one study demonstrating this bias, male college students were asked to take the roles of both actors and observers. As actors they were asked to explain why they chose to major in a particular subject or why they were dating a particular woman. For the most part, the reasons they gave had to do with external causes—the inherent interest of the subject matter or the attractiveness of their date. One subject wrote, "Chemistry is a very fascinating field." Thus, the subjects saw their behavior as natural responses to objects and people in the environment. However, when these same subjects were asked to play the role of observer and explain why a friend made the same choices, they tended to explain their friend's behavior in terms of internal needs, interests, and traits. One subject commented, "He needs someone he can relax with" (Nisbett, Caputo, Legant, & Marecek, 1973). Another study showed that people writing to advice columnists "Ann Landers" and "Dear Abby" blame their own difficulties on other people, that is, external factors. When they write about other people's problems they do not blame them on external factors (Fischer, Schoeneman & Rubanowitz, 1987).

Why do we use the actor-observer bias? First, we tend to attribute behavior to causes that are *salient* or especially noticeable. Because the forces and constraints of our environment are salient to us, we tend to see our behavior as being caused by them (Taylor & Fiske, 1978). When we are observers, other people are salient parts of our environment. We want to understand them and so we tend to attribute traits to them. Second, we have different information about ourselves and others (Monson & Snyder, 1977). As actors, we know our behavior is different in different situations. As observers, we see others in a limited number of situations, but we assume they are likely to behave similarly in other situations. Thus, we infer traits that will account for these presumably consistent choices. Third, people resist labeling themselves. We all hate to be pigeonholed, so we usually do not explain our behavior in terms of trait labels. But we have no objection to pigeonholing other people. We like to view ourselves as flexible and adaptive and others as understandable and predictable (Sande, Goethals, & Radloff, 1988).

Behavior
Actor A walks down the street whistling.

Actor's attribution	Observer's attribution
"I'm whistling because it's such a beautiful day." (External attribution)	"A's whistling because A is a relaxed, cheerful person." (Internal attribution)

Figure 12.2
The Actor-Observer Bias in Attribution. (Based on Jones & Nisbett, 1971)

Interim Summary

We form an impression of a person by combining disparate pieces of information. Our first impressions can be strongly affected by a few key elements.

Schemata influence what we attend to, how we interpret information, and how we remember. Our initial schema about a person can affect our expectations about and interpretations of the person's behavior and our own behavior as well.

If new information is incongruent with one of our schema, we may change the new information to assimilate it into the existing schema, or we may change our schema to accommodate the new information.

Our overall impressions are strongly affected by primacy effects, or the influence of first impressions. Recency effects, in which later information has greater effect, are rarer but can occur in some specific circumstances.

Attribution is the process of explaining the causes of behavior, other people's and our own. The covariation principle attributes causation to events that occur together. Distinctiveness, consistency, and consensus are three criteria that we use to make attributions about another's behavior. The discounting principle states that people discount internal causes of others' behavior when there are plausible external causes.

Biases that affect attribution are the correspondence bias, which is the tendency to ignore external causes of others' behavior, and the actor-observer bias, which is the tendency to attribute our own behavior to external causes and the behavior of others to internal causes.

••••••••••••••••••••••••••
ATTITUDES AND BELIEFS

Attitudes and beliefs help us organize the overwhelming information input we receive every waking moment of our lives. **Beliefs** can be defined as perceptions of factual matters, of what is true or false. For example, our ideas about how many teeth alligators have, what causes unemployment, and whether artichokes grow on trees are *beliefs*. **Attitudes** can be defined as positive or negative evaluations of people, objects, ideas, or events (Bem, 1970). For example, a person's opposition to abortion or support for affirmative action is an *attitude*. A belief does not indicate liking or disliking; it is merely our idea of what is true or not true. An attitude adds an evaluative component to a belief: for example, an artichoke is an herb (belief), and it has a wonderful taste (attitude).

Although attitudes and beliefs are different, what we say about one applies to the other. To avoid repetition, we will generally refer to attitudes, but you should remember that our discussion also applies to beliefs.

Attitude Formation and Change

Psychologists have identified three major influences on the formation and change of attitudes: social influences, or the influence of other people; cognitive influences, or the influence of our reasoning; and behavioral influences, or the influence of our own behavior. These influences jointly mold our earliest attitudes, and they can change our attitudes throughout our lives (Bem, 1970).

SOCIAL INFLUENCES ON ATTITUDES
Attitudes strongly affect how we perceive and respond to other people. But other people strongly influence the formation of our attitudes. Our early attitudes are influenced by our parents (Oskamp, 1977). Later on, attitudes are influenced by peers. Both parents and peers influence attitudes through three processes: providing information, reinforcement, and identification.

When we are young, parents influence our attitudes by providing information about people, objects, policies, ideas, and events in the world. Parents tell children what is good and what is bad. Young children, having no information to the contrary, believe what their parents say. For example, if children are told

Parents have a great deal of influence on their children's attitudes about the world.

that they can have fun from playing with children of other religions, they will probably develop positive attitudes toward these children. We base many attitudes on the information our parents provide when we are young.

Very often, parents praise children for expressing certain attitudes and disapprove when they express others. Such approval or disapproval has been shown to have a strong impact on the formation of people's attitudes. Thus a second means by which parents influence attitudes is by administering rewards and punishments (McGinnies, 1970). Rewards and punishments affect the expression of attitudes through the principles of operant conditioning (see Chapter 6) just as they affect other behaviors. As research on operant conditioning shows, people engage in the behaviors for which they are rewarded, and these include the expression of particular attitudes.

Even mild reinforcements can shape attitudes. Students at Harvard University were contacted by telephone and asked to comment on various aspects of Harvard's educational system. Some students were reinforced with the response "Good!" every time they made a critical comment about Harvard. Others were reinforced when they made positive comments. Students who were reinforced for being critical made more negative comments than students who heard "Good!" after positive comments (Hildum & Brown, 1956). A later study followed a similar procedure, except that attitudes were measured in a classroom survey 1 week after the reinforcement procedure. Even after a time delay and in a different situation, subjects showed the attitudes that had been reinforced on the telephone (Insko, 1965).

A third social influence on attitudes is *identification* (Kelman, 1961). In the course of growing up, we often try to emulate other people we admire. That is, we identify with them. Part of this process of identification is adopting their attitudes. Freud suggested that the first people we identify with are our parents, especially the parent of the same sex. Erik Erikson emphasizes that throughout childhood and adolescence we identify with many other people, such as relatives, celebrities, or older peers, in the process of forming an identity. Through these identifications we adopt many attitudes. A study of peer influence at different ages suggests that it increases through the elementary school years, reaches its peak in junior high school (ages 12 and 13), and then begins to decrease (see **Figure 12.3**).

Though somewhat diminished, the influence of peers can be profound during high school and college years. This was shown in Theodore Newcomb's classic study of attitude formation and change among students at Bennington College during the 1930s (Newcomb, 1943). At that time, Bennington was a

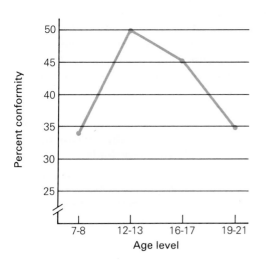

Figure 12.3
Peer Conformity as a Function of Age. (From Costanzo, 1970)

progressive school for women that drew most of its students from wealthy and conservative families. However, because of the progressive attitudes of the faculty, many Bennington seniors had dropped their original conservative attitudes and had become quite liberal. New students entering as freshmen also began to change in the liberal direction. Newcomb found that the more liberal the freshmen became, the more the older students liked them. Acceptance was a powerful reinforcer that strongly affected the newer students' attitudes. This same kind of peer influence has been found for the issue of smoking marijuana. High school students become notably more or less in favor of smoking marijuana depending on the attitudes of their friends (Kandel, 1978).

COGNITIVE INFLUENCES ON ATTITUDES
Another important source of attitudes is judgment based on our own direct experience and reasoning (Fazio, Lenn, & Effrein, 1984; Gerard & Orive, 1987). Very often we go beyond what we have been told by other people and figure things out for ourselves. Many studies have shown that one attitude can be logically derived from others.

In one study, conducted by social psychologist William McGuire (1960), high school students completed a questionnaire indicating whether they believed 48 different statements were true. Many of these statements were logically related, although related statements were dispersed throughout the questionnaire. For example, three related statements were:

Any form of recreation that constitutes a serious health menace will be outlawed by the City Health Authority.

The increasing water pollution in this area will make swimming a serious health hazard.

Swimming at the local beaches will be outlawed by the City Health Authority.

As you can see, the third statement is logically derived from the first two.

About a week after completing the questionnaire, some subjects who did not believe the first statement read essays that tried to persuade them that it was true. The other two statements were not mentioned in the essay. A questionnaire given immediately after the subjects read the essay showed that they were influenced by it and had come to believe the first statement. In addition, the questionnaire showed that those who had come to believe the first statement and already believed the second statement, subsequently came to believe the third statement, a derivation from the first two. A third questionnaire given a week later indicated that the subjects still believed this conclusion. From this we see that if people's beliefs are changed, other logically related beliefs will change as well (see Wyer & Hartwick, 1980).

BEHAVIORAL INFLUENCES ON ATTITUDES

A third influence on people's attitudes is their own behavior. This may seem strange, since you may feel that attitudes influence behavior rather than vice versa. How can behavior influence attitudes? Leon Festinger's (1957) theory of cognitive dissonance helps explain how this happens.

Cognitive dissonance is defined as the unpleasant state of tension that exists when a person holds any two inconsistent cognitions. Festinger borrowed the term dissonance from music, where it refers to sounds that are jarring, grating, or inharmonious. According to his theory, two thoughts can also grate, and whenever we have two inconsistent cognitions, the person is motivated to reduce the resulting dissonance. This can be done by changing one of the inconsistent cognitions.

Dissonance also results if someone's behavior is inconsistent with his or her attitude. An experiment by Jonathan Freedman (1965) shows how this kind of process leads to attitude formation in young children. The hypothesis of this experiment was that children who were prevented from playing with an attractive toy would experience dissonance. The two cognitions "That is a great toy" (attitude) and "I'm not playing with it" (behavior) would be inconsistent. Furthermore, Freedman predicted that the children would reduce dissonance by changing their attitude and coming to dislike the toy—unless they had a good reason for avoiding it.

Young children were brought into a laboratory where an experimenter asked them a series of questions about their toy preferences. In the room were five toys—a Tonka tractor, a Dick Tracy toy rifle, a cheap plastic submarine, a child's baseball glove, and an extremely expensive, battery-controlled robot. After a period of time the experimenter said that he had to leave the room for several minutes but that while he was gone the child could play with some of the toys that were there. The only restriction, the experimenter stated, was that the child was not to play with the robot, which happened to be the most attractive toy!

The experimenter created two conditions by stating this restriction in one of two ways. In the mild-threat condition he said, "It is wrong to play with the robot." In the strong-threat condition he added, "If you play with the robot, I'll be very angry and will have to do something about it." Almost none of the children in either condition played with the robot.

The theory of cognitive dissonance predicts that the children should come to dislike the robot, a negative attitude consistent with their behavior—unless there is a good reason for them not to play with the toy. Clearly, the group that heard the strong threat has a better reason not to play with the robot. In the words of dissonance theorists, subjects in this group have *sufficient external justification* for not playing with the toy because they were warned of serious consequences if they played with it. However, children in the mild-threat condition did not have a good reason, or sufficient justification, for their behavior. These children would need to provide their own justification by deciding that they really did not like the toy. In this way, dissonance would be reduced.

About 3 months after the first session, the children were brought back to the laboratory and told they could play with any toy they wanted. Fewer children in the mild-threat condition than those in the strong-threat condition played with the robot. They had formed a more negative attitude. This attitude was consistent with their earlier behavior of not playing with the robot in the face of only a mild threat. As **Table 12.1** shows, the results of the study supported cognitive dissonance theory.

Table 12.1   **Results of the Freedman (1965) Toy Study**

Condition	Percentage of Subjects Playing with Attractive Toy in Second Session
Strong threat	67%
Mild threat	29%
Control	66%

After Freedman (1965).

Research on dissonance theory has provided many demonstrations that people will form attitudes that justify their behavior (Aronson, 1992; Cooper & Fazio, 1984). For example, when parents make sure that their children do not hit each other or that they do their homework, the children should form attitudes consistent with these behaviors, especially if the tangible rewards for the behaviors are small. The less the external justification, the more the children will adopt an attitude that is consistent with their actions.

Festinger's theory of cognitive dissonance has stimulated more research than nearly any other theory in social psychology (Sande & Zanna, 1987). Hundreds of studies seem to show that when there is an inconsistency between our attitudes and our behavior, we feel stupid or guilty. These unpleasant feelings cause us to change our attitudes to make them consistent with our behavior (Aronson, 1988). So, if we decide to spend a great deal of money on a vacation trip to Las Vegas, we come to feel that gambling and the night life are exhilarating. If we stand in line for 3 hours to buy tickets to a play, we justify that effort by judging the production to be the best we've ever seen.

Two recent theories have challenged the basic assumptions of dissonance theory: self-perception theory and impression-management theory. Both of these theories offer alternative explanations for the many findings that seem to support dissonance theory.

The theory of cognitive dissonance shows that if we spend a great deal of money on a trip to Las Vegas, we are likely to change our attitude to match our behavior and come to believe that gambling is exhilarating.

Self-perception theory (Bem, 1972) holds that there is no evidence that we have an internal need to be consistent or that we are bothered by violating our principles. Instead, it suggests that the reason our attitudes turn out to be consistent with our behavior is that we simply infer what our attitudes must be from our actions. As Bem says, if you ask a friend how he knows he likes brown bread, he is likely to say, "Because I eat it."

Impression-management theory (Baumeister & Hutton, 1987; Schlenker, 1982; Tedeschi, Schlenker, & Bonoma, 1971) suggests that subjects in dissonance experiments operate from a need to appear consistent rather than from a drive to be consistent. According to impression-management theory, credibility is very important in relationships with other people and we can have credibility only if we are seen as consistent. Because a person who changes his or her mind all the time can never be counted on, it may be very important to us to appear consistent to others. Although we may agree that foolish consistency is the "hobgoblin of little minds," we still feel we must appear consistent.

Which theory is correct? Research on dissonance has strongly supported Festinger's theory. Clear evidence shows that behaving inconsistently creates an unpleasant physiological arousal, which people are motivated to reduce through attitude change (Croyle & Cooper, 1983). At the same time, self-perception theory has been very important in pointing to the many things we infer about our behavior, such as the fact that we must have been very hungry because we ate a big meal. It is also clear that many people want to be seen in a positive light and that being consistent is one way of doing this. Thus, the debate about the validity of dissonance theory has shed light on our need to be consistent, how we perceive ourselves, and how we try to control other people's impressions of us.

The Power of Persuasion

In the course of growing up, we form many attitudes. These attitudes are useful in organizing information about other people and the world around us. They rarely escape pressures to change. Others may attempt to persuade us, or change our attitudes, for a variety of reasons. They may want us to validate their opinions, buy their products, or support their political goals. Social psychologists are interested in persuasion and attitude change because of its relationship to a number of long-standing social problems. For example, racial discrimination is rooted in stereotypes and racist attitudes. Changing these attitudes can help eliminate discrimination.

A theory of persuasion called the Elaboration Likelihood Model (ELM) has identified two distinct routes to persuasion, called the *central route* and the *peripheral route* (Petty & Cacioppo, 1986). The central route involves producing attitude change by inducing a person to think carefully about the arguments contained in a message. This means getting the person to elaborate the arguments in the message and to generate thoughts that are favorable to it. The peripheral route refers to influencing attitudes by associating the message being advanced with an unrelated cue that makes the person more likely to believe the message. For example, an attractive communicator, a good mood, and a neatly typed manuscript are all cues that might signal that a message should be believed. A communicator's attractiveness does not make the argument better, but attractiveness is a cue that can make the listener want to accept the message. One of the major hypotheses of the Elaboration Likelihood Model is that the attitude change produced through the central route, that is, through thought and elaboration of arguments, is more enduring and resistant to change than attitude change produced by a peripheral cue.

The distinction between attitude change through the central route and attitude change through the peripheral route helps us understand several important factors that affect whether attempts to change attitudes are successful. These are the characteristics of the communicator, the nature of the communicator's message, and the situation in which the attempt to persuade occurs.

COMMUNICATOR CHARACTERISTICS

Often certain positive characteristics of the communicator are a cue to the listener that the message being presented should be believed. For example, if the communicator is an expert, that is a signal that he or she commands facts about the issue and can be believed. It is also possible for an expert to stimulate the listener to think carefully about a set of recommendations. So, an expert communicator can affect persuasion through both the peripheral and

central route. Three important communicator characteristics can be identified: credibility, attractiveness, and similarity. Communicators with high credibility, that is, a reputation for expertise and honesty, produce more attitude change than communicators with low credibility (Hennigan, Cook, & Gruder, 1982; Olson & Cal, 1984). For example, one study showed that an article describing a cure for the common cold was believed more if subjects thought it was printed in the *New England Journal of Medicine* rather than in *Life* magazine (Hovland & Weiss, 1951).

Attractive sources are often more effective than unattractive ones, possibly because we like to please attractive people by doing what they want, including adopting specific attitudes. In one study, a woman was more successful in changing the attitudes of subjects about education when she was dressed attractively than when she appeared unkempt and homely (Mills & Aronson, 1965). Other research shows that attractive communicators are more effective at using emotional arguments (Pallak, Murroni, & Koch, 1983).

Another factor in the communicator's effectiveness is his or her similarity to the listener. If someone seems to be facing the same problems and situations as we are, we tend to feel they share our interests and we are more likely to believe them. This was shown in a study in which paint salespeople in a hardware store attempted to influence the brand of paint their customers bought. The salespeople were more successful when the extent of their own painting experience was described as similar to that of the customers' (Brock, 1965).

MESSAGE CHARACTERISTICS

Communicators who are credible, attractive, and similar to their audiences are more persuasive than those who lack these qualities. However, the characteristics of the communicator are only one determinant of persuasion. Obviously, it does not matter who is trying to be persuasive if what he or she is saying is not convincing What makes a message persuasive, and do characteristics of the message affect persuasion through the central route or the peripheral route? As we will see, a number of factors make a message work and they operate through both routes. For example, both the number and quality of arguments are important (Petty & Cacioppo, 1984). The number of arguments can be impressive in itself and can be a peripheral cue that enhances the impact of the message. The quality of an argument can make listeners think more about the issue and enhance persuasion through the central route.

In general, the message must appear unbiased and it must motivate the listeners to change their minds or take action. Research on the influence of one- versus two-sided communications demonstrates the importance of making a message seem unbiased. A one-sided communication puts forth arguments for only one position. A two-sided communication discusses arguments on both sides of the issue. In a classic experiment with American soldiers in the Pacific during World War II, soldiers heard arguments about how long the war would last. Some communications were one-sided, presenting only reasons why the war would be long. Other communications were two-sided, giving reasons why the war might be long and why it might be won quickly. The results showed that soldiers with a high school education were more persuaded by the two-sided communication. To them, the one-sided communication seemed biased, since they knew there were arguments on the other side of the issue. Soldiers with less than a high school education were more persuaded by a one-sided communication. To them, the two-sided communication seemed confusing (Hovland, Lumsdaine, & Sheffield, 1949). More recent experiments are generally consistent with these findings (McGuire, 1985).

Another message characteristic that can affect persuasion is fear. In the presidential election of 1988, the Bush campaign ran an ad about Willie Horton, a black man convicted of murder in Massachusetts. It told how Horton had raped a woman while he was out of jail on a weekend furlough. The purpose of the ad was to make voters afraid of the crime-fighting policies of Bush's opponent, Michael Dukakis, then Governor of Massachusetts (Germond & Witcover, 1989). The ad was extremely controversial. Many commentators argued that it played on racial fears and prejudices. But it was very effective. Focus group studies indicated that the ad led many people to vote for Bush rather than Dukakis. Similarly, ads for commercial products often raise fears in order to persuade potential buyers. Fears like being in the dark with dead flashlight batteries, having bad breath at a party, or being rejected by our peers can be used effectively to change attitudes and related behavior. Ads of this kind and

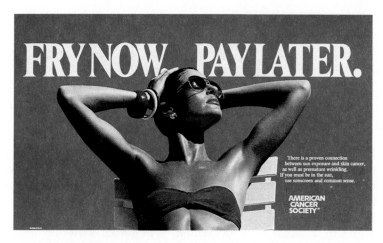

Fear is a persuasive message characteristic and is often used effectively in advertising campaigns.

many other persuasive communications state that unless you act or think in a certain manner, harmful consequences will follow.

The first study on fear was conducted by Irving Janis and Seymour Feshbach (1953), who predicted that high fear would increase attitude change by catching the audience's attention and motivating change. In this experiment, messages about the consequences of tooth decay were used in an attempt to make high school students brush their teeth more often. One group of students, the low-fear group, was given a calm talk about the dangers of decay. A second group, the high-fear group, saw gory slides and was told that infections from tooth decay could spread and cause serious illness, including blindness. Quite surprisingly, the results showed that subjects in the low-fear group showed the most change in attitude.

Other experiments, however, have shown opposite results, which support Janis and Feshbach's original hypothesis that high fear is more persuasive (Maddux & Rogers, 1983). For example, in one study, subjects in a high-fear condition saw frightening films about the dangers of smoking. The films showed diseased lungs and actual surgery on lungs. Subjects in a low-fear condition saw milder, more clinical films with charts and graphs. Smokers were more persuaded about the dangers of smoking in the high-fear condition (Leventhal, Watts, & Pagano, 1967).

Most studies of fear show that high fear is more persuasive than low fear, but there are

Psychology in the News

A CRUSHING VERDICT

By William Nack

The hour had come at last, and with it the final silence that so many had been awaiting since the proceedings had begun two weeks before. It was 10:52 on Monday night, and the scene in Courtroom 4 of Marion County Superior Court was frozen into an eerie diorama. The lawyers sat staring fixedly into space. The jurors gazed blankly across the white light of the room. And Don King, carrying a Bible, sat as still as a statue in the front row of the spectator section.

At the very center of it all, with the corners of his mouth turned down and his eyebrows furrowed, Mike Tyson sat motionless at the defense table. It had been here, in this courtroom, that the central drama of Tyson's life had been played out. It had been here that the former heavyweight champion of the world had watched as the state of Indiana built a compelling case that he had raped a college-bound 18-year-old last July 19 in room 606 of Indianapolis's Canterbury Hotel. And it had been here that he had watched as his $5,000-a-day attorney, Vincent Fuller, fumbled his way through a closing argument. At one point Judge Patricia Gifford had to remind Fuller that an exhibit he was seeking to display to the jury—a floor plan of room 606—had never been officially admitted into evidence; he could not use it. And it had been here that Tyson acquiesced as Fuller took the extraordinary gamble of not only putting him on the stand, but also of depicting him as a notorious sexual predator in an attempt to persuade the jury that the accuser should have known better than to go out with him and accompany him to his room. In effect, Fuller asked the jury to believe that Tyson was so sexually ravenous that no woman would go out with him except to have sex but not so ravenous that he would commit rape. It was a tough sell.

Now all of that was done, and the man widely regarded as the toughest fighter on the planet took one deep breath as bailiff Ed Atwood turned and carried three white sheets of paper from the jury foreman to Gifford. The judge riffled through the papers and began reading:

"We the jury find the defendant, Michael G. Tyson, guilty of the crime of rape...." Tyson's head snapped back slightly, but his face betrayed no emotion.

Hours earlier, in his summation to the jury, prosecutor Greg Garrison had pounded on the major elements of Tyson's defense. Garrison's presentation was masterly, as it had to be. So-called acquaintance-rape cases are difficult to win; because of the absence of eyewitnesses, these cases boil down to which principal witness, the accused or the accuser, is more persuasive. In his efforts to cast reasonable doubt on the complainant's account, Fuller argued in his summation that Tyson's accuser, who had come to Indianapolis to compete in the Miss Black America pageant, was a gold digger. He also contended that Tyson, who was in town to attend the Indiana Black Expo, was telling the truth when he testified that, after the young woman had consensual sex with him in his hotel room, she spurned his invitation to spend the rest of the night with him.

In his closing argument Garrison mocked the defense's contentions. He proclaimed the gold-digger argument "a ridiculous fairy tale," pointing out that if the young woman had truly been after Tyson's wealth, she would have accepted his invitation to spend the night as a prelude to a more enduring relationship.

As it turned out, Garrison was accurate in his reading of a trial that had twisted like a slalom course, cresting in its first week with the accuser's wrenching account of the alleged rape and cresting again in the second week with Tyson setting forth his version of the same events. Fuller's decision to have Tyson take the stand was risky, though the lawyer obviously concluded that it was a gamble he had to take. In addition to the accuser's account, the defense had to overcome the testimony of Tyson's limousine driver, who described in detail how the accuser had rushed in agitation and disarray from the hotel after the rape and that of the victim's moth-

436

er. At least two jurors had tears in their eyes as they listened to the woman relate how the alleged attack had become her daughter's recurring nightmare.

Garrison ended the state's presentation by playing a tape recording of the accuser's call to 911, in which she reported the assault approximately 24 hours after she had left Tyson's room. All the jurors had listened raptly as the young woman was heard describing how Tyson had raped her.

Tyson testified that about 20 minutes after they had met, the young woman consented to having a sexual encounter with him. He said, "I grabbed the girl and pushed her to me. 'Would you like to go out, do you want to go out?' And she said 'Sure,' " Later, Tyson testified, "I said, I had told her—she said, 'Yes, we'll go out, we can go to a movie or dinner.'... I said, 'That's not what I want to do.... I want you.' "

"What did she say?" asked Fuller.

"She said, 'Sure, just give me a call," Tyson testified.

Fuller then asked his client if the woman had made any comment about his direct approach. "She said, 'That's kind of bold,' " Tyson testified. Asked by Fuller how he responded to that, Tyson replied, "I said, 'That's the way I am. I just

want to know what I'm getting before I'm getting into it.' "

According to Tyson's testimony, the victim then gave him her room number at the Omni. That night, Tyson said, he reached the accuser in her hotel room on his limo phone. Although she was already in bed, he persuaded her to join him. In his limo, Tyson said, they began kissing and touching. The limo took them to the Canterbury, a block away, and they went to Tyson's sixth-floor room. Tyson testified that he and the young woman went into the bedroom, sat on the bed and talked for 10 minutes about his pigeons and about her home and then started kissing. The only time she got irritated with him, Tyson testified, was when, after they had had sex, she asked him to walk her downstairs and he said he was too tired. She left his room alone.

The accuser's account of those events had been dramatically different from Tyson's. He did not speak lustfully to her the afternoon before the alleged rape, she had testified, and when he reached her on the phone after midnight, he promised to take her around town in the limo. She pulled back, she had said, when Tyson tried to kiss her in the limo. The accuser had testified that she went to Tyson's room alone with

him after he said something to her about getting his bodyguard, and that Tyson lured her into his bedroom by saying he merely wanted to talk. She had said that after several minutes of conversation he removed all but his underwear while she was using the bathroom, attacked her when she came out and, despite her pleas to stop, raped her.

Tyson's testimony was lacking in plausibility and loaded with contradictions, and on cross-examination Garrison hammered away at Tyson's assertion that the accuser—who had been presented to the jury as a model citizen, an honor student and Sunday school teacher—had chirpily agreed to have sex with him 20 minutes after they met.

Fuller's gambit had failed miserably; Tyson was his own worst witness. "Whenever they have to put the defendant on the stand, you know things are going well," said coprosecutor Barbara Trathen after the verdict was announced. Ultimately, with no eyewitness testimony to consider, the jury was left to weight the accounts of the accuser and the accused.

Questions

1. What characteristics of Mike Tyson and his accuser affect each one's credibility?
2. How would you compare the persuasiveness of the argument that Mike Tyson's lawyer used compared to the one used by the accuser's lawyer?
3. Do you think the jury was more influenced by central route or peripheral route persuasion?
4. What does attribution theory suggest about the way jurors might have assessed the testimony of Mike Tyson and his accuser?
5. What impressions of Mike Tyson and his accuser were the jurors likely to form? How could these impressions affect their deliberations?

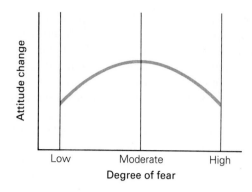

Figure 12.4
The Inverted-U Relationship Between Fear and Attitude Change. (From Worchel & Cooper 1983)

exceptions such as the Janis and Feshbach findings. Psychologists are now studying the possibility that moderate fear is most persuasive because of its motivating qualities (see **Figure 12.4**). Intense fear may lead listeners to attack the communicator or ignore the message. Other research shows that fear works best when subjects are given explicit recommendations on how to escape from danger (Harris & Jellison, 1971; Leventhal, 1970).

THE SITUATION

The degree to which we are affected by persuasive messages depends in part on the situations in which we receive them. Sometimes people are distracted by other thoughts, sounds, or activities while they are reading or listening to a persuasive message. These distractions can have a considerable impact on the effect of a persuasive message. A number of studies have indicated that if people are distracted while they are listening to a message they will actually show more attitude change. This occurs because distraction interferes with silent counterarguing, the debate a listener carries on while a message is being received (Petty, Wells, & Brock, 1976).

In one study, college students listened to a speaker arguing against fraternities. In one condition they simultaneously watched a film of the speech. In a second condition they watched an amusing but irrelevant film, an Academy Award–winning short called *The Day of the Painter*. Subjects in the second condition were more influenced by the speech (Festinger & Maccoby, 1964).

Distraction is just one of the many situational factors that can increase persuasion.

Another factor is simply pleasant surroundings that can become associated with the message and thus serve as a peripheral cue that the message is one that should be accepted (Petty & Cacioppo, 1986). This phenomenon was shown in a study in which students read essays while they ate peanuts and drank soda. Other subjects did not have these enjoyable refreshments. The subjects who ate while they read showed more attitude change than the other subjects (Janis, Kaye, & Kirschner, 1965).

The Persistence of Attitudes

Generally, research indicates that people will maintain the attitudes they have at any particular time, whether they are new or old, unless there are pressures to change. Thus, a person who changes his or her attitude is likely to maintain that new attitude unless some force, such as peer pressure, induces a change (McGuire, 1969).

Theodore Newcomb's studies of Bennington students demonstrate the persistence of changed attitudes (Newcomb, Koenig, Flacks, & Warwick, 1967). After the 1960 and 1964 presidential elections, Newcomb surveyed women who had been students at Bennington in the 1930s and had become liberals at that time. He wanted to see whether, 30 years later, they were still more liberal than were similar women who went to other colleges. In the 1960 election, 60 percent of the Bennington graduates favored the Democrat, Kennedy. Only 30 percent of women who were similar in terms of social class, education, region, religion, and so forth supported Kennedy. In the 1964 election, 90 percent of the Bennington graduates supported the Democrat, Johnson, while about 65 percent of the comparison women did. The Bennington graduates became more liberal than their peers in the 1930s and remained so 30 years later.

Newcomb et al. (1967) suggest this happened because the Bennington women tended to marry liberal husbands (or they converted their husbands), who reinforced their liberal attitudes. Women who had reverted to their earlier conservative beliefs had married men who did not support liberal attitudes. Thus, the Bennington studies show that new attitudes will persist if there is continuing support for them.

Another important factor in the maintenance of new attitudes is the distortion of memory. When people change their minds, they can experience cognitive dissonance if they recognize that they have been inconsistent over time. One way to reduce this dissonance is to distort the memory of their old attitude and to believe that the new attitude is the one they have always held. An interesting demonstration of this point occurred in a study of attitude change among high school students.

A week before the actual experiment, the students were asked to complete a questionnaire dealing with several political issues. Using these surveys, the experimenter formed groups composed of all probusing or all antibusing students. These groups were then called in for discussion of the busing issue. In each discussion, one of their peers, who was actually a confederate of the experimenter, tried to change the students' minds. The confederate spoke first, using clever two-sided statements and countering typical arguments from the other side of the issue. A second questionnaire handed out after the discussion showed that the confederate had been remarkably successful in changing the attitudes of his peers. The students were then asked to recall as accurately as they could how they had answered the first questionnaire. Their memory was very accurate except on the busing issue (see **Table 12.2**). Nearly every subject remembered his or her initial attitude on busing as having been identical to what it was *after* the discussion (Goethals & Reckman, 1973).

Interim Summary

Attitudes, positive or negative evaluations of people, objects, events, or ideas, are formed by social, cognitive, and behavioral influences.

Parents and peers influence attitudes by providing information and reinforcement and by serving as figures for identification.

People's attitudes are also influenced by their own logic and reasoning. McGuire showed that if people changed one belief they would also change logically related beliefs.

People make their attitudes consistent with their behavior. The theory of cognitive dissonance predicts that the less external justification there is for behavior, the more people will form attitudes consistent with their behavior.

Table 12.2   **Error in Recall Scores**

All subjects were asked to duplicate their earlier responses on a 31-point scale; the higher the score, the higher the error. These results indicate that subjects whose attitudes about busing had been changed as a result of group discussion recalled those earlier attitudes very inaccurately. However, the same subjects recalled their attitudes on other issues quite accurately. Furthermore, control subjects, who had not participated in a persuasive group discussion, recalled their busing attitudes and other attitudes highly accurately.

Condition	Busing Issue	Other Issues
Experimental subjects (mean)	13.06	3.96
Control subjects (mean)	3.25	2.75

After Goethals & Reckman (1973).

The Elaboration Likelihood Model of persuasion proposes a central route and a peripheral route to persuasion. The central route involves getting listeners to think carefully about the arguments of the message. The peripheral route involves associating the message with cues designed to make the message more acceptable.

The effectiveness of a persuasive communication is affected by the communicator, the nature of the message, and the situation. Some persuasive communicator characteristics are credibility, attractiveness, and similarity to the listeners.

Message characteristics include both the number and the quality of the arguments. The knowledge of the audience determines whether one-sided or two-sided communications are more persuasive. Two-sided communications appear less biased than one-sided communications to people aware of opposing viewpoints. One-sided communications are clearer to people unaware of opposing arguments. Fear can arouse motivation to change, but fear that is too strong can produce negative reactions. Thus, communications that arouse moderate fear seem to be most effective.

Distractions can increase persuasion, as can a pleasant setting.

New attitudes often remain stable, partly because people may forget their old attitudes. Generally, pressures to change are required to change attitudes.

PREJUDICE AND STEREOTYPES

All the elements of social cognition that we have discussed—impression formation, schemata, and attitudes and beliefs—are important in understanding the negative and oversimplified perceptions many people hold about members of groups to which they do not belong. The problems of intergroup hostility and conflict are pronounced both within our own country and within the world at large. For example, within the United States tensions between blacks, whites, Latinos, and Asians exploded in Los Angeles following the Rodney King verdict. Conflict between Sunni and Shiite moslems in Iraq and other Arab countries has escalated sharply, and the nation of Yugoslavia is on the verge of total disintegration because of conflict between various ethnic groups. Social psychologists have approached the problem of prejudice in a number of ways during the past 50 years and modern research on stereotypes lies at the heart of social cognition. In this section we will explore various approaches to these problems.

The distinction between prejudice and stereotypes is the same as the distinction between attitudes and beliefs. A **stereotype** is a set of beliefs about the characteristics of people in a particular group that is generalized to almost all group members. A **prejudice** is a negative attitude toward or evaluation of a person due solely to his or her membership in a group. Also important is the concept of **discrimination,** defined as the expression of prejudice in behavior. In this section we will highlight the way cognitive factors contribute to the formation and maintenance of stereotypes. We will also consider a range of psychological factors that lead to prejudice and the forms that racism takes in modern society.

The Origins of Racial Prejudice

Clearly, a number of factors produce racial prejudice. Prejudice results from a range of cultural, historical, social, and psychological conditions. We will emphasize cognitive factors that produce and perpetuate racist stereotypes. First, however, we will discuss the role of learning cultural attitudes, competition and conflict, and in-group favoritism.

Learning Cultural Attitudes

Most psychologists have argued that prejudice comes from culture, not personality. People adopt prejudiced attitudes, just as they adopt other attitudes, on the basis of identification and the information and reinforcement provided by parents and peers. One psychologist with this viewpoint, Thomas Pettigrew, examined the role of both culturally learned attitudes and personality in prejudice. Pettigrew (1959) measured levels of prejudice among whites in the northern and southern United States and in South Africa. He found much higher levels of prejudice against black people in South Africa and the southern United States than he did in the northern United States. Yet personality traits supposedly linked to prejudice did not differ among white people in these three regions. Prejudice grew out of a white cultural heritage that led to negative stereotypes about black people. In turn, white parents taught these cultural beliefs to their children. Pettigrew found that white Northerners most attached to their cultural beliefs were the *least* prejudiced, while white Southerners most attached to their culture were the *most* preju-

Most psychologists agree that prejudice comes from culture, not personality. People adopt prejudiced attitudes on the basis of identification and reinforcement provided by parents and peers.

diced. Thus, the extent to which people adopted their cultural beliefs determined how prejudiced they were. This was also true in South Africa, where the white people who most accepted the cultural beliefs were most prejudiced.

COMPETITION AND CONFLICT

Pettigrew's research demonstrates the importance of culture and learning. But how do racist beliefs and attitudes creep into cultures in the first place? Many psychologists have proposed what is called **realistic conflict theory**, arguing that conflict resulting from competition for scarce resources generates prejudice. For example, Kinder and Sears (1981) proposed that many whites feel threatened by blacks whom they perceive as competing for jobs, with prejudice as the result. Also consistent with realistic conflict theory is the finding that religious groups in Israel discriminate against each other in direct proportion to the extent to which they perceive conflict of interests. When people perceived their group in conflict with other groups, they supported discriminatory action against those other groups (Struch & Schwartz, 1989.)

IN-GROUP FAVORITISM AND SOCIAL IDENTITY

Clearly, people develop hostilities and prejudices when their groups are in conflict. But something even more basic than actual conflict may create hostility and prejudice between groups. According to a recent theory in social psychology known as **social identity theory,** people have a basic tendency to, first, categorize individuals into groups and, second, prefer their own group (Tajfel & Turner, 1986). These two groups become the "in-group" and the "out-group." The preference for members of the in-group leads to preferential treatment of in-group members in the allocation of resources. In fact, a classic social identity study showed that if people must decide between allocating large amounts to both in-group members and out-group members versus allocating moderate amounts to in-group members and small amounts to out-group members, they will choose the latter alternative. People seem to place more emphasis on their group doing relatively better than other groups than on how their own group does in absolute terms (Tajfel, Flament, Billig, and Bundy, 1971).

Why should people categorize individuals in this way? Categorization is a basic and automatic cognitive process that helps us manage a complex world of information (Hamilton & Trollier, 1986). Preferring the in-group seems to be tied to self-esteem (Oakes & Turner, 1980). Our self-concept is based in part on how we compare ourselves to other individuals and in part on how the groups we belong to compare to other groups (Tajfel & Turner, 1986; Goethals & Darley, 1987). In some cases people can boost their self-concepts by derogating and mistreating members of out-groups, especially when their own self-esteem is threatened (Crocker, Thompson, McGraw, & Ingerman, 1987).

In conclusion, prejudice comes from learning prejudiced attitudes from the culture. Those attitudes often reflect real conflicts of interest as well as more basic human tendencies to raise the value of one's own group by derogating out-groups and their members. Combined with cognitive processes that help form and maintain stereotypes, these processes make prejudice very difficult to overcome.

Cognitive Processes in Stereotyping

Researchers concerned with cognitive processes and information processing have in recent years contributed important fresh perspectives to our understanding of stereotypes and intergroup behavior (Hamilton, 1981). According to the cognitive processes approach, stereotypes are best thought of as schemata about groups or individuals belonging to those groups that are reinforced by the way we process information about people. For example, simply categorizing a person as belonging to an out-group, that is, a group different than the one we belong to, can lead us to accentuate the differences between that person and ourselves (Eiser, 1984). Furthermore, we tend to perceive members of our own group, the in-group, as more heterogeneous or diverse than members of other groups and we perceive the characteristics of members of other groups as extreme (Judd & Park, 1988; Quattrone, 1986) One interesting consequence of seeing members of out-groups as less diverse than members of our own group is that we perceive people in the out-group as being "all alike." Not surprisingly, research on eyewitness identification shows that white students identifying faces in a photographic lineup can make correct identifications of other whites more easily than they can of blacks. The reverse is true of black students (Brigham & Malpass, 1985). Our schemata for people belonging to different groups are apparently not as sensitive to differences among them as are our schemata for members of our own group.

Not only are our schemata for members of out-groups less sensitive to differences between them, they are also less complex. We tend to have rich and differentiated schemata about members of our own group but relatively simple schemata about members of other groups. This means that we have less cognitive context for weighing information about members of out-groups, and as a result we tend to be very heavily influenced by small pieces of information about them. As a consequence, our evaluations of individual out-group members are more extreme than our evaluations of in-group members (Linville, 1982). For example, in one study white subjects judging law school applicants made more negative evaluations of a poorly qualified black student than a similar white student, while they made more positive evaluations of a strong black applicant than an equally strong white student (Linville & Jones, 1980). The evaluations of the out-group member were more polarized.

Research on the formation of stereotypes also illustrates the importance of cognitive processes. Let us consider, for example, how the memory for salient stimuli contributes to stereotyping. Salient stimuli are those that are especially noticeable, such as rare or unusual stimuli. For example, if blacks are in a minority they are more noticeable. Furthermore, let us assume that socially undesirable behaviors are more unusual and noticeable than socially desirable behaviors. This means that, as a member of a minority group, a black person performing a socially undesirable behavior will be an especially salient stimulus. Whites may perform socially undesirable behaviors in exactly the same proportion as blacks, but blacks doing so will be more memorable if they are in the minority. Thus, one might recall that blacks perform socially undesirable behaviors more frequently than they actually do.

An experiment by Hamilton and Gifford (1976) showed exactly this kind of error in memory. Subjects read approximately 40 statements describing individuals from two groups, A and B, who performed behaviors that were either socially desirable or socially undesirable. For example, one statement read "John, a member of group A, visited a sick friend in the hospital." Individuals belonging to group A were always described more frequently. Group B was the minority.

There were two conditions in the experiment. In both conditions, group A and group B performed an equal proportion of desirable or undesirable behaviors. In the first condition, one third of the behaviors for both groups were socially desirable. In the second condition, one third of the behaviors for both groups were undesirable.

After subjects read all the statements, they were asked to recall whether a member of group A or group B performed each behavior. As predicted, subjects tended to remember that a member of the minority group, group B, performed the more unusual behavior more frequently than was the case (see **Table 12.3**). Thus, when desirable behaviors were less common (variation 1), group B was given more credit for performing them than was deserved. When undesirable behaviors were less common (variation 2), group B was also recalled as having performed them more frequently than was the case. Thus, if black people are in the minority, one might recall that they perform undesirable behaviors more than they actually

Table 12.3   **Comparison of Statements Describing and Later Attributed to Groups in Hamilton and Gifford's Study of Stereotyping**

Groups and Types of Behaviors	Number of Statements Describing Each Type of Behavior	Number of Statements Attributed to Each Group
Variation 1		
Group A		
Desirable behaviors	8	5.87
Undesirable behaviors	16	15.71
Group B (minority)		
Desirable behaviors	4	6.13
Undesirable behaviors	8	8.29
Variation 2		
Group A		
Desirable behaviors	18	17.52
Undesirable behaviors	8	5.79
Group B (minority)		
Desirable behaviors	9	9.48
Undesirable behaviors	4	6.21

After Hamilton & Gifford (1976).

do. In this way, our memory for salient stimuli can contribute to stereotypes and prejudice.

Not only do cognitive processes contribute to the formation of stereotypes, they also affect the maintenance of stereotypes. Recall that stereotypes are schemata and that we remember especially well information that fits our schemata. Thus if a rich person has the stereotype, or schema, that poor people are lazy, he or she might remember poor people taking a coffee break on the job more than the fact that their job requires long hours of back-breaking labor. People think about information that is consistent with stereotypes more extensively than information that is inconsistent (Bodenhausen, 1988). And when they do think about inconsistent information, it is often with the purpose of explaining it away (Hastie, 1984). Furthermore, recent research shows that people sometimes imagine behaviors that are consistent with their stereotypes and are then unable to recall accurately whether a statement about someone's behavior was something they actually read or something they just imagined (Slusher & Anderson, 1987). In short, there are powerful tendencies to ignore, distort, and fabricate information in ways that maintain our stereotypes. These tendencies, though they may have very damaging consequences, simply reflect the most basic attributes of human information processing.

Stereotypes and Self-Fulfilling Prophecies

Whatever the causes of prejudices and stereotypes, they can have the further perverse effect of making themselves come true. This effect can be understood in terms of the important concept of the self-fulfilling prophecy. A **self-fulfilling prophecy** is an expectancy that leads to a certain pattern of behavior whose consequences confirm the expectancy. A classic hypothetical example is that a rumor spreads in a small town that the bank is about to collapse. This information may be totally false, but consider its consequences. The townspeople descend on the bank and demand their money. As a result, all the bank's funds are withdrawn and, indeed, it collapses. Similar self-fulfilling prophecies can occur in interpersonal relations. If we expect another person to be friendly, we will act friendly ourselves and elicit friendly behavior from the other person. Our expectation leads to behavior that confirms the expectancy.

In one study of self-fulfilling racial stereotypes, white subjects were hired to act as interviewers of students applying for jobs. Actually, the job applicants were confederates of the experimenter and were carefully trained to act in certain ways during the interview. In some cases these confederates were black and in other cases they were white. The behavior of the interviewers was carefully recorded and analyzed. When the applicant was black, the interviewers maintained more distance and terminated the interview more quickly. Apparently their behavior was affected by their perceptions of black people.

How might the interviewer's behavior in such a setting affect the performance of the applicants? A second experiment answered this question. White confederates were trained as interviewers and instructed to behave either in the relatively friendly manner that was used with white subjects in the first experiment or in the relatively distant manner that had been used with blacks. Then these confederates interviewed white subjects using either the friendly manner or the distant manner. Finally, the performance of these white subjects was rated by judges who did not know the procedures or hypotheses of the study. The subjects who were interviewed in the distant manner used with black subjects in the first experiment were judged to have performed less well in the interview than the subjects who were interviewed warmly (Word, Zanna, & Cooper, 1974). Other studies have shown similar results (Snyder, Tanke, & Berscheid, 1977).

What do these experiments show? Perhaps people perform less well in a variety of situations because of self-fulfilling prophecies. Because people in one group expect people from another group to perform poorly, they may treat them with less interest and warmth. This negative treatment in turn brings out the other group's worst. Their behavior is guarded, inhibited, and unimpressive. The expectancy that particular people will be unimpressive leads the holder of this expectancy to behave in a way that elicits unimpressive behavior in those people.

There have been many other studies of self-fulfilling prophecies in interpersonal relations. In one well-known but controversial study called "Pygmalion in the Classroom" (Rosenthal & Jacobson, 1968), teachers were told that certain pupils in sixth-grade classes, making up about 20 percent of these classes, had been identified by intelligence tests as potential "late bloomers." Unbeknownst to the teachers, these students had been randomly selected by the experimenters. No expectation was created for the rest of the students, who thus served as a control group. At the end of the year the students who had been identified earlier as "late bloomers" actually showed greater gains in IQ scores than the control subjects. In the "Pygmalion" study expectancy was manipulated by the experimenters, but in thousands of classrooms across the country teachers could clearly bring with them expectancies based on racial and ethnic stereotypes that could have similar results.

Just what are the processes that produce these expectancy effects? Recent research supports a four-factor theory. This theory identifies factors of *climate, feedback, input,* and *output* (Harris & Rosenthal, 1985; Rosenthal, 1973). According to this theory, teachers provide a warmer climate for pupils whom they expect to do well. This warmth is conveyed through both verbal and nonverbal communication. Second, more careful, detailed feedback is given to students who are expected to do well. That is, they are given more guidance about what is good and bad about the work they are doing. Third, teachers tend to provide more input for such students. They give them more time and instruction in explaining classroom materials. Finally, high-expectancy students are given more opportunity to generate their own output. For example, they are given more time to ask questions and to respond in class. Thus they learn to produce and to obtain the rewards for being productive. In short, there are various important ways in which high expectancy students are given advantages by teachers, and it is no surprise that they perform better than students from whom teachers expect less.

Are there ways to avoid making expectations self-fulfilling? Clearly, being aware of the "self-fulfilling prophecy" phenomenon is helpful. If we remind ourselves that our expectations may be wrong and try to assess whether or not they are correct when we interact with other people, we are much less likely to fall into the trap of the self-fulfilling prophecy (Darley, Hilton, Fleming, & Swan, 1988). Being open-minded reduces the tendency for other people to act in accord with our expectations (Neuberg, 1989). In short, a little effort can make a significant difference in avoiding false confirmation of prejudices and stereotypes.

Interim Summary

Research by Pettigrew shows that people in highly prejudiced regions do not have different personalities than those in other regions. Their prejudice has its origins in culturally learned attitudes traceable to historical conditions. Competition and conflict also contribute to prejudice and hostility between groups, as does people's tendency to discriminate against out-group members in the interest of raising their own self-esteem.

Stereotypes can be thought of as schemata about groups or persons belonging to those groups. Our schemata about members of such groups are less sensitive to differences among them, less complex, and lead to more extreme evaluations of them.

Prejudices and stereotypes about members of certain groups can lead to self-fulfilling prophecies in which expectations come to produce behavior that confirms the expectations. The four factors of climate, feedback, input, and output have been hypothesized to produce the expectancy effects that lead to self-fulfilling prophecies.

INTERPERSONAL ATTRACTION

We have seen how the processes of social cognition can sometimes result in negative perceptions and evaluations of other people. But there is also a warm side of human relations. In this section we consider some of the factors that determine whether people become attracted, fall in love, and establish enduring relationships.

Before we begin, let us distinguish liking from three types of love: romantic love, companionate love, and consummate love (Sternberg, 1988). **Liking** usually involves respect or high regard for another person. In addition, it often involves seeing the other as similar to oneself. **Romantic love** usually combines liking and several other factors. Three of these are great attachment to and dependence on the other person, caring for or desiring to help the other person, and the desire for an exclusive, intimate relationship (Rubin, 1973). In addition, romantic love often includes physiological arousal, sexual desire, and intense preoccupation with the loved person (Walster & Walster, 1979). Companionate love is slightly harder to define. To distinguish it from roman-

People who are near and become familiar to us stand a good chance of becoming friends.

tic love we can define **companionate love** as the enduring attachment that remains once the passion of romantic love dissipates over time (Berscheid, 1985). It is sometimes referred to as the warm afterglow of romantic love or the affection we feel for those with whom our lives are intertwined. Recently, psychologists have begun to identify **consummate love**, a kind of love that seems to combine the elements of both romantic and companionate love.

In this section we will consider the determinants of attraction and love and a crucial aspect of building and maintaining relationships—self-disclosure.

The Determinants of Attraction

Some of the factors that have been identified as influencing interpersonal attraction are proximity and familiarity, physical attractiveness, competence, reciprocal liking, and attitude similarity.

PROXIMITY AND FAMILIARITY

We can only come to like or love those whom we have a chance to meet and get to know. The people we encounter and interact with most often are those who live or work close to us. Not surprisingly, many studies have shown that nearness or *proximity* is a key factor in liking others. For example, a study of married couples in student housing showed that people chose friends on the basis of proximity. The closer one couple lived to another, the more

they tended to like each other. Their best friends were usually the couple in the next apartment, and it was unusual for people to be very friendly with others who were more than four apartment units away. It was easy to predict who a couple's friends were on the basis of where they lived (Festinger, Schachter, & Back, 1950).

How can we explain the power of proximity? One important factor is sheer *familiarity* (Moreland & Zajonc, 1982). The common wisdom that "familiarity breeds contempt" is more accurately translated to "familiarity breeds content" (Rubin, 1973). We like both people and objects more after we have been exposed to them for a long period of time. The exception is someone or something we truly detest, in which case repeated exposure can lead to even more dislike (Grush, 1976). Still, repeated exposure does lead to increased liking if we originally felt neutral or slightly positive toward the person or object (Swap, 1977). In short, people who are near and become familiar stand a strong chance of becoming good friends.

PHYSICAL ATTRACTIVENESS

Another important factor in the early stages of a relationship is appearance or physical attractiveness. In one study of the importance of physical attractiveness, students were randomly matched for a dancing date that they believed was part of a study of computer dating and attraction. At the beginning of the study,

Physical attractiveness is important in dating and marriage choices.

each subject's physical attractiveness was rated by student judges. In addition, each subject completed several personality questionnaires measuring a range of traits, interests, and abilities. After the dance, subjects were asked how much they had liked their date. There was a clear tendency for simple physical appearance to determine how much the students liked their dates. None of the personality traits that were measured played a significant role during this single-encounter situation. Only attractiveness mattered (Walster, Aronson, Abrahams, & Rottman, 1966).

Is physical attractiveness important in ways other than initial attraction? As it turns out, physical attractiveness continues to be important in dating and even in marriage choice. People who are seriously dating or engaged are often much more similar in their level of attractiveness than would be predicted by chance (Murstein, 1972b). The same is true for married couples (Price & Vandenberg, 1979). That is, handsome men and beautiful women tend to pair off, as do average-looking men and average-looking women.

Perhaps this phenomenon can be understood in terms of a "matching process" (Folkes, 1982). Although almost everyone will want to date those who are very attractive, they may also think that they will probably be rejected by those who are significantly more attractive. Thus they limit their choices accordingly. Another reason for limiting choices may be that people feel it is equitable to date someone who has equal social assets—in this case, attractiveness—and feel that it would be unfair to date

someone of significantly more or less social desirability (Greenberg & Cohen, 1982). Still another possibility is that all of us attempt to attract the best-looking partners we can but only succeed with those who are similar. The evidence suggests that caution and realism probably limit some of our attempts at love (Shanteau & Nagy, 1979).

COMPETENCE

How do we react to a blunderer as opposed to someone who is always competent? Obviously, we generally like adept people more. Some research suggests, however, that if highly talented individuals commit embarrassing errors, the error can make them liked more (Aronson, Willerman, & Floyd, 1966). Their failure shows that they are "human" and not beyond the reach of ordinary people. On the other hand, if a person of average talent and ability commits blunders, it is just another sign of ineptness. Thus, the average blunderer should be liked less. To test this reasoning, Aronson and his colleagues conducted an experiment in which subjects heard a tape recording of a student being interviewed for a prestigious position on campus. In the interview, the student had to answer some difficult questions measuring his intelligence and had to tell about his background. In the high-ability condition, his answers to the questions were superb and he revealed a record of great talent and achievement. In the low-ability condition, his credentials appeared average. In both conditions, some interviews ended routinely and in others there was a bang and splatter and the student said, "My God, I've spilled coffee all over my new suit." The tape ended with the sounds of a frantic cleanup. When subjects subsequently indicated their impressions of the student, they showed more liking overall for the highly talented individual. As we might have predicted, however, the blunder had a strong effect on their reactions. When the average individual spilled coffee, he was liked even less. This seemed to be just one more indication of his incompetence. But when the "superstar" spilled coffee on himself, he was liked better. His blunder apparently humanized him. A further study by Deaux (1972) indicates that the blunder effect works only with male subjects, perhaps because they are more competitive and like other competent persons less when they show a weakness.

Table 12.4 Subjects' Liking for Confederate in Different Conditions

Confederate's Attitude Toward Subjects	Subjects' Liking of Confederate Rated on a −10 to +10 Scale
Negative to positive	7.67
Positive to positive	6.42
Negative to negative	2.52
Positive to negative	0.87

After Aronson & Linder (1965).

RECIPROCAL LIKING

One of the most valued rewards people can offer each other is their affection. If people like us, they will probably help us. Not surprisingly, research has shown that liking is *reciprocal.* We like those who like us in return. Because other people's liking for us is important, however, it can operate in subtle ways to influence just how much we like other people in return.

For example, long-term compatibility depends on *when* someone likes us as well as *how much* they like us. In a study of this question, Aronson and Linder (1965) proposed that we like people more if they first dislike us and then come to like us than if they liked us all along. They also predicted that we have the least affection for people who like us at first but later do not like us. In a test of these predictions, college women overheard a series of seven evaluations of them by an attractive young woman who was either (1) consistently positive, (2) consistently negative, (3) at first positive and then negative, or (4) at first negative and then positive. The results confirmed the predictions. As **Table 12.4** shows, subjects liked the woman most when she went from negative to positive evaluations and liked her least when she went from positive to negative evaluations.

There are several possible explanations for these findings. One is that people who change their evaluations are perceived as being discerning. Perhaps they have more credibility, so their liking (or disliking) means more. Another possible explanation for preferring the negative-to-positive evaluator is that the early

critical remarks create a need for affection or liking. Later positive evaluations fulfill this need and thus are much more satisfying than the evaluations of the consistently positive person.

Do these findings imply that husbands or wives who have been consistently positive toward their spouses in the past cannot satisfy their spouses to a greater degree in the future? Perhaps a stranger who has been neutral, or even critical, arouses more liking when he or she is positive than does the reliable spouse. These concerns have led to the formulation of Aronson's law of marital infidelity (Aronson, 1988), which says that strangers are liked for their compliments more than are spouses, while critical remarks hurt more from the spouse than from the stranger. These ideas are intriguing, but Aronson goes on to say that this law probably does not apply in good marriages where communication is honest and open.

ATTITUDE SIMILARITY

One very important factor in determining how compatible two partners will be in a relationship is their degree of attitude similarity. People with similar attitudes like each other in the short run and get along well over the long run. Laboratory studies of interpersonal attraction have shown that when students were told the attitudes of hypothetical strangers, there was a strong and direct relationship between attitude similarity and the students' reports of liking the stranger. It seems that we like people who share our attitudes about many issues more than those who share our attitudes on only a few issues (Byrne, 1971).

Theodore Newcomb (1961) conducted some important studies at the University of Michigan to investigate whether similarity is important in real, long-term relationships. He randomly assigned rooms to students who had agreed to live in an experimental dormitory for a year. At the end of one semester, Newcomb found that attitude similarity was a very strong predictor of how much the students reported that they liked each other.

Why should this be true? There are probably two major reasons. The first reason is suggested by *balance theory,* which states that people like to have an ordered, clear, and consistent view of their environment that enables all the parts to fit together. It seems natural or *balanced* that you will agree with your friends and disagree with your enemies (see **Figure**

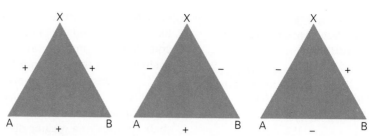

Figure 12.5
Balance Theory
Balance theory predicts that two people, A and B, will like each other (as indicated by the plus sign) if their opinions about some object, person, idea, or event are the same. This situation is illustrated in the first two triangles where A and B both like X (Triangle 1) or dislike X (Triangle 2). Balance theory also predicts that A and B will dislike each other if they have different evaluations of X (Triangle 3). If A and B like each other but disagree about X, the resulting imbalance can be resolved either by A or B changing his or her opinion about X or by A and B coming to dislike each other. (Based on Heider, 1946; Newcomb, 1953)

12.5). In fact, it seems so natural that there is a norm, or group standard, to like people who agree and dislike those who disagree (Jellison & Oliver, 1983). We expect good to go with good and bad with bad. Friends and agreement are good, enemies and dissent are not. Also, people who hold attitudes similar to ours tend to confirm our own beliefs and thus validate our own view of the world (Byrne, 1977).

Research suggests our disliking for people who are dissimilar may be even stronger than our liking for people who are similar (Rosenbaum, 1986). The explanation for this "repulsion hypothesis" employs the concepts of balance theory outlined in Figure 12.5 and dissonance theory. According to the repulsion hypothesis, although others with attitudes similar to our own do provide balance or consonance, these psychological states are relatively bland compared to the arousal and discomfort that accompany the imbalance and dissonance generated by disagreeing opinions. Thus disagreement hurts more than agreement helps. Although there is controversy about whether our attraction to similar others or our repulsion by dissimilar others is stronger, it is clear that both attraction and repulsion are psychologically significant aspects of our interpersonal relationships (Byrne, Clore, & Smeaton, 1986).

Love

At the beginning of this section, we distinguished liking, based on respect and feelings of similarity, from romantic, companionate, and consummate love. In the remainder of this section we will consider how people fall in love, some key aspects of maintaining an enduring relationship, and the importance of self-disclosure both for ourselves and for our intimate relationships.

ROMANTIC LOVE

What is involved in falling in love and in experiencing the emotional feelings of romantic or passionate attachment? One recent theory suggests that there are three conditions for experiencing romantic love (Berscheid & Walster, 1974; Walster & Walster, 1979). The first condition is some culturally based expectation that one will fall in love. Since the Middle Ages, literature and art have made much of romantic love, and many people expect that they will experience this emotion. Second, there must be some appropriate person to fall in love with. The expectation that one will fall in love combined with meeting the right person often leads to "love at first sight" (Averill & Boothroyd, 1977). Berscheid and Walster report that 50 percent of adult males and females surveyed said that they have at least once fallen in love at first sight.

The third, and most complex, condition for romantic love is that once we meet the appropriate person, the emotion that we feel in the presence of that person must be interpreted as love. Emotional arousal from a variety of different stimuli or events in the environment can be channeled into passionate feelings for a loved person if that person is frequently on your mind. Suppose, for example, that some-

For centuries, literature and art have extolled romantic love. In this illustration from the 14th century, a troubadour is bound with the gold thread of love.

one in your dormitory insults you. You are aroused and feeling angry and hostile. Then your thoughts turn to your lover. This theory suggests that the arousal due to the insult can be experienced as strong love or passion for your loved one. This explanation for romantic love grows out of Schachter's (1964) two-factor theory of emotion. As we discussed in Chapter 4, this theory proposes that emotions are based on some kind of physiological arousal and a labeling of that arousal as being a specific emotion, depending on cues in the environment.

There is evidence supporting the idea that arousal from other sources can be labeled as love and can lead to increased attraction. In a study by Dutton and Aron (1974), male subjects who had walked across a bridge were stopped and interviewed by an attractive woman. Half the men met the woman after crossing a rickety and unsafe bridge, which may have caused them to feel anxious. Others met her after crossing a strong and perfectly safe bridge. The men who met the woman after crossing the rickety bridge were more likely to

call her for a date later on. Apparently fear caused arousal, which was labeled as attraction to the woman. However, more research is needed to determine just how arousal from other sources leads to increased feelings of love or attraction (Berscheid, 1985). For example, it may be that the attractive woman in the study above served to reduce the negative arousal of fear and thus served as a reinforcement (Riordan & Tedeschi, 1983).

COMPANIONATE AND CONSUMMATE LOVE:
THE IMPORTANCE OF COMMITMENT
Romantic love can be seen as a kind of "liking plus," specifically, "liking plus passion," where passion includes physical attraction, emotional absorption, and mental preoccupation. Companionate love, which we have described as the affection that remains after the passion of romantic love subsides, can also be thought of as a kind of "liking plus." In this case "liking plus commitment," where commitment means a person's firm and lasting decision to maintain a loving relationship even when passion fades.

The key to an enduring relationship is each person's attitude about his or her partner, commitment, and a desire to make the relationship last.

As a result of commitment, many relationships starting out as romantic love (liking plus passion) evolve into companionate love (liking plus commitment).

Although it is important to distinguish romantic and companionate love, you might question whether commitment must *replace* passion. Isn't it possible to have a relationship involving, liking, passion, *and* commitment? The answer is clearly yes, and the name consummate love has been given to the relationship involving all three (Sternberg, 1986, 1988).

Clearly, commitment is essential if a loving relationship is to endure. What do we know about the chances of romantic relationships enduring and the factors that increase those chances? There are now more than one million divorces in the United States each year. The divorce rate has increased dramatically during the last three decades and now hovers around 50 percent. Although there are some recent indications that the divorce rate is no longer increasing and may actually be dropping, the fact remains that nearly half the marriages in the United States end in divorce. What have studies of committed love and enduring relationships taught us about the factors that help relationships survive?

One important factor is learning how to manage conflict and anger (Peterson, 1983). Relationships are not conflict free. After the early stages of a relationship, constant adjust-ment and readjustment are necessary as the individuals in the relationship and the relationship itself change. These adjustments entail conflict. Couples need to develop successful ways of minimizing conflict or using it constructively. Equity and fairness are also of critical importance in maintaining intimate relationships (Hatfield, Traupman, Sprecher, Utne, & Hay, 1984). There must be a willingness to trust that the relationship will be fair in the long run and not to worry about immediately demanding a benefit in exchange for every compromise or reward that one provides (Clark, 1984). That is, taking the long-term perspective is important.

Perhaps the key to enduring relationships is the couple's attitudes about each other. A study of marriages that had lasted more than 15 years showed that simply liking one's spouse, and regarding him or her as one's best friend, is of paramount importance (Lauer & Lauer, 1985). Commitment and a fierce desire to make the relationship last are also essential. Managing conflict and establishing equity take time and energy. Couples have to be willing to make the effort. A recent study shows that husbands especially must take the time to talk about and understand the relationship (Acitelli, 1992). Both husbands and wives who have made the effort find their intimate relationships the most satisfying part of their lives.

Self-Disclosure and Intimate Relationships

Self-disclosure is defined as talking to another person about your own needs, thoughts, feelings, behavior, and background (Archer, 1980). Using the measures of self-disclosure in **Table 12.5,** psychologists have explored who discloses what to whom and some of the differences between people who disclose a great deal and those who do not. For example, Sidney Jourard (1971) has shown that college student subjects, both males and females, disclose more to their mothers than to their fathers. He also found that groups of people who disclose more as determined by their scores on the self-disclosure scale rated higher on measures of interpersonal competence. In general, psychologists who have studied self-disclosure argue that it is a very rewarding and self-actualizing experience. People learn a great deal about themselves and others through mutual self-disclosure and find that self-disclosure leads

Table 12.5   **Sample Items from Jourard's Self-Disclosure Questionnaire**

The answer sheet that accompanied the questionnaire had columns headed "Mother," "Father," "Male Friend," "Female Friend," and "Spouse." Subjects indicated whether they had told the other person nothing about this aspect of self (0), had talked in general terms about the item (1), or had talked in full and complete detail about it (2).

1. My personal views on sexual morality—how I feel that I and others ought to behave in sexual matters.

2. What I would appreciate most for a present.

3. What I enjoy most, and get the most satisfaction from in my present work.

4. How I really feel about the people that I work for, or work with.

5. All of my present sources of income—wages, fees, allowance, dividends, etc.

6. The facts of my present sex life—including knowledge of how I get sexual gratification; any problems that I might have, with whom I have relations, if anybody.

7. Things in the past or present that I feel guilty or ashamed and guilty about.

8. My present physical measurements, for example, height, weight, waist, etc.

After Jourard (1971).

to intimacy (Jourard, 1971). In this section we will consider five factors that determine how much individuals disclose to others: reciprocity, appropriateness norms, trust, the quality of relationships, and gender.

Many studies of self-disclosure have indicated that it is reciprocal (Cohn & Strassberg, 1983; Cozby, 1972). That is, the more personal information one person discloses to a companion, the more personal information the companion will disclose in return. Sometimes others reveal what we regard as too much information, which may lead us to feel uncomfortable and to dislike those persons. But we still disclose more to them, in accordance with the reciprocity principle.

Norms, or group standards, indicate how much disclosure is appropriate for different people in different situations (Kleinke & Kahn, 1980). People strive to disclose the normative or appropriate amount in different situations. Sometimes other people disclose matters that

are too personal. In such a case, we will compromise between the tendency to reciprocate and the desire to follow appropriateness norms. Thus we may disclose a good deal to them but not match their level of self-disclosure exactly.

Another determinant of self-disclosure is how much we trust the other person (Chaiken & Derlega, 1976). If we do not trust others, we might not fully reciprocate what they reveal to us. We may fear that they will betray our confidences or somehow use them against us.

A fourth determinant of self-disclosure is the quality of a relationship. Altman and Taylor (1973) have developed a social-penetration theory which suggests that the more intimate we are with another person, the more different topics we disclose to that person and the more deeply we discuss any particular topic. Furthermore, not only does the quality of a relationship affect the degree of self-disclosure, but the opposite can be true too. A high degree of self-disclosure can lead to a more intimate relationship.

Finally, studies of men's and women's self-disclosure indicate that the two sexes do not disclose to the same degree. Generally, women disclose more than men (Cozby, 1973). Jourard (1971) has suggested that men's limited self-disclosure prevents healthy expression and adds stress to their lives. It seems, however, that both men and women respond to stereotypes that represent women as more intimate and self-disclosing than men and turn these stereotypes into self-fulfilling prophecies.

Interim Summary

We like others who are near, familiar, and attractive. We also like competent people, though we like very competent people more when they err or blunder.

In general, we like others who like us. However, we may like someone more who doesn't like us at first but then comes to like us. We like least people who like us at first but then come to dislike us. We like those whose attitudes are similar to our own and we strongly dislike those whose attitudes are different.

Romantic love depends on expectations, finding an appropriate person to fall in love with, and interpreting arousal felt in the presence of that person as love. Companionate love, an essential ingredient of an enduring relationship, is the affection that remains after the passion of romantic love subsides.

Self-disclosure is sharing with another person one's needs, thoughts, feelings, behavior, and background. The type of self-disclosure is determined by reciprocity, norms, trust, relationship quality, and gender.

SUMMARY

1. Impressions are based on combining disparate pieces of information.
2. Schemata influence what we attend to, how we interpret information, and what we remember. Sometimes we interpret information to fit our schemata. At other times information changes our schemata.
3. People often show primacy effects in impression formation, being more influenced by early information.
4. The covariation and discounting principles and the correspondence and actor observer biases are important aspects of attribution.
5. Attitudes are influenced by other people, by our own logic and reasoning, and by our behavior.
6. There are two routes to persuasion, the central route and the peripheral route.
7. Attitude change depends on the communicator, the message, and the situation.
8. In order to understand prejudice we must understand how prejudiced attitudes are learned, how self-esteem is raised by discriminating against members of out-groups, and how stereotypes are formed and maintained.
9. Sometimes prejudices are maintained by self-fulfilling prophecies.
10. We like people who are familiar, attractive, and competent, and also those who like us and who have attitudes similar to our own.
11. Romantic love depends on expectations, finding the right person, and interpreting arousal as love.
12. Self-disclosure is determined by reciprocity, norms, trust, relationship quality, and gender.

KEY INDIVIDUALS

Fritz Heider
Jonathan Freedman
Daniel T. Gilbert
Harold Kelley
Irving Janis
Edward E. Jones
Theodore Newcomb
Seymour Feshbach
William McGuire
Leon Festinger
Thomas Pettigrew
Sidney Jourard

KEY RESEARCH

"warm-cold" study of impression formation
assimilation and accommodation of information into schemata
primacy and recency effects in impression formation (paragraphs about Jim)
attitude formation and change among Bennington College students
Elaboration Likelihood Model (ELM) of persuasion
the effectiveness of one-sided versus two-sided communications in persuasion
fear as a motivator in persuasive communications
the persistence of changed attitudes among Bennington College graduates
the role of culturally learned attitudes in the development of prejudice
"Pygmalion in the Classroom"

KEY TERMS

social cognition
social influence
schema
scripts
assimilation
accommodation
primacy effect
recency effect
attribution
covariation principle
discounting principle
correspondence bias

fundamental attribution error

actor-observer bias

beliefs

attitudes

cognitive dissonance

self-perception theory

impression-management theory

stereotype

prejudice

discrimination

realistic conflict theory

social identity theory

self-fulfilling prophecy

liking

romantic love

companionate love

consummate love

self-disclosure

13 Social Influence

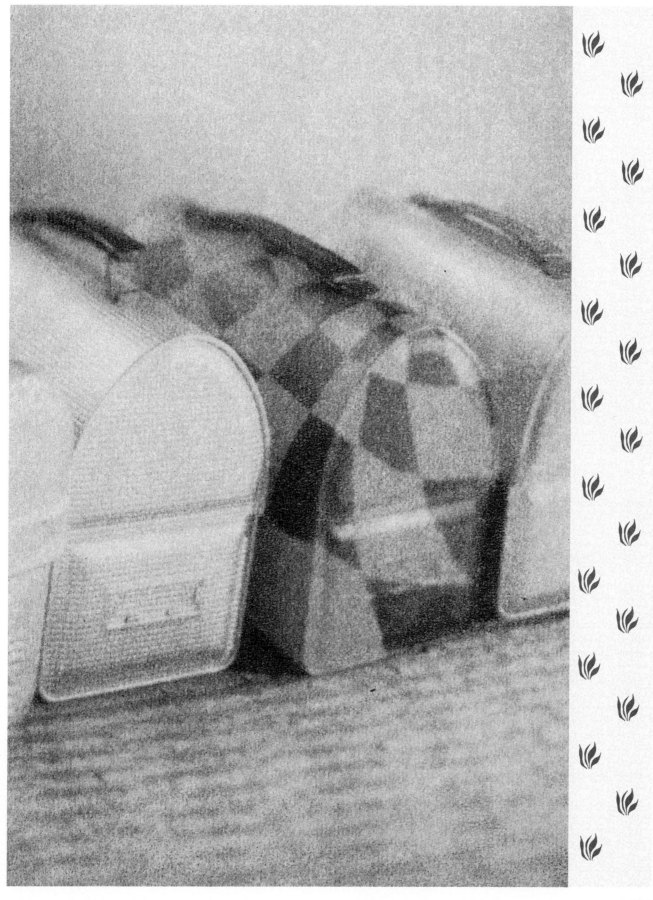

455

During the times of year when the Supreme Court is in session, Monday is the day on which it announces its decisions. Men and women of the press from the world over await the release of these announcements. Sometimes the Court's decisions are momentous, and much is said and written about their impact on our lives. Other times its decisions seem esoteric and trivial. In either case, the way the nine members of the Court reach their judgment is hidden from public view. All that we know is that the individual justices must combine their various points of view and attempt to make a decision, sometimes unanimous, more often split. How do individual justices respond to the opinions and personalities of other members of the Court? How does the group as a whole decide the way to act?

The area of psychology that considers the ways individuals influence each other and the ways groups make decisions is *social influence,* the subject of this chapter. Throughout our lives we are influenced by others in many ways. Some of these ways are direct and obvious; others are quite subtle. In this chapter we will consider the full range of influences that act on us as individuals and as members of groups.

In the first section we will consider the strong and direct pressures of group standards and authority figures, which lead individuals to conform and comply. This type of influence is quite obvious.

At other times, social influence is indirect and barely noticeable. However, these more subtle influences exert a strong impact on many kinds of individual behaviors. Two important behaviors that are strongly affected by social influence are aggression and altruism, or hurting and helping others. These will be discussed in the second section of this chapter.

Next, we will discuss how some of the influence processes that affect individuals, as well as several additional ones, also affect important aspects of group functioning. We will consider how decision making occurs in groups. Of special interest will be recently discovered group processes that give insight into how people make choices, good and bad, that can affect entire nations. In the final section, we will consider how leaders influence followers and the problem of coordinating and directing individuals in groups.

CONFORMITY AND COMPLIANCE

Experiments by social psychologists Solomon Asch and Stanley Milgram subjected people to strong influence pressures. In one experiment subjects were pressured to conform to the judgments of other group members. In the other, subjects were pressured to obey the somewhat disturbing commands of an authority figure. The results of these studies have revealed a great deal about how human beings act and react to each other.

The Asch Experiments

We define **conformity** as going along with other people's attitudes and behaviors as a result of real or imagined pressure. How strong are the pressures in a group to make an individual conform to group ideas and standards for behavior? This is one of the foremost questions about group behavior. Can people think independently, make rational judgments, and plan effective action in groups, or do they respond unthinkingly and irrationally to group pressures?

When Solomon Asch became a social psychologist in the 1940s, a prevalent view was that people, like rats, were easily influenced by simple rewards and punishments. This view was influenced by Freud's claim that much of human behavior was irrational and by Watson's behaviorist perspective that conditioning could mechanically influence people to do or become anything. Asch, on the other hand, believed that people were rational and deliberative. Research that seemed to suggest otherwise was, he thought, open to alternative interpretations. Even though earlier work by Muzafer Sherif (1935) had shown that people would conform in an ambiguous situation, as when they were judging the apparent movement of a stationary point of light, Asch felt that individuals would not conform when reality was clear. To show that people would not be influenced by others when they could rely on their own good sense and judgment, Asch devised a now-classic experiment (1952).

In Asch's experiment, the only advance information given to the male subjects was that they would be participating in a study of "visual discrimination." Let us describe the experience of a typical subject in this experiment.

He arrives at the laboratory to find several other subjects waiting for the experiment.

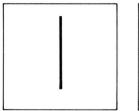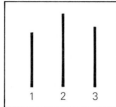

Figure 13.1
Line Comparison Cards Used in Asch's Experiment.
Subjects were asked to state which of the three
comparison lines (right) matched the standard line (left)
(After Asch, 1952)

When it is time to get started, the experimenter seats the subjects around a table and explains the purpose of the study. It concerns people's ability to make visual discriminations by matching one of three comparison lines shown on one board to a standard line shown on another (see **Figure 13.1**). The subjects' job will be to say which of the three comparison lines—1, 2, or 3—is the same as the standard.

The experimenter remarks that, since the task is easy, he will save time and simply ask subjects to announce their judgments out loud in order of their seating position. Beginning on his left, the experimenter asks the first person for his judgment on the first trial. Our subject sees that he will be announcing his decision next to last and awaits his turn. The first two trials are routine. The judgments are easy and everyone agrees on the answers. On the third trial, however, our subject hears the first person give what clearly seems to be the wrong answer. Quickly, the next four people all say the same seemingly wrong number. The subject is completely baffled, but he feels positive that the others are wrong. Yet when his turn to state his decision comes, he feels panicked. He asks the experimenter if he should say what he thinks is really the right answer or just how it looks to him. The experimenter replies that the subject should just say which line he thinks is the same as the standard. The subject gives the answer he thinks is correct—the one that is different from all the others. Then the last person agrees with the rest of the subjects. Our subject feels that he's sticking out like a sore thumb. He wishes he could understand why the others gave such an odd answer (see **Figure 13.2**).

On the next trial the subject looks carefully to form his own judgment before he hears anyone else give theirs. But it happens again. The first subject gives an answer that seems wrong, and the others calmly report the same. Our subject doesn't want everyone to think he's playing games or losing his mind, and he wishes that he could sit in the others' chairs or see the board differently. If you were in our subject's place, what would you say?

Although our subject wasn't able to figure out why the other participants were giving such implausible answers, you might have

Figure 13.2
Subject Reaction in Asch's Experiment.
The sole true subject in Asch's experiment looked bewildered and concerned
when confronted by an obviously incorrect unanimous majority. Here he looks
carefully to check his judgment.

guessed what was really happening. The subject we have been discussing was the only real subject in the entire experiment. The others were confederates of the experimenter and were instructed to give correct answers on the first two trials and then incorrect answers on 12 of the next 16 trials. Asch's main concern was how many subjects would go along with the unanimous and incorrect majority on the "conformity trials." In a control group, where subjects had made judgments in isolation, there had been virtually no errors. Asch therefore had hypothesized that the experimental groups would show very little conformity.

The results were quite surprising, both to Asch and to other people who had overestimated the individual's independence. About 37 percent of the responses in the conformity trials agreed with the majority, even though these responses were incorrect. However, this does not mean that everyone conformed about a third of the time. There were large individual differences. About a quarter of the subjects were completely independent and never "yielded" to the majority. On the other hand, about a third of the subjects conformed on half the trials or more.

It is often tempting to conclude from these results that Asch's research identified two types of people, conformers and nonconformers. But as Asch discovered in interviews with subjects after the experiment, people conformed or defied the majority for many different reasons. For example, sometimes subjects

People have a need to be accepted by others. This may in part explain our inclination toward conformity.

actually "saw" what the majority reported, sometimes they believed that their own deviant perception was wrong, and sometimes they believed that they were correct but conformed anyway. Overall, Asch found a great deal more conformity than he had predicted, great variation in how people behaved, and even more variation in why the subjects acted as they did and how they felt about it.

Conformity, Nonconformity, and Rejection

Asch's original experiments had a great impact on the field of social psychology. There seemed to be an unending series of questions about when and why people conformed in the line judgment situation and what this meant about human nature and social interaction. Subsequent research showed that majorities as small as 3 or 4 produced as much conformity as groups as large as 16, but conformity dropped sharply if the incorrect majority was not unanimous (Asch, 1955). These and other follow-up studies quickly began to get at the basic questions of why people conform at all, what kinds of people are likely to conform more or less than average, and what kinds of situations elicit the most conformity. The issue of foremost importance was why people conform at all. Asch's postexperimental interviews and later research led social psychologists to consider two key motives for conformity (Deutsch & Gerard, 1955). One is people's need to be correct. The other is their need to be accepted by others. Both of these needs operated in the original Asch experiment. Because we are often not sure of the right thing to do, say, or believe, we often rely on other people's judgments and actions to guide our own behavior. In the interviews after Asch's experiment, some of the conforming subjects reported they were so used to relying on others that they decided the others must be correct, no matter how the lines looked. Still, analyses of Asch's interviews showed that the main reason subjects conformed in the line judgment situation was that they were worried about what others might think of them for deviating from the majority. Additional evidence for this explanation was that when subjects wrote their responses on a piece of paper rather than announcing their responses out loud, conformity-induced errors dropped drastically. During 12 conformity trials subjects averaged only 1.5 errors when the responses were written. When they were announced publicly, however, the average number of errors rose to 4.4.

Is the fear that others will reject, dislike, or mistreat us simply for holding different opinions actually warranted? A famous experiment by Stanley Schachter (1951) suggests it may be. Schachter investigated group reactions to individuals who conformed or deviated from the majority's opinion. In this study, groups of male college students read and discussed the case of a troubled delinquent boy named Johnny Rocco. Johnny had had a very difficult childhood, growing up in an urban slum, and he often got into trouble. Subjects in the experiment were asked to recommend that Johnny receive either a great deal of love and affection, harsh discipline and punishment, or some combination of the two. The case was written sympathetically and the subjects made lenient recommendations. To study the consequences of nonconformity, Schachter included in each discussion group a confederate who sometimes agreed with the real subjects and sometimes recommended that Johnny needed severe punishment. When the confederate took the deviant opinion, he maintained it and defended it as best he could. How did the majority treat this deviant?

The results were quite clear. The subjects' communications were immediately directed at the deviating confederate in an effort to get him to agree to a lenient recommendation. When it became clear that the deviant would stick to his position, communication dropped off sharply. He was largely ignored. After the discussion, when subjects had a chance to assign group members to tasks and to recommend who should be included in the group, the nonconforming confederate was clearly rejected. However, in groups where the same confederate took the majority opinion, he was viewed positively and not rejected. Thus, holding to an unpopular opinion even in a short discussion of a case study caused an individual to be ostracized. At least under some circumstances, fear of rejection due to nonconformity is justified.

Compliance with Authority

Compliance is agreeing to another person's direct requests or commands to behave in specific ways. To study the extent to which people will comply and *why* they comply, Stanley Milgram (1974) conducted some ingenious but highly controversial experiments on "obedience to authority."

The subjects in Milgram's experiments were adult men of various ages, occupations, and social positions in the area of New Haven, Connecticut. They had answered advertisements requesting participants in an experiment on learning. When each subject arrived at the laboratory, he was introduced to another participant in the study. The experimenter explained that one of the two would play the role of "learner" and the other "teacher." According to the experimenter, the focus of the experiment was the effect of punishment on learning. Whenever the learner made a mistake, he was to be punished with an electrical shock. Then the subjects were shown the apparatus that was to be used to administer the punishment. This shock-generating machine had thirty switches on it, the first delivering 15 volts, the second 30, and so on up to 450 volts, where the switches were labeled "Danger—Severe Shock—X X X." At this point names were drawn from a hat and one subject discovered he was to be the teacher and the other person the learner. The learner was taken to a different room, strapped into a chair, and wired with electrodes. The teacher then returned to the shock generator, where he could not see the learner, and was instructed to move up the row of switches every time the learner made a mistake, thereby giving the learner an increasingly severe shock (see **Figure 13.3** on page 460).

Finally, the experiment started. It quickly became bizarre and frightening. The learner made many mistakes and the experimenter told the teacher to give increasingly severe shocks. At 75 volts the teacher could hear the learner grunting in the next room. At 150 volts the learner shouted, "Let me out" and said his heart couldn't stand the pain. He began to yell. He let out an agonizing scream at 285 volts and refused to answer after that. Then there was nothing.

Most teachers became very upset. Some asked the experimenter if they should continue, and others told him they wanted to stop. Sometimes they asked the experimenter to look in on the learner and sometimes asked if he would take complete responsibility for what happened. No matter what the teacher asked or how he protested, the experimenter only said, "The experiment requires that we go on," or "Please continue, teacher," or "Although the shocks may be painful, they are not danger-

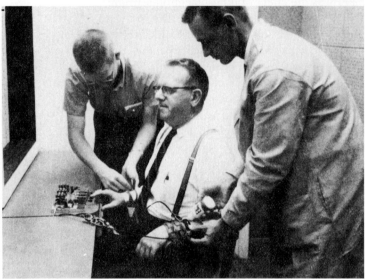

Figure 13.3
Milgram's Experiment.
The top photo shows the fake shock-generating machine Milgram used. The bottom photo shows the subject receiving a sample shock from the generator.

ous," or "Go on to the next trial, please," or "It is absolutely essential that you go on." The experimenter mechanically continued to give these replies, assuring the teachers that they would not be responsible. If the teacher adamantly refused to continue, the experimenter said, "You have no choice but to go on." Milgram wanted to know how many subjects would defy the orders of the experimenters and stop. How would you behave in this situation?

As you might have guessed, the "learner" in Milgram's experiments was not a real subject but a confederate, and the shock machine did not really deliver shocks. After the experiment, the real subjects, the teachers, were told the truth. However, during the experiment they

were convinced that the learner was another subject just like themselves.

Of those who knew about Milgram's proposed work before he started, few felt that he would learn very much. They felt that no one would continue shocking the learner once it was clear he was suffering. In fact, 40 psychiatrists at a leading medical school predicted that less than one tenth of 1 percent of the subjects would comply completely (Milgram, 1974).

We now know how wrong these experts were. In an earlier version of this experiment, the learner did not complain or scream. It never occurred to Milgram that this embellishment would be necessary to make some teachers stop. However, if the teacher was completely out of contact with the learner, obedience was nearly total. In a variation called the *remote condition,* the subject could hear pounding on the walls but could not hear the learner's voice. Under these conditions 65 percent of the subjects were fully obedient. In the previously described voice *feedback condition,* 62.5 percent of the teachers continued to the end.

What happens when the victim is positioned closer to the teacher? In the *proximity condition,* the learner, portrayed by a professional actor who kicked and screamed, was seated only 1 1/2 feet away. Here, 40 percent of the subjects were fully obedient. Going one step further, Milgram conducted a *touch-proximity condition,* where the teacher actually had to push the learner's arm down on an electric grid. In this situation, obedience dropped to 30 percent (see **Figure 13.4**).

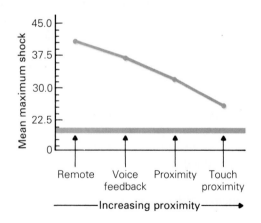

Figure 13.4
Amount of Shock Delivered to "Learners" in the Four Experimental Conditions.
The curve shows that as learners moved closer to the subjects, subjects were less willing to obey orders and deliver the shocks. (After Milgram, 1974)

How can we best explain the totally unexpected degree of obedience in this research? While there are particular aspects of Milgram's situation, such as the gradual increase in the level of shock, that entrap its subjects, research has shown that obedience to authority is actually quite general. It occurs in different cultures, affecting children as well as adults (Gilbert, 1981; Shanab & Yahya, 1977). A key factor in obedience to authority is the concept of responsibility. In Milgram's experiments subject after subject raised the issue of responsibility should harm come to the learner. Although the experimenter did not always discuss it, when he did say "I'm responsible for what goes on here," the subjects showed visible relief. Thus the idea that "I am not responsible" is crucial in convincing subjects to obey. Other studies show that obedience is sharply reduced when the authority tells subjects that they are responsible for any negative consequences (Hamilton, 1978). What is surprising is that subjects will so readily assign responsibility to someone else and deny it themselves. This process is called the **diffusion of responsibility,** defined as the phenomenon whereby being part of a group lowers each person's sense of responsibility. Milgram believed that diffusion of responsibility is crucial in understanding the murder of six million Jews in Europe during World War II. Individuals involved in this massacre often stated that they were just "carrying out orders." The Jonestown massacre in 1978 shows, again, the extremes that people will go to in following orders.

The Reverend Jim Jones started his People's Temple Full Gospel Church in Indiana during the 1960s. He was known as a flamboyant and charismatic leader who performed seemingly miraculous feats of faith healing and contributed large amounts of money to the civil rights and other liberal causes in the Midwest. In 1965 Jones took his church to California. He became an important figure in San Francisco, providing a refuge for minorities, the elderly, drug addicts, and others who needed help and protection. The People's Temple had an important impact on many elections in the Bay Area and was responsible for turning out large crowds for political rallies. But after rumors started to spread about beatings, forced marriages, and staged faith healings, Jones and his followers decided to leave the United States and establish the People's Temple in Jonestown, Guyana.

Jim Jones demanded unquestioned obedience to his authority. Trouble began when people tried to leave the temple. Jones resisted all such challenges to his supremacy. By 1978 there was enough concern about Jonestown that Congressman Leo Ryan of California decided to investigate firsthand.

We don't know what Leo Ryan was going to report to the Congress and the press about his findings. We do know that he offered to take back to the United States anyone who wanted to go. Several people said they wanted to return, and none of Jim Jones' exhortations could change their minds. However, neither Ryan nor the defectors ever left South America. A group of Jones' lieutenants shot them down at the airstrip. Then came the ultimate horror.

Jones had maintained a high level of fear in his colony. He kept preaching that outside forces were threatening the work of the People's Temple and that its members had to be prepared for the worst. He said they must die rather than let outsiders subvert their work. Several times Jones ordered his followers to "rehearse" a mass suicide, in which they were to drink Kool-Aid laced with cyanide and prepare to die within 5 minutes. After Ryan had been shot, Jones ordered his followers to line up and drink the poisoned Kool-Aid. This time it was no rehearsal or practice run. Most people obeyed Jones' orders freely and conformed with the group, but some apparently tried to resist or escape. Most of them were forced to join the mass death ritual. More than 900 people died in the mass murder-suicide at Jonestown.

The Guyana incidents show the extreme destruction that powerful authority can direct when people turn over responsibility for their actions to others (Osherow, 1984). Later in this chapter we will see that diffusion of responsibility has been used to explain several other kinds of group behavior including the decision on whether to help a person in need.

Compliance without Pressure

Milgram's research shows us that people can be induced to comply with the directives of authority even when the behavior required is against their wishes and values. In our day-to-day experience, however, we are seldom exposed to such direct pressure to perform such disagreeable acts. Often the pressure to conform or comply is more subtle (Cialdini, 1988).

In this section we shall consider research on three subtle yet powerful techniques that can lead people to comply without feeling pressured.

THE FOOT-IN-THE-DOOR TECHNIQUE

One method of obtaining compliance, sometimes used by salespeople, is called the **foot-in-the-door technique.** This technique involves getting people to comply with small requests before asking them to comply with larger ones. For example, a life insurance salesperson may ask you to discuss your financial plans, sign a form to make a small change in your policy, or give some information. After you have agreed to these small requests, the salesperson may ask you to purchase more insurance. Are you more likely to buy after the salesperson has gotten a "foot in the door" by obtaining your compliance with small requests?

An experiment designed to answer this question showed that people were more likely to agree to a large request after they had agreed to a small one (Freedman & Fraser, 1966). The subjects in this experiment were housewives who lived in a suburban area of California. There were two groups. Subjects in one group were simply asked to put up a huge sign on their front lawns that said, "DRIVE CAREFULLY." Subjects in the second group were first asked to put up a small sign in a window of their home encouraging people to drive safely. Most of the women in the second group complied with this request. Whether or not they had complied, several days later they were asked to put up the large lawn sign.

Only 16.7 percent of the subjects in the first group, who were not asked to put up the small sign, agreed to put up the large sign. However, 76 percent of those in the second group, who were first asked to put up the small sign, put up the large one. Thus, complying with a small request made people more likely to agree to a large one.

One reason for this might be that agreeing to the first request makes people feel committed to being nice to the person making that request. A second reason might be that agreeing to the first request makes people feel committed to the specific cause of safe driving. However, Freedman and Fraser showed that neither of these reasons is a sufficient explanation. Even when people who had been asked to comply with a small request were later approached by an entirely different person to comply with an entirely unrelated large request, they were much more likely to agree to this large request than were people who had not been asked to agree to some small request.

What, then, is the explanation for the foot-in-the-door findings? According to self-perception theory (Bem, 1972), we infer our attitudes and traits from our behavior, as long as we feel that our behavior has been freely chosen. For example, we know that we like spinach if we freely eat it. How does this work with the foot-in-the-door situation? When people agree to a small request, they come to see themselves as the kind of person who helps out and gets involved in causes. To act consistently with this new self-image, they agree to the subsequent large requests (De Jong, 1979; Snyder & Cunningham, 1975).

THE DOOR-IN-THE-FACE TECHNIQUE

Foot-in-the-door research shows that people are more likely to comply with a large request if they have previously complied with a smaller one. Therefore it may surprise you to learn that people are also more likely to comply with a request if they have previously *turned down* a larger request.

Consider the following situation. A person collecting money for a charity you support asks you to make a $100 donation. Most of us would probably gasp and say no. Suppose the person then said, "Well, all right, can you give us $10?" What would happen then? You would probably sigh with relief and say yes. You have just been caught by the **door-in-the-face technique,** in which a person who has refused to comply with a large request is more likely to comply with a small or moderate one (Cialdini, Vincent, Lewis, Catalan, Wheeler, & Darby, 1975). Later research has shown that this result occurs only when the same person makes the second request and when he or she makes it immediately (Cann, Sherman, & Elkes, 1975).

This pattern of findings can be explained in terms of self-perceptions and considerations of fairness and equity (Walster, Walster, & Berscheid, 1978). By giving up on the large request and asking for a smaller favor, the asker has, so to speak, met you halfway. People usually feel that it seems only fair to agree to the small request since the asker has made a concession and not pushed them to comply with the big favor. However, these "equity" considerations operate only if the same person makes the second request. Furthermore, if several days go by, the asker's concession is forgotten, and self-perception ("I am not the kind of person who agrees to this kind of favor") sets in. (See **Table 13.1**)

LOWBALLING

A third technique for gaining compliance without pressure is referred to as the lowball technique (Cialdini, 1988). Suppose you have agreed to take part in a psychological experiment, without knowing too much about the details. Then you are informed that you have to show up at 7 A.M. to participate. Would you still do it? Research has indicated that people are more likely to show up at 7 A.M. if they had first made a general agreement to participate than if they were told about the 7 A.M. starting time at the beginning (Cialdini, Cacioppo, Bassett, & Miller, 1978). Getting people to participate in a 7 A.M. experiment by getting a general commitment and then giving them the bad news about the starting time is an example of the lowball technique. In general, **lowballing** can be defined as getting people to agree to an action and then changing the agreement by telling them that the action will be less rewarding or more costly than was originally stated or implied. An auto salesperson might use this technique to sell a car by agreeing on a favorable price and then changing it to a higher price, perhaps telling the customer that the salesperson's manager had disapproved the deal or that some of the options the customer had wanted wouldn't be available at the agreed-on price.

Why does the lowball technique work? Some evidence suggests that people form a commitment to performing an action, such as buying a car or showing up for an experiment, and that the commitment makes them carry through even when the desirability of performing the action is reduced (Cialdini et al., 1978). Another possibility is that the initial commitment creates an obligation to a specific person rather than to a specific action. Consistent with this hypothesis is a study showing that lowballing works only if the person who presents the later "bad news" that changes the agreement is the same person who elicited the original commitment.

In this study, subjects were asked to participate in a study even though extra course credit that had been promised originally was suddenly made unavailable. This attempt at lowballing worked only when the person who explained that the extra credit would no longer

Table 13.1 — Percentage of Subjects Complying with a Moderate Request Under Various Conditions

This table illustrates both the foot-in-the-door and the door-in-the-face phenomenon. Compliance to a moderate request is increased if subjects have previously agreed to a small request. This is true whether or not there has been a 7- to 10-day delay between requests (foot-in-the-door effect). Compliance to a moderate request also increases after subjects have previously refused a large request, but only if there has been no delay between requests (door-in-the-face effect).

Size of Initial Request	Second, Moderate Request Made Immediately	Second, Moderate Request, Delayed
Small	78% comply (foot-in-the-door effect)	70% comply (foot-in-the-door effect)
Large	90% comply (door-in-the-face effect)	29% comply
No initial request (control)	50% comply	

After Cann, Sherman, & Elkes (1975).

be available was the same person who had elicited the original commitment (Burger & Petty, 1981). When a different person explained that there would be no extra credit but asked subjects to participate anyway, very few of them complied. Thus, like the door-in-the-face technique, lowballing is successful only when a person is able to create an obligation through his or her interaction with another person. In all three of these compliance-without-pressure techniques, apparently people's initial agreement—or refusal—to comply with a request makes them more likely to agree to perform a subsequent, distinctly more costly behavior.

Interim Summary

Asch's studies of conformity showed that people sometimes conform to majority opinion, even when that opinion is clearly in error. Individuals vary greatly in how much they conform to group pressure.

One reason for conforming is the need to be correct. Another is the need to be well treated by others. Schachter's study of conformity and deviation showed that people who deviate from group opinion are sometimes rejected by the group.

In a study of obedience to authority, Milgram showed that some people will obey an experimenter's command to shock another person, even if that person is suffering and in apparent danger. However, obedience decreased when the person receiving the shocks was closer to the subject. One explanation for the subjects' obedience was that they felt the experimenter was responsible for what happened to the person receiving the shocks.

According to the foot-in-the-door technique, if people agree to a small request, they are then more likely to agree to a larger one. As a result of agreeing to the small request they come to see themselves as helpers.

According to the door-in-the-face technique, people who have refused a large request are more likely to agree to a moderate request from the same requester. They believe that it is equitable to agree to the moderate request since the asker has abandoned the large request.

In the lowball technique, people are led into a less desirable action than they originally agreed to.

• •

AGGRESSION AND ALTRUISM

During the recent conflict between Serbia and Bosnia, world opinion was outraged when Serbian snipers fired on a bus load of Muslin orphans. At about the same time a man in the United States was killed when he stepped into the path of an oncoming truck to rescue two children. Taking lives and saving lives are our most dramatic examples of aggression and altruism. They make us wonder how the same creature, the human being, could be capable of both actions, and they call to mind William Blake's haunting lines in his poem about the deadly tiger:

> Did he smile his work to see? Did he who made the Lamb make thee?

How is it possible for living beings to be created so differently, and how could individuals of one species, *Homo sapiens,* display such

divergent behavior? Even more puzzling, how can we account for the fact that a single person, for example, U.S. Army General and President Andrew Jackson, can lead a life full of acts of both barbarous cruelty and tenderness, self-sacrifice, and sensitivity? Although we may never be able to fully answer these questions, social psychological research on aggression and altruism gives us some important insights.

Aggression can be defined as behavior that one person enacts with the intention of harming or destroying another person or object. Psychologists have debated the causes of aggression for many years. These debates have centered around the nature-nurture question: is aggression innate, that is, programmed into human beings from birth, or is it learned from various environmental influences? Older theories of aggression suggested in one way or another that aggressive behavior is innate. Later study has emphasized the way the environment influences us to be aggressive. We shall present both views and attempt to tie together some of the strands of evidence.

Instinct Theories of Aggression

Seventeenth-century political philosopher Thomas Hobbes argued that people are naturally competitive and hostile. They are interested only in their own power and in advantage over others. For this reason, they need government to prevent constant conflict and mutual destruction.

Sigmund Freud's theories echoed Hobbes' pessimistic view of human nature. For many years Freud's writings emphasized eros, the human drive for pleasure. However, after observing the unprecedented and seemingly interminable carnage of World War I, Freud postulated a second drive, *thanatos,* directed toward self-destruction and death. Freud felt that this drive to return to an inanimate, lifeless state conflicted with the pleasure drive and was satisfied by being turned outward. The result was aggression toward others. Unless there was a more acceptable way to express thanatos, Freud felt people would act aggressively from time to time. Thus Freud implied that people need to express hostile and destructive impulses periodically, just as they need to eat, drink, and express sexual needs.

Freud was not the only person to propose that aggression is inborn. In his well-known book *On Aggression* (1966), Konrad Lorenz proposed that aggression in all animals,

Research shows that learning plays an important part in the development of aggression. The parents of these cats did not teach them to hunt and they did not develop aggressive behavior toward rats.

human beings included, is instinctive. He argued that because aggressive behavior is adaptive for animals, they evolved with an inborn tendency to aggress. He noted, however, that most animals have "built-in safety devices" (Lorenz, 1966). These include rituals, such as exposing their throats, which signal submission and end conflicts. These safety devices prevent animals from killing members of their own species when they fight for territory or dominance. Human beings, Lorenz argued, are biologically weaker, "basically harmless," and therefore do not have strong, compensating safety devices. However, once we acquire the ability to kill other human beings through our weapons technology, we have no compensating biological safety devices to stop us short of using those weapons. We do not, for example, follow submission gestures from our fellow human beings by stopping our attacks.

There are many difficulties with instinct theories of aggression. First, there is considerable evidence that learning plays a very important role in aggression. One classic study showed that kittens who were not permitted to observe their mothers hunting rats or who were raised with rats would not attack these animals (Kuo, 1930). Furthermore, it may be that animals are reinforced for aggressive behavior by gaining dominance and sexual privileges in their group. Thus their fighting could be explained by external rewards rather than internal drives. Finally, instinct theories do not

explain why aggression is more prevalent in some situations than others. One approach that does try to explain when people will be aggressive is the frustration-aggression hypothesis.

The Frustration-Aggression Hypothesis

In 1939, the year of Freud's death, psychologist John Dollard and his colleagues at Yale University published a book entitled *Frustration and Aggression* (Dollard, Doob, Miller, Mowrer, & Sears, 1939). This well-known work was influenced both by Freudian thinking and by developments in learning theory. The authors proposed the **frustration-aggression hypothesis,** the view that "frustration always leads to aggression" and that "aggression is always a consequence of frustration." Thus the authors argue that while aggression was an innate response, it would be elicited only in specific situations. Whenever an important need, such as for food, water, recognition, or achievement, is thwarted, the resulting frustration produces an aggressive response.

Research conducted soon after the publication of *Frustration and Aggression* showed some evidence that aggression does increase under frustrating circumstances. In one study, young children were shown an attractive set of toys but were prevented from playing with them. After an agonizing period of frustration, the children were eventually allowed access to the toys, which they threw, stomped, and smashed. In comparison, children who had not been frustrated did not throw, stomp, or smash the toys. In this case, frustration did lead to aggression (Barker, Dembo, & Lewin, 1941).

The research on frustration and aggression suggested many hypotheses about how and when people will behave aggressively. For example, the aggressive response may not always be directed at the persons or objects causing the frustration. This may be too dangerous or inconsistent with moral values. Instead, the aggression may be temporarily held in and later *displaced* against someone or something else in a safe and socially approved way. The target of this displaced aggression is called a *scapegoat*. The concept of displaced aggression, or scapegoating, is often used to account for racial or ethnic discrimination. People who are frustrated by economic or other circumstances, this viewpoint holds, will express their anger against certain groups who are powerless and who are deemed to deserve hostile treat-

When frustrated by poor economic circumstances, people sometimes use scapegoating to express their anger against certain groups, who are powerless, but who are deemed to warrant hostility.

ment (Allport, 1954). A correlational study of lynchings of blacks is consistent with this view. Hovland and Sears (1940) found that from 1882 to 1930 the number of lynchings per year in southern states was highly correlated with the price of cotton. When prices were low, indicating frustrating economic conditions, the number of lynchings increased.

Later research has qualified the frustration-aggression hypothesis. Leonard Berkowitz (1980) has suggested that frustration produces anger and a readiness to aggress. However, Berkowitz has also shown that certain cues are needed to convert this readiness into actual aggression. These cues are environmental stimuli associated either with aggressive behavior or with the frustrating object or person. In one study, for example, subjects were insulted and berated by a confederate for failing to complete a jigsaw puzzle. Then the subjects watched a film in which the actor Kirk Douglas was brutally beaten. After the film the subjects were given an opportunity to show aggression by electrically shocking the confederate. By this time the subjects had learned that the confederate's name was either Bob or Kirk. Subjects used higher-intensity shocks against the confederate if his name turned out to be Kirk. Because of its association with the brutality in the film, the name Kirk served as a cue to aggressive behavior (Geen & Berkowitz, 1967).

Although the results of this and other studies lend powerful support to the frustration-aggression hypothesis, other research has revealed shortcomings (Krebs & Miller, 1985). For example, some research has shown that

frustration does not always lead to aggression (Gentry, 1970). Other studies have shown that frustration can produce different responses in different people in different situations (Kulik & Brown, 1979). Overall, research suggests that frustration and aggression are related. Frustration does not always lead to aggression, and many nonfrustrating circumstances and situations can also elicit aggression.

One of the most interesting extensions of the original frustration-aggression hypothesis is the idea that any unpleasant, or what psychologists call *aversive*, event can produce anger, which in turn can produce aggression (Berkowitz & Heimer, 1989). The aversive events that can increase human aggression include "irritable cigarette smoke, foul odors, high room temperatures, and disgusting scenes" (Berkowitz & Heimer, 1989, p. 1). Thus aggression can be produced not only by frustration, the thwarting of needs, but also by any unpleasant event that produces annoyance, anger, or irritation. Several other factors, such as the reason for the aversive event, determine whether aggression will actually occur following an aversive event. But it is important to remember that the simple fact of unpleasantness increases the probability of aggression.

Arousal and Aggression

Suppose you are out riding a bicycle, attempting to get to the top of a steep hill without getting off your bike and walking. You are already breathing hard from a strenuous ride as you pedal with all your strength to get to the top. You are feeling exhilarated and proud of yourself until a motorist yells at you to get out of the road. Naturally, the motorist makes you angry, but much to your surprise, you uncharacteristically yell back and say something distinctly aggressive. Why would you react in such a way? It may be that the arousal from your hard bike riding was transferred or channeled into your aggressive reaction to the motorist. This transferred arousal may increase the probability that your anger will cause you to act aggressively or it may magnify whatever aggressive response you make. The idea that arousal can be transferred from one source to another is called the theory of *excitation transfer* (Zillman, 1982). The basic concept is that arousal from one source is channeled into and energizes some other response. For example, a young woman might react more joyously to a beautiful symphony if she is already aroused by romantic feelings for her date. There is evidence that aggression can be fueled by the arousal generated from exercise, playing competitive games, or certain kinds of music.

Aggression does not always follow such arousal. The person must have some disposition to react aggressively to the situation, and he or she must incorrectly attribute the arousal to the aggression-producing event rather than to the correct source, such as exercise (Zillman, 1984). Even though arousal does not always produce aggression, it is of utmost importance that we fully understand how it can. We will see shortly that aggression produced by arousal can have very serious social consequences.

Social Learning and Aggression

The social learning theory explanation for aggression is quite different from the instinct and frustration-aggression approaches. Social learning theory rejects the idea that aggressive behavior is inborn. Instead, social learning theory attempts to specify just how people learn aggressive behavior and which social conditions produce and maintain aggressiveness.

Social learning theorists have suggested that aggressive behaviors are learned through *reinforcement* and the *imitation* of aggressive models (Bandura, 1973). People may be reinforced or rewarded for aggressive behavior in a number of ways. Children who succeed in getting to the head of a line or in playing with the most desirable toys by being pushy will quickly learn to act aggressively. In this case, aggressive behavior is directly reinforced.

Children also learn through the process of imitation, a type of learning called observational learning that we discussed in Chapter 6. This involves observing other people who serve as models for behavior. For example, an adult who is successful in being aggressive may become a model for a child, and the child's own aggressive tendencies will be strengthened through *vicarious reinforcement.* The child will come to expect reinforcement or a reward for behaving like the aggressive model. In a classic study by Albert Bandura and his colleagues, children observed models attacking an inflated plastic Bobo doll (Bandura, Ross, & Ross, 1963). Later the children were allowed to play with the doll themselves. Those who had observed an aggressive model were aggressive toward the doll and directly imitated many of the model's specific behaviors (see **Figure 13.5**).

Transferred arousal may increase the likelihood that these athletes, already aroused from their game, will behave aggressively during a conflict.

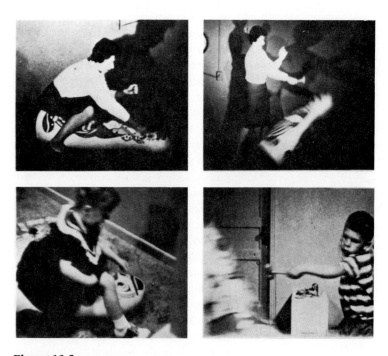

Figure 13.5
Learning Through Imitation.
Social learning theorists suggest that aggression can be learned through imitation. In Bandura's experiments, young children first observed an adult attacking an inflated Bobo doll (top photos). Later, these children showed similar aggression toward the doll (bottom photos).

One consistent finding in later research was that children will imitate the behavior of live models, filmed humans, and cartoon characters all to about the same degree (Bandura, 1973). These findings relate to a crucially important social issue: what are the effects of frequently watching televised violence? Is it possible that children are being taught to express aggressiveness? We will discuss research on this issue shortly.

Applying Theories of Aggresson: Understanding Violence in Society

There is more than just an academic interest in understanding aggression. Violence in the United States is an ever-increasing problem. It is one of our more intractable social ills. In recent years a number of psychologists who have studied aggression have begun applying the theories we have just discussed to understanding several important forms of violence and aggression in our society. In this section we would like to discuss what we have learned about three important questions, the roots of family violence, the impact of violent pornography on aggression toward women, and the role of television in stimulating aggression.

FAMILY VIOLENCE

The phenomenon of family violence, particularly child abuse and spouse abuse, is a problem of major proportions in our society (Emery, 1989; Walker, 1989). In almost any moderate or large-sized community, almost any issue of a daily newspaper will report an instance of family violence or sexual abuse in its local news section. Occasionally the story is so stunning that it attracts national attention. A few years ago Joel Steinberg, a lawyer in New York City, was sentenced to a jail term of 8¹/₂ to 25 years for killing Lisa, a baby girl he and his wife had taken into custody. Steinberg had had a long history of beating his wife. On one occasion he broke her nose. On another she needed surgery to repair her spleen, which had been injured in a beating. While the arrival of Lisa ended the beatings temporarily, soon Steinberg fell into a pattern of beating both wife and child. He believed that Lisa was trying to hypnotize him and one night he beat her to stop her. When Steinberg discovered that Lisa was not breathing, she was taken to the hospital. After several days Lisa died from a brain hemorrhage.

Because many instances of family violence go unreported, it is impossible to know

Attorney Joel Steinberg and his wife Hedda were charged with second-degree murder, first-degree assault, and endangering the welfare of a child after abusing their two adopted children.

how large a problem it is. Based on what we do know, it is reasonable to estimate that the there are between 5 million and 25 million cases of family violence each year in the United States. What basis is there for such an estimate? We know that in 1986 more than 1000 children died as a result of family violence and that 1700 women died as a result of spouse abuse. Clearly, many people who are killed in explosions of family violence have suffered many beatings before they are killed, and many, many people are beaten but not killed. Thus we do know about some of the most dramatic instances of family violence, but there is a great deal we do not know.

How can theories of aggression help explain family violence? Studies of family violence suggest that at least two of the theories we discussed above are relevant. First, family violence is learned and reinforced. Thus the principles of social learning are certainly important. For example, many men find that being abusive to their wives wins compliance (Walker, 1989). Thus abusive behavior is reinforced. In addition, the principles of frustration and aggression are clearly involved as well. As we pointed out earlier, a wide range of aversive events can produce anger and aggression, and those who have studied family violence believe that while much of it is learned and reinforced, a great deal of it is "aversively stimulated," that is, produced by frustration and other unpleasant stimuli (Emery, 1989). More work needs to be done to explain and then control family violence. As we attempt to make progress, we know that basic principles of aggression will be relevant.

VIOLENT PORNOGRAPHY AND AGGRESSION TOWARD WOMEN

Earlier we discussed the idea of excitation transfer, the notion that arousal from one source, such as exercise or competition, can be channeled into and energize aggression (Zillman, 1982). Sexual arousal is of particular concern to excitation transfer researchers and others. Can sexual arousal be channeled into aggressive behavior? This question has taken on increased importance with the debate over the effects of pornography. Some opponents of pornography have argued that in addition to degrading women, pornography may have the harmful consequence of creating arousal in its observers, an arousal which is subsequently transferred into aggressive behavior. Is this true?

Research on the effects of watching sexually explicit films has yielded contradictory results. Some studies have indicated that exposure to erotica decreases aggression; others have indicated the opposite. At present, social psychologists believe that mild forms of erotica, such as nudes from *Playboy* magazine, decrease or have no effect on aggression and do not have a significant effect on attitudes or beliefs about women (Donnerstein, Linz, & Penrod, 1987). However, there is also evidence that violent pornography, including the type seen in R-rated slasher movies, can lead to a desensitization to violence and an increase in aggressive behavior (Donnerstein et al., 1987). For example, in one study, after watching a film containing violent and explicit sex, subjects watched film clips of a man behaving extremely violently toward a woman. Compared to control subjects, these subjects were less physiologically aroused by the violent film clips, less disturbed by them, and saw the woman in the film clips as having suffered less injury. In short, the film containing violent and explicit sex desensitized people to subsequent violence against women (Linz, Donnerstein, & Adams, 1989). Since desensitization can lead people to become less inhibited from behaving aggressively, it may be responsible for the increase in aggression that violent pornography produces.

One research study in this area indicates how complex the relationship between sexually arousing films and aggression can be. Male subjects were shown one of four films: a neutral film of a talk show, an erotic but nonviolent film depicting a couple making love, or one of two violent, aggressive films in which two men assaulted and had sex with a woman. In one version of the violent film, the woman suffered throughout the assault. In the other, she was shown to become a willing participant in the violent sex. After seeing one of these four films, a second condition was introduced: subjects in one group were insulted and angered by a female confederate; subjects in a second group were not. Finally, all subjects were presented with the opportunity to retaliate against the female confederate. There was little aggression following the neutral film and no increased aggression following the nonviolent erotic film—for either angered or nonangered subjects. However, both groups of subjects, angered and nonangered, behaved more aggressively when they had seen the violent film in which the woman seemed to enjoy the sexual assault. And when subjects had seen the violent film in which the woman suffered throughout the sexual assault, nonangered subjects did not behave more aggressively but angered subjects did. In short, viewing violent sexual films increased aggression for all subjects if the woman seemed to enjoy the violence and had the same effect for angered subjects, even when the assaulted woman was obviously suffering (Donnerstein & Berkowitz, 1981). The results of the study are shown in **Table 13.2** on page 469. From these studies, researchers concluded that sexual excitement, when combined with the observation of aggressive behavior in the sexually arousing material, can lead to an increase in aggression. Both the concept of excitation transfer and the principles of social learning theory help explain these findings. As we shall see in the next section, social learning theory also helps explain the relation between violent television and aggression.

TELEVISION AND AGGRESSION

In 1982 the National Institute of Mental Health (NIMH) released its analysis of more than 10 years of research into the effects of watching television. The major conclusion is by now a familiar one. Watching violence on television causes children and adolescents to behave

Table 13.2   Degree of Aggression Shown Toward Female Confederate by Angered and Nonangered Male Subjects after Watching Various Films

| | FILM | | | |
Subjects	Neutral Talk Show	Nonviolent, Erotic	Violent, Woman Enjoys	Violent, Woman Suffers
Nonangered	Low	Low	High	Low
Angered	Low	Low	High	High

Based on Donnerstein & Berkowitz (1981).

more aggressively. The response of the television networks is also familiar. They claim that the report is filled with inaccuracies and that NIMH's review of the 2500 studies was biased and uncritical. We should recognize from the outset that people are of two minds about this issue.

First, let us consider some basic data about what is on television and how much people watch it. Since 1967, the percentage of television shows containing violent episodes has remained about the same, but the number of violent episodes per show has steadily increased. Prime-time shows that portray violence currently average about 5 violent acts per hour. On children's weekend shows, mostly cartoons, the count is 18 violent acts per hour. In 1979 the networks agreed to a code limiting the amount of violence in cartoons. However, a study by Cramer and Mechem (1982) found no decrease in the amount of violence shown in cartoons. If anything, the newer cartoons are even more violent and less entertaining.

A steady increase in television viewing closely parallels the rising proportion of violence. In 1965–66, the Nielsen ratings reported that the average American household watched television 5 hours and 30 minutes a day. By 1980–81, the daily average had risen to 6 hours and 44 minutes (Burger, 1982). In 1987 twelve-year-old children alone watched about 4 hours of television every day (Liebert & Sprafkin, 1988).

It certainly is not implausible, then, to think that people—adults and children—might be influenced by the violence they watch on television. In other domains, certainly, television producers claim that their medium does influence behavior. For example, they sell 30-second segments of air time for many thousands of dollars, based on their claim that commercials influence behavior. But what evidence

is there that televised violence influences children and adolescents to become aggressive?

Essentially, two kinds of studies address this issue (Liebert & Sprafkin, 1988). First are laboratory studies, whose crucial contribution is to show a causal relationship between watching televised violence and behaving aggressively. The study by Liebert and Baron (1972) discussed in Chapter 1 is a good example. Subjects were randomly assigned to two groups. One group watched a violent television show, "The Untouchables," while a second group watched an equally engaging and arousing, but nonviolent, sports competition. Afterward the children were allowed to play, while observers recorded their aggressive acts. The children who had watched the violent program behaved more aggressively than those who had watched the sports competition. This kind of study shows that televised violence does lead directly to aggressive behavior.

The second kind of study, the field study, tells us whether there is a correlation between televised violence and aggression outside the lab. Hundreds of these studies generally show the same results: children who watch more televised violence at home are reported to behave more aggressively (Eron & Huesmann, 1985). One important study of this kind was conducted on several hundred subjects over a 10-year period (Lefkowitz, Eron, Walder, & Huesmann, 1972). Lefkowitz and his colleagues showed that boys who watched more violent television in the third grade were rated as more aggressive by their peers and teachers at age 19—ten years later. Follow-up studies with the same subjects showed that the group of third-graders that was more likely to watch violent television at age 8 was also more likely to be convicted of a serious crime by age 30 (Eron & Huesmann, 1984). Another study demonstrated that during the 1970s homicide rates in the

United States increased during the week after a heavyweight championship fight (Phillips, 1983, 1986). These findings suggest the long-term effects of watching televised violence. Because they are correlational, these studies do not prove that televised violence *causes* aggressive behavior. A review of these studies concludes that we need more evidence before deciding that viewing televised violence causes people in natural settings to be more aggressive (Freedman, 1984, 1986).

The reason the debate continues is that no study can combine the best features of both kinds of study, the demonstration of cause and effect found in the laboratory experiments and the demonstration of a general, real-world relationship found in field studies. Just as no experimenter can ethically investigate the connection between smoking and lung cancer by randomly assigning some people to smoke two packs of cigarettes a day for 15 years and others to abstain completely from smoking, the television-watching habits of children cannot be controlled. Thus there will be continued debate. Eventually parents will have to decide if the results of laboratory experiments and field studies give sufficient support to the idea that violence on television is harmful. Then parents will have to decide whether they want to do anything about it, such as controlling the kind and amount of television their children watch.

In the meantime, some other findings of the NIMH study (1982) can be pondered. People who watch television very frequently are more likely to view the world as a "mean and scary" place and to trust other people less. Also, children who watch more television than their peers have lower reading and IQ scores. In one town, children's reading scores fell sharply two years after television was first introduced. Cause and effect have not been conclusively demonstrated, but these findings must give us pause.

Helping and Altruism

Altruism is defined as the unselfish helping of other people. We have seen that people can be influenced to behave aggressively merely by observing other people behave aggressively. Can observing others' unselfish behavior also influence people to behave altruistically? Unlike the case for aggression, no comprehensive general theories have been proposed to explain

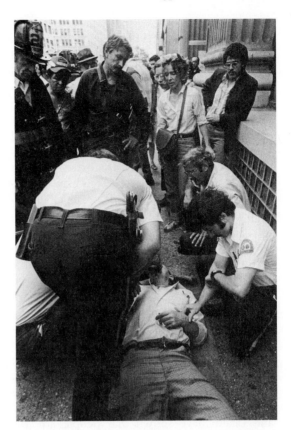

The presence of other bystanders in an emergency situation can lead to a diffusion of responsibility.

altruism. Nevertheless, psychologists remain interested in altruism partly because helping others is often seen as an ideal. Ironically, the modern study of altruism began with a distressing instance of people's failure to help.

In 1964, a woman named Kitty Genovese was brutally stabbed to death near her apartment in Queens, New York. At one point, the assailant ran away and then came back to stab her again to make sure she was dead. During the 30 minutes that the attack took place, Kitty Genovese cried out for help and begged for someone to intervene. Out of the 38 people who heard or watched from their apartments, not one even called the police. The incident gained national publicity. People wondered how the apparent indifference and apathy of so many people in our society could be explained. Are we really that uncaring?

Two social psychologists, John Darley and Bibb Latané, felt that the best way to understand situations like the Kitty Genovese murder is to find out why normally helpful people might not intervene and help in specific situations. One of the factors that Darley and Latané thought was important in the Kitty Genovese incident was the number of bystanders. While the news media focused on the number of people who didn't help as the most astonishing aspect of the case, Darley and Latané felt that perhaps Kitty Genovese was not helped precisely *because* there were so many bystanders. Their research has considered several ways in which the presence of other people can inhibit helping. For example, other people's behavior can lead us to define an ambiguous situation as not serious or dangerous. In addition, the presence of other bystanders in an emergency situation can lead to the diffusion of responsibility.

DEFINING THE SITUATION

When a potential emergency occurs, people must clarify what is happening. Is the situation dangerous? Does that person need help? These critical questions have a substantial impact on how people respond. Several studies by Darley and Latané have shown that people are less likely to define a situation as dangerous if other people are present. In one study, subjects were shown into a room to fill out some questionnaires. In some cases they were alone, in other cases other subjects were present. Then, as part of the experiment, steam, which resembled smoke, began to pour through a vent in the wall. Darley and Latané measured how quickly subjects reacted to what was happening. They found that subjects reacted most quickly when they were alone. The more people there were in the room, the slower anyone was to act. Sometimes no one reacted until the steam was so thick that it was difficult to see the questionnaire (Latané & Darley, 1968). In another study, subjects heard a female experimenter fall, cry out, and moan for nearly a minute. Sometimes the subjects were alone, sometimes they were with one other person. Again, subjects were slower to respond and offer help when they were with another person (Latané & Rodin, 1969).

How can we account for these results? Subjects unintentionally influenced each other to define the situation as not dangerous. In post-experimental interviews, the subjects reported feeling very hesitant about showing anxieties and uncertainties. Most subjects looked to others to see if they seemed upset. Of course, the others were trying to conceal their own concerns and so they appeared calm. It looked as if they were not worried and did not think the situation was an emergency. Thus the individual defined the situation as safe. In this way each subject influenced the others to think there was no cause for alarm.

DIFFUSING RESPONSIBILITY

Even if people define a situation as an emergency, they still may decide that they have no responsibility to take action. This is especially likely to take place if there are other people around who could help. People may reason that someone else should and probably will intervene. Thus no single individual feels responsible for helping. As we have seen before, the term for this phenomenon is *diffusion of responsibility*.

Darley and Latané (1968) conducted an experiment to see whether the number of bystanders in an emergency situation can create diffusion of responsibility and thus reduce the frequency of help given to a victim in need. In this study, female subjects participated in a group discussion with other men and women. The subjects were isolated from one another and communicated over an intercom system. One of the participants, who was actually a confederate of the experimenter, mentioned that he had epilepsy. Later in the discussion, this same person began to have a mock seizure and begged for help. The independent variable in the study was the number of other people the subjects believed were involved in the discussion. Some women thought they were the only other person, others thought there was one other person besides themselves and the victim. A third group thought there was a total of six people: themselves, the victim, and four others. Darley and Latané measured the number of subjects who had responded by the end of the seizure and the average amount of time it took them to respond in each of the three conditions. The results can be seen in **Figure 13.6**. Quite clearly, subjects generally responded and responded quickly when they thought they were the only potential helper. Here there could be no diffusion of responsibility. If there was one or four other potential helpers, subjects responded neither as frequently nor as quickly.

AROUSAL AND REWARD-COST ANALYSIS

Even when a bystander defines a situation as dangerous and accepts responsibility, he or she may not necessarily take action. An emergency situation can be defined as a frightening, arousing event. According to one theory, how people act in the emergency depends on how they appraise the rewards and costs associated with various ways of reducing their arousal (Piliavin, Dovidio, Gaertner, & Clark, 1981). Let us consider the two aspects of what has come to be called the arousal theory of behavior in emergencies. First, how does arousal operate in emergencies, and second, how do rewards and costs affect emergency behavior?

Arousal theory proposes that the arousal generated by seeing an emergency situation becomes more and more unpleasant the longer it continues; the bystander becomes motivated to reduce this arousal. The way a person chooses to reduce the arousal varies according to the rewards and costs in the situation, but in many cases helping directly is the best way to reduce the arousal quickly and completely. Consistent with the arousal theory, a study demonstrated that the more physiologically aroused that subjects in an emergency situation become, the more likely they are to help—and that when they do help, they help more quickly (Sterling & Gaertner, 1984).

While high arousal generates rapid helping in many situations, the precise method of reducing emergency-produced arousal depends on rewards and costs. What are the rewards and costs involved in helping and not helping? The rewards of helping would include good feelings about yourself and perhaps praise from others. The costs of helping might include getting involved in what could be an embarrassing, distasteful, or even dangerous situation. The reward of not helping would be the freedom to go about your normal business; the costs would be guilt or the disapproval of others. Psychologists have learned about the importance of rewards and, particularly, costs, in emergencies from several fascinating studies done on the subway systems of New York City and Philadelphia.

In the first study, student experimenters pretended to collapse in subway cars moderately full of people. They would simply fall to the floor and wait to see if they were helped. In some cases the student collapsing carried a cane, suggesting that he collapsed because he was lame. In other cases the student wore a jacket reeking of liquor and carried a bottle in a brown paper bag. In this case there was a different, but equally obvious, cause of the student's collapse. Observers who were part of the experiment watched to see what hap-

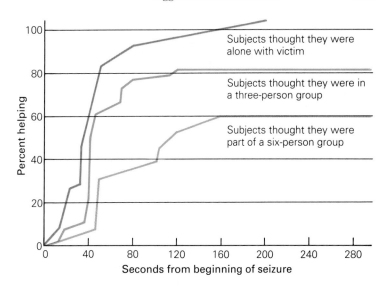

Figure 13.6
Helping Responses in the Emergency of an Epileptic Seizure.
When subjects were alone with the victim or in a small group, there was less diffusion of responsibility. More subjects responded, and their responses were quicker. (After Darley & Latané, 1968)

pened. As predicted by the reward-cost analysis, help was offered much less often in the "drunk" trials than in the "lame" trials. A full 90 percent of the "lame" victims were helped within 70 seconds. Only 20 percent of the "drunk" victims were helped within 70 seconds. It is easy to see how passengers on the subway might think that the costs of not helping a drunk person would be low (who would really blame me for not getting involved with a drunk?) and the costs of helping as relatively high (he might get physically ill, make a fuss, or act violently) (Piliavin, Rodin, & Piliavin, 1969).

In two follow-up studies, the effect of other personal characteristics on helping was investigated. In one, the person who collapsed bit off a capsule of red dye resembling blood and let it trickle down his chin. Here the rate of helping was reduced from about 90 to 60 percent. People were much more likely to try to get someone else to help, perhaps someone who was more knowledgeable and competent in emergency situations (Piliavin & Piliavin, 1972). An interesting but depressing result emerged from a second follow-up study. When the victim had an ugly facial birthmark, help was significantly reduced, from about 86 to 61 percent. Interacting with a stigmatized person is very costly for some individuals, which can lead them to ignore these people (Piliavin, Piliavin, & Rodin, 1975).

Table 13.3   **Predictions of Typical Bystander's Response, Depending on Costs of Helping or Not Helping the Victim**

Cost of Not Helping Victim	Response if Cost of Direct Help Is Low	Response if Cost of Direct Help Is High*
High	(a) Direct intervention	(b) Indirect intervention or redefinition of the situation, disparagement of the victim, etc.**
Low	(c) Varies, depending on the perceived norms of the situation	(d) Leaving scene, ignoring victim, using denial, etc.

*There are some situations, generally those in which victims themselves are very likely to perish, such as severe fires, explosions, cave-ins, and ship accidents, in which the costs of helping become so high that they will be perceived as total, incalculable, or infinite. Under these limiting conditions, the actions and reactions of bystanders will deviate somewhat from these predictions.
** This lowers the cost of helping, leading to (d).
After Piliavin et al. (1975).

The data from these and other studies suggest that the rewards and costs involved in specific emergency situations greatly affect whether help is forthcoming. **Table 13.3** suggests how these rewards and costs operate. When the costs of helping are low (there's no danger or difficulty) and the costs of not helping are high (others would blame and criticize you), people are likely to intervene directly and help. When the costs of both helping (this might be dangerous or this person seems very strange) and not helping (something needs to be done) are high, the most likely response is to help indirectly, usually by getting someone who is trained to act in such situations. An alternative response is to redefine the situation in ways that make it less costly not to help. When the costs of helping are high (this drunk might be violent) and the costs of not helping are low (no one will blame me for not helping this person), people generally will ignore the victim or leave the scene. When the costs of both helping and not helping are low, the norms of the situation will determine what people do. Responses can vary greatly here.

HELPING: EGOISM OR ALTRUISM?
One of the critical questions in the research on helping is, why exactly do people help in emergency situations (Dovidio, 1984; Krebs & Miller, 1985)? What is the motivation? Most researchers agree that emergency situations create negative emotional states, but they disagree

about why these feelings lead to helping. Some argue that the reason people help is basically selfish or egoistic—they help the person in trouble to relieve their own negative feelings, such as moods of sadness or anxiety (Manucia, Baumann, & Cialdini, 1984). Others argue that people are genuinely altruistic—they want to help even though they receive no benefit in return (Batson, 1987). This "empathy-altruism" theory holds that people feel empathic concern when other people are in difficulty and help to relieve the distress of the person in trouble, not to relieve their own emotional distress.

Research addressing the question of whether altruistic or egoistic motives influence people to help is continuing and it is difficult to say at present which theory is correct. The most recent research supports the empathy-altruism theory, but the final answer is not yet in (Schroeder, Dovidio, Sibicky, Matthews, & Allen, 1988). One important factor seems to be whether people respond to emergency situations predominantly with reactions of personal distress or reactions of empathic concern. People who respond with reactions of empathic concern are more likely to help. That is, concern for the other person rather than one's own distress seems to be a more powerful motivation to help.

What then can we conclude about helping and altruism? When people do help, they usually feel very good about themselves. The anticipation of such feelings motivates the giving of assistance in many circumstances. Still, we have seen that often people do not help because they are unsure and afraid. They are fearful of acting inappropriately and they are fearful of getting involved in something that might be time-consuming, dangerous, or upsetting. As Maslow (1962) suggests, our need for safety takes precedence over our need for esteem. We would rather be safe than a Good Samaritan. This does not mean that people have little capacity for goodness and kindness. It does mean that this capacity can be deflected by concerns about safety and, to some extent, convenience. The impulse to help does not flourish in a busy, demanding, and often threatening world.

Interim Summary

Freud and Lorenz proposed an instinct view of aggression, the view that people are innately aggressive. Another explanation of aggressive behavior is that people are aggressive when they have been frustrated or annoyed by unpleasant events. Berkowitz suggested that frustration produces a readiness to aggress, but cues associated with aggressive behavior are needed to elicit aggression.

Excitation transfer research shows that arousal from other events, such as exercise, can be transferred to aggression if the person does not perceive the actual cause of the arousal. Highly pornographic material increases aggression.

Social learning theory holds that aggression is not innate but learned through direct reinforcement, observation, and vicarious reinforcement. Many studies show that watching violence on television can lead to aggressive behavior.

Research by Darley and Latané showed that other people's outward calm in an emergency situation can lead people to define the situation as not serious. It also showed that when several people observe an emergency situation, individuals are slower to intervene because of diffusion of responsibility. People's assessments of the rewards and costs of various ways of reducing arousal also influence their reactions in an emergency situation.

Concern for the person in distress is a more powerful motivator to help than the desire to relieve one's own negative feelings.

- -

DECISION MAKING IN GROUPS

In the preceding sections we considered how individuals are influenced by other people. In this section we will consider how a group of people as a whole is influenced by several processes that occur within the group, including some of the processes we have already discussed, such as conformity pressures and the tendency to act aggressively.

Our major concern is how individuals in groups combine their various perspectives and talents to make decisions. How do they construct a single policy or plan out of their individual concerns and biases? Does the group output reflect the best of the individual inputs, or do pressures to conform and to obey the orders of authority figures lead to poor collective decision making?

Some of the very early thinking about groups was extremely negative. For example, in his book *The Crowd* (1895), Gustave Le Bon argued that human beings had a two-part personality. The top, conscious part was unique to the individual. The bottom part was unconscious and was the same for everyone. This unconscious half of the personality was thought to contain base desires and instincts. Only the conscious part of the human psyche contained any semblance of dignity and virtue.

Ordinarily, according to Le Bon, the conscious aspect of the personality guides behavior. But in a large group or a crowd this layer of functioning is somehow stripped away and the seething instincts from below take over.

Accounts of persons in panic situations, such as theatre fires, make us think that Le Bon was right. So does the violence, such as in lynchings, occasionally observed in certain large crowds. On the other hand, some studies show that even large groups can coordinate work effectively and correct for individual biases and errors (Steiner, 1972). How exactly do individuals in groups work together?

Group Polarization

During the Korean War, President Truman, Secretary of State Acheson, and General MacArthur met in the Pacific to discuss military strategy. All three were known to oppose a certain tactic that might draw the Chinese into the war. However, after discussing the options, they chose that particular tactic. As a result, the war expanded, dragged on for several more years, and ended inconclusively (DeRivera, 1968). How can their decision be understood? It may have resulted from what is known as a "shift to risk" or "risky shift" (Wallach, Kogan, & Bem, 1962). A **risky shift** is defined as the tendency of a group to make decisions that are riskier than those that the members of the group would recommend individually. Recent research shows that just as groups sometimes become more risky, they can in other instances become more cautious, and in still other situations become more extreme in any of a number of directions. For example, a group of environmentalists might make a decision favoring stricter, that is, more extreme, air pollution standards than they had favored individually. The risky shift and other instances of groups making extreme decisions are all examples of "group polarization" or "choice shifts." **Group polarization** occurs when a group of people,

Group polarization occurs when a group of people, each member of which has a moderate stance on an issue, discuss the issue and conclude by taking an extreme position.

each member taking a moderate stance on an issue related to a shared value, discusses that issue and in the end takes an extreme stance. In this section we will consider how psychologists, essentially by accident, discovered the risky shift and later discovered that it was best understood as a specific instance of a group polarization.

Several years ago there was considerable interest in the relationship between risk taking and other personal characteristics such as self-esteem and creative thinking. To explore these issues, psychologists Michael Wallach and Walter Kogan developed a questionnaire to

Table 13.4   **A Sample Item from the Choice Dilemma Questionnaire**

Mr. J., an American prisoner-of-war in World War II, has the choice of possible escape with the risk of execution if apprehended, or of continuing to endure the severe privations of the camp.

Imagine that you are advising Mr. J. Listed below are several probabilities or odds his escape would succeed. Please check the *lowest* probability that you would consider acceptable for an escape to be attempted.

_____ Place a check here if you think Mr. J. should try to escape, no matter what the probabilities

_____The chances are 9 in 10 that the escape would succeed.
_____The chances are 7 in 10 that the escape would succeed.
_____The chances are 5 in 10 that the escape would succeed.
_____The chances are 3 in 10 that the escape would succeed
_____The chances are 1 in 10 that the escape would succeed.

From Wallach & Kogan (1959).

measure how much risk individuals were willing to take in a variety of situations (Kogan & Wallach, 1967). This measuring device was called the *Choice Dilemma Questionnaire* or the *CDQ*. It posed problems such as the one shown in **Table 13.4.** Subjects were asked to indicate the lowest odds (1, 3, 5, 7, or 9 out of 10) they would accept and still recommend that Mr. J attempt the escape. Subjects could also decide not to take the risk. Subjects who recommended the risky move, even if the odds of making it were only 3 in 10, took a greater risk than those who demanded a 5 in 10, or 50-50 chance of success.

A second example involved an engineer with a heart ailment who could either curtail his activities or undergo a heart operation, which might restore him to perfect health or might kill him. A third example described a college student who had to choose between going to graduate school at a very prestigious university, where the degree would be difficult to achieve but would be very valuable, and another university where the student would be guaranteed a degree but the degree would have much less value. Kogan and Wallach devised 12 dilemmas in all. In every case, subjects were asked to indicate the lowest chances of success they would require before they would recommend the riskier but potentially more rewarding course of action.

Kogan and Wallach originally predicted that groups asked to make unanimous recommendations about risk would simply hit on a compromise position or perhaps make a decision that was slightly more conservative than the average individual recommendation. These predictions were based on books such as William Whyte's *The Organization Man* (1955), which emphasized how cautious and uncreative people become in groups. However, when people met in groups to discuss and decide the CDQ items, their decisions were riskier than the average of their individual recommendations. This "risky shift" has been shown to occur in many different situations. If we look back at the Truman, Acheson, and MacArthur decision about Korea, we see that they collectively chose a course of action that was riskier than what they individually would have recommended before their meeting. Their decision is an instance of the risky shift with historical importance.

At first researchers thought that "diffusion of responsibility" within the group accounted for the shift to risk. Later, psychologists proposed that risky individuals are dominant and lead the group toward risk. Most recently it has been proposed that various implicit or explicit decision-making schemes, such as the majority rules, can account for risky shifts (Zuber, Crott, & Werner, 1992). A great deal of research indicates that the risky shift occurs because taking risks is valued in our culture (Brown, 1986). This value leads to two kinds of pressures toward group shifts to risk.

The first kind of pressure is *social comparison*. Since people think that it is good to be risky, they compare their recommendations. To some degree they compete to become at least as risky as the others, or slightly more so (Goethals & Zanna, 1979). The second kind of pressure stemming from the value on risk is in the form of *persuasive arguments*. Because risk is valued, the arguments most often raised in group discussion favor the risky alternative. Thus group members hear more new arguments favoring risk than caution. The predominance of those arguments helps persuade people to become riskier (Burnstein, 1983). Both of these pressures probably operate together. People are motivated by comparison and competition to become riskier. This motivation makes them receptive to the arguments favoring risk that are likely to dominate the discussion (Myers, 1983).

The risky shift was an important discovery in the attempt to understand decision making in groups. We know now that the risky shift is just one instance of the more general phenomenon called group polarization. Let us first consider the fact that there can be group polarization, or choice shifts, toward caution as well as toward risk. Then we will show that groups can polarize toward other values as well.

Two of the items on the original CDQ did not consistently produce shifts to risk. In addition, several investigators have written dilemmas that regularly produce shifts in the direction of caution (Fraser, Gouge, & Billig, 1971). Whether there is a shift to risk or caution seems to depend on the values made salient or important in specific dilemmas. Since risk is a general value in the culture, it is usually salient. However, when life or the security and welfare of dependent children are at stake, risk can seem foolhardy. Then a value toward protecting others can predominate and produce a shift toward caution.

Other values can also lead to group polarization. A study was conducted with secondary-school students in France who admired Charles de Gaulle and disliked Americans. After the discussions their attitudes were again assessed. The students who discussed de Gaulle became more positive toward him. The students who discussed Americans became more negative (Moscovici & Zavalloni, 1969). In a similar study conducted in the United States, prejudiced high school students became more prejudiced after group discussion of racial issues. Unprejudiced students became less prejudiced (Myers & Bishop, 1970). Whenever a group makes a decision involving a cherished value, whether it be risk, care for others, the environment, or its own rights, the chances are that the decision will be extreme. No individual wants to be in the position of not being as risky, patriotic, or concerned as his or her peers.

The tendency toward group polarization can lead to irrational decisions in groups. The group might take a biased look at the problems they face and ignore important issues that conflict with its values. Can this happen in real groups, and are there other self-defeating, group decision-making tendencies? We will consider these questions in the following sections.

Groupthink

Irving Janis, a psychologist at Yale University, has written some disheartening analyses of group processes and decision making (Janis, 1972, 1982; Janis & Mann, 1977). Janis notes that many of the "fiascoes" of United States foreign policy during the last several decades resulted from sloppy decision making by people who fell victim to groupthink. Janis, who coined the term, defines *groupthink* as a mode of decision making marked by "deterioration of mental efficiency, reality testing, and moral judgment that results from ingroup pressures" (Janis, 1972, p. 9). These pressures include the tendency to preserve friendly relations and to seek complete group consensus on important topics. In other words, there is often mindless conformity, as shown in the Asch (1955) experiments, and collective misjudgment of risk, as shown by demonstrations of the risky shift. We can define **groupthink** more simply as a mode of group decision making in which group coherence takes precedence over efficiency. Groupthink occurs because members tend to boost each other's self-esteem and protect each other's ego by seeking concurrence, especially if the stakes are high and there is stress. This drive to seek concurrence, which we saw so clearly in Schachter's (1951) Johnny Rocco study, causes groupthink and, in many cases, disastrous policy recommendations and decisions.

How can a group know when it is becoming a victim of groupthink? Janis mentions several symptoms. First, there is an illusion of invulnerability. Because each member in the group supports everyone else, individuals believe they are all smart and talented. Thus they feel they can do anything. Nothing can stop them. Le Bon (1895) observed these same feelings in crowds. Second, and perhaps most important, there is an illusion of unanimity. Individual decision makers who have doubts about an idea don't mention them in order to preserve the consensus and not hurt other group members' feelings. Other symptoms include stereotyping opponents or enemies and seeing them as ineffectual and morally inferior, a fear of disapproval, an unquestioned belief in the group's moral superiority, and a shared effort to rationalize and dismiss negative feedback from the outside.

What is the evidence that groupthink has been a problem for decision makers in the United States? Janis discusses several foreign policy fiascoes, including the failure to anticipate the Japanese attack on Pearl Harbor in 1941, the Bay of Pigs disaster in 1961, and the escalation of the Vietnam War in the 1960s. In his analyses of these decisions, Janis finds much evidence of groupthink.

Consider, for example, the Bay of Pigs. This occurred in the first three months of John F. Kennedy's administration. The plan was to overthrow the Cuban government of Fidel Castro by landing a group of Cuban exiles at a spot known as the Bay of Pigs and having them lead a mass uprising against Castro. The invasion force was destroyed by the Cuban army. The affair humiliated the United States and might have led to war with the Soviet Union. How could the United States have undertaken such an ill-advised action?

The group in charge of planning made several erroneous assumptions. First, they believed no one would ever know that the United States was responsible for the invasion. Second, they thought the Cuban air force was totally ineffective. They also assumed the landings would touch off popular uprisings against Castro. And finally, they believed the invaders could retreat into the mountains if they were strongly opposed. All of these assumptions were totally false and all could have been discredited with only a limited investigation. For example, most newspapers knew the United States government was planning some kind of move against Cuba. CIA polls showed Castro to be very popular. And by simply looking at a good map, the planners would have realized that the invaders would be trapped if they met with resistance. Although the Kennedy administration blamed the failure on its own inexperience and the difficulties involved in executing an operation planned in the previous administration, it is clear that many of the symptoms of groupthink were present (Janis, 1982). Consequently, alternatives were not discussed, expert opinion was not consulted, and alternative plans—should there be problems—were not made. Instead, the urge to protect each other's egos and not disturb the consensus led the people in the group to feel they had might and right on their side. The conformity that we saw in Solomon Asch's laboratory at the beginning of the chapter made its way into the highest decision-making centers of the United States government.

Janis thinks that groupthink can be prevented, although policymakers rarely take the

During the Cuban missile crisis, President Kennedy took steps to avoid groupthink, which had lead to disastrous results during the Bay of Pigs Invasion. This photo of the United Nations Security Council shows a presentation of the evidence that the Soviets had missile bases in Cuba.

necessary steps. One instance in which group-think was avoided again involved the Kennedy administration and Cuba.

In October 1962, spy planes over Cuba revealed that Soviet technicians and engineers were deploying offensive nuclear weapons aimed at the United States. The Soviet foreign minister had promised the United States that this was not happening and that the Soviet Union had no intention of using Cuba as a base from which to threaten America. When the evidence of the Russian actions became known to President Kennedy, he began a series of meetings with his top advisers to plan an appropriate response to the Soviet action. Because of the Bay of Pigs experience, Kennedy was concerned about the sloppy decisions that can evolve in group policymaking bodies. Consequently, several steps were taken to avoid a recurrence of the Bay of Pigs disaster. These steps were successful. After several days of extreme tension, the Russians agreed to take their missiles from Cuba. In return, the United States promised not to invade Cuba. The situation was resolved in a successful way from the American point of view. The missile crisis represents the Kennedy administration at its best, just as the Bay of Pigs showed it at its worst.

How was groupthink avoided in the missile crisis? There were four major changes. First, there was a new definition of roles for those involved in the planning. No one was regarded as an expert and everyone was regarded as responsible for each issue being discussed. In addition, each member of the group was to play "devil's advocate" and challenge other' statements to make sure they were sound. Second, there were procedural changes. The group did not isolate itself and adopt a self-confident attitude. New people were brought in to challenge what the group had decided thus far and to offer new suggestions. Third, President Kennedy did not attend all sessions. During these leaderless sessions, participants did not have to defer to his authority or conform to his suggestions to avoid being rejected. Finally, moral considerations were discussed. Instead of just stereotyping the adversary as weak and evil, the group recognized that the Russians were powerful and that it would be inconsistent with American values to launch a surprise attack on Cuba. These steps made the discussions very uncomfortable and tense. Group members were constantly challenged and repeatedly forced to rethink their positions.

However, the result was a thorough consideration of the alternatives, their advantages and disadvantages, and various contingency plans. Overall, the quality of decision making was much higher (Janis, 1982).

Minority Influence on Group Decisions

The tendency to seek concurrence in groups and the illusion of unanimity that results from it lie at the heart of groupthink. In order to prevent groupthink, doubters must be willing to express their views. Individuals who don't agree with the evolving group consensus must make their voices heard. At least in fiction the isolated individual can affect, and even change, the group decision. In the movie *Twelve Angry Men,* a lone juror, portrayed by Henry Fonda, changed the guilty votes of the eleven other jurors and persuaded them to acquit the defendant. While *Twelve Angry Men* is not based on fact, in his portrayal Henry Fonda actually performed a number of behaviors that research on minority influence shows to be important in group decision making (Moscovici, 1985; Nemeth, 1986).

If a minority in a group wants to have an impact, it must do two things. It must *become visible,* and it must *create tension* (Moscovici & Mugny, 1983). That is, it must take a position that other people are aware of. This means overcoming the illusion of unanimity that is so crucial in producing groupthink. Minorities must make themselves heard and make others take notice. Second, the minorities must create tension that will motivate those in the majority to try to deal with their ideas. In *Twelve Angry Men* Henry Fonda made himself noticed by raising his hand to vote not guilty, and he created tension by continuing to press his arguments. Other research on minority influence identifies other important factors. It is essential for the minority to be *consistent* in its stand. It cannot simply take a variety of positions that disagree with the majority. Finally, the minority must be firm and unyielding (Papastamov & Mugny, 1985). It has to be willing to dig in its heels and be uncompromising.

When a minority makes itself noticed and creates tension by taking an uncompromising and consistent position, it can have a strong impact on the group and stop the typical pattern of conforming to the majority. Studies suggest that the minorities have their effect through different processes than the majority. The majority typically influences through overt conformity. As we discussed earlier in this chapter, people often go along with the majority, even if they do not believe it, due to their fear of being rejected. On the other hand, people do not fear the minority. When they are confronted with a consistent, firm minority other people begin to listen carefully to its arguments, to focus on the issues. They try to understand why the minority feels the way it does. As the group begins to think about the issues and the problems it faces, without fear of rejection, it is more likely to think of novel solutions to problems and to consider a broad range of options (Nemeth, 1986). Even if the minority does not persuade the group of its own position, it is likely to make it think carefully and help it avoid the pitfalls of groupthink.

Interim Summary

Groups polarize or shift in the direction of their values when they discuss issues relevant to those values. Thus, group recommendations are often extreme. Because risk is seen as a value in our culture, group decisions often reflect a risky shift; that is, the group decision is often riskier than the individual recommendations of group members. Pressures to preserve friendly relations in groups lead to a reduction of criticism of others' ideas. This leads to less efficient, less realistic, and less moral reasoning, which in turn leads to poor decisions. Such decision making is the result of groupthink.

For a minority to have an impact on group decisions, it must become visible and create tension. It must also be consistent, firm, and unyielding in its stand.

LEADERSHIP

People in groups influence each other in many ways. Le Bon's theory of crowds and the research on groupthink suggest that influence in groups often leads people to aggression, self-destruction, and chaos. Yet we know that groups can also function well, sometimes as a result of minority influence and often as a result of one person leading the group in productive directions. Leaders come in many shapes and sizes, and they influence groups in extremely varied ways. There are few similarities between columnist Ann Landers and politician

Jesse Jackson, but they are both leaders. So are Queen Elizabeth and Boris Yeltsin. What is it that these leaders have and do in common? We can define a **leader** as the person who exerts the most influence in a group (Hollander, 1985; Shaw, 1981) and **leadership** as the exercise of influence or power over others. One particularly interesting kind of leader has been identified by psychologists and political scientists who have studied the United States presidency. These are "transformational leaders," people who can sense and express the unexpressed desires of the nation and change the political system (Burns, 1984). In the United States, both Franklin Roosevelt and Ronald Reagan were transformational leaders, as was Mikhail Gorbachev in the former Soviet Union. Despite the fact that there are many different kinds of leaders, they all have in common the characteristic of exerting the most influence in their groups.

In this section we consider four key questions about leaders and leadership. First, what are the characteristics of successful leaders? Second, what precisely do leaders do? Third, are there different kinds of leaders, or do they all fit a common mold? Finally, what kinds of leaders are most effective or successful?

Characteristics of Leaders

Psychologists have studied leaders and leadership for many years. They started with the most direct question: what kinds of people rise to the top and become leaders? They assumed a "great person" or *trait theory* of leadership when they began with this question. The trait theory holds that most leaders are likely to have certain traits that make them "natural leaders." Is this assumption correct?

Hundreds of studies have investigated the traits of leaders in myriad situations, including the military, Indian tribes, nursery schools, factories, political parties, and nations. The traits that are generally associated with leadership are quite interesting. One is height. Leaders are typically taller than other people. Sheer stature seems to give people authority. Leaders are also older and more intelligent. An especially strong finding is that leaders are verbally fluent and more talkative than followers (Stogdill, 1974). Leaders are also generally sociable, highly motivated, and energetic (Gibb, 1969). They must combine these various characteristics into the ability to persuade and motivate followers (Nixon, 1982).

A number of studies have added to our understanding of leaders' characteristics. For example, people who emerge as leaders combine an orientation toward success with an orientation toward affiliating with other people (Sorrentino & Field, 1986). They also score high on measures of self-confidence, achievement, and dominance (Costantini & Craik, 1980). In addition, like the transformational leader discussed above, they must be able to perceive the needs and goals of their group members and then adapt their behavior accordingly (Kenny & Zaccaro, 1983). One important question is whether, in most instances, leaders are male. Although there are numerous examples of outstandingly successful women leaders, is it true that people generally expect leaders to be men and that it is difficult for women to become leaders? A number of studies have addressed this question.

Twenty years ago both men and women expected leaders to be males, and women were less likely to view themselves as potential leaders (Megargee, 1969). The expectation that leaders should be men makes it extra difficult for women to succeed as leaders. They must "be like gold to be seen as silver" (Hollander, 1985). However, studies show that expectations are changing slowly. In a 1980 study of men and women leaders among cadets at the United States Military Academy at West Point, women performed as well as men and had equally good morale in their units, but their success was attributed to luck. The men's successes were attributed to ability. However, a 1984 study showed some differences. Women's successes were no longer attributed to luck, though there remained a stubborn pattern of women subordinates rating female leaders negatively (Rice, Bender, & Vitters, 1980; Rice, Instone, & Adams, 1984). Although stereotypes of leaders as male continue to hamper women leaders, the data do suggest that gender discrimination in the area of leadership is waning (Hollander, 1985).

The research on the personal characteristics associated with leadership has generated some consistent findings. However, there are plenty of exceptions. For example, Napoleon was very short and Calvin Coolidge was far from talkative. Because of these exceptions, many psychologists believe that the trait approach is limited. They argue that different kinds of leaders are needed in different situations. This *situational theory* assumes that the demands of the situation determine the charac-

In a 1980 study of men and women leaders at the United States Military Academy at West Point, women performed as well as men and had equally good morale in their units, but their success was attributed to luck. The men's success, however, was attributed to ability. Just four years later, this attitude had changed. This and other studies suggest that gender discrimination in leadership is waning.

teristics of the leader (Stogdill, 1974). At times a group may need a leader who can give rousing speeches. Then the leader who emerges will be a charismatic orator. At other times the group may need a leader who can show that he or she meets important moral standards (see "Psychology in the News"). More recently, both the trait theory and situational theory have given way to the *transactional theory* (Shaw, 1981). This theory assumes that both the characteristics of persons and the demands of the situation determine who will become a leader. Consistent with this approach is a study of presidential leadership in the United States showing that when a strong motive in a candidate, such as for power or achievement, matches a strong need in the electorate, the candidate tends to get more votes and to be re-elected (Winter, 1987). We will see an example of the transactional theory when we discuss leadership effectiveness at the end of this section.

The Behavior of Leaders

As psychologists became frustrated with trying to identify the particular traits of leaders, they began to ask a different question. What do lead-

Psychology in the News

CHARACTER COMES THROUGH AS MAJOR ISSUE

By Robert Shogan

The 1992 New Hampshire Democratic primary was the campaign that was supposed to be all about issues and ideas. Victory in this recession ridden state, most people thought, would go to the candidate with the most convincing agenda of economic remedies.

But, instead, the campaign is turning on something very different: the vexing questions of character that go to the heart of the American political process, and for which there are no easy answers.

No one is unhappier about this than Arkansas Gov. Bill Clinton. "For too much of the last couple of weeks this election has been about me," he complained recently as he watched his once-commanding lead in the polls fade in the wake of unsubstantiated allegations of infidelity and questions about his draft status 22 years ago.

Mr. Decency

On the other hand, former Massachusetts Sen. Paul E. Tsongas, the principal beneficiary of Clinton's decline, had reason to be de-lighted with the emergence of the character issue. He was praised in a recent Boston Herald editorial for his "decency and strength of character." In an apparent allusion to the unfortunate Clinton, the Herald added: "At a time when voters are weary of candidates with feet of clay, Paul Tsongas is a man whose integrity is unquestioned."

All of this should come as no surprise. Despite repeated vows by the media, voters and candidates to pay strict attention to the issues facing the country, recent events are just the latest demonstration of the dominating effect of questions about character and personality in shaping the outcome of presidential campaigns.

"Over the last 20 years we've spent a lot of time and resources understanding how people factor out various traits they want to see in a president," says GOP pollster Richard Wirthlin, who helped Ronald Reagan win two terms in the White House. "That research clearly points to the fact that you have to have credibility, there has to be a sense of integrity and consistency. Those are the greens fees that a candidate has to pay simply to get onto the golf course called presidential politics."

No better way?

Moreover, given the highly personalized nature of the U.S. political system, politicians and scholars alike argue that there is no better way of choosing a candidate for president than by evaluating what kind of human being he or she really is.

"Voters know that the issues a president will have to face will change in time," Robert Teeter, a GOP pollster and senior Bush campaign strategist, has observed. "But his character will always be there."

"Character isn't everything, but it's very important," says Thomas C. Reeves, a University of Wisconsin history professor and author of "A Question of Character," a critique of the Kennedy presidency. "The American people expect a president to be not just a political leader, but also a role model of personal behavior."

---

ers actually do? Greater progress in understanding was made by considering this question rather than the traits of leaders.

In one of the largest studies of leadership ever conducted, individuals in many different kinds of groups were asked to indicate what they felt were the most important leadership behaviors (Halpin & Winer, 1952). This and many other studies of leaders show two major categories of behavior. The first category is called *initiating structure*. This means that leaders define the goals of the group, plan how to achieve them, indicate how each member will participate, and, in general, direct the action of the group. The second category of leader behavior is called *showing consideration*. This means communicating with individual followers, showing trust, explaining actions, and demonstrating positive regard for group members. In addition to initiating structure and showing consideration, leaders clearly perform a range of other different behaviors in different situations. For example, taking overall responsibility in the group is an important leader behav-

However, disagreement abounds about which aspects of character matter most and which not at all.

Take the case of Franklin D. Roosevelt, founder of the modern presidency. Many felt that his legendary personality, which allowed him to inspire the nation and manipulate his political allies and adversaries, had more to do with his success than his often erratic approach to public policy, a judgment reflected by the verdict handed down by Justice Oliver Wendell Holmes on his first meeting with F.D.R.: "A second-class intellect but a first-class temperament."

"He must have been psychoanalyzed by God," an admiring associate once said of Roosevelt, according to University of North Carolina historian William Leuchtenberg.

But for all his character strengths, Roosevelt had some notable defects that only came to light years after his death. He was dis-loyal to his wife, with whose social secretary he apparently conducted a prolonged romance. He also systematically undercut his boss at the Navy Department—where he served as an assistant secretary during World War I—in his ambition to make a name for himself.

"Had these things been known about him at the time, he probably would not have been elected president," says Geoffrey Ward, author of "The First Rate Temperament," a chronicle of F.D.R.'s rise to national prominence.

"Now we want to know everything about a politician," Ward says. And he worries that the result "is to reduce all our leaders to the lowest common denominator."

Context, he cautions

But Duke University's James David Barber, author of "The Presidential Character," contends that "no single episode" discloses much that is relevant to a politician's fitness to be president. "You have to look at any revelation in the context of the politician's whole life and of the duties of the presdient," he said.

Thus the fact that President Harding, who led America into the Roaring '20s, had a mistress means little by itself, Barber says. But the mistress' revelation made after Harding's death that their relationship reflected Harding's obsessive need of approval and affection might have served as a warning of the scandalous corruption that ultimately engulfed his presidency.

"Character Comes Through as Major Issue" by Robert Shogan, LOS ANGELES TIMES, February 17, 1992. Copyright © 1992 Los Angeles Times. Reprinted by permission.

Questions

1. What does this article suggest about the qualities people want in leaders besides the qualities that psychologists have studied?
2. How does the article support the *situational theory* of leadership?
3. Is it surprising that character was so important during the presidential election in the United States in 1992?
4. How does the article support the idea of *leadership schema* discussed below?
5. What does the article suggest about the key role that the mass media play in shaping our perceptions of leaders?

---

ior. One study shows that when a leader assumes responsibility, the group's tendency to help in emergencies increases (Baumeister, Chesner, Senders, & Tice, 1988).

The Perception of Leaders

In recent years psychologists have proposed that how individuals emerge as leaders and how effectively they perform as leaders depend on more than their personal characteristics and their behavior. In addition, it is very important how they are perceived (Kinder & Fiske, 1986). In his book the *Mask of Command*, historian John Keegan (1987) suggests that leaders must have a theatrical impulse so that they will be perceived as having the traits people expect in leaders. What are the important elements in the way we perceive leaders?

Research suggests that people have an overall image or idea of what a leader is and how a leader should behave. This general idea is known as a **leadership schema** (Simonton, 1986, 1987). The leadership schema provides most people with an image of the ideal leader as someone who is strong, active, and good. When we interact with or observe leaders, some aspect of their behavior can activate, or call to mind, part of the leadership schema. As a consequence, we tend to judge the person in comparison to the overall leadership schema. Sometimes this means that we perceive their behavior as more consistent with the the leadership schema than it actually is. This erroneous perception is called the **halo error** (Saal, Downey, & Lahey, 1980). For example, during the August 1991 attempted coup in the Soviet Union, Russian President Boris Yeltsin made a dramatic move in standing on a tank and defying the men who tried to oust President Gorbachev. Yeltsin's act was clearly strong and active. His strong and active behavior may have called the leadership schema to mind for many people, with the result that they perceived Yeltsin as good as well as strong and active. Studies of cadet leaders at the United States Military Academy at West Point showed that their subordinates tended to perceive the leaders as having a more consistent range of leadership qualities than the leaders perceived themselves as having (Frone, Adams, Rice, & Instone-Noonan, 1987).

Types of Leaders

The two central leadership behaviors discussed above, initiating structure and showing consideration, can be difficult, though not impossible, for one person to manifest. They are inherently incompatible with each other. Initiating structure involves giving orders, telling people what to do, getting them moving, and, perhaps, ruffling their feathers. Showing consideration means listening and explaining, making people feel better, and perhaps, smoothing their feathers. This incompatibility, along with the findings that leaders have somewhat different traits in different situations, raises an important question. Can we identify different types of leaders, perhaps according to whether they primarily initiate structure or show consideration? Research by Bales and Slater (1955) indicated this was possible.

Robert Bales and Philip Slater (1955) were interested in the leadership patterns that emerged in small, unstructured groups. They studied a group of college students who spent approximately an hour a day for about 5 days discussing and trying to resolve labor-manage-

ment conflicts. At the end of each day subjects were asked to indicate which member in the group had the best ideas, who had most effectively guided the discussion, and how much they liked each group member.

At the end of the first day, the person who was rated as having the best ideas and as having been most helpful in moving the group toward a solution was also most liked. However, the tendency for the same person to be best liked and rated as having the best ideas dropped sharply after the first day. In subsequent days, it seemed as if two leaders emerged, one referred to as the *task leader,* who specialized in making suggestions, giving information, and expressing opinions, and the other referred to as the *socioemotional leader,* who helped others express themselves, made jokes, released tension, and expressed positive feelings for others. Thus, leadership split into two channels.

The relation between the two kinds of leaders is interesting. Although some rivalry might be expected between them, they get along very well and cooperate extensively. In a family, one parent might be the task leader and the other the socioemotional leader. Together they might very effectively lead the family group. In an army platoon, the commanding officer and the chaplain might also make a good leader combination. In former heavyweight champion Muhammad Ali's training camp, manager Angelo Dundee was the task leader who saw that Ali got his work done and that the camp ran smoothly. But Ali's friend Bundini Brown was the socioemotional leader, keeping everyone loose and relaxed.

The general tendency to split leadership in unstructured groups has one qualification. Bales and Slater found the split happens only after the task leader is identified and agreed on. Once it has been decided who will lead the group in its pursuit of external goals, the group can afford the luxury of a socioemotional leader.

Leadership Effectiveness

When we think of the range of people who have been successful leaders, it seems hard to make any generalizations about what kind of leader is the most effective. However, we do know that there are task leaders, who often initiate structure. This style of leadership is often called *directive leadership.* We also know that there are socioemotional specialists, who show consideration. This style is called *democratic leadership.* In most situations where a single leader is elected or appointed, he or she will adopt either a directive or a democratic style.

An early experiment conducted by Kurt Lewin and his colleagues attempted to show which style was more effective—directive leadership, democratic leadership, or a third style (Lewin, Lippitt, & White, 1939). Three groups of 10-year-old boys worked on different tasks and club activities. Each group was led by an adult. In one group, the adult behaved in an autocratic, directive style. In a second group, the leader behaved in a democratic style. In the final group, the leader acted in a *laissez-faire style,* in which he passively watched the boys and permitted them to do as they pleased. He was "hands off." The directive leaders produced apathetic or rebellious group atmospheres, neither of which was enjoyable or productive. The laissez-faire groups, lacking adult supervision, were cheerful enough, but they were not at all productive. The groups led by democratic leaders were, however, both happy and productive. This study suggested that democratic leaders are more effective (see **Figure 13.7**).

Other studies have shown that the situation is much more complicated. Some studies indicate that democratic leaders are more effective, whereas other studies show that directive leaders are more effective. After reviewing many of these studies, Shaw (1981) suggested the following conclusions. It is clear that followers are happier in groups with democratic leaders. If we consider group productivity, however, we find that *on the average* directive leaders are more successful. But this conclusion needs to be qualified. The productivity of groups with democratic leaders is highly variable. Both the most productive and the least productive groups have democratic leaders. Thus, we can conclude that being a democratic leader is risky. If a democratic leader can show regard for personal problems and interpersonal relations and at the same time coordinate, direct, and give structure—that is, if the leader can combine initiating structure and showing consideration—he or she will be highly effective. Although this is very difficult, it is what the best leaders do.

Because some studies show democratic leaders to be more effective and others show directive leaders to be more effective, psychologists have explored the possibility that each

Figure 13.7
Three Leadership Styles.
These photos show the three leadership styles used in the Lewin, Lippitt, and White study (1939). They are, autocratic (top), democratic (middle), and laissez-faire (bottom).

style may be more advantageous in different circumstances. An intriguing transactional theory, offered by Fred Fiedler (1964, 1978), suggests that one needs first to consider how favorable the group situation is for the leader. Favorability is determined by three factors in the situation: the quality of leader-follower rela-

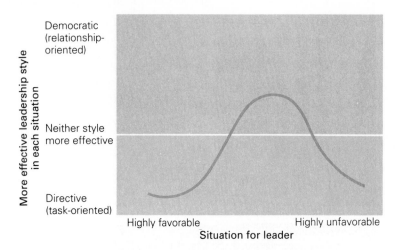

Figure 13.8
Relationship Between Favorability of Situation for Leader and Effective Leadership Style (After Fiedler, 1967)

tions, the clarity of the task, and the authority of the leader's position. A highly favorable situation occurs when relations with followers are good, the requirements of the task are clear, and the leader's position is one of great authority and prestige. An unfavorable situation would be the opposite.

Fiedler has studied leadership in groups such as postal workers, basketball players, Belgian naval officers, store managers, research chemists, furnace workers, and bomber crews. After classifying the situation in these groups as favorable or unfavorable to leadership, Fiedler predicted and found that when the situation is either very favorable or very unfavorable to leadership, the directive or task-oriented leader is most effective (see **Figure 13.8**). If the situation is very favorable, the leader can be assertive and commanding without upsetting anyone. Group members can see that what the leader is asking is necessary and that success will result. When the situation is very unfavorable, chaos is likely to rule. Here a strong minded, directive, authoritative person is needed to "take over" and guide the group away from disaster. In the middle range of situations, which are the most common, the democratic leader is more effective. In such situations, in which there is usually some tension and people need to be treated with respect, the careful coordination of interpersonal relations characteristic of democratic leadership is necessary.

Fiedler's theory is very complex, as are the data collected to test it. Reviews of the research suggest that the original theory was well grounded in data when it was proposed. Subsequent tests of the theory suggest that it is well supported by laboratory studies but not as clearly supported by field studies. Although it has a great deal of merit and is fundamentally correct, there are variables other than leadership style and favorability of the situation that must be considered before we fully understand leadership effectiveness (Peters, Hartke, & Pohlmann, 1985; Rice & Kastenbaum, 1983).

Interim Summary

Leaders are often, but not always, tall, talkative, energetic, and sociable. They are also most often male, though there is some evidence that gender discrimination in the area of leadership is waning. The characteristics of leaders also depend partly on the needs of the group.

Many leadership behaviors fall into two categories: initiating structure and showing consideration. Some leaders emphasize the successful completion of tasks. Others emphasize warm personal relationships within the group.

Groups with democratic leaders are happier and generally more productive than those with directive leaders. Fiedler's work suggests that directive leaders are more effective in situations that are either very favorable or very unfavorable to leaders. Democratic leaders are more effective in situations of middling favorability.

SUMMARY

1. Asch's studies show that people conform because of the need to be correct and the need to be well treated by others.
2. Milgram's studies show that many people will obey an authority if they feel that the person in authority is responsible for whatever happens.
3. If people agree to a small request, they are more likely to agree to a larger request later. This phenomenon is called the "foot-in-the-door" technique.

4. If people refuse a large request, they are more likely to agree to a moderate request later. This is called the "door-in-the-face" technique.

5. In the "lowball" technique, people are led into a less desirable action than they originally agreed to.

6. Aggression is often produced by frustration.

7. Following the excitation transfer principle, arousal from other events can be transferred to aggression.

8. Social learning theory holds that aggression is learned through observation and vicarious reinforcement.

9. People are less likely to help in an emergency if there are other bystanders present.

10. Groups often make extreme or polarized decisions, including decisions that are riskier than those favored by the average group member.

11. Groupthink is caused by the pressure to preserve friendly relations in a group.

12. Leaders initiate structure and show consideration. Some emphasize task completion and others emphasize interpersonal relations. The leadership style that is more effective depends on the situation.

KEY INDIVIDUALS

Solomon Asch
Bibb Latané
Stanley Schachter
Gustave Le Bon
Stanley Milgram
Michael Wallach
Sigmund Freud
Walter Kogan
Konrad Lorenz
Irving Janis
John Dollard
Robert Bales
Leonard Berkowitz
Philip Slater
Kitty Genovese

Kurt Lewin
John Darley
Fred Fiedler

KEY RESEARCH

Asch's experiments on conformity
the Johnny Rocco study
Milgram's obedience to authority studies
an experiment demonstrating the foot-in-the-door technique
an experiment demonstrating the door-in-the-face technique
an experiment demonstrating the lowballing technique
instinct theories of aggression
the frustration-aggression hypothesis of aggression and modifications
sexually arousing films and aggression
factors affecting behavior in emergencies
reward-cost analysis and behavior in emergencies
the Choice Dilemma Questionnaire
categories of leaders' behavior
types of leaders
styles of leadership
effect of favorability of situation on leader's effectiveness

KEY TERMS

conformity
compliance
diffusion of responsibility
foot-in-the-door technique
door-in-the-face technique
lowballing
aggression
frustration-aggression hypothesis
altruism
risky shift
group polarization
groupthink
leader
leadership
leadership schema
halo error

14 Personality and Assessment

CHAPTER OUTLINE

In the fall of 1991 the 100 members of the United States Senate had to make a difficult assessment of two people who were intelligent and articulate and who seemed sincere and honest. Yet one of them was clearly lying. One individual was Clarence Thomas, nominee for the Supreme Court of the United States. The other was Anita Hill, a law professor at the University of Oklahoma. Hill had accused Thomas of sexually harassing her. According to Hill, when she worked for Thomas at the Department of Education and then later at the Equal Employment Opportunity Commission (EEOC) he persistently engaged in unwanted sexual advances. Hill stated that Thomas made remarks about his capacity to satisfy women sexually, the size of his penis, and the details of a pornographic movie, "Long Dong Silver." She detailed a number of other crude sexual comments allegedly made by Thomas as well. Most people watching Hill's televised testimony to the Senate Judiciary Committee felt that she was controlled, direct, responsive, and truthful. Clarence Thomas was given a chance to reply. He denied Ms. Hill's accusations in the strongest terms, and, bringing race into the controversy, characterized this whole aspect of the confirmation process as a "high-tech lynching." Many people felt that Thomas was strong, straightforward, and candid.

A full understanding of the personalities of both Anita Hill and Clarence Thomas could give us a better picture of the reliability of their testimony during the Supreme Court Confirmation Hearings held in the fall of 1991.

Citizens watching all or parts of several days of televised Committee proceedings tried to assess both Hill and Thomas. While they both seemed highly credible, one was not telling the truth and might be seriously disturbed or dangerous. Many of these citizens communicated their beliefs about the two individuals to their senators. When it came to a vote, no doubt influenced by letters and phone calls from constituents, the Senate confirmed Clarence Thomas by the narrowest of margins, 52–48.

How do we make a judgment about whether Anita Hill or Clarence Thomas is lying? How do we assess what kind of Supreme Court justice Clarence Thomas would actually make? In order to answer these questions we need to understand how people behave, how consistent they are from one situation to another, and how overt behavior corresponds to underlying personality traits. We need to have a general understanding of the way the character of each individual human being develops and functions. And we need to have a full understanding of both Hill and Thomas. How have their actions, their beliefs, and their lives formed and changed? The field of psychology that considers the complexities of individual character is called *personality*. In exploring personality we ask such questions as: Why would someone engage in sexual harassment? Why would someone lie about it? Can we predict from a person's past behavior the kinds of contributions he or she will make on the Supreme Court over the next 30 years?

People have discussed the nature of personality for centuries. We have always been curious about the basic qualities of human nature, whether we are essentially good or bad, rational or irrational, skilled or incompetent. These questions about human nature and human differences were of concern to the ancients, and they continue to fascinate and challenge twentieth-century psychologists. The study of personality thrives today because it considers these basic questions: What are the basic qualities of people in general? What are the important differences between individuals? What are the differences between different kinds of people? In asking why individuals behave as they do, personality lies at the heart of psychology.

Personality can be defined as the unique patterning of behavioral and mental processes that characterizes an individual and the individual's interactions with the environment. The key word in the definition of personality is *individual*. Personality psychology is the study of individuals, with special emphasis on understanding what makes a person unique. Henry Murray once stated that every person is in some ways like all other people, in other ways like some other people, and in still other ways like no other person (Murray & Kluckhohn, 1953). While personality psychology considers all these aspects of the person, at present it gives more attention to how people differ.

Our goal in this chapter is to understand what psychology can tell us about the psychological characteristics of the individual. Throughout history people have put forth various explanations of personality. In the following section, we will consider how the different approaches to personality have evolved.

•
PERSPECTIVES ON PERSONALITY

The Greeks and Romans discussed a fourfold personality classification scheme based on the four cosmic elements—earth, air, fire, and water. Both Hippocrates and the Roman physician Galen suggested that these elements are represented in the personality by four kinds of human temperament—melancholic, sanguine,

choleric, and phlegmatic—corresponding to earth, air, fire, and water (see **Figure 14.1**).

The modern psychological study of personality has been marked by the development of four major perspectives. The first and major milestone was the work of Sigmund Freud. Freud's consistent emphasis was on unconscious, biologically rooted drives, especially sexual and aggressive drives, and the ways they are channeled by external forces. Freud's theories grew out of his work with psychologically disturbed individuals. From his observation of their difficulties, he formulated a theory of the structures of the personality, how they develop, and how they interact. His theory outlines the many ways that individuals satisfy their basic unconscious drives within an array of social and physical constraints.

Freudian theory and the theories of other psychologists basically sympathetic to Freud, called neo-Freudians, make up the psychodynamic perspective on personality. These theories all emphasize the dynamic forces within the personality that give rise to specific psychological characteristics.

The second major perspective on personality, the trait perspective, grew out of two criticisms of the Freudian approach. First, a disillusioned follower of Freud, Carl Jung, felt that not all people, or even most, were primarily

Figure 14.1
The Four Temperaments.
The Greeks and Romans discussed four types of temperament, each one corresponding to the four cosmic elements. This figure presents a medieval woodcut illustrating the temperaments and the characteristics associated with each temperament type.

motivated by sexual or destructive drives. He and others felt that humans had other needs and interests and that people could be divided into personality types according to their different characteristics. A second group of critics felt that Freud's theories were not sufficiently supported by evidence. They felt that observations of psychologically disturbed people in a therapy setting were not sufficient data on which to build a theory. They also felt that more attention should be paid to measuring personality characteristics and describing people in terms of their individual traits, whether these traits be related to sex, aggression, or anything else. In short, the trait perspective attempts to consider a broad range of human characteristics and to devise ways of measuring the traits that individuals possess.

The third major perspective on personality is the behavioral perspective, which originally grew out of the work of J. B. Watson and B. F. Skinner. This perspective criticizes both the psychodynamic and trait perspectives. First, it objects to the psychodynamic concepts of intrapsychic structures and stages of development because they cannot be directly observed or operationalized. Furthermore, it rejects the emphasis of both the psychodynamic and trait perspectives on internal determinants of behavior. The psychodynamic perspective emphasizes inner drives; the trait perspective emphasizes internal traits. In contrast, the behavioral perspective emphasizes how external factors shape behavior and ultimately, through learning, a person's characteristics. Furthermore, because the behavioral perspective emphasizes people's responsiveness to external events and stimuli, it also emphasizes that people will behave differently in different situations and that personality characteristics vary from time to time and place to place. Today the behavioral perspective is represented by social learning theory with its emphasis on the importance of cognitive processes in guiding behavior.

The fourth perspective is the humanistic perspective. Like the trait and behavioral perspectives, it grew out of dissatisfaction with other perspectives. Humanistic psychology especially rejects the psychodynamic and behavioral perspectives, primarily because they emphasize too strongly the determination of behavior, whether by internal drives or external stimuli, and do not consider sufficiently the extent to which people exercise free will and voluntarily direct their own lives.

Interim Summary

Personality is the unique patterning of behavior and mental processes that characterizes an individual. There are four main perspectives in the study of personality: the psychodynamic perspective, the trait perspective, the behavioral perspective, and the humanistic perspective.

THE PSYCHODYNAMIC PERSPECTIVE

The work of Sigmund Freud and his followers makes up the specific psychodynamic perspective known as the psychoanalytic theory of personality. We have already considered some of Freud's ideas. In Chapter 1 and Chapter 4 we briefly noted that Freud explored people's unconscious motives and conflicts using the techniques of dream interpretation and free association. His central idea was that personality characteristics, including the symptoms of psychological disorders, grow out of unconscious conflicts about sexual and aggressive drives. In addition, Freud emphasized that personality is largely determined during the first 5 years of life, when the person develops characteristic ways of dealing with internal drives and conflicts. In this section we will discuss in more detail Freud's ideas about the structure, development, and dynamics of personality (Freud, 1933/1964, 1940/1964).

The Structure of Personality

From his work with people suffering from various psychological disorders, Freud developed a configuration of personality as composed of three different mental structures. He called these the *id*, the *ego,* and the *super ego*. What a person thinks, feels, and does is a function of the actions or interactions of these three hypothetical structures. Freud proposed further that each of these structures develops at a different time.

THE ID
Freud held that at birth the child's personality consists solely of unconscious drives for pleasure and destruction. Freud called this hypothetical mental structure the **id,** that portion of the mind in which these instinctual drives reside. The id strives for immediate satisfaction of

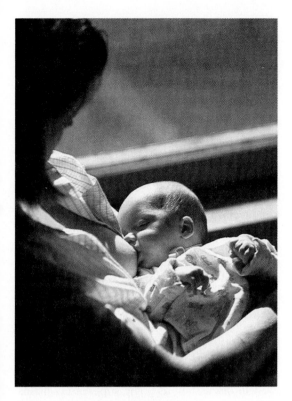

Freud believed that the id could reduce tension either through reflex actions (such as sucking) or through primary-process thinking.

its drives. According to Freud, this satisfaction is obtained by the elimination of tension. When the id's tensions accumulate, satisfaction is achieved by a reduction in tension levels.

Freud specified two ways in which the id tries to achieve the reduction of tension. One mechanism is *reflex action,* or simply responding reflexively to stimuli in the environment. For example, a child's sucking on a nipple is reflex action. This reflex reduces tension and quiets an aroused and unhappy child. A second mechanism that the id uses is **primary-process thinking,** the type of thinking that involves creating a fantasy about the object or behavior that serves to reduce tension and satisfy the id's drives. For example, a child might fantasize about nursing in order to partially reduce tension. Not only children use primary-process thinking. College students engage in daydreaming sexual fantasies—sometimes during class (Cameron, Frank, Lifter, & Morrissey, 1968) and perhaps even while studying.

THE EGO

Primary-process thinking alone cannot ensure the survival of the child. Imagining feeding is pleasurable, but it does not satisfy nutritional requirements. For this reason, a second mental structure, which Freud termed the *ego,* develops. The **ego** is the portion of the mind that is largely conscious and reality oriented. It comprises information that the child perceives and remembers, along with the cognitive processes that develop to process this information, such as thinking, reasoning, and planning. The ego is conscious of what happens in the child's world and, by perceiving the difference between the child and the external environment, it is also responsible for the child's capacity for self-awareness.

One important characteristic of the ego is that it develops in order to help the id obtain real rather than imaginary satisfaction. It is able to do this because it follows the *reality principle* rather than the pleasure principle. The **reality principle** is the idea that behavior must be dictated by the constraints and demands of external reality to obtain complete and immediate satisfaction of drives. In attempting to follow the reality principle the ego uses **secondary-process thinking,** or realistic thinking, rather than simple fantasy, or primary-process thinking. Although it is more realistic than the id, the ego derives all its energy from the unconscious drives of the id and exists only to find effective ways of satisfying those drives. In short, the id is not suitably adapted to satisfy its own drives. The ego, on the other hand, is a reality-oriented mental structure that develops out of early experience to help the id obtain satisfaction.

THE SUPEREGO

The ego has to consider more than reality in obtaining satisfactions for the id. During the phallic period, which we will discuss later, the third major structure of the personality develops. This structure is called the **superego** and it contains moral principles and values that have been acquired from the child's parents and society. It actually consists of two subparts. One part is the *conscience,* which contains moral prohibitions against certain behaviors, especially those expressing the sexual and aggressive drives of the id. The other part of the superego is the *ego-ideal.* This is the image of what one ideally can be and how one ought to behave. We can think of the conscience as con-

The superego is the storehouse for moral principles and values.

taining dictates about what is immoral, or about what one should not do, and the ego-ideal as containing models about what is moral, or about what one *should* do.

THE KEY ROLE OF THE EGO

If you have the feeling that the ego is caught in the middle, you are correct. It is this rational, reality-oriented portion of the personality that directs behavior. Unless it is overwhelmed by id tensions or superego dictates, the ego determines final decisions and actions. But in doing so it must provide some gratification for the id's drives and must also act within the moral constraints of the superego. Furthermore, it must choose behaviors that fit the constraints

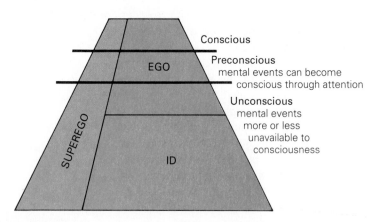

Figure 14.2
The Relationship of the Three Structures of Personality to Levels of Awareness. (After Liebert & Spiegler, (1982)

of reality. It is the executive of the personality, but it must serve three masters: the id, the superego, and external reality. Later we will discuss some of the tools the ego uses in its dealings with the id, the superego, and reality.

CONSCIOUS, PRECONSCIOUS, AND UNCONSCIOUS REGIONS

Freud felt that the three structures of personality—the id, ego, and superego—function within overlapping portions of the conscious, preconscious, and unconscious regions of the mind (see **Figure 14.2**).

As noted before, the id is unconscious. Its drives operate only in unconscious form. The ego is largely conscious but has preconscious and unconscious portions as well. The preconscious portion of the mind contains thoughts, memories, and other kinds of information that are not conscious but that can easily be brought into consciousness. In addition, a portion of the ego is unconscious. This portion contains the ego-defense mechanisms, which we will discuss shortly. The superego contains all three areas—its dictates can be felt in consciousness, or they can be preconscious, or they can operate unconsciously.

The Development of Personality

The energy the id produces to obtain pleasure is called **libido.** As we have noted above, the id strives to obtain pleasure by reducing tension. Freud believed that at different ages, human beings experience tension most intensely in different areas of the body. Known as **erogenous zones,** these areas require pleasure-producing stimulation to reduce or eliminate the tension. Freud named the different psychological stages of development according to the zone that at a particular age is most sensitive to tension and most in need of tension-reducing stimulation.

THE ORAL STAGE

Freud proposed that during the first 18 months of life, the most sensitive zone is the mouth. Thus the first stage is called the **oral stage,** the period in which the mouth experiences the most tension and requires the most tension-reducing stimulation. The id strives to reduce tension in and around the mouth by sucking, even on a thumb or pacifier. The first thing that the child perceives and remembers is often related to feeding or obtaining care and feeding from parents.

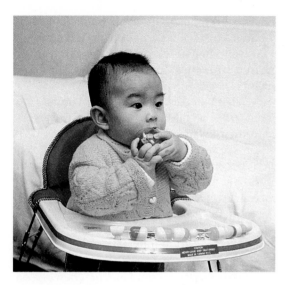

During the oral stage, the id strives to reduce tension in and around the mouth.

THE ANAL STAGE

At about the age of 18 months, the child enters the **anal stage,** when the locus of gratification changes to the anal region. The child derives satisfaction from stimulation in the anal region, either from the retention or elimination of feces. Also, parents begin to toilet train their children at this age. Parents want to control when and where the child eliminates feces. Given the child's desires, this imposition of control comes at exactly the wrong time. A child's pleasure in retaining or eliminating feces at his or her choice of time and place can lead to conflict with the parents' efforts to dictate new times and places.

THE PHALLIC STAGE

At about the age of 3 or 4 years, the child enters the **phallic stage,** during which the genitals become the most sensitive area and the child derives pleasure from manipulating them. Again, there is likely to be conflict with parental wishes. Parents typically try to curb behaviors such as masturbation or at least confine them to private settings.

Whether or not there is conflict about masturbation, the phallic stage is marked by the Oedipus or Electra complexes, sets of desires that produce conflict and discord within the family. The Oedipus complex is experienced by boys and the Electra complex by girls. Both Oedipus and Electra are names derived from Greek drama. *Oedipus Rex,* for ex-

ample, is a play by Sophocles about a man who fulfills a prophecy that he will kill his father and marry his mother. Freud's theories about these complexes are among his most central, yet controversial, ideas.

Freud proposed that all children experience a desire to have a sexual relationship with their parent of the opposite sex. Boys want to have a sexual relationship with their mothers, and girls with their fathers. These sexual wishes are one key aspect of the Oedipus and Electra complexes. The second key aspect of these complexes is a related wish to eliminate the parent of the same sex, who stands as a rival for the affections of the opposite-sex parent. For example, a young boy may wish that his father were dead so that he could have his mother to himself.

Like other desires emanating from the id, the Oedipus and Electra complexes are unconscious. The ego fears the consequences of expressing them and realizes that these drives cannot be satisfied directly. As a result, it holds the original sexual wish in the unconscious and seeks partial satisfaction for it. The ego obtains partial satisfaction by identifying with the parent of the same sex, the parent who has been the rival. Boys try to be as much like their fathers as they can, and girls try to be like their mothers. By being similar to the same-sex parent, children can vicariously enjoy the love that

Freud proposed that during the phallic stage, children try to resolve the Electra or Oedipus complex by identifying with the parent of the same sex.

the opposite-sex parent expresses for the same-sex parent. For example, a little girl might be as much like her mother as possible and then enjoy the fact that she is very similar to the one the father loves. This process is known as *identification.*

In identifying with a parent, an important part of the personality is set in place. Many of our characteristic ways of behaving are determined by our identification with our mothers and fathers. One specific aspect of identifying with a parent is adopting, or *introjecting,* their values and morals. These incorporated values and morals form the third part of the personality, the superego. When the Oedipal conflict is resolved and the superego has been formed through incorporation of parental morality, the major structures of the personality are in place and the phallic stage is over.

THE LATENCY PERIOD

Freud proposed that once the phallic stage is over, at about age 5, there is a long **latency period** during which no major unconscious drives press the ego for satisfaction. This period extends through late childhood to puberty. During this time children may learn a good deal about the world around them, other people, and their own skills, capacities, and interests. However, there is little pressure from the id and little internal conflict.

THE GENITAL STAGE

When the young person reaches puberty, or sexual maturation, he or she enters the final stage of development. This is the **genital stage,** during which the person feels strong and adult sexual desires for the first time. There may also be a reawakening of old Oedipal sexual and aggressive feelings. From this point on, the ego will have to work hard to balance the demands of the id for sexual gratification with the constraints of reality and the prohibitions and exhortations of the superego. The adult personality reflects how well the ego manages to do this.

THE CONCEPT OF FIXATION

We have noted in discussing Freud's stages of development that the desires of the id change from age to age. However, Freud noted that sometimes individuals never lose their desire for a particular kind of gratification, such as oral stimulation. When this happens, the person is said to be fixated. **Fixation** is thus a fail-

ure of development in which the individual continues to seek a particular kind of gratification even after he or she has passed through the stage in which that kind of pleasure normally is sought.

What causes fixation? According to Freud, when a child is either extremely frustrated in the pursuit of a pleasure or overgratified, he or she may become fixated. The person then becomes continuously concerned with obtaining the pleasure, and this concern becomes an enduring personality characteristic. For example, a person fixated at the oral stage will show continuous concern with getting some kind of oral gratification. Such a person might engage in behaviors that give direct oral stimulation, such as smoking or chewing on pencils, or the person might symbolically pursue oral gratification. For example, he or she might want to acquire a lot of money or knowledge, which may be compared to taking in nourishment through the mouth during the oral stage. A person fixated on the pleasures of expelling feces in the anal stage might be extremely sloppy, late, and disorganized as an adult. A person fixated on the pleasure of retaining feces might be excessively neat or orderly as an adult. Such a person might also be miserly, withholding money just as he or she withheld feces as a child. **Table 14.1** indicates the kinds of behaviors or characteristics that are associated with oral, anal, and phallic fixa-

Table 14.1 **Characteristics Associated with Fixations at Freudian Stages of Development**

Stage	Characteristic
Oral	Optimistic
	Dependent
	Generous
	Demanding
	Sarcastic
Anal	Orderly
	Frugal
	Punctual
	Obstinate
	Rebellious
Phallic	Proud
	Self-assured
	Vain
	Timid
	Bashful

Based on Fenichel (1945).

tions. In short, the concept of fixation was Freud's way of explaining how important psychological characteristics and individual differences in personality develop.

The Ego-Defense Mechanisms

As the "executive" of the personality, the ego strives to direct behavior in ways that satisfy the id, the superego, and the demands of reality. In attempting to achieve this goal, the ego develops several defense mechanisms. These **ego-defense mechanisms** are unconscious strategies by the ego to shield itself from threatening perceptions, feelings, and impulses. The defense mechanisms help keep the demands of the id and the dictates of the superego under control. In doing so, they reduce feelings of anxiety and keep other feelings, such as guilt, conflict, and anger, from overwhelming the ego. However, the ways of behaving and viewing the world that result from these mechanisms are not always effective or realistic. The defense mechanisms can be divided into three groups: (1) the behavior-channeling defense mechanisms, (2) the primary reality-distorting mechanisms, and (3) the secondary reality-distorting mechanisms.

BEHAVIOR-CHANNELING DEFENSES

The three behavior-channeling defenses are *identification, displacement*, and *sublimation*. These mechanisms direct behavior in ways that protect the person from conflict, anxiety, or harm. For the most part, they produce realistic behavior that the person feels is moral.

Identification, first used in resolving the Oedipal conflict, involves attempting to resolve conflicts about one's behavior by identifying with another person who appears successful, realistic, and moral—trying to act as much like that person as possible. Freud regarded identification as a relatively healthy defense mechanism. Conflicts about behavior are generally accompanied by anxiety. By resolving conflicts, identification also reduces anxiety.

Displacement directs aggressive behavior away from someone or something that has aroused anger toward someone against whom it is both safe and morally acceptable to aggress. For example, a man who has been angered by his boss might fear being hostile toward him and might therefore honk his horn at a fellow commuter on the way home, shout at his wife, ridicule his son, or kick his dog. In all of these instances, he is displacing aggression in a way that he feels is safe and acceptable.

Sublimation entails expressing drives for pleasure or aggression in socially acceptable ways. In this way, the id obtains partial satisfaction while the superego's dictates are followed. For example, a person might sublimate his sexual drives into painting highly respectable representations of nudes. Aggressive drives might be channeled into studying military history or playing contact sports. Freud felt that sublimation was extremely important for civilized existence and social achievement.

PRIMARY REALITY-DISTORTING DEFENSES

One of the most basic ways the ego protects itself from feelings or perceptions that cause anxiety is simply not to feel or perceive them. The two defense mechanisms that protect the ego by keeping threatening feelings or perceptions out of awareness are *repression* and *denial*. They are called primary reality-distorting mechanisms because they are the first line of defense. They protect the ego from even being aware of threats.

Repression entails blocking from awareness unacceptable unconscious drives such as sexual feelings or impulses, aggressive thoughts or wishes, or feelings of guilt emanating from the superego. For example, a person who feels guilty for cheating on an exam may simply repress these feelings and not consciously experience them.

Denial is the defense mechanism used to keep threatening perceptions of the external world, rather than internal drives and feelings, out of awareness. For example, a person living in California may simply refuse to admit that earthquakes threaten his life and home, or a smoker may deny that cigarettes are hazardous to her health.

SECONDARY REALITY-DISTORTING DEFENSES

Repression and denial simply push threatening feelings and perceptions out of awareness. However, other defense mechanisms often are called into play following denial or repression (White & Watt, 1981). The three secondary reality-distorting mechanisms we will discuss are *projection, reaction formation,* and *rationalization.*

Projection involves perceiving personal characteristics in other people that you cannot admit in yourself. For example, a man might repress his own sexual feelings toward his brother's wife and then project those feelings onto her. Thus, the man will perceive that his brother's wife is sexually interested in him. Another common example is projecting feelings of anger toward others onto those other people. A student who is angry with her roommate might project her anger and perceive the roommate as angry or hostile.

Reaction formation is consciously feeling or acting the strong opposite of one's true unconscious feelings because the true feelings are threatening. For example, a girl who hates her father may repress those feelings and consciously experience strong feelings of affection for him instead. These feelings are due to reaction formation.

Rationalization, a very common defense mechanism, involves generating a socially acceptable explanation for behavior that may be caused by unacceptable drives. For example, a person may rationalize aggression by saying that another person deserved to be punished or harmed. A man may rationalize sexually harassing a woman by telling himself that she really wants to have sex with him, even if she does not admit it.

Table 14.2   Sample Items from Adorno's E and F Scales

Items from the Ethnocentrism (E) Scale

One trouble with Jewish business people is that they stick together and prevent other people from having a fair chance in competition.

Negroes have their rights, but it is best to keep them in their own districts and schools and to prevent too much contact with whites.

The worst danger to real Americanism during the last 50 years has come from foreign ideas and agitators.

America may not be perfect, but the American Way has brought us about as close as human beings can get to a perfect society.

Items from the Fascism (F) Scale

Obedience and respect for authority are the most important virtues children should learn.

When a person has a problem or worry, it is best not to think about it but to keep busy with more cheerful things.

People can be divided into two distinct classes: the weak and the strong.

What the youth needs most is strict discipline, rugged determination, and the will to work and fight for family and country.

An insult to our honor should always be punished.

After Adorno et al. (1950).

The Authoritarian Personality

One of Freud's most enduring influences is shown in a book dealing with prejudice called *The Authoritarian Personality* (Adorno, Frenkel-Brunswik, Levinson, & Sanford, 1950). The authors of this book were initially concerned with anti-Semitism, or prejudice against Jews. They had seen the slaughter of Jews that had taken place in Europe under Nazi fascism, and they wondered whether Americans had the same potential for fascism that Germans had. They wanted to find what larger pattern of attitudes and personality characteristics was associated with prejudice and fascist tendencies. The authors of the book were very strongly influenced by Freudian personality theory. Thus, they believed that prejudice is an expression of unconscious needs, conflicts, and defense mechanisms.

During the course of the study, a measure of prejudice called the *E-scale* was developed. *E* stands for ethnocentrism, a glorification of one's own ethnic group and a hostility toward other groups. It was found that E-scale scores correlated with a measure of personality structure, the *F*-scale (see **Table 14.2**). People scoring high on the F-scale were said to have "authoritarian personalities," which gave them a potential for fascism (thus the name *F-scale).*

What are the characteristics of the authoritarian personality? Adorno et al. showed that authoritarians had a strong interest in power and authority. They tended to be very submissive and obedient toward those with more authority but very harsh and demanding toward those with less authority. They also held very conventional values, with little independent examination of moral questions. They were intolerant of weakness in others and refused to admit weakness in themselves. They also were unable to accept sexuality and aggressiveness in themselves. Finally, they were thought to have the potential to accept fascist political appeals.

Adorno et al. formulated a theory to explain how the characteristics of authoritarian individuals develop and lead people to become prejudiced. The unconscious ego-defense mechanisms which we have just discussed play a large role in their theory. The process begins when parents who demand that their children live up to rigid standards of conventional morality and competence use harsh discipline to enforce these standards and to enforce obedience and respect at home. The children, afraid to express any personal inadequacy or anger and aggression toward the harsh discipline, *repress* these feelings. Instead, inadequacies are *projected* onto members of minority ethnic groups, and aggression felt toward the parents is *displaced* onto these groups. Finally, authoritarian individuals rationalize their hostility by thinking that these ethnic groups deserve harsh treatment in light of the perceived inadequacies that have been projected onto them.

The theory of the development of the prejudiced and authoritarian personality has been very controversial (Altmeyer, 1988; Forbes, 1985). Research, however, has demonstrated its utility in understanding politics and public policy. The theory of authoritarianism predicts that people are most likely to show the authoritarian side of their personality when they are threatened. Studies by Sales (1973) and Doty, Peterson, and Winter (1991) have examined levels of authoritarian behaviors in the United States during periods of relatively high or low social threat. Periods of high threat are those characterized by high crime, strikes, and a poor economy. Periods of low threat have less crime, fewer strikes, and a better economy. The results show that authoritarian behaviors, such as Ku Klux Klan activity and expressions of racial prejudice, were higher in a high-threat period in our history, 1978–82, than in the subsequent low-threat period, 1983–87. Also, it is interesting that President Reagan used more authoritarian rhetoric in his 1980 campaign for election than in his 1984 campaign for reelection (Doty et al, 1991).

Modern Psychoanalytic Theory

In the more than five decades since Freud's death, psychoanalytic thought has continued to develop. A large number of theorists and therapists continue to discuss both the normal personality and psychological disorders using many of Freud's key concepts. However, most of these psychologists have modified Freud's ideas. The work of one psychoanalyst, Heinz Kohut (1971, 1978), is representative. Kohut's theories about the self and narcissistic disorders are highly influential in psychoanalytic circles.

Kohut's key ideas center on the development and influence of the self—one's sense of who one is and of one's worth. Positive experiences may lead one to have a stable, effective, and vigorous self, called the *autonomous self*; negative experiences can produce a weak or in-effective self that manifests itself in various narcissistic disorders. Narcissism is a Freudian concept meaning attachment to one's self. Narcissistic disorders develop when one's self attachment is too strong, too weak, or unrealistic.

Kohut developed the concept of the self because he felt that Freud's view of the structure of the personality was incomplete. Kohut proposed that in addition to the id, ego, and superego, the self was important in guiding behavior and organizing experience. The self begins in early childhood as the *nuclear self*, a sense of self-esteem. It grows out of the mother's treatment of the child. If the mother responds to the child's behaviors warmly, the child experiences him- or herself as joyful, happy, and worthy. If the mother is rejecting, the child experiences him- or herself as unworthy and empty. These initial experiences of one's self as worthy or unworthy are the first aspects of the nuclear self.

Two other parts of the nuclear self are ambitions and goals. Ambitions develop from mirroring by parents. Mirroring means approval, recognition, and admiration of a child's behaviors and efforts. On the basis of mirroring, children discover that certain of their thoughts, feelings, and actions are appreciated—ambitions arise to develop these aspects of the self. In addition, children need to idealize other people, often their parents. They develop ideals or goals to become like their parents in positive ways. Thus the nuclear self consists of self-esteem, ambitions, and goals. Later, other ideas and feelings about who one is are added to the nuclear self.

The self is strongest if parents accept, or mirror, their children and provide models of behavior and self-acceptance for the children to idealize and pursue. However, most parents cannot constantly mirror or provide objects of idealization. This inability creates tension and frustration. To some extent these reactions can produce positive growth in the child by leading to active behaviors and an expanded sense of abilities and self-esteem. However, too much frustration of the needs for mirroring and idealization can lead to narcissistic personality or behavior disorders. Sometimes these disorders can be truly pathological. At other times, they fall well within normal ranges, meaning they simply represent less than ideal patterns of experience and behavior.

Another illustration of Kohut's thinking and its relation to Freud is Kohut's view of the Oedipus complex. Freud felt that the sexual and aggressive drives of the Oedipal conflict were unpleasant and traumatic. Kohut feels that the Oedipal period is marked primarily by assertive, possessive, and affectionate feelings toward the opposite-sex parent and by self-confident and competitive feelings toward the same-sex parent. He argues that both the parents and the child can view and experience this period in a positive way. Parents can "react with pride and joy to the child's developmental achievement, to his vigor and assertiveness" (Kohut, 1977, p. 230).

Overall, Kohut's theory is closely allied with Freud's basic concepts, but it modifies Freud's ideas in unique and original ways. Kohut's work is widely respected among psychoanalysts today.

The Freudian Legacy

Freud's two great contributions to psychology were (1) to suggest that behavior is strongly determined by unconscious sexual and aggressive drives interacting with the constraints of reality and the dictates of morality and (2) to suggest that childhood events, such as the resolution of the Oedipus complex, strongly shape the personality. Freud's distinct view of personality was that it was determined by fixations, identification with parental figures in childhood, and behavior and thinking patterns derived from the use of defense mechanisms. How do psychologists today evaluate these views?

There is no doubt that Freudian theory very much influences the way people in our culture think about personality and behavior. People commonly talk about individuals being repressed or fixated, as lacking in ego strength, or having a rigid superego. However, there is less agreement among psychologists themselves about the value or correctness of Freud's ideas. Few psychologists would agree with Freud that people are motivated predominantly by sex and aggression. On the other hand, many would agree that unconscious drives of many kinds, and conflicts about these drives, strongly affect personality. Others claim that Freud's theories are of little value. Some claim that his ideas are highly implausible, and some argue that his theories cannot be adequately tested. Still others argue that his theories gener-

alize too much from disturbed patients, that they cannot be applied to other people.

But despite these criticisms, psychoanalytic theory is still developing, and new research often supports the usefulness of many of Freud's ideas. This has prompted one psychologist, Lloyd Silverman, to write regarding psychoanalytic theory, "The reports of my death are greatly exaggerated" (Silverman, 1976). Research by Silverman and others (Silverman, Ross, Adler, & Lustig, 1978) shows that the psychoanalytic approach is very much alive. For example, a study of repression shows that speech disturbances during the discussion of highly emotional topics improve right after brief instances of forgetting (Luborsky, 1977). The repression, shown by forgetting, temporarily reduces anxiety, which in turn leads to speech that is less halting. Similarly, studies and reviews of research support many psychoanalytic concepts, such as evidence for clusters of "oral" and "anal" traits (Erdelyi & Goldberg, 1979; Fisher & Greenberg, 1977; Kline, 1981).

Interim Summary

Freud's theories, which are part of the psychodynamic perspective, emphasize unconscious sexual and aggressive drives. These drives come from the unconscious id. The ego is largely conscious and uses realistic thinking to obtain gratification for the id, but it strives to do so in ways that are realistic and within the moral dictates of the superego.

Freud proposed that personality develops through the oral, anal, phallic, latency, and genital stages. Personality is determined in part by identification with the same-sex parent and by fixations at one of the early stages of development.

Freud proposed that the ego uses several defense mechanisms to minimize anxiety produced by demands of the id, dictates of the superego, and external threats. These defenses include both those that direct behavior and those that distort some aspect of self or reality.

Research on the authoritarian personality considers how the ego-defense mechanisms of repression, projection, displacement, and rationalization can be related to ethnocentric attitudes.

EXPLORING PERSONALITY DYNAMICS: PROJECTIVE TESTING

According to Freudian and other psychodynamic theories, understanding people's personalities may require indirect methods to get information about unconscious motives and conflicts, which subjects cannot report directly. One way to gain this kind of access is to use a projective test. In this section we will outline the general assumptions underlying the use of projective tests and discuss some of the specific techniques that are widely used.

The Assumptions of Projective Testing

The word *projective* holds the key to understanding these tests. In general, **projective tests** are based on the assumption that people will *project* their needs, feelings, and conflicts onto ambiguous stimuli. Thus, many psychologists believe that if people are asked to respond to ambiguous stimuli such as inkblots or drawings, to give their associations to words, or to draw objects without specific instructions, their responses will reveal these unconscious needs, feelings, and conflicts. For example, if a woman is asked to say the first word that comes into her mind when she hears the word "mother," the answer will give a clue about her unconscious concerns. Thus, the response "rage" could be an indication of hostility between the subject and her mother. Two of the best-known projective tests are the *Rorschach test* and the *Thematic Apperception Test* (TAT).

Rorschach's Test

In 1911 a Swiss psychiatrist named Hermann Rorschach published the first in a series of studies later compiled in a book called *Psychodiagnostics* (1942). These studies reported Rorschach's investigation of psychiatric patients' responses to ambiguous inkblots. Rorschach assumed that patients' perceptions of these ambiguous figures would reveal a great deal about their personalities and their manner of thinking. Unfortunately, Rorschach died at a young age, long before his work was complete. However, other psychiatrists and psychologists who were interested in projective testing continued his work.

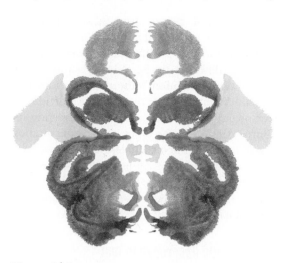

Figure 14.3
An Image Similar to Those Used in Rorschach's Test.

Rorschach's test consists of 10 symmetrical inkblots, which are presented to subjects on cardboard cards. **Figure 14.3** is similar to what a subject would see. As you might imagine, different individuals see many different kinds of objects in this and other cards. Some cards generate certain common responses called "populars." Popular responses include witches, clowns, monkeys, cannibals, bats, Indians, baby faces, and climbing animals. In a Rorschach test, it is always assumed that people's responses reflect their particular needs, feelings, and conflicts. For example, a psychologist would take note if a person saw blood and destruction in many different cards.

The interpretation of responses is based on various scoring systems and an examiner's experience, that is, his or her careful comparison of one person's responses with those of many other people (Beck, Beck, Levitt, & Molish, 1961; Klopfer, Ainsworth, Klopfer, & Holt, 1954). Among the variables that are considered are the number of responses, how much human form is seen, and the ways colors are perceived.

Many psychologists are satisfied that an experienced practitioner can make valid inferences using this test. However, because there is no agreed way to interpret any particular set of responses, the Rorschach test has been widely criticized. Some psychologists feel it constitutes little more than "reading tea leaves."

Empirical studies have also questioned the reliability and validity of the Rorschach test. Subjects often give different responses when tested at different times, indicating low retest reliability. In addition, different psychologists make different inferences about an individual's personality based on the same responses (Buros, 1965). On the other hand, other studies show that the Rorschach test can assess personality dimensions such as introversion-extroversion, anxiety, aggressiveness, and defensiveness, especially in regard to present functioning (Exner, 1974; Singer, 1981, 1984a).

The Thematic Apperception Test

Another projective test that seems somewhat less mysterious than Rorschach's inkblot test is one that was developed by Christiana Morgan and Henry Murray (1935). This test is called the Thematic Apperception Test or TAT. The test is composed of 19 pictures of people with ambiguous expressions in ambiguous situations and 1 blank card. The term *apperception* refers to the contention that people being tested do more than perceive what is there. They apperceive, which means that they bring their own interpretations into play in understanding the pictures. It is assumed that what people apperceive in the TAT cards will reflect central *themes* or motives, concerns, interests, and fears in their personalities.

Figure 14.4 is a sample TAT card. Subjects are asked to look at this and other cards and to make up stories about what is going on in each picture. They are told each story should have a separate beginning, middle, and end, as well as a clear conclusion.

One key assumption about the test is that the subject will identify with one of the figures in each picture and will make this person the central figure or "hero." Then, many of the subject's own feelings will be projected onto this person. For example, if several heroes in a subject's stories have difficulties with their fathers or are extremely worried about sexual relations, an examiner might suppose that these matters are important problems for the subject.

The TAT is open to the same kinds of criticisms as the Rorschach. There are no objectively established criteria for interpreting overall personality structure from the TAT, and its reliability and validity have been challenged. Still, many experienced psychologists do feel that they get a great deal of information from

Figure 14.4
A Sample Card from a TAT Test.
When taking a TAT test, subjects are asked to make up a story about the card and to give the story a beginning, a middle, and an end.

TAT stories, and studies have supported their validity in measuring an individual's needs (Atkinson, 1981).

Interim Summary

Psychodynamic psychologists often use projective tests to assess the psychological functioning of individuals. These tests assume that a person will project unconscious drives and conflicts onto ambiguous stimuli such as inkblots, which are used in the Rorschach test, or pictures, which are used in the TAT.

• •

THE TRAIT PERSPECTIVE

In this section we will consider the trait perspective on personality. This perspective rejects the psychodynamic view that personality characteristics reflect unconscious drives, conflicts, fixations, and defenses. It assumes that personalities are defined by the various combinations of traits people possess. **Traits** are relatively stable characteristics of a person that can be measured. The trait perspective assumes that people's behavior in many different situations will reflect these personal traits. That is, behavior is generally caused by internal factors, traits, rather than external pressures and situations. Furthermore, this approach assumes that the appropriate way to study personality is to measure the amount of various traits that people possess, rather than inferring their unconscious needs and fears with projective tests.

Modern trait theories grew out of earlier type theories. Type theories and trait theories differ in two key respects. First, type theories focused more on groups, such as extroverts, while trait theories emphasize individuals, some of whom may have high degrees of extroversion. Second, type theories assumed people fall into one particular category or another—they are either introverts or they are extroverts. On the other hand, trait theorists do not categorize individuals but assume that a given person may have any amount of a particular trait. Someone may be highly introverted, somewhat extroverted, or not distinctly introverted or extroverted. To illustrate the trait approach, we will begin by discussing an influential type theory that classified individuals into a limited number of psychological categories. Then we will discuss three trait theories and current controversies over the assumptions of trait theory.

Type Theories

Type theorists assume that individuals can be assigned to one of a small number of types or groups. All individuals within each type are assumed to be similar to each other on dimensions that define the type, and they are assumed to be quite different from individuals of another type. For example, a type theorist might hold that people can be divided into either active or passive types. Such a theorist would hold that active and passive people form two groups and that members of each group share many similarities.

One representative type theory was proposed by one of Sigmund Freud's most distinguished followers, the Swiss analyst Carl G. Jung. As a young physician, Jung admired Freud's work and began to research Freud's theory of dreams. In time, Jung became Freud's close colleague and was the heir apparent to the psychoanalytic school. However, after 1909, when Freud and Jung visited the United States together, both theoretical and personal differences separated them. From 1914 to 1939, when Freud died, they never communicated again. After their split, Jung went on to develop his own extensive and sophisticated theoretical system and published many books, one of which, *Psychological Types* (1921/1971), is relevant here.

Carl Jung
(1875–1961)

In this book, Jung presented the idea that people could be grouped into one of two basic types, introverts and extroverts, on the basis of their attitude. *Attitude* was Jung's term for an individual's orientation toward experience. People who are introverted can be thought of as looking inward, whereas extroverts can be thought of as looking outward. The **introvert** is generally shyer and more withdrawn, cares less about other people, and is more oriented toward his or her own inner experiences. **Extroverts** are more oriented toward the people, objects, and events around them, and are more relaxed and cheerful around other people.

In addition, Jung discussed four *functions,* Jung's term for the ways the individual reacts to experience. Sensation and intuition are methods of taking in information about the world. Sensation refers to use of the five senses to perceive objects and persons. Intuition is going beyond the five senses to seek the ultimate philosophical meaning of experience and its potential. Two other functions, thinking and feeling, are used to make judgments about experience. Thinking refers to the use of reason in making judgments, while feeling refers to the use of emotions and values.

Generally, each individual will tend to rely primarily on one function, although Jung felt that the other functions could develop as the person matured. Combining the distinction between the introversion-extroversion attitude with the four functions produces eight types in all, such as the introverted-feeling type. Interestingly, Jung considered himself an introverted-intuitive type.

Jung's work was an ambitious attempt to understand personality in terms of the characteristics of different types of people. However, the trait perspective has changed considerably since Jung's early work. We will see how in the next section on trait theories.

Trait Theories

The primary assumption of any trait theory is that personality can be described in terms of how much of various traits individuals possess. It considers many different traits and the unique combinations that characterize individu-

Gordon Allport
(1897–1967)

als. Most modern trait theories owe a great deal to the pioneering work of Gordon Allport (1961). Allport contributed to the study of individuals and their traits from the 1930s through the 1960s. We will consider his contribution first. Then we discuss the theories of Hans Eysenck and the research his work inspired.

ALLPORT'S TRAIT THEORY

Allport thought of traits as internal structures that direct the behavior of an individual in consistent and characteristic ways. He distinguished several different kinds of traits. First, he distinguished common traits from unique traits, depending on whether they characterized many people or few. Second, he distinguished cardinal, central, and secondary traits, depending on how pervasively they manifested themselves in an individual's personality.

Common traits are characteristics such as friendliness or dominance, which are common to many people and by which individuals can be compared. For example, responsibility is a common trait. One can measure the extent to which different people show it. More important than common traits, Allport felt, were what he called *unique traits*. These are unusual traits or trait combinations that characterize individuals and give them their unique personalities. They can include a particular style of humor or wit, a unique kind of ebullience and

optimism, or a deep and crude cynicism and hostility that is shown under pressure.

Both common and unique traits can be either cardinal, central, or secondary, depending on how pervasively they are manifested. The most pervasive of a person's characteristics are said to be *cardinal traits.* These traits direct behavior in consistent ways in many situations and thus make those situations "functionally equivalent." That is, a cardinal trait leads a person to behave in similar ways in very different situations. For one individual, assertiveness may be a cardinal trait. Such a person might be loud and active with a friend, authoritative with a subordinate in a work situation, bold and outgoing with strangers, self-satisfied when praised. Thus, if assertiveness is a cardinal trait, it will show up in many different situations and will be an enduring characteristic of the person.

People generally have only one cardinal trait, if any, but several central and secondary traits. *Central traits* are similar to cardinal traits but are not as consistently manifested. Some common central traits are shyness, optimism, cheerfulness, and introversion. There are unique central traits as well. *Secondary traits* are seen only in particular situations or at particular times. They are important characteristics of individuals, but they are not as pervasive as central or cardinal traits. Instead, they help give a more complete picture of the person.

EYSENCK'S STUDIES OF PERSONALITY TRAITS

Hans Eysenck is an English psychologist who has spent the last four decades studying the basic dimensions of personality. Using the techniques of factor analysis (see Chapter 9) to analyze many measures of personality, behavior, and self-reported feelings and beliefs, Eysenck concluded that there are two basic dimensions of personality (Eysenck, 1953). The first is the key dimension identified many years before by Jung, *introversion* versus *extroversion,* but Eysenck defines these traits slightly differently. Introversion according to Eysenck is composed of reserve, lack of sociability, caution, and emotional control. Extroversion is composed of sociability, activity, daring, and expressiveness. There may be few, if any, perfect introverts or extroverts, but there is an introversion-extroversion dimension. People may be near one of the extremes or at any point between them.

Eysenck's second dimension is *stability* versus *instability,* sometimes called *neuroti-*

Introverts are generally shy and withdrawn. Extroverts interact more with the people, objects, and events around them.

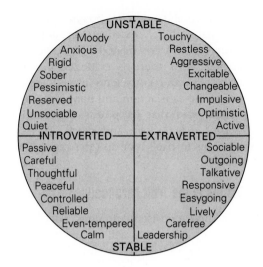

Figure 14.5
Eysenck's Dimensions of Personality. (After Eysenck, 1964)

cism. The stable individual is well adjusted, calm, relaxed, and easygoing. The unstable or neurotic person is moody, anxious, restless, and temperamental. Different individuals can be characterized on the basis of how much introversion-extroversion and how much stability they show in their personalities. All of your friends and classmates can be located on these dimensions. **Figure 14.5** will help you understand the different personality characteristics that Eysenck has classified along the two dimensions of stability and introversion-extroversion.

RESEARCH ON THE "BIG FIVE"

For more than three decades psychologists have extended the research of Eysenck and Raymond Cattell (1950, 1966, 1973) in an effort to identify the basic trait dimensions of personality. The basic question was whether extroversion and stability are really the only important dimensions of personality, or whether there might be more. An early study by Tupes and Christal (1961), replicated by Norman (1963), identified five qualities thought to be basic traits: extroversion, agreeableness, conscientiousness, emotional stability, and cultural interest. As you can see, extroversion and emotional stability are the same as the basic dimensions identified by Eysenck. However, Norman argued that agreeableness, conscientiousness, and cultural interest are also independent trait dimensions. Norman's research was ignored for a number of years, but it has received a great

deal of attention in recent years (McCrae & Costa, 1987). Most psychologists now refer to the Big Five as basic dimensions of personality. These factors are typically numbered and labeled as follows: (I) Surgency (or Extroversion), (II) Agreeableness, (III) Conscientiousness (or Dependability), (IV) Emotional Stability (vs. Neuroticism), and (V) Culture (Goldberg, 1990). The last factor, number V, has also been labeled Intellect (Digman & Inouye, 1986) and Openness (McCrae & Costa, 1991). We will refer to the Big Five traits as *extroversion, agreeableness, conscientiousness, stability,* and *openness.*

What, specifically, does each of these factor labels mean? Table 14.3 lists the factors and some of the scales that make up each one. The scales listed with each factor give a more complete idea of what each label means. They tell us that in addition to varying in how *extroverted* or sociable and how *stable* versus unsta-

Table 14.3   The Big Five Factors and Scales Commonly Making up Each One (After Norman)

Factor 1: Extroversion
Talkative–Silent
Sociable–Reclusive
Adventurous–Cautious
Sociable–Reclusive

Factor 2: Agreeableness
Good-natured–Irritable
Mild, Gentle–Headstrong
Cooperative–Negativistic
Not Jealous–Jealous

Factor 3: Conscientiousness
Responsible–Undependable
Persevering–Quitting, Fickle
Fussy, Tidy–Careless
Scrupulous–Unscrupulous

Factor 4: Stability
Calm–Anxious
Composed–Excitable
Not hypochondriacal–Hypochondriacal
Poised–Nervous, Tense

Factor 5: Openness
Imaginative–Simple, Direct
Artistically sensitive–Insensitive
Intellectual–Nonreflective, Narrow
Polished, Refined–Boorish

Adapted from Digman & Inouye (1986).

Studies have shown that the friendliness dimension of personality corresponds to the agreeableness factor.

ble or neurotic we are, people also differ in how *conscientious* (that is, responsible, persevering, scrupulous, and fussy) they are, how *agreeable* (that is, good natured, gentle, cooperative, and not jealous) they are, and how *open* (that is, imaginative, artistically sensitive, intellectual, and refined) they are. Studies have shown that when people rate themselves and when they rate others, using as many as 1710 trait terms, the ratings show the Big Five to be the basic dimensions of personality (Goldberg). This has been shown with sixth-grade children in Hawaii (Digman & Inouye) and adults around 60 years of age in Baltimore (Piedmont, McCrae, and Costa, 1991).

Two studies show the importance and pervasiveness of the Big Five approach to personality. First, for many years psychologists have identified dominance and friendliness as the two principal dimensions of interpersonal behavior (Leary, 1957). People's behavior toward others varies according to whether it is dominant or submissive, or in between, and whether it is friendly or hostile, or in between. Studies have shown that the dominance dimension of interpersonal behavior corresponds to the extroversion factor of personality and that the friendliness dimension of interpersonal behavior corresponds to the agreeableness factor of personality (Trapnell & Wiggins, 1990). Thus extroverted people are likely to act dominant in their relations with others, and, not surprisingly, agreeable people are likely to be friendly.

Second, several studies in recent years have shown that stability, extroversion, and openness (or culture) are related to psychological well-being. Now there is evidence that both agreeableness and conscientiousness are also related to life satisfaction and happiness. Years ago Freud said that happiness depended on *liebe und arbeit*, love and work. This new study seems to back him up (McCrae & Costa, 1991).

Evaluation of the Trait Perspective

Despite these consistent findings, social learning theorists, whom we will discuss in the next section, have criticized the trait perspective. They feel behavior is caused more by external factors, or the characteristics of specific situations, than by internal factors, or personality traits. Allport argued that traits render situations functionally equivalent and that people will consistently manifest their traits in different situations. The critics, as we shall see, argue that this has not been empirically demonstrated. For example, the critics argue that labeling an individual "aggressive" or "responsible" does not really predict how he or she will act in a specific situation. Will an aggressive woman blow her horn in traffic jams, be rude to waitresses, or be insensitive to her employees? The critics of the trait approach suggest that the answer is probably "not always." They feel that human beings are too unpredictable for the simple listing of their traits to have much meaning.

In this section we will consider three different kinds of research that address the question of whether people's behavior is consistently related to personality traits. This research considers whether people behave consistently over time, whether they behave consistently across situations, and whether people are consistent if both traits and situations are considered together.

CONSISTENCY ACROSS TIME

The most impressive evidence in support of trait theory comes from longitudinal studies of how people behave over a long time period. An important study of 100 subjects who were tested and retested over 25 years found high levels of consistency on some important traits. Men showed consistent levels of dependability, emotional control, and aesthetic interest. Women showed the same degrees of submissiveness, gregariousness, and nonconformity over time (Block, 1971). Thus, according to these studies, people are consistent. However, such studies do not show that we are all consistent all the time in all ways. As we shall see in the next section, while people generally may be consistent over time, that does not mean that they behave the same way in different situations.

INCONSISTENCY ACROSS SITUATIONS

One of the leading critics of the trait approach has been Stanford University psychologist Walter Mischel (1968; Mischel & Mischel, 1980). Mischel reviewed research on people's behavior in different situations and found that there is a rather low degree of consistency. For example, the person who is honest in one situation, for example, school, may not be honest at home. Similarly, people can show varying amounts of other traits, such as dependency and self-control, in different situations. Mischel also reported that the correlation between a person's standing on personality tests and his or her behavior in specific situations is often very low. That is, even if a person has a high score on a trait like extroversion, you cannot be sure that he or she will wave to a neighbor.

More recent work by Mischel (1984) shows that while self-control and adaptive behavior generally vary across situations so that individuals respond effectively to the changing demands of the environment, there is some cross-situational consistency when people are highly stressed. When demands in situations exceed their abilities, people may respond consistently with certain nonadaptive behaviors such as aggression or withdrawal.

Mischel's work suggests that an individual's high or low standing on various traits is not always a good predictor of behavior. Many other factors determine how people act. One of these factors is individual differences in consistency.

CONSIDERING BOTH PERSON AND SITUATION

Work by Magnusson and Endler (1977, 1980) suggests that three key factors must be taken into account in order to fully predict behavior. First, we must consider the traits of the person. Is the individual often hostile and aggressive, generally kind, or perhaps anxious? Second, we need to consider the situation as perceived by the person. Does the person perceive a situa-

tion to be threatening or merely competitive? Finally, we need to ask how the person generally manifests particular traits in particular situations. That is, what is the person's characteristic mode of response to a given situation? For example, Endler and Hunt (1969) and Endler and Rosenstein (1962) have identified 14 different manifestations of anxiety in various situations. These reactions include perspiration, immobilization, nausea, and dry mouth. Their research shows that people's behavior in a particular situation can be predicted accurately if we know their traits, how they perceive the situation, and how they characteristically manifest their traits in such situations. In short, both the person and the situation need to be considered, as well as how varied the expressions of a trait can be.

Interim Summary

The trait perspective assumes that personality is best described in terms of traits, that is, relatively stable and measurable characteristics of people. Jung proposed that people fall into one of eight psychological types. He argued that they are either introverted or extroverted and that they primarily use either thinking, feeling, sensation, or intuition in experiencing the world.

Allport classified traits as either common or unique traits, and as either cardinal, central, or secondary traits. Eysenck's studies using factor analysis suggest that introversion-extroversion and stability-instability are the two major trait dimensions along which individuals differ. Researchers studying the Big Five personality traits have identified extroversion, agreeableness, conscientiousness, stability, and openness as the major traits that describe individuals.

Critics of the trait perspective argue that behavior is not consistent across time and situation as trait theorists assume. Research suggests that individuals are consistent over time but are not impressively consistent across situations. Research also suggests that some people may be consistent across situations for only some traits. Other research by Endler suggests that traits and the situation must both be considered to predict behavior.

• •
MEASURING PERSONALITY TRAITS

In this section we will consider several **personality inventories,** tests that psychologists have devised to measure the extent to which individuals possess particular traits. Personality inventories differ from projective tests in two ways. First, they use unambiguous stimuli, often in the form of true-false questions about personal characteristics or behavior. In contrast, projective tests use stimuli that are purposely ambiguous and open to interpretation. Second, personality inventories are constructed and the results scored on the basis of research findings about the characteristics of individuals who give certain responses. Psychologists using projective tests, on the other hand, depend less on established findings and more on professional experience and insight. For both of these reasons, personality inventories are called *objective tests.*

The first personality inventories were devised many years ago, shortly after tests of intelligence began to flourish. During World War I a test known as the *Woodworth Personal Data Sheet* was used to determine which soldiers were most likely to be disabled by stress in combat. Recruits were asked whether they had had symptoms such as bad dreams or fainting spells. Persons with high scores were singled out for further evaluation. In the years since the end of that war many other tests have been developed. We shall consider three of them here: the *MMPI*, the *CPI*, and the *16 PF.*

The MMPI

Probably the most famous and widely used inventory of personality traits is the *Minnesota Multiphasic Personality Inventory*, or *MMPI.* The MMPI was designed in the 1940s to help diagnose patients with psychological disorders. Since then it has been widely used with both normal and abnormal individuals to assess their personalities. We shall outline the steps involved in constructing the various scales of the MMPI and then discuss how it is used.

THE CLINICAL SCALES
The first step in constructing the MMPI was to choose several groups, each made up of people diagnosed as having a specific psychological disorder (such as depression, hysteria, and schizophrenia) as well as a group of people

Table 14.4   **Some Illustrative MMPI Items**

I smile at everyone I meet.

There is an international plot against me.

I usually feel that life is interesting and worthwhile.

I save nearly everything I buy even after I have no use for it.

At times I feel very "high" or very "low" for no apparent reason.

with no previous history of psychological disorders. The latter group was called the "Minnesota normals." Second, sets of true-false questions, or items (see **Table 14.4**), were submitted to the normals and each of the diagnostic groups. Third, items that were answered differently by the normals and any one of the diagnostic groups were identified and selected for inclusion on the test. In selecting items, no interpretation was made of the individual's answer. All that was significant was that the item distinguished the two groups. For example, if the item, "I like poetry" was answered differently by depressed individuals and normals, it would be included in the test. Items that were not answered differently were discarded. Fourth, new questions were tested and old ones were retested to find which ones reliably differentiated the normals from the diagnostic groups. Finally, on the basis of this testing and retesting, items were organized into ten *clinical scales,* with eight being composed of sets of items answered differently by the normals and a particular diagnostic group. The clinical scales also included a *masculinity-femininity* (Mf) scale composed of items answered differently by men and women, and a social introversion scale composed of items answered differently by introverts and extroverts. The ten clinical scales, numbered 1 to 0, are shown in **Table 14.5.**

THE VALIDITY SCALES
When personality inventories are constructed, the issues of reliability and validity need to be addressed just as in the construction of intelligence tests (see Chapter 9). That is, there needs to be evidence that (1) people's responses are consistent at different times (reliability) and (2) scores on the test measure what they are intended to measure (validity). In addi-

tion, personality inventories present a special validity problem. Sometimes individuals responding to such a test will try to present a certain image of themselves by lying or distorting their answers. Three scales, called *validity scales,* were thus added to the MMPI to measure these tendencies. They are the *lie (L), frequency (F)*, and *correction (K)* scales.

The lie scale includes statements about standards of socially desirable behaviors that almost no one measures up to. An example would be "I sometimes feel angry." If people answer "false" to this statement, they are probably lying. If a person endorses more than a few items on this scale, psychologists assume that the person is trying too hard to present a favorable self-image. This suggests that other responses on the test may be distorted and that the results as a whole may not be valid for this individual.

The frequency scale consists of statements about negative or highly unusual behaviors. If persons admit to such behaviors or feelings, it probably indicates that they were careless or confused in answering the questions, or that they are "faking bad," perhaps to attract attention and help.

The correction scale is similar to the lie scale in that it considers how much people deny common but negative behaviors or claim praiseworthy but unlikely actions. However, the statements on the correction scale are less extreme. It measures not lying so much as the extent to which people try to present themselves favorably and the extent to which they have adaptive psychological defenses. Moderate scores on the K scale are consistent with being psychologically healthy. It should also be noted that psychologists note the number of unanswered responses on the MMPI and score them simply as "Cannot say" or "?." A high number of unanswered questions may indicate evasiveness or indecisiveness. Table 14.5 lists the clinical and validity scales of the MMPI, their abbreviations, and the characteristics of high scorers.

Table 14.5   MMPI Scales and Interpretation of High Scores

Scale and Abbreviation	Interpretation of High Score
Validity Scale	
Cannot say (?)	Subject is evasive or indecisive.
Lie (L)	Subject tends to present self in idealized or overly virtuous manner.
Frequency (F)	Subject is confused, answering randomly, or trying to fake symptoms. A high score on this scale suggests the profile is invalid.
Correction (K)	Subject is defensive and attempting to obscure symptoms.
Clinical Scale	
1. Hypochondriasis (Hs)	Subject is unrealistically concerned with physical complaints.
2. Depression (D)	Subject is unhappy, depressed, and pessimistic.
3. Hysteria (Hy)	Subject focuses on vague physical symptoms to avoid dealing with severe psychological stress.
4. Psychopathic deviate (Pd)	Subject's social interactions indicate emotional shallowness, rebelliousness, and disregard for law or conventional morality.
5. Masculinity-Feminity (Mf)	Subject shows interests and behaviors usually associated with opposite sex role.
6. Paranoia (Pa)	Subject is strong, irrational suspicions and overestimates own importance.
7. Psychasthenia (Pt)	Subject is tense, rigid, anxious and may have obsessive thoughts and compulsive behaviors.
8. Schizophrenia (Sc)	Subject is withdrawn, experiences distortions of reality, and dresses and acts bizarrely.
9. Hypomania (Ma)	Subject is outgoing, impulsive, overly active, and excited.
0. Social introversion-extroversion (Si)	Subject is withdrawn, shy, inhibited, and self-effacing.

USING THE MMPI

It is probably apparent to you by now how the MMPI is used. For example, a person would score high on a scale for depression if answers to many of the scale 2 (Depression) items matched those of the depressed diagnostic group. Thus a psychologist could compare a person's scores with those of individuals with specific psychological disorders and predict whether the person has those disorders.

Actually, after four decades of experience with the MMPI, psychologists have learned that certain behavior and trait patterns correspond to various patterns of scores. For example, it is common to find people with high hypochondriasis (Hs) and hysteria (Hy) scores but low depression (D) scores. Such people do not admit or experience psychological distress but show many physical signs of psychological distress, such as pain and headache. Similarly, experience has shown that severely disturbed people have high scores on scales 6, 7, and 8, whereas less disturbed people have higher scores on scales 1, 2, and 3. Today the MMPI can be computer scored and interpreted. **Figure 14.6** shows a printout accompanied by a computer-generated analysis of the scores. In addition, Gilberstadt and Duker (1965) have developed an atlas describing the characteristics of people with certain psychological profiles.

The MMPI was developed to determine the likelihood that people were suffering from certain psychological disorders, but it has been widely used with normal people as well. Normal people also show typical profiles or patterns. Profiles for both these groups can be very informative.

Figure 14.6
The MMPI.
This is a computer printout of a profile and its interpretation for the Minnesota Multiphasic Personality Inventory (MMPI).

THE MINNESOTA REPORT™   Page 1

for the Minnesota Multiphasic Personality Inventory™: Adult System

By James N. Butcher, Ph.D.

Client No. : 22222222222   Gender : Female
Setting : Medical   Age : 44
Report Date : 18-JUL-84
PAS Code Number : 00011657 844 0004

PROFILE VALIDITY

This is a valid MMPI profile. The client was quite cooperative with the evaluation and appears to be willing to disclose personal information. There may be some tendency on the part of the client to be overly frank and to exaggerate her symptoms in an effort to obtain help. She may be open to the idea of psychological counseling if her clinical scale pattern reflects psychological symptoms in need of attention.

SYMPTOMATIC PATTERN

The client is exhibiting much somatic distress and may be experiencing a problem with her psychological adjustment. Her physical complaints are probably extreme, possibly reflecting general lack of effectiveness in life. She is probably feeling quite tense and nervous, and may be feeling that she cannot get by without help for her physical problems. She is likely to be reporting a great deal of pain, and feels that others do not understand how sick she is feeling. She may be quite irritable and may become hostile if her symptoms are not given "proper" attention.

Many individuals with this profile have a history of psychophysical disorders. They tend to overreact to minor problems with physical symptoms. Ulcers and gastrointestinal distress are common. The possibility of actual organic problems, therefore, should be carefully evaluated.

Her response content indicates that she is preoccupied with feeling guilty and unworthy, and feels that she deserves to be punished for wrongs she has committed. She feels regretful and unhappy about life, complains about having no zest for life, and seems plagued by anxiety and worry about the future. She has difficulty managing routine affairs, and the item content she endorsed suggests a poor memory, concentration problems, and an inability to make decisions. She appears to be immobilized and withdrawn and has no energy for life. According to her response content, there is a strong possibility that she has seriously contemplated suicide. A careful evaluation of this possibility is suggested. She views her physical health as failing and reports numerous somatic concerns. She feels that life is no longer worthwhile and that she is losing control of her thought processes.

INTERPERSONAL RELATIONS

She appears to be somewhat passive-dependent in relationships. She may manipulate others through her physical symptoms, and become hostile if sufficient attention is not paid to her complaints. Marital unhappiness is likely to be a factor in her present clinical picture. She is a rather introverted person who has some difficulties meeting other people.

NOTE: This MMPI interpretation can serve as a useful source of hypotheses about clients. This report is based on objectively derived scale indexes and scale interpretations that have been developed in diverse groups of patients. The personality descriptions, inferences and recommendations contained herein need to be verified by other sources of clinical information since individual clients may not fully match the prototype. The information in this report should most appropriately be used by a trained, qualified test interpreter. The information contained in this report should be considered confidential.

THE MINNESOTA REPORT   Page 3

for the Minnesota Multiphasic Personality Inventory : Adult System

By James N. Butcher, Ph.D.

CLINICAL PROFILE

Client No. : 22222222222   Gender : Female
Setting : Medical   Age : 44
Report Date : 18-JUL-84

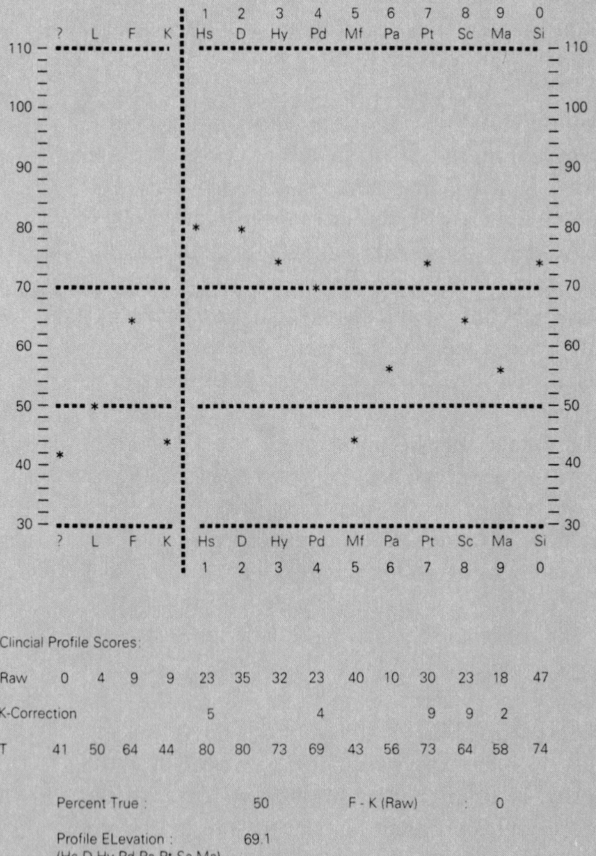

Clincial Profile Scores:

		?	L	F	K	Hs	D	Hy	Pd	Mf	Pa	Pt	Sc	Ma	Si
Raw		0	4	9	9	23	35	32	23	40	10	30	23	18	47
K-Correction					5				4			9	9	2	
T		41	50	64	44	80	80	73	69	43	56	73	64	58	74

Percent True :   50   F - K (Raw)   :   0

Profile ELevation :   69.1
(Hs,D,Hy,Pd,Pa,Pt,Sc,Ma)

Welsh Code :   12" 037'48-96/5:   F-L/K?:

Table 14.6	CPI Scales
Dominance	Communality
Capacity for status	Achievement via
Sociability	conformity
Social presence	Achievement via
Self-acceptance	independence
Sense of well-being	Intellectual efficiency
Responsibility	Psychological-
Socialization	mindednesses
Self-control	Flexibility
Tolerance	Feminity
Good impression	

Table 14.7 **Cattell's 16 Traits**

Terms in parentheses are Cattell's technical names for these traits.

(*Sizothymia*) Reserved ←——→	Outgoing (*Affectothymia*)
(*Low 'g'*) Less intelligent ←——→	More intelligent (*High 'g'*)
(*Low ego strength*) Emotional ←——→	Stable (*High ego strength*)
(*Submissiveness*) Humble ←——→	Assertive (*Dominance*)
(*Desurgency*) Sober ←——→	Happy-go-lucky (*Surgency*)
(*Low super-ego*) Expedient ←——→	Conscientious (*High super-ego*)
(*Threctia*) Shy ←——→	Venturesome (*Parmia*)
(*Harria*) Tough-minded ←——→	Tender-minded (*Premsia*)
(*Alaxia*) Trusting ←——→	Suspicious (*Protension*)
(*Praxternia*) Practical ←——→	Imaginative (*Autia*)
(*Artlessness*) Forthright ←——→	Shrewd (*Shrewdness*)
(*Assurance*) Placid ←——→	Apprehensive (*Guilt-proneness*)
(*Conservatism*) Conservative ←——→	Experimenting (*Radicalism*)
(*Group adherence*) Group-tied ←——→	Self-sufficient (*Self-sufficiency*)
(*Low integration*) Casual ←——→	Controlled (*High self-concept*)
(*Low ergic tension*) Relaxed ←——→	Tense (*Ergic tension*)

After Cattell (1965).

The CPI

The California Psychological Inventory, or *CPI,* was constructed with the same procedures used to create the MMPI. In fact, the CPI and the MMPI use some identical items. But, unlike the MMPI, the focus of the CPI is on identifying traits that differentiate normal individuals. It measures 18 traits, such as dominance, sociability, sense of well-being, self-control, flexibility, intellectual efficiency, and achievement via independence.

Like the MMPI test items, items on the CPI were selected if they distinguished between two reference groups. Items selected to be on the MMPI scales generally must differentiate normal individuals from people with particular psychological disorders. Items selected to be on the CPI scales, however, must differentiate between two normal groups. For example, in order to compile items for the sociability scale, students of high school and college age who were viewed by their peers as either sociable or nonsociable were compared. Items that were answered differently by these two groups were retained for the scale. **Table 14.6** lists the scales for the CPI.

The 16 PF

The MMPI and the CPI were both constructed by the empirical method of selecting items that discriminate different groups of people. A somewhat different approach was taken to develop a test called the *Sixteen Personality Factor Questionnaire,* or *16 PF.* Before psychologists took seriously the Big Five approach to personality traits, Raymond Cattell (1972) identified 16 personality traits that he felt were basic and developed the 16 PF to measure the degree to which people have these traits. The

traits are presented in **Table 14-7.** The questionnaire that measures them consists of more than 100 items to which people give responses such as "yes," "no," "sometimes," or "practically always." The scale has been shown to be a valid measure of people's standings on the 16 traits. Cattell has done a great deal of research using the 16 PF, showing, for example, that airline pilots are more tough-minded, practical, self-assured, and controlled than artists or writers. In contrast, artists and writers showed sensitivity, imagination, and intelligence. The 16 PF is often used by high school and college counselors to help students make personal and vocational decisions.

Interim Summary

Personality inventories assess the extent to which people have traits or other characteristics by measuring how similar their responses are to reference groups of individuals known to have the trait or characteristic. Two such tests are the MMPI, which was developed to help diagnose psychological disorders, and the CPI, which was developed to measure how much normal individuals possess particular traits. The 16 PF was developed by Cattell to measure how much people possess each of his 16 basic traits.

THE BEHAVIORAL PERSPECTIVE

The fundamental assumption of the behavioral perspective on personality is that the characteristics of individuals result from external events, especially reinforcement. As a result of external forces, people learn specific patterns of behavior in specific situations and generalize them to similar situations. Also, the behavioral perspective does not assume that people will be consistent. They may learn quite different patterns of behavior in different situations. Furthermore, though patterns of behavior learned early in life may persist, personality is not necessarily stable. People can have new experiences and learn new patterns of behavior that will change their personality. The behavioral view of personality as constellations of learned behaviors maintained by reinforcement was a reaction to the Freudian approach, which postulated unobservable, unverifiable psychic structures and dynamics. It also contrasts sharply with both the psychodynamic and trait perspectives in its contention that changeable, external factors rather than stable, internal factors shape personality and behavior.

B. F. Skinner's Radical Behaviorism

One of the most forceful proponents of the behavioral approach is B. F. Skinner (1953, 1959). Skinner, whose views are rooted in J. B. Watson's philosophy of behaviorism, argues that we can make a great deal of progress in understanding people by focusing exclusively on their behavior and the external forces that have shaped it throughout their lives.

Skinner's key concept is that behavior is determined by its consequences. As we saw in Chapter 6, Skinner's movement, the experimental analysis of behavior, uses the concepts of reinforcement, generalization, and extinction to explain in detail how behavior is shaped by consequences. The most important factor in shaping behavior, according to Skinner, is rein-

According to Skinner, children who are reinforced for sharing will learn to share.

forcement. For example, a young boy who is reinforced for sharing rather than taking toys for himself will learn to share toys. Next, the boy may generalize his tendency to share toys and thereby share and cooperate in many other situations. Furthermore, even if his sharing behavior does not receive immediate reinforcement in every situation, it may still persist because it is on a schedule of partial reinforcement.

Skinner suggests that most behavior that we observe in people is maintained because it is reinforced in some way. The reinforcers in a person's life situations may not be readily apparent, but the behavioral viewpoint suggests that if one looks carefully enough, one is likely to find them. Specifically, Skinner suggests that we must conduct a *functional analysis* of an individual's behavior. This means analyzing both situations and behaviors to identify the events that function as discriminative stimuli and reinforcers.

One of the great advantages of the behavioral perspective, and especially of the functional analysis of behavior, is that it can be readily applied to change behavior. Once it has been discovered that a person's behavior is maintained by certain reinforcers, these reinforcers can be withdrawn, leading to extinction, or used to reinforce alternative forms of behavior. Such processes, known as *behavior modification,* will be discussed in Chapter 17.

Social Learning Theory

Many psychologists have found Skinner's basic emphasis on behavior and reinforcement welcome but have found the exclusive focus on behavior too extreme. Among these people are social learning theorists, who have added to their behavioral account of personality many cognitive factors (Bandura, 1977). As we shall see, variables such as a person's expectancies and values are important in the social learning perspective on personality.

BASIC PRINCIPLES

Perhaps the social learning theorists' most important departure from strict behaviorism has been to argue that people can learn by means other than direct reinforcement. To account for this, they have devised the important notion of **observational learning,** the view that people often learn not only by having their own behaviors reinforced but also by observing other people perform behaviors and receive reinforcement. These other people are called *models.* For example, from observing models we can learn how to serve a tennis ball, insult strangers, or draw tulips. Sometimes we can learn how to perform a behavior by simply watching another person perform it once. In other instances we must observe many times and practice the behavior on our own extensively, as may be the case in learning how to nurture others or how to be assertive.

Observational learning is one way we might *learn* behaviors without reinforcement, but reinforcement remains very important in determining whether a person will actually *perform* a behavior. A person may have learned how to influence a group but may not engage in this behavior until some kind of reinforcement is available. This is often enough to induce the person to begin performing the behavior. However, the person will also perform the behavior because of *vicarious reinforcement* (Bandura, Ross, & Ross, 1963). Vicarious reinforcement takes place when we observe another person being reinforced for an action. It often leads us to expect that we too will be reinforced for performing the same action. For example, if we see that one of our neighbors earns money by recycling bottles, we may engage in this behavior too, assuming of course that through observation we have learned how to perform it.

These children are learning to swim by observing their teacher and practicing the behavior.

RECIPROCAL INTERACTION AND SELF-EFFICACY

Social learning theorists see people as highly active, especially as processors of information and as self-regulating organisms actively involved in perception and interpretation. This idea is best expressed in the social learning concept of *reciprocal interaction* (Bandura, 1977), which holds that the person and the environment affect each other. Clearly the environment affects us. We cannot ignore it. But at the same time our behavior changes the environment. For example, our friendliness produces similar reactions in others. A far different environment would be produced if we were cynical or arrogant. This implies of course that, if we wish, we can choose how we would like to affect that environment. We can try to affect it in ways that will make certain behaviors of ours more adaptive or reinforcing. For example, we can attempt to interest others in art, perhaps by showing them a few interesting paintings. If we are successful, we will have friends who like to discuss art with us, thereby creating reinforcers for our interest in art. In short, we respond to the environment but the environment responds to us as well. **Figure 14.7** illustrates the concept of reciprocal interaction. An important determinant of the way people respond to their environment is their perception of their *self-efficacy.* Albert Bandura (1982, 1983) has argued that perceived self-efficacy, defined as people's judgments of how

Albert Bandura

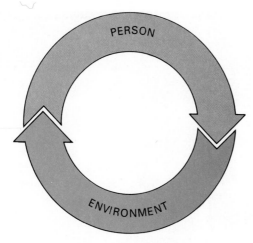

Figure 14.7
Bandura's Concept of Reciprocal Interaction.
Bandura proposed that both the person and the
environment affect each other in reciprocal interaction.
The person's behavior changes the environment, and the
environment influences the person's behavior.

well they can organize and bring to bear their cognitive, social, and behavioral skills in particular activities, is a major determinant of how fearful they are in threatening situations. Perceived self-efficacy also influences whether people will attempt to cope with problems or challenges despite their fears. One study shows that people who have higher perceived self-efficacy will respond to threatening communications more than will people who have lower perceived self-efficacy. Those with higher self-efficacy feel that protective actions will be effective, and so they are willing to take them (Maddux & Rogers, 1983). In short, the principle of reciprocal interaction argues that people can affect their environment. Whether they attempt to take effective action depends largely on their sense of perceived self-efficacy. Bandura is currently investigating how the modeling of mastery and dependable coping strategies can raise perceived self-efficacy.

COGNITIVE SOCIAL LEARNING THEORY
By introducing concepts such as observational learning and vicarious reinforcement, social learning theorists have demonstrated that cognitive processes are important in a full account of learning. For example, we have to consider attention, memory, and expectancy in order to understand how people learn and to predict how they will behave. This view has been spelled out in Walter Mischel's (1973, 1984)

"cognitive social learning theory." Part of Mischel's theory is that five "person variables" are important in understanding how people interact with their environment. These person variables are:

1. *Competencies.* Each person has different capacities and abilities. These may be mental abilities, such as intelligence, creativity, or memory; physical capacities, such as running speed or the ability to pitch a baseball; or artistic ability, such as singing, painting, or dancing. Our competencies affect what we can do and often what we attempt to do.
2. *Encoding strategies and personal constructs.* These terms refer to the ways we take in or encode information about objects and events in the environment and to the concepts or *constructs* individuals use to perceive and categorize other people. None of us pays attention to everything or perceives everyone else entirely accurately. However, our perceptions, accurate or not, strongly influence our behavior.
3. *Expectancies.* It has already been noted that expectancies are key variables in determining action. Because of our experience and behavior and what we see, hear, and read about others, we have expectancies about the consequences of our actions. Most important, of course, are expectancies about whether certain actions will lead to reinforcement. If we expect that they will, we are more likely to perform them.
4. *Values.* What we value or find reinforcing is critical in determining our behavior. Behaviors that produce the most valued outcomes for us are the behaviors we will pursue.
5. *Self-regulatory system and plans.* Self-regulatory systems include self-imposed goals and aspirations, which affect behavior. They also include the standards by which we assess our behaviors. Many people regulate their own behavior by rewarding or not rewarding themselves for certain actions. Some students decide that they will treat themselves to a movie or a chocolate ice cream soda *after* they finish each term paper. If they stick to these plans, they have good incentive to get their work done. Giving themselves a reward for doing the work is likely to establish a behavior pattern that matches personal standards and leads to many valued outcomes in the long run.

Although social learning theorists have integrated the variety of capacities and abilities each person has into their understanding of behavior, their focus remains on the reciprocal interaction of the person and the environment. This focus is clear in the next section, where we will consider how individuals perceive the influence of their own behavior versus the influence of the environment on their lives.

Perceptions of the Locus of Control

Some people believe that they are masters of their own fate, while others feel that they are controlled by forces beyond their control. This idea has been studied extensively by social learning theorists Julian Rotter (1966), Jerry Phares (1984), and Herbert Lefcourt (1982). Rotter suggested that, on the basis of their experience, individuals develop "generalized expectancies" that their reinforcements are controlled either by internal or external forces (see **Figure 14.8**). He has devised a scale to identify whether people are "internal" or "external." The scale contains 29 pairs of statements concerning the causes of success, failure, misfortune, and political events. One statement reflects a belief in internal control, the other a belief in external control. For each pair, subjects are asked to pick the statement they most agree with. The items in **Table 14.8** will give you a good idea of the kind of statements on the scale. You might try choosing between the statements yourself.

In scoring, subjects are given one point for every *external* choice. What are some of

Table 14.8 **Sample Items from an Early Version of Rotter's Test of Internal-External Locus of Control**

1a Promotions are earned through hard work and persistence.
1b Making a lot of money is largely a matter of getting the right breaks.
2a When I am right, I can convince others.
2b It is silly to think that one can really change another person's basic attitudes.
3a In my case the grades I make are the results of my own efforts; luck has little or nothing to do with it.
3b Sometimes I feel that I have little to do with the grades I get.
4a Getting along with people is a skill that must be practiced.
4b It is almost impossible to figure out how to please some people.

From "Internal Control—External Control" by Julian B. Rotter in *Psychology Today,* June 1971. Copyright © by American Psychological Association. Reprinted with permission from *Psychology Today Magazine.*

the ways that internals and externals differ? Generally, internals are more likely to strive to achieve. The slogan "We try harder" would fit internals more than externals. This has been shown in a number of studies. One interesting example involves tuberculosis patients in a hospital. Internals made more effort to find out about their disease, for example, what caused it and what could be done about it, and then actually tried to do something. The externals sought less information and took fewer steps to deal with their illness (Seeman & Evans, 1962).

Perceived locus of control has been linked to effort in many other domains. For ex-

Julian Rotter

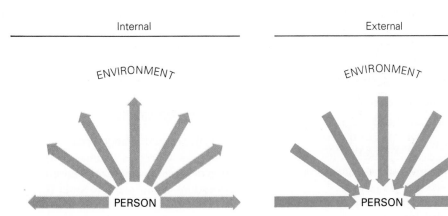

Figure 14.8
Internal Versus External Locus of Control.
Different individuals perceive different determinants of their outcomes or reinforcements. Some (internals) believe that their own efforts and behaviors determine their outcomes and their successes and failures. Others (externals) believe that outside forces, such as luck, chance, or fate, determine what happens to them.

ample, passive behavior patterns among the elderly are frequently interpreted to be senile behavior. Langer (1981), however, argues that these patterns often reflect elderly people's feeling that they have lost personal control over their environment. Studies in other areas indicate that people who perceive an internal locus of control are more likely to be involved in politics and social action (Strickland, 1977).

A representative study by Davis and Phares (1967) gives further support to the idea that internals are more self-initiating. In this study subjects were asked to attempt to change another person's attitudes about a controversial political issue. Before they met with the person, subjects were told to jot down any questions they had about the person since the answers to these questions might prove very useful in an attempt to influence someone. In addition, subjects were told what would determine success in this situation. One group was told that whether the person could be influenced was simply a matter of chance. A second group was told that persuasion depended on their own skill. A third group was not given any information about the factors determining their success in the experiment. The experimenters predicted that, overall, internals would want more information about the person they had to persuade. They would try to act as effectively as possible because they thought that their success was based on their own efforts and behavior. The externals would not bother to find out about the person because they would tend to believe that success or failure in persuasion rested on chance (see **Table 14.9**).

The results of the experiment confirmed this general prediction and told a little more be-

sides. When no information was given about the determinants of persuasion, internals asked for more information than externals, apparently assuming, as previously suggested, that their own efforts determined success. When subjects were told that success depended on skill, internals still tried harder than externals. Perhaps even this information could not overcome the externals' generalized expectancy that there is little correlation between effort and success. In the condition where subjects were told that persuasion depended on luck, there was no difference in the amount of information sought by internals and externals. The internals' tendency to work harder for success was counteracted when they were given the specific expectancy that luck reigned in this particular situation.

These studies and many others show that there are important differences between people who believe that reinforcements are due to their own behavior and those who believe that outcomes are random. Most important, the perception of an internal locus of control leads people to expend more effort to achieve their goals. Externals protect themselves to some degree by being able to blame their failures on the environment. Unfortunately, their belief that the world is beyond their control leads them to try less and fail more. You should think about your own perceptions of how outcomes are controlled. Do you sometimes give less than your best effort because you feel your best efforts won't make any difference? Do you satisfy yourself with less than your best performance by blaming the environment? These behavior patterns are typical of people who perceive an external locus of control. Internals work harder and by and large are better adjusted. Sometimes, however, they blame themselves too much (Phares, 1984) and may persist in efforts that only make undesirable situations worse (Strickland, 1978).

Gender and Personality

The 1991 United States Senate confirmation hearings for Clarence Thomas to be Associate Justice of the Supreme Court raised fundamental questions about gender. Anita Hill's accusations of sexual harassment spurred discussion of the relations between women and men, the treatment of women in our society, stereotypes about male and female behavior, and the real differences between men and women. Do men and women differ in their sex drive? Are they

Table 14.9   A Demonstration of the Difference Between Internals and Externals

Hypothesis: internals will seek more information about the person they have to persuade than will externals.

Subjects Were Told	Behavior of Internals Versus Externals
Chance determines success.	Both sought same amount of information.
Skill determines success.	Internals sought more information than externals.
Nothing about determinants of success.	Internals sought more information than externals.

Based on Davis & Phares (1967).

likely to express sexual interests differently? Why do men sexually harass and rape? Similar questions were raised in the rape trial of Mike Tyson, former heavyweight champion. In recent years psychologists have done a great deal of research on gender differences. Despite hundreds of studies, there is very little agreement on their significance. In particular, psychologists disagree sharply over whether we should be more impressed with the similarities between the sexes or the differences. In this section, we will review the debate over gender differences and examine some of the most recent research findings about personality differences between men and women.

Before going on we should remind you that the topic of gender differences is a broad one, and that we have discussed it earlier in the book in a number of places. For example, in Chapter 2, Brain and Behavior, we discussed gender differences in the human brain, in Chapter 10 we talked about boys and girls differing in cognitive and social development, and in Chapter 11 we discussed the possibility that men and women judge behavior using different moral principles. In this section we want to focus exclusively on personality. Also, as we begin this topic it is important to keep in mind that there are widespread stereotypes about personality differences between men and women. Many of these stereotypes take male behavior as a norm and point to female departures from these norms as in some way inferior. For example, one recent review of stereotypes shows that women are often seen as incompetent, weak, dependent, passive, and lacking in confidence (American Psychological Association, 1988). One wonders how such stereotypes influenced people's assessments of Professor Anita Hill when she testified that Clarence Thomas had sexually harassed her. We think it is important to emphasize that none of the stereotypes about gender differences provides a basis for knowledge. Although there are many intriguing studies of gender differences, it is difficult to be certain of fundamental personality differences between men and women.

What do we actually know about gender differences in personality? One of the most careful reviews of research on this topic was published nearly twenty years ago by Maccoby and Jacklin (1974). At that time only four differences were found to be reliable. Three of these were cognitive differences: girls were found to

Studies over the last twenty years have consistently shown that the only personality difference between males and females is that males tend to be more aggressive.

be have higher verbal abilities, boys had higher mathematical abilities and spatial abilities. The only personality difference was aggression. Boys were more aggressive. A much more recent review of subsequent studies by Maccoby suggests that aggression is still the only major area of personality difference between males and females (Maccoby, 1990). Nevertheless, studies on gender differences appear in the literature with great frequency, and Maccoby herself has suggested that some of the findings of no differences between men and women are "partly illusory." (Maccoby, 1990, p. 513). What are some of the differences suggested by recent research?

GENDER AND INFLUENCE

One difference in personality between men and women is in the area of influence and leadership. Generally, women are more easily influenced than men (Eagly, 1987). Also, despite some waning of the stereotype that leaders are men, recent studies confirm that men more often emerge as leaders in groups that do not have a leader at the outset (Eagly & Karau, 1991). How can these findings be explained? The roles that men and women play in groups are strongly influenced by social learning. Men are often expected to be more powerful and more concerned with accomplishing a group's goals. They are rewarded for behaving in accord with those expectations. Women, on the other hand, are typically expected to be inter-

The roles that men and women play in groups are strongly influenced by social learning. In a group setting, men are often expected to be more powerful while women are expected to be nurturing and supportive.

personally supportive and nurturing. Like men, they are rewarded for behaving in accord with those expectations. Not surprisingly, then, even very recent studies show that women act less like powerful people and more like warm and supportive people. For instance, women are likely to be significantly more apologetic and helpful after they have accidentally spilled a soft drink into someone else's bag of possessions (Gonzalez, Pederson, Manning, & Wetter, 1990). Also, in interview situations, women are more likely than men to adopt the low-status behavior of smiling (Deutsch, 1990). That is, women apologize, help, and smile more than men, confirming their position of less status and power. These behavioral tendencies, conditioned by social learning, give men an advantage in exerting influence and taking control of group tasks.

The social role expectations that allow men to be more influential and to lead have interesting effects on the language people actually use when they are trying to influence each other. When women try to influence men they speak more tentatively than when they are trying to influence women (Carli, 1990). For example, when talking to men, women are more likely to use *tag questions*, such as "People are basically friendly, aren't they." Women are also more likely to use *disclaimers* such as "I may be wrong ..." or "I don't know but ..."

Interestingly, this tentative style seems to work for women in influencing men. Men respond to the opinions of a woman if she does not challenge them but approaches issues tentatively. When trying to influence other women, women are just as assertive as men. They seem to have learned the fact that other women are more influenced by women who are assertive rather than tentative. That is, women have learned to use their assertiveness selectively. It works with other women, but not with men (Carli, 1990).

GENDER AND MATE PREFERENCE

Another difference between men and women that has been studied for many years is the importance they attach to different aspects of their partner's personality in heterosexual romantic relationships. A great deal of research shows that men find physical attractiveness in women more important than women find it in men and that women attach greater importance to their mate's earning power and his capacity to be a good provider (Buss, 1989; Feingold, 1990). This effect has been shown in many different societies around the world using many different methods of study.

Consistent with the finding that men care about women's attractiveness more than vice versa is a recent finding that the quality of an interaction between a man and a woman is more affected by the woman's physical attractiveness than the man's (Garcia, Stinson, Ickes, & Bissonnette, 1991). If the woman is not attractive, the interaction does not go well. Although women like attractive men more than unattractive men, the quality of the interaction is not affected as much by the man's attractiveness. Furthermore, women seem to respond to the importance men place on women's physical attractiveness. Over the entire life span, from age 10 to age 79, women are more concerned with their weight and physical appearance than men (Pliner, Chaiken, & Flett, 1990). As in many other domains, women respond to the expectations men have for the way they look and the way they behave.

Why should men care more about their potential mate's physical attractiveness and women care more about earning potential? There is a lively debate about this question. One view is that the difference is determined by evolution (Buss, 1989). According to this approach, both men and women are concerned with "reproductive success," that is, having as many healthy offspring as they can. Men can be reproductively successful by having sexual relations often and impregnating as many women as they can. Therefore, they have evolved to be attracted to physically attractive women, who are likely to be young and healthy and therefore likely to bear children. Women can be reproductively successful by making sure that the relatively few children they are able to bear are well protected. Therefore women have evolved to be attracted to men who can provide for and protect them. This "sociobiological" or evolutionary view is very controversial. Another theory is that men have more power and they have been taught to regard women as objects or commodities. Therefore, they are attracted to women who are externally attractive. Women have less power and are therefore attracted to men who themselves have power and can be good providers (Howard, Blumstein, & Schwartz, 1987). There is no way to know which explanation is closer to the truth. But we can count on there being a good deal of debate about this question in the future.

GENDER AND SELF-EVALUATION

Men are more aggressive than women and are generally less easy to influence. They are expected to dominate and to lead. These characteristics and expectations often give men a degree of power and privilege. Is this advantage likely to affect the way they evaluate themselves and their performances? A few recent studies suggest that men are sold on the idea that they are superior—even when they are not—and that they evaluate themselves less accurately than women. In one study men and women answered multiple-choice questions about sports, politics, movie stars, and fashion. They also answered practical questions and solved anagrams. After performing these tasks, the subjects were asked to evaluate their performance. Although the results varied somewhat according to the specific task, the overall results were clear. Men tended either to be accurate or to overestimate their performance. Women, in contrast, were either accurate or underestimated their performance. Most of the gender difference is explained by another gender difference, one of confidence and expectations. Men expect to do better and consequently overestimate their performance. Women do not expect as much success and subsequently underestimate their performance (Beyer, 1990). Similar results were found in a study of peo-

ple's evaluations of their intellectual, creative, athletic, and moral behaviors. Both males and females view themselves as superior to their peers. However, this inaccurate self-evaluation is much more prominent in males, from kindergarten through middle age, than in females (Goethals, Allison, & Messick, 1991). In short, another gender difference is that men evaluate themselves more favorably, and less accurately, than women.

GENDER AND PERSONALITY: A NOTE OF CAUTION

In conclusion, there are at least some traits—such as aggression, mate preferences, and influence—on which men and women differ. Although biology plays some role in gender differences, it is clear that many of these differences are shaped by social learning. Thus, it is possible for the differences to become larger or smaller. It may not always and everywhere be the case, for example, that women are more easily influenced than men. Furthermore, no matter what the cause of gender differences, the possibility that they do or do not exist provides no basis, in our opinion, to justify differential treatment of people based on their gender. We believe that psychologists should continue to explore the similarities and differences between the sexes, and we continue to argue that findings of similarities or differences should have no implications for how men and women are treated in our society.

Evaluation of the Behavioral Perspective

The research on locus of control and gender differences makes clear that the behavioral perspective on personality has evolved a great deal since Skinner first proposed radical behaviorism. One form of the behavioral approach, social learning theory, is widely accepted and continues to evolve rapidly. This is especially true, as we have just seen, as it is applied to such topics as gender differences. The fact that social learning theory is closely tied to empirical research contributes to its applicability, acceptability, and adaptability. On the other hand, as social learning theory has adapted itself to new research and new ideas, the behavioral approach has become less distinct. There seem to be converging developments in the behavioral and trait perspectives on personality. Whether the proponents of various approaches explicitly acknowledge it, agreement on the best ways to understand individuals seems to

Psychology in the News

TOP FEMALE RUNNERS GAINING ON MEN

By Boyce Rensberger

On the track, perhaps more than in other fields, women are catching up to men and, if trends continue, may pull even and perhaps eventually outrun them.

According to two scientists who study athletic performance, the speed of champion female runners in recent decades has been increasing so much faster than that of top male competitors that by 1998, both sexes could complete a marathon in the same time: 2 hours and 2 minutes.

That is about 5 minutes faster than the current men's world record, and 19 minutes less than the women's record.

In shorter races, where running speeds are higher and men now have a greater advantage, it will take women until the second quarter of the next century to catch up, if present projections hold.

Around 2027, the scientists predict, both the men's and the women's world records for the 1,500-meter event will be 3 minutes 13.6 seconds.

To reach that time, men would have to better the current record by about 16 seconds while women will have to cut a full 39 seconds from their current best.

Parity in the 200-meter race would come around 2050 with a time of 18.6 seconds—more than a second faster than the current men's record and nearly 3 seconds under the women's record.

The scientists, who are publishing their findings in today's Nature, concede that the idea of women running as fast as men flies in the face of conventional thinking. For one thing, as matters stand now, not one of the world's record-holding women could meet the qualifying standard for men to compete in the 1992 Olympics.

"If it weren't for the imperative of the data forcing me to this conclusion, I would have called this implausible and outlandish," said Brian J. Whipp, a physiologist at the medical school of the University of California at Los Angeles. He specializes in research on how the body controls oxygen use during athletic activity. Whipp made the projections with Susan A. Ward, also at UCLA.

Whipp and Ward emphasize that they made a simple-minded extrapolation that assumes no limiting factors will come into play as records continue to be broken. "We know there have to be limits, but there's no way to tell when they might be reached," Whipp said.

When he and Ward began their eight-decade study of world track records, they assumed that they would find the rate of improvement slowing down.

"We hoped to see a sign that runners were approaching a limit. That would have told us something about the limits of human physiology," Whipp said. "We were quite surprised to see straight lines" of consistent improvement when the records were graphed.

Most previous studies have plotted the world record times for each event. This yields a curve that does seem to be flattening. But the UCLA pair argue that this can be misleading because of the arithmetic relationship between time and speed.

To get a better measure of physical exertion, they calculated the

be emerging. As you will recall, the behavioral perspective at first considered only observable variables and external determinants of behavior, such as reinforcers. Then this position was extended into the social learning approach, which began to consider important "person variables," which are very similar to traits. In contrast, the trait perspective began by considering only the internal dispositions of a person but then integrated some consideration of situational variables. Thus, at present both social learning and trait proponents agree that internal and external variables must be considered in order to understand fully human action. Social learning theorists still emphasize concepts of reinforcement and situational control; trait theorists still emphasize what is inside the person. But there is much more agreement now than in the past. There may be even greater shared understanding in the future.

520

runners' average speeds during their record-breaking races. This approach overcomes the fact that as times get shorter, each record tends to better the previous one by smaller increments, even though the increase in physical effort may be as great as ever.

In other words, the amount of increase in speed that was enough to cut the record by two-hundredths of a second last time may shave off only one-hundredth this time.

For men, Whipp and Ward plotted the world's record speeds from 1905 through 1985 for seven standard Olympic running events, from the 200-meter to the marathon. In each event, the speeds increased at a nearly steady rate, and the graph showed a virtual straight line sloping upward with time.

For women, only five events had enough data to graph—four shorter races and the marathon. Again, the speeds increased in a straight-line graph, but the slope for each was about twice as steep as that for the men. Women, in other words, were improving their performances twice as fast as men were.

"Despite potential pitfalls," the researchers wrote in their Nature report, "we could not resist extrapolating these record progressions into the future."

The chief pitfall is that absolute limits on what the human body can do—even the best body with the best training—may be reached before the straight lines intersect.

Whipp recalled that in 1954, when Briton Roger Bannister broke the 4-minute mile, Diane Leather, also British, broke the 5-minute mile, then a record for female runners. Had the two run together, Leather would have finished 320 meters behind Bannister.

The current men's world record miler is another Briton, Steve Cram. If he were to run against the fastest women miler, Paula Ivan of Romania, he would finish only 180 meters ahead of her.

"That gives you a sense of how women are catching up," Whipp said.

Why are women improving faster than men?

The UCLA researchers suspect the reason lies in the growing numbers of people who take up running in the first place. The more people who try running, the better the chance of finding someone with superior ability and training.

"Top Female Runners Gaining on Men," by Boyce Rensberger, THE WASHINGTON POST, January 2, 1992. Copyright © 1992 The Washington Post. Reprinted by permission.

Questions

1. What are some of the reasons the improvements in running speed for women have been twice as fast as the improvements for men?
2. How might the differences in self-evaluation between men and women affect the likelihood of women running marathons as fast as men by the end of this century?
3. What are some of the pitfalls in extrapolating from the existing records?
4. How might a reader's stereotypes about the personality differences between men and women affect his or her reaction to this article?
5. How might self-efficacy or person variables affect the likelihood of women running as fast as men?
6. How might perceptions of the locus of control affect an individual woman's chances of running as fast as men?

Interim Summary

The behavioral perspective on personality assumes that personality is a constellation of behaviors that has been learned through reinforcement. It assumes that people may behave differently in different situations and that their behavior is influenced more by situational variables than by internal variables.

B. F. Skinner's radical behaviorism argues that only behavior should be studied. Mental processes that cannot be observed or measured should not be discussed. Social learning theorists believe that personality and behavior are influenced by more than reinforcement. They cite the importance of models, observational learning, and perceptions of self-efficacy. They also argue that persons and environments affect each other. Cognitive social learning theory stresses the importance of person variables in behavior. These variables include competencies, cognitive strategies, expectancies, values, and self-regulatory systems. Social learning theorists have contributed to our understanding of perceptions of locus of control and the similarities and differences between the sexes.

• •

THE HUMANISTIC PERSPECTIVE

The humanistic perspective highlights the ideas that people's behavior is shaped by their unique perceptions of the world around them and that people have the potential for growth. We will illustrate this perspective by discussing the work of Carl Rogers and Abraham Maslow, two leading figures in the humanistic movement. We will see that their emphasis is on the person's internal world, his or her perceptions and feelings, and on the individual's capacity for self-actualization. **Self-actualization,** for humanistic psychologists, is the process by which a person attempts to realize fully all of his or her inner potentials.

Humanistic psychology developed largely in reaction to the perceived imbalances of the Freudian and strict behavioral perspectives on understanding the person. Psychologists such as Rogers and Maslow believed that there is more to human behavior than simple repetition of patterns determined by unconscious dynamics during childhood, as emphasized by Freudians, and that there is more to psychology than simply predicting and controlling behavior, as emphasized by behaviorists. They felt that there needed to be more emphasis on what a person is like as an adult, how people perceive the world around them, how they feel, how they understand their own behavior, and how they grow and develop their full capacities. In addition, humanistic psychologists feel that more needs to be said about the positive side of human nature. They feel that within every human being there is a capacity for good and a richness and depth to personality slighted by Freudians and behaviorists. Various psychological factors, especially pressures to conform and the need to gain approval, may suppress this rich potential. Humanistic psychologists felt it important to create a "third force" that would supplement the Freudian and behavioral perspectives, explore human potential, and learn how this potential can be more effectively realized.

Carl Rogers

One of Carl Rogers' central concepts is that of the organism or the individual person (Rogers, 1951, 1959). Rogers contends that the organism strives toward maintaining, enhancing, and actualizing itself. In doing so it is drawn toward, and evaluates positively, all those experiences, feelings, and behaviors that further this goal. In contrast, the organism avoids and values negatively those experiences that constrict, reduce, or block development. In short, the organism has a strong tendency toward enhancing and actualizing inner potential.

The organism's enhancement and actualization do not happen easily or without interference. In growing up, a child may learn a set of values from his or her parents that restrict the tendency toward self-actualization. Parents do not allow all the behaviors that feel good and seem enhancing to their children. Parents will not approve of behaviors such as hitting a sibling when angry, dressing exactly as one pleases, or singing loudly during a church sermon. Children have strong needs for approval and affection, or, as Rogers puts it, *positive regard*. They quickly see that receiving positive regard may be *conditional* on behaving according to parental standards. Thus, behaving in ways that promote self-actualization can conflict with the need for positive regard, cramping the child's self-actualization (see **Figure 14.9**).

A further development is that children construct a self-concept consistent with the values they learn from their parents. The **self-concept** is an image of the self or the way one thinks about one's self. Children come to see themselves as people who generally meet parental standards. When their behavior and feelings are consistent with parental standards, their self-concept is enhanced and they feel worthy. When they behave in unapproved ways they feel unworthy. Thus, the fact that approval is conditional on certain kinds of behavior creates *conditions of worth*. Feelings of being worthy, and of being a good person, exist only when behavior is consistent with conditions of worth.

What are the consequences of conditional positive regard, conditions of worth, and the self-concept? The organism may strive for experiences that are inconsistent with the self-concept. The self-concept, in turn, may not recognize or accept these strivings. In this way the

Figure 14.9
Conditions of Worth.
Rogers argued that parents express positive regard only when their children's behavior meets certain conditions. This conditional positive regard strongly influences children's behavior and inhibits those self-actualizing tendencies that do not elicit positive regard.

self-concept can frustrate or block the organism's tendency toward self-actualization. It will deny feelings or urges that are contrary to the learned rules of the self-concept. There can be a great deal of conflict between the two central aspects of the person: the organism (with its tendency toward self-actualization) and the self-concept.

How much opposition between these two aspects of the personality typically exists? It is difficult to answer this question because there are great differences between individuals. In the well-adjusted or *fully functioning* person, all the organism's experiences are admitted and recognized. They are seen as consistent with the overall self-concept. However, when there is substantial inconsistency between the self-concept and the organism, serious psychological problems can result. People may be out of touch with their internal worlds. They can be unable to admit what is inconsistent with their self-concept. Under these circumstances, anxiety and other disturbing symptoms may develop and therapy may be required. Rogers is perhaps best known for the widely used therapy that he developed from his theories. Its central concept is unconditional positive regard, which, unlike conditional positive regard, fosters self-actualization. We will discuss Rogerian, or humanistic, therapy further in Chapter 17.

Abraham Maslow

Abraham Maslow is another humanistic psychologist whose ideas have been very influential. He is best known for two contributions. The first is his theory of the hierarchy of motives. This theory of motivation views the human personality as fundamentally oriented toward self-actualization and the development of potential. Self-actualization occurs naturally once other, more basic motives have been satisfied. Maslow's other major contribution is his research on the characteristics of self-actualized people (Maslow, 1968, 1970). In this section, we will consider both of Maslow's contributions.

THE HIERARCHICAL THEORY OF MOTIVATION
As we noted in Chapter 4, Maslow proposed a hierarchical theory of motivation in which "lower" needs had to be satisfied before "higher" ones could be addressed. There are five kinds of needs: physiological needs, safety needs, belongingness and love needs, esteem needs, and finally, the need for self-actualization.

Maslow's theory of motivation views the human personality as fundamentally oriented toward self-actualization and the development of potential.

Physiological needs are basic life needs, such as hunger and thirst, that must be satisfied before all others. If they are not met, people will direct all their resources toward satisfying them. Once physiological needs are fulfilled, *safety needs* can be addressed. Both physical and psychological safety are necessary to meet these needs. Maslow believed that, in general, children need safety more than adults. He noted, however, that an unfulfilled need for safety in children can become a permanent problem, since these people may continue to be highly concerned with safety as adults. These adults may feel less safe than others in identical situations and direct much of their energy into building safety and security. This will prevent them from trying to satisfy higher needs.

People who have satisfied their physiological and safety needs can attempt to meet *belongingness* and *love needs*. These form the third step in the hierarchy. These needs include the need to be accepted by and included in groups and the need for affection from parents, peers, and other loved ones. People who feel loved and who feel their needs to be gratified can move to the next step in the hierarchy. People who do not feel that these needs have been met will focus their energies on being accepted and being loved. These people may conform excessively or act in other ways to gain acceptance and approval. As we noted in discussing the need for social approval in Chapter 4, these kinds of behavior may seem unbecoming to others and thus may fail to gain positive responses.

Esteem needs are next in Maslow's hierarchy. Essentially, these needs relate to a desire to have a positive self-concept. They include the need to be competent, to achieve, to be effective, and to be free, autonomous, and independent. In addition, esteem needs include the desire to have one's achievements and competencies recognized and appreciated by others. This recognition gives one the added capacity to be effective in interactions with other people. As with other needs, people who lack positive self-esteem will be excessively concerned with gaining recognition.

The final step on the motivational hierarchy is the *need for self-actualization*. This is the need to develop all of one's potentials and capacities and to be all that one can be. It includes the need to appreciate the intrinsic worth of our surroundings and to experience the world deeply. It also includes the need to grow in harmony with the world around us.

The need for self-actualization is an entirely different kind of need from the lower needs in the hierarchy. Maslow refers to the lower needs as *deficiency motives*. They are all stimulated by a lack or a deficit. The person experiencing them strives to get whatever it is he or she feels is missing. On the other hand, self-actualization is called a *being motive* or a *growth motive*. With this need, no specific deficit needs to be filled. The person simply wants to be and to grow as fully as possible. The need for self-actualization is never satisfied, as the other needs can be, because more growth and experiencing of the world are always possible. The need for self-actualization pulls people toward positive states rather than away from negative ones.

THE CHARACTERISTICS OF SELF-ACTUALIZERS
According to Maslow, very few people satisfy all their lower needs and reach the state where they experience no deficits, but only the need to grow, develop, experience, and appreciate. One of the most important studies in the humanistic tradition is Maslow's investigation of individuals whom he believed were self-actualized (Maslow, 1968).

Maslow began by selecting historical and contemporary figures who were, in his estimation, self-actualized. These were healthy people whom Maslow felt had fully used their potentials. They included American social worker Jane Addams, physicist Albert Einstein, German composer Ludwig van Beethoven, psychologist William James, American presidents Thomas Jefferson and Abraham Lincoln, first lady Eleanor Roosevelt, and American writer Henry David Thoreau. In general, Maslow found that these people had satisfied their needs for safety, belongingness, love, respect, and self-esteem and were thus primarily motivated to achieve self-actualization. He felt that they were concerned with fulfilling all their potentials and talents and that, compared to others, they had achieved a greater knowledge and acceptance of inner human nature. More specifically, Maslow found these healthy, self-actualized people to have the following characteristics when compared to others:

1. A superior perception of the real world around them.
2. A greater acceptance of themselves, other people, and their environment.
3. Greater spontaneity in their feelings and actions.

Two examples of self-actualizers are scientist Albert Einstein and social worker Jane Addams.

4. Greater focus on problems and tasks around them rather than on themselves.
5. More detachment from mundane matters and a desire for privacy.
6. More autonomy and more resistance to social pressures to conform.
7. Fresh appreciation of all that is around them, and rich emotional reactions.
8. Increased identification with all of humankind.
9. Strong and intimate interpersonal relationships with a few other people.
10. More democratic, egalitarian, and nonprejudiced attitudes.
11. Superior creativity.
12. A more deeply developed sense of values.

LOVE FOR SELF-ACTUALIZERS

Maslow has done other research on the characteristics of self-actualizers. One of his particularly interesting studies explored what self-actualized people are like in their relationships with others, especially in their intimate relationships. The subjects for the study were adults Maslow knew whom he judged to be self-actualized. He compared their relationships to those of persons who were not self-actualized.

First, Maslow found that people's needs generally determine the quality of their interpersonal relationships. For example, people primarily motivated by safety needs will seek protection and security from other people.

Those motivated by esteem needs will seek recognition and respect. What does the self-actualized person look for? Maslow (1962) found that self-actualizers want only to love for the sake of experiencing love. He stated that the self-actualized person loves another "because he is loveworthy rather than because he gives out love" (p. 34). What differences in behavior follow from loving simply for the sake of love rather than loving to fill a specific need? One difference is that self-actualized people are more open with other people. They have less tendency to conceal information or to reveal information selectively in the interests of making a favorable impression. Other people's opinions matter relatively little to them.

Another difference is that self-actualized persons are regarded as more loving and more lovable than persons who are not self-actualized. Also, self-actualizers feel sex is an integral part of love and in the context of a love relationship experience more intense and profound enjoyment of sex than do non–self-actualized people. They are not interested in sex for sex's sake and they can get along without sex. In short, they have less need for sex but enjoy it more deeply than others.

Self-actualized persons prefer being with others who are also self-actualized, and they enjoy sharing the other person's needs and trying to find similar gratifications. Thus their relationships are characterized by mutual goals and interests and by "fun, merriment, elation, feelings of well-being, and gaiety" (Maslow, 1970, p. 194). Their relationships are playful and cheerful, but they still take love seriously. They experience it deeply and feel awed by its power and beauty.

Overall, self-actualized people enjoy love and experience it profoundly. At the same time, they do not need love and are not looking for anything specific from it. Love is an end in itself, to be treasured when it happens. The self-actualized person enjoys love when it comes along but in the meantime relishes life's other opportunities.

ASSESSING SELF-ACTUALIZATION

In many of Maslow's studies he used his own judgment to decide which individuals were self-actualized. However, a personality inventory has also been devised in an attempt to measure self-actualization more precisely. It is called the *Personal Orientation Inventory* or POI (Knapp, 1976; Shostrom, 1964, 1974). Like the internal versus external locus of control measure, it asks people to indicate which statement in a series of pairs of statements they most agree with. For example, one pair might be "My moral values are dictated by society" versus "My moral values are self-determined" or "I worry about the future" versus "I do not worry about the future." Two of the major scales of the POI measure *time competence* and the degree to which individuals are *inner directed*. Time competence refers to whether people are more concerned with the present than worried about the past or future, and whether they can integrate the present with the past and future and see how they are connected. Being inner directed means being concerned with the significance of life and with values. Self-actualizing people are thought to be both more time competent and more inner directed. Although the POI scale is promising, more research is needed. There is evidence that people who have been in group therapy get higher scores on the POI, but more convincing support for the scale as a measure of self-actualization still needs to be collected (Dosamantes-Alperson & Merrill, 1980).

Evaluation of the Humanistic Perspective

The humanistic approach has interested many psychologists who value its emphasis on the positive potential of human beings. The research supporting humanistic ideas, however, has been widely criticized. For example, many critics of Maslow's research on the characteristics of self-actualized people have argued that his selection of self-actualized people is somewhat arbitrary. Although they are all individuals who achieved great things and fulfilled some potentials, many of them had severe personal problems as well. Eleanor Roosevelt, for example, had extremely distressing relationships with her husband and her children, and William James and Abraham Lincoln both had many periods of deep depression. Some did not possess all of the characteristics of self-actualizers. Moreover, many of these characteristics are very difficult to define objectively and to assess. This is true of many of the concepts in humanistic psychology, such as the self-actualization concept itself. Thus, while the humanistic perspective has played a very important role in encouraging psychology to consider the whole person and the way he or she experiences the world and strives to grow, it lacks some of the empirical objective research of the trait and social learning perspectives. In short, the ideals of humanistic psychology are notable, but its conclusions cannot be accepted uncritically.

Interim Summary

The humanistic perspective on personality assumes that people strive for self-actualization, that is, the development of their potentials, and that psychologists must pay more attention to how people experience themselves and their worlds.

Rogers' theory suggests that children learn conditions of worth and that these conditions can impede self-actualization. Self-actualization flourishes in an atmosphere of unconditional positive regard.

Maslow proposed a hierarchical theory of motivation in which lower needs must be satisfied before the person can attempt to satisfy higher needs. The hierarchy progresses from physiological needs, to safety needs, to belongingness and love needs, to esteem needs, and finally to self-actualization needs.

The characteristics of self-actualized persons include greater self-acceptance, spontaneity, detachment, autonomy, fresh appreciation, creativity, and appreciation of what is around them. The Personal Orientation Inventory is a scale designed to measure self-actualization, though research is still needed to validate the scale. In general, the humanistic approach has been criticized for its lack of empirical, objective research.

SUMMARY

1. The four major perspectives on personality are the psychodynamic, trait, behavioral, and humanistic perspectives.
2. Freud's psychodynamic approach emphasizes the unconscious drives of the id, the reality orientation of the ego, and the moral orientation of the superego. It also considers the oral, anal, phallic, latency, and genital stages of development and the defense mechanisms of the ego.
3. Projective tests such as the Rorschach and TAT are often used to assess unconscious drives and conflicts.
4. Within the trait perspective, Jung considered types of individuals, such as introverts and extroverts, while Eysenck considered the two specific trait dimensions of introversion-extroversion and stability-instability. The big five factor approach considers extroversion, agreeableness, conscientiousness, stability, and openness.
5. Two widely used personality inventories are the MMPI and the CPI.
6. Within the behavioral perspective, radical behaviorists discuss the reinforcement principles that account for the learning of observable behavior, social learning theorists also consider observational learning, and cognitive social learning theorists discuss important "person variables."
7. The humanistic perspective emphasizes the phenomenology of individuals and the drive toward self-actualization.

KEY INDIVIDUALS

Sigmund Freud
Hans Eysenck
Raymond Cattell
Walter Mischel
B. F. Skinner
J. B. Watson
Heinz Kohut
Albert Bandura
Hermann Rorschach
Julian Rotter
Christiana Morgan
Jerry Phares
Henry Murray
Herbert Lefcourt
Carl Jung
Carl Rogers
Gordon Allport
Abraham Maslow

KEY RESEARCH

the Rorschach inkblot test
the Thematic Apperception Test (TAT)
two basic dimensions of personality
surface and source traits underlying individual differences in personality
a study of individual differences in consistency
the Minnesota Multiphasic Personality Inventory (MMPI)
the California Psychological Inventory (CPI)
the Sixteen Personality Factor Questionnaire (16 PF)
five "person variables" in cognitive social learning theory
perceived locus of control ("internals" versus "externals")
the hierarchical theory of motivation
the characteristics of self-actualizers
a scale to measure self-actualization

KEY TERMS

personality
latency period
rationalization
id
genital stage
projective tests
primary-process thinking
fixation
traits
ego
ego-defense mechanisms
introvert
reality principle
identification

extroverts
secondary-process thinking
displacement
personality inventories
superego
sublimation
observational learning
erogenous zones
repression

self-actualization
oral stage
denial
self-concept
libido
anal stage
phallic stage
projection
reaction formation

Part Five
....

PSYCHOLOGICAL DISORDERS AND TREATMENT

Chapter 15

Health and Stress

Chapter 16

Major Psychological Disorders

Chapter 17

Treatment of Psychological Disorders

Martin Seligman is Professor of Psychology at the University of Pennsylvania and Director of Clinical Training in the Department of Psychology. A distinguished teacher and researcher, he has published numerous books and articles in a wide range of subject areas including depression, learned helplessness, and explanatory style.

Q What can we learn about psychology by studying psychological and stress-related disorders?

A The most obvious justification for studying psychological and stress-related disorders is that they are important in their own right. And to the extent that we want to help people who are depressed or schizophrenic or suffering post-traumatic stress or who have been raped, then we have to understand these problems in order to treat them. In addition, we can learn something about normal people by understanding abnormal people. For example, a hundred years ago we found out where in the brain speech was located by studying people with pathology, that is, people who lost their speech after a stroke. We found that Broca's and Wernicke's areas of the cortex were damaged. From that knowledge about disordered people we could infer where in the brain speech was localized in normal people. And so, if we want to understand people who are cheerful and happy, we can begin by studying depressed people to find out what has gone wrong. We might then understand what goes right to keep most of us from being depressed.

Q Your work on learned helplessness has been very important to the field. What is learned helplessness?

A Learned helplessness is a question of how people under conditions of uncontrollability—in which nothing they do matters—break down and in what specific ways they break down. When human beings and animals encounter problems that are unsolvable, in which no response they make matters, they break down. Specifically, they become passive and lethargic, they become stupid and have trouble learning, and they become sad. These are the three primary psychological consequences of uncontrollability.

Q What are some of the important applications of learned helplessness?

A By creating learned helplessness in the laboratory and finding out what cures it, what prevents it, and who is especially prone to it, we learn about the cure, prevention, and risk factors for helpless people in the real world. For example, there is a class of drugs that relieves and prevents learned helplessness in the laboratory. These very same drugs relieve clinical depression in the real world. As another example, people who are especially at risk for learned help-

Martin Seligman

lessness in the laboratory are pessimistic. They see bad events as lasting forever, as undermining everything they do, and as their own fault. In parallel, people who are at risk for becoming depressed have the same beliefs. If you have the habit of saying, when a bad event occurs, "It's my fault, it's going to hurt me in everything I do, and it's going to last forever," you are at special risk for depression.

Finally, we know from the laboratory how to prevent learned helplessness, and this allows us to ask if we can prevent depression from occurring in the normal course of life. The approach taken by my research group is to teach college freshmen—people like the readers of this book—the skills of thinking about setbacks as temporary, specific, and caused by external forces and how to make this a habitual way of thinking about setbacks in life. By learning these skills in their freshman year, it is our hope that as our students go through college and beyond, they will suffer less depression, enjoy better physical health, and have higher achievement.

Q What do you think the exciting new developments in the future will be?

A I just described a development in the prevention of learned helplessness that excites me. A second area of learned helplessness that excites me has to do with physical health. Because helplessness, depression, and pessimism are related to second heart attacks, more infectious disease, and faster growth of tumors, it is possible that teaching people the skills of combatting depression, optimism, and coping with helplessness may save lives. Teaching these skills may prevent second heart attacks, may lower the risk of breast cancer, and may lower the risk of infection. So within the field of learned helplessness, I'd say prevention and enhancing physical health are two of the most exciting future hopes.

Let me make a very general statement about psychopathology and its future that returns to the first question. I think that psychopathology by definition concentrates on making sick people normal. But I think the principles that have come out of the study of psychopathology and therapy are eminently applicable to making normal people much better, helping them to higher achievement, better health, more happiness, and the like. So I believe the entire field of psychopathology will, in the lifetime of readers of this book, expand from the treatment of sick people, trying to bring them up to some minimal standard, to greatly enhancing the well-being of people in general.

15 Health and Stress

CHAPTER OUTLINE

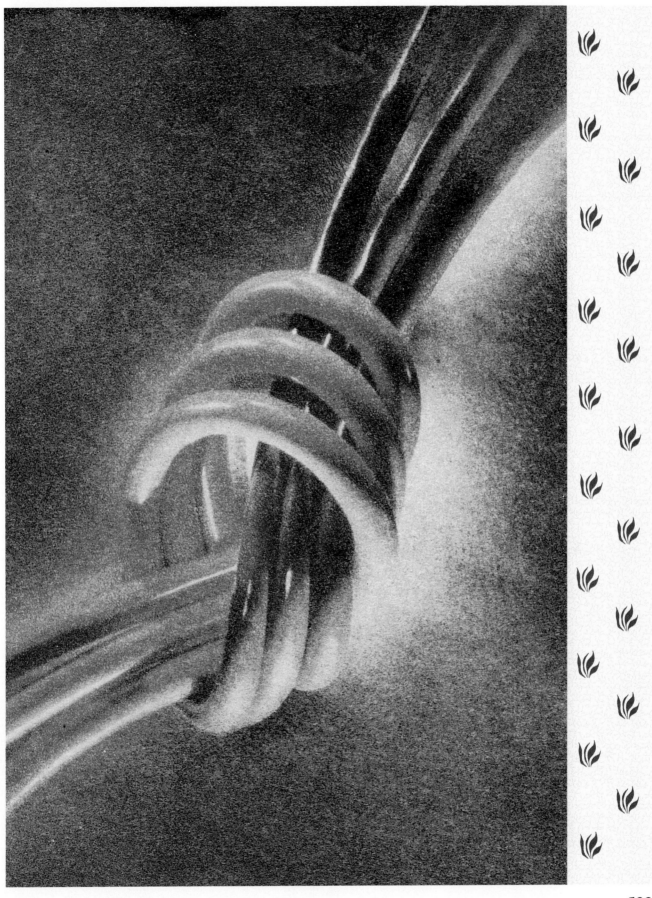

Stress is part of the normal fabric of human existence. It is an inevitable accompaniment of the challenges we undertake in developing new skills, abilities, and competencies. In most cases we grow by mastering the challenge. In some cases, however, the challenge exceeds our ability to cope. Then stress develops. **Stress** can be defined as a disruption of our normal psychological and physiological functioning that occurs when a challenge threatens our ability to cope adequately. Long-term stress is an important factor in the development of physical illness, including such leading causes of death as heart disease and high blood pressure. The costs of stress in terms of human suffering, social and occupational impairment, and illness are enormous. The need for better understanding and management of stress is a high priority in our increasingly complex society, which continuously challenges our coping abilities.

In this chapter we will introduce the major concepts and findings in the rapidly growing area of stress research. We begin by examining the relatively new field of health psychology and by exploring the health-related implications of stress. We will then discuss the nature of stress more generally, examining the characteristics of stressful situations, the psychological determinants of stress, and the effects of stress on our emotions, our thinking, and our bodies. We will conclude with a discussion of methods of coping with stress.

HEALTH PSYCHOLOGY

Psychology has long been involved in questions of *mental* health and mental illness. More recently, psychology has extended its domain to address problems of *physical* health and illness. This is entirely fitting, since mental and physical illness often go hand in hand. Surveys have shown that about half of mentally ill patients also have a significant physical illness (Koran, 1989). Conversely, medical patients have higher than normal levels of psychological problems. Other surveys have found that about 25 percent of patients being treated for physical illness also have a serious psychological disorder needing treatment (Barrett, Barrett, Oxman, & Gerber, 1988; Wells, Golding, & Burnam, 1988). Some hospitals now prescribe

psychological evaluation and counseling as part of the treatment program for many patients. This often leads to marked reductions in the use of medical services by these patients. After psychological counseling, patients spend less time in the hospital, use fewer drugs, and make fewer outpatient and emergency-room visits (Holder & Blose, 1987; Schlesinger, Mumford, Glass, Patrick, & Sharfstein, 1983).

The field of psychology concerned with the role of psychological factors in health and illness is known as **health psychology.** The aims of health psychology are threefold: to employ psychological knowledge and expertise to help identify the factors responsible for health and illness, to promote health, and to prevent and treat illness (Matarazzo, 1982).

A major factor behind the development of health psychology is a profound shift in the leading causes of death in North America during this century (see **Figure 15.1**). In 1900 the leading causes of death, such as pneumonia, influenza, and tuberculosis, could often be traced to single disease-causing agents such as bacteria or viruses. The control of such diseases was due to improved public health practices, which reduced sources of infection, and to the development of infection-controlling drugs like penicillin. By 1980 the only leading causes of death due to infection were influenza and pneumonia, which ranked sixth among the ten leading causes of death. Most leading causes of death are now due to the convergence of many different causes, known as *risk factors.* These risk factors often reflect unhealthy behavior patterns and practices. A landmark U.S. Surgeon General's report, *Healthy People* (Califano, 1979), pointed out that mortality from seven of the ten leading causes of death could be reduced by one half if people were to change their behavior in five ways: eliminate smoking, exercise regularly, use less alcohol, eat a balanced diet, and control high blood pressure. For example, each of these five factors contributes to the development of heart disease, by far the leading cause of death today. In other words, behavior and lifestyle are today among the sources of major forms of disease and disability.

Stressful Life Events and Illness

In addition to unhealthy behaviors like smoking, poor diet, and lack of exercise, psychological stress is a major risk factor in the develop-

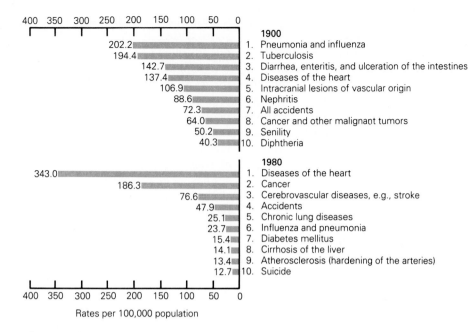

Figure 15.1
Leading Causes of Death in the United States: 1900 and 1980. (From Levy & Moskowitz, 1982)

ment of illness. This is not to say that stress by itself directly causes illness and death. Stress, however, appears to lower resistance to many different illnesses. When combined with other risk factors, stress increases the probability of subsequent illness. For example, studies show that divorce and marital separation contribute to both psychological and physical ailments. Divorced and separated people are more anxious and depressed, they have more medical illnesses, and they are more likely to commit suicide than married people (Asher & White, 1978).

Like divorce and separation, bereavement is also known to be associated with heightened rates of illness and death. Scientific evidence suggests that "dying of grief" is more than merely folklore. One study compared the death rates of nearly 4500 widowers over the age of 54 with death rates of married men of the same age. As seen in **Figure 15.2,** the death rates of the widowers increased over 40 percent in the first 6 months of bereavement and remained slightly elevated for several years thereafter (Young, Benjamin, & Wallis, 1963). Similar findings have been reported in many subsequent investigations (Kapiro, Koskenvuo, & Rita, 1987; Stroebe & Stroebe, 1987). Of course, people do not actually die from grief *per se.*

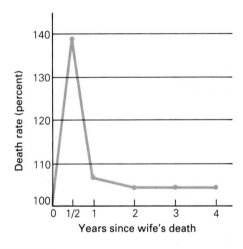

Figure 15.2
Relative Death Rates of Widowers. (Based on Young, Benjamin, & Wallis, 1963)

They die from a variety of specific medical causes. Yet many experts believe that grief can be an emotional trigger that combines with biological factors to cause death from heart attacks or strokes (Engel, 1971; Lynch, 1977). Other factors leading to higher mortality among the bereaved include reduced physical activity, poor eating habits, and higher consumption of alcohol.

Divorce, separation, and bereavement are

only three among many stressful life events known to have harmful health consequences. Several years ago, two stress researchers, Thomas Holmes and Richard Rahe, combined a number of such life events into one list, which they called the **Social Readjustment Rating Scale,** or **SRRS** (Holmes & Rahe, 1967). Holmes and Rahe generated the list by asking medical patients to describe stressful life events they had experienced in a period of several

months prior to becoming ill. The results showed that 43 different life events were frequently cited by the patients (see **Table 15.1**).

Holmes and Rahe reasoned that each of the 43 SRRS life events was stressful because it required a change, or *social readjustment*, in people's lives. The SRRS ranks the 43 life events from the most to least stressful. This ranking was determined by asking people from all walks of life to estimate the amount of social readjustment required by each of the events. Holmes and Rahe first assigned an arbitrary value of 50 "life change units" (LCUs) to marriage and then asked their subjects to assign a proportionately larger or smaller number to each of the remaining events. The numbers people assigned varied from an average of 100 for death of a spouse (rank 1) to an average of 11 for minor violations of the law (rank 43).

One study using the SRRS examined the relationship between stressful life events and illness among the naval personnel on three ships during a 6-month cruise. Before the cruise, each subject reported the life changes experienced in the previous 6 months. At the end of the cruise, the sick-bay records of the sailors were compared with their life-change scores. As seen in **Figure 15.3,** the higher the life-change score, the greater the number of sick-bay visits (Rahe, 1975).

Unfortunately, studies like the above are often misinterpreted as proving that stress *causes* illness. This is an overstatement. The most that such studies can demonstrate is that stressful life events are *risk* factors for the development of medical symptoms. In other words, stress seems to lower resistance to illness and to motivate people to seek medical care. In addition, the relationship between stress and symptom development is far from perfect. Many people with high life stress do not become ill, and many people with low life stress do. We know, for example, that people differ in their ability to cope effectively with stressful events. Many individuals possess psychological resources that help them cope with and ward off the health-impairing effects of stress.

Suzanne Kobasa (1979) conducted an important study demonstrating that personal coping resources need to be taken into account when considering the stress-illness relationship. Kobasa's subjects were a large group of business executives who showed higher than normal levels of stressful life events as mea-

Table 15.1   **The Social Readjustment Rating Scale**

Rank	The Event	LCU Value
1	Death of spouse	100
2	Divorce	73
3	Marital separation	65
4	Jail term	63
5	Death of close family member	63
6	Personal injury or illness	53
7	Marriage	50
8	Fired at work	47
9	Marital reconciliation	45
10	Retirement	45
11	Change in health of family member	44
12	Pregnancy	40
13	Sex difficulties	39
14	Gain of new family member	39
15	Business readjustment	39
16	Change in financial state	38
17	Death of close friend	37
18	Change to different line of work	36
19	Change in number of arguments with spouse	35
20	Mortgage over $10,000	31
21	Foreclosure of mortgage or loan	30
22	Change in responsibilities at work	29
23	Son or daughter leaving home	29
24	Trouble with in-laws	29
25	Outstanding personal achievement	28
26	Wife begins or stops work	26
27	Begin or end school	26
28	Change in living conditions	25
29	Revision of personal habits	24
30	Trouble with boss	23
31	Change in work hours or conditions	20
32	Change in residence	20
33	Change in schools	20
34	Change in recreation	19
35	Change in church activities	19
36	Change in social activities	18
37	Mortgage or loan less than $10,000	17
38	Change in sleeping habits	16
39	Change in number of family get-togethers	15
40	Change in eating habits	15
41	Vacation	13
42	Christmas	12
43	Minor violations of the law	11

From Holmes & Rahe (1967)

sured by the SRRS. She divided the executives into two groups: those who showed a high rate of subsequent illness and those who showed little or no subsequent illness. Kobasa referred to the latter group as "hardy" because they were able to manage life stress without suffering negative health consequences. The major question addressed by the study was: how do hardy people differ from the nonhardy? By analyzing the results of extensive psychological testing, Kobasa found that **hardiness** could be described by three C's:

Challenge: Hardy people are open to change. They regard life events as challenges rather than threats to their well-being.

Commitment: Rather than being alienated from their life situations, hardy people show an active and vigorous involvement in their environment.

Control: Hardy people have a sense that their own actions and beliefs largely determine their fate. In other words, they have an internal locus of control, as discussed in Chapter 14.

In brief, when potentially stressful events occur in the lives of hardy people, they view the events as a challenge, they meet the challenge with active involvement, and they believe they have control over their own lives (Maddi & Kobasa, 1984).

In addition to personal hardiness, an **optimistic disposition** can serve as a buffer against stressful events. According to psychologists Michael Scheier and Charles Carver (1985), optimists agree with such statements as "In uncertain times, I usually expect the best" and "I always look on the bright side of things." By contrast, pessimists tend to agree with such statements as "If something can go wrong for me, it will" and "I rarely count on good things happening to me." Research has shown that an optimistic disposition is associated with better health and greater ability to cope with stress. In one study, for example, 51 middle-aged men were assessed for optimism or pessimism before undergoing coronary artery bypass surgery. The optimists were faster to recover from the surgery and returned to their normal activities sooner than the pessimists (Scheier et al., 1989).

Many refinements in our understanding of stressful life events have been suggested in the

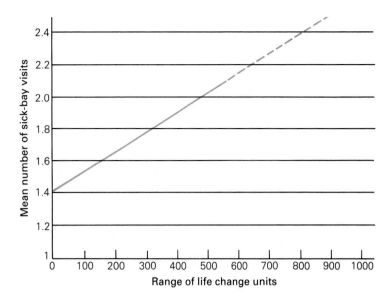

Figure 15.3
Mean Number of Sick-Bay Visits As A Function of Life-Change Scores. (After Rahe, 1975)

two decades since the development of the SRRS. We now know, for example, that life change *per se* is not necessarily stressful, as Holmes and Rahe assumed. Rather, life change is stressful if the person perceives the change as *undesirable*. In other words, it is necessary to take into account the individual's negative appraisal of life change in order to predict its stress potential (Sarason, Levine, & Sarason, 1982). Hardy individuals, as well as those with an optimistic disposition, are able to buffer the impact of potentially stressful events by adopting positive appraisals of life events.

Despite its limitations, the SRRS has played an important role in alerting both the general public and health-care professionals to the psychological costs of events we often take for granted. By isolating particular life events, the SRRS helps identify groups of people, such as the recently divorced or recently unemployed, who may be at high risk for stress-related illness. It thus opens the possibility of offering assistance to such high-risk groups before illness and psychological disability can escalate.

Probing the Stress-Illness Relationship

The link between stressful life events and heightened risk of illness raises an intriguing question: How does a psychological problem (stress) become translated into a physical problem (illness)? This question restates a classic is-

Psychology in the News

COMFORTING MAKES A COMEBACK

By Daniel Goleman

"Comfort always, cure rarely," was a motto of medicine in times long gone, when bedside manner was far more potent than any medicines.

Now, in a movement that counters the rush to high-technology, high-turnover medicine, some physicians are urging that the lost art of comforting be revived. They are spurred by a steady march of scientific findings demonstrating how heavily patients' emotional states can affect the course of their diseases.

For example, among 100 patients preparing to go through bone marrow transplants for leukemia, 13 were found to be highly depressed and 12 of them indeed died within a year of the transplant. But 34 out of the 87 who were not depressed were still alive after two years, a recent study at the University of Minnesota showed.

Of the patients who felt they had strong emotional support from their spouses, family or friends, 54 percent survived the transplants after two years. But the two-year survival rate of those who said they had little social support was only 20 percent.

In another study, 122 men were evaluated for the pessimism or optimism they had felt at the time of suffering a heart attack. Their state of mind was found to be a better predictor of death from heart attack eight years later than were any of the standard medical risk factors, including damage to the heart in the first episode, artery blockage, cholesterol levels or blood pressure.

Of the 25 most pessimistic men, 21 had died after eight years; of the 25 most optimistic, just 6 died.

No one is suggesting that emotional distress outweighs biological factors in disease or that psychologi-

cal help can replace medical care. But the bottom line from these and other studies seems to be that attending to patients' emotional distress along with ordinary medical care can add an extra margin of healing in many cases.

The very idea that emotions can play any role at all in disease is anathema to many people in the field of medicine. That notion, a much-cited 1985 editorial in The New England Journal of Medicine proclaimed, is nothing but "folklore." But more and more medical researchers are finding the new data too compelling to ignore.

For example, the study of pessimists and heart attacks is one of a series done by different researchers on people's attitudes and their health. In one of the first, reported by Dr. Martin Seligman at the University of Pennsylvania in 1988,

---

sue in psychology, that is, the relationship between mind and body. Probing the mind-body relationship is at the forefront of contemporary stress research.

Psychologists do not yet completely understand the mechanisms by which stress affects health. We do know, however, that stress produces striking changes in the body's physiological activity. Under nonstressful conditions, physiological activity is maintained within certain limits. These limits are so predictable that we can speak of "normal" levels of heart rate, blood pressure, body temperature, and so forth. Almost a century ago, Walter B. Cannon coined the term **homeostasis** ("equal state") to describe the tendency of the body to maintain its internal equilibrium. Under stress, however, homeostasis is disrupted. Changes occur in all of the major physiological systems of the body, including the cardiovascular, gastroin-

testinal, and endocrine (hormonal) systems. We will describe these effects in more detail in our discussion of physiological reactions to stress later in this chapter. For now it is sufficient to note that disrupted homeostasis appears to set the stage for the development of illness.

A good example of stress-induced disruption of homeostasis is the relatively recent discovery that stress interferes with the body's immune system. The **immune system** protects against illness by recognizing and destroying disease-causing substances like viruses, bacteria, and cancer cells. Such foreign substances are known collectively as *antigens*. When an antigen invades the body, white blood cells, or *lymphocytes,* begin to proliferate. Some lymphocytes, known as *T cells,* attack and destroy antigens directly. Others, known as *B cells,* produce *antibodies* that combine with and neutralize antigens. We now know that stress can

members of the Harvard University classes of 1939 to 1944 were evaluated as being pessimistic or optimistic on the basis of essays they had written in college about their wartime experiences.

"Pessimists" tend to explain setbacks in their lives as resulting from some trait of theirs that cannot change and will blight other things, too. By contrast, "optimists" tend to explain an unfortunate turn of events as resulting from something in the situation that can be changed, rather than as their fault.

The more pessimistic the Harvard men had been as students, the more likely they were to have got a serious chronic disease like atherosclerosis by the age 45.

Medical scientists are already looking for possible physical mechanisms that could link people's emotional states to their state of health.

Dozens of research teams are pursuing the possibility that negative emotional states may adversely affect the ability of the immune system to fight disease.

Although some of these researchers have established that anxiety and depression can hamper the activity of crucial cells within the immune system, no research has yet been able to show that these changes are clinically significant for the course of disease or healing.

Dr. Eduardo Colon, a psychiatrist at the University of Minnesota, said his own study showing that depression in recipients of bone marrow transplants for leukemia led to a high death rate "raises more questions than it answers."

Noting that the bone marrow transplants are psychologically trying as well as physically difficult, Dr. Colon said, "If you're depressed, you may not do the things that could help you recover—get out of bed and move around, care for mouth sores the treatment causes, and so on. Or it may make you less compliant in taking your medication. Or, perhaps, the depression may cause changes in the immune system."

From "Doctors Find Comfort Is a Potent Medicine" by Daniel Goleman, THE NEW YORK TIMES, November 26, 1991. Copyright © 1991 by The New York Times Company. Reprinted by permission.

Questions

1. This article cites three studies showing that patients' "state of mind" can influence the course of their disease. Exactly how would you describe this state of mind?
2. Discuss both a behavioral and a physiological explanation for the link between negative emotions and poor health.
3. After reading the entire chapter, discuss two or three coping methods that might be useful in improving patients' health following serious illness.

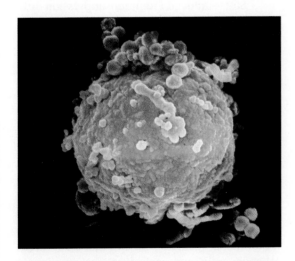

Stress suppresses the ability of the body's immune system to protect against disease-causing agents. B cells, like this specimen covered with bacteria, produce antibodies that combine with and neutralize antigens.

suppress the number of lymphocytes in the body as well as suppress their ability to multiply in the presence of antigens. The *immunosuppressive* effects of stress therefore point to a mechanism that links stress to illness.

The field of research that explores the effects of stress and other psychological states on the immune system is known as **PNI,** which is short for the rather awkward word **psychoneuroimmunology** (*psycho* = mind; *neuro* = brain; *immunology* = study of immunity). Pioneering PNI research on the immunosuppressive effects of stress in animals was conducted by Vernon Riley (1981). Riley induced stress in mice by placing them in a cage on a turntable that rotated at 45 RPM. In a variety of experiments he examined the effects of this rotation stress on different measures of immune system functioning. The results of two such studies are shown in **Figure 15.4.** One study

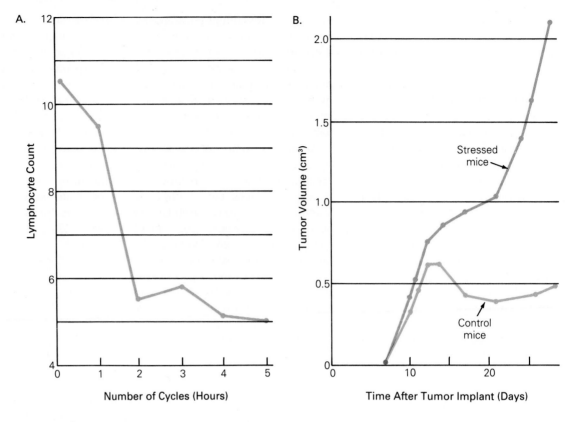

Figure 15.4
The Influence of Stress on Lymphocytes and Tumor Growth.
Panel A shows a decrease in lymphocyte counts in mice stressed 10 minutes per
hour for 5 hours. Panel B shows the growth of an implanted tumor in stressed and
control mice over a 30-day period. (After Riley, 1981)

measured lymphocytes in mice given 10 minutes of rotation stress each hour for 5 hours. As
seen in **Figure 15.4A,** lymphocyte counts decreased markedly over the 5-hour period. In another study, Riley examined the effects of
stress on the growth of malignant tumors. He
first implanted cancer cells under the skin in a
group of mice. The group was then subdivided
into a control group, which received no stress,
and an experimental group given 10 minutes
per hour of rotation stress for 3 days. Following
this, he examined tumor growth in both
groups over several weeks. **Figure 15.4B**
shows tumor growth in both the control and
stressed mice during this period. In the control
group, tumor size stabilized after a short period, presumably due to the antitumor activity of
an intact immune system. In contrast, the
stressed animals showed a rapid increase in tumor size over the period. Taken together, these
two studies demonstrated that stress impairs
immune system functioning and that this im-

pairment is associated with a rapid progression
of implanted cancer cells.

Stress-induced immunosuppression can
also be observed in humans. Recall that bereavement is a highly stressful experience associated with an increased risk of illness and
death. One group of investigators asked
whether bereavement was also associated with
alterations in immune system activity. The subjects of this study were 15 spouses of women
with a terminal disease. Blood samples were
drawn from the spouses both before and within 2 months after the deaths of their wives. At
each time, blood lymphocytes were combined
with an antigen that normally stimulates lymphocytes to multiply. Lymphocyte activity was
measured in response to five different dose levels of the antigen. As seen in **Figure 15.5,** lymphocyte activity at each dose level was less in
the postbereavement than in the prebereave-
ment period. The stress of bereavement was associated with immunosuppression in human

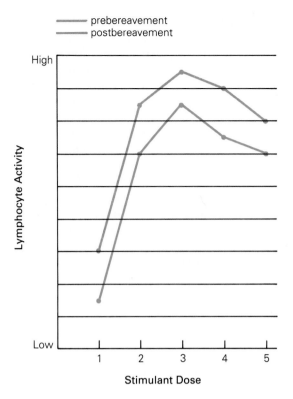

Figure 15.5
Lymphocyte Stimulation in Widowers Before and After Wife's Death.
Each point represents an increasing dose of the lymphocyte-stimulating compound. (After Schleifer et al., 1983)

subjects much as rotation stress produced immunosuppression in laboratory animals (Schleifer, Keller, Camerino, Thornton, & Stein, 1983).

Similar immunosuppressive effects have been reported in human subjects in other kinds of stressful situations, including academic examinations, unemployment, and marital separation (Kiecolt-Glaser & Glaser, 1988; Halley, 1991). PNI findings like these represent a major development in health psychology because they promise to uncover the underlying mechanisms that link psychological stress to physical illness. They are only a beginning, however. Researchers still need to determine if the stress-induced immunosuppression observed in PNI studies is large enough to explain illness onset and, if so, the specific illnesses that can be explained by this mechanism. Nevertheless, the mind-body relationship is fast yielding many of its secrets to PNI researchers (Plotnikoff, Faith, Murgo, & Wybran, 1991).

Personality and Illness

As we have seen, stress can be a risk factor for subsequent illness. But people do not fall ill in general; they develop specific illnesses. The interesting question then becomes: is there a relationship between *specific* ways of reacting to stressful events and the development of *specific* illnesses? In other words, do different ways of coping with stress help determine the different kinds of illness people will develop? This question is known as the problem of **psychosomatic specificity.** According to the psychosomatic specificity hypothesis, people who share similar ways of coping with stressful events will also be likely to develop similar illnesses.

The term *psychosomatic* is often misunderstood. One erroneous belief is that "psychosomatic" means that the person is not really sick, that his or her problems are "all in the head." On the contrary, the symptoms of psychosomatic illness reflect physiological disturbances associated with tissue damage (as in ulcers), pain (as in migraine headaches), and even early death (a frequent sequel to heart disease). A second erroneous belief is that patients with psychosomatic illnesses do not need medical treatment. In fact, medical treatment is always required. The term *psychosomatic* simply points to the operation of psychological factors along with physiological factors in certain illnesses.

Research on the psychosomatic specificity hypothesis has been conducted for many years. A good example of such research is that of David Graham and his colleagues (Graham, 1962, 1972). These researchers first asked patients to describe their ways of coping with stressful events surrounding their illnesses. They found that patients with the same illness tended to describe and cope with the stressful events in their lives in a similar manner. For example, when under stress patients with hypertension tended to feel that they were being threatened with serious harm and therefore had to be on guard at all times. Patients with intestinal ulcers felt they were being deprived of what was rightfully theirs and wanted to get even. Patients with hives felt they were being unfairly treated by others but also felt helpless to do anything about it. Other specific attitudes about stress and ways of coping were found for more than a dozen different illnesses. Note that Graham did not ask about the specific events that preceded attacks of illness. Rather, he asked about patients' attitudes toward these events and about their coping strategies.

Graham then tested his findings on a second group of patients. To do this, the characteristic attitudes and coping strategies associated with several different illnesses were depicted in cartoon form. Four of these cartoons are shown in **Figure 15.6.** Patients with different illnesses were then asked to choose the cartoon that best illustrated their current life situation. In general, patients tended to choose the cartoon illustrating the attitude and coping strategy that had been identified in the first group of patients, which supported the generality of Graham's findings.

What is the current status of the psychosomatic specificity hypothesis? Although it is a

Figure 15.6
Cartoons from Graham's Study.
Graham asked hospital patients to choose the cartoon that most reminded them of their life situation. Cartoon 1, most often chosen by patients with hives, shows a person who is taking a beating that he is unable to prevent. Cartoon 2, typically chosen by patients with Raynaud's disease, shows an angry person who wants to take aggressive action. Cartoon 3, often chosen by patients with essential hypertension, shows a person who feels threatened and on guard. Cartoon 4, the choice of patients with duodenal ulcers, shows a person who feels deprived of his due and wants to get even. (From Graham, 1962; in Sternbach, 1966)

very intriguing idea from a psychological perspective, it has not in general made a major impact on medical practice. One reason is that medical illnesses can often be controlled by drugs or surgical procedures, which do not require patients to examine their coping strategies. A second reason is that there is as yet no single method of assessing the psychological component of a psychosomatic illness. Some investigators use self-report tests, others projective tests, and still others the interview method. For example, the work of Graham and his associates has never been replicated by other investigators using the same methods, so the Graham findings must still be considered tentative. In the absence of standardized assessment procedures, the results of different studies often appear to be in conflict, and progress in this field is slow. In sum, the psychosomatic specificity hypothesis has neither been completely confirmed nor refuted as an approach to understanding illness. An important exception is research on coronary heart disease and the Type A behavior pattern, to which we now turn.

CORONARY HEART DISEASE
Coronary heart disease (CHD) is a major cause of death in North America. In any one year, about 1.3 million Americans suffer from CHD and about 500,000 die from heart attacks due to CHD. One fourth of all heart-attack victims are relatively young people under the age of 65 (Levy & Moskowitz, 1982).

CHD develops gradually over many years as one or more of the three coronary arteries supplying blood to the heart muscle harden and lose their flexibility. Hardening of the arteries is known as *atherosclerosis*, which refers to the growth of hard, fatty *plaques* on the inside of artery walls. A heart attack occurs when these plaques block one of the coronary arteries. This cuts off the supply of blood, oxygen, and nutrients to a portion of the heart muscle, causing the heart attack. A heart attack is fatal if a large part of the heart is damaged in this way.

Three major factors have long been known to increase the risk of developing CHD: (1) high blood pressure, (2) smoking, and (3) high levels of cholesterol, a fatty substance in the blood. People with any one of these factors have about twice the normal risk of developing CHD; people with all three have many times the normal risk (Brand, 1978). A more recently identified risk factor is the so-called Type A behavior pattern.

THE TYPE A BEHAVIOR PATTERN

The **Type A behavior pattern** is a cluster of traits identified in the 1960s by two medical researchers, Meyer Friedman and Ray Rosenman. The person exhibiting Type A behavior is highly ambitious, excessively hard working, intensely competitive, and always under time pressure. In addition, the Type A person easily becomes impatient, irritable, and hostile, especially when distracted from whatever task he or she is currently occupied with. According to Friedman and Rosenman, the Type A person is engaged in a never-ending struggle to achieve as much as possible in the shortest period of time. Never satisfied with past accomplishments, the Type A person continuously sets new and higher goals and so is in a constant whirlwind of activity (Friedman & Rosenman, 1974).

The Type A behavior pattern can be assessed by means of a standardized interview or by a self-report test. These methods have generated a large amount of research linking Type A behavior to CHD. For example, Rosenman conducted an 8-year follow-up study of over 1000 healthy men who had been assessed for Type A behavior. At the end of the 8-year period, CHD was 2½ times more common in Type A men than in those lacking Type A traits (Rosenman, Brand, Jenkins, Friedman, Straus, & Wurm, 1975).

Type A personalities tend to be ambitious, hard-working, and competitive. They become impatient and hostile if distracted from the task at hand. Here, Chicago Bears Coach Mike Ditka during a 1989 football game against the Redskins.

Why does the Type A person develop such traits? According to David Glass (1977), the Type A person has an unusually high need for control over the environment. This sort of person will be particularly threatened by potentially uncontrollable situations. Life, however, is full of situations over which one has less than complete control. The Type A person is unable to accept this and employs Type A behavior in a constant attempt to assert control. The Type A person is like a juggler who has too many balls in the air at one time but cannot allow himself to let go of even one of them.

Not all studies find a relationship between the Type A behavior pattern and CHD. This suggests that the concept of Type A behavior needs to be further refined. In particular, some researchers report that hostility is a particularly deleterious component of the Type A behavior pattern: people who have Type A traits but lack hostility may not be particularly at risk. On the other hand, people who have a distrustful and cynical attitude toward others and who are therefore likely to become hostile and angry when stressed have been shown to be more than normally susceptible to CHD and heart attacks (Carver, Diamond, & Humphries, 1985; Houston & Vavak, 1991). For example, a study conducted in Finland found that middle-aged men with CHD *and* high levels of hostility were more likely to die of a heart attack than men with CHD and low levels of hostility. In this study, 316 men with CHD were asked via a questionnaire whether they tended to be irritable, easily angered, or argumentative. The sample was then divided into four groups defined by increasing levels of hostility. Three years later, 34 of the 316 men had died of a heart attack. In this group of 34, the men with the highest level of hostility were more than twice as likely to have died than men with the lowest level of hostility (Koskenvuo, Kaprio, Rose, Kesaniemi, Sarna, Heikkila, & Langinvainio, 1988).

Interim Summary

The field of health psychology is concerned with the role of psychological factors in health and illness. Health psychology attempts to identify factors responsible for health and illness, to promote healthy behavior, and to prevent and treat illness when it occurs.

Today's leading causes of death are strongly influenced by unhealthy behavior patterns. Modifying these causes of death requires psychological and behavioral interventions to help people pursue health-promoting behavior in their daily lives.

A major factor in the development of illness is psychological stress. Though stress alone does not cause illness, it does appear to lower resistance to many different illnesses.

Many stressful life events are known to have harmful health consequences. The Social Readjustment Rating Scale (SRRS) is a device for ranking and measuring 43 major life events that are frequently identified as stressful. However, to predict the stress potential of any event, it is necessary to take into account the individual's appraisal of the event as threatening. So-called hardy individuals, as well as those with an optimistic disposition, buffer stress by adopting positive appraisals of life events.

Stress disrupts homeostasis and induces changes in the body's cardiovascular, gastrointestinal, and endocrine systems. In addition, stress appears to reduce the ability of the immune system to protect against disease-causing agents.

The psychosomatic specificity hypothesis states that people who share similar ways of coping with stress will also be likely to develop similar illnesses. Although this hypothesis has never been confirmed in a general way, it is supported by the relationship between the Type A behavior pattern and coronary heart disease (CHD). In particular, people who show the Type A trait of becoming excessively angry and hostile when stressed are at higher than normal risk of developing CHD.

The more we learn about stress, its effects on the body, and more effective ways of managing stress, the greater will be our ability to treat illness when it occurs.

●●●●●●●●●●●●●●●●●●●●●●●●●●●●●

A CLOSER LOOK AT STRESS

Although impaired health can be a significant outcome of stress, illness is not the only way in which stress exerts a disruptive influence over our lives. At this point we want to take a closer look at the nature of stress and its effects on

both our minds and bodies. To begin to understand how stress affects our everyday lives, consider the following vignette:

You are a high-school senior. You have wanted to attend college since you were a child. For many years you have worked hard in school to maintain a record that will allow you to attend a college of your choice. But today you must take the Scholastic Aptitude Test, an examination used by many colleges to screen applicants. You know that if you do poorly, you are unlikely to be admitted, despite your commitment and good grade-point average. The problem is that you are not a good test taker and you have never done very well on standardized tests. Your hopes for the future are riding on the outcome of today's exam.

Last night at dinner you were preoccupied with thoughts about the test and hardly said a word. After dinner you tried to relax but found it difficult to concentrate. Even though you were tired, you had trouble falling asleep. You slept poorly and woke several times following vaguely troubling dreams. At breakfast your stomach was in knots.

As you walk to the exam room, your breath is short, your hands feel clammy and cold, and your heart begins to pound against your chest. You feel anxious and

A stress reaction to taking an exam might include anxiety, poor concentration, shortness of breath, cold and clammy hands, or heart palpitations.

panicky. Now, waiting for the exam to begin, you try to focus on the subjects you have studied. But all that comes to mind are thoughts of failing the exam and ruining your life. The monitor hands out the exam, and . . .

If this example is even somewhat familiar to you, you already have an intuitive understanding of stress. In this example of a student undergoing examination stress we can identify three separate components that together make up what we mean by stress. The first component is the examination situation itself, or the **stressful event.** A stressful event is, simply, any situation that the individual perceives as threatening. Thus, a critical determinant of stress is the individual's perception or **appraisal** of an event. An event will be appraised as threatening if it challenges important personal goals and taxes one's ability to cope. In this case, the student appraised the examination as a threat to the goal of attending college. Appraisals of threat thus constitute a second component of stress. The third component of stress is the **stress reaction.** In the above example, the stress reaction includes the disruptive emotion of anxiety, cognitive disruptions such as poor concentration and impaired thinking, and signs of physiological disruption such as shortness of breath, cold and clammy hands, and heart palpitations.

We are now in a position to combine these three components—stressful events, appraisals, and stress reactions—into a comprehensive definition: *Stress is a pattern of disruptive psychological and physiological functioning that occurs when an environmental event is appraised as a threat to important goals and taxes one's ability to cope.* Let us examine each of these three components of stress in greater detail.

Stressful Events

As we have noted, almost any event can be stressful if the individual appraises it as threatening. Thus it is not possible to specify in advance every situation that people may find stressful. What we can do, however, is survey individuals to discover events that the average person is likely to find stressful. We have seen one example of this approach in the *Social Readjustment Rating Scale* (Table 15.1). The SRRS consists of major life changes that have been linked to subsequent illness. Note, however, that the SRRS consists of many events that occur relatively infrequently in any one person's life, such as death of a spouse, retirement, or change in occupation. Thus, the SRRS is far from an exhaustive list of stressful events. A complete picture must also take into account two other sources of stress: minor daily frustrations and long-term, or chronic, stressful situations.

For example, day in and day out frustrations, which have been dubbed **"daily hassles,"** constitute a source of stress over and above the relatively infrequent crises that make up the SRRS. Examples of such hassles include annoying practical problems like misplacing belongings—books, keys, etc.—as well as minor disappointments, arguments, or money worries. **Table 15.2** lists what people report as their ten most frequent daily hassles (Kanner, Coyne, Schaefer, & Lazarus, 1981).

In contrast to daily hassles, **chronic sources of stress** include ongoing life difficulties such as low income, poor housing, strains in a relationship, unsatisfying work, or inadequate child care. In sum, the total amount of stress experienced by an individual is made up of daily hassles, chronically stressful situations, and SRRS-type life changes (De Longis, Coyne, Dakof, Folkman, & Lazarus, 1982; Eckenrode, 1984).

Rather than simply calculate stress as the total of daily hassles, chronic sources of stress, and major life changes, it is often more fruitful to ask: "What is it about these situations that renders them stressful?" Specifying the characteristics of stressful events allows us to predict in advance if any given situation has the poten-

Table 15.2   The 10 Most Frequent Daily Hassles

1. Concerns about weight
2. Health of a family member
3. Rising prices of common goods
4. Home maintenance
5. Too many things to do
6. Misplacing or losing things
7. Yard work or outside home maintenance
8. Property, investment, or taxes
9. Crime
10. Physical appearance

After Kanner, Coyne, Schaeffer, & Lazarus (1981)

tial to produce stress. Let us turn to three important characteristics of stressful events: helplessness, overload, and conflict.

HELPLESSNESS

Most people prefer to have control over the events in their lives, even when these events are unpleasant. **Helplessness** occurs when unpleasant events happen regardless of anything we do or do not do, that is, independently of our ability to control them. As we saw in Chapter 6, experience with uncontrollable negative events produces a phenomenon known as *learned helplessness,* which is a generalized expectation that events are independent of our control.

Uncontrollable events are highly stressful. For example, one study investigated the effects of uncontrollable aversive stimuli on the development of stomach ulcers in rats. Three conditions were compared (see **Figure 15.7**). In one condition the animals were able to control the onset and duration of a series of electric shocks. In the second condition the animals were helpless to control the shocks. However, both groups received the same number of shocks. A third group received no shocks. At the end of the experiment, the helpless animals

In one study, nursing home residents who were given more control over their lives were found to be more alert and active, and showed greater improvements in health than a control group.

showed more weight loss and a higher frequency of stomach ulcers than animals in the other two groups. Because the first group received the same number of shocks as the helpless group, the physiological changes must have been due to uncontrollability, not the experi-

Figure 15.7
Helplessness Training Procedure.
Rats are randomly assigned to one of three conditions: escapable shock, inescapable shock, and no shock. The escapable shock animal (left) can terminate programmed shocks to the tail by turning the wheel. The inescapable shock animal (center) is wired in series to the first animal. When the first animal receives a shock, the animal in the center is unable to control the wheel. The animal on the right is placed in the cage and hooked up but does not receive shocks at any time. (From "Psychological Factors in Stress and Disease" by Jay M. Weiss, SCIENTIFIC AMERICAN, June 1972. Copyright © 1972 by Scientific American, Inc. Reprinted with permission. All rights reserved.)

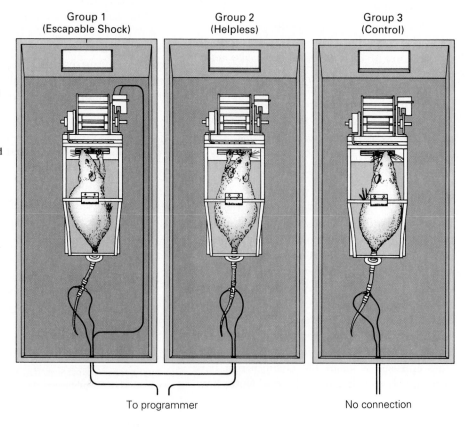

ence of shock itself (Weiss, 1972). Other animal studies using the same experimental technique have shown that helplessness also suppresses the ability of the immune system to produce lymphocytes in response to antigens (Laudenslager et al., 1983). Studies like these show that uncontrollable negative events are intensely stressful as well as damaging to health.

Psychologists Ellen Langer and Judith Rodin discovered equally profound effects of helplessness in elderly nursing home residents. One reason that elderly people sometimes resist living in nursing homes is that they fear losing their ability to exert control over their lives because the staff tends to take complete responsibility for them. In the Langer-Rodin study, a group of nursing home residents was encouraged to make choices about the details of their living arrangements and to exert control over day-to-day events in their lives. A second group, called the "attention" group, was encouraged to believe the staff would look after them and care for their needs. The group encouraged to exert control over their lives was found to be more alert and active and also showed greater improvements in health than the "attention" group. A dramatic finding was that the simple method of giving residents more control led to a reduced death rate. A death rate of 25 percent was recorded in the 18 months before the study began. The death rate in the 18 months following the study was 15 percent for the group given greater control and 30 percent for the "attention" group. These results suggest that the psychological and physical decline observed in many elderly people may have as much to do with their sense of control over their lives as with the aging process (Langer & Rodin, 1976; Rodin & Langer, 1977).

The stressful impact of uncontrollable events can even be lessened if we merely believe we have control. In a study of this phenomenon, subjects in one group were exposed to loud noise and told they could stop the noise by pressing a button. However, the experimenters urged the subjects *not* to press the botton. Subjects in a second group were exposed to the same noise but had no control button to press. Even though subjects in the first group never pressed the button, they showed less evidence of stress than subjects in the second group, who lacked the option of control (Glass & Singer, 1972). A belief in our ability to control what happens to us may be as important as actually exercising that control.

OVERLOAD

Overload occurs when an event becomes so intense that we can no longer adapt to it. People can adapt to a wide range of intensities of physical stimuli such as heat, cold, and noise. Yet there are limits to adaptability, and we therefore experience stress when these limits are exceeded. For example, in many laboratory studies the "cold-pressor test" is used to assess stress reactions. The subject is asked to immerse an arm or foot in a tank of water maintained to just above the freezing point. In only a matter of seconds the subject begins to show overload in the form of pain and physiological reactions such as increased heart rate and blood pressure.

Another form of overload is work overload, a particular problem among employees and some students. Work overload takes two different forms. One form occurs when there are too many things to do in too little time. (For the Type A person, this is a chronic source of stress.) A second form occurs when performance standards are so high that the work cannot be satisfactorily completed, regardless of the time allowed (Ivancevich & Matteson, 1980). Surveys show that one-third to one-fourth of workers see their work as often stressful; work overload is major source of such reports (Sauter, Murphy, & Hurrell, 1990).

Time pressure can be a major cause of stress.

Time pressure is the psychological experience of work overload. Time pressure is the appraisal that not enough time is available to complete one's work in a satisfactory manner. The major symptom of time pressure is constant worry over deadlines. Time pressure is especially severe in occupations such as newspaper or textbook publishing, where deadlines are constant. But much time pressure is self-imposed and so can occur in any occupation. Some people are never quite satisfied with the quality of their work and thus have difficulty bringing a project to a conclusion. Others are "workaholics," who constantly take on more and more projects and thus create for themselves both work overload and time pressure. Still others have a poor sense of priorities. They may waste time on unimportant tasks and then find they have run out of time to do the important ones. In sum, time pressure is a psychological phenomenon that is based partly on objective work overload and partly on the individual personality.

CONFLICT

Conflict occurs when environmental stimuli arouse two or more incompatible response tendencies, or motives. Conflict situations require the person to make choices among alternative courses of action in which some motives will be satisfied but others will be frustrated. Psychologists distinguish among several different forms of conflict, including *approach-approach conflict, avoidance-avoidance conflict,* and *approach-avoidance conflict* (Lewin, 1946; Miller, 1951).

The simplest kind of conflict is approach-approach conflict. In such a conflict, the person is pulled toward two desirable goals or behaviors. One goal can be obtained only by giving up the other. For example, a little boy in a candy store whose grandmother tells him he can have a vanilla or a chocolate ice-cream cone, but not both, is in an approach-approach conflict. Either course of action is satisfying, but something must be given up.

A second kind of conflict involves the opposite situation. This is an avoidance-avoidance conflict, in which the person must choose between two undesirable alternatives. A woman who has fallen in love with a man of a different religion may have to choose between terminating the relationship or telling her parents about it. Both of these courses of action are threatening.

A third type of conflict involves only one goal or course of action. This is an approach-avoidance conflict, in which the person is both drawn to and repelled by a goal or course of action. For example, a child flying in an airplane for the first time may be very eager and excited to board the plane but may also be frightened by the noisy jet engines.

Fenz and Epstein (1967) studied sport parachuting as an approach-avoidance conflict. In sport parachuting, the actual jump is approached because of the anticipated thrill and avoided because of the threat of injury. Fenz and Epstein predicted that physiological signs of stress would increase as the actual jump grew closer in time. They tested this hypothesis by recording parachutists' heart rates at a series of points leading up to and following a jump. They divided their subjects into novice and experienced parachutists, with the hypothesis that experience in jumping would reduce conflict-induced stress reactions. **Figure 15.8** shows that both hypotheses were confirmed: novice parachutists showed increasing heart rates between arriving at the airport and the jump, while experienced parachutists showed an initial heart rate increase that then remained steady to the time of the jump.

In brief, knowing the characteristics of stressful situations allows us to predict the kinds of events people will find stressful. In addition, stress reactions can often be reduced or eliminated by reducing or eliminating helpless-

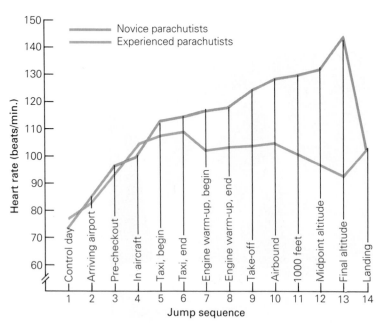

Figure 15.8
Stress in Sport Parachutists. (After Fenz & Epstein, 1967)

ness, overload, and conflict. Still, we should recognize that not all people find the same events equally stressful. For example, a course assignment may constitute work overload for one student, but another student will experience no difficulty with the task. People also differ in their ability to tolerate conflict and uncontrollability. Thus we need to take individual appraisals into account to know whether a given event will produce a stress response.

Appraisals

Appraisal refers to the cognitive process by which the individual perceives situations as either benign or threatening. Richard Lazarus of the University of California, a leading stress researcher who has written extensively on this aspect of stress, divides appraisals into *primary appraisals* and *secondary appraisals*. A primary appraisal of stress occurs when the individual perceives a threat to his or her well-being, that is, when events threaten the attainment of important goals. Secondary appraisals, according to Lazarus, are judgments concerning what can be done to meet the challenge posed by the stressful event. Secondary appraisals include evaluations of available *coping resources* and the likelihood that they can be effectively employed. In other words, stress will depend on two factors: (1) perceptions of threat and (2) judgments of the adequacy of coping resources (Lazarus, 1991; Lazarus & Folkman, 1984).

PRIMARY APPRAISAL

A pioneering study of students preparing for a medical school admission exam illustrates the role of perceived threat in determining the stressfulness of events. The investigator compared the levels of stomach acidity (an index of stress) in eight students immediately before the exam with acidity levels during a less stressful period. As you would expect, stomach acidity was greatly elevated in the group as a whole just before the exam. However, two of the eight students actually showed slightly lower levels of stomach acidity before the exam. It turned out that one of the two had already been admitted to medical school and the other had little interest in going in the first place. In other words, the exam did not pose a threat to these students' personal goals, was not appraised as stressful, and thus did not affect levels of stomach acidity (Mahl, 1949).

A second example of the stress-determining role of primary appraisals comes from an experiment by Lazarus and his colleagues. Subjects were assigned to different appraisal conditions while their physiological reaction to a stressful event was monitored. The stressful event was an industrial safety film that depicted gruesome accidents arising from carelessness at work, such as the loss of a finger in a machine. Before watching the film, subjects were divided into three appraisal groups: a denial group, an intellectualization group, and a control group. Subjects in the *denial* group were told that the people in the film were really actors and that nobody was actually injured. These subjects were therefore encouraged to deny the reality of the events depicted in the film. Subjects in the *intellectualization* group were asked to take an analytical approach to the film and to examine it in terms of the success of its cinematic techniques in promoting industrial safety. This group was therefore encouraged to block out the emotional impact of the events depicted. Finally, subjects in the *control* group were given no specific instructions and therefore provided a baseline for the stressfulness of the film. The measure of stress in this study was electrodermal (sweat gland) activity of the hands, which reflects arousal of the sympathetic nervous system. **Figure 15.9** shows the aver-

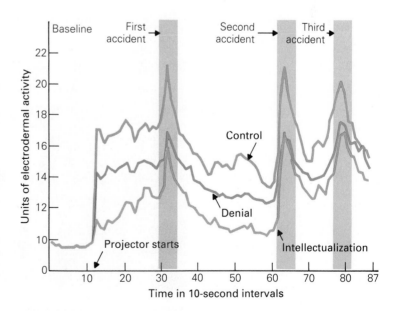

Figure 15.9
Effects of Denial and Intellectualization on Electrodermal Activity. (After Lazarus et al., 1965)

age electrodermal activity levels in the three groups while watching the film. As you can see, both the denial and the intellectualization groups showed less physiological arousal than the control group. These results show that appraisals that distort the full significance of stressful events can correspondingly reduce the ability of such events to produce stress reactions (Lazarus, Opton, Nomikos, & Rankin, 1965).

SECONDARY APPRAISAL

This form of appraisal refers to an individual's judgment of the adequacy of the coping resources he or she brings to a situation. Coping involves a wide variety of potential strategies, skills, and abilities for acting on the environment and for managing disruptive emotional, cognitive, and physiological reactions to stressful events. Stress will be high when the person judges that there is a disparity between coping resources and environmental events; stress will be reduced to the extent that coping resources more closely match environmental events.

For example, most people would probably conclude that being placed in a capsule on top of a rocket and shot into space is highly stressful. Yet intense assessments of the astronauts in the Mercury space program of the 1960s revealed almost no evidence of stress reactions during the flights. Because of a combination of their professional flying background and their intense training, the astronauts' coping skills were equal to the demands of space flight. The astronauts were also intelligent, self-confident, and persevering people. Their approach to difficult situations was to pause, assess the situation, decide on a course of action, and then follow through (Cox, 1978; Wolfe, 1979).

Lazarus' theory of primary and secondary appraisals suggests that both are necessary conditions for experiencing an event as stressful. This means that it is possible for an individual to appraise an event as threatening but to be so confident in his or her coping resources that little or no stress is actually experienced. This may account for the coolness of the Mercury astronauts in an objectively difficult situation. The opposite may also be true. A person may have no particular coping skills in a given situation but not perceive the situation as threatening and therefore experience little stress. For example, a person who is relatively unskilled in a given sport but who is not threatened by losing is free to enjoy the activity regardless of ability. Only when a primary appraisal of threat is matched by a secondary appraisal of inadequate coping resources will stress be experienced. Later in this chapter we discuss in more detail some methods of effective coping under stressful circumstances.

Assessments of astronauts revealed almost no evidence of stress reactions during space flights. Effective training contributed to their excellent coping skills.

Stress Reactions

As we have seen, appraisal processes interact with situations to produce stress reactions. Stress reactions are the disruptive effects of stressful events on psychological and physiological functioning. We shall see that there are many ways in which stress disrupts emotional, cognitive, and physiological activity. Although we describe stress reactions as occurring on three distinct levels, you should realize that stress produces a variety of simultaneously occurring *psychological* and *physiological* changes.

EMOTIONAL DISRUPTION

When people are asked how they feel when under stress, they usually respond with terms like *anxious, irritable, angry, depressed*, or *guilty*. Some people experience only one of these emotions, while others experience mixed emotions, either simultaneously or in succession. Stress emotions are unpleasant or *negative* emotions, as opposed to positive emotions such as joy, happiness, and love.

The most common of the stress emotions are anxiety and depression. The anxious person is worried, apprehensive, and fearful. The depressed person feels blue, worthless, fatigued, and pessimistic. One study found that people who had recently experienced a stressful event, such as the death of a spouse or a severe accident, showed a high frequency of anxiety and depression. **Table 15.3** lists the various symptoms used to identify these two emotions and the percentage of subjects showing each symptom (Horowitz, Wilner, Kaltreider, & Alvarez, 1980).

Anxiety is usually experienced in *anticipation* of a stressful encounter. Waiting to give a talk, take an exam, or engage in athletic competition are all examples of anxiety-provoking situations. In contrast, depression usually occurs after stressful changes in our lives (Costello, 1976). Breaking up a relationship, death in the family, or severe illness are examples of depression-provoking situations. Many stressful events, such as moving or going away to college, involve a combination of anticipation and loss, and so mixed feelings of anxiety and depression are not uncommon.

Anxiety and depression disrupt people's lives, but they are also informative. By attending to these feelings as they occur, the individual can begin to identify the stressful events that provoke them and then take steps to correct

Table 15.3   Percentage of Subjects Showing Symptoms of Depression and Anxiety Following Severe Life Stress

Symptom	Percentage
Depression	
Feeling blue	97
Worrying too much about things	97
Feeling lonely	92
Feeling low in energy or slowed down	91
Blaming yourself for things	89
Crying easily	84
Feeling everything is an effort	81
Feeling no interest in things	78
Feeling hopeless about the future	75
Feelings of worthlessness	72
Loss of sexual interest or pleasure	66
Feeling of being trapped or caught	62
Thoughts of ending your life	45
Anxiety	
Feeling tense or keyed-up	95
Nervousness or shakiness inside	94
Feeling fearful	75
Feeling so restless you couldn't sit still	72
Feeling pushed to get things done	70
Heart pounding or racing	67
Trembling	66
Suddenly scared for no reason	56
Spells of terror and panic	48
Feeling that familiar things are strange or unreal	36

After Horowitz, Wilner, Kaltreidr, & Alvarez (1980)

Anxiety is usually experienced in anticipation of a stressful encounter.

Table 15.4   Physiological Symptoms of Stress

Headaches	Loss of sexual functioning
Constipation	Excessive urination
Loose bowel movements	Cold hands or feet
Faintness or dizziness	Blushing
Hot flashes	Twitches, tics, spasms
Voice quavering or shaking	Lump in throat
Dry mouth	Grinding of teeth
Tightness in jaw	Lower back pain
Soreness of muscle	Heart racing
Weakness in parts of the body	Tightness in stomach
Pains in heart or chest	Nausea or upset stomach
Sweaty palms	Trouble getting your breath
Shakiness	Fatigue

After Fuller (1977)

the situation. These feelings are signals that important needs are not being met and that one's ability to cope is being taxed. Recognizing these feelings and identifying their underlying sources are often the first steps in devising methods to cope with stress (Costello, 1976).

COGNITIVE DISRUPTION

Cognitive functioning is a second category of psychological activity that is disrupted under stress. This disruption is seen in many specific cognitive functions, such as thinking, concentration, and memory.

Under stress our ability to organize our thoughts in a logical and coherent way is impaired. Thinking tends to be dominated by worries about the consequences of our actions and by negative self-evaluations. For example, students who are especially prone to examination anxiety tend to worry about possible failure and their own inadequacies. This in turn interferes with clear thinking during the exam (Spielberger, 1979). Psychologists often use the term *obsessive* to describe this kind of thinking. Obsessive thinking means that repetitive thought sequences emerge involuntarily into consciousness.

The ability to concentrate on specific stimuli while ignoring other stimuli not related to the task at hand is lessened under stress. The person is distracted, both by obsessive thoughts and by external stimuli. It is as if the person were continually on guard for any sign of danger. As stress mounts, the person becomes "jumpy" and overreactive. Poor concentration impairs the individual's performance and coping ability.

Finally, people under stress are often confused and forgetful. As one person who lost his home in a flood reported:

To me it seems like I can remember but three hours later I don't remember what happened.... I go places, I don't even know where in hell I'm at, you know. I have to sit down and think, "What the hell am I doing down here, where am I at?" (K. Erikson, 1976, p. 213)

In summary, stress can disrupt a variety of cognitive functions. This means that problem solving, which often requires a combination of flexible thinking, good concentration, and intact memory will be significantly affected by stress. Indeed, both clinical and research psychologists often use impaired problem-solving ability as an indicator of stress.

PHYSIOLOGICAL DISRUPTION

Just as emotional stability and cognitive functioning are disrupted by stress, so too is the body's normal homeostatic balance. People under stress experience a variety of symptoms of disrupted physiological functioning. Examples of some of the physiological symptoms that can occur with stress are listed in **Table 15.4.**

The physiological bases of the symptoms in Table 15.4 are well understood. We owe this understanding to work initiated by Walter B. Cannon, the founder of homeostasis, and by Hans Selye, a Canadian endocrinologist. Cannon's studies of stress date back to the early part of the twentieth century; Selye's work began about a generation later, in the 1930s.

Cannon's "Fight or Flight" Response. Look again at Table 15.4. Notice that the symptoms fall into two major groups. The first group consists of symptoms of muscle tension, such as shakiness, soreness, and tightness of muscles. The second group consists of symptoms that reflect excessive arousal of internal organs and glands, such as dry mouth, sweaty palms, cold hands, racing heart, and upset stomach. Both groups of symptoms tell us that the body is in a highly activated state and is expending a large amount of energy. This is striking, because coping with stressful events does not usually require strenuous physical activity and energy expenditure. For example, taking an examination or adjusting to a breakup of a relationship requires psychological coping efforts but no great expenditure of energy. How can we explain the presence of physiological activation under stress even when overt physical activity is not called for?

Cannon explored this problem as part of his investigations of homeostasis and its disruption. He was interested in physiological changes that occur when an animal's survival is at stake. In a classic experiment, Cannon studied the reaction of cats when suddenly confronted by a threatening dog. Cannon observed that blood circulated more rapidly through the body, muscular tension increased, breathing became more rapid, and unnecessary digestive activity slowed or ceased. Cannon also discovered that adrenaline was released into the bloodstream to support these physiological adjustments (Cannon, 1929).

Cannon noted that each of these changes was adaptive in preparing the animal for intense activity aimed at survival. He called the entire reaction the **"fight or flight" response** because it prepared the animal for the behaviors of either attacking or fleeing the source of threat. The central notion is that the body's physiological resources are mobilized for vigorous physical activity to deal with threats to survival.

We understand today, however, that threats to survival are not the only cause of this reaction. As we have seen, any threat to personally important motives that taxes coping abilities is sufficient to trigger this reaction. In other words, a response pattern that probably originated to help ensure survival has been carried over as part of our reaction to many different kinds of stressful events—even those to which "fight or flight" is neither an appropriate nor a possible response. Thus our bodies become mobilized without the possibility of subsequent vigorous action, like a parked car with a racing engine. If sustained for long periods, this mobilization can lead to symptoms such as those listed in Table 15.4.

Cannon was the first to clearly demonstrate that stress affects the body. Cannon did this in a series of short-term, or acute, experiments in which animals' survival was abruptly threatened. Cannon's experiments, however, did not explicitly link stress to subsequent illness. It was Hans Selye who, a generation af-

ter Cannon, convincingly demonstrated that long-term, or chronic, stress could damage body tissue, producing disease and even death.

Selye's General Adaptation Syndrome. Selye's experimental method was to expose animals to long periods of continued stress, such as physical exertion, hot or cold environments, or injections of toxic substances. Selye found that chronic exposure to such situations severely taxed animals' ability to adapt, leading eventually to observable changes in internal organs. Specifically, he found that chronic stress routinely produced (1) enlargement of the adrenal glands, (2) stomach ulcers, and (3) atrophy (shrinking) of the lymph glands (Selye, 1956). Whereas Cannon had shown that acute stress produced changes in the *functioning* of internal organs, Selye showed that chronic stress produced changes in the *structure* of these organs.

Selye believed that the body's ability to resist stressful situations was limited. He called the ability to resist stress "adaptation energy." As adaptation energy is expended in resisting stress, exhaustion and then death may ensue. Selye's concept of the **general adaptation syndrome (GAS)** describes three stages in the body's resistance to chronic stress: an alarm stage, a stage of resistance, and a stage of exhaustion. The *alarm stage* occurs when a stressful event is first encountered. This stage corresponds to Cannon's "fight or flight" response and is marked by a rapid mobilization of physiological resources to help deal with the stressful event. No organism can maintain itself for long in this activated stage of alarm. What happens, then, if exposure to the stressor continues? According to Selye, the organism passes into a second stage, the *stage of resistance.* In this stage the body returns to normal levels of activity and resistance rises. In other words, the organism has learned to adapt to the stressful event. With still further exposure, this ability to adapt is lost. The loss of adaptation energy is known as the *exhaustion stage.* Here, the organism's resistance to the stressful event gradually declines and illness or death ensue (see **Figure 15.10** on page 554).

The GAS was developed to describe the physiological changes produced in experimental animals by various forms of stress. But Selye suggested that the GAS also describes the psychological response to any prolonged stressful

Hans Selye
(1907–1982)

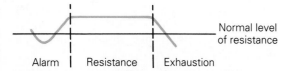

Figure 15.10
The General Adaptation Syndrome.
Initially, a stressful event causes a stage of alarm and
mobilization, and resistance drops below normal. If stress
continues to be present, resistance rises well above normal
until eventually exhaustion sets in and resistance falls
below normal again. (After Selye, 1973)

experience. Consider, for example, our own response to most strenuous tasks. At first the experience is a hardship that requires much psychological energy. A period of adaptation then
occurs as we learn to manage the task and resist the stress. Finally, we lose our ability to tolerate the burden and become exhausted by its
continued demands (Selye, 1973).

POST-TRAUMATIC STRESS DISORDER
Sometimes people in intensely stressful situations show few signs of stress, only to experience a prolonged stress reaction after the event
has passed. A **post-traumatic stress disorder
(PTSD)** is a disabling reaction to stress that first
makes its appearance following a traumatic
event. By traumatic event we mean a highly
stressful situation that is outside the normal
range of human experience. A stressful event
becomes traumatic when it poses a severe
threat to basic needs, including the individual's
very survival, and when the victim has little or
no control over the event.

The major symptoms of PTSD represent a
fluctuation between two distinct psychological
states. In the first, the person involuntarily re-
experiences the traumatic event in the form of
disturbing flashbacks and nightmares. This
state alternates with periods of "emotional
numbing," in which the person is unresponsive, withdrawn, and depressed. This second
state can be seen as an attempt to avoid and deny the emotionally charged, involuntary memories of the first state. A third kind of symptom
is a general hyperalertness and jumpiness, in
which the person is easily startled, especially by
sights and sounds reminiscent of the traumatic
event. These three types of symptoms can be
seen in the following case vignette:

The patient is a Vietnam veteran seen in
the late 1970s, ten years after combat

duty. During his year in the army his platoon was repeatedly ambushed, and in
one of those ambushes his closest friend
was killed while he stood a few feet
away.... He admits that his mind keeps
returning to these events, and he still has
nightmares about them, but he insists he
does not want to talk about any of that.
He is constantly anxious and agitated, and
he jumps at the sound of a firecracker or
backfiring automobile.... He says he feels
constantly bored and depressed and is
'only going through the motions' at work
and at home. (Harvard Mental Health
Letter, 1991)

PTSD often occurs after natural disasters
such as hurricanes and earthquakes or after hu-
man-made disasters such as fires, airplane
crashes, and explosions. Studies of disasters
have shown that only a small percentage of
people experience stress reactions during the
immediate impact of the event. However, a delayed PTSD may then occur after the immediate threat has passed. For example, a follow-up
study two years after a flood devastated a West
Virginia community found that every survivor
had experienced a more or less severe form of
PTSD (K. Erikson, 1976).

PTSD is also frequently observed among
rape victims, prisoners of war, and hostages
held by terrorists. One group among whom
PTSD is particularly frequent are veterans of
the Vietnam conflict. According to a U.S.
Veterans Administration study, 15 percent of
males and 9 percent of females who served in
Vietnam are victims of PTSD. Veterans who experienced the heaviest combat or were exposed to other traumatic events such as wit-
nessing atrocities or losing comrades are three
to five times more likely to have PTSD than veterans exposed to less tramatic events (Roberts,
1988).

Both Vietnam veterans and others suffering from PTSD can benefit from professional
help. Psychotherapy to help the person come
to grips with the traumatic event and drug
therapy to relieve physiological arousal are often employed. Group therapy, in which victims
of PTSD can share their experiences and gain
support from others, is especially helpful. In
general, the sooner the victim of PTSD receives
treatment, the greater are the chances of complete recovery.

Delayed stress reactions are frequently observed among rape victims as well as victims of natural disasters, prisoners of war, and hostages taken in terrorist incidents.

Interim Summary

Stress is a pattern of disruptive psychological and physiological functioning that occurs when an environmental event is appraised as a threat to important personal goals and to one's ability to cope.

Any event that the person appraises as threatening can be stressful. In most cases people will be stressed by events that produce helplessness, overload, or conflict.

Appraisal refers to the cognitive process by which the individual perceives situations as benign or threatening. Primary appraisal of stress involves the individual's perception of an event as a threat to well-being. Secondary appraisal refers to the individual's judgment of the adequacy of personal coping resources.

Stress reactions are the disruptive effects of stressful events on psychological and physiological functioning. Stress pro-

duces negative emotions such as anxiety and depression, impairs cognitive functioning, and disrupts physiological functioning.

One model of disturbed physiological functioning is Cannon's fight or flight response, which describes the reaction to acute and immediate threats. Another model is Selye's general adaptation syndrome (GAS), which is concerned with the effects of long-term, chronic stress.

A post-traumatic stress disorder (PTSD) is a chronic stress reaction that occurs following psychological trauma. Traumatic events such as natural disasters, rape, or military combat pose severe threats to well-being and are essentially uncontrollable. The symptoms of PTSD fluctuate between periods of reliving the trauma and periods of emotional numbing. Vietnam veterans and other victims of PTSD can be helped by psychological and medical treatment.

METHODS OF COPING WITH STRESS

We have seen that stressful events produce negative emotions, impaired cognitive functioning, and a general mobilization of bodily response systems. We should not assume, however, that people are passive victims of these unpleasant stress reactions. Indeed, the experience of stress can motivate people to reassert control over themselves and their environment. **Coping methods** are the strategies people use to control stressful events or their reactions to them.

Coping methods fall into two broad categories (Lazarus,1991). The first includes methods that alter an individual's reactions to stressful events. These are known as *emotion-focused* methods because they deal with an individual's reactions to stressful events rather than with the events themselves. The three emotion-focused methods we will discuss are defense mechanisms, reappraisal of the situation, and arousal reduction. The second broad category consists of *problem-focused* methods that aim to change the stressful event through direct action or problem-solving activities. In this second category we will discuss the two methods of anticipatory coping and seeking social support.

Defense Mechanisms

As we saw in Chapter 14, the concept of **defense mechanisms** is a central feature of psychoanalytic theory. Freud saw defense mechanisms as a means of warding off anxiety and other negative feelings caused by the threat of unacceptable sexual and aggressive drives. Today most psychologists view defense mechanisms as psychological maneuvers for coping with both internal and external events that threaten the individual's well-being. People under stress do not consciously "choose" a particular defense mechanism. Rather, defense mechanisms are usually unconscious and automatic methods of reducing stress when the situation does not allow for more direct coping methods. Any and all of the defense mechanisms discussed in Chapter 14 may be employed by people under stress. Perhaps the two most frequently cited by stress researchers are *denial* and *intellectualization.*

Denial is a reality-distorting defense because it blocks the ability to perceive accurately, and thus to act on, external threats. Denial is seen in the patient dying of cancer who makes plans for a retirement home or in the person living in the path of a hurricane who fails to heed evacuation warnings.

In intellectualization, perception is not distorted, but the emotional arousal that normally accompanies stress is blocked from conscious awareness. What remains is a calm and detached approach to the stressful situation. The following example is from a civilian survivor of a wartime bombing attack:

> After a while [the corpses] became just like objects or goods that we handled in a very businesslike way.... We had no emotions.... Because of the succession of experiences I had been through, I was temporarily without feeling. (Lifton, 1967, p. 31)

Defense mechanisms reduce stress by distorting feelings and/or perceptions of external reality. They change the person, not the stressful situation. Most psychologists regard excessive use of defense mechanisms as a sign of psychological disturbance. For example, the woman who denies a lump in her breast and avoids seeing a physician may be putting her life in jeopardy.

On the other hand, in certain situations defense mechanisms provide the only means of coping. When a severe crisis such as a natural disaster or the death of a loved one occurs, defense mechanisms can often help the person get through the early period of intense threat. As the threat recedes, the individual can slowly adjust to the reality of the situation and can cope in more direct ways. In addition, recent research has shown that "positive illusions" can be surprisingly beneficial when a person is under stress. For example, people who are unrealistically optimistic or who exaggerate their degree of control over stressful events are likely to cope better than those who are doggedly realistic (Taylor & Brown, 1988).

Generally, defense mechanisms are not beneficial when they interfere with other methods of coping that can improve the situation. When nothing constructive can be done anyway, defense mechanisms can at least help the person feel better and attend to problems that can be dealt with (R. Lazarus, 1983).

Reappraising the Situation

We have noted that one condition for the occurrence of stress is the person's perception that the event threatens important needs or motives. If stress depends on the perception of events, it should be possible to reduce stress by modifying the perception of threat. This method of coping is known as reappraising the situation, or **cognitive reappraisal.** To reappraise means to reexamine one's initial perception of a situation. This method of coping thus relies on the ability to weigh evidence and to convert a negative appraisal into a positive one.

Methods of cognitive reappraisal are often used to help hospitalized patients deal with the stress of medical procedures (Turk, 1982). An example comes from a study involving surgical patients. Prior to the operation, a team of psychologists taught patients how to reduce stress. The psychologists first explained that it is rarely events themselves that cause stress but rather the views people take of them. Then they explained that no situation is either all positive or all negative and that people who cope effectively try to look at the positive side. Finally, they encouraged the patients to consider the positive aspects of undergoing surgery, such as improved health, the extra care and attention that goes along with being hospitalized, and the rare opportunity to relax, take stock of

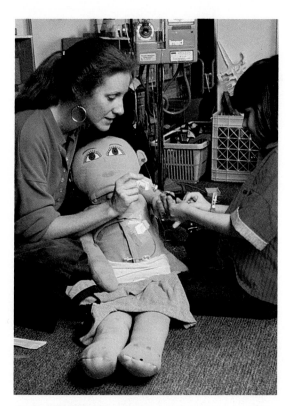

This psychologist is helping a child cope with the stress of illness and hospitalization by using a doll to explain the procedures she will undergo.

themselves, and have a vacation from outside pressures. The patients were encouraged to re-hearse these positive aspects whenever they began to feel anxious about the upcoming surgery. This group was compared with a con-trol group on several measures of postoperative stress. The results showed that the reappraisal group requested pain-relieving medication about one third as often as the control group and also tended to leave the hospital sooner. These results suggest that reappraising the situ-ation not only reduces stress but also helps medical patients cope with physical pain and speeds their recovery (Langer, Janis, & Wolfer, 1975).

Reappraising the situation is an effective coping method for several reasons. First of all, focusing on positive aspects of life crises dis-tracts the person from dwelling on threatening negative aspects. Second, positive appraisal generates positive emotional states, which block negative emotions. And, finally, reap-praisal increases the person's sense of control in a threatening situation.

Arousal Reduction

We have seen that stress reactions are associat-ed with physiological arousal. Some symptoms of this arousal are muscular tension, headaches, a racing heart, stomach upset, and cold, clam-my palms. Arousal reduction can be defined as any voluntary method of directly inhibiting stress-induced physiological arousal and its as-sociated symptoms. Three such methods are taking sedative drugs, getting physical exercise, and relaxation training.

SEDATIVE DRUGS
As we saw in Chapter 5, the sedative drugs in-clude ethyl alcohol, the barbiturates, and the benzodiazepines. Each of these types of drug reduces physiological arousal and induces sleep more or less rapidly, depending on the particu-lar drug and dosage. There is no question that sedatives provide a quick and effective method of dampening stress-induced physiological arousal.

Although sedatives can often help in the short-term control of stress reactions, their use as a long-term coping method is questionable. In the first place, long-term use of sedatives of-ten leads to *substance abuse,* which produces an entirely new set of problems for the user. We will have more to say about substance abuse in Chapter 16. In the second place, in-gesting chemicals does not teach the person any skills for mastering stress. Indeed, overus-ing sedatives may encourage a passive accep-tance of stressful events and a passive approach to controlling one's stress reactions. For long-term control of stress reactions, sedatives are best replaced by more active coping methods.

PHYSICAL EXERCISE
Physical exercise is a highly effective technique for reducing stress. This statement is attested to by people who build regular exercise into their daily lives, as well as by controlled studies of the physiological and psychological benefits of exercise (Davidson & Schwartz, 1976). For ex-ample, McCann and Holmes (1984) studied the effects of aerobic exercise on feelings of de-pression in a group of mildly depressed college women. The subjects were assigned to one of three groups: (1) a group following an exercise program of dancing, jogging, and running; (2) a pseudotreatment group given relaxation in-structions but no direct training; and (3) a con-

Physical exercise is one very effective way to reduce stress.

trol group that received no treatment. At the end of 10 weeks, subjects in the aerobic exercise condition showed significantly greater reductions in feelings of depression than did subjects in the other two groups.

Given that exercise arouses the body, how can it be an effective method of dealing with stress-induced arousal? One answer is provided by Cannon's classic research: Stress-induced arousal has no adaptive function, while exercise-induced arousal supports vigorous musclar activity. In addition, the person who is exercising controls arousal levels by actively deciding when to be active and when to relax. The voluntary nature of exercise therefore provides a sense of mastery and self-control that is lacking in stress-induced arousal. Finally, regular, vigorous exercise actually produces a relaxed state following the exercise. This "rebound" relaxation may last for several hours, during which time it blocks any stress-induced arousal (Girdano & Everly, 1979). In sum, physical exercise is an adaptive form of arousal, it promotes a sense of self-control over arousal levels, and it produces a postexercise state of relaxation.

RELAXATION TRAINING

Relaxation training, sometimes known as deep relaxation, is a third form of tension reduction. Deep relaxation is one end of a continuum of physiological arousal that stretches from the highly aroused state of the stress reaction, through the quiet state of ordinary relaxation, to a state of extremely low arousal achieved by relaxation training. In deep relaxation, the skeletal muscles become loose and supple, and both the autonomic nervous system and the endocrine system are at low levels of activity. Deep relaxation is acquired through practice. After it is acquired, it can then be used as a method of controlling stress-induced arousal.

There are a number of techniques for learning deep relaxation. Two of these—*hypnosis* and *meditation*—have already been discussed in Chapter 5. In hypnosis, deep relaxation is achieved by direct suggestion and by the use of relaxing mental images, such as imagining one's self lying on a quiet beach. A person who has learned the appropriate suggestions and images from a hypnotist can then use the same methods for self-relaxation. In meditation, deep relaxation is produced by focusing attention on a mental image for several minutes. Continued practice with either hypnotic or meditative techniques often produces an altered state of consciousness in which the person feels temporarily disengaged from the immediate environment. Many people find this altered state of consciousness highly useful in combating stress-induced tension and fatigue (Benson 1975).

A third method of producing deep relaxation is through **progressive relaxation.** Progressive relaxation involves alternately tensing and relaxing each of the major muscles of the body. This method teaches the person to recognize the difference between tension and relaxation and to voluntarily produce a state of deep relaxation. The following exercise may help you appreciate the pleasant feelings produced by progressive relaxation.

While seated, place your right hand on your right knee and close your eyes. Make a fist with your right hand. Focus your attention on the cramped sensations in your right hand and forearm for about 5 seconds. Then relax by letting your fingers extend slowly. Feel the contrast as

Table 15.5   Progressive Relaxation Instructions

Sit down or lie down in a comfortable position. Take a few deep breaths, in and out, and let your body become loose and pleasantly heavy. Now try to tense every muscle in your body. Tense up every muscle. . . . Now let go of the tension. Let go and switch off all the tension. Notice the feeling of relief. . . . Let's do that again. Tense up every muscle . . . hold the tension . . . relax, let go, ease up, and enjoy the relief. . . . Take in a deep breath now and hold it . . . right in, breathe deeply in . . . and exhale, breathe it all out, and feel the tension going out of the body. . . . Just continue breathing normally, in and out. Each time you exhale, every time you breathe out, feel the tension going out of your body. . . . Now relax the rest of your body, but clench your jaws and close your eyes very tightly. Jaws are tense. Eyes are tight . . . . Keep the rest of the body relaxed, but study the tense feelings in the jaws and in the eyes and face. . . . Relax the jaws and stop tightening up your eyes. Let the jaws and the eyes and the face relax with the rest of your body . . . enjoy the contrast. . . . Now push your head back until you feel tension in your neck. . . . Shrug your shoulders, lift them up. Your

neck and shoulders and your upper back should feel tense. Keep the rest of your body relaxed. Study the difference between the tension in your neck and back and the relaxation elsewhere. All right, relax your shoulders, drop them gently down, and let your head return to a comfortable position. Enjoy the sensations and let yourself relax even deeper. . . . As you relax the rest of your body, tighten your fists and also tighten your stomach . . . try to get tension in your hands, your arms, and your stomach. . . . Study that tension. . . . Let go of it. Ease up and allow the tension to disappear. . . . Finally flex your buttocks and thighs, and point your toes downward so that your calves tense up. Feel the tension in your hips, buttocks, thighs, and calf muscles. . . . Keep the rest of the body relaxed. . . . Every part above the hips is relaxed; feel the tension only in and below the hips. . . . And now stop tensing, relax, ease up, and allow the calm sensations to develop and spread. Relax your entire body. As you inhale think the word *"in"* silently to yourself, and as you exhale think the word *"out"* to yourself. Carry on relaxing like this for as long as you like, gently and easily breathing in and out.

From A. Lazarus (1977)

the tension flows out and pleasant feelings of relaxation flow in. After repeating this two or three times, you may begin to notice a warm, heavy, or tingling sensation as the hand and forearm become deeply relaxed.

Progressive relaxation training proceeds by teaching the person to tense and relax in turn the muscles of the head, neck, abdomen, arms, and legs. **Table 15.5** contains typical progressive relaxation instructions.

Progressive relaxation, if practiced regularly, can be highly effective. It is used routinely in stress-management courses and has proved beneficial in reducing symptoms in many stress-related disorders. In addition to its value in reducing stress-induced arousal, progressive relaxation also appears to enhance immune system functioning (Green, Green, & Santoro, 1988). Therefore progressive relaxation may combat the immunosuppression produced by stressful life events discussed earlier in the chapter.

Anticipatory Coping

Stress reactions are due in part to a lack of effective coping skills. Therefore, stress reactions can be lessened by increasing people's ability to cope. Anticipatory coping involves developing skills in preparation for meeting stressful situations. Three components of anticipatory coping are (1) gaining information, (2) developing a plan of action, and (3) self-monitoring.

GAINING INFORMATION

A first step in anticipatory coping is acquiring as much information as possible about an impending stressful event. For example, if you are to give a talk before a group, you may find it helpful to know what kind of audience you will be addressing, its needs and expectations, and the physical setting of the talk. Gaining information provides a basis for developing a plan of action for meeting a stressful event.

DEVELOPING A PLAN OF ACTION

To develop a plan of action the person must first anticipate the demands to be placed on him or her and then practice appropriate responses to these demands (Martin & Poland, 1980). One way to anticipate demands is to imagine being in the stressful situation in as realistic a way as possible. Closing one's eyes and visualizing the situation from beginning to end allows one to anticipate possible difficulties. Once these difficulties have been determined, the person can then practice, or *rehearse,* appropriate responses.

Role playing—acting out the stressful situation with another person—is a helpful form of rehearsal. Consider, for example, the problem of asking the boss for a raise. By having a friend play the role of the boss, a person can practice appropriate responses to a number of possible reactions.

SELF-MONITORING

Advance information and preparation can do much to reduce the imbalance between demands and abilities in a stressful situation. Nevertheless, some degree of stress reaction is still likely. Therefore, practice in self-monitoring is a third element of anticipatory coping. Self-monitoring involves the ability first to recognize and then to control signs of a stress reaction. The first step in this process is to learn to interpret negative emotions, cognitive disruption, and physiological arousal as compo-nents of a stress reaction. For example, fearfulness, poor concentration, and a racing heart are indicators that stress is mounting. Once these signs are recognized, one can take steps to reduce the stress reaction. Thus the person may be able to employ a brief form of the relaxation response or engage in some reassuring reappraisals of the situation. In turn, blocking stress reactions by such means frees the person to confront stress more efficiently and effectively (Meichenbaum, 1977).

A number of studies have demonstrated the effectiveness of anticipatory coping in dealing with stressful situations (Turk, 1982). A now classic study involving surgical patients awaiting an operation provides a good example. The patients in this study were divided into an anticipatory-coping and a control group. On the night before their operations were scheduled, subjects in the control group were given routine information about the duration of the operation and the anesthetic to be used. Subjects in the anticipatory-coping group, in addition to this information, were informed that postoperative pain was a normal consequence of such operations and were told in detail how the pain might be experienced. These subjects were also taught how to relax muscles to reduce pain and were reassured that painkilling medication would be available if needed. What difference did this special preparation make? As shown in **Figure 15.11**, subjects in the anticipatory-coping group required only half the amount of painkilling medication

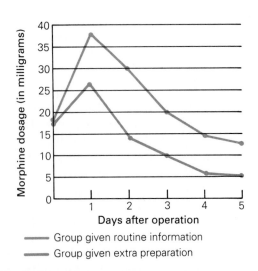

Figure 15.11
Effects of Anticipatory Coping on the Postoperative Use of Painkilling Drugs (After Egbert et al., 1964)

and left the hospital about 3 days sooner than control-group subjects (Egbert, Battit, Welch, & Bartlett, 1964). In other words, providing advance information, allowing people to prepare a plan of action, and teaching a simple technique of stress reduction can markedly reduce the impact of a stressful situation.

Seeking Social Support

Thus far we have discussed coping with stress as if it were a purely individual matter. But one highly predictable reaction of people under stress is to seek out the company of other people (Schachter, 1959). The help that others can provide in coping with stress is known as **social support.**

Social support takes three major forms, each of which performs a crucial function. One form consists of giving the individual information and practical problem-solving guidance in dealing with stressful events. This is important because, as we have seen, stress impairs cognitive functioning. A second form of social support consists of giving care, affection, and nurturance. This form of social support helps maintain self-esteem and bolsters confidence. Finally, social support can provide encouragement and reassurance—encouragement that one is able to master the stressful situation and reassurance that one's life will return to normal (Caplan, 1981; Cohen, 1990).

The importance of social support in moderating the impact of stressful events is considerable. For example, one study investigated the effects of social support in two groups of men hospitalized after serious automobile accidents. The men in one group were given routine hospital care and discharged. Men in the second group were given routine hospital care plus informational and emotional support by trained social workers. Three months after discharge from the hospital, subjects from the first group showed major psychological problems, ill-health, and social maladjustment, whereas subjects from the second group had returned to their previous level of functioning (Bordow & Porritt, 1979). This study demonstrated that social support can reduce or eliminate the adverse psychological and medical consequences of stressful events by helping people cope more effectively.

At the begining of this chapter we noted the "broken heart" effect of increased rates of death in widowers following the loss of a

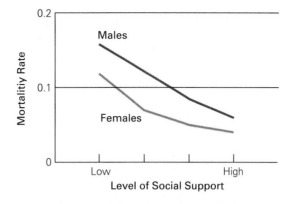

Figure 15.12
Social Support and Health.
Mortality rates for both men and women are affected by the amount of social support in their lives. Note that women also have an overall lower mortality than men. (House, Landis, & Umberson, 1988)

spouse. The opposite is also true: Longitudinal studies show that men and women who enjoy strong social networks (e.g. supportive family and friends, formal and informal group membership) have lower death rates than men and women who are lonely and socially isolated (House, Landis, & Umberson, 1988). This effect is illustrated in **Figure 15.12.** Studies like these dramatically illustrate that the quality of one's social relationships is a risk factor for disease and death of the same relative magnitude as physical risk factors like smoking, poor diet, and lack of exercise. As we have seen throughout this chapter, health and illness are inseparable from our psychology and our social relationships.

Interim Summary

Coping methods are the strategies people use to control stressful events or their reactions to them. Emotion-focused coping methods are used to deal with reactions to stressful events rather than with the events themselves. Problem-focused coping methods are aimed at directly altering or controlling the environment.

Three emotion-focused methods of coping with stress are use of defense mechanisms, cognitive reappraisal, and arousal reduction. Arousal reduction methods include the use of sedative drugs, exercise, and deep relaxation.

Two problem-focused methods of coping with stress are anticipatory coping and seeking social support. Anticipatory coping includes the steps of gaining information, developing a plan of action, and self-monitoring. Social support may take the form of information and guidance to overcome the cognitive impairment brought on by stress; care, affection, and nurturance to maintain self-esteem and bolster confidence; and encouragement and reassurance for dealing directly with the stressful event.

SUMMARY

1. The field of health psychology is concerned with the role of psychological factors in health and illness. Many stressful life events are known to have harmful health consequences. Stress is a pattern of disruptive psychological and physiological functioning that occurs when an environmental event is appraised as a threat to important personal goals and to one's ability to cope. So-called hardy individuals, as well as those with an optimistic disposition, buffer stress by adopting positive appraisals of life events.

2. Stress induces changes in the body's cardiovascular, gastrointestinal, and endocrine systems. In addition, stress appears to reduce the ability of the immune system to protect against disease-causing agents.

3. According to the psychosomatic specificity hypothesis, people who share similar ways of coping with stressful events will also be likely to develop similar illnesses. This hypothesis is supported by the relationship between the Type A behavior pattern and coronary heart disease (CHD): People who show the Type A trait of becoming excessively angry and hostile when stressed are at higher than normal risk of developing CHD.

4. Appraisal refers to the cognitive process by which the individual perceives situations as benign or threatening. Primary appraisal of stress involves the individual's perception of an event as a threat to well-being. Secondary appraisal refers to the individual's judgment of the adequacy of personal coping resources.

5. One model of disturbed physiological functioning under stress is Cannon's fight or flight response, which describes the reaction to acute and immediate threats. Another model is Selye's general adaptation syndrome (GAS), which is concerned with the effects of long-term, chronic stress.

6. A post-traumatic stress disorder (PTSD) is a chronic stress reaction that occurs following psychological trauma. Traumatic events such as natural disasters, rape, or military combat pose severe threats to well-being and are essentially uncontrollable.

7. Coping methods are the strategies people use to control stressful events or their reactions to them. Emotion-focused coping methods are used to deal with reactions to stressful events rather than with the events themselves. Problem-focused coping methods are aimed at directly altering or controlling the environment. Three emotion-focused methods of coping with stress are: use of defense mechanisms, cognitive reappraisal, and arousal reduction. Two problem-focused methods of coping with stress are anticipatory coping and seeking social support.

KEY INDIVIDUALS

Thomas Holmes
Richard Rahe
Suzanne Kobasa
Vernon Riley
David Graham
Meyer Friedman
Ray Rosenman
Richard Lazarus
Walter B. Cannon
Hans Selye

KEY RESEARCH

development of the Social Readjustment Rating Scale (SRRS)
role of hardiness and of optimism in the stress-illness relationship
immunosuppressive effects of stress
psychosomatic specificity hypothesis
the Type A behavior pattern

sport parachuting as an approach-avoidance
 conflict
primary and secondary appraisals and the stress
 response
the "fight or flight" response
the general adaptation syndrome (GAS)
effects of aerobic exercise on mild depression

KEY TERMS

stress
health psychology
Social Readjustment Rating Scale (SRRS)
hardiness
optimistic disposition
homeostasis
immune system

psychoneuroimmunology (PNI)
psychosomatic specificity
Type A behavior pattern
stressful event
appraisals
stress reaction
daily hassles
chronic sources of stress
helplessness
overload
conflict
fight-or-flight response
general adaptation syndrome (GAS)
post-traumatic stress disorder (PTSD)
coping methods
defense mechanisms
cognitive reappraisal
progressive relaxation
social support

16 Major Psychological Disorders

CHAPTER OUTLINE

Criteria of Abnormality

Abnormal as Infrequent
Abnormal as Deviant
Abnormal as Maladaptive
Abnormal as Personal Distress

Diagnosis of Psychological Disorders

Diagnostic Tools
Benefits and Costs of Diagnosis

Perspectives on Psychological Disorders

The Medical Perspective
The Psychodynamic Perspective
The Behavioral Perspective
The Cognitive Perspective
The Humanistic Perspective

Anxiety, Somatoform, and Dissociative Disorders

Anxiety Disorders
Somatoform Disorders
Dissociative Disorders

Mood Disorders

Major Depressive Episode
Manic Episode
Depressive and Bipolar Disorders
Suicide
Women and Depression
Understanding Mood Disorders

Schizophrenia

Symptoms of Schizophrenia
Types of Schizophrenia
Understanding Schizophrenia

Substance-Use Disorders

When Substance Use Becomes Abuse
Alcoholism
Understanding Substance Abuse

Personality Disorders

Paranoid Personality Disorder
Histrionic Personality Disorder
Obsessive-Compulsive Personality
 Disorder
Antisocial Personality Disorder

Summary

The following three cases are examples of some of the psychological disorders we will discuss in this chapter. By the end of the chapter you should have little difficulty recognizing the disorder exemplified by each vignette and should also have an understanding of the nature and causes of each.

A 28-year-old housewife is afraid she can no longer care for her three young children. Over the past year she has had recurrent episodes of "nervousness," lightheadedness, rapid breathing, trembling, and dizziness, during which things around her suddenly feel strange and unreal. Formerly active and outgoing, she has become afraid to leave home unless accompanied by her husband or mother. She now avoids supermarkets and department stores and says any crowded place makes her uneasy. When unable to avoid such situations, she tries to get near the doorways and always checks for windows and exits. Neither she nor her family can understand what is happening to her. Recently she has wanted her mother to stay with her when the children are at home as she worries about what would happen if an accident occurred and she, immobilized by one of her nervous episodes, were unable to help them. (Adapted from Spitzer, Skodol, Gibbon, & Williams, 1989, pp. 268–69)

The patient, a 25-year-old female graduate student in physical chemistry, was brought to the emergency room by her roommates, who found her sitting in her car with the motor running and the garage door closed. The patient had entered psychotherapy 2 years previously, complaining of long-standing unhappiness, feelings of inadequacy, low self-esteem, chronic tiredness, and a generally pessimistic outlook on life. During the 2 months before her emergency-room visit, she had become increasingly depressed, developed difficulty falling asleep and concentrating, and lost 10 pounds. The onset of these symptoms coincided with a rebuff she had received from a chemistry laboratory instructor to whom she had become attracted. (Adapted from Spitzer et al., 1989, pp. 258–59).

Emilio is a 40-year-old man who looks 10 years younger. He was brought to the hospital, his 12th hospitalization, by his mother because she was afraid of him. He was dressed in a ragged overcoat, bedroom slippers, and a baseball cap and wore several medals around his neck. His emotions range from anger at his mother—"she feeds me shit"—to a giggling, fawning seductiveness toward the interviewer. His speech and manner have a childlike quality, and he walks with a mincing step and exaggerated hip movements. His mother reports that he stopped taking his medication about a month ago and has since begun to hear voices and to look and act more bizarrely. When asked what he has been doing, he says "eating wires and lighting fires." His speech is often incoherent and marked by frequent rhyming associations. (Adapted from Spitzer et al., 1989, pp. 51-52)

As these vignettes indicate, there are many forms of psychological disorder. Psychological problems can range from mild to severe, can cause different degrees of incapacitation, and can have a variety of underlying causes. As we shall see, it is not at all uncommon for people to experience psychological difficulties at one time or another in their lives. Knowing something about these problems and the solutions to them can be an important benefit of studying psychology. In this chapter we

Many people will experience psychological difficulties sometime in life, and about 30 percent will develop a psychological disorder.

will consider questions about the definition and understanding of the more common forms of psychological disorder. In the next chapter we will discuss the variety of treatments available to people experiencing psychological difficulties.

CRITERIA OF ABNORMALITY

Most people would agree that the behavior described in the three cases at the beginning of the chapter is abnormal. But exactly how do we distinguish normal from abnormal behavior? Abnormal behavior is fairly easy to recognize but difficult to define precisely. Various psychologists have suggested the following four major criteria of abnormality, although no single criterion is completely satisfactory.

Abnormal as Infrequent

One criterion of abnormality states that any behavior that occurs infrequently is abnormal. This criterion is known as a *statistical defini-*

Table 16.1   **Percentages of Selected Psychological Disorders in U.S. Adult Population**

Disorder	At Any One Time	Over a Lifetime
Any disorder	15.4	32.2
Anxiety disorders	7.3	14.6
Mood disorders	5.1	8.3
Substance-abuse disorders	3.8	16.4
Schizophrenic disorders	0.7	1.5
Antisocial personality disorder	0.5	2.5

(From Regier et al., 1988)

tion because it defines abnormality in terms of the relative frequency of behavior in a population.

The statistical definition of abnormality has two major limitations. First, many socially valued human characteristics, such as artistic or scientific creativity, are relatively infrequent but can scarcely be considered psychologically abnormal. The second problem with this definition is that psychological disorders are not as infrequent as a purely statistical definition would imply (see **Table 16.1**). A recent survey of U.S. adults (over 18) found that 15.4 percent have a psychological disorder at any given time and that 32.2 percent will be afflicted at some time during their lives (Regier et al., 1988). A purely statistical criterion, therefore, has both logical and factual shortcomings.

Abnormal as Deviant

A second criterion of abnormality holds that behavior is abnormal if it is socially deviant. Every society has numerous rules, known as social norms, that govern the behavior of people in various social roles, such as student, professor, or parent. Deviant behavior can be defined as behavior that violates social norms. If you examine the case histories at the beginning of the chapter, you will see that the behaviors described strike us as bizarre or unusual because the people deviate from the way we expect them to behave.

This criterion also has two major limitations. First, it implies that abnormality is culturally relative. Because social norms vary from society to society, corresponding definitions of abnormality should also vary. Modern anthropological research has shown, however, that certain behavior patterns are considered abnor-

"Why doesn't he just snap out of it."

mal in both industrialized and tribal societies, even though social norms in these two societies are quite different (Murphy, 1976).

Second, not all deviant behavior is unusual or harmful enough to be considered truly abnormal. Belching at the dinner table or holding unpopular political views may be socially unacceptable, but such behaviors hardly qualify as psychological disorders. Most psychologists thus distinguish between behavior that is merely socially deviant and behavior that reflects a psychological disorder.

Abnormal as Maladaptive

The third criterion holds that behavior that is maladaptive for the individual or the group is abnormal. In biology, maladaptive refers to behavior that fails to promote survival of the species. When applied to psychology, maladaptive refers to behavior that fails to promote the well-being, growth, and fulfillment of the person and, ultimately, the group. This view, then, makes a judgment about the consequences of behavior (Carson, Butcher, & Coleman, 1988).

Most people with psychological disorders meet this criterion. Symptoms such as anxiety, depression, or bizarre, irrational beliefs distort or block one's personal development and lead to impaired social functioning. The people described in the beginning of the chapter did not merely behave deviantly; their behavior interfered with their ability to function effectively and to enhance others' well-being.

The criterion of maladaptiveness is generally accepted among mental-health professionals. However, maladaptiveness cannot serve as a sole criterion of abnormality. That is, some behavior is maladaptive but not abnormal. For example, inability to function effectively because of a chronic physical illness may be maladaptive but is not psychologically abnormal. Thus abnormality includes, but must go beyond, maladaptiveness.

Abnormal as Personal Distress

The infrequent, deviant, and maladaptive criteria approach abnormality from an independent observer's perspective. Most people with psychological disorders also experience subjective distress. They may experience anxiety, depression, pain, and other physical symptoms, as well as impairment of attention, memory, and other cognitive functions. Some people may in fact suffer from acute subjective distress while functioning more or less adequately in their social, occupational, and family roles. There are many examples of prominent people who have continued to function at a high level while acutely distressed. Both Abraham Lincoln and Winston Churchill were periodically beset by feelings of deep despondency and depression, even at the height of their public careers (Fieve, 1975).

The major limitation of this criterion is that it reflects an ideal of normality that is rarely met. As we saw in the previous chapter, stressful life events are part of the fabric of daily existence and often produce disorganized emotional, cognitive, and physiological functioning. Surveys indicate that at any one time as much as 80 percent of the population suffers from one or more symptoms of personal distress, such as feelings of anxiety or depression (Srole, Langner, Michael, Opler, & Rennie, 1962). Only about 15 percent, however, develop symptoms severe enough to be described as a psychological disorder.

Still, this criterion of abnormality conveys an important point: abnormality is on a continuum, with ideal functioning at one extreme and severe psychological disorganization at the other (see **Figure 16.1**). At any one time, most people will fall somewhere in the middle between the 15 percent of people with a diagnosable disorder and those completely without symptoms. Most people will also tend to move back and forth along the continuum depending on life stresses and their ability to cope. We should therefore not think of normality and abnormality as sharply defined terms.

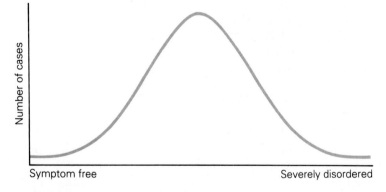

Figure 16.1
The Continuum of Normality and Abnormality

Interim Summary

No single criterion of abnormality is completely satisfactory, either logically or factually. In practice, abnormal behavior is usually defined by the convergence of four criteria: (1) relative infrequency, (2) social deviance, (3) maladaptiveness, and (4) personal distress. When these criteria converge, the person can be considered a candidate for professional diagnosis and treatment.

DIAGNOSIS OF PSYCHOLOGICAL DISORDERS

The diagnostic process involves matching information about a person's symptoms, life history, and current functioning to preestablished categories of psychological disorders.

The chief method of obtaining such information is a *diagnostic interview* conducted by a psychologist or other professional. The diagnostic interview includes questions about the patient's social, occupational, and psychological functioning, as well as questions about family background, developmental history, and previous psychological disorders. Equally important, the diagnostic interview gives the interviewer a chance to observe the patient's appearance, mood, speech, and cognitive functioning. In addition to the interview, information may be gathered from projective tests, personality inventories such as the Minnesota Multiphasic Personality Inventory, and interviews with the patient's family and friends. The information thus gathered can then be used to arrive at a formal diagnosis, which is a shorthand description of the person's psychological disorder.

Diagnostic Tools

The Diagnostic and Statistical Manual of Mental Disorders (DSM), published by the American Psychiatric Association, is a classification system that lists and describes specific categories of psychological disorder. The first edition, known as DSM-I, was published in 1952. DSM-II was published in 1968, and DSM-III in 1980. The 1980 edition was revised in 1987 and is known as **DSM-III-R.** DSM-III-R includes 17 major categories of psychological disorder, which in turn are broken down into more than 200 specific disorders (see **Table 16.2** on page

The diagnostic interview includes questions about the patient's social, occupational, and psychological functioning, as well as questions about the family background, developmental history, and previous psychological disorders.

570). Although some of the diagnostic prescriptions in DSM-III-R are controversial, the manual is generally regarded as a significant advance in diagnostic practice. DSM-I and DSM-II were little more than listings of diagnostic categories with vague descriptions of each. The vagueness often led to disagreement, or unreliability, in assigning a specific diagnosis to a particular patient. This disagreement meant that therapists and researchers often used different terms to describe patients with similar problems, thus impairing both treatment and research accuracy. The solution in DSM-III-R is to describe specific criteria that must be observed before a diagnosis can be assigned. Although the reliability of diagnosing all DSM-III-R categories is not yet established, preliminary results are encouraging (Mannuzza et al., 1989).

A second innovation of DSM-III-R is the use of a comprehensive "multiaxial" system of diagnosis. In this system, each patient is described on five separate axes, each of which represents an aspect of the individual's functioning.

Axis I is used to record the patient's specific psychological disorder from one of the major categories listed in Table 16.2.

Axis II is used to record any personality disorder that may occur with the Axis I diagnosis. A *personality disorder* is a set of deeply in-

Table 16.2   DSM-III-R Classification of Psychological Disorders

This table lists the major categories of psychological disorders according to DSM-III-R and provides an example of each type of disorder. Each of the 17 major categories includes a number of subcategories.

Major Category	Specific Example
1. Disorders of infancy, childhood, or adolescence	Mental retardation
2. Organic mental disorders	Alzheimer's disease
3. Substance-use disorders	Alcohol abuse
4. Schizophrenia	Schizophrenia
5. Delusional disorder	Paranoid delusions
6. Psychotic disorders not elsewhere classified	Schizophreniform disorder
7. Mood disorders	Depression
8. Anxiety disorders	Phobia
9. Somatoform disorders	Conversion disorder
10. Dissociative disorders	Multiple personality disorder
11. Sexual disorders	Premature ejaculation
12. Sleep disorders	Insomnia
13. Factitious disorders	Feigned illness
14. Impulse control disorders	Pathological gambling
15. Adjustment disorder	Stress-related anxiety
16. Psychological factors affecting physical condition	Stress-related hypertension
17. Personality disorders	Histrionic personality disorder

(DSM-III-R, 1987)

grained, inflexible, and maladaptive traits that significantly impair an individual's psychological and social functioning. DSM-III-R describes 11 personality disorders, some of which are discussed in the final section of this chapter.

Axis III is used to record any medical disorder. Patients with psychological disorders have higher than normal rates of physical illness (Wells et al., 1989), and this axis calls attention to the possible need of medical treatment.

Axis IV is used to estimate the severity of stressful life events related to the patient's Axis I disorder. The events considered here are much like those that make up the Social Readjustment Rating Scale discussed in the previous chapter. An overall rating of severity is made on a six-point scale.

Axis V is used to indicate the patient's level of psychological, social, and occupational functioning, both at the time of evaluation and at its highest point during the past year. For this purpose the interviewer uses a rating scale, known as the Global Assessment of Functioning (GAF) Scale, to give a numerical estimate from 1 to 100 of the level of functioning. For example, a student experiencing temporary examination stress but otherwise functioning effectively would be given a GAF rating of 90. A person unable to function effectively and requiring hospitalization because of a suicide attempt would be given a GAF rating of 20. Comparing the patient's highest level of functioning over the past year with his or her current level helps the interviewer to predict the patient's potential for recovery.

A complete multiaxial diagnosis for a hypothetical patient might look like this:

Axis I	Major depressive episode
Axis II	Histrionic personality disorder
Axis III	Hypertension
Axis IV	Marital separation severity: 3-moderate
Axis V	Current GAF: 50
	Highest GAF past year: 80

In sum, the DSM-III-R multiaxial system is a brief and efficient method of communicating a good deal of information about a patient. In addition to describing the patient's current symptoms (Axis I), the multiaxial system is used to provide a shorthand description of the patient's personality (Axis II), of any medical conditions that also need to be treated (Axis III), of stressful events that have contributed to the psychological disorder (Axis IV), and of both past and current levels of psychological, social, and occupational functioning (Axis V).

Benefits and Costs of Diagnosis

Arriving at an accurate diagnosis is important for both therapeutic and scientific reasons. As we shall see in the following chapter, there is a wide range of psychological and medical therapies for treating psychological disorders. Therefore, an accurate diagnosis is crucial to matching the patient with the most effective treatment program.

Diagnosis is also the first step in scientific research on the nature, causes, and treatment of psychological disorders. In such research, particular disorders are usually considered independent variables, while tests or other measures are considered dependent variables. For example, we may wish to test the hypothesis that patients with anxiety disorders are more physiologically aroused under stress than nonanxious patients. Unless we define "anxiety disorder" as precisely as possible, anxious patients may end up in the nonanxious group and vice versa, decreasing the probability of detecting differences in arousal between the two groups.

Psychological diagnosis can also have negative effects. One cost of diagnosis stems from the consequences of labeling people as having a psychological disorder. Despite the efforts of psychologists and other professionals to enlighten the public about the nature of psychological disorders, a social stigma remains. For example, studies have shown that people tend to react more negatively to a person described as "a former mental patient" than they do to a person described in the same words but without the designation of "mental patient" (Farina, 1976).

Even mental-health professionals are not immune to such stereotyping. In a now classic study by David Rosenhan (1973), eight volunteers gained admission to 12 different mental hospitals by claiming they had heard a bizarre, disembodied voice, a symptom known as an *auditory hallucination*. Based on the alleged hallucination, each pseudopatient was diagnosed as schizophrenic. Once admitted, however, each pseudopatient acted in his or her

normal fashion. Rosenhan and his colleagues found that the diagnosis biased the staff's interpretation of the pseudopatients' past and present behavior. Some instances were minor, as when one pseudopatient took to pacing the corridors out of boredom, which was misinterpreted as a sign of anxiety. Other distortions were massive, as when the fairly typical middle-class upbringing of one pseudopatient was interpreted in his case report as filled with conflict and pathology, apparently to "explain" his current "schizophrenia." Rosenhan's study is a convincing reminder of the power of diagnostic labels to stereotype individuals by biasing perceptions of their behavior.

A second cost of diagnosis lies in its potential to blame the victim for his or her problems. For example, the authors of DSM-III-R debated the wisdom of including a diagnosis of "self-defeating personality disorder." The authors had in mind people who seem to seek out failure and suffering, as in substance abuse, deliberately poor job performance, or hurtful relationships. But feminist critics objected that the diagnosis could be turned against battered wives and other abused women. According to the feminist critique, an abusive relationship might be attributed to the woman's "self-defeating personality" rather than to the social and economic realities that often trap women in such relationships. In the end, the diagnosis of self-defeating personality disorder was *not* included in DSM-III-R. But the controversy revealed that a diagnosis can have unintended negative consequences if it implies that the person with a problem is a problem person (Holden, 1986).

Interim Summary

Diagnosis is the process of matching information about a person to categories of psychological disorder. Accurate diagnosis is necessary for both therapeutic and scientific reasons. The potential costs of diagnosis include stigmatization and blaming the victim for his or her problems.

DSM-III-R is an innovative classification system that includes specific diagnostic criteria for each of more than 200 disorders, as well as a multiaxial system used to describe patients on five separate dimensions of functioning.

PERSPECTIVES ON PSYCHOLOGICAL DISORDERS

A diagnosis describes a patient's psychological disorder but does not explain its cause. Explaining psychological disorders requires extensive hypothesis testing guided by one or more of the theoretical perspectives discussed in Chapter 1. Here we will discuss how five prominent perspectives—the medical, the psychodynamic, the behavioral, the cognitive, and the humanistic—attempt to explain the causes of psychological disorders.

The Medical Perspective

The medical perspective assumes that abnormal behaviors are *symptoms of mental illness,* which can be *diagnosed* and *treated.* The language of symptoms, syndromes, and diagnostic categories, as well as terms like *mental health* and *mental illness,* all reflect the impact of the medical perspective.

One corollary of the medical perspective assumes that the causes of psychological disorders can be found in underlying impairments of the brain's functioning. In this respect, the medical perspective joins the biopsychological perspective discussed in Chapters 1 and 2. For example, those with a medical orientation would tend to view anxiety as a result of faulty

Thomas Szasz

According to the behavioral perspective, anxiety occurs when an individual encounters a stimulus that has, in the past, been associated with a stressful event.

neurochemical activity at specific brain synapses. Advocates of this perspective point to the ability of certain sedative drugs (known as antianxiety agents) to alleviate anxiety, as well as to the recent discovery of specific synaptic receptors for these drugs, as discussed in Chapter 5. The medical perspective has generated important findings on the neurochemical correlates of several psychological disorders, as we shall see in this chapter, as well as on a variety of drug and other therapies discussed in the following chapter.

The medical perspective is not, however, without its critics. For example, Thomas Szasz (1961), an outspoken psychiatrist, points out that the medical perspective generally promises more than it has delivered and that most psychological disorders cannot be explained by brain impairments. Szasz and other critics argue that the medical perspective obscures the fact that mental-health professionals constantly make ethical judgments about what constitutes normal or abnormal behavior. In this view, mental-health professionals are "social engineers" who decide which behaviors and beliefs are socially appropriate and which must be treated. The debate initiated by Szasz a generation ago has helped to sensitize mental-health professionals to the ethical context of their work and to the tentativeness of their overall understanding of psychological disorders.

The Psychodynamic Perspective

The psychodynamic perspective stems from Sigmund Freud's development of psychoanalytic theory at the turn of the century. Freud was trained as a physician and, early in his career, hoped that psychological disorders could be reduced to underlying brain impairments (Pribram & Gill, 1976). But because the neuroscience of his day was too undeveloped to support such research, Freud turned instead to psychology to explain disordered behavior and mental activity.

As you have already learned, Freud theorized that behavior and conscious mental activity were to a great extent determined by the dynamic balance among largely unconscious structures of the personality. For Freud, the ego, as the executive of the personality, had to allow for the expression of unconscious drives in a way that took into account both external reality and internal moral standards. To accomplish its goals, the ego relied on a variety of unconscious defense mechanisms, which allowed for at least partial discharge of drive tensions in socially and personally acceptable ways.

As you also know, theorists who followed Freud modified many of his concepts. But they shared with Freud a general psychodynamic orientation that saw psychological disorder as the result of unconscious conflicts between motives and defense mechanisms. In the psychodynamic perspective, psychological problems develop when basic motives that are unacceptable to the conscious portion of the personality are blocked from expression by rigid and inflexible defense mechanisms. For example, psychodynamic theorists see anxiety as occurring when defense mechanisms against unacceptable motives begin to break down and allow conscious expression of the underlying motives. In this perspective, basic motives are unacceptable to the conscious portion of the personality because their expression has led to frustration and punishment, usually in childhood. Such negative experiences endow the motives with the ability to create anxiety when later aroused in adulthood.

The psychodynamic perspective has exerted a major influence on the study and treatment of psychological disorders for nearly a century. However, many psychologists reject the psychodynamic perspective for two major reasons: (1) it emphasizes internal determinants of behavior to the relative exclusion of external determinants, and (2) many of its concepts, such as unconscious motivation, are extremely difficult to operationalize and test empirically. The scientific problems of this approach prompted the development of a third major approach, the behavioral perspective.

The Behavioral Perspective

Unlike the medical and psychodynamic perspectives, which grew out of direct clinical contact with patients, the behavioral perspective grew out of laboratory research on conditioning and learning, which was then applied to psychological disorders. The behavioral perspective does not look for internal, psychodynamic causes for psychological disorders. Instead, it focuses on the patient's symptoms as behaviors to be modified through the techniques of classical and operant conditioning.

More specifically, this perspective analyzes behavior—whether normal or abnormal—as a function of situational cues (stimuli) and consequences (reinforcers). This is what B. F. Skinner has called a *functional analysis of behavior*. By applying a *functional* analysis, the behavioral psychologist attempts to isolate both the stimuli for and the reinforcers of abnormal behavior. For example, anxiety would be analyzed in terms of the stimuli that cue anxiety and the reinforcers that strengthen it. More specifically, anxiety is seen as a classically conditioned response to a stimulus that has been reinforced by being paired with an aversive or stressful event. According to this perspective, anxiety occurs when the person encounters stimuli that in the past have been associated with stressful events.

The behavioral perspective is criticized by many psychologists because of its self-imposed limitations. Because it uses very few concepts, it often fails to make important distinctions among qualitatively different kinds of behavior and environmental events. In addition, many psychologists feel the behavioral perspective ignores important cognitive processes.

The Cognitive Perspective

The cognitive perspective is an outgrowth of the behavioral perspective and is, in fact, sometimes known as the cognitive-behavioral perspective. This perspective attempts to supplement the behavioral perspective by taking cognitive factors into account in explaining disordered behavior.

According to this perspective, an objective functional analysis of the stimuli for and consequences of behavior is necessary but not sufficient for explaining psychological disorders. The way in which people attend to, perceive, and think about environmental events is as important as the events themselves. To return to our example of anxiety, a person confronted with anxiety-provoking stimuli may focus on these stimuli rather than distract his or her attention and may allow thoughts of impending danger to dominate his or her cognitive activity instead of engaging in problem-solving solutions to the threatening stimuli.

The cognitive perspective forms a sort of bridge between the behavioral and the psychodynamic perspectives. It is oriented both to the controlling influence of external events and to the person's unique perceptions and interpretations of these events. However, the cognitive perspective remains loyal to its behavioral roots by regarding cognitive activities as potentially observable behaviors that can be modified. For this reason, the cognitive perspective is often referred to as the cognitive-behavioral perspective.

The Humanistic Perspective

The humanistic perspective is quite different from the intellectual style of the other four perspectives. Advocates of this perspective tend to be skeptical about the diagnostic process because it represents a description based on pre-existing categories rather than the person's own perception of his or her inner and outer worlds. Advocates also decry "treatment" to the extent that it represents manipulating or changing people's behavior for "their own good." Because an objective, professional assessment of a person's difficulties may be at variance with the person's own assessment, effective helping requires an ability to understand and work with the person's self-perceptions and unique needs.

The humanistic perspective regards psychological disorders as temporary blocks in the person's growth toward self-actualization. The symptoms of psychological disorder arise when a person's efforts toward self-actualization are blocked by external demands or the conditional positive regard of others. In this perspective anxiety occurs when there is a conflict between a person's self-actualizing tendencies and the conditional positive regard of parents and other important figures in the person's life. Anxiety is overcome when the person becomes more fully in touch with his or her internal world and less dependent on externally imposed conditions of worth. Thus, psychological disorders may often occur at important life transitions, when the person is attempting to grow out of accustomed roles and toward greater autonomy and individuality.

Interim Summary

Theoretical approaches to psychological disorders include the medical, psychodynamic, behavioral, cognitive, and humanistic perspectives. These differing perspectives guide research and theories on the nature, causes, and treatment of psychological disorders.

ANXIETY, SOMATOFORM, AND DISSOCIATIVE DISORDERS

In this section we discuss three types of psychological disorders that have traditionally been considered together because they share certain similarities. In general, anxiety, somatoform, and dissociative disorders are less debilitating than other psychological disorders we will consider. The person suffering from one of these disorders is distressed by his or her symptoms, but the symptoms do not involve gross distortions of reality, as is the case with more severe disorders. Although these three disorders interfere with the person's ability to function up to his or her potential, the person does not necessarily engage in bizarre behavior that violates social norms. For example, a person with a phobia of airplane travel may show no unusual behavior unless compelled to fly. The person's desire to avoid flying, however, exacts a cost in personal distress and loss of flexibility in adaptive functioning. The anxiety, somatoform, and dissociative disorders can therefore be contrasted with the more severe and incapacitating mood disorders and schizophrenia, which we will discuss later in this chapter.

Anxiety Disorders

The **anxiety disorders** include several conditions in which the person attempts to cope with overwhelming levels of anxiety that go well beyond everyday apprehension and jitters. The level of anxiety seen in these disorders includes both cognitive components such as thoughts of death and destruction and physical conponents such as dizziness, heart pounding, and shortness of breath. This anxiety tends to be out of proportion to the particular event that elicits it, or it may even occur in the absence of any specific event. In addition, this anxiety may persist and generalize to many areas of the person's life. In this section, we will discuss four types of anxiety disorders: panic disorders, phobic disorders, generalized anxiety disorder, and finally, obsessive-compulsive disorder.

PANIC DISORDER

A person suffering from a **panic disorder** experiences repeated attacks of abrupt, extreme anxiety, usually lasting for several minutes. People with this disorder describe their attacks as extreme discomfort associated with a feeling of impending doom and an intense desire to flee from the present situation. In some cases the person even believes he or she is about to die.

> Susan, a 25-year-old legal secretary, was about to leave her office one night when she was suddenly overwhelmed by anxiety she had never experienced before— an intense panicky sensation that something dreadful and frightening was going to happen to her. She became flushed and found breathing difficult, almost as though she were choking. She struggled to maintain her composure, but within seconds she felt dizzy and lightheaded. Waves of fear coursed through Susan. The sound of her heart beating fast and strong and the sensation of blood rushing through her body at great pressure made her think she might be dying. Gradually the feelings subsided. Relieved but still shaky, she made her way home. (Fishman & Sheehan, 1985, p. 26)

The extreme discomfort of panic attacks is due to a massive arousal of the sympathetic nervous system in what Cannon (1929) first called the "fight or flight" response, which we discussed in Chapter 15. The fight or flight response is experienced by the person as shortness of breath, dizziness, heart palpitations, choking sensations, nausea, and other symptoms of high sympathetic nervous system arousal (**Table 16.3**). Because these panic attacks are unexpected and seem to come out of the blue, they are sometimes called *spontaneous* panic attacks. Their unexpected nature often leads the person to attribute them not to psychological sources, but to a physical problem such as a heart attack or an undiagnosed illness.

People with panic disorder can often be successfully treated with drugs, which leads medically oriented investigators to believe that the basic problem lies in some instability of the sympathetic nervous system. On the other hand, psychologists note that panic attacks often occur when the person is under a great deal of stress that is unacknowledged. The psychological approach to treatment therefore aims to discover and address problems in the person's life that may be the underlying source of the attacks.

Anxiety disorders include several conditions in which the person suffers from overwhelming anxiety. These members of the SOAR Program are learning to overcome their fear of flying.

PHOBIC DISORDER

A person with a **phobic disorder,** or **phobia,** experiences anxiety only in specific settings or when confronted with a specific stimulus. Phobias are defined by three criteria. First, the person experiences anxiety out of proportion to any objective danger. Second, the person

Table 16.3   **DSM-III-R Criteria for Panic Disorder (at least four of the following must be present)**

1. shortness of breath
2. dizziness or faintness
3. palpitations (tachycardia)
4. trembling or shaking
5. sweating
6. choking
7. nausea or abdominal distress
8. depersonalization or derealization
9. numbness or tingling sensations (paresthesias)
10. flushes (hot flashes) or chills
11. chest pain or discomfort
12. fear of dying
13. fear of going crazy or of doing something uncontrolled

(DSM-III-R, 1987)

usually recognizes that the anxiety is irrational. And, third, the anxiety motivates a compelling desire to avoid the feared setting or stimulus.

Many people are troubled by *simple phobias* such as fear of snakes, mice, or needle injections. Avoiding or minimizing contact with such objects usually does not constrict one's life or impair social functioning. *Social phobias,* such as fear of public speaking or of eating in restaurants, cause greater impairment in that such activities are expected of adults in many occupational and social roles.

Agoraphobia (from the Greek word *agora,* meaning "open space") is an example of a complex phobic disorder that can be extremely debilitating. Unlike a simple phobia, in which the phobic stimulus is quite specific, the person with agoraphobia fears a variety of situations. He or she may fear being anywhere outside the safe confines of home, such as traveling in a car, being in public places, or being in a crowd. In the extreme, the agoraphobic cannot tolerate being alone, not only outdoors but also within his or her own home. Many agoraphobics are made hostage to their fears. The vignette of the 28-year-old housewife on page 566 is a case of agoraphobia.

Agoraphobia is sometimes known as "fear of fear" because it usually develops after a person has experienced one or more spontaneous panic attacks. Depending on where the initial panic attack occurred, the person develops a fear of being in that same situation again. A panic attack occurring in a shopping mall, for

Agoraphobics may fear being anywhere outside the safe confines of their home.

example, will cause the person to fear shopping malls. Because panic attacks can occur in different situations, the person may eventually refuse to leave home or to be alone for fear of experiencing another panic attack (Barlow & Mavissakalian, 1981).

In sum, phobias range from simple to complex and from mild to severe. A person with a simple phobia of small animals may, by avoidance, show only mild impairment, while a person with agoraphobia may experience a severe loss of adaptive functioning.

GENERALIZED ANXIETY DISORDER

The person with a **generalized anxiety disorder** suffers from persistent anxiety, stemming from no specific identifiable threat. People with a generalized anxiety disorder tend to be extremely sensitive in their interpersonal relations, have difficulty making decisions, and worry excessively about past mistakes and possible future calamities (Carson et al., 1988). At times the anxiety may escalate into a panic attack, in which the person experiences an overwhelming sense of dread accompanied by massive visceral symptoms. The following is a personal account of a generalized anxiety disorder with panic attacks:

> I could barely get myself to the office or stay in it until it was time to go. I was always exhausted, always cold; my hands were clammy with sweat; I cried weakly and easily. I was afraid to go to sleep; but I did sleep, to wake with a constricting headache, dizziness and tachycardia (rapid heartrate). To these now familiar symptoms were added waves of panic fear followed by depression. The panics almost overwhelmed me. I felt very much more frightened when I was alone and but little less frightened with other people. ("Disabilities," 1952)

OBSESSIVE-COMPULSIVE DISORDER

Obsessive-compulsive disorder, or OCD, is a form of anxiety disorder characterized by persistent and irresistible urges to engage in repetitive thoughts and/or actions. **Obsessions** are recurrent thoughts that are experienced as involuntary intrusions into consciousness. Common obsessions include fears that one will harm another person, destroy property, or be contaminated by germs. For example, one patient stopped cooking for fear he would poison his wife and stopped using electrical appliances for fear of causing a fire. **Compulsions** are ritualistic and rigid actions that the person feels compelled to carry out. Common compulsions include handwashing, checking that doors are locked and stoves turned off, and counting objects. Compulsive behavior often occurs in response to obsessions as a way of temporarily banishing the troubling thoughts. For example, a patient might spend hours in the bathroom repeatedly washing himself because of the thought he might pass germs on to anything or anyone he touches.

The following illustrates a severe case of OCD:

> Mrs R. was a 37-year-old housewife...She usually washed her hands four or five times per day, but each session lasted between three and four hours. She also washed her face excessively, and when first seen both face and hands were raw and bleeding. Compulsive repetition, it transpired, characterized many other of her daily activities. All doors, bolts, and locks had to be checked three times before she could leave her home. Electric switches for lights and appliances had always to be turned on or off twice.... While dressing, each piece of underwear had to be put on, taken off, and put on again three times....She did not admit for some time that she also found it necessary to repeat everything she said three times—once aloud, twice *sotto voce*. (Reed, 1985, p. 157)

It may seem curious that OCD is classified as an anxiety disorder, because people with OCD do not appear to experience anxiety symptoms like those described above. However, people with OCD become extremely anxious if not allowed to carry out their compulsive rituals. Compulsive behavior thus appears to serve as a means of avoiding the experience of anxiety. As with phobic avoidance patterns, compulsions reduce anxiety at the cost of severely disrupting day-to-day living. Fortunately, a combination of drug therapy and behavior therapy (Chapter 17) has proved to be effective in treating this often bizarre form of anxiety disorder (Rapoport, 1989).

Somatoform Disorders

Somatoform means "bodylike" and refers to physical symptoms that have no physiological basis. In **somatoform disorders,** the person complains of medical problems for which no underlying physical cause can be found. Patients with somatoform disorders may suffer from a variety of symptoms, including muscular aches and pains, headaches, abdominal pain, menstrual difficulties, limb paralyses, and impaired hearing or vision.

Hypochondriasis is a type of somatoform disorder in which the person has converted psychological distress into physical symptoms. The person will often go from physician to physician until he or she finds a physician who is willing to prescribe some form of treatment. Such people are both convinced they have a dread disease and terrified at the prospect. They reject any suggestion that their problem has an emotional basis and are often critical of their physicians for not being able to find the physical cause of their symptoms. Such people are often unhappy in their jobs or marriages and have poor interpersonal relationships. They may lead the lives of virtual invalids as a way of giving some legitimacy to their suffering. The clever physician will schedule regular visits with hypochondriacs so the patient does not need the excuse of having a physical problem in order to receive a sympathetic hearing (Barsky & Klerman, 1985).

Conversion disorder is the DSM-III-R term for a somatoform disorder traditionally known as *hysteria*. This disorder was first described in the medical literature by Hippocrates in the fifth century B.C. A conversion disorder is characterized by symptoms that suggest a disorder of the central nervous system, such as seizures, paralysis of the arms or legs, and loss of the ability to speak. The patient may temporarily lose the ability to see or to hear or may lose the sense of touch or pain in discrete body areas. Because they so clearly resemble symptoms of known medical disorders but have no physiological basis, conversion symptoms have confused and mystified physicians over the centuries.

> A 29-year-old physician in the first year of a psychiatric residency was experiencing a great deal of stress from problems in both his personal life and his hospital work. His marriage was deteriorating and he was being heavily criticized by the rather authoritarian chief of psychiatry for allegedly mismanaging some treatment cases.
>
> Shortly before he was to discuss his work in an important hospital-wide con-

ference being conducted by the chief psychiatrist, he had an "attack" in which he developed difficulty in speaking and severe pains in his chest. He thought his condition was probably related to a viral infection, but physical findings were negative. (Carson et al., 1988, p. 200)

Unlike medical patients with similar symptoms, the patient with conversion symptoms often seems unconcerned by his or her disability. This lack of concern suggests that the patient is using the symptoms to avoid a difficult life situation while gaining the attention normally bestowed on sick people. Freud called this source of motivation the *secondary gain* of having symptoms. A behavioral psychologist would interpret the same phenomenon as an example of *positive reinforcement* for sick behavior. However, such patients are not consciously faking. They cannot voluntarily produce or eliminate their symptoms on command.

Dissociative Disorders

The essential feature of a **dissociative disorder** is an abrupt but usually temporary loss of voluntary cognitive activity. For example, the dissociative disorder known as *psychogenic amnesia* (psychologically caused forgetfulness) is a sudden inability to remember personally important information to an extent that goes well beyond everyday forgetfulness. The amnesia usually follows an intensely stressful event and may terminate as abruptly as it began. These points are illustrated in the following case:

> Susan H., a young woman of 18, was brought to the hospital in a state of confusion. Her mental clouding rapidly cleared after admission, but it was then evident that her mind was completely blank for the events of the 7 hours prior to coming to the hospital. . . . It was only when she was put into a state of light hypnosis that her memory was restored. It was then discovered that the period covered by the amnesia had been one in which she had suffered an intolerable disappointment—abandonment by her boyfriend at a time when she desperately needed his help. (Adapted from Nemiah, 1978, p. 156)

In a 1978 court case, defendant William Milligan was acquitted of rape when he was

Severe abuse in childhood is often associated with multiple personality disorder in adulthood, as in the case of Truddi Chase, pictured here.

judged not responsible for his actions because he possessed multiple personalities. **Multiple personality** is a rare but dramatic type of dissociative disorder in which entire segments of the person's cognitive activity and behavior are split off from conscious awareness so that the person seems to fluctuate between two or more distinct personalities. Each personality has its own memories, behavior patterns, and interests. One personality is usually dominant but may be abruptly replaced by one or more secondary personalities. The dominant personality is usually conventional, moralistic, and dull, while the secondary personality or personalities are more individualistic, carefree, and irresponsible. For example, in the Billy Milligan case, the lesbian personality Adelena was thought to be the personality who committed the rapes. The dominant personality is usually unaware of the secondary personality or personalities, but the latter are usually aware of the dominant personality.

Although it is a rare disorder, multiple personality has been the subject of fiction, television, and motion pictures. Popular case study accounts, such as *The Three Faces of Eve* and *Sybil*, continue to capture the public imagination. Psychologists have intensely studied the few existing documented cases of multiple personality in a search for clues to the nature of consciousness and to the altered states of consciousness associated with this disorder (Ross, 1989).

According to some investigators, patients with multiple personality are highly susceptible to hypnosis. For example, Bliss (1980) found that 14 patients with multiple personalities spontaneously learned self-hypnosis as children to protect themselves from parental abuse. According to Bliss, self-hypnosis was used to develop alternate personalities who could better cope with the abuse; these personalities then continued to be called on when other kinds of threats were experienced later in life. Because multiples are so hypnotically susceptible, hypnosis is often used therapeutically to bring the various dissociated personalities into one fully functioning person with more mature coping skills.

Interim Summary

The symptoms of the anxiety, somatoform, and dissociative disorders are usually distressing to the patient but do not involve major distortions of reality. They can be understood as maladaptive ways of coping with anxiety and/or relating to other people.

In the anxiety disorders, the person experiences overwhelming levels of anxiety that are out of proportion to the specific event provoking the anxiety. Panic disorders, phobic disorders, generalized anxiety, and obsessive-compulsive disorders are types of anxiety disorders.

Somatoform disorders lie on the border between psychological and medical ailments. In these disorders, which include hypochondriasis and conversion disorder, the person exhibits physical symptoms for which no underlying physiological cause can be found.

A dissociative disorder is characterized by an abrupt but usually temporary loss of voluntary cognitive activity. Multiple personality is a type of dissociative disorder in which entire portions of a person's cognitive activity and behavior are split off from conscious awareness. Another type of dissociative disorder is psychogenic amnesia.

MOOD DISORDERS

We all experience changes in mood. On our bad days, we feel "down," tend to withdraw from social contact, and can't seem to muster the energy to engage in our usual pursuits. On our good days, we feel "up," enjoy the company of others, and pursue our activities with interest and enthusiasm. These variations in mood, however, bear only slight resemblance to the extremes of mood associated with the mood disorders.

The term **mood** refers to a pervasive and sustained emotional state that colors the person's perceptions, thoughts, and behavior. The **mood disorders** are so named because the primary symptoms involve persistent and extreme disturbances of mood. At one extreme is **depression,** which is marked by intense feelings of sadness, hopelessness, despondency, and lowered self-esteem. At the opposite extreme is **mania,** which is characterized by feelings of euphoria, elation, well-being, and heightened self-esteem. These extremes of mood grossly interfere with the person's ability to function effectively.

Mood disorders are among the most prevalent of mental-health problems in Western societies. Using DSM-III-R criteria, a recent investigation found that over the course of a lifetime, 8 to 12 percent of men and 20 to 26 percent of women will experience a major depressive episode. The rates for manic episodes are much lower, in the range of about 1 percent for both sexes (Boyd & Weissman, 1981). In addition, the prevalence of mood disorders has been increasing in Western industrialized countries for the last 50 years. For example, young people between the ages of 15 and 40 in North America and Europe were about twice as likely to show depression in the 1960s and 1970s as they were before World War II (Klerman & Weissman, 1989). It would appear that affluence and technological advance do not protect against depression and may in fact be risk factors for it.

Major Depressive Episode

A person experiencing a **major depressive episode** shows a depressed mood, slowed behavior, and such biological signs as difficulties in eating and sleeping. Severely depressed people tend to regard the past as a series of failures, the present as devoid of interest and pleasure, and the future as hopeless. They may cry easily and frequently, speak and move about slowly, and wear a sorrowful expression. At times they may feel tense and restless and attempt to discharge these feelings by wringing

Psychology in the News

RECESSION FEARS HAVE SOME PEOPLE DEPRESSED AND ACTING ERRATICALLY

By Ron Suskind

Symptoms: Fitful sleep. Feelings of dread. Sluggishness. A decline in self-esteem. Irregular diet. Addictive behavior. Avoidance of problems. A desperate desire for relief.

Diagnosis: Clinical depression.

The condition is affecting much of the U.S. as recession fever spreads across the land. New England was among the first to come down with it and has a bad case. The region led the nation in prosperity in the 1980s (remember the Massachusetts Miracle?). Now hard-times epidemiologists have something to study there again.

Recession may or may not be on the way, but recessionary psychology is already here. Economic problems are real enough, but the mood is disproportionately dark. Because it is, it could well make any downturn deeper.

"We're learning that economics is not a fiscal science," says Harvard economist Robert Reich, "but about psychology and sociology. What we're dealing with up here, and increasingly in the rest of the country, are fast deflating expectations becoming self-fulfilling prophesies. In some ways, it's as Roosevelt said, 'We have nothing to fear but fear itself.' "

Ignored Realities

The depressed patient, caught up in the gloom, ignores what good news there is. New England's per capita income is still the highest in the nation—$22,215 this year. Growth in New England's exports increased 13.6% the first half of this year.

"People who are depressed respond to stimuli that confirm their darkening world view, rather than anything that confirms the positive," says psychologist William Roiter of Hurst Associates Inc., one of a growing number of Boston-area firms that proffer psychologi-

---

their hands, pacing, or complaining—a syndrome called *agitated depression.*

In depression, self-esteem is low. Depressed people may feel guilty over real or imagined past misdeeds and regard themselves as worthless human beings. At times these feelings may develop into **delusions,** which are false beliefs held with great conviction in the absence of objective evidence. For example, depressed people may believe that God or the devil is punishing them for their sins or that they are solely responsible for evil in the world.

Depression is often signaled by certain changes in the person's habits. Waking early in the morning and being unable to fall back asleep is a frequent sign. A loss of appetite leading to weight loss and a decline in sexual drive may also occur. These biological signs usually accompany severe depression. **Table 16.4** lists the DSM-III-R criteria for a diagnosis of major depressive episode.

Table 16.4   **DSM-III-R Criteria for Major Depressive Episode (at least five of the following must be present)**

1. depressed mood
2. markedly diminished interest or pleasure in all, or almost all activities
3. significant weight loss or weight gain when not dieting
4. insomnia or hypersomnia
5. psychomotor agitation or retardation
6. fatigue or loss of energy
7. feelings of worthlessness or excessive or inappropriate guilt
8. diminished ability to think or concentrate, or indecisiveness
9. recurrent thoughts of death, recurrent suicidal ideation without a specific plan, or a suicide attempt or a specific plan for committing suicide

(DSM-III-R, 1987)

cal counseling to companies. Their business isn't at all depressed.

Mr. Roiter of Hurst Associates says his seminar called "Take Control of Your Life" is by far the most requested by corporations. "When you lose the sense of being able to control your life, you stop trying to solve problems and instead just end up seeking relief."

Candy Is Dandy

Some people seem to be drowning their sorrows in chocolate. The hottest business in Boston's financial district may be The Chocolate Dipper. Sales are up at least 20% since summer. "It has been a great October," says manager Pat Waggett from behind mounds of candy. "They come in here and tell me their troubles. I say, 'Take two truffles and call me in the morning.' "

Drugstores report robust sales in Maalox, Rolaids and Sominex. Among prescription drugs, pharmacists say, Tagamet (for ulcers), Prozac (for depression) and Halcyon (for insomnia) are moving briskly.

Even accountants have started talking like Jungians: "You combine recession and depression—and you've got a giant repression of fears," says Kenneth Freed, of Freed, Sanderson & Co. "First off, I tell clients you can't be creative and do business when you're this depressed. So we try to pull them up off the floor. We have no choice." Mr. Freed says that among his 125 business clients, "there isn't one budgeting for growth, not even the businesses that are doing fine. They're being overwhelmed by the general gloom."

From "Dark Mood: Recession Fears Have Some People Depressed And Acting Erratically" by Ron Suskind, THE WALL STREET JOURNAL, 10/31/90. Copyright © 1990 Dow Jones & Company, Inc. Reprinted by permission of The Wall Street Journal. All Rights Reserved Worldwide.

Questions

1. This article is supposed to be about clinical depression. But is it? Compare the symptoms described in the first paragraph with the diagnostic criteria for Major Depressive Episode in Table 16.4 What might be a better way of describing the symptoms listed in the first paragraph?
2. The theme of this article is that economic depression and psychological depression are linked. How does the author of the article explain this linkage? Do you agree?
3. The comments of psychologist William Roiter are a good reflection of a major perspective on depression. Which one? Explain your choice.

The following case illustrates many of these symptoms, including feelings of worthlessness, loss of interests, agitation, biological signs, and a delusional belief of impending death from disease.

A 55-year-old man has suffered from loss of appetite and a 50-pound weight loss over the past 6 months. His loss of appetite has been accompanied by a burning pain in his chest, back, and abdomen, which he has become convinced indicates a fatal abdominal cancer. He is withdrawn and isolated, unable to work, uninterested in friends and family, and unresponsive to their attempts to make him feel better. He awakes at 4:00 A.M. and is unable to fall back asleep. He claims to feel worse in the mornings and to improve slightly as the day wears on. He is markedly agitated and speaks of feelings of extreme unworthiness. He says that he would be better off dead and that he welcomes his impending demise from cancer. (Adapted from Spitzer et al., 1989, p. 252)

Manic Episode

A person experiencing a **manic episode** shows a euphoric mood, extreme excitement, and hyperactivity. In many respects, mania is the polar opposite of depression (see **Table 16.5**). A manic person's mood may vary from extremely cheerful to elated to euphoric. Far from feeling worthless, the manic person's self-esteem is limitless. These people may undertake tasks, such as writing a novel or composing music, for which they have no particular talent:

I feel no sense of restriction or censorship whatsoever. I am afraid of nothing and no one. During this elated state,

Table 16.5   **DSM-III-R Criteria for Manic Episode (at least four of the following must be present)**

1. persistently elevated, expansive, or irritable mood
2. inflated self-esteem or grandiosity
3. decreased need for sleep
4. more talkative than usual or pressure to keep talking
5. flight of ideas or racing thoughts
6. distractibility
7. increase in goal-directed activity, or psychomotor agitation
8. excessive involvement in pleasurable activities which have a high potential for painful consequences

(DSM-III-R, 1987)

when no inhibition is present, I feel I can race a car with my foot on the floorboard, fly a plane, when I have never flown a plane before, and speak languages I hardly know. Above all, as an artist I feel I can write poems and paint paintings that I could never dream of when just my normal self. (Fieve, 1975, p. 52)

The manic person is in a constant whirlwind of activity. He or she finds it difficult to

sit still and instead constantly moves about—talking, gesticulating, and investigating. Manic people may call friends at all hours of the day or night and may even accost complete strangers, usually to relate their enthusiasm for a world-beating scheme or a sure-fire business deal. They may go on shopping sprees, dress flamboyantly, and even withdraw their money from the bank and hand it out to strangers on the street.

Mania is often accompanied by rapid, incessant talking, a phenomenon known as *pressure of speech.* When severe, the person's speech jumps from one topic to another, with only a tenuous relationship to an underlying theme. This phenomenon, known as *flight of ideas,* is seen in the following excerpt:

> Then I left San Francisco and moved to.... Where did you get that tie? It looks like it's left over from the fifties. I like the warm weather in San Diego. Is that a conch shell on your desk? Have you ever gone scuba diving? (Andreasen, 1979, p. 13–18)

Mania can escalate to delusional proportions. Self-confidence may be replaced by *grandiose delusions,* such as feeling all-powerful and all-knowing. Hyperactivity may pass into a state of uncontrolled excitement in which patients throw off their clothes, bang on walls, and break up furniture. Behavior in such extreme cases approaches the popular stereotype of the "raving maniac."

Depressive and Bipolar Disorders

Episodes of depression and mania are usually of limited duration. Even without treatment, most cases of depression improve within 6 months. Attacks of mania are usually even briefer. And with the development of modern treatment methods, episodes of depression and mania can now be effectively treated within weeks rather than months. However, patients often reexperience problems following recuperation. After recovering from an episode of depression, about 50 percent of these patients will again become depressed within a few years. However, there is a good chance of complete recovery after several years of recurrent episodes (Klerman, 1978).

When patients are followed over several years of recurrent episodes, we find two major types of mood disorder. In the first, episodes of

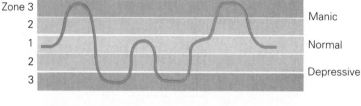
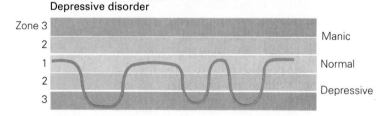

Figure 16.2
Depressive and Bipolar Mood Disorders
Zone I indicates the normal "ups and downs" most people experience, while zones 2 and 3 indicate the manic and depressive episodes that characterize mood disorders. As shown in this diagram, the time between episodes can vary. (After Webb et al., 1981)

depression last a few weeks or months and are followed by periods of normal mood, often lasting for months or years. This type is known as *depressive disorder.* In the second and much rarer type, called *bipolar disorder,* a period of depression is followed by a transition to normal mood and then to a period of mania. **Figure 16.2** is a diagram of these variations in mood in depressive and bipolar disorders. The lengths of the depressive, normal, and manic periods are quite variable from patient to patient. In some cases a switch from mania to depression or vice versa may occur very rapidly and with only a brief passage through a normal mood level:

> For 4 months Mrs. S. has spent most of her time lying in bed. She appears sad and deep in thought and often states, "I'm no good to anyone; I'm going to be dead soon." She expresses many feelings of hopelessness and worthlessness and has difficulty concentrating. Suddenly, one day, her mood seems to be remarkably better. She is pleasant, verbalizes more, and appears somewhat cheerful. The following day, however, the rate of her

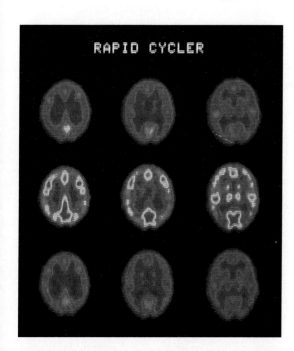

Shown here are PET scans of identical planes of the brain of a rapid cycling bipolar patient. The top and bottom sets of planes were obtained on days during which the patient was depressed. The middle set was obtained on a hypermanic day.

speech is increased, she is moving rapidly, shows a flight of ideas, and intrudes into everyone's activities. Over a couple of days this activity increases to the point where she is unable to control her actions and attempts to break the furniture. (Adapted from NIMH, 1978, p. 1)

Suicide

Depression is a major risk factor in suicide. The suicide rate for patients with a major depressive episode is about 25 times greater than in the general population (Beck, 1967). Thus depressed people contribute overwhelmingly to the conservatively estimated 25,000 deaths due to suicide each year in the United States alone. About three times more women than men attempt suicide. However, about three times more men than women actually succeed in killing themselves. Part of the reason for this is that men tend to use more certain methods such as firearms, where women tend to use less certain methods, such as drug overdose (Goodstein & Calhoun, 1982).

Figure 16.3 on page 584 illustrates U.S. suicide rates for men and women at different ages. The figure also illustrates how ethnicity influences suicide by showing rate for blacks and whites. (Blacks have the lowest overall rate of suicide of any American ethnic group, while whites have one of the highest. Notice that white males show the highest overall rate of the four groups. For black males and females and for white females, suicide rates tend to increase during adolescence and early adulthood and then to decline over the life span. White males are again the exception; their rate of suicide shows a gradual increase over the entire life span. Older white males have a higher rate of suicide than any of the other groups. You may find it instructive to devise explanations for these gender, ethnic, and age differences. For example, the relatvely lower rates of black suicide have been attributed to the supportive influence of the black church, especially in the southern United States where a majority of blacks reside (GAP, 1989).

A majority of severely depressed patients contemplate suicide, but few patients actually attempt it and fewer still are successful. Curiously, the risk of suicide is greater during recovery from depression than during the depths of a depressive episode. The major reason for this is that severely depressed patients

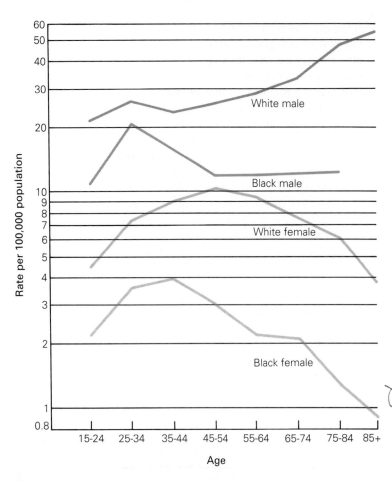

Figure 16.3
Suicide Death Rates in the United States (1982) By Age, Race, and Sex (From Weed, 1985)

may lack the physical and mental energy to carry out their suicidal intentions. As their depression lifts, they gain the physical and psychological wherewithal to follow through on their suicidal intentions.

The vignette of the 25-year-old graduate student on page 566 illustrates a suicide attempt in a case of severe depression.

Women and Depression

One of the more intriguing facts about depression is that women are twice as likely as men to be or to become depressed. This gender difference is not due to any greater willingness on the part of women to admit and seek help for depression, because community surveys find the same 2 to 1 ratio among people who have never been treated for depression (Weissman & Klerman, 1977). One interesting explanation

of the difference is known as the *rumination-distraction hypothesis.* In this view, men and women are equally susceptible to the onset of depression but cope differently once it occurs. Women are thought to cope with depression by dwelling on their negative mood and its possible causes. Through constant rumination, women may amplify their depression and make matters worse. Men, on the other hand, are thought to cope with depression by engaging in distracting activities like sports, which damp negative moods (Nolen-Hoeksema, 1987). You may want to test this hypothesis by surveying the ways in which your male and female friends cope with "the blues."

A report sponsored by the American Psychological Asociation concluded that women are at greater risk for depression because of their life experience in certain critical areas, including the following:

Marriage and childrearing. Married women are three times as likely to be depressed as married men or single women. Women with more and younger children are more likely to be depressed than women with fewer and older children.

Sexual and physical abuse. Victimization of women is probably more prevalent than generally acknowledged and is likely to be a significant cause of depression.

Poverty. Poverty is a "pathway to depression," and 75 percent of the U.S. poor are women and children.

The report acknowledges that our understanding of depression in women is as yet incomplete, and it calls for an increased focus on the special needs of women, societal changes to reduce women's risk of becoming depressed, and more effective use of existing treatment options when depression occurs (McGrath, Keita, Strickland, & Russo, 1990).

Understanding Mood Disorders

There are two major approaches to understanding mood disorders: the biological and the psychological. The biological approach considers research on biochemical and genetic factors in depression and mania. The psychological approach focuses on the role of environmental and intrapsychic factors in generating these disturbed moods. We will consider two psychological perspectives: the psychoanalytic and the cognitive-behavioral. We should note, though, that the biological and psychological approaches are not mutually exclusive. They are best considered complementary approaches addressing a complex biopsychological phenomenon.

THE BIOLOGICAL APPROACH

One line of research in the biological approach seeks to determine whether biochemical disturbances occur during depressed and manic episodes. Specifically, this research centers on possible abnormalities in brain neurotransmitter systems. This work has led to the *biogenic amine hypothesis* of mood disorders.

Biogenic amines are a class of neurotransmitters that includes *norepinephrine* and *serotonin*. The biogenic amine hypothesis holds that depression is associated with lower than normal levels of norepinephrine and serotonin, whereas mania is associated with higher than normal levels of one or both of these neurotransmitters.

The biogenic amine hypothesis grew out of the discovery that certain drugs, first developed for the treatment of medical disorders, also produced mood changes. In the 1950s, physicians observed that patients treated for high blood pressure with *reserpine* often became severely depressed. *Iproniazid*, which was developed to treat tuberculosis, had the opposite effect, producing elation and euphoria in some patients. Reserpine exerts its effects on the brain by *reducing* brain levels of norepinephrine and serotonin. In contrast, iproniazid works by *increasing* levels of norepinephrine and serotonin. Research on the neurotransmitters affected by drugs used to treat depression also supports the biogenic amine hypothesis, as we discuss in Chapter 17.

Most experts agree that the biogenic amine hypothesis of mood disorders is sound but incomplete. Some depressed patients do not seem to have lowered brain amine activity, and it has not been firmly established that manic patients have heightened amine activity. More research is needed before a complete biochemical understanding of these disorders is possible (Goodwin, 1982; Siever & Uhde, 1984).

Many biological investigators also feel that mood disorders may be due in part to a genetically inherited vulnerability. Research evidence, while incomplete, does support this hypothesis. For example, an identical twin of a patient with a mood disorder has about a 70

percent chance of also developing a mood disorder, a rate many times greater than that of the general population (Gershon, Bunney, Leckman, Van Eerdewegh, & De Bauche, 1976). Parents or children of patients with bipolar disorder are six times more likely to develop the disorder than members of the general population (Plomin, 1990). Interpretation of these data is somewhat controversial because the increased vulnerability of close relatives of patients with mood disorders may also be due to the stress of living with these patients.

THE PSYCHOANALYTIC PERSPECTIVE

The psychoanalytic perspective on depression was first developed in a famous paper by Freud entitled "Mourning and Melancholia" (1917/1957). Freud emphasized the similarity between the state of grief that occurs following the death of a loved one and the symptoms of depression. Grief involves pervasive feelings of sadness, a tendency to withdraw from others, and lowered self-esteem. Freud suggested that we take grief as a model of clinical depression.

According to Freud, grief is complicated by inevitable mixed feelings. In addition to affection, the mourner is also likely to have had occasional angry feelings toward the deceased. But because such feelings are unacceptable to the mourner, the anger is redirected toward the self, leading to lowered self-esteem and feelings of guilt. Freud thus suggested that depression is likely to be caused by losses of valued people or objects, as well as symbolic losses, such as the loss of social prestige, the loss of one's health through illness, or the loss of a job—in short, anything in which one has a great deal of emotional investment. Research offers some support for this theory by showing that depressed patients as a group have a higher than normal frequency of life changes involving death, separation, and career disappointments in the period before the onset of their depression (Paykel, 1974).

THE COGNITIVE-BEHAVIORAL PERSPECTIVE

The cognitive-behavioral perspective can be traced to research on *learned helplessness*. As we saw in Chapter 6, the concept of learned helplessness stems from the observation that cognitive deficits can be produced in animals by prior experience with uncontrollable stress. In Seligman's (1975) experiments, exposure to uncontrollable stress appeared to cause animals to form negative expectations about their ability to master subsequent difficult situations. After exposure to uncontrollable stress, the animals did not even try to avoid new stressors that were in fact controllable. The animals appeared passive, depressed, and unmotivated. Thus learned helplessness is often known as an *animal model* of human depression.

At approximately the same time that the concept of learned helplessness was being formulated, Aaron Beck theorized that depressed patients suffered primarily from self-defeating beliefs (Beck, 1974; Beck, Rush, Shaw, & Emery, 1979). According to Beck, depressed patients share a **cognitive triad** of negative beliefs that distort their perception and thinking, which in turn cause the symptoms of depression. The cognitive triad consists of:

1. A negative view of the self
2. A negative view of the world
3. A negative view of the future

These negative views mean that depressed patients will blame themselves for their misfortunes, see the world as ungratifying, and lack hope for the future. Beck theorized that this cognitive triad is constantly reinforced by faulty thinking in depressed patients. For example, patients may ignore evidence that

contradicts their negative views, or they may draw sweeping general conclusions about their hopeless situation from one negative experience.

Both learned helplessness and the negative cognitive triad emphasize cognitive factors in depression. Learned helplessness suggests that uncontrollable stressors produce cognitive distortions, and the cognitive triad describes specific negative cognitions in depressed patients. These two concepts have more recently lead to an approach to depression known as the *attribution theory* of depression. As you already know, an attribution is an inference about the underlying causes of our own or other people's behavior. The attribution theory of depression suggests that depressed patients differ from nondepressed people in the attributions they make about the causes of negative events in their lives. According to this theory, there are three types of relevant attributions that can be made. Negative events can be attributed to (1) internal or external causes, (2) stable or unstable causes, or (3) global or specific causes. Depressed patients tend to attibute negative events to personal inadequacy (internal), to factors that persist across time (stable), and to factors that generalize across situations (global). Nondepressed people tend to blame misfortune on the environment (external), on transient factors (unstable), and on the immediate situation (specific). Thus a depressed student who fails an exam may blame herself for not understanding the material, think that she will never be able to understand, and believe she will fail all exams she takes. A nondepressed student who also fails may blame a lack of study time, chalk it up to a bad day, and resolve to do better on the next exam (Abramson, Seligman, & Teasdale, 1978; Peterson & Seligman, 1984). **Table 16.6** illustrates this theory by describing possible attributions for the negative event of having a cold.

As you can see, the attributional style of depressed patients has the cumulative effect of lowering their self-esteem and feelings of efficacy, while the attributional style of nondepressed people has the effect of bolstering their self-esteem and sense of efficacy. Note that external, unstable, and specific attributions for negative events are not necessarily more objective or accurate than internal, stable, and global attibutions; they are simply different. This raises the interesting question as to whether it is nondepressed or depressed peo-

Table 16.6   **Differing Causal Attributions for the Negative Event: "I Have a Cold"**

	Internal	External
Stable		
Global	"My life is always terrible."	"Medical care in the twentieth century is not as good as most people believe."
Specific	"I always have difficulties with congestion when I have a hectic vacation."	"Doctors still don't know how to tell who is at risk for a cold."
Unstable		
Global	"I've been really tired; I volunteered to work overtime until my boss comes back from her honeymoon."	"When it doesn't rain, the pollution builds up and screws up everything."
Specific	"I forgot to take any Vitamin C for a couple of days."	"The rain last week was really unpredictable."

(Adapted from Peterson, 1982)

ple who are the more objective in their views of the world. This question was addressed in a famous study that compared depressed and nondepressed students' perceptions of control in a situation in which they actually had no control. The task was simple: both groups of subjects had to decide, on a series of trials, whether to push a button or refrain from pushing the button in order to turn on a light. In fact, pushing or not pushing the button was irrelevant because the light was programmed to turn on for 75 percent of the trials no matter which choice as made. When later asked, the depressed students accurately reported that they had very little control over the light. Surprisingly, the nondepressed students wildly overestimated the amount of control they exerted over the light (Alloy & Abramson, 1979). In other words, the nondepressed students showed an *illusion of control* compared with the nondepressed students' more realistic perceptions.

The contrast between nondepressed peoples' tendency to see the world through rose-colored glasses and the often brutally frank judgments of depressed people has been repeatedly demonstrated. This phenomenon has come to be known as *depressive realism* (Alloy & Abramson, 1988). It is as if nondepressed people maintain their self-esteem with protective illusions that place a more optimistic cast on situations than is objectively warranted. Many years ago Sigmund Freud (1917/1957) made a similar observation:

> When in his [the depressed person's] heightened self-criticism he describes himself as petty, egoistic, dishonest, lacking in independence, one whose sole aim has been to hide the weakness of his own nature, it may be, so far as we know, that he has come pretty near to understanding himself; we only wonder why a man has to be ill before he can be accessible to a truth of this kind. (p. 246)

Interim Summary

The dominant feature of the mood disorders is a disturbance of mood, resulting in severe depression or mania. Patients with a depressive disorder may experience repeated episodes of depression followed by normal mood levels. Patients with bipolar disorder may pass through episodes of de-

pression and mania before returning to normal mood levels. Depression is a major risk factor in suicide. Women are twice as likely as men to be depressed, for several reasons.

The biological approach to understanding mood disorders centers on the biogenic amine hypothesis, which holds that depression and mania are associated with abnormally low or high levels of certain brain neurotransmitters. The psychological approach to understanding mood disorders includes the psychoanalytic and the cognitive-behavioral perspectives, which differ in their view of the core symptoms and thus the causes of depression.

SCHIZOPHRENIA

No other psychological disorder is as widely misunderstood as schizophrenia. The public often equates schizophrenia with multiple personality, assuming that schizophrenic patients fluctuate between a placid, conventional personality and a monstrous, violent one, as in the famous story of Dr. Jekyll and Mr. Hyde. Nothing could be further from the truth. Although *schizo-phrenic* literally means "split-mind," the term refers to the fragmentation or splitting up of normally integrated psychological functioning (Bleuler, 1950). A schizophrenic patient has only one personality, but his or her cognitive activity is often severely disorganized. **Schizophrenia** is a serious and severe psychological disorder marked by disorganization of thinking, perception, and emotion. The case vignette of Emilio on page 566 is an example of schizophrenia.

At any one time less than 1 percent of the population suffers from schizophrenia. This rate is lower than those for most other major disorders discussed in this chapter. But because schizophrenia is a severe disorder requiring intensive treatment, schizophrenic patients constitute about 20 percent of all patients in mental-health facilities (NIMH, 1977).

Symptoms of Schizophrenia

In most cases the first appearance of schizophrenic symptoms occurs sometime between the ages of 15 and 45. The symptoms may then fluctuate in severity over a period of many years. During active phases of the disorder, patients are said to be **psychotic**, which means that they experience severe symptoms that greatly impair their ability to interpret and test reality. During less active periods of the disorder the number and severity of symptoms is much reduced, and patients are said to be in a *residual* phase.

Schizophrenic patients manifest a wide variety of unusual and often bewildering symptoms. Many clinicians and researchers find it helpful to categorize schizophrenic symptoms as either positive symptoms or negative symptoms (Andreasen, 1988). Positive symptoms represent exaggerations or distortions of normal psychological functions. Prominent among the positive symptoms we will discuss are *hallucinations* (perceptions, such as hearing voices, that occur in the absence of external stimuli), *delusions* (bizarre beliefs held with great conviction without objective evidence), and

thought disorder (disjointed thought and speech). In contrast, negative symptoms represent a loss of normal psychological functions. We will discuss two negative symptoms, *blunted affect* (emotional unresponsiveness) and *anhedonia* (inability to experience pleasure).

HALLUCINATIONS

Hallucinations can be considered strong mental images that are experienced as if they were perceptions of external reality. Hallucinations may correspond to any of the five senses. The patient may experience an *auditory hallucination* of voices, a *visual hallucination* of objects or people, a *tactile hallucination* of skin sensations, or even *hallucinations of taste and smell*. Auditory hallucinations are the most common form seen in schizophrenia. Patients may experience voices talking to them, commenting on their behavior, or telling them what to do and how to do it. Often the patient will talk back to the voices.

The following is an example of an auditory hallucination reported by a patient with delusions of death and destruction:

> You know Virginia's dead. You know your father's dead. You know the world is ending. You know you're dead. You know you've killed a lot of people. You know you're responsible for the California earthquake, the death of the planet. You know you have a mission. You know you're the messiah. (Vonnegut, 1975, p. 139)

DELUSIONS

While delusions occur in psychological disorders other than schizophrenia, those of schizophrenics are usually quite bizarre. Some patients may believe, for example, that mysterious forces are controlling their thoughts. At times they may feel that ideas are being inserted into their minds. At other times their minds may go completely blank, leading them to believe that their thoughts are being siphoned off. Other patients may believe their minds are like radios, broadcasting their thoughts over long distances. **Figure 16.4** is a patient's drawing of his delusional experience.

Patients will understandably try to make some sense of these bizarre and often frightening delusions by developing elaborate explanations. These explanations are known as *systematized delusions* because they incorporate

Figure 16.4
A Delusional Drawing Produced By a Schizophrenic Patient (As presented in Schizophrenia Bulletin, Issue 7, Winter 1973)

simpler delusions into a more complex belief system. A common example is a *delusion of persecution,* in which the patient develops a plausible but ultimately unrealistic theory of being victimized by conspiratorial forces:

> A young woman was sent to a hospital because she complained that she was being tortured and persecuted and that there were wires around her. For a month before admission, she had heard the voices of three men, especially at night. These men talked about her in such an insulting way that she put cotton in her ears in order to shut out their voices. She also had the idea that electricity was passing through her body, that "they" were experimenting on her with television, and that someone was trying to seduce her by means of electric vibrations. (Kisker, 1977, p. 256)

THOUGHT DISORDER

Normal communication and thought require us to place one idea after another in a logical sequence of related ideas. The schizophrenic patient has difficulty maintaining this orderly flow of ideas. Thought and speech are more likely to resemble a tangled mass of only marginally related themes. Because the patient is unable to keep on the track of one related theme, this symptom is known as *derailment.* The following example of a patient's response to the question "What do you think of the Watergate affair?" illustrates the fractured language of schizophrenia:

> You know I didn't tune in on that, I felt so bad about it. I said, boy, I'm not going to know what's going on in this. But it seemed to get so murky, and everybody's reports were so negative. Huh, I thought, I don't want any part of this, and I was I don't care who was in on it, and all I could figure out was Artie had something to do with it. Artie was trying to flush the bathroom toilet of the White House or something. The tour guests stuck or something. She got blamed because of the water overflowed, went down in the basement, down, to the kitchen. They had a, they were going to have to repaint and restore the White House room, the enormous living room. And then it was at this reunion they were having.... (Andreasen, 1979, pp. 13–19)

Schizophrenic patients seem to be unable to "filter out" distracting associations in their flow of ideas. Their thought and speech therefore become fragmented by involuntary intrusions of normally inhibited thoughts (Chapman & Chapman, 1973; Grillon et al., 1990). This fragmentation is graphically illustrated in the page of writing from a patient seen in **Figure 16.5**.

BLUNTED AFFECT

The term "affect" refers to the outward expression of a person's feelings or emotions. Patients with **blunted affect** show a reduction in the intensity of emotional expression. Even when discussing normally arousing topics, their voices may be monotonous and their facial expres-

Figure 16.5
Drawing By a Schizophrenic Patient
This drawing illustrates thought disorder in a young man with schizophrenia. (As presented in Rosen, Fox, & Gregory, 1972)

sion rigid and immobile. The following description of blunted affect comes from the classic work of Eugen Bleuler, who coined the term "schizophrenia" at the turn of the twentieth century:

> During a lengthy clinical presentation a paranoid (patient) complains constantly about his persecutions but sits very calmly and nonchalantly as he tells his story. Asked if he thought his hallucinations were real, he answers with a shrug of his shoulders: "Perhaps they are pathological, perhaps they are real." The question very obviously does not interest him. . . (Another patient) comes to the doctor to ask him, please, not to kill her. Although she really believes that it is a matter of life and death, she remains completely affectless. (Bleuler, 1950, p.41)

ANHEDONIA

Schizophrenia often involves loss of the ability to experience pleasure, a symptom known as **anhedonia** (an = without, hedonia = pleasure). Together with the symptom of blunted affect, anhedonia points to a severe disturbance in the emotional life of schizophrenic patients. Because of their lack of fellow-feeling, patients with anhedonia tend to be socially withdrawn and isolated. They also tend to be indifferent to activities others find rewarding, including basic activities like sex and eating. The following account of schizophrenic anhedonia is from the work of Emil Kraepelin, the German psychiatrist who first described schizophrenia a century ago:

> The singular indifference of the patients towards their former emotional relations, the extinction of affection for relatives and friends, of satisfaction in their work and vocation, in recreation and pleasures, is not seldom the first and most striking symptom of the onset of the disease. The patients have no real joy in life, "no human feelings"; to them "nothing matters, everything is the same"; they "feel no grief and no joy," "their heart is not in what they say." A patient said he was childish and without interest, as he had never been before. Another said that nothing gave him pleasure, he was sad and yet not sad. . . . (Another) said "I am as cold as it is possible to be." (Kraepelin, 1919/1971, p.33)

Types of Schizophrenia

Individual schizophrenic patients may show a prominence of one or more of the foregoing symptoms during the active phase of the disorder. Such patients may be further diagnosed as having a particular type of schizophrenia. DSM-III-R recognizes four such types. The prominent symptoms of the *disorganized type* are thought disorder and blunted affect. Systematized delusions are absent. Usually this type of patient also shows a variety of bizarre mannerisms such as outlandish dress or peculiar gestures.

The *paranoid type* is marked by highly elaborate delusions of persecution without marked thought disorder or blunted affect. This type may appear rather normal until an unwary person becomes entangled in the patient's argumentativeness and suspiciousness.

The *catatonic type* is rare today, and probably reflected an advanced stage of schizophrenia before the advent of modern treatment methods. Catatonia is a disorder of voluntary movement, in which patients assume a rigid, inflexible posture for lengthy periods of time. At other times these patients may explode into an excited, activated state marked by purposeless, repetitive movements.

Because relatively few schizophrenic patients fit readily into any of these types, a fourth category, known as the *undifferentiated type* is also used for diagnostic purposes. This is a category for patients with multiple psychotic symptoms that do not exactly match the criteria of the other three categories.

The disorder of voluntary movement known as catatonia probably reflected an advanced stage of schizophrenia rarely seen today.

Some patients show many, if not all, of the schizophrenic symptoms we have described. Unlike more typical schizophrenic patients, however, these patients usually experience symptoms briefly, sometimes for only a few days, and then recover completely. The DSM-III-R term for this disorder is *schizophreniform* disorder, meaning "having the appearance of schizophrenia." Many experts believe that schizophreniform disorder should be considered a form of mania with hallucinations and delusions. (Kendler, 1991). In short, DSM-III-R reserves the term *schizophrenia* for patients with lengthy active phases of the disorder and a poor prognosis for complete recovery.

Understanding Schizophrenia

Researchers have uncovered much important information about the causes of schizophrenia in recent years. The disorder cannot be explained by any single factor but is the result of many psychological and biological influences working in combination. One prominent area of research centers on the possibility that disorders of brain functioning underlie schizophrenic symptoms. Many other studies have strenghtened the conviction that an interaction of genetic and environmental factors is ultimately responsible for the development of schizophrenia. We will examine both of these broad areas of research.

THE DOPAMINE HYPOTHESIS

A variety of evidence suggests that at least some of the symptoms of schizophrenia are associated with abnormal activity in brain regions that use *dopamine* as a neurotransmitter. Dopamine is an important neurotransmitter in both the frontal lobes of the cortex and the subcortical area known as the limbic system (for a review see Chapter 2). The dopamine hypothesis stems from research with two classes of drugs, amphetamines and antipsychotics, that affect both the activity of dopamine and the intensity of schizophrenic symptoms.

Amphetamines increase dopamine activity in the brain. When taken by schizophrenic patients in even small doses, amphetamines also increase the severity of their symptoms. Moreover, large doses of amphetamines can, over a period of days, produce a psychotic state even in people who are not schizophrenic. The symptoms of this so-called *amphetamine psychosis,* often seen in abusers of amphetamines, are almost identical to such positive symptoms of schizophrenia as hallucinations and delusions (Snyder, 1974).

Antipsychotic drugs reduce dopamine activity in the brain. As we shall see in the next chapter, antipsychotics are used therapeutically to reduce or eliminate schizophrenic symptoms. In sum, drugs that increase dopamine activity also produce positive schizophrenic symptoms; drugs that decrease dopamine activity ameliorate these symptoms. Therefore, the dopamine hypothesis holds that the positive symptoms of schizophrenia are the result of heightened activity at dopamine synapses in the brain (Snyder, 1981; Seeman & Niznik, 1990).

Many investigators regard the dopamine hypothesis as sound but incomplete. They point out that numerous neurotransmitters influence synaptic transmission in the human brain. In addition, antipsychotic drugs do not actually cure schizophrenia even though they control the positive symptoms seen in the active phase of the disorder. It is unlikely, then, that a disorder of dopamine neurotransmission can by itself account for all the symptoms, both positive and negative, of schizophrenia (Crider, 1979).

BRAIN ATROPHY

As we saw in Chapter 2, major new brain imaging technologies now allow scientists to visualize both the structure and the functioning of the human brain. These technologies have been applied to the study of the brains of schizophrenic patients with often dramatic results. An important finding using both computerized tomography (CT) scans and magnetic resonance imaging (MRI) is that 10 to 40 percent of schizophrenic patients show a significant shrinking, or *atrophy,* of the brain. Atrophy of brain tissue produces enlargements of the cerebral *ventricles,* which are fluid-containing cavities inside the brain. Enlarged venticles can be clearly seen on brain scans (see **Figure 16.6** on page 592). Brain atrophy in schizophrenic patients is most pronounced in the temporal lobes of the cortex, which lie over the dopamine-rich limbic system. Some, but not all, studies also suggest that atrophy also occurs in the frontal lobes (Andreasen et al., 1990; Delisi et al., 1991).

Other studies have profitably employed regional cerebral blood flow (RCBF) measure-

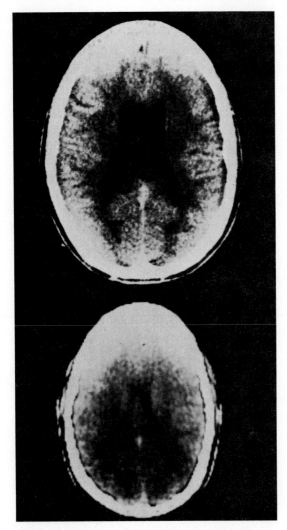

Figure 16.6
CT Scans
These computerized tomography (CT) scans show the
differences in the brains of a schizophrenic patient (top)
and a nonschizophrenic patient (bottom). Note that the
shaded, long-shaped ventricles in the schizophrenic patient
are noticeably larger than those shown in the
nonschizophrenic patient

ments to observe brain activity in schizophrenic patients. In this method, subjects inhale a radioactive gas that is picked up by sensors on the skull as blood flows through the brain. The amount of blood flow indicates the degree of metabolic activity in the brain's neurons. An important study by Weinberger, Berman, & Zec (1986) found that the frontal cortex of schizophrenic patients showed abnormally low activity when patients were challenged by a cognitive task. Specifically, both schizophrenic and normal subjects were given two tests while RCBF measurements were made. One task was a simple test requiring little cognitive activity. The second task, known as the Wisconsin Card Sorting (WCS) test, requires an ability to make abstractions from data and to be cognitively flexible. Schizophrenic patients are known to perform poorly on the WCS. The results of this study are shown in **Figure 16.7.** No difference between schizophrenic and normal subjects was seen in cortical activity during the number matching task. During performance on the WCS test, however, normal subjects showed a dramatic increase in the activty of the frontal cortex, while schizophrenic subjects showed no change. In sum, this study showed that schizophrenic patients have a specific frontal cortex impairment that is correlated with a specific cognitive impairment.

ARE THERE TWO TYPES OF SCHIZOPHRENIA?

Crow (1980; 1985) has proposed a hypothesis that takes into account the distinction between positive and negative symptoms, the dopamine hypothesis, and the evidence for brain atrophy in schizophrenia. According to this hypothesis, there are two major types of schizophrenia. Type I patients show predominantly positive symptoms, which are due to heightened dopamine activity. These patients respond well to antipsychotic drug therapy, and they have normal-sized ventricles and normal cognitive abilities. Type II patients show predominantly negative symptoms and poor response to antipsychotic drug therapy. These patients have enlarged ventricles and impaired cognitive abilities. Type I patients are more likely to recover from schizophrenia than are type II patients.

Critics think Crow is mistaken in positing two distict types of schizophrenia. They point out that only a minority of patients show exclusively positive or negative symptoms, most show an admixture of both kinds of symptoms. These critics are more likely to think of schizophrenia as occurring along a continuum of severity from positive to negative symptoms. Patients with only positive symptoms are less severely affected and more likely to recover than patients with only negative symptoms or with an admixture of both. In this view, enlarged ventricles increase the severity of the disorder (Grinspoon & Bakalar, 1990b). Whatever the ultimate view of schizophrenia, there is no question that brain research has made great progress in understanding this most mysterious disorder.

THE ROLES OF HEREDITY AND ENVIRONMENT

Most experts now believe that schizophrenia develops out of an interaction between genetic and environmental influences. This view is known as the **diathesis-stress** model of schizophrenia. *Diathesis* refers to a genetic predisposition and *stress* to environmental events that cause the predisposition to be expressed in schizophrenic symptoms. In this model, both genetic and environmental factors must be present for the disorder to occur.

The role of genetic factors has been demonstrated by numerous studies showing that a person's chances of becoming schizophrenic increase with the degree of genetic relatedness to a known schizophrenic patient (see **Table 16.7** on page 594). A person unrelated to a schizophrenic patient has about a 1 percent chance of becoming schizophrenic at some time in life. By comparison, first-degree relatives, such as siblings or parents, have a 5 to 15 percent chance of becoming schizophrenic. The identical twin of a schizophrenic patient has a 25 to 50 percent chance of becoming schizophrenic.

While these figures strongly suggest that schizophrenia has a genetic component, they do not absolutely prove it. People who share a high degree of genetic relatedness are also more likely to share the same environment. For example, first-degree relatives are more likely to live in the same home than second-degree relatives. Thus, it can be argued that children who are raised by a schizophrenic parent are more likely to become schizophrenic for social and psychological, rather than genetic, reasons. By this interpretation, the degree of environmental similarity, rather than the degree of genetic similarity, is the crucial factor in determining schizophrenia.

To overcome this interpretive difficulty, Heston (1966) examined the development of schizophrenia in children whose mothers were schizophrenic but who were placed in *adoptive* families shortly after birth. By the time these children reached adulthood, about 10 percent had become schizophrenic, which is about the same as the rate of schizophrenia among children actually raised by their schizophrenic mothers. A similar study by Kety (1983) examined both the biological and the adoptive families of schizophrenic patients who had been adopted in infancy. They found that schizophrenia was much more likely to occur in the biological families, rather than the

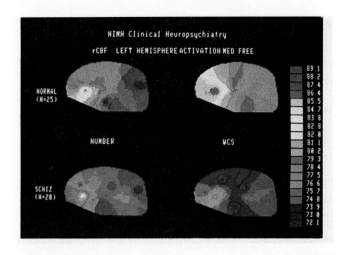

Figure 16.7
Cerebral Blood Flow Measurement
Cerebral blood flow measurement shows no difference between schizophrenic and normal subjects in cortical activity during the simple number matching task on the left. During performance on the WCS cognitive task on the right, however, normal subjects show a dramatic increase in the activity of the frontal cortex but schizophrenic subjects show no change. (As presented in Weinberger et al., 1986)

adoptive families, of schizophrenic patients. To summarize, both of these studies capitalized on the practice of adoption to separate hereditary influences from the influence of being raised by a schizophrenic parent. Both showed that similar heredity, rather than similar environment, accounted for the higher rates of schizophrenia in the offspring of schizophrenic parents. These findings indicate a genetic predisposition is undoubtedly an important factor in the development of schizophrenia.

Heredity is not the whole answer, however. The figures for identical twins in Table 16.7 show that if a person is genetically *identical* to a schizophrenic patient his or her chances of also developing schizophrenia are somewhere between 25 percent and 50 percent. If genes alone determined schizophrenia, the chances should be 100 percent. Thus, there must also be nongenetic, or environmental, factors that determine whether a person with the genetic predisposition for schizophrenia in fact becomes schizophrenic.

At this time researchers do not know with certainty if preschizophrenic children experience specific types of environmental stress more frequently than other children. One theory holds that the mothers of schizophrenic patients may have experienced complications during pregnancy and delivery. These cause the

Table 16.7   Probability of Schizophrenia in Relatives of Schizophrenic Patients

Relationship to Schizophrenic Patient	Percent of Genes in Common	Probability of Becoming Schizophrenic
None	None	About 1%
Second-degree relative (for example, niece, nephew, grandchild)	25%	2–3%
First-degree relative (for example, child, brother, sister, fraternal twin)	50%	5–15%
Identical twin	100%	25–50%

Based on Gottesman & Shields (1972); Slater & Cowie (1971)

preschizophrenic child to be less healthy and robust and thus more susceptible to the deleterious effects of his or her genetic predisposition (Stabenau & Pollin, 1970; McNeil & Kay, 1987). Another theory holds that the genetic predisposition in such children is often brought out by unsupportive and psychologically destructive parents. According to this view, the parents of preschizophrenic children are themselves very disturbed, and they create a stressful and conflict-ridden environment. Irrational behavior may be a way of life in such families, so that the susceptible child finds it increasingly easy to fall into schizophrenia (Lidz, 1973; Wynne, 1968).

A search to confirm these and other theories of the *stress* component of the diathesis-stress model is now being conducted in a series of very ambitious longitudinal studies. These are known as *high-risk studies* because they follow the children of schizophrenic mothers from birth into adulthood. As shown in Table 16.7, 5 to 15 percent of these children will become schizophrenic at some time in life. These children therefore constitute a "high-risk" group. By comparing the life histories of the 5 to 15 percent who go on to become schizophrenic with those who do not, it should be possible to isolate environmental factors leading to schizophrenia. Unfortunately such studies require 20 or more years to complete, so final answers are not yet available.

However, one high-risk study has shown that different environmental stressors in the backgrounds of schizophrenic patients lead to different forms of schizophrenia. In this study, high-risk children who later developed predominantly negative symptoms were more likely to have experienced birth complications, whereas high-risk children who later developed predominately positive symptoms were more likely to have experienced unstable early family environments. In addition, the children who later developed negative symptoms were rated by their school teachers as passive and socially isolated, whereas the children who developed positive symptoms were rated as overactive, aggressive, and irritable. This study therefore indicates that a genetic diathesis is a precondition for schizophrenia but that the type of symptoms shown by the patient depend on specific kinds of environmental stressors (Cannon, Mednick, & Parnas, 1990).

We should not be misled into concluding that birth complications and unstable family environments exhaust all possible stressors in the development of schizophrenia. This is because many schizophrenic patients have experienced neither of these two background factors (Crider, 1979). Future research is likely to uncover other kinds of stressors capable of influencing the development of schizophrenia in susceptible children.

Interim Summary

The symptoms of schizophrenia can be grouped into positive (behaviorally excessive) and negative (behaviorally deficient) syndromes. Positive symptoms include hallucinations, delusions, and thought disorder; negative symptoms include anhedonia and blunted affect. DSM-III-R lists four types of schizophrenia: disorganized, paranoid, catatonic, and undifferentiated.

The dopamine hypothesis holds that schizophrenic symptoms are associated with hyperactivity at dopamine synapses in the brain, which may account for positive symptoms. Some schizophrenic patients show a generalized atrophy of the brain due to a progressive loss of neurons, which may account for negative symptoms. The diathesis-stress model regards the psychological and neurochemical disturbances in schizophrenia as the outcome of an interaction between a genetic predisposition to the disorder and environmental stressors. Longitudinal studies of genetically at-risk individuals suggest that different kinds of environmental stressors produce different types of symptoms.

SUBSTANCE-USE DISORDERS

The **substance-use disorders** include a variety of syndromes caused by the abuse of chemical substances such as alcohol, drugs, tobacco, and caffeine. In Chapter 5 we described the psychoactive effects of several of these substances. Many of these psychoactive substances, such as the sedative drugs, are prescribed under medical supervision for the relief of pain, anxiety, and other symptoms of psychological disorder. Others, such as alcohol and marijuana, are used as recreational drugs by millions precisely because of the alteration in normal modes of consciousness they produce. For large numbers of people, however, the medical or recreational use of drugs develops into chronic patterns of *substance abuse.* This abuse leads to a variety of psychological disorders, which take an appalling toll on individual well-being and severely tax treatment facilities.

When Substance Use Becomes Abuse

Substance abuse occurs when the use of psychoactive substances produces chronic changes in behavior patterns and brain activity that are both personally and socially debilitating. These changes may include one or more of the following: (1) psychological dependence, (2) physical dependence, and (3) substance-induced organic mental disorders. **Table 16.8** on page 596 sets out the major effects observed with abuse of various drugs. Finally, substance abuse will sooner or later result in (4) impaired social functioning.

PSYCHOLOGICAL DEPENDENCE
Prolonged use of chemical substances may lead to psychological dependence: a compelling craving for the substance and an inability to discontinue its use. The psychologically dependent person may go through repeated cycles of drug use followed by attempts to abstain that end in failure and renewed heavy use. Compulsive use may continue in spite of severe threats to health, as illustrated in the following famous case:

> A prominent physician was informed that his heart arrhythmia was due to his heavy cigar smoking. He stopped for 14 months, but the torture, he said, "was beyond human power to bear." Eventually, he developed cancer of the jaw and mouth that was also attributed to smoking. Despite 33 operations for cancer and construction of a clumsy artificial jaw, he continued to smoke. He died at the age of 83. His many efforts to stop smoking, and the persistence of his craving and suffering, make him a tragic example of tobacco addiction. His name was Sigmund Freud. (Adapted from Altrocchi, 1980)

PHYSICAL DEPENDENCE
Prolonged use of many drugs can also lead to physical dependence marked by tolerance and withdrawal symptoms. *Tolerance* develops when increasing amounts of the drug are necessary to achieve the desired state of intoxication. For example, the alcoholic may find it necessary to drink increasingly greater amounts in order to experience the effects originally produced by one or two drinks. *Withdrawal* is a syndrome of distressing symptoms that occurs following the cessation of regular use of certain drugs. The nature of the withdrawal syndrome varies somewhat from drug to drug, but the most common symptoms include anxiety, irritability, restlessness, and impaired concentration. Some substances, such as marijuana and the psychedelics, have not been shown to produce withdrawal syndromes.

ORGANIC MENTAL DISORDERS
An **organic mental disorder** is a psychological or behavioral abnormality due to known impairment of brain functioning. Organic mental disorders can be caused by injury, disease, or abnormal aging (senility). When an organic mental disorder is caused by a psychoactive substance, it is known as a *substance-induced organic mental disorder.*

Whether a psychoactive substance will cause an organic mental disorder depends on several factors, such as the type of substance used, the dose, the duration of use, and individual differences in susceptibility to the effects of the particular substance. Among the more common substance-induced organic mental disor-

Table 16.8   Drugs of Abuse

Drugs	DEPENDENCE Physical	Psychological	Possible Effects	Effects of Overdose	Withdrawal Syndrome
Narcotics					
Opium	High	High	Euphoria,	Slow and shallow	Watery eyes,
Morphine	High	High	drowsiness,	breathing,	runny nose,
Codeine	Moderate	Moderate	respiratory	clammy skin,	yawning,
Heroin	High	High	depression,	convulsions,	loss of appetite,
Hydromorphone	High	High	constricted pupils,	coma,	irritability,
Meperidine (Pethidine)	High	High	nausea	possible death	tremors, panic,
Methadone	High	High-low			cramps, nausea, chills and sweating
Sedatives					
Chloral Hydrate	Moderate	Moderate	Slurred speech,	Shallow respiration,	Anxiety,
Barbiturates	High-mod	High-mod	disorientation,	clammy skin,	insomnia,
Benzodiazepines	Low	Low	drunken behavior	dilated pupils,	tremors,
Methaqualone	High	High	without odor of	weak and rapid pulse,	delirium,
Glutethimide	High	Moderate	alcohol	coma	convulsions
Stimulants					
Cocaine	Possible	High	Increased alertness,	Agitation,	Apathy,
Amphetamines	Possible	High	excitation, euphoria,	increase in body	long periods of
Phenmetrazine	Possible	High	increased pulse rate	temperature,	sleep,
Methylphenidate	Possible	Moderate	and blood pressure,	hallucinations,	irritability,
			insomnia	convulsions	depression, disorientation
Psychedelics					
LSD	None	Unknown	Illusions and	Longer, more intense	Withdrawal
Mescaline and peyote	None	Unknown	hallucinations,	"trip" episodes,	syndrome
Amphetamine variants	Unknown	Unknown	poor perception	psychosis,	not reported
Phencyclidine	Unknown	High	of time	possible death	
Phencyclidine analogues	Unknown	High	and distance		
Cannabis					
Marijuana	Unknown	Moderate	Euphoria,	Fatigue,	Insomnia,
Tetrahydrocannabinol	Unknown	Moderate	relaxed inhibitions,	paranoia,	hyperactivity,
Hashish	Unknown	Moderate	increased appetite	possible psychosis	and decreased appetite occasionally reported
Alcohol	Repeated use of alcohol can lead to dependence		Impaired judgment and coordination, increased incidence of aggressive acts	Respiratory depression, death	Severe anxiety, tremors, hallucinations, convulsions

Excerpted from U.S. Department of Justice Bulletin, Drug Enforcement Administration Drugs of Abuse 1989

ders are *delirium, organic hallucinations,* and *organic delusions.*

The chief symptom of **delirium** is a disturbance of attention, in which the person finds it difficult to focus on an external stimulus or to shift attention from one stimulus to another. The person may be unable to speak or think coherently or to engage in simple activities like watching television. Consciousness may fluctuate from drowsiness to a coma. Memory is also impaired to the extent that the person cannot recall the day or date, where he or she is, or even his or her name.

Common *organic hallucinations* include the sensation of "bugs" crawling under the skin, angry voices, or frightening visual images. Organic hallucinations occur most commonly with alcohol, opiate, and psychedelic drug abuse. *Organic delusions,* varying from suspiciousness to a full-blown delusion of persecution, may be caused by the psychedelic or stimulant drugs.

Substance-induced organic mental disorders usually subside as the body metabolizes and excretes the offending substance. In the interim, the person can be helped by calming reassurance, reminders of the cause of the symptoms, and by tranquilizing medication.

IMPAIRED SOCIAL FUNCTIONING

A person who is dependent on and chronically intoxicated by drugs is less able, or often unable, to carry out normal social expectations. Occupational functioning may deteriorate, and absences from work or school may be common. The person's interactions with others may become erratic and troubled, leading to a decline in the number and quality of social and occupational relationships. The deterioration of the person's ability to function is often the first hard evidence of hidden substance abuse.

Alcoholism

Alcoholism, or alcohol abuse, is a substance-use disorder characterized by psychological and physical dependence and impaired social functioning. It is by far the most common form of substance abuse in North America. About 3 to 5 percent of the population suffers from alcoholism at some time in the life span (Goodwin & Guze, 1979). In the following discussion, we will consider alcoholism as an example of the way in which substance abuse can affect the user's health and well-being and seriously distort his or her personal relationships.

The consequences of alcoholism are catastrophic. Drunken driving accounts for more than half of the approximately 50,000 traffic fatalities each year in the United States. Experts estimate that violent behavior associated with alcohol abuse accounts for approximately 65 percent of murders, 40 percent of assaults, 35 percent of rapes, 30 percent of suicides, and 60 percent of child-abuse cases. In the United States alone the annual cost of alcohol abuse runs to tens of billions of dollars, due to lost productivity, accidents, crime, and the direct costs of health care for alcoholics, which itself is about $44 billion (Grinspoon & Bakalar, 1990a; Stone, 1980). Nor is alcoholism any less destructive for the individual alcoholic, who risks organic mental disorders, cirrhosis of the

liver, cancer, and organ damage. **Figure 16.8** illustrates the physical organs most susceptible to damage from long-term alcohol abuse.

There are many types of problem drinkers, including the "binge" drinker, who alternates long periods of sobriety with briefer periods of intoxication, and the "instant alcoholic," who becomes an abuser on first being introduced to alcohol. In most cases, however, alcoholism progresses over a long period divided into early, middle, and chronic phases (see **Table 16.9** on page 598).

In the *early phase,* the prealcoholic drinks socially for mild mood alteration and relief of tension. But he or she begins to develop a tolerance for alcohol and requires more than the usual drink or two to achieve the desired effects. The person progresses to psychological dependence as he or she becomes preoccupied with drinking and irritable if the daily intake is missed.

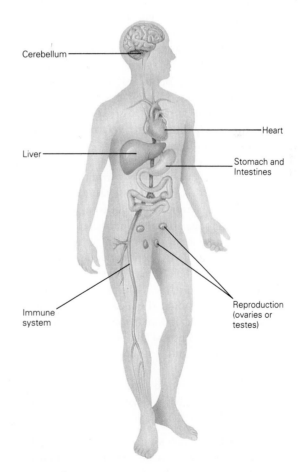

Figure 16.8
Organs Affected By Alcohol

Table 16.9   Signs of Alcohol Abuse Among 100 Alcoholic Subjects

Sign	Percent of Subjects
1. Frequent drunks	98
2. Weekend drunks	82
3. Morning drinking	84
4. Benders	76
5. Neglecting meals	86
6. "Shakes"	88
7. Job loss from drinking	69
8. Separation or divorce because of drinking	44
9. Blackouts	64
10. Joined A.A.	39
11. Hospitalization for drinking	100
12. Delirium tremens	45

Excerpted from Goodwin & Guze (1979)

In the *middle phase,* the person begins to lose control over drinking. The emerging alcoholic may regard a drink as increasingly necessary to begin the day and become irritable when friends question the increased use of alcohol. In an effort to control drinking, the person may begin to switch brands, make and then break promises to self and family to stop, and even change jobs or move to a new location for "a new start." Periods of abstinence broken by "falling off the wagon" are frequent in this phase.

In the *chronic phase,* the person may begin to drink continuously throughout the day, remaining intoxicated for several days on end. Withdrawal symptoms begin to appear. At this stage, drinking no longer alleviates tension but leads to attacks of depression or anxiety. Even without complete abstinence, a lowering of blood-alcohol levels may precipitate *delirium tremens,* an organic delirium with hallucinations. By this point, the alcoholic's psychological and physical dependence are often compounded by physical illness, accidents, loss of employment, and estrangement from family and friends.

The following vignette illustrates the long-term, progressive nature of alcohol abuse and repeated failures to control use.

Tom began drinking at the age of 13. He said he had no problems with alcohol in college, but he did admit occasional blackouts. He was drunk often while an officer in World War II and for the first time suffered morning tremors. Still, at the age of 29 he wrote, "Alcohol is very nice to me. It convinces me that the world is better than it seems. I never have hangovers." Four years later he wrote, "I don't think I am an alcoholic but I drink maybe a quart a week. I am unhappy with less." At the age of thirty-five he said, "I am changing from a heavy to a moderate drinker." But two years later: "I drink too much, a major worry, maybe a pint of whiskey a day." At this time his alcohol consumption had gone from four drinks to ten drinks a day. At age 44: "I drink all day and half the night." Three years later he began a serious attempt to quit. He attended alcohol clinics as an outpatient and by age 50 his drinking had become more intermittent: "I really do quit for a period of weeks or months." But four to five years later he admitted increasing loss of control, fear, and hopelessness: "I have been an alcoholic for at least ten years." (Vaillant, 1983, as abridged by Grinspoon & Bakalar, 1990a, p. 4)

Some alcoholics give up drinking without treatment. More typically, however, intense efforts are required, Treatment is often difficult because the alcoholic may deny there is any problem to be treated. If this resistance can be overcome, treatment usually begins with a hospital-based *detoxification* program, in which alcohol is metabolized from body tissues and

There is no sure way to cure alcoholism. However, support groups like Alcoholics Anonymous often help.

withdrawal symptoms are controlled with tranquilizing medications. Following detoxification, the most effective treatment includes (1) counseling to deal with the many family, social, and occupational problems caused by the patient's alcohol abuse and (2) membership in support groups like Alcoholics Anonymous.

However, there is no sure cure for alcoholism. A number of studies show that most alcoholics who undergo treatment begin drinking again (relapse) within a few months. About 50 percent of alcoholics relapse within six months of treatment, and about 70 percent relapse within 2 years. Yet many alcoholics do recover eventually. Those who recover typically do so after many years of trying and many unsuccessful treatment programs (De Soto, O'Donnell, & De Soto, 1989; Vaillant, 1983).

Understanding Substance Abuse

The causes of substance abuse are not fully understood. What is clear, however, is that substance abuse is the result of social, psychological, and physiological factors operating in concert. Psychologists and other researchers distinguish between factors associated with initial use of a psychoactive substance and factors associated with its continued use and abuse.

INITIAL USE

Two factors are associated with initial use. One is access to the substance. No substance can be used unless it is available. As examples, illegal substance use occurs at higher than normal rates in the inner city, where drug dealing is a major commercial activity, as well as among physicians and other medical workers, who have access to drugs through their occupations (Ausubel, 1980).

Peer influences are a second major factor in initial use. Future abusers are almost always introduced to both legal and illegal substances in adolescence by friends who hold favorable attitudes toward drugs and, often, corresponding rebellious attitudes toward prevailing cultural values. Peer-group initiation usually begins with marijuana and progresses to more potent illegal drugs (Johnson, 1980).

Peer influence against drug use may account for the recent decline in illegal drug use among high school and college students, as compared with marked increases in the 1960s and 1970s. For example, one study surveyed illegal drug use among seniors at the same college in 1969, 1978, and 1989. As can be seen in **Figure 16.9,** the 1989 students reported strikingly lower frequencies of virtually all forms of drug use than their counterparts in 1969 and 1978. The one exception was for alcohol use, which remained around 40 percent in all three surveys (Pope, Ionescu-Pioggia, Aizley, & Varma, 1990).

ABUSE

Exposure to psychoactive substances and peer-group pressure does not explain continued use and abuse, however. Many researchers feel that the difference between experimentation and regular use is due to personality factors. Although no single personality type is associated with regular use and abuse, a number of studies using personality inventories have

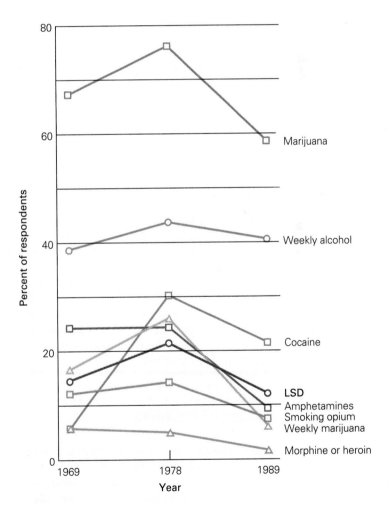

Figure 16.9
College Seniors Reporting Use of Various Drugs in 1969, 1978, and 1989.
All rates represent the percent of students who had ever used a given drug, except for the categories of weekly marijuana and weekly alcohol use. (As presented in Pope et al., 1990)

found that abusers score lower than non-abusers on scales measuring social conformity and social responsibility. Substance abuse appears to be correlated with social alienation and poor impulse control (Gorsuch, 1980; Shedler & Block, 1990).

Once regular use becomes established, the substance itself often changes motivational patterns, leading to abuse. For example, substance use is positively reinforced by desired changes in mood and consciousness and negatively reinforced by reductions in anxiety and other undesired mood states. These reinforcing changes will tend to promote further use. In addition, giving up drug use will be experienced as aversive, so that drugs are used in order to avoid negative feelings associated with cessation. In addition, abstinence from certain drugs will also produce unpleasant withdrawal symptoms. Thus, the substance abuser becomes caught in a vicious cycle of regular use leading to psychological and physical dependence that motivates continued use. Addiction occurs over time as the pattern of dependence becomes increasingly difficult to break (Baker, 1988; Gawin, 1991).

Interim Summary

Substance-use disorders are caused by the abuse of psychoactive substances such as drugs, alcohol, and tobacco. Problems associated with substance abuse may include impaired social functioning, psychological dependence, physical dependence, or various organic mental disorders. Each of these problems typically occurs in alcoholism, the most common form of substance abuse in our society. Causes of substance abuse include access, peer influence, and personality factors, as well as motivational changes induced by long-term use.

PERSONALITY DISORDERS

A *personality trait,* as we learned in Chapter 14, is a relatively stable behavioral or cognitive characteristic that an individual exhibits in a wide range of situations. A **personality disorder,** on the other hand, is a particular combination of traits that is extremely inflexible and therefore results in impaired psychological, social, and occupational functioning (Millon, 1981).

Personality disorders are often apparent by adolescence and tend to endure through the life span, although they may become muted in later life (DSM-III-R, 1987). Personality disorders therefore contrast with the more episodic and "colorful" symptoms of the disorders already discussed. DSM-III-R recognizes this distinction by identifying personality disorders on Axis II of its multiaxial diagnostic scheme.

Individuals with personality disorders may also have any of the Axis I disorders and thus may receive both an Axis I and Axis II diagnosis. Such individuals are likely to develop depressive episodes or an anxiety disorder when their inflexibility interferes with their ability to cope with stressful events. In fact, personality disorders are usually first diagnosed when the individual seeks treatment for an Axis I disorder. Otherwise, individuals with personality disorders are not especially unhappy with themselves. Indeed, they tend to regard other people as the source of any interpersonal conflicts they experience.

The entire diagnostic category of personality disorders is somewhat controversial for two reasons. First, some psychologists argue that the criteria for diagnosing such disorders are both vague and difficult to observe reliably. In addition, they object to labeling an enduring personality configuration, as opposed to an Axis I syndrome, as abnormal. Other psychologists argue that the concept of personality disorder aids in understanding patients for whom it is an appropriate, though sometimes imprecise, description. They further argue that the psychological inflexibility and troubled interpersonal relations characteristic of such patients are sufficient criteria for diagnosing psychological abnormality.

DSM-III-R describes 11 different personality disorders, and we will discuss four of the more prominent ones: the paranoid, histrionic, obsessive-compulsive, and antisocial personalities.

Paranoid Personality Disorder

An individual with a paranoid personality disorder can be likened to a detective who single-mindedly searches for the clue that will solve his or her case. Always suspicious and mistrustful, these persons resolutely seek out the "truth." The usual goal of their search is evidence that others are disloyal, disrespectful, or contemplating trickery. They are often perceptive regarding details but generally misevaluate information that does not conform to their suspicions. Those affected with a paranoid personality disorder are seen by others as secretive, scheming, and humorless. They are argumentative and quick to take offense. At times their suspiciousness may escalate into pathological jealousy or rage. Because of their inability to trust others, their interpersonal and occupational functioning is severely constricted (DSM-III-R, 1987; Shapiro, 1965). The following vignette illustrates manipulation and hostility in a paranoid personality:

> A middle-aged lawyer sued his wife for divorce and custody of his daughters. He somehow induced the children to lodge far-fetched charges of child abuse and to testify in court that their mother had had oral sex with neighborhood men. The judge, not deceived, awarded the mother custody, and soon after received valuable jewelry bought in the wife's name by an anonymous third party. The judge returned the jewelry immediately, but the husband, who presumably had sent it, spread the story of a "bribe" in the newspapers. The court called in a psychiatrist who said the husband was a paranoid personality. (Goldstein, 1987)

Histrionic Personality Disorder

Histrionic means theatrical or dramatic, two terms that aptly characterize people with this disorder. They constantly call attention to themselves by behaving in an exaggerated and colorful manner. When feeling well, they crave excitement and variety; when feeling poorly, they may behave like virtual invalids. They usually have a rich fantasy life, in which other people are endowed with romantic, stereotyped attributes, such as those of a prince charming or wicked witch.

The cognitive style of individuals with a histrionic personality disorder is unreflective and impulsive. Their perceptions and ideas are relatively vague, lacking detail or qualification. They tend to come quickly to decisions and have strong opinions but are unable to specify why they hold these opinions. This cognitive style can be seen in the following vignette from a therapist:

> Once, for example, in taking a case history from an exceedingly [histrionic] patient, I made repeated efforts to obtain a description of her father from her. She seemed, however, hardly to understand

Dramatic and colorful behavior like this is also often seen in histrionic personality disorder.

the sort of data I was interested in, and the best she could provide was, "My father? He was wham-bang! That's all—just wham-bang!" (Shapiro, 1965, p. 111)

In interpersonal situations, these persons are often charming, sexy, and seductive. Once a relationship is established, however, they may become increasingly demanding and manipulative. If the other person threatens to break off the relationship, the histrionic person may engage in tearful pleading, or even suicidal gestures as a means of ensuring continued sympathy and concern. Such stormy, conflict-ridden relationships often place a great burden on others.

Obsessive-Compulsive Personality Disorder

The individual with an obsessive-compulsive personality disorder is a perfectionist. He or she will strive to make sure things are "just right" before letting go of a project. Because perfection is rarely achieved in human affairs, these persons are usually dissatisfied with their own and others' work. They usually see others as irresponsible if not actually immoral and conduct their own lives according to rigid prescriptions for appropriate behavior.

The cognitive style associated with this disorder is highly analytical and intellectual. The individuals pay extraordinary attention to detail, often failing to grasp the overall significance of the situation. Their propensity to make elaborate distinctions and to qualify all ideas impedes their ability to make decisions. The following is an example of an obsessive-compulsive professor-scientist:

> Professor Edwards was well known as a lecturer who went into extraordinary detail on minor points, "usually missing the forest for the trees" as one student publication put it. To his colleagues, he was a perfectionist who drove himself in preparing manuscripts for publication. He demanded twice as many subjects, three times as many statistical tests, and extraordinary controls before he would write up an experiment. Even then he could not let the manuscript go until he put it through innumerable revisions. When it came time to type the final version, he would not allow the typist to make a single erasure for fear that the editor would think him hasty in his scientific work. (Nathan & Harris, 1980, p. 367)

The interpersonal relationships of those with an obsessive-compulsive personality disorder are strained. Guided by strict notions of right and wrong, they will often strive to make others conform to their view of the world. In addition, they tend to be cold and aloof in their relationships with others, who see them as mechanical and intolerant.

Antisocial Personality Disorder

The essential feature of this disorder is a long history of frequent antisocial behavior that violates the rights of others. The DSM-III-R criteria for this disorder emphasize an adolescent history of truancy, delinquency, and violations of the law, plus an adult history of occupational instability, failure to meet financial obligations, and criminal behavior. In addition to such relatively objective criteria, most psychologists add several personality characteristics. For example, Martin (1981) lists the following six traits:

1. *Lack of conscience.* Individuals with an antisocial personality disorder are devoid of moral scruples or feelings of remorse following transgressions against others.
2. *Impulsiveness.* Although they are not intellectually deficient, these individuals seem incapable of planning ahead or delaying immediate gratification for longer-term gains. Instead they act on impulses, which lead to a chaotic and irresponsible lifestyle.
3. *Inability to profit from mistakes.* These

persons are often abandoned by former friends, fired from jobs, or arrested for criminal activity. Yet they learn little from such negative experiences and often return to the same patterns that caused past difficulties.
4. *Lack of emotional ties to others.* Such people tend to be callous and manipulative in their relations with others. Lacking sensitivity, they treat others as objects for gratifying their own needs.
5. *Stimulus seeking.* These individuals are easily bored by routine activities. They constantly search out exciting and often hazardous activities, such as daring crimes or the use of powerful psychoactive drugs.
6. *Ability to make a good impression.* In the service of manipulating others or getting out of difficult situations these persons can be likable and charming. Many an unsuspecting person has been cheated or deceived by these most skillful of "con artists."

A neighboring family was on vacation, and X knew the contents of the house. He figured that he could burglarize the place successfully because the family regarded him as a friend and would never suspect him. (He) proceeded to steal cameras, radios, piggy banks, and a diamond ring. When the family returned, the police were called. He made himself available to go through the list of what was missing and what was untouched; this gave him ideas for the future. He also offered police the names of people he said might be responsible for the thefts... Through his gift of gab, X was offered a job with a drug treatment agency...and impressed others by his polished appearance and speech. He was selected for a permanent position and appeared on television as a "rehabilitated addict" While serving as a model of a cured man, he was chipping heroin, smoking marihuana, and drinking considerable amounts of alcohol. (Mental Health Letter, 1985)

A good deal of research has been conducted on the sources of the behavior patterns associated with an antisocial personality disorder. One clear finding is that this disorder tends to run in families. For example, Robins (1966) found that one third of the fathers and one tenth of the mothers of people with an antisocial personality disorder also had the same disorder and or suffered from alcoholism.

Both genetic and environmental factors are probably involved in the transmission of this disorder from generation to generation. A genetic factor has been demonstrated in a number of studies shoving that when children of people with an antisocial personality disorder are adopted into normal families early in life, they are more likely to become antisocial than are adopted children whose natural parents are normal. Environmental factors are implicated by the higher-than-normal incidence of broken families, parental neglect, and early death of parents in the background of people with an antisocial personality disorder (Goodwin & Guze, 1979). As in schizophrenia, a diathesis-stress model of causation seems to be appropriate.

Psychological research has focused on the trait of fearlessness in those with antisocial personality disorder (see **Table 16.10**). In laboratory studies, for example, such people are slower to learn a simple response to avoid pain than are normal subjects; however, they learn as rapidly as normals if positively reinforced. Thus the antisocial personality is associated with a specific deficit in fear-motivated learning (Fowles, 1988; Lykken, 1957). There is some evidence that the relative fearlessness associated with antisocial personality disorder is due to lowered levels of physiological arousal in response to physically threatening stimuli (Hare, 1978; Raine, Venables, & Williams, 1990).

Lykken (1982) theorizes that fearlessness may be a necessary but not a sufficient condition for the development of an antisocial personality disorder. According to Lykken, many military heroes, adventurers, and dare-devils are also fearless in the face of physical threats. He suggests that fearless children will develop an antisocial personality disorder if they are deprived of positive childrearing experiences that teach empathy and respect for others. The chaotic family backgrounds found among those with an antisocial personality disorder, mentioned previously, are consistent with this view.

Interim Summary

A personality disorder is a combination of inflexible traits resulting in impaired psychological and social functioning. Prominent types of this disorder include the paranoid, histrionic, compulsive, and antisocial personality disorders. Personality disorders are often first recognized when the individual seeks treatment for some other psychological problem, such as anxiety, depression, or substance abuse.

Table 16.10   Measuring Fearlessness

According to David Lykken (1982), the trait of fearlessness is shared by both heroes and antisocial personalities. If forced to choose between two unpleasant alternatives, the fearless person will opt for a frightening or socially embarrassing alternative over a tedious or uncomfortable alternative. The following questions are from a test developed by Lykken to measure fearlessness. For each question, the person is to choose the lesser evil.

1. (a) Cleaning up your house after floodwaters have left it filled with mud.
   (b) Making a parachute jump.
2. (a) Having to walk around all day on a blistered foot.
   (b) Sleeping out on a camping trip in an area where rattlesnakes have been reported.
3. (a) You're in a bank and suddenly three masked men with guns come in and make everyone raise their hands.
   (b) Sitting through a 2-hour concert of bad music.
4. (a) Having the pilot announce that there is engine trouble and he may have to make an emergency landing.
   (b) Working a week in the fields digging potatoes.
5. (a) Finding out people have been gossiping about you.
   (b) Working all day in the hot sun.
6. (a) Being at a circus when suddenly two lions get loose down in the ring.
   (b) Arriving at the circus and discovering that you've forgotten your tickets.
7. (a) Washing a car.
   (b) Driving a car at 95 miles an hour.
8. (a) Asking someone to pay you money that he owes you.
   (b) Sleeping one night on the floor.

From "Fearlessness: Its Carefree Charm and Deadly Risks" by David T. Lykken in Psychology Today, September 1982. Copyright © 1982 by American Psychological Association. Reprinted with permission from Psychology Today Magazine.

SUMMARY

1. Abnormal behavior is usually defined by the convergence of four criteria: (1) relative infrequency, (2) social deviance, (3) maladaptiveness, and (4) personal distress.
2. Diagnosis is the process of matching information about a person to categories of psychological disorder. DSM-III-R is an innovative diagnostic system that includes specific criteria for each of more than 200 psychological disorders. Reliable diagnoses facili-

tate treatment decisions and research, but a diagnostic label can become stigmatizing.

3. Theoretical approaches to psychological disorders include the medical, psychodynamic, behavioral, cognitive, and humanistic perspectives on their causes and treatment.

4. The symptoms of the anxiety, somatoform, and dissociative disorders are usually distressing to the patient but do not involve major distortions of reality. In the anxiety disorders, the person experiences overwhelming levels of anxiety out of proportion to any objective threat. In the somatoform disorders, which include hypochondriasis and conversion disorder, the person exhibits physical symptoms for which no underlying physiological cause can be found. A dissociative disorder is characterized by an abrupt but usually temporary loss of voluntary cognitive activity, as in multiple personality and psychogenic amnesia.

5. Patients with major depressive disorder experience repeated episodes of depression followed by normal mood levels. Patients with bipolar disorder pass through episodes of depression and mania before returning to normal mood levels. Depression is a major risk factor in suicide and occurs more frequently in women than in men. The biological approach to understanding mood disorders holds that depression and mania are associated with abnormally low or high levels of certain brain neurotransmitters. The psychological approach includes the psychoanalytic and the cognitive-behavioral perspectives, which differ in their view of the core symptoms and thus the causes of depression.

6. The symptoms of schizophrenia can be grouped into positive (behaviorally excessive) and negative (behaviorally deficient) syndromes. The dopamine hypothesis, which may account for the positive symptoms, holds that schizophrenic symptoms are associated with hyperactivity at dopamine synapses in the brain. Some schizophrenic patients show a generalized atrophy of the brain due to the progressive loss of neurons, which may account for negative symptoms. The diathesis-stress model regards the psychological and neurochemical disturbances in schizophrenia as the outcome of an interaction between a genetic predisposition to the disorder and environmental stressors.

7. Substance-use disorders are caused by the abuse of psychoactive substances such as drugs, alcohol, and tobacco. Causes of substance abuse include access, peer influence, and personality factors, as well as motivational changes induced by long-term use of the substances themselves.

8. A personality disorder is a combination of inflexible traits resulting in impaired psychological and social functioning, as seen for example in the paranoid, histrionic, compulsive, and antisocial personality disorders.

KEY INDIVIDUALS

David Rosenhan
Thomas Szasz
Sigmund Freud
B. F. Skinner
Aaron Beck

KEY RESEARCH

the power of diagnostic labels to stereotype individuals
multiple personality and self-hypnosis
biogenic amine hypothesis of mood disorders
"Mourning and Melancholia"
cognitive triad of depressed patients
learned helplessness and depression
women and depression
depressive attributions and depressive realism
dopamine hypothesis of schizophrenia
brain imaging techniques in schizophrenia
genetic influences in development of schizophrenia
"high risk" studies of schizophrenia
fearlessness and antisocial personality disorder

KEY TERMS

Diagnostic and Statistical Manual of Mental Disorders (DSM)
DMS-III-R
anxiety disorders
panic disorder
phobic disorder
phobia
generalized anxiety disorder

obsessive-compulsive disorder
obsessions
compulsions
somatoform disorders
hypochondriasis
conversion disorder
dissociative disorder
multiple personality
mood
mood disorders
depression
mania
major depressive episode
delusions

manic episode
cognitive triad
schizophrenia
psychotic
hallucinations
blunted affect
anhedonia
diathesis-stress
substance-use disorders
organic mental disorder
delirium
alcoholism
personality disorder

17 Treatment of Psychological Disorders

CHAPTER OUTLINE

The Beginnings of Modern Treatment

Psychoanalytic Therapy

Classical Psychoanalysis
Psychodynamic Psychotherapy

Behavior Therapy

Desensitization Procedures
Biofeedback Therapy
Assertion Training
Cognitive Behavior Therapy
Behavior Modification
Self-Control Procedures

Humanistic Therapy

The Variety of Humanistic Therapies
Client-Centered Therapy

Therapeutic Groups

Family Therapy
Support Groups

The Effectiveness of Psychotherapy

Evaluating Psychotherapy
Comparing Psychotherapies

Medical Treatments

Drug Therapy
Electroconvulsive Therapy

Community Mental Health

Deinstitutionalization
Community Care
The Homeless Mentally Ill

Summary

607

I n 1431, Joan of Arc, age 19, was burned at the stake for heresy. For 3 years she had led an army of the King of France against English invaders. After being captured and put on trial, she told the court that she had become a soldier following visitations from Saint Michael, Saint Catherine, and Saint Margaret. She insisted that she could see, hear, and even touch the three saints, who urged her to take up arms for the King. The court offered her her life in return for denying the visitations. She refused to do so and was condemned as a witch. Joan of Arc is the most famous of tens of thousands of people put to death over the next 300 years because their interpretation of their private experiences

Joan of Arc was burned at the stake for heresy in 1431. She is the best-known of the people put to death during the Middle Ages because their interpretation of their private experiences ran counter to the accepted religious doctrine.

and beliefs ran counter to religious doctrine. It was believed that witches gave the possession of their souls to the devil in exchange for magical powers. The "treatment" for possession was to drive out the devil by beatings, torture, and, if necessary, death.

In the seventeenth century, many people with psychological disorders fell victim to a process known as the Great Confinement. This was an attempt by European governments to rid their countries of social deviants such as beggars and petty criminals by placing them in prisonlike institutions known as royal hospitals. Because psychologically disturbed people were also considered social deviants, they too were often confined in such institutions. Conditions were appalling. The inmates were locked and chained, deprived of adequate fresh air, food, and exercise, and often brutalized by their keepers. Our word bedlam, which conveys a sense of chaos and noisy uproar, is derived from the name of one such institution in London—Bethlehem Royal Hospital. Fashionable Londoners would visit Bethlehem Royal Hospital during their Sunday outings to be amused by the antics of the inmates (Foucault, 1965; Rosen, 1968).

These two vignettes illustrate the major ways in which people with psychological disorders have been "treated" throughout most of human history. The first method, seen in the history of witchcraft, is punishment, sometimes including execution. Punishment was usually administered to rid the victim of evil spirits, which were thought to be the cause of disturbed behavior. The second method, used in the royal hospitals, is confinement, an attempt to control people with psychological disorders by putting them away in special institutions. If you think these methods are merely historical curiosities, try to imagine the average person's reaction to, say, a psychotic person standing on a street corner in your town. When confronted by someone acting "crazy," the average person is likely to recommend "knocking some sense into" or "locking up" the person.

It is important to understand that punishment and confinement were not employed arbitrarily or merely maliciously. They were used because they reflected prevailing beliefs about the causes of and the best ways of dealing with abnormal behavior.

The same holds true today. Because we are relatively enlightened about the causes of abnormal behavior, our methods of treatment are relatively humane and enlightened. However, mental-health professionals do not completely understand or agree about the causes of psychological disorders. As we discuss the various forms of modern treatment, we will see how they have developed from different ways of thinking about the causes of abnormal behavior.

This chapter begins with a brief discussion of the contributions of two pioneers of modern treatment: Philippe Pinel and Sigmund Freud. We will then consider the various forms of individual and group psychotherapy that have been developed over the past century. Our next major topic, medical treatments for psychological disorders, includes drug therapy and electroconvulsive therapy. We end by discussing the community mental health movement—an unprecedented attempt to treat mental patients by humane methods in their home communities.

THE BEGINNINGS OF MODERN TREATMENT

The confinement of people with psychological disorders in so-called royal hospitals began to decline at the end of the eighteenth century. The modern era was ushered in by Philippe Pinel, a French physician who became the superintendent of a royal hospital in Paris in 1792. Pinel believed that "the mentally sick, far from being guilty people deserving of punishment, are sick people whose miserable state deserves all the consideration that is due to suffering humanity" (Zilboorg & Henry, 1941, pp. 323-24). Amid great skepticism, Pinel replaced chains, brutality, and confinement with a method called moral treatment. Moral treatment depended on a fundamental respect between doctor and patient, in which the doctor's kindness, firmness, and good example were used to teach the patient to control and eventually to overcome his or her disturbed behavior. Moral treatment proved to be a great success and soon spread throughout Europe and America.

Moral treatment was carried out in a new kind of institution—the mental hospital. American mental hospitals of the early 1800s

The word "bedlam" is derived from the name of Bethlehem Royal Hospital in London. Fashionable Londoners would visit the hospital as an amusement to watch the behavior of the insane.

were usually small institutions. Patients were encouraged to continue their vocations even while hospitalized, and recreation, including dancing, was prescribed as "good medicine." The majority of patients recovered and were able to return to normal life (Grob, 1966).

The close and continued contact between doctors and patients required by moral treatment eventually made it impractical. With increases in population during the nineteenth century, greater numbers of people required treatment in mental hospitals, and doctors were able to spend less and less time with each patient. After about 1850, mental hospitals developed into large, impersonal institutions housing thousands of patients who often received only minimal treatment. By the mid-twentieth century, mental hospitals themselves were ripe for reform. As we shall see at the end of this chapter, we are today undergoing yet another revolution in the treatment of mental patients, one that even surpasses Pinel's reforms.

A second major advance in treatment occurred at the end of the nineteenth century. A young Viennese doctor by the name of Sigmund Freud became interested in hysterical disorders, now called conversion disorders. Patients with these disorders often suffer from

Phillipe Pinel
(1745-1826)

Freud had patients recline on this couch while he sat out of view.

Joseph Breuer
(1842-1925)

physical symptoms such as loss of sensation or muscular paralysis. Freud's clients were not hospitalized mental patients. Rather, they were often successful men and women struggling as best they could with their symptoms.

Freud was interested in learning more about hysterical disorders and so traveled to Paris to study with the leading expert on the subject, Pierre Charcot. Charcot advocated the use of hypnosis for treating hysterical disorders. Impressed with the results of Charcot's research, Freud returned to Vienna where he and a colleague, Joseph Breuer, began to use hypnosis in the treatment of their patients.

With hypnosis, Freud and Breuer were able to place patients in a relaxed state in which patients were more willing to talk about their symptoms. Freud and Breuer discovered that patients would often trace their symptoms back to a particularly stressful, or traumatic, experience in childhood. Talking about such episodes often generated a great deal of emotion, following which the troubling symptom would disappear. Freud and Breuer tentatively concluded that hysterical disorders were caused by memories of traumatic events in the patient's childhood. These memories were so painful that they were repressed into the unconscious mind, where, even though unconscious, they continued to cause tension and anxiety. Freud and Breuer also concluded that the best treatment for these symptoms was to

encourage the patient to uncover the painful childhood memories and to experience their full emotional force (Breuer & Freud, 1895/1955).

Somewhat later, Freud, working without Breuer, was obliged to develop other methods of therapy. There were two important reasons behind his decision. First, he discovered that not all patients could be hypnotized. Second, he found that merely uncovering painful memories did not always produce a lasting cure. In his search for more effective therapies, Freud gradually developed *classical psychoanalysis.* Classical psychoanalysis became for many years the most important form of psychotherapy. **Psychotherapy** is the treatment of psychological disorders or other personal problems by psychological methods. Since Freud's time, many other forms of psychotherapy have been developed, including *behavior therapy, humanistic therapy*, and *group therapy*. We will discuss each of these in the following sections.

Psychotherapy is practiced by various professional groups. The three major professions involved in psychotherapy are *psychiatry, clinical psychology*, and *clinical social work*. Psychiatrists are physicians holding an M.D. degree who specialize in the treatment of mental illness. Clinical psychologists hold a doctoral degree from a graduate program in psychology that combines academic and clinical training. Some psychiatrists and clinical psychologists choose to become *psychoanalysts* through postgraduate training in psychoanalytic institutes, which teach the theory and therapeutic methods developed by Freud and his followers. Clinical social workers, who make up the largest of the three basic mental-health professions, earn a M.S.W. (master of social work) degree following a 2- or 3-year program in a school of social work. Psychiatrists, clinical psychologists, and clinical social workers receive extensive graduate and postgraduate training in hospitals, clinics, counseling centers, or other mental-health facilities. They often continue to practice in such settings, but they also engage in private practice.

In addition to these traditional mental health professions, psychotherapy is increasingly practiced by people with a variety of other professional backgrounds. *Educational* and *counseling psychologists,* with either master's or doctor's degrees, and *psychiatric nurses,* with either R.N. or master's degrees, are prime examples. Most of these therapists work in schools, hospitals, or clinics, but an increasing number are also engaged in private practice.

Interim Summary

The treatment of psychological disorders in any era reflects prevailing views of their causes. The modern era has replaced punishment and confinement with a large variety of more humane psychological, medical, and community-based treatments.

The modern era began about 200 years ago with the work of Philippe Pinel, who replaced confinement of the mentally ill with moral treatment based on a fundamental respect between doctor and patient. A century later, Sigmund Freud developed classical psychoanalysis to treat so-called neurotic disorders. Today many different forms of psychotherapy are practiced by psychologists, psychiatrists, social workers, and other professional groups.

PSYCHOANALYTIC THERAPY

Psychoanalytic therapy stems from Freud's pioneering attempts to understand and treat patients with anxiety and somatoform disorders such as we discussed in the previous chapter. Freud believed that his patients' symptoms resulted from sexual and aggressive drives that had never been satisfactorily integrated into the patients' personalities during childhood. For Freud, the cure lay in helping patients understand how their symptoms were related to childhood conflicts over the expression of sexual and aggressive drives and then in helping patients develop more mature and adaptive ways of expressing these motives.

The therapeutic techniques developed by Freud are known collectively as *classical psychoanalysis*. Classical psychoanalysis is a relatively rare form of treatment today. Most contemporary therapists who subscribe to psychoanalytic theory practice what is known as *psychodynamic psychotherapy*, which is a more modern and flexible version of the method developed by Freud. Because of its theoretical and historical importance, the bulk of our discussion is devoted to classical psychoanalysis.

Classical Psychoanalysis

Classical psychoanalysis is a very intensive and probing form of psychotherapy that includes the six key processes of free association, dream analysis, resistance, transference, insight, and working through. This form of therapy can require several sessions each week for many years. In classical psychoanalysis, the patient must be willing to look at his or her problems from a psychological perspective and to talk about these problems as accurately and honestly as possible.

What actually goes on during psychoanalysis is a good deal more complex than the popular stereotype of a patient on a couch chattering away about his or her childhood. To understand this complex process, let us examine its six key concepts.

FREE ASSOCIATION

How does the psychoanalyst encourage the patient to talk about memories and feelings? As we discussed earlier, Freud experimented with hypnosis as a means of relaxing patients. When he found that not all patients could be hypnotized, he hit upon the idea of having them recline on a couch while he sat out of view so as not to be a distraction. Freud instructed his patients to say whatever came to mind, no matter how trivial or embarrassing it seemed. This was the method of **free association.**

Classical psychoanalysis is a lengthy and intensive form of psychotherapy that uses the six key processes of free association, dream analysis, resistance, transference, insight, and working through.

This method worked so well that Freud called it the "fundamental rule of psychoanalysis." The basic notion behind free association is that unconscious material may be reached through a chain of associated ideas, beginning with those that are currently in awareness and progressing to those that have been repressed into the unconscious.

DREAM ANALYSIS

The topics patients talk about in psychoanalysis can be drawn from many sources, including childhood memories, current relationships and problems, and future hopes and plans. Freud also found dreams to be a rich source of material for analysis. Freud felt that dreams were a distorted expression of unconscious drives. He referred to a dream's unconscious sexual or aggressive meaning as its **latent content;** the conscious and remembered aspects of the dream were called its **manifest content.** Through the psychoanalytic technique of **dream analysis,** the manifest content of a dream is interpreted to yield its latent content. Freud felt that inferring the latent content of a dream from its manifest content provided "a royal road to the unconscious."

An example of Freudian dream analysis is contained in the famous case of "Little Hans" (Freud, 1909/1955). Hans was a 5-year-old boy with a horse phobia. Freud suspected that Hans' phobia was really a defense against his true feelings—that the fear of horses was really a displaced fear of his father. Why should Hans fear his father? Freud believed that Hans was in the midst of an Oedipus complex. Unconsciously, Hans was competing with his father for his mother's love. Consequently, Hans feared being harmed by his father.

Freud's interpretation of the case was supported by the following dream, which Hans said he "saw" while in bed one night:

> In the night there was a big giraffe in the room and a crumpled one; and the big one called out because I took the crumpled one away from it. Then it stopped calling out; and then I sat down on the top of the crumpled one. (Freud, 1909/1955, p. 37)

Freud interpreted the dream's manifest content as follows: the big giraffe represented Hans' father and the crumpled giraffe his mother. (The adjective "crumpled" is a key, because Freud thought it could represent Hans' concep-

Table 17.1 **Manifest and Latent Contents of Little Hans' Dream**

Manifest Content	Latent Content
Big giraffe	Father
Crumpled giraffe	Mother
Sitting down on	Sexual intercourse

Based on Freud (1909/1955)

tion of the female genitals.) In the dream Hans took the mother away from the father and "sat down" on it. Freud concluded that "sat down" could represent a child's conception of sexual intercourse. The manifest and latent contents of the dream are listed in **Table 17.1.** The action of the dream thus appeared to confirm Freud's hypothesis of rivalry, typical of the Oedipus complex, between Hans and his father for the mother's sexual attentions.

RESISTANCE

Uncovering repressed wishes is not simple. Some memories may be so charged with anxiety that the patient avoids discussing them. The patient might suddenly "change the topic" or "forget" the details of an important experience. The patient might develop a headache or even ask to end the session. All such maneuvers are considered forms of **resistance** by which the patient avoids becoming aware of unconscious conflicts by refusing to acknowledge and deal with important topics. Although these maneuvers temporarily disrupt the flow of associations, evidence of resistance gives the analyst important clues about topics that need to be pursued in greater depth.

TRANSFERENCE

In psychoanalysis, the patient is the active partner in the therapeutic interaction. The patient's personality and motivations are the subject under investigation. The analyst establishes the rules under which the sessions proceed and may even direct the patient's talk with subtle encouragement. However, the analyst consciously refrains from imposing his or her own personality and needs on the relationship in order to understand the patient as objectively as possible. Despite the analyst's emotional neutrality, the patient's relationship with the analyst soon becomes extremely intense. For example, the patient may begin to develop romantic notions about the therapist. When these feelings are not reciprocated, the patient may begin to express anger, resentment, or jealousy.

The assumption is that the patient's reactions to the analyst mirror the ways he or she has learned to react to other important people. This phenomenon is known as **transference,** which means that the patient re-creates, within the therapeutic session, the interpersonal patterns that have caused his or her psychological difficulties in the first place. *Positive transference* occurs when feelings of love, admiration, or esteem are displaced onto the analyst. *Negative transference* refers to the displacement of destructive feelings like anger or jealousy.

Transference is a crucial aspect of psychoanalysis. Far from disrupting the therapy, it tells both parties exactly what they must come to understand. By analyzing the patient's behavior and feelings and relating them to childhood conflicts, the analyst helps the patient learn more adaptive and mature ways of relating to others.

INSIGHT

The goal of psychoanalysis is to make the patient aware of the unconscious conflicts responsible for his or her difficulties. This process is known as gaining **insight.** Insight does not come as a flash of recognition, after which all the patient's problems are solved. Rather it is achieved in bits and pieces as different aspects of the patient's needs, defenses, and behavior patterns are revealed and analyzed in the transference relationship.

The major method by which the analyst helps the patient gain insight is known as interpretation. An **interpretation** is a hypothesis that summarizes a large segment of the patient's behavior and offers an explanation of its unconscious motivation. The analyst may observe, for example, that the patient is incapable of expressing anger in the transference relationship. The analyst might then offer this interpretation: "You are afraid to be angry with me because you feel guilty about being angry with anyone who is like a parent to you" (Morse & Watson, 1977, p. 39).

Interpretation must be skillfully timed. If offered before the patient is able to accept it, an interpretation may only arouse anxiety and defensiveness. The best interpretation is one that is just beyond the patient's current level of awareness and moves the therapy to a new level of insight.

WORKING THROUGH

With increasing insight, the patient is in a position to give up maladaptive patterns of interaction for more mature ways of behaving. The patient first begins to behave in a less childish way with the therapist. Gradually he or she uses these new behaviors in interactions with others. This process of acquiring new behavior patterns and attitudes following insight is known as the process of **working through.** A successful psychoanalysis does not mean that the patient becomes a superhuman, immune to the inevitable stresses of daily living. All Freud ever promised was freedom from the misery caused by the burden of long-repressed conflicts.

Psychodynamic Psychotherapy

You should be aware that classical psychoanalysis is a very esoteric form of psychotherapy. Only about one person in ten thousand ever undergoes psychoanalysis, and there is increasing question as to whether psychoanalysis is even an effective treatment for most of the major psychological disorders discussed in the previous chapter. Some students of psychoanalysis even suggest that the procedure is more appropriate for increasing self-understanding in already healthy people—analogous, say, to a college education—than for treating psychological problems (Michels, 1990).

Since Freud's death in 1939, psychoanalytic theory has developed to reflect changing intellectual and societal influences. Two major trends are evident (Bernstein & Nietzel, 1980). The first is an increased recognition of the importance of social and cultural factors in human development and behavior. Neo-Freudians like Horney, Adler, and Fromm, discussed in Chapter 14, represent this trend. The second trend is an increased emphasis on the role of the rational, problem-solving ego in directing behavior, and a corresponding deemphasis of the role of unconscious sexual and aggressive drives. Erik Erikson's work, discussed in Chapter 11, is an example of this trend.

Although classical psychoanalytic therapists can still be found, most therapists who subscribe to psychoanalytic theory practice what is known as **psychodynamic psycho-**

therapy. This more modern form of therapy is briefer, more flexible, and more oriented to the patient's current concerns than is classical psychoanalysis. The analyst's couch is replaced by face-to-face contact between patient and therapist. Free association and dream analysis give way to a more direct discussion of critical issues. Less emphasis is placed on a thorough reconstruction of the childhood experiences contributing to the patient's difficulties, and greater emphasis is placed on issues arising from his or her current style of interacting with others. On the other hand, transference feelings provide an important source of information about the patient's interpersonal problems, and the therapist will also deal with and interpret the patient's resistance to change. The concepts of insight and of working through are also important therapeutic goals. In sum, the style of psychodynamic psychotherapy differs from classical psychoanalysis, but many of Freud's original concepts of the therapeutic process remain as core ingredients.

Interim Summary

In classical psychoanalysis, the therapist uses free association and the interpretation of dreams, resistance, and transference to help the patient gain insight into the unconscious conflicts underlying his or her symptoms. By means of the working-through process, the patient gradually replaces unhealthy patterns of interaction with more mature ways of behaving.

Contemporary psychodynamic psychotherapy reflects developments in therapeutic style and methods since Freud's time. This form of therapy is usually briefer, more flexible, and more oriented to current conflicts in the patient's life than is classical psychoanalysis, although concepts such as transference, resistance, and insight remain central to the therapy.

BEHAVIOR THERAPY

Behavior therapy is a general term for a large number of specific techniques derived from psychological research. The earliest forms of behavior therapy were derived from the principles of classical and operant conditioning.

Today, however, behavior therapy also borrows ideas and methods from other areas of psychology, especially cognitive psychology and social psychology (Craighead, 1990). The background of behavior therapy is therefore quite different from that of psychoanalytic therapy.

In addition, there are several important differences between behavior therapy and psychoanalytic therapy. First of all, they differ in their explanations of psychological disorders. Psychoanalytic therapy regards psychological disorders as essentially failures in personality development. Troubling behaviors are seen as symptoms of unresolved conflicts among different areas of the personality. Therefore, the therapeutic emphasis is on analyzing and resolving these underlying conflicts. Behavior therapy, on the other hand, regards psychological disorders as essentially failures in learning. Troubling behaviors are seen as learned responses that are not adaptive in the patient's current environment. Thus, psychoanalytic therapy regards symptoms as expressions of more deeply seated problems, while behavior therapy regards symptoms as troubling behaviors that are themselves the problem.

Second, each theory has different therapeutic goals. Psychoanalytic therapy aims to help the patient gain insight into his or her problems. After insight is achieved and the working-through process is completed, the patient should be able to behave more maturely and adaptively. In contrast, behavior therapy emphasizes the goal of directly replacing maladaptive behavior patterns with more adaptive ones. Patients and therapists need to arrive at a thorough understanding of the patient's problems and how they can be modified. But this form of understanding is different from the psychoanalytic concept of insight. Whereas insight implies tracing problems to their origins, the behavior therapy approach is to identify, and then change, the personal and social factors that support maladaptive behavior patterns.

Third, the two approaches differ in therapeutic methods. Psychoanalytic therapy emphasizes the importance of the relationship between patient and therapist. Insight comes about in part through an analysis of the transference relationship—the specific ways in which the patient relates to the therapist and, by extension, to other important people in his or her life. In contrast, behavior therapy aims to establish a good working relationship primarily as the basis for teaching patients new ways of behaving. After the problem is understood, the patient and therapist usually work together to establish a learning program with specific goals. In effect, each behavioral therapy method we will discuss is a learning program for a specific kind of problem. The therapist instructs the patient in new ways of behaving, provides feedback concerning the patient's success, and encourages the patient to experiment with new behaviors.

Modern behavior therapy stems, in large part, from the work of Joseph Wolpe and of B. F. Skinner and his students. In 1958, Wolpe developed a procedure for treating phobias called *systematic desensitization* (Wolpe, 1958). The term *systematic* referred to a step-by-step learning program; the term *desensitization* referred to eliminating the ability of phobic stimuli to elicit anxiety responses. At about the same time, Skinner and his students began to use operant conditioning methods with hospitalized mental patients (Lindsley, Skinner, & Solomon, 1953). This led to the rapid development of many operant procedures for teaching new behavior patterns to institutionalized children and adults (Ayllon & Azrin, 1968).

Behavior therapy methods are today routinely used in all facets of mental-health treatment, and the field is continuously enriched by new contributions from research in general psychology. To give you some idea of the variety of behavior therapy, we will discuss several well-developed methods: (1) desensitization procedures, (2) biofeedback therapy, (3) assertion training, (4) cognitive behavior therapy, (5) operant procedures, and (6) self-control procedures.

Desensitization Procedures

Janet K. suffers from examination anxiety. She is a bright, hard-working college student, but her grades do not reflect her ability. She begins to feel uneasy when an exam is announced and is in a near panic on the day of the test. Looking at the exam, she has difficulty focusing her attention, is distracted by her racing heart, and is unable to recall the details of what she has studied.

Janet's problem is not unique. Like millions of others, she suffers from a phobia. To deal with such problems, behavior therapists

Psychiatrist Joseph Wolpe is shown here helping a client through the use of systematic desensitization.

have developed a number of desensitization methods. Among the most widely used are *systematic desensitization* and *in vivo desensitization*.

SYSTEMATIC DESENSITIZATION

Systematic desensitization is a three-step method for treating anxiety in which relaxation training is paired with successive visualizations of anxiety-provoking situations, from least to most intense. The first step is training in progressive relaxation, a method of inhibiting anxiety. The second step consists of constructing a series of anxiety-provoking scenes on the basis of the patient's description of his or her problem. Third, while the patient is deeply relaxed, the therapist asks the patient to imagine being in each scene. This exercise is repeated until all feelings of anxiety have disappeared. Wolpe (1958) originally proposed that visualizing anxiety-provoking scenes without negative consequences served as a form of extinction and that a nonanxious response to these scenes could then be learned through the use of progressive relaxation.

In progressive relaxation, the therapist instructs the patient in tensing and then relaxing muscles of the arms, legs, abdomen, neck, and head. By practicing at home, most patients become adept in quickly achieving a deep state of

PHOBIC DRIVERS GO TO CLASS TO LEARN MASTERY OVER FEAR

By Glenn Ruffenach

Louis Hertz has a problem on the road: left turns. They scare him to death. Waiting to turn, "I'm afraid I'll pass out," he says. "I'm afraid I'll get out of the car and run."

Forget fear of flying. Mr. Hertz, a 58-year-old advertising executive, shares with as many as four million other Americans one of the most debilitating of anxiety disorders: a fear of driving. He is talking about it in the middle of a 20-week class that he and eight others have paid $1,000 each to attend. The course, led by psychologist Charles Melville, is one of hundreds of programs that have sprung up around the country in recent years to help people cope with phobias and other disorders.

Once dismissed as a form of hypochondria, anxiety disorders are now considered the most prevalent mental-health problem in the country, by some estimates affecting as many as one out of every 10 people. Fears linked to driving are thought to be among the most common.

Some individuals, like Mr. Hertz, can get on the road but quail at the thought of being trapped in traffic or driving on freeways. Others recoil from retaining walls or from stretches of deserted road, or from tunnels or bridges. (Each month, patrolmen at the Chesapeake Bay Bridge Tunnel in Virginia end up taking the wheel for several drivers who can't bring themselves to cross the 21-mile span.) Heredity seems to play a part in the problem, but no one is immune: Butchers, bakers and compact-disc makers all may be affected.

What follows is a look at one group's efforts to tackle its fears.

WEEK ONE: "I feel like I'm going to collapse and die."

"I have to fight to stay conscious."

"I thought I was going to have a stroke."

One by one, each participant describes the common experience that fanned their individual fears:

panic attacks. In the brief moments of terror, hearts gallop, arms and legs turn to stone, and lungs seem to collapse. Most of the nine seated around Mr. Melville had their first attack while they were driving. It occurred for no apparent reason.

"I began hyperventilating driving home from work," says Cindy Flanary, a 32-year-old businesswoman. Pulling into her driveway, "I couldn't let go of the steering wheel," she says. "I finally leaned on the horn with my elbow so someone would come and help me."

That was in 1985. For five years, she couldn't bring herself to drive again.

Mr. Melville, who has dealt with phobias for 20 years, says such attacks are often an "accumulation of life stresses." Worries about a series of events, such as a divorce, loss of a job, and death of a friend, will erupt in the form of a panic attack. A car is the perfect incubator: A

---

relaxation. This technique was discussed in Chapter 15.

The patient and therapist jointly develop the series of anxiety-provoking scenes, known as an **anxiety hierarchy.** For example, Janet K. and her therapist might work out an anxiety hierarchy like this (Bellack & Hersen, 1980).

1. Instructor announcing an exam in 1 week.
2. Studying the night before the exam.
3. Eating breakfast the morning of the exam.
4. Walking to the exam room.
5. Standing in the hall waiting to enter the exam room.

6. Entering the exam room.
7. Sitting down in the exam room.
8. Instructor passes out exam.

In subsequent sessions, the two steps are put together: while the patient is deeply relaxed, the therapist presents each scene, working from the least to most anxiety provoking. The therapist helps the patient experience each scene by describing its associated sights and sounds in detail. Each item is repeated until the patient is free from anxiety. Then the next item is presented. The average systematic desensitization procedure takes 10 to 15 ses-

driver is often alone, usually at some distance from a "safe" place, such as home, and suddenly feels isolated and trapped. The intensity of the attacks can quickly lead to obsession.

The class listens with frustration. "I just want to feel safe *anywhere*," says Paula Cox, 34, a Ph.D. candidate. "I don't trust my body. I want to trust my body."

WEEK EIGHT: The class isn't sleeping—it just looks that way. People are slouched in chairs. One hand on chest. One hand on stomach. They're practicing controlled breathing (through the diaphragm) as a way of dealing with panic.

Between deep breaths and filling out "panic reports" (a diary of the time, place, severity and symptoms of attacks), participants are becoming more open about their struggles.

WEEK 14: Progress. Mr. Hertz announces to gasps from the group that he has driven on Atlanta's

downtown freeways for the first time in about seven years. But "I haven't yet approached the left-turn business," he concedes.

The drivers are "desensitizing" themselves to panic attacks, Mr. Melville explains. The trick is to put oneself in situations, starting with something as simple as running up a flight of stairs to get the heart racing, that produce sensations of panic, and then progress to tougher situations. The drivers gradually work themselves up to situations that caused the greatest panic.

For Mr. Hertz, Mr. Melville plots a "hierarchy" of bigger and bigger risks to enable him to make a left turn: A left turn in a quiet neighborhood with no stoplight. A left turn on a quiet street with a stoplight. A left turn at a light with a special lane for turns. A left turn at a light on a four-lane road.

"You have to be willing to risk

some degree of fear," says Karen Healy, 47, a psychiatric social worker who teaches the course with Mr. Melville and who spent eight years conquering her own fears of driving. "That's the variable that's difficult to control."

WEEK 20: More victories, and some lingering concerns. Ms. Desjardin allows herself a smile and says she has managed a short drive by herself, which draws applause. Ms. Cox is still wary. "My toughest problem is still believing that this is not going to hurt me," she says.

Says Mrs. Healy: "We give them the tools. After that, It's very individualized as to how much you'll improve."

Questions

1. How does the therapy described in this article exemplify the concepts of *desensitization* and *anxiety hierarchy*?
2. Why do the patients have to be "willing to risk some degree of fear" in order to benefit from this form of therapy?

---

sions. It has proved remarkably effective in the treatment of phobias and similar anxiety reactions (Paul & Bernstein, 1973).

IN VIVO DESENSITIZATION

Sometimes anxiety reactions can be treated by exposing the patient directly to anxiety-provoking situations, rather than to imagined scenes. This is known as ***in vivo*** (live) **desensitization.** Consider for example agoraphobia, a fear of leaving one's home because of past panic attacks. The patient may report that anxiety increases the farther he or she gets from home.

The therapist might then suggest an anxiety hierarchy in which the patient walks one block from home on the first day, two blocks on the second day, three blocks on the third day, and so forth. On each occasion, the patient would be asked to stay in the situation until all feelings of discomfort subside. Thus, the anxiety response is gradually extinguished along a hierarchy of distance from home.

A great deal of research supports the effectiveness of desensitization procedures for the treatment of phobias. For example, Marks (1981) has developed an innovative program in

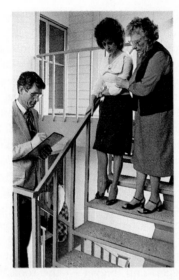

This woman is being helped overcome her fear of heights (acrophobia) through the use of in vivo desensitization.

which nurses are trained to guide phobic patients in graduated *in vivo* exposure to phobic situations. In this program the patient is encouraged to remain in the phobic situation until feelings of discomfort have subsided. Marks reports that this procedure results in the reduction of the target phobia, as well as increased well-being in other aspects of the patient's life.

Biofeedback Therapy

The essence of biofeedback therapy lies in guiding the patient toward self-regulation of his or her own physiological activity in order

Figure 17.1
Biofeedback Therapy
Office training sessions usually last about 30 to 45 minutes.

to overcome troubling symptoms. There are many different forms of biofeedback therapy, depending on the specific problem being treated. However, all forms of biofeedback therapy share in common the use of electronic instruments to record and to feed back to the patient precise information on his or her own physiological activity. Biofeedback therapy has proved to be especially helpful in the treatment of stress-related disorders such as muscle tension headaches, migraine headaches, irritable bowel syndrome, and high blood pressure.

Different kinds of biofeedback instruments are designed to detect, amplify, and display different forms of physiological activity. Thus, the electrical activity generated by a tense muscle can picked up by small metal sensors placed over a muscle; the amount of blood circulating in the hand can be indirectly detected by measuring the warmth of a finger with a heat-sensitive probe, and blood pressure can be detected from an inflated cuff wrapped around the arm. These different forms of activity are then amplified by biofeedback instruments much as a stereo set amplifies disks or tapes. Finally, the amplified signals are used to power a display—such as a graph on a video monitor, a bank of lights, or a musical tone—which signals increases or decreases in the underlying physiology. Biofeedback instruments thus create a *feedback loop* from the body through the instument and back to the observing patient.

Figure 17.1 shows a patient attached to a biofeedback instrument that simultaneously records forehead muscle activity and finger temperature. Because tense forehead muscles and cold hands are often seen in headache sufferers, this patient is learning to reduce his headaches by relaxing his forehead and warming his hands. He does this by listening to the activity of his muscles over the earphones and by observing his finger temperature on the paper chart.

Why should biofeedback therapy be helpful for what are generally considered medical disorders? One answer is that biofeedback is a method of restoring homeostasis, the tendency of physiological systems to function within fairly narrow limits. Homeostasis depends on the body's own feedback mechanisms to detect deviations from normal functioning and to return physiological activity to an optimal level. When internal feedback loops malfunction, symptoms such as poor circulation, intestinal distress, or muscle spasms and pain can develop. Biofeedback may function by providing an artificial feedback loop that aids in restoring homeostasis.

It has been found that the use of biofeedback instruments is usually most effective when combined with other self-regulation strategies. In treating stress-related disorders, for example, biofeedback is often combined with a relaxation technique such as progressive relaxation or meditation. The patient is asked to practice the relaxation technique between biofeedback sessions. Biofeedback instruments are then used to monitor the degree of relaxation achieved by home practice and to teach increasingly precise regulation of physiological activity. Thus biofeedback therapy is really a package of self-regulation strategies that includes instrument biofeedback as a key component. Research indicates that this multicomponent form of biofeedback therapy can be an effective treatment for various stress-related disorders (Ford, Stroebel, Strong, & Szarek, 1983; Hatch, Fisher, & Rugh, 1987; Shellenberger, Amar, Schneider, & Stewart, 1989).

Assertion Training

How would you react in each of the following situations?

1. You have just moved into a new apartment with two friends and are looking for a fourth roommate. The two friends come to you and inform you that they have found a fourth person—someone whom you secretly dislike.
2. You are dining in a very nice restaurant with some friends. You order a steak cooked "rare." A little later the waiter brings you your steak, and it is well done. The waiter asks, "Will there be anything else?" (Adapted from Bernstein & Nietzel, 1980, p. 375)

We all know people who handle situations like this extremely well. They know how to resolve social conflicts by expressing themselves in a direct but tactful way that preserves everyone's self-esteem. Psychologists refer to such people as "appropriately assertive." We also know others who are incapable of expressing their feelings and wishes because they fear others will take exception or cease to like them. Instead, they may say nothing and hold their feelings in check. Sometimes the feelings may be expressed in indirect ways, ranging from malicious gossip to kicking the proverbial

These people attending an assertion training class are learning to express their feelings in a direct way.

dog. At other times they may, after a series of incidents in which they say nothing, surprise everyone by exploding in an angry tirade. People like this do not know how to assert themselves appropriately.

Assertion training teaches people to express their feelings in a direct and honest way that neither humiliates nor degrades other people. Acting assertively lets other people know how you see the problem, how you feel about it, and what you would like to do about it. An assertive response to our second example above might be: "There must be some mistake. I ordered a rare steak and this is well done. I would feel better if you returned this steak to the kitchen for a rare one."

Assertion training has proved especially effective for patients who tend to be anxious in social situations and who react by withdrawing and feeling helpless. The following case gives an example of such a patient and the techniques used to teach appropriate assertion:

Mrs. T., a 37-year-old housewife, was troubled by long-standing depression and anxiety. During the initial interview with the behavior therapist, she complained of feeling uneasy in nearly all social situations. She was even unable to establish eye contact with the therapist.

The therapist suggested a graded program of assertion training. The first steps were simple: maintaining eye contact with herself in a mirror and then maintaining eye contact with the therapist. They then rehearsed a variety of situations in the office, such as asking a stranger on the street for directions, expressing and defending an opinion, and discussing a controversial topic. When these tasks were completed, Mrs. T. rehearsed a similar series of increasingly assertive interactions in the presence of two colleagues of the therapist. The therapist then accompanied Mrs. T. on a shopping trip, where he encouraged her to initiate a conversation with a salesgirl and to return an item she had just bought. She needed little encouragement and in fact initiated several assertive interactions on her own. After 28 sessions, Mrs. T.'s husband said the change in his wife was "amazing" and that she was happier than he had ever known her to be. (Adapted from Piaget & Lazarus, 1969)

Cognitive Behavior Therapy

In many places in this book, we have discussed research into the ways in which our beliefs and thoughts influence our emotional reactions. For example, dental patients can be divided into calm, collected "copers" and frantic "catastrophisers." When asked what was going through their minds while their teeth were being worked on, the copers say such things as, "I was imagining being on a peaceful beach," or "I told myself to calm down and take it easy." The catastrophisers tend to say such things as, "I was imagining the drill going through my cheek" or "I was thinking how awful, painful, and terrible the whole experience was" (Chaves & Barber, 1974).

The goal of **cognitive behavior therapy** is to help people control disturbing emotional reactions like anxiety and depression by teaching them more effective ways of interpreting and thinking about their experiences. The "catastrophisers" in our example could benefit from learning some of the cognitive strategies employed by the "copers."

One of the best-known forms of cognitive therapy is known as *rational-emotive therapy*. Its originator, Albert Ellis, stresses that the emotional difficulties of many patients in psychotherapy are due to what he calls the "irrational beliefs" they bring to bear on their experiences. His goal is to teach patients more effec-

Albert Ellis

tive "rational beliefs." According to Ellis, the following three "irrational" beliefs are frequently encountered among patients (Ellis & Harper, 1975; Lange & Jakobowski, 1976):

Irrational Belief No. 1 "You *must* have sincere love and approval almost all the time from all the people you find significant."

People with this belief are likely to become extremely anxious whenever their needs or opinions deviate even slightly from those of friends, neighbors, or social groups. Such people may even withdraw completely from social interaction out of fear of offending anyone.

Irrational Belief No. 2 "You must prove yourself thoroughly competent, adequate, and achieving, or you must at least have real competence or talent at something important."

People with this belief are likely to be constantly driven to achieve perfection and to become depressed when their unrealistic goals are not met. They may eventually avoid challenges or not undertake new initiatives because they fear not being perfectly competent and skilled.

Irrational Belief No. 3 "You have to view life as awful, terrible, horrible, or catastrophic when things do not go the way you would like them to go."

People like this are constant complainers. They may become angry and bitter when the world and other people do not live up to their expectations.

In rational-emotive therapy, patients are first taught to recognize and then question their irrational beliefs. Patients are shown how to ask themselves questions such as, "*Where* is the evidence that I am a worthless person if not universally approved? *Who* says I must be perfect? *Why* must things go exactly the way I would like?" After recognizing and analyzing their irrational beliefs, patients are then taught to substitute more realistic alternatives. For example, rational alternatives to the three foregoing irrational beliefs are:

Alternative Belief No. 1 "I would *like* to be approved, but I do not *need* such approval."

Alternative Belief No. 2 "What I do doesn't have to be perfect to be good; I will be happier if I achieve at a realistic level rather than strive for perfection."

Alternative Belief No. 3 "If I can't change the situation, it may be unfortunate but not catastrophic. I can make plans to make my life as enjoyable as possible." (Adapted from Lange & Jakubowski, 1976, pp. 128–29)

Aaron T. Beck and his colleagues have developed a cognitive therapy specifically designed for work with depressed patients (Beck, Rush, Shaw, & Emery, 1979; Beck, 1991). As you will recall from Chapter 16, Beck finds that depressed patients suffer from a "cognitive triad" of negative beliefs about themselves, their future, and their experiences. These negative beliefs, in turn, are based on faulty information processing and faulty logic, such as ignoring positive information or overgeneralizing from single negative instances. Cognitive therapy for depression therefore consists of isolating, challenging, and changing erroneous patterns of information processing and thinking.

The following example consists of a brief exchange between a cognitive therapist and a depressed student who believed that she would not get into the college to which she had applied. Notice how the therapist challenges her all-or-nothing belief that any grade less than an A is a failure, as well as her faulty perception of her class standing:

Therapist Why do you think you won't be able to get into the university of your choice?

Patient Because my grades were really not so hot.

T Well, what was your grade average?

P Well, pretty good up until the last semester in high school.

T What was your grade average in general?

P A's and B's.

T Well, how many of each?

P Well, I guess, almost all of my grades were A's but I got terrible grades my last semester.

T What were your grades then?

P I got two A's and two B's.

T Since your grade average would seem to me to come out to almost all A's, why do you think you won't be able to get into the university?

P Because of competition being so tough.

T Have you found out what the average grades are for admissions to the college?

Aaron Beck and his colleagues have developed a cognitive therapy specifically designed to help depressed patients.

P Well, somebody told me that a B average would suffice.

T Isn't your average better than that?

P I guess so. (Beck et al., 1979, p. 153)

Beck's form of cognitive therapy has consistently proved to be an effective treatment for depression. For example, a review of 27 separate studies reported that depressed clients treated with Beck's approach were significantly more improved than clients receiving no therapy and somewhat more improved than clients receiving other forms of psychotherapy (Dobson, 1989). In addition, depressed patients treated with cognitve therapy over a 3- or 4- month period do very well in maintaining their improvement and not relapsing after the end of therapy. This outcome compares very favorably to depressed clients treated with drug therapy, who tend to relapse at a fairly high rate unless the drug is continued for several months (Craighead, 1990).

Behavior Modification

Principles derived from operant conditioning have been applied to a wide range of clinical problems. This form of treatment is sometimes called *behavior modification* to distinguish it from other forms of behavior therapy. Like operant conditioning, **behavior modification** focuses on the control of behavior by discriminative, reinforcing, and punishing stimuli. Behavior modification has been applied most widely in training programs in prisons, mental hospitals, institutions for the mentally retarded, and nursery schools. Various behavior-modification techniques have proved valuable in strengthening adaptive behavior and weakening destructive behavior in many patients often considered "hopeless" cases.

STRENGTHENING ADAPTIVE BEHAVIOR

The principle of positive reinforcement holds that a positive reinforcer will increase the frequency of any behavior it follows. This principle has been widely used in establishing new behaviors in adults and children lacking self-care and social skills. One example of this is the use of *token economies.* **Token economies** are systems in which behaviors are reinforced with tokens (often plastic poker chips) that can later be traded in for certain privileges. In a sense, the tokens serve as a form of money.

In one such application, chronic mental patients earned tokens for desirable behaviors. These *target behaviors* were set up by the psychologists in charge of the program. They included self-care behaviors, such as brushing teeth and bathing, as well as work assignments, such as kitchen chores, laundry, or janitorial tasks. Each time a patient exhibited one of these behaviors, he or she received a specified number of tokens. The patients could later cash in the tokens for privileges such as movies, supervised walks around the hospital grounds, television, or items from the hospital commissary (see **Figure 17.2**). From all indications this program was a success. Both the patients' behavior and the general morale of the hospital staff improved (Ayllon & Azrin, 1968).

Another behavior-modification technique is the use of *shaping* to teach the patient a new skill. Recall our discussion in Chapter 6 of using the process of shaping to train a dog to ring a doorbell. The following study demonstrates how shaping can also be used to teach new skills to human clients.

This study involved a nursery school pupil who had regressed to the point where she crawled almost all the time. In an attempt to teach the girl to walk, a team of psychologists established a reinforcement program in which the teacher would pay attention to the girl whenever she walked. But because the girl never walked, they could not immediately rein-

Figure 17.2
Use of Tokens in Therapy.
In token economies, patients receive tokens for performing desirable behaviors, as shown on this patient's record. The tokens can then be used to obtain special privileges.

force the target behavior. To deal with this problem, they decided to shape her behavior by reinforcing successive approximations to the target behavior. First they reinforced the behavior of standing up to get her coat. Next they reinforced the behavior of simply standing, then of walking a few steps, and then of walking progressively longer distances. After about a week of such shaping, the child exhibited a nearly normal pattern of standing and walking (Harris, Johnston, Kelly, & Wolf 1964).

WEAKENING PROBLEM BEHAVIOR

At times patients engage in behaviors that may injure themselves or others. A number of behavior-modification techniques have been developed for reducing or eliminating such undesirable behavior patterns.

One technique is based on the principle of operant extinction, which states that a response will decrease in frequency if it is not reinforced. For example, a team of psychologists was faced with the problem of a disturbed 7-year-old boy, John, who continually hit himself.

When first seen, John's head was scarred and his ears were swollen and bleeding. The therapists hoped to eliminate John's self-inflicted injuries by withholding all attention and social reinforcement whenever the behavior occurred. John was observed via a one-way mirror for eight 90-minute extinction sessions. During the first session, he hit himself nearly 3000 times. Over the next seven sessions, this behavior gradually declined in frequency until it was entirely eliminated (Bucher & Lovaas, 1968).

Although extinction can be useful in such situations, it often works very slowly, as in John's case. When it is necessary to eliminate undesirable behavior quickly, other methods must be used. One such method is known as *reinforcement of alternative behavior.* In this method the patient is positively reinforced for behavior that is incompatible with the problem behavior. In one case, the disruptive behavior of a hyperactive child named Crystal was markedly reduced by reinforcing academic performance. Before the therapy began, Crystal engaged in disruptive behaviors such as running around the room and hitting other pupils about 90 percent of the time. The behavior-modification program consisted in part of reinforcing correct answers on a math program with check marks that could be exchanged for toys and candy. Crystal's disruptive behavior quickly dropped to about 10 percent of the time spent in each math session, and she worked on math problems 65 percent of each session (Ayllon, Layman, & Kandel, 1975). Thus a problem behavior can often be reduced or eliminated by strengthening an alternative, incompatible behavior.

Self-Control Procedures

A **self-control procedure** is a special form of behavior modification in which the client actively participates in designing and carrying out the behavior-modification program. For the behavior therapist, self-control means that the client arranges cues (discriminative stimuli) and consequences (reinforcers) in his or her environment to support new forms of behavior.

Self-control procedures are especially helpful in changing ingrained habits like overeating or smoking. But they can also be used to support more effective studying, a regular program of exercise, or any other goal. There are three main steps in devising a self-control program: (1) analyzing the situation, (2) managing discriminative stimuli, and (3) managing consequences (Reese, Howard, & Reese, 1978).

ANALYZING THE SITUATION

Before starting any self-control program, a behavioral analysis of the problem is necessary. In controlling overeating, for example, the client should keep a log of all meals and snacks, noting when and where they occurred, what was eaten, and the consequences in terms of calories taken in or actual weight gained. **Figure 17.3** on page 624 shows a log prepared by a student interested in losing weight. As you can see, the student eats reasonably at regular meals but adds unnecessary calories by eating fattening foods during snacks with friends. Eliminating snacking is an obvious place to begin the weight-reduction program.

MANAGING DISCRIMINATIVE STIMULI

One way to eliminate behavior that occurs in certain situations is to avoid those situations or discriminative stimuli. Our overeating student would do well to stay out of the snack bar, engaging instead in some equally satisfying alternative behavior such as attending a psych lecture or visiting the student lounge. People who wish to lose weight can also avoid stimuli for eating by clearing the cupboards of fattening foods or taking smaller portions at each meal. Sometimes overeating can be controlled by setting up new discriminative stimuli for eating. For example, students can make sure they only eat at a specific table during specific hours in which the dining room is open. This effectively cuts down the number of opportunities to eat and gain weight. Each of these methods is a way of gaining control over eating by avoiding long-established discriminative stimuli for eating.

MANAGING CONSEQUENCES

The best reinforcers of new behavior are the natural consequences of self-control, such as weight loss from eating less, better health from giving up smoking, or better grades from improving study habits. One problem with natural consequences is that they are often delayed and so are not very effective in supporting the behavior of the moment.

To establish new behavior patterns, temporary support from artificial reinforcers is often necessary. Keeping a graph of day-by-day

Day Th Date 10/11 WEIGHT 138 GOAL 118							CALORIES, eaten 3828		
Baseline X Program ___ Maintenance ___							Calories, exercise 100		
Amt. sleep last night 6 hrs. Weather Cold							Total meals 7		
Time	Place	Activity	People	Mood	Amount		FOOD Calories		Sum
7:30	Dorm	Breakfast	People ?	Bitchy	1	O.J.	120		448
					1	H.B. egg	78		
					1	revolting coffee c; s	40		
					2	toast, butter	210		
10:30	College Inn	Break	Debbie, Neal Dinny, Barb	BORED	1	Danish	125		165
					1	Coffee	40		
Noon	Dorm	Lunch	Jill, Pearl Eva, Stephanie	OK	1	Milk	160		660
					1	Spaghetti	Couldn't eat		
					2	Cake ☹	500		
4:30	Snack Bar	After Lab	Ed, David Gerrilynn	Ravenous	1	Cheeseburger	470		720
					1	Fr. Fries (make up for lunch)	250		
6:30	Dorm	Dinner	Gerri, Betsy Denise, Chip, Cathy	good	2	Meat (lamb ??)	470		805
					1	Peas	115		
					2	Sm. potatoes	120		
					1	Choc. ice cream	100		
10:30	Snack Bar	A well-deserved break	Tim; Marci, Andy, Richard, Skye; Talley, Tom	Tired	2	Beer	300		530
					1	Sm. potato chips	230		
11-12	Room	Studying	Rhea for a while, Esther; Madeline came by.	Zonked	½ box (maybe 10?) Choc. Chip cookies		500 ?	448 165 1380 1835 3828	500
							Total meals 7 Total Cal. 3828		

Figure 17.3
Managing Food Intake.
Keeping a log like this is the first step in a self-control program. (After Reese et al., 1978)

progress in self-control is one good way of providing immediate reinforcement. Another method is to plan rewarding activities, such as going to a movie or buying a new item of clothing, when self-control subgoals are met. After a new behavior pattern becomes established, these artificial reinforcers are no longer necessary because they are replaced by the natural reinforcers of healthier and more effective behavior patterns.

Interim Summary

Behavior therapy is a general term for a number of specific techniques derived from research in learning, cognition, and social psychology. Behavior therapists see disordered behavior as a failure of learning and

aim to modify maladaptive patterns of thought, feeling, and behavior by identifying and then changing the environmental factors responsible for them.

The methods of behavior therapy include desensitization procedures for eliminating anxiety, biofeedback therapy as a remedy for stress-related disorders, and assertion training for teaching people to express their feelings in a direct but nonthreatening manner. Cognitive behavior therapy aims to teach patients more effective ways of interpreting and thinking about their experiences, and has proved especially effective in treating depression.

A variety of behavior modification procedures exist for strengthening adaptive behavior and weakening problem behavior.

Self-control procedures are a form of behavior modification in which the client participates actively in analyzing and changing the discriminative stimuli and reinforcers that support maladaptive behavior patterns.

HUMANISTIC THERAPY

Humanistic therapy offers an alternative to both psychoanalytic and behavioral therapies. Humanistic theorists object to the psychoanalytic assumption that human behavior is determined by unconscious drives and conflicts, as well as to the behavioral assumption that a person's reinforcement history is the central determinant of current behavior. The humanistic therapist sees a person as a set of *potentials* that continuously unfold as he or she seeks to achieve self-actualization. Psychological disorders occur when the process of becoming a unique human being is blocked by parents, teachers, spouses, and others who, often unwittingly, try to channel the person's development along lines they find acceptable. When this occurs, the person begins to deny and distort his or her true feelings, beliefs, and perceptions. The person's awareness of his or her own uniqueness becomes narrowed and the potential for growth is reduced.

The goals of **humanistic therapy** are to remove the blocks to self-actualization, to put the person in touch with his or her true self, and to promote continued growth. The therapist consciously avoids giving advice or assuming the role of "expert" since this would only serve to impose the therapist's own views on the patient.

The Variety of Humanistic Therapies

There are many different forms of humanistic psychotherapy. Some humanistic therapists differ only slightly from psychoanalytic therapists in their approach to treatment. They may use interpretations and analyze resistances, as does the psychoanalytic therapist. The major difference is that the humanistic therapist sees the patient's behavior as an expression of his or her current feelings rather than as simply a clue to past conflicts (Morse & Watson, 1977).

Other humanistic therapists actively attempt to put the patient in touch with his or her true feelings and perceptions. In *Gestalt* (German for "whole") *therapy*, for example, the therapist will often challenge patients to give up their facades, resistances, and "phony games" in order to experience underlying feelings directly. The Gestalt therapist may ask the patient to act out a dream or a problem with another person in order to increase the patient's awareness of his or her immediate feelings. For example, a man who tapped the table while other people spoke was asked by a Gestalt therapist if others' talking annoyed him. When he denied that it did, the therapist asked him to experience the feeling behind his habit by tapping more vigorously. As he did, his anger mounted until he was pounding the table. The exercise made him aware of his anger at others' talking as well as of his inhibited and unassertive response to it (Altrocchi, 1980).

The best-known and most widely practiced humanistic therapy is Carl Rogers' client-centered therapy. We will examine this style of therapy as an example of the alternative offered by the humanistic approach.

Carl Rogers

Client-Centered Therapy

Client-centered therapy focuses on the client's conscious experience rather than on the therapist's theory or techniques. Clients are treated as fully responsible individuals capable of understanding and directing their own lives.

For Rogers, a warm, trusting, and accepting relationship between therapist and client is the chief ingredient of therapeutic change. Such a relationship helps the client become conscious of those aspects of experience that have been denied or distorted in the past. In recognizing and accepting his or her individuality, the client sets the stage for continued growth as a person. In order to facilitate these changes, the therapist must adopt and communicate three interrelated attitudes: (1) unconditional positive regard, (2) empathy, and (3) congruence (Rogers, 1951; 1961).

UNCONDITIONAL POSITIVE REGARD
By *positive regard*, Rogers means a warm and caring attitude that expresses a genuine interest in the client and communicates a sense of trust in his or her ability to change and grow. *Unconditional* means that the therapist is willing to accept the person for what he or she is without reservation. This does not mean that the therapist will necessarily approve of every-

thing the client says or does. It simply means that the therapist's liking for the client does not depend on the client's behaving in a specific way. Thus **unconditional positive regard** is the therapist's wholehearted acceptance of the client. It is the way in which the therapist lets the client know that there are no conditions attached to the relationship.

EMPATHY

Empathy is the process of seeing the world from the other person's perspective and understanding what he or she is experiencing. For Rogers, the therapist must constantly strive for an empathic understanding of the client. For example:

> **Client** I don't know exactly what to say—at times I get real jumpy, and can't sit still; that never happened before... and I even get shaky.
> **Therapist** That sounds like it's pretty unpleasant and worrisome for you.
> **C** I don't know what to make of it, really—I don't know whether it means I'm going crazy, or what to think....
> **T** So when you feel this way, sometimes the thought goes through your mind that it would mean something really bad is going on, like you're going crazy or something?
> **C** (Nods yes, looks somewhat frightened.)
> **T** I imagine that's a pretty frightening thought in itself, isn't it?
> **C** It sure is, yes, it really is. (Strayhorn, 1979, p. 19)

Empathy results from a process of **active listening,** in which the therapist tries to grasp both the content of what the client is saying and the feeling behind it. The therapist communicates empathy by the technique of reflection. In **reflection,** the therapist summarizes the client's message—including content and feeling—and communicates it back to the client. Sometimes accurate empathy does not even require a verbal message, as in the following response of a parent to a child's success:

> *Hey, you used to have training wheels, and now look at you, you can ride a bike without training wheels!* A few minutes later the young cyclist is overheard telling the three-year-olds, *I used to have training wheels. I don't have training wheels now, see? I used to.* (Brothers, 1989).

It requires a great deal of skill to set aside one's own preconceptions and put oneself in an-

other's shoes. Accurate and effective reflection enables the client to clarify his or her own feelings and to move to higher levels of self-understanding.

CONGRUENCE

According to Rogers, **congruence** on the part of the therapist requires that the therapist be genuine and honest in the relationship with the client. The therapist must truly value the client and continually strive for empathy. These attitudes cannot be faked or used as mere therapeutic techniques. In Rogers' terms, the therapist must be "dependably real" if the relationship is to be therapeutic. This means that the therapist must also be in touch with his or her own immediate feelings and must communicate these feelings to the client. It would be destructive for the therapist to feign interest in the patient while actually feeling bored. It would be equally destructive for the therapist to maintain a cool professional front while feeling liking and affection for a client. The therapeutic relationship thrives when both client and therapist express and communicate both positive and negative feelings of the moment. **Table 17.2** summarizes clients' views of therapists who show unconditional positive regard, empathy, and congruence.

In Rogers' view, the therapist's attitudes of unconditional positive regard, empathy, and

---

Table 17.2   **Client Statements Reflecting Therapist's Unconditional Positive Regard, Empathy, and Congruence**

Unconditional Positive Regard

His feeling toward me didn't depend on how I felt toward him.

How much he liked or disliked me was not altered by anything that I told him about myself.

I didn't think that anything I said or did really changed the way he felt toward me.

Empathy

He wanted to understand how I see things.

He usually sensed or realized what I felt.

He realized what I meant even when I had difficulty saying it.

Congruence

He was comfortable and at ease in our relationship.

I felt that he was real and genuine with me.

He was openly himself in our relationship.

After Barrett-Leonard (1962)

congruence initiate a process of growth in the client. As the client realizes someone is listening and understanding, perhaps for the first time in any real sense, he or she becomes aware of long-denied feelings and thoughts. The client finds that these feelings and thoughts are accepted by the therapist and moves toward accepting them also. Gradually, the client becomes a more fully functioning person, able to change and grow in ways that express his or her true personality (Rogers, 1961; Meador & Rogers, 1984).

Interim Summary

Humanistic therapy developed as an alter-native to both psychoanalytic and behavior therapies. Humanistic therapy aims to help the patient achieve his or her full potential by removing blocks to growth. In Carl Roger's client-centered therapy, these changes are facilitated by unconditional positive regard, empathy, and congruence on the part of the therapist.

THERAPEUTIC GROUPS

A group can powerfully influence the behavior, attitudes, and feelings of its members. Therapy in a group setting is a way of harnessing this influence to help people overcome psychological difficulties and achieve more fulfilling lives.

Therapeutic groups have several advantages over individual therapy. First, in individual therapy there is no guarantee that the patient's newly acquired insights or behavior patterns will transfer from therapy sessions to daily interactions in the outside world. A therapeutic group gives the person an opportunity to test out new attitudes and behaviors in a relatively sheltered and supportive social situation. With feedback from the therapist and other group members, the person can further modify and strengthen new ways of interacting. Second, the group participant can learn new ways of coping with personal problems by observing other group members as they work to become more effective people. Third, group members can facilitate problem solving by pooling information and experience and by supporting individual attempts to change. Fourth, membership in a group of people with common problems can inspire confidence and

overcome loneliness for people who may have thought their problem was unique.

Some therapeutic groups are extensions of well-developed individual therapies. Groups may be conducted on psychoanalytic, behavioral, or humanistic principles, for example. Psychoanalytic group therapy, with goals of insight and working through, were among the earliest of therapeutic groups. Certain behavior therapies, especially systematic desensitization and assertion training, are often conducted in group settings. Encounter groups, popular in the 1960s and 1970s, were devised by humanistic psychologists as a means of promoting self-awareness and personal growth. Such groups are often composed of strangers and may last several hours or days. The goal is to develop trust and openness among members as the basis for honest expression of feelings and heightened awareness of how others perceive one's behavior. Most people find the encounter group to be a liberating experience, although the emotional intensity may negatively affect a small percentage of participants (Yalom, 1986).

Other therapeutic groups have their own rationales that are independent of any associated individual therapy. Two good examples, which illustrate the diversity of goals and methods in therapeutic groups, are *family therapy* and *support groups*.

Family Therapy

Family therapy represents an increasingly popular departure from traditional methods of psychotherapy. Most psychotherapies, including most group therapies, assume that *individuals* have problems to be solved. By contrast, **family therapy** sees the *family unit*, rather than any one of its members, as the focus of treatment. Family therapy assumes that a disturbance in one family member reflects a more general difficulty in the family's interactions. The family literally becomes the patient.

Families usually enter therapy because one member, known as the "identified patient," has a psychological problem. For example, a child may be expressing fears, wetting the bed, or showing disruptive behavior. The family therapist assumes that this problem reflects some difficulty in the interactions among family members. In a situation where the parents are threatening to divorce, for instance, such symptoms can operate to keep the parents together out of concern for the child. In other words, a

Family therapy sees the family unit, rather than any one of its members, as the focus of treatment.

symptom in one family member is assumed to have an adaptive function in maintaining family stability, even though the symptom is a less than optimal solution to the initial family problem. The goal of family therapy is to rearrange the family's interactions so that the symptoms of the "identified patient" are no longer required to maintain family stability (Haley, 1976).

Like behavior therapists, family therapists are often less interested in uncovering the reasons behind a particular kind of family interaction than in directly intervening to modify it. *Experiential* family therapists attempt to provide new experiences within therapy sessions so that the family becomes more aware of troubling interactions and more able to adopt new patterns. For instance, the therapist might ask the family to reenact a particular incident they have been discussing abstractly. The reenactment will be followed by questions such as "How did that make you feel?" or "Why does Dad always stay in the background?" After problems are acknowledged and understood, the therapist might ask the family to practice new ways of interacting. With a family that has difficulty expressing affection, the therapist might ask the parents to hold hands in front of the children or might ask each member to say something affectionate to each other. This form of family therapy emphasizes breaking of rigid family "rules," expression of emotion, and development of more adaptive interaction patterns (Madanes, 1981).

In *structural* family therapy, the focus is on the component "subsystems" of the family, such as the subsystem comprising the two parents, the subsystem comprising the children, or a subsystem comprising one parent and one child. According to family therapists, the various subsystems should have clear, but not rigid, boundaries, especially between children and parents. However, some families may be too *enmeshed*, having few or no distinctions among subsystems. In such families, for example, the adults may have relinquished their parental roles, which creates confusion among the children as to how they should behave. Other families may be too *disengaged,* with every member an autonomous unit and a virtual absense of famility solidarity (Minuchin, 1974).

One form of enmeshed family structure is known as a "triangle." The triangle is formed by the relationships among the two parents and a child. In this structure, the mother and child typically form an enmeshed subsystem that blurs boundaries between them and simultaneously strains the parental relationship, or parental subsystem. The following account is an example of such a triangle, in which Billy is the identified patient.

Billy, a bright student, has suddenly become "school-phobic." He is skipping classes, flunking tests, fighting with classmates. A few weeks ago, he suffered a fainting spell in the school cafeteria. Although the school doctor could find nothing physically wrong with him, Billy continues to complain of dizziness and refuses to attend school. Alarmed over Billy's problem, Ellen Cooper, with her husband, Fred, reluctantly tagging along, has consulted school counselors, the family pediatrician and a child psychologist—who finally advised a measure that until then the Coopers never heard of—psychotherapy for the whole family.

Billy and his parents form what therapists call a triangle. It frequently consists of a mother overinvolved with one child and a father who is distant and overinvolved in his work. The classic technique is to pull the mother out and make the father take more responsibility for the problem child. Therapists might do that by assigning a "family task." In the Coopers' case, Ellen is instructed to relax and try to enjoy her children while Fred takes over the disciplinary role for a week.

This small stroke produces surprising results. Relieved of her burden, Ellen begins relating more cheerfully to her children and Fred spends more time at home. A process has begun that eases the flow of anxiety in the household. Within weeks, Billy's symptoms subside or vanish. (Gelman, 1978)

Family therapy is intuitively reasonable because it brings together the major participants in an identified patient's problem into a joint effort at solution. Although subscribed to by an increasing number of therapists, family therapy is as yet too recent to have been thoroughly evaluated. A major question is whether treating the family as a unit is more effective than treating its members individually, as in conventional psychotherapy (Gurman & Kniskern, 1981).

Support Groups

Support groups, also known as self-help or mutual-help groups, have proliferated in recent years. Today there are an estimated half-million support groups, involving millions of participants, in existence in North America. Unlike most other types of therapeutic groups, support group meetings are usually conducted by its members without the presence of a professional therapist. Support groups are voluntary organizations of people who meet regularly to exchange information about, and to support each other's efforts to overcome, a problem they have in common. Support groups tend to fall into one of four broad categories: (1) reform groups that address addictive behavior, such as Alcoholics Anonymous and Narcotics Anonymous, (2) self-care groups for people with medical or psychological disorders, such as the Alzheimer's Disease Association and Recovery, Inc. for former mental patients, (3) transition groups for people in crisis, such as the Compassionate Friends for bereaved parents, and (4) advocacy groups of friends and relatives of people with psychological or medical problems, such as the National Alliance for the Mentally Ill (NIMH, 1989; Silverman, 1978). **Table 17.3** lists a variety of support groups from each of these categories.

The grandparent of the support group movement is Alcoholics Anonymous (AA), which was founded in the 1930s by a recovered alcoholic. The goals of AA include informing participants of the nature of alcoholism, teaching new ways of coping with the problem, and supporting efforts to remain abstinent. Membership in AA is now frequently advised by mental-health professionals for their alcoholic clients. Like AA, other support groups often work in tandem with therapists and physicians, who have found that their patients and clients are helped by the support group experience. Support group members say they benefit from the knowledge that they are not alone in having a particular problem, from helping and receiving help from their peers, and from learning more effective ways to cope with their problems (Leerhsen, 1990).

Scientific evaluation of the effectiveness of support groups has lagged behind their rapid growth. However, the limited number of studies that have been conducted suggest considerable impact. For example, a study of cancer patients showed marked benefits of the support group experience. The subjects were 86 women with metastatic breast cancer, in which the breast cancer spreads to other areas of the body and is usually fatal. The women were randomly assigned either to a control group which received conventional medical treatment or an experimental group which received conventional medical treatment plus membership in a support group led by a professional therapist. The group meetings were designed to help the women confront and deal with such issues as the social isolation that often accompanies a diagnosis of cancer, fears of death and dying, poor doctor-patient communication, and establishing supportive family and social networks. In addition, support group members were taught a simple self-hypnosis technique for pain control. The results of the study showed that stress emotions like depression and anxiety increased over time in the control group but decreased in the experimental group. Support group members also reported half as much pain as the controls. A striking and unanticipated finding was that support group members lived longer than the controls. Control group subjects lived an average of 18.9 months after the time they entered the study; subjects in the support group lived an average of 36.6 months (Spiegel, 1991; Spiegel, Bloom, Kraemer, & Gottheil, 1989).

The results of this study are consistent with our earlier discussion in Chapter 16 regarding the negative effects on health and well-

Table 17.3   Selected Self-Help Groups

The following organizations offer support to people with mental or behavioral problems.

AIDS REFERRAL

The U.S. Conference of Mayors publishes a brochure, *Local AIDS-Related Services National Directory,* a listing of over 2000 AIDS groups.

AL-ANON FAMILY GROUP HEADQUARTERS

For relatives and friends of persons with alcohol problems.

ALCOHOLICS ANONYMOUS

For men and women who share the common problems of alcoholism.

ALZHEIMER'S DISEASE AND RELATED DISORDERS ASSOCIATION

Offers assistance and information to Alzheimer's families through its 188 chapters nationwide.

AMERICAN ASSOCIATION OF SUICIDOLOGY

For those who have experienced the suicide of someone close.

ASSOCIATION FOR CHILDREN AND ADULTS WITH LEARNING DISABILITIES

For individuals—children and adults—who suffer from a learning disability.

AMERICAN NARCOLEPSY ASSOCIATION

Provides information and referrals to people with sleep disorders.

AUTISM SOCIETY OF AMERICA

For both adults and children who have autism.

THE COMPASSIONATE FRIENDS

For bereaved parents: peer support.

DEPRESSION AFTER DELIVERY

For women experiencing Post Partum Depression.

EMOTIONS ANONYMOUS

For persons with emotional problems: a Twelve-Step Program adapted from the Alcoholics Anonymous Program.

FAMILIES ANONYMOUS

For concerned relatives and friends of youthS with drug abuse or related behavior problems.

NARCOTICS ANONYMOUS

For narcotic addicts: peer support for recovered addicts.

THE NATIONAL ALLIANCE FOR THE MENTALLY ILL

For families and friends of seriously mentally ill individuals; provides information, emotional support, and advocacy through local and state affiliates.

NATIONAL ASSOCIATION OF ANOREXIA NERVOSA AND ASSOCIATED DISORDERS

Offers assistance to anorexics/bulimics and their families.

NATIONAL COALITION AGAINST DOMESTIC VIOLENCE

National organization of shelters and support services for battered women and their children.

NATIONAL DEPRESSIVE AND MANIC DEPRESSION ASSOCIATION

For depressed persons and their families.

NATIONAL FOUNDATION FOR DEPRESSIVE ILLNESS, INC.

Provides referrals to support groups.

NATIONAL MENTAL HEALTH ASSOCIATION

Citizens advocacy group concerned with all aspects of mental health and mental illnesses.

OCD FOUNDATION, INC.

For sufferers of obsessive-compulsive disorder and their families and friends.

ORTON DYSLEXIA SOCIETY

For persons interested in the study, treatment, and prevention of the problems of specific language disability.

PARENTS ANONYMOUS

For parents who have abused their children.

PARENTS UNITED

For abused children and for adults who were abused as children.

PHOBIA SOCIETY OF AMERICA

For people who suffer from phobia and panic attacks.

RECOVERY, INC.

For former mental patients: peer support.

TARDIVE DYSKINESIA/TARDIVE DYSTONIA NATIONAL ASSOCIATION

For tardive dyskinesia or tardive dystonia sufferers.

(NIMH, 1989)

being of a *lack* of social support and social integration. By providing such support and integration, support groups may work to decrease stress and to increase physical and psychological well-being in their members.

Interim Summary

Therapeutic groups attempt to harness the behavior-influencing power of groups to help people overcome difficulties and lead more fulfilling lives. Some therapeutic groups are extentions of individual therapies, such as group therapies based on psychoanalytic, behavioral, or humanistic concepts. Other therapeutic groups have their own rationale and techniques. Family therapy aims to help families adopt more open and supportive styles of interaction as a means of reducing psychopathology in particular family members. Support groups, often led by their members, aim to provide social support and effective coping skills to help people deal with specific psychological or medical problems.

THE EFFECTIVENESS OF PSYCHOTHERAPY

How effective is psychotherapy? Most therapists probably think the answer is obvious, because they know that most of their patients are better off *after* treatment than they were *before* treatment. Few therapists would continue to practice if they were not convinced of the effectiveness of psychotherapy. Testimonials, however, are no substitute for scientific proof. And both private and governmental health-insurance programs are today asking for hard evidence of psychotherapy's effectiveness before spending millions of dollars for this form of treatment. In this section we will discuss major problems that arise in evaluating psychotherapy and the current state of knowledge regarding its effectiveness.

Evaluating Psychotherapy

Evaluating psychotherapy is an enormous undertaking with many potential pitfalls. One major problem is that a substantial percentage of people with psychological problems get better without any professional assistance. This phenomenon is known as *spontaneous remission*. A number of studies have shown that the rate of spontaneous remission ranges from about 30 to 50 percent, depending on the particular disorder in question (Bergin, 1971; Lambert, 1976). Spontaneous remission requires that any evaluation of psychotherapy compare a treated group with an untreated control group. Psychotherapy, then, is effective to the extent that improvement after therapy is greater than any improvement occurring without therapy over the same time period.

Another problem in evaluating psychotherapy is measuring its outcome. Simply asking patients or therapists how much improvement has occurred may not yield reliable answers, because both parties have vested interests in the outcome. Instead, it is preferable to have a third party do the evaluation. Possible criteria for evaluating therapy include decreases in symptoms, improvement on psychological tests, and improved school or work effectiveness. A good evaluation study will include several such measures.

Despite these problems, many evaluation studies of psychotherapy have been conducted. A review of this research by Mary Lee Smith, Gene Glass, and Thomas Miller (1980) located 475 studies in which a therapy group had been compared with an untreated control group. A large variety of evaluation measures had been used in these studies. Smith et al. found that on 88 percent of the measures the therapy groups showed greater improvement than the control groups. This survey indicates, then, that psychotherapy is effective in general, although it does not tell us the specific ways in which different therapies are effective.

Smith et al. also compared the amount of improvement shown by the average psychotherapy patient with that shown by the average control-group patient. **Figure 17.4** on page 632 shows that the average improvement of patients receiving psychotherapy is higher than the average spontaneous remission of control-group patients. The average psychotherapy patient shows greater improvement than 80 percent of untreated control-group patients.

Comparing Psychotherapies

Psychotherapy produces improvement rates consistently superior to the rate of spontaneous remission. But is one form of psychotherapy superior to other forms? Smith et al. (1980) exam-

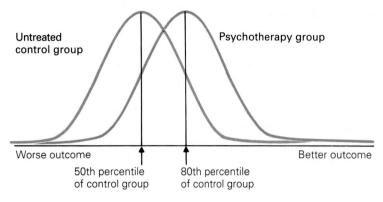

Untreated control group

Psychotherapy group

Worse outcome

Better outcome

↑ 50th percentile of control group

↑ 80th percentile of control group

Figure 17.4
The Improvement of Patients in Control Groups Versus the Improvement of Patients Receiving Psychotherapy. Based on 475 Controlled Studies. (After Smith, Glass, & Miller, 1980)

ined this question by analyzing the results from approximately 50 studies in which a behavioral therapy was compared with some other form of therapy. Both types of therapy were in turn compared with an untreated control group. The researchers found that both behavior and nonbehavior therapies were superior to no treatment but that there was virtually no difference between the two types of therapies on the average.

How can different forms of therapy produce such similar results? This question is at the forefront of contemporary research on psychotherapy. There are two major approaches to answering this question (Stiles, Shapiro, & Elliott, 1986).

One possibility is that certain therapies are effective for certain problems or disorders but relatively ineffective for others. For example, systematic desensitization is very effective for phobias (Paul, 1969) but probably cannot help alleviate depression. Biofeedback combined with relaxation training is effective for migraine headache (Blanchard, Theobald, Williamson, Silver, & Brown, 1978) but is unlikely to cure schizophrenia. When specific therapies are pitted against a wide range of disorders, their *relative* strengths are hidden while their *average* strengths look very similar. Just as we do not expect penicillin to cure all kinds of disease, we should not expect one therapy to be effective for every psychological disorder. Arnold Lazarus (1981) has long argued that psychotherapists should employ a "multimodal"

approach to their clients. Just as clients may have problems in several areas, including behavior, emotion, cognition, and interpersonal relationships, the therapist should have a range of specific methods effective for specific problem areas. Matching the right method to the right problem may increase the overall effectiveness of psychotherapy.

A second possibility is that different forms of psychotherapy may have more in common than is generally acknowledged. They may all share *nonspecific factors* over and above their differences in treatment goals and methods. As Jerome Frank (1973) points out, all therapies share three ingredients: the patient, the therapist, and the relationship between them. According to Frank, these three factors account for much of the change that takes place in psychotherapy. The *patient* is a person in distress. He or she suffers from symptoms that are difficult or impossible to control and, most likely, has also experienced some decline in personal and social effectiveness. The patient is looking for help and guidance. The *therapist*, on the other hand, is in a position to meet the patient's needs. He or she has spent many years studying about and treating similar problems. The therapist holds a complex and extensive theory of human behavior and is an expert in diagnosing and offering remedies for psychological problems. The *relationship* is one in which the therapist offers understanding, respect, acceptance, and encouragement in order to influence the patient to adopt more effective attitudes, feelings, and behaviors.

According to Frank, these three ingredients awaken in the patient an *expectation of success*, a faith in the therapist's power to alleviate the patient's distress. Faith is a powerful motivator that operates in many helping and healing situations. You have undoubtedly heard of the "miracle" cures of religious faith healing. A similar phenomenon in medical practice is known as the **placebo effect.** A placebo is a treatment, such as a sugar pill or an injection of water, with no curative powers of its own. Yet many medical patients improve with a placebo simply because they *believe* they are receiving effective treatment. Every form of treatment, medical or psychological, thus has a built-in placebo effect. The placebo effect may account for a portion of the similarity in outcome among differing psychotherapies (Waterhouse & Strupp, 1984).

Interim Summary

A large number of studies have compared the effectiveness of different psychotherapies with untreated control groups and with each other. Psychotherapy is routinely more effective than no treatment, but there is as yet little evidence that one form of psychotherapy is routinely superior to other forms. However, certain therapies may be better than others for particular problems. All therapies share the ability to offer hope, acceptance, and encouragement to people in distress.

MEDICAL TREATMENTS

Psychotherapy alters disordered behavior by helping patients replace ineffective and self-defeating patterns of thinking and interacting with more realistic and effective patterns. Medical treatments alter disordered behavior by directly altering the underlying activity of the brain. We have already discussed the pros and cons of one medical treatment—psychosurgery—in Chapter 2. Although psychosurgery is rarely used today for psychological disorders, both *drug therapy* and *electroconvulsive therapy* (ECT) are routinely prescribed for certain types of disorders.

Drug Therapy

Pharmacology is the science of drugs—their preparation, use, and effects. *Psychopharmacology* deals specifically with drugs directly affecting mental activity and behavior. As you learned in Chapter 5, these drugs are known as *psychoactive drugs.*

Over the last generation, great progress has been made in developing drugs to treat psychological disorders. Today we have drugs to combat anxiety, psychosis, depression, and mania. Although these drugs are not without their hazards, millions of people benefit from chemical substances that effectively control the symptoms of psychological disorder.

Modern psychopharmacology began with the twin discoveries of the psychoactive effects of *chlorpromazine* and *lithium* around 1950. Chlorpromazine was developed in the search for a sedative to prepare patients for surgery. However, it was soon discovered that chlor-

promazine effectively controlled psychotic symptoms, and it became the first of a large number of *antipsychotic* medications. The discovery of the psychoactive properties of lithium was even more accidental. An animal researcher noted that lithium—a simple metal—had a tranquilizing effect on rats. He decided to administer it to patients in a state of manic excitement and found that their mania was rapidly controlled. Today lithium is the best single treatment for mania. By 1960 drugs for the treatment of depression and anxiety were also developed. In the following sections, we will consider how each of these types of drugs works and the benefits and risks associated with each.

ANTIANXIETY DRUGS

Few people today are unaware of Valium, Librium, and Xanax. They are among the most widely used of a large class of antianxiety medications known as *benzodiazepines.* Approximately $1\frac{1}{2}$ percent of the U.S. population use benzodiazepines on a regular basis (Salzman, 1991). The benzodiazepines are known as antianxiety drugs because of their use in treating anxiety disorders such as panic attacks and agoraphobia. But they also have other uses. Some are used primarily as sleeping pills. Because they induce muscle relaxation, they are also useful in the treatment of muscle spasms. Finally, they are used to control the symptoms of withdrawal from alcohol dependence.

As with any drug, benzodiazepine use has its risks. Because the benzodiazepines act swiftly and effectively, many users are tempted to "pop a pill" at the first sign of tension or stress. This can create a psychological dependence much like alcohol dependence. Critics charge that some physicians help create this dependence by prescribing antianxiety drugs for minor emotional problems instead of helping the patient deal with the source of the discomfort. Prolonged use of benzodiazepines for several months can also lead to physical dependence, which produces a withdrawal reaction if the drug is abruptly discontinued. The withdrawal reaction, which is marked by restlessness, irritability, insomnia, and muscle tension, can be avoided if the daily dose is slowly tapered off over time. The best use of these drugs, which is also the best way to avoid physical and psychological dependence, is for a brief period to treat specific problems like anxiety attacks or insomnia (Harvard Mental Health Letter, 1988).

ANTIPSYCHOTIC DRUGS

The chief use of antipsychotic drugs like chlorpromazine is in combating the symptoms of schizophrenia. Antipsychotics are especially useful in relieving schizophrenic thought disorder, emotional flatness, and auditory hallucinations. They are also effective against psychotic states occurring in other disorders such as mania and amphetamine abuse (Baldessarini, 1977; Lickey & Gordon, 1991). The effects of antipsychotic drugs and placebos are compared in **Figure 17.5.**

Antipsychotic drugs work primarily by interfering with the activity of the neurotransmitter dopamine at synapses in the brain. Molecules of the antipsychotic drug become attached to dopamine receptors. By blocking these receptors, dopamine is no longer able to excite the postsynaptic neuron. As we saw in the previous chapter, the fact that antipsychotic drugs block dopamine receptors has led many researchers to conclude that schizophrenia may be due, at least in part, to excessive dopamine activity in the brain.

Antipsychotic drugs are not without their side effects. They can cause muscle rigidity, tremors, and restlessness, which must in turn be controlled by an additional drug. Some patients who have taken antipsychotic drugs over many years develop *tardive dyskinesia,* the major symptom of which is an involuntary, repetitive, chewing movement of the mouth and lips. This unsightly and embarrassing disorder can often be avoided if the dose is reduced as soon as the patient's psychotic symptoms decrease. Despite these limitations, antipsychotic drugs have greatly helped to improve the lives of hundreds of thousands of schizophrenic patients, who are now often able to live in their home communities rather than in mental hospitals.

ANTIDEPRESSANT DRUGS

The major class of drug used to treat depression are the *tricyclic antidepressants,* so called because of their three-ring chemical structure. The tricyclics are effective with about 70 percent of depressed patients. They improve mood, relieve sleeping difficulties, improve appetite, and eliminate suicidal thinking. A major investigation sponsored by the U.S. National Institute of Mental Health found that 16 weeks of tricyclic antidepressant therapy was as effective as 16 weeks of psychotherapy for less severely depressed patients but more effective than psychotherapy for severely depressed patients (Elkin et al., 1989).

The tricyclics have two major limitations, both of which require careful supervision of the patient. The first is that the tricyclics usually are not effective until 2 to 4 weeks after drug treatment begins. Patients need to be supported and encouraged to continue to take what at first seems to be an ineffective drug. Second, the tricyclics can be fatal if taken in overdose. If the patient is suicidal and not under hospital supervision, it is wise to prescribe only a limited supply of the drug.

The tricyclic drugs work primarily by increasing the amount of two neurotransmitters, *norepinephrine* and *serotonin,* in the brain. Because these drugs relieve depression by increasing levels of these neurotransmitters, many researchers believe that depression may be due to low levels of norepinephrine and/or serotonin at certain brain synapses. A major role for serotonin in depression is suggested by the effectiveness of a relatively new antidepressant, fluoxetine (Prozac). Fluoxetine is a nontricyclic drug that appears to work mainly by increasing brain serotonin levels (Baldessarini, 1990).

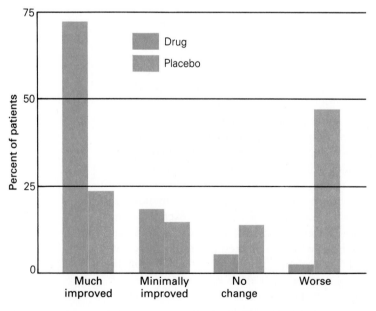

Figure 17.5
Physicians' Ratings of Patients' Responses to Treatment with Antipsychotic Drugs or Placebo. (From Berger, 1978)

LITHIUM

Curiously, lithium is not really a drug in the conventional sense of the term. It is a simple chemical, the third element in the periodic table of elements. In addition to its therapeutic use, lithium is an industrial material used in such applications as the manufacture of batteries.

Lithium is taken in the form of lithium carbonate. It has two major therapeutic uses. The first is in the control of mania. Within 2 weeks, 70 to 80 percent of manic patients show improvement. Even more important, lithium is used to prevent future episodes of mania and depression in patients with bipolar mood disorder. After hospital discharge, patients who take lithium daily have one half to one third as many relapses as patients who are not treated with lithium. Many patients with recurrent depressions (major depression) also seem to benefit from lithium (Baldessarini, 1977). We might think of lithium as a *mood stabilizer* because it appears to smooth out the extremes of elation and depression in affective disorders.

Lithium has few side effects, which makes it easy for patients to take their daily dose. However, an overdose of lithium can be very serious and even fatal. To guard against overdose, patients must have a periodic blood test to check lithium concentration levels in the body (Lickey & Gordon, 1991).

Table 17.4 lists some examples of therapeutic drugs and their effects.

Electroconvulsive Therapy

One of the most controversial treatments in all of medicine, **electroconvulsive therapy (ECT)** involves passing an electrical current through the head to induce a temporary brain seizure similar to an epileptic seizure. The story of ECT is one of paradox: It was originally developed for schizophrenia but works best for severe depression; it is more effective than antidepressant drugs but is given to a relatively small percentage of depressed patients; it has probably saved tens of thousands of lives that might have been lost to suicide but is regarded by many as an inhumane and barbaric procedure.

ECT was developed in the 1930s after it was noted that schizophrenic patients who also suffered from epilepsy often improved temporarily following an epileptic seizure. This observation led some investigators to conclude

Table 17.4   Examples of Therapeutic Drugs

Class	Trade Names	Effects
Antianxiety Benzodiazapines	Valium Librium Xanax	Sedation, muscle relaxation, decreased anxiety
Antipsychotic	Thorazine Prolixin Haldol	Reduced hallucinations, thought disorder, withdrawal, and emotional flatness
Antidepressant	Elavil Tofranil Prozac	Improved mood, sleep, and appetite; decreased negative thinking
Antimanic Lithium	Eskalith	Reduced manic excitement

that an *artificially* induced seizure might be an effective treatment for schizophrenia. The procedure of passing an electrical current through the brain in order to induce such a seizure was first used in 1938. While ECT did *not* prove to be very effective in treating schizophrenia, it was also tried on depressed patients, who often showed a dramatic improvement following a series of 6 to 10 ECT treatments spaced over a period of 2 or 3 weeks.

The ECT procedure is relatively brief. The patient lies on a table, is given an injection of a fast-acting sedative, and quickly passes into unconsciousness. A second injection of a muscle-relaxing drug is then given to block the muscu-

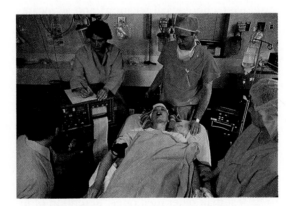

Electroconvulsive therapy, ECT, involves passing an electronic current through the head to produce a temporary brain seizure.

lar contractions that would otherwise accompany the brain seizure. Two electrodes are then placed on the temporal area of the head. One electrode may be placed on each temporal area (bilateral ECT), or both electrodes may be placed on one temporal area, usually on the right or nondominant side (unilateral ECT). A current, ranging from 70 to 170 volts, is passed between the electrodes for approximately half a second. The brain seizure itself usually lasts less than a minute and often only a few seconds. The sedative and muscle-relaxing drugs wear off soon afterward, and the patient is usually able to resume his or her activities within 15 to 60 minutes. Many pa-tients feel somewhat groggy and confused immediately following treatment, but this feeling gradually passes within a day (Salzman, 1978; Weiner, 1979).

ECT is generally reserved for the 20 to 30 percent of depressed patients who do not improve with antidepressant drugs or who are so suicidal that rapid relief from depression is of prime importance. ECT is most effective with the more severe forms of depression. Improvement occurs in as much as 80 to 90 percent of such cases. Although ECT speeds recovery from a depressive episode, it does not forestall *future* episodes. It is thus not a permanent cure for mood disorders (Janicak, Davis, Gibbons, Ericksen, Chang, & Gallagher, 1985).

There are two major reasons why the use of ECT is limited. The first is that many people are repulsed by the idea of passing electricity through the brain. One can easily conjure up images of present-day Dr. Frankensteins maliciously experimenting with the brains and minds of helpless victims. An organization called The Network Against Psychiatric Assault describes ECT as a "bogus, barbaric, and destructive technological weapon" and advocates banning its use. Defenders of ECT argue that its negative image is undeserved. They claim that ECT does not damage the brain and that it rescues thousands of patients from the agony of depression. Controlled studies show that the suicide rate of depressed patients given ECT is lower than for patients receiving any other treatment (Avery, 1977; Endler, 1989).

The second limiting factor in the use of ECT is that it can cause a temporary memory impairment. Recent memories are more likely to be lost than older memories. Retention of information learned soon after ECT is also impaired. Research on this problem indicates that memory functioning improves gradually follow-ing ECT treatment. After a few weeks, the average patient performs as well on memory tests as do patients who have not received ECT. However, some patients continue to complain of a "patchy" loss of memory for particular events surrounding their ECT treatment. Research, however, suggests that memory impairment occurs primarily with bilateral ECT and can be significantly reduced by using unilateral ECT (Crowe, 1984; Endler & Persad, 1988; Squire, Slater, & Miller, 1981; Weiner, 1979).

Interim Summary

Medical treatments aim to alter disordered behavior by directly altering underlying brain activity. In recent years, an increasing number of psychoactive drugs has proved to be effective in treating anxiety, psychosis, depression, and mania. The benefits of drugs in relieving the symptoms of psychological disorder must always be weighed against their costs in terms of unwanted side effects. Research into the way in which psychoactive drugs alter brain functioning to produce therapeutic effects often leads to hypotheses about the neurochemical bases of psychological disorders. Electroconvulsive therapy (ECT) is an effective treatment, but not a cure, for depression. It is controversial because it involves inducing a brain seizure and because it can cause a temporary memory impairment.

COMMUNITY MENTAL HEALTH

Until the 1960s, mental hospitals were the primary setting for the care and treatment of patients with major psychological disorders such as schizophrenia, severe affective disorders, chronic alcoholism, and organic mental disorders. But the mental hospital is fast becoming a vestige of the past. Mental patients have been returned to their home communities and fewer patients are being sent to institutions in the first place. This process is known as *deinstitutionalization*. Services formerly provided by the mental hospital are now being provided by a variety of community-based treatment facilities. This is known as *community care*. The change from institutional to community care has been dramatic. For example, in 1955 over 60 percent of all U.S. mental patients were treated in mental hospitals. By 1980 this number had declined 15 percent, while the remaining 85 percent were treated in community mental health centers or general medical hospitals (U.S. Department of Commerce, 1984). This trend is still continuing. Many mental hospitals have experienced an 80 to 90 percent decline in the number of patients; some have even closed. In the future, public mental hospitals will undoubtedly treat only a small number of very disturbed patients on a short-term basis, although a number of private mental hospitals will continue to exist for those who can afford them.

Deinstitutionalization

During the first half of the nineteenth century, mental patients benefited greatly from the moral therapy inaugurated by Pinel and practiced in the early mental hospitals. The majority of patients eventually recovered and were discharged (Grob, 1966). But with increases in the general population, mental hospitals soon became overcrowded. The population of mental hospitals increased year after year, growing to more than half a million people in the United States alone by the mid-1950s. Once admitted, patients could spend many years, sometimes their entire lives, in the hospital. In the process, they tended to lose whatever contact they had with families, communities, or employers. They tended to become chronic patients who knew little about the world except how to live in a mental hospital.

By the 1960s the mental hospital system was ripe for reform. In 1963 the U.S. Congress established a national network of *community mental-health centers* (CMHCs) designed to treat patients in their home communities and to return them to their former lives as quickly as possible. CMHCs provide a variety of mental-health services, including: *counseling and psychotherapy* on an hourly basis, *day care* programs for more severely disturbed patients who can nevertheless return home in the evening, *early intervention* programs for the diagnosis and treatment of children with mental and emotional problems, and *crisis intervention* programs for the rapid treatment of patients in acute turmoil. *Follow-up care* for discharged mental patients is also an important service provided by CMHCs. Through *consultation and educational services* to schools, courts, and other community agencies, CMHCs also aim to prevent psychological problems from developing in the first place. When problems do occur, the goal is to prevent them from escalating into more serious and chronic disabilities. Today there are approximately 2000 community mental health centers, supported by a combination of federal, state, and private sources, which offer a variety of mental health services to communities (National Council of Community Mental Health Centers, 1991).

THE ROLE OF PSYCHOACTIVE DRUGS

Most experts believe that deinstitutionalization would not have been possible without the development of psychoactive drugs in the 1950s and 1960s. By controlling the severity of patients' symptoms, psychoactive drugs have allowed patients to participate in community-based programs. For example, several studies have shown that antipsychotic medication reduces the frequency of relapses in schizophrenic patients. Within a 30-month period after treatment, the great majority of schizophrenic patients will relapse if not continued on antipsychotic medication. The drugs reduce this relapse rate by about one half (Baldessarini, 1977).

THE LEGAL RIGHTS OF MENTAL PATIENTS

Deinstitutionalization has also been supported by numerous rulings of state and federal courts. The message is clear: the mentally ill are protected by constitutional guarantees as much as other citizens. The courts have repeatedly affirmed, for example, that a person cannot be involuntarily committed to a mental hospital without "due process of law." In most states, this means that the mental hospital superintendent must prove in court, beyond a reasonable doubt, that the person is likely to harm himself or others if not committed. The result is that increasingly fewer people are committed to mental hospitals.

Thousands of former mental patients have been discharged into the community under *right-to-treatment rulings* by the courts. The right to treatment means that a mental patient has the right to receive a therapeutic program aimed at remedying his or her psychological difficulties. If such a program is not available, the patient must be discharged. In many cases, the courts have found that mental patients were not receiving adequate treatment and therefore ordered that they be discharged. Many courts have also held that patients have a further right to treatment in the *least restrictive alternative.* If, for example, a patient's condition is not serious enough to justify hospitalization, the patient should receive treatment in a CMHC or other community facility.

Community Care

Community care is the other side of the coin to deinstitutionalization. It refers to the package of services provided by federal, state, and local governments to replace mental hospitalization. In fact, community care is an ideal goal that has not yet been reached. Nevertheless, most communities provide a number of options for former mental-hospital patients and for people who would have been sent to a mental hospital in the past.

Many former mental patients have been transferred to private *nursing homes,* especially if they are chronically ill or elderly. In some states, a system of private *board-and-care homes* has also been developed. Like nursing homes, these facilities must be licensed by the

Community mental health centers offer a number of services including day programs, counseling, and job training. This highly successful center is Fountain House in New York City.

state, although the range of medical services that they offer is not as wide. Other discharged patients may live in *halfway houses,* which are state-supported community residences offering shelter and professional treatment until the patient can make a full transition to community living. Of course, many former patients simply live with their family or friends. Patients who are not gainfully employed or who are chronically disabled because of their psychological condition are likely to be supported by some combination of medicare, medicaid, social security, or welfare benefits (Grinspoon & Bakalar, 1990b).

Community mental-health centers also provide many services for former and would-be mental-hospital patients. General hospitals often have a *psychiatric unit* that provides intensive care and supervision when emergencies arise. Medication and individual, group, or recreational therapy are available for persons suffering episodes of psychological disorders.

The Homeless Mentally Ill

Unfortunately, the process of deinstitutionalization has often proceeded more rapidly than the development of adequate community care resources. The *homeless mentally ill* have become victims of this disparity. The homeless mentally ill are people with chronic psychological disorders such as schizophrenia and alcoholism who are not dangerous and therefore cannot be involuntarily treated, yet who have not found their way into community care programs. Some find their way to shelters that provide a bed for the night but are closed during the day; others simply live and sleep on city streets or in parks. According to one expert (Torrey, 1988), there are twice as many schizophrenic individuals in the United States living in shelters and on the streets (about 130,000) than there are in public mental hospitals (about 60,000).

Few mental health professionals believe that the solution lies in returning to the old mental hospital system. We know from 200 years of experience that mental hospitals do not solve the problem of chronic mental illness; mental hospitals simply hide the problem from public view. What, then, can be done for the homeless mentally ill?

Many experts believe that the solution lies in strengthening the system of community care (Okin, 1987). Unfortunately, no single level of government is responsible for community care. Instead, community agencies depend on a combination of local, state, and federal support. In turn, each level of government acts as if the other levels are ultimately responsible for community care. Clearly, money needs to be targeted more directly to support community mental health centers, halfway houses, and other community services. In addition, affordable low-income housing needs to be made available to the chronically mentally ill who are able to manage on their own (NIMH, 1991).

Finally, others believe that legal changes are needed to allow for the involuntary treatment of nondangerous but severely disturbed individuals. For example, some states now allow the mentally ill to be hospitalized for a brief period when the person is obviously irrational, unable to make competent treatment decisions, and shows clear symptoms of mental illness such as hallucinations and delusions (Stone, 1987). Critics fear that this approach will erode the civil liberties gained by mental patients in the past quarter-century. Defenders argue that the freedom to be mentally ill and homeless is a cruel hoax perpetrated on the mentally ill in the name of legal principles. As you can appreciate, there are no easy answers in the continuing search for both humane and effective programs for the homeless mentally ill (Geller, Fisher, Simon, & Wirth-Cauchon, 1990).

Interim Summary

Community mental health promises a revolution in the care and treatment of mental patients even more extensive than Pinel's reforms of 200 years ago. The development of community mental health centers and the discovery of effective psychoactive drugs have allowed mental hospital patients to be discharged and to be treated in the community. Community care is also consistent with newly acquired legal safeguards such as the right to treatment and treatment in the least restrictive alternative. Unfortunately, the promise of community care is as yet unfulfilled. Deinstitutionalization has created its own problem of the homeless mentally ill. The solution to this problem requires the development of specific community care programs for this group of people.

SUMMARY

1. The modern era in the treatment of psychological disorders began about 200 years ago with Philippe Pinel's development of moral treatment of the mentally ill. A century later Sigmund Freud developed classical psychoanalysis to treat less severe psychological disorders. Today many different types of psychological and medical therapies are available to people with psychological disorders.

2. In classical psychoanalysis, the therapist uses free association and the interpretation of dreams, resistance, and transference to help the patient gain insight into the unconscious conflicts underlying his or her symptoms. Contemporary psychodynamic psychotherapy is briefer, more flexible, and more oriented to current difficulties in the patient's life than is classical psychoanalysis.

3. Behavior therapy is a general term for a number of specific therapies derived from psychological research. Behavior therapy includes desensitization procedures, biofeedback therapy, assertion training, and cognitive behavior therapy. Behavior modification and self-control procedures aim to strengthen adaptive behavior and weaken problem behavior.

4. Humanistic therapy aims to help the patient achieve his or her full potential. In client-centered therapy, change and growth are facilitated by the therapist's unconditional positive regard, empathy, and congruence.

5. Therapeutic groups attempt to harness the behavior-influencing power of groups to help people overcome personal difficulties. Family therapy helps families adopt more open and supportive styles of interaction as a means of overcoming difficulties in a particular family member. Suppport groups, often led by their members, aim to provide social support and effective coping skills to people with specific psychological or medical problems.

6. Psychotherapy is more effective than no treatment, but there is no evidence that one form of psychotherapy is routinely superior to other forms. However, certain therapies may be superior to others for particular problems.

7. In recent years, an increasing number of psychoactive drugs has proved to be effective in treating anxiety, psychosis, depres-

sion, and mania. The benefits of drugs in relieving the symptoms of psychological disorder must always be weighed against their costs in terms of unwanted side effects. Electroconvulsive therapy (ECT) is an effective treatment, but not a permanent cure, for depressive disorder.

8. The development of community mental health centers and the discovery of effective psychoactive drugs have allowed mental hospital patients to be deinstitutionalized and to be treated in the community. Community care is also required by legal safeguards such as patients' right to treatment and right to treatment in the least restrictive alternative. However, deinstitutionalization has also led to the problem of homelessness among former patients.

KEY INDIVIDUALS

Philippe Pinel
Pierre Charcot
Sigmund Freud
Joseph Breuer
B. F. Skinner
Joseph Wolpe
Albert Ellis
Aaron T. Beck
Carl Rogers

KEY RESEARCH

the practice of moral treatment
development of classical psychoanalysis
systematic desensitization
rational-emotive therapy
Beck's cognitive therapy for depression

client-centered therapy
psychotherapy evaluation study
discovery of chlorpromazine and lithium
development of electroconvulsive therapy (ECT)
development of community mental-health centers

KEY TERMS

psychotherapy
classical psychoanalysis
free association
latent content
manifest content
dream analysis
resistance
transference
insight
interpretation
working through
psychodynamic psychotherapy
behavior therapy
systematic desensitization
anxiety hierarchy
in vivo desensitization
assertion training
cognitive behavior therapy
behavior modification
token economies
self-control procedure
humanistic therapy
client-centered therapy
unconditional positive regard
empathy
active listening
reflection
congruence
family therapy
support groups
placebo effect
electroconvulsive therapy (ECT)

APPENDIX

Methods and Statistics in Psychology

by

Keith E. Stanovich

Ontario Institute for Studies in Education

author of

How to Think Straight About Psychology

APPENDIX OUTLINE

ost of the results presented throughout this text have depended on carefully conducted psychological research. In many ways, research in psychology is similar to research in other sciences. It involves careful observation and control of variables that might influence the results but which are not of primary interest to the investigator. To prevent these irrelevant variables from obscuring the effects of the relevant variables, psychologists use the methods of random assignment and experimental control. To determine whether relations between variables are real or are merely the result of chance fluctuations in the data, psychologists use methods derived from a branch of mathematics called statistics. Here we will describe in detail the most frequently used methods of psychological research and examine how psychologists use statistics to summarize data and to determine what inferences can be drawn from the data.

· ·

RESEARCH METHODS: DISCOVERING RELATIONSHIPS

In Chapter 1 we described several methods that psychologists use in their research. Among these were naturalistic observation, the case study, surveys, correlational studies, and the experiment. All of these methods make use of statistical procedures in some way. Many of the research studies described in this text are correlational studies or experiments. Therefore, in this discussion we will focus on these two methods. We will examine the characteristics that differentiate experiments from correlational studies and learn why both methods are used in psychological investigations.

The True Experiment

You will recall from the discussion in Chapter 1 that the unique strength of the experiment as a method of investigation is that it allows the researcher to identify cause and effect, that is, to make a causal inference. The causal inference is the inference that the independent variable caused any changes that were observed in the dependent variable. Other potential causes of changes in the dependent variable are eliminated as possible candidates by one of two methods: random assignment and experimental control.

RANDOM ASSIGNMENT

As we learned in Chapter 1, **random assignment** is a method of assigning subjects to the experimental and control groups so that each subject in the experiment has the same chance of being assigned to either of the groups. Flipping a coin is one way to decide to which group each subject will be assigned. In actual experimentation a computer-generated table of random numbers is most often used. By using random assignment, the investigator is attempting to equate the two groups on all behavioral and biological variables prior to the investigation. One of the important properties of random assignment, and one that is often overlooked, is that it also equates the groups on all other extraneous variables (that is, variables other than the independent variable)—even ones that the investigator has not explicitly measured.

How well random assignment works depends on the number of subjects in the experiment. As you might expect, the more the better. That is, the more subjects there are to assign to the experimental and control groups, the closer the groups will be matched on all variables prior to the manipulation of the independent variable. Fortunately for researchers, random assignment works pretty well even with relatively small numbers (e.g., 15–20) in each of the groups.

The use of random assignment ensures that there will be no systematic bias in how the subjects are assigned to the two groups. The groups will always be matched fairly closely on any variable, but to the extent that they are not matched, random assignment removes any bias toward either the experimental or the control group. Perhaps it will be easier to understand how random assignment eliminates the problem of systematic bias if we focus on the concept of **replication:** the repeating of an experiment in all of its essential features to see if the same results are obtained.

Imagine an experiment conducted by a developmental psychologist who is interested in the effect of early enrichment experiences for preschool children. Children randomly assigned to the experimental group receive the enrichment activities designed by the psychologist during their preschool day-care period. Children randomly assigned to the control group participate in more traditional playgroup activities for the same period. The dependent variable is the children's school achievement, which is measured at the end of the children's first year in school to see whether children in the experimental group have outperformed those in the control group.

The use of random assignment attempts to ensure that the groups start out relatively closely matched on all other extraneous variables that could affect the dependent variable of school achievement. These extraneous variables are sometimes called *confounding* variables. Some possible confounding variables are intelligence test scores and home environment. Random assignment will *roughly* equate the two groups on these variables. However, particularly when the number of subjects is small, there may still be some differences between the groups. For example, if after random assignment the intelligence test scores of children in the experimental group were 105.6 and those of children in the control group were 101.9 (this type of difference could occur even if random assignment has been properly used), we might worry that any difference in academic achievement in favor of the experimental group was due to the higher intelligence test scores of children in that group rather than to the enrichment program. Here is where the importance of replication comes in. Subsequent studies may again show IQ differences between the groups after random assignment, but the lack of systematic bias in the random assignment procedure ensures that the difference will not always be in favor of the experimental group. In fact, what the property of no systematic bias ensures is that, across a number of similar studies, any IQ differences will occur approximately half of the time in favor of the experimental group and half of the time in favor of the control group.

Thus, there are really two strengths in the procedure of random assignment. One is that in any given experiment, as the sample size gets larger, random assignment ensures that the two groups are relatively matched on all extraneous variables. However, even in experiments where the matching is not perfect, the lack of systematic bias in random assignment allows us to be confident in any conclusions about cause—as long as the study can be replicated. Thus, while random assignment is no guarantee of absolute subject group equality in any one experiment, it is nevertheless the best insurance available against nonequivalent groups.

Finally, there is a procedure termed *matched random assignment*, which, when used, usually results in groups being even more closely matched. In matched random assign-

ment, two subjects are matched on certain characteristics such as age, sex, and intelligence. One member of the pair is then randomly assigned to either the experimental or the control group. Once one member is assigned, the other member of the pair is automatically assigned to the other group. This procedure results in more closely equated groups than does pure random assignment.

EXPERIMENTAL CONTROL

Although random assignment equates the two subject groups of the experiment, the environmental conditions under which the two groups are observed and measured must also be controlled. This means that the researcher must try to control all of the variables in the experimental environment that might reasonably be thought to have a link to the dependent variable. For example, in the preschool enrichment experiment, the investigator would certainly try to hold constant the children's supervisors, the amount of attention the children received, and the number of books and toys in their rooms.

The key aspects of an experiment are thus manipulation, random assignment, and control. The investigator manipulates the variable thought to be the cause (the independent variable) and equates the groups on all variables except the dependent variable. The equating of the groups is accomplished through the procedures of random assignment and experimental control. Random assignment ensures the equality of the two groups on all variables linked to the subjects. Control of the experimental situation ensures that environmental variables are equivalent across the two groups. Finally, the investigator looks to see whether there is a difference in the dependent variable between the two groups. If there is, then the investigator can infer that the independent variable was the cause of the difference. Variation in the dependent variable must have been caused by the independent variable because nothing else was varying in a systematic manner. In short, the independent variable is linked with the dependent variable and nothing else is.

The Correlational Study

In an experiment the investigator attempts to isolate the factor (the independent variable) that is hypothesized to cause the change in the dependent variable. The independent variable is isolated because it is the only variable that is allowed to vary between the experimental and the control group. Correlational studies, however, do not isolate variables in this way. Instead, correlational studies measure relationships between variables as they naturally occur, without the imposed manipulation and random assignment of the true experiment. Thus, in a correlational study many variables may be varying together.

While this degree of "naturalness" might seem to be a strength of a correlational study, it in fact represents a severe limitation. Merely measuring, without manipulation or randomness, does not isolate the causal path connecting two variables. The relationships observed in correlational studies may come about in a variety of ways. Thus, we repeat here the caution expressed in Chapter 1: *correlation does not imply causation.*

MEASUREMENT, NOT MANIPULATION

Consider, for example, an educational researcher who wanted to determine whether a new, nontraditional reading series (call it New Series) that has recently been adopted by a few school districts leads to better achievement among second-grade children than an older, widely used series (call it Old Series). First of all, notice that the researcher has made a causal hypothesis. This is true even though the word cause does not appear in the hypothesis just presented. It is important that you recognize that causal hypotheses can be expressed in many different ways. The phrase "leads to better achievement" is a causal phrase. It is the same as saying "I hypothesize that the New Series causes increases in achievement."

Now imagine that this investigator measured the reading achievement of second graders in some school districts using the New Series and some using the Old Series and found that achievement scores were considerably higher in districts using the New Series. Can the investigator conclude that the New Series leads to ("causes") better achievement scores? If you have followed the discussion so far, you will realize that the answer is clearly no. This investigator did not carry out an experiment—where an independent variable is manipulated—but instead simply measured two variables (the achievement scores and which reading series was used) as they occurred naturally and determined if the two variables went together (were "co-related"). The researcher carried out

a correlational study and thus cannot make a causal inference.

Why is a causal inference not justified in this case? You should be able to think of many ways in which the school districts using the New Series may have differed from those using the Old Series and it should be fairly obvious that several of these factors might have effects on school achievement. For example, maybe the school districts using the New Series were richer and could afford to replace their reading series more often. Perhaps the teachers using the New Series were more experienced. Perhaps these teachers were more amenable to curriculum change. Perhaps the teachers using the Old Series resisted change. Perhaps children in the districts using the New Series had higher scores on intelligence tests. Perhaps the student/teacher ratio was lower in districts using the New Series. All of these variables are potentially linked to higher achievement scores. Merely observing a difference between the districts using the two series does not allow us to decide whether the difference is indeed due to the New Series or to any of these other factors that may be varying along with it.

This example illustrates the type of problem that occurs when we measure variables as they occur naturally rather than manipulating them. So many variables are related to each other that it becomes extremely difficult to disentangle the critical causal linkages. An experiment attempts to isolate specific relationships to test in a context in which all other potential linkages are removed (via random assignment). Experiments are often criticized for being unnatural, because they create situations that are unlike anything occurring in "real life." We should realize from the discussion here why such criticisms are unfounded. The artificiality and "unnaturalness" of experiments is precisely what the researcher is seeking. The investigator does not want to reproduce the situation occurring in the real world because, as the example above illustrated, that situation is ambiguous. In order to reduce this ambiguity, the investigator conducting an experiment deliberately separates the naturally occurring correlations among variables in order to isolate a specific variable to test.

THE THIRD VARIABLE PROBLEM

The example of the correlational study on the old and new reading series illustrates a particular difficulty in interpreting correlational research that is sometimes called the third variable problem. The **third variable problem** refers to the fact that a correlation between two variables (call them A and B) may arise in situations in which there is no causal connection at all between them. Thus, it is possible for variables A and B to be correlated even though it is not true that changes in variable A are causing changes in variable B, nor is it true that changes in variable B are causing changes in variable A. The third variable problem refers to the possibility that the link between the two variables occurs because both are linked to some third variable, which may be an unknown variable not even measured by the investigator.

Consider a simple example. If on every day of one summer we recorded how many pounds of ice cream were consumed in the United States on that day and we also recorded how many drownings took place in the nation's lakes and rivers on that same day, we would find a correlation between these two variables. Days having a high number of drownings would be those on which large amounts of ice cream were consumed and days having few drownings would be days on which relatively small amounts of ice cream were consumed. Few of us would want to infer, however, that there is a causal connection between these two variables. It is unlikely that the drownings are causing people to eat more ice cream and it is almost as unlikely that eating ice cream is causing people to drown. Yet it is easy to see that there might be a third variable that probably accounts for the connection: the variable of the weather and/or temperature. On hot, sunny days a lot of people eat ice cream and a lot of people swim. The more swimmers there are in the water on any one day, the higher the probability of a drowning. Thus, ice cream consumption will be linked with the number of drownings through the third variable of weather conditions. Correlations of the ice cream–drownings type are often called spurious. A **spurious correlation** is one that does not result from a direct causal connection between the variables.

A second example of a spurious correlation comes from an actual research study that took place several years ago in Taiwan (Li, 1975). In this case, the researchers were studying the factors related to the tendency to use contraceptive devices. A large team of investigators measured a wide range of behavioral and environmental variables. The variable that correlated the highest with contraceptive use was the number of electrical appliances (toasters, fans, etc.) in the home. Does this mean, then, that if the Taiwanese government wishes to encourage population control it should distribute free toasters in post offices? We hope you realize that this would be a mistake, because the correlation between contraceptive use and the number of appliances in the home is spurious. The likely third variable is socioeconomic status. In many countries of the world there is a tendency for people from higher socioeconomic levels to use contraception to a greater extent than people from low socioeconomic levels. Also, the larger incomes of people in the higher groups often result in the purchase of more electrical appliances. So the two variables of contraceptive use and number of appliances are linked through a third variable rather than through any direct causal connection between them. Electrical appliances are not causing people to use contraceptives and neither is the use of contraceptives causing people to buy more appliances.

THE DIRECTIONALITY PROBLEM

The third variable problem is not the only factor that prevents us from drawing causal inferences from correlational data. Even if we were to eliminate the third variable problem, we would be left with another difficulty: the directionality problem. The **directionality problem** refers to an ambiguity that remains even when we know that a relation between two variables, A and B, is not spurious. Are changes in A causing changes in B? Or is it the reverse? Are there causal paths running in both directions? In short, if there is a causal path between the two variables, in what direction does it run?

When a researcher in developmental psychology reports a correlation between an aspect of parental behavior and a behavioral characteristic of their infants or young children, it is quite common for people immediately to start generating explanations for why the parents' behavior might have affected the children's behavior. There is often a tendency to ignore the possibility of the opposite causal path. We are so used to thinking of the direction of cause as running from parents to children that this dominates our thinking. But recent research in developmental psychology has uncovered the sometimes very subtle ways in which children shape the behavior of their parents. There are causal paths running in both directions. The lesson here is not to be easily seduced into considering only one causal path because of the nature of the variables involved. This can lead to mistaken inferences and such false inferences can have very negative consequences.

Some years ago experimental psychologists and educational psychologists began studying eye movements to determine what they could tell about how children process information while carrying out academic tasks. For example, it was demonstrated that children who were poor readers displayed eye movement patterns that differed from those of better readers. The poor readers made more fixations (times when the eyes were not moving but instead were focused on a certain spot) per line of text, they fixated for longer periods, and they had more regressions (movements from right to left instead of left to right). However, before the relationship between eye movement patterns and reading ability had been fully explored, some people drew a causal inference. They assumed that inefficient eye movements were the cause of the children's reading problems. This inference led in turn to the design of many different "eye movement training" programs in which children were given practice at tasks like rapidly fixating moving lights and fixating in the left-to-right direction. The idea was to increase the efficiency of the presumed cause (eye movements) and expect to see an improvement in the thing it affects (reading skill).

Unfortunately, the assumption about the causal path was premature. When researchers finally did the proper research, it turned out that the causal path ran in precisely the opposite direction: from reading ability to eye movements. The fact is not that efficient eye movements lead to good reading but rather that skill in reading leads to the eye movement patterns that are characteristic of good readers. Since there is no causal path running from eye movements to reading skill, the attempt to train eye movements was futile.

This example illustrates the harm that can be done (in this case in the form of wasted effort, squandering of scarce resources, wasting of children's learning time) when a premature causal inference is made from data that is merely correlational. These educational interventions were initiated when all researchers had was a correlational connection—that certain eye movement patterns were associated with certain levels of reading ability.

This example also illustrates how correlational studies can be turned into experiments by exercising manipulation and control. The initial investigations had simply measured eye movements and reading skill as they occurred naturally. Later experimental investigations manipulated each of the relevant variables in turn, controlled for extraneous variables, and then looked for an effect on the other variable. That is, in separate experiments, each variable was manipulated as the independent variable and each was treated as the dependent variable. For example, some investigators formed experimental groups who received eye movement training and control groups who performed some neutral activity. They observed that the group receiving the training did not read more efficiently. Other investigators manipulated the ease with which subjects read by manipulating the difficulty of the text. One group might read easy text composed of short, frequently used, and easily understood words. Another group might read difficult text composed of long, infrequently used words with obscure meanings. Manipulation of this text difficulty variable had a profound effect on the eye movement patterns of the subjects. Subjects who read the difficult text had more fixations per line of text, longer fixation durations, and more regressions than the subjects who read the easy text. In fact, good readers of difficult text displayed eye movement patterns similar to those of poor readers of normal text. These experiments established the causal direction as running from reading ability to eye movements—something that could never have been demonstrated by correlational studies alone.

WHY USE CORRELATIONAL STUDIES?

You may wonder why researchers bother with correlational studies at all if such studies cannot determine causation. There are actually several reasons. First is the simple fact that correlational work often precedes experimental work. Correlational studies are often easier to conduct and thus often serve as preliminary investigations. Although they cannot definitively answer the question of why certain relationships occur, they can point to where important relationships exist. These important relationships then become the focus of experimental investigations.

A second reason for correlational studies is that researchers are sometimes interested in many variables that are difficult to manipulate. A researcher in educational psychology would rarely be in a position where it would be possible to randomly assign subjects to particular school curricula. Children are nonrandomly assigned to such groups on the basis of geographic, economic, social, and political factors that are not under the control of the researcher. Thus, there are some variables that could, in principle, be manipulated but are not because the practical problems in doing so are too great. Research on some of these variables is usually correlational.

There are other variables that could be manipulated but are not because of ethical considerations. Surely no researcher studying the effects of malnutrition on brain development would randomly assign some newborns to a "healthy diet" condition and others to a "starvation diet" condition. Likewise, no researcher studying drug dependence would randomly assign subjects to a "heavy cocaine use" condition. Such research with humans must be correlational. However, true experiments with nonhuman animals are frequently carried out on these variables, and in many cases the results of these experiments do generalize to human behavior.

There are also some variables that are inherently correlational. Called **organismic variables,** these are variables that are properties of the organism being studied. Variables such as a person's sex, age, and race are organismic variables. They are properties of people as individuals and cannot be assigned as an experimental condition. For example, an investigator could not pull a number out of a random number table and assign you to the "12-year-old" condition if you are 23 years old. The age variable is inherently correlational—it cannot be manipulated. Yet such organismic variables are often of great interest to psychologists. Research is done on them, but that research is correlational.

Finally, there are many situations in which prediction rather than a causal explanation is the goal. University admissions directors and high school counselors would like to have testing instruments that predict how likely a student is to succeed in a particular type of college. Personnel directors would like to have devices that predict how well a person will do in a particular job category within an organization. Insurance companies would like to have instruments that predict the likelihood that a person of a certain age and background will have an automobile accident or will die. Market researchers would like to have instruments that predict the degree of public acceptance of particular products. Military recruiters would like

to have assessment devices that predict the likelihood that a potential recruit will succeed in a particular training program. In each of these cases the primary focus is on the accuracy of the prediction itself. The primary requirement is that the predictive instrument *works,* regardless of why it works. For this purpose, correlational evidence is just fine. If the interest is simply in prediction and not in the underlying explanation of *why* a relationship occurs, then correlational evidence—which simply documents a relationship—is completely sufficient. Correlational work will thus be common in many applied situations where the focus is on predicting behavioral relationships rather than on explaining them.

A final reason why correlational studies are important and useful in science is because research on a particular problem often proceeds from weaker methods to ones that allow more powerful conclusions to be drawn. For example, interest in a particular hypothesis may originally stem from a particular case study of unusual interest. This is the proper role for case studies; to suggest hypotheses for further study with more powerful techniques and to motivate scientists to apply more rigorous methods to a research problem. Following the case studies, researchers might undertake correlational investigations to verify whether the link between variables is real rather than the result of the peculiarities of a few case studies. If the correlational studies support the relationship between relevant variables, then researchers will attempt experiments in which variables are manipulated in order to isolate a causal relationship between the variables. The progression, then, is from case studies, to correlational studies, to experiments with manipulated variables. While this gradual progression toward more powerful research methods is not always followed in every research area (sometimes different types of investigations go on in parallel), the progression quite commonly occurs. Correlational studies thus often represent an important intermediate step in a research program.

The Strength of the Scientific Method

All of the methods used in psychology—the experiment and the correlational study described in detail here, as well as the survey, the case study, and naturalistic observation—are based on the idea of **empiricism,** the view that knowledge is obtained through observation. Of course, observation in science must be structured in certain specific ways; recall, for example, our previous discussion of manipulation, random assignment, and control. This concern for structured observation pervades all the methods that psychologists use and it is what differentiates the scientific method of acquiring knowledge from other methods.

The eye movement and reading ability example discussed earlier illustrates some of the broader implications of the systematic empiricism fundamental to scientific thinking. It is important to realize that the hypothesis that eye movements affect reading efficiency has some plausibility. It happens to be wrong, but it is not an implausible idea. What this example illustrates is the important point that plausibility is not enough in science. There is plenty of plausible "commonsense wisdom" around, but much of it is wrong. It is logical that much commonsense wisdom about human behavior is wrong simply because much of it is contradictory. Consider some "commonsense" cliches about human behavior that we often hear: "Absence makes the heart grow fonder" or "Opposites attract." Both cliches are actually behavioral predictions. Stated in more formal language the first says, "The tendency for two people to be attracted to each other will increase if they undergo physical separation." The second is also a behavioral prediction that could be stated in scientific terms. That is, the key concepts in the statement could be given in **operational definitions:** definitions in terms of observable events that can be measured.

The problem with much "commonsense" folk wisdom is that it blatantly contradicts other "commonsense" maxims. If indeed "Absence makes the heart grow fonder," then what about "Out of sight, out of mind?" If "Opposites attract," why do "Birds of a feather flock together?" There are numerous examples of such contradictory "commonsense" notions about human behavior. "Look before you leap" but "He who hesitates is lost." "Better safe than sorry" but "Nothing ventured, nothing gained." These cliches show the problem of using mere plausibility as a criterion of truth. They are all somewhat plausible. In general, there are many more things that are plausible than are true. Plausibility comes cheap. In contrast, the methodologies of science are often difficult to carry out. Nevertheless, the use of the scientific method is necessary if we are to separate the true from the merely plausible.

The scientific method provides a way of deciding between contradictory claims, many of which might be equally plausible. This is particularly true in the area of human behavior where plausible "wisdom" is in large supply but established facts are much harder to come by. Indeed, when psychologists have examined how the evidence about human behavior squares with what people *believe* about human behavior they have found many contradictions. Many examples of these contradictions are contained in Alfie Kohn's book *You Know What They Say . . . : The Truth About Popular Beliefs* (1990). For example, contrary to what many people believe, it turns out that there is no evidence indicating that highly religious people are more altruistic than less religious people (Paloutzian, 1983; Smith, Wheeler, & Diener, 1975). Many people believe that a full moon affects human behavior. It doesn't (see Coates, Jehle, & Cottington, 1989; Culver, Rotton, & Kelly, 1988; Rotton & Kelly, 1985). Some people believe that "opposites attract." They don't (see Buss, 1985; Buss & Barnes, 1986; Murstein, 1980). Some people believe that blind people are blessed with supersensitive hearing. They're not (see Niemeyer & Starlinger, 1981; Stankov & Spilsbury, 1978). And the list goes on and on and on (see Kohn, 1990). In summary, we need the scientific method because not all plausible hypotheses are true, not even those that are "commonsense" or that "everybody knows."

STATISTICS: ASSESSING RELATIONSHIPS

In our discussion of experiments and correlational studies we have glossed over a very important point that we must now consider in detail: How does an investigator know when the performance of two groups are different or when there is a relationship between two variables? It is in answering this question that we enter the domain of statistics, which is an integral part of psychology.

Recall from Chapter 1 that the concepts in psychological hypotheses and theories must be operationally defined, that is, defined in terms of observable variables that can be measured. The phrase "that can be measured" takes us into the realm of statistics. **Measurement,** which is fundamental to all sciences, involves assigning numbers to observable events via some rule.

The end result of a psychological investigation, whether experimental or correlational, is a set of numbers. These numbers are sometimes termed **raw data** because they have not yet undergone condensation or transformation. In an experiment, for example, each subject in both the experimental and control groups (whose difference defines the independent variable) will have a score—a number that reflects the subject's performance on the dependent variable. Thus, the outcome of such an investigation will be a set of scores in the control condition and a set of scores in the experimental condition.

A correlational study, on the other hand, might involve the measurement of two variables for each subject. Consider an investigator who wants to determine whether there was a relationship between performance on an aptitude test and the amount of anxiety experienced by the subjects at the time of the test. The investigator would assess the aptitude test performance and each subject would receive an aptitude test score. Similarly, anxiety would be assessed and each subject would also receive an anxiety score. The raw data, then, would be a list of *pairs* of scores: a list of paired aptitude and anxiety scores for each subject. Thus, both experiments and correlational studies result in lists of numbers—the raw data. What do we do with these data?

First, we make use of descriptive statistics, one of the two branches of statistics that we will discuss. Describing the results and putting them into some easily understandable form is usually the first stage in the statistical treatment of any data. **Descriptive statistics** is the name for the category of procedures used to condense and summarize raw data so that they can be more easily inspected and understood. Presenting the results of an experiment as simply a list of say, 500 numbers (a number of scores that is not uncommon in psychological research) does not display the data in a form that is very comprehensible to most readers. Most of us cannot scan down a list of 500 numbers and discern all of the subtle patterns that may be there. Use of descriptive statistics allows us to arrange and summarize the data so that they are comprehensible.

After psychologists have used descriptive statistics to make data understandable, they will frequently turn to a second branch of statistics. Known as **inferential statistics,** these are procedures that help determine what conclusions can be drawn from the data.

Inferential statistics aid the researcher in making the decision about whether the results obtained are replicable or are due simply to chance. In all research there is always some probability that chance factors alone might have produced the research outcome. However, if this probability is sufficiently low, the psychologist will be willing to believe that a particular result was due to the factors of interest in the research and not merely to unknown chance factors. If the psychologist concludes that the result is due to the factors of interest, he or she will then be willing to conclude that the result is replicable. That is, the study could be repeated on another group of individuals observed in similar conditions and the result would be similar.

Descriptive Statistics

In this section, we will look at some of the most important ways in which psychologists summarize and condense groups of measurements in order to get them into a form that is understandable. First we will discuss frequency distributions, tables and graphs that organize collections of measurements, and we will discuss the most important distribution, the normal distribution. Following that, we will consider measures of the two most important characteristics of a collection of scores, the central tendency and variability of the scores. Next we will consider a method for computing standardized scores, called *z*-scores, and the relationship of these standard scores to the normal distribution. Finally, we will look at a measure of the correlation between pairs of scores.

FREQUENCY DISTRIBUTIONS

The first step in summarizing a collection of scores involves looking at how the scores are distributed across the range of possible values for that variable. A **frequency distribution** is a table or graph that represents how many times each particular score appeared in the raw data. Let's look at an example of how raw data is turned into a frequency distribution. Suppose a psychologist attempted to repeat Pavlov's original demonstration of classical conditioning with 12 dogs. After attaching appropriate instruments to measure the amount of salivation, the researcher subjected each animal to a standard classical conditioning procedure. The hypothetical raw data obtained from the procedure are presented in **Table 1** on page 650. Do not forget that most experimentation in psy-

Table 1   Hypothetical Classical Conditioning Data

Dog	Amount of Salivation(cc)
Fido	.5
Lassie	.8
Tramp	.6
Rivets	.4
King	.6
Rin Tin Tin	.5
Benji	1.6
Marmaduke	.7
Tige	.6
Lad	.7
Arfy	.9
Lady	.5

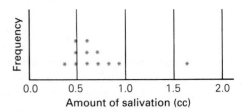

Figure 1
Simple Graphical Frequency Distribution of Hypothetical Classical Conditioning Data.

chology will involve many more data points than you see displayed in Table 1. Thus, it will help you to visualize how the use of descriptive statistics solves the problem of condensing a large set of raw data into a comprehensible form if you imagine that Table 1 contained 200 scores rather than 12 scores.

These data become more understandable when they are displayed in a *tabular frequency distribution* as in **Table 2.** Notice that each possible score value from a low of .3 to a high of 1.6 is represented on the left. On the right is

Table 2   Simple Tabular Frequency Distribution of Hypothetical Classical Conditioning Data

Amount of Salivation (cc)	Frequency
1.6	1
1.5	0
1.4	0
1.3	0
1.2	0
1.1	0
1.0	0
.9	1
.8	1
.7	2
.6	3
.5	3
.4	1
.3	0

the frequency with which each particular score appears. For example, only one dog (Benji) received a score of 1.6, so the value to the right of 1.6 in the tabular frequency distribution is 1. No dog received a score of 1.5, so the number to the right of it is 0. On the other hand, three dogs received a score of .6 (Tramp, King, and Tige), so the number to the right of .6 is 3.

Another way to represent the data is in a simple *graphical frequency distribution,* shown in **Figure 1.** Here the possible score values are labeled on the horizontal *x*-axis. Each score is represented by an asterisk that appears above its value. The frequency of occurrence is thus represented by the height of the column of asterisks at each score value. For example, we can easily read from the graph that the score of .5 occurred three times (three asterisks are above .5). Notice how the properties of the set of scores are revealed by this graph. For example, we can see that, with one exception, the values are fairly closely clustered around .5 or .6. We can also see clearly that one of the points (Benji's) is quite different from the others. The identification of unusual or extreme scores such as this is one of the reasons psychologists create frequency distributions. Extreme scores such as the one in Figure 1 are sometimes called *outliers.* Can you see why?

Table 2 and Figure 1 are examples of simple frequency distributions. Sometimes the data require representations that are more condensed. For example, if the range of scores in the raw data was so large that it would be inconvenient to list all values, a psychologist would group adjacent score values together and form a *grouped frequency distribution.* **Table 3** is an example of a grouped frequency distribution. The data represent the hypothetical distribution of resting heart rates of 50 persons selected to participate in a special exercise program. Notice that once a score value is

Table 3   Grouped Frequency Distribution of Hypothetical Resting Heart Rates for 50 Persons

Heart Rate (beats per minute)	Frequency
95–99	2
90–94	3
85–89	5
80–84	3
75–79	9
70–74	15
65–69	8
60–64	4
55–59	1

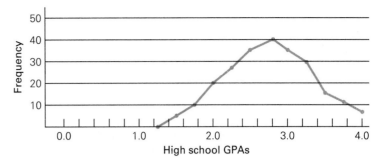

Figure 2
Distribution of High School Student GPAs.

placed in a group, its specific identity is lost. For example, we know there are three scores in the 80–84 interval, but we don't know the precise value of each score. Within that interval might be the three scores 81, 81, and 83 or perhaps the scores 81, 83, and 84, or any of a number of other combinations of three scores that fall within the interval.

In some studies where an extremely large number of scores makes up the raw data a simple graphical frequency distribution such as Figure 1 would take too long to construct. In such a case, a graph such as **Figure 2** would be more appropriate. This type of graph is called a *frequency polygon.* These hypothetical data represent the distribution of grade-point averages (GPAs) of a group of high school students. As in Figure 1, the *x*-axis labels are the possible values for the variable. In this case, the values run from 0.0 (the lowest possible GPA) to 4.0 (the highest possible GPA). A single point (rather than a column of asterisks) represents the frequency of occurrence of each particular score. The line connecting the points results in a shape that gives us a visual representation of the distribution of scores. The height of the line above a score value represents the frequency with which that score value occurred. For example, we can see that a GPA of 1.8 occurred slightly more than 10 times and a GPA of 2.8 occurred approximately 40 times.

Inspection of a graph such as Figure 2 can tell the psychologist much about the data. For example, the shape of the distribution communicates information. Some shapes are of special interest to researchers. One is a **symmet-**

ric distribution, which can be folded vertically in the middle and each side would approximately match the other opposite side. Figure 2 is approximately symmetric. Another shape of interest is a **skewed distribution** in which one "tail," or extreme end, of the distribution is much longer than the other. **Figure 3,** which represents the scores on an easy exam, is an example of a skewed distribution. The maximum possible score on the exam was 50 and most people did very well on it. The majority of the scores are bunched together above 40. More people scored 48 than any other score. Note, however, the long tail of the distribution stretching out on the left. Thus, although the exam was easy for most people, there were a few low scorers. In a case like this, where the tail of the distribution is on the left, we say that the distribution is skewed negatively (or "skewed left"). If the long tail pointed to the right, we would say that the distribution was positively skewed (or "skewed right").

Another factor of interest to researchers is the number of points of maximum frequency. In Figures 2 and 3 there is only one point of maximum frequency in each. The score with

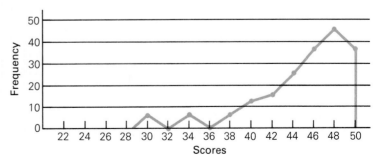

Figure 3
Distribution of Scores on an Easy Examination.

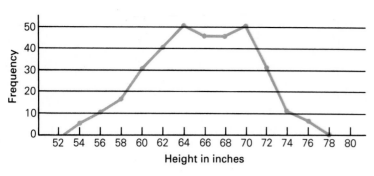

Figure 4
Frequency Polygon of Distribution of Hypothetical Heights of Males and Females.

maximum frequency in Figure 2 is 2.8 and the score with maximum frequency in Figure 3 is 48. These are called **unimodal distributions** because there is only one point of greatest frequency. In contrast, consider **Figure 4,** where a hypothetical distribution of heights of males and females is presented. It illustrates what is termed **bimodal distribution,** a distribution with two points of greatest frequency. The scores of 64 and 70 both occurred more frequently than neighboring score values. Such distributions are often encountered when measurements from two or more distinct groups, such as heights of males and females, are combined.

THE NORMAL DISTRIBUTION

The most important type of frequency distribution is called the **normal distribution,** a symmetric and unimodal distribution that is de-

fined by a specific formula. An example of a normal distribution is displayed in **Figure 5.** Most of the time the shape of a normal distribution resembles that of a bell (as in the example in Figure 5). For this reason, the normal distribution is sometimes referred to as the bell curve. However, these distributions can sometimes take on shapes that are not very "bell-like" (although they will always be symmetrical and unimodal). This is because a simple scale change on the *x*-axis could make the distribution either much "thinner" or much "fatter" than the one in Figure 5. Thus, because the distribution might not always be plotted in a way that makes it look like a "bell," the term *normal distribution* is preferred to "bell curve."

The normal distribution is considered the most important type of frequency distribution for two reasons. First, the distributions of many biological, psychological, and physical variables in the world are often approximately normal. Second, the normal distribution allows us to calculate the most powerful types of inferential statistics, the branch of statistics that helps us determine what conclusions can be drawn from data.

MEASURES OF CENTRAL TENDENCY

The term **central tendency** refers to the location of a group of scores on the *x*-axis or the tendency of scores in a frequency distribution to cluster around a central point. Measures of central tendency help us answer questions like: Where is the center of the distribution of scores? Where do most scores cluster? What

Figure 5
Hypothetical Normal Distribution of IQ Scores.

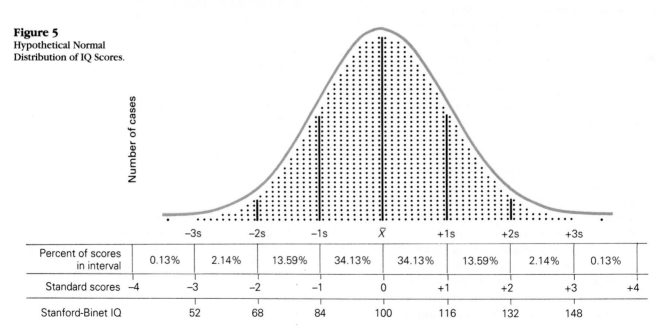

	−3s	−2s	−1s	X̄	+1s	+2s	+3s	
Percent of scores in interval	0.13%	2.14%	13.59%	34.13%	34.13%	13.59%	2.14%	0.13%
Standard scores −4	−3	−2	−1	0	+1	+2	+3	+4
Stanford-Binet IQ	52	68	84	100	116	132	148	

score is in the middle of the distribution? What is a typical score?

You might wonder whether we are talking about the "average" here. The answer is that we are, but that psychologists and statisticians prefer not to use that term. The reason is not, as you might think, that psychologists just want to create more jargon for you to learn. In fact, "jargon" too often gets a bad rap. There are often quite good reasons for its use. Jargon is often created because the technical distinctions in a particular field are not captured by words that are already in the language. This is one of those cases. Statisticians do not use the word *average* because it is ambiguous. Simply put, there are many different kinds of "averages." When you see the word *average* in the media, for example, it is impossible to tell which particular kind of average is being referred to. As we will see, this makes it possible for different types of "averages" to be used in misleading ways. It is for this reason that statisticians prefer the term *central tendency* to refer to a class of measures and to use specific terms to refer to particular examples of measures of central tendency. The three measures of central tendency most often computed by psychologists are the mean, the median, and the mode.

The most frequently employed measure of central tendency is called the mean. If you have been using the term *average* and calculating *averages* but have never before heard the term central tendency, chances are that what you have really been calculating is the mean. For example, if you are a bowler and have been calculating your bowling average, you have been computing the mean. How do you compute a bowling average? You add up all the scores of all your games and then you divide by the number of games you bowled. The **mean** is the sum of the scores in a distribution divided by the number of scores. For example, for the data in Table 1, the mean amount of salivation is .7 cc. This was obtained by adding up the individual scores (to obtain 8.4) and dividing this sum by 12 to get .7. Because the mean is used so frequently, psychologists often represent it with a special symbol. Both M and $\overline{X}$ (pronounced "X bar") have been used as symbols for the mean. $\overline{X}$ is more frequently used in psychology. The mean is one of the most commonly used measures when inferential statistics are calculated.

The median is another measure of central

List of Scores in Rank Order	The Middle Scores	Median
1.6		
.9		
.8		
.7		
.7		
.6	.6	$\frac{.6 + .6}{2} = .6$
.6	.6	
.6		
.5		
.5		
.5		
.4		

Figure 6
Computing the Median from the Data of Table 1.

tendency but it is derived in a different way from the mean. The **median** is simply the value in the middle of the distribution—at the fiftieth percentile. It is obtained by listing the values in numerical order and then finding the value below which and above which half the scores fall. When there is an odd number of scores, the median is simply the middle value in the ordered list. When the number of score values is even, most psychologists would use the mean of the two scores in the middle of the ordered list. **Figure 6** illustrates how the median is computed from the hypothetical classical conditioning data. This figure simply puts the same data that are displayed in Table 1 into numerical order. Note that the mean (.7) and the median (.6) of this set of scores are not equal.

Usually the mean and the median will be close in value if the distribution is approximately symmetric, although they may not be precisely equal. In the case of a skewed distribution, the mean and the median may differ substantially. For example, suppose the annual incomes of employees of a small manufacturing plant were $9,000, $11,000, $12,000, $13,000, and $50,000. The mean income is $19,000, but the median income is $12,000, which is $7,000 less than the mean. The value of $50,000 creates a long tail to the right, skewing the distribution positively. Usually the value of the mean will be displaced in the direction of the longer "tail" of a skewed distribution. In situations in which the distribution is markedly skewed, the median is often the preferred measure of central tendency. From this example, you can see how using the term *average,* which includes both the mean and the median, can be confusing. Two people can be talking about the *same* data and yet come up with different "averages." For example, imagine that you are a corporate executive engaged in wage negotiations with the union in one of your plants. A representative of the media asks you for the average wage paid to workers in your company. Which measure of central tendency do you pick? Undoubtedly the mean. Why? Because the distribution of wages in most corporations is highly positively skewed. There are a few very high wage earners compared to the majority. The mean would be affected by these extreme scores and would have a higher value than the median.

The third measure of central tendency is the **mode,** the value that occurs most frequently in the data. The mode is the least used measure of central tendency. One reason is that in a small group of scores, there may be several modes or no mode at all. For example, in the hypothetical income example discussed above, there is no mode because each value occurred just once.

Each of these three measures of central tendency conveys somewhat different information about the center of the distribution. When researchers want to compare the central tendencies of different entities, these measures will give somewhat differing weights to different properties. For example, imagine that a researcher wanted to compare the family incomes in different countries of the world. After correcting for currency exchange values and condensing incomes into frequency groupings (because of the vast amount of data, the researcher would deal with income categories $18,000–$20,000, etc., rather than with individual values, $21,123, $23,456, etc.), which measure of central tendency should be used to compare family incomes in the different countries? The mode would reflect the income category that is most common in a given country—the income category that most families fall in. The median is the family income that is above that of 50 percent of the families in that country and below that of 50 percent of the families. Recall, however, that the median would not take into account whether there were any extremely high incomes in the distribution. To take a small example, the median of $15,100, $16,700, $18,300, $18,900, and $19,700 is $18,300 and the median of $15,100, $16,700, $18,300, $79,000, and $250,000 is *also* $18,300. The mean, on the other hand, is quite sensitive to the extreme scores of skewed dis-

tributions. The mean would give a lot more weight to the higher incomes and thus result in a considerably higher value than the median for those countries with more skewed income distributions. For example, the income distribution in the United States is more skewed than that in Japan (there is a larger disparity of incomes in the United States). Thus, using the mean as a measure of central tendency would tend to favor the United States over Japan and using the median would tend to favor Japan over the United States.

This example illustrates the complexities involved in characterizing the central tendencies in distributions. It also illustrates how extremely important it is to know which measure of central tendency is being used in a particular comparison. Now it should be clear why the terms *central tendency, mean, median,* and *mode,* are not just "jargon"—instead, they provide very necessary distinctions in our vocabularies.

CENTRAL TENDENCY AND THE
NORMAL DISTRIBUTION

In a perfectly symmetrical distribution, the mean and the median are equal. If the distribution is perfectly symmetric and unimodal, then the mean, median, and the mode all have the same value. The normal distribution is one example of a symmetric and unimodal distribution. In a normal distribution, the mean, median, and mode will have the same value. Thus, when the distribution is normal questions about which measure of central tendency to use do not arise because the mean, median, and mode will be the same.

MEASURES OF VARIABILITY

The term **variability** refers to the separation, dispersion, or spread of the scores on the *x*-axis in a frequency distribution. Look at the two distributions presented in **Figure 7.** They are equal in central tendency; the mean, median, and mode all have the same value. But the two distributions differ quite a bit in variability. In the bottom figure, there are large differences between the score values. The data in the bottom figure are much more variable than the data in the top. The more spread out the scores are, the more variable they are.

Variability can be discerned visually by looking at frequency distributions like those in Figure 7. But as was the case with central tendency, researchers often need a more precise mathematical index of this property of distributions. The measures of central tendency took all of the scores in the distribution and boiled them down to one measure that reflected the centrality property. Measures of variability do the same thing for the property of spread, or dispersion. These measures condense the data into one score that reflects the variability of the distribution. The larger a measure of variability is, the more spread out is the distribution. Thus, for the data in Figure 7 we would want a measure of variability to be higher for the distribution on the bottom, reflecting the fact that the scores are more spread out there than in the distribution at the top. Several numerical measures of variability have been devised. We will discuss only two here: the range and the standard deviation.

The measure of variability that is easiest to compute is the **range,** the difference between the largest and smallest score in a collection. However, the range is not often used because it is a very crude measure of variability. By taking account of only the highest and lowest values, it ignores how dispersed the scores are between these two values.

The most frequently employed measure of variability is the standard deviation. Because the standard deviation is employed so often, it is designated by special symbols. Usually the lowercase Greek letter σ, SD, or the lowercase letter s are used to represent the standard deviation.

The **standard deviation** is obtained by finding the sum of the squared deviations from the mean, dividing by the number of scores, and then taking the square root. The steps to compute the standard deviation are:

1. compute the mean (recall that the mean is the sum of score values divided by the number of score values);
2. subtract the mean from each score in order to find each score's deviation from the mean;
3. square each of these deviations;
4. add the squares;
5. divide the result by the number of scores;
6. find the square root of the result.

The final result is the standard deviation. An example of the computations is given in **Figure 8.** Note that the key to the computation is step 2. This step calculates how far from the mean a score is (in either direction, above or below). The farther the scores are from the

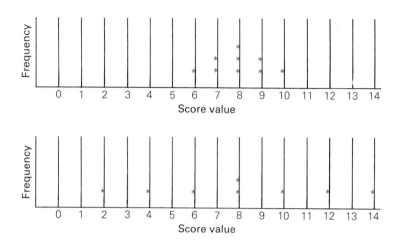

Figure 7
Two Distributions with the Same Central Tendency But Different Variability.

mean, the larger the standard deviation. The more spread out or dispersed the scores are from the mean, the more variability there is in the distribution.

We can interpret the standard deviation much more precisely if the scores form a normal distribution. All normal distributions are characterized by fixed relationships between a score's frequency of occurrence and its distance from the mean in units of the standard deviation. For example, for all normal distributions, 34.13 percent of the scores fall between the mean and one standard deviation above the mean (see Figure 5). And, since the normal distribution is symmetric, 34.13 percent also fall

Scores	Mean	Deviation from Mean	Squared Deviation
.5	.7	−.2	.04
.8	.7	.1	.01
.6	.7	−.1	.01
.4	.7	−.3	.09
.6	.7	−.1	.01
.5	.7	−.2	.04
1.6	.7	.9	.81
.7	.7	0	0
.6	.7	−.1	.01
.7	.7	0	0
.9	.7	.2	.04
.5	.7	−.2	.04
			Sum = 1.10

$$SD = \sqrt{\frac{1.10}{12}} = 0.30$$

Figure 8
Computing the Standard Deviation from the Data of Table 1.

between the mean and one standard deviation below the mean. So, for all normal distributions, 68.26 percent (that is, about two thirds) of the scores fall within one standard deviation of the mean. In addition, for all normal distributions, slightly over 95 percent of the scores fall within two standard deviations above and below the mean.

Let's examine this last characteristic. If we know the mean and the standard deviation of a collection of scores, and if we know that the scores are normally distributed, then we can tell immediately between which two points 95 percent of the scores fall. For example, scores on the SAT test are approximately normally distributed with mean equal to approximately 450 and standard deviation equal to 100. This means that approximately 95 percent of the SAT scores fall between 250 and 650. This is because two standard deviations above the mean is 650 and two standard deviations below the mean is 250 and 95 percent of the scores are within two standard deviations of the mean in a normal distribution. Looking at it another way, we can say that only 5 percent of the scores are more than two standard deviations from the mean. That is, only 5 percent of the SAT scores are either less than 300 or greater than 700. These types of relationships hold when the distribution of scores is normal. When distributions are skewed, or nonnormal in other ways, these relations will not hold.

z-Scores

The standard deviation, along with the mean can be used to form a standardized measure called a *z*-score. A **z-score**, or standard score, is a score's distance from the mean of the group, expressed in units of the standard deviation. The *z*-score is obtained by subtracting the mean from the original, or raw, score and dividing by the standard deviation. Symbolically, if x is the raw score:

$$z = \frac{x - \bar{X}}{\text{SD}}$$

A *z* of zero represents a score right at the mean (for $x - \bar{X}$ to be zero, the raw score must be at the mean). A negative *z* represents a score below the mean, and a positive *z* represents a score above the mean. So, for example, a *z* of +1 represents a score one standard deviation above the mean, while a *z* of -1 represents a score one standard deviation below the mean.

Recall that about 68 percent of the scores in a normal distribution are within one standard deviation of the mean and that about 95 percent of the scores are within two standard deviations of the mean. If all the scores from a normal distribution were converted to *z*-scores, about 68 percent of them would be between -1 and +1 and 95 percent of them would be between -2 and +2. Since this fact applies to any normal distribution, psychologists often convert raw scores to *z*-scores. By doing this, they can quickly identify unusual scores (for example, any larger than 2). You may have seen test results posted in terms of *z*-scores as well as raw scores. If, for example, your *z*-score was +2.5, you could be confident that you did extremely well on the test (unless performance was measured in number of errors). Finally, we should mention that *z*-scores can be calculated and are quite useful even in distributions that are nonnormal.

Z-scores are often used to compare performance in distributions that have different central tendencies and variabilities. For example, imagine that a child, Bill, received a raw score of 80 on a mathematics test and a score of 60 on a history test. Can we conclude that Bill is better in math than in history? The answer is no. If the national mean on the mathematics test is 90 and that on the history test is 50 and both are normally distributed, then Bill is actually better in history than in math, even though his raw score on the math test is higher. He would be above the mean in history but below it in math.

Even if the means were the same on both of the tests—say, 40—we still could not conclude that Bill did better on the math test. This is because it is possible that the variability is greater on the math test and that Bill is actually farther above the mean on the history test. This would be the case if the standard deviation of the math test was 20 and that of the history test was 5. In this case, Bill's *z*-score on the math test would be 2 (80 - 40 divided by 20) and his *z*-score on the history test would be 4 (60 - 40 divided by 5). Bill is actually better in history, even though his raw score on this test was lower. Thus, *z*-scores solve the problem of comparing performance on variables having differing means and/or standard deviations.

Correlation

Psychologists are interested in more than merely summarizing the characteristics of a single collection of scores. There are many situations in which two or more measurements have been taken on the same individuals, and psychologists may be interested in examining the relationship or correlation between the values of the two measurements.

Correlation refers to the extent to which pairs of score values vary together (covary). Consider height and weight, for example. Suppose we observe a person who is 6 feet tall and weighs 180 pounds. Now suppose we found another person who was shorter than the first, say 5 feet 6 inches tall. We would probably find that the second person also weighed less than the first, perhaps 140 pounds. And if we found a very tall person, say one who was 6 feet 8 inches tall, we would most likely find that the third person was also heavier, perhaps 240 pounds. If we observed several persons, we would likely see that as we moved from one person to the next, measuring both height and weight, the measures would tend to covary. If we found a tall person, that person would most likely weigh more than most. And if we came across a short person, that person would probably weigh less than most.

The covariation in pairs of measures, such as the covariation in height and weight, represents a situation in which we would say that the measures are correlated. In the case of height and weight, we would say that they are *positively correlated,* since increases in height are usually associated with increases in weight, and decreases in height are associated with decreases in weight.

Two variables can also be correlated when large values of one are paired with small values of the other. Consider vehicle weight and gas mileage. Suppose we found a car that weighed 3000 pounds and got 20 miles per gallon (mpg). If we then found a much larger car, say one that weighed 4000 pounds, we would probably find that it got poorer gas mileage, maybe only 12 mpg. And if we then found a very light vehicle, one that weighed only 2000 pounds, we would probably see that the mileage for it was much greater, perhaps 30 mpg. In this case, weight and mileage covary, but they covary differently from height and weight. An increase in vehicle weight would be associated with a *decrease* in gas mileage, and vice versa. For this situation, we would say that the two characteristics are inversely or *negatively correlated.*

Let us consider one final example involving two variables, a person's weight and the

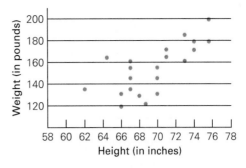

Figure 9
Scatter Plot of Hypothetical Weights versus Heights Showing a Positive Correlation.

score on an intelligence test. Suppose we found someone who weighed 195 pounds and had a score of 106 on an intelligence test. Now, suppose we found someone who weighed much less, say 130 pounds. Would we expect the intelligence test score of the 130-pound person to be less than the intelligence test score of the 195-pound person? Obviously not. We do not expect the intelligence test score of the light person to be necessarily less than that of the heavy person, nor do we expect it to be larger. These two variables do not covary, as do weight and height or vehicle weight and gas mileage.

A **scatter plot** is a plot of the values of one variable against the values of another variable. This simple graphical technique is used so that the correlation between two variables can be examined visually. For example, suppose we took a sample of 20 persons and measured the weight and height of each. We would use the 20 pairs of values to form the scatter plot shown in **Figure 9.** Each person is represented by one point in the plot. For example, the point with the coordinates of 76 and 200 represents the data of a person who is 76 inches tall and weighs 200 pounds.

Notice that as we move from one point to the next in Figure 9 from left to right, we also move in an upward direction. In fact, the points tend to group about a line with a positive, or upward slope. This is characteristic of scatter plots representing positive correlations.

Figure 10 presents the scatter plot of a negative correlation. In this case, hypothetical gas mileage values have been plotted against vehicle weights, two characteristics that are negatively correlated. Here the points tend to

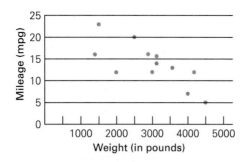

Figure 10
Scatter Plot of Hypothetical Gas Mileage versus Vehicle Weights Showing a Negative Correlation.

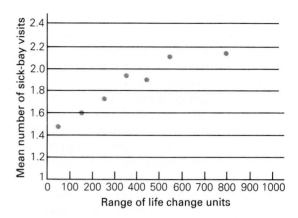

Figure 12
Scatter Plot of Number of Sick-Bay Visits versus Life-Change Scores.

group about a line with negative, or downward slope.

Finally, what would a scatter plot of two uncorrelated characteristics look like? **Figure 11** presents the scatter plot of 15 hypothetical pairs of weights and intelligence test scores. Look at the differences between this figure and those representing positive and negative correlations. Note that in this figure the points tend to form an undifferentiated mass, rather than group about a line with either a positive or a negative slope.

As we have seen, pairs of variables differ in the direction of correlation. They also differ in the strength of correlation. For example, in Chapter 15 we discussed a study of naval personnel in which the number of visits to a sick bay and the subjects' life-change scores were correlated. **Figure 12** reproduces the scatter plot. Compare it with Figure 9, the scatter plot of weight and height. Note that the points of Figure 12 cluster very close to a straight line, while the points of Figure 9 are much less tightly clustered. In general, the closer a set of points clusters to a line, the stronger the corre-

lation between the variables. This is equally true for negative correlations, only in this case the slope of the line would be negative, or from upper left to lower right.

Statistics that measure the strength and direction of correlations between pairs of variables are called **correlation coefficients.** Several are used in psychology, but the most commonly used is the Pearson product moment correlation coefficient. The symbol for this correlation coefficient is *r,* and it is usually referred to as the Pearson *r.*

The formula for calculating the Pearson *r* always yields a number whose value is between −1 and +1. A value of −1 represents a perfect negative correlation between two variables. A value of +1 represents a perfect positive correlation. The points of a scatter plot representing a correlation of +1 or −1 would lie on a straight line. A value of 0 represents no linear correlation between the two. Values between −1 and 0 or between 0 and +1 represent correlations of intermediate strength. For example, the correlation coefficient for Figure 9 is approximately .6, while that for Figure 12 is over .8. On the other hand, the correlation coefficient for Figure 10 is about −.6. Students sometimes think that negative correlations are not as good or as strong as positive correlations. However, the sign of a correlation coefficient tells nothing about the strength of a relationship, just its direction. A correlation coefficient of −1 represents just as perfect a correlation as does a coefficient of +1. Thus, it is the absolute value (magnitude, independent of sign) that represents the strength of the correlation (how closely the points approximate a straight line).

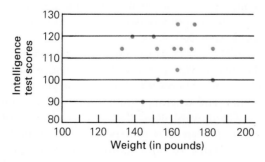

Figure 11
Scatter Plot of Hypothetical Intelligence Test Scores versus Weight. The Two Variables Are Not Correlated

The sign of the correlation represent its direction (either a direct relation if the sign is positive or an inverse relation if the sign is negative).

It should be noted that the Pearson correlation measures the extent of the linear ("straight-line") correlation between two variables. If the relationship is strongly curvilinear then other statistical procedures are necessary. This is why it is important for researchers to examine scatter diagrams before calculating correlation coefficients. The shape of the scatter diagram will indicate to the researcher whether the Pearson coefficient is appropriate.

One final point to be aware of is that not all correlational studies employ the Pearson *r*. A correlational study is such because of the lack of a manipulated variable. It is correlational whether or not a Pearson *r* is conducted on the data. Do not fall into the trap of thinking that a study is not correlational simply because you do not see a Pearson *r*.

Inferential Statistics

In the preceding sections we have discussed how psychologists summarize and condense collections of scores. We have covered some of the basic procedures of descriptive statistics such as examining the shapes of the distributions and obtaining measures of central tendency and variability. We have also seen how psychologists look at relationships between pairs of measurements using scatter plots and correlation coefficients. In this section we will discuss how psychologists determine the generalizability or replicability of their research findings. The methods employed here involve the use of inferential statistics.

Let us return to the example of the investigator who was interested in the new and old reading series. Suppose that this researcher had been able to randomly assign children to reading series and to conduct a true experiment. Children in group 1 use the New Series and children in group 2 use the Old Series. The investigator is interested in the relationship between the type of reading series used and reading achievement. The type of reading series used is the independent variable, and the dependent variable is reading achievement at the end of second grade. Suppose the researcher chose to summarize the performance of the two groups by using the mean scores on a standardized reading achievement test. If there

were a difference in the means of the two groups, we would say that a relationship between the independent and the dependent variables existed. On the other hand, if there were no difference between the means, we would say that the type of reading series used is not related to reading achievement.

Notice that the existence of a relationship between the dependent and independent variables is reflected by the difference between the means of the two groups. A difference in the means indicates that there is a relationship between the dependent variable and the independent variable. No difference in the means indicates that there is *no* relationship between the two variables.

Suppose in the reading series experiment, the mean of the scores of the subjects in the New Series group was 82.7 and the mean of the scores of the subjects in the Old Series group was 74.7. We can see that there is a difference in the means of the two groups, so we can say that for these particular subjects there is a relationship between reading series and reading achievement. How can this finding be extended beyond the small group of subjects actually studied? Here the concept of replication comes in again. Recall that the issue of replicability concerns the question of whether the same relationship would result if the experiment were repeated with another two groups of subjects. The concern with replicability stems from the fact that psychologists wish to be able to make general statements about all persons who could have been included in a research project, not just those who actually participated. Thus, the subjects in an experiment are actually samples from a much larger population. The psychologist is interested not only in the behavior of the particular sample studied, but also in whether the observed relationship holds for the population as well. If the psychologist concludes that results are replicable, this means that essentially the same results would be obtained if another sample from the same population were selected to participate in the research—in short, it means that the results would generalize to that particular population.

The determination of replicability involves deciding whether the differences observed between groups are real or whether they could have been due merely to chance factors. In our earlier discussion of random assignment we mentioned that it is likely, particularly with small sample sizes, that random assignment will not *exactly* match the two groups on any particular variable before the experiment begins (the differences may be small, but they will probably exist). The key point here is that this will apply to the dependent variable itself; that is, before the manipulation takes place, chance fluctuations in random assignment will have created differences between the groups.

Measurement error also contributes to these chance fluctuations between the groups. That is, even if random assignment has worked perfectly, and even if the independent variable really has no effect, we may *still* observe differences between the groups. Why? Because if two perfectly equal groups are measured with less than perfect accuracy (as is always the case), then they may become unmatched due to the chance fluctuation that measurement itself introduces. What all of this boils down to is something really very simple, but with profound implications: There will always be differences between the groups even when the independent variable is not a causal factor because chance factors of sampling and measurement will always create differences.

These facts about measurement and random sampling obviously create a problem in making inferences. We cannot simply look to see if there is a difference in the means of the two groups and, if there is, conclude that the independent variable had an effect. Why? Because the difference that we observed might be due simply to chance factors rather than to the independent variable. We are actually faced with a much more complex decision. Since there will always be differences between the two groups whether or not the independent variable has an effect, we have to assess when the difference between our groups gets so large that we cannot reasonably attribute it to chance. That is, when the differences are small we will chalk them up to chance, because factors like variation in random assignment and measurement error could easily cause small differences. But at some point the differences will get so large that we will doubt whether chance alone could have been producing them. Then we will assume that something else must be operating. If the experiment is designed properly the only candidate for that "something else" is the independent variable. So it is only when the difference between the means is so great that chance alone is not a likely explanation that we will claim that we have evidence that the independent variable is related to the dependent variable.

What the procedures of inferential statistics actually do is to formalize and quantify the decision-making logic of the previous paragraph. Researchers use certain formulas called test statistics to help them determine whether the results obtained were due to chance alone. These test statistics help the investigator to calculate the probability that the results were due to chance alone. If that probability turns out to be high, the investigator will conclude that any differences obtained were probably due to chance and that there is no evidence that the independent variable is linked to the dependent variable. On the other hand, if the probability that the differences obtained were due to chance alone is low, then the investigator will conclude that the independent variable must also be having an effect. The latter result is an indication that the results would be replicable: if the investigator sampled another group of subjects from the same population and randomly assigned them to the same conditions of the experiment it is likely that a difference between groups in the same direction would be obtained.

How low does the probability the difference was due to chance alone have to be before the investigator will conclude that the independent variable had an effect? In psychology the probability of a difference being due to chance alone must be less than .05 before the difference will be considered replicable. When the probability that chance alone was operating is less than this we say that the difference is *statistically significant* at the .05 level. Then we can conclude that the independent variable did have an effect.

SUMMARY

1. Research methods in psychology are based on empiricism, the view that knowledge is obtained through observation. Two methods of psychological research that make particularly heavy use of statistics are the true experiment and the correlational study. The key aspects of an experiment are manipulation of the independent variable, random assignment of subjects, and control of the experimental environment. An experiment is the method that allows a researcher to make a strong inference about cause.

2. Correlational studies, which measure relationships between variables as they occur naturally, are used when it would be diffi-

cult to manipulate the variables of interest. They are also employed in the earlier stages of scientific investigations. Correlational studies often suggest which variables should be examined with true experiments. Correlational studies are also useful when the goal of the research is prediction rather than a causal explanation.

3. Psychologists use statistics in two ways: to summarize or describe data and to determine what conclusions or inferences can be drawn from the data. Psychologists begin by summarizing their data using the methods of descriptive statistics. They create distributions of scores and examine the characteristics of those distributions. They compute measures of central tendency—the mean, median, and mode—and measures of variability, such as the range and standard deviation. They inspect the data to determine the extent to which they are normally distribut-

ed and they may convert raw scores to z-scores. If pairs of scores have been collected, psychologists may create scatter plots of the data and compute the value of a Pearson r to determine the strength of correlation between the pairs.

4. Once the data have been summarized, psychologists use inferential statistics to determine if any difference between groups was due to chance alone or to the effects of the independent variable. Test statistics are used to arrive at the probability that any difference obtained was due to chance alone. If that probability is less than .05, the result is deemed to be statistically significant and the investigator can conclude that the difference observed was due to a replicable effect of the independent variable.

Glossary

Abnormal behavior Behavior that is characterized by the convergence of the four criteria of relative infrequency, social deviance, impaired social functioning, and personal distress.

Absolute threshold The minimum amount of stimulation necessary to produce a sensation.

Accommodation The process by which schemata are revised completely or developed further and made more complex to fit new incoming information.

Acquisition During conditioning, the process by which an organism learns a new response.

Action potential The neural impulse, or wave of electrical energy, that is transmitted down the axon when the neuron is stimulated beyond threshold.

Active listening In humanistic psychotherapy, the process by which the therapist tries to grasp both the content of what the client is saying and the feeling behind it.

Actor-observer bias The tendency to attribute one's own behavior to external or situational causes but to attribute others' behavior to internal dispositions and traits.

Adaptation The process of changing behavior to fit changing circumstances.

Adolescence The period that begins with the onset of puberty and ends somewhere around age 18 or 19.

Adult An individual who is capable of assuming the responsibility of daily work and committed love.

Aerial haze A monocular (one-eye) cue for distance by which objects appear less distinct (hazy) as they get farther away.

Affective disorders See *mood disorders.*

Afterimage A visual experience that persists for a brief period after the stimulus has been removed.

Aggression Behavior that one person enacts with the intention of harming or destroying another person or object.

Alcoholism Alcohol abuse, characterized by psy-chological dependence, physical dependence, and impaired social functioning.

Algorithm A procedure by which an individual considers all the possible solutions to a problem.

All-or-none response The neuron's response to an excitatory potential. Once a certain threshold is reached, the neuron always fires an impulse down its axon with the same intensity.

Alpha waves An 8–10 cycle per second pattern detected in the electroencephalogram. Alpha waves are characteristic of a waking, relaxed state.

Altruism The unselfish helping of other people.

Amnesia A psychological disorder in which memories for certain events are unavailable to recall.

Amplitude In light and sound waves, the height of a wave. In light, amplitude corresponds to the psychological property of brightness; in sound, it corresponds to the psychological property of loudness.

Amygdala The part of the limbic system located at the base of the temporal lobe that is involved in appetite, sexuality, and aggression.

Analgesic Any agent that produces insensitivity to pain without loss of consciousness.

Anal stage In Freudian theory, the second stage of development, lasting from approximately age 1 or 1-1/2 to 3, in which the anal region is the most sensitive to tension.

Anchor A starting value or point based on a recent experience.

Androgens The general name for male sex hormones, of which testosterone is the most important.

Anesthesia Loss of sensation with or without loss of consciousness.

Anhedonia A symptom of schizophrenia in which the patient loses the ability to experience pleasure.

Anterograde amnesia A memory disorder in which humans lose the ability to store information.

Anxiety disorders The group of psychological disorders that includes panic, phobic, generalized anxiety, and obsessive-compulsive disorders. A person suffering from an anxiety disorder experiences an overwhelming level of anxiety.

Anxiety hierarchy A rank ordering of anxiety-provoking situations used in systematic desensitization.

Aphasia An impairment in the ability to speak or to understand spoken language.

Appraisal Cognitive process by which the individual perceives situations as either benign or threatening.

Arousal An internal (physiologically based) state of excitement or tension. Drive theorists believe that a state of arousal demands the reduction or elimination of tension (see *drive*).

Artificial intelligence Computer programs that are designed to make the kinds of judgments and problem-solving decisions that humans make.

Assertion training A variety of therapeutic techniques designed to teach people to express their feelings directly and honestly.

Assimilation The process by which incongruent information is fit into an existing schema by being shaped or distorted so that it is seen as consistent with the schema.

Association cortex All areas of the cortex that are not classified as either sensory or motor areas.

Association neurons All neurons in the nervous system that are not classified as sensory or motor neurons.

Attachment An intense emotional relationship, specific to two people, that endures over a long period of time.

Attention The process that determines which sensations will be perceived; i.e., which information will be transferred from sensory to short-term memory.

Attitudes Positive or negative evaluations of people, objects, events, and ideas.

Attribution The process of understanding behavior, our own and other people's, by making inferences about its underlying causes.

Attribution theory of depression A theory of depression suggesting that depressed people make different attributions about the causes of events in their lives than nondepressed people.

Auditory nerve Axons from neurons within the cochlea that conduct neural impulses to the auditory areas of the brain.

Automatic processing The effortless (without rehearsal) transfer of information to long-term memory.

Autonomic nervous system (ANS) The division of the peripheral nervous system that regulates the involuntary muscles and internal organs.

Autonomous morality According to Piaget, a stage in moral development when the child believes that rules and regulations are the product of social agreements rather than sacred and unchangeable laws. Also called *morality of cooperation*.

Avoidance learning A conditioning procedure in which an aversive stimulus is signaled by a warning stimulus. Organisms learn to avoid the aversive stimulus by emitting the appropriate response to the warning stimulus.

Axon The portion of a neuron that transmits neural impulses away from the soma toward the synapse.

Axon terminal The portion of the axon farthest from the soma that contains the stored neurotransmitters.

Babbling stage A period in the first year when infants produce a mixture of the phonemes that adults use.

Backward conditioning A form of classical conditioning in which the US begins before the CS.

Basilar membrane A membrane within the cochlea. Movement of the basilar membrane produces bending of hair cells, which in turn transduce sound waves into neural impulses.

Behavior Any activity that can be observed, recorded, and measured.

Behavioral psychology Psychological perspective which states that the only proper subject of the science of psychology is that which is observable-behavior.

Behaviorism A philosophy of psychological study holding that only observable behavior is the proper subject of psychological investigation.

Behavior modification A form of behavior therapy utilizing principles and methods derived from operant conditioning.

Behavior therapy A general term for a variety of therapeutic techniques derived originally from learning principles but now including methods derived from other psychological research areas.

Beliefs Perception of factual matters, about what is true and false.

Bimodal distribution Distribution which has two points of greatest frequency.

Binocular cues In depth perception, cues that rely on both eyes working together, such as convergence and retinal disparity.

Biofeedback The therapeutic method of teaching voluntary control over muscular and visceral activity through the use of monitoring instruments.

Biopsychology The psychological perspective which assumes that for every behavior, feeling, and thought, there is a corresponding physical event that takes place in the brain. The psychological specialty that studies physiological processes and the way such processes relate to behavior and experience.

Blind spot A portion of the retina through which the optic nerve exits from the eye and travels to the brain. This area has no rods or cones and is not responsive to light.

Brain graft A surgical procedure in which tissue from one brain is removed and placed into another brain.

Brain stem The bottommost portion of the brain, an enlarged extension of the spinal cord consisting of the medulla, pons, midbrain, and thalamus.

Brightness The psychological dimension of light that corresponds to the amplitude of the light wave.

Broca's area A portion of the frontal lobe critical to the production of speech.

❦

Case study The extensive study of all or part of the life history of an individual.

Catharsis Term used in psychoanalytic psychology referring to a cleansing or reduction of a feeling through the expression of that feeling.

Central core The innermost and evolutionary oldest portion of the brain. It consists of the brain stem, the thalamus, and the cerebellum, the structures that regulate basic life processes.

Central nervous system (CNS) The brain and the spinal cord.

Central tendency The location of a group of scores on the *x*-axis; the tendency of scores to cluster around a central point.

Cerebellum Attached to the rear of the brain stem, this brain structure is involved in the control of complex and coordinated muscle movements and maintenance of muscle tone.

Cerebral cortex The outer covering of the mammalian brain in which higher processes are mediated.

Chaining A technique in operant conditioning by which organisms learn complex sequences of behavior by learning a series of operantly conditioned responses that are reinforced with conditioned reinforcers.

Chronological age (CA) An individual's actual age in years and months. One element used in the calculation of IQ.

Circadian rhythm A daily cycle in behavioral or physiological activity. The 24-hour sleep/wake cycle is an example.

Classical conditioning Learning that results from the association of two stimuli. In classical conditioning a neutral stimulus (CS) is paired with a stimulus (US) that reflexively elicits a response (UR) until the neutral stimulus also comes to elicit that response (CR).

Classical psychoanalysis An intense, probing form of psychotherapy developed by Sigmund Freud, which involves the processes of free association, dream analysis, resistance, transference, interpretation, insight, and working through.

Client-centered therapy A form of humanistic therapy developed by Carl Rogers which focuses on the client's conscious experience and regards the client as a responsible individual capable of understanding and directing his or her own life.

Clinical psychology The psychological specialty involving the assessment and treatment of persons with psychological difficulties.

Closure A principle of Gestalt organization by which a figure is perceived as a whole even though part of the figure is missing.

Cochlea The snail-shaped part of the inner ear that contains the receptors for hearing.

Cognition The processing of information about the world around us; the mental processes of thinking, knowing, perceiving, attending, remembering, and the like.

Cognitive behavior therapy A form of behavior therapy that tries to help people control anxiety and depression by teaching them more effective ways of interpreting and thinking about their experiences.

Cognitive dissonance An uncomfortable tension created by an inconsistency between any two cognitions.

Cognitive psychology Psychological perspective that is primarily concerned with mental processes, or cognitions.

Cognitive reappraisal A method of coping in which one reevaluates the meaning of stressful events.

Cognitive triad Three negative beliefs common to depressed people: a negative view of the self, a negative view of the world, and a negative view of the future.

Color blindness A condition in which individuals lack the ability to discriminate among different wavelengths of light (colors).

Color constancy The tendency for a familiar object to be perceived as a constant color even though the light that it reflects changes the sensation.

Coma A state of deep unconsciousness below normal sleep.

Companionate love The enduring attachment that remains after the passion of romantic love dissipates over time.

Competence The knowledge or skill that a person possesses.

Complementary colors Pairs of primary colors that, when mixed, produce a neutral gray.

Complex cells Cells in the visual cortex that respond to lines of a particular orientation located anywhere in the visual field. These cells receive input from many simple cells and may be important for detecting movement.

Complexity The combination of sound waves making up a sound, which is sensed as the sound's timbre.

Compliance Agreeing to behave according to the requests or commands of another person.

Compulsion Recurrent, ritualistic behavior sequence experienced as irresistable.

Computer-assisted axial tomography (CAT) Brain imaging technique in which many individual images are obtained by passing X-rays through the head. The computer then assembles these individual pictures into an image.

Concept A categorization of the salient people, objects, and events in the environment.

Concrete operational period The third of Piaget's four major periods of cognitive development. According to Piaget, the child begins to understand logical concepts, such as conservation, during this period.

Concurrent validity That form of validity established when the scores on a new test correlate highly with the scores on an existing test.

Conditioned reinforcer A stimulus that becomes reinforcing by being associated with a primary reinforcer.

Conditioned response (CR) In classical conditioning, the response that results from pairing the conditioned stimulus (CS) with the unconditioned stimulus (US).

Conditioned stimulus (CS) In classical conditioning, the stimulus that is paired with the unconditioned stimulus (US) and eventually comes to elicit the conditioned response (CR).

Conduction deafness Deafness that occurs because the bones of the middle ear do not transmit sound waves properly. Also known as middle ear deafness.

Cones Cells in the retina responsible for transducing light into neural impulses. Cones are sensitive to color and are primarily used in daylight or artificial light.

Confabulation The fabrication of memory for events the person is unable to recall.

Conformation bias Searching for evidence that supports one's initial ideas.

Conformity Adopting the attitudes and behaviors of other people as a result of real or imagined pressure from others.

Congruence In humanistic psychotherapy, the therapist's attempt to maintain empathy and honesty in his or her relationship with a client.

Consciousness The totality of sensations, perceptions, thoughts, feelings, and images in awareness at any given time.

Conservation The recognition that certain properties of objects, such as number, volume, length, or weight, remain unchanged despite transformations in the shape or size of the objects. According to Piaget, this knowledge is acquired during the concrete operational period of cognitive development.

Constructive memory The process whereby inaccurate information is added to that already in memory.

Construct validity That form of validity established when the test yields results that are consistent with what is known about the concept under investigation.

Consummate love A kind of love that combines the elements of both romantic and compassionate love.

Content validity That form of validity established when the test questions adequately sample the concept under investigation.

Continuous reinforcement schedule (CRS) A schedule of reinforcement in which the reinforcer is delivered each time the organism emits the response.

Control group Subjects in an experiment who are not exposed to the independent variable being studied.

Convergence A binocular (two-eye) cue for distance through which the eyes rotate toward the nose as an object comes closer.

Conversion disorder A form of somatoform disorder characterized by symptoms such as seizures, motor paralyses, and sensory impairments lacking any physiological basis.

Convolutions The irregular "hills and valleys" that make up the surface of the cortex in humans and other complex animals.

Coping methods Strategies for reducing stress by controlling stressors or one's reactions to them.

Cornea The transparent, domelike, outer covering of the lens and iris that allows light to enter the eye.

Corpus callosum A massive band of axons connecting the two hemispheres of the brain.

Correlation A relationship between any two variables; the statistical technique used to investigate whether two variables are associated.

Correlation coefficient A value representing the strength and direction of correlation between two variables.

Correspondence bias The tendency for observers to underestimate the role of external causes and to overestimate the role of internal or dispositional causes of other people's behavior. Also called *fundamental attribution error.*

Cortex See *cerebral cortex.*

Counseling psychology The psychological specialty which helps disturbed persons whose disorders are less serious than the ones dealt with by clinical psychologists.

Covariation principle In Kelley's attribution theory, a principle stating that behavior is attributed to causes which are present when the behavior occurs and absent when the behavior does not occur.

Critical period Periods in the development of the embryo and fetus in which the risk to particular organs of the body is greatest.

Cross-sectional method Research design in which the investigator observes or tests people of varying ages at approximately the same point in time.

Data Records of the observations or measurements in an empirical study.

Decay theory A theory of forgetting which holds that memory for an item spontaneously fades or decays with the passage of time.

Decibel (dB) Unit used to measure loudness.

Declarative memory Storage system in long-term memory in which memory for specific information or "fact" memory is stored.

Deductive reasoning The ability to draw logical conclusions from available evidence.

Defense mechanism In Freudian psychology, the means of warding off anxiety and other negative feelings caused by the threat of unacceptable sexual and aggressive drives. Today, considered to be psychological maneuvers for coping with internal and external events that threaten the individual's well-being.

Delay conditioning A form of classical conditioning in which there is a delay between the onset of the CS and the onset of the US. The two stimuli partially overlap and typically end at the same time.

Delayed stress reaction A stress syndrome occurring some time after a traumatic stress experience.

Delirium An organic mental disorder characterized by disturbance of attention, disorientation, and fluctuating level of awareness.

Delta waves Low frequency, high voltage EEG waves characteristic of stage 4 sleep.

Delusion A false, idiosyncratic belief held with great conviction in the absence of objective evidence.

Dementia A psychological disorder characterized by impairment of abstract thinking, memory, and judgment and often accompanied by confusion and disorientation. Alzheimer's disease is a primary cause of dementia.

Dendrites The portions of the neuron that receive impulses from other neurons and carry them toward the soma and axon.

Denial In Freudian theory, the ego-defense mechanism that blocks from consciousness threatening perceptions of the external world.

Dependent variables The variables that are measured by an experimenter. They are hypothesized to be affected by changes in an independent variable.

Depersonalization A state in which the body is experienced as separate from the self.

Depression An extreme mood of despondency, hopelessness, and lowered self-esteem.

Descriptive statistics The category of procedures used to describe, condense, and summarize raw data.

Development The changes that occur in cognitive and social abilities throughout life.

Developmental psychology The psychological specialty that studies how individuals grow and change throughout life

Diagnostic and Statistical Manual of Mental Disorders See *DSM-III*

Diathesis-stress model A hypothesis holding that particular psychological disorders, for example schizophrenia, result from the interaction of a specific genetic predisposition (diathesis) and specific environmental factors (stress).

Difference threshold The minimum amount of stimulus change needed for two stimuli to be perceived as different.

Diffusion of responsibility A process by which being part of a group lowers each person's sense of responsibility.

Directionality problem The ambiguity or difficulty in knowing the direction of the causal path between two variables that are causally related.

Discounting principle In Kelley's attribution theory, a principle stating that behavior cannot be attributed to any one cause if other, equally plausible causes for the behavior exist.

Discrimination In conditioning, a process whereby the organism learns to respond differently to stimuli that are differentially reinforced. In social psychology, the expression of prejudice in hostile behavior toward members of a particular group.

Discriminative stimulus In conditioning, a stimulus that signals that a response will be reinforced.

Displacement In language, the ability to convey information about events that occurred at another time or in a different place. In Freudian theory, the ego-defense mechanism by which aggressive feelings toward someone or something that has aroused anger are expressed toward someone against whom it is safe and morally acceptable to aggress.

Dissociated consciousness A state in which two or more conscious activities are performed independently of each other.

Dissociative disorders The group of psychological disorders that includes psychogenic amnesia and multiple personality. These disorders are characterized by a dissociation of cognitive activities, for example, specific memories or self-identity.

Distortion The process by which information in memory is altered, making it inaccurate.

DNA The molecules of deoxyribonucleic acid that make up the gene. DNA directs and controls the complex cellular reactions necessary for life.

Dominant gene A member of a gene pair that controls the expression of a physical trait regardless of the nature of the other member of the gene pair (see *recessive gene*).

Door-in-the-face technique A technique for obtaining compliance in which a person asks for an extremely large favor, and after being refused, asks for and obtains compliance to a moderate request.

Double-blind technique Control measure in a research study by which both the subjects and the researcher analyzing the data of the study are kept uninformed about the hypothesis.

Down syndrome A form of organic retardation resulting from an abnormality in which the child has one more chromosome than normal.

Dream analysis In psychoanalytic therapies, the process of analyzing dreams for their manifest and latent contents.

Drive A hypothetical state of tension or arousal that motivates organisms to perform certain activities that reduce the tension. The tension typically arises from some form of deprivation that results in a physiological or tissue-based need.

Drive reduction Hull's term for the behavior that organisms exhibit when they are in an aroused state (see *drive*).

DSM-III The third edition of the *Diagnostic and Statistical Manual of Mental Disorders*, a classification of psychological disorders published by the American Psychiatric Association. The revision of *DSM-III*, published in 1987, is referred to as *DSM-III-R*.

Educational psychologists Psychologists who specialize in studying the educational process.

EEG See *electroencephalogram.*

Effortful processing Information processing that is voluntary, slow, and limited in capacity.

Ego In Freudian theory, the portion of the mind that is largely conscious and reality oriented. It functions as the executive of the personality, striving to achieve satisfaction for the id in ways that are both moral and realistic.

Ego-defense mechanisms In Freudian theory, unconscious strategies used by the ego to shield itself from threatening perceptions, feelings, and impulses.

Elaborative rehearsal A control process for transferring information from short- to long-term memory. Elaborative rehearsal involves analyzing information for meaning.

Electroconvulsive therapy (ECT) A treatment of mood disorders in which a brain seizure is induced by passing an electric current through the head.

Electroencephalogram (EEG) Recording of electrical brain waves made by placing disc-shaped electrodes on the surface of the skull.

Embedded sentence A more complex sentence constructed by the insertion of one simple sentence within another. This speech characteristic begins to appear when the child is roughly 3 or 4 years old.

Embryo Term for the developing human organism from the second through the eighth week of development.

Emmert's law Principle stating that the closer an object is, the larger the image cast on the retina.

Emotion A state made up of a characteristic subjective experience, a characteristic pattern of physiological arousal, and a characteristic pattern of overt expression.

Empathy In humanistic therapy, the process of taking another person's perspective.

Empiricism The view that all knowledge is obtained through observation.

Encoding In the information-processing approach to human memory, the way information is "put into" memory.

Encounter group Form of group interaction that emphasizes becoming aware of one's inner feelings and experience, taking responsibility for one's life, and pursuing life actively and productively.

Endocrine system The glandular system that uses hormones to transmit messages throughout the body.

Endorphins Chemicals that occur naturally in the brain and act as neurotransmitters. These substances are thought to be involved in the inhibition of pain.

Engram A hypothetical physical change that occurs in the brain when a piece of information is stored.

Episodic memory A type of declarative memory, episodic memory is an autobiographical memory system responsible for storing a record of the events of our lives.

Equilibrium The sense that keeps us informed about the position of our body in space.

Erogenous zones In Freudian theory, those areas of the body which experience great tension and which require pleasure-producing stimulation.

Eros In Freudian theory, the drive for bodily pleasure.

Escape learning Another name for operant conditioning with negative reinforcement. In this procedure, the organism learns to emit a response to terminate an aversive stimulus.

Ethology The study of the behavior of animals in their natural habitats.

Excitatory potential An event that occurs in the dendrites of a neuron and has the effect of pushing the neuron closer to the threshold of firing.

Expectancy One aspect of the cognitive view of conditioning, which holds that the organism comes to expect a reinforcer.

Experiment A study in which a scientist treats an object of study in a specific way and then observes the effects of the treatment.

Experimental group Subjects in an experiment who are exposed to the independent variable being studied.

Experimental psychology The psychological specialty that studies basic psychological processes such as sensation, perception, motivation, emotion, learning, memory, and cognition.

Experimenter bias Type of bias that occurs when researchers who are aware of the hypothesis of a study subtly influence the subjects to behave according to prediction.

Extinction The gradual disappearance of a learned response when the reinforcer or US is removed.

Extrovert As first suggested by Jung, a personality type characterized by cheerfulness and an orientation toward object, people, and events in the environment.

Facial feedback hypothesis Hypothesis that the muscles of the face both express a given emotion and contribute to the feeling that characterizes that emotion.

Factor analysis A statistical technique used in constructing and evaluating intelligence tests. By computing the correlations of each test question with every other test question, it is possible to determine which questions measure the same mental ability.

Family therapy Treatment of more than one member of a family simultaneously on the assumption that a disturbance in one family member reflects a more general difficulty in the family's interactions.

Fetal alcohol syndrome (FAS) A group of physical deformities that appear frequently in the offspring of alcoholic women.

Fetus Term for the developing human organism from the third month after conception until birth.

Fight-or-flight response Cannon's term for the physiological changes that occur in response to a stressful or threatening event. These changes prepare the organism for the behaviors of either attacking or fleeing the source of stress.

Figure-ground relationship A principle of Gestalt organization by which we organize stimuli into objects that stand out (figure) and those that form the background (ground).

Fixation In Freudian theory, a failure of development in which the individual continues to seek a particular kind of gratification even after he or she has passed through that stage.

Fixed-action pattern A term used by ethologists to describe the species-specific responses that are elicited or released in the presence of naturally occurring events known as sign stimuli.

Fixed-interval (FI) schedule A partial reinforcement schedule in which the reinforcer is delivered after the first response that occurs following a set amount of time.

Fixed-ratio (FR) schedule A partial reinforcement schedule in which the reinforcer is delivered after a fixed number of nonreinforced responses.

Foot-in-the-door technique A technique for obtaining compliance in which a person first asks a very small favor and then asks for and obtains compliance with a moderate request.

Forgetting The inability to recall a particular piece of information accurately.

Formal operational period Piaget's final stage of cognitive development in which the individual is able to reason about hypothetical or abstract (formal) situations in the absence of concrete materials.

Form perception The process by which sensory stimuli are organized into meaningful shapes and patterns.

Forward classical conditioning All forms of classical conditioning in which the CS begins at the same time as or before the US. These include trace, delay, and simultaneous conditioning.

Fovea A small indentation in the center of the retina that contains only cones and produces the most acute vision.

Free association In psychoanalysis, the method of uncovering unconscious conflicts by having the patient report any and all ideas that come into consciousness.

Frequency The physical characteristic of sound that corresponds to the number of cycles per second, measured in Hertz (Hz); corresponds to the psychological property of pitch.

Frequency distribution A table or graph that represents the frequency of each value's occurrence

Frequency theory A theory of hearing that suggests that the entire basilar membrane vibrates at the same frequency as the auditory stimulus.

Frontal lobe The frontmost portion of the cerebral cortex

Frustration-aggression hypothesis The view that frustration always leads to aggression and that aggression is always a consequence of frustration

Functional fixedness An idea about the way objects should be used, based on past experience, that is relatively difficult to modify.

Fundamental attribution error See *correspondence bias.*

℞

Gender An awareness and understanding of the differences that distinguish males from females.

Gender constancy A stage of development occurring at about age 6 or 7 when children recognize that gender does not change.

Gender roles The attitudes, beliefs, and behavior patterns that people associate with being male or female.

Gender stability A stage of development occurring between ages 4 and 5 in which children recognize the superficial signs of gender differences but still do not understand the immutability of gender.

General Adaptation Syndrome (GAS) Selye's description of an organism's reaction to a stressor, made up of the stages of alarm and mobilization, resistance, and exhaustion.

Generalization A process in conditioning by which once a CR has been established to a stimulus, similar stimuli will also evoke that response.

Generalized anxiety disorder An anxiety disorder characterized by persistent anxiety stemming from no specific identifiable threat.

Generativity The ability to use language in a highly creative way so that an almost infinite number of sentences can be created from a limited number of words.

Genes The basic unit of hereditary transmission inherited at birth. Genes typically come in pairs and are located on tiny cellular particles known as chromosomes.

Genital stage In Freudian theory, the final stage of development, beginning in puberty, during which the person experiences strong, adult sexual desires for the first time.

Glia cell A type of cell within the brain that supplies support and nutrients to the neurons.

Good continuation A principle of Gestalt organization by which stimuli are organized into continuous lines of patterns.

Grammar The set of rules that allow us to speak and comprehend our language.

Group polarization A phenomenon in which a group of people discussing an issue related to a shared value makes a decision that is more extreme than the average of the stands of the individual members of the group.

Groupthink A mode of group decision making in which group coherence takes precedence over efficiency.

℞

Hair cells Very fine hairs embedded in the basilar membrane that bend as fluid travels through the cochlea. It is the bending of the hair cells that tranduces sound vibration into neural impulses.

Hallucination A perceptual experience occurring in the absence of appropriate external stimuli; a mental image experienced as a perception.

Halo error Bias in which we judge a person more favorably on many traits because we have favorable information about the person's standing on a few traits.

Hardiness A personality disposition characterized by being open to change, actively involved in one's environment, and believing that one has control over one's life.

Health psychology Field of psychology concerned with the role of psychological factors in health and illness.

Helplessness A state occurring when unpleasant events occur independently of our ability to control them.

Hemisphere Either the left or the right half of the brain.

Heritability ratio An estimate of how much of the total variance in a given trait is due to genetic factors.

Hertz (Hz) The unit (cycles per second) used to measure the frequency of a sound wave.

Heuristic A shorthand solution to a problem relying on rules of thumb that have helped an individual solve problems in the past.

Hippocampus The part of the limbic system situated between the thalamus and cortex which is involved in certain aspects of memory.

Homeostasis An ideal or optimal level of physiological functioning that maintains an organism on an even keel.

Homosexuality Sexual preference for partners of the same sex.

Hormones Chemical substances produced by the glands of the endocrine system and secreted into the bloodstream where they are carried to various target locations.

Hue The psychological dimension of light that corresponds to wavelength and is often referred to as "color."

Humanistic psychology A philosophy of psychological study that emphasizes the whole person and the importance of each person's subjective experience.

Humanistic therapy A form of psychotherapy which regards the person as a continuously unfolding set of potentials. The goals of humanistic therapy are to remove blocks to self-development, to put the person in touch with his or her true self, and to promote continued growth.

Hypercomplex cells Cells in the visual cortex that respond to particular shapes. These cells receive input from complex cells.

Hypermnesia Heightened ability to recall past experiences.

Hypnosis A state of hypersuggestibility characterized by focused attention, reduced reality testing, and imaginative involvement.

Hypnotic susceptibility test A standardized procedure for determining a person's responsiveness to hypnosis.

Hypochondriasis A type of somatoform disorder in which a person both fears and is mistakenly convinced that he or she is ill.

Hypothalamus A small area of the limbic system located directly beneath the thalamus. The hypothalamus contains centers that regulate motivated behaviors such as eating, drinking, and sexual behavior. It also controls the endocrine system and helps maintain homeostasis.

Hypothesis A proposition or assertion about the possible relationship between variables.

🌿

Id In Freudian theory, the portion of the mind that contains unconscious drives for pleasure.

Identification In Freudian theory, a defense mechanism by which a person attempts to be like another who seems to be successful. Identification with the same-sex parent is used to resolve the Oedipal conflict in the phallic stage.

Illusion A perception that does not agree with the true physical characteristic of an object.

Imagery coding A technique for encoding information in long-term memory by creating a mental image of an object or scene.

Immune system A complex of organs and cells that function to protect the body against disease agents such as viruses, bacteria, and pollutants.

Impression-management theory Theory that suggests people operate from a need to appear consistent rather than a drive to be consistent.

Incentives Environmental events that motivate or "pull" the organism in certain directions, as opposed to internal, physiological states that "push" the organism in certain directions.

Incus The middle of the three small bones that make up the middle ear.

Independent variable A variable that is manipulated by an experimenter and is hypothesized to cause changes in a dependent variable.

Inductive reasoning Type of reasoning that involves the discovery of a general rule or principle derived from specific observations.

Industrial psychology The psychological specialty involving the study of behavior in the workplace, especially industry.

Infancy The first two years of human life.

Inference A form of constructive memory by which we fill in information missing from memory using general knowledge about a situation already stored in memory.

Inferential statistics The procedures used to indicate the relationship between dependent and independent variables, to determine the significance level of observed differences, and to indicate causation. Inferential statistics help determine what conclusions can be drawn from the data.

Information processing A model that views cognitive development as the gradual acquisition of skills and rules necessary to solve complex problems.

Inhibitory potential An event which occurs in the cell body of a neuron and has the effect of pushing the neuron away from the threshold of firing (i.e., making it more difficult for excitatory potentials to fire the neuron).

Insight In psychoanalysis, the process of becoming aware of the relation of unconscious conflicts to current difficulties.

Insomnia Inability to obtain adequate sleep because of difficulty falling asleep, difficulty staying asleep, or early morning wakening.

Instinct An innate or genetically predetermined disposition to behave in a particular way when confronted with certain stimuli.

Instrumental conditioning A form of learning in which the organism's response is instrumental in determining the consequences of its behavior. Also called *operant conditioning*.

Intelligence The capacity to understand the world and the resourcefulness to cope with its problems.

Intelligence quotient (IQ) The relationship between mental age and chronological age, expressed as MA/CA × 100

Interference theory A theory of forgetting which holds that information cannot be recalled because other information stored in memory interferes with retrieval.

Interposition A monocular (one-eye) cue for distance by which closer objects block our vision for objects that are farther away.

Interpretation In psychoanalysis, a hypothesis offered by the therapist to summarize and explain the unconscious motivation of the patient's behavior. Through the interpretation the therapist helps the patient gain insight.

Interval schedules In operant conditioning, schedules of reinforcement in which a reinforcer is delivered only after a certain amount of time has passed.

Intoxication The state in which an excess of a sedative poisons the body, leading to uncoordinated actions, slowed reaction times, and slurred speech.

Introspection A method of studying consciousness whereby subjects report on their subjective experience.

Introvert As first suggested by Jung, a personality type characterized by shyness and an orientation toward inner experiences.

***In vivo* desensitization** A form of desensitization therapy in which the patient is directly exposed to anxiety-provoking situations.

James-Lange theory Theory of emotion stating that an eliciting stimulus triggers an internal physiological response that sends feedback to the brain to create the feeling of a specific emotion.

Just noticeable difference (j.n.d.) The amount of stimulus change needed before a difference threshold can be detected.

Keyword method A mnemonic device often used to help learn the vocabulary of a foreign language in which a keyword is chosen which sounds like the foreign word and then that keyword is associated with the English equivalent by imagery or a related process.

Kinesthesis The sense of the position and movement of body parts.

Language A form of communication characterized by semanticity, generativity, and displacement.

Latency period In Freudian theory, the long, quiet period from age 5 to puberty, in which no major unconscious drives press for satisfaction.

Latent content In psychoanalytic theory, the unconscious motives or drives expressed in the manifest content of dreams.

Lateral hypothalamus (LH) An area of the hypothalamus that is part of a system for the control of eating. Destruction of this area causes an animal to stop eating.

Law of effect A principle proposed by Thorndike, which states that acts followed by a satisfying state of affairs will be more likely to recur and acts followed by an annoying state of affairs will be less likely to recur.

Leader Person in a group who has the greatest amount of influence over others.

Leadership The exercise of influence or power over others.

Leadership schema The overall idea people have of how a leader looks and behaves.

Learned helplessness A condition produced when organisms are subjected to an unescapable aversive stimulus (e.g., electric shock). The inability to escape the aversive event produces a hypothetical state of helplessness that transfers to other situations in which the organism could escape the aversive situation but no longer tries.

Learning A relatively permanent change in immediate or potential behavior that results from experience.

Lens The transparent, flexible structure in the eye that focuses light on the retina.

Libido The energy the id produces to obtain pleasure.

Liking Respect or high regard for another person and often seeing the other as similar to oneself.

Limbic system The set of related anatomical structures, including the hippocampus, amygdala, and hypothalamus, which surround the brain stem and are involved in a number of processes including emotion, motivation, and aspects of memory.

Linear perspective A monocular (one-eye) cue for distance by which parallel lines (e.g., railroad tracks) appear to converge as they get farther away.

Linguistic-relativity hypothesis The notion that the language of a particular culture determines the way in which people perceive and understand the world they live in.

Longitudinal method A research design in which the same subjects are observed over an extended period of time.

Long-term memory The third stage of human memory (after sensory and short-term memory). This relatively permanent storage system holds vast amounts of information for long periods of time.

Loudness The psychological dimension of hearing related to the amplitude (height) of a sound wave.

Lowballing Getting people to agree to an action and then telling them that the action will be more costly or less rewarding than was originally stated.

Magnetic resonance imaging (MRI) A technique used for exploring the living brain, MRI uses magnetic fields to generate a three-dimensional picture of the brain.

Maintenance rehearsal A technique for keeping information in short-term memory by continually repeating (rehearsing) the information.

Major depressive episode A psychological disorder characterized by depressed mood, slowed behavior, and such biological signs as sleeping and eating difficulties.

Major hemisphere Sometimes used to refer to the left hemisphere because it controls language, an important human skill.

Malleus The outermost of the three small bones that make up the middle ear.

Mania An extreme mood of elation, well-being, and heightened self-esteem.

Manic episode A psychological disorder characterized by elevated mood, excitement, and hyperactivity.

Manifest content In psychoanalytic theory, the conscious or remembered aspects of a dream (see *latent content*).

Mean The sum of the scores in a distribution divided by the number of scores, abbreviated M or X.

Mean length of utterance (MLU) An estimate of the average length of a young child's utterances, using either words or morphemes as the basic unit of measurement.

Measurement The process of assigning numbers to observable events via some rule.

Median The value in the middle of a distribution below which and above which half the values fall.

Meditation A method for voluntarily producing an altered state of consciousness distinct from waking or sleeping.

Memory The ability to store information so that it can be used at a later time.

Menarche The beginning of the menstrual cycle, occurring around puberty. Indicative of sexual maturity in girls.

Menopause The cessation of the menstrual cycle.

Mental age (MA) A measure of an individual's performance on an intelligence test expressed in terms of months and years.

Mental processes Processes that are experienced in or take place in consciousness, including thoughts, memories, emotions, dreams, perceptions, and beliefs.

Mental set In problem solving, a particular way of looking at a problem based on past successes, which may interfere with solving new and different problems.

Metamemory Knowledge about the actual process of remembering, such as how much one can remember or how long it takes to commit something to memory.

Method of loci A mnemonic device that involves imagining items to be remembered and then associating each image with a place that is already stored in memory.

Mindfulness Choosing to be more aware of the environment and responses to it.

Mindlessness Following routines or carrying out orders automatically.

Minor hemisphere Sometimes used to refer to the right hemisphere, which controls spatial skills.

Mnemonic A technique for improving memory. Mnemonics typically involve methods for organizing and associating information in long-term memory.

Mode The value that occurs most frequently in a distribution.

Modeling Learning by imitating the behavior of others. See also *observational learning*.

Monocular cues In depth perception, cues that can be registered by each eye working independently. These include aerial haze, relative size, interposition, and linear perspective.

Mood A sustained emotional state that colors perception, thought, and behavior.

Mood disorders A class of psychological disorders in which the primary symptom is persistent and extreme disturbances of mood, ranging from depression at one extreme to mania at the other.

Morality of cooperation See *autonomous morality*.

Moral realism According to Piaget, a stage in moral development when the child believes that rules are sacred and unchangeable.

Morphemes The smallest meaningful elements of a spoken language.

Motivation The desires, needs, and interests that arouse an organism and direct it toward a specific goal.

Motor cortex The area of the cortex located at the border to the frontal and parietal lobes which sends impulses to voluntary muscles.

Motor development The ability of infants to use their arms and legs to move about and explore the environment.

Motor neuron A neuron that makes synaptic contact with a muscle or gland.

Multiple personality A form of dissociative disorder in which large segments of the personality are split off from conscious awareness, so that the person seems to fluctuate between two or more distinct personalities.

Narcolepsy A sleep disorder characterized by sudden and irresistible attacks of sleep during the day.

Naturalistic observation The study of behavior in its natural environment where the observer attempts not to interfere with the natural behavior of the subject.

Need for achievement (n Ach) The need to accomplish something difficult, to meet a standard of excellence, or to excel.

Negative identity According to Erikson, an extreme form of acting out that occurs when the adolescent cannot resolve the identity crisis successfully. A negative identity may result in delinquency, drug abuse, or even suicide.

Negative reinforcement The procedure used to increase the probability that a response will recur by removing an aversive stimulus after the response occurs.

Negative reinforcer In operant conditioning, any

stimulus whose removal increases the probability that the behavior it follows will recur.

Nerve deafness Deafness resulting from damage to the cochlea, the hair cells, or the auditory nerve. Also known as inner ear deafness.

Neuron The type of cell that is the basic unit of the nervous system, responsible for conducting information throughout the nervous system.

Neuroscience The branch of the life sciences that studies the relationship between the central nervous system and behavior.

Neurotransmitter A chemical substance involved in the transmission of neural impulses from one neuron to another. Neurotransmitters are released when an action potential reaches the end of the axon (axon terminal). Upon release, neurotransmitters cross the synapse and attach to receptors on either the dendrite or cell body of the adjacent neuron.

Noise In sensation, irrelevant or distracting stimuli.

Nonstate theory Any theory that attributes hypnotic responsiveness to psychological processes occurring in normal waking consciousness (see *state theory*).

Normal distribution A perfectly symmetrical and unimodal frequency distribution in which the mean, median, and mode all have the same value. Because the normal distribution frequently resembles the shape of a bell, it is sometimes called a "bell curve."

Norms Standards of performance that are used to compare an individual's score with the scores of others from a similar background; statistical guidelines that indicate both what is average and how much variation around the average one can expect.

NREM sleep All sleep states other than REM sleep.

Object permanence The recognition that an object continues to exist even though it is no longer visible. According to Piaget, achievement of object permanence occurs during the sensorimotor period of cognitive development.

Observational learning Learning that results from watching the behavior of others and observing the consequences of that behavior. See also *modeling*.

Obsessions Recurrent thoughts or images experienced as involuntary intrusions into consciousness.

Obsessive-compulsive disorder A form of anxiety disorder characterized by a compelling urge to engage in repetitive, stereotyped thoughts (obsessions) and/or actions (compulsions).

Occipital lobe The rearmost portion of the cerebral cortex, located behind the parietal and temporal lobes.

Olfactory mucosa The area within the nasal cavity that contains the receptors for smell.

Operant conditioning Learning that occurs when an organism learns to associate its behavior with the consequences or results of that behavior. The frequency of a response is increased or decreased depending upon the consequence of the response. Also called *instrumental conditioning*.

Operational definition A definition of a variable in terms of observable events that can be measured.

Opponent-process theory A theory of color vision that postulates three pairs of opposing color receptors, red-green, blue-yellow, and black-white. The pattern of stimulation of these receptors accounts for the perception of all colors. Also, a theory of motivation which claims that every emotional experience leads to an opposite emotional experience that persists long after the primary emotion has passed.

Optimistic disposition A personality trait that protects against illness and its effects.

Oral stage In Freudian theory, the first stage of development, lasting from birth to about age 1-1/2, in which the mouth experiences the most tension and requires the most tension-reducing stimulation.

Organic delusional syndrome An organic mental disorder characterized by delusions with or without other psychotic symptoms.

Organic hallucinosis An organic mental disorder characterized by hallucinations in the absence of other psychotic symptoms.

Organic mental disorder A psychological or behavioral abnormality due to known impairment of brain functioning.

Organismic variables Variables, such as age, sex, and race, that are properties of the organism being studied.

Ossicles Collectively, the three small bones that make up the middle ear: the malleus, incus, and stapes.

Oval window The thin membrane that separates the middle ear and inner ear and transmits sound waves from the ossicles to the cochlea.

Panic disorder A form of anxiety disorder in which the person experiences bouts of abrupt, extreme anxiety, usually lasting for several minutes.

Papillae Small bumps on the surface of the tongue that contain the taste buds.

Parallel search A procedure for searching through short-term memory in which all items are examined simultaneously.

Parietal lobe The portion of the cerebral cortex between the frontal lobe and the occipital lobe.

Partial reinforcement effect The finding that behaviors which are reinforced only part of the time take longer to extinguish than behaviors which are continuously reinforced.

Partial reinforcement schedule (PRF) A general term to describe schedules of reinforcement in which the reinforcer is delivered only part of the time the organism emits the response.

Pattern recognition A control process in human memory that regulates the flow of information from sensory to short-term memory. By this process, raw, meaningless information in sensory memory is compared with meaningful patterns in long-term memory, recognized, and then transferred to short-term memory.

Perception The process by which the organism selects, organizes, and interprets sensations.

Perceptual constancy The ability to perceive objects as relatively stable in terms of shape, size, and color despite changes in sensory information.

Perceptual context The tendency for our perception of an object to be influenced by other stimuli that are present.

Perceptual set The tendency for our perception of an object to be influenced by what we expect to encounter.

Performance The knowledge a person demonstrates in a particular setting at a given moment in time.

Peripheral nervous system (PNS) The part of the nervous system outside the brain and spinal cord. Its function is to transmit sensory impulses from the sense organs to the central nervous system and to transmit motor impulses from the central nervous system to the muscles and glands.

Personality The unique patterning of behavioral and mental processes that characterizes an individual and the individual's interactions with the environment. Also, the psychological specialty which studies these processes.

Personality disorder A combination of personality traits that is extremely inflexible and impairs psychological, social, and occupational functioning.

Personality inventories Inventories of true-false questions about personal characteristics of behavior that are used to measure the extent to which individuals possess particular traits.

Personality psychology The specialty concerned with how individuals differ and the traits that make people unique.

PET scan See *positron emission tomography.*

Phallic stage In Freudian theory, the third stage of development, lasting from approximately age 3 to age 5 in which the genital region experiences the most tension and requires the most tension-reducing stimulation.

Phobic disorder A form of anxiety disorder characterized by excessive fear of particular objects or situations.

Phonemes The smallest unit of sound in a spoken language. Phonemes have no meaning of their own and must be combined with one another to produce a meaningful sound.

Phonology The study of how sounds are combined to produce words and sentences.

Pinna The fleshy visible parts of the outer ear.

Pitch The psychological dimension of hearing corresponding to the frequency of a sound wave.

Pituitary gland Located at the base of the brain, the pituitary gland secretes hormones that influence growth and the secretion of other hormones in the endocrine system.

Placebo effect Improvement of a medical or psychological problem due solely to the belief that a treatment is effective.

Place theory A theory of hearing which holds that tones of different pitches cause different areas of the basilar membrane to vibrate.

Polygraph An electronic recording device that simultaneously records several channels of physiological information from electrical signals generated by autonomic nervous system activity, skeletal muscle activity, or brain activity.

Positive reinforcement The procedure used to increase the probability that a response will recur by following the response with a reinforcer.

Positive reinforcer In operant conditioning, any stimulus whose presentation increases the probability that the behavior it follows will recur.

Positron emission tomography (PET) A brain-imaging technique in which the amount of glucose used in thousands of small brain areas is measured. This information is then fed into a computer that produces a picture of the level of activity throughout the brain.

Posthypnotic suggestion A suggestion received under hypnosis and carried out when no longer hypnotized.

Post-traumatic stress disorder (PTSD) A psychological disorder caused by an uncontrollable traumatic event.

Preconscious processes Subconscious mental activities that are potentially available to consciousness (see also *consciousness, subconscious processes, unconscious processes*).

Predictive validity That form of validity established when a test accurately predicts performance on some future task.

Prejudice A negative attitude toward or negative evaluation of a person due solely to his or her membership in a particular group.

Preoperational period The second of Piaget's four major periods of cognitive development (roughly from ages 2 to 7). During this period children show limitations in their understanding of certain logical principles, such as conservation or reversibility.

Primacy effect Common tendency for our impression of a person to be more strongly influenced by early information about the person than by recent information about the person.

Primary colors Three monochromatic light sources (corresponding to red, blue, and green) that, when mixed in the appropriate amounts, can produce any other color.

Primary mental abilities Thurstone's analysis of the seven basic factors that constitute intelligence: verbal comprehension, numerical skills, word fluency, spatial visualization, memory, reasoning, and perceptual skills.

Primary-process thinking In Freudian theory, the method of thinking used by the id to create in fantasy an image of the object or events that will satisfy its drives.

Primary reinforcer In operant conditioning, a reinforcer that is necessary to survival.

Primary sex characteristics The physical characteristics of males and females that make sexual union and procreation possible.

Proactive interference The process by which the recall of new information is interfered with by previously learned material.

Procedural memory Storage system in long-term memory in which memory of how to do things or "skill" memory is stored.

Progressive relaxation A method for producing deep relaxation, relying on alternately tensing and relaxing each of the major muscles of the body.

Projection In Freudian theory, the ego-defense mechanism by which people perceive in others traits or feelings they cannot accept in themselves.

Projective tests Psychological tests such as the Rorschach inkblot test and the TAT which assume that individuals will project their own unconscious needs and feelings onto ambiguous stimuli.

Prototype The best example of a concept.

Proximity A principle of Gestalt organization by which objects that are near each other tend to be perceived as a group.

Psychedelics Psychoactive drugs that produce alterations in perception, thought, and imagination.

Psychoactive drug Any chemical compound that produces a change in behavior or mental activity by altering brain functioning.

Psychoanalytic psychotherapy A briefer, more flexible adaptation of classical psychoanalysis, which places more emphasis on the patient's current style of interacting than on unresolved childhood conflicts.

Psychodynamic psychology A philosophy of psychological study that assumes that unconscious forces influence human behavior.

Psychodynamic psychotherapy A modern form of psychotherapy derived from psychoanalysis that is shorter, more flexible, and more oriented toward a patient's concerns than classical psychoanalysis.

Psychology The scientific study of behavior and mental processes.

Psychoneuroimmunology (PNI) The field of research that explores the effects of stress and other psychological factors on the immune system.

Psychosis A disordered state of consciousness occurring in various psychological disorders. It is characterized by impaired ability to interpret and test reality, as seen, for example, in hallucinations and delusions.

Psychosomatic specificity The hypothesis that people who share similar ways of coping with stressful events are likely to develop similar illnesses.

Psychosurgery A surgical procedure which involves destroying selected areas of the brain with the intention of changing maladaptive behavior.

Psychotherapy The treatment of psychological disorders or other personal problems by psychological methods.

Punisher In operant conditioning, any stimulus whose presentation decreases the probability that the behavior it follows will recur.

Punishment The procedure used to decrease the probability that a response will recur by presenting an aversive stimulus (punisher) after the response.

Pupil The opening in the iris that regulates the amount of light that enters the eye.

Purity In light, the number of different wavelengths making up a light; corresponds to the psychological property of saturation.

Random assignment A method of assigning subjects to the experimental and control groups by chance so that each subject has an equal chance of being assigned to either of the groups; often involves using a procedure such as flipping a coin or following a computer-generated list of random numbers.

Range In a frequency distribution, the difference between the largest and the smallest values in a collection.

Rationalization In Freudian theory, the ego-defense mechanism by which people give socially acceptable explanations for behavior which may in actuality be motivated by socially unacceptable drives and feelings.

Ratio schedule In operant conditioning, a schedule of reinforcement in which a reinforcer is delivered only after a certain number of responses.

Raw data Numbers obtained in a psychological investigation which have not yet undergone condensation or transformation.

Reaction formation In Freudian theory, the ego-defense mechanism by which a person consciously feels or acts the opposite of his or her true unconscious feelings because the true feelings arouse anxiety.

Realistic conflict theory Theory that conflict resulting from competition for scarce resources generates prejudice.

Reality principle In Freudian theory, the principle governing the ego, which states that behavior must be dictated by the constraints and demands of external reality as well as by the desire to obtain complete and immediate satisfaction of drives.

Recency effect Occasional tendency for our impression of a person to be more strongly influenced by recent information about the person than by early information.

Receptor The portion of a dendrite into which a neurotransmitter fits, breaking down the semipermeable membrane.

Recessive gene A member of a gene pair that controls the expression of a physical trait only if it is paired with a similar gene (see *dominant gene*).

Reflection In humanistic psychotherapy, the process by which the therapist summarizes the client's message and communicates it back to the client.

Reflex A specific, involuntary response to a stimulus that does not require learning.

Relative size A monocular (one-eye) cue for distance by which larger objects appear closer and smaller objects appear farther away.

Reliability The extent to which a test yields a consistent, reproducible measure of an individual's performance.

REM sleep A periodic state during sleep identified by rapid eye movements and correlated with vivid dreaming.

Replication The repeating of an experiment in all of its essential features to see if the same results will be obtained.

Repression In Freudian theory, the ego-defense mechanism by which unacceptable unconscious drives are kept from conscious awareness.

Residual The phase of schizophrenia in which psychotic symptoms are reduced.

Resistance In psychoanalysis, any means by which the patient avoids becoming aware of unconscious conflicts.

Resting potential The electrical potential (voltage) that exists between the inside and the outside of the neuron when it is not conducting a neural impulse.

Retina The rear portion of the eye that contains the rods and cones and is responsible for transducing light into neural impulses.

Retinal disparity A binocular (two-eye) cue for distance by which each eye sees a slightly more disparate (different) view of an object as it comes closer.

Retrieval In the information-processing approach to human memory, the process by which stored information is recalled.

Retrieval cues Stimuli that help locate information in long-term memory.

Retrieval failure A theory of forgetting which holds that information cannot be recalled because the proper cues are not available.

Retroactive interference The process by which recall of previously learned material is interfered with by newly learned material.

Risky shift A group decision that is riskier than the average decision made individually by the members of the group. Also called *shift to risk.*

Rods Cells in the retina responsible for transducing low levels of light into neural impulses. Rods only sense black and white and are most useful for peripheral and night vision.

Role confusion In Erikson's theory, the failure to synthesize past experiences and develop a clear and consistent self-identity.

Romantic love Type of love that involves the desire for an exclusive, intimate relationship with another person, great attachment to and dependence on the other person, and care for and the desire to help the other person.

Saturation The psychological dimension of a color that corresponds to its purity (i.e., how many hues make up the color).

Scatter plot A graph used to plot the values of one variable versus the values of another variable. The shape of the resulting cluster of dots can be used to make a preliminary estimate of correlation.

Schema General knowledge, acquired from experience, about any object, event, person, or group. Schemata influence the organization and storage of new memories.

Schizophrenia A serious and severe psychological disorder characterized by disorganization of thinking, perception, and emotion.

School psychology The psychological specialty involving work with students in school settings.

Scientific method Method of investigation used by psychologists involving the use of systematic procedures for collecting and reporting scientific data.

Script General knowledge that we have about what happens in particular situations.

Secondary-process thinking In Freudian theory, the realistic thought processes used by the ego to satisfy the drives of the id.

Secondary sex characteristics The visible physical characteristics, other than genitalia, that distinguish the mature male and female.

Sedation The calm, tranquil state produced by sedatives.

Sedatives Psychoactive drugs that calm, decrease activity, and induce sleep.

Selective attention The cognitive process by which only a limited range of stimuli is allowed into consciousness at any one time.

Self-actualization In humanistic personality theory, a key process by which a person attempts to develop to the full all his or her potentials.

Self-concept In Carl Rogers' personality theory, an image of the self that children develop, based on parental values.

Self-control procedure A special form of behavior modification in which the client actively participates in designing and carrying out the behavior modification program.

Self-disclosure Telling another person about one's own needs, thoughts, feelings, behavior, and background. Self-disclosure typically involves the sharing of highly personal information.

Self-fullfilling prophecy An expectancy that leads to a certain pattern of behavior whose consequences confirm the expectancy.

Self-perception theory Theory that people infer what their attitudes must be from their actions.

Semantic encoding A technique for encoding information in long-term memory by remembering the general meaning of words and sentences.

Semanticity Meaningful information expressed through language.

Semantic memory Type of declaratice memory in which general information about the world, such as rules, concepts, and facts, is stored.

Semantics The study of how meaning is expressed through words and sentences.

Sensation The process by which sense organs gather information about the environment.

Sensorimotor period The first of Piaget's four major periods of cognitive development. During this period, which lasts from birth to about age 2, the infant discovers relationships between sensations and motor behavior.

Sensory memory The first stage of human memory. This storage system holds a very nearly literal image of the stimulus for a very brief period of time.

Sensory neuron A cell that responds directly to an external stimulus such as light, sound, or touch.

Serial search A process for searching through short-term memory in which items are examined one at a time.

Set point theory A theory of human weight regulation and obesity which holds that each individual has a predetermined weight which the body tries to maintain. Obese individuals are thought to have a higher set point than normal-weight individuals.

Sex typing Process through which children acquire knowledge about the expected or stereotypic attitudes, beliefs, and behaviors associated with their gender in their culture.

Shape constancy The tendency for a familiar object to be perceived as a constant shape even though the retinal image changes as the object changes its orientation.

Shaping A technique used in operant conditioning that involves reinforcing behaviors that are increasingly similar to the desired behavior until the desired behavior finally occurs.

Shift to risk See *risky shift.*

Short-term memory The second stage of human memory (after sensory memory). This temporary storage system holds small amounts of information (5–9 chunks) for a maximum of 20 seconds.

Signal detection theory A theory that states that detecting a stimulus depends not just on the stimulus intensity but also on the interaction of many factors such as motivation and experience.

Sign stimuli Naturally occurring events in the habitat of animals, which elicit specific responses important to the survival of the organism (see *fixed-action pattern*).

Similarity One of the Gestalt laws of perception, which holds that similar elements within the perceptual field will tend to be grouped together.

Simple cells Cells in the visual cortex that respond to lines in a particular place in the visual field and of a particular orientation.

Simplicity A principle of Gestalt organization by which complex stimulus patterns are perceived as a combination of their simpler components.

Simultaneous conditioning A form of classical conditioning in which the CS and the US begin and end at the same time.

Single-blind procedure Control measure in which subjects in a study are kept uninformed about the hypothesis so that this knowledge does not unconsciously affect their behavior.

Size constancy The tendency for a familiar object to be perceived as a constant size even though the retinal image changes as the object moves closer or farther away.

Skewed distribution Distribution in which one "tail," or extreme end, of the distribution is much longer than the other.

Sleep apnea A sleep disorder characterized by repeated, temporary cessations of breathing (apnea).

Sleep spindles Bursts of rapid EEG waves characteristic of stage 2 sleep.

Sleepwalking A sleep disorder in which complex behaviors such as walking about are performed in a state of sleep.

Social cognition The study of the ways human beings process information about their social world, including themselves, other people, and social issues.

Social identity theory Theory stating that people have a tendency to categorize individuals into groups and to prefer their own group.

Social influence The study of the ways people influence each other's judgments, actions, and decisions.

Social psychology The psychological specialty that studies social interaction and the way one person affects another.

Social readjustment rating scale (SRRS) A list of 43 different life events used to gauge the amount of stress an individual has recently undergone.

Social support The nurturance, information, and example that others can provide in helping a person to cope with stress.

Sociobiology A theory which contends that social behavior, such as altruism, can best be understood in terms of the genetic principle of kin selection. This principle asserts that the self-sacrifice of an individual increases the probability that its genes will endure through the survival of its closest relatives.

Soma The cell body of the neuron, located between the dendrite and axon, that produces nutrients and other necessary chemicals for the neuron.

Somatic nervous system The division of the peripheral nervous system that regulates the voluntary muscles.

Somatization disorder A form of somatoform disorder in which the person experiences physical symptoms for which no physical cause can be found.

Somatosensory cortex The area of the cortex located at the border of the frontal and parietal lobes which receives sensory information from the touch receptors in the skin.

Spinal reflex An automatic response to a stimulus which is completely controlled by neurons in the spinal cord.

Spontaneous recovery In conditioning, a process related to extinction in which a learned response recurs after apparent extinction.

Spurious correlation Correlation that does not result from a direct causal connection between variables.

SQ3R method A technique for remembering information involving five steps: survey, question, read, recite, and review.

Standard deviation (SD) The average distance of each score from the mean.

Standardization A procedure in which questions intended to be used on an intelligence test are pretested on people of varying ages, races, and social backgrounds.

Stapes The innermost of the three small bones that make up the middle ear.

State theory Any theory that attributes hypnotic responsiveness to an altered state of consciousness (see *nonstate theory*).

Statistical analysis A set of techniques, borrowed from mathematics, that can be used to describe data, determine the probability that results are due to chance, and guide the inferences that can be made from the data.

Stereotype A set of beliefs about the characteristics

of people in a particular group that is generalized to almost all group members.

Stimulants Psychoactive drugs that increase activity, alertness, and positive mood.

Stimulus Any form of energy that is capable of exciting the nervous system.

Storage In the information-processing approach to human memory, the way a memory system maintains information.

Stress A pattern of disruptive psychological and physiological functioning that occurs when an environmental event is appraised as a threat to important goals and one's ability to cope.

Stressful event Any event that produces negative appraisals and stress reactions.

Stress reactions The disruptive effects of stressful events on psychological and physiological functioning.

Subconscious processes Mental or behavioral activities that take place outside of conscious awareness (see also *preconscious processes, unconscious processes*).

Subgoal analysis A problem-solving strategy that involves reducing a complex problem to a series of smaller problems.

Subjects Participants in a research study.

Sublimation In Freudian theory, an ego-defense mechanism by which people channel socially unacceptable drives into acceptable behaviors.

Substance-use disorders A variety of syndromes caused by the abuse of chemical substances, such as alcohol, drugs, tobacco, and coffee.

Superego In Freudian personality theory, the portion of the mind that contains moral principles and values, including the conscience—moral prohibitions against certain behaviors—and the ego-ideal—dictates about behavior one should perform.

Support groups Voluntary organizations of people who meet regularly to exchange information about, and to support each other's efforts to overcome a problem they have in common.

Surveys Questionnaires conducted in person, by telephone, or through the mail, inquiring into the ways a group of people thinks or acts.

Syllogism An argument consisting of two statements assumed to be true (premises) and a conclusion that follows logically from the premises.

Symmetric distribution Distribution in which, if folded vertically in the middle, each side would approximately match the opposite side.

Synapse The space between the axon of one neuron and the dendrites of another neuron.

Synaptic vesicles Small, hollow, pea-shaped structures located in the axon terminal. These structures contain stored neurotransmitters waiting to be released across the synapse.

Syntax Rules that determine how morphemes are combined to produce grammatically correct sentences.

Systematic desensitization A behavior therapy method for treating anxiety by pairing deep relaxation with successive visualizations of anxiety-provoking situations from least to most intense.

Tag question A question produced by the addition of a short ending, such as "isn't it," to a declarative sentence.

Taste buds Groups of cells located on the papillae of the tongue that contain the receptors for taste.

Temporal lobe The portion of the cerebral cortex located on the side of the brain below the parietal lobe and in front of the occipital lobe.

Teratogen A group of toxins that are able to permeate the placenta and disrupt the development of the fetus.

Thalamus A portion of the brain stem located in the exact geographic center of the brain. It is involved in channeling sensory messages to the cortex.

Thanatos In Freudian theory, the self-destructive drive or death instinct.

Theory A coherent group of assumptions and propositions than can explain data.

Thinking Mental activity involving organizing, categorizing, planning, reasoning, and problem solving.

Third variable problem Difficulty that sometimes occurs in correlational studies in which a correlation between two variables may arise even though there is no causal connection at all between them; the correlation arises because the two are linked to some third variable.

Timbre The psychological dimension of hearing related to the complexity of a sound. Pure sounds consist of a sound wave of a single frequency. Complex sounds consist of a combination of frequencies.

Token economy In a behavior modification program, a system in which behaviors are reinforced with tokens that can later be traded in for certain privileges.

Tolerance The phenomenon whereby increasing doses of a drug are required to produce the same effect.

Trace conditioning A form of classical conditioning in which there is a fixed period of time between the offset of the CS and the onset of the US.

Trait In trait theories of personality, a relatively stable personal characteristic that can be measured.

Transactional analysis (TA) A form of psychotherapy developed by Eric Berne, which holds that all interpersonal interactions are governed by one of three aspects of the personality: the Child, the Parent, or the Adult, which correspond roughly to the id, the ego, and the superego.

Transcendental Meditation (TM) A meditative technique adopted from Yoga, the Hindu spiritual discipline.

Transduction The process by which receptor cells in the nervous system transform stimuli into neural impulses.

Transference In psychoanalysis, the development toward the therapist of positive or negative emotional reactions originally developed toward other significant figures in the patient's life.

Trichromatic theory A theory of color vision

which holds that color vision relies on three different types of cones (see also *Young-Helmholtz, theory*).

Two-factor theory Theory stating that emotion is the joint effect of physiological arousal and cognitive appraisal.

Two-process theory An explanation of avoidance learning, which states that both classical and operant conditioning are involved.

Tympanic membrane The thin membrane that separates the outer and the middle ears and transmits sound waves from the outer ear to the ossicles; the eardrum.

Type A behavior pattern A coronary-prone behavior pattern characterized by ambition, competitiveness, time urgency, and hostility.

Unconditional positive regard In humanistic psychotherapy, the therapist's whole-hearted acceptance of the client.

Unconditioned response (UR) In classical conditioning, an unlearned response to a stimulus (US).

Unconditioned stimulus (US) In classical conditioning, the stimulus that elicits an unlearned response (UR).

Unconscious processes Subconscious mental activities that are more or less permanently unavailable to consciousness (see also *consciousness, preconscious processes* and *subconscious processes*).

Unimodal distribution Distribution in which there is only one point of greatest frequency.

Validity The extent to which a test measures what it was designed to measure.

Variability In a frequency distribution, the separation, dispersion, or spread of the scores on the *x*-axis

Variable Any factor in a study that can vary or change.

Variable-interval (VI) schedule A partial reinforcement schedule in which the reinforcer is delivered after the first response that occurs following an unpredictable amount of time.

Variable-ratio (VR) schedule A partial reinforcement schedule in which the reinforcer is delivered after a variable number of nonreinforced responses.

Ventromedial hypothalamus (VMH) An area of the hypothalamus that is part of a system for the control of eating. Destruction of this area produces excessive eating, eventually leading to obesity.

Visual agnosia The inability to recognize visual objects.

Wavelength In measuring light and sound waves, the distance from the crest of one wave to the crest of the next.

Weber's law Principle stating that the amount by which a stimulus must be increased or decreased to be perceived as different is always a constant proportion of the initial stimulus intensity.

Wernicke's area A portion of the temporal lobe critical in the formation and understanding of meaningful language.

Withdrawal A syndrome of distressing symptoms, for example, anxiety, irritability, and restlessness, that occurs following cessation of regular use of certain drugs.

Working through In psychoanalysis, the gradual process of acquiring new behavior patterns and attitudes following insight.

Young-Helmholtz theory A theory of color perception which postulates that there are three basic color receptors: red, green, and blue. The pattern of stimulation of these receptors accounts for the perception of all colors. Also referred to as *trichromatic theory*.

z-score A score's distance from the mean of the group, expressed in units of the standard deviation used to identify unusual values.

References

Abbey, A. (1987). Misperceptions of friendly behavior as sexual interest: A survey of naturally occurring incidents. *Psychology of Women Quarterly, 11,* 173-194.

Abel, E. L. (1980). Fetal alcohol syndrome: Behavioral teratology. *Psychology Bulletin, 87,* 29-50.

Abrahamson, P. R., Perry, L. B., Rothblatt, A., Seeley, T. T., & Seeley, D. M. (1979). *Negative attitudes toward masturbation and pelvic vasocongestion: A thermographic analysis.* Unpublished manuscript, UCLA.

Abramson, L. Y., Seligman, M. E. P., & Teasdale, J. D. (1978). Learned helplessness in humans: Critique and reformulation. *Journal of Abnormal Psychology, 87,* 49-74.

Acitelli, L. K. (1992). Gender differences in relationship awareness and marital satisfaction among young married couples. *Personality and Social Psychology Bulletin, 18,* 102-110.

Acredolo, L., & Hake, J. L. Infant perception. In B. B. Wolman (Ed.), *Handbook of developmental psychology.* Englewood Cliffs, NJ: Prentice-Hall.

Ader, R., & Cohen, N. (1982). Behaviorally conditioned immunosuppression and murine systemic lupus erythematosus. *Science, 215,* 1534-1536.

Ader, R., & Cohen, N. (1985). CNS-immune system interactions: Conditioning phenomena. *Behavioral and Brain Sciences, 8,* 379-426.

Adler, A. (1927). *The practice and theory of individual psychology.* New York: Harcourt, Brace & World.

Adler, A. (1939). *Social interest.* New York: Putnam.

Adorno, T. W., Frenkel-Brunswik, E., Levinson, D. J., & Sanford, R. N. (1950). *The authoritarian personality.* New York: Harper.

Adrian, E. D. (1928). *The basis of sensation.* New York: Norton.

Adrian, E. D. (1940). Double representation of the feet in the sensory cortex of the cat. *Journal of Physiology, 98,* 16.

Akil, H., Watson, S. J., Young, E., Lewis, M. E., Khachaturian, H., & Walker, M. W. (1984). Endogenous opiates: Biology and function. *Annual Review of Neuroscience, 7,* 223-256.

Alba, J. W., & Hasher, L. (1983). Is memory schematic? *Psychological Bulletin, 93,* 203-231.

Albert, D. J., Dyson, E. M., Walsh, M. L., & Wong, R. (1988). Defensive aggression and testosterone-dependent intermale social aggression are each elicited by food competition. *Physiology and Behavior, 43,* 21-28.

Alexander, M. P., & Albert, M. A. (1983). The anatomical basis of visual agnosia. In A. Kertesz (Ed.), *Localization in neuropsychology.* New York: Academic Press.

Alloy, L. B., & Abramson, L. Y. (1979). Judgment of contingency in depressed and nondepressed students: Sadder but wiser? *Journal of Experimental Psychology, 108,* 441-485.

Alloy, L. B., & Abramson, L. Y. (1988). Depressive realism: Four theoretical perspectives. In L. B. Alloy (Ed.), *Cognitive processes in depression.* New York: Guilford Press.

Allport, G. W. (1961). *Pattern and growth in personality.* New York: Holt, Rinehart & Winston.

Allport, G. W., Vernon, P. E., & Lindzey, G. (1960). *A study of values* (3rd ed.). Boston: Houghton Mifflin.

Altemeyer, B. (1988). *Enemies of Freedom.* San Francisco: Jossey-Bass.

Altman, I., & Taylor, D. A. (1973). *Social penetration: The development of interpersonal relationships.* New York: Holt, Rinehart & Winston.

Altrocchi, J. (1980). *Abnormal behavior.* New York: Harcourt Brace Jovanovich.

The American Medical Association Family Medical Guide. (1982). New York: Random House.

American Psychiatric Association. (1980). *Diagnostic and statistical manual of mental disorders* (3rd ed.). Washington, DC: Author.

American Psychiatric Association. (1987). *Diagnostic and statistical manual of mental disorders* (3rd ed. rev.). Washington, DC: Author.

American Psychiatric Association. (1991). *Benzodiazepine dependence, toxicity, and abuse.* Washington, D.C.: American Psychiatric Association.

American Psychological Association. (1981). Ethical principles of psychologists. *American Psychologist, 36,* 633-638.

American Psychological Association. (1984, August). *Behavioral research with animals* (pamphlet distributed at APA convention). Toronto.

American Psychological Association. (1988). Brief in *Price Waterhouse v. Hopkins,* no. 87-1167, U.S. Supreme Court.

Amoore, J. E. (1982). Odor theory and odor classification. In E. T. Theimer (Ed.), *Fragrance chemistry: The science of the sense of smell.* New York: Academic Press.

Amoore, J. E., Johnston, J. W., Jr., & Rubin, M. (1964). The stereochemical theory of odor. *Scientific American, 210,* 42-49.

Amoore, J. E., & Venstrum, D. (1967). Correlations between stereochemical assessments and organoleptic analysis of odorous compounds. In T. Hayaslu (Ed.), *Olfaction and taste.* Oxford: Pergamon Press.

Anand, B. K., & Brobeck, B. R. (1951). Localization of the feeding center in the hypothalamus of the rat. *Proceedings for the Society of Experimental Biology and Medicine, 77,* 323-324.

Anastasi, A. (1958). Heredity environment and the question "how?" *Psychological Review, 65,* 197-208.

Anderson, D. R., Lorsch, E. P., Field, D. F., Collins, P. A., & Nathan, J. G. (1986). Television viewing at home: Age trends in visual attention and times with TV. *Child Development, 57,* 1024-1033.

Anderson, J. R. (1984). Spreading activation. In J. R. Anderson & S. M. Kosslyn (Eds.), *Tutorials in learning and memory: Essays in honor of Gordon Bower.* San Francisco: Freeman.

Anderson, J. R., & Bower, G. H. (1973). *Human associative memory.* Washington, DC: V. H. Winston & Sons.

Anderson, P. (1983). Cerebellar synaptic plasticity—putting theories to the test. *Trends in the Neurosciences, 52,* 324-325.

Andersson, B. (1992). Effects of day-care on cognitive and socioemotional competence of thirteen year old Swedish school children. *Child Development, 61,* 20-36.

Andreasen, N. C. (1979). Thought, language, and communication disorders. *Archives of General Psychiatry, 36*, 1315-1321.

Andreasen, N. C. (1988). Brain imaging: Applications in psychiatry. *Science, 239*, 1381-1388.

Andreasen, N. C., Swayze, V. W., Flaum, M., Yates, W. R., Arndt, S., & McChesney, C. (1990). Ventricular enlargement in schizophrenia evaluated with computed tomographic scanning. *Archives of General Psychiatry, 47*, 1008-1015.

Andrews, K. H., & Kandel, D. B. (1979). Attitude and behavior: A specification of the contingent consistency hypothesis. *American Sociological Review, 44*, 298-310.

Anglin, J. M. (1977). *Word, object, and conceptual development.* New York: Norton.

Anisfeld, E., Casper, V., Nozyce, M., & Cunningham, N. (1990). Does infant carrying promote attachment? An experiment study of the effects of increased physical contact on the development of attachment. *Child Development, 61*, 1617-1627.

Annis, R. C., & Frost, B. (1973). Human visual ecology and orientation anisotropies in acuity. *Science, 182*, 729-731.

Archer, R. L. (1980). Self-disclosure. In D. M. Wegner & R. R. Vallacher (Eds.), *The self in social psychology.* New York: Oxford Press.

Aronson, E. (1977). Research in social psychology as a leap of faith. *Personality and Social Psychology Bulletin, 3*, 190-195.

Aronson, E. (1988). *The social animal* (5th ed.). San Francisco: Freeman.

Aronson, E. (1992). The return of the repressed: Dissonance Theory. *Psychological Inquiry.* Santa Cruz, CA.

Aronson, E., Blaney, N. T., Stephan, C., Sikes, J., & Snapp, M. (1978). *The jigsaw classroom.* Beverly Hills, CA: Sage.

Aronson, E., Brewer, M., & Carlsmith, J. M. (1963). Experimentation in social psychology. In G. Lindzey & E. Aronson (Eds.), *Handbook of social psychology. Vol. 1* (3rd ed.). New York: Random House.

Aronson, E., & Bridgeman, D. (1979). Jigsaw groups and the desegregated classroom: In pursuit of common goals. *Personality and Social Psychology Bulletin, 5*, 438-466.

Aronson, E., & Linder, D. (1965). Gain and loss of esteem as determinants of interpersonal attraction. *Journal of Experimental Social Psychology, 1*, 156-171.

Aronson, E., Willerman, B., & Floyd, J. (1966). The effect of a pratfall on increasing attractiveness. *Psychonomic Science, 4*, 227-228.

Asch, S. E. (1946). Forming impressions of abnormality. *Journal of Abnormal and Social Psychology, 41*, 258-290.

Asch, S. (1952). *Social psychology.* Englewood Cliffs, NJ: Prentice-Hall.

Asch, S. (1955). Opinions and social pressure. *Scientific American, 11*, 32.

Aserinsky, E., & Kleitman, N. (1953). Regularly occurring periods of eye mobility and concomitant phenomena during sleep. *Science, 118*, 273-274.

Aslin, R. N. (1987). Visual and auditory development in infancy. In J. D. Osofsky (Ed.), *Handbook of infant development.* New York: Wiley.

Aslin, R. N., Pisoni, D. B., & Jusczyk, P. W. (1983). Auditory development and speech perception in infancy. In M. M. Haith & J. J. Campos (Eds.), *Handbook of child psychology: Vol. 2. Infancy and developmental psychobiology* (pp. 573-688). New York: Wiley.

Atkinson, J. W. (1977). Motivation for achievement. In T. Blass (Ed.), *Personality variables in social behavior.* Hillsdale, NJ: Erlbaum.

Atkinson, J. W. (1981). Studying personality in the context of an advanced motivational psychology. *American Psychologist, 36*, 117-128.

Atkinson, J. W., & Litwin, G. H. (1960). Achievement motive and test anxiety conceived as motive to approach success and motive to avoid failure. *Journal of Abnormal and Social Psychology, 60*, 52-63.

Atkinson, K., MacWhinney, B., & Stoel, C. (1970). An experiment on the recognition of babbling. *Papers and Reports on Child Language Development*, Stanford University, No. 1.

Atkinson, R. C. (1975). Mnemotechnics in second language learning. *American Psychologist, 30*, 821-828.

Atkinson, R. C. & Raugh, M. R. (1975). An application of the mnemonic keyword method to acquisition of a Russian vocabulary. *Journal of Experimental Psychology: Human Learning and Memory, 104*, 126-133.

Atkinson, R. C. & Shiffern, R. M. (1968). Human memory: A control system and its control processes. In K. W. Spence and J. T. Spence (Eds.), *The psychology of learning and motivation, (Vol. 2).* New York: Academic Press.

Ausubel, D. P. (1980). An interactional approach to narcotic addiction. In D. J. Letteri, M. Sayers, & H. W. Pearson, *Theories on drug abuse: Selected contemporary perspectives* (NIDA Monograph No. 30, DHHS Publication No. ADM 80-967). Washington, DC: Government Printing Office.

Averill, J. R. (1969). Autonomic response patterns during sadness and mirth. *Psychophysiology, 5*(4), 399-414.

Averill, J. R., & Boothroyd, P. (1977). On falling in love in conformance with the romantic ideal. *Motivation and Emotion, 1*, 235-247.

Avery, D. (1977, August). The case for "shock" therapy. *Psychology Today,* p. 104.

Ax, A. F. (1953). The physiological differentiation between fear and anger in humans. *Psychosomatic Medicine, 15*, 433-442.

Ayllon, T., & Azrin, N. (1968). *The token economy: A motivational system for therapy and rehabilitation.* New York: Appleton-Century-Crofts.

Ayllon, T., Layman, D., & Kandel, H. J. (1975). A behavioral educational alternative to drug control of hyperactive children. *Journal of Applied Behavior Analysis, 8*, 137-146.

Azrin, N. H., & Holtz, W. C. (1966). Punishment. In W. K. Honig (Ed.), *Operant behavior: Areas of research and application* (pp. 380-447). New York: Appleton-Century-Crofts.

Backer, T. E., Batchelor, W. F., Jones, J. M., & Mays, V. M. (1989). Introduction to the special issue Psychology and Aids. *American Psychologist, 43*, 835-836.

Backlund, E. O., Grandburg, P. O., & Hamberger, B. (1985). Transplantation of adrenal medullary tissue to striatum in Parkinsonianism: First clinical trials. *Journal of Neurosurgery, 62*, 169-173.

Baddeley, A. (1988). Cognitive psychologfy and human memory. *Trends in neurosciences, 11*, 176-181.

Bahrick, H. P. (1984). Semantic memory store content in permastore: Fifty years of memory for Spanish learned in school. *Journal of Experimental Psychology: General, 113*, 1-29.

Bahrick, H. P., Bahrick, P. O., & Wittlinger, R. P. (1975). Fifty years of memory for names and faces: A cross-sectional approach. *Journal of Experimental Psychology: General, 104*, 54-75.

Bahrick, H. P., Hall, L. K. (1991). Lifetime maintenance of high school mathematics content. *Journal of Experimental Psychology—General, 120*, 20-33.

Bailey, J. M., & Pillard, R. C. (1991). A genetic study of male sexual orientation. *Archives of genetic psychiatry, 48*, 1089-1096.

Baker, A. J., Rierden, J., & Wapner, S. (1974). Age

changes in size-value phenomena. *Child Development, 45,* 257-268.

Baker, T. B. (1988). Models of addiction. *Journal of Abnormal Psychology, 97,* 115-117.

Baldessarini, R. J. (1977). *Chemotherapy in psychiatry.* Cambridge, MA: Harvard University Press.

Baldessarini, R. J. (1990).Update on antidepressants. *Harvard Mental Health Letter, 6,* 4-6.

Bales, R. F., & Slater, P. (1955). Role differentiation in small decision-making groups. In T. Parsons & R. F. Bales (Eds.), *Family, socialization and interaction processes.* New York: Free Press.

Baltes, P. (1983). *New perspectives on the development of intelligence.* Paper presented at the meeting of the American Psychological Association, Anaheim, CA.

Bandura, A. (1973). *Aggression: A social learning analysis.* Englewood Cliffs, NJ: Prentice-Hall.

Bandura, A. (1977). *Social learning theory.* Englewood Cliffs, NJ: Prentice-Hall.

Bandura, A. (1982). Self-efficacy mechanism in human agency. *American Psychologist, 37,* 122-147.

Bandura, A. (1983). Self-efficacy determinants of anticipated fears and calamities. *Journal of Personality and Social Psychology, 45,* 464-469.

Bandura, A. (1986). *Social foundations of thought and action: A cognitive theory.* Englewood Cliffs, NJ: Prentice-Hall.

Bandura, A., Ross, D., & Ross, S. A. (1963a). Imitation of fil-mediated aggressive models. *Journal of Abnormal and Social Psychology, 66,* 3-11.

Bandura, A., Ross, D., & Ross, S.A. (1963b). Vicarious reinforcement and imitative behavior. *Journal of Abnormal and Social Psychology, 67,* 601-607.

Bandura, A., & Walters, R. H. (1963). *Social learning and personality development.* New York: Holt, Rinehart & Winston.

Banks, M. S., & Salapatek, P. (1983). Infant and visual perception. In M. M. Heath & J. J. Campos (Eds.), *Handbook of child psychology: Vol. 2. Infancy and developmental psychobiology* (pp. 435-572). New York: Wiley.

Baratz, J. C. (1970). Teaching reading in an urban Negro school system. In F. Williams (Ed.), *Language and poverty.* Chicago: Markham.

Barber, T. X. (1965). Measuring "hypnotic-like" suggestibility with and without "hypnotic induction"; psychometric properties, norms, and variables influencing response to the Barber Suggestibility Scale (BSS). *Psychological Reports, 16,* 809-844.

Barber, T. X. (1969). *Hypnosis: A scientific approach.* New York: Van Nostrand Reinhold.

Barber, T. X. (1979). Suggested ("hypnotic") behavior: The trance paradigm versus an alternative paradigm. In E. Fromm & R. E. Shor (Eds.), *Hypnosis: Developments in research and new perspectives.* Chicago: Aldine.

Barchas, J. D., Berger, P. A., Ciaranello, R. D., & Elliott, G. R. (1977). *Psychopharmacology: From theory to practice.* New York: Oxford University Press.

Bard, P. A. (1928). A diencephalic mechanism for the expression of rage with special reference to the sympathetic nervous system. *American Journal of Physiology, 84,* 490-515.

Barker, R., Dembo, T., & Lewin, K. (1941). Frustration and regression: An experiment with young children. *University of Iowa Studies in Child Welfare, 18,* 1-314.

Barlow, D., & Mavissakalian, M. (1981). *Phobia.* New York: Guilford.

Baron, R. A., & Byrne, D. (1984). *Social psychology: Understanding human interaction.* Boston: Allyn & Bacon.

Barrett, G. V., & Depinet, R. L. (1990). A reconsideration of testing for competence rather than for intelligence. *American Psychologist, 46,* 1012-1024.

Barrett, J. E., Barrett, J. A., Oxman, T. E. & Gerber, P. D. (1988). The prevalence of psychiatric disorders in a primary care practice. *Archives of General Psychiatry, 45,* 1100-1106.

Barrett-Lennard, G. J. (1962). Dimensions of therapist response as causal factors in therapeutic changes. *Psychological Monographs, 76* (Whole No. 563).

Barsalou, L. W. (1985). Ideals, central tendency, and frequency of instantiation as determinants of graded structure in categories. *Journal of Experimental Psychology: Learning, Memory, and Cognition, 12,* 116-134.

Barsky, A. J. & Klerman, G. L. (1985). Hypochondriasis. *Harvard Mental Health Letter, 2,* 4-6.

Bartlett, F. E. (1932). The war of the ghosts. In *Remembering: A study in experimental social psychology.* Cambridge: Cambridge University Press.

Bartochuk, L. M. (1982, September). Separate worlds of taste. *Psychology Today,* pp. 48-56.

Bartus, R. T., Dean, R., III, Beer, D., & Lippa, A. S. (1982). The cholinergic hypothesis of geriatric memory dysfunction. *Science, 217,* 408-417.

Basbaum, A. I., & Besson, (Eds.) (1991). *Towards a new pharmacology of pain.* New York: Wiley.

Basbaum, A. I., & Fields, H. L. (1984). Endogenous pain control systems: Brainstem spinal pathways and endorphin circuitry. *Annual Review of Neuroscience, 7,* 309-338.

Bassili, J. N., & Smith, M. C. (1986). On the spontaneity of trait attribution: Converging evidence for the role of cognitive strategy. *Journal of Personality and Social Psychology, 50,* 239-245.

Bates, E., Benigni, L., Bretherton, L., Camaroni, L., & Volterra, V. (1979). *The emergence of symbols: Cognition and communication in infancy.* New York: Academic Press.

Batson, C. D. (1987). Prosocial motivation: Is it ever truly altruistic? In L. Berkowitz (Ed.), *Advances in experimental social psychology. Vol. 20.* New York: Academic Press.

Baumeister, R. F., Chesner, S. P., Senders, P. S., & Tice, D. M. (1988). Who's in charge here? Group leaders tend to lend help in emergencies. *Personality and Social Psychology Bulletin, 14,* 17-22.

Baumeister, R. F., & Hutton, D. G. (1987). Self-presentation theory: Self-construction and audience pleasing. In B. Mullen & G. R. Goethals (Eds.), *Theories of group behavior.* New York: Springer-Verlag.

Baumeister, R. F., Hutton, D. G., & Tice, D. M. (1989). Cognitive processes during deliberate self-presentation: how self-presenters alter and misinterpret the behavior of their interaction partners. *Journal of Experimental Social Psychology, 25,* 59-78.

Baumrind, D. (1967). Child care practices anteceding three patterns of preschool behavior. *Genetic Psychological Monographs, 75,* 43-88.

Baumrind, D. (1975). Early socialization and adolescent competence. In S. E. Dragustin & G. H. Elder, Jr. (Eds.), *Adolescence in the life cycle.* Washington, DC: Hemisphere.

Baumrind, D. (1983). Rejoinder to Lewis' reinterpretation of parental firm control effects: Are authoritative families really harmonious? *Psychological Bulletin, 94,* 132-142.

Bayley, N. (1970). Development of mental abilities. In P. H. Mussen (Ed.), *Carmichael's manual of child psychology. Vol. 1.* New York: Wiley.

Bayliss, G. C., Rolls, E. T., & Leonard, C. M. (1985). Selectivity between faces in the responses of a population of neurons in the cortex in the superior temporal sulcus of the monkey. *Brain Research, 342,* 91-102.

Beck, A. T. (1967). *Depression: Causes and treatment.* Philadelphia: University of Pennsylvania Press.

Beck, A. T. (1974). The development of depression: A cognitive model. In R. J. Friedman & M. M. Katz (Eds.), *The psychology of depression: Contemporary theory and research.* New York: Wiley.

Beck A. T. (1991). Cognitive therapy: A 30-year retrospective. *American Psychologist, 46,* 368-375.

Beck, A. T., Rush, A. J., Shaw, B. F., & Emery, G. (1979). *Cognitive therapy of depression.* New York: Guilford Press.

Beck, S. J., Beck, A. G., Levitt, E. E., & Molish, H. B. (1961). *Rorschach's test: Basic processes.* New York: Grune & Stratton.

Beckhard, R. (1977). Managerial careers in transition: Dilemmas and directions. In J. Van Maanen (Ed.), *Organizational careers: Some new perspectives.* New York: Wiley.

Beecher, H. K. (1959). *Measurement of subjective responses.* Oxford: University Press.

Beets, J. G. T. (1978). Odor and stimulant structure. In E. C. Carterette & M. P. Friedman (Eds.), *Handbook of perception. Vol. 6A.* New York: Academic Press.

Beidler, L. M. (1978). Biophysics and chemistry of taste. In E. C. Carterette & M. P. Friedman (Eds.), *Handbook of perception. Vol. 6A.* New York: Academic Press.

Békèsy, G. von. (1960). *Experiments in hearing.* New York: McGraw-Hill.

Bell, A. P., Weinberg, M. S., & Hammersmith, S. K. (1981). *Sexual preference: Its development in men and women.* Bloomington, IN: Indiana University Press.

Bell, R. Q., & Harper, I. V. (1977). *Child effects on adults.* Hillsdale, NJ: Erlbaum.

Bellack, A. S., & Hersen, M. (1980). *Introduction to clinical psychology.* New York: Oxford.

Bellugi, U., & Klima, E. S. (1972). The roots of language in the sign talk of the deaf. *Psychology Today, 4,* 32-35, 66.

Belluzi, J. D., & Stein, L. S. (1981). Facilitation of long-term memory by brain endorphins. In J. C. Martinez, R. A. Jensen, R. B. Messing, H. Rigter, & J. L. McGaugh, *Endorphins, peptides, learning, and memory processes* (pp. 291-303). New York: Academic Press.

Belsky, J., & Rovine, M. J. (1988). Nonmaternal case in the first year of life and security of infant-parent attachment. *Child Development, 59,* 157-167.

Bem, D. J. (1970). *Beliefs, attitudes, and human affairs.* Belmont, CA: Brooks/Cole.

Bem, D. J. (1972). Self-perception theory. In L. Berkowitz (Ed.), *Advances in experimental social psychology. Vol. 6.* New York: Academic Press.

Bem, D. J., & Allen, A. (1974). On predicting some of the people some of the time: The search for cross-situational consistencies in behavior. *Psychological Review, 81,* 506-520.

Bem, S. L. (1985). Androgyny and gender schema theory. In T. B. Sonderegger (Ed.), *Nebraska symposium on motivation: Psychology and gender.* Lincoln, NE: University of Nebraska Press.

Bem, S. L. (1981). Gender schema theory: A cognitive account of sex typing. *Psychological Review, 88,* 354-364.

Benbow, C. P. (1988). Sex differences in mathematical reasoning ability in intellectually talented preadolescents: Their nature, effects, and possible causes. *Behavioral and Brain Sciences, 11,* 169-232.

Bennett, W., & Gurin, J. (1982, March). Do diets really work? *Science 82,* pp. 42-50.

Benson, F. D., Metter, E. J., Kuhl, D. E., & Phelps, M. E. (1983). Positron-computed tomography in neurobehavioral problems. In A. Kertesz (Ed.), *Localization in neuropsychology* (pp. 121-139). New York: Academic Press.

Benson, H. (1975). *The relaxation response.* New York: Morrow.

Benzing, W. C., & Squire, L. R. (1989). Preserved learning and memory in amnesia: Intact adaptation-level ef-fects and learning of stereoscopic depth. *Behavioral Neuroscience, 103,* 538-547.

Berger, P. A. (1978). Medical treatment of mental illness. *Science, 200,* 977.

Berger, T. W., Berry, S. D., & Thompson, R. F. (1986). The role of the hippocampus in classical conditioning of aversive and appetitive behaviors. In R. L. Isaacson & K. H. Probram (Eds.) *The hippocampus.* New York: Plenum.

Bergin, A. E. (1971). The evaluation of therapeutic outcomes. In A. E. Bergin & S. L. Garfield (Eds.), *Handbook of psychotherapy and behavior change: An empirical analysis.* New York: Wiley.

Berkowitz, L. (1980). *A survey of social psychology.* New York: Holt, Rinehart & Winston.

Berkowitz, L., & Heimer, K. (1989). On the construction of the anger experience: aversive events and the negative priming in the formation of feelings. In L. Berkowitz (Ed.), *Advances in experimental social psychology,* Volume 22, (pp. 1-37). San Diego: Academic Press.

Berlyne, D. E. (1960). *Conflict, arousal, and curiosity.* New York: McGraw-Hill.

Berlyne, D. E. (1971). *Aesthetics and psychobiology.* New York: Appleton-Century-Crofts.

Berne, E. (1964). *Games people play.* New York: Grove Press.

Bernstein, D. A., & Nietzel, M. T. (1980). *Introduction to clinical psychology.* New York: McGraw-Hill.

Bernstein, I. (1978). Learned taste aversion in children receiving chemotherapy. *Science, 200,* 1302-1303.

Berridge, K. C., & Fentress, J. C. (1985). Trigeminal-taste interaction in palatability processing. *Science, 248,* 747-749.

Berscheid, E. (1985). Interpersonal attraction. In G. Lindsay & E. Aronson (Eds.), *Handbook of social psychology* (2nd ed.). *Vol. 2.* (pp. 413-484). New York: Random House.

Berscheid, E., & Walster, E. (1974). A little bit about love. In T. H. Huston (Ed.), *Foundations of interpersonal attraction.* New York: Academic Press.

Besson, J. A., Corrigan, F. M., & Foreman, I. (1985). Nuclear magnetic resonance (NMR). II. Imaging in dementia. *British Journal of Psychiatry, 146,* 31-35.

Beyer, S. (1990). Gender differences in the accuracy of self-evaluations of performance. *Journal of Personality and Social Psychology, 59,* 960-970.

Biernat, M., & Wortman, C. B. (1991). Sharing of home responsibilities between professionally employed women and their husbands. *Journal of Personality and Social Psychology, 60,* 844-860.

Binet, A., & Simon, T. (1916). *The development of intelligence in children* (E. Kite, Trans.). Baltimore: Williams & Wilkins.

Bjorklund, A. (1991). Neural Transplanation—an experimental tool with clinical possibilities. *Trends in the Neurosciences, 14,* 319-322.

Bjorklund, A., & Steveni, A. (1984). Intracerebral neural implants: Neuronal replacement and reconstruction of damaged circuits. *Annual Review of Neuroscience, 7,* 279-308.

Blakemore, C. (1977). Genetic instructions and developmental plasticity in the kitten's visual cortex. *Philosophical Transactions of the Royal Society of London, 278,* 425-434.

Blakemore, C. (1977). *Mechanics of mind.* Cambridge: University Press.

Blakemore, C., & Cooper, G. F. (1970). Development of the brain depends upon the visual environment. *Nature, 228,* 477-478.

Blanchard, E. B., Theobald, D. E., Williamson, D. A., Silver, B. V., & Brown, D. A. (1978). Temperature biofeedback in treatment of migraine headaches. *Archives of General Psychiatry, 35,* 581-588.

Blanchard, K., & Johnson, S. (1982). *The one minute manager*. New York: Morrow

Blasi, A. (1980). Bridging moral cognition and moral action: A critical review of the literature. *Psychological Bulletin, 88*, 1–45.

Bleier, R., Houston, L., & Byne, W. (1986). Can the corpus callosum predict gender, age, handiness, or cognitive differences? *Trends in the Neurosciences, 99*, 391–394.

Bleuler, E. (1950). *Dementia praecox or the group of schizophrenias* (J. Zinkin, Trans.). New York: International Universities Press.

Bliss, E. L. (1980). Multiple personalities: A report of 14 cases with implications for schizophrenia and hysteria. *Archives of General Psychiatry, 37*, 1388–1397.

Block, E. B. (1976). *Hypnosis: A new tool in crime detection*. New York: McKay, 1976.

Block, J. (1971). *Lives through time*. Berkeley, CA: Bancroft Books.

Block, J. (1983). Differential premises arising from differential socialization of the sexes: Some conjectures. *Child Development, 54*, 1335–1354.

Blood, R. O. (1972). *The family*. New York: Free Press.

Bloom, B. L., Asher, S. J., & White, S. W. (1978). Marital disruption as a stressor: A review and analysis. *Psychological Bulletin, 85*, 867–894.

Bloom, B. S. (1964). *Stability and change in human characteristics*. New York: Wiley.

Blumer, D., & Benson, D. F. (Eds.). (1975). *Psychiatric aspects of neurologic diseases*. New York: Grune and Stratton.

Bodenhausen, G. V. (1988). Stereotypic biases in social decision making and memory: testing process models of stereotype use. *Journal of Personality and Social Psychology, 55*, 726–737.

Bodmer, W. F., & Cavalli-Sforza, L. L. (1970). Intelligence and race. *Scientific American, 223*(4), 19–29.

Bogen, J. E., & Vogel, P. J. (1963). Treatment of generalized seizures by cerebral commissurotomy. *Surgical Forum, 14*, 431.

Bolles, R. C. (1972). Reinforcement, expectancy, and learning. *Psychological Review, 79*, 394–409.

Bootzin, R. R., & Nicassio, P. M. (1978). Behavioral treatments for insomnia. In M. Hersen, R. M. Eisler, & P. M. Miller (Eds.), *Progress in behavior modification. Vol. 6*. New York: Academic Press.

Bordow, S., & Porritt, D. (1979). An experimental evaluation of crisis intervention. *Social Science and Medicine, 13*, 251–256.

Borgida, E., & Nisbett, R. E. (1977). The differential impact of abstract vs. concrete information on decisions. *Journal of Applied Social Psychology, 7*, 258–271.

Boring, E. G. (1930). A new ambiguous figure. *American Journal of Psychology, 42*, 109–116.

Borkovec, T. D. (1982). Insomnia. *Journal of Consulting and Clinical Psychology, 50*, 880–895.

Bornstein, M. H., & Sigman, M. D. (1986). Continuity in mental development from infancy. *Child Development, 57*, 251–274.

Botwick, J., & Storandt, M. (1974). *Memory, related functions and age*. Springfield, IL: Charles C. Thomas.

Bouchard, C. (1989). Genetic factors in obesity. *Medical Clinics of North America, 73*, 67–81.

Bouchard, T. J., & McGue, M. (1981). Familial studies of intelligence: A review. *Science, 212*, 1055–1059.

Bourne, L. E., Dominowski, R. L., & Loftus, E. F. (1979). *Cognitive processes*. Englewood Cliffs, NJ: Prentice-Hall.

Bousfield, W. A. (1953). The occurrence of clustering in the recall of randomly arranged associates. *Journal of General Psychology, 49*, 229–240.

Bower, G. H. (1970). Organizational factors in memory. *Cognitive Memory, 1*, 18–46.

Bower, G. H. (1972). Mental imagery and associative learning. In L. Gregg (Ed.), *Cognition in learning and memory*. New York: Wiley.

Bower, G. H., Clark, M. C., Lesgold, A. M., & Winzenz, D. (1969). Hierarchical recall schemes in categorized word lists. *Journal of Verbal Learning and Verbal Behavior, 8*, 323–343.

Bower, G. H., & Springston, F. (1970). Pauses as recoding points in letter series. *Journal of Experimental Psychology, 83*, 421–430.

Bowers, K. (1976). *Hypnosis for the seriously curious*. Monterey, CA: Brooks/Cole.

Bowlby, J. (1973). *Attachment and loss. Vol. 2. Separation*. New York: Basic Books.

Bowlby, J. (1980). *Attachment and loss. Vol. 3: Loss, sadness, and depression*. New York: Basic Books.

Bowlby, J. (1982). *Attachment and loss: Vol. 1. Attachment*. New York: Basic Books.

Boyd, J. H., & Weissman, M. M. (1981). Epidemiology of affective disorders. *Archives of General Psychiatry, 38*, 1039–1046.

Bozarth, M. A. (1986). Neural basis of psychomotor stimulant and opiate reward: Evidence suggesting the involvement of a common dopaminergic system. *Behavioral Brain Research, 22*, 107–116.

Bradburn, N. M. (1963). Achievement and father dominance in Turkey. *Journal of Abnormal and Social Psychology, 67*, 464–468.

Bradley, D. R., & Petry, H. M. (1977). Organizational determinants of subjective contour: The subjective Necker cube. *American Journal of Psychology, 90*, 253–262.

Brand, R. J. (1978). Coronary-prone behavior as an independent risk factor for coronary heart disease. In T. M. Dembroski, S. M. Weiss, J. L. Shields, S. G. Haynes, & M. Feinleib (Eds.), *Coronary-prone behavior*. New York: Springer-Verlag.

Bransford, J. D., & Johnson, M. K. (1973). Considerations of some problems of comprehension. In W. G. Chase (Ed.), *Visual information processing*. New York: Academic Press.

Breggin, P. R. (1973). Psychosurgery (letter to the editor). *Journal of the American Medical Association, 226*, 1121.

Breland, K., & Breland, M. (1960). The misbehavior of organisms. *American Psychologist, 16*, 681–684.

Brett, D. J., & Cantor, J. (1988). The portrayal of men and women in U.S. television commercials: A recent content analysis and trends over 15 years. *Sex Roles, 18*, 595–609.

Breuer, J., & Freud, S. (1955). *Studies on hysteria* (J. Strachey, Ed. and trans.). London: Hogarth Press. (Originally published 1895)

Briggs, G. E. (1957). Retroactive inhibition as a function of the degree of original and interpolated learning. *Journal of Experimental Psychology, 53*, 60–67.

Brigham, T. C., & Malpass, R. S. (1985). The role of experience and context in the recognition of faces of own and other-race. *Journal of Social Issues, 41*, 139–155.

Brobeck, J. R., Tepperman, T., & Long, C. N. (1943). Experimental hypothalamic hyperphagia in the albino rat. *Yale Journal of Biology and Medicine, 15*, 831–853.

Brock, T. C. (1965). Communicator-recipient similarity and decision change. *Journal of Personality and Social Psychology, 1*, 650–654.

Bronfenbrenner, U. (1970). *Two worlds of childhood: U.S. and U.S.S.R.* New York: Russell Sage.

Bronson, G. (1974). The postnatal growth of visual capacity. *Child Development, 45*, 873–890.

Brooks-Gunn, J. (1986). Pubertal processes and girls' psychological adaptation. In R. M. Lerner & T. Foch (Eds.), *Biological-psychological interactions in early adolescence: A life-span perspective*. Hillsdale, NJ: Erlbaum.

Brooks-Gunn, J., & Furstenberg, F. F. (1989). Adolescent sexual behavior. *American Psychologist, 44,* 249-257.

Brothers, L. (1989). Empathy. *Harvard Mental Health Letter, 6,* 4-6.

Brown, R. (1965). *Social psychology.* New York: Free Press.

Brown, R. (1973). *A first language: The early stages.* Cambridge, MA: Harvard University Press.

Brown, R. (1986). *Social psychology* (2nd ed.). New York: Free Press.

Brown, R., & Kulik, J. (1982). Flashbulb memories. In U. Neisser (Ed.), *Memory observed.* San Francisco: Freeman.

Brown, R., & McNeill, D. (1966). The tip of the tongue phenomena. *Journal of Verbal Learning and Verbal Behavior, 5,* 325-327.

Bruner, J. S. (1983). *Child's talk.* New York: Norton.

Bryan, J. H., & Walbeck, N. H. (1970). Preaching and practicing self-sacrifice: Children's actions and reactions. *Child Development, 41,* 329-353.

Bucher, B., & Lovaas, O. I. (1968). Use of aversive stimulation in behavior modification. In M. R. Jones (Ed.), *Miami symposium on the prediction of behavior, 1967: Aversive stimulation.* Coral Gables, FL: University of Miami Press.

Buckout, R. (1975). Eyewitness testimony. *Scientific American, 231,* 23-31.

Budiansky, S. (1987, June 29). Taking the pain out of pain. *U.S. News and World Report,* pp. 50-57.

Buhler, C. (1972). The course of life as a psychological problem. In W. R. Looft (Ed.), *Developmental psychology: A book of readings.* New York: Holt, Rinehart & Winston.

Burch, P. R. J. (1979). Huntington's disease: Types, frequency, and progression. In T. N. Chase, N. S. Wexler, & A. Barbeau (Eds.), *Advances in neurology.* New York: Raven Press.

Bureau of the Census. (1982). *Statistical abstract of the United States, 1982-1983.* Washington, DC: U.S. Government Printing Office.

Burger, F. (1982, May 2). The 46-hour-a-week habit. *The Boston Globe.*

Burger, J. M., & Petty, R. E. (1981). The low-ball compliance technique: Task or person commitment? *Journal of Personality and Social Psychology, 40,* 492-500.

Burns, J. M. (1984). *Leadership.* New York: Harper & Row.

Burnstein, E. (1983). Persuasion as argument processing. In M. Brandstatter, J. H. Davis, & G. Stocker-Kreichgauer (Eds.), *Group decision processes.* London: Academic Press.

Buros, O. K. (Ed.). (1965). *The sixth mental measurement yearbook.* Highland Park, NJ: Gryphon Press.

Buss, A. H. (1966). *Psychopathology.* New York: Wiley.

Buss, D. M. (1985). Human mate selection. *American Scientist, 73,* 47-51.

Buss, D. M. (1989). Sex differences in human mate preferences: evolutionary hypotheses tested in 37 cultures. *Behavioral and Brain Sciences, 12,* 1-49.

Buss, D. M., & Barnes, M. (1986). Preferences in human mate selection. *Journal of Personality and Social Psychology, 50,* 559-570.

Butler, R. A. (1954). Incentive conditions which influence visual exploration. *Journal of Experimental Psychology, 48,* 19-23.

Butters, N., & Brody, B. A. (1968). The role of the left parietal lobe in the mediation of intra- and cross-modal associations. *Cortex, 4,* 328-343.

Butters, N., & Squire, L. (Eds.). (1984). *The neuropsychology of memory.* New York: Guilford Press.

Byrne, D. (1971). *The attraction paradigm.* New York: Academic Press.

Byrne, D. (1977). Social psychology and the study of sexual behavior. *Personality and Social Psychology Bulletin, 3,* 3-30.

Byrne, D., Clore, G. L., & Smeaton, G. (1986). The attraction hypothesis: Do similar attitudes affect anything? *Journal of Personality and Social Psychology, 51,* 1167-1170.

Cahill, & Akil, L. (1982). Plasma beta-endorphin-like immunoreactivity, self-reported pain perception and anxiety levels in women during pregnancy and labor. *Life Sciences, 31,* 1879-1882.

Califano, J. (1979). *Healthy people: The Surgeon General's report on health promotion and disease prevention.* Washington, DC: Government Printing Office.

Calne, S., Schoenberg, B., Martin, W., Vitt, R. J., Spencer, P., & Calne, D. B. (1987). Familial Parkinson's disease. *Canadian Journal of Neurological Science, 14,* 303-305.

Cameron, P., Frank, F., Lifter, M., & Morrissey, P. (1968). *Cognitive functionings of college students in a general psychology class.* Paper presented at a meeting of the American Psychological Association.

Campfield, L. A., Brandon, P., & Smith, F. J., (1985). On-line continuous measurement of blood glucose and meal pattern in free-feeding rats: The role of glucose in meal initiation. *Brain Research Bulletin, 14,* 605-617.

Campos, J. J., Bertenthal, B. I., & Caplovitz, K. (1982). The interrelationship of affect and cognition in the visual cliff situation. In C. Izard, J. Kagan, & R. Zajonc (Eds.), *Emotion and cognition.* New York: Plenum.

Campos, J. J., Langer, A., & Krowitz, A. (1970). Cardiac response on the visual cliff in prelocomotor human infants. *Science, 170,* 196-197.

Campos, J. J., Svedja, M., Bertenthal, B., Benson, N., & Schmid, D. (1981). *Self-produced locomotion and wariness of heights: New evidence from training studies.* Paper presented at the meeting of the Society for Research in Child Development, Boston, MA.

Cann, A., Sherman, S. J., & Elkes, R. (1975). Effects of initial request size and timing of a second request on compliance: The foot-in-the-door and the door-in-the-face. *Journal of Personality and Social Psychology, 32,* 774-782.

Cannon, T. D., Mednick, S. A., & Parnas, J. (1990). Antecedents of predominately negative and predominately positive-symptom schizophrenia in high-risk population. *Archives of General Psychiatry, 47,* 622-632.

Cannon, W. B. (1927). The James-Lange theory of emotions: A critical examination and an alternative theory. *American Journal of Psychology, 39,* 106-124.

Cannon, W. B. (1929). *Bodily changes in pain, hunger, fear, and rage* (2nd ed.). New York: Appleton-Century-Crofts.

Cannon, W. B., & Washburn, A. L. (1912). An explanation of hunger. *American Journal of Psychology, 29,* 441-454.

Caplan, G. (1981). Mastery of stress: Psychosocial aspects. *American Journal of Psychiatry, 138* (4), 413-420.

Caplan, P. J., MacPherson, G. M., & Tobin, P. (1985). Do sex-related differences in spatial abilities exist? *American Psychologist, 40,* 786-799.

Carli, L. (1990) Gender, language, and culture. *Journal of Personality and Social Psychology, 59,* 941-951.

Carr, D. B., Bullen, B. A., Skrinar, G. S., Arnold, M. A., Rosenblatt, M., Beitins, I. Z., Martin, J. B., & McArthur, J. W. (1981). Physical conditioning facilitates the exercise-induced secretion of beta-endorphin and betalipotropin. *The New England Journal of Medicine, 305,* 560-562.

Carroll, L. (1988). Concern with Aids and the sexual behavior of college students. *Journal of Marriage and the Family, 50,* 405-411.

Carson, R. C., Butcher, J. N., & Coleman, J. C. (1988). *Abnormal psychology and modern life* (8th ed.). Glenview, IL: Scott, Foresman.

Carter, H., & Glick, P. C. (1976). *Marriage and divorce.* Cambridge, MA: Harvard University Press.

Cartwright, R. D. (1978). *A primer on sleep and dreaming.* Reading, MA: Addison-Wesley.

Carver, C. S., Diamond, E. L., & Humphries, C. (1985). Coronary prone behavior. In Schneiderman, N. & Tapp, J. T. (Eds.). *Behavioral medicine: the biopsychosocial approach.* Hillsdale, N.J.: L. Erlbaum.

Casey, K. L. (1973). Pain: Current view of neural mechanisms. *American Scientist, 61,* 194-200.

Casler, L. (1967). Perceptual deprivation in institutional settings. In G. Newton & S. Levine (Eds.), *Early experience and behavior.* New York: Springer.

Cattell, R. B. (1949). *The culture free intelligence test.* Champaign, IL: Institute for Personality and Ability Testing.

Cattell, R. B. (1950). *Personality: A systematic, theoretical, and factual study.* New York: McGraw-Hill.

Cattell, R. B. (1965). *The scientific analysis of personality.* Baltimore: Penguin.

Cattell, R. B. (1966). *The scientific analysis of personality.* Chicago: Aldine.

Cattell, R. B. (1972). The 16 PF and basic personality structure: A reply to Eysenck. *Journal of Behavioral Science, 1,* 169-187.

Cattell, R. B. (1973). *Personality and mood by questionnaire.* San Francisco: Jossey-Bass.

Ceraso, J. (1967). The interference theory of forgetting. *Scientific American, 217,* 117-124.

Cernoch, J. M., & Porac, R. H. (1985). Recognition of maternal maxillary odors by infants. *Child Development, 56,* 1593-1598.

Chaiken, A. L., & Derlega, V. J. (1976). Self-disclosure. In J. W. Thibaut, J. T. Spence, & R. C. Carson (Eds.), *Contemporary topics in social psychology.* Morristown, NJ: General Learning Press.

Chang, T. M. (1986). Semantic memory: Facts and models. *Psychological Bulletin, 99,* 199-220.

Chapman, C. R., Wilson, M. E., & Gehrig, J. D. (1976). Comparative effects of acupuncture and transcutaneous stimulation of the perception of painful dental stimuli. *Pain, 2,* 265-283.

Chapman, L. J., & Chapman, J. P. (1973). *Disordered thought in schizophrenia.* Englewood Cliffs, NJ: Prentice-Hall.

Chaves, J. F., & Barber, T. X. (1974). Cognitive strategies, experimenter modeling, and expectation in the attenuation of pain. *Journal of Abnormal Psychology, 83* (4), 356-363.

Cherry, E. C. (1953). Some experiments on the recognition of speech with one and two ears. *Journal of the Acoustical Society of America, 25,* 975-979.

Chevalier-Skolnikoff, S. (1973). Facial expression of emotion in nonhuman primates. In P. Ekman (Ed.), *Darwin and facial expression.* New York: Academic Press.

Chi, M. T. H., & Glaser, R. (1985). Problem-solving ability. In R. J. Sternberg (Ed.), *Human abilities: An information processing approach.* New York: Freeman.

Chiesi, H. L., Spilich, G. J., & Voss, J. F. (1979). Acquisition of domain-related information in relation to high and low domain knowledge. *Journal of Verbal Learning and Verbal Behavior, 18,* 257-273.

Cho, A. K. (1990). Ice: A new dosage form of an old drug. *Science, 249,* 631-634.

Chomsky, N. (1968). *Language and mind.* New York: Harcourt, Brace & World.

Chomsky, N. (1975). *Reflections on language.* New York: Pantheon.

Chomsky, N. (1976). The fallacy of Richard Herrnstein's I.Q. In N. J. Block & G. Dworkin (Eds.), *The I.Q. controversy.* New York: Pantheon.

Christopher, F. S., & Cate, R. M. (1985). Premarital sexual pathways and relationship development. *Journal of Social and Personal Relationships, 2,* 271-288.

Cialdini, R. B. (1988). *Influence: Science and practice* (2nd ed.). Glenview, IL: Scott, Foresman.

Cialdini, R. B., Cacioppo, J. T., Bassett, R., & Miller, J. A. (1978). Low-ball procedure for producing compliance: Commitment then cost. *Journal of Personality and Social Psychology, 36,* 463-476.

Cialdini, R. B., Vincent, J. E., Lewis, S. K., Catalan, J., Wheeler, D., & Darby, B. L. (1975). A reciprocal concessions procedure for inducing compliance: The door-in-the-face technique. *Journal of Personality and Social Psychology, 21,* 206-215.

Clark, M. S. (1984). Record keeping in two kinds of relationships. *Journal of Personality and Social Psychology, 47,* 549-557.

Clarke, A. M., & Clarke, A. D. B. (1976). *Early experience: Myth and evidence.* New York: Free Press.

Clarke-Stewart, A., & Fein, G. (1983). Early childhood programs. In M. M. Haith & J. J. Campos (Eds.), *Handbook of child psychology. Vol. 2: Infancy and developmental psychology.* New York: Wiley.

Clarke-Stewart, K. A. (1978). And daddy makes three: The father's impact on the mother and the young child. *Child Development, 49,* 466-478.

Clarke-Stewart, K. A. (1989). Infant day care: Maligned or malignant? *American Psychologist, 44,* 266-273.

Cleland, C. C. (1978). *Mental retardation: A developmental approach.* Englewood Cliffs, NJ: Prentice-Hall.

Clement, U., Schmidt, G., & Kruse, M. (1984). Changes in sex differences in sexual behavior: a replication of a study in West German students (1966-81). *Archives of sexual behavior, 13,* 99-120.

Coe, W. C., & Sarbin, T. R. (1977). Hypnosis from the standpoint of a contextualist. *Annals of the New York Academy of Sciences, 296,* 2-13.

Cohen, D. B. (1979). *Sleep and dreaming: Origins, nature and functions.* Oxford: Pergamon Press.

Cohen, N. J., & Squire, L. (1980). Preserved learning and retention of pattern analyzing skill in amnesia: Dissociation of knowing how and knowing that. *Science, 210,* 207-210.

Cohen, S. (1990). Social support and physical illness. *Advances, 7,* 35-47.

Cohn, N. B., & Strassberg, D. S. (1983). Self-disclosure reciprocity among preadolescents. *Personality and Social Psychology Bulletin, 9,* 97-102.

Colby, A., Kohlberg, L., Gibbs, J., & Lieberman, M. (1983). A longitudinal study of moral development. *Monographs of the Society for Research in Child Development, 48* (Serial No. 200).

Colegrove, F. W. (1899). The day they heard about Lincoln. *American Journal of Psychology, 10,* 228-255.

Coleman, J. C. (1980). *The nature of adolescence.* London: Methuen.

Coleman, R. M. (1986). *Wide awake at 3:00 A.M.* New York: W. H. Freeman.

Collerton, D. Cholinergic function and intellectual decline in Alzheimer's disease. *Neuroscience, 19,* 1-28.

Collins, A. M., & Loftus, E. F. (1975). A spreading activation theory of semantic processing. *Psychological Review, 82,* 407-428.

Collins, A. M., & Quillian, M. R. (1969). Retrieval time from semantic memory. *Journal of Verbal Learning and Verbal Behavior, 8,* 240-247.

Committee on Children, Youth, and Families. (1983). Washington, DC: The White House.

Constantinople, A. (1969). An Eriksonian measure of personality development in college students. *Develop-mental Psychology, 1,* 357-372.

Cooper, J. R. (Ed.). (1978). *Sedative-hypnotic drugs: Risks and benefits* (DHEW Publication No. ADM 79-592). Washington, DC: Government Printing Office.

Cooper, J. R., Bloom, F. E., & Roth, R. H. (1987). *The biochemical basis of neuropharmacology* (5th ed.). New York: Oxford University Press.

Cooper, J., & Fazio, R. (1984). A new look at dissonance theory. In L. Berkowitz (Ed.), *Advances in experimental social psychology. Vol. 17.* Orlando, FL: Academic Press.

Cordua, G. D., McGraw, K. O., & Drabman, R. S. (1979). Doctor or nurse: Children's perception of sex typed occupations. *Child Development, 50,* 590-593.

Coren, S. (1969). Brightness contrast as a function of ground relation. *Journal of Experimental Psychology, 80,* 517-524.

Coren, S., & Girgus, J. (1978). *Seeing is deceiving: The psychology of visual illusions.* Hillsdale, NJ: Erlbaum.

Coren, S., & Ward, L. M. (1989). *Sensation and perception* (third edition). San Diego: Harcourt, Brace, & Jovanovich.

Corkin, S. (1982). Some relationships between global amnesias and the memory impairments in Alzheimer's disease. In S. Corkin, K. L. Davis, J. H. Growdon, E. Usdin, & R. J. Wurtman (Eds.), *Alzheimer's disease: A report of progress in research.* New York: Raven Press.

Corkin, S., Davis, K. L., Growdon, J. H., Usdin, E., & Wurtman, R. J. (1982). *Alzheimer's disease: A report of progress in research.* New York: Raven Press.

Cornell, E. H., & McDonnell, P. M. (1986). Infants' acuity at twenty feet. *Investigative Opthalmology and Visual Science, 27,* 1417-1420.

Corrigan, R. (1978). Language development as related to stage 6 object permanence development. *Journal of Child Language, 5,* 173-189.

Corso, J. F. (1977). Auditory perception and communication. In J. E. Birren & K. W. Schaie (Eds.), *Handbook of the psychology of aging.* New York: Van Nostrand Reinhold.

Corso, J. F. (1985). Communication, presbycusis, and technological aids. In H. K. Ulatowska (Ed.), *The aging brain: Communication in the elderly* (pp. 33-51). San Diego, CA: College Hill.

Costantini, E., & Craik, K. H. (1980). Personality and politicians: California party leaders, 1960-76. *Journal of Personality and Social Psychology, 38,* 641-661.

Costanzo, P. R. (1970). Conformity development as a function of self-blame. *Journal of Personality and Social Psychology, 14,* 366-374.

Costanzo, P. R., & Shaw, M. E. (1966). Conformity as a function of age level. *Child Development, 37,* 967-975.

Costello, C. G. (1976). *Anxiety and depression.* Montreal: McGill-Queens.

Cotman, C. W., & McGaugh, J. L. (1980). *Behavioral neuroscience.* New York: Academic Press.

Courchesne, C. E., Hesselink, J. R., Jerigan, T. L., & Yeung, C. R. (1987). Abnormal neurology in a non-retarded person with autism: Unusual findings with MRI. *Archives of neurology, 44,* 335-341.

Cowan, N. (1984). On short and long auditory stores. *Psychological Bulletin, 96,* 341-370.

Cowan, W. M. (1979). The development of the brain. *Scientific American, 241,* 112-133.

Cox, T. (1978). *Stress.* Baltimore: University Park.

Coyle, J. T., Price, D. L., & Delong, M. H. (1983). Alzheimer's disease: A disorder of central cholinergic innervation. *Science, 219,* 1184-1189.

Cozby, P. C. (1972). Self-disclosure, reciprocity and liking. *Sociometry, 35,* 151-160.

Cozby, P. C. (1973). Self-disclosure: A literature review. *Psychological Bulletin, 79,* 73-91.

Craighead, W. E. (1990). There's a place for us: All of us. *Behavior Therapy, 21,* 3-23.

Craik, F. I. M. (1977). Depth of processing in recall and recognition. In S. Dornic (Ed.), *Attention and performance. Vol. 6.* Hillsdale, NJ: Erlbaum.

Craik, F. I. M., & Tulving, E. (1975). Depth of processing and the retention of words in episodic memory. *Journal of Experimental Psychology: General, 104,* 268-294.

Cramer, P., & Mechem, M. B. (1982). Violence in children's animated television. *Journal of Applied Developmental Psychology, 3,* 23-29.

Crider, A. (1979). *Schizophrenia: A biopsychological perspective.* Hillsdale, NJ: Erlbaum.

Crites, J. (1969). *Vocational psychology.* New York: McGraw-Hill.

Crocker, J., Fiske, S. T., & Taylor, S. (1984). Schematic bases of belief change. In J. Richard Eiser (Ed.), *Attitudinal judgment.* New York: Springer-Verlag.

Crocker, J., Hannah, D. B., & Weber, R. (1983). Person memory and causal attributions. *Journal of Personality and Social Psychology, 44,* 55-66.

Crocker, J., Thompson, L. L., McGraw, K. M., & Ingerman, C. (1987). Downward comparison, prejudice, and evaluation of others: effects of self-esteem and threat. *Journal of Personality and Social Psychology, 52,* 907-916.

Crowe, R. R. (1984). Electroconvulsive therapy-a current perspective. *New England Journal of Medicine, 311,* 163-167.

Crow, T. J. (1980). Molecular pathology of schizophrenia: More than one disease process? *British Medical Journal, 280,* 1-9.

Crow, T. J. (1985).The two-syndrome concept: Origins and current status. *Schizophrenia Bulletin, 11,* 471-486.

Crowne, D. P., & Marlowe, D. (1964). *The approval motive.* New York: Wiley.

Croyle, R. T., & Cooper, J. (1983). Dissonance arousal: Physiological evidence. *Journal of Personality and Social Psychology, 45,* 782-791.

Crutcher, D. M. (1991). Family support in the home: home visiting and public law 99-457. *American Psychologist, 46,* 138-140.

Culliton, B. J. (1976). Psychosurgery: National commission issues surprisingly favorable report. *Science, 194,* 299-301.

❧

Dale, P. (1976). *Language development: Structure and function.* New York: Holt, Rinehart & Winston.

Dallenbach, K. M. (1927). The temperature spots and end organs. *American Journal of Psychology, 54,* 431-433.

Damasio, A. R., & Van Hoesin, G. W. (1983). Emotional disturbances associated with focal lesions of the limbic frontal lobe. In K. M. Heilman & P. Staz (Eds.), *Neuropsychology of human emotion* (pp. 85-110). New York: Guilford Press.

Darley, J. M., Fleming, J. H., Hilton, J. L., & Swan, W. B. (1988). Dispelling negative expectancies: the impact of interaction goals and target characteristics on the expectancy confirmation process. *Journal of Experimental Social Psychology, 44,* 19-36.

Darley, J. M., & Latané, B. (1968). Bystander intervention in emergencies: Diffusion of responsibility. *Journal of Personality and Social Psychology, 44,* 20-33.

Darwin, C. (1872). *The expression of emotion in man and animals.* New York: Philosophical Library.

Darwin, C. I., Turvey, M. I., & Crowder, R. G. (1972). An auditory analogue of the Sperling partial report procedure: Evidence for brief auditory storage. *Cognitive Psychology, 3,* 255-267.

Davidson, R. J. (1978). Specificity and patterning in biobehavioral systems. *American Psychologist, 33* (5), 430-436.

Davidson, R. J., & Schwartz, G. E. (1976). The psychobiology of relaxation and related states: A multiprocess theory. In D. I. Mostofsky (Ed.), *Behavior control and modification of physiological activity*. New York: Prentice-Hall.

Davis, A., & Eells, K. (1953). *Davis-Eells games.* Yonkers, NY: World Book.

Davis, W. L., & Phares, E. J. (1967). Internal-external control as a determinant of information-seeking in a social influence situation. *Journal of Personality, 35,* 547-561.

Deaux, K. (1972). To err is humanizing: But sex makes a difference. *Representative Research in Social Psychology, 3,* 20-28.

DeCastro, J. M., & DeCastro, E. S. (1989). Spontaneous meal patterns of humans: Influence of the presence of other people. *American Journal of Clinical Nutrition, 50,* 237-247.

Deci, E. L. (1975). *Intrinsic motivation.* New York: Plenum.

Deci, E. L., & Ryan, R. M. (1980). The empirical exploration of intrinsic motivational processes. *Advances in Experimental Social Psychology, 13,* 39-80.

De Jong, W. (1979). An examination of self-perception mediation of the foot-in-the-door effect. *Journal of Personality and Social Psychology, 37,* 2221-2239.

De Lacoste-Utamsing, C., & Holloway, R. L. (1982). Sexual dimorphism in the human corpus callosum. *Science, 216,* 1431-1432.

DeLisi, L. E., Hoff, A. L., Schwartz, J. E., Shields, G. W., Srinivas, N. H., Simhadri, M. G., Henn, F. A., & Anand, A. K. (1991). Brain morphology in first-episode schizophrenic-like psychotic patients: A quantitative magnetic resonance imaging study. *Biological Psychiatry, 29,* 159-175.

Delk, J. L., & Fillenbaum, S. (1965). Differences in perceived color as a function of characteristic color. *American Journal of Psychology, 78,* 290-293.

Delmonte, M. M. (1985). Meditation and anxiety reduction: A literature review. *Clinical Psychology Review, 5,* 91-102.

De Longis, A., Coyne, J. C., Dakof, G., Folkman, S., & Lazarus, R. S. (1982). Relations of daily hassles, uplifts, and major life events to health status. *Health Psychology, 1,* 119-136.

Dement, W. C. (1978). *Some must watch while some must sleep.* New York: W. W. Norton.

Denney, D. W. (1980). Task demands and problem-solving strategies in middle-age and older adults. *Journal of Gerontology, 35,* 559-564.

DeRivera, J. (1968). *The psychological dimension of foreign policy.* Columbus, OH: Merrill.

De Sota, C. B., O'Donnell, W. E., & De Soto, J. L. (1989). Long-term recovery in alcoholics. *Alcoholism: Clinical and Experimental Research, 13,* 693-697.

Deutsch, F. M. (1990). Status, sex, and smiling: the effect of role on smiling in men and women. *Personality and Social Psychology Bulletin, 16,* 531-540.

Deutsch, M. (Ed.). (1967). *The disadvantaged child.* New York: Basic Books.

Deutsch, M., & Gerard, H. (1955). A study of normative and informational influence upon individual judgment. *Journal of Abnormal and Social Psychology, 51,* 629-636.

Deutscher, I. (1968). Socialization to postparental life. In A. Rose (Ed.), *Human behavior and social processes.* Boston: Little, Brown.

DeValois, R. L. (1965). Behavioral and electrophysiological studies of primate vision. In W. D. Neff (Ed.), *Contributions to sensory physiology. Vol. 1.* New York: Academic Press.

DeValois, R. L., Albrecht, D. G., & Thorell, L. G. (1982). Spatial frequency selectivity in the macaque visual cortex. *Vision Research, 22,* 545-559.

DeValois, R. L., & DeValois, K. K. (1975). Neural coding of color. In E. C. Carterette & M. P. Friedman (Eds.), *Handbook of perception. Vol. 5.* New York: Academic Press.

de Villiers, J. G., & de Villiers, P. A. (1973). A crosssectional study of the acquisition of grammatical morphemes in child speech. *Journal of Psycholinguistic Research, 2,* 331-341.

de Villiers, J. G., & de Villiers, P. A. (1978). *Language acquisition.* Cambridge, MA: Harvard University Press.

Digman, J. M., & Inouye, J. (1986). Further specification of the five robust factors of personality. *Journal of Personality and Social Psychology Bulletin, 50,* 116-123.

Dilalla, L. F., Thompson, L. A., Plomin, R., Phillips, K., Fagan, J. F., Haith, M., Cyphers, L. H., & Fulker, D. W. (1990). Infant predictors of preschool and adult IQ: A study of infant twins and their parents. *Developmental Psychology, 26,* 759-769.

DiMatteo, M. R., & Friedman, H. S. (1984). *Social psychology and medicine.* Cambridge, MA: Oeigeschlager, Gunn, & Hain.

Disabilities and how to live with them. (1952). *Lancet,* pp. 79-83.

Dixon, N. F. (1981). *Preconscious processing.* Chichester: John Wiley.

Dobson, K. S. (1989). A meta-analysis of the efficacy of cognitive therapy for depression. *Journal of Consulting and Clinical Psychology, 57,* 414-419.

Dollard, J., Doob, L., Miller, N., Mowrer, O., & Sears, R. (1939). *Frustration and aggression.* New Haven, CT: Yale University Press.

Donnerstein, E., & Berkowitz, L. (1981). Victim reactions in aggressive erotic films as a factor in violence against women. *Journal of Personality and Social Psychology, 41,* 710-724.

Donnerstein, E., Linz, D., & Penrod, S. (1987). *The question of pornography: research findings and policy implications.* New York: Free Press.

Dosamantes-Alperson, E., & Merrill, N. (1980). Growth effects of experiential movement psychotherapy. *Psychotherapy: Theory, Research, and Practice, 17,* 63-68.

Doty, R. M., Peterson, B. E., & Winter, D. G. (1991) Threat and authoritarianism in the United States, 1978-1987. *Journal of Personality and Social Psychology, 61,* 629-640.

Douglas, J. W. B., & Ross, J. M. (1964). Age of puberty related to educational ability, attainment, and school leaving age. *Journal of Child Psychology and Psychiatry, 5,* 185-196.

Dourish, C. T., Rycroft, W., & Iverson, S. D. (1989). Postponement of satiety by blockade of cholecystokinein (CCK-B) receptors. *Science, 245,* 1509-1511.

Douvan, E., & Adelson, J. B. (1966). *The adolescent experience.* New York: Wiley.

Dovidio, J. F. (1984). Helping behavior and altruism: An empirical and conceptual overview. In L. Berkowitz (Ed.), *Advances in experimental social psychology. Vol. 17* (pp. 361-427). New York: Academic Press.

Dreyer, P. H. (1982). Sexuality in adolescence. In B. B. Wolman (Ed.), *Handbook of developmental psychology.* Englewood Cliffs, NJ: Prentice-Hall.

Drinkall, J., & Martin, E. G. (1980, August 4). The pot trade: U.S. marijuana output rivals Hawaiian sugar and California grapes. *Wall Street Journal,* pp. 1, 6.

DSM-III, 1980. See American Psychiatric Association, 1980.

DSM-III-R, 1987. See American Psychiatric Association, 1987.

DuBois, N. F. (1987, April). Training students to become autonomous learners. Paper presented at American Educational Research Association, Washington, D.C.

DuBois, N. F., Kiewra, K. A., & Fraley, J. (1988, April). Differential effects of a learning strategy course. Paper presented at American Educational Research Association, New Orleans, LA.

Duncker, K. (1939). The influence of past experience upon perceptual properties. *American Journal of Psychology, 52,* 255-265.

Duncker, K. (1945). On problem solving. *Psychological Monographs, 58* (5, Whole No. 270).

Dunphy, D. C. (1963). The social structure of urban adolescent peer groups. *Sociometry, 26,* 230-246.

Dutton, D. G., & Aron, A. P. (1974). Some evidence for heightened sexual attraction under conditions of high anxiety. *Journal of Personality and Social Psychology, 30,* 510-517.

Dywan, J., & Bowers, K. (1983). The use of hypnosis to enhance recall. *Science, 222,* 184-185.

Eagly, A. H. (1987). *Sex differences in social behavior: a social role interpretation.* Hillsdale, NJ: Erlbaum.

Eagly, A. H., & Karau, S. J. (1991). Gender and the emergence of leaders: a meta-analysis. *Journal of Personality and Social Psychology, 60,* 685-710.

Ebbinghaus, H. (1885). *Uber das Gedachtnis.* Leipzig: Dunker & Humboldt.

Eccles, J. C. (1973). The cerebellum as a computer: Patterns in space and time. *Journal of Physiology, 229,* 1-32.

Eccles, J. S. (1985). Sex differences in achievement patterns. In T. Sonderegger (Ed.), *Nebraska symposium on motivation: Psychology and gender.* Lincoln, NE: University of Nebraska Press.

Eckenrode, J. (1984). Impact of chronic and acute stressors on daily reports of mood. *Journal of Personality and Social Psychology, 46,* 907-918.

Edwards, B. (1979). *Drawing on the right of the brain.* Los Angeles, CA: J. P. Tarcher.

Edwards, C. P. (1982). Moral development in comparative cultural perspective. In D. A. Wagner & H. W. Stevens (Eds.), *Cultural perspectives on child development.* San Francisco, CA: Freeman.

Egan, D. E., & Greeno, J. G. (1974). Theory of rule induction: Knowledge acquired in concept learning, serial pattern learning, and problem solving. In L. W. Gregg (Ed.), *Knowledge and cognition.* Potomac, MD: Erlbaum.

Egan, J. P. (1975). *Signal detection theory and ROC analysis.* New York: Academic Press.

Egbert, L. D., Battit, G. E., Welch, C. E., & Bartlett, M. K. (1964). Reduction of postoperative pain by encouragement and instruction of patients. *The New England Journal of Medicine, 270,* 825-827.

Ehrlich, I. (1975). The deterrent effects of capital punishment. *American Economic Review, 65,* 397-417.

Eibl-Eibesfeldt, I. (1975). *Ethology: The biology of behavior.* New York: Holt, Rinehart & Winston.

Eibl-Eibesfeldt, I. (1989). *Human ethology.* Hawthorne, NY: Aldine de Gruyter.

Eisenberg, N., & Lennon, R. (1983). Sex differences in empathy and related capacities. *Psychological Bulletin, 94,* 100-131.

Eiser, J. R. (Ed.). (1984). *Attitudinal judgment.* New York: Springer-Verlag.

Ekman, P. (1973). Cross-cultural studies of facial expression. In P. Ekman (Ed.), *Darwin and facial expression.* New York: Academic Press.

Ekman, P., & Friesen, W. V. (1971). Constants across cultures in the face and emotion. *Journal of Personality and Social Psychology, 17* (2), 124-129.

Ekman, P., Levenson, R. W., & Friesen, W. V. (1983). Autonomic nervous system activity distinguishes among emotions. *Science, 221,* 1208-1210.

Ekstrom, R. B., French, J. W., Harmon, H. H., & Derman, D. (1976). *Manual for kit of factor-referenced cognitive tests.* Princeton, NJ: Educational Testing Service.

Elkin, I., Shea, T., Watkins, J. T., et al. (1989). National Institute of Mental Health treatment of depression collaborative research program: General effectiveness of treatments. *Archives of General Psychiatry, 46,* 971-982.

Ellis, L., Ames, M. A., Peckham, W., & Burke, D. (1988). Sexual orientation of human offspring may be altered by severe maternal stress during pregnancy. *Journal of Sex Research, 25,* 152-157.

Ellis, A., & Harper, R. A. (1975). *A new guide to rational living.* Englewood Cliffs, NJ: Prentice-Hall.

Emery, R. E. (1989). Family violence, special issue: children and their development: knowledge base, research agenda, and social policy application. *American Psychologist, 44,* 321-328.

Endler, N. S., & Hunt, J. McV. (1969). Generalizability of contributions from sources of variance in the S-R inventories of anxiousness. *Journal of Personality, 37,* 1-24.

Endler, N. S., & Rosenstein, A. J. (1962). An S-R inventory of anxiousness. *Psychological Monographs,* Whole No. 536.

Endler, N. S. & Persad, E. (1988). *Electroconvulsive therapy: The myths and the realities.* Toronto: Hans Huber Publishers.

Endler, N. S. (1989). *Holiday of darkness: A psychologist's personal journey out of his depression.* Toronto: Wall & Thompson.

Engel, G. L. (1971). Sudden and rapid death during psychological stress. *Annals of Internal Medicine, 74,* 771-782.

Engel, J., Jr. (1983). Functional localization of epileptogenic lesions. *Trends in the Neurosciences, 63,* 60-65.

Erdelyi, M. H., & Goldberg, B. (1979). Let's not sweep repression under the rug: Toward a cognitive psychology of repression. In J. F. Kihlstrom & F. J. Evans (Eds.), *Functional disorders of memory.* Hillsdale, NJ: Erlbaum.

Ericsson, K. A., & Polson, P. G. (1985). Memory for restaurant orders. In M. T. T. Chi, R. Glaser, & M. J. Farr (Eds.), *The nature of expertise.* Columbus, OH: National Center for Research in Vocational Education.

Erikson, E. (1963). *Childhood and society.* New York: Norton.

Erikson, K. (1976). *Everything in its path: Destruction of community in the Buffalo Creek flood.* New York: Simon & Schuster.

Erikson, R. P., & Covey, E. (1980). On the singularity of taste sensations: What is a taste primary? *Physiology and Behavior, 25,* 527-533.

Eron, L. D., & Huesmann, L. R. (1984). The control of aggressive behavior by changes in attitude, values, and the conditions of learning. In R. J. Blanchard & C. Blanchard (Eds.), *Advances in the study of aggression. Vol. 1.* Orlando, FL: Academic Press.

Eron, L. D., & Huesmann, L. R. (1985). The role of television in the development of prosocial and antisocial behavior. In D. Olweus, M. Radke-Yarrow, & J. Block (Eds.), *Development of antisocial and prosocial behavior.* Orlando, FL: Academic Press.

Evans, R. B. (1969). Childhood parental relationships of homosexual men. *Journal of Consulting and Clinical Psychology, 33,* 129-135.

Evarts, E. V. (1972). Contrasts between activity of precentral and postcentral neurons of cerebral cortex during movement in the monkey. *Brain Research, 40,* 25-31.

Evarts, E. V. (1979). Brain mechanisms of movement. In *The brain.* San Francisco: Freeman.

Exner, J. E. (1974). *The Rorschach: A comprehensive system.* San Francisco: Freeman.

Eysenck, H. J. (1953). *The structure of human personality.* New York: Wiley.

Eysenck, H. J. (1964). Principles and methods of personality description, etc.: Eysenck on extraversion. *The British Journal of Psychology, 55,* 284-294.

Eysenck, H. J. & Eysenck, M. W. (1985). *Personality and individual differences.* New York: Plenum.

Fallon, A. E., & Rozin, P. (1985). Sex differences in perceptions of desirable body shape. *Journal of Abnormal Psychology, 94,* 102-105.

Fantino, E. (1973). Aversive control. In *The study of behavior: Learning, motivation, emotion, and instinct.* Glenview, IL: Scott, Foresman.

Fantz, R. L. (1963). Pattern vision in newborn infants. *Science, 140,* 296-297.

Farina, A. (1976). *Abnormal psychology.* Englewood Cliffs, NJ: Prentice-Hall.

Fay, R. E., Turner, C. F., Klassen, A. D., & Gagnon, J. H. (1989). Prevalence and patterns of same-gender sexual contact among men. *Science, 243,* 338-348.

Fazio, R. H., Lenn, T. M., & Effrein, E. A. (1984). Spontaneous attitude formation. *Social Cognition, 2,* 217-234.

Fechner, G. T. (1860). *Elemente de psychophysik. Vol. 1* (H. E. Adler, D. H. Howes, & E. G. Borwg, Eds. and Trans.). Leipzig: Breitkopf and Hartel. New York: Holt, Rinehart & Winston.

Feder, H. H. (1984). Hormones and sexual behavior. *Annual Review of Psychology, 35,* 165-200.

Feingold, A. (1988). Cognitive gender differences are disappearing. *American Psychologist, 43,* 95-103.

Feingold, A. (1990). Gender differences in effects of physical attractiveness on romantic attraction: a comparison across five research paradigms. *Journal of Personality and Social Psychology, 59,* 981-993.

Feldman, M. W., & Lewonton, R. C. (1975). The heritability hang-up. *Science, 190,* 1163-1168.

Feldman, R. S., & Quenzer, L. F. (1984). *Fundamentals of neuropharmacology.* Sunderland, MA: Sinauer Associates.

Fenichel, O. (1945). *The psychoanalytic theory of neurosis.* New York: Norton.

Fenz, W. D., & Epstein, S. (1967). Gradients of physiological arousal in parachutists as a function of an approaching jump. *Psychosomatic Medicine, 29,* 33-50.

Festinger, L. (1957). *A theory of cognitive dissonance.* New York: Harper & Row.

Festinger, L., & Maccoby, N. (1964). On resistance to persuasive communications. *Journal of Abnormal and Social Psychology, 68,* 359-366.

Festinger, L., Schachter, S., & Back, K. (1950). *Social pressures in informal groups: A study of a housing community.* Stanford, CA: Stanford University Press.

Fiedler, F. E. (1964). A contingency model of leadership effectiveness. In L. Berkowitz (Ed.), *Advances in experimental social psychology.* New York: Academic Press.

Fieldler, F. E. (1978). Recent developments in research on the contingency model. In L. Berkowitz (Ed.), *Group processes.* New York: Academic Press.

Fieve, R. R. (1975). *Moodswing: The third revolution in psychiatry.* New York: Morrow.

Fischer, K. W. (1983). Illuminating the process of moral development: Commentary of Colby et al., a longitudinal study of moral development. *Monographs of the Society for Research in Child Development, 48* (Serial No. 200).

Fischer, K., Schoeneman, T. L., & Rubanowitz, D. E. (1987). Attributions in advice columns. II. The dimensionality of actors' and observers' explanations for inter-

personal problems. *Personality and Social Psychology Bulletin, 13,* 458-466.

Fisher, S., & Greenberg, R. P. (1977). *The scientific credibility of Freud's theories and therapy.* New York: Basic Books.

Fisher, W. A., & Byrne, D. (1978). Individual differences in affective, evaluative, and behavioral responses to an erotic film. *Journal of Applied Social Psychology, 8,* 355-365.

Fisher, W. A., & Byrne, D. (1978). Sex differences in response to erotica: Love versus lust. *Journal of Personality and Social Psychology, 36,* 119-125.

Fishman, S. M., & Sheehan, D. V. (1985 April). Anxiety and panic: Their cause and treatment. *Psychology Today,* pp. 26-32.

Fisk, A. D., & Schneider, W. (1984). Memory as a function of attention, level of processing, and automatization. *Journal of Experimental Psychology; Learning, Memory, and Cognition, 10,* 181-197.

Fiske, S. T., & Taylor, S. E. (1984). *Social cognition.* Reading, MA: Addison-Wesley.

Fiske, S. T., & Taylor, S. E. (1991). *Social cognition.* New York: McGraw-Hill.

Flavell, J. (1985). *Cognitive development.* Englewood Cliffs, NJ. Prentice Hall.

Flavell, J. H., Beach, D. H., & Chinsky, J. M. (1966). Spontaneous verbal rehearsal in a memory task as a function of age. *Child Development, 37,* 283-299.

Flavell, J. H., & Wellman, H. M. (1976). Metamemory. In R. V. Kail & J. W. Hagen (Eds.), *Memory in cognitive development.* Hillsdale, NJ: Erlbaum.

Fletcher, H., & Munson, W. A. (1933). Loudness: Its definition, measurement, and calculation. *Journal of the Acoustical Society of America, 5,* 82-102.

Folkes, V. S. (1982). Communicating the reasons for social rejection. *Journal of Experimental Social Psychology, 18,* 235-252.

Forbes, H. A. (1988). *Nationalism, ethnocentrism and personality.* Chicago: University of Chicago Press.

Ford, M. R., Stroebel, C. F., Strong, P., & Szarek, B. L. (1983). Quieting response training: Long-term evaluation of a clinical biofeedback practice. *Biofeedback and Self-Regulation, 8,* 265-278.

Foucault, M. (1965). *Madness and civilization.* New York: Random House.

Foulkes, D. (1985). *Dreaming: A Cognitive-psychological analysis.* Hillsdale, NJ: Erlbaum.

Fouts, R. S. (1973). Acquisition and testing of gestural signs in four young chimpanzees. *Science, 180,* 978-980.

Fouts, R. S., Hirsch, A. D., & Fouts, D. H. (1982). Cultural transmission of human language in a chimpanzee mother/infant relationship. In H. E. Fitzgerald, J. A. Mullins, & P. Page (Eds.), *Psychological perspectives: Child nurturance series. Vol. 4.* New York: Plenum.

Fowles, D. C. (1988). Psychophysiology and psychopathology: A motivational approach. *Psychophysiology, 25,* 373-391.

Fox, G. L. (1981). The family's role in adolescent sexual behavior. In T. Ooms (Ed.), *Teenage pregnancy in a family context: Implications for policy.* Philadelphia: Temple University Press.

Fox, J. L. (1983). Debate on learning theory is shifting. *Science, 222,* 1219-1222.

Frank, J. D. (1973). *Persuasion and healing: A comparative study of psychotherapy* (rev. ed.). New York: Schocken.

Frankenburg, W. K., & Dodds, J. B. (1967). The Denver developmental screening test. *Journal of Pediatrics, 71,* 181-191.

Fraser, S., Gouge, C., & Billig, M. (1971). Risky shifts, cautious shifts, and group polarization. *European Journal of Social Psychology, 1,* 7-29.

Freed, W. F., de Mendinaceli, L., & Wyatt, R. J. (1985).

Promoting functional plasticity in the damaged nervous system. *Science, 227,* 1544–1552.

Freedman, J. (1965). Long-term behavioral effects of cognitive dissonance. *Journal of Experimental Social Psychology, 1,* 145–155.

Freedman, J. (1984). Effect of television violence on aggressiveness. *Psychological Bulletin, 96,* 227–246.

Freedman, J. L. (1986) Television violence and aggression: a rejoinder. *Psychological Bulletin, 100,* 372–378.

Freedman, J. L., & Fraser, S. C. (1966). Compliance without pressure: The foot-in-the-door technique. *Journal of Personality and Social Psychology, 4,* 195–202.

Freud, S. (1950). Mourning and melancholia. In J. Strachey (Ed. and Trans.), *The standard edition of the complete works of Sigmund Freud. Vol. 4.* London: Hogarth Press. (Original work published 1917).

Freud, S. (1953). *A general introduction to psychoanalysis.* New York: Permabooks.

Freud, S. (1953). The interpretation of dreams. In J. Strachey (Ed. and Trans.), *The standard edition of the complete works of Sigmund Freud. Vols. 4 and 5.* London: Hogarth Press. (Original work published 1900).

Freud, S. (1955). Analysis of a phobia in a five-year-old boy (J. Strachey, Ed. and Trans.). London: Hogarth Press. (Original work published 1909).

Freud, S. (1957). Three essays on the theory of sexuality. In J. Strachey (Ed. and Trans.), *The standard edition of the complete works of Sigmund Freud, Vol. 7.* London: Hogarth Press. (Original work published 1905).

Freud, S. (1961). Civilization and its discontents. In J. Strachey (Ed. and Trans.), *The standard edition of the complete works of Sigmund Freud. Vol. 21.* London: Hogarth Press. (Original work published 1930).

Freud, S. (1964). New introductory lectures on psychoanalysis. In J. Strachey (Ed. and Trans.), *The standard edition of the complete works of Sigmund Freud. Vol. 22.* London: Hogarth Press. (Original work published 1933).

Freud, S. (1964). An outline of psychoanalysis. In J. Strachey (Ed. and Trans.), *The standard edition of the complete works of Sigmund Freud. Vol. 23.* London: Hogarth Press. (Original work published 1940).

Fried, P. A., & Watkinson, M. A. (1990). 36- and 48-month neurobehavioral follow-up of children prenatally exposed to marijuana, cigarettes, and alcohol. *Developmental and Behavioral Pediatrics, 11,* 49–58.

Friedman, M. D., & Rosenman, R. H. (1974). *Type A behavior and your heart.* New York: Knopf.

Friedman, M. I., & Stricker, E. M. (1976). The physiological psychology of hunger: A physiological perspective. *Physiological Review, 83,* 409–431.

Frietsch, G., & Hitzig, E. (1870). Veber die elektrische errebarkeit des grosshiens. *Archiv Anatomie, Physiologie und Wissenschaftliche, 37,* 308–332.

Frieze, I. H., Parsons, J. E., Johnson, P. B., Ruble, D. N., & Zellman, G. L. (1978). *Women and sex roles: A social psychological perspective.* New York: Norton.

Frolich, A. (1902). Dr. Alfred Frolich stellt einen Fall von Tumor der Hypophyse ohme Akromegalie vor. *Wierner Klinische Rundschau, 15,* 883.

Fromm, E. (1941). *Escape from freedom.* New York: Rinehart.

Fromm, E. (1956). *The art of loving.* New York: Harper & Row.

Frone, M. R., Adams, J., Rice, R. W., & Instone-Noonan, D. (1987) Halo error: a field study of comparison of self- and subordinate evaluations of leadership process and leader effectiveness. *Personality and Social Psychology Bulletin, 12,* 454–461.

Fuchs, V. R. (1986). Sex differences in economic well being. *Science, 232,* 459–464.

Fuller, G. D. (1977). *Biofeedback: Methods and procedures in clinical practice.* San Francisco: Biofeedback Press.

Furman, W., Rahe, D., & Hartup, W. W. (1979). Rehabilitation of socially withdrawn preschool children through mixed-age and same-age socialization. *Child Development, 50,* 915–922.

Furrow, D., Nelson, K., & Benedict, H. (1979). Mothers' speech to children and syntactic development: Some simple relationships. *Journal of Child Language, 6,* 423–442.

Furstenberg, F. F., Brooks-Gunn, J. B., & Chase-Lindsdale, (1989). Teenaged pregnancy and childbearing. *American Psychologist, 44,* 313–320.

❦

Gaither, N. S., & Stein, B. E. (1979). Reptiles and mammals use similar sensory organizations in the midbrain. *Science, 205,* 595–597.

Galanter, E. (1962). Contemporary psychophysics. In R. Brown, E. Galanter, H. Hess, & G. Mandler (Eds.), *New directions in psychology.* New York: Holt.

Gallatin, J. (1980). Political thinking in adolescence. In J. Adelson (Ed.), *Handbook of adolescent psychology,* New York: Wiley.

Garcia, J. (1984). Evolution of learning mechanisms. In B. L. Hammond (Ed.), *Psychology and learning.* Washington, DC: APA.

Garcia, J., Brett, L. P., & Rusiniak, K. W. (1989). Limits of darwinian conditioning. In S. B. Klein & R. R. Mowrer (eds.) *Contemporary learning theories.* Hillsdale, N.J.: Erlbaum, 181–204.

Garcia, J., McGowan, G. K., & Green, K. F. (1972). Biological constraints on conditioning. In A. H. Black & W. F. Prokasy (Eds.), *Classical conditions. II. Current research and theory.* New York: Appleton-Century-Crofts.

Garcia, S., Stinson, L., Ickes, W., & Bissonnette, V. (1991). Shyness and physical attractiveness in mixed-sex dyads. *Journal of Personality and Social Psychology, 61,* 35–49.

Gardner, H. (1983). *Frames of mind: A theory of multiple intelligences.* New York: Basic Books.

Gardner, H. (1985). *The mind's new science.* New York: Basic Books.

Gardner, R. A., & Gardner, B. T. (1969). Teaching sign language to a chimpanzee. *Science, 165,* 664–672.

Gardner, R. A., & Gardner, B. T. (1977). Comparative psychology and language acquisition. In K. Salzinger & R. Denmark (Eds.), *Psychology: The state of the art. Annals of the New York Academy of Sciences.*

Gardner, W., Millstein, S. G., & Wilcox, B. (1991). *Adolescents in the Aids epidemic: New directions for child development.* San Francisco: Jossey-Bass.

Garn, S. M. (1975). Bone loss and aging. In R. Goldman & M. Rockstein (Eds.), *The physiology and pathology of human aging.* New York: Academic Press.

Garner, D., Garfinkel, P., Schwartz, D., & Thompson, M. (1980). Cultural expectations of thinness in women. *Psychological Reports, 47,* 483–491.

Garner, W. R. (Ed.). (1982). *Ability testing: Uses, consequences, and controversies.* Report of the National Academy of Sciences.

Gawin, F. H. (1991). Cocaine addiction: Psychology and neuropsychology. *Science, 251,* 1580–1586.

Gazzaniga, M. S. (1970). *The bisected brain.* New York: Appleton-Century-Crofts.

Gazzaniga, M. S., & LeDoux, J. E. (1978). *The integrated mind.* New York: Plenum.

Geen, R. G., & Berkowitz, L. (1967). Some conditions facilitating the occurrence of aggression after the observation of violence. *Journal of Personality, 35,* 666–676.

Geiselman, R., & Padilla, J. (1988) Cognitive interviewing with child witnesses. *Journal of Police Science and Administration, 16*, 236-242.

Geldard, F. A. (1972). *The human senses* (2nd ed.). New York: Wiley.

Geller, J. L., Fisher, W. H., Simon, L. J. & Wirth-Cauchon J. L. (1990). Second-generation deinstitutionalization, II: The impact of Brewster v. Dukakis on correlates of community and hospital utilization. *American Journal of Psychiatry, 147*, 988-933.

Gelman, D. (1978, May 15). Families on the couch. *Newsweek*, pp. 80-84.

Gelman, R. (1969). Conservation acquisition: A problem of learning to attend to relevant attributes. *Journal of Experimental Child Psychology, 7*, 167-187.

Gelman, R. (1978). Accessing one-to-one correspondence: Still another paper on conservation. *British Journal of Psychology, 73*, 209-220.

Gelman, R. (1982). Basic numeric abilities. In R. J. Sternberg (Ed.), *Advances in the psychology of human intelligence: Vol. 1*. Hillsdale, NJ: Erlbaum.

Gelman, R., & Baillargeon, R. (1983). A review of Piagetian concepts. In J. H. Flavell & E. M. Markman (Eds.), *Handbook of child psychology. Vol. 3: Cognitive development*. New York: Wiley.

Gentry, W. D. (1970). Effects of frustration, attack, and prior aggressive training on overt aggression and vascular processes. *Journal of Personality and Social Psychology, 16*, 718-725.

Gerard, H. B., & Orive, R. (1987). The dynamics of opinion formation. In L. Berkowitz (Ed.), *Advances in experimental social psychology. Vol. 20*. New York: Academic Press.

Gergen, K. J., & Marlowe, D. (1970). *Personality and social behavior*. London: Addison-Wesley.

Germond, J., & Witcover, J. (1989). *Whose broad stripes and bright stars?: the trivial pursuit of the presidency, 1988*. New York: Warner Books.

Gerrard, M. (1987). Sex, sex guilt, and contraceptive use revisited: the 1980's. *Journal of Personality and Social Psychology, 52*, 975-980.

Gershon, E. S., Bunney, W. E., Jr., Leckman, J. F., Van Eerdewegh, M., & De Bauche, B. A. (1976). The inheritance of affective disorders: A review of data and of hypotheses. *Behavior Genetics, 5* (3), 227-261.

Geschwind, N. (1970). The organization of language and the brain. *Science, 170*, 940-944.

Geschwind, N. (1979). Specializations of the human brain. In *The brain*. San Francisco: Freeman.

Getchell, T. V., & Getchell, M. L. (1987). Peripheral mechanisms of olfaction: Biochemistry and neurophysiology. In T. E. Finger & W. L. Silver (Eds.). *Neurobiology of taste and smell*. New York: Wiley 91-124.

Ghanta, V. K., Hiramoto, R. N., Salvason, H. B., & Spector, N. H. (1985). Neural and environmental influences on neoplasia and conditioning of NK activity. *Journal of Immunology, 135*, 848-852.

Gibb, C. A. (1969). Leadership. In G. Lindzey & E. Aronson (Eds.), *Handbook of social psychology. Vol. 4* (2nd ed.). Reading, MA: Addison-Wesley.

Gibbons, B. (1986). The inate sense of smell. *National Geographic 170*, 324-361.

Gibson, E. J., & Walk, R. D. (1960). The "visual cliff." *Scientific American, 202*, 64-71.

Gibson, J. J. (1966). *The senses considered as a perceptual system*. Boston: Houghton Mifflin.

Gilberstadt, H., & Duker, J. A. (1965). *A handbook for clinical and actuarial MMPI interpretation*. Philadelphia: Saunders.

Gilbert, D. T., Pelham, B. W., & Krull, D. S. (1988). On cognitive busyness: when person perceivers meet self-regulation of behavior. *Journal of Personality and Social Psychology, 54*, 733-740.

Gilbert, A. N., & Wysocki, C. J. (1987, October). The smell survey results. *National Geographic*, pp. 514-525.

Gilbert, D. T., & Jones, E. E. (1986). Perceiver-induced constraint: Interpretations of self-generated reality. *Journal of Personality and Social Psychology*.

Gilbert, J. H. V. (1982). Babbling and the deaf child: A commentary on Lenneberg et al. (1964) and Lenneberg (1967). *Journal of Child Language, 9*, 511-515.

Gilbert, S. J. (1981). Another look at the Milgram obedience studies: The role of the gradated series of shocks. *Personality and Social Psychology Bulletin, 7*, 690-695.

Gilligan, C. (1982). *In a different voice*. Cambridge, MA: Harvard University Press.

Gilligan, C., & Belenky, M. (1980). A naturalistic study of abortion decisions. In R. Selman & R. Yando (Eds.), *Clinical developmental psychology*. San Francisco: Jossey-Bass.

Gilling, D., & Brightwell, R. (1982). *The human brain*. New York: Facts on File.

Ginsburg., B. E. (1971). Developmental behavioral genetics. In N. B. Talbot, J. Kagan, & L. Eisenberg, *Behavioral science in pediatric medicine*. Philadelphia: Saunders.

Gintzler, A. R. (1980). Endorphin-mediated increase in pain threshold during pregnancy. *Science, 210*, 193-195.

Girdano, D., & Everly, G. (1979). *Controlling stress and tension: A holistic approach*. Englewood Cliffs, NJ: Prentice-Hall.

Gladue, B. A., Green, R., & Hellman, R. E. (1984). Neuroendocrine response to estrogen and sexual orientation. *Science, 225*, 1496-1499.

Glass, A. L., Holyoak, K. J., & Santa, J. L. (1979). *Cognition*. Reading, MA: Addison-Wesley.

Glass, D. C. (1977). *Behavior patterns, stress, and coronary disease*. Hillsdale, NJ: Erlbaum.

Glass, D. C., & Singer, J. (1972). *Urban stress*. New York: Academic Press.

Goethals, G. R., & Darley, J. M. (1987). Social comparison theory: self-evaluation and group life. In B. Mullen & G. R. Goethals (Eds.), *Theories of group behavior*. New York: Springer-Verlag.

Goethals, G. R., Messick, D. M., & Allison, S. T. (1991). The uniqueness bias: studies of constructive social comparison. In J. Suls & T. A. Wills (Eds.), *Social comparison: contemporary theory and research*. Hillsdale, NJ: Erlbaum.

Goethals, G. R., & Reckman, R. F. (1973). Recalling previously held attitudes. *Journal of Experimental Social Psychology, 9*, 491-501.

Goethals, G. R., & Solomon, P. R. (1988). Interdisciplinary perspectives on the study of memory. In P. R. Solomon, G. R. Goethals, C. M. Kelley, & B. Stephens (Eds.), *Memory: Interdisciplinary approaches*. New York: Springer-Verlag.

Goethals, G. R., & Zanna, M. P. (1979). The role of social comparison in choice shifts. *Journal of Personality and Social Psychology, 37*, 1179-1185.

Gold, P. E. (1987). Sweet memories. *American Scientist, 75*, 151-155.

Gold, P. E., & Stone, W. S. (1988). Neuroendocrine effects on memory in aged rodents and humans. *Neurobiology of Aging 9*, 709-718.

Gold, P. E., Vogt, J., & Hall, L. J. (1986). Posttraining glucose effects on memory: Behavioral and pharmacological characteristics. *Behavioral and Neural Biology, 46*, 145-155.

Gold, R. (1978). On the meaning of nonconservation. In A. M. Lesgold, J. W. Pellegrino, S. D. Fokkema, & R. Glasser (Eds.), *Cognitive psychology and instruction*. New York: Plenum.

Goldberg, L. R. (1990). An alternative "description of personality": the big-five factor structure. *Journal of Personality and Social Psychology, 59*, 1216-1229.

Goldstein, A. (1978). Opiate receptors and opiod peptides: A ten year overview. In M. A. Lipton, A. DiMascio, & K. F. Killam (Eds.), *Psychopharmacology: A generation of progress.* New York: Raven Press.

Goldstein, E. B. (1984). *Sensation and perception* (2nd ed.). Belmont, CA: Wadsworth.

Goldstein, R. L. (1987). Litigious paranoids and the legal system: The role of the forensic psychiatrist. *Journal of Forensic Sciences, 32,* 1009-1015.

Goleman, D. (1987, November 24). Teenage risk-taking: Rise in death prompts new research effort. *New York Times.*

Gonzales, M. H., Pederson, J. H., Manning, D. J., & Wetter, D. W. (1990). Pardon my gaffe: effects of sex, status, and consequence severity on accounts. *Journal of Personality and Social Psychology, 58,* 610-621.

Gonzalez, M. F., & Deutsch, J. A. (1981). Vagotomy abolishes cues of satiety produced by gastric distension. *Science, 212,* 1283-1284.

Goode, E., & Haber, L. (1977). Sexual correlates of homosexual experience: An exploratory study of college women. *Journal of Sex Research, 13,* 12-21.

Goodglass, H., & Kaplan, E. (1983). *Assessment of aphasia and related disorders* (2nd ed.). Philadelphia: Lean & Fibiger.

Goodstein, L. D., & Calhoun, J. F. (1982). *Understanding abnormal behavior.* Reading, MA: Addison-Wesley.

Goodwin, C. J. (1991). Misportraying Pavlov's apparatus. *American Journal of Psychology, 104,* 135-141.

Goodwin, D. W., & Guze, S. B. (1979). *Psychiatric diagnosis* (2nd ed.). New York: Oxford.

Goodwin, F. K. (1982). *Depression and manic-depressive illness.* Washington, DC: Government Printing Office.

Gordun, S., & Gilgun, J. F. (1987). Adolescent sexuality. In V. B. Van Hasselt & M. Hersen (Eds.), *Handbook of adolescent psychology.* New York: Pergamon Press.

Gorsuch, R. L. (1980). Interactive models of non-medical drug use. In D. J. Letteri, M. Sayers, & H. W. Pearson, *Theories on drug abuse: Selected contemporary perspectives* (NIDA Monograph No. 30, DHHS Publication No. ADM 80-967). Washington, DC: Government Printing Office.

Gottesman, I. (1963). Genetic aspects of intelligent behavior. In N. Ellis (Ed.), *Handbook of mental deficiency.* New York: McGraw-Hill.

Gottesman, I. I., & Shields, J. (1972). *Schizophrenia and genetics: A twin study vantage point.* New York: Academic Press.

Gottesman, I. I., & Shields, J. (1982). *Schizophrenia: The epigenetic puzzle.* Cambridge: Cambridge University Press.

Gottlieb, G. (1970). Conceptions of prenatal behavior. In L. R. Aronson, E. Toback, D. S. Lehrman, & J. S. Rosenblatt (Eds.), *Development and evolution of behavior: Essays in memory of T. C. Schneirla.* San Francisco: Freeman.

Gottlieb, G. (1975). Development of species identification in ducklings. III. Maturational rectification of perceptual deficit caused by auditory deprivation. *Journal of Comparative and Physiological Psychology, 89,* 899-912.

Goy, R. W. (1968). Organizing effect of androgen on the behavior of rhesus monkeys. In R. P. Michael (Ed.), *Endocrinology of human behavior.* London: Oxford University Press.

Goy, R. W., & Goldfoot, D. A. (1973). Hormonal influences on sexually dimorphic behavior. In R. O. Green (Ed.), *Handbook of physiology* (Section 7, Vol. 2, Part 1). Washington, DC: American Physiological Society.

Graham, D. T. (1962). Some research on psychophysiologic specificity and its relation to psychosomatic disease. In R. Roessler & N. Greenfield (Eds.), *Physiological correlates of psychological disorder.* Madison: University of Wisconsin Press.

Graham, D. T. (1972). Psychosomatic medicine. In N. S. Greenfield & R. A. Sternbach (Eds.), *Handbook of psychophysiology.* New York: Holt, Rinehart & Winston.

Graziadei, P. P. C. (1969). The ultrastructure of vertebrate taste buds. In C. Pfaffman (Ed.), *Olfaction and taste. Vol. 3.* New York: The Rockefeller University Press.

Green, D. M., & Swets, J. A. C. (1974). *Signal detection theory and psychophysics.* New York: Wiley, 1966. (Reprinted, New York: Krieger)

Green, G., & Osborne, G. (1985). Does vicarious instigation provide support for observational learning theories? A critical review. *Psychological Bulletin, 97,* 3-17.

Green, M. L., Green, R. G., & Santoro, W. (1988). Daily relaxation modifies serum and salivary immunoglobulins and psychophysiologic symptom severity. *Biofeedback and Self-Regulation, 13,* 187-199.

Greene, R. L. (1987). Effects of maintenance rehearsal on human memory. *Psychological Bulletin, 102,* 402-413.

Greenberg, J., & Cohen, R. L. (Eds.). (1982). *Equity and justice in social behavior.* New York: Academic Press.

Greenfield, P. M., & Savage-Rumbaugh, E. S. (1984). Perceived variability and symbol use: A common language-cognition interface in children and chimpanzees (Pan Troglodytes). *Journal of Comparative Psychology, 98,* 201-218.

Greif, E. B. (1977). Peer interactions in preschool children. In R. A. Webb (Ed.), *Social development in childhood: Day care programs and research.* Baltimore: The Johns Hopkins University Press.

Greif, E. G., & Ullman, K. J. (1982). The psychological impact of menarche on early adolescent families: A review of the literature. *Child Development, 53,* 1413-1430.

Grillon, C., Courchesne, E., Ameli, R., Geyer, M. A., & Braff, D. L. (1990). Increased distractibility in schizophrenic patients. *Archives of General Psychiatry, 47,* 171-179.

Grinspoon, L., & Bakalar, J. B. (1990a). Alcohol abuse and dependence. Boston: *The Harvard Medical School Mental Health Review.*

Grinspoon, L., & Bakalar, J. B. (1990a). Drug abuse and dependence. Boston: *The Harvard Medical School Mental Health Review, 1,* 1-26.

Grinspoon, L., & Bakalar, J. B. (1990b). *Schizophrenia.* Boston: *The Harvard Medical School Mental Health Review.*

Grisso, T., Baldwin, E., Blanck, P. D., Rotheram-Borus, M. J., Schooler, N. R., & Thompson, T. (1991) Standards in research: APA's mechanism for monitoring the challenges. *American Psychologist, 46,* 758-766.

Grob, G. N. (1966). The state mental hospital in mid-nineteenth-century America: A social analysis. *American Psychologist, 21,* 510-523.

Grossberg, S., & Stone, G. (1986). Neural dynamics of word recognition and recall: Attentional priming, word recognition, and recall. *Psychological Review, 93,* 46-74.

Grossman, H. J. (1983). *Manual on terminology and classification in mental retardation.* Washington, DC: American Association on Mental Deficiency.

Grossman, S. P. (1979). The biology of motivation. *Annual Review of Psychology, 30,* 209-242.

Group for the Advancement of Psychiatry. (1989). *Suicide and ethnicity in the United States.* New York: Bruner/Mazel.

Grush, J. E. (1976). Attitude formation and mere exposure phenomena: A nonartifactual explanation of empirical findings. *Journal of Personality and Social Psychology, 33,* 281-290.

Guilford, J. P. (1959). Three faces of intellect. *American Psychologist, 14,* 469-479.

Gurman, A. S., & Kniskern, D. P. (1981). Family therapy outcome research: Knowns and unknowns. In A. Gurman & D. Kniskern (Eds.), *Handbook of family therapy.* New York: Brunner/Mazel.

Gustavson, C. (1977). Comparative and field aspects of learned food aversions. In L. M. Barker, M. R. Best & M. Domjan (Eds.), *Learning mechanisms in food selection.* Baylor, TX: Baylor University Press.

Haefely, et al. (1990). *Trends in Pharmacological Sciences, 11,* 452+.

Haley, J. (1976). *Problem solving therapy: New strategies for effective family therapy.* San Francisco: Jossey-Bass.

Hall, C. S., & Van de Castle, R. L. (1966). *The content analysis of dreams.* New York: Appleton-Century-Crofts.

Hall, G. S. (1904). *Adolescence.* New York: Appleton.

Halley, F. M. (1991). Self-regulation of the immune system through biobehavioral strategies. *Biofeedback and Self-Regulation, 16,* 55-74.

Halpern, D. F. (1986). *Sex differences in cognitive abilities.* Hillsdale, NJ: Erlbaum.

Halpin, A., & Winer, B. (1952). *The leadership behavior of the airplane commander.* Columbus, OH: Ohio State University Research Foundation.

Hamilton, D. L. (1981). *Cognitive processes in stereotyping and intergroup behavior.* Hillsdale, NJ: Erlbaum.

Hamilton, D. L. (1988). Person memory and impression formation. In P. R. Solomon, G. R. Goethals, C. M. Kelley, & B. S. Stephens (Eds.), *Memory: Interdisciplinary approaches. The G. Stanley Hall symposium.* New York: Springer-Verlag.

Hamilton, D. L. (1989). Understanding impression formation: what has memory research contributed? In P. R. Solomon, G. R. Goethals, C. M. Kelley, and B. R. Stephens (Eds.). *Memory: interdisciplinary approaches.* New York: Springer-Verlag.

Hamilton, D. L., & Gifford, R. K. (1976). Illusory correlation in interpersonal perception: A cognitive basis of stereotypic judgments. *Journal of Experimental Social Psychology, 32,* 47-67.

Hamilton, D. L., & Trollier, T. (1986). Stereotypes and stereotyping: an overview of the cognitive approach. In J. Dovidio & S. L. Gaertner, S. L. (Eds.), *Prejudice, discrimination, and racism.* New York: Academic Press.

Hamilton, V. L. (1978). Obedience and responsibility: A jury simulation. *Journal of Personality and Social Psychology, 36,* 126-146.

Hare, R. D. (1978). Psychophysiological studies of psychopathy. In D. C. Forles (Ed.), *Clinical applications of psychophysiology.* New York: Columbia University Press.

Harlow, H. F. (1958). The nature of love. *American Psychologist, 13,* 673-685.

Harlow, H. F. (1971). *Learning to love.* San Francisco: Albion.

Harlow, H. F., & Harlow, M. K. (1965). The affectional system. In A. M. Schrier, H. F. Harlow, & F. Stollnitz (Eds.), *Behavior of nonhuman primates. Vol. 2.* New York: Academic Press.

Harlow, H. F., & Suomi, S. J. (1970). The nature of love—simplified. *American Psychologist, 25,* 161-168.

Harlow, J. M. (1868). Recovery from the passage of an iron bar through the head. *Publications of the Massachusetts Medical Society* (Boston), *2,* 327-346.

Harnishfeger, K. K., & Bjorklund, D. F. (1990). Children's strategies: A brief history. In D. F. Bjorklund (Ed.), *Children's strategies: Contemporary views of cognitive development.* Hillsdale, NJ: Erlbaum.

Harris, B. (1979). Whatever happened to Little Albert? *American Psychologist, 34,* 151-160.

Harris, F. R., Johnston, M. K., Kelley, C. S., & Wolf, M. M. (1964). Effects of positive social reinforcement on regressed crawling of a nursery school child. *Journal of Educational Psychology, 55,* 35-41.

Harris, J. E. (1980). Memory aids people use: Two interview studies. *Memory and Cognition, 8,* 31-38.

Harris, J. E., & Morris, P. E. (Eds.). (1984). *Everyday memories, actions, and absent-mindedness.* New York: Academic Press.

Harris, L. (1971, January). Change, yes—upheaval, no. *Life,* p. 70.

Harris, L., et al. (1975). *The myth and reality of aging in America.* Washington, DC: National Council on the Aging.

Harris, M. J., & Rosenthal, R. (1985). Mediation of interpersonal expectancy effects: 31 Meta-analyses. *Psychological Bulletin, 97,* 363-386.

Harris, P. L. (1983). Infant cognition. In M. M. Harth & J. J. Campos (Eds.), *Handbook of child psychology, Vol. 3, Infancy and developmental psychobiology.* New York: Wiley.

Harris, R. J., & Monaco, G. E. (1978). Psychology of pragmatic implication: Information processing between the lines. *Journal of Experimental Psychology: General, 107,* 1-22.

Harris, T. (1969). *I'm o.k.—you're o.k.: A practical guide to transactional analysis.* New York: Harper & Row.

Harris, V. A., & Jellison, J. M. (1971). Fear-arousing communications, false physiological feedback, and the acceptance of recommendations. *Journal of Experimental Social Psychology, 7,* 269-279.

Hart, J. H., Berndt, R. S., & Caramazza, A. (1985). Category-specific naming deficit following cerebral infarction. *Nature, 316,* 385-398.

Hart, S. N. (1991). From property to person status: historical perspective on children's rights. *American Psychologist, 46,* 53-59.

Hartmann, E. L. (1973). *The functions of sleep.* New Haven, CT: Yale University Press.

Harvard Mental Health Letter (1988). Sleeping pills and anti-anxiety drugs. *Author, 5,* 1-4.

Harvard Mental Health Letter (February 1991). *Post-traumatic stress: Part 1, Harvard Medical School, 7,* 1-4.

Hascher, L., & Zachs, R. T. (1979). Automatic and effortful processing in memory. *Journal of Experimental Psychology: General, 108,* 365-388.

Hass, A. (1979). *Teenage sexuality: A survey of teenage sexual behavior.* New York: Macmillan.

Hassett, J. (1980). Acupuncture is proving its points. *Psychology Today, 14,* 81-89.

Hastie, R. (1984). Causes and effects of causal attribution. *Journal of Personality and Social Psychology, 46,* 44-56.

Hatch, J. P., Fisher, J. G., & Rugh, J. D. (1987). *Biofeedback: Studies in clinical efficacy.* New York: Plenum Press.

Hatfield, E., Traupman, J., Sprecher, S., Utne, M., & Hay, T. (1984). Equity and intimate relations. In W. Ickes (Ed.), *Compatible and incompatible relationships.* New York: Springer-Verlag.

Hawkins, R. D., & Kandel, E. R. (1984). Is there a cell biological alphabet for simple forms of learning? *Psychological Review, 91,* 375-391.

Hayes, C. (1951). *The ape in our house.* New York: Harper.

Hayes, C. D. (1987). *Risking the future: Adolescent sexuality, pregnancy and childbearing (Vol. 1).* Washington, DC: National Academy Press.

Heath, R. G. (1964). Pleasure response of human subjects to direct stimulation of the brain: Physiologic and psychodynamic considerations. In R. G. Heath (Ed.), *The role of pleasure in behavior.* New York: Harper & Row.

Hebb, D. O. (1949). *Organization of behavior.* New York: Wiley.

Heider, F. (1944). Social perception and phenomenal causality. *Psychological Review, 51,* 358-374.

Heider, F. (1946). Attitudes and cognitive organization. *Journal of Psychology, 21,* 107-112.

Heider, F. (1958). *The psychology of interpersonal relations.* New York: Wiley.

Heilman, K. M., Watson, R. T., & Valenstein, E. (1985). Neglect and related disorders. In K. M. Heilman & E. Valenstein (Eds.), *Clinical neuropsychology* (2nd ed.). New York: Oxford University Press.

Helmholtz, H. von. (1852). On the theory of compound colours. *Philosophical Magazine, 4,* 519-534.

Helmholtz, H. von. (1863). *Die Lehre von den tonempfindungen als physiologischegrundlage fur die theorie der musik.* Brunswick: Vieweg-Verlag.

Helson, H., Judd, D. B., & Wilson, M. (1956). Color rendition with fluorescent sources of illumination. *Illuminating Engineering, 51,* 329-346.

Henderson, N. D. (1982). Human behavior genetics. *Annual Review of Psychology, 33,* 403-440.

Hendricks, J., & Hendricks, C. D. (1975). *Aging in mass society.* Cambridge, MA: Winthrop.

Hennigan, K. M., Cook, T. D., & Gruder, C. L. (1982). Cognitive tuning set, source credibility, and the temporal persistence of attitude change. *Journal of Personality and Social Psychology, 42,* 412-425.

Henry, K. R. (1984). Cochlear damage resulting from exposure to four different octave bands of noise at three different ages. *Behavioral Neuroscience, 1,* 107-117.

Hentall, I. D., & Fields, H. L. (1978). Segmental and descending influences on intraspinal thresholds of single C fibers. *Journal of Neurophysiology, 42,* 1527-1537.

Hering, E. (1878). *Zur lehre vom lichtsinne.* Vienna: Gerold.

Hershey, D. (1974). *Life span and factors affecting it.* Springfield, IL: Charles C. Thomas.

Herzog, A. R., Rogers, W. L., & Woodworth, J. (1982). *Subjective well-being among different age groups.* Ann Arbor, MI: University of Michigan Press.

Heston, L. H., & White, J. A. (1983). *Dementia: A practical guide to Alzheimer's disease and related illness.* San Francisco: Freeman.

Heston, L. L. (1966). Psychiatric disorder in foster home reared children of schizophrenic mothers. *British Journal of Psychiatry, 112,* 819-825.

Heston, L. L., & White, J. A. (1991). *The vanishing mind.* San Francisco: Freeman.

Hildum, D., & Brown, R. (1956). Verbal reinforcement and interview bias. *Journal of Abnormal and Social Psychology, 53,* 108-111.

Hilgard, E. R. (1956). *Theories of learning.* New York: Appleton-Century-Crofts.

Hilgard, E. R. (1965). *Hypnotic susceptibility.* New York: Harcourt, Brace and World.

Hilgard, E. R., & Hilgard, J. R. (1975). *Hypnosis in the relief of pain.* Los Altos, CA: W. Kaufmann.

Hilgard, J. R. (1970). *Personality and hypnosis: A study of imaginative involvement.* Chicago: University of Chicago Press.

Hill, R., Foote, N., Aldous, J., Carlson, R., & McDonald, R. (1970). *Family development in three generations.* Cambridge, MA: Schenkman.

Hilton, H. (1986). *The executive memory guide.* New York: Simon & Schuster.

Hinsz, V. B. & Tomhave, J. A. (1991). Smile and (half) the world smiles with you, frown and you frown alone. *Personality and Social Psychology Bulletin, 17,* 586-592.

Hiroto, D. S., & Seligman, M. E. P. (1975). Generality of learned helplessness in man. *Journal of Personality and Social Psychology, 31,* 311-327.

Hobson, J. A. (1988). *The dreaming brain.* New York: Basic Books.

Hobson, J. A. (1989). *Sleep.* New York: Scientific American Library.

Hobson, J. A., & McCarley, R. W. (1977). The brain as a dream state generator: An activation-synthesis hypothesis of the dream process. *American Journal of Psychiatry, 134* (12), 1335-1348.

Hochberg, J. (1970). Attention, organization, and consciousness. In D. I. Mostofsky (Ed.), *Attention: Contemporary theory and analysis.* New York: Appleton-Century-Crofts.

Hoffer, B. J., & Olson, L. (1991). Ethical issues in brain-cell transplantation. *Trends in the Neurosciences, 14,* 384-388.

Hoffert, S. L., & Hayes, C. D. (1987) *Risking the future: Adolescent sexuality, pregnancy, and childbearing* (Vol. 2). Washington, DC: National Academy Press.

Hoff-Ginsberg, E., & Shatz, M. (1982). Linguistic input and the child's acquisition of language. *Psychological Bulletin, 92,* 3-26.

Hoffman, L. (1984). Work, family, and the socialization of the child. In R. D. Parke (Ed.), *Review of child development research. Vol. 3: The family.* Chicago, IL: University of Chicago Press.

Hohmann, G. W. (1962). Some effects of spinal cord lesions on experienced emotional feelings. *Psychophysiology, 3,* 143-156.

Holden, C. (1982). NAS backs cautious use of ability tests. *Science, 215,* 950.

Holden, C. (1986). Proposed new psychiatric diagnoses raise charges of gender bias. *Science, 231,* 327-328.

Holder, H. D. & Blose, J. O. (1987). Changes in health care costs and utilization associated with mental health treatment. *Health and Community Psychiatry, 38,* 1070-1075.

Holender, D. (1986). Semantic activation without conscious identification in dichotic listening, parafoveal vision, and visual masking: A survey and appraisal. *The Behavioral and Brain Sciences, 9,* 1-66.

Hollander, E. P. (1985). Leadership and power. In G. Lindsay & E. Aronson (Eds.), *Handbook of social psychology* (3rd ed.) (pp. 485-538). New York: Random House.

Hollis, K. E. (1984). The biological function of Pavlovian conditioning: The best defense is a good offense. *Journal of Experimental Psychology: Animal Behavior Processes, 10,* 413-425.

Holmes, D. S. (1984). Meditation and somatic arousal reduction: A review of the experimental evidence. *American Psychologist, 39,* 1-10.

Holmes, T. H., & Rahe, R. H. (1967). The social readjustment rating scale. *Journal of Psychosomatic Research, 11,* 213-218.

Horn, J. L. (1978). The nature and development of intellectual abilities. In R. T. Osborne, C. E. Noble, & N. Weyl (Eds.), *Human variation.* New York: Academic Press.

Horn, J. L. (1982). The aging of human abilities. In B. B. Wolman (Ed.), *Handbook of developmental psychology.* Englewood Cliffs, NJ: Prentice-Hall.

Horn, J. M. (1983). The Texas adoption project: Adopted children and their intellectual resemblance to biological and adoptive parents. *Child Development, 54,* 268-275.

Horney, K. (1939). *New ways in psychoanalysis.* New York: Norton.

Horney, K. (1950). *Neurosis and human growth.* New York: Norton.

Horowitz, M. J., Wilner, N., Kaltreidr, N., & Alvarez, W. (1980). Signs and symptoms of post-traumatic stress disorder. *Archives of General Psychiatry, 37,* 85-92.

Horton, D. L., & Mills, C. B. (1984). Human learning and memory. *Annual Review of Psychology, 35,* 361-394.

House, J. S., Landis, K. R. & Umberson, D. (1988). Social relationships and health, *Science, 241,* 540-545.

Householder, J., Hatcher, R., Burnes, W., & Chasnoff, I. (1982). Infants born to narcotic-addicted mothers. *Psychological Bulletin, 92,* 453-468.

Houston, B. K. & Vavak, C. R. (1991). Cynical hostility: Developmental factors, psycho-social correlates, and health behaviors. *Health Psychology, 10,* 9-17.

Hovland, C. I., Lumsdaine, A. A., & Sheffield, F. D. (1949). *Experiments on mass communication.* Princeton, NJ: Princeton University Press.

Hovland, C. I., & Sears, R. (1940). Minor studies of aggression: Correlation of lynchings with economic indices. *Journal of Psychology, 9,* 301-310.

Hovland, C. I., & Weiss, W. (1951). The influence of source credibility on communication effectiveness. *Public Opinion Quarterly, 15,* 635-650.

Howard, A., Pion, G. M., Gottfredson, G. D., Flattau, P. E., Oskamp, S. P., Bray, S. M., Douglas, W., & Burstein, A. G. (1986). The changing face of American psychology: A report from the Committee on Employment and Human Resources. *American Psychologist, 41,* 1311-1327.

Howard, J. A., Blumstein, P., & Schwartz, P. (1987). Social or evolutionary theories? Some observations on preferences in human mate selection. *Journal of Personality and Social Psychology, 53,* 194-200.

Hubel, D. H., & Wiesel, T. N. (1962). Receptive fields, binocular interaction and functional architecture in the cat's visual cortex. *Journal of Physiology, 160,* 106-154.

Hughes, J., Smith, T. W., Kosterlitz, A. W., Fothergill, L. A., Morgan, B. A., & Morris, H. R. (1975). Identification of two related pentapeptides from the brain with potent opiate against activity. *Nature* (London), *258,* 577-579.

Hull, C. L. (1943). *Principles of behavior.* New York: Appleton-Century-Crofts.

Hulse, S. H., Fowler, H., & Honig, W. K. (1978). *Cognitive processes in animal behavior.* Hillsdale, NJ: Erlbaum.

Hunt, J. McV. (1969). Has compensatory education failed? Has it been tried? *Harvard Educational Review, 39,* 130-152.

Hunt, M. (1974). *Sexual behavior in the 1970s.* Chicago: Playboy.

Hunt, W. A., & Matarazzo, J. D. (1973). Recent developments in the modification of smoking behavior. *Journal of Abnormal Psychology, 81,* 107-114.

Hurvich, L. M., & Jameson, D. (1957). An opponent process theory of color vision. *Psychological Review, 64,* 384-404.

Huston, A. C. (1983). Sex-typing. In P. H. Mussen (Ed.), *Handbook of developmental psychology. Vol. 4.* New York: Wiley.

Huston, A. C. (1985). The development of sex typing: Themes from recent research. *Developmental Review, 5,* 1-17.

Hyde, J. S., & Linn, M. C. (1988). *The psychology of gender: Advances through meta-analysis.* Baltimore: The Johns Hopkins University Press.

Hyman, B. T., Damasio, H., Damasio, A. R., & Van Hoesin, G. W. (1989). Alzheimer's disease. *Annual Review of Public Health, 10,* 115-140.

Ingalls, Z. (1980, July 21). We're not dead yet. *The Chronicle of Higher Education,* pp. 3-4.

Ingelfinger, F. J. (1944). The late effects of total and subtotal gastrectomy. *The New England Journal of Medicine, 231,* 321-327.

Inhelder, B., & Piaget, J. (1958). *The growth of logical thinking from childhood to adolescence.* New York: Basic Books.

Insko, C. (1965). Verbal reinforcement of attitude. *Journal of Personality and Social Psychology, 2,* 621-623.

Intons-Peterson, M. J., & Fourner, J. (1986). External and internal memory aids: When and how often do we use them. *Journal of Experimental Psychology: General, 115,* 267-280.

Intons-Peterson, M. J., & Reddel, M. (1984). What do people ask about a neonate? *Developmental Psychology, 20,* 358-359.

Isabella, R. A., & Belsky, J. (1991). Interactional synchrony and the origins of infant-mother attachment: A replication study. *Child Development, 62,* 373-384.

Ivancevich, J. M., & Matteson, M. T. (1980). *Stress and work: A managerial perspective.* Glenview, IL: Scott, Foresman.

Iverson, S. D., & Iverson, S. D. (1981). *Behavioral pharmacology* (2nd ed.). New York: Oxford University Press.

Izard, C. E. (1971). *The face of emotion.* New York: Appleton-Century-Crofts.

Izard, C. E. (1977). *Human emotions.* New York: Plenum.

Izard, C. E. (1979). Emotions as motivations: An evolutionary developmental perspective. In H. E. Howe, Jr., & R. A. Dienstbier (Eds.), *Nebraska symposium on motivation. Vol. 26.* Lincoln: University of Nebraska Press.

Jacobson, J. L. (1981). The role of inanimate objects in early peer interaction. *Child Development, 52,* 618-626.

Jacobson, J. L., & Wille, D. E. (1986). The influence of attachment pattern on developmental changes in peer interaction from the toddler to the preschool period. *Child Development, 57,* 338-347.

Jakobson, R. (1968). *Child language, aphasia, and phonological universals.* The Hague: Mouton.

James, W. (1890). *Principles of psychology.* New York: Holt.

James, W. (1902). *The varieties of religious experience.* New York: Longmans, Green.

Janicak, P. G., Davis, J. M., Gibbons, R. D., Ericksen, S., Chang, S., & Gallagher, P. (1985). Efficacy of ECT: A meta-analysis. *American Journal of Psychiatry, 142,* 297-302.

Janis, I. L. (1972). *Victims of groupthink: A psychological study of foreign policy decisions and fiascoes.* Boston: Houghton Mifflin.

Janis, I. L. (1982). *Victims of groupthink.* Boston: Houghton Mifflin.

Janis, I. L., & Feshbach, S. (1953). Effects of fear-arousing communications. *Journal of Abnormal and Social Psychology, 48,* 78-92.

Janis, I. L., Kaye, D., & Kirschner, P. (1965). Facilitating effects of "eating-while-reading" on responsiveness to persuasive communications. *Journal of Personality and Social Psychology, 1,* 181-186.

Janis, I. L., & Mann, L. (1977). *Decision making.* New York: Free Press.

Jellison, J. M., & Oliver, D. F. (1983). Attitude similarity and attraction: An impression management approach. *Personality and Social Psychology Bulletin, 9,* 111-115.

Jenkins, J. G., & Dallenbach, K. M. (1924). Oblivisence

during sleep and waking. *American Journal of Psychology, 35,* 605–612.

Jensen, A. R. (1969). How much can we boost IQ and scholastic achievement? *Harvard Educational Review, 39,* 1–123.

Jensen, A. R. (1972). The heritability of intelligence. *Saturday Evening Post, 244,* 2, 9, 149.

Jensen, A. R. (1973). *Genetics and education.* New York: Harper & Row.

Jensen, A. R. (1980). *Bias in mental testing.* New York: Free Press.

Jessor, R., Costa, F., Jessor, L., & Donovan, J. E. (1983). Time of first intercourse: A prospective study. *Journal of Personality and Social Psychology, 44,* 608–626.

Joffe, J. M. (1969). *Prenatal determinants of behavior.* Oxford: Pergamon Press.

John, E. R., Prichep, L. S., Fridman, J., & Easton, P. (1988). Neurometrics: Assisted differential diagnosis of brain dysfunction. *Science, 239,* 162–169.

Johnson, B. P. (1980). Toward a theory of drug subcultures. In D. J. Letteri, M. Sayers, & H. W. Pearson, *The ories on drug abuse: Selected contemporary perspectives* (NIDA Monograph No. 30, DHHS Publication No. ADM 80-967). Washington, DC: Government Printing Office.

Johnson, D., & Denrick, E. J. (1977). Therapeutic fasting in morbid obesity: Long-term follow-up. *Archives of Internal Medicine, 137,* 1381–1382.

Johnson, K. M. (1987). *Neurochemistry and neurophysiology of phencyclidine: The third generation of progress* (pp. 1581–1588). New York: Raven Press.

Johnson, M. K., & Hasher, L. (1987). Human learning and memory. *Annual Review of Psychology, 38,* 631–668.

Johnson-Laird, P. N., & Wason, P. C. (1977). A theoretical analysis of insight into a reasoning task, and postscript. In P. N. Johnson-Laird & P. C. Wason (Eds.), *Thinking: Readings in cognitive science* (pp. 143–157). Cambridge, England: Cambridge University Press.

Jones, E. E. (1990). *Interpersonal perception.* New York: Freeman.

Jones, E. E., & Nisbett, R. E. (1971). *The actor and the observer: Divergent perceptions of the causes of behavior.* Morristown, NJ: General Learning Press.

Jones, E. E., Rock, L., Shaver, K. G., Goethals, G. R., & Ward, L. M. (1968). Pattern of performance and ability attribution: An unexpected primacy effect. *Journal of Personality and Social Psychology, 10,* 317–341.

Jones, J. M., Levine, I. S., & Rosenberg, A. A. (1991). *American Psychologist, 46,* Special Issue on Homelessness, 1107–1264.

Jones, R. T. (1980). Human effects: An overview. In R. C. Peterson (Ed.), *Marijuana research findings: 1980* (NIDA Research Monograph No. 31, DHHS Publication No. ADM 80-1001). Washington, DC: Government Printing Office.

Jourard, S. M. (1971). *The transparent self* (2nd ed.). New York: Van Nostrand Reinhold.

Jouvet, M. (1973). Serotonin and sleep in the cat. In J. Barchus & E. Usdin (Eds.), *Serotonin and behavior.* New York: Academic Press.

Joyce, J. (1934). *Ulysses.* New York: Modern Library.

Judd, C. M., & Park, B. (1988). Out-group homogeneity: judgments of variability at the individual and group levels. *Journal of Personality and Social Psychology, 54,* 778–788.

Jung, C. G. (1971). Psychological types. In H. Read, M. Fordham, & G. Adler (Eds.), *Collected works. Vol. 6.* Princeton, NJ: Princeton University Press. (Originally published 1921)

Kagan, J. (1969). Inadequate evidence and illogical conclusions. *Harvard Educational Review, 39,* 274–277.

Kagan, J. (1971). *Understanding children: Behavior, motives, and thought.* New York: Harcourt Brace Jovanovich.

Kagan, J. (1973). What is intelligence? *Social Policy, 4,* 88–94.

Kagan, J., Kearsley, R. B., & Zelazo, P. R. (1978). *Infancy: Its place in human development.* Cambridge, MA: Harvard University Press.

Kahana, E., & Coe, R. M. (1969). *Perceptions of grandparenthood by community and institutionalized aged.* Proceedings of the 77th Annual Convention of the American Psychological Association, 735–736.

Kahneman, D., & Tversky, A. (1973). On the psychology of prediction. *Psychology Review, 80,* 237–251.

Kahneman, D., & Tversky, A. (1984). Choices, values, and frames. *American Psychologist, 39,* 341–350.

Kalat, J. W. (1984). *Biological psychology* (2nd ed.). Belmont, CA: Wadsworth.

Kales, A., Soldatos, C. R., & Kales, J. D. (1981). Sleep disorders: Evaluation and management in the office setting. In S. Arieti (Ed.), *American handbook of psychiatry* (2nd ed.) (pp. 423–454). New York: Basic Books.

Kalish, H. I. (1981). *From behavioral science to behavior modification.* New York: McGraw-Hill.

Kalish, R. A. (1979). The new ageism and the failure models: A polemic. *The Gerontologist, 19,* 398–402.

Kalish, R. A. (1982). *Late adulthood: Perspectives on human development.* Monterey, CA: Brooks/Cole.

Kamin, L. J. (1974). *The science and politics of I.Q.* Hillsdale, NJ: Erlbaum.

Kamin, L. J. (1976). Heredity, intelligence, politics, and psychology. In N. J. Block & G. Dworkin (Eds.), *The I.Q. controversy.* New York: Pantheon.

Kamin, L. J. (1981). Some historical facts about IQ testing. In H. J. Eysenck vs. L. J. Kamin, *The intelligence controversy.* New York: Wiley.

Kandel, D. (1973). The role of parents and peers in adolescent marijuana use. *Science, 181,* 1067–1070.

Kandel, D. B. (1978). Similarity in real-life adolescent friendship pairs. *Journal of Personality and Social Psychology, 36,* 306–312.

Kanizsa, G. (1976). Subjective contours. *Scientific American, 234,* 48–52.

Kanner, A. D., Coyne, J. C., Schaefer, C., & Lazarus, R. S. (1981). Comparison of two modes of stress measurement: Daily hassles and uplifts versus major life events. *Journal of Behavioral Medicine, 4,* 1–39.

Kapiro, J., Koskenvuo, M., & Rita, H. (1987). Mortality after bereavement: A prospective study of 95,647 widowed persons. *American Journal of Public Health, 773,* 283–287.

Kassajarjian, H. H. (1963). Voting intentions and political perceptions. *Journal of Psychology, 56,* 85–88.

Kassin, S. M. (1985). Eyewitness identification: Retrospective self-awareness and the accuracy-confidence correlation. *Journal of Personality and Social Psychology, 49,* 878–893.

Katz, I. (1968). Factors influencing Negro performance in the desegregated school. In M. Deutsch, I. Katz, & A. R. Jensen (Eds.), *Social class, race, and psychological development.* New York: Holt, Rinehart & Winston.

Katzell, R. A., & Guzzo, R. A. (1983). Psychological approaches to productivity improvement. *American Psychologist, 38,* 468–472.

Kaufman, A. S. (1983). Some questions and answers about the Kaufman Assessment Battery for Children (K-ABC). *Journal of Psychoeducational Assessment, 1,* 205–218.

Keegan, J. (1987). *The mask of command.* New York: Viking.

Keller, F. S. (1968). Goodbye teacher. . . . *Journal of Applied Behavior Analysis, 1,* 79-88.

Kelley, H. H. (1950). The warm-cold variable in first impressions of personality. *Journal of Personality, 18,* 431-439.

Kelly, H. H. (1972). Attribution in social interaction. In E. E. Jones, D. E. Kanouse, H. H. Kelley, R. E. Nisbett, S. Valins, & B. Weiner (Eds.). *Attribution: Perceiving the causes of behavior.* Morristown, N.J.: General Learning Press.

Kelley, H. H. (1973). The processes of causal attribution. *American Psychologist, 28,* 107-128.

Kellogg, W. N. (1968). Communication and language in the home-raised chimpanzee. *Science, 162,* 423-427.

Kelman, H. (1961). Processes of opinion change. *Public Opinion Quarterly, 25,* 57-58.

Kempler, D., & Van Lancker, D. (1987, April). The right turn of phrase. *Psychology Today,* pp. 20-22.

Kendler, K. S. (1991). Mood-incongruent psychotic affective illness. *Archives of General Psychiatry, 48,* 362-369.

Kenny, D. A., & Zaccaro, S. J. (1983). An estimate of variance due to traits in leadership. *Journal of Applied Psychology, 68,* 678-685.

Kesner, R. P., & Olton, D. S. (1990). *Neurobiology of comparative cognition.* Hillsdale, NJ: Erlbaum.

Kety, S. S. (1979). Disorders of the human brain. In *The brain.* San Francisco: Freeman.

Kety, S. S. (1983). Mental illness in the biological and adoptive relatives of schizophrenic adoptees: Findings relevant to genetic and environmental factors in etiology. *American Journal of Psychiatry, 140,* 720-727.

Kiecolt-Glaser, J. K., & Glaser, R. (1988). Psychological influences on immunity, *American Psychologist, 43,* 892-898.

Kielcolt-Glaser, J. K., & Glaser, R. (1989). Psychological influences on immunity: Implications for AIDS. *American Psychologist, 43,* 892-898.

Kiester, E., Jr. (1980, May). Images of the night. *Science 80,* pp. 36-43.

Kihlstrom, J. F. (1979). Hypnosis and psychopathology: Retrospect and prospect. *Journal of Abnormal Psychology, 88* (5), 459-473.

Kihlstrom, J. F. (1987). The cognitive unconscious. *Science, 237,* 1445-1452.

Kimble, G. A. (1984). Psychology's two cultures. *American Psychologist, 39,* 833-839.

Kinder, D. R., & Fiske, S. T. (1986). Presidents in the public mind. In M. G. Hermann (Ed.), *Political psychology.* San Francisco: Jossey-Bass.

Kinder, D. R., & Sears, D. O. (1981). Prejudice and politics: symbolic racism versus racial threats to the good life. *Journal of Personality and Social Psychology, 40,* 414-431.

King, W. L. (1961). An experience in Buddhist meditation. *Journal of Religion, 41,* 51-61.

Kinnaman, A. J. (1902). Mental life of two *Macacus Rhesus* monkeys in captivity. *American Journal of Psychology, 13,* 98-148.

Kinsey, A., Pomeroy, W. B., & Martin, C. E. (1948). *Sexual behavior in the human male.* Philadelphia: Saunders.

Kinsey, A., Pomeroy, W. B., Martin, C. E., & Gebhard, P. H. (1953). *Sexual behavior in the human female.* Philadelphia: Saunders.

Kintsch, W. (1974). *The representation of meaning in memory.* Hillsdale, NJ: Erlbaum.

Kisker, G. W. (1977). *The disorganized personality* (3rd ed.). New York: McGraw-Hill.

Klatzky, R. L. (1980). *Human memory* (2nd ed.). San Francisco: Freeman.

Klatzky, R. L. (1984). *Memory and awareness: An information-processing perspective.* New York: Freeman.

Kleinke, C. L., & Kahn, M. L. (1980). Perceptions of self-disclosers: Effects of sex and physical attractiveness. *Journal of Personality, 48,* 190-205.

Klerman, G. L. (1978). Affective disorders. In A. M. Nicholi, Jr. (Ed.), *The Harvard guide to modern psychiatry.* Cambridge, MA: Belknap.

Klerman, G. L., & Weissman, M. M. (1989). Increasing rates of depression. *Journal of the American Medical Association, 261,* 2229-2235.

Kline, P. (1981). *Fact and fantasy in Freudian theory* (2nd ed.). London: Metheun.

Klineberg, O. (1938). Emotional expression in Chinese literature. *Journal of Abnormal and Social Psychology, 33,* 517-520.

Klinnert, M., Campos, J. J., Sorce, J., Emde, R. N., & Svedja, M. (1983). Emotions as behavior regulators: Social referencing in infancy. In R. Plutchik & H. Kellerman (Eds.), *Emotions in early development. Vol. 2: The emotions.* New York: Academic Press.

Klopfer, B., Ainsworth, M. D., Klopfer, W. G., & Holt, R. R. (1954). *Developments in the Rorschach technique. Vol. 1.* New York: Harcourt, Brace & World.

Kluver, H., & Bucy, P. (1937). "Psychic blindness" and other symptoms following bilateral temporal lobectomy in Rhesus monkeys. *American Journal of Physiology, 119,* 352-353.

Knapp, R. R. (1976). *Handbook for the personal orientation inventory.* San Diego, CA: Edits.

Knittle, J. L. (1975). Early influences on the development of adipose tissue. In G. A. Bray (Ed.), *Obesity in perspective.* Washington, DC: Government Printing Office.

Knittle, J. L., & Hirsch, J. (1968). Effect of early nutrition on the development of rat epididymal fat pads: Cellularity and metabolism. *Journal of Clinical Investigation, 47,* 2091-2098.

Knox, V. J., Gekoski, W. L., Shum, K., & McLaughlin, D. M. (1981). Analgesia for experimentally induced pain: Multiple sessions of acupuncture compared to hypnosis in high- and low-susceptible subjects. *Journal of Abnormal Psychology, 90* (1), 28-34.

Kobasa, S. C. (1979). Stressful life events, personality, and health. An inquiry into hardiness. *Journal of Personality and Social Psychology, 37* (1), 1-11.

Kogan, N., & Wallach, M. A. (1967). Risk taking as a function of the situation, the person, and the group. In G. Mandler, P. Mussen, N. Kogan, & M. A. Wallach (Eds.), *New directions in psychology. Vol. 3.* New York: Holt, Rinehart & Winston.

Kohlberg, L. (1963). The development of children's orientation toward a moral order: I. Sequence in the development of moral thought. *Vita Humana, 6,* 11-33.

Kohlberg, L. (1966). A cognitive-developmental analysis of children's sex-role concepts and attitudes. In E. E. Maccoby (Ed.), *The development of sex differences.* Stanford, CA: Stanford University Press.

Kohlberg, L. (1967). Moral and religious education and the public schools: A developmental view. In T. Sizer (Ed.), *Religion and public education.* Boston: Houghton Mifflin.

Kohlberg, L. (1969). Stage and sequence: The cognitive-developmental approach to socialization. In D. A. Goslin (Ed.), *Handbook of socialization: Theory and research.* Boston: Houghton Mifflin.

Kohlberg, L., & Ullian, D. Z. (1974). Stages in the development of psychosexual concepts and attitudes. In R. C. Van Wiele (Ed.), *Sex differences in behavior.* New York: Wiley.

Köhler, W. (1925). *The mentality of apes.* New York: Harcourt, Brace.

Kohn, A. (1990). *You know what they say . . . . The truth about popular beliefs.* New York: HarperCollins.

Kohut, H. (1971). The analysis of the self: A systematic approach to the psychoanalytic treatment of narcissistic personality disorders. *Monographs Series of the Psychoanalytic Study of the Child,* No. 41. (New York: International Universities Press.)

Kohut, H. (1977). *The restoration of the self.* New York: International Universities Press.

Kohut, H. (1978). *The psychology of the self* (A. Goldberg, Ed.). New York: International Universities Press.

Kolata, G. (1985). Obesity declared a disease. *Science, 227,* 1019-1020.

Kolers, P. A. (1983). Perception and representation. *Annual Review of Psychology, 34,* 129-166.

Komisurak, B. R., & Whipple, B. (1986). Vaginal stimulation produced analgesia in rats and women. *Annals of the New York Academy of Sciences, 467,* 30-39.

Konĕcni, V. J., & Ebbesen, E. B. (1986). Courtroom testimony by psychologists on eyewitness identification issues: Critical notes and reflections. *Law and Human Behavior, 10,* 117-126.

Koran, L. M. (1989). Medical evaluation of psychiatric patients. *Archives of General Psychiatry, 46,* 733-740.

Kornhauser, A., & Reid, O. M. (1965). *Mental health of the industrial worker.* New York: Wiley.

Koskenvuo, M., Kaprio, J., Rose, R. J., Kesaniemi, A., Sarna, S., Heikkila, K., & Langinvainio, H. (1988). Hostility as a risk factor for mortality and ischemic heart disease in men. *Psychosomatic Medicine, 50,* 330-340.

Kotovsky, K., & Simon, H. (1973). Empirical tests of a theory of human acquisition of concepts for sequential patterns. *Cognitive Psychology, 4,* 399-424.

Kowall, N. E., McKee, A. C., Yanker, B. A., & Beal, M. F. (1992). In vivo neurotoxicity of beta amyloid [$\beta(1-40)$ and the $\beta(25-35)$] fragment. *Neurobiology of Aging, 13,* 537-542.

Kozielecki, J. (1981). *Psychological decision theory.* Warsaw, Poland: Polish Scientific Publishers.

Kraepelin, E. (1971/1919). *Dementia praecox and paraphrenia.* Huntington, NY: Robert E. Krieger.

Krebs, D. L., & Miller, D. T. (1985). Altruism and aggression. In G. Lindzey & E. Aronson (Eds.), *Handbook of social psychology* (3rd ed.) (pp. 1-72). New York: Random House.

Krieger, D. T. (1983). Brain peptides: Why, where, why. *Science, 222,* 975-985.

Kries, J. von (1895). Uber die Natur gewisser mit den psychischen Vorgangen verknupfter Ghirnzustande. *Zeitschrift fur Psychologie 8,* 1-33.

Kruuk, H. (1966). A new view of the hyaena. *New Scientist, 30,* 849-851.

Kubler-Ross, E. (1969). *On death and dying.* New York: Macmillan.

Kuffler, S. W., Nicholls, J. G., & Martin, A. R. (1984). *From neuron to brain* (2nd ed.). Sunderland, MA: Sinauer Associates.

Kugel, R. B. (1967). Familial mental retardation—fact or fancy? In J. Hellmuth (Ed.), *Disadvantaged child. Vol. 1.* New York: Bruner/Mazel.

Kulik, J. A., & Brown, R. (1978). Frustration, attribution of blame, and aggression. *Journal of Applied Social Psychology, 8,* 66-140.

Kuo, Aing Yang. (1930). The genesis of the cat's responses to the rat. *Journal of Comparative Psychology, 11,* 1-35.

Labov, W. (1970). The logic of nonstandard English. In F. Williams (Ed.), *Language and poverty.* Chicago: Markham.

Lackner, J. R., & Garrett, M. F. (1972): Resolving ambiguity: Effects of biasing content in the unattended ear. *Cognition, 1,* 359-372.

Laing, K. C., Juler, R. G., & McGaugh, J. L. (1986). Mod-

ulating effects of posttraining epinephrine on memory: Involvement of the amygdala noradrenergic system. *Brain Research, 368,* 125-133.

Lamb, M. E. (1976). Interactions between 8-month-old children and their mothers and fathers. In M. E. Lamb (Ed.), *The role of the father in child development.* New York: Wiley.

Lamb, M. E. (1981). The development of father-infant relationships. In M. E. Lamb (Ed.), *The role of the father in child development.* New York: Wiley.

Lamb, M. E., & Sternberg, K. J. (1990). Do we really know how day care affects children? *Journal of Applied Developmental Psychology, 11,* 351-379.

Lambert, M. J. (1976). Spontaneous remission in adult neurotic disorders: A revision and summary. *Psychological Bulletin, 83* (1), 107-119.

Landauer, T. K. (1986). How much do people remember? Some estimates of quantity of learned information in long-term memory. *Cognitive Science, 10,* 477-493.

Landers, S. (1986). Judge reiterates IQ test ban. American Psychological Association *Monitor,* December 18.

Landesman-Dwyer, S., Ragozin, A. S., & Little, R. E. (1981). Behavioral correlates of prenatal alcohol exposure: a four-year follow-up study. *Neurobehavioral Toxicology and Teratology, 3,* 187-193.

Lange, A. J., & Jakobowski, P. (1976). *Responsible assertive behavior: Cognitive/behavioral procedures for trainers.* Champaign, IL: Research Press.

Lange, C. (1887). *Uber Gemutsbewegungen: Eine psycho-physiologische Studie.* Leipzig: Thomas.

Langer, E. J. (1981). Old age: An artifact? In J. McGaugh & S. Kiesler (Eds.), *Aging: Biology and behavior.* New York: Academic Press.

Langer, E. J., Janis, I. L., & Wolfer, J. A. (1975). Reduction of psychological stress in surgical patients. *Journal of Experimental Social Psychology, 11,* 155-165.

Langer, E. J., & Rodin, J. (1976). The effects of choice and enhanced personal responsibility for the aged: A field experiment in an institutional setting. *Journal of Personality and Social Psychology, 34,* 191.

Lashley, K. S. (1950). In search of the engram. *Society for Experimental Biology, Symposium 4,* 454-482.

Latané, B., & Darley, J. M. (1968). Group inhibition of bystander intervention in emergencies. *Journal of Personality and Social Psychology, 10,* 215-221.

Latané, B., & Rodin, J. (1969). A lady in distress: Inhibiting effects of friends and strangers on bystander intervention. *Journal of Experimental Social Psychology, 5,* 189-202.

Laudenslager, M. L., Ryan, S. M., Drugan, R. C., Hyson, R. L., & Maier, S. R. (1983). Coping and immunosuppression: Inescapable but not escapable shock suppresses lymphocyte proliferation. *Science, 221,* 568-571.

Lauer, J. C., & Lauer, R. H. (1985, June). Marriages made to last. *Psychology Today,* pp. 22-26.

Laurence, J., & Perry, C. (1983). Hypnotically created memory among highly hypnotizable subjects. *Science, 222,* 523-524.

Lawler, E. (1975). Expectancy theory. In R. M. Steers & L. W. Porter (Eds.), *Motivation and work behavior.* New York: McGraw-Hill.

Lazarus, A. A. (1977). *In the mind's eye: The power of imagery for personal enrichment.* New York: Rawson Associates.

Lazarus, A. A. (1981). *The practice of multimodal therapy.* New York: McGraw-Hill.

Lazarus, R. S. (1983). The costs and benefits of denial. In S. Breznitz (Ed.), *The denial of stress* (pp. 1-30). New York: International Universities Press.

Lazarus, R. S. (1991). *Emotion and adaptation.* New York: Oxford, 1991.

Lazarus, R. S., & Folkman, S. (1984). *Stress, appraisal, and coping.* New York: Springer-Verlag.

Lazarus, R. S., Opton, E. M., Nomikos, M. S., & Rankin, N. O. (1965). The principle of short-circuiting of threat: Further evidence. *Journal of Personality, 33,* 622-635.

Leary, T. (1957). *Interpersonal diagnoses of personality.* New York: Ronald Press.

Le Bon, G. (1903). *The crowd* (Trans.). London: Allen & Unwin. (Originally published 1895)

Lee, L. C. (1973, August). *Social encounters of infants: The beginnings of popularity.* Paper presented at the International Society for the Study of Behavioral Development, Ann Arbor.

Leerhsen, C. (1990). Unite and conquer. *Newsweek,* February 5, 50-55.

Lefcourt, H. M. (1982). *Locus of control: Current trends in theory and research* (2nd ed.). Hillsdale, NJ: Erlbaum.

Lefkowitz, M. M., Eron, L. D., Walder, L. O., & Huesmann, L. R. (1972). Television violence and child aggression: A follow-up study. In G. A. Comstock & E. A. Rubinstein (Eds.), *Television and social behavior. Vol. 3. Television and adolescent aggressiveness.* Washington, DC: Government Printing Office.

Lefrancois, G. R. (1980). *Of children.* Belmont, CA: Wadsworth.

Lehn, W. H. (1979). Atmospheric refraction and lake monsters. *Science, 205,* 183-185.

Lehrman, D. S. (1970). Some semantic and conceptual issues in the nature-nurture problem. In L. A. Aronson, E. Tobach, D. S. Lehrman, & J. S. Rosenblatt (Eds.), *Development and evolution of behavior: Essays in memory of T. C. Schneirla.* San Francisco: Freeman.

Leibowitz, H. W. (1974). Multiple mechanisms of size perception and size constancy. *Hiroshima Forum for Psychology, 1,* 47-53.

Lenneberg, E. H. (1967). *Biological foundations of language.* New York: Wiley.

Lennie, P. (1984). Recent developments in the physiology of color vision. *Trends in the Neurosciences, 73,* 245-248.

Leon, G. R., & Roth, R. (1977). Obesity: Psychological causes, correlations, and speculations. *Psychological Bulletin, 84,* 117-139.

Leonard, L. B., Chapman, K., Rowan, L. E., & Weiss, A. L. (1983). Three hypotheses concerning young children's imitations of lexical items. *Developmental Psychology, 19,* 591-601.

Lepper, M. R., & Greene, D. (Eds.). (1978). *The hidden costs of reward.* Hillsdale, NJ: Erlbaum.

Lepper, M. R., Greene, D., & Nisbett, R. E. (1973). Undermining children's intrinsic interest with extrinsic rewards: A test of the overjustification hypothesis. *Journal of Personality and Social Psychology, 28,* 129-137.

Lerner, R. M. (1984). *On the nature of human plasticity.* New York: Cambridge University Press.

LeVay, S. (1991). A difference in hypothalamic structure between heterosexual and homosexual men. *Science, 253,* 1034-1037.

Levenson, R. W., Ekman, P. & Friesen, W. V. (1990). Voluntary facial action generates emotion-specific autonomic nervous system activity. *Psychophysiology, 27,* 363-384.

Leventhal, H. (1970). Findings and theory in the study of fear communications. *Advances in Experimental Social Psychology, 5,* 119-186.

Leventhal, H., Watts, J. C., & Pagano, F. (1967). Effects of fear and instructions on how to cope with danger. *Journal of Personality and Social Psychology, 6,* 313-321.

Levin, I. (1987). Associative effects of information framing. *Bulletin of the Psychonomic Society, 25,* 85-86.

Levy, J., Trevarthen, C., & Sperry, R. W. (1972). Perception of bilateral chimeric figures following hemispheric disconnection. *Brain, 95,* 61-78.

Levy, R. I., & Moskowitz, J. (1982). Cardiovascular research: Decades of progress, a decade of promise. *Science, 217,* 121-129.

Lewin, K. (1946). Behavior and development as a function of the total situation. In D. Cartwright (Ed.), *Field theory in social science.* New York: Harper & Row.

Lewin, K., Lippitt, R., & White, R. (1939). Patterns of aggressive behavior in experimentally created social climates. *Journal of Psychology, 10,* 271-299.

Lewin, R. (1987). Dramatic results with brain grafts. *Science, 237,* 245-247.

Lewin, R. (1988). Cloud over Parkinson's therapy. *Science, 240,* 390-391.

Lewin, T. (1987, August 16). Medical use of fetal tissue spurs new abortion debate. *New York Times,* p. 30.

Lewis, R. A. (1973). A longitudinal test of a developmental framework for premarital dyadic formation. *Journal of Marriage and the Family, 35,* 16-25.

Ley, R. (1991). *A whisper of espionage.* Garden City Park, NY: Avery.

Lezak, M. D. (1983). *Neuropsychological assessment* (2nd ed.). New York: Oxford University Press.

Li, C. (1975). *Path analysis: A primer.* Pacific Grove, CA: Boxwood Press.

Liang, J. C., Juler, R., & McGaugh, J. L. (1986). Modulating effects of posttraining epinephrine on memory: Involvement of the amygdala noradrenergic system. *Brain Research, 368,* 125-133.

Lickey, M. E. & Gordon, B. (1991). *Medicine and mental illness: The use of drugs in psychiatry.* New York: W. H. Freeman.

Lidz, T. (1973). *The origin and treatment of schizophrenic disorders.* New York: Basic Books.

Liebert, R. M., & Baron, R. A. (1972). Some immediate effects of televised violence on children's behavior. *Developmental Psychology, 6,* 469-475.

Liebert, R. M., & Spiegler, M. D. (1974). *Personality: Strategies for the study of man.* Homewood, IL: Dorsey.

Liebert, R. M., & Sprafkin, J. (1988). *The early window: Effects of television on children and youth.* New York: Pergamon Press.

Lifton, R. J. (1967). *Death in life: Survivors of Hiroshima.* New York: Random House.

Lifton, R. J. (1986). *The Nazi doctors.* New York: Basic Books.

Lilly, J. C. (1967). *The mind of the dolphin.* New York: Doubleday.

Limber, J. (1977). Language in child and chimp. *American Psychologist, 32,* 280-295.

Lindsay, D. S., & Johnson, M. K. (1987). Reality monitoring and suggestibility: Children's ability to discriminate among memories from different stories. In S. J. Ceci, M. P. Toglia, & D. F. Ross (Eds.), *Children's eyewitness memory.* New York: Springer-Verlag.

Lindsay, P. H., & Norman, D. A. (1977). *Human information processing.* New York: Academic Press.

Lindsley, O. R., Skinner, B. F., & Solomon, H. C. (1953). *Studies in behavior therapy: Status report 1.* Waltham, MA: Metropolitan State Hospital.

Lindvall, O., Brundin, P., Swidner, H., Rehncrona, S., Gustavii, B., et al. (1990). Grafts of fetal dopamine neurons survive and improve motor function in Parkinson's disease. *Science, 247,* 574-577.

Linville, P. W. (1982). The complexity-extremity effect and age-based stereotyping. *Journal of Personality and Social Psychology, 42,* 193-211.

Linville, P. W., & Jones, E. E. (1980). Polarized appraisals of outgroup members. *Journal of Personality and Social Psychology, 38,* 689-703.

Linz, D., Donnerstein, E., & Adams, S. M. (1989). Physiological desensitization and judgments about female victims. *Human Communication Research, 15,* 509– 522.

Livingstone, M., & Hubel, D. (1988). Segregation of form, color, movement, and depth: Anatomy, physiology, & perception. *Science, 240,* 740–749.

Lloyd, K. E. (1978). Behavior analysis and technology in higher education. In A. C. Carania & T. A. Brigham (Eds.), *Handbook of applied behavior analysis.* New York: Irvington.

Lloyd, K. E., & Lloyd, M. E. (1987). Personalized system of instruction. In L. A. Haerlynck & R. P. West (Eds.), *Design for excellence in education: Legacy of B. F. Skinner.* Hillsdale, NJ: Erlbaum.

Loeb, G. E. (1985). The functional replacement of the ear. *Scientific American, 252,* 104–111.

Loehlin, J. C., Lindzey, G., & Spuhler, J. N. (1975). *Race differences in intelligence.* San Francisco: Freeman.

Loftus, E. F. (1979). The malleability of human memory. *American Scientist, 67,* 313–320.

Loftus, E. F. (1980). *Eyewitness testimony.* Cambridge, MA: Harvard University Press.

Loftus, E. F. (1984). Eyewitness on trial. In B. D. Sales & A. Alwork (Eds.), *With liberty and justice for all.* Englewood Cliffs, NJ: Prentice-Hall.

Loftus, E. F. (1986). Experimental psychologist as advocate or impartial educator. *Law and Human Behavior, 10,* 63–78.

Loftus, E. F. (1991). Resolving legal questions with psychological data. *American Psychologist, 46,* 1046– 1048.

Loftus, E. F., & Hoffman, H. G. (1989). Misinformation and memory: The creation of new memories. *Journal of Experimental Psychology: General, 118,* 100–104.

Loftus, E. F., & Loftus, G. R. (1980). On the permanance of stored information in the human brain. *American Psychologist, 35,* 409–420.

Loftus, E. F., & Zanni, G. (1975). Eyewitness testimony: The influence of wording of a question. *Bulletin of the Psychonomic Society, 5,* 86–88.

Londerville, S., & Main, M. (1981). Security of attachment, compliance, and maternal training methods in the second year of life. *Developmental Psychology, 17,* 289–299.

Long, G. M. (1980). Iconic memory: A review and critique of the study of short-term visual storage. *Psychological Bulletin, 88,* 785–820.

Longnet-Higgins, H. D. (1987). *Mental processes.* Cambridge, MA: MIT Press.

Lord, C. G., Ross, L., & Lepper, M. R. (1979). Biased assimilation and attitude polarization: The effects of prior theories on subsequently considered evidence. *Journal of Personality and Social Psychology, 27,* 2098–2109.

Lorenz, K. (1966). *On aggression.* New York: Harcourt Brace Jovanovich.

Luborsky, L. (1977). New directions in research on neurotic and psychosomatic symptoms. In I. L. Janis (Ed.), *Current trends in psychology: Readings from the American Scientist.* Los Altos, CA: Kaufmann.

Luchins, A. (1942). Mechanization in problem solving. *Psychological Monographs, 54* (6, Whole No. 248).

Luchins, A. (1957). Primacy-recency effects in impression formation. In C. Hovland et al. (Eds.), *The order of presentation in persuasion.* New Haven, CT: Yale University Press.

Luckey, E. G., & Bain, J. K. (1970). Children: A factor in marital satisfaction. *Journal of Marriage and the Family, 32,* 43–44.

Luddens, H., Pritchett, D. B., Kohler, M., Killish, I., Keinananen, K., Monyer, H., Sprengel, R., & Seeberg, P. H. (1990). Cerebellar GABA, receptor selective for a behavioral alcohol antagonist. *Nature, 346,* 648–651.

Luria, A. R. (1968). *The mind of mnemonist.* New York: Basic Books.

Luria, A. R. (1973). *The working brain: An introduction to neuropsychology* (B. Haigh, Trans.). New York: Basic Books.

Lykken, D. T. (1957). A study of anxiety in the sociopathic personality. *Journal of Abnormal and Social Psychology, 55,* 6–10.

Lykken, D. T. (1979). The detection of deception. *Psychological Bulletin, 86* (1), 47–53.

Lykken, D. T. (1981). *A tremor in the blood: Uses and abuses of the lie detector.* New York: McGraw-Hill.

Lykken, D. T. (1982, September). Fearlessness: Its carefree charm and deadly risks. *Psychology Today,* pp. 20–28.

Lynch, J. (1977). *The broken heart.* New York: Basic Books.

Macauley, R. K. (1980). *Generally speaking: How children learn language.* Rowley, MA: Newbury House.

Maccoby, E. E. (1990) Gender and relationships: A developmental account. *American Psychologist, 45,* 513–520.

Maccoby, E. E., & Jacklin, C. N. (1974). *The psychology of sex differences.* Stanford, CA: Stanford University Press.

Maccoby, E. E., & Jacklin, C. N. (1980). Sex differences in aggression: a regainer and reprise. *Child Development, 51,* 964–980.

MacFarlane, J. W. (1964). Perspectives on personality consistency and change from the guidance study. *Vita Humana, 7,* 115–126.

Mack, S. (1981). Novel help for the handicapped. *Science, 212,* 26–27.

Mackenzie, J. (1886). The production of so called "rose cold" by means of an artificial rose. *American Journal of Medical Science 91,* 45–57.

Mackintosh, N. J. (1974). *The psychology of animal learning.* London: Academic Press.

Mackintosh, N. J. (1983). *Conditioning and associative learning.* New York: Oxford University Press.

MacQueen, G., Marshall, J., Perdue, M., Siegal, S., & Bienenstock, J. (1989). Pavlovian conditioning of rat mucosal mast cells to secrete rat mast cell protease II. *Science, 234,* 83–85.

Madanes, C. (1981). *Strategic family therapy.* San Francisco: Jossey-Bass.

Maddi, S. R., & Kobasa, S. C. (1984). *The hardy executive: Health under stress.* Homewood, IL: Irwin.

Maddux, J. E., & Rogers, R. W. (1983). Protection motivation and self-efficacy: A revised theory of fear appeals and attitude change. *Journal of Experimental Social Psychology, 19,* 469–479.

Madrazo, I., Drucker-Colin, R., Diaz, V., Martinez-Mata, J., Torres, C., & Becerril, J. J. (1987). Open microsurgical autograft of adrenal medulla to the right caudate nucleus in two patients with intractable Parkinson's disease. *New England Journal of Medicine, 316,* 831–834.

Maeir, S. F. (1989). Learned helplessness: Event covariation and cognitive changes. In S. B. Klein & R. R. Mowrer (Eds.) *Contemporary learning theories.* Hillsdale, N.J.: Erlbaum, 73–110.

Magnusson, D., & Endler, N. S. (1977). *Personality at the crossroads: Current issues in interactional psychology.* New York: Halsted Press.

Mahl, G. F. (1949). Anxiety, HCL secretion, and peptic ulcer etiology. *Psychosomatic Medicine, 11,* 30–44.

Maier, N. R. (1931). Reasoning in humans. Journal of *Comparative Psychology, 12,* 181–194.

Main, M., & Weston, D. (1981). The quality of the toddler's relationship to mother and father: Related to conflict behavior and readiness to establish new relationships. *Child Development, 52,* 932–940.

Mandler, G. (1975). *Mind and emotion.* New York: Wiley.

Mann, D. M. A. (1988). Neuropathological and neurochemical aspects of Alzheimer's disease. In: L. L. Iverson & S. D. Iverson (Eds.) *Handbook of psychopharmacology.* New York: Plenum.

Mannuzza, S., Fyer, A. J., Martin, L. Y., Gallops, M. S., Endicott, J., Gorman, J., Liebowitz, M. R., & Klein, D. F. (1989). Reliability of anxiety assessment. *Archives of General Psychiatry, 46,* 1093-1101.

Manucia, G. K., Baumann, D. J., & Cialdini, R. B. (1984). Mood influences on helping: Direct effects or side effects? *Journal of Personality and Social Psychology, 46,* 357-364.

Maraschark, M., Richman, C. L., Yuille, J. C., & Hunt, R. R. (1987). The role of imagery in memory. *Psychological Bulletin, 102,* 28-41.

Marcel, A. J. (1983). Conscious and unconscious perception: Experiments on visual masking and word recognition. *Cognitive Psychology, 15,* 197-237.

Marcia, J. E. (1967). Ego identity status: Relationship to change in self-esteem, "general maladjustment," and authortarianism. *Journal of Personality, 35,* 118-133.

Marcia, J. E., & Freedman, M. L. (1970). Ego identity status in college women. *Journal of Personality, 38,* 249-263.

Marek, G. R. (1982). Toscanini's memory. In U. Neisser (Ed.), *Memory observed* (pp. 414-417). San Francisco: Freeman.

Mark, V., & Erwin, F. (1970). *Violence and the brain.* New York: Harper & Row.

Mark, V., Sweet, W. H., & Ervin, F. (1972). The effect of amygdalectomy on violent behavior in patients with temporal lobe epilepsy. In E. Hitchcock, L. Laitinen, & K. Vaernet (Eds.), *Psychosurgery.* Springfield, IL: Charles C. Thomas.

Marks, I. (1981). Behavioral treatment plus drugs in anxiety syndromes. In D. F. Klein & J. Rabkin (Eds.), *Anxiety: New research and changing concepts.* New York: Raven Press.

Marks, I. M., & Gelder, M. G. (1967). Transvestism and fetishism: Clinical and psychological changes during faradic aversion. *British Journal of Psychiatry, 113,* 711-729.

Marsh, J. (Ed.) (1990). The biology of nicotine dependence. Ciba Foundation.

Marshall, G. P., & Zimbardo, P. G. (1979). Affective consequences of inadequately explained physiological arousal. *Journal of Personality and Social Psychology, 37,* 970-988.

Martin, B. (1981). *Abnormal psychology: Clinical and scientific perspectives* (2nd ed.). New York: Holt, Rinehart & Winston.

Martin, J. A. (1977). The effects of positive and negative adult-child interactions on children's task performance and task preferences. *Journal of Experimental Child Psychology, 23,* 493-502.

Martin, J. H., & Brust, J. C. M. (1985). Imaging the living brain. In E. R. Kandel & J. H. Schwartz (Eds.), *Principles of neural science.* New York: Elsevier.

Martin, R. A., & Poland, E. Y. (1980). *Learning to change: A self-management approach to adjustment.* New York: McGraw-Hill.

Maslach, C. (1979). Negative emotional biasing of unexplained arousal. *Journal of Personality and Social Psychology, 37,* 359-369.

Masland, R. H. (1986). The functional architecture of the retina. *Scientific American, 255,* 102-111.

Maslow, A. H. (1954). *Motivation and personality.* New York: Harper.

Maslow, A. H. (1962). *Toward a psychology of being.* Princeton, NJ: Van Nostrand.

Maslow, A. H. (1968). *Toward a psychology of being* (2nd ed.). Princeton, NJ: Van Nostrand.

Maslow, A. H. (1970). *Motivation and personality* (2nd ed.). New York: Harper.

Masters, J. C. & Keil, L. S. (1987). Generic comparison process in human judgement and behavior. In Masters, J. C. and Smith, W. P. (Eds.), *Social Comparison, Social Justice, and Relative Deprivation,* 11-54. Hillsdale, NJ: Erlbaum.

Masters, W. H., & Johnson, V. E. (1966). *Human sexual response.* Boston: Little, Brown.

Masters, W. H., & Johnson, V. E. (1970). *Human sexual inadequacy.* Boston: Little, Brown.

Masters, W. H., & Johnson, V. E. (1979). *Homosexuality in perspective.* Boston: Little, Brown.

Matarazzo, J. D. (1982). Behavioral health's challenge to academic, scientific, and professional psychology. *American Psychologist, 36,* 1-14.

Matlin, M. W. (1983). *Perception.* Boston: Allyn & Bacon.

Matsuda, L. A., Lolait, S. J., Brownstein, M. J., Young, A. C. & Bonner, T. I. (1990). Structure of a cannabinoid receptor and functional expression of the cloned cDNA. *Nature, 346,* 561-564.

Matthies, H. (1989). Neurobiological aspects of learning and memory. *Annual Review of Psychology, 1989, 40.*

Maugh, T. A. (1990, Feb. 19) Love, American style: Surveys say risks overstated. *Los Angeles Times.*

Maurer, D., & Salapatek, P. (1976). Developmental changes in the scanning of faces by young infants. *Child Development, 47,* 523-527.

Mazziota, J. C., & Phelps, M. E. (1985). Human neuropsychological imaging studies of local brain metabolism: Strategies and results. *Research Publication of the Association for Research on Nervous and Mental Disorders, 63,* 121-137.

McArthur, L. A. (1972). The how and what of why: Some determinants and consequences of causal attribution. *Journal of Personality and Social Psychology, 22,* 171-193.

McCall, R. B., Appelbaum, M. I., & Hogarty, P. S. (1973). Developmental changes in mental performance. *Monographs of the Society for Research in Child Development, 38* (Serial No. 150).

McCann, I. L., & Holmes, D. S. (1984). Influence of aerobic exercise on depression. *Journal of Personality and Social Psychology, 46,* 1142-1147.

McCaul, K. D., & Malott, J. M. (1984). Distraction and coping with pain. *Psychological Bulletin, 95,* 516-533.

McClean, P. (1977). The triune brain in conflict. *Psychotherapy and Psychosomatics, 28,* 207-220.

McClelland, D. C. (1971). *Motivational trends in society.* Morristown, NJ: General Learning Press.

McClelland, D. C. (1973). Testing for competence rather than for intelligence. *American Psychologist, 28,* 1-14.

McClelland, D. C., Atkinson, J. W., Clark, R. A., & Lowell, E. L. (1953). *The achievement motive.* New York: Appleton-Century-Crofts.

McClelland, D. C., & Steele, R. S. (1972). *Motivation workshops.* New York: General Learning Press.

McClelland, D. C., & Winter, D. G. (1969). *Motivating economic achievement.* New York: Free Press.

McClelland, J. L., & Rumelhart, D. E. (1981). An interactive activation model of context effects on letter perception: Part 1. An account of basic findings. *Psychological Review, 88,* 375-407.

McClosky, M., Wible, C. G. & Cohen, N. J. (1988). Is there a special flashbulb memory mechanism? *Journal of Experimental Psychology: General, 117,* 171-181.

McCloskey, M., & Zaragoza, M. (1985). Misleading postevent information and memory for events: Arguments and evidence against memory impairment hypothesis. *Journal of Experimental Psychology: General, 114,* 1-16.

McDougall, W. (1908). *Social psychology.* New York: G. P. Putnam's Sons.

McFadden, D., & Wightman, F. L. (1983). Audition:

Some relations between normal and pathological hearing. *Annual Review of Psychology, 34,* 95-128.

McGaugh J. L. (1983). *Annual review of psychology.*

McGaugh J. L. (1988). Modulation of memory storage processes. In P. R. Solomon, G. R. Goethals, C. M. Kelley, & B. Stephens (Eds.), *Memory: Interdisciplinary approaches.* New York: Springer-Verlag.

McGaugh, J. L. (1989). Involvement of hormonal and neuromodulatory systems in the regulation of memory storage. *Annual Review of Neuroscience, 12,* 255-288.

McGhee, P. E., & Frueh, T. (1980). Television viewing and the learning of stereotypes. *Sex Roles, 6,* 179-188.

McGhie, A., & Chapman, J. (1961). Disorders of attention and perception in early schizophrenia. *British Journal of Medical Psychology, 34,* 103-117.

McGill, T. (1977). *Readings in animal behavior.* New York: Holt.

McGinnies, E. (1970). *Social behavior: A functional analysis.* Boston: Houghton Mifflin.

McGinniss, J. M. (1991). Health objectives for the nation. *American Psychologist, 46,* 520-524.

McGovern, T. V., Furumoto, L., Halpern, D. F., Kimble, G. A., & McKeachie, W. J. (1991). Liberal education, study in depth, and the arts and sciences major—psychology. *American Psychologist, 46,* 598-605.

McGrath, E., Keita, G. P., Strickland, B. & Russo, N. F. (Eds.) (1990). *Women and Depression: Risk Factors and Treatment Issues.* Washington, D.C.: American Psychological Association.

McGuire, W. J. (1960). A syllogistic analysis of cognitive relationships. In M. J. Rosenberg & C. I. Hovland (Eds.), *Attitude organization and change.* New Haven, CT: Yale University Press.

McGuire, W. J. (1969). The nature of attitudes and attitude change. In G. Lindzey & E. Aronson (Eds.), *Handbook of social psychology. Vol. 3.* Reading, MA: Addison-Wesley.

McGuire, W. J. (1985). Attitudes and attitude change. In G. Lindzey & E. Aronson (Eds.), *Handbook of social psychology* (3rd ed.). *Vol. 2* (pp. 233-346). New York: Random House.

McKay, D. G. (1973). Aspects of the theory of comprehension, memory, and attention. *Quarterly Journal of Experimental Psychology, 25,* 22-40.

McMinn, M. R. (1984). Mechanisms of energy balance in obesity. *Behavioral Neuroscience, 98,* 375-393.

McNally, R. J. (1987). Preparedness and phobias. *Psychological Review, 101,* 283-303.

McNeil, D. (1970). *The acquisition of language.* New York: Harper & Row.

McNeil, T. F., & Kay, L. (1987). Swedish high-risk study: Sample characteristics at age 6. *Schizophrenia Bulletin, 13,* 373-381.

McRae, R. R., & Costa, P. T., Jr. (1987). Validation of the five-factor model of personality across instruments and observers. *Journal of Personality and Social Psychology, 52,* 81-90.

McRae, R. R., & Costa, P. T., Jr. (1991). Adding *liebe und arbeit:* the full five-factor model and well-being. *Personality and Social Psychology Bulletin, 17,* 227-232.

McShane, J. (1991). *Cognitive development.* Oxford: Basil Blackwell.

Mead, M. (1935). *Sex and temperament in three primitive societies.* New York: Morrow.

Meador, B. D., & Rogers, C. R. (1984). Person-centered therapy. In R. J. Corsini (Ed.), *Current psychotherapies* (3rd ed.). Itasca, IL: Peacock.

Megargee, E. I. (1976). The prediction of dangerous behavior. *Criminal Justice and Behavior, 3,* 3-22.

Meichenbaum, D. (1977). *Cognitive-behavior modification: An integrative approach.* New York: Plenum.

Meltzer, H. Y., & Stahl, S. M. (1976). The dopamine hypothesis of schizophrenia. *Schizophrenia Bulletin, 2,* 19-76.

Melzack, R. (1973). *The puzzle of pain.* London: Penguin.

Melzack, R., & Wall, P. D. (1965). Pain mechanisms: A new theory. *Science, 150,* 971-979.

Mental Health Letter (1985). *The antisocial personality.* (Vol. 2, pp. 1-4). Boston: Harvard Medical School.

Menyuk, P. (1983). Language development and reading. In T. M. Gallagher & C. A. Prutting (Eds.), *Pragmatic assessment and intervention issues in language.* San Diego: College-Hill Press.

Menzel, E. W. (1978). Cognitive mapping in chimpanzees. In S. H. Hulse, H. Fowler, & W. K. Honig (Eds.), *Cognitive processes in animal behavior.* Hillsdale, NJ: Erlbaum.

Mercer, J. R. (1984). What is a racially and culturally nondiscriminatory test? A sociological and pluralistic perspective. In C. R. Reynolds & R. T. Brown (Eds.), *Perspectives on bias in mental testing.* New York: Plenum.

Meredith, H. V. (1975). Somatic changes during prenatal life. *Child Development, 46,* 603-610.

Mesalum, M. M. (1983). The functional anatomy and hemispheric specialization for directed attention. *Trends in the Neurosciences, 63,* 345-387.

Mezibov, D. (1981). Cited in *Behavior Today, 12* (31), 2-3.

Michels, R. (1990). Psychoanalysis: The second century. *Harvard Mental Health Letter, 7,* 5-7.

Milgram, S. (1974). *Obedience to authority.* New York: Harper & Row.

Miller, C. T., Byrne, D., & Fisher, J. D. (1980). Order effects on sexual and affective responses to erotic stimuli by males and females. *Journal of Sex Research, 16,* 131-147.

Miller, G. A. (1956). The magical number seven, plus or minus two: Some limits on our capicity for information processing. *Psychological Review, 63,* 81-87.

Miller, J. A. (1983). Lessons for the lab. *Science News, 124,* 394-396.

Miller, L. J., & Branconnier, R. J. (1983). Cannabis: Effects on memory and the cholingeric limbic system. *Psychological Bulletin, 93,* 441-456.

Miller, N. E. (1951). Comments on theoretical models: Illustrated by the development of a theory of conflict behavior. *Journal of Personality and Social Psychology, 20,* 82-100.

Miller, P. H., Haynes, V. F., DeMarie-Dreblow, D., & Woody-Ramsey. (1986). Children's strategies for gathering information in three tasks. *Child Development, 57,* 1429-1439.

Millon, T. (1981). *Disorders of personality.* New York: Wiley.

Mills, J., & Aronson, E. (1965). Opinion change as a function of communicator's attractiveness and desire to influence. *Journal of Personality and Social Psychology, 1,* 173-177.

Milner, B. A. (1963). Effects of different brain lesions on card sorting. *Archives of Neurology* (Chicago), *9,* 90-100.

Milner, B. (1966). Amnesia following operation on the temporal lobe. In C. M. Whitty & O. L. Zangwill (Eds.), *Amnesia.* London: Buttersworth.

Milner, B. (1972). Disorders of learning and memory after temporal lobe lesions in man. *Clinical Neurosurgery, 19,* 421-446.

Milner, B., & Petrides, M. (1984). Behavioral effects of frontal lobe lesions in man. *Trends in the Neurosciences, 7* (11), 403-407.

Milstein, R. M. (1980). Responsiveness in newborn infants of overweight and normal weight parents. *Appetite, 1,* 65-74.

Minuchin, S. (1974). *Families and family therapy.* Cambridge, MA: Harvard University Press.

Mischel, W. (1968). *Personality and assessment.* New York: Wiley.

Mischel, W. (1973). Toward a cognitive social learning reconceptualization of personality. *Psychological Review, 80,* 252-283.

Mischel, W. (1984). Convergences and challenges in the search for consistency. *American Psychologist, 39,* 351-364.

Mischel, W., & Mischel, H. N. (1980). *Essentials of psychology.* New York: Random House.

Mishkin, M., & Appenzeller, T. (1987). The anatomy of memory. *Scientific American, 256,* 80-89.

Mitchell, D. E., & Wilkinson, F. (1974). The effect of early astigmatism on the visual resolution of gratings. *Journal of Psychology, 243,* 739-756.

Moerk, E., & Moerk, C. (1979). Quotations, imitations, and generalizations: Factual and methodological analyses. *International Journal of Behavioral Development, 2,* 43-72.

Mogenson, G. J. (1976). Neural mechanism of hunger: Current status and future prospects. In D. Novin, W. Wyrwicka, & G. Bray (Eds.), *Hunger: Basic mechanisms and clinical applications.* New York: Raven Press.

Mollon, J. D. (1982). Colour vision and colour blindness. In H. B. Barlow & J. D. Mollon, *The senses* (pp. 165-191). New York: Cambridge University Press.

Money, J., & Ehrhardt, A. (1972). *Man and woman, boy and girl.* Baltimore: The Johns Hopkins University Press.

Monson, T. C., & Snyder, M. (1977). Actors, observers, and the attribution process: Toward a reconceptualization. *Journal of Experimental Social Psychology, 13,* 89-111.

Montermayor, R. (1982). The relationship between parent-adolescent conflict and the amount of time parents spend alone with parents and peers. *Child Development, 53,* 1512-1519.

Moore, J. W., & Solomon, P. R. (Eds.). (1980). The role of the hippocampus in learning and memory [Special issue]. *Physiological Psychology, 2.*

Moore, R. Y. (1987). Parkison's disease—a new therapy. *New England Journal of Medicine, 316,* 872-873.

Moreland, R. K., & Zajonc, R. B. (1982). Exposure effects in person perception: Familiarity, similarity, and attraction. *Journal of Experimental Social Psychology, 18,* 395-415.

Morgan, C. D., & Murray, H. A. (1935). A method for investigating fantasies. *Archives of Neurological Psychiatry, 34,* 289-306.

Morgan, C. T., & Morgan, J. D. (1940). Studies in hunger. II. The relation of gastric denervation and dietary sugar to the effects of insulin upon food intake in the rat. *Journal of General Psychology, 57,* 153-163.

Morin, S. F., & Rothblum, E. D. (1991). Removing the stigma: fifteen years of progress. *American Psychologist, 46,* 947-949.

Morrison, D. M. (1985). Adolescent contraceptive behavior: A review. *Psychological Bulletin, 98,* 538-568.

Morse, S. J., & Watson, R. I., Jr. (1977). *Psychotherapies: A comparative casebook.* New York: Holt, Rinehart & Winston.

Moscovici, S. (1985). Social influence and conformity. In G. Lindzey & E. Aronson (Eds.), *Handbook of social psychology* (3rd ed.) (pp. 347-412). New York: Random House.

Moscovici, S., & Mugny, G. (1983). Minority influences. In P. Paulus (Ed.), *Basic group process.* New York: Springer-Verlag.

Moscovici, S., & Zavalloni, M. (1969). The group as a polarizer of attitudes. *Journal of Personality and Social Psychology, 12,* 125-135.

Mowrer, O. H. (1947). On the dual nature of learning—a reinterpretation of "conditioning" and "problem solving." *Harvard Educational Review, 17,* 102-148.

Mueller, E., & Lucas, T. (1975). A developmental analysis of peer interaction among toddlers. In M. Lewis & L. A. Rosenblum (Eds.), *Friendship and peer relations.* New York: Wiley.

Mueller, E., & Vandall, D. (1979). Infant-infant interaction. In J. Osofsky (Ed.), *Handbook of infant development.* New York: Wiley.

Muir, D., & Field, J. (1979). Newborn infants orient to sound. *Child Development, 50,* 431-436.

Munsinger, H. (1975). The adopted child's I.Q.: A critical review. *Psychological Bulletin, 82,* 623-659.

Murphy, J. M. (1976). Psychiatric labeling in crosscultural perspective. *Science, 191,* 1019-1028.

Murphy, T. N. (1982). Pain: Its assessment, and management. In R. J. Gatchel, A. Baum, & A. E. Singer (Eds.), *Handbook of psychology and health. Vol. 1. Clinical psychology and behavioral medicine: Overlapping disciplines.* Hillsdale, NJ: Erlbaum.

Murray, H. A. (1938). *Explorations in personality.* New York: Oxford.

Murray, H. A., & Kluckhohn, C. (1953). Outline of a conception of personality. In C. Kluckhohn, H. A. Murray, & D. Schneider (Eds.), *Personality in nature, society, and culture* (2nd ed.). New York: Knopf.

Murray, J. D., & Keller, P. A. (1991). Psychology and rural America: current status and future directions. *American Psychologist, 46,* 220-231.

Murstein, B. I. (1972a). Person perception and courtship progress among premarital couples. *Journal of Marriage and the Family, 34,* 621-626.

Murstein, B. I. (1972b). Physical attractiveness and marital choice. *Journal of Personality and Social Psychology, 22,* 8-12.

Murstein, B. I. (1980). Mate selection in the 1970s. *Journal of Marriage and Family, 42,* 51-66.

Mussen, P. H., Conger, J. J., & Kagan, J. (1979). *Child development and personality.* New York: Harper & Row.

Mussen, P. H., Conger, J. J., Kagan, J., & Geiwitz, J. (1979). *Psychological development: A life-span approach.* New York: Harper & Row.

Myers, D. G. (1983). Polarizing effects of social interaction. In H. Brandstatter, J. H. Davis, & G. Stocker-Kreichgauer (Eds.), *Group decision processes.* London: Academic Press.

Myers, D. G., & Bishop, G. D. (1970). Discussion effect of racial attitudes. *Science, 169,* 778-779.

🕊

Napolitan, D. A., & Goethals, G. R. (1979). The attribution of friendliness. *Journal of Experimental Social Psychology, 15,* 105-133.

NAS calls tests fair but limited. (1982, April). *American Psychological Association Monitor,* p. 9.

Nathan, P. E., & Harris, S. L. (1980). *Psychopathology and society* (2nd ed.). New York: McGraw-Hill.

Nathans, J., Piantanidu, T. P., Eddy, R. L., Shows, T. B., & Hogness, D. S. (1986). Molecular genetics of inherited variation in human color vision. *Science, 232* 203-210.

National Academy of Sciences. (1982). *Marijuana and health.* Washington, DC: National Academy Press.

National Center for Health Statistics. (1977, September). *Monthly vital statistics report: Natality statistics.* Washington, DC: Department of Health, Education and Welfare.

National Council of Community Mental Health Centers. (1991). *National registry of community mental health services.* Rockville, MD: Author.

National Institute on Drug Abuse. (1982). *Marijuana*

and health. Washington, DC: Government Printing Office.

National Institute of Mental Health. (1977). *Psychiatric services and the changing institutional scene, 1950-1985* (DHEW Publication No. ADM 77-433). Washington, DC: Government Printing Office.

National Institute of Mental Health. (1978). *The switch process in manic-depressive illness* (DHEW Publication No. ADM 78-633). Washington, DC: Government Printing Office.

National Institute of Mental Health. (1982). *Television and behavior: Ten years of scientific progress and implications for the eighties* (DHHS Publication No. ADM 82-1195). Washington, DC: Government Printing Office.

National Institute of Mental Health (1989). *Mutual help groups.* Rockville, MD: U.S.. Department of Health and Human Services.

National Institute of Mental Health. (1991). *Caring for people with severe mental disorders: A national plan of research to improve services.* Washington, D.C.: U.S. Government Printing Office.

Natsoulas, T. (1978). Consciousness. *American Psychologist, 33,* 906-914.

Nebes, R. D. (1974). Hemispheric specialization in commissurotomized man. *Psychological Bulletin, 81,* 1-14.

Neisser, U. (1967). *Cognitive psychology.* New York: Appleton-Century-Crofts.

Neisser, U. (Ed.). (1982). *Memory observed: Remembering in natural contexts.* San Francisco: Freeman.

Neisser, U. (1988). Domains of memory. In P. R. Solomon, G. R. Goethals, C. M. Kelley, & B. Stephens (Eds.), *Memory: Interdisciplinary approaches.* New York: Springer-Verlag.

Nelson, K. (1973). Structure and strategy in learning to talk. *Monographs of the Society for Research in Child Development, 38* (Serial No. 149).

Nelson, T. O. (1977). Repetition and depth of processing. *Journal of Verbal Learning and Verbal Behavior, 16,* 151-171.

Nemeth, C. (1986). Differential contributions of majority and minority influences. *Psychological Review, 93,* 23-32.

Nemiah, J. C. (1978). The dynamic bases of psychopathology. In A. M. Nicholi, Jr. (Ed.), *The Harvard guide to modern psychiatry.* Cambridge, MA: Belknap.

Neuberg, S. L. (1989). The goal of forming accurate impressions during social interactions: attenuating the impact of negative expectancies. *Journal of Personality and Social Psychology, 56,* 374-386.

Neugarten, B. L. (1968). The awareness of middle age. In B. L. Neugarten (Ed.), *Middle age and aging.* Chicago: University of Chicago Press.

Neugarten, B. L. (1977). Personality and aging. In J. E. Birren & K. W. Schaie (Eds.), *Handbook of the psychology of aging.* New York: Van Nostrand Reinhold.

Neugarten, B. L. (1980, April). Acting one's age: New rules for old. *Psychology Today,* pp. 66-80.

Newcomb, T. M. (1943). *Personality and social change.* New York: Dryden Press.

Newcomb, T. M. (1953). An approach to the study of communication. *Psychological Review, 60,* 393-404.

Newcomb, T. M. (1961). *The acquaintance process.* New York: Holt, Rinehart & Winston.

Newcomb, T. M., Koenig, K. E., Flacks, R., & Warwick, D. P. (1967). *Persistence and change: Bennington College and its students after twenty-five years.* New York: Wiley.

Newll, A., & Simon, H. (1972). *Human problem solving.* Englewood Cliffs, NJ: Prentice-Hall.

Newman, B. P. (1982). In B. B. Wolman (Ed.), *Handbook of developmental psychology.* Englewood Cliffs, NJ: Prentice-Hall.

Newman, B. P., & Newman, P. R. (1983). *Understanding adulthood.* New York: Holt, Rinehart & Winston.

Nickerson, R. S., & Adams, M. J. (1979). Long-term memory for a common object. *Cognitive Psychology, 11,* 287-307.

Nielson, S. L., & Sarason, I. G. (1981). Emotion, personality, and selective attention. *Journal of Personality and Social Psychology, 41,* 945-960.

Niemeyer, W., Starlinger, I. (1981). Do the blind hear better? *Audiology 20,* 503-515.

Nina, P. T., Insel, T. M., Cohen, R. M., Cook, J. M., Skolnick, P., & Paul, S. M. (1982). Benzodiazepine receptor-mediated experimental "anxiety" in primates. *Science, 218,* 1332-1334.

Nisbett, R. E., Caputo, C., Legant, P., & Maracek, J. (1973). Behavior as seen by the actor and as seen by the observer. *Journal of Personality and Social Psychology, 27,* 154-164.

Nisbett, R. E., & Wilson T. D. (1977). Telling more than we can know: Verbal reports on mental processes. *Psychological Review, 84,* 231-.

Nixon, R. (1982). *Leaders.* New York: Warner.

Noise pollution. (1986, June). *Harvard Health Letter,* pp. 1-4.

Nolen-Hoeksema, S. (1987). Sex differences in unipolar depression: Evidence and theory. *Psychological Bulletin, 101,* 259-282.

Norman, W. T. (1963). Toward an adequate taxonomy of personality attributes: Replicated factor structure in peer nomination personality ratings. *Journal of Abnormal and Social Psychology, 66,* 574-583

Oakes, P. J., & Turner, J. C. (1980). Social categorization and intergroup behavior: does minimal intergroup discrimination make social identity more positive? *European Journal of Social Psychology, 10,* 295-301.

O'Brien, M., & Huston, A. C. (1985). Development of sex-typed play behavior in toddlers. *Developmental Psychology, 21,* 866-871.

Oetting, E. R., & Beauvais, F. (1987). Peer cluster theory, socialization characteristics, and adolescent drug use: A path analysis. *Journal of Counseling Psychology, 34,* 205-213.

Offer, D. (1969). *The psychological world of the teenager: A study of normal adolescent boys.* New York: Basic Books.

Offer, D., & Offer, J. (1975). *From teenage to young manhood: A psychological study.* New York: Basic Books.

Offer, D., Ostrov, E., & Howard, K. I. (1981). *The adolescent: A psychological self portrait.* New York: Basic Books.

Ohman, A., Dimberg, U., & Ost, L. G. (1985). Animal and social phobias: Biological constraints on learned fear response. In S. Reiss & R. R. Bootzin (Eds.), *Theoretical issues in behavior therapy* (pp. 123-175). New York: Academic Press.

Ohman, A., Eriksson, A., & Olofsson, C. (1975). One trial learning and resistance to extinction of autonomic responses to potentially phobic stimuli. *Journal of Comparative and Physiological Psychology, 88,* 619-627.

Okin, R. L. (1987). The case for deinstitutionalization. *Harvard Medical School Mental Health Letter, 4* (4), 5-7.

Olds, J. M. (1958). Self stimulation experiments and differentiated reward systems. In H. H. Jasper, L. D. Proctor, R. S. Knighton, W. C. Noshay, & R. T. Costello (Eds.), *Reticular formation of the brain.* Boston: Little, Brown.

Olds, J. M., & Milner, P. M. (1954). Positive reinforcement produced by electrical stimulation of the septal area and other areas of the rat brain. *Journal of Comparative and Physiological Psychology, 46,* 419–427.

Olds, M. E., & Forbes, J. L. (1981). The central basis of motivation: Intercranial self-stimulation studies. *Annual Review of Psychology, 32,* 523–574.

Olson, G. M. (1981). The recognition of specific persons. In M. E. Lamb & L. R. Sherrod (Eds.), *Infant social cognition: Empirical and theoretical considerations.* Hillsdale, NJ: Erlbaum.

Olson, G. M., & Sherman, T. (1983). Attention, learning, and memory in infants. In P. H. Mussen (Ed.), *Handbook of child psychology: Vol. 2. Infancy and developmental psychobiology* (pp. 1001–1080). New York: Wiley.

Olson, J. M. & Cal, A. V. (1984). Source credibility, attitudes, and the recall of past behavior. *European Journal of Social Psychology, 14,* 203–210.

Olson, J. M., Herman, C. P., & Zanna, M. P. (1986). *Relative deprivation and social comparison: The Ontario symposium. Vol. 4.* Hillsdale, NJ: Erlbaum.

Olton, D. S., & Wenk, G. L. (1987). Dementia: Animal models of the cognitive impairments produced by degeneration of the basal forebrain cholinergic system. In H. Y. Meltzer (Ed.) *Psychopharmacology: third generation of progress.* New York: Raven Press.

Opton, E. (1979, December). A psychologist takes a closer look at the recent landmark *Larry P.* opinion. *American Psychological Association Monitor.*

Orne, M. R., Whitehouse, W. G., Dinges, D. F., & Orne, E. C. (1988). Reconstructing memory through hypnosis: Forensic and clinical implications. In H. M. Pettinati (Ed.), *Hypnosis and memory* (pp. 21–63). New York: Guilford Press.

Orne, M. T. (1966). Mechanisms of post-hypnotic amnesia. *International Journal of Clinical and Experimental Hypnosis, 14,* 121–134.

Orne, M. T. (1972). Can a hypnotized subject be compelled to carry out otherwise unacceptable behavior? *International Journal of Clinical and Experimental Hypnosis, 20,* 101–117.

Orne, M. T., Soskis, D. A., Dinges, E. F., & Orne, D. C. (1984). Hypnotically induced testimony. In G. Wells & E. F. Loftus (Eds.), *Eyewitness Testimony; Psychological Perspective* (pp. 171–213). New York: Cambridge University Press.

Ornstein, R. E. (1977). *The psychology of consciousness* (2nd ed.). New York: Harcourt Brace Jovanovich.

Osborne, R. E., & Gilbert, D. T. (1992). The preoccupational hazards of social life. *Journal of Personality and Social Psychology, 62,* 219–228.

Osherow, N. (1984). Making sense of the nonsensical: An analysis of Jonestown. In E. Aronson (Ed.), *Readings about the social animal.* New York: Freeman.

Oskamp, S. (1977). *Attitudes and opinions.* Englewood Cliffs, NJ: Prentice-Hall.

Ouchi, W. G. (1981). *Theory Z.* New York: Avon Books.

Overmier, J. B., & Hollis, K. (1990). Fish in the think tank: Learning, memory, and integrated behavior. In Kesner, R. P., & Olton, D. S. (Eds.), *Neurobiology of Comparative Cognition.* Hillsdale, NJ: Erlbaum.

Paivio, A. (1971). *Imagery and verbal processes.* New York: Holt, Rinehart & Winston.

Paivio, A. (1986). *Mental representations: A dual coding approach.* New York: Oxford University Press.

Paivio, A., & Desrochers, A. (1980). A dual coding approach to bilingual memory. *Canadian Journal of Psychology, 34,* 388–399.

Palca, J. (1989). Sleep researchers awake to possibilities. *Science, 245,* 351–352.

Pallak, S. R., Murroni, E., & Koch, J. (1983). Communicator attractiveness and expertise, emotional versus rational appeals, and persuasion: A heuristic versus systematic processing interpretation. *Social Cognition, 2,* 122–141.

Palmore, E. B. (1981). The facts on aging quiz: Part two. *The Gerontologist, 21,* 431–437.

Paloutzian, R. F. (1983). *Invitaton to the psychology of religion.* Glenview, IL: Scott, Foresman.

Pandya, D. N., & Seltzer, B. (1982). Association areas of the cerebral cortex. *Trends in the Neurosciences, 53,* 386–390.

Papastamov, S., & Mugny, G. (1985). Rigidity and minority influences: The influence of the social in social influence. In S. Moscovici & E. van Avermaet (Eds.), *Perspectives on minority influence.* Cambridge: Cam-bridge University Press.

Parke, R. D. (1981). *Fathers.* Cambridge, MA: Harvard University Press.

Parkin, A. J. (1987). *Memory and amnesia.* Oxford: Blackwell.

Parssingham, R. E. (1973). Anatomical differences between the neocortex of man and other primates. *Brain, Behavior, and Emotion, 7,* 337–359.

Paschkis, K. E., Rakoff, A. E., Cantarow, A., & Rupp, J. J. (1967). *Clinical endocrinology.* New York: Harper & Row.

Patterson, F. G. (1978). The gestures of a gorilla: Language acquisition in another pongid. *Brain and Language, 5,* 72–97.

Patterson, F. G. (1980). Innovative uses of language by a gorilla: A case study. In K. E. Nelson (Ed.), *Children's language. Vol. 2.* New York: Gardner Press.

Paul, G. L. (1969). Outcome of systematic desensitization. In C. M. Franks (Ed.), *Behavior therapy: Appraisal and status.* New York: McGraw-Hill.

Paul, G. L., & Bernstein, D. A. (1973). *Anxiety and clinical problems: Systematic desensitization and related techniques.* Morristown, NJ: General Learning Press.

Paul, S. M., Hulihan-Giblin, B., & Skolnick, P. (1982). (+)-Amphetamine binding to rat hypothalamus: Relation to anorexic potency of phenylethylamines. *Science, 218,* 487–490.

Pavlov, I. P. (1927). *Conditioned reflexes.* London: Clarendon Press.

Paykel, E. S. (1974). Life stress and psychiatric disorder: Applications of the clinical approach. In B. S. Dohrenwend & B. P. Dohrenwend (Eds.), *Stressful life events: Their nature and effects.* New York: Wiley.

Payne, J. W. (1985). Psychology of risky decisions. In G. Wright (Ed.), *Behavioral decision making* (pp. 3–23). New York: Plenum.

Payne, S., Summers, D. A., & Stewart, T. R. (1973). Value differences across three generations. *Sociometry, 36,* 20–30.

Pearce, J. M. (1987). A model for stimulus generalization in Pavlovian conditioning. *Psychological Review, 1,* 61–73.

Pendlebury, W. W., Beal, M. F., Kowall, N. W., & Solomon, P. R. (1987). Results of immunocytochemical, neurochemical, and behavioral studies in aluminum-induced neurofilamentous degeneration. In R. J. Wurtman, S. H. Corkin, and J. H. Growdon (Eds.), *Alzheimer's disease: Advances in basic research and therapies* (pp. 529–533). Boston, MA: Center for Brain Sciences and Metabolism Charitable Trust.

Penfield, W. (1947). Some observations on the cerebral cortex of man. *Proceedings of the Royal Society, 134,* 349.

Penfield, W., & Perot, P. (1963). The brain's record of auditory and visual experience. *Brain, 86,* 595–697.

Penfield, W., & Rasmussen, T. (1950). *The cerebral cortex of man.* New York: Macmillan.

Perlmutter, M., & Hall, E. (1985). *Adult development and aging.* New York: Wiley.

Perlow, M. J., Freed, W. J., Hoffer, B. J., Seiger, A., Olson, L., & Wyatt, R. J. (1979). Brain grafts reduce motor abnormalities produced by destruction of nigrostriatal dopamine system. *Science, 204,* 643–646.

Pert, C. B., & Snyder, S. H. (1973). Opiate receptor: Demonstration in nervous tissue. *Science, 179,* 1011–1014.

Peterhans, E. & von der Heydt, R. (1991). Subjective contours—bridging the gap between psychophysics and physiology. *Trends in Neuroscience, 14,* 112–119.

Peters, L. H., Hartke, D., Pohlmann, J. T. (1985). Fiedler's contingency theory of leadership: An application of the meta-analysis procedures of Schmidt and Hunter, *Psychological Bulletin, 97.*

Petersen, R. C. (1984). Marijuana overview. In M. D. Glantz, (Ed.), *Correlates and consequences of marijuana use.* Washington, D.C.: U.S. Department of Health and Human Services.

Petersen, R. C., & Stillman, R. C. (1978). Phencyclidine: An overview. In R. C. Petersen & R. C. Stillman (Eds.), *Phencyclidine (pcp) abuse: An appraisal* (NIDA Research Monograph No. 21, DHEW Publication No. ADM 78-728). Washington, DC: Government Printing Office.

Peterson, C. (1982). Learned helplessness and health psychology. *Health Psychology, 1,* 153–168.

Peterson, D. R. (1983). Conflict. In H. H. Kelley, E. Berscheid, A. Christensen, J. Harvey, T. L. Huston, G. Levinger, E. McClintock, A. Peplau, & D. R. Peterson, *Close relationships.* San Francisco: Freeman.

Peterson, L. R., & Peterson, M. J. (1959). Short-term retention of individual verbal items. *Science, 53,* 193–198.

Peterson, C. & Seligman, M. E. P. (1984). Causal explanations as a risk factor for depression: Theory and evidence. *Psychological Review, 91,* 347–374.

Pettigrew, J. D. (1978). The paradox of the critical period for striate cortex. In C. W. Cotman (Ed.), *Neuronal plasticity.* New York: Raven Press.

Pettigrew, T. F. (1959). Regional differences in anti-Negro prejudice. *Journal of Abnormal and Social Psychology, 59,* 28–36.

Petty, R. E., & Cacioppo, J. T. (1984). The effects of involvement on responses to argument quantity and quality: Central and peripheral routes to persuasion. *Journal of Personality and Social Psychology, 1,* 69–81.

Petty, R. E., & Cacioppo, J. T. (1986). The elaboration likelihood model of persuasion. In L. Berkowitz (Ed.), *Advances in experimental social psychology. Vol. 20* (pp. 123–205). New York: Academic Press.

Petty, R. E., Wells, G. L., & Brock, T. C. (1976). Distraction can enhance or reduce yielding to propaganda: Thought disruption versus effort justification. *Journal of Personality and Social Psychology, 34,* 874–884.

Pfaff, D. W. (1982). *The physiological mechanisms of motivation.* New York: Springer-Verlag.

Pfaff, D. W. (Ed.). (1985). *Taste, olfaction, and the central nervous system.* New York: Rockefeller University Press.

Phares, E. J. (1984). *Introduction to personality.* Columbus, OH: Merrill.

Phelps, M. E., Hoffman, E. J., Mullani, N. A., & Ter-Pogossian, M. M. (1975). Application of annihilation coincidence detection to transaxial reconstruction tomography. *Journal of Nuclear Medicine, 16,* 210–214.

Phillips, D. P. (1983). The impact of mass media violence on U.S. homicides. *American Sociological Review, 50,* 364–371.

Phillips, D. P. (1986). National experiments on the effects of mass media violence on fatal aggression: Strengths and weaknesses of a new approach. In L. Berkowitz (Ed.), *Advances in experimental social psy-*

chology. Vol. 19 (pp. 361–427). New York: Academic Press.

Piaget, G. W., & Lazarus, A. A. (1969). The use of rehearsal desensitization. *Psychotherapy: Theory, Research, and Practice, 6,* 264–266.

Piaget, J. (1932). *The moral judgment of the child.* New York: Harcourt, Brace & World.

Piaget, J. (1952). *The origins of intelligence in children.* New York: International Universities Press.

Piaget, J. (1972). Intellectual evolution from adolescence to adulthood. *Human Development, 15,* 1–12.

Piaget, J., & Inhelder, B. (1969). *The child's conception of space.* New York: Basic Books.

Piedmont, R. L., McRae, R. R., & Costa, P. T., Jr. (1991). Adjective check list scales and the five-factor model. *Journal of Personality and Social Psychology, 60,* 630–637.

Pierce, N. R. (1985, July 12). Main street learns to love pot. *The Berkshire Eagle,* p. 5.

Pierrel, R., & Sherman, J. G. (1968, February). Train your pet the Barnabus way. *Brown Alumni Monthly,* pp. 8–14.

Piliavin, I. M., Piliavin, J. A., & Rodin, J. (1975). Costs, diffusion, and the stigmatized victim. *Journal of Personality and Social Psychology, 32,* 429–438.

Piliavin, I. M., Rodin, J., & Piliavin, J. A. (1969). Good Samaritanism: An underground phenomenon? *Journal of Personality and Social Psychology, 13,* 289–299.

Piliavin, J. A., Dovidio, J. F., Gaertner, S. L., & Clark, R. D., III. (1981). *Emergency intervention.* New York: Academic Press.

Piliavin, J. A., & Piliavin, I. M. (1972). Effects of blood on reactions to a victim. *Journal of Personality and Social Psychology, 23,* 353–361.

Pliner, P., Chaiken, S., & Flett, G. L. (1990). Gender differences in concern with body weight and physical appearance over the life span. *Personality and Social Psychology Bulletin, 16,* 263–273.

Plomin, R. (1983). Developmental behavioral genetics. *Child Development, 54,* 253–259.

Plomin, R. (1990). The role of inheritance in behavior. *Science, 248,* 183–188.

Plomp, R., & Levelt, W. J. M. (1965). Tonal consonance and critical band width. *Journal of the Acoustical Society of America, 38,* 548–560.

Plotnikoff, N. P., Faith, R. E., Murgo, A. J., & Wybran, J. (1991). *Stress and immunity.* Boca Raton, Fl: CRC Press.

Plutchik, R. (1980a). *Emotion: A psycho-evolutionary synthesis.* New York: Harper & Row.

Plutchik, R. (1980b, February). A language for the emotions, *Psychology Today,* pp. 68–78.

Polivy, J., Garner, D. M., & Garfinkel, P. E. (1986). Causes and consequences of present preference for thin female physiques. In C. P. Herman, M. P. Zanna & E. T. Higgins (Eds.), *Physical appearance, stigma, and social behavior: Proceedings of the third Ontario symposium on personality and social psychology.* Hillsdale, NJ: Erlbaum.

Polivy, J., & Herman, C. P. (1985). Dieting and binging: A causal analysis. *American Psychologist, 40,* 193–201.

Pope, H. G., Jr., Ionescu-Pioggia, M., Aizley, H. G., & Varma, D. E. (1990). Drug use and life style among college undergraduates in 1989: A comparison with 1969 and 1978. *American Journal of Psychiatry, 147,* 998–1001.

Posner & Synder, 1974 (Ed: Reference in Zimbardo, 12th ed.)

Power, T. G., & Parke, R. D. (1983). Patterns of mother and father play with their 8-month old infant: A mutiple analysis approach. *Infant Behavior and Development, 6,* 453–459.

Premack, D. (1971). Language in chimpanzees. *Science, 172,* 808–822.

Pressley, M., Heisel, B. E., McCormick, C. G., & Makamura, G. V. (1982). Memory strategy instruction with children. In C. J. Brainerd & M. Pressley (Eds.), *Progress in cognitive development research: Vol. 2. Verbal processes in children.* New York: Springer-Verlag.

Pribram, K. H., & Gill, M. M. (1976). *Freud's "project" reassessed.* New York: Basic Books.

Price, R. A., & Vandenberg, S. G. (1979). Matching for physical attractiveness in married couples. *Personality and Social Psychology Bulletin, 5,* 398–400.

Provence, S., & Lipton, R. C. (1962). *Infants in institutions.* New York: International Universities Press.

Pugliese, M. T., Weyman-Daum, M., Moses, N., & Lifshitz, F. (1987). Parental health beliefs as a cause of nonorganic failure to thrive. *Pediatrics, 80,* 175–182.

Quattron, G. A. (1986). On the perception of a group's variability. In S. Worchel & W. G. Austin (Eds.), *Psychology of intergroup relations.* Chicago: Nelson-Hall.

Quigley, S. P., & Kretschmer, R. E. (1982). *The education of deaf children: Issues, theory, and practice.* Baltimore: University Park Press.

Quinton, D., Rutter, M., & Liddle, C. (1984). Institutional rearing, parenting difficulties, and marital support. *Psychological Medicine, 14,* 107–124.

Rahe, R. H. (1975). Life changes and near-future illness reports. In L. Levi (Ed.), *Emotions: Their parameters and measurement.* New York: Raven Press.

Raichle, M. E. (1986). Neuroimaging. *Trends in the Neurosciences, 9,* 525–529.

Raine, A., Venables, P. H., & Williams, M. (1990). Relationship between central and autonomic measure of arousal at age 15 years and criminality at age 24 years. *Archives of General Psychiatry, 46,* 1003–1007.

Rapoport, J. L. (1989). *The boy who couldn't stop washing: The experience and treatment of obsessive-compulsive disorder.* New York: Dutton.

Raskin, D. C. (1987). Methodological issues in estimating polygraph accuracy in field applications. *Canadian Journal of Behavioral Science, 19,* 393+.

Raskin, D. C. (1988). Does science support polygraph testing? In A. Gale (Ed.), *Lies, Truth, and Science.* London: Sage.

Raskin, M., Bali, L. R., & Peeke, H. V. (1980). Muscle biofeedback and transcendental meditation. *Archives of General Psychiatry, 37,* 93–97.

Ray, O. S. (1983). *Drugs, society, and human behavior* (3rd ed.). St. Louis, MO: Mosby.

Reed, G. (1972). *The psychology of anomalous experience: A cognitive approach.* London: Hutchinson.

Reed, G. F. (1985). *Obsessional experience and compulsive behavior: A cognitive-structural approach.* Orlando, FL: Academic Press.

Reese, E., Howard, J., & Reese, T. W. (1978). *Human operant behavior: Analysis and application.* Dubuque, IA: Wm. C. Brown.

Regier, D. A., Boyd, J. H., Burke, J. D., Jr., Rae, D. S., Myers, J. K., Kramer, M., Robins, L. N., George, L. K., Karno, M., & Locke, B. Z. (1988). One-month prevalence of mental disorders in the United States. *Archives of General Psychiatry, 45,* 977–986.

Reifman, A. S., Larrick, R. P., & Fein, S. (1991). Temper and temperature on the diamond: the heat-aggression relationship in major league baseball. *Personality and Social Psychology Bulletin, 17,* 580–585.

Reiman, E. M., Fusselman, M. J., Fox, P. T., & Raichle, M. E. (1989). Neuroanatomical correlates of anticipatory anxiety. *Science, 243,* 1071–1074.

Reiman, E. M., Raichle, M. E., Butler, F. K., Herscovitch, P., & Robins, E. (1984). A focal brain abnormality in panic disorder, a severe form of anxiety. *Nature, 310,* 683–685.

Reiman, E. M., Raichle, M., Robins, E., Butler, F. K., Herscovitch, P., Fox, P., & Perlmutter, J. (1986). The application of positron emission tomography to the study of panic disorder. *American Journal of Psychiatry, 143,* 469–477.

Reisenzein, R. (1983). The Schachter theory of emotion: Two decades later. *Psychological Bulletin, 94,* 239–264.

Rescorla, R. A. (1978). Some implications of a cognitive perspective on Pavlovian conditioning. In S. Hulse, H. Fowler, & W. K. Honig (Eds.), *Cognitive processes in animal behavior.* Hillsdale, NJ: Erlbaum.

Rescorla, R. A. (1988). Pavlovian conditioning. *American Psychologist, 43,* 151–160.

Rescorla, R. A., & Holland, P. C. (1982). Behavioral studies of associative learning in animals. *Annual Review of Psychology, 33,* 265–308.

Rescorla, R. A., & Solomon, R. L. (1967). Two-process learning theory: Relationships between Pavlovian conditioning and instrumental learning. *Psychological Review, 74,* 151–182.

Restak, R. (1984). *The brain.* New York: Bantam.

Reynolds, A. G., & Flagg, P. W. (1983). *Cognitive psychology.* Boston: Little, Brown.

Reynolds, G. S. (1975). *A primer of operant conditioning.* Glenview, IL: Scott, Foresman.

Reynolds, R. I., & Taksooshian (1988). Where were you on August 8, 1985? *Bulletin of the Psychonomic Society, 26,* 23–25.

Rheingold, H. L., & Cook, K. V. (1975). The contents of boys' and girls' rooms as an index of parents' behavior. *Child Development, 46,* 459–463.

Rice, R. W., Bender, L. R., & Vitters, A. G. (1980). Leader sex, follower attitudes toward women, and leadership effectiveness: A laboratory study. *Organizational Behavior and Human Performance, 25.*

Rice, R. W., Instone, D., & Adams, J. (1984). Leader sex, leader success, and leadership process: Two field studies. *Journal of Applied Psychology, 69.*

Rice, R. W., & Kastenbaum, D. R. (1983). The contingency model of leadership: Some current issues. *Basic and Applied Social Psychology, 4.*

Riley, V. (1981). Psychoneuroendocrine influences on immuno-competence and neoplasia. *Science, 212,* 1100–1109.

Riordan, C. A., & Tedeschi, J. T. (1983). Attraction in aversive environments: Some evidence for classical conditioning and negative reinforcement. *Journal of Personality and Social Psychology, 44,* 683–692.

Riotblat, H. (1987). *Introduction to comparative cognition.* San Francisco: Freeman.

Ritz, M. E., Lamb, R. J., Goldberg, S. R., & Kuhar, M. J. (1987). Cocaine receptors on dopamine transporters are related to self-administration of cocaine. *Science, 237,* 1219–1222.

Robbins, L. N., Helzer, J. E., Weissman, M. M., Orvaschel, H., Gruenberg, E., Burke, J. D., & Regier, D. A. (1984). Lifetime prevalence of specific psychiatric disorders in three sites. *Archives of General Psychiatry, 41,* 941–958.

Robbins, T. W., & Fray, P. J. (1980). Stress induced eating: Fact, fiction or misunderstanding? *Appetite, 1,* 103–133.

Roberts, L. (1988). Study raises estimate of Vietnam war stress. *Science, 241,* 788.

Robins, L. N. (1966). *Deviant children grow up.* Baltimore: Williams & Wilkins.

Robinson, F. P. (1970). *Effective study.* New York: Harper & Row.

Robinson, J. O. (1972). *The psychology of visual illusion.* London: Hutchinson.

Rock, I. & Palmer, S. (December 1990). The legacy of gestalt psychology. *Scientific American,* 84–90.

Rockstein, M. (1975). The biology of aging in humans: An overview. In R. Goldman & M. Rockstein (Eds.), *The physiology and pathology of human aging.* New York: Academic Press.

Rodin, J. (1985). Insulin levels, hunger, and food intake: An example of feedback loops in body weight regulation. *Health Psychology, 4,* 1–18.

Rodin, J. & Langer, E. J. (1977). Long-term effects of a control-relevant intervention with the institutionalized aged. *Journal of Personality and Social Psychology, 35,* 897–902.

Roffwarg, H. P., Muzio, J. N., & Dement, W. C. (1966). Ontogenetic development of the human sleep-dream cycle. *Science, 152,* 604–619.

Rogers, C. R. (1951). *Client-centered therapy: Its current practice, implications, and theory.* Boston: Houghton Mifflin.

Rogers, C. R. (1959). A theory of therapy, personality, and interpersonal relationships, as developed in the client-centered framework. In S. Koch (Ed.), *Psychology: A study of a science. Vol. 3.* New York: McGraw-Hill.

Rogers, C. R. (1961). *On becoming a person: A therapist's view of psychotherapy.* Boston: Houghton Mifflin.

Rollins, B. C., & Feldman, H. (1970). Marital satisfaction over the life cycle. *Journal of Marriage and the Family, 32,* 20–28.

Rollins, B. C., & Galligan, R. (1978). The developing child and marital satisfaction of parents. In R. M. Lerner & G. B. Spanier (Eds.), *Child influences on marital and family interaction: A life-span approach.* New York: Academic Press.

Ronnett, G. V., Hester, L. D., Nye, J. S., Connors, K., & Snyder, S. H. (1990). Human cortical neuronal cell line: Establishment from a patient with unilateral megalencephaly. *Science, 248,* 603–604.

Roosa, M. W., Fitzgerald, H. E., & Carson, N. A. (1982). Teenage and older mothers and their infants: A descriptive comparison. *Adolescence, 17,* 1–17.

Rorschach, H. (1942). *Psychodiagnostics.* Berne, Switzerland: Verlag Hans Huber.

Rosch, E. (1974). Linguistic relativity. In A. Silverstein (Ed.), *Human communication: Theoretical perspectives.* New York: Halstead Press.

Rosch, E. (1975). Cognitive representations of semantic categories. *Journal of Experimental Psychology: General, 104,* 192–233.

Rosch, E. H. (1973). Natural categories. *Cognitive Psychology, 4,* 328–350.

Rosch, E. H. (1975). Cognitive reference points. *Cognitive Psychology, 7,* 532–547.

Rose, S. A., & Wallace, I. F. (1985). Visual recognition memory: A predictor of later cognitive functioning in preterms. *Child Development, 56,* 843–852.

Rosen, B. C. (1961). Family structure and achievement motivation. *American Psychological Review, 26,* 574–585.

Rosen, E., Fox, R. W., & Gregory, I. (1972). *Abnormal psychology* (2nd ed.). Philadelphia: Saunders.

Rosen, G. (1968). *Madness in society: Chapters in the historical sociology of mental illness.* New York: Harper & Row.

Rosenbaum, M. E. (1986). The repulsion hypothesis: On the nondevelopment of relationships. *Journal of Personality and Social Psychology, 51,* 1156–1166.

Rosenhan, D. L. (1973). On being sane in insane places. *Science, 179,* 250–258.

Rosenman, R. H., Brand, R. J., Jenkins, D., Friedman, M., Straus, R., & Wurm, M. (1975). Coronary heart disease in the Western Collaborative Group study: Final follow-up experience of 8 1/2 years. *Journal of the American Medical Association, 233,* 872–877.

Rosenthal, R. (1966). *Experimenter effects in behavioral research.* New York: Appleton-Century-Crofts.

Rosenthal, R. (1973). On the social psychology of the self-fulfilling prophecy: Further evidence for pygmalion effects and their mediating mechanisms. *MSS Modular Publication, 53,* 1–28.

Rosenthal, R., & Jacobson, L. (1968). *Pygmalion in the classroom.* New York: Holt, Rinehart & Winston.

Ross, C. A. (1989). *Multiple personality disorder: Diagnosis, clinical features, and treatment.* New York: Wiley.

Ross, D., & Mesalum, M. M. (1979). Dominant language functions of the right hemisphere. *Archives of Neurology, 31,* 144–148.

Rothbart, M., Dawes, R., & Park, B. (1984). Stereotyping and sampling biases in intergroup perception. In J. Richard Eiser (Ed.), *Attitudinal judgment.* New York: Springer-Verlag.

Rothstein, J. D., Garland, W., Puia, G., Guidotti, A., & Costa, E. (1990). Naturally occurring endogenous benzodiazepines: purification, synthesis, and physiology. *Society for Neuroscience Abstracts, 16,* 806.

Rotter, J. B. (1966). Generalized expectancies for internal versus external control of reinforcement. *Psychological Monographs, 80* (Whole No. 609).

Rotter, J. B. (1971, June). External control and internal control. *Psychology Today,* pp. 37ff.

Routtenberg, A. (1968). The two-arousal hypothesis: Reticular formation and the limbic system. *Psychological Review, 75,* 51–80.

Rowland, N. E., & Antelman, S. E. (1976). Stress induced hyperphagia and obesity in rats: A possible model for understanding human obesity. *Science, 191,* 310–312.

Rubenstein, J., & Howes, C. (1976). The effects of peers on toddler interaction with mother and toys. *Child Development, 47,* 597–605.

Rubin, D. (1986). *Autobiographical memory.* New York: Cambridge University Press.

Rubin, J. L., Provenzano, F. J., & Luria, Z. (1974). The eye of the beholder: Parents' views on sex of newborns. *American Journal of Orthopsychiatry, 43,* 720–731.

Rubin, Z. (1973). *Liking and loving.* New York: Holt, Rinehart & Winston.

Ruble, D. N. (1984). Sex role development. In M. C. Bornstein & M. E. Lamb (Eds.), *Developmental psychology: An advanced textbook.* Hillsdale, NJ: Erlbaum.

Ruble, D. N., Balaban, T., & Cooper, J. (1981). Gender constancy and the effects of sex-typed televised toy commercials. *Child Development, 52,* 667–673.

Rumbaugh, D. M. (1977). *Language learning by a chimpanzee: The Lana project.* New York: Academic Press.

Rutter, M. (1979). Maternal deprivation, 1972–1978: New findings, new concepts, new approaches. *Child Development, 50,* 283–305.

Rutter, M. (1982). Social-emotional consequences of day care for preschool children. *American Journal of Orthopsychiatry, 51,* 4–28..

Saal, F. E., Downey, R. G., & Lahey, M. A. (1980). Rating the ratings: assessing the psychometric quality of rating data. *Psychological Bulletin, 88,* 413–423.

Sachs, J. (1977). The adaptive significance of linguistic input to prelinguistic infants. In C. E. Snow & C. A. Ferguson (Eds.), *Talking to children: Language input and acquisition.* Cambridge: Cambridge University Press.

Sachs, J. D. S. (1967). Recognition memory for syntactic and semantic aspects of connected discourse. *Perception and Psychophysics, 2,* 437–442.

Sachs, J. D. S. (1979). Topic selection in parent-child discourse. *Discourse Processes, 2,* 145-153.

Sacks, O. (1985). *The man who mistook his wife for a hat.* New York: Summit Books.

Saghir, M. T., & Robins, E. (1973). *Male and female homosexuality: A comprehensive investigation.* Baltimore: Williams & Wilkins.

Salapatek, P., & Kessen, W. (1966). Visual scanning of triangles by the human newborn. *Journal of Experimental Child Psychology, 3,* 155-167.

Sales, S. M. (1973). Threat as a factor in authoritarianism: an analysis of archival data. *Journal of Personality and Social Psychology, 28,* 44-57.

Salzman, C. (1978). Electroconvulsive therapy. In A. M. Nicholi (Ed.), *The Harvard guide to modern psychiatry.* Cambridge, MA: Harvard University Press.

Salzman, C. (1991). The APA task force report of benzodiazepine dependence, toxicity and abuse. *American Journal of Psychiatry, 148,* 151-152.

Sande, G. N., Goethals, G. R., & Radloff, C. E. (1988). Perceiving one's own traits and others': The multifaceted self. *Journal of Personality and Social Psychology, 54,* 13-20.

Sande, G. W., & Zanna, M. P. (1987). Cognitive Dissonance: Collective Actions and Individual Reactions. In Mullen, B. & Goethals, G. R. (Eds.), *Theories of Group Behavior.* New York: Springer-Verlag.

Sanford, R. H. (1935). The effects of abstinence from food upon imaginal processes: A preliminary experiment. *Journal of Psychology, 2,* 129-136.

Sarason, I. G. (1984). Stress, anxiety, and cognitive interference: Reactions to tests. *Journal of Personality and Social Psychology, 46,* 929-938.

Sarason, I. G., Levine, H. M., & Sarason, B. R. (1982). Assessing the impact of life changes. In T. Miller, C. Green, & R. Meagher (Eds.), *Handbook of clinical health psychology* (pp. 377-401). New York: Plenum.

Sarbin, T. R., & Coe, W. C. (1972). *Hypnosis: A social psychological analysis of influence communication.* New York: Holt, Rinehart & Winston.

Satow, K. L. (1975). Social approval and helping. *Journal of Experimental Social Psychology, 11,* 501-509.

Sauter, S. L., Murphy, L. R., & Hurrell, J. J. (1990). Prevention of work-related psychological disorders: A national strategy proposed by the national institute for occupational safety and health (NIOSH). *American Psychologist, 45,* 1146-1158.

Savage-Rumbaugh, E. S., Pate, J. L., Lawson, J., Smith, S. T., & Rosenbaum, S. (1983). Can a chimpanzee make a statement? *Journal of Experimental Psychology: General, 112,* 457-492.

Saxe, L., Dougherty, D., & Cross, T. (1985). The validity of polygraph testing: Scientific analysis and public controversy. *American Psychologist, 40,* 355-366.

Scarr, S., & Weinberg, R. A. (1976). I.Q. test performance of black children adopted by white families. *American Psychologist, 31,* 726-739.

Scarr, S., & Weinberg, R. A. (1986). The early childhood enterprise: Care and education of the young. *American Psychologist, 41,* 1140-1146.

Schachter, S. (1951). Deviation, rejection, and communication. *Journal of Abnormal Psychology, 46,* 190-207.

Schachter, S. (1959). *The psychology of affiliation.* Stanford, CA: Stanford University Press.

Schachter, S. (1964). The interaction of cognitive and physiological determinants of emotional state. In L. Berkowitz (Ed.), *Advances in experimental social psychology. Vol. 1.* New York: Academic Press.

Schachter, S., & Singer, J. (1962). Cognitive, social and physiological determinants of emotional state. *Psychological Review, 69,* 379-399.

Schaie, K. W., & Labouvie-Vief, G. (1974). Generational versus ontogenetic components of change in adult cognitive behavior: A fourteen year cross-sequential study. *Developmental Psychology, 10,* 305-320.

Schaie, K. W., & Willis, S. L. (1986). *Adult development and aging.* Boston: Little, Brown.

Scheier, M. R., & Carver, C. S. (1985). Optimism, coping and health: Assessment and implications of generalized outcome expectancies. *Health Psychology, 4,* 219-247.

Scheier, M. F., Matthews, K. A., Owens, J. F., Magovern, G. J., Lefebvre, R. C., Abbott, R. A., & Carver, C. S. (1989). Dispositional optimism and recovery from coronary artery bypass surgery: The beneficial effects on physical and psychological well-being. *Journal of Personality and Social Psychology, 57,* 1024-1040.

Schein, E. (1980). *Organizational psychology.* Englewood Cliffs, NJ: Prentice-Hall.

Schemmel, R., Michelsen, P., & Gill, J. L. (1970). Dietary obesity in rats. *Journal of Nutrition, 100,* 1041-1048.

Schiffman, H. (1976). *Sensation and perception.* New York: Wiley.

Schleifer, S. J., Keller, S. E., Camerino, M., Thornton, J. C., & Stein, M. (1983). Suppression of lymphocyte stimulation following bereavement. *Journal of the American Medical Association, 250,* 364-377.

Schlenker, B. R. (1982). Translating actions into attitudes: An identity-analytic approach to the explanations of social conduct. In L. Berkowitz (Ed.), *Advances in experimental social psychology. Vol. 15.* New York: Academic Press.

Schlesinger, H. J., Mumford, E., Glass, G. V., Patrick, C., & Sharfstein, S. (1983). Mental health treatment and medical care utilization in a fee-for-service system: Outpatient mental health treatment following the onset of a chronic disease. *American Journal of Public Health, 73,* 422-429.

Schnapf, J., & Baylor, D. A. (1987). How photoreceptor cells respond to light. *Scientific American, 256,* 40-47.

Schneider, D. J., Hastorf, A. H., & Ellsworth, P. C. (1979). *Person perception.* Reading, MA: Addison-Wesley.

Schroeder, D. A., Dovidio, J. F., Sibicky, M. E., Matthews, L. L., & Allen, J. L. (1988). Empathic concern and helping behavior: Egoism or altruism? *Journal of Experimental Social Psychology, 24,* 333-353.

Schulz, R., & Aderman, D. (1974). Clinical research and the stages of dying. *Omega, 5,* 137-143.

Schuman, M. (1980). The psychophysiological model of meditation and altered states of consciousness: A critical review. In J. M. Davidson & R. J. Davidson (Eds.), *The psychobiology of consciousness.* New York: Plenum.

Schwarz, B. (1989). *Psychology of learning and behavior.* (3rd ed.) New York: Norton.

Schwarz, G. E., Weinberger, D. A., & Singer, J. A. (1981). Cardiovascular differentiation of happiness, sadness, anger, and fear following imagery and exercise. *Psychosomatic Medicine, 43* (4), 343-364.

Schwartz, S., & Griffin, T. (1986). *Medical thinking: The psychology of medical judgment and decision making.* New York: Springer-Verlag.

Scoville, W. B., & Milner, B. (1957). Loss of recent memory after bilateral hippocampal lesions. *Journal of Neurology, Neurosurgery, and Psychiatry, 20,* 11-21.

Sebald, H. (1986). Adolescents' shifting orientation toward parents and peers: A curvilinear trend over recent decades. *Journal of Marriage and the Family, 48,* 5-13.

Seeley, T. T., Abramson, P. R., Perry, L. B., Rothblatt, A. B., & Seeley, D. M. (1980). Thermographic measurement of sexual arousal: A methodological note. *Archives of Sexual Behavior, 9,* 77-85.

Seeman, M., & Evans, J. W. (1962). Alienation and learning in a hospital setting. *American Psychological Review, 27,* 772-783.

Seeman, P., & Niznik, H. B. (1990). Dopamine receptors

and transporters in Parkinson's disease and schizophrenia. *The FASEB Journal, 4,* 2737-2744.

Seligman, M. E. P. (1970). On the generality of the law of learning. *Psychological Review, 77,* 406-418.

Seligman, M. E. P. (1975). *Helplessness: On depression development and death.* San Francisco: Freeman.

Seligman, M. E. P., & Maier, S. F. (1967). Failure to escape traumatic shock. *Journal of Experimental Psychology, 74,* 1-9.

Seligman, M. E. P., Maier, S. F., & Solomon, R. L. (1971). Unpredictable and uncontrollable aversive events. In F. R. Brush (Ed.), *Aversive conditioning and learning.* New York: Academic Press.

Selye, H. (1956). *The stress of life.* New York: McGraw-Hill.

Selye, H. (1973). The evolution of the stress concept. *American Scientist, 61,* 692-699.

Sem-Jacobson, C. W. (1968). *Depth-electroencephalographic stimulation of the human brain and behavior.* Springfield, IL: Charles C Thomas.

Shanab, M. E., & Yahya, K. A. (1977). A behavioral study of obedience in children. *Journal of Personality and Social Psychology, 35,* 530-536.

Shanteau, J., & Nagy, G. (1976). Decisions made about other people: A human judgment analysis of dating choice. In J. S. Carroll & J. W. Payne (Eds.), *Cognition and social behavior.* Hillsdale, NJ: Erlbaum.

Shapiro, D. (1965). *Neurotic styles.* New York: Basic Books.

Shapiro, D. H. (1980). *Meditation: Self-regulation strategy and altered states of consciousness.* New York: Aldine.

Shapiro, D. H. (1985). Clinical uses of meditation as a self-regulation strategy: Comments on Holmes's (1984) conclusions and implications. *American Psychologist, 40,* 719-722.

Shapiro, L. R., Crawford, P. B., Clark, M. J., Pearson, D. J., Raz, J., & Huenemann, R. L. (1984). Obesity prognosis: A longitudinal study of children from age 6 months to 9 years. *American Journal of Public Health, 74,* 968-972.

Shaw, M. E. (1981). *Group dynamics: The psychology of small group behavior.* New York: McGraw-Hill.

Shedler, J., & Block, J. (1990). Adolescent drug use and psychological health: A longitudinal inquiry. *American Psychologist, 45,* 612-630.

Sheehan, P. W., & Perry, C. W. (1976). *Methodologies of hypnosis.* Hillsdale, NJ: Erlbaum.

Sheffield, F. D., & Roby, T. B. (1950). Reward value of a nonnutritive sweet taste. *Journal of Comparative and Physiological Psychology, 43,* 471-481.

Shellenberger, R., Amar, P., Schneider, C., & Stewart, R. (1989). *Clinical efficacy and cost effectiveness of biofeedback therapy: Guidelines for third party reimbursement.* Wheat Ridge, CO: Association of Applied Psychophysiology and Biofeedback.

Shepherd, G. (1988). *Neurobiology* (2nd ed.). New York: Oxford Press.

Sherif, M. (1935). A study of some social factors in perception. *Archives of Psychology, 27,* 187.

Shettleworth, S. J., & Jeurgensen, M. R. (1980). Reinforcement and the organization of behavior in golden hamsters: Brain stimulation reinforcement for seven action patterns. *Journal of Experimental Psychology: Animal Behavior Processes, 6,* 352-375.

Shiffrin, R. M., & Schneider, W. (1977). Controlled and automatic human information processing. II. Perceptual learning, automatic attending, and general theory. *Psychological Review, 84,* 127-190.

Shirley, M. M. (1931). *The first two years.* Minneapolis: University of Minnesota Press.

Shneidman, E. S. (1973). *Deaths of man.* New York: Quadrangle.

Shockley, W. (1972). Dysgenics, geneticity, and raceology: A challenge to the responsibility of educators. *Phi Delta Kappan, 53,* 297-307.

Shostrom, E. L. (1964). An inventory for the measurement of self-actualization. *Educational and Psychological Measurement, 24,* 207-218.

Shostrom, E. L. (1974). *Manual for the personal orientation inventory.* San Diego, CA: Edits.

Siegel, J. M., Nienhuis, R., Fahringer, H. M., Paul, R., Shiromani, P., Dement, W. C., Mignot, E., & Chiu, C. (1991). Neuronal activity in narcolepsy: Identification of cataplexy-related cells in the medial medulla. *Science, 252,* 1315-1318.

Siegler, R. S. (1991). *Children's thinking.* (2nd ed.). Englewood Cliffs, NJ: Prentice-Hall.

Siever, L. J., & Uhde, T. W. (1983). New studies and perspectives on the noradrenergic receptor system in depression: Effects of the adrenergic agonist clonidine. *Biological Psychiatry, 19,* 131-156.

Signorelli, N. (1989). Television and conceptions about sex roles: Maintaining conventionality and the status quo. *Sex Roles, 21,* 341-360.

Silverman, L. H. (1976). Psychoanalytic theory: "The reports of my death are greatly exaggerated." *American Psychologist, 31,* 621-637.

Silverman, L. H., Ross, D. C., Adler, J. M., & Lustig, D. A. (1978). Simple research paradigm for demonstrating subliminal psychodynamic activation: Effects of Oedipal stimuli on dart-throwing accuracy in college males. *Journal of Abnormal Psychology, 87,* 341-357.

Silverman, P. R. (1978). *Mutual help groups: A guide for mental health workers* (DHEW Publication No. ADM 78-646). Washington, DC: GPO.

Silverstein, B., Peterson, B., & Perdue, L. (1986). Some correlates of the thin standard of bodily attractiveness in women. *International Journal of Eating Disorders, 5,* 145-155.

Simonton, D. K. (1986) Dispositional attributions of (presidential) leadership: an experimental simulation of historiometric results. *Journal of Experimental Social Psychology, 22,* 389-418.

Simonton, D. K., (1987) Presidential inflexibility and veto behavior: two individual-situational interactions. *Journal of Personality, 55,* 1-18.

Singer, J. L. (1977). Ongoing thought: The normative baseline for alternate states of consciousness. In N. E. Zinberg (Ed.), *Alternate states of consciousness* (pp. 89-120). New York: Free Press.

Singer, J. L. (1981). Research implications of projective methods. In A. I. Rabin (Ed.), *Assessment with projective techniques.* New York: Springer.

Singer, J. L. (1984a). *The human personality.* San Diego, CA: Harcourt, Brace, & Jovanovich.

Singer, J. L. (1984b). The private personality. *Personality and Social Psychology Bulletin, 10,* 7-30.

Singular, S. (1982, October). A memory for all seasons. *Psychology Today,* pp. 54-63.

Sizemore, C. C., & Pitillo, E. S. (1978). *I'm Eve.* New York: Doubleday.

Sjostrom, J. (1980). Fat cells and body weight. In A. J. Stunkard (Ed.), *Obesity.* Philadelphia: Saunders.

Skeels, H. M. (1966). Adult status of children with contrasting early life experiences: A follow-up study. *Monographs of the Society for Research in Child Development, 31* (Whole No. 105).

Skinner, B. F. (1938). *The behavior of organisms: An experimental analysis.* Englewood Cliffs, NJ: Prentice-Hall.

Skinner, B. F. (1948). Superstition in the pigeon. *Journal of Experimental Psychology, 38,* 168-172.

Skinner, B. F. (1953). *Science and human behavior.* New York: Macmillan.

Skinner, B. F. (1959). *Contingencies of reinforcement: A theoretical analysis.* New York: Appleton-Century-Crofts.

Skinner, B. F. (1961, November). Teaching machines. *Scientific American,* pp. 91-102.

Skodak, M., & Skeels, H. M. (1949). A final follow-up study of one hundred adopted children. *Journal of Genetic Psychology, 75,* 85-125.

Slater, E., & Cowie, V. (1971). *The genetics of mental disorder.* London: Oxford University Press.

Slobin, D. I. (1970). Universals of grammatical development in children. In G. B. Flores d'Arcais & W. J. M. Levelt (Eds.), *Advances in psycholinguistics.* New York: American Elsevier.

Slobin, D. I. (1979). *Psycholinguistics.* Glenview, IL: Scott, Foresman.

Slochower, J. (1976). Emotional labelling of over-eating in obese and normal weight individuals. *Psychosomatic Medicine, 38,* 131-139.

Slusher, M. P., & Anderson, C. A. (1987). When reality monitoring fails: the role of imagination in stereotype maintenance. *Journal of Personality and Social Psychology, 52,* 653-662.

Smith, D. A., & Graesser, A. C. (1981). Memory for actions in scripted activity as a function of typicality, retention interval, and retrieval task. *Memory and Cognition, 109,* 373-392.

Smith, D. E., Wesson, D. R., Buxton, M. E., Seymour, R., & Kramer, H. M. (1978). The diagnosis and treatment of the pcp abuse syndrome. In R. C. Petersen & R. C. Stillman (Eds.), *Phencyclidine (pcp) abuse: An appraisal* (NIDA Research Monograph No. 21, DHEW Publication No. ADM 78-728). Washington, DC: Government Printing Office.

Smith, E. E., & Medin, D. L. (1981). *Categories and concepts.* Cambridge, MA: Harvard University Press.

Smith, M. C. (1983). Hypnotic memory enhancement of witnesses: Does it work? *Psychological Bulletin, 94,* 387-407.

Smith, M. L., Glass, G. V., & Miller, T. I. (1980). *The benefits of psychotherapy.* Baltimore: Johns Hopkins University Press.

Smith, R. E., Wheeler, G., & Diener, E. (1975). Faith without works. *Journal of Applied Social Psychology, 5,* 320-330.

Smith, S. M. (1979). Remembering in and out of context. *Journal of Experimental Psychology: Human Learning and Memory, 5,* 460-471.

Snodgrass, V. (1973). Medical news. *Journal of the American Medical Association, 225,* 1035-1046.

Snow, C. E. (1981). The uses of imitation. *Journal of Child Language, 8,* 205-212.

Snow, C. E. (1983). Saying it again: The role of expanded and deferred imitations in language acquisition. In K. E. Nelson (Ed.), *Children's language. Vol. 4.* Hillsdale, NJ: Erlbaum.

Snyder, F. (1970). The phenomenology of dreaming. In L. Madow & L. H. Snow (Eds.), *The psychodynamic implications of the physiological studies on dreams.* Springfield, IL: Charles C Thomas.

Snyder, M., & Cunningham, M. R. (1975). To comply or not to comply: Testing the self-perception explanation of the "foot-in-the-door" phenomenon. *Journal of Personality and Social Psychology, 31,* 64-67.

Snyder, M., Tanke, E. D., & Berscheid, E. (1977). Social perception and interpersonal behavior: On the selffulfilling nature of social stereotypes. *Journal of Personality and Social Psychology, 31,* 64-67.

Snyder, S. H. (1971). *Uses of marijuana.* New York: Oxford University Press.

Snyder, S. H. (1974). *Madness and the brain.* New York: McGraw-Hill.

Snyder, S. H. (1981). Dopamine receptors, neuroleptics, and schizophrenia. *American Journal of Psychiatry, 138,* 460-464.

Snyder, S. H. (1984). Drug and neurotransmitter receptors in the brain. *Science, 224,* 22-31.

Soldatos, C. R., & Kales, A. (1986). Treatment of sleep disorders. In R. M. Berlin & C. R. Soldatos (Eds.), *Sleep disorders in psychiatric practice.* Orlando, FL: Rylandic.

Solomon, P. R. (1980). Perception, illusion, and magic. *Teaching of Psychology, 7,* 3-8.

Solomon, P. R., Solomon, S. D., Vander Schaaf, E. R., & Perry, H. E. (1983). Altered activity in hippocampus is more detrimental to classical conditioning than removing the structure. *Science, 220,* 329-331.

Solomon, R. L. (1980). The opponent-process theory of acquired motivation: The costs of pleasure and the benefits of pain. *American Psychologist, 35,* 691-712.

Sorensen, R. (1973). *Adolescent sexuality in contemporary America.* New York: World.

Sorrentino, R. M., & Field, N. (1986). Emergent leadership over time: The functional value of positive motivation. *Journal of Personality and Social Psychology, 50,* 1091-1099.

Spady, D., Atrens, M. A., & Szymanski, W. (1986). Effects of mothers' smoking on their infants' body composition as determined by total body potassium. *Pediatric Research, 20,* 716-719.

Spanos, N. P. (1986). Hypnotic behavior: A social-psychological interpretation of amnesia, analgesia, and "trance logic." *Behavioral and Brain Sciences, 9,* 449-467.

Spanos., N. P., Gwynn, M. I., & Stam, H. J. (1983). Instructional demands and ratings of overt and hidden pain during hypnotic analgesia. *Journal of Abnormal Psychology, 92,* 479-488.

Spear, N. E., & Miller, R. (1982). *Information processing in animals: Memory mechanisms.* Hillsdale, NJ: Erlbaum.

Spearman, C. (1904). "General intelligence": Objectively determined and measured. *American Journal of Psychology, 15,* 201-291.

Spence, K. W. (1951). Theoretical implications of learning. In S. S. Stevens (Ed.), *Handbook of experimental psychology.* New York: Wiley.

Sperling, G. (1960). The information available in brief visual presentations. *Psychological Monographs, 74* (Whole No. 498).

Sperry, R. W. (1968a). Hemisphere disconnection and unity in conscious awareness. *American Psychologist, 23,* 723-733.

Sperry, R. W. (1968b). Mental unity following surgical disconnection of the cerebral hemispheres. *The Harvey lectures. Series 62* (pp. 306-327). New York: Academic Press.

Sperry, R. W. (1974). Lateral specialization in the surgically separated hemispheres. In F. O. Schmitt & F. G. Worden (Eds.), *The neurosciences: Third study program.* Cambridge, MA: MIT Press.

Sperry, R. W. (1982). Some effects of disconnecting the cerebral hemispheres. *Science, 217,* 1223-1226.

Spiegal, D. (1991) A psychosocial intervention and survival time patients with metastatic breast cancer. *Advances, 7,* 10-19.

Spiegal, D., Bloom, J., Kraemer, H. C. & Gottheil, (1989). Effect of psychosocial treatment on survival of patients with metastatic breast cancer. *Lancet, 2,* 888-891.

Spiegal, D. & Spiegal, H. (1985). Hypnosis. In H. I. Kaplan & B. J. Sadock (Eds.) *Comprehensive Textbook of psychiatry/*IV. Baltimore: Williams & Wilkens.

Spielberger, C. (1979). *Understanding stress and anxiety.* New York: Harper & Row.

Spiro, R. J. (1977). Remembering information from text: The "state of schema approach." In R. C. Anderson, R. J. Spiro, & W. E. Montague (Eds.), *Schooling and the acquisition of knowledge.* Hillsdale, NJ: Erlbaum.

Spiro, R. J. (1980). Accommodative reconstruction in prose recall. *Journal of Verbal Learning and Verbal Behavior, 19,* 84-95.

Spitzer, R. L., Skodol, A. E., Gibbon, M., & Williams,

J. B. W. (1989). *DSM-III casebook*. Washington, DC: American Psychiatric Association.

Springer, J. P., & Deutsch, G. (1989). *Left brain, right brain* (3rd ed.). San Francisco: Freeman.

Squire, L. R. (1982). The neuropsychology of human memory. *Annual Review of Neuroscience, 5,* 241-273.

Squire, L. R. (1987). *Memory and brain.* New York: Oxford University Press.

Squire, L. R., Slater, P. C., & Miller, P. L. (1981). Retrograde amnesia and bilateral electroconvulsive therapy. *Archives of General Psychiatry, 38,* 89-95.

Squire, L. R., & Zola-Morgan, S. (1988). Memory: Brain systems and behavior. *Trends in the Neurosciences, 11,* 170-175.

Srole, L., Langner, T. S., Michael, S. T., Opler, M. K., & Rennie, T. A. C. (1962). *Mental health in the metropolis.* New York: McGraw-Hill.

Sroufe, L. A., Fox, N., & Pancake, V. (1983). Attachment and dependency in developmental perspective. *Child Development, 54,* 1615-1627.

Stabenau, J. R., & Pollin, W. (1970). Experiential differences for schizophrenics as compared with their non-schizophrenic siblings: Twin and family studies. In M. Roff & D. F. Ricks (Eds.), *Life history research in psychopathology.* Minneapolis: University of Minnesota Press.

Stankov, L., & Spilsbury, G. (1978). The measurement of auditory abilities of blind, partially sighted, and sighted children. *Applied Psychological Measurement, 2,* 491-503.

Stapp, J., & Fulcher, R. (1981). The employment of APA members. *American Psychologist, 36,* 1263-1314.

Stapp, J., & Fulcher, R. (1982). The employment of 1979 and 1980 doctorate recipients in psychology. *American Psychologist, 37,* 1159-1185.

Stauss, D. T., & Benson, D. F. (1983). Frontal lobe lesions and behavior. In A. Kertesz (Ed.), *Localization in neuropsychology* (pp. 429-454). New York: Academic Press.

Stechler, G., & Halton, A. (1982). Prenatal influences on human development. In B. B. Wolman (Ed.), *Handbook of developmental psychology.* Englewood Cliffs, NJ: Prentice-Hall.

Steiner, I. D. (1972). *Group process and productivity.* New York: Academic Press.

Stemmler, G. (1989). The autonomic differentiation of emotions revisited: Convergent and discriminant validation. *Psychophysiology, 26,* 617+.

Stephan, W. G. (1973). Parental relationships and early social experience of activist male homosexuals and male heterosexuals. *Journal of Abnormal Psychology, 32,* 506-513.

Sterling, B., & Gaertner, S. L. (1984). The attribution of arousal and emergency helping: A bidirectional process. *Journal of Experimental Social Psychology, 20,* 586-596.

Stern, D. (1977). *The first relationship: Mother and infant.* Cambridge, MA: Harvard University Press.

Sternbach, R. A. (1966). *Principles of psychophysiology.* New York: Academic Press.

Sternberg, R. J. (1985). *Beyond IQ: A triarchic theory of human intelligence.* New York: Cambridge University Press.

Sternberg, R. J. (1986). A triangular theory of love. *Psychological Review, 93,* 119-135.

Sternberg, R. J. (1986). *Intelligence applied: Understanding and increasing your intellectual skills.* San Diego, CA: Harcourt Brace Jovanovich.

Sternberg, R. J. (1988). Triangulating love. In R. J. Sternberg & M. J. Barnes (Eds.) *The psychology of love* (pp. 119-138). New Haven, CT: Yale University Press.

Sternberg, R. J. (1990). *Metaphors of mind: Perceptions of the nature of intelligence.* New York: Cambridge University Press.

Sternberg, R. J., & Detterman, D. K. (1986). *What is intelligence: Contemporary viewpoints on its nature and definition.* Norwood, NJ: Ablex.

Sternberg, S. (1966). High speed scanning in human memory. *Science, 153,* 652-654.

Stevenson, H. W., & Lee, S. (1990). Contexts of achievement. *Monographs of the Society for Research in Child Development, 55,* No. 1-2.

Stewart, D. B. (1987). *Report of the Scholastic Aptitude Test (SAT) to College Board Members.* New York: The College Board.

Stiles, W. B., Shapiro, D. A. & Eliott., R. (1986). "Are all psychotherapies equivalent?". *American Psychologist, 41,* 165-180.

Stillings, N., Feinstein, M., Garfield, J., Rissland, E., Rosenbaum, D., Weisler, S., & Baker-Ward, L. (1987). *Cognitive science.* Cambridge, MA: MIT Press.

Stogdill, R. M. (1974). *Handbook of leadership: A survey of theory and research.* New York: Free Press.

Stone, A. A. (1987, June 3). Civil rights for mentally ill must be redefined. *Wall Street Journal.*

Stone, A. A., & Neale, J. M. (1984). New measure of daily coping: Development and preliminary results. *Journal of Personality and Social Psychology, 46,* 892-906.

Stone, M. (1980, January). Recognizing and treating the alcoholic. *Behavioral Medicine,* pp. 14-17.

Storms, M. S. (1980). Theories of sexual orientation. *Journal of Personality and Social Psychology, 38,* 783-792.

Storms, M. S. (1981). A theory of erotic orientation development. *Psychological Review, 88,* 340-353.

Strack, F., Martin, L., & Stepper, S. (1988). Inhibiting and facilitating conditions of facial expressions: A nonobtrusive test of the facial feedback hypothesis. *Journal of Personality and Social Psychology, 54,* 768-777.

Strayhorn, J. M., Jr. (1979, September). How doctors can talk more effectively with patients. *Behavioral Medicine,* pp. 17-24.

Streissguth, A. P., Barr, H. M., Sampson, P. D., Darley, B. L., & Martin, D. C. (1989). IQ at age 4 in relation to maternal alcohol use and smoking during pregnancy. *Developmental Psychology, 25,* 3-11.

Streissguth, A. P., Martin, D. C., Barr, H. M., Sandman, B. M., Kirchner, G. L., & Darby, D. L. (1984). Intrauterine alcohol and nicotine exposure: Attention and reaction time in 4-year-old children. *Developmental Psychology, 20,* 533-541.

Stricker, E. (1990). Handbook of Behavioral Neurobiology. Volume 10: Neurobiology of Food and Water Intake. New York: Plenum.

Strickland, B. R. (1977). Internal-external control of reinforcement. In T. Bass (Ed.), *Personality variables in social behavior.* Hillsdale, NJ: Erlbaum.

Strickland, B. R. (1978). Internal-external expectancies of health-related behaviors. *Journal of Consulting and Clinical Psychology, 46,* 1192-1211.

Stroebe, W., & Stroebe, M. S. (1987). *Bereavement and health: The psychological and physical consequences of partner loss.* Cambridge: Cambridge University Press.

Struch, N., & Schwartz, S. H. (1989). Intergroup aggression: its predictors and distinctiveness from in-group bias. *Journal of Personality and Social Psychology, 56,* 364-373.

Stunkard, A. J. (1982). Obesity. In M. Belak & A. Kazdan (Eds.), *International handbook of behavior modification and therapy.* New York: Plenum.

Stunkard, A. J., Sorensen, T. I. A., Hanis, C., Teasdale, T. W., Chakraborty, R., Schull, W. J., & Schulsinger, F. (1986). An adoption study of human obesity. *New England Journal of Medicine, 314,* 193-198.

Stuss, D. T., & Benson, D. F. (1987). The frontal lobe and control of cognition and memory. In E. Perecman

(Ed.), *The frontal lobes revisited*. New York: IRBN Press.

Summers, W. K., Majovski, L. V., Marsh, G. M., Tachiki, K., & Kling, A. K. (1986). Oral tetrahydroaminoacridine in long-term treatment of senile dementia, Alzheimer's type. *New England Journal of Medicine, 315,* 1241-1245.

Suomi, S. J., & Harlow, H. F. (1972). Social rehabilitation of isolate-reared monkeys. *Developmental Psychology, 6,* 487-496.

Susman, E. J., Inoff-Germain, G., Nottelmann, E. D., Loriaux, D. L., Cutler, G. B., & Chouros, G. S. (1987). Hormones, emotional dispositions, and aggressive atributes in young adolescents. *Child Development, 58,* 1114-1134.

Suzdak, P. D., Schwartz, R. D., & Skolnick, P. (1986). Ethanol stimulates Y-aminobutyric acid receptor mediated chloride transport in rat brain synaptoneurosomes. *Proceedings of the National Academy of Science U.S.A., 83,* 4071-4075.

Svaetchin, G. (1956). Spectral response curves from single cones. *Acta Physiological Scandanivica Supplementum, 134,* 17-46.

Svare, B., & Kinsley, C. H. (1987). Hormones and sex-related behavior: A comparative analysis. In K. Kelley (Ed.), *Females, males, and sexuality*. Albany: State University of New York Press.

Swanson, J. M., & Kinsbourne, M. (1979). State-dependent learning and retrieval: Methodological cautions against theoretical considerations. In J. F. Kihlstrom & F. J. Evans (Eds.), *Functional disorders of memory*. Hillsdale, NJ: Erlbaum.

Swap, W. C. (1977). Interpersonal attraction and repeated exposure to rewarders and punishers. *Personality and Social Psychology Bulletin, 3,* 248-251.

Szasz, T. (1961). *The myth of mental illness*. New York: Paul B. Hoeber.

Tajfel, H., Flament, C., Billig, M. G., & Bundy, F. F. (1971). Social categorization and intergroup behavior. *European Journal of Social Psychology, 1,* 149-177.

Tajfel, H., & Turner, J. C. (1986). The social identity theory of intergroup behavior. In S. Worchel & W. G. Austin (Eds.), *The psychology of intergroup relations*. Chicago: Nelson-Hall.

Talland, G. A. (1968). *Disorders of memory and learning*. Baltimore: Penguin.

Tallman, J. F., & Gallagher, D. W. (1985). The GABA-ergic system: A locus of benzodiazepine action. *Annual Review of Neuroscience, 8,* 21-44.

Tanabe, T., Iino, M., & Tagaki, S. F. (1975). Discrimination of odors in olfactory bulb, pyriformamygdaloid areas and orbito-frontal cortex of the monkey. *Journal of Neurophysiology, 38,* 1284-1296.

Tanner, J. M. (1970). Physical growth. In P. H. Mussen (Ed.), *Carmichael's manual of child psychology*. New York: Wiley.

Tanner, J. M. (1978). *Fetus into man: Physical growth from conception to maturity*. Cambridge, MA: Harvard University Press.

Tanner, J. M. (1981). Growth and maturation during adolescence. *Nutrition Review, 39,* 43-55.

Tanner, J. M., Whitehouse, R. H., & Takaishi, M. (1966). Standards from birth to maturity for height, weight, height velocity, and weight velocity: British children, 1965. *Archives of Diseases in Childhood, 41,* 454-471, 613-635.

Tate, B. G., & Baroff, G. W. (1966). Aversive control of self injurious behavior in a psychotic boy. *Behavior Research and Therapy, 4,* 281-287.

Taulbee, P. (1983). Solving the mystery of anxiety. *Science News, 124,* 45-46.

Tavris, C., & Sadd, S. (1977). *The Redbook report on female sexuality*. New York: The Redbook Publishing Co.

Taylor, S. E., & Brown, J. D. (1988). Illusion and self-being: A social psychological perspective on mental health. *Psychological Bulletin, 103,* 193-210.

Taylor, S., & Fiske, S. T. (1978). Salience, attention, and attribution: Top of the head phenomena. In L. Berkowitz (Ed.), *Advances in experimental social psychology. Vol. 11*. New York: Academic Press.

Tedeschi, J. T., Schlenker, B. R., & Bonoma, T. V. (1971). Cognitive dissonance: Private ratiocination or public spectacle? *American Psychologist, 26,* 685-695.

Teevan, R. C., & McGhee, P. E. (1972). Childhood development of fear of failure motivation. *Journal of Personality and Social Psychology, 21,* 345-348.

Teitelbaum, P. H. (1955). Sensory control of hypothalamic hyperphagia. *Journal of Comparative and Physiological Psychology, 48,* 156-163.

Teitelbaum, P. H., & Epstein, A. N. (1962). The lateral hypothalamic syndrome: Recovery of feeding and drinking after lateral hypothalamic lesions. *Psychological Review, 69,* 74-90.

Terenius, L. (1982). Endorphins and modulation of pain. *Advances in Neurology, 33,* 59-64.

Terman, L. M. (1925). *Genetic studies of genius. Vol. 1. Mental and physical traits of a thousand gifted children*. Stanford, CA: Stanford University Press.

Terman, L. M., & Oden, M. H. (1947). *The gifted child grows up*. Stanford, CA: Stanford University Press.

Terman, L. M., & Oden, M. H. (1959). *The gifted child at midlife*. Stanford, CA: Stanford University Press.

Terrace, H. S., Petitto, A., Sanders, R. J., & Bever, T. G. (1979). Can an ape create a sentence? *Science, 206,* 891-902.

Tesser, A. (1984). Self-evaluation maintenance processes: Implications for relationships and development. In J. Masters & K. Yarkin (Eds.), *Boundary areas of psychology: Social and developmental*. New York: Academic Press.

Tesser, A. (1985). Some effects of self-evaluation maintenance cognition and action. In R. M. Sorrentino & E. T. Higgins (Eds.), *The handbook of motivation and cognition: Foundations of social behavior*. New York: Guilford Press.

Tesser, A. (1988). Toward a self-evaluation maintenance model of social behavior. In L. Berkowitz (Ed.), *Advances in experimental social psychology* (Volume 21, pp. 181-227). San Diego, Academic Press.

Tesser, A., Campbell, J., & Campbell, J. (1985). A self-evaluation maintenance model of student motivation. In C. Ames & R. Ames (Eds.), *Research on motivation in education: The classroom milieu*. New York: Academic Press.

Thigpen, C. H., & Cleckley, H. (1957). *The three faces of Eve*. New York: McGraw-Hill.

Thompson, J. K., Jarvie, G. J., Lakey, B. B., Cureton, J. J. (1982). Exercise and obesity: Etiology, physiology, and intervention. *Psychological Bulletin, 91,* 55-79.

Thompson, R. F. (1986). The neurobiology of learning and memory. *Science, 233,* 941-947.

Thompson, R. F., Berger, T. W., & Madden, J. (1983). Cellular processes of learning and memory in the mammalian CNS. *Annual Review of Neuroscience, 6,* 447-491.

Thorndike, E. L. (1898). Animal intelligence: An experimental study of the associative process in animals. *Psychological Review Monograph Supplement, 2* (4, Whole No. 8).

Thorndike, E. L., et al. (1921). Intelligence and its measurement: A symposium. *Journal of Educational Psychology, 12,* 123-247.

Thorndyke, P. W., & Hayes-Roth, B. (1979). The use of

schemata in the acquisition and transfer of knowledge. *Cognitive Psychology, 11,* 82-106.

Thurstone, L. L. (1938). *Primary mental abilities.* Chicago: University of Chicago Press.

Tinbergen, N. (1951). *The study of instinct.* Oxford: Clarendon Press.

Tinklepaugh, O. L. (1928). An experimental study of representative factors in monkeys. *Journal of Comparative and Physiological Psychology, 8,* 197-236.

Tolman, E. C. (1948). Cognitive maps in rats and men. *Psychological Review, 55,* 189-208.

Tomita, T. (1986). Retrospective review of retinal circuitry. *Vision Research, 26,* 1339-1350.

Tomkins, S. S. (1970). A theory of memory. In J. S. Antrobus (Ed.), *Cognition and affect.* Boston: Little, Brown.

Tomkins, S. S. (1980). Affect as amplification: some modifications in theory. In R. Plutchik, & H. Kellerman (Eds.), *Emotion: Theory, Research and Experience.,* pp. 141-144. New York: Academic.

Torrey, E. F. (1988). *Nowhere to Go: The tragic odyssey of the homeless mentaly ill.* New York: Harper & Row.

Townsend, B., Cotter, N. Van Compernolled, & White, R. L. (1987). Pitch perception of cochlear implant subjects. *Journal of the Acoustcal Society of America, 82,* 106-114.

Trapnell, P. D., & Wiggins, J. S. (1990). Extension of the interpersonal adjective scales to include the big five dimensions of personality. *Journal of Personality and Social Psychology, 59,* 781-790.

Troll, L. E. (1971). The family of later life: A decade review. *Journal of Marriage and the Family, 33,* 263-290.

Troll, L. E. (1975). *Early and middle adulthood.* Monterey, CA: Brooks/Cole.

Trope, Y., Cohen, O., & Moaz, Y. (1988). The perceptual and inferential effects of situational inducements on dispositional attribution. *Journal of Personality and Social Psychology, 55,* 165-177.

Tulving, E. (1968). Theoretical issues in free recall. In T. R. Dixon & D. L. Horton (Eds.), *Verbal behavior and general behavior theory.* Englewood Cliffs, NJ: Prentice-Hall.

Tulving, E. (1972). Episodic and semantic memory. In E. Tulving & W. Donaldson (Eds.), *Organization of memory.* New York: Academic Press.

Tulving, E. (1985). How many memory systems are there? *American Psychologist, 40,* 385-398.

Tulving, E., & Pearlstone, Z. (1966). Availability versus accessibility of information in memory for words. *Journal of Verbal Learning and Verbal Behavior, 5,* 381-391.

Tupes, E. C., & Christal, R. E. (1961). *Recurrent personality factors based on trait ratings* (Technical Report ASD-TR-61-97). Lackland Air Force Base, TX: U.S. Air Force.

Turk, D. C. (1982). Cognitive learning approaches: Applications in health care. In Doleys, D. M., Meredith, R. L. & Ciminero, A. R. (Eds.) *Behavioral medicine: Assessment and strategies.* New York: Plenum.

Turkkan, J. S. (1989). Classical conditioning: The new hegemony. *Behavioral and Brain Sciences, 12, 121-179.*

Tversky, A., & Kahneman, D. (1973). Availability: A heuristic for judging frequency and probability. *Cognitive Psychology, 5,* 207-232.

Tversky, A., & Kahneman, D. (1973). Judgment under uncertainty: Heuristics and biases. *Science, 185,* 1124-1131.

Tversky, A., & Kahneman, D. (1974). Judgments under uncertainty: Heuristics and biases. *Science, 185,* 1124-1131.

Tversky, A., & Kahneman, D. (1982). Judgment under uncertainty: Heuristics and biases. In D. Kahneman, P. Slovic, & A. Tversky (Eds.), *Judgment under uncertainty: Heuristics and biases* (pp. 3-20). New York: Cambridge University Press.

Udry, J. R. (1971). *The social context of marriage.* Philadelphia: Lippincott.

Uleman, J. S. (1987). Consciousness and control: the case of spontaneous trait inferences. *Personality and Social Psychology Bulletin, 13,* 337-354.

Underwood, B. J. (1957). Interference and forgetting. *Psychological Review, 54,* 49-60.

U.S. Children and Their Families. Current conditions and recent trends (1989). Select Committee on Children, Youth and Families. Washington, DC: U..S. Government Printing Office.

U.S. Department of Commerce, Bureau of the Census. (1984). *Statistical abstract of the United States.* Washington, DC: Government Printing Office.

Valenstein, E. S. (1980). *The psychosurgery debate.* San Francisco: Freeman.

Valliant, G. E. (1983). *The natural history of alcoholism.* Cambridge, MA: Harvard University Press.

van de Poll, N. E., Taminian, M. S., Endert, E., & Louiverse, A. L. (1988). Gonadal steroid influence upon sexual and aggressive behavior of female rats. *International Journal of Neuroscience, 41,* 271-286.

Van Hosesin, G. W. (1982). The parahippocampal gyrus. *Trends in the Neurosciences, 52,* 345-350.

Van Maanen, J. (1977). Summary: Toward a theory of the career. In J. Van Maanen (Ed.), *Organizational careers: Some new perspectives.* New York: Wiley.

Van Osdol, W. R., & Shane, D. G. (1977). *An introduction to exceptional children.* Dubuque, IA: Wm. C. Brown.

Veevers, J. E. (1973). Voluntarily childless wives: An exploratory study. *Sociology and Social Research, 57,* 356-365.

Veterans Administration. (1981). *Legacies of Vietnam: Comparative adjustment of veterans and their peers.* Washington, DC: Government Printing Office.

von Frisch, K. (1974). Decoding the language of the bee. *Science, 185,* 663-668.

Vonnegut, M. (1975). *The Eden express.* New York: Praeger.

Waddell, K. J., & Rogoff, B. (1981). Effect of contextual organization on spatial memory of middle-aged and older women. *Developmental Psychology, 17,* 878-885.

Wadden, T. A., & Stunkard, A. J. (1985). Adverse social and psychological consequences of obesity. *Annals of Internal Medicine, 103,* 10620-10670.

Wagstaff, G. F. (1981). *Hypnosis, compliance, and belief.* New York: St. Martin's Press.

Wald, G. (1964). The receptors of human color vision. *Science, 145,* 1007-1017.

Walker, L. E. (1989). Psychology and violence against women. *American Psychologist, 44,* 695-702.

Wallach, M. A., & Kogan, N. (1959). Sex differences and judgment processes. *Journal of Personality, 27,* 555-564.

Wallach, M. A., Kogan, N., & Bem, D. (1962). Group influence on individual risk taking. *Journal of Abnormal and Social Psychology, 65,* 75-86.

Wallach, M. A., & Wallach, L. (1983). *Psychology's sanction for selfishness: The error of egoism in theory and therapy.* San Francisco: Freeman.

Walster, E., Aronson, V., Abrahams, D., & Rottman, L. (1966). Importance of physical attractiveness in dating behavior. *Journal of Personality and Social Psychology, 4,* 508-516.

Walster, E. H., & Walster, G. W. (1979). *A new look at love.* Reading, MA: Addison-Wesley.

Walster, E., Walster, G. W., & Berscheid, E. (1978). *Equity: Theory and research.* Boston: Allyn & Bacon.

Walters, L. (1988). Ethical issues in fetal research. *Clinical Research, 36,* 209.

Ward, I. L. (1972). Prenatal stress feminizes and demasculinizes the behavior of males. *Science, 175,* 82-84.

Warren, M. M., & Ackert, K. (Eds.) (1964). *The frontal granular cortex and behavior.* New York: McGraw-Hill.

Wason, P. C., & Johnson-Laird, P. N. (1972). *Psychology of reasoning: Structure and content.* Cambridge, MA: Harvard University Press.

Waterhouse, G. J., & Strupp, H. H. (1984). The patient-therapist relationship: Research from the psychodynamic perspective. *Clinical Psychology Review, 4,* 77-92.

Watkins, C. R., & Mayer, D. J. (1982). Organization of endogenous opiate and nonopiate pain control system. *Science, 216,* 1185-1192.

Watkings, M. J. (1975). Inhibition of recall with extralist "cues." *Journal of Verbal Learning and Verbal Behavior, 14,* 294-303.

Watson, J. B. (1913). Psychology as the behaviorist views it. *Psychological Review, 20,* 158-177.

Watson, J. B., & Raynor, R. (1920). Conditioned emotional reactions. *Journal of Experimental Psychology, 3,* 1-14.

Watson, R. I. (1963). *The great psychologists.* Philadelphia: Lippincott.

Webb, W. B. (1975). *Sleep, the gentle tyrant.* Englewood Cliffs, NJ: Prentice-Hall.

Wechsler, D. (1958). *The measurement and appraisal of adult intelligence.* Baltimore: Williams & Wilkins.

Wechsler, D. (1975). Intelligence defined and undefined. *American Psychologist, 30,* 135-159.

Weed, J. A. (1985). Suicide in the United States: 1958-1982. In C. A. Taube & Barrett (Eds.), *Mental health, United States 1985* (DHHS Pub. No. ADM 85-1378). Washington, DC: Government Printing Office.

Weinberger, D. R., Berman, K. F., & Zec, R. F. (1986). Physiologic dysfunction of dorsolateral prefrontal cortex in schizophrenia. *Archives of General Psychiatry, 43,* 114-124.

Weiner, R. D. (1979). The psychiatric use of electrically induced seizures. *American Journal of Psychiatry, 136* (12), 1507-1517.

Weingarten, H. P. (1982). Diet palability modulates sham feeding in VMH-lesioned and normal rats: Implications finickiness and evaluation of sham feeding data. *Journal of Comparative and Physiological Psychology, 96,* 223-233.

Weinraub, M., Jaeger, E., & Hoffman, L. W. (1988). Predicting infant outcomes in families of employed and non-employed mothers. *Early Childhood Research Quarterly, 3,* 361-378.

Weinsenberg, M. (1977). Pain and pain control. *Psychological Bulletin, 84,* 1008-1084.

Weiss, J. (1972). Psychological factors in stress and disease. *Scientific American, 226,* 104-113.

Weissman, M. M., & Klerman, G. L. (1977). Sex differences and epidemiology of depression. *Archives of General Psychiatry, 34,* 98-111.

Weitzenhoffer, A. M., & Hilgard, E. R. (1962). *Stanford Hypnotic Susceptibility Scale, Form C.* Palo Alto, CA: Consulting Psychologists Press.

Wells, K. B., Golding, J. M., & Burnam, M. A. (1988). Psychiatric disorder in a sample of the general population with and without chronic medical conditions. *American Journal of Psychiatry, 145,* 976-981.

Wells, K. B., Stewart, A., Hays, R. D., Burnam, M. A., Rogers, W., Daniels, M., Berry, S., Greenfield, S., & Ware, J. (1989). The functioning and well-being of depressed patients. *Journal of the American Medical Association, 262,* 914-919.

Wertheimer, M. (1912). Experimentalle studien uber das sehen von beuegung. *Zeitschrift Fuer Psychologie, 61,* 161-265.

Wheeler, L., Deci, E. L., Reis, H. T., & Zuckerman, M. (1978). *Interpersonal influence.* Boston: Allyn & Bacon.

Whelan, R. E., & Simon, N. G. (1984). Biological motivation. *Annual Review of Psychology, 35,* 257-276.

White, R. W., & Watt, N. F. (1981). *The abnormal personality.* New York: Wiley.

Whitehouse, P. J., Price, D. L., Clark, A. W., Coyle, J. T., & DeLong, M. H. (1981). Alzheimer's disease: Evidence for selective loss of cholinergic neurons in the nucleus basalis. *Annals of Neurology, 10,* 122-126.

Who is minding the children? (1987). Bureau of the Census. Washington, DC: U.S. Government Printing Office.

Whorf, B. L. (1956). Science and linguistics. In J. B. Carroll (Ed.), *Language, thought, and reality: Selected writings of Benjamin Whorf.* Cambridge, MA: MIT Press.

Whyte, W. H. (1955). *The organization man.* New York: Simon & Schuster.

Wilson, B. A. (1987). *Rehabilitation of memory.* New York: Guilford Press.

Wilson, E. O. (1975). *Sociobiology: The new synthesis.* Cambridge, MA: Belknap.

Wilson, E. O. (1978). *On human nature.* Cambridge, MA: Harvard University Press.

Wingfield, A. (1979). *Human learning and memory.* New York: Harper & Row.

Winter, D. G. (1987). Leader appeal, leader performance, and the motive profiles of leaders and followers: a study of American presidents and elections. *Journal of Personality and Social Psychology, 52,* 196-202.

Winter, L., & Uleman, J. S. (1984). When are social judgments made? Evidence for the spontaneousness of trait inferences. *Journal of Personality and Social Psychology, 47,* 237-252.

Winter, L., Uleman, J. S., & Cunniff, C. (1985). How automatic are social judgments? *Journal of Personality and Social Psychology, 49,* 904-917.

Winterbottom, M. R. (1958). The relation of need for achievement to early learning experiences in independent and mastery. In J. W. Atkinson (Ed.), *Motives in fantasy, action and society.* Princeton, NJ: Van Nostrand.

Wise, R. A., & Bozarth, M. A. (1984). Brain reward circuitry: Four circuit elements wired in apparent series. *Brain Research Bulletin, 12,* 203-208.

Wolfe, J. B. (1936). Effectiveness of token rewards for chimpanzees. *Comparative Psychology Monographs, 12* (60, 294).

Wolfe, T. (1979). *The right stuff.* New York: Farrar, Straus & Giroux.

Wolpe, J. (1958). *Psychotherapy by reciprocal inhibition.* Stanford, CA: Stanford University Press.

Woodruff, D. S. (1983). A review of aging and cognitive processes. *Research on Aging, 5,* 139-153.

Woodworth, R. S. (1938). *Experimental psychology.* New York: Holt.

Woolsey, C. N. (1958). Organization of somatic and sensory motor areas of the cerebral cortex. In H. F. Harlow

& C. N. Woolsey (Eds.), *Biological and biochemical basis of behavior.* Madison: University of Wisconsin Press.

Worchel, S., & Cooper, J. (1983). *Understanding social psychology* (3rd ed.). Homewood, IL: Dorsey.

Word, C. H., Zanna, M. P., & Cooper, J. (1974). The nonverbal mediation of self-fulfilling prophecies in intersocial interaction. *Journal of Experimental Social Psychology, 10,* 109-120.

World Health Organization. (1980). *World health statistics annual.* Geneva: Author.

Wrightsman, L. S., Willis, C. E., & Kassin, S. M. (Eds.). (1987). *On the witness stand: Controversies in the courtroom.* Newbury Park, CA: Sage.

Wyer, R. S., & Hartwick, J. (1980). The role of information retrieval and conditional inference processes in belief formation and change. In L. Berkowitz (Ed.), *Advances in experimental social psychology. Vol. 13.* New York: Academic Press.

Wynne, L. C. (1968). Methodologic and conceptual issues in the study of schizophrenics and their families. In D. Rosenthal & S. S. Kety (Eds.), *The transmission of schizophrenia.* Oxford: Pergamon.

Yalom, I. D. (Ed.) (1986). Group psychotherapy. *American Psychiatric Association Annual Review, Vol. V.* Washington, DC: American Psychiatric Press.

Yang, B. (1979). The research in the forecast of acupuncture anesthesia. In *National symposia of acupuncture and moxibustion and acupuncture anesthesia.* Bejing, China.

Yarbus, A. L. (1967). *Eye movements and vision.* New York: Plenum.

Young, M., Benjamin, B., & Wallis, C. (1963). The mortality of widowers. *Lancet, 2,* 454-457.

Young, T. (1802). On the theory of light and colors. *Philosophical Transactions of the Royal Society of London, 92,* 12-48.

Youniss, J., & Smollar, J. (1985). Adolescent relations with mothers, fathers, and friends. Chicago: University of Chicago Press.

Zaika, R. (1975). *Perception and photography.* Englewood Cliffs, NJ: Prentice-Hall.

Zelnick, M., & Kanter, J. F. (1980). Sexual activity, contraceptive use, and pregnancy among metropolitan teenagers: 1971-1979. *Family Planning Perspectives, 12,* 230-237.

Zigler, E., Abelson, W. D., & Seitz, V. (1973). Motivational factors in the performance of economically disadvantaged children on the Peabody Picture Vocabulary Test. *Child Development, 44,* 294-303.

Zigler, E., & Butterfield, E. C. (1968). Motivational aspects of changes in I.Q. test performance of culturally deprived nursery school children. *Child Development, 39,* 1-14.

Zilboorg, G. S., & Henry, G. W. (1941). *A history of medical psychology.* New York: Norton.

Zillman, D. (1984). *Connections between sex and aggression.* Hillsdale, NJ: Erlbaum.

Zimmer, J. (1984). Courting the gods of sport: Athletes use superstition to ward off devils of injury and bad luck. *Psychology Today, 18,* 36-39.

Zillman, D. (1978). Attribution and misattribution of excitatory reactions. In J. H. Harvey, W. J. Ickes, & R. F. Kidd (Eds.), *New directions in attribution research, Vol. 2.* Hillsdale, NJ: Erlbaum.

Zillman, D. (1982). Transfer of excitation in emotional behavior. In J. T. Cacioppo & R. E. Petty (Eds.), *Social psychophysiology: A sourcebook.* New York: Guilford Press.

Zuber, J. A., Crott, H. W., & Werner, J. (1992). Choice shift and group polarization: an analysis of the status of arguments and social decision schemes. *Journal of Personality and Social Psychology, 62,* 50-61.

Zwislocki, J. J. (1981). Sound analysis in the ear: A history of discoveries. *American Scientist, 69,* 184-192.

Credits

FIGURES AND TABLES

Page

22 Table 1.3. Division and State Association membership. Copyright © 1991 by the American Psychological Association. Reprinted by permission.

51 Figure 2.6. Pamela Taulbee, "Solving the Mystery of Anxiety," *Science News,* July 16, 1983.

58 Figure 2.11. From *Biological Psychology,* Second Edition, by James W. Kalat. Copyright © 1984 by Wadsworth, Inc. Reprinted by permission of the publisher.

58 Figure 2.11. From "The Brain" by David H. Hubel. Copyright © 1979 by Scientific American, Inc. All rights reserved.

63 Figure 2.16. From *Brain and Conscious Experience,* edited by John C. Eccles. Copyright © 1966 by Pontifica Academia Scientarium. Reprinted by permission of Springer-Verlag and the author.

63 Figure 2.17. From *The Frontal Granular Cortex and Behavior* by Warren and Akert. Copyright © 1964 by McGraw-Hill, Inc. Used with permission of McGraw-Hill Book Company.

66 Figure 2.18. From *Functional Neuroscience* by Michael Gazzaniga et al. Copyright © 1979 by Harper & Row Publishers, Inc. Reprinted by permission of HarperCollins Publishers.

66 Figure 2.19. From *Functional Neuroscience* by Michael Gazzaniga et al. Copyright © 1979 by Harper & Row Publishers, Inc. Reprinted by permission of HarperCollins Publishers.

70 Figure 2.21. From Wilder Penfield, M.D. and Herbert Jasper, M.D., *Epilepsy and the Functional Anatomy of the Human Brain,* published by Little Brown and Company. Copyright © 1954, by Wilder Penfield and Herbert Jasper.

77 Figure 2.28. From "The Split Brain in Man" by Michael Gazzaniga in *Scientific American,* August 1967. Copyright © 1967 by Scientific American, Inc. Reprinted by permission of the author.

85 Table 3.1. From "Contemporary Psychophysics" by Eugene Galanter in *New Directions in Psychology* edited by R. Brown, et al. Copyright © 1962 by Holt, Rinehart and Winston. Reprinted by permission of the author.

87 Table 3.2. From *Fundamentals of Psychology* by F. A. Geldard. Copyright © 1962 by John Wiley & Sons, Inc. Reprinted by permission.

98 Table 3.7. "Decibel Ratings and Hazardous Time Exposures in Common Noises," from American Academy of Otolaryngology—Head & Neck Surgery Inc., Washington, D.C.

104 Figure 3.17. Adapted from "Tuning a Deaf Ear" by Patricia J. Wynne from "Science and the Citizen," *Scientific American,* November 1984, p. 76. Copyright © by Scientific American, Inc. Reprinted by permission. All rights reserved.

116 Figure 3.25. From "Gestalt Laws of Form Perception" from *Perception,* Third Edition, by Margaret W. Matlin. Copyright © 1992 Allyn & Bacon. Reprinted by permission.

116 Figure 3.26. From "Organizational Determinants of Subjective Contour" by D. R. Bradely and H. M. Petry in *American Journal of Psychology,* Vol. 90, 1977. Copyright © 1977 by the American Journal of Psychology. Reprinted by permission of the University of Illinois Press.

117 Figure 3.28. From *Sensation and Perception* by H. Schiffman. Copyright © 1976 by John Wiley & Sons, Inc.

124 Figure 3.40. From *Sensation and Perception* by Stanley Coren and Ward Porac. Copyright © 1979 by Academic Press, Inc. Reprinted by permission.

126 Figure 3.42. Reprinted by permission from *Nature,* Vol. 228, No. 477. Copyright © 1970 Macmillan Journals Limited.

139 Figure 4.3. From *Physiological Psychology* by Mark Rosenzweig and Arnold Leiman. Copyright © 1982 by D. C. Heath and Company. Reprinted by permission.

155 Table 4.2. From *Explorations in Personality,* edited by Henry A. Murray. Copyright 1938 by Oxford University Press, Inc. Renewed 1966 by Henry A. Murray. Reprinted by permission of the publisher.

163 Figure 4.15. Reprinted by permission of the Penny & Stermer Group.

168 Figure 4.19. From "Cardiovascular Differentiation of Happiness, Sadness, Anger, and Fear Following Imagery and Exercise" by Gary E. Schwartz, et al. from *Psychosomatic Medicine,* Vol. XLIII, No. 4, p. 349. Reprinted by permission of Elsevier Publishing Company, Inc.

171 Figure 4.21. From *Darwin and Facial Expressions: A Century of Research in Review* edited by Paul Ekman. Copyright © 1973 by Academic Press, Inc. Reprinted by permission of the author.

181 Figure 5.1. From *Human Information Processing,* Second Edition, by Peter H. Lindsay and Donald A. Norman. Copyright © 1977 by Academic Press, Inc. Reprinted by permission.

182 Figure 5.2. From *The Human Brain* by Dick Gilling and Robin Brightwell. Copyright © 1982 by Dick Gilling and Robin Brightwell. Reprinted by permission of Forbis Publishers Ltd.

183 Figure 5.5. From *Cognition* by Arnold Lewis Glass, Keith James Holyoak, and John Lester Santa. Copyright © 1979 by Random House, Inc. Reprinted by permission.

187 Figure 5.11. Dymond Cartwright, *A Primer on Sleep and Dreaming.* Copyright © 1978 by Addison-Wesley, Reading, MA. Reprinted with permission.

189 Figure 5.12. From "Are you wide awake at 3:00 A.M. by choice or chance?" by Richard M. Coleman. Reprinted by permission of W.H. Freeman and Company.

192 Figure 5.13. From "The Brain as a Dream State Generator" by Alan Hobson and Robert W. McCarley from *The American Journal of Psychiatry,* December 1977. Copyright © 1977 by The American Psychiatric Association. Reprinted by permission.

Thinking" by James R. Rest; Doctoral Thesis, The University of Chicago, 1969. Copyright © 1969 by James R. Rest. Reprinted by permission.

369 Table 10.2. Adapted from *Childhood and Society,* Second Edition, by Erik H. Erikson. Copyright © 1950, 1963 by W. W. Norton & Company, Inc. Copyright renewed, 1978 by Erik H. Erikson. Reprinted by permission of W. W. Norton & Company, Inc.

377 Figure 10.3. From "Marital Satisfaction Over the Family Life Cycle" by B. C. Rollins and H. Feldman in *Journal of Marriage and the Family,* Vol. 32, No. 1, February, 1970. Reprinted by permission.

402 Figure 11.3. From *Stability and Change in Human Characteristics* by Benjamin S. Bloom. Copyright © 1964 by John Wiley & Sons, Inc. Reprinted by permission of the author.

404 Table 11.5. From *Mental Retardation: A Developmental Approach,* by Charles Carr Cleland. Copyright © 1978. Adapted by permission of Prentice-Hall, Inc., Englewood Cliffs, NJ.

408 Figure 11.4. From S. Scarr and R. A. Weinberg, "I.Q., Test Performance of Black Children Adopted by White Families," *American Psychologist,* 1976. Vol. 31, pp. 727–39. Copyright © 1976 by The American Psychological Association. Adapted by permission of the author.

411 Figure 11.6. From the Culture-Fair Intelligence Test, Scale 2, Form A, test booklet. Copyright © 1949, 1960, renewed, 1977 by The Institute for Personality and Ability Testing, Inc. Reproduced by permission.

431 Figure 12.3. From "Conformity Development as a Function of Self-Blame" by Philip R. Constanzo in *Journal of Personality and Social Psychology,* April, 1970. Copyright © 1970 by The American Psychological Association. Reprinted by permission.

432 Table 12.1. From "Long-Term Behavioral Effects of Cognitive Dissonance" by Johnathan L. Freedman in *Journal of Experimental Social Psychology,* Vol. 1, 1965. Copyright © by Academic Press, Inc. Reprinted by permission.

438 Figure 12.4. From *Understanding Social Psychology,* Fourth Edition, by Stephen Worchel and Joel Cooper. Copyright © 1988 by The Dorsey Press. Reprinted by permission.

439 Table 12.2. From "The Perception of Consistency in Attitudes" by G. R. Goethals and R. F. Reckman in *Journal of Experimental Social Psychology,* Vol. 9, No. 6, November 1973. Copyright © 1973 by Academic Press, Inc. Reprinted by permission.

442 Table 12.3. From "Illusory Correlation in Interpersonal Perception" by David H. Hamilton and Robert Gifford in *Journal of Experimental Social Psychology,* Vol. 12, No. 4, July, 1976. Copyright © 1976 by Academic Press, Inc. Reprinted by permission.

447 Table 12.4. From "Gain and Loss of Esteem as Determinants of Interpersonal Attractiveness" by Elliot Aronson and Darwyn Linder in *Journal of Experimental Social Psychology,* Vol. 1, No. 2. Copyright © 1965 by Academic Press, Inc. Reprinted by permission.

451 Table 12.5. From *The Transparent Self* by Sidney Jourard. Copyright © 1971 by Van Nostrand Reinhold Company. Reprinted by permission of the publisher.

457 Figure 13.1. From *Social Psychology* by Solomon E. Asch. Copyright © 1952 by Prentice-Hall, Inc. Reprinted by permission of the author.

460 Figure 13.4. From *Obedience to Authority* by Stanley Milgrim. Copyright © 1974 by Stanley Milgrim. Reprinted by permission of Harper & Row Publishers and Tavistock Publications.

463 Table 13.1. From "Effects of Initial Request Size and Timing of Second Request" by Cann, Sherman, and Elkes, in *Journal of Personality and Social Psychology,* Vol. 32, No. 5, November, 1975, p. 777. Copyright © 1975 by The American Psychological Association. Adapted by permission of the publisher and the author.

473 Figure 13.6. From "Bystander Intervention in Emergencies: Diffusion of Responsibility" by John Darley and Bibb Latane in *Journal of Personality and Social Psychology,* April, 1968. Copyright © 1968 by The American Psychological Association. Reprinted by permission.

474 Table 13.3. From I. M. Piliavin, et al., p. 430, *Journal of Personality and Social Psychology,* Vol. 32, No. 5, November 1975. Copyright 1975 by the American Psychological Association. Adapted by permission of the author.

476 Table 13.4. From "Sex differences in judgment" by Michael A. Wallach and Nathan Kogan from *Journal of Personality,* March-December 1959. Copyright © 1959. Duke University Press (Durham, N.C.). Reprinted by permission.

486 Figure 13.8. From *A Theory of Leadership Effectiveness* by Fred E. Fiedler. Copyright © 1967 by McGraw-Hill, Inc. Reprinted by permission.

493 Figure 14.2. From *Personality—Strategies and Issues,* sixth edition, by Robert M. Liebert and Michael D. Spiegler. Copyright © 1990 by Brooks/Cole Publishing Company. Reprinted by permission.

505 Figure 14.5. From "Eysenck on Extraversion" by H. J. Eysenck in *British Journal of Psychology,* Vol. 55, 1964. Copyright © 1964 by The British Psychological Society. Reprinted by permission.

509 Table 14.4. Table "Descriptions of MMPI Scales and Simulated Items" from *Psychological Testing and Assessment* by Lewis R. Aiken. Copyright 1943, renewed © 1970 by the University of Minnesota.

510 Figure 14.6. From *Minnesota Multiphase Personality Inventory.* Copyright 1943, renewed © 1970 by The University of Minnesota. Reprinted by permission.

515 Table 14.6. From "Internal Control–External Control" by Julian B. Rotter from *Psychology Today,* June 1971. Copyright © 1971 Ziff-Davis Publishing Company. Reprinted by permission.

535 Figure 15.1. From "Cardiovascular Research: Decades of Progress A Decade of Promise" by Robert I. Levy and Jay Moskowitz, *Science,* Vol. 240, July 9, 1982. Copyright © 1982 by the American Association for the Advancement of Science. Reprinted by permission.

536 Table 15.1. "Social Readjustment Rating Scale" by Holmes & Rahe, *Journal of Psychosomatic Research,* Vol. 11. Copyright © 1967 Pergamon Press Ltd. Reprinted by permission.

537 Figure 15.3. Reprinted with permission from *Journal of Psychosomatic Research,* Vol. 14, R. H. Rahe, et al., "Prediction of near-future health change from subjects' preceding life changes." Copyright © 1970, Pergamon Press, Ltd.

540 Figure 15.4. Adapted from "The influence of stress on lymphocytes and tumor growth" from "Psychoneuroendocrine influences on immunocompetence and neoplasma" by Vernon Riley, *Science,* June 5, 1981. Copyright © 1981 by the American Association for the Advancement of Science. Reprinted by permission.

541 Figure 15.5. "Lymphocyte proliferation in widowers" from "Suppression of lymphocyte stimulation following be-

reavement" by S. J. Schleifer et al., *Journal of the American Medical Association*, 1983, pp. 374-377.

542 Figure 15.6. From David T. Graham, "Some Research on Psychophysiologic Specificity," *Physiological Correlates of Psychological Disorder*, pp. 222-223. Copyright © 1962 by the Regents of the University of Wisconsin.

545 Table 15.2. "Ten most frequent hassles" from "Comparison of two modes of stress measurement" by A. D. Kanner et al., *Journal of Behavioral Medicine*, Vol. 4, No. 1. Copyright © 1981 Plenum Publishing Corporation. Reprinted by permission.

546 Figure 15.7. From "Psychological Factors in Stress and Disease" by Jay M. Weiss in *Scientific American*, June 1972. Copyright © 1972 by Scientific American, Inc. All rights reserved.

548 Figure 15.8. Reprinted by permission of Elsevier Science Publishing Co., Inc. from "Gradients of Physiological Arousal in Parachutists as a Function of an Approaching Jump" by W. D. Fenz and S. Epstein in *Psychosomatic Medicine*, Vol. XXIX, No. 1, p. 38. Copyright © 1967 by The American Psychosomatic Association.

549 Figure 15.9. From Lazarus, Opton, Nomikos, and Rankin, "The Principle of Short-Circuiting Threat: Further Evidence," *Journal of Personality*, Vol. XXXIII, March 1965-December 1965, p. 628. Copyright © 1965, Duke University Press (Durham, N.C.).

551 Table 15.3. From "Signs and Symptoms of Post-traumatic Stress Disorder" by Mardi J. Horowitz, et al., in *Archives of General Psychiatry*, Vol. 37, January 1980. Copyright © 1980 by the American Medical Association. Reprinted by permission.

552 Table 15.4. From *Biofeedback: Methods & Procedures in Clinical Practice* by George D. Fuller. Copyright © 1977 by George D. Fuller. Reprinted by permission.

554 Figure 15.10. From *Stress Without Distress* by Hans Selye, M.D. Copyright © 1974 by Hans Selye, M.D. Reprinted by permission of HarperCollins Publishers.

559 Table 15.5. From *In the Mind's Eye* by Arnold Lazarus. Copyright © 1977 by Rawson Associates Publishers, Inc. Reprinted by permission of Mary Yost Associates, Inc.

560 Figure 15.11. From "Reduction of Postoperative Pain by Encouragement and Instruction of Patients" by L. D. Egbert, G. E. Battit, and C. E. Welch in *New England Journal of Medicine*, Vol. 270, No. 16, 1964. Copyright © 1964 by the Massachusetts Medical Society. Reprinted by permission.

567 Table 16.1. From "One-month Prevalence of Mental Disorder in the United States" by D. A. Regrer et al., *Archives of General Psychiatry*, 1988, 45, pp. 977-986. Copyright © 1988 American Medical Association. Reprinted by permission.

582 Figure 16.2. From *DSM-III Training Guide*, edited by Linda J. Webb, et al. Copyright © 1981 by Brunner/Mazel, Inc. Reprinted by permission.

584 Figure 16.3. Mental Health, United States 1985, ed. by Carl A. Taube and Sally A. Barrett. U.S. Department of Health and Human Services. DHHS Publication No. (ADM) 85-1378.

586 Table 16.6. From "Differing Causal Attributions for the Negative Event" by C. Peterson, *Health Psychology*, 1982, 1, pp. 153-168. Copyright © 1982 by Health Psychology. Reprinted by permission of Lawrence Erlbaum Associates, Inc.

589 Figure .16.5. From *Abnormal Psychology*, Second Edition, by Ephraim Rosen, Ronald E. Fox, and Ian Gregory.

Copyright © 1972 by Holt, Rinehart and Winston, Inc. Reprinted by permission of the publisher.

598 Table 16.9. From *Psychiatric Diagnosis*, 2/E by Donald W. Goodwin and Samuel B. Guze. Copyright © 1979 by Oxford University Press, Inc. Reprinted by permission.

599 Figure 16.9. From "Drug Use and Life Style Among College Undergraduates in 1989: A Comparison With 1969 and 1978 by H. G. Pope, Jr., et al., *American Journal of Psychiatry*, 147:8, August 1990. Copyright © by the American Psychiatric Association. Reprinted by permission.

624 Figure 17.3. "Diet Log" from *Human Behavior: Analysis and Application*, 2/E by Ellen P. Reese, et al. Copyright © 1978 by Ellen P. Reese. Reprinted by permission of the author.

632 Figure 17.4. From *The Benefits of Psychotherapy* by Mary Lee Smith, et al. Copyright © 1980 by The Johns Hopkins University Press. Reprinted by permission.

634 Figure 17.5. From "Medical Treatment of Mental Illness" by Philip A. Berger, *Science*, Volume 200, pp. 974-981, May 26, 1978. Copyright © 1978 by American Association for the Advancement of Science. Reprinted by permission.

PHOTO CREDITS

Positions of the photographs are indicated in the abbreviated form as follows: top (t), bottom (b), center (c), left (l), right (r). Unless otherwise acknowledged, all photographs are the property of Scott Foresman.

Page

4 Shirley Rosicke/The Stock Market
5 (l) Gabe Palmer/The Stock Market; (r) Charles Gupton/Southern Light
9 (t) Institute for Intercultural Studies/Library of Congress; (b) Courtesy of Chris Costner Sizemore, author of *I'm Eve*, Doubleday, 1977.
15 John Coletti/Stock, Boston
20 Archives of the History of American Psychology
21 (t) The Bettmann Archive; (b) Clark University Archives
23 Roe DiBona
24 (l) The Bettmann Archive; (r) Ron Sherman/TSW, Chicago
25 The Bettmann Archive
26 (t) The Granger Collection, New York; (b) Historical Pictures Service
27 The Bettmann Archive
29 Rick Friedman/Black Star
30 D&I MacDonald/The Picture Cube
32 UPI/Bettmann
37 Courtesy Dr. James L. McGaugh
45 Figure 2.3 Photo: Carolina Biological Supply
49 Jean-Claude Lejeune
54 (t) From *Some Account of the Life and Labors of Dr. Francois Joseph Gall, Founder of Phrenology* by Charlotte Fowler Wells, 1896; (b) The Bettmann Archive
55 (both) Jean-Loup Charmet
57 The Natural History Museum, London
59 Montreal Neurological Institute
61 From *The Excitable Cortex in Conscious Man* by Wilder Penfield. Liverpool University Press, 1958 (Second impression 1967)
63 From *American Journal of Medical Sciences*, Vol. 20, 1850

71 Courtesy of Dr. Eric Courchesne, UCSD Magnetic Resonance Institute

72 Figure 2.23 and Figure 2.24 Courtesy Drs. Michael E. Phelps and John C. Mazziotta, UCLA School of Medicine

75 Courtesy California Institute of Technology

78 Figure 2.29 From "Perception of Bilateral Chimeric Figures Following Hemispheric Deconnexion" by Jerre Levy, Colwyn Trevarthen and R. W. Sperry. *Brain,* Vol. 95, page 68, 1972

79 Figure 2.30 Courtesy Drs. Michael E. Phelps and John C. Mazziotta, UCLA School of Medicine

85 The Granger Collection, New York

87 The Granger Collection, New York

89 Figure 3.3 Photo: Courtesy Munsell Color, Baltimore, Maryland

91 Figure 3.5 Photo: Courtesy Deric S. Bownds and Dr. S. Carlson

93 Historical Pictures Service

94 Figure 3.10 (both) MacMillan Science Co., Inc.

105 J. Guichard/Sygma

106 Bruno Barbey/Magnum

110 (both) J. P. Laffont/Sygma

111 Joseph Nettis/Stock, Boston

117 Ira Wyman/Sygma

119 Figure 3.29 (tl) Cy Furlan and (br) Milt & Joan Mann/Cameramann International

121 Figure 3.33 Phil Schermeister

123 Figure 3.36 © M. C. Escher Heirs c/o Cordon Art—Baarn—Holland. Collection Haags Gemeentemuseum—The Hague; Figure 3.37 Milt & Joan Mann/Cameramann International

124 Figure 3.40 (both) Courtesy Dr. Peter Thompson, University of York, England

132 Lenore Weber

135 M. Stouffer/Animals Animals

136 Stanley Rowin/The Picture Cube

138 John Sanderson

139 Figure 4.4 Courtesy Dr. Neal Miller

141 Yoav Levy/Phototake

143 Arlene Collins/Monkmeyer Press

147 Photograph by Dellenback. Reproduced by permission of The Kinsey Institute for Research in Sex, Gender, and Reproduction, Inc.

148 Gil Dupuy

151 Figure 4.10 Harlow Primate Laboratory, University of Wisconsin

152 (l) M. L. Miller/Sipa; (r) Deborah Davis/PhotoEdit

157 Figure 4.13 Courtesy Dr. David C. McClelland, from *Motivation Workshops* by D. C. McClelland and R. S. Steele. New York: General Learning Press, 1972

158 Ellis Herwig/The Picture Cube

160 REPRINTED FROM PSYCHOLOGY TODAY MAGAZINE Copyright © 1986 American Psychological Association

162 Lee White/West Light

171 Figure 4.21 Photos Courtesy Dr. Paul Ekman, from UNMASKING THE FACE by Paul Ekman and Wallace V. Friesen; (b) The Bettmann Archive

179 Nathan Bilow/Stock Imagery

185 Figure 5.7 © Ted Spagna

186 Figure 5.8 Photos: © Ted Spagna. From DREAMSTAGE Scientific Catalog, Copyright © 1977 J. Allan Hobson and Hoffmann-La Roche Inc.; Figure 5.9 From DREAMSTAGE Scientific Catalog, Copyright © 1977 J. Allan Hobson and Hoffman-La Roche Inc.

187 Figure 5.10 Photo: © Ted Spagna. From DREAMSTAGE

Scientific Catalog, Copyright © 1977 J. Allan Hobson and Hoffman-La Roche Inc.

191 © The Detroit Institute of Arts, Gift of Mr. and Mrs. Bert L. Smokler and Mr. and Mrs. Lawrence A. Fleishman

194 Barbara Alper/Stock, Boston

196 (1) The Bettmann Archive; (r) Mary Evans Picture Library

197 John Ficara/Woodfin Camp & Associates

206 (all) Courtesy Dr. Albert Hofmann

213 Courtesy Dr. Elizabeth F. Loftus

217 The Granger Collection, New York

218 John Chase

222 (both) Courtesy of Professor Benjamin Harris, from Watson's 1919 film *Experimental Investigation of Babies*

225 Steve Starr/Stock, Boston

226 Joe McNally

227 Figure 6.11 Photo: Richard Wood/The Picture Cube

231 James Pozarik/Gamma-Liaison

235 Yerkes Regional Primate Research Center of Emory University

238 Denny Baily/Unicorn

240 Figure 6.19 Photo: Courtesy Dr. Philip G. Zimbardo

244 (all) Courtesy Dr. Stuart Ellins, California State University, San Bernardino

245 Animal Behavior Enterprises, Inc.

247 Courtesy Department of Psychology, University of California, Berkeley

248 Historical Pictures Service

249 (both) From *The Mentality of Apes* by Wolfgang Köhler. Routledge & Kegan Paul Ltd., London, 1927 (Reprinted 1948, 1973)

257 Courtesy Compaq Computer Corp.

264 Richard Pasley/Stock, Boston

273 (both) AP/Wide World

275 The Bettmann Archive

288 (all) Philip-Lorca diCorcia

294 Joseph Gianetti/Stock, Boston

296 Michael Weisbrot

299 Charles Gupton/Southern Light

306 Spencer Grant/The Picture Cube

307 Bob Daemmrich

309 Jerry Howard/Stock, Boston

316 Bryan & Cherry Alexander

319 Paul Fusco/Magnum

324 Courtesy Dr. Sandra Scarr

328 (t) Courtesy Gesell Institute; (b) *Two Boys in a Garden* attributed to John Durand, c. 1765. Courtesy Connecticut Historical Society

329 Jeffry W. Myers/Stock, Boston

336 Figure 9.4 From J. L. Conel: *The Postnatal Development of the Human Cerebral Cortex,* Vols. I-VIII, 1939-1967. Cambridge: Harvard University Press. Reprinted by permission

337 Paul Damien/TSW, Chicago

338 Figure 9.6 From L. A. Stroufe and R. G. Cooper; *Child Development: Its Nature and Course,* 1988. McGraw-Hill, Inc. Reprinted by permission

339 Figure 9.7 Enrico Ferorelli

340 Yves De Braine/Black Star

341 Figure 9.8 (both) George Zimbel/Monkmeyer Press

344 Figure 9.11 From the film *Formal Thought.* Davidson Films, Inc.

347 (l) Elizabeth Crews/The Image Works; Figure 9.12 Harlow Primate Laboratory, University of Wisconsin

348 Myrleen Ferguson/PhotoEdit

356 Bob Daemmrich/The Image Works
367 Bob Daemmrich
369 Jon Erikson
371 Don Smetzer/TSW, Chicago
372 Frank Siteman/The Picture Cube
373 Bob Daemmrich
375 Bob Daemmrich/Stock, Boston
377 Ellis Herwig
379 David Young-Wolff/PhotoEdit
380 Capital Features/The Image Works
381 Bob Daemmrich/The Image Works
383 Benn Mitchell/The Image Bank
384 Dan McCoy/Rainbow
385 Rhoda Sidney/PhotoEdit
390 Jeffry W. Myers/Stock, Boston
391 Byron, 1906
392 (t) Library of Congress; (c) Historical Pictures Service
394 REPRINTED FROM PSYCHOLOGY TODAY MAGAZINE Copyright © 1985 American Psychological Association
401 Focus on Sports
404 Lester Sloan/Woodfin Camp & Associates
405 Loren Santow/TSW, Chicago
409 Ben Simmons/The Stock Market
411 Brown Brothers
419 Stanford University Visual Art Services/Steve Gladfelter
422 Stacy Pick/Stock, Boston
424 Nina Berman/Sipa
426 Ed Kashi
428 Patsy Davidson/The Image Works
430 Bob Daemmrich/Stock, Boston
433 J. Barry O'Rourke/The Stock Market
435 Courtesy American Cancer Society
440 UPI/Bettmann
445 Don Smetzer/TSW, Chicago
446 Gabe Palmer/The Stock Market
449 Courtesy Universitätsbibliothek, Heidelberg. Codex Manesse, Cod. Pal. Germ. 848, fol. 251r
450 © Joel Gordon 1988
457 Figure 13.2 William Vandivert
458 Herb Snitzer/Stock, Boston
460 Figure 13.3 (both) Copyright 1965 by Stanley Milgram. From the film OBEDIENCE, distributed by the Pennsylvania State University, PCR
465 Courtesy Dr. Loh Seng Tsai
466 Bob Daemmrich/Sygma
467 (t) Focus on Sports; Figure 13.5 (all) Courtesy Dr. Albert Bandura
468 UPI/Bettmann
471 Martin A. Levick
476 Gabe Palmer/The Stock Market
478 UPI/Bettmann
481 Robert McElroy/Woodfin Camp & Associates
485 Figure 13.7 (all) Courtesy Ronald Lippitt
490 Robert Trippet/Sipa
491 Figure 14.1 (both) Courtesy Zentralbibliothek, Zürich. MS. C 101, fol. 25-26
493 Bruce McAllister/The Image Works
494 © Joel Gordon 1986
495 (1) Sybil Shackman/Monkmeyer Press; (r) R. Kopstein/Monkmeyer Press
502 Figure 14.4 Sepp Seitz/Woodfin Camp & Associates
503 The Bettmann Archive
504 (t) Courtesy Harvard University News Office; (bl) Frank Siteman/The Picture Cube; (br) Stuart Cohen/Stock, Boston

506 Jacques Chenet/Woodfin Camp & Associates
510 Figure 14.6 From *Minnesota Multiphasic Personality Inventory.* Copyright © 1943 and renewed 1970 by the University of Minnesota. Reprinted by permission of the University of Minnesota Press
512 Myrleen Ferguson/PhotoEdit
513 (t) Jim Bradshaw; (b) Courtesy Dr. Albert Bandura
515 Courtesy Dr. Julian Rotter
517 IPA/The Image Works
518 Okoniewski/The Image Works
523 Mikki Ansin/The Picture Cube
525 (l) Library of Congress; (r) Courtesy University of Illinois at Chicago, The Library, Jane Addams Memorial Collection
531 Courtesy Dr. Martin Seligman
543 Focus on Sports
544 Susan Van Etten/PhotoEdit
546 Jim Pickerell/TSW, Chicago
547 Jeffry W. Myers/Stock, Boston
550 NASA
551 Kolvoord/The Image Works
553 © Laszlo
555 Billy E. Barnes/Southern Light
557 Will & Deni McIntyre/Science Source/Photo Researchers
558 Mimi Forsyth/Monkmeyer Press
566 Willie Hill Jr./The Image Works
567 Courtesy The Advertising Council Inc. and the American Mental Health Fund
569 Stacy Pickerell/TSW, Chicago
572 (t) UPI/Bettmann
575 Rick Friedman/Black Star
576 Linc Cornell/Stock, Boston
578 Carolyn Brown
583 Courtesy Drs. Michael E. Phelps and John C. Mazziotta, UCLA School of Medicine
588 Figure 16.4 NIMH
589 Figure 16.5 From *Abnormal Psychology,* Second Edition, by Ephraim Rosen, Ronald E. Fox, and Ian Gregory. © 1972 by W. B. Saunders Company. Copyright 1965 by W. B. Saunders Company. Reprinted by permission of Holt, Rinehart and Winston, CBS College Publishing
590 Grunnitus/Monkmeyer Press
592 Figure 16.6 NIMH
593 Figure 16.7 Courtesy of Dr. Daniel R. Weinberger/NIMH. From *Archives of General Psychiatry,* Vol. 43, February 1986, page 117
598 Hank Morgan/Rainbow
601 Menzies/The Image Works
608 Giraudon/Art Resource, NY
609 (t) By Courtesy of the Trustees of Sir John Soane's Museum; (b) Culver Pictures
610 (t) Historical Pictures Service; (b) Culver Pictures
611 Ann Chwatsky/The Picture Cube
615 Courtesy Dr. Joseph Wolpe
618 (t) James Wilson/Woodfin Camp & Associates; Figure 17.1 Owen Franken/Stock, Boston
619 Alex Webb/Magnum
620 UPI/Bettmann
621 REPRINTED FROM PSYCHOLOGY TODAY MAGAZINE Copyright © 1985 American Psychological Association
622 Figure 17.2 Courtesy California Department of Mental Health
625 Carl Rogers Memorial Library
628 Joseph Nettis/Photo Researchers
635 James Wilson/Woodfin Camp & Associates
638 Christopher Morris/Black Star

Name Index

Abel, E. L., 333
Abelson, W. D., 399, 409
Abrahams, D., 446
Abrahamson, P. R., 151
Abramson, L. Y., 586, 587
Acheson, Dean, 475, 476
Acitelli, L. K., 450
Adams, J., 484
Adams, Marilyn, 276
Adams, S. M., 469
Addams, Jane, 524, 525
Ader, Robert, 223
Aderman, D., 386
Adler, Alfred, 613
Adler, J. M., 500
Adler, Jerry, 17-19
Adorno, Theodore W., 12, 498
Adrian, E. D., 60, 105
Ainsworth, M. D., 501
Aizley, H. G., 599
Akil, H., 48, 49
Akil, L., 49
Alba, J. W., 272
Albert, M. A., 60
Albrecht, D. G., 118
Aldous, J., 376
Alexander, M. P., 60
Ali, Muhammad, 484
Allen, J. L., 474
Alloy, L. B., 587
Allport, Gordon W., 12, 466, 504, 506
Altman, I., 451
Altrocchi, J., 595, 625
Alvarez, W., 551
Alzheimer, Alois, 384
Ames, M. A., 153
Amoore, J. E., 105, 106
Anand, B. K., 140
Anderson, C. A., 443
Anderson, J. R., 260, 269
Anderson, P., 68
Andreasen, N. C., 71, 72, 582, 588, 589, 591
Anglin, J. M., 294
Annis, Robert C., 125
Appelbaum, M. I., 402
Appenzeller, T., 287
Archer, R. L., 450
Aristotle, 16, 106, 261

Arnold, Roseanne, 280, 281
Aron, A. P., 449
Aronson, E., 6, 7, 433, 434, 446, 447
Aronson, V., 446
Asch, Solomon E., 422-423, 456-458, 477, 478
Aserinsky, Eugene, 185-186
Atkinson, John W., 157, 158, 502
Atkinson, K., 310
Atkinson, R. C., 261, 284
Ausubel, D. P., 599
Averill, J. R., 168, 448
Avery, D., 636
Ax, A. F., 163
Ayllon, T., 615, 622, 623
Azrin, N. H., 241, 615, 622

Back, K., 445
Backer, T. E., 223
Backlund, E. O., 74
Bahrick, Harry P., 265, 275, 282, 375
Bahrick, P. O., 265, 375
Bailey, J. M., 153
Bain, J. K., 377
Bakalar, J. B., 205, 207, 592, 597, 598, 638
Baker, A. J., 125
Baker, T. B., 600
Baker-Ward, L., 306
Balaban, T., 355
Baldessarini, R. J., 634, 635, 637
Bales, Robert F., 484
Bali, L. R., 195
Ballargeon, R., 344, 345
Baltes, P., 382
Bandura, Albert, 249, 266, 366, 467, 468, 513
Bannister, Roger, 521
Baratz, J. C., 309
Barber, James David, 483
Barber, T. X., 200, 201, 620
Barchas, J. D., 48, 203
Bard, Philip, 167
Barglow, P., 350, 351
Barker, R., 465
Barlow, D., 576
Baroff, G. W., 242

Baron, Robert A., 13-15, 470
Barrett, G. V., 406
Barrett, J. A., 534
Barrett, J. E., 534
Barrett-Lennard, G. J., 626
Barsalou, L. W., 296
Bartlett, Frederick E., 271, 272
Bartlett, M. K., 561
Bartochuk, L. M., 106
Basbaum, A. I., 109
Bassett, R., 463
Bassili, J. N., 426
Batchelor, W. F., 223
Bates, E., 315
Batson, C. D., 474
Battit, G. E., 561
Baumann, D. J., 474
Baumeister, R. F., 428, 433, 483
Baumrind, D., 349-350
Baxter, Jeff, 103
Bayley, N., 402
Bayliss, G. C., 118
Baylor, D. A., 90
Beach, D. H., 346
Becerril, J. J., 74
Beck, A. G., 501
Beck, Aaron T., 583, 586, 621
Beck, S. J., 501
Beckhard, R., 379
Beecher, H. K., 108
Beethoven, Ludwig van, 524
Beets, J. G. T., 106
Beidler, L. M., 106
Bekesy, George von, 99-100
Belenky, M., 366
Bell, A. P., 153
Bell, Alexander Graham, 97
Bellugi, U., 308
Belluzi, J. D., 49
Bem, D. J., 430, 433, 462, 475
Bem, S. L., 356
Benedict, H., 315
Benigni, L., 315
Benjamin, B., 535
Bennett, W., 141
Benson, D. F., 62, 63
Benson, F. D., 72
Benson, H., 194, 558

Haber, L., 153
Haith, M., 403
Haley, J., 628
Hall, C. S., 192
Hall, E., 380
Hall, G. Stanley, 21–23, 363
Hall, Lynda J., 282, 288
Halley, F. M., 541
Halpern, D. F., 80
Halpin, A., 482
Halton, A., 333
Hamberger, B., 74
Hamilton, D. L., 423, 441, 442
Hamilton, V. L., 461
Hammersmith, S. K., 153
Hannah, D. B., 424
Harding, Warren, 483
Hare, R. D., 603
Harlow, Harry F., 150, 347
Harlow, J. M., 63
Harlow, M. K., 150
Harmon, H. H., 400
Harper, R. A., 28, 620
Harris, B., 223
Harris, F. R., 622
Harris, J. E., 284
Harris, L., 370, 383
Harris, M. J., 444
Harris, R. J., 271
Harris, S. L., 602
Harris, V. A., 438
Hart, J. H., 269
Hart, S. N., 33
Hartmann, E. L., 193
Hartwick, J., 432
Hascher, Lynn, 257
Hasher, L., 272
Hassett, J., 110
Hastie, R., 426, 443
Hastorf, A. H., 426
Hatcher, R., 333
Hatfield, E., 450
Hawkins, R. D., 222
Hay, T., 450
Hayes, Cathy, 318
Hayes, Keith, 318
Heath, R. G., 65
Hebb, D. O., 136
Heider, Fritz, 426, 448
Heikkila, K., 543
Heilman, K. M., 61
Heimer, K., 466
Hellman, R. E., 153
Helmholtz, Hermann von, 19, 20, 21, 93–94, 99
Helson, H., 120
Hendricks, C. D., 380, 384
Hendricks, J., 380, 384
Hennigan, K. M., 434
Henry, G. W., 609
Henry, K. R., 98
Hentall, I. D., 111
Herbert, J. F., 85
Hering, Ewald, 95
Herman, C. P., 143, 144
Herrnstein, Richard J., 232
Hershey, D., 373
Hertz, Heinrich, 97
Herzog, A. R., 382
Heston, L. H., 384
Heston, L. L., 593

Hildum, D., 431
Hilgard, Ernst R., 26, 198, 200–202
Hilgard, Josephine R., 198, 200–202
Hill, Anita, 280, 281, 490, 516–517
Hill, R., 376
Hilton, H., 284
Hilton, J. L., 444
Hinsz, Verlin, 13
Hippocrates, 19, 23, 491, 577
Hiramoto, R. N., 224
Hiroto, D. S., 250
Hirsch, A. D., 319
Hirsch, J., 141
Hitler, Adolf, 10
Hitzig, E., 59, 62
Hobbes, Thomas, 464
Hobson, J. A., 187, 191–194
Hobson, J. Allan, 192, 193
Hochberg, J., 122
Hoffer, B. J., 73, 74
Hoff-Ginsberg, E., 315
Hoffman, E. J., 71
Hoffman, H. G., 273–274
Hoffman, L., 351
Hofman, Albert, 205
Hogarty, P. S., 402
Hogness, D. S., 94
Hohmann, G. W., 169
Holden, C., 411, 413, 571
Holder, H. D., 534
Holender, D., 183
Holland, P. C., 217, 247
Hollander, E. P., 480, 481
Hollis, Karen E., 246
Holloway, R. L., 80
Holman, R. B., 48
Holmes, D. S., 195, 557
Holmes, Oliver Wendell, 483
Holmes, Thomas H., 536, 537
Holt, R. R., 501
Holtz, W. C., 241
Holyoak, K. J., 181, 183, 299
Honig, W. K., 247
Horn, J. L., 380, 400
Horn, J. M., 407
Horney, Karen, 613
Horowitz, M. J., 551
Horton, D. L., 258, 272
Horton, Willie, 435
House, J. S., 561
Householder, J., 333
Houston, B. K., 543
Houston, L., 80
Houston, Patrick, 17–19
Hovland, C. I., 406, 434, 435
Howard, J., 623
Howard, J. A., 30, 519
Hubel, David H., 117–118, 126
Huesmann, L. R., 470
Hughes, J., 49
Hulihan-Giblin, B., 50
Hull, Clark L., 134–135
Hulse, S. H., 247
Humphries, C., 543
Hunt, J. McV., 409, 507
Hunt, M., 10, 147, 151, 152
Hunt, R. R., 260
Hunt, W. A., 243
Hurrell, J. J., 547
Hurvich, L. M., 96
Huston, A. C., 355, 357
Hutton, D. G., 428, 433

Ickes, W., 518
Iino, M., 105
Ingalls, Z., 383
Ingelfinger, F. J., 138
Ingerman, C., 441
Inhelder, B., 315, 340, 343, 344
Inouye, J., 505, 506
Insel, T. M., 51
Insko, C., 431
Instone-Noonan, D., 484
Intons-Peterson, Margaret J., 284, 352
Ionescu-Pioggia, M., 599
Ivan, Paula, 521
Ivancevich, J. M., 547
Iverson, S. D., 139
Izard, C. E., 163, 170, 171

Jacklin, C. N., 353, 517
Jackson, Andrew, 464
Jackson, Jesse, 18, 480
Jacobson, L., 443
Jacobson, R., 310
Jakubowski, P., 620, 621
James, Henry, 21
James, William, 20–23, 26, 166–169, 172, 178, 181, 202, 278, 279, 282, 524, 526
Jameson, D., 96
Janicak, P. G., 636
Janis, Irving L., 303, 435, 438, 477–479, 557
Jarvie, G. J., 144
Jefferson, Thomas, 524
Jellison, J. M., 438, 448
Jenkins, D., 543
Jenkins, John G., 276–277, 284
Jensen, Arthur R., 405, 406, 408–410, 412
Jessor, L., 11
Jessor, R., 11
Joan of Arc, 608
John, E. R., 70
Johnson, B. P., 599
Johnson, D., 143
Johnson, K. M., 207
Johnson, Lyndon B., 438
Johnson, M. K., 272, 273
Johnson, Magic, 151
Johnson, P. B., 354
Johnson, Spencer, 231
Johnson, Virginia E., 147–149, 151, 152
Johnson-Laird, P. N., 301
Johnston, J. W., Jr., 105
Johnston, M. K., 622
Jones, E. E., 425, 426, 428, 429, 442
Jones, J. M., 33, 223
Jones, Jim, 461
Jones, R. T., 206, 207
Jordan, Michael, 17
Jourard, Sidney M., 450, 451
Joyce, James, 179
Judd, C. M., 441
Judd, D. B., 120
Juergensen, M. R., 244
Jung, Carl G., 21, 491–492, 503

Kagan, Jerome, 29, 346, 348, 379, 390, 409, 410

Subject Index